STRATEGIC BRAND MANAGEMENT

BUILDING, MEASURING, AND MANAGING BRAND EQUITY

THIRD EDITION

Kevin Lane Keller

Amos Tuck School of Business
Dartmouth College

Upper Saddle River, NJ 07458

Library of Congress Cataloging-in-Publication Data

Keller, Kevin Lane
Strategic brand management : building, measuring, and managing brand equity / Kevin Lane Keller. — 3rd ed.
p. cm.
Includes bibliographical references and index.
ISBN 978-0-13-188859-3 (casebound)
1. Brand name products—Management. I. Title.
HD69.B7K45 2008
658.8'27—dc22

2007003552

Editor in Chief: David Parker
Project Manager: Melissa Pellerano
Editorial Assistant: Christine Ietto
Product Development Manager: Ashley Santora
Development Editor: Elisa Adams
Marketing Manager: Jodi Bassett
Marketing Assistant: Ian Gold
Managing Editor, Production: Renata Butera
Production Editor: Marcela Boos
Permissions Coordinator: Charles Morris
Manufacturing Buyer: Diane Peirano
Design/Composition Manager: Christy Mahon
Art Director: Pat Smythe
Cover Design: Bruce Kensalaar
Manager, Visual Research: Beth Brenzel
Image Permission Coordinator: Debbie Latronica
Photo Researcher: Teri Stratford
Composition: Integra Software Services
Full-Service Project Management: Thistle Hill Publishing Services, LLC
Printer/Binder: Courier/Kendallville
Typeface: Times 10/12

Credits and acknowledgments borrowed from other sources and reproduced, with permission, in this textbook appear on appropriate page on pages 677–678.

Pearson Education LTD.
Pearson Education Singapore, Pte. Ltd
Pearson Education, Canada, Ltd
Pearson Education–Japan
Pearson Education Australia PTY, Limited
Pearson Education North Asia Ltd
Pearson Educación de Mexico, S.A. de C.V.
Pearson Education Malaysia, Pte. Ltd.

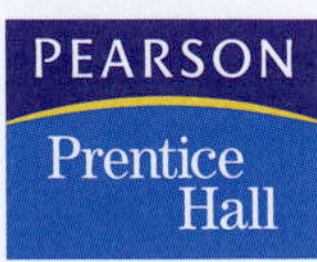

10 9 8 7
ISBN-13: 978-0-13-188859-3
ISBN-10: 0-13-188859-5

This book is dedicated to
my mother and the memory of my father
with much love, respect, and admiration.

BRIEF CONTENTS

CONTENTS

PROLOGUE: BRANDING IS NOT ROCKET SCIENCE

Although the challenges in branding can be immense and difficult, branding is not necessarily rocket science. I should know. I am not a rocket scientist—but my dad was. He was a physicist in the Air Force for 20 years, working on various rocket fuels. Always interested in what I did, he once asked what the book was all about. I explained the concept of brand equity and how the book addressed how to build, measure, and manage it. He listened, paused, and remarked, "That's very interesting but, uh, that's not *exactly* rocket science."

He's right. Branding is not rocket science. In fact, it is an art and a science. There's always a creativity and originality component involved with marketing. Even if someone were to follow all the guidelines in this book—and all the guidelines were properly specified—the success or failure of a brand strategy would still depend largely on how, exactly, this strategy would be implemented.

Nevertheless, good marketing is all about improving the odds for success. My hope is that this book adds to the scientific aspect of branding, illuminating the subject and providing guidance to those who make brand-related decisions.

PREFACE

Let me answer a few questions as to what this book is about, how it's different from other books about branding, what's new with this third edition, who should read it, how it's organized, and how you can get the most out of it.

What Is the Book About?

This book deals with brands—why they are important, what they represent to consumers, and what firms should do to manage them properly. As many business executives now recognize, perhaps one of the most valuable assets a firm has are the brands it has invested in and developed over time. Although competitors can often duplicate manufacturing processes and factory designs, it's not so easy to reproduce strongly held beliefs and attitudes established in the minds of consumers. The difficulty and expense of introducing new products, however, puts more pressure than ever on firms to skillfully launch their new products as well as manage their existing brands.

Although brands may represent invaluable intangible assets, creating and nurturing a strong brand poses considerable challenges. Fortunately, the concept of *brand equity*—the main focus of this book—can provide marketers with valuable perspective and a common denominator to interpret the potential effects and tradeoffs of various strategies and tactics for their brands. Think of brand equity as the marketing effects uniquely attributable to the brand. In a practical sense, brand equity is the added value a product accrues as a result of past investments in the marketing activity for the brand. It's the bridge between what happened to the brand in the past and what should happen to it in the future.

The chief purpose of this book is to provide a comprehensive and up-to-date treatment of the subjects of brands, brand equity, and s*trategic brand management*—the design and implementation of marketing programs and activities to build, measure, and manage brand equity. One of the book's important goals is to provide managers with concepts and techniques to improve the long-term profitability of their brand strategies. We'll incorporate current thinking and developments on these topics from both academics and industry participants, and combine a comprehensive theoretical foundation with enough practical insights to assist managers in their day-to-day and long-term brand decisions. And we'll draw on illustrative examples and case studies of brands marketed in the United States and all over the world.

Specifically, we'll provide insights into how to create profitable brand strategies by building, measuring, and managing brand equity. We address three important questions:

1. How can we create brand equity?
2. How can we measure brand equity?
3. How can we sustain brand equity to expand business opportunities?

Readers will learn:

- The role of brands, the concept of brand equity, and the advantages of creating strong brands
- The three main ways to build brand equity by properly choosing brand elements, designing marketing programs and activities, and leveraging secondary associations
- Different approaches to measuring brand equity, and how to implement a brand equity measurement system
- Alternative branding strategies and how to devise brand hierarchies and brand portfolios

- The role of corporate brands, family brands, individual brands, modifiers, and how to combine them into sub-brands
- How to adjust branding strategies over time and across geographic boundaries to maximize brand equity

What's Different about This Book?

My objective in writing this book was to satisfy three key criteria by which any marketing text could be judged:

- *Depth:* The material in the book had to be presented in the context of a conceptual framework that was comprehensive, internally consistent and cohesive, and well grounded in the academic and practitioner literature.
- *Breadth:* The book had to cover all those topics that practicing managers and students of brand management found intriguing and/or important.
- *Relevance:* Finally, the book had to be well grounded in practice and easily related to past and present marketing activities, events, and case studies.

Although a number of excellent books have been written about brands, no book has really maximized those dimensions to the greatest possible extent. This book set out to fill that gap by accomplishing three things.

First, we develop a framework that provides a definition of brand equity, identifies sources and outcomes of brand equity, and provides tactical guidelines about how to build, measure, and manage brand equity. Recognizing the general importance of consumers and customers to marketing—understanding and satisfying their needs and wants—this framework approaches branding from the perspective of the consumer; it is called *customer-based brand equity*.

Second, besides these broad, fundamentally important branding topics, for completeness, numerous Science of Branding boxes provide in-depth treatment of cutting-edge ideas and concepts, and each chapter contains a Brand Focus case study that delves into detail on specific, related branding topics, such as brand audits, legal issues, brand crises, and corporate name changes.

Finally, to maximize relevance, numerous examples illuminate the discussion of virtually every topic, and over 100 Branding Briefs provide more in-depth examinations of selected topics or brands.

Thus, this book can help readers understand the important issues in planning and evaluating brand strategies, as well as providing appropriate concepts, theories, and other tools to make better branding decisions. We identify successful and unsuccessful brand marketers—and why they have been so—to offer readers a greater appreciation of the range of issues in branding, as well as a means to organize their own thoughts about those issues.

Who Should Read the Book?

A wide range of people can benefit from reading this book:

- Students interested in increasing both their understanding of basic branding principles and their exposure to classic and contemporary branding applications and case studies
- Managers and analysts concerned with the effects of their day-to-day marketing decisions on brand performance
- Senior executives concerned with the longer-term prosperity of their brand franchises and product or service portfolios
- All marketers interested in new ideas with implications for marketing strategies and tactics

The perspective we adopt is relevant to any type of organization (public or private, large or small), and the examples cover a wide range of industries and geographies. To illuminate branding concepts across different settings, we review specific applications to industrial, high-tech, online, service, retailer, and small business in both Chapters 1 and 15.

How Is the Book Organized?

The book is divided into six major parts, adhering to the "three-exposure opportunity" approach to learning new material. Part I introduces branding concepts; Parts II, III, IV, and V provide all the specific details of those concepts; and Part VI summarizes and applies the concepts in various contexts. The specific chapters for each part and their contents are as follows.

Part I sets the stage by providing the "big picture" of what strategic brand management is all about. The goal is to provide a sense for the content and context of strategic brand management by identifying key branding decisions and suggesting some of the important considerations for those decisions. Specifically, Chapter 1 introduces some basic notions about brands, and the role they've played and continue to play in marketing strategies. It defines what a brand is, why brands matter, and how anything can be branded, and provides an overview of the strategic brand management process.

Part II addresses the topic of brand equity and provides a blueprint for the rest of the book. Chapter 2 introduces the concept of customer-based brand equity, outlines the customer-based brand equity framework, and summarizes guidelines for building, measuring, and managing customer-based brand equity. With Chapter 1, it provides a useful overview or top-line summary of the scope of topics covered in the book. Chapter 3 develops a conceptual model of brand knowledge and addresses the critically important issue of competitive brand positioning.

Part III examines the three major ways to build customer-based brand equity, taking a single product–single brand perspective. Chapter 4 addresses the first way to build customer-based brand equity and how to choose brand elements (brand names, logos, symbols, slogans), and the role they play in contributing to brand equity. Chapters 5 and 6 outline the second way to build brand equity and how to optimize the marketing mix to create customer-based brand equity. Chapter 5 covers product, pricing, and distribution strategies; Chapter 6 is devoted to creating integrated marketing communication programs to build brand equity. Although most readers are probably familiar with these "4 P's" of marketing, it's illuminating to consider them from the standpoint of brand equity and the effects of brand knowledge on consumer response to marketing mix activity and vice versa. Finally, Chapter 7 examines the third major way to build brand equity—by leveraging secondary associations from other entities like company, geographical region, person, and other brands.

Part IV looks at how to measure customer-based brand equity. These chapters take a detailed look at what consumers know about brands, what marketers want them to know, and how marketers can develop measurement procedures to assess how well they're doing. Chapter 8 provides a big-picture perspective of these topics, introducing the brand value chain and examining how to develop and implement a brand equity measurement system. Chapter 9 examines approaches to measuring customers' brand knowledge structures, in order to identify and quantify potential sources of brand equity. Chapter 10 looks at measuring potential outcomes of brand equity in terms of the major benefits a firm accrues from these sources of brand equity.

Part V addresses how to manage brand equity, taking a broader, multiple product–multiple brand perspective as well as a longer-term, multiple-market view of brands. Chapter 11 considers issues related to branding strategies—which brand elements a firm chooses to apply across the various products it sells—and how to maximize brand equity across all the different brands and products that a firm might sell. It also describes two important tools to help formulate branding strategies—the brand–product matrix and the brand hierarchy. Chapter 12 outlines the pros and cons of brand extensions and develops guidelines for introducing and naming new products and brand extensions. Chapter 13 considers how to reinforce, revitalize, and retire brands, examining a number of specific topics in managing brands over time, such as the advantages of maintaining brand consistency, the importance of protecting sources of brand equity, and tradeoffs in fortifying vs. leveraging brands. Chapter 14 examines the implications of differences in consumer behavior and different types of market segments for managing brand equity. We pay particular attention to international issues and global branding strategies.

Finally, Part VI considers some implications and applications of the customer-based brand equity framework. Chapter 15 highlights managerial guidelines and key themes that emerged in earlier chapters of the book. This chapter also summarizes success factors for branding, applies the customer-based brand equity framework to address specific strategic brand management issues for different types of products (industrial goods, high-tech products, online, services, retailers, and small businesses), and relates the framework to several other popular views of brand equity.

Revision Strategy for Third Edition

The overarching goal of the revision of *Strategic Brand Management* was to preserve the aspects of the text that worked well, but to improve it as much as possible and add new material as needed. We retained the customer-based brand equity framework that was the centerpiece of the second edition, and the three dimensions of depth, breadth, and relevance. Given all the academic research progress that has been made in recent years, however, as well as all the new market developments and events, the book required—and got—some important updates.

1. *Updated Branding Briefs and academic references:* Over half the 100-plus Branding Briefs and other examples within the text have been replaced with more current material. The goal was to blend classic and contemporary examples, so some appropriate examples remain. The academic references throughout the book are newly updated.
2. *Streamlined chapters:* Lengthy passages and examples have been edited and the text now employs a more active voice.
3. *Updated original as well as additional new cases:* To provide broader, more relevant coverage, three new cases have been added to the *Best Practices in Branding* casebook – GE, American Express, and iPod. Each of the 12 other cases has been updated and more tightly edited.
4. *Better presentation of text material and stronger supplementary support:* The text now includes more colorful graphics. All critical figures are reprinted in the Instructor's Manual, which has been expanded to provide more help for classroom instruction and guidance for experiential learning.

How Can You Get the Most out of the Book?

Branding is a fascinating topic that receives much attention in the popular press. The ideas presented in the book will help you interpret current branding developments. One good way to better understand branding and the customer-based brand equity framework is to apply the concepts and ideas presented in the book to current events, or to any of the more detailed branding issues or case studies presented in the Branding Briefs. The Discussion Questions at the end of the chapters often ask you to pick a brand and apply one or more concepts from that chapter. Focusing on one brand across all the questions—perhaps as part of a class project—permits some cumulative and integrated learning and is an excellent way to become more comfortable with and fluent in the material in the book.

This book truly belongs to you, the reader. Like most marketing, branding doesn't offer "right" or "wrong" answers, and you should question things you don't understand or don't believe. The book is designed to facilitate your understanding of strategic brand management and present some "best practice" guidelines. At the end of the day, however, what you get out of it will be what you put into it, and how you blend the ideas contained in these pages with what you already know or believe.

Faculty Resources

Instructors can access a variety of print, media, and presentation resources through www.prenhall.com/kevinlanekeller. Additionally, a DVD Video Library is available to accompany the textbook.

ACKNOWLEDGMENTS

I have been gratified by the acceptance of the first two editions of *Strategic Brand Management*. It has been adopted by numerous universities and used by scores of marketing executives around the world. The success of the text is in large part due to the help and support of others whom I would like to acknowledge and thank.

The Prentice Hall team on the third edition was a huge help in the revision—many thanks to Jeff Shelstad, Katie Stevens, Melissa Pellerano, and Christine Ietto. Elisa Adams gave the text a thorough overhaul. Keith Richey, Jackson Womack, and Jennifer Seaton provided additional research assistance and help with the text, as did Jon Michaels and Lowey Sichol with the cases. John Lin has been a steady contributor about what is happening in the tech world. Marcia Diefendorf provided her usual superb administrative assistance in a number of areas.

I have learned much about branding in my work with industry participants, who have unique perspectives on what is working and not working (and why) in the marketplace. Our discussions have enriched my appreciation for the challenges in building, measuring, and managing brand equity and the factors affecting the success and failure of brand strategies.

I have benefited from the wisdom of my colleagues at the institutions where I have held academic positions: Dartmouth College, Duke University, the University of California at Berkeley, Stanford University, the Australian Graduate School of Management, and the University of North Carolina at Chapel Hill.

Over the years, the doctoral students I advised have helped in my branding pursuits in a variety of useful ways, including Sheri Bridges, Christie Brown, Jennifer Aaker, Meg Campbell, and Sanjay Sood. The following set of dedicated reviewers also provided insightful feedback and help on the third edition: Michael L. Barretti, Suffolk University; Olan Farnall, California State University, Fullerton; and Timothy W. Aurand, Northern Illinois University.

Finally, thanks go to my wife, Punam Anand Keller, and two daughters, Carolyn and Allison, for their continual patience and understanding.

ABOUT THE AUTHOR

Kevin Lane Keller is the E. B. Osborn Professor of Marketing at the Tuck School of Business at Dartmouth College. Professor Keller has degrees from Cornell, Carnegie-Mellon, and Duke universities. At Dartmouth, he teaches MBA courses on marketing management and strategic brand management and lectures in executive programs on that topic.

Previously, Professor Keller was on the faculty of the Graduate School of Business at Stanford University, where he also served as the head of the marketing group. Additionally, he has been on the marketing faculty at the University of California at Berkeley and the University of North Carolina at Chapel Hill, been a visiting professor at Duke University and the Australian Graduate School of Management, and has two years of industry experience as Marketing Consultant for Bank of America.

Professor Keller's general area of expertise lies in marketing strategy and planning. His specific research interest is in how understanding theories and concepts related to consumer behavior can improve marketing strategies. His research has been published in three of the major marketing journals—the *Journal of Marketing*, the *Journal of Marketing Research*, and the *Journal of Consumer Research*. He also has served on the Editorial Review Boards of those journals. With over sixty published papers, his research has been widely cited and has received numerous awards.

Professor Keller is acknowledged as one of the international leaders in the study of brands, branding, and strategic brand management. Actively involved with industry, he has worked on a host of different types of marketing projects. He has served as a consultant and advisor to marketers for some of the world's most successful brands, including Accenture, American Express, Disney, Ford, Intel, Levi Strauss & Co., Procter & Gamble, and SAB Miller. Additional brand consulting activities have been with other top companies such as Allstate, Beiersdorf (Nivea), BlueCross BlueShield, Campbell's, Eli Lilly, ExxonMobil, General Mills, Goodyear, Kodak, Mayo Clinic, Nordstrom, Shell Oil, Starbucks, Unilever, and Young & Rubicam. He has also served as an academic trustee for the Marketing Science Institute. A popular speaker, he has conducted marketing seminars to top executives in a variety of forums.

Professor Keller is currently conducting a variety of studies that address strategies to build, measure, and manage brand equity. In addition to *Strategic Brand Management*, as of the twelfth edition, he is also the co-author with Philip Kotler of the all-time best selling introductory marketing textbook, *Marketing Management*.

An avid sports, music, and film enthusiast, in his so-called spare time, he has served as executive producer for one of Australia's great rock and roll treasures, The Church, as well as American power-pop legends Dwight Twilley and Tommy Keene. He is also on the Board of Directors for The Doug Flutie, Jr. Foundation for Autism. Professor Keller lives in Etna, New Hampshire, with his wife, Punam (also a Tuck marketing professor), and his two daughters, Carolyn and Allison.

1 BRANDS AND BRAND MANAGEMENT

Preview

Ever more firms and other organizations have come to the realization that one of their most valuable assets is the brand names associated with their products or services. In our increasingly complex world, all of us, as individuals and as business managers, face more choices with less time to make them. Thus a strong brand's ability to simplify consumer decision making, reduce risk, and set expectations is invaluable. Creating strong brands that deliver on that promise, and maintaining and enhancing the strength of those brands over time, is a management imperative.

This text will help you reach a deeper understanding of how to achieve those branding goals. Its basic objectives are

1. To explore the important issues in planning, implementing, and evaluating brand strategies
2. To provide appropriate concepts, theories, models, and other tools to make better branding decisions

We place particular emphasis on understanding psychological principles at the individual or organizational level in order to make better decisions about brands. Our objective is to be relevant for any type of organization regardless of its size, nature of business, or profit orientation.

With these goals in mind, this first chapter defines what a brand is. We consider the functions of a brand from the perspective of both consumers and firms and discuss why brands are important to both. We look at what can and cannot be branded and identify some strong brands. The chapter concludes with an introduction to the concept of brand equity and the strategic brand management process. Brand Focus 1.0 at the end of the chapter traces some of the historical origins of branding.

What Is a Brand?

Branding has been around for centuries as a means to distinguish the goods of one producer from those of another. In fact, the word *brand* is derived from the Old Norse word *brandr,* which means "to burn," as brands were and still are the means by which owners of livestock mark their animals to identify them.[1]

According to the American Marketing Association (AMA), a ***brand*** is a "name, term, sign, symbol, or design, or a combination of them, intended to identify the goods and services of one seller or group of sellers and to differentiate them from those of competition." Technically speaking, then, whenever a marketer creates a new name, logo, or symbol for a new product, he or she has created a brand.

In fact, however, many practicing managers refer to a brand as more than that—as something that has actually created a certain amount of awareness, reputation, prominence, and so on in the marketplace. Thus we can make a distinction between the AMA definition of a "brand" with a small *b* and the industry's concept of a "Brand" with a big *B*. The difference is important for us because disagreements about branding principles or guidelines often revolve around what we mean by the term.

Thus, the key to creating a brand, according to the AMA definition, is to be able to choose a name, logo, symbol, package design, or other characteristic that identifies a product and distinguishes it from others. These different components of a brand that identify and differentiate it are ***brand elements.*** We'll see in Chapter 4 that brand elements come in many different forms.

For example, consider the variety of brand name strategies. Some companies, like General Electric and Samsung, use their names for essentially all their products. Other manufacturers assign new products individual brand names that are unrelated to the company name, like Procter & Gamble's Tide, Pampers, Iams, and Pantene product brands. Retailers create their own brands based on their store name or some other means; for example, Macy's has its own Alfani, INC, Charter Club, and Club Room brands.

Brand names themselves come in many different forms.[2] There are brand names based on people's names, like Estée Lauder cosmetics, Porsche automobiles, and Orville Redenbacher popcorn; names based on places, like Sante Fe cologne, Chevrolet Tahoe SUV, and British Airways; and names based on animals or birds, like Mustang automobiles, Dove soap, and Greyhound buses. In the category of "other," we find Apple computers, Shell gasoline, and Carnation evaporated milk.

Some brand names use words with inherent product meaning, like Lean Cuisine, JustJuice, and Ticketron, or suggesting important attributes or benefits, like DieHard auto batteries, Mop & Glo floor cleaner, and Beautyrest mattresses. Other names are made up and include prefixes and suffixes that sound scientific, natural, or prestigious, like Intel microprocessors, Lexus automobiles, and Compaq computers.

Not just names but other brand elements like logos and symbols also can be based on people, places, things, and abstract images. In creating a brand, marketers have many choices about the number and nature of the brand elements they use to identify their products.

Brands versus Products

How do we contrast a brand and a product? A ***product*** is anything we can offer to a market for attention, acquisition, use, or consumption that might satisfy a need or want. Thus, a product may be a physical good like a cereal, tennis racquet, or automobile; a service such as an airline, bank, or insurance company; a retail outlet like a department store, specialty store, or supermarket; a person such as a political figure, entertainer, or professional athlete; an organization like a nonprofit, trade organization, or arts group; a place including a city, state, or country; or even an idea like a political or social cause. This very broad definition of product is the one we adopt in the book. We'll discuss the role of brands in some of these different categories in more detail later in this chapter and in Chapter 15.

We can define five levels of meaning for a product:[3]

1. The ***core benefit level*** is the fundamental need or want that consumers satisfy by consuming the product or service.
2. The ***generic product level*** is a basic version of the product containing only those attributes or characteristics absolutely necessary for its functioning but with no distinguishing features. This is basically a stripped-down, no-frills version of the product that adequately performs the product function.
3. The ***expected product level*** is a set of attributes or characteristics that buyers normally expect and agree to when they purchase a product.
4. The ***augmented product level*** includes additional product attributes, benefits, or related services that distinguish the product from competitors.
5. The ***potential product level*** includes all the augmentations and transformations that a product might ultimately undergo in the future.

Figure 1-1 illustrates these different levels in the context of air conditioners and portable MP3 players. In many markets most competition takes place at the product augmentation level, because most firms can successfully build satisfactory products at the

Level	Air Conditioner
1. Core Benefit	Cooling and comfort.
2. Generic Product	Sufficient cooling capacity (BTU per hour), an acceptable energy efficiency rating, adequate air intakes and exhausts, and so on.
3. Expected Product	*Consumer Reports* states that for a typical large air conditioner, consumers should expect at least two cooling speeds, expandable plastic side panels, adjustable louvers, removable air filter, vent for exhausting air, power cord at least 60 inches long, R-22 HCFC refrigerant (less harmful to the earth's ozone layer than other types), one year parts-and-labor warranty on the entire unit, and a five-year parts-and-labor warranty on the refrigeration system.[a]
4. Augmented Product	Optional features might include electric touch-pad controls, a display to show indoor and outdoor temperatures and the thermostat setting, an automatic mode to adjust fan speed based on the thermostat setting and room temperature, a toll-free 800 number for customer service, and so on.
5. Potential Product	Silently running, completely balanced throughout the room, and energy self-sufficient.

Level	Portable MP3 Player
1. Core Benefit	Musical entertainment on the move.
2. Generic Product	Ability to play music downloaded from the Web or "ripped" from CD collections.
3. Expected Product	*Consumer Reports* states that for a typical MP3 player, consumers should expect a solid-state device with no moving parts (which eliminates skipping) and 64 to 128 megabytes of memory. Most standard-capacity players have expansion slots to add more memory and software to interface with a computer.[b]
4. Augmented Product	Optional features might include color LCD screen, audio equalizer, and the ability to store files other than digital-audio files, including text, image, or video files.
5. Potential Product	Voice-controlled programming; extended "infinite life" batteries.

[a] *Consumer Reports*, July 2005.
[b] *Consumer Reports*, Annual Buying Guide, 2004.

FIGURE 1-1

Examples of Different Product Levels

expected product level. Harvard's Ted Levitt has argued that "the new competition is not between what companies produce in their factories but between what they add to their factory output in the form of packaging, services, advertising, customer advice, financing, delivery arrangements, warehousing, and other things that people value.[4]

A brand is therefore more than a product, because it can have dimensions that differentiate it in some way from other products designed to satisfy the same need. These differences may be rational and tangible—related to product performance of the brand—or more symbolic, emotional, and intangible—related to what the brand represents. One marketing observer put it this way:

> . . . what distinguishes a brand from its unbranded commodity counterpart and gives it equity is the sum total of consumers' perceptions and feelings about the product's attributes and how they perform, about the brand name and what it stands for, and about the company associated with the brand.[5]

Extending our previous example, a branded product may be a physical good like Kellogg's Corn Flakes cereal, Prince tennis racquets, or Ford Taurus automobiles; a service such as United Airlines, Bank of America, or Allstate insurance; a store like Bloomingdale's department store, Body Shop specialty store, or Safeway supermarket; a person such as Warren Buffett, Julia Roberts, or David Beckham; a place like the city of London, state of California, or country of Australia; an organization such as the Red Cross, American Automobile Association, or the Rolling Stones; or an idea like corporate responsibility, free trade, or freedom of speech.

Some brands create competitive advantages with product performance. For example, brands such as Gillette, Merck, and others have been leaders in their product categories for decades, due, in part, to continual innovation (see Figure 1-2 for a list of 20 innovative companies). Steady investments in research and development have produced leading-edge products, and sophisticated mass marketing practices have ensured rapid adoption of new technologies in the consumer market.

Other brands create competitive advantages through non-product-related means. For example, Coca-Cola, Chanel No. 5, and others have been leaders in their product categories for decades by understanding consumer motivations and desires and creating relevant and appealing images surrounding their products. Often these intangible image associations may be the only way to distinguish different brands in a product category.

Brands, especially strong ones, carry a number of different types of associations, and marketers must account for all of them in making marketing decisions. The marketers behind some brands have learned this lesson the hard way. Branding Brief 1-1 describes the problems Coca-Cola encountered in the introduction of "New Coke" when it failed to account for all of the different aspects of the Coca-Cola brand image. Not only are there many different types of associations to link to the brand, there are many different means to create them—the entire marketing program can contribute to consumers' understanding of the brand and how they value it.

By creating perceived differences among products through branding and by developing a loyal consumer franchise, marketers create value that can translate to financial profits for the firm. The reality is that the most valuable assets many firms have may not be tangible ones, such as plants, equipment, and real estate, but *intangible* assets such as management skills, marketing, financial and operations expertise, and, most important, the brands themselves. This value was recognized by John Stuart, CEO of Quaker Oats from 1922 to 1956, who famously said, "If this company were to split up I would give you the property, plant and equipment and I would take the brands and the trademarks and I would fare better than you."[6] Let's see why brands are so valuable.

Twenty Innovative Companies

1. Apple
2. 3M
3. Microsoft
4. GE
5. Sony
6. Dell
7. IBM
8. Google
9. P&G
10. Nokia
11. Virgin
12. Samsung
13. Wal-Mart
14. Toyota
15. eBay
16. Intel
17. Amazon
18. Ideo
19. Starbucks
20. BMW

Based on poll of 940 senior executives in 68 countries by Boston Consulting Group.

FIGURE 1-2

Twenty Innovative Companies

Source: Bruce Nussbaum, "Get Creative," *Business Week*, August 1, 2005, pp. 61–68.

BRANDING BRIEF 1-1

Coca-Cola's Branding Lesson

One of the classic marketing mistakes occurred in April 1985 when Coca-Cola replaced its flagship cola brand with a new formula. The motivation behind the change was primarily a competitive one. Pepsi-Cola's "Pepsi Challenge" promotion had posed a strong challenge to Coke's supremacy over the cola market. Starting initially just in Texas, the promotion involved advertising and in-store sampling showcasing consumer blind taste tests between Coca-Cola and Pepsi-Cola. Invariably, Pepsi won these tests. Fearful that the promotion, if taken nationally, could take a big bite out of Coca-Cola's sales, especially among younger cola drinkers, Coca-Cola felt compelled to act.

Coca-Cola's strategy was to change the formulation of Coke to more closely match the slightly sweeter taste of Pepsi. To arrive at a new formulation, Coke conducted taste tests with an astounding number of consumers—190,000! The findings from this research clearly indicated that consumers "overwhelmingly" preferred the taste of the new formulation to the old one. Brimming with confidence, Coca-Cola announced the formulation change with much fanfare. Consumer reaction was swift but, unfortunately for Coca-Cola, negative. In Seattle, retired real estate

Coca-Cola made a mistake in changing the formulation of its Coke brand.

Why Do Brands Matter?

An obvious question is, why are brands important? What functions do they perform that make them so valuable to marketers? We can take a couple of perspectives to uncover the value of brands to both customers and firms themselves. Figure 1-3 provides an overview of the different roles that brands play to these two parties. We'll talk about consumers first.

Consumers

As with the term *product*, this book uses the term ***consumer*** broadly to encompass all types of customers, including individuals as well as organizations. To consumers, brands provide important functions. Brands identify the source or maker of a product and allow consumers to assign responsibility to a particular manufacturer or distributor. Most important, brands take on special meaning to consumers. Because of past experiences with the product and its marketing program over the years, consumers find out which brands satisfy their needs and which ones do not. As a result, brands provide a shorthand device or means of simplification for their product decisions.[7]

If consumers recognize a brand and have some knowledge about it, then they do not have to engage in a lot of additional thought or processing of information to make a product decision. Thus, from an economic perspective, brands allow consumers to lower the search costs for products both internally (in terms of how much they have to think) and

investor Gay Mullins founded the "Old Cola Drinkers of America" and set up a hotline for angry consumers. A Beverly Hills wine merchant bought 500 cases of "Vintage Coke" and sold them at a premium. Meanwhile, back at Coca-Cola headquarters, roughly 1,500 calls a day and literally truckloads of mail poured in, virtually all condemning the company's actions. Finally, after several months of slumping sales, Coca-Cola announced that the old formulation would return as "Coca-Cola Classic" and join "new" Coke in the marketplace (see the accompanying photo).

The new Coke debacle taught Coca-Cola a very important, albeit painful and public, lesson about its brand. Coke clearly is not just seen as a beverage or thirst-quenching refreshment by consumers. Rather, it seems to be viewed as more of an American icon, and much of its appeal lies not only in its ingredients but also in what it represents in terms of Americana, nostalgia, and its heritage and relationship with consumers. Coke's brand image certainly has emotional components, and consumers have a great deal of strong feelings for the brand. Although Coca-Cola made a number of other mistakes in introducing New Coke (e.g., both its advertising and packaging probably failed to clearly differentiate the brand and communicate its sweeter quality), their biggest slip was losing sight of what the brand meant to consumers in its totality. The *psychological* response to a brand can be as important as the *physiological* response to the product. At the same time, American consumers also learned a lesson—just how much the Coke brand really meant to them. As a result of Coke's marketing fiasco, it is doubtful that either side will take the other for granted from now on.

Source: Reprinted by permission from Patricia Winters, "For New Coke, 'What Price Success?'" *Advertising Age,* 20 March 1989, S1–S2. Copyright Crain Communications Inc.

externally (in terms of how much they have to look around). Based on what they already know about the brand—its quality, product characteristics, and so forth—consumers can make assumptions and form reasonable expectations about what they may *not* know about the brand.

Consumers

Identification of source of product
Assignment of responsibility to product maker
Risk reducer
Search cost reducer
Promise, bond, or pact with maker of product
Symbolic device
Signal of quality

Manufacturers

Means of identification to simplify handling or tracing
Means of legally protecting unique features
Signal of quality level to satisfied customers
Means of endowing products with unique associations
Source of competitive advantage
Source of financial returns

FIGURE 1-3

Role That Brands Play

The meaning imbued in brands can be quite profound, allowing us to think of the relationship between a brand and the consumer as a type of bond or pact. Consumers offer their trust and loyalty with the implicit understanding that the brand will behave in certain ways and provide them utility through consistent product performance and appropriate pricing, promotion, and distribution programs and actions. To the extent that consumers realize advantages and benefits from purchasing the brand, and as long as they derive satisfaction from product consumption, they are likely to continue to buy it.

These benefits may not be purely functional in nature. Brands can serve as symbolic devices, allowing consumers to project their self-image. Certain brands are associated with certain types of people and thus reflect different values or traits. Consuming such products is a means by which consumers can communicate to others—or even to themselves—the type of person they are or would like to be.

Pulitzer Prize–winning author Daniel Boorstein asserts that, for many people, brands serve the function that fraternal, religious, and service organizations used to serve—they help people define who they are and then help people communicate that definition to others. As Susan Fournier notes:

> Relationships with mass [market] brands can soothe the "empty selves" left behind by society's abandonment of tradition and community and provide stable anchors in an otherwise changing world. The formation and maintenance of brand-product relationships serve many culturally-supported roles within post-modern society.[8]

Brands can also play a significant role in signaling certain product characteristics to consumers. Researchers have classified products and their associated attributes or benefits into three major categories: search goods, experience goods, and credence goods.[9] With ***search goods*** like grocery produce, consumers can evaluate product attributes like sturdiness, size, color, style, design, weight, and ingredient composition by visual inspection. The product attributes of ***experience goods*** like automobile tires cannot be assessed so easily by inspection, and actual product trial and experience is necessary to judge durability, service quality, safety, and ease of handling or use. For ***credence goods*** like insurance coverage, consumers may rarely learn product attributes. Given the difficulty of assessing and interpreting product attributes and benefits for experience and credence goods, brands may be particularly important signals of quality and other characteristics to consumers for these types of products.[10]

Brands can reduce the risks in product decisions.[11] Consumers may perceive many different types of risks in buying and consuming a product:

- *Functional risk:* The product does not perform up to expectations.
- *Physical risk:* The product poses a threat to the physical well-being or health of the user or others.
- *Financial risk:* The product is not worth the price paid.
- *Social risk:* The product results in embarrassment from others.
- *Psychological risk:* The product affects the mental well-being of the user.
- *Time risk:* The failure of the product results in an opportunity cost of finding another satisfactory product.

Consumers can certainly handle these risks in a number of ways, but one way is obviously to buy well-known brands, especially those with which consumers have had favorable past experiences. Thus, brands can be a very important risk-handling device, especially in business-to-business settings where risks can sometimes have quite profound implications.

In summary, to consumers, the special meaning that brands take on can change their perceptions and experiences with a product. The identical product may be evaluated differently depending on the brand identification or attribution it carries. Brands take on unique, personal meanings to consumers that facilitate their day-to-day activities and enrich their lives. As consumers' lives become more complicated, rushed, and time starved, the ability of a brand to simplify decision making and reduce risk is invaluable.

Firms

Brands also provide a number of valuable functions to their firms.[12] Fundamentally, they serve an identification purpose, to simplify product handling or tracing. Operationally, brands help to organize inventory and accounting records. A brand also offers the firm legal protection for unique features or aspects of the product. A brand can retain intellectual property rights, giving legal title to the brand owner.[13] The brand name can be protected through registered trademarks; manufacturing processes can be protected through patents; and packaging can be protected through copyrights and designs. These intellectual property rights ensure that the firm can safely invest in the brand and reap the benefits of a valuable asset.

We've seen that these investments in the brand can endow a product with unique associations and meanings that differentiate it from other products. Brands can signal a certain level of quality so that satisfied buyers can easily choose the product again.[14] This brand loyalty provides predictability and security of demand for the firm and creates barriers of entry that make it difficult for other firms to enter the market.

Although manufacturing processes and product designs may be easily duplicated, lasting impressions in the minds of individuals and organizations from years of marketing activity and product experience may not be so easily reproduced. One advantage that brands such as Crest toothpaste, Cheerios cereal, and Levi's jeans have is that consumers have literally grown up with them. In this sense, branding can be seen as a powerful means to secure a competitive advantage.

In short, to firms, brands represent enormously valuable pieces of legal property, capable of influencing consumer behavior, being bought and sold, and providing the security of sustained future revenues.[15] For these reasons, huge sums, often representing large multiples of a brand's earnings, have been paid for brands in mergers or acquisitions, starting with the boom years of the mid-1980s. The merger and acquisition frenzy during this time led Wall Street financiers to seek out undervalued companies from which to make investment or takeover profits. One of the primary undervalued assets of such firms was their brands, given that they were off-balance-sheet items. Implicit in Wall Street's interest was a belief that strong brands result in better earnings and profit performance for firms, which, in turn, creates greater value for shareholders.

The price premium paid for many companies is clearly justified by the opportunity to earn and sustain extra profits from their brands, as well as by the tremendous difficulty and expense of creating similar brands from scratch. For a typical fast-moving consumer goods company, net tangible assets may be as little as 10 percent of the total value (see Figure 1-4). Most of the value lies in intangible assets and goodwill, and as much as 70 percent of intangible assets can be supplied by brands.

Brand	Brand Value (billions)	Percentage of Market Capitalization
Coca-Cola	$67.5	64%
Microsoft	59.9	22
IBM	53.4	44
GE	47.0	12
Intel	35.6	21
Nokia	26.5	34
Disney	26.4	46
McDonald's	26.0	71
Toyota	24.8	19
Marlboro	21.2	15

Sources: Interbrand and Business Week, "Best Global Brands by Value," 2005. Used with permission of Interbrand.

FIGURE 1-4a

Brand Value as a Percentage of Market Capitalization (2005)

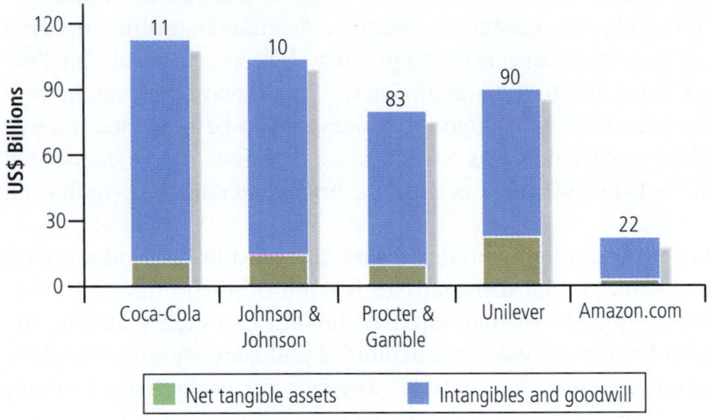

Source: Used with permission of Interbrand.

FIGURE 1-4b

Brands on the Balance Sheet

Can Everything Be Branded?

Brands clearly provide important benefits to both consumers and firms. An obvious question, then, is, how are brands created? How do you "brand" a product? Although firms provide the impetus for brand creation through their marketing programs and other activities, ultimately *a brand is something that resides in the minds of consumers*. A brand is a perceptual entity rooted in reality, but it is more than that—it reflects the perceptions and perhaps even the idiosyncrasies of consumers.

To brand a product it is necessary to teach consumers "who" the product is—by giving it a name and using other brand elements to help identify it—as well as what the product does and why consumers should care. In other words, marketers must give consumers a *label* for the product ("here's how you can identify the product") and provide *meaning* for the brand ("here's what this particular product can do for you, and why it's special and different from other brand name products").

Branding creates mental structures and helps consumers organize their knowledge about products and services in a way that clarifies their decision making and, in the process, provides value to the firm. *The key to branding is that consumers perceive differences among brands in a product category*. These differences can be related to attributes or benefits of the product itself, or they may be related to more intangible image considerations.

Whenever and wherever consumers are deciding between alternatives, brands can play an important decision-making role. *Accordingly, marketers can benefit from branding whenever consumers are in a choice situation*. Given the myriad choices consumers make each and every day, it is no surprise how pervasive branding has become.

For example, consider how marketers have been able to brand what were once commodities. A ***commodity*** is a product so basic that it cannot be physically differentiated in the minds of consumers. Over the years, a number of products that at one time were seen as essentially commodities have become highly differentiated as strong brands have emerged in the category.[16] Some notable examples are: coffee (Maxwell House), bath soap (Ivory), flour (Gold Medal), beer (Budweiser), salt (Morton), oatmeal (Quaker), pickles (Vlasic), bananas (Chiquita), chickens (Perdue), pineapples (Dole), and even water (Perrier).

These products became branded in various ways. The key success factor in each case, however, was that consumers became convinced that all the product offerings in the category were not the same and that meaningful differences existed. In some instances, such as with produce, marketers convinced consumers that a product was *not* a commodity and could actually vary appreciably in quality. In these cases, the brand was seen as ensuring uniformly high quality in the product category on which consumers could depend. Intel has spent vast sums of money on its "Intel Inside" promotion to brand its microprocessors or computer chips as delivering the highest level of performance and safety or confidence possible.

In other cases, like Perrier bottled mineral water, because product differences were virtually nonexistent, brands have been created by image or other non-product-related considerations. One of the best examples of branding a commodity in this fashion is diamonds (see Branding Brief 1-2).

We can recognize the universality of branding by looking at some different product applications in the categories we defined previously—physical goods, services, retail stores, online businesses, people, organizations, places, and ideas. For each of these different types of products, we will review some basic considerations and look at examples. (We consider some of these special cases in more detail in Chapter 15.)

Physical Goods

Physical goods are what are traditionally associated with brands and include many of the best-known and highly regarded consumer products, like Coca-Cola, Mercedes-Benz, Nescafé, and Sony. As more and more different kinds of products are sold or promoted directly to consumers, the adoption of modern marketing practices and branding has spread further.

THE PHARMACEUTICAL INDUSTRY

In the United States, prescription drugs are increasingly being branded and sold to consumers with traditional marketing tactics such as advertising and promotion.[17] Direct-to-consumer advertising for prescription drugs also grew from $242 million in 1994 to $4.2 billion in 2005. In 2005, a number of pharmaceutical brands received more than $100 million in ad support; the most competitive drug categories were related to cholesterol and erectile dysfunction. AstraZeneca's acid reflux drug Nexium has been the most highly advertised in recent years, with a media budget of over $200 million for four years running.[18]

More and more companies selling industrial products or durable goods to other companies are recognizing the benefits of developing strong brands. Brands have begun to emerge among certain types of physical goods that never supported brands before. Let us consider the role of branding in industrial and technologically intensive or "high-tech" products.

Business-to-Business Products. Business-to-business branding creates a positive image and reputation for the company as a whole. Creating such goodwill with business customers is thought to lead to greater selling opportunities and more profitable

BRANDING BRIEF 1-2

Diamond Industry Creates New Niches to Increase Sales

Diamond marketers have been able to create emotional associations to their products and uncover new market segments.

De Beers Group added the phrase "A Diamond is Forever" as the tagline in its ongoing ad campaign in 1948. The diamond supplier, which was founded in 1888 and sells about 60 percent of the world's rough diamonds, wanted to attach more emotion and symbolic meaning to the purchase of diamond jewelry. "A Diamond is Forever" became one of the most recognized slogans in advertising and helped fuel a diamond jewelry industry that's now worth nearly $25 billion per year in the United States alone.

Nearly all women who get engaged receive an engagement ring. But that ring may be the only diamond ring they ever own. De Beers has faced the challenge of creating more demand for something that the company once urged customers to think of as a once-in-a-lifetime, "forever" purchase.

In 2001, De Beers used the tagline "for your past, present, and future" to increase sales of three-stone diamond rings. The company promoted three-stone rings as meaningful anniversary gifts. The goal was to turn engagement ring buyers into repeat customers—and the three-stone ring could work just as well for a three-year anniversary

relationships. A strong brand can provide valuable re-assurance to business customers who may be putting their company's fate—and perhaps their own careers!—on the line. A strong business-to-business brand can thus provide a strong competitive advantage.

Business-to-business brands are often corporate brands, so understanding branding from a corporate brand perspective is critical. Business-to-business branding is complex because there are many people involved, both on the company side and in the many different market segments the company could be targeting within and across companies. Such complexity requires adjustments in marketing programs and marketing communications. One challenge for many business-to-business brands is de-commoditizing themselves to create product and service differences. The Science of Branding 1-1 describes some particularly important guidelines for business-to-business branding.

Eaton is a business-to-business marketer that believes in the importance of marketing.

EATON

Cleveland-based Eaton Corporation is a diversified industrial manufacturer with sales of more than $12 billion through its electrical, fluid power, truck, and automotive businesses. Eaton pioneered the concept that electricity is a tangible and highly manageable resource—a Power Chain™ that can be managed to help companies, institutions, and homeowners optimize the use of electrical power. In the Fluid Power business, Eaton provides hydraulic systems and components for use in aerospace, mining, forestry, utility, and other industries.

gift as a 25-year gift. Until then, sales of the three-stone pieces had been only modest, but U.S. sales of the rings rose 74 percent in 2002.

Now De Beers wants customers to start thinking about their right hand, as well as their left. The company is succeeding in changing the perception of diamond rings as limited to engagement rings and wedding bands. It's spicing up the stagnant right-hand ring category with fashionable, affordable options.

Industry experts say De Beers isn't only hoping to expand ring sales but also striving to create a new market for the smaller diamonds that manufacturers have in abundance, as consumers favor increasingly bigger diamonds for engagement rings. Aimed at 30- to 54-year-old women with household incomes of more than $100,000, the right-hand rings are usually platinum, with multiple diamonds and open space in the design that is intended to make the rings look bigger without pumping up the cost. Vertical designs distinguish right-hand rings from solitaire engagement rings worn on the left hand.

Ads for right-hand rings launched in 2003 include statements capturing the symbolism of right and left hands. One declares, "Your left hand says 'we.' Your right hand says 'me.'" All the ads end with the tagline, "Women of the World, Raise Your Right Hand." The print ads, created by The Diamond Trading Company, De Beers's London-based marketing arm, feature 16 different right-hand ring designs.

Sources: Sandra O'Loughlin, "Sparkler on the Other Hand," *Brandweek,* 19 April 2004; Blythe Yee, "Ads Remind Women They Have *Two* Hands," *Wall Street Journal*, 14 August 2003; Lauren Weber, "De Beers to Open First U.S. Retail Store," *Newsday*, 22 June 2005.

The truck business produces intelligent drivetrain systems for safety and fuel economy, while automotive develops market-moving innovations that deliver improved fuel economy, safety, and performance. An important part of Eaton's business focus is to develop products that help customers protect the environment by conserving energy, reducing emissions, and managing resources.

Eaton sells literally tens of thousands of products to customers around the world. It carefully segments each market and identifies all the relevant parties in a buying decision to understand their differing needs and wants. Eaton's brand strategy emphasizes the strength of the corporate brand with distinctive attributes that customers find important for all its products and services—innovation, professionalism, involvement, quality, reliability, and integrity. In focusing on critical competencies, Eaton's brand strategy speaks to the company's particular way of interacting with customers—as a whole and business unit by business unit—which helps to build relationships beyond products and pricing.

High-Tech Products. Many technology companies have struggled with branding. Managed by technologists, they often lack any kind of brand strategy and sometimes see branding as simply naming their products. In many of their markets, however, financial success is no longer driven by product innovation alone, or by the latest and greatest product specifications and features. Marketing skills are playing an increasingly important role in the adoption and success of high-tech products.

THE SCIENCE OF BRANDING 1-1

Understanding Business-to-Business Branding

1. ***The role and importance of branding should be tied directly into the industrial marketer's business/profit model and value-delivery strategy.*** The starting point for the business model should be the firm's distinctive competence, its target market and customers, its position in the value chain, and its strategy for delivering superior value to those chosen customers.
2. ***Understand the role of the brand in the organizational buying process.*** Use market research to identify the composition of the buying center (decision-making unit) and the decision criteria used by the organization members who occupy the key roles in the decision-making unit.
3. ***Be sure the basic value proposition has relevance for all significant players in the decision-making unit and decision-making process.*** There will be many people involved in any buying decision and they all must find the brand promise both relevant and responsive to their needs and concerns.
4. ***Emphasize a corporate branding approach.*** It is important to remember the importance of the buyer-seller relationship and the central role played by the buyer's corporate credibility and reliability.
5. ***Build the corporate brand around brand intangibles.*** Maximize expertise, trustworthiness, ease of doing business, and likeability as a means to establish corporate credibility, reputation, and distinctiveness.[19]
6. ***Avoid confusing corporate communication strategy and brand strategy and carefully manage the relationship between the two sets of activities to avoid potential conflict.*** The focus of brand strategy should be on the brand as a strategic entity and what it means for the customer, not on the broader issues of corporate citizenship that may or not be relevant for buyers.

INTUIT

Intuit makes the highly successful Quicken personal-finance software package. In discussing the origins of his company, Intuit's founder Scott Cook comments: "We started with the belief that it is a consumer market, not a technology market. We'd run it like Procter & Gamble."[20] Applying classic package-goods marketing techniques, Intuit first conducted extensive research with consumers and then designed a product to satisfy the unmet needs and wants of the market. Because research revealed that most consumers did not like doing financial management and found it a necessary evil, Intuit designed the Quicken software package to offer two key benefits—ease of use and speed—that were not currently offered by other products in the market.

The speed and brevity of technology product life cycles cause unique branding challenges. Trust is critical, and customers often buy into companies as much as products. CEOs of technology companies can become dominant components of their brands, as did Apple's Steve Jobs, Microsoft's Bill Gates, and Cisco's John Chambers. Marketing

7. ***Apply detailed segmentation analysis within and across industry-defined segments, based on differences in the composition and functioning of buying centers within those segments.*** Brand positioning within those sub-segments must then be tailored to the unique needs of the individuals in those segments but, just as importantly, must build upon and be consistent with the overall corporate brand positioning.
8. ***Build brand communications around the interactive effects of multiple media,*** recognizing that: (a) budgets are usually smaller than in consumer marketing; (b) "mass" media are likely to be very limited in terms of reach and availability; and (c) specialized media such as industry trade shows, educational activities, and professional journals may be most effective in reaching specific sub-segments of buyers within customer organizations.
9. ***Adopt a top-down and bottom-up brand management approach. Top-down brand management*** involves marketing activities that capture the "big picture" and recognize the possible synergies across products and markets to brand products accordingly. ***Bottom-up brand management,*** on the other hand, requires that marketing managers primarily direct their marketing activities to maximize brand equity for individual products for particular business units and markets.
10. ***Educate all members of the organization as to the value of branding and their role in delivering brand value.*** Whereas a few individuals may be responsible for developing brand strategy, the whole organization is responsible for its implementation. Industrial products and brands are likely to have multiple customer "touch points," each of which must be managed consistently with the brand image.

Source: Kevin Lane Keller and Frederick E. Webster, Jr., "A Roadmap for Branding in Industrial Markets," *Journal of Brand Management* 11 (May 2004): 388–402.

budgets may be small, although high-tech firms' adoption of package-goods marketing techniques has increased expenditures on mass market advertising. The Science of Branding 1-2 provides a set of guidelines for marketing managers at high-tech companies. (Chapter 15 also considers aspects of high-tech branding in greater detail.)

Services

Although strong service brands like American Express, British Airways, Hilton Hotels, Merrill Lynch, and Federal Express have existed for years, the pervasiveness of service branding and its sophistication have accelerated in the past decade. As Interbrand's John Murphy noted, "In the last 30 years, some of the greatest branding successes have come in the area of services." Branding Brief 1-3 describes the ascent of the Southwest Airlines brand.

One of the challenges in marketing services is that they are less tangible than products and more likely to vary in quality, depending on the particular person or people

THE SCIENCE OF BRANDING 1-2

Understanding High-Tech Branding

Marketers operating in technologically intensive markets face a number of unique challenges, for example, an accelerated product life cycle due to continual R&D advances and innovations. Here are 10 guidelines that managers for high-tech companies can use to improve their company's brand strategy

1. ***It is important to have a brand strategy that provides a roadmap for the future.*** Technology companies too often rely on the faulty assumption that the best product based on the best technology will sell itself. As the market failure of the Sony Betamax illustrates, the company with the best technology does not always win.
2. ***Understand your brand hierarchy and manage it appropriately over time.*** A strong corporate brand is vital in the technology industry to provide stability and help to establish a presence on Wall Street. Since product innovations provide the growth drivers for technology companies, however, brand equity is sometimes built in the product name to the detriment of corporate brand equity.
3. ***Know who your customer is and build an appropriate brand strategy.*** Many technology companies understand that when corporate customers purchase business-to-business products or services, they are typically committing to a long-term relationship. For this reason, it is advisable for technology companies to establish a strong corporate brand that will endure over time.
4. ***Realize that building brand equity and selling products are two different exercises.*** Too often, the emphasis on developing products leads to an overemphasis on branding them. When a company applies distinct brand names to too many products in rapid succession, the brand portfolio becomes cluttered and consumers may lose perspective on the brand hierarchy. Rather than branding each new innovation separately, a better approach is to plan for future innovations by developing an extendable branding strategy.
5. ***Brands are owned by customers, not engineers.*** In high-tech firms, CEOs in many cases work their way up the ladder through the engineering divisions. Although engineers have an intimate knowledge of products and technology, they may lack the big-picture brand view. Compounding this problem is the fact that technology companies typically

providing them. For that reason, branding can be particularly important to service firms as a way to address intangibility and variability problems. Brand symbols may also be especially important, because they help to make the abstract nature of services more concrete. Brands can help to identify and provide meaning to the different services provided by a firm. For example, branding has become especially important in financial services, to help organize and label the myriad new offerings in a manner that consumers can understand.

Branding a service can also be an effective way to signal to consumers that the firm has designed a particular service offering that is special and deserving of its name. For

spend less on consumer research compared with other types of companies. As a result of these factors, tech companies often do not invest in building strong brands.

6. ***Brand strategies need to account for the attributes of the CEO and adjust accordingly.*** Many of the world's top technology companies have highly visible CEOs, especially compared with other industries. Some notable high-tech CEOs with prominent public personas include Oracle's Larry Ellison, Apple's Steve Jobs, Cisco's John Chambers, and Dell's Michael Dell. In each case, the CEO's identity and persona are inextricably woven into the fabric of the brand.
7. ***Brand building on a small budget necessitates leveraging every possible positive association.*** Technology companies typically prioritize their marketing mix as follows, in order from most important to least important: industry analyst relations, public relations, trade shows, seminars, direct mail, and advertising. Often, direct mail and advertising are discretionary items in a company's marketing budget and may in fact receive no outlay.
8. ***Technology categories are created by customers and external forces, not by companies themselves.*** In their quest for product differentiation, new technology companies have a tendency to reinvent the wheel and claim they have created a new category. Yet only two groups can truly create categories: analysts and customers. For this reason, it is important for technology companies to manage their relationships with analysts in order to attract consumers.
9. ***The rapidly changing environment demands that you stay in tune with your internal and external environment.*** The rapid pace of innovation in the technology sector dictates that marketers closely observe the market conditions in which their brands do business. Trends in brand strategy and marketing change almost as rapidly as the technology.
10. ***Invest the time to understand the technology and value proposition and do not be afraid to ask questions.*** It is important for technology marketers to ask questions in order to educate themselves and build credibility with the company's engineering corps and with customers. To build trust among engineers and customers, marketers must strive to learn as much as they can about the technology.

Source: Patrick Tickle, Kevin Lane Keller, and Keith Richey, "Branding in High-Technology Markets," *Market Leader* 22 (Autumn 2003): 21–26.

example, British Airways not only branded its premium business class service as "Club Class"; it also branded its regular coach service as "World Traveler," a clever way to communicate to the airline's regular passengers that they are also special in some way and that their patronage is not taken for granted. Branding has clearly become a competitive weapon for services.

Retailers and Distributors

To retailers and other channel members distributing products, brands provide a number of important functions. Brands can generate consumer interest, patronage, and loyalty in a

BRANDING BRIEF 1-3

Flying High with the Southwest Airlines Brand

Southwest Airlines instills tremendous customer loyalty.

Southwest Airlines, originally called Air Southwest, was founded by Texans Rollin King and Herb Kelleher in 1967. Southwest started as a commuter carrier with flights between Dallas, Houston, and San Antonio, but today it operates in 55 cities across the nation. Southwest is famous for its cheap fares and no-frills service. Seats on its planes are all the same class, and the in-flight service offers neither movies nor meals.

Southwest knew from an early stage that it could not differentiate on price alone, because competitors could easily muscle into the market with their own cheaper versions. To promote customer loyalty, the airline sought to create a unique flying experience for its customers. Early flights featured Jet Bunnies—flight attendants dressed in hot pants and go-go boots—who served beverages known as Love Potions and snacks called Love Bites. Southwest encouraged its pilots and cabin crew members to entertain the passengers with jokes and snappy patter during in-flight announcements.

store, as consumers learn to expect certain brands and products. To the extent "you are what you sell," brands help retailers create an image and establish positioning. Retailers can also create their own brand image by attaching unique associations to the quality of their service, their product assortment and merchandising, and their pricing and credit policy. Finally, the appeal and attraction of brands, whether manufacturers' brands or the retailers' own brands, can yield higher price margins, increased sales volumes, and greater profits.

Retailers can introduce their own brands by using their store name, creating new names, or some combination of the two. Many distributors, especially in Europe, have actually introduced their own brands, which they sell in addition to—or sometimes even instead of—manufacturers' brands. Products bearing these ***store brands*** or ***private label*** brands offer another way for retailers to increase customer loyalty and generate higher margins and profits. In Britain, five or six grocery chains selling their own brands account for roughly half the country's food and packaged-goods sales, led by Sainsbury and Tesco. Another top British retailer, Marks & Spencer, sells only its own-brand goods, under the label St. Michael. Several U.S. retailers also emphasize their own brands. Branding Brief 1-4 describes some of the branding developments at Wal-Mart. (Chapter 5 considers store brands and private labels in greater detail.)

One of the company's early recruitment bulletins specified that applicants should have a sense of humor. Even CEO Herb Kelleher got into the act. On several occasions, Kelleher donned an Elvis Presley costume to meet passengers at the gate, and once on an Easter flight he served drinks and snacks while dressed in a bunny suit. Another passenger-pleasing feature of Southwest flights is the first-come, first-served open seating, whereby passengers are given numbered cards that reflect the boarding order based on when they arrive at the gate.

Southwest's advertising has always been informational, yet inflected with humor at the same time. For several years, the airline has used as its tagline a clever play on the standard message from a captain telling passengers they are free to move about the plane's cabin. Southwest's version, which emphasizes its national route coverage, declares, "You are now free to move about the country." Recent ads highlighted Southwest's low fares with humorous television spots in which a character commits some egregious social blunder, after which a voiceover asks "Wanna Get Away?"

Today, Southwest is the nation's fourth-largest airline, flying nearly 3,300 daily flights to 63 cities in 32 states. It holds the distinction of being the only low-fare airline to achieve long-term success. By offering a low-cost, convenient, and customer-friendly alternative to major carriers, Southwest has attracted passengers in droves and, after its first profitable year in 1969, achieved profitability in each of the 37 years that followed.

Sources: Jane Woolridge, "Baby-Boom Airline Is Unknown, Cheap," *San Diego Union-Tribune*, 30 December 1984; Katrina Brooker, "The Chairman of the Board Looks Back," *Fortune*, 28 May 2001; Wendy Zellner, "Holding Steady," *BusinessWeek*, 3 February 2003, 66–68.

Online Products and Services

The number of people in the United States with access to the Internet from their homes surpassed 75 percent of the population in 2004. Other countries have experienced similarly rapid adoption. The end of the twentieth century saw an unprecedented headlong rush by new and existing businesses to create online brands. Quickly, these businesses learned the complexities and challenges of the task.

Many online marketers made serious—and sometimes fatal—mistakes during this heady time. Some oversimplified the branding process, equating flashy or unusual advertising with building a brand. Although such marketing efforts sometimes caught consumers' attention, more often than not, they failed to create awareness of what products or services the brand represented, why those products or services were unique or different, and most important, why consumers should buy the brand.

What realities of brand building did online marketers miss? First, as for any brand, it is critical to create unique aspects of the brand on some dimension important to consumers, such as convenience, price, variety, and so forth. At the same time, the brand needs to perform satisfactorily in other areas, such as customer service, credibility, and personality. For instance, customers increasingly began to demand higher levels of service both during and after their Web site visits. As a consequence, to be competitive, many firms have had to improve their online service by making customer service agents

BRANDING BRIEF 1-4

Branding the Wal-Mart Way

Wal-Mart, which first opened in Rogers, Arkansas, in 1962, is the world's number-one retailer, with more than 5,700 stores, including some 1,350 discount stores, nearly 2,000 combination discount and grocery stores (Wal-Mart Supercenters in the United States and ASDA in the United Kingdom), and 550 warehouse stores (Sam's Club). Wal-Mart's founder, Sam Walton, sought to build conveniently located retail outlets that offered wide selection, low prices, and quality customer service.

Wal-Mart is one of the most powerful and successful retailer brands.

Wal-Mart's low prices have always been a key to pleasing consumers. The chain innovated the everyday-low-pricing strategy popular in many retail stores. The slogan "We Sell for Less. Always" illustrates Wal-Mart's dedication to underselling the competition. Its reputation for friendly service is another way the company creates customer satisfaction. At the

available in real time, shipping products promptly and providing tracking updates, and adopting liberal return policies.[21] Such improvements have been critical to overcoming the low opinion some customers had about online businesses' service. Successful online brands were those that were well positioned and found unique ways to satisfy consumers' unmet needs.

GOOGLE

Founded in 1998 by two Stanford University Ph.D. students, the search engine Google takes its name from a play on the word *googol*—the number 1 followed by 100 zeroes—a reference to the huge amount of data online. Google's stated mission is "To organize the world's information and make it universally accessible and useful." The company has become the market leader in the search engine industry through its business focus and constant innovation. Its home page focuses on searches alone and is not cluttered with other services, as are many other portals. By focusing on plain text, avoiding pop-up ads, and using sophisticated search algorithms, Google provides fast and reliable service. By September 2006, it was the Internet's most-used search engine, performing almost half of all searches. Google's revenue is driven by search ads, little text-based boxes that advertisers pay for only when users click on them.[22]

Online brands also learned the importance of off-line activities to draw customers to Web sites, and many of the most successful business ventures came about when off-line brands like Pampers diapers, British Airways, and the *New York Times* leveraged their strong reputations and marketing muscle online. Home page Web addresses, or URLs, began to

entrances to its stores, Wal-Mart stations "people greeters" who welcome and assist customers. The company employs helpful and knowledgeable sales associates who are positioned throughout the store to answer questions and help customers find items. These gestures foster trust: According to a company survey that asked,' "What does Wal-Mart mean to you?" more customers responded "trust" than "low prices."

A less well-known contributor to the company's success is its implementation of sophisticated logistics. Sam Walton was something of a visionary when it came to logistics. He had the foresight to realize, as early as the 1960s, that the company growth he was striving for required the installation of advanced information systems to manage the volumes of merchandise. By 1998, Wal-Mart's computer database was second only to the Pentagon's in terms of capacity. One business writer recently proclaimed Wal-Mart to be "the king of store logistics."

Wal-Mart today bears little resemblance to the Arkansas store that started it all. The company is an indelible part of the U.S. retail landscape, and has expanded into South America and Europe. Wal-Mart's annual sales in 2005 reached a colossal $316 billion, earning the company the top spot in the Fortune 500 ranking.

Sources: Wendy Zelner, "Someday, Lee, This May All Be Yours," *Business Week*, 15 November 1999; Wendy Zelner, "Will WalMart.com Get It Right This Time?" *Business Week*, 6 November 2000; Anthony Bianco and Wendy Zellner, "Is Wal-Mart Too Powerful," *Business Week*, 6 October 2003; Aaron Bernstein, "Wal-Mart Under Attack," *Business Week*, 20 October 2005.

appear on all collateral and marketing material. Partnerships became critical as online brands developed networks of online partners and links. Online marketers also began to target specific customer groups—often geographically widely dispersed—for which the brand could offer unique value propositions. Web site designs have finally begun to maximize the benefits of interactivity, customization, and timeliness and the advantages of being able to inform, persuade, and sell all at the same time. Branding Brief 1-5 describes how Amazon.com has built a strong online brand. (Chapter 6 examines Web site and interactive advertising issues.)

People and Organizations

The naming aspect of branding, at least, is generally straightforward when the product category is people and organizations. These often have well-defined images that are easily understood and liked (or disliked) by others. That's particularly true for public figures such as politicians, entertainers, and professional athletes. All these compete in some sense for public approval and acceptance, and all benefit from conveying a strong and desirable image.

Paul Newman has parlayed his engaging image to brand a number of products whose sales benefit social causes.

PAUL NEWMAN

Legendary actor Paul Newman has translated his likable, down-to-earth image into a multi-million-dollar business. Newman's Own was launched after many of the actor's friends and neighbors requested more of the special-recipe salad dressing he made and gave as gifts. Since then, the brand has extended into pasta sauce, salsa, steak sauce, lemonade, and popcorn. As sole owner, Newman donates all profits and royalties after taxes to educational

BRANDING BRIEF 1-5

Building the Amazon.com Brand

Jeffrey Bezos left his job on Wall Street as a hedge fund manager in 1994 to return to his home in suburban Seattle and found online retailer Amazon.com, despite the fact that he had no previous retail experience. Bezos did, however, have a vision of making Amazon.com "the earth's biggest bookstore." Within a year of opening, Amazon.com offered a selection of more than one million book titles, which made it the world's largest book broker.

In addition to offering unparalleled selection, Bezos also wanted Amazon.com to provide a unique shopping experience and the highest level of customer service. He aimed for Amazon.com to be "the world's most customer-centric company." To this end, the site was designed so that when shoppers viewed a book title, a list of related titles that might interest them would instantly appear on the same Web page. For customers that submitted information on their favorite authors and subjects, Amazon.com sent them periodic recommendations and reviews via e-mail. Another personal touch included the development of personalized front pages that opened whenever registered customers visited the site. Of these customized features, Bezos said, "We want Amazon.com to be the right store for you as an individual. If we have 4.5 million customers, we should have 4.5 million stores." To further promote goodwill among its customers, Amazon.com automatically upgraded many of its orders to priority shipping at no extra cost. These consumer-focused efforts yielded the desired results: In 1998, over 60 percent of orders on the site were from repeat customers.

and charity purposes, totaling $150 million since 1982. He also founded the Hole in the Wall Gang Camp to allow children with cancer or serious blood diseases to have a normal summer camp experience free of charge. Considering his corporate slogan, "Shameless Exploitation in Pursuit of the Common Good," it's not surprising that Newman says on his company Web site, "It started out as a joke and got out of control."

That's not to say that only the well-known or famous can be thought of as a brand. Certainly, one key for a successful career in almost any area is that co-workers, superiors, or even important people outside the company know who you are and your skills, talents, attitude, and so forth. By building up a name and reputation in a business context, you are essentially creating your own brand.[23] The right awareness and image can be invaluable in shaping the way people treat you and interpret your words, actions, and deeds.[24]

Similarly, organizations often take on meanings through their programs, activities, and products. Nonprofit organizations such as the Sierra Club, the American Red Cross, Amnesty International, and UNICEF have increasingly emphasized marketing.

NATIONAL GEOGRAPHIC

Founded in 1888 by 33 highly regarded scientists, the National Geographic Society is a nonprofit scientific and educational membership organization with a mission related to "the increase and diffusion of geographic knowledge."[25] The distinctive yellow border it uses is one of the world's most recognizable brand symbols. The Society's products include

Much of Amazon.com's early growth was credited to word-of-mouth sources such as testimonials from satisfied customers and media stories. Before long, Amazon.com had top-of-mind awareness among consumers looking to buy products online. As one industry analyst said in 1998, "When you think of Web shopping, you think of Amazon first." The company's ad spending was small compared with other dot-coms: During the fourth quarter of 1998, Amazon.com spent $3.7 million, most of which went to radio commercials. The company began advertising more extensively the following year, when it spent $50 million on a series of holiday-themed advertisements.

Once the bookselling strategy had proved successful, Amazon.com expanded into other product categories, such as CDs, videos, and gifts. Between 1998 and 2001, the site added numerous other product categories including baby products, electronics, kitchen and housewares, tools and hardware, toys, and even barbecues. During that time, the company also expanded its global reach by establishing sister sites in the United Kingdom, Germany, France, Japan, Spain, and Austria. Bezos declared his company's intention of providing "the earth's biggest selection." With more than 29 million customers and about $8.5 billion in annual sales in 2005, the Amazon.com brand is stronger than ever.

Sources: www.amazon.com; Alice Z. Cuneo, "Amazon Unleashes $50 Million for the Holidays," *Advertising Age*, 15 November 1999; Rachel Beck, "Amazon.com Moves Beyond Books and Music with Gift Shop, Video Launch," AP Newswire, 17 November 1998; Robert D. Hof, "Amazon.com: The Wild World of E-commerce," *Business Week*, 14 December 1998.

National Geographic magazines, books, maps, television shows, and gift items. The National Geographic Channel, launched in January 2001, ranks as one of the more desired networks, according to viewer surveys. With a tagline, "Dare to Explore," the channel showcases science, technology, and history in addition to its traditional emphasis on natural history and a stable of explorers, scientists, and photographers. Its companion Web site has won many awards. National Geographic Enterprises includes licensing, a catalog business, travel expeditions, e-commerce, and retail. These units oversee the merchandise related to the National Geographic brand worldwide. All National Geographic's net proceeds from licensing support vital exploration, conservation, research, and education programs.

Sports, Arts, and Entertainment

A special case of marketing people and organizations as brands exists in the sports, arts, and entertainment industries. Sports marketing has become highly sophisticated in recent years, employing traditional package-goods techniques. No longer content to allow won-loss records to dictate attendance levels and financial fortunes, many sports teams are marketing themselves through a creative combination of advertising, promotions, sponsorship, direct mail, and other forms of communication. By building awareness, image, and loyalty, these sports franchises are able to meet ticket sales targets regardless of what their team's actual performance might turn out to be. Brand symbols and logos in particular have become an important financial contributor to professional sports through licensing agreements. Branding Brief 1-6 describes how Manchester United built a powerhouse soccer team—and a powerful brand.

BRANDING BRIEF 1-6

Building a Brand Winner with Manchester United

Manchester United, the wealthiest soccer club in the English League (the club is valued at $750 million) and one of the most popular sports organizations in the world, has a tradition of winning on the field and in the business world. The club was founded in 1878 and reached the pinnacle of sport with two consecutive English League titles in the 1950s. A tragic plane crash in 1958 that killed seven players gave the club international attention. In 1968, a rebuilt team won another European title. It was not until the 1990s, however, that Manchester United grew into its current role as one of the most popular and lucrative sports franchises in the world. In 1999, a year in which the team won a "treble"—three major English and European soccer titles—its stock market value surpassed $2 billion.

One sports brand that engenders tremendous consumer loyalty is Manchester United.

Branding plays an especially valuable function in the arts and entertainment industries that bring us movies, television, music, and books. These offerings are good examples of experience goods: Prospective buyers cannot judge quality by inspection and must use cues such as the particular people involved, the concept or rationale behind the project, and word-of-mouth and critical reviews.

Think of a movie as a product whose "ingredients" are the plots, actors, and director.[26] Certain movie titles such as *Austin Powers*, *Batman*, and *Harry Potter* have established themselves as strong brands by combining all these ingredients into a formula that appeals to consumers and allows the studios to release sequels (essentially brand extensions) that rely on the title's initial popularity. For years, some of the most valuable movie franchises have featured recurring characters or ongoing stories, and many of the successful recent films have been sequels. Their success is due to the fact that moviegoers know from the title and the actors, producers, directors, and other contributors that they can expect certain things—a classic application of branding.

Star Wars

When the first Star Wars movie opened on May 25, 1977, the movie licensing industry barely existed. But by the release of the final episode in the series, *Star Wars: Episode III—Revenge of the Sith*, *Star Wars* merchandising had generated a staggering $9 billion in retail sales,

Television is credited with much of Manchester United's financial success. With the advent of satellite television in recent years, fans all over the world can enjoy live coverage of all the best matches. Soccer was already a global game played on every inhabited continent, but the game's visibility has never been higher as a result of this increased media coverage. One analyst described Manchester United's recent financial fortunes as follows, "Basically, they got really lucky. The success on the field has coincided with the success of soccer as pure media content." As one of the most successful club teams in the 1990s, Manchester United received a large share of this burgeoning media coverage.

The club's visibility, combined with its accomplishments, has won it legions of foreign fans. In addition to roughly 7.3 million fans in Britain, Manchester United estimates it has 75 million fans worldwide, with growing interest in Asia. Although soccer is not nearly as popular in the United States as in other countries—the number of people playing soccer has held steady at 18 million for a decade—American companies have shown an increased interest in Manchester United. In 2001, the club signed a $500 million, 13-year licensing deal with Nike. But when an American, Malcolm Glazer, purchased the team for $1.5 billion in 2005, a storm of protest from local fans ensued. Their loyalties were further tested later that year when the team failed to qualify for the Champions League or even the UEFA playoffs.

Sources: Bill Glauber, "Meet Manchester United Marketing," *Baltimore Sun*, 19 March 2001; Andy Dworkin, "Nike Scores Soccer Sponsorship," *Portland Oregonian*, 7 November 2000; "Red Devil," *The Economist*, 21 May 2005, 70; and Laura Cohn, "Can Glazer Put This Ball in the Net," *BusinessWeek*, 30 May 2005, 40.

almost triple the movies' worldwide box office of $3.4 billion. The force was also certainly with the final *Star Wars* film, as Lucas Licensing had deals with about 400 licensees in more than 30 countries covering thousands of products, with expected proceeds of an additional $1.5 billion. The licensing success of Stars Wars transformed the toy industry too, making it more focused on television and film entertainment properties.[27]

A strong brand is valuable in the entertainment industry because of the fervent feelings that names generate as a result of pleasurable past experiences. A new album release from Walter Becker and Donald Fagen would probably not have caused a ripple in the marketplace, but when *Two Against Nature* was hailed as coming from Steely Dan (their original band), the album won four Grammy awards and achieved platinum sales status.

Geographic Locations

Increased mobility of both people and businesses, and growth in the tourism industry, have contributed to the rise of place marketing. Cities, states, regions, and countries are now actively promoted through advertising, direct mail, and other communication tools. These campaigns aim to create awareness and a favorable image of a location that will entice temporary visits or permanent moves from individuals and businesses alike. The brand name is usually preordained by the name of the location. Branding Brief 1-7 describes how the city of Las Vegas has marketed itself.

A strong entertainment brand like Star Wars has numerous licensing opportunities.

BRANDING BRIEF 1-7

Ad Campaigns Entice Visitors with a Glimpse of Freedom, Fun

Las Vegas has cultivated a reputation as an exciting adult playground, and promoters have tried to capture that reputation to lure visitors. With the opening of family-friendly hotels such as the MGM, Treasure Island, and Excalibur in the mid-1990s, Las Vegas tried to move in on the family resort business and tested the catch-all ad theme: "It's anything and everything." The theme accurately represented what the city had become, but other tourism destinations tried to make the same claim in varying ways so the line was not singularly differentiating. After 9/11, the pitch focused on the city's emerging restaurant and resorts scene with "What you want. When you want." That campaign fell flat, too.

Las Vegas has been very successfully marketed as a visitor destination.

Prior to 9/11, we actually did an extensive brand planning exercise to determine a singularly defining and relevant positioning. The outcome of that effort was the positioning of "Adult Freedom—a place where you can do things you couldn't or wouldn't do at home." Essentially, the challenge was to portray the Las Vegas experience as something completely different from anywhere else. The line "What You Want, When You Want" was the first campaign from this new positioning. The effort did not fall flat—in fact, we saw a very positive response in consumer awareness and perception analysis, and visitor levels still rose. However, while these campaigns helped raise visitor levels, the line still lacked the resonance and impact we were looking for. There is successful, and there is wildly successful—we were going for the latter.

Immediately after 9/11, we developed a campaign that was a variation of the Adult Freedom positioning called "It's Time for You"—research told us that people needed a break, and that they needed to be told it was okay for them to take one. This campaign ran for only a short time after the tragic event—and simply invited "you" to take some time.

Ideas and Causes

Finally, numerous ideas and causes have been branded, especially by nonprofit organizations. They may be captured in a phrase or slogan and even be represented by a symbol, such as AIDS ribbons. By making ideas and causes more visible and concrete, branding can provide much value. As Chapter 11 describes, cause marketing increasingly relies on sophisticated marketing practices to inform or persuade consumers about the issues surrounding a cause. Branding Brief 1-8 describes the activities of the World Wildlife Fund.

"What Happens Here, Stays Here" (WHHSH) was the second campaign we developed based on the Adult Freedom positioning. We weren't just looking to change perceptions—we were attempting to change the actual behavior associated with the vacation experience. If Las Vegas stood for Adult Freedom—we wanted to give visitors *permission* to enjoy and indulge. WHHSH is implicitly permissive, even encouraging, to visitors, challenging them to make the most of their experience and push their personal boundaries.

WHHSH, while provocative in its execution, is really very individualistic—its meaning is derived from the viewer; for one person pushing their boundaries might be going to sleep at midnight when they're usually in bed by nine. The formula for the campaign is to never tell the complete story—to allow the viewer to inject their own experience and interpretation based on that.

On "Vegas Alibi"

We developed this campaign for two primary reasons—first, the opening of the Wynn Hotel in 2005 signified a new era for Las Vegas with an explosion of investment in the destination. Billions of dollars of investment were being put into the market for new hotels, high-end shopping, world-class dining, and new entertainment offerings. WHHSH was designed for one thing—to get people excited about Las Vegas—but not necessarily to tell this *product* story.

Secondly, we found that consumer awareness of this new growth was limited. We conducted a research program to determine the *depth* of consumer knowledge and its relationship with their desire to visit the city. We came up with a new proprietary research model called "Vegas IQ" that not only provided a market-by-market indication of how "smart" people are about Las Vegas but also showed if we can *raise their IQ*, we could increase propensity to travel to the destination.

"Vegas Alibi" was the campaign designed to address this need—but do so in a way that wouldn't conflict or otherwise derail the highly successful WHHSH. "Alibi" actually complements WHHSH—if what happens here truly stays here, what are you going to tell people when you get home? We also address the product knowledge challenge with a highly aggressive PR program and initiated a multi-faceted branded entertainment/integration program that inserted Las Vegas product into television shows, movies, and other popular entertainment.

Sources: Michael McCarthy, "Vegas Goes Back to Naughty Roots," *USA Today,* 11 April 2005; Julie Dunn, "Vegas Hopes for Payoff with Denverites," *The Denver Post,* 16 June 2005; John M. Broder, "The Pied Piper of Las Vegas Seems to Have Perfect Pitch," *The New York Times,* 4 June 2004; www.visitlasvegas.com.

What Are the Strongest Brands?

It's clear from these examples that virtually anything can be and has been branded. Which brands are the strongest, that is, the best-known or most highly regarded? Figure 1-5 reveals *Business Week*'s ranking of the world's 25 most valuable brands in 2005 based on Interbrand's brand valuation methodology (see Chapter 10).

We can easily find some of the best known brands by simply walking down a supermarket aisle. It's also easy to identify a number of other brands with amazing staying power that have been market leaders in their categories for decades. According to research

BRANDING BRIEF 1-8

Branding a Cause: World Wildlife Fund

The World Wildlife Fund (WWF), founded in 1961, is today the world's largest private organization dedicated to nature conservation. The WWF boasts more than 4.7 million supporters in 100 countries. Its familiar logo, which depicts a panda, represents its enduring efforts to protect that species.

In the United States, its annual budget does not allow for lavish marketing expenditures, so the WWF relies primarily on direct marketing campaigns to bring its message to the public and solicit contributions. One recent mailing offered recipients a chance to win one of several trips, including an African safari and an Alaskan cruise, in a sweepstakes.

The WWF also earns revenue through corporate partnerships. It offers four different business partnership options:

1. *Conservation Partner:* Major global sponsorship from multinational corporations; partners include Canon and Ogilvy & Mather.
2. *Corporate Supporter:* Financial or in-kind support from medium or large corporations; supporters include INRA and Delverde
3. *Corporate Club:* Support from environmentally aware local businesses; only offered in Hungary, Russia, Poland, and United Arab Emirates.
4. *Product Licensing:* Corporate licensing agreements to use WWF trademarks. Groth AG manufactures WWF branded stamps and coins and IBTT BV makes toy animals bearing the WWF panda logo.

To help spread its message, the WWF developed a Web site. The site contains pages for its national chapters, membership information, updates on current environmental issues, and information on special WWF projects. In 2000, the Web Marketing Association honored the site by naming it the best for any nonprofit organization on the Internet. In addition to its award-winning central Web site, the WWF developed a number of cause-specific Web sites, such as its Amazon rain forest relief site (www.worldwildlife.org/amazon) and a site dedicated to its clean water campaign (www.panda.org/livingwaters).

The group changed its name to the Worldwide Fund for Nature in 1986, but it is still known by the original World Wildlife Fund name in the United States and Canada. The original name and the accompanying acronym became a source of controversy when the WWF sued the World Wrestling Federation in 2001 over use of the initials WWF. The major point of contention was the similarity between the Web sites for the two organizations, because the World Wildlife Fund URL was www.wwf.org and the World Wrestling Federation used www.wwf.com. The High Court in London decided in favor of the World Wildlife Fund, giving the wildlife group exclusive rights to the WWF initials and ordering the wrestling group to abandon its Web site address.

Source: www.wwf.org; "World Wrestling Federation Loses Court Case over Rights to WWF Name," *Dow Jones Business News*, 10 August 2001.

Rank		2005 Brand Value ($ billions)	2004 Brand Value ($ billions)	Percent Change	Country of Ownership
1	Coca-Cola	67.53	67.39	0	U.S.
2	Microsoft	59.94	61.37	−2	U.S.
3	IBM	53.37	53.79	−1	U.S.
4	GE	46.97	44.11	7	U.S.
5	Intel	35.59	33.50	6	U.S.
6	Nokia	26.45	24.04	10	Finland
7	Disney	26.44	27.11	−2	U.S.
8	McDonald's	26.01	25.00	4	U.S.
9	Toyota	24.84	22.67	10	Japan
10	Marlboro	21.19	22.13	−4	U.S.
11	Mercedes	20.01	21.33	−6	Germany
12	Citibank	19.97	19.97	0	U.S.
13	Hewlett-Packard	18.87	20.98	−10	U.S.
14	American Express	18.56	17.68	5	U.S.
15	Gillette	17.53	16.72	5	U.S.
16	BMW	17.13	15.89	8	Germany
17	Cisco	16.59	15.95	4	U.S.
18	Louis Vuitton	16.08	NA	NA	France
19	Honda	15.79	14.87	6	Japan
20	Samsung	14.96	12.55	19	S. Korea
21	Dell	13.23	11.5	15	U.S.
22	Ford	13.16	14.48	−9	U.S.
23	Pepsi	12.24	11.89	3	U.S.
24	Nescafé	13.25	13.68	3	Switzerland
25	Merrill Lynch	12.02	11.50	5	U.S.

Source: Robert Berner and David Kiley, "Global Brands," *Business Week*, 1 August 2005, 86–94.

FIGURE 1-5

Business Week's Twenty-Five Most Valuable Global Brands

by marketing consultant Jack Trout, in 25 popular product categories, 20 of the leading brands in 1923 are still leading brands today—only five have lost their leadership position (see Figure 1-6).[28]

Similarly, many brands that were number one in the United Kingdom in 1933 also remain strong today: Hovis bread, Stork margarine, Kellogg's Corn Flakes, Cadbury's chocolates, Gillette razors, Schweppes mixers, Brooke Bond tea, Colgate toothpaste, and Hoover vacuum cleaners. These brands have evolved over the years and made a number of changes. Most of them barely resemble their original forms.

At the same time, just as many brands have lost their market leadership and, in some cases, their very existence! Winston, after years of dominance in the cigarette category, lost its leadership position to Marlboro in 1975 and now trails that brand by a large margin. Other seemingly invincible brands, such as Levi-Strauss, General Motors, Montgomery Ward, Polaroid, and Xerox, have run into difficulties and seen their market preeminence challenged or even lost.

Although some of these failures are related to factors beyond the control of the firm, such as technological advances or shifting consumer preferences, in other cases the blame could probably be placed on the actions or inaction of the marketers behind the brands. Some failed to account for changing market conditions and continued to operate with a "business as usual" attitude or, perhaps even worse, recognized that changes were necessary but reacted inadequately or inappropriately. The Science of Branding 1-3 provides some academic insights into factors affecting market leadership.

Product Categories		Leading Brands in 1923		Leading Brands of Today	
1	Bacon	1	Swift	1	Swift
2	Batteries	2	Eveready	2	Duracell
3	Breakfast cereal	3	Kellogg's Corn Flakes	3	Cheerios
4	Cameras	4	Kodak	4	Kodak
5	Canned fruit	5	Del Monte	5	Del Monte
6	Canned milk	6	Carnation	6	Carnation
7	Chewing gum	7	Wrigley's	7	Wrigley's
8	Chocolate	8	Hershey's	8	Hershey's
9	Crackers	9	Nabisco	9	Nabisco
10	Flour	10	Gold Medal	10	Gold Medal
11	Mint candies	11	Life Savers	11	Life Savers
12	Paint	12	Sherwin-Williams	12	Sherwin-Williams
13	Paper	13	Hammermill	13	Hammermill
14	Pipe tobacco	14	Prince Albert	14	Prince Albert
15	Razors	15	Gillette	15	Gillette
16	Sewing machines	16	Singer	16	Singer
17	Shirts	17	Manhattan	17	Arrow
18	Soap	18	Ivory	18	Dove
19	Soft drinks	19	Coca-Cola	19	Coca-Cola
20	Soup	20	Campbell's	20	Campbell's
21	Shortening	21	Crisco	21	Crisco
22	Tea	22	Lipton	22	Lipton
23	Tires	23	Goodyear	23	Goodyear
24	Toilet soap	24	Palmolive	24	Dial
25	Toothpaste	25	Colgate	25	Colgate

Source: Proprietary research by Jack Trout, based on industry share data. As summarized in Jack Trout, "Branding Can't Exist without Positioning," *Advertising Age*, 14 March 2005, 28. Reprinted with permission from the *Brand Leaders: Then and Now*. Copyright Crain Communications Inc.

FIGURE 1-6

Brand Leaders: Then and Now

The bottom line is that any brand—no matter how strong at one point in time—is vulnerable and susceptible to poor brand management. The next section discusses why it is so difficult to manage brands in today's environment. Figure 1-9 displays an analysis of fast-growing brands by leading marketing consultant firm Vivaldi Partners. Brand Focus 1.0 at the end of the chapter describes some of the historical origins of branding and brand management.

Branding Challenges and Opportunities

Although brands may be as important as ever to consumers, in reality *brand management may be more difficult than ever*. Let's look at some recent developments that have significantly complicated marketing practices and pose challenges for brand managers (see Figure 1-10).[29]

Savvy Customers

Increasingly, consumers and businesses have become more experienced with marketing, more knowledgeable about how it works, and more demanding. A well-developed media market pays increased attention to companies' marketing actions and motivations. Consumer information and support exists in the form of consumer guides (*Consumer Reports*), Web sites (Epinions.com), influential blogs, and so on. Consulting firm Brand Keys conducts annual surveys and has found that consumer expectations of what they want from brands are on average 13 percent higher than what they think brands will deliver for them, and the gap is growing.[30]

THE SCIENCE OF BRANDING 1-3

Understanding Market Leadership

The extent of the enduring nature of market leadership has been the source of much debate. According to a study by New York University's Stern School of Business Professor Peter Golder, leading brands are more likely to *lose* their leadership position over time than retain it. Golder evaluated more than 650 products in 100 categories and compared the category leaders from 1923 with the category leaders in 1997 (see Figure 1-7). His study found that only 23 of the top brands in the 100 categories remained market leaders in 1997, and 28 percent of the leading brands had failed by 1997. The clothing and fashion category experienced the greatest percentage of failures (67 percent) and had no brands that remained leaders in 1997. Leaders in the food and beverage category fared better, with 39 percent of brands maintaining leadership while only 21 percent failed.

One 1923 leader that did not maintain leadership was Underwood typewriters. Underwood's primary mistake was lack of innovation. Rather than invest in research and development, Underwood followed a harvesting strategy that sought the highest margin possible for its products. By 1950, several competitors had already invested in computer technology, whereas Underwood only acquired a small computer firm in 1952. Subsequent developments in the market further damaged Underwood's position. Between 1956 and 1961, lower-priced foreign competitors more than doubled their share of manual typewriter sales. Sales of electric typewriters, which Underwood did not make, overtook sales of manual typewriters in the early 1960s. Olivetti acquired Underwood in the mid-1960s, and the brand name was dropped in the 1980s.

Golder uses Wrigley, which has dominated the chewing gum market for nine decades, as an example of a long-term leader. According to Golder, Wrigley's success is based on three factors: "maintaining and building strong brands, focusing on a single product, and being in a category that has not changed much." Wrigley has consistently marketed its brand with high-profile sponsorship and advertising. It also used subsidiaries to extend into new product categories like sugarless gum and bubblegum, so as not to dilute the brand. Wrigley's sole focus on chewing gum enables the company to achieve maximum results in what is considered a mature category. During the 1990s, sales of Wrigley's products grew almost 10 percent annually. Finally, the chewing gum market is historically stable and uncomplicated. Still, Wrigley's makes considerable investments in product and packaging improvement to maintain its edge.

Golder and his co-author Gerard Tellis argue that dedication to the brand is vital for sustained brand leadership, elucidating five factors for enduring market leadership (see Figure 1-8). They comment:

> The real causes of enduring market leadership are vision and will. Enduring market leaders have a revolutionary and inspiring vision of the mass market, and they exhibit an indomitable will to realize that vision. They persist under adversity, innovate relentlessly, commit financial resources and leverage assets to realize their vision.

(*Continued*)

(*Continued*)

Category	1923 Leaders	1997 Leaders
Cleansers	Old Dutch	Comet Soft Scrub Ajax
Chewing gum	Wrigley Adams	Wrigley's Bubble Yum Bubblicious
Motorcycles	Indian Harley-Davidson	Harley-Davidson Honda Kawasaki
Five cent mint candies	Life Savers	Breath-Savers Tic Tac Certs
Peanut butter	Beech-Nut Heinz	Jif Skippy Peter Pan
Razors	Gillette Gem Ever ready	Gillette Bic Schick
Soft drinks	Coca-Cola Cliquot Club Bevo	Coca-Cola Pepsi Dr. Pepper/Cadbury
Coffee	Arbuckle's Yuban White House Hotel Astor	Folger's Maxwell House Hills Bros.
Laundry soap	Fels Naptha Octagon Kirkman	Tide Cheer Wisk
Cigarettes	Camel Fatima Pall Mall	Marlboro Winston Newport
Shoes	Douglas Walkover	Nike Reebok
Candy	Huyler's Loft Page & Shaw	Hershey M&M/Mars Nestlé
Jelly or jam	Heinz	Smucker's Welch's Kraft

Source: Used with permission of Journal of Marketing Research/American Marketing Association.

FIGURE 1-7

Brands Then and Now

Tellis and Golder identify the following five factors and rationale as the keys to enduring brand leadership.

Vision of the Mass Market
Companies with a keen eye for mass market tastes are more likely to build a broad and sustainable customer base. Although Pampers was not the market leader in the disposable diaper category during its first several years, it spent significantly on research and development in order to design an affordable and effective disposable diaper. Pampers quickly became the market leader.

Managerial Persistence
The "breakthrough" technology that can drive market leadership often requires the commitment of company resources over long periods of time. For example, JVC spent 21 years researching the VHS video recorder before launching it in 1976 and becoming a market leader.

Financial Commitment
The cost of maintaining leadership is high because of the demands for research and development and marketing. Companies that aim for short-term profitability rather than long-term leadership, as Rheingold Brewery did when it curtailed support of its Gablinger's light beer a year after the 1967 introduction of the product, are unlikely to enjoy enduring leadership.

Relentless Innovation
Due to changes in consumer tastes and competition from other firms, companies that wish to maintain leadership positions must continually innovate. Gillette, both a long-term leader and historically an innovator, typically has at least 20 shaving products on the drawing board at any given time.

Asset Leverage
Companies can become leaders in some categories if they hold a leadership position in a related category. For instance, Coca-Cola leveraged its success and experience with cola (Coke) and diet cola (Tab) to introduce Diet Coke in 1982. Within one year of its introduction, Diet Coke became the market leader.

Source: Gerard J. Tellis and Peter N. Golder, "First to Market, First to Fail? Real Causes of Enduring Market Leadership," *MIT Sloan Management Review*, 1 January 1996. Used by permission of the publisher.

FIGURE 1-8

Factors Determining Enduring Leadership

Sources: Peter N. Golder, "Historical Method in Marketing Research with New Evidence on Long-Term Market Share Stability," *Journal of Marketing Research* (May 2000): 156–172; Peter N. Golder and Gerard J. Tellis, "Growing, Growing, Gone: Cascades, Diffusion, and Turning Points in the Product Life Cycle," *Marketing Science* 23, no. 2 (Spring 2004): 207–218; Laurie Freeman, "Study: Leading Brands Aren't Always Enduring," *Advertising Age,* 28 February 2000; Gerald J. Tellis and Peter N. Golder, "First to Market, First to Fail? Real Causes of Enduring Market Leadership," *MIT Sloan Management Review,* 1 January 1996.

FIGURE 1-9

Vivaldi Partners Study: Next Generation Growth Brands

		Current ($ billion)	Four-Year percentage Change
1	Apple	5.3	38
2	BlackBerry	1.2	36
3	Google	8.7	36
4	Amazon.com	2.7	35
5	Yahoo!	6.8	34
6	eBay	7.4	31
7	Red Bull	1.7	31
8	Starbucks	3.0	25
9	Pixar	2.9	24
10	Coach	3.9	23
11	Whole Foods	0.7	22
12	EA Sports/Games	6.9	22
13	MTV	7.0	22
14	Samsung	14.3	18
15	Victoria's Secret	6.8	17
16	Nike	7.1	16
17	Toyota	25.8	15
18	Formula One	3.2	14
19	ESPN	9.3	14
20	Harley-Davidson	7.6	12

Sources: "Next Generation Growth Brands," Vivaldi Partners, June 2005.
Kurt Badenhausen and Maya Roney, "Next Generations," *Forbes*, 20 June 2005, 121–122.

In this postmodern marketing world, many believe that it is more difficult to persuade consumers with traditional communications than it used to be. As one commentator put it:

> The dollars that were spent on advertising in the 1950s and 1960s are still paying off. The advertising done 30 years ago for the Marlboro Man is still paying off all around the world. It was so cheap to get a large share of voice in the 1950s—it would be impossible to duplicate that now. There was also more receptivity in the marketplace. Now there is a more world-weary, seen-it-all attitude. People are more likely not to believe what they see on TV, to tune things out. The more you turn up the

FIGURE 1-10

Challenges to Brand Builders

Savvy customers
More complex brand families and portfolios
Maturing markets
More sophisticated and increasing competition
Difficulty in differentiating
Decreasing brand loyalty in many categories
Growth of private labels
Increasing trade power
Fragmenting media coverage
Eroding traditional media effectiveness
Emerging new communication options
Increasing promotional expenditures
Decreasing advertising expenditures
Increasing cost of product introduction and support
Short-term performance orientation
Increasing job turnover

volume, the more people resist, and it becomes harder and harder to implant in people's minds that things are desirable.[31]

Other marketers believe that what consumers want from products and services and brands has changed. For example, Kevin Roberts of Saatchi and Saatchi argues that companies must transcend brands to create "trustmarks"—a name or symbol that emotionally binds a company with the desires and aspirations of its customers—and ultimately "lovemarks." He argues that it is not enough for a brand to be just respected.

> Pretty much everything today can be seen in relation to a love-respect axis. You can plot any relationship – with a person, with a brand – by whether it's based on love or based on respect. It used to be that a high respect rating would win. But these days, a high love rating wins. If I don't love what you're offering me, I'm not even interested.[32]

A passionate believer in the concept, Roberts reinforces the point that trustmarks truly belong to the people who offer the love to the brand and that an emotional connection is critical.[33]

Brand Proliferation

Another important change in the branding environment is the proliferation of new brands and products, in part spurred by the rise in line and brand extensions. As a result, a brand name may now be identified with a number of different products with varying degrees of similarity. Marketers of brands such as Coke, Nivea, Dove, and Virgin have added a host of new products under their brand umbrellas in recent years. There are few single (or "mono") product brands around, which complicates the decisions that marketers have to make.

Media Fragmentation

Another important change in the marketing environment is the erosion or fragmentation of traditional advertising media and the emergence of interactive and nontraditional media, promotion, and other communication alternatives. For several reasons, marketers have become disenchanted with traditional advertising media, especially network television:[34]

- *Cost:* The price of network TV has risen dramatically in many countries. Since the mid-1970s, the price of network TV advertising in the United States has far out-paced the rate of inflation but without accompanying increases in audience size.
- *Clutter:* Commercial breaks on network TV have become more cluttered as advertisers increasingly choose to advertise with 10- or 15-second spots rather than the traditional 30- or 60-second spots.
- *Fragmentation:* The growth of independent stations and cable channels has resulted in a dramatic erosion of the network share of audience (from 91 percent in 1975 to barely over 50 percent by 2005).
- *Technology:* The increase in the use of remote controls, VCRs, and PVRs such as TiVo—and the resulting zapping, grazing, and channel surfing, in the popular vernacular—has further reduced TV advertising's effectiveness.

For these and other reasons, the percentage of the communication budget devoted to advertising has shrunk over the years. In its place, marketers are spending more on nontraditional forms of communication and on new and emerging forms of communication such as interactive electronic media; sports and event sponsorship; in-store advertising; mini-billboards in transit vehicles, parking meters, and other locations; and product placement in movies.

McDonald's

In 2004, McDonald's devoted a third of its U.S. marketing budget to television, compared with two-thirds five years before that. Instead of 30-second ads, McDonald's spent on diverse marketing activities such as athletic shoe retailer Foot Locker's in-store video network; closed-circuit sports programming piped into Hispanic bars; and ads in *Upscale*, a custom-published magazine distributed to black barber shops. To target mothers, McDonald's advertises in women's magazines such as *O: The Oprah Magazine* and *Marie Claire* and on Web sites such as Yahoo! and iVillage.[35]

Increased Competition

One reason marketers have been forced to use so many financial incentives or discounts is that the marketplace has become more competitive. Both demand-side and supply-side factors have contributed to the increase in competitive intensity. On the demand side, consumption for many products and services has flattened and hit the maturity stage, or even the decline stage, of the product life cycle. As a result, marketers can achieve sales growth for brands only by taking away competitors' market share. On the supply side, new competitors have emerged due to a number of factors, such as the following:

- *Globalization:* Although firms have embraced globalization as a means to open new markets and potential sources of revenue, it has also increased the number of competitors in existing markets, threatening current sources of revenue.
- *Low-priced competitors:* Market penetration by generics, private labels, and low-priced "clones" imitating product leaders has increased on a worldwide-basis. Retailers have gained power and often dictate what happens within the store. Their chief marketing weapon is price, and they have introduced and pushed their own brands and demanded greater compensation from trade promotions to stock and display national brands.
- *Brand extensions:* We've noted that many companies have taken their existing brands and launched products with the same name into new categories. Many of these brands provide formidable opposition to market leaders.
- *Deregulation:* Certain industries like telecommunications, financial services, health care, and transportation have become deregulated, leading to increased competition from outside traditionally defined product-market boundaries.

Increased Costs

At the same time that competition is increasing, the cost of introducing a new product or supporting an existing product has increased rapidly, making it difficult to match the investment and level of support that brands were able to receive in previous years. By 2000, an estimated 30,000 new consumer products were introduced in the United States, at a failure rate estimated around 93 percent. Given the millions of dollars spent on developing and marketing a new product, the total failure cost was conservatively estimated by one group to exceed $20 billion.[36]

Greater Accountability

Finally, marketers often find themselves responsible for meeting ambitious short-term profit targets because of financial market pressures and senior management imperatives. Stock analysts value strong and consistent earnings reports as an indication of the long-term financial health of a firm. As a result, marketing managers may find themselves in the dilemma of having to make decisions with short-term benefits but long-term costs (such as cutting advertising expenditures). Moreover, many of these same managers have experienced rapid job turnover and promotions and may not anticipate being in their current positions for very long. One study found that the average tenure of a CMO is only 23 months, suggesting they have little time to make an impact.[37] These different organizational pressures may encourage quick-fix solutions with perhaps adverse long-run consequences.

The Brand Equity Concept

Marketers now face a number of competitive challenges, and some critics feel the response of many has been ineffective or, worse, has further aggravated the problem. In the rest of this book we'll present theories, models, and frameworks that accommodate and reflect marketing's new challenges in order to provide useful managerial guidelines and suggest promising new directions for future thought and research. We'll introduce a "common denominator" or unified conceptual framework, based on the concept of brand equity, as a tool to interpret the potential effects of various brand strategies.

One of the most popular and potentially important marketing concepts to arise in the 1980s was ***brand equity.*** Its emergence, however, has meant both good news and bad news to marketers. The good news is that brand equity has elevated the importance of the brand in marketing strategy and provided focus for managerial interest and research activity. The bad news is that, confusingly, the concept has been defined a number of different ways for a number of different purposes. No common viewpoint has emerged about how to conceptualize and measure brand equity.

Fundamentally, branding is all about endowing products and services with the power of brand equity. Despite the many different views, most observers agree that brand equity consists of the marketing effects uniquely attributable to a brand. That is, brand equity explains why different outcomes result from the marketing of a branded product or service than if it were not branded. That is the view we take in this book. As a stark example of the transformational power of branding, consider the following.

Christie's Auctions

A May 2000 auction by Christie's East shows just how profoundly a brand can change people's opinions—and the prices they are willing to pay for products. Actress Judy Garland's slippers from *The Wizard of Oz*, which cost only $12.50 to make in 1938, sold for over

Christie's capitalizes on the power of branding to conduct its auctions.

$800,000! Actor Christopher Reeve's Superman suit fetched over $30,000; *Gilligan's Island*'s skipper's hat sold for more than $8,000; and Penny Marshall's pajamas from *Laverne & Shirley* went for $1,500. At an earlier auction, the dress that Marilyn Monroe wore when she sang "Happy Birthday" to President John F. Kennedy on May 19, 1962 was sold for a staggering $1,150,000. Without such celebrity associations, it is doubtful that any of these items would cost more than a few hundred dollars at a flea market.

Branding is all about creating differences. Most marketing observers also agree with the following basic principles of branding and brand equity:

- Differences in outcomes arise from the "added value" endowed to a product as a result of past marketing activity for the brand.
- This value can be created for a brand in many different ways.
- Brand equity provides a common denominator for interpreting marketing strategies and assessing the value of a brand.
- There are many different ways in which the value of a brand can be manifested or exploited to benefit the firm (in terms of greater proceeds or lower costs or both).

Fundamentally, the brand equity concept reinforces how important the brand is in marketing strategies. It clearly builds on many previously identified principles about brand management. By virtue of the fact that it adapts current theorizing and research advances to address the new challenges in brand management created by a changing marketing environment, the concept of brand equity can also provide useful new insights.

Chapters 2 and 3 in Part II of the book provide an overview of brand equity and a blueprint for the rest of the book. The remainder of the book addresses in much greater depth how to build brand equity (Chapters 4 to 7 in Part III), measure brand equity (Chapters 8 to 10 in Part IV), and manage brand equity (Chapters 11 to 14 in Part V). The concluding Chapter 15 in Part VI provides some additional applications and perspective.

The remainder of this chapter provides an overview of the strategic brand management process that helps to pull all these various concepts together.

Strategic Brand Management Process

Strategic brand management involves the design and implementation of marketing programs and activities to build, measure, and manage brand equity. In this text, we define the ***strategic brand management process*** as having four main steps (see Figure 1-11):

1. Identifying and establishing brand positioning
2. Planning and implementing brand marketing programs
3. Measuring and interpreting brand performance
4. Growing and sustaining brand equity

Let's briefly highlight each of these four steps.[38]

Identifying and Establishing Brand Positioning

The strategic brand management process starts with a clear understanding of what the brand is to represent and how it should be positioned with respect to competitors. Brand positioning can be defined as the "act of designing the company's offer and image so that it occupies a distinct and valued place in the target customer's mind," such that the potential benefit to the firm is maximized. Competitive brand positioning is all about creating brand superiority in the minds of consumers. Fundamentally, positioning convinces

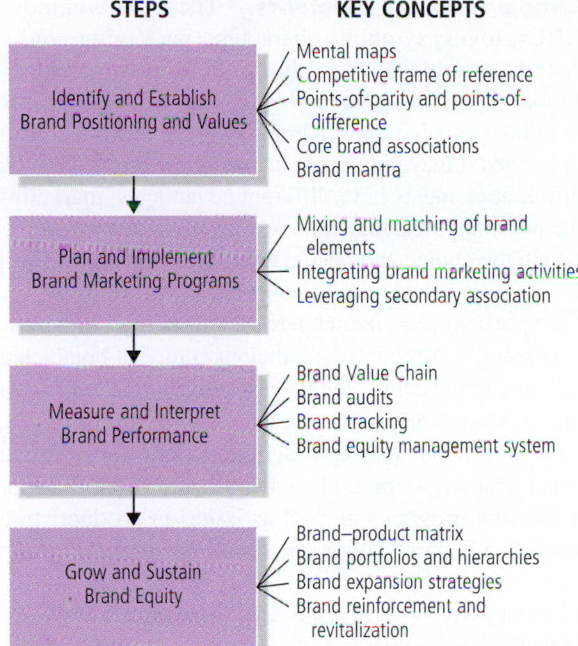

FIGURE 1-11

Strategic Brand Management Process

consumers of the advantages or ***points of difference*** a brand has over competitors, while at the same time alleviating concerns about any possible disadvantages (establishing ***points of parity***).

Positioning also often specifies the appropriate core brand associations and brand mantra. A ***mental map*** is a visual depiction of the different types of associations linked to the brand in the minds of consumers. ***Core brand associations*** are that subset of associations (attributes and benefits) that best characterize a brand. To further focus what a brand represents, it is also often useful to define a ***brand mantra,*** also known as a brand essence or core brand promise. A brand mantra is a short three- to five-word expression of the most important aspects of a brand and its core brand associations, the enduring "brand DNA" and the most important aspects of the brand to the consumer and the company. Core brand associations, points of parity, points of difference, and a brand mantra are thus an articulation of the heart and soul of the brand.

Planning and Implementing Brand Marketing Programs

As Chapter 2 outlines, building brand equity requires creating a brand that consumers are sufficiently aware of and with which they have strong, favorable, and unique brand associations. In general, this knowledge-building process will depend on three factors:

1. The initial choices of the brand elements or identities making up the brand and how they are mixed and matched
2. The marketing activities and supporting marketing program and the way the brand is integrated into them
3. Other associations indirectly transferred to or leveraged by the brand as a result of linking it to some other entity (such as the company, country of origin, channel of distribution, or another brand)

Some important considerations of each of these three factors are as follows.

Choosing Brand Elements. The most common brand elements are brand names, URLs, logos, symbols, characters, packaging, and slogans. A number of options and criteria are relevant for choosing them to enhance brand awareness or facilitate the formation of strong, favorable, and unique brand associations. The best test of the brand-building contribution of a brand element is what consumers would think about the product or service if they knew only its brand name or its associated logo or other element. Because different elements have different advantages, marketing managers often use a subset of all the possible brand elements or even all of them. Chapter 4 examines in detail the means by which the choice and design of brand elements can help to build brand equity.

Integrating the Brand into Marketing Activities and the Supporting Marketing Program. Although the judicious choice of brand elements can make some contribution to building brand equity, the biggest contribution comes from marketing activities related to the brand. Marketing programs can create strong, favorable, and unique brand associations in a variety of ways. This text highlights only some particularly important marketing program considerations for building brand equity. Chapter 5 addresses new developments in designing marketing programs as well as issues in product strategy, pricing strategy, and channels strategy. Chapter 6 addresses issues in communications strategy.

Leveraging Secondary Associations. The third and final way to build brand equity is to leverage secondary associations. Brand associations may themselves be linked to other entities that have their own associations, creating these secondary associations. For example, the brand may be linked to certain source factors, such as the company (through branding strategies), countries or other geographical regions (through identification of product origin), and channels of distribution (through channel strategy), as well as to other brands (through ingredients or co-branding), characters (through licensing), spokespeople (through endorsements), sporting or cultural events (through sponsorship), or some other third-party sources (through awards or reviews).

Because the brand becomes identified with another entity, even though this entity may not directly relate to the product or service performance, consumers may *infer* that the brand shares associations with that entity, thus producing indirect or secondary associations for the brand. In essence, the marketer is borrowing or leveraging some other associations for the brand to create some associations of the brand's own and thus help to build its brand equity. Chapter 7 describes the means of leveraging brand equity.

Measuring and Interpreting Brand Performance

The task of determining or evaluating a brand's positioning often benefits from a brand audit. A ***brand audit*** is a comprehensive examination of a brand to assess its health, uncover its sources of equity, and suggest ways to improve and leverage that equity. A brand audit requires understanding sources of brand equity from the perspective of both the firm and the consumer. Chapter 3 describes the conceptual foundations of competitive brand positioning and provides detailed guidelines on how to develop such positioning strategies.

Once marketers have determined the brand positioning strategy, they are ready to put into place the actual marketing program to create, strengthen, or maintain brand associations. To understand the effects of these brand marketing programs, marketers should measure and interpret brand performance through marketing research. A useful tool for the task is the brand value chain. The ***brand value chain*** is a means to trace the value creation process for brands, to better understand the financial impact of brand marketing expenditures and investments. Chapter 8 describes this planning tool and Chapters 9 and 10 describe a number of measures to operationalize it.

To manage their brands profitably, managers must successfully design and implement a brand equity measurement system. A ***brand equity measurement system*** is a set of research procedures designed to provide timely, accurate, and actionable information for marketers so that they can make the best possible tactical decisions in the short run and the best strategic decisions in the long run. As described in Chapter 8, implementing such a system involves two key steps—conducting ***brand tracking*** and implementing a ***brand equity management system***.

Growing and Sustaining Brand Equity

Maintaining and expanding on brand equity can be quite challenging. Brand equity management activities take a broader and more diverse perspective of the brand's equity—understanding how branding strategies should reflect corporate concerns and be adjusted, if at all, over time or over geographical boundaries or market segments. Managing brand equity can mean managing brands within the context of other brands, as well as over multiple categories, over time, and across multiple market segments.

Defining the Branding Strategy. The firm's branding strategy provides general guidelines about which brand elements to apply across its products. Two main tools in defining the corporate branding strategy are the brand–product matrix and the brand hierarchy. The ***brand–product matrix*** is a graphical representation of all the brands and products sold by the firm. The ***brand hierarchy*** displays the number and nature of common and distinctive brand components across the firm's products. By capturing the potential branding relationships among the different products sold by the firm, it graphically portrays the firm's branding strategy. The ***brand portfolio*** is the set of all brands and brand lines that a particular firm offers for sale to buyers in a particular category. Chapter 11 reviews issues concerning branding strategies and the concepts of the brand–product matrix, brand hierarchy, and brand portfolio. Chapter 12 concentrates on the topic of brand extensions in which an existing brand is used to launch a product in an existing category.

Managing Brand Equity over Time. Effective brand management also requires taking a long-term view of marketing decisions. Because consumers' responses to marketing activity depend on what they know and remember about a brand, short-term marketing mix actions, by changing brand knowledge, *necessarily* increase or decrease the success of future marketing actions. A long-term perspective of brand management recognizes that any changes in the supporting marketing program for a brand may, by changing consumer knowledge, affect the success of future marketing programs. A long-term view also produces proactive strategies designed to maintain and enhance customer-based brand equity over time, in the face of external changes in the marketing environment and internal changes in a firm's marketing goals and programs. Chapter 13 outlines issues related to managing brand equity over time.

Managing Brand Equity over Geographic Boundaries, Cultures, and Market Segments. Another important consideration in managing brand equity is recognizing and accounting for different types of consumers in developing branding and marketing programs. International factors and global branding strategies are particularly important in these decisions. In expanding a brand overseas, managers need to build equity by relying on specific knowledge about the experience and behaviors of those market segments. Chapter 14 examines issues related to broadening of brand equity across market segments.

Review

This chapter began by defining a brand as a name, term, sign, symbol, or design, or some combination of these elements, intended to identify the goods and services of one seller or group of sellers and to differentiate them from those of competitors. The different components of a brand (brand names, logos, symbols, package designs, and so forth) are brand elements. Brand elements come in many different forms. A brand is distinguished from a product, which is defined as anything that can be offered to a market for attention, acquisition, use, or consumption that might satisfy a need or want. A product may be a physical good, service, retail store, person, organization, place, or idea.

A brand is a product, but one that adds other dimensions that differentiate it in some way from other products designed to satisfy the same need. These differences may be rational and tangible—related to product performance of the brand—or more symbolic, emotional, or intangible—related to what the brand represents. Brands themselves are valuable intangible assets that need to be managed carefully. Brands offer a number of benefits to customers and the firms. The key to branding is that consumers perceive differences among brands in a product category. Marketers can brand virtually any type of product by giving the product a name and attaching meaning to it in terms of what it has to offer and how it differs from competitors. A number of branding challenges and opportunities faced by present-day marketing managers were outlined related to changes in customer attitudes and behavior, competitive forces, marketing efficiency and effectiveness, and internal company dynamics.

Brand positioning is defining and establishing brand vision and positioning. Building brand equity depends on three main factors: (1) the initial choices of brand elements or identities making up the brand; (2) the way the brand is integrated into the supporting marketing program; and (3) the associations indirectly transferred to the brand by linking the brand to some other entity (such as the company, country of origin, channel of distribution, or another brand).

Measuring brand equity requires measuring aspects of the brand value chain and implementing a brand equity measurement system as well as understanding how branding strategies should reflect corporate concerns and be adjusted, if at all, over time or over geographical boundaries. Effectively managing brand equity includes defining the corporate branding strategy—by defining the brand hierarchy and brand–product matrix—and devising a policy for brand fortification and leverage over time and over geographical boundaries.

Discussion Questions

1. What do brands mean to you? What are your favorite brands and why? Check to see how your perceptions of brands might differ from those of others.
2. Who do you think has the strongest brands? Why? What do you think of the *Business Week* list of the 25 strongest brands in Figure 1-5? Do you agree with the rankings? Why or why not?
3. Can you think of anything that cannot be branded? Pick an example that was not discussed in each of the categories provided (services; retailers and distributors; people and organizations; sports, arts, and entertainment) and describe how each is a brand.
4. Can you think of yourself as a brand? What do you do to "brand" yourself?
5. What do you think of the new branding challenges and opportunities that were listed in the chapter? Can you think of any other issues?

BRAND FOCUS 1.0

Historical Origins of Branding[39]

Branding, in one form or another, has been around for centuries. The original motivation for branding was for craftsmen and others to identify the fruits of their labors so that customers could easily recognize them. Branding, or at least trademarks, can be traced back to ancient pottery and stonemason's marks, which were applied to handcrafted goods to identify their source. Pottery and clay lamps were sometimes sold far from the shops where they were made, and buyers looked for the stamps of reliable potters as a guide to quality. Marks have been found on early Chinese porcelain, on pottery jars from ancient Greece and Rome, and on goods from India dating back to about 1300 B.C.

In medieval times, potters' marks were joined by printers' marks, watermarks on paper, bread marks, and the marks of various craft guilds. In some cases, these were used to attract buyers loyal to particular makers, but the marks were also used to police infringers of the guild monopolies and to single out the makers of inferior goods. An English law passed in 1266 required bakers to put their mark on every loaf of bread sold, "to the end that if any bread bu faultie in weight, it may bee then knowne in whom the fault is." Goldsmiths and silversmiths were also required to mark their goods, both with their signature or personal symbol and with a sign of the quality of the metal. In 1597, two goldsmiths convicted of putting false marks on their wares were nailed to the pillory by their ears. Similarly harsh punishments were decreed for those who counterfeited other artisans' marks.

When Europeans began to settle in North America, they brought the convention and practice of branding with them. The makers of patent medicines and tobacco manufacturers were early U.S. branding pioneers. Medicine potions such as Swaim's Panacea, Fahnestock's Vermifuge, and Perry Davis' Vegetable Pain Killer became well known to the public prior to the Civil War. Patent medicines were packaged in small bottles and, because they were not seen as a necessity, were vigorously promoted. To further influence consumer choices in stores, manufacturers of these medicines printed elaborate and distinctive labels, often with their own portrait featured in the center.

Tobacco manufacturers had been exporting their crop since the early 1600s. By the early 1800s, manufacturers had packed bales of tobacco under labels such as Smith's Plug and Brown and Black's Twist. During the 1850s, many tobacco manufacturers recognized that more creative names—such as Cantaloupe, Rock Candy, Wedding Cake, and Lone Jack—were helpful in selling their tobacco products. In the 1860s, tobacco manufacturers began to sell their wares in small bags directly to consumers. Attractive-looking packages were seen as important, and picture labels, decorations, and symbols were designed as a result.

The history of branding in the United States since 1860 to its more modern developments from 1985 on (reviewed earlier in the chapter) can be divided into four main periods. We next consider some of the important developments in each.

Emergence of National Manufacturer Brands: 1860 to 1914

In the United States after the Civil War, a number of forces combined to make widely distributed, manufacturer-branded products a profitable venture:

- Improvements in transportation (e.g., railroads) and communication (e.g., telegraph and telephone) made regional and even national distribution increasingly easy.
- Improvements in production processes made it possible to produce large quantities of high-quality products inexpensively.
- Improvements in packaging made individual (as opposed to bulk) packages that could be identified with the manufacturer's trademark increasingly viable.
- Changes in U.S. trademark law in 1879, the 1880s, and 1906 made it easier to protect brand identities.
- Advertising became perceived as a more credible option, and newspapers and magazines eagerly sought out advertising revenues.
- Retail institutions such as department and variety stores and national mail order houses served as effective middlemen and encouraged consumer spending.
- The population increased due to liberal immigration policies.
- Increasing industrialization and urbanization raised the standard of living and aspirations of Americans, although many products on the market still were of uneven quality.
- Literacy rose as the percentage of illiterate Americans dropped from 20 percent in 1870 to 10 percent in 1900.

All of these factors facilitated the development of consistent-quality consumer products that could be efficiently sold to consumers through mass market advertising campaigns. In this fertile branding environment, mass-produced merchandise in packages largely replaced locally produced merchandise sold from bulk containers. This change brought about the widespread use of trademarks. For example, Procter & Gamble made candles in Cincinnati and shipped them to merchants in other cities along the Ohio and Mississippi rivers. In 1851, wharf hands began to brand crates of Procter & Gamble candles with a crude star. The firm soon noticed that buyers downriver relied on the star as a mark of quality, and merchants refused the candles if the crates arrived without the mark. As a result, the candles were marked with a more formal star label on all packages, branded as "Star," and began to develop a loyal following.

The development and management of these brands was largely driven by the owners of the firm and their top-level management. For example, the first president of National Biscuit was involved heavily in the introduction in 1898 of Uneeda Biscuits, the first nationally branded biscuit. One of their first decisions was to create a pictorial symbol for the brand, the Uneeda biscuit slicker boy, who appeared in the supporting ad campaigns. H. J. Heinz built up the Heinz brand name through production innovations and spectacular promotions. Coca-Cola became a national powerhouse due to the efforts of Asa Candler, who actively oversaw the growth of the extensive distribution channel.

National manufacturers sometimes had to overcome resistance from consumers, retailers, wholesalers, and even employees from within their own company. To do so, these firms employed sustained "push" and "pull" efforts to keep both consumers and retailers happy and accepting of national brands. Consumers were attracted through the use of sampling, premiums, product education brochures, and heavy advertising. Retailers were lured by in-store sampling and promotional programs and shelf maintenance assistance.

As the use of brand names and trademarks spread, so did the practice of imitation and counterfeiting. Although the laws were somewhat unclear, more and more firms sought protection by sending their trademarks and labels to district courts for registration. Congress finally separated the registration of trademarks and labels in 1870 with the enactment of the country's first federal trademark law. Under the law, registrants were required to send a facsimile of their mark with a description of the type of goods on which it was used to the Patent Office in Washington along with a $25 fee. One of the first marks submitted to the Patent Office under the new law was the Underwood Devil, which was registered to William Underwood & Company of Boston on November 29, 1870 for use on "Deviled Entremets." By 1890, most countries had trademark acts, establishing brand names, labels, and designs as legally protectable assets.

Dominance of Mass Marketed Brands: 1915 to 1929

By 1915, manufacturer brands had become well established in the United States on both a regional and national basis. The next 15 years saw increasing acceptance and even admiration of manufacturer brands by consumers. The marketing of brands became more specialized under the guidance of functional experts in charge of production, promotion, personal selling, and other areas. This greater specialization led to more advanced marketing techniques. Design professionals were enlisted to assist in the process of trademark selection. Personal selling became more sophisticated as salesmen were carefully selected and trained to systematically handle accounts and seek out new businesses. Advertising combined more powerful creativity with more persuasive copy and slogans. Government and industry regulation came into place to reduce deceptive advertising. Marketing research became more important and influential in supporting marketing decisions.

Although functional management of brands had these virtues, it also presented problems. Because responsibility for any one brand was divided among two or more functional managers—as well as advertising specialists—poor coordination was always a potential problem. For example, the introduction of Wheaties cereal by General Mills was nearly sabotaged by the company's salesmen, who were reluctant to take on new duties to support the brand. Three years after the cereal's introduction and on the verge of its being dropped, a manager from the advertising department at General Mills decided to become a product champion for Wheaties, and the brand went on to great success in the following decades.

Challenges to Manufacturer Brands: 1930 to 1945

The onset of the Great Depression in 1929 posed new challenges to manufacturer brands. Greater price sensitivity swung the pendulum of power in the favor of retailers who pushed their own brands and dropped nonperforming manufacturer brands. Advertising came under fire as manipulative, deceptive, and tasteless and was increasingly being ignored by certain segments of the population. In 1938, the Wheeler Amendment gave power to the Federal Trade Commission (FTC) to regulate advertising practices. In response to these trends, manufacturers' advertising went beyond slogans and jingles to give consumers specific reasons why they should buy advertised products.

There were few dramatic changes in marketing of brands during this time. As a notable exception, Procter & Gamble put the first brand management system into place, whereby each of their brands had a manager assigned only to that brand who was responsible for its financial success. Other firms were slow to follow, however, and relied more on their long-standing reputation for good quality—and a lack of competition—to sustain sales. During World War II, manufacturer brands became relatively scarce as resources were diverted to the war effort. Nevertheless, many brands continued to advertise and helped to bolster consumer demand during these tough times.

The Lanham Act of 1946 permitted federal registration of service marks (marks used to designate services rather than products) and collective marks such as union labels and club emblems.

Establishment of Brand Management Standards: 1946 to1985

After World War II, the pent-up demand for high-quality brands led to an explosion of sales. Personal income grew as the economy took off, and market demand intensified as the rate of population growth exploded. Demand for national brands soared, fueled by a burst of new products and a receptive and growing middle class. Firm after firm during this time period adopted the brand management system.

In the brand management system, a brand manager took "ownership" of a brand. A brand manager was responsible for developing and implementing the annual marketing plan for his or her brand, as well as identifying new business opportunities. The brand manager might be assisted, internally, by representatives from manufacturing, the sales force, marketing research, financial planning, research and development, personnel, legal, and public relations and, externally, by representatives from advertising agencies, research suppliers, and public relations agencies.

Then, as now, a successful brand manager had to be a versatile jack-of-all trades. For example, a marketing manager at Gillette once identified the following factors for being a successful brand manager:[40]

- A dedication to the brand, reflected in an effort to do what was best for the business
- An ability to assess a situation and see alternative solutions
- A talent for generating creative ideas and a willingness to be open to others' ideas
- An ability to make decisions in a highly ambiguous environment
- An ability to move projects through the organization
- Good communication skills
- A high energy level
- A capacity for handling many tasks simultaneously

Notes

1. Interbrand Group, *World's Greatest Brands: An International Review* (New York: John Wiley, 1992).
2. Adrian Room, *Dictionary of Trade Greatest Brands: An International Review* (New York: John Wiley, 1992); Adrian Room, *Dictionary of Trade Name Origins* (London: Routledge & Kegan Paul, 1982).
3. The second through fifth levels are based on a conceptualization in Theodore Levitt, "Marketing Success Through Differentiation—of Anything," *Harvard Business Review* (January–February 1980): 83–91.
4. Theodore Levitt, "Marketing Myopia," *Harvard Business Review* (July–August 1960): 45–56.
5. Alvin A. Achenbaum, "The Mismanagement of Brand Equity," ARF Fifth Annual Advertising and Promotion Workshop, 1 February 1993.
6. Thomas J. Madden, Frank Fehle, and Susan M. Fournier, "Brands Matter: An Empirical Investigation of Brand-Building Activities and the Creation of Shareholder Value," Harvard Business School working paper, 2002.
7. Jacob Jacoby, Jerry C. Olson, and Rafael Haddock, "Price, Brand Name, and Product Composition Characteristics as Determinants of Perceived Quality," *Journal of Consumer Research* 3, no. 4 (1971): 209–216; Jacob Jacoby, George Syzbillo, and Jacqueline Busato-Sehach, "Information Acquisition Behavior in Brand Choice Situations," *Journal of Marketing Research* 11 (1977): 63–69.
8. Susan Fournier, "Consumers and Their Brands: Developing Relationship Theory in Consumer Research," *Journal of Consumer Research* 24, no. 3 (1997): 343–373.
9. Philip Nelson, "Information and Consumer Behavior," *Journal of Political Economy* 78 (1970): 311–329; and Michael R. Darby and Edi Karni, "Free Competition and the Optimal Amount of Fraud," *Journal of Law and Economics* 16 (April 1974): 67–88.
10. Allan D. Shocker and Richard Chay, "How Marketing Researchers Can Harness the Power of Brand Equity." Presentation to New Zealand Marketing Research Society, August 1992.
11. Ted Roselius, "Consumer Ranking of Risk Reduction Methods," *Journal of Marketing* 35 (January 1971): 56–61.

12. Leslie de Chernatony and Gil McWilliam, "The Varying Nature of Brands as Assets," *International Journal of Advertising* 8 (1989): 339–349.
13. Constance E. Bagley, *Managers and the Legal Environment: Strategies for the 21st Century*, 2nd ed. (St. Paul, MN: West, 1995).
14. Tulin Erdem and Joffre Swait, "Brand Equity as a Signaling Phenomenon," *Journal of Consumer Psychology* 7, no. 2 (1998): 131–157.
15. Charles Bymer, "Valuing Your Brands: Lessons from Wall Street and the Impact on Marketers," ARF Third Annual Advertising and Promotion Workshop, February 5–6, 1991.
16. Levitt, "Marketing Success."
17. Yumiko Ono, "Prescription-Drug Makers Heighten Hard-Sell Tactics," *Wall Street Journal*, 29 August 1994, B-1.
18. Christine Bittar, "Prescription Drugs," *Brandweek*, 25 April 2005, SR26.
19. P. Mitchell, J. King, and J. Reast, J. "Brand Values Related to Industrial Products," *Industrial Marketing Management* 30, no. 5 (2001): 415–425.
20. Tom Clark, "Package-Goods Execs Flood into Software," *Advertising Age*, 16 May 1994, S-4.
21. Lorrie Grant, "Web Sites Look to Customer Service," *USA Today,* 29 September 1999, B3.
22. Julie Schlosser, "Google," *Fortune*, 31 October 2005, 168-69. Jefferson Graham, "Google's Profit Sails Past Expectations," *USA Today*, 21 October 2005, 1B.
23. David Lidsky, "Me Inc.: the Rethink," *Fast Company*, March 2005, 16.
24. University professors are certainly aware of the power of the name as a brand. In fact, one reason why many professors choose to have students identify themselves on exams by student numbers of some type is so that they will not be biased in grading by their knowledge of the student who prepared it. Otherwise, it may be too easy to give higher grades to those students that the professor likes or, for whatever reason, expects to have done well on the exam.
25. Robert P. Parker, "If You Got It Flaunt It," ARF Brand Equity Workshop, February 15–16.
26. Joel Hochberg, "Package Goods Marketing vs. Hollywood," *Advertising Age*, 20 January 1992.
27. Ben Pappas, "Star Bucks," *Forbes*, 17 May 1999, 53; Gail Schiller, "Licensed 'Star Wars' Merchandise to Make Killing," HollywoodReporter.com, 18 May 2005; Todd Waserman, "Star Wars: Then & Now," *Brandweek*, 16 May 2005, 44–46.
28. Jack Trout, "Branding Can't Exist Without Positioning," *Advertising Age*, 14 March 2005, 28.
29. Allan D. Shocker, Rajendra Srivastava, and Robert Ruekert, "Challenges and Opportunities Facing Brand Management: An Introduction to the Special Issue," *Journal of Marketing Research* 31 (May 1994): 149–158.
30. Kenneth Hein, "The Expectation Epidemic," *Brandweek*, 23 May 2005, 34–37.
31. B. G. Yovovich, "What Is Your Brand Really Worth?" *Adweek's Marketing Week*, 8 August 1988, 18–21.
32. Alan M. Webber, "Trust in the Future," *Fast Company*, September 2000, 210–220.
33. Kevin Roberts, *Lovemarks: The Future Beyond Brands* (New York: Powerhouse Books, 2004).
34. Alvin A. Achenbaum, "The Implication of Price Competition on Brands, Advertising and the Economy," ARF Fourth Annual Advertising and Promotion Workshop, 12–13 February 1992. Zipping and zapping refer to the practice of fast-forwarding through ad breaks while watching taped TV programs and switching to other channels during commercial breaks while watching live TV programs. Channel grazing or surfing refers to watching snatches or a few minutes of one program, then another, and so on.
35. Anthony Bianco, "The Vanishing Mass Market," *BusinessWeek*, 12 July 2004, 61–72.
36. www.bases.com/news/news03052001.html.
37. Gail J. McGovern and John A. Quelch. "The Fall and Rise of the CMO," *Strategy and Business* 37 (Winter 2004): 44–51.
38. For discussion of other approaches to branding, see David A. Aaker, *Managing Brand Equity* (New York: Free Press, 1991); David A. Aaker, *Building Strong Brands* (New York: Free Press, 1996); David A. Aaker and Erich Joachimsthaler, *Brand Leadership* (New York: Free Press, 2000); Jean-Noel Kapferer, *Strategic Brand Management*, 2nd ed. (New York: Free Press, 2005); Scott M. Davis, *Brand Asset Management* (New York: Free Press, 2000).
39. Much of this section is adapted from an excellent article by George S. Low and Ronald A. Fullerton, "Brands, Brand Management, and the Brand Manager System: A Critical-Historical Evaluation," *Journal of Marketing Research* 31 (May 1994): 173–190; and an excellent book by Hal Morgan, *Symbols of America* (Steam Press, 1986).
40. Shirley Spence and Thomas Bonoma, "The Gillette Company: Dry Idea Advertising," Case 9-586-042 (Boston: Harvard Business School, 1986).

2 CUSTOMER-BASED BRAND EQUITY

Preview

Chapter 1 introduced some basic notions about brands, particularly brand equity, and the roles they have played and are playing in marketing strategies. Part II of the text explores brand equity and how to identify and establish an effective brand positioning.

This chapter more formally examines the brand equity concept, introducing one particular view—the concept of customer-based brand equity—that will serve as the organizing framework for the rest of the book.[1] We'll consider the sources of customer-based brand equity and the outcomes or benefits that result from those sources. We then present the customer-based brand equity model in detail and discuss some of the main implications of that model. Brand Focus 2.0 at the end of the chapter provides a detailed overview of the advantages of creating a strong brand. Chapter 3 concentrates on brand positioning.

Customer-Based Brand Equity

Two questions often arise: What makes a brand strong? and How do you build a strong brand? To help answer both, we introduce the customer-based brand equity (CBBE) model. This model incorporates theoretical advances and managerial practices in understanding and influencing consumer behavior. Although a number of useful perspectives concerning brand equity have been put forth, the CBBE model provides a unique point of view as to what brand equity is and how it should best be built, measured, and managed.

The CBBE model approaches brand equity from the perspective of the consumer—whether the consumer is an individual or an organization. Understanding the needs and wants of consumers and organizations and devising products and programs to satisfy them are at the heart of successful marketing. In particular, two fundamentally important questions marketers face are: What do different brands mean to consumers? and How does the brand knowledge of consumers affect their response to marketing activity?

The basic premise of the CBBE model is that the power of a brand lies in what customers have learned, felt, seen, and heard about the brand as a result of their experiences over time. In other words, *the power of a brand lies in what resides in the minds of customers.* The challenge for marketers in building a strong brand is ensuring that customers have the right type of experiences with products and services and their accompanying marketing programs so that the desired thoughts, feelings, images, beliefs, perceptions, opinions, and so on become linked to the brand.

We formally define ***customer-based brand equity*** as the differential effect that brand knowledge has on consumer response to the marketing of that brand. A brand has positive customer-based brand equity when consumers react more favorably to a product and the way it is marketed when the brand is identified than when it is not (say, when the product is attributed to a fictitious name or is unnamed). Thus, customers might be more accepting of a new brand extension for a brand with positive customer-based brand equity, less sensitive to price increases and withdrawal of advertising support, or more willing to seek the brand in a new distribution channel. On the other hand, a brand has *negative* customer-based brand equity if consumers react less favorably to marketing activity for the brand compared with an unnamed or fictitiously named version of the product.

Let's look at the three key ingredients to this definition: (1) "differential effect," (2) "brand knowledge," and (3) "consumer response to marketing." First, brand equity arises from differences in consumer response. If no differences occur, then the brand-name product can essentially be classified as a commodity or a generic version of the product. Competition, most likely, would then just be based on price. Second, these differences in response are a

Improved perceptions of product performance
Greater loyalty
Less vulnerability to competitive marketing actions
Less vulnerability to marketing crises
Larger margins
More inelastic consumer response to price increases
More elastic consumer response to price decreases
Greater trade cooperation and support
Increased marketing communication effectiveness
Possible licensing opportunities
Additional brand extension opportunities

FIGURE 2-1

Marketing Advantages of Strong Brands

result of consumers' knowledge about the brand, that is, what they have learned, felt, seen, and heard about the brand as a result of their experiences over time. Thus, although strongly influenced by the marketing activity of the firm, brand equity ultimately depends on what resides in the minds of consumers. Third, customers' differential responses, which make up brand equity, are reflected in perceptions, preferences, and behavior related to all aspects of brand marketing, including their choice of a brand, recall of copy points from an ad, response to a sales promotion, and evaluations of a proposed brand extension. Brand Focus 2.0 provides a detailed account of these advantages, as summarized in Figure 2-1.

The simplest way to illustrate what we mean by customer-based brand equity is to consider one of the typical results of product sampling or comparison tests. For example, in blind taste tests, two groups of consumers sample a product. One group knows which brand it is, the other doesn't. Invariably the two groups have different opinions despite consuming the same product.

For example, Larry Percy reports the results of a beer tasting experiment that showed how discriminating consumers could be when given the names of the well-known brands of the beer they were drinking, but how few differences consumers could detect when they did not know the brand names. Figure 2-2 displays the perceptual maps—visual tools to portray perceptual differences among brands expressed by consumers—that the researchers derived from the two types of responses. As it turns out, even fairly knowledgeable consumers can have difficulty distinguishing different brands of beer.

When consumers report different opinions about branded and unbranded versions of identical products, it must be the case that knowledge about the brand, created by whatever means (past experiences, marketing activity for the brand, or word of mouth), has somehow changed their product perceptions. This result has occurred with virtually every type of product—conclusive evidence that consumers' perceptions of product performance are highly dependent on their impressions of the brand that goes along with it. In other words, clothes may seem to fit better, a car may seem to drive more smoothly, the wait in a bank line may seem shorter, and so on, depending on the particular brand.

Brand Equity as a Bridge

Thus, according to the customer-based brand equity model, consumer knowledge drives the differences that manifest themselves in terms of brand equity. This realization has important managerial implications. For one thing, brand equity provides marketers with a vital strategic bridge from their past to their future.

Brands as a Reflection of the Past. Marketers should consider all the dollars spent on manufacturing and marketing products each year not so much as "expenses" but as

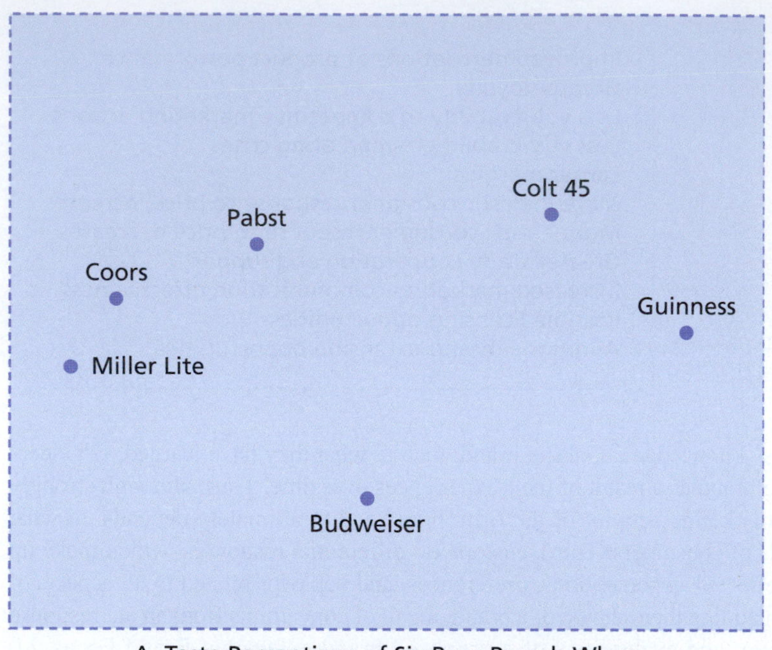

A. Taste Perceptions of Six Beer Brands When the Drinker Knows What He Is Drinking

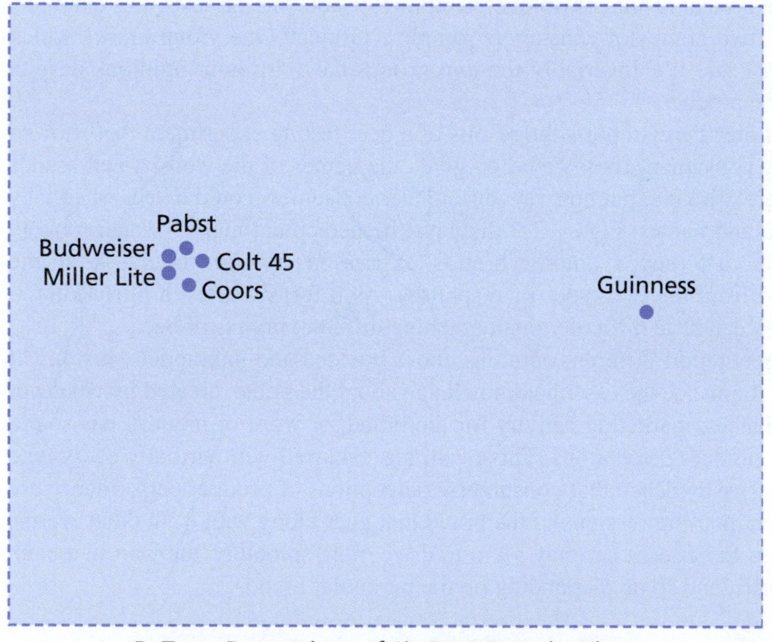

B. Taste Perceptions of Six Beer Brands When the Drinker Does **Not** Know What He Is Drinking

FIGURE 2-2

Results of Blind Beer Taste Tests

"investments"—investments in what consumers learned, felt, and experienced about the brand. If not properly designed and implemented, these expenditures may not be good investments, in that they may not have created the right knowledge structures in consumers' minds, but we should consider them investments nonetheless. Thus, the *quality* of the investment in brand building is the most critical factor, not the *quantity* beyond some minimal threshold amount. In fact, it is possible to "overspend" on brand building if money is not being spent wisely. Conversely, as we'll see throughout the book, some brands are considerably outspent but amass a great deal of brand equity through marketing activities that create valuable, enduring memory traces in the minds of consumers.

Brands as a Direction for the Future. The brand knowledge that marketers create over time dictates appropriate and inappropriate future directions for the brand. Consumers will decide, based on their brand beliefs and attitudes, where they think the brand should go and grant permission (or not) to any marketing action or program. Thus, at the end of the day, the true value and future prospects of a brand rest with consumers and their knowledge about the brand.

No matter how we define brand equity, though, its value to marketers as a concept ultimately depends on how they use it. Brand equity can offer focus and guidance, providing a means to interpret past marketing performance and design future marketing programs. Everything the firm does can help to enhance or detract from brand equity. Those marketers who build strong brands have embraced the concept and use it to its fullest as a means of clarifying, communicating, and implementing their marketing actions. The process of creating such brand power is not without its critics, however, as described in The Science of Branding 2-1. Other factors can influence brand success, and brand equity has meaning for other constituents besides customers, such as employees, suppliers, channel members, media, and the government.[2] Nevertheless, success with customers is often crucial for success for the firm, so the next section considers brand knowledge and CBBE in more detail.

Making a Brand Strong: Brand Knowledge

From the perspective of the CBBE model, brand knowledge is the key to creating brand equity, because it creates the differential effect that drives brand equity. What marketers need, then, is an insightful way to represent how brand knowledge exists in consumer memory. An influential model of memory developed by psychologists is helpful for this purpose.[3] The ***associative network memory model*** views memory as consisting of a network of nodes and connecting links, in which nodes represent stored information or concepts, and links represent the strength of association between the information or concepts. Any type of information can be stored in the memory network, including verbal, visual, abstract, or contextual information.

Using the associative network memory model, let's think of brand knowledge as consisting of a brand node in memory with a variety of associations linked to it. We can consider brand knowledge as having two components: brand awareness and brand image. ***Brand awareness*** is related to the strength of the brand node or trace in memory, which we can measure as the consumer's ability to identify the brand under different conditions.[4] It is a necessary, but not always sufficient, step in building brand equity. Other considerations, such as the image of the brand, often come into play.

Brand image has long been recognized as an important concept in marketing.[5] Although marketers have not always agreed about how to measure it,[6] one generally accepted view is that, consistent with our associative network memory model, ***brand image*** is consumers' perceptions about a brand, as reflected by the brand associations held in consumer memory.[7] In other words, brand associations are the other informational nodes linked to the brand node in memory and contain the meaning of the brand for consumers. Associations come in all forms and may reflect characteristics of the product or aspects independent of the product.

For example, consider Apple computers. If someone asked you what came to mind when you thought of Apple computers, what would you say? You might reply with

THE SCIENCE OF BRANDING 2-1

No Logo

In her book *No Logo,* Naomi Klein details the aspects of global corporate growth that have led to consumer backlash against brands. She explains the subject of her book as follows:

> The title *No Logo* is not meant to be read as a literal slogan (as in No More Logos!), or a post-logo logo (there is already a No Logo clothing line, I'm told). Rather, it is an attempt to capture an anti-corporate attitude I see emerging among many young activists. This book is hinged on a simple hypothesis: that as more people discover the brand-name secrets of the global logo web, their outrage will fuel the next big political movement, a vast wave of opposition squarely targeting those with very high name-brand recognition.

Klein cites marketing campaigns that exist within schools and universities, among other examples of advertising encroaching on traditionally ad-free space. She asserts that as marketers compete for "eyeballs" using unconventional and unexpected means, fewer ad-free spaces remain, and consumer resentment builds. Klein then argues that the vast number of mergers and acquisitions in the past two decades, and the increasing number of brand extensions, have severely limited consumer choice and engendered additional consumer resentment. She cautions that an inherent danger of building a strong brand is that the public will be all the more eager to see the brand tarnished once unseemly facts surface.

Klein also details the numerous movements that have arisen to protest the growing power of corporations and the proliferation of branded space that accompanies this growth. The author

associations such as "user friendly," "creative," "for desktop publishing," "used at many schools," and so forth. Figure 2-3 displays some commonly mentioned associations for Apple computers that consumers have expressed in the past. The associations that came to *your* mind make up your brand image for Apple. Through skillful marketing, Apple has been able to achieve a rich brand image made up of a host of brand associations. Many are likely to be shared by a majority of consumers, so we can refer to "the" brand image of Apple, but at the same time, we recognize that this image varies, perhaps even considerably, depending on the consumer or market segment.

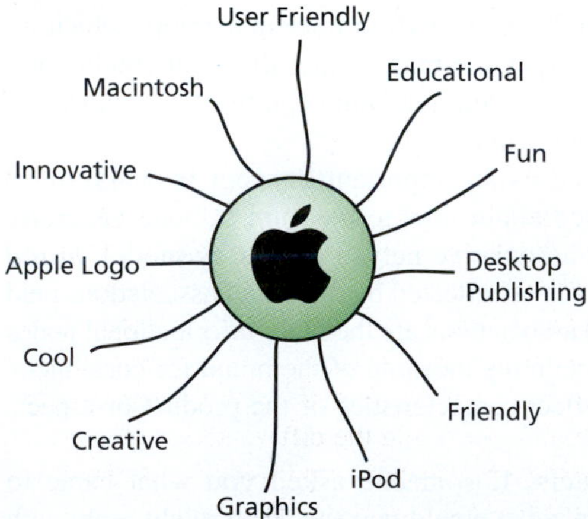

FIGURE 2-3

Possible Apple Computer Associations

highlights such anticorporate practices as "culture jamming" and "ad-busting," which serve to subvert and undermine corporate marketing by attacking the marketers on their own terms. She also discusses the formation of labor activist organizations such as Essential Action and the International Labour Organization, which perform labor monitoring and hold companies accountable for the treatment of their labor forces. Klein observes that the issues of corporate conduct are now highly politicized. As a result, she notes, "Political rallies, which once wound their predicable course in front of government buildings and consulates, are now just as likely to take place in front of the stores of the corporate giants."

Her follow-up book, *Fences and Windows,* reviews newspaper columns written from late 1999 to 2002 covering a wide range of antiglobalization topics related to corporate behavior, unions, and public protests to summits. *Publishers Weekly* observed: "The two title images recur throughout: the fences are real, steel cages keeping protesters from interfering with summits, but they are also metaphorical, such as the 'fence' of poverty that prevents the poor from receiving adequate education or health care. Klein argues that globalization has only delivered its promised benefits to the world's wealthiest citizens and that its emphasis on privatization has eroded the availability of public services around the globe."

Sources: Naomi Klein, *No Logo: Taking Aim at the Brand Bullies* (New York: Picador, 1999); Naomi Klein, *Fences and Windows: Dispatches from the Front Lines of the Globalization Debate* (New York: Picador, 2002); Review, *Publishers Weekly,* 2002.

Other brands, of course, carry a different set of associations. For example, McDonald's marketing program attempts to create brand associations in consumers' minds between its products and "quality," "service," "cleanliness," and "value." McDonald's rich brand image probably also includes strong associations to "Ronald McDonald," "golden arches," "for kids," and "convenient," as well as perhaps potentially negative associations such as "fast food." Coca-Cola's marketing program strives to link brand associations in consumers' minds to "refreshment," "taste," "availability," "affordability," and "accessibility." Whereas Mercedes-Benz has achieved strong associations to "performance" and "status," Volvo has created a strong association to "safety." We'll return in later chapters to the different types of associations and how to measure their strength.

Sources of Brand Equity

What causes brand equity to exist? How do marketers create it? *Customer-based brand equity occurs when the consumer has a high level of awareness and familiarity with the brand and holds some strong, favorable, and unique brand associations in memory.* In some cases, brand awareness alone is enough to create favorable consumer response, for example, in low-involvement decisions when consumers are willing to base their choices on mere familiarity. In most other cases, however, the strength, favorability, and uniqueness of brand associations play a critical role in determining the differential response that makes up brand equity. If customers perceive the brand as only representative of the product or service category, then they'll respond as if the offering were unbranded.

Thus marketers must also convince consumers that there are meaningful differences among brands. Consumers must not think all brands in the category are the same. Establishing a positive brand image in consumer memory—strong, favorable, and unique brand associations—goes hand-in-hand with creating brand awareness to build customer-based brand equity. Let's look at both these sources of brand equity.

Brand Awareness

Brand awareness consists of brand recognition and brand recall performance. ***Brand recognition*** is consumers' ability to confirm prior exposure to the brand when given the brand as a cue. In other words, when they go to the store, will they be able to recognize the brand as one to which they have already been exposed?

Brand recall is consumers' ability to retrieve the brand from memory when given the product category, the needs fulfilled by the category, or a purchase or usage situation as a cue. In other words, recall of Kellogg's Corn Flakes will depend on consumers' ability to retrieve the brand when they think of the cereal category or of what they should eat for breakfast or a snack, whether at the store when making a purchase or at home when deciding what to eat.

If research reveals that many consumer decisions are made at the point of purchase, where the brand name, logo, packaging, and so on will be physically present and visible, then brand recognition will be important. If consumer decisions are mostly made in settings away from the point of purchase, on the other hand, then brand recall will be more important.[8] For this reason, creating brand recall is critical for service and online brands: Consumers must actively seek the brand and therefore be able to retrieve it from memory when appropriate. Note, however, that even though brand recall may be less important at the point of purchase, consumers' brand evaluations and choices will still often depend on what else they recall about the brand given that they are able to recognize it there. As is the case with most information in memory, we are generally more adept at recognizing a brand than at recalling it.

Advantages of Brand Awareness. What are the benefits of creating a high level of brand awareness? There are three—learning advantages, consideration advantages, and choice advantages.

Learning advantages: Brand awareness influences the formation and strength of the associations that make up the brand image. To create a brand image, marketers must first establish a brand node in memory, the nature of which affects how easily the consumer learns and stores additional brand associations. The first step in building brand equity is to register the brand in the minds of consumers. If the right brand elements are chosen, the task becomes easier.

Consideration advantages: Second, as we suggested earlier, consumers must consider the brand whenever they are making a purchase for which it could be acceptable or fulfilling a need it could satisfy. Raising brand awareness increases the likelihood that the brand will be a member of the ***consideration set,*** the handful of brands that receive serious consideration for purchase.[9] Much research has shown that consumers are rarely loyal to only one brand but instead have a set of brands they would consider buying and another—possibly smaller—set of brands they actually buy on a regular basis. Because consumers typically consider only a few brands for purchase, making sure that the brand is in the consideration set also makes other brands less likely to be considered or recalled. Research in psychology on "part-list cuing effects" has shown that recall of some information can inhibit recall of other information.[10] In a marketing context, that means that if a consumer thinks of going to Burger King for a quick lunch, he or she may be less likely to think of going to other types of fast-food restaurants, such as Kentucky Fried Chicken or Taco Bell.[11]

Choice advantages: The third advantage of creating a high level of brand awareness is that it can affect choices among brands in the consideration set, even if there are essentially no other associations to those brands.[12] For example, consumers have been shown to adopt a decision rule in some cases to buy only more familiar, well-established brands.[13] Thus, in low-involvement decision settings, a minimum level of brand awareness may be sufficient for product choice, even in the absence of a well-formed attitude.[14] One influential model of attitude change and persuasion, the elaboration-likelihood model, is consistent with the notion that consumers may make choices based on brand awareness considerations when they have low involvement. Low involvement results when consumers lack either purchase motivation (they don't care about the product or service) or purchase ability (they don't know anything else about the brands in a category).[15]

1. *Consumer purchase motivation:* Although products and brands may be critically important to marketers, choosing a brand in many categories is not a life-or-death decision for most consumers. For example, despite millions of dollars spent in TV advertising over the years to persuade consumers of product differences, 40 percent of consumers in one survey believed all brands of gasoline were about the same or did not know which brand was best. A lack of perceived differences among brands in a category is likely to leave consumers unmotivated about the choice process.
2. *Consumer purchase ability.* Consumers in some product categories just do not have the necessary knowledge or experience to judge product quality even if they so desired. The obvious examples are products with a high degree of technical sophistication, like telecommunications equipment with state-of-the-art features. But consumers may be unable to judge quality even in low-tech categories. Consider the college student who has not really had to cook or clean before, roaming the supermarket aisles for the first time, or a new manager forced to make an expensive capital purchase for the first time. The reality is that product quality is often highly ambiguous and difficult to judge without a great deal of prior experience and expertise. In such cases, consumers will use whatever shortcut or ***heuristic*** they can come up with to make their decisions in the best manner possible. Sometimes they simply choose the brand with which they are most familiar and aware. We discuss the role of perceived quality in consumer decisions in greater detail later.

Establishing Brand Awareness. How do you create brand awareness? In the abstract, creating brand awareness means increasing the familiarity of the brand through repeated exposure, although this is generally more effective for brand recognition than for brand recall. That is, the more a consumer "experiences" the brand by seeing it, hearing it, or thinking about it, the more likely he or she is to strongly register the brand in memory. Thus, anything that causes consumers to experience a brand name, symbol, logo, character, packaging, or slogan—including advertising and promotion, sponsorship and event marketing, publicity and public relations, and outdoor advertising—can increase familiarity and awareness of that brand element. And the more elements marketers can reinforce, usually the better. For instance, in addition to its name, Intel uses the "Intel Inside" logo and its distinctive symbol to enhance awareness.

Repetition increases recognizability, but improving brand recall also requires linkages in memory to appropriate product categories or other purchase or consumption cues. A slogan or jingle creatively pairs the brand and the appropriate cues (and, ideally, the brand positioning as well, helping build a positive brand image). Oher brand elements like logos, symbols, characters, and packaging also aid recall.

The way marketers pair the brand and its product category, such as with an advertising slogan, helps determine the strength of product category links. For brands with strong category associations, like Ford cars, the distinction between brand recognition and recall may not matter much—consumers thinking of the category are likely to think of the brand. In competitive markets or when the brand is new to the category, it is more important to emphasize category links in the marketing program. Strong links between the brand and the category or other relevant cues may become especially important over time if the product meaning of the brand changes through brand extensions, mergers, or acquisitions.

Many marketers have attempted to create brand awareness through so-called shock advertising with bizarre themes.[16] For example, at the height of the dot-com boom, online retailer Outpost.com used ads featuring gerbils shot through cannons, wolverines attacking marching bands, and preschoolers having the brand name tattooed on their foreheads. The problem with such approaches is that they invariably fail to create strong category links because the product is just not prominent enough in the ad. They also can generate a fair amount of ill will. Often coming across as desperate measures, they rarely provide a foundation for long-term brand equity. In the case of Outpost.com, most potential customers did not have a clue what the company was about.

In short, we can create brand awareness by increasing the familiarity of the brand through repeated exposure (for brand recognition) and forging strong associations with the appropriate product category or other relevant purchase or consumption cues (for brand recall).[17]

Brand Image

Creating a positive brand image takes marketing programs that link strong, favorable, and unique associations to the brand in memory. The definition of customer-based brand equity does not distinguish between the source of brand associations and the manner in which they are formed; all that matters is their favorability, strength, and uniqueness. This means that consumers can form brand associations in a variety of ways other than marketing activities: from direct experience; through information from other commercial or nonpartisan sources such as *Consumer Reports* or other media vehicles; from word of mouth; and by assumptions or inferences consumers make about the brand itself, its name, logo, or identification with a company, country, channel of distribution, or person, place, or event.

Marketers should recognize the influence of these other sources of information by both managing them as well as possible and by adequately accounting for them in designing communication strategies. Consider how The Body Shop was able to build brand equity.

The Body Shop

The Body Shop created a global brand image without using conventional advertising. Its strong associations to personal care and environmental concern occurred through its products (natural ingredients only, never tested on animals), packaging (simple, refillable, recyclable), merchandising (detailed point-of-sale posters, brochures, and displays), staff (encouraged to be enthusiastic and informative concerning environmental issues), sourcing policies (using small local producers from around the world), social action program (requiring each franchisee to run a local community program), and public relations programs and activities (taking visible and sometimes outspoken stands on various issues).

Strength of Brand Associations. The more deeply a person thinks about product information and relates it to existing brand knowledge, the stronger the resulting brand associations will be. Two factors that strengthen association to any piece of information are its personal relevance and the consistency with which it is presented over time. The particular associations we recall and their salience will depend not only on the strength of association, but also on the retrieval cues present and the context in which we consider the brand. Let's consider the factors that, in general, affect the strength and recallability of a brand association.

Consumers form beliefs about brand attributes and benefits in different ways. ***Brand attributes*** are those descriptive features that characterize a product or service. ***Brand benefits*** are the personal value and meaning that consumers attach to the product or service attributes. In general, direct experiences create the strongest brand attribute and benefit associations and are particularly influential in consumers' decisions when they accurately interpret them. Word of mouth is likely to be particularly important for restaurants, entertainment, banking, and personal services. Figure 2-4 shows how consumers evaluate the importance of different reasons for brand choice.

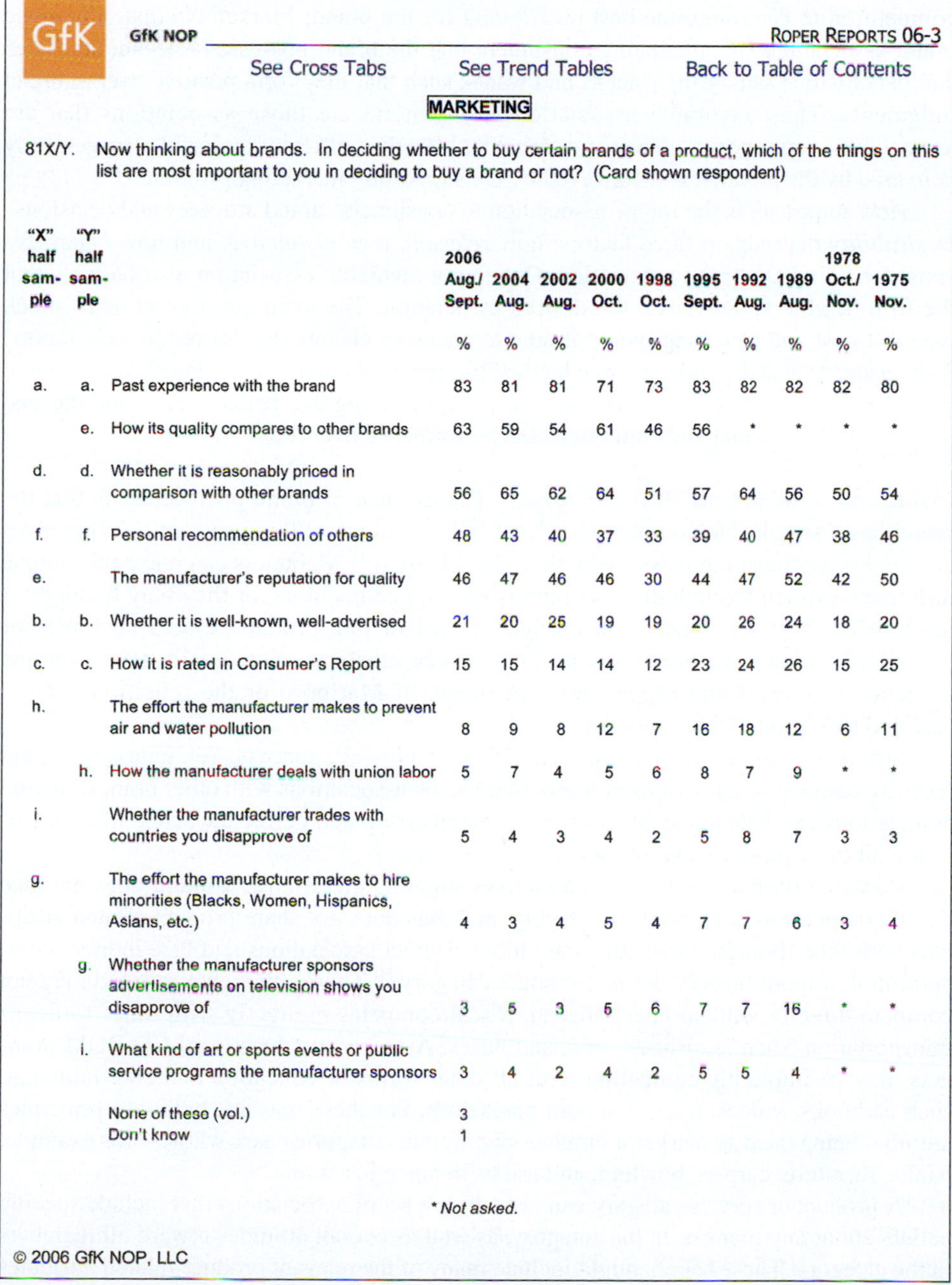

GfK GfK NOP — ROPER REPORTS 06-3

See Cross Tabs See Trend Tables Back to Table of Contents

MARKETING

81X/Y. Now thinking about brands. In deciding whether to buy certain brands of a product, which of the things on this list are most important to you in deciding to buy a brand or not? (Card shown respondent)

"X" half sample	"Y" half sample		2006 Aug./ Sept.	2004 Aug.	2002 Aug.	2000 Oct.	1998 Oct.	1995 Sept.	1992 Aug.	1989 Aug.	1978 Oct./ Nov.	1975 Nov.
			%	%	%	%	%	%	%	%	%	%
a.	a.	Past experience with the brand	83	81	81	71	73	83	82	82	82	80
	e.	How its quality compares to other brands	63	59	54	61	46	56	*	*	*	*
d.	d.	Whether it is reasonably priced in comparison with other brands	56	65	62	64	51	57	64	56	50	54
f.	f.	Personal recommendation of others	48	43	40	37	33	39	40	47	38	46
e.		The manufacturer's reputation for quality	46	47	46	46	30	44	47	52	42	50
b.	b.	Whether it is well-known, well-advertised	21	20	25	19	19	20	26	24	18	20
c.	c.	How it is rated in Consumer's Report	15	15	14	14	12	23	24	26	15	25
h.		The effort the manufacturer makes to prevent air and water pollution	8	9	8	12	7	16	18	12	6	11
	h.	How the manufacturer deals with union labor	5	7	4	5	6	8	7	9	*	*
i.		Whether the manufacturer trades with countries you disapprove of	5	4	3	4	2	5	8	7	3	3
g.		The effort the manufacturer makes to hire minorities (Blacks, Women, Hispanics, Asians, etc.)	4	3	4	5	4	7	7	6	3	4
	g.	Whether the manufacturer sponsors advertisements on television shows you disapprove of	3	5	3	5	6	7	7	16	*	*
	i.	What kind of art or sports events or public service programs the manufacturer sponsors	3	4	2	4	2	5	5	4	*	*
		None of these (vol.)	3									
		Don't know	1									

* Not asked.

Source: GfK Roper Reports® US, Q3 2006, GfK Roper Consulting.

FIGURE 2-4

GFK Roper Reports

Company-influenced sources of information, such as advertising, are often likely to create the weakest associations and thus may be the most easily changed. To overcome this hurdle, marketing communication programs use creative communications that cause consumers to elaborate on brand-related information and relate it appropriately to existing knowledge. They expose consumers to communications repeatedly over time, and ensure that many retrieval cues are present as reminders. Starbucks, Google, Red Bull, and Amazon.com are recent examples of companies that created amazingly rich brand images without the benefit of intensive advertising programs.

Favorability of Brand Associations. To choose which favorable and unique associations to link to the brand, marketers carefully analyze the consumer and the competition to determine the best positioning for the brand. Marketers create favorable brand associations by convincing consumers that the brand possesses relevant attributes and benefits that satisfy their needs and wants, such that they form positive overall brand judgments. Thus, favorable associations for a brand are those associations that are *desirable* to consumers—convenient, reliable, effective, efficient, colorful—successfully *delivered* by the product, and conveyed by the supporting marketing program

How important is the image association to consumers' brand attitudes and decisions? ***Desirability*** depends on three factors: how *relevant,* how *distinctive,* and how *believable* consumers find the brand association. Creating a favorable association also requires that the firm be able to deliver on the desired association. The main question is, How much would it cost and how long would it take to create or change the desired association(s)? ***Deliverability*** also depends on three factors: the actual or potential ability of the product to perform, the current or future prospects of communicating that performance, and the sustainability of the actual and communicated performance over time.

Uniqueness of Brand Associations. The essence of brand positioning is that the brand has a sustainable competitive advantage or "unique selling proposition" that gives consumers a compelling reason why they should buy it.[18] Marketers can make this unique difference explicit through direct comparisons with competitors, or they may highlight it implicitly. They may base it on product-related or non-product-related attributes or benefits. In some categories, non-product-related attributes more easily create unique associations—recall the rugged western image of Marlboro or the rebellious nature ascribed to Virginia Slims smokers.

Strong and unique associations are critical to a brand's success. Yet, unless the brand faces no competition, it will most likely share some associations with other brands. Shared associations can help to establish category membership and define the scope of competition with other products and services.[19]

Research on noncomparable alternatives suggests that even if a brand does not face direct competition in its product category, and thus does not share product-related attributes with other brands, it can still share more abstract associations and face indirect competition in a more broadly defined product category.[20] Thus, although a railroad may not compete directly with another railroad, it still competes indirectly with other forms of transportation, such as airlines, cars, and buses. A maker of educational CD-ROM products may be implicitly competing with all other forms of education and entertainment, such as books, videos, television, and magazines. For these reasons, branding principles are now being used to market a number of different categories as a whole—for example, banks, furniture, carpets, bowling, and trains, to name just a few.

A product or service category can also share a set of associations that include specific beliefs about any member in the category, as well as overall attitudes toward all members in the category. These beliefs might include many of the relevant product-related attributes for brands in the category, as well as more descriptive attributes that do not necessarily relate to product or service performance, like the color of a product, such as red for ketchup. Consumers may consider certain attributes or benefits prototypical and essential to all brands in the category, and a specific brand an exemplar and most representative.[21] For example, they might expect a running shoe to provide support and comfort and to be built well enough to withstand repeated wearings, and they may believe that Asics, New Balance, or some other leading brand best represents a running shoe. Similarly, consumers might expect an online retailer to offer easy navigation, a variety of offerings, reasonable shipping options, secure purchase procedures, responsive customer service, and strict privacy guidelines, and they may consider Amazon.com or some other market leader to be the best example of an online retailer.

Because the brand is linked to the product category, some category associations may also become linked to the brand, either specific beliefs or overall attitudes. Product category attitudes can be a particularly important determinant of consumer response. For example, if a consumer thinks that all brokerage houses are basically greedy and that brokers are in it for themselves, then he or she probably will have similarly unfavorable beliefs about and negative attitudes toward any particular brokerage house, simply by virtue of its membership in the category. Thus, in almost all cases, some product category associations will be shared with all brands in the category. Note that the strength of the brand associations to the product category is an important determinant of brand awareness.[22]

In short, to create the differential response that leads to customer-based brand equity, marketers need to make sure that some strongly held brand associations are not only favorable but also unique and not shared with competing brands. Unique associations help consumers choose the brand.

Consumers will not hold all brand associations to be equally important, nor will they view them favorably or value them equally across different purchase or consumption situations. And they are right. Brand associations may be situation- or context-dependent and vary according to what consumers want to achieve in that purchase or consumption decision.[23] An association may thus be valued in one situation but not another.[24]

For example, the associations that come to mind when consumers think of FedEx may be "fast," "dependable," and "convenient," with "purple and orange packages." The color of the packaging may matter little to most consumers when actually choosing an overnight delivery service, although it may perhaps play an important brand awareness function. Fast, dependable, and convenient service may be more important, but even then only under certain situations. A consumer who needs delivery only "as soon as possible" may consider less expensive options like Express Mail.

We're now ready to outline a more complete version of the customer-based brand equity model.

Building a Strong Brand: The Four Steps of Brand Building

The CBBE model looks at building a brand as a sequence of steps, each of which is contingent on successfully achieving the objectives of the previous one. The steps are as follows:

1. Ensure identification of the brand with customers and an association of the brand in customers' minds with a specific product class or customer need.
2. Firmly establish the totality of brand meaning in the minds of customers by strategically linking a host of tangible and intangible brand associations with certain properties.

3. Elicit the proper customer responses to this brand identification and brand meaning.
4. Convert brand response to create an intense, active loyalty relationship between customers and the brand.

These four steps represent a set of fundamental questions that customers invariably ask about brands—at least implicitly. The four questions (with corresponding brand steps in parentheses) are:

1. Who are you? (brand identity)
2. What are you? (brand meaning)
3. What about you? What do I think or feel about you? (brand responses)
4. What about you and me? What kind of association and how much of a connection would I like to have with you? (brand relationships)

Notice the ordering of the steps in this "branding ladder," from identity to meaning to responses to relationships. That is, we cannot establish meaning unless we have created identity; responses cannot occur unless we have developed the right meaning; and we cannot forge a relationship unless we have elicited the proper responses.

Brand Building Blocks

To provide some structure, let us think of establishing six "brand building blocks" with customers that we can assemble in a pyramid, with significant brand equity only resulting if brands reach the top of the pyramid. This brand-building process is illustrated in Figures 2-5 and 2-6. We'll look at each of these steps and corresponding brand building blocks and their subdimensions in the following sections. As will become apparent, building blocks up the left side of the pyramid represent a more "rational route" to brand building, whereas building blocks up the right side of the pyramid represent a more "emotional route." Most strong brands were built by going up both sides of the pyramid.

Brand Salience

Achieving the right brand identity means creating brand salience with customers. ***Brand salience*** measures awareness of the brand, for example, how often and how easily the brand is evoked under various situations or circumstances. To what extent is the brand top-of-mind and easily recalled or recognized? What types of cues or reminders are necessary? How pervasive is this brand awareness?

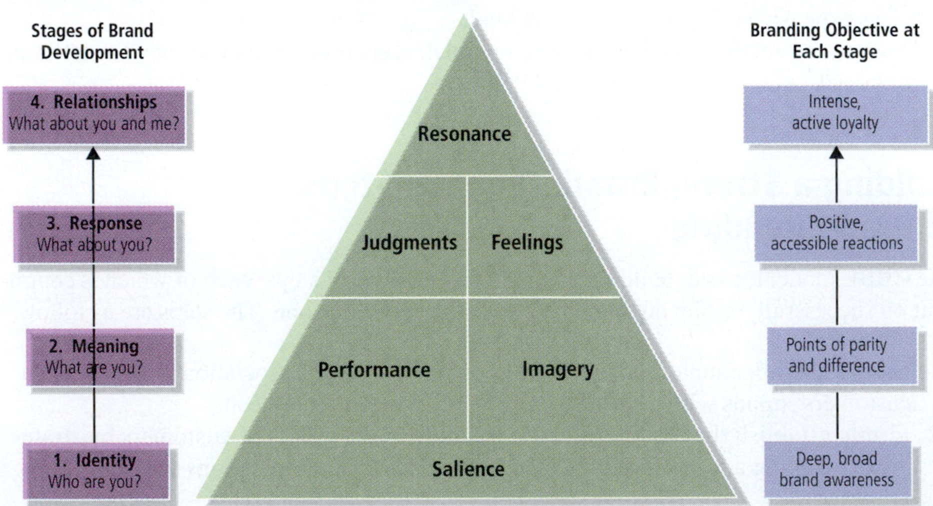

FIGURE 2-5

Customer-Based Brand Equity Pyramid

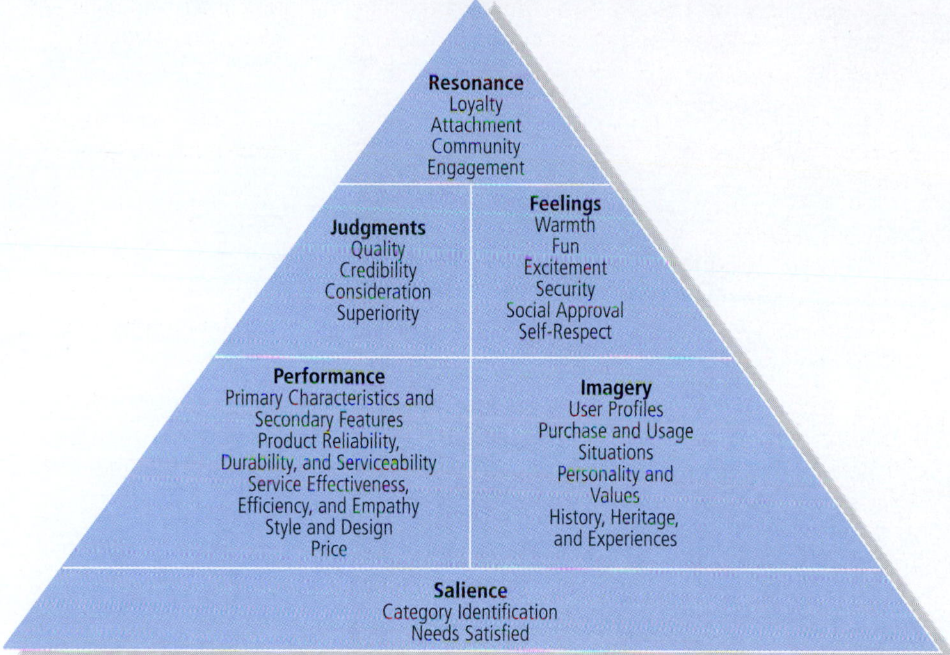

FIGURE 2-6

Subdimensions of Brand Building Blocks

We've said that brand awareness refers to customers' ability to recall and recognize the brand under different conditions and to link the brand name, logo, symbol, and so forth to certain associations in memory. In particular, building brand awareness helps customers understand the product or service category in which the brand competes and what products or services are sold under the brand name. It also ensures that customers know which of their "needs" the brand—through these products—is designed to satisfy. In other words, what basic functions does the brand provide to customers?

Breadth and Depth of Awareness. Brand awareness thus gives the product an identity by linking brand elements to a product category and associated purchase and consumption or usage situations. The *depth* of brand awareness measures how likely it is for a brand element to come to mind, and the ease with which it does so. A brand we easily recall has a deeper level of brand awareness than one that we recognize only when we see it. The *breadth* of brand awareness measures the range of purchase and usage situations in which the brand element comes to mind and depends to a large extent on the organization of brand and product knowledge in memory.[25] To see how this works, consider the breadth and depth of brand awareness for Tropicana orange juice.

TROPICANA

We want consumers at least to recognize the Tropicana brand when it is presented to them. Beyond that, they should think of Tropicana whenever they think of orange juice, particularly when they are considering buying orange juice. Ideally, consumers would think of Tropicana whenever they were deciding which type of beverage to drink, especially when seeking a "tasty but healthy" beverage. Thus, consumers must think of Tropicana as satisfying a certain set of needs whenever those needs arise. One of the challenges for any provider of orange juice is to link the product to usage situations beyond the traditional one of breakfast—hence the industry campaign to boost consumption of Florida orange juice that used the slogan "It's not just for breakfast anymore."

WITH A TASTE THIS FRESH,
YOUR JUICER WILL BE JEALOUS.
Tropicana
ORIGINAL
AMAZING, STRAIGHT-FROM-THE-ORANGE TASTE.
Have a Tropicana Morning.

Product Category Structure. As the Tropicana example suggests, to fully understand brand recall, we need to appreciate ***product category structure***, or how product categories are organized in memory. Typically, marketers assume that products are grouped at varying levels of specificity and can be organized in a hierarchical fashion.[26] Thus, in consumers' minds, a product hierarchy often exists, with product class information at the highest level, product category information at the second-highest level, product type information at the next level, and brand information at the lowest level.

The beverage market provides a good setting to examine issues in category structure and the effects of brand awareness on brand equity. Figure 2-7 illustrates one hierarchy that might exist in consumers' minds. According to this representation, consumers first distinguish between flavored and nonflavored beverages (water). Next, they distinguish between nonalcoholic and alcoholic flavored beverages. They further distinguish nonalcoholic beverages into hot drinks like coffee or tea, and cold drinks like milk, juices, and soft drinks. Alcoholic beverages are distinguished by whether they are wine, beer, or distilled spirits. We can make even further distinctions. For example, we can divide the beer category into no-alcohol, low-alcohol (or "light"), and full-strength beers, and divide full-strength beers by variety (ale or lager), by brewing method (draft, ice, or dry), by price and quality (discount, premium, or super-premium), and so on.

The organization of the product category hierarchy that generally prevails in memory will play an important role in consumer decision making. For example, consumers often make decisions in a top-down fashion, first deciding whether to have water or some type of flavored beverage. If the consumer chose a flavored drink, the next decision would be whether to have an alcoholic or a nonalcoholic drink, and so on. Finally, consumers might then choose a particular brand within the product category in which they are interested. The depth of brand awareness will influence the likelihood that the brand comes to mind, whereas the breadth of

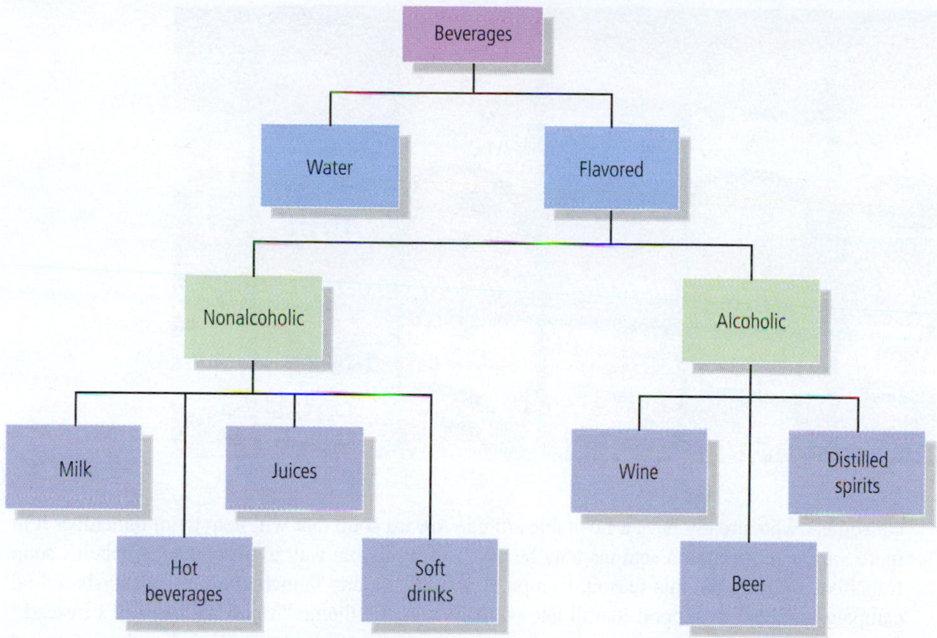

FIGURE 2-7

Beverage Category Hierarchy

brand awareness describes the different types of situations in which the brand might come to mind. In general, soft drinks have great breadth of awareness in that they come to mind in a variety of different consumption situations. A consumer may consider drinking one of the different varieties of Coke virtually any time, anywhere. Other beverages, such as alcoholic beverages, milk, and juices, have much more limited perceived consumption situations.

Strategic Implications. The product hierarchy shows us that not only the depth of awareness matters but also the breadth. In other words, the brand must not only be top-of-mind and have sufficient "mind share," but it must also do so at the right times and places.

Breadth is an oft-neglected consideration, even for brands that are category leaders. For many brands, the key question is not *whether* consumers can recall the brand but *where* they think of it, *when* they think of it, and how easily and how often they think of it. Many brands and products are ignored or forgotten during possible usage situations. Increasing brand salience in those settings can drive consumption and increase sales volume. For example, tax preparer H&R Block launched a marketing campaign that attempted to establish the company in the minds of consumers as a "year-round financial services provider" that could provide help with mortgages, insurance, investments, banking, and financial planning services at any time and not just at tax time.[27]

In some cases, the best route for improving sales for a brand is not improving consumer attitudes toward the brand but, instead, increasing the breadth of brand awareness and situations in which consumers would consider using the brand. Consider the marketing challenges for Campbell's soup.

Campbell's Soup

Ads for Campbell's soup through the years have emphasized either taste, with its long-time advertising slogan "Mmm, Mmm, Good," or nutrition—"Never Underestimate the Power of Soup." Part of Campbell's challenge in increasing sales may lie not so much in the consumer attitudes these slogans address as with memory considerations, and the fact that people do not think of eating soup as often as they should for certain meal occasions. For example, although soup is often eaten as a side dish or appetizer when people dine at restaurants, it is probably often overlooked for more common dinner occasions at home. Creating a communication program for those

Campbell's Soup is driving sales by making its product line more salient.

> consumers who already have a favorable attitude toward soup that will help them remember it in more varied consumption settings may be the most profitable way to grow the Campbell's soup franchise. Perhaps for this reason, Campbell Soup Company launched a new, reality-based ad campaign in 2003 to support its full line of soups with the theme "Make It Campbell's Instead." TV host Gordon Elliott was shown intercepting consumers at home, at work, and on the streets and urging them to enjoy a delicious meal featuring soup rather than other meal and snack options.[28]

In other words, it may be harder to try to *change* existing brand attitudes than to *remind* people of their existing attitudes toward a brand in additional, but appropriate, consumption situations.

Summary. A highly salient brand is one that has both depth and breadth of brand awareness, such that customers always make sufficient purchases as well as always think of the brand across a variety of settings in which it could possibly be employed or consumed. Brand salience is an important first step in building brand equity, but is usually not sufficient. For many customers in many situations, other considerations, such as the meaning or image of the brand, also come into play.

Creating brand meaning includes establishing a brand image—what the brand is characterized by and should stand for in the minds of customers. Brand meaning is made up of two major categories of brand associations related to performance and imagery. These associations can be formed directly, from a customer's own experiences and contact with the brand, or indirectly, through advertising or by some other source of information, such as word of mouth. The next section describes the two main types of brand meaning—brand performance and brand imagery—and the subcategories within each of those two building blocks.

Brand Performance

The product itself is at the heart of brand equity, because it is the primary influence on what consumers experience with a brand, what they hear about a brand from others, and what the firm can tell customers about the brand in their communications. Designing and delivering a product that fully satisfies consumer needs and wants is a prerequisite for successful marketing, regardless of whether the product is a tangible good, service, organization, or person. To create brand loyalty and resonance, marketers must ensure that consumers' experiences with the product at least meet, if not actually surpass, their expectations. As Chapter 1 noted, numerous studies have shown that high-quality brands tend to perform better financially and yield higher returns on investment.

Brand performance describes how well the product or service meets customers' more functional needs. How well does the brand rate on objective assessments of quality? To what extent does the brand satisfy utilitarian, aesthetic, and economic customer needs and wants in the product or service category?

Brand performance transcends the product's ingredients and features to include dimensions that differentiate the brand. Often, the strongest brand positioning relies on performance advantages of some kind, and it is rare that a brand can overcome severe performance deficiencies. Five important types of attributes and benefits often underlie brand performance, as follows:[29]

1. Primary ingredients and supplementary features
2. Product reliability, durability, and serviceability
3. Service effectiveness, efficiency, and empathy
4. Style and design
5. Price

Customers often have beliefs about the levels at which the primary ingredients of the product operate (low, medium, high, or very high), and about special, perhaps even patented, features or secondary elements that complement these primary ingredients. Some attributes are essential ingredients necessary for a product to work, whereas others are supplementary features that allow for customization and more versatile, personalized usage. Of course these vary by product or service category.

How do customers view performance? ***Reliability*** measures the consistency of performance over time and from purchase to purchase. ***Durability*** is the expected economic life of the product, and ***serviceability*** the ease of repairing the product if needed. Thus, perceptions of product performance are affected by factors such as the speed, accuracy, and care of product delivery and installation; the promptness, courtesy, and helpfulness of customer service and training; and the quality of repair service and the time involved.

Customers often have performance-related associations with service. ***Service effectiveness*** measures how well the brand satisfies customers' service requirements. ***Service efficiency*** describes the speed and responsiveness of service. Finally, ***service empathy*** is the extent to which service providers are seen as trusting, caring, and having the customer's interests in mind.

Consumers may have associations with the product that go beyond its functional aspects to more aesthetic considerations such as its size, shape, materials, and color involved. Thus, performance may also depend on sensory aspects such as how a product looks and feels, and perhaps even what it sounds or smells like.

Finally, the pricing policy for the brand can create associations in consumers' minds about how relatively expensive (or inexpensive) the brand is, and whether it is frequently or substantially discounted. Price is a particularly important performance association because consumers may organize their product category knowledge in terms of the price tiers of different brands.[30]

Brand Imagery

The other main type of brand meaning is brand imagery. Brand imagery depends on the extrinsic properties of the product or service, including the ways in which the brand attempts to meet customers' psychological or social needs. It is the way people think about a brand abstractly, rather than what they think the brand actually does. Thus, imagery refers to more intangible aspects of the brand, and consumers can form imagery associations directly from their own experience or indirectly through advertising or by some other source of information, such as word of mouth. Many kinds of intangibles can be linked to a brand, but four main ones are:

1. User profiles
2. Purchase and usage situations
3. Personality and values
4. History, heritage, and experiences

For example, take a brand with rich brand imagery, such as Nivea skin cream in Europe. Some of its intangible associations include: family/shared experiences/maternal; multipurpose; classic/timeless; and childhood memories.

One set of brand imagery associations is about the type of person or organization who uses the brand. This imagery may result in customers' mental image of actual users or more aspirational, idealized users. Consumers may base associations of a typical or idealized brand user on descriptive demographic factors or more abstract psychographic factors. Demographic factors might include the following:

- *Gender.* Venus razors and Secret deodorant have "feminine" associations, whereas Marlboro cigarettes and Right Guard deodorant have more "masculine" associations.
- *Age.* Pepsi Cola, Powerade energy sports drink, and Fuji film have positioned themselves as younger than Coke, Gatorade, and Kodak, respectively.
- *Race.* Goya foods and the Univision television network have a strong identification with the Hispanic market.
- *Income.* Sperry Topsider shoes, Polo shirts, and BMW automobiles have been associated with yuppies—young, affluent, urban professionals.

Psychographic factors might include attitudes toward life, careers, possessions, social issues, or political institutions; for example, a brand user might be seen as iconoclastic or as more traditional and conservative.

In a business-to-business setting, user imagery might relate to the size or type of organization. For example, buyers might see Microsoft as an "aggressive" company, and Patagonia or Timberland as "caring" companies. User imagery may focus on more than characteristics of just one type of individual and center on broader issues in terms of perceptions of a group as a whole. For example, customers may believe that a brand is used by many people and therefore view the brand as "popular" or a "market leader."

A second set of associations tells consumers under what conditions or situations they can or should buy and use the brand. Associations can relate to type of channel, such as department stores, specialty stores, or the Internet; to specific stores such as Macy's, Foot Locker, or Bluefly.com; and to ease of purchase and associated rewards (if any).

Associations to a typical usage situation can relate to the time of day, week, month, or year to use the brand; location—for instance, inside or outside the home; and type of activity during which to use the brand—formal or informal. For example, advertising for Snickers emphasizes that the candy bar is "Most Satisfying" and therefore "satisfies" as a filling snack. For a long time, pizza chain restaurants had strong associations to their channels of distribution and the manner by which customers would purchase and eat the pizza—Domino's was known for delivery, Little Caesar for carryout, and Pizza Hut for dine-in service—although in recent years each of these major competitors has made inroads in the traditional markets of the others.

Through consumer experience or marketing activities, brands may take on personality traits[31] and, like a person, appear to be "modern," "old-fashioned," "lively," or "exotic." Brands may also take on values. Five dimensions of brand personality (with corresponding subdimensions) are sincerity (down-to-earth, honest, wholesome, and cheerful), excitement (daring, spirited, imaginative, and up-to-date), competence (reliable, intelligent, successful), sophistication (upper class and charming), and ruggedness (outdoorsy and tough).[32]

How does brand personality get formed? Although any aspect of the marketing program may affect brand personality, advertising may be especially influential because of the inferences consumers make about the underlying user or usage situation depicted in an ad. Advertisers may imbue a brand with personality traits through anthropomorphization and product animation techniques, as with the famous California Raisins; through personification and the use of brand characters like the Geico Gecko; through user imagery such as the Mountain Dew "dudes," and so on.[33] More generally, the actors in an ad, the tone or style of the creative strategy, and the emotions or feelings evoked by the ad can affect brand personality. Once brands develop a personality, it can be difficult for consumers to accept information they see as inconsistent with that personality.[34]

Still, user imagery and brand personality may not always be in agreement. When performance-related attributes are central to consumer decisions, as they are for food products, for example, brand personality and user imagery may be less closely related. Differences between personality and imagery may arise for other reasons too. For example, at one point in time, Perrier's brand personality was "sophisticated" and "stylish," whereas its actual user imagery was not as flattering or subdued but "flashy" and "trendy."

When user and usage imagery are important to consumer decisions, however, brand personality and imagery are more likely to be related, as they are for cars, beer, liquor, cigarettes, and cosmetics. Thus, consumers often choose and use brands that have a brand personality consistent with their own self-concept, although in some cases the match may be based on consumers' desired rather than their actual image.[35] These effects may also be more pronounced for publicly consumed products than for privately consumed goods.[36] On the other hand, consumers who are high "self-monitors" and sensitive to how others see them are more likely to choose brands whose personalities fit the consumption situation.[37]

Finally, brands may take on associations to their past and certain noteworthy events in the brand history. These types of associations may recall distinctly personal experiences and episodes or past behaviors and experiences of friends, family, or others. Thus they can be highly personal and individual, or more public and shared by many people. For example, there may be associations to aspects of the marketing program for the brand such as the color of the product or look of its package, the company or person that makes the product and the country in which it is made, the type of store in which it is sold, the events for which the brand is a sponsor, and the people who endorse the brand. In either case, associations to history, heritage, and experiences involve more specific, concrete examples that transcend the generalizations that make up the usage imagery. In the extreme case, brands become iconic by combining all these types of associations into what is in effect a myth, tapping into enduring consumer hopes and dreams.[38] For example, Mountain Dew has developed a "rebel myth" with advertising showing "exciting, vital men who are far from the ideological model of success."[39]

Summary. A number of different types of associations related to either performance or imagery may become linked to the brand. We can characterize the brand associations making up the brand image and meaning according to three important dimensions—strength, favorability, and uniqueness—that provide the key to building brand equity. Successful results on these three dimensions produce the most positive brand responses, the underpinning of intense and active brand loyalty.

To create brand equity, it is important that the brand have some strong, favorable, and unique brand associations *in that order.* In other words, it doesn't matter how unique a brand association is unless customers evaluate the association favorably, and it doesn't matter how desirable a brand association is unless it is sufficiently strong that customers actually recall it and link it to the brand. At the same time, not all strong associations are favorable, and not all favorable associations are unique.

Creating strong, favorable, and unique associations is a real challenge to marketers, but essential to building customer-based brand equity. Strong brands typically have firmly established favorable and unique brand associations with consumers. Brand meaning is what helps to produce ***brand responses,*** or what customers think or feel about the brand. We can distinguish brand responses as either brand judgments or brand feelings, that is, in terms of whether they arise from the "head" or from the "heart," as the following sections describe.

Brand Judgments

Brand judgments are customers' personal opinions about and evaluations of the brand, which consumers form by putting together all the different brand performance and imagery associations. Customers may make all types of judgments with respect to a brand, but four types are particularly important: judgments about quality, credibility, consideration, and superiority.

Brand Quality. Brand attitudes are consumers' overall evaluations of a brand[40] and often form the basis for brand choice. Brand attitudes generally depend on specific attributes and benefits of the brand. For example, consider Sheraton hotels. A consumer's attitude toward Sheraton depends on how much he or she believes the brand is characterized by certain associations that matter to the consumer for a hotel chain, like location; room comfort, design, and appearance; service quality of staff; recreational facilities; food service; security; prices; and so on.

Consumers can hold a host of attitudes toward a brand, but the most important relate to its perceived quality and to customer value and satisfaction. Perceived quality measures are inherent in many approaches to brand equity. In the annual EquiTrend survey by Total Research, 20,000 consumers rate 1,000 brands across 35 categories on five dimensions: familiarity, quality, purchase intent, brand expectations, and distinctiveness. Total Research then creates an Equity Score based on the first three measures.[41]

Brand Credibility. Customers may also form judgments about the company or organization behind the brand. ***Brand credibility*** describes the extent to which customers see the brand as credible in terms of three dimensions: perceived expertise, trustworthiness, and likability. Is the brand seen as (1) competent, innovative, and a market leader (brand expertise); (2) dependable and keeping customer interests in mind (brand trustworthiness); and (3) fun, interesting, and worth spending time with (brand likability)? In other words, credibility measures whether consumers see the company or organization behind the brand as good at what it does, concerned about its customers, and just plain likable.

Brand Consideration. Favorable brand attitudes and perceptions of credibility are important but not enough if customers don't actually consider the brand for possible purchase or use. Consideration depends in part on how personally relevant customers find the brand and is a crucial filter in terms of building brand equity. No matter how highly they regard the brand or how credible they find it, unless they also give it serious consideration and deem it relevant, customers will keep a brand at a distance and never closely embrace it. Brand consideration depends in large part on the extent to which strong and favorable brand associations can be created as part of the brand image.

Brand Superiority. Superiority measures the extent to which customers view the brand as unique and better than other brands. Do customers believe it offers advantages that other brands cannot? Superiority is absolutely critical to building intense and active relationships with customers and depends to a great degree on the number and nature of unique brand associations that make up the brand image.

Brand Feelings

Brand feelings are customers' emotional responses and reactions to the brand. Brand feelings also relate to the social currency evoked by the brand. What feelings are evoked by the marketing program for the brand or by other means? How does the brand affect customers' feelings about themselves and their relationship with others? These feelings can be mild or intense and can be positive or negative.

The emotions evoked by a brand can become so strongly associated that they are accessible during product consumption or use. Researchers have defined ***transformational advertising*** as advertising designed to change consumers' perceptions of the actual usage experience with the product.[42] For example, Herbal Essence shampoo has been positioned

The Ten Commandments of Emotional Branding

1. From Consumers to People
   Consumers buy. People live.

2. From Product to Experience
   Products fulfill needs. Experiences fulfill desires.

3. From Honesty to Trust
   Honesty is expected. Trust is engaging and intimate. It needs to be earned.

4. From Quality to Preference
   Quality is a given. Preference creates the sale.

5. From Notoriety to Aspiration
   Being known does not mean that you are also loved.

6. From Identity to Personality
   Identity is recognition. Personality is about character and charisma.

7. From Function to Feel
   Function is about practical qualities. Sensorial design is about experiences.

8. From Ubiquity to Presence
   Ubiquity is seen. Presence is felt.

9. From Communication to Dialogue
   Communication is selling. Dialogue is sharing.

10. From Service to Relationship
    Service is selling. Relationship is awknowledgement.

Source: Marc Gobe, *Emotional Branding: The New Paradigm for Connecting Brands to People* (Watson-Guptill, 2001). © 2001, Marc Gobe (Allworth Press, www.allworth.com)

FIGURE 2-8

The Ten Commandments of Emotional Branding

as offering a revitalizing, sensual shampoo experience. In a parody of a famous scene from the film *When Harry Met Sally,* ads showed scenes of women reaching heights of pleasure while lathering, exclaiming "Yes, yes, YES."

More and more firms are attempting to tap into more consumer emotions with their brands. Figure 2-8 summarizes one point of view with respect to emotional branding. Branding Brief 2-1 describes how Hallmark has engendered brand feelings with consumers.

The following are six important types of brand-building feelings.[43]

1. *Warmth:* The brand evokes soothing types of feelings and makes consumers feel a sense of calm or peacefulness. Consumers may feel sentimental, warmhearted, or affectionate about the brand. Hallmark is a brand typically associated with warmth.
2. *Fun:* Upbeat types of feelings make consumers feel amused, lighthearted, joyous, playful, cheerful, and so on. Disney is a brand often associated with fun.
3. *Excitement:* The brand makes consumers feel energized and that they are experiencing something special. Brands that evoke excitement may generate a sense of elation, of "being alive," or being cool, sexy, or so on. MTV is a brand seen by many teens and young adults as exciting.
4. *Security:* The brand produces a feeling of safety, comfort, and self-assurance. As a result of the brand, consumers do not experience worry or concerns that they might have otherwise felt. Allstate insurance is a brand that communicates security to many.

BRANDING BRIEF 2-1

Eliciting Feelings for the Hallmark Brand

Hallmark was launched in 1910 when Joyce C. Hall distributed through the mail a number of postcards he had stored in two shoeboxes under his bed. From his room at the Kansas City YMCA, Hall sent packets containing a hundred of his postcards, along with invoices, to vendors throughout the Midwest. When a third of the vendors returned a check to him, Hallmark was in business. Hallmark quickly expanded into greeting cards, and over the course of the next 95 years moved into other categories characterized by emotional connections to celebration and commemoration such as wrapping paper, gifts, party decorations, and ornaments. By 2005, the $4.4 billion company was the leading greeting card company in the United States, with domestic market share exceeding 50 percent.

Hall demonstrated his knack for branding in 1928 when he began printing the Hallmark name on all cards the company produced. In 1932, the company became a pioneer in licensing when it struck an agreement with Disney to license Disney characters, the first licensing contract for either company. In 1944, the company added the slogan that appears on the back of every card, "When you care enough to send the very best."

One of the company's longest-lasting and highest-profile marketing programs is its sponsorship of the Hallmark Hall of Fame television series, which was introduced in 1951. The Hallmark Hall of Fame has won more Emmy awards than any other television program, including the first-ever Emmy given to a sponsor. A natural extension was the highly succcessful launch of the Hallmark Channel on television in 2001. Focusing on family-friendly entertainment, the channel shows original movies and entertainment as well as popular network favorites from years gone by. In addition to reaching more than 69 million homes in the United States, the Hallmark Channel is

Hallmark has tapped into consumer emotions to create a wide-ranging business.

5. *Social approval:* Consumers feel that others look favorably on their appearance, behavior, and so on. This approval may be a result of direct acknowledgment of the consumer's use of the brand by others or may be less overt and a result of attribution of product use to consumers. Mercedes is a brand that may signal social approval to consumers.
6. *Self-respect:* The brand makes consumers feel better about themselves; consumers feel a sense of pride, accomplishment, or fulfillment. A brand like Tide laundry detergent is able to link its brand to "doing the best things for the family" to many homemakers.

also seen in over 122 international markets. Its success led to the later introduction of the Hallmark Movie Channel

Hallmark products can be found at more than 43,000 retail outlets domestically and online at Hallmark.com. Hallmark Gold Crown stores, the company's flagship network of 4,000 independently owned card and gift specialty stores, carry the most extensive selection of gift and personal expression products. Hallmark's creative staff consists of around 800 artists, designers, stylists, writers, editors, and photographers. Together they generate more than 19,000 new and redesigned greeting cards and related products per year. The company offers more than 48,000 products in its model line at any one time. Today, the company publishes in 30 languages and its products are available in more than 120 countries around the globe.

The company researches the latest consumer trends in color, fashion, design, and lifestyles. It conducts focus groups and surveys, facilitates online consumer communities, and utilizes a sophisticated point-of-sale network to understand consumer needs today. Hallmark has also created an official loyalty program, called Gold Crown Card, that rewards frequent buyers with discounts and special incentives. All this marketing activity, however, is directed to a very singular purpose, defined as its brand essence:

Hallmark is here to help people define and express the very best in themselves, to serve their spirit of kindness, their need to comfort and to heal, to love and be loved, to laugh and to celebrate, to reach out and to remember.

We are here to offer gifts of thoughtfulness, messages of care, moments of beauty created to heighten the pleasure of giving, the thrill of receiving and the joy of sharing.

We are here to commemorate the smallest events and the largest milestones, to affirm our respect for humanity, our belief in its future and our unwavering reverence for the sweetness and fullness of life.

We are here to make connections with timely humor and timeless inspiration, with gentle affection and genuine surprise, with light and music and color, with stirring images and powerful stories that speak to what is universal in the human heart.

We are here to enhance relationships, to enrich lives, to play our unique and cherished role in the always changing, never changing seasons of friendship and family and love.

Sources: Kate Fitzgerald, "Hallmark Casts for New Role," *Advertising Age*, 29 August 1994; Kipp Cheng, "Hallmark.com Revamps Consumer-Targeted Site," *Adweek*, 24 May 1999; Carol Krol, "Hallmark Uses Loyalty Effort for Segmenting Consumers," *Advertising Age*, 1 February 1999; www.hallmark.com.

The first three types of feelings are experiential and immediate, increasing in level of intensity. The latter three types of feelings are private and enduring, increasing in level of gravity.

Summary. Although all types of customer responses are possible—driven from both the head and heart—ultimately what matters is how positive they are. Responses must also be accessible and come to mind when consumers think of the brand. Brand judgments and feelings can favorably affect consumer behavior only if consumers internalize or think of positive responses in their encounters with the brand.

Brand Resonance

The final step of the model focuses on the ultimate relationship and level of identification that the customer has with the brand. ***Brand resonance*** describes the nature of this relationship and the extent to which customers feel that they are "in sync" with the brand. Examples of brands with high resonance include Harley-Davidson, Apple, and eBay. Resonance is characterized in terms of intensity, or the depth of the psychological bond that customers have with the brand, as well as the level of activity engendered by this loyalty (repeat purchase rates and the extent to which customers seek out brand information, events, and other loyal customers). We can break down these two dimensions of brand resonance into four categories:

1. Behavioral loyalty
2. Attitudinal attachment
3. Sense of community
4. Active engagement

We can gauge ***behavioral loyalty*** in terms of repeat purchases and the amount or share of category volume attributed to the brand, that is, the "share of category requirements." In other words, how often do customers purchase a brand and how much do they purchase? For bottom-line profit results, the brand must generate sufficient purchase frequencies and volumes. The lifetime value of behaviorally loyal consumers can be enormous.[44] For example, a loyal General Motors customer could be worth $276,000 over his or her lifetime (assuming 11 or more vehicles bought and word-of-mouth endorsement that makes friends and relatives more likely to consider GM products). Similarly, experts have estimated that the lifetime value of a sophisticated computer user (defined as one who buys a new machine and software about every two years) is approximately $45,000. A nonsophisticated user who postpones purchases as long as possible was estimated to provide $25,000 in lifetime value.

Behavioral loyalty is necessary but not sufficient for resonance to occur.[45] Some customers may buy out of necessity—because the brand is the only product stocked or readily accessible, the only one they can afford, or other reasons. Resonance, however, requires a strong personal ***attachment***. Customers should go beyond having a positive attitude to viewing the brand as something special in a broader context. For example, customers with a great deal of attitudinal attachment to a brand may state that they "love" the brand, describe it as one of their favorite possessions, or view it as a "little pleasure" that they look forward to.

Prior research has shown that mere satisfaction may not be enough.[46] Xerox found that when customer satisfaction was ranked on a scale of 1 (completely dissatisfied) to 5 (completely satisfied), customers who rated Xerox products and services as "4"—and thus were satisfied—were six times more likely to defect to competitors than those customers who provided ratings of "5."[47] Similarly, loyalty guru Frederick Reichheld points out that although more than 90 percent of car buyers are satisfied or very satisfied when they drive away from the dealer's showroom, fewer than half buy the same brand of automobile the next time.[48] Creating greater loyalty requires creating deeper attitudinal attachment, through marketing programs and products and services that fully satisfy consumer needs.

The brand may also take on broader meaning to the customer by conveying a sense of ***community***.[49] Identification with a brand community may reflect an important social phenomenon in which customers feel a kinship or affiliation with other people associated with the brand, whether fellow brand users or customers, or employees or representatives of the company. A brand community can exist online or off-line.[50] Branding Brief 2-2 profiles three company-initiated programs to help build brand communities.

BRANDING BRIEF 2-2

Building Brand Communities

Apple

Apple encourages owners of its computers to form local Apple user groups. By 2005, there were over 700 groups, ranging in size from fewer than 25 members to over 1,000 members. The user groups provide Apple owners with opportunities to learn more about their computers, share ideas, and get product discounts, as well as sponsor special activities and events and perform community service. A visit to Apple's Web site helps customers find nearby user groups.

Harley-Davidson

The world-famous motorcycle company sponsors the Harley Owners Group (HOG), which by 2005 had 900,000 members in chapter groups all over the world sharing a very simple mission, "To Ride and Have Fun." The first-time buyer of a Harley-Davidson motorcycle gets a free one-year membership. HOG benefits include a magazine called *Hog Tales*, a touring handbook, emergency road service, a specially designed insurance program, theft reward service, discount hotel rates, and a Fly & Ride program enabling members to rent Harleys while on vacation. The company also maintains an extensive Web site devoted to HOG, which includes information about club chapters and events and features a special members-only section.

Camp Jeep allows owners to live the brand's promise.

Jeep

In addition to joining the hundreds of local Jeep enthusiast clubs throughout the world, Jeep owners can convene with their vehicles in wilderness areas across America as part of the company's official Jeep Jamborees and Camp Jeep. Since the inaugural Camp Jeep in 1995, over 28,000 people have attended the three-day sessions, where they practice off-road driving skills and meet other Jeep owners. Jeep Jamborees bring Jeep owners and their families together for two-day off-road adventures in more than 30 different locations from spring through autumn each year. Promising to be "every bit as muddy," Camp Jeep on the Road hit eight cities in 2005 to allow existing and prospective Jeep 4x4 owners to put the vehicles through their paces on- and off-road.

A stronger sense of community among loyal users can engender favorable brand attitudes and intentions.[51]

Finally, perhaps the strongest affirmation of brand loyalty occurs when customers are ***engaged***, or willing to invest time, energy, money, or other resources in the brand beyond those expended during purchase or consumption of the brand. For example, customers may choose to join a club centered on a brand, receive updates, and exchange correspondence with other brand users or formal or informal representatives of the brand itself. They may choose to visit brand-related Web sites, participate in chat rooms, and so on. In this case, customers themselves became brand evangelists and ambassadors and help to communicate about the brand and strengthen the brand ties of others. Strong attitudinal attachment or social identity or both are typically necessary, however, for active engagement with the brand to occur.

In summary, brand resonance and the relationships consumers have with brands have two dimensions: ***intensity*** and ***activity***. Intensity measures the strength of the attitudinal attachment and sense of community. Activity tells us how frequently the consumer buys and uses the brand, as well as engages in other activities not related to purchase and consumption.

Brand-Building Implications

The customer-based brand equity model provides a road map and guidance for brand building, a yardstick by which brands can assess their progress in their brand-building efforts as well as a guide for marketing research initiatives. With respect to the latter, one CBBE application aids in brand tracking and providing quantitative measures of the success of brand-building efforts (see Chapter 8). Figure 2-9 contains a set of candidate measures for the six brand building blocks.

The model also reinforces a number of important branding tenets, five of which are particularly noteworthy. We discuss them in the following sections.

Customers Own Brands. The basic premise of the CBBE model is that the true measure of the strength of a brand is the way consumers think, feel, and act with respect to that brand. The strongest brands will be those to which consumers become so attached and passionate that they, in effect, become evangelists or missionaries and attempt to share their beliefs and spread the word about the brand. *The power of the brand and its ultimate value to the firm reside with customers.* It is through learning about and experiencing a brand that customers end up thinking and acting in a way that allows the firm to reap the benefits of brand equity. Although marketers must take responsibility for designing and implementing the most effective and efficient brand-building marketing programs possible, the success of those marketing efforts ultimately depends on how consumers respond. This response, in turn, depends on the knowledge that has been created in their minds for those brands.

Don't Take Shortcuts with Brands. The CBBE model reinforces the fact that there are no shortcuts in building a brand. A great brand is not built by accident but is the product of carefully accomplishing—either explicitly or implicitly—a series of logically linked steps with consumers. The more explicitly marketers recognize the steps and define them as concrete goals, the more likely they will give them the proper attention and fully realize them so they can provide the greatest contribution to brand building. *The length of time to build a strong brand will therefore be directly proportional to the amount of time it takes to create sufficient awareness and understanding so that firmly held and felt beliefs and attitudes about the brand are formed that can serve as the foundation for brand equity.*

I. Salience

What brands of product or service category can you think of? (using increasingly specific product category cues)
Have you ever heard of these brands?
Which brands might you be likely to use under the following situations . . . ?
How frequently do you think of this brand?

II. Performance

Compared with other brands in the category, how well does this brand provide the basic functions of the product or service category?
Compared with other brands in the category, how well does this brand satisfy the basic needs of the product or service category?
To what extent does this brand have special features?
How reliable is this brand?
How durable is this brand?
How easily serviced is this brand?
How effective is this brand's service? Does it completely satisfy your requirements?
How efficient is this brand's service in terms of speed, responsiveness, and so forth?
How courteous and helpful are the providers of this brand's service?
How stylish do you find this brand?
How much do you like the look, feel, and other design aspects of this brand?
Compared with other brands in the category with which it competes, are this brand's prices generally higher, lower, or about the same?
Compared with other brands in the category with which it competes, do this brand's prices change more frequently, less frequently, or about the same amount?

III. Imagery

To what extent do people you admire and respect use this brand?
How much do you like people who use this brand?
How well do the following words describe this brand: down-to-earth, honest, daring, up-to-date, reliable, successful, upper class, charming, outdoorsy?
What places are appropriate to buy this brand?
How appropriate are the following situations to use this brand?
Can you buy this brand in a lot of places?
Is this a brand that you can use in a lot of different situations?
To what extent does thinking of the brand bring back pleasant memories?
To what extent do you feel you grew up with the brand?

IV. Judgments

Quality
What is your overall opinion of this brand?
What is your assessment of the product quality of this brand?
To what extent does this brand fully satisfy your product needs?
How good a value is this brand?

Credibility
How knowledgeable are the makers of this brand?
How innovative are the makers of this brand?
How much do you trust the makers of this brand?
To what extent do the makers of this brand understand your needs?
To what extent do the makers of this brand care about your opinions?
To what extent do the makers of this brand have your interests in mind?

(Continued)

FIGURE 2-9

Possible Measures of Brand Building Blocks

Credibility (cont.)

How much do you like this brand?

How much do you admire this brand?

How much do you respect this brand?

Consideration

How likely would you be to recommend this brand to others?

Which are your favorite products in this brand category?

How personally relevant is this brand to you?

Superiority

How unique is this brand?

To what extent does this brand offer advantages that other brands cannot?

How superior is this brand to others in the category?

V. Feelings

Does this brand give you a feeling of warmth?

Does this brand give you a feeling of fun?

Does this brand give you a feeling of excitement?

Does this brand give you a feeling of security?

Does this brand give you a feeling of social approval?

Does this brand give you a feeling of self-respect?

VI. Resonance

Loyalty

I consider myself loyal to this brand.

I buy this brand whenever I can.

I buy as much of this brand as I can.

I feel this is the only brand of this product I need.

This is the one brand I would prefer to buy/use.

If this brand were not available, it would make little difference to me if I had to use another brand.

I would go out of my way to use this brand.

Attachment

I really love this brand.

I would really miss this brand if it went away.

This brand is special to me.

This brand is more than a product to me.

Community

I really identify with people who use this brand.

I feel as if I almost belong to a club with other users of this brand.

This is a brand used by people like me.

I feel a deep connection with others who use this brand.

Engagement

I really like to talk about this brand to others.

I am always interested in learning more about this brand.

I would be interested in merchandise with this brand's name on it.

I am proud to have others know I use this brand.

I like to visit the Web site for this brand.

Compared with other people, I follow news about this brand closely.

It should be recognized that the core brand values at the bottom two levels of the pyramid—brand salience, performance, and imagery—are typically more idiosyncratic and unique to a product and service category than other brand values.

The brand-building steps may not be equally difficult. Creating brand identity is a step that an effectively designed marketing program often can accomplish in a relatively short period of time. Unfortunately, this step is the one that many brand marketers tend to skip in their mistaken haste to quickly establish an image for the brand (as is evident by the numerous failed dot-com brands whose target market had no inkling what they did). It is difficult for consumers to appreciate the advantages and uniqueness of a brand unless they have some sort of frame of reference for what the brand is supposed to do and with whom or what it is supposed to compete. Similarly, consumers cannot have highly positive responses without a reasonably complete understanding of the brand's dimensions and characteristics.

Finally, due to circumstances in the marketplace, consumers may actually start a repeated-purchase or behavioral loyalty relationship with a brand without much underlying feeling, judgment, or associations. Nevertheless, these other brand-building blocks will have to come into place at some point to create true resonance. That is, although the start point may differ, the same steps in brand building eventually must occur to create a truly strong brand.

Brands Should Have a Duality. One important point reinforced by the model is that a strong brand has a duality—it appeals to both the head and the heart. Thus, although there may be two different ways to build loyalty and resonance—going up the left-hand and right-hand sides of the pyramid—strong brands often do both. *Strong brands blend product performance and imagery to create a rich, varied, but complementary set of consumer responses to the brand.*

Chewing Gum

Chewing gum marketers used to employ conventional advertising images, such as Wrigley's Doublemint gum ads featuring a wholesome set of twins. Not any more. Targeting "socially bold 18–24 year olds," an ad campaign for Dentyne Fire emphasized the ability of the gum to light the passions of the other sex. Juicy Fruit has gone online to spread the word on its "grapermelon" and "strappleberry" flavors. Expanding salience by broadening the perceptions of when gum-chewing is appropriate and employing more compelling imagery and emotional appeals has paid off. After experiencing flat sales in prior years, gum sales rose 6 percent in 2004.[52]

By appealing to both rational and emotional concerns, a strong brand provides consumers with multiple access points while reducing competitive vulnerability. Rational concerns can satisfy utilitarian needs, whereas emotional concerns can satisfy psychological or emotional needs. Combining the two allows brands to create a formidable brand position. Consistent with this reasoning, a McKinsey study of 51 corporate brands found that having distinctive physical *and* emotional benefits drove greater shareholder value, especially when the two were linked.[53]

Brands Should Have Richness. The level of detail in the CBBE model highlights the number of possible ways to create meaning with consumers and the range of possible avenues to elicit consumer responses. Collectively, these various aspects of brand meaning and the resulting responses produce strong consumer bonds to the brand. The various associations making up the brand image may be reinforcing, helping to strengthen or increase the favorability of other brand associations, or they may be unique, helping to add distinctiveness or offset some potential deficiencies. Strong brands thus have both breadth (in terms of duality) *and* depth (in terms of richness).

At the same time, brands should not necessarily be expected to score highly on all the various dimensions and categories making up each core brand value. Building blocks can have hierarchies in their own right. For example, with respect to brand awareness, typically marketers should first establish category identification in some way before considering strategies to expand brand breadth via needs satisfied or benefits offered. With brand performance, they may wish to first link primary characteristics and related features before attempting to link additional, more peripheral associations. Similarly, brand imagery often begins with a fairly concrete initial articulation of user and usage imagery that, over time, leads to broader, more abstract brand associations of personality, value, history, heritage, and experience. Brand judgments usually begin with positive quality and credibility perceptions that can lead to brand consideration and then perhaps ultimately to assessments of brand superiority. Brand feelings usually start with either experiential ones (warmth, fun, and excitement) or inward ones (security, social approval, and self-respect.) Finally, resonance again has a clear ordering, whereby behavioral loyalty is a starting point but attitudinal attachment or a sense of community is almost always needed for active engagement to occur. Here is a clever way one company went about eliciting active engagement from its customers

Weldbond Adhesives

With claims that it "bonds almost anything!" the marketers of Weldbond Adhesives decided to put their product to the test. For a one-year period, they ran a contest, "You Glued What?" that asked customers to submit their most outrageous product applications. Demonstrating the product's versatility and inspiring creativity in use, winning entries appeared in photos and stories on hang tags attached to the product's packaging for all to see. Devotees of the brand described how they glued a 1,452-pound wooden bowl (which used 1,213 gallons of Weldbond), created Weldbond-sealed giant sand sculptures, and assembled the largest model of the *Titanic* ever constructed.[54]

Brand Resonance Provides Important Focus. As Figure 2-5 shows, brand resonance is the pinnacle of the CBBE model and provides important focus and priority for decision making about marketing. Marketers building brands should use brand resonance as a goal and a means to interpret their brand-related marketing activities. The question to ask is, To what extent is marketing activity affecting the key dimensions of brand resonance—consumer loyalty, attachment, community, or engagement with the brand? Is marketing activity creating brand performance and imagery associations and consumer judgments and feelings that will support these brand resonance dimensions? In an application of the CBBE model, the marketing research firm Knowledge Networks found that brands that scored highest on loyalty and attachment dimensions were not necessarily the same ones that scored high on community and engagement dimensions (see Figure 2-10).

Yet, it is virtually impossible for consumers to experience an intense, active loyalty relationship with all the brands they purchase and consume. Thus, some brands will be more meaningful to consumers than others, because of the nature of their associated product or service, the characteristics of the consumer, and so on. When it is difficult to create a varied set of feelings and imagery associations, marketers might not be able to obtain the deeper aspects of brand resonance like active engagement. Nevertheless, by taking a broader view of brand loyalty, they may be able to gain a more holistic appreciation for their brand and how it connects to consumers. And by defining the proper role for the brand, they should be able to obtain higher levels of brand resonance. Branding Brief 2-3 describes how Jones Soda created extraordinary brand resonance with its users.

Rank Order	Brand Loyalty	Brand Attachment	Brand Community	Brand Engagement
1	Harley-Davidson	Harley-Davidson	Harley-Davidson	Harley-Davidson
2	Hershey's	Hershey's	Lifetime Television	Lifetime Television
3	Campbell's	Campbell's	Public Broadcasting	Lexus
4	Clorox	Discovery Channel	Fidelity Investments	Discovery Channel
5	Heinz	BMW	MSN	Public Broadcasting
6	Kodak	Wal-Mart	Lexus	Wal-Mart
7	Kraft	Public Broadcasting	Discovery Channel	BMW
8	Wal-Mart	Kraft	AOL.com	Dell
9	Duracell	Kodak	Chevrolet	Toyota
10	Discovery Channel	NBC	Hershey's	Fidelity Investments

FIGURE 2-10

Brand Rankings on Resonance Dimensions (United States, Fall 2001)

Creating Customer Value

Customer–brand relationships are the foundation of brand resonance and building a strong brand. Marketers have recognized the importance of adopting a strong consumer and customer orientation for years. The customer-based brand equity model certainly puts that notion front and center, making it clear that the power of a brand resides in the minds of consumers and customers. The Science of Branding 2-2 describes some criteria to determine whether a company is consumer-centric.

Too many firms, however, still find themselves paying the price for lacking a customer focus. Even the biggest firms can stumble.

VOLKSWAGEN

After a remarkable revival in the 1990s when it enjoyed 50 percent growth for seven straight years, Volkswagen AG did not fare well around the turn of the century. By 2005, the company was experiencing stagnant sales and losing money in its critical U.S. market. The culprit? According to VW CEO Bernd Pischetsrieder, "The biggest failure in Volkswagen is too little customer focus." In his view, the company was paying too much attention to technology and features that he felt customers didn't necessarily want to pay for. According to Pischetsrieder, "The first question is, how does it help the customer and will the customer pay for it? When we have a test drive, the question is not whether I like it. It's will the customer pay for it? Or will the customer not even notice it?"[55]

Volkswagen is not alone in its recognition of the financial value of customer experiences. Many firms are now more carefully defining the financial value of prospective and actual customers and devising marketing programs to optimize that value.

Customer Relationship Management

Customer relationship marketing (CRM) uses a company's data systems and applications to track consumer activity and manage customer interactions with the company:

> CRM synthesizes all of a company's customer "touchpoints"—including e-mail, call centers, retail stores, and sales reps—to support subsequent customer interactions as well as to inform financial forecasts, product design, and supply-chain management.[56]

BRANDING BRIEF 2-3

Putting a Face to the Customer at Jones Soda

Jones Soda Company injects customer input into almost every aspect of the brand. Because the beverage market is a crowded field, founder and CEO Peter van Stolk says Jones Soda Co. needs to go out of its way to find reasons for customers to care about the brand. The company, which was launched with six flavors in 1996, uses its Web site to solicit comments, conduct polls, and collect suggestions.

Jones Soda creates resonance in part by personalizing the brand experience.

Although many companies ask for feedback, Jones puts customer ideas into practice all the time. Suggestions to the Seattle-based company have yielded flavors such as chocolate fudge and green apple and offbeat names like Bohemian Raspberry and D'Peach Mode. And the Web site encourages fans to submit their own photos for the bottle labels. The ever-changing black-and-white label photos have become a Jones signature. When the company became inundated with more photos than it could ever use, it launched myjones.com, where customers can order custom 12-packs of soda with personal photo labels for $34.95.

Distribution of Jones Soda began with an alternative distribution strategy. The company placed its own coolers, bearing its signature flames, in some unique venues, such as skate, surf, and snowboarding shops, tattoo and piercing parlors, and individual fashion stores and national retail clothing and music

For instance, CRM can help customer service representatives give better service by enabling them to instantly view and analyze pertinent information, such as the customer's entire purchase record or the availability of product replacements, and to determine the most cost-efficient course for both parties.

CRM projects usually require the installation of sophisticated hardware and complicated software. Once they have CRM systems in place, companies expect to harness the data-mining power of the system to trim costs or increase profits and make back their investment. As an alternative to expensive in-house CRM systems, several companies are marketing Web-based CRM applications that are considerably cheaper and easier to use.

Experts agree, however, that technology is only part of the CRM equation. If the company intends to build a relationship, it must do more than mine a customer's data in order to extract more money from that customer. CRM can increase value for both the company and the customer. As one marketing executive cautioned, "CRM isn't a bad idea, but companies should be sure to take their customers' point of view into account." In other words, employing the proper human touch is as important as installing the best CRM system.

stores. Then the company began branching out to convenience and food stores. Jones is now available in larger chain stores such as Starbucks, Barnes & Noble, Safeway, Target, and 7-Eleven stores.

Jones Soda has also incorporated unique marketing initiatives in its strategy. Professional athletes in sports such as BMX bike riding and surfing promote Jones Soda at extreme sporting events like the X-Games. And two Jones Soda Co. RVs are on the road nine months a year visiting venues like skate parks and high schools. The RVs attract crowds full of the company's 12-to-24-year-old target demographic. The fans get Jones stickers and buttons while the drivers scan the crowd on the lookout for trends.

The strategy has worked well so far. The company has produced 30 percent yearly revenue growth in a flat beverage market and brought in $30 million in annual revenue. After running Jones Soda for eight years, van Stolk has established his own ideas about branding. He says strong brands take time, not money, to develop. He emphasizes looking outside the company, at companies that are leaders in other industries, for inspiration. He doesn't put too much trust in focus groups, preferring to conduct simple taste tests where answer choices are strictly limited. Van Stolk says the company's target demographic is younger than its target customer because trends tend to drift up from young people to older groups. He values input but doesn't cater to every customer whim and says absorbing all the suggestions puts him in a position to make well-informed choices.

Sources: Ryan Underwood, "Cracking Jones Soda's Secret Formula," *Fast Company,* March 2005; "Made to Order: Brands Are Tailoring Their Packages to Niche Markets and, Even, Markets of One," *BrandPackaging,* May 2005; www.jonessoda.com.

Customer Equity

Many firms have introduced customer relationship marketing programs to improve customer interactions. Some marketing observers encourage firms to formally define and manage the value of their customers. The concept of customer equity can be useful in that regard. Although we can define customer equity in different ways, one definition calls it "the sum of lifetime values of all customers."[57] Customer lifetime value (CLV) is affected by revenue and by the cost of customer acquisition, retention, and cross-selling. Several different concepts and approaches have been put forth that are relevant to the topic of customer equity. Let's look at a few.

Blattberg and Colleagues. Blattberg and Deighton have defined customer equity as the optimal balance between what marketers spend on customer acquisition and what they spend on customer retention.[58] They calculated customer equity as follows.

> We first measure each customer's expected contribution toward offsetting the company's fixed costs over the expected life of that customer. Then we discount the expected contributions to a net present value at the company's target rate of return for marketing investments. Finally, we add together the discounted, expected contributions of all current contributions.

THE SCIENCE OF BRANDING 2-2

Putting Customers First

At most companies, employees don't have any idea what their firm's return on invested capital is, let alone the returns on specific customer segments—and even if they knew, they'd be powerless to do anything about it. But according to authors Larry Selden and Geoffrey Colvin, a few companies, such as Dell, Best Buy, and Royal Bank of Canada, have been solid stocks for shareholders because of their customer-centric approach. According to these authors, ***customer-centricity*** means that all employees understand how their actions affect share price. Selden and Colvin maintain that customer-centric companies are a good bet for investors because they hold an advantage that can lead to a jump in share price. To determine whether a company is truly customer-focused, Selden and Colvin suggest customers ask themselves the following five questions:

1. ***Is the company looking for ways to take care of you?*** Only a few companies identify customer needs first, and then create ways to meet them. Too many companies try to make customers buy the products and services they already offer. Royal Bank of Canada is an example of a company that found a customer segment with unique needs and met those needs. Many of the bank's customers were Canadians who spent winters in Florida or Arizona. Those customers, who tended to be affluent, wanted to borrow money in the United States for homes and get a U.S. credit rating that reflected their Canadian record. They also wanted to be served by employees who knew the United States as well as Canada. To serve those customers, the bank opened a branch in Florida through its U.S. subsidiary. The results have been exceptional: Customers are signing up in droves and the new branch will be profitable in months rather than the typical years. Opening new branches aimed at specific customer segments represented a growth opportunity for the bank's shareholders.

The authors offer the following observation:

> Ultimately, we contend that the appropriate question for judging new products, new programs, and new customer-service initiatives should not be, Will it attract new customers? or, Will it increase our retention rates? but rather, Will it grow our customer equity? The goal of maximizing customer equity by balancing acquisition and retention efforts properly should serve as the star by which a company steers its entire marketing program.

Blattberg and Deighton offer eight guidelines as a means of maximizing customer equity:

1. Invest in highest-value customers first.
2. Transform product management into customer management.
3. Consider how add-on sales and cross-selling can increase customer equity.
4. Look for ways to reduce acquisition costs.
5. Track customer equity gains and losses against marketing programs.

2. ***Does the company know its customers well enough to differentiate between them?*** True differentiation means knowing who your various customer segments are, what each group wants, where the groups are shopping, and how to serve the customers individually. For example, Best Buy configures some stores to serve its "soccer-mom" customer segment and others to entice a segment of affluent entertainment lovers with stores that have home-theater demo rooms.
3. ***Is someone accountable for customers?*** At most companies various departments own pieces, but no one owns any specific customer segment. But at companies with customer-centric approaches, things are different. At Best Buy, for example, an individual is accountable for the "soccer-mom" segment across multiple stores.
4. ***Is the company managed for shareholder value?*** If a company is managed for shareholder value, employees know about earning a return on invested capital that exceeds the cost of capital, plus investing increasing amounts of capital at that positive spread and maintaining that spread for as long as possible. Customer-centric companies apply those criteria to customer segments. They know how much capital they've invested in a segment and how much return they earn on it. They maintain the positive spread by creating and reinventing enduring customer relationships.
5. ***Is the company testing new customer offers and learning from the results?*** Constant learning about what customers want and a formal process for sharing it are critical to customer-centricity. 7-Eleven Japan does this well. Every week employees from all over Japan meet to discuss hypotheses tested and verified in the stores. Ideas such as changing the lunch menu for the next day based on the predicted weather (like serving hot noodles on a cool day) are heard throughout the company.

Sources: Larry Selden and Geoffrey Colvin, "5 Rules for Finding the Next Dell," *Fortune*, 12 July 2004; Larry Selden and Geoffrey Colvin, *Angel Customers and Demon Customers: Discover Which Is Which and Turbo-Charge Your Stock* (New York: Portfolio, 2003).

6. Relate branding to customer equity.
7. Monitor the intrinsic retainability of your customers.
8. Consider writing separate marketing plans—or even building two marketing organizations—for acquisition and retention efforts.

Rust, Zeithaml, and Lemon. Rust, Zeithaml, and Lemon define customer equity as the discounted lifetime values of a firm's customer base.[59] According to their view, customer equity is made up of three components and key drivers:

- *Value equity:* Customers' objective assessment of the utility of a brand based on perceptions of what is given up for what is received. Three drivers of value equity are quality, price, and convenience.
- *Brand equity:* Customers' subjective and intangible assessment of the brand, above and beyond its objectively perceived value. Three key drivers of brand equity are customer brand awareness, customer brand attitudes, and customer perception of brand ethics.

- *Relationship equity:* Customers' tendency to stick with the brand, above and beyond objective and subjective assessments of the brand. Four key drivers of relationship equity are loyalty programs, special recognition and treatment programs, community-building programs, and knowledge-building programs.

Note that this definition of brand equity differs from the customer-based brand equity definition proposed in this chapter, which puts the focus on the beneficial differential response to marketing activity that strong brands produce.

These authors propose that the three components of customer equity vary in importance by company and industry. For example, they suggest that brand equity will matter more with low-involvement purchases involving simple decision processes (like facial tissues), when the product is highly visible to others, when experiences associated with the product can be passed from one individual or generation to the next, or when it is difficult to evaluate the quality of a product or service prior to consumption. On the other hand, value equity will be more important in business-to-business settings, whereas retention equity will be more important for companies that sell a variety of products and services to the same customer.

Rust and colleagues advocate customer-centered brand management to firms with the following directives that, they maintain, go against current management convention:

1. Make brand decisions subservient to decisions about customer relationships.
2. Build brands around customer segments, not the other way around.
3. Make your brands as narrow as possible.
4. Plan brand extensions based on customer needs, not component similarities.
5. Develop the capability and the mind-set to hand off customers to other brands in the company.
6. Take no heroic measures to try to save ineffective brands.
7. Change how you measure brand equity to make individual-level calculations.

Kumar and Colleagues. In a series of studies, Kumar and his colleagues explore a number of questions concerning customer lifetime value and how firms should allocate their marketing spending to customer acquisition and retention efforts.[60] The authors show that marketing contacts across various channels influence CLV nonlinearly. Customers who are selected on the basis of their lifetime value provide higher profits in future periods than do customers selected on the basis of several other customer-based metrics. Kumar and his colleagues show how each customer varies in his or her lifetime value to a firm, and how customer lifetime value computations require different approaches depending on the business application. They also demonstrate how their framework, which incorporates projected profitability of customers in the computation of lifetime duration, can be superior to traditional methods such as the recency, frequency, and monetary value framework and past customer value.

Relationship of Customer Equity to Brand Equity

Brand equity management can be related to customer equity management in different ways. One way to reconcile the two points of view is to think of a matrix where all the brands and sub-brands and variants that a company offers are rows, and all the different customer segments or individual customers that purchase those brands are columns (see Figure 2-11). Effective brand and customer management would necessarily take into account both the rows and the columns to arrive at optimal marketing solutions.

As they have been developed conceptually and put into practice, however, the two perspectives tend to emphasize different aspects (see Figure 2-12). The customer equity perspective puts much focus on the bottom-line financial value created by customers. Its

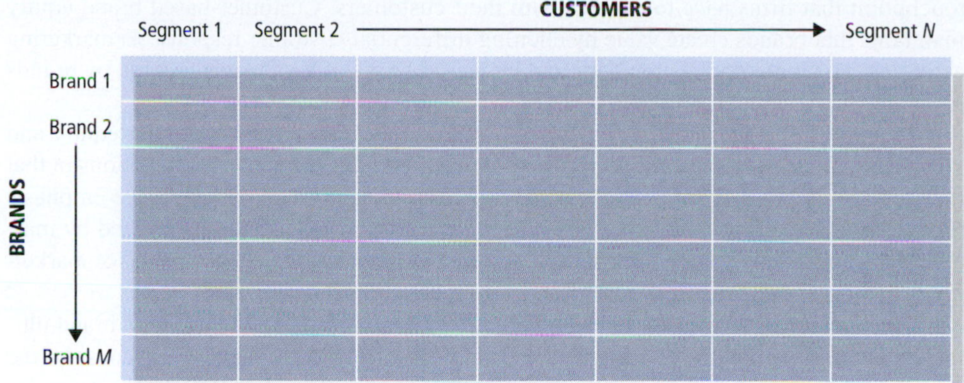

FIGURE 2-11

Brand and Customer Management

clear benefit is the quantifiable measures of financial performance it provides. In its calculations, however, the customer equity perspective largely ignores some of the important advantages of creating a strong brand, such as the ability of a strong brand to attract higher quality employees, elicit stronger support from channel and supply chain partners, create growth opportunities through line and category extensions and licensing, and so on.

The customer equity perspective also tends to be less prescriptive about specific marketing activities beyond general recommendations toward customer acquisition, retention, and cross-selling. The customer equity perspective does not always fully account for competitive response and the resulting moves and countermoves, nor does it fully account for social network effects, word of mouth, and customer-to-customer recomendations.

Thus, customer equity approaches can overlook the "option value" of brands and their potential impact on revenues and costs beyond the current marketing environment. Brand equity, on the other hand, tends to put more emphasis on strategic issues in managing brands and how marketing programs can be designed to create and leverage brand awareness and image with customers. It provides much practical guidance for specific marketing activities.

With a focus on brands, however, managers do not always develop detailed customer analyses in terms of the brand equity they achieve with specific consumers or groups of consumers and the resulting long-term profitability that is created. Brand equity approaches could benefit from sharper segmentation schemes.

There is no question that customer equity and brand equity are related. In theory, both approaches can be expanded to incorporate the other point of view and they are clearly inextricably linked. Customers drive the success of brands, but brands are the necessary

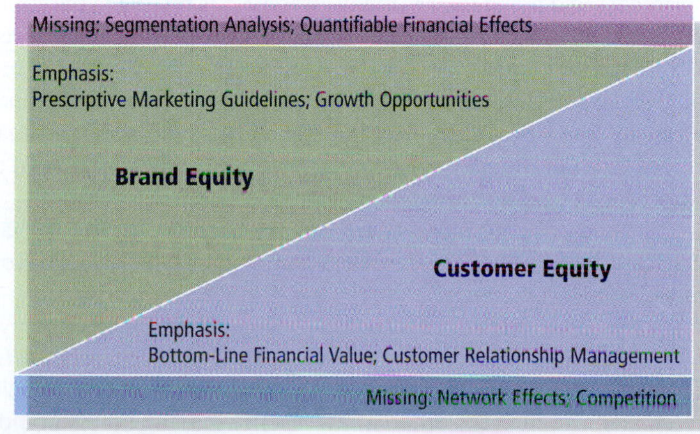

FIGURE 2-12

Brand Equity vs. Customer Equity

touchpoint that firms have to connect with their customers. Customer-based brand equity maintains that brands create value by eliciting differential customer response to marketing activities. The higher price premiums and increased levels of loyalty engendered by brands generates incremental cash flows.

Many of the actions that will increase brand equity will increase customer equity and vice versa. In practice, customer equity and brand equity are complementary notions in that they tend to emphasize different considerations. Brand equity tends to put more emphasis on the "front end" of marketing programs and intangible value potentially created by marketing programs; customer equity tends to put more emphasis on the "back end" of marketing programs and the realized value of marketing activities in terms of revenue.

The two concepts go hand-in-hand: Customers need and value brands; but a brand ultimately is only as good as the customers it attracts. As evidence of this duality, consider the role of the retailer as "middleman" between firms and consumers. Retailers clearly recognize the importance of both brands and customers. A retailer chooses to sell those brands that are the best "bait" for those customers it wants to attract. Retailers essentially assemble brand portfolios to establish a profitable customer portfolio. Manufacturers make similar decisions, developing brand portfolios and hierarchies to maximize their customer franchises.

But effective brand management is critical, and it is a mistake to ignore its important role in developing long-term profit streams for firms. Some marketing observers have perhaps minimized the challenge and value of strong brands to overly emphasize the customer equity perspective, for example, maintaining that "our attitude should be that brands come and go—but customers . . . must remain."[61] Yet, that statement can easily be taken to the logical, but opposite, conclusion: "Through the years, customers may come and go, but strong brands will endure." Perhaps the main point is that both are really crucial, and the two perspectives can help to improve the marketing success of a firm. The customer-based brand equity concept is an attempt to do just that.

Review

Customer-based brand equity is the differential effect that brand knowledge has on consumer response to the marketing of that brand. A brand has positive customer-based brand equity when customers react more favorably to a product and the way it is marketed when the brand is identified than when it is not.

We can define brand knowledge in terms of an associative network memory model, as a network of nodes and links wherein the brand node in memory has a variety of associations linked to it. We can characterize brand knowledge in terms of two components: brand awareness and brand image. Brand awareness is related to the strength of the brand node or trace in memory, as reflected by consumers' ability to recall or recognize the brand under different conditions. It has both depth and breadth. The depth of brand awareness measures the likelihood that consumers can recognize or recall the brand. The breadth of brand awareness measures the variety of purchase and consumption situations in which the brand comes to mind. Brand image is consumer perceptions of a brand as reflected by the brand associations held in consumers' memory.

Customer-based brand equity occurs when the consumer has a high level of awareness and familiarity with the brand and holds some strong, favorable, and unique brand associations in memory. In some cases, brand awareness alone is sufficient to result in more favorable consumer response—for example, in low-involvement decision settings where consumers are willing to base their choices merely on familiar brands. In other cases, the strength, favorability, and uniqueness of the brand associations play a critical role in determining the differential response making up the brand equity.

To create the differential response that leads to customer-based brand equity, marketers should associate unique, meaningful points of difference to the brand to provide a competitive advantage and a "reason why" consumers should buy it. For some brand associations, however, it may be enough to rank roughly equally with competing brand associations in order to negate potential points of difference for competitors.

The CBBE model lists a series of steps for building a strong brand: (1) establishing the proper brand identity, (2) creating the appropriate brand meaning, (3) eliciting the right brand responses, and (4) forging appropriate brand relationships with customers. Specifically, according to this model, building a strong brand requires establishing breadth and depth of brand awareness; creating strong, favorable, and unique brand associations; eliciting positive, accessible brand responses; and forging intense, active brand relationships. Achieving these four steps, in turn, means establishing six brand building blocks: brand salience, brand performance, brand imagery, brand judgments, brand feelings, and brand resonance.

The strongest brands excel on all six of these dimensions and thus fully execute all four steps of building a brand. In the CBBE model, the most valuable brand building block, brand resonance, occurs when all the other core brand values are completely "in sync" with respect to customers' needs, wants, and desires. In other words, brand resonance reflects a completely harmonious relationship between customers and the brand. With true brand resonance, customers have a high degree of loyalty marked by a close relationship with the brand and actively seek means to interact with the brand and share their experiences with others. Firms that are able to achieve resonance and affinity with their customers should reap a host of valuable benefits, such as greater price premiums and more efficient and effective marketing programs.

Thus, the basic premise of the CBBE model is that the true measure of the strength of a brand depends on how consumers think, feel, and act with respect to that brand. Achieving brand resonance requires eliciting the proper cognitive appraisals and emotional reactions to the brand from customers. That, in turn, necessitates establishing brand identity and creating the right meaning in terms of brand performance and brand imagery associations. A brand with the right identity and meaning can make a customer believe it is relevant and "my kind of product." The strongest brands will be those to which consumers become so attached and passionate that they, in effect, become evangelists or missionaries and attempt to share their beliefs and spread the word about the brand

Customer relationship marketing (CRM) refers to a company's use of data systems and applications to track consumer activity and manage customer interactions with the company. Customer equity relates to the lifetime value to a firm of its customer relationships and is enhanced through strategies that attract and retain profitable customers and cross-sell additional products and services to them.

Discussion Questions

1. Pick a brand. Attempt to identify its sources of brand equity. Assess its level of brand awareness and the strength, favorability, and uniqueness of its associations.
2. Which brands do you have the most resonance with? Why?
3. Can every brand achieve resonance with its customers? Why or why not?
4. Pick a brand. Assess the extent to which the brand is achieving the various benefits of brand equity.
5. What do you think of Naomi Klein's positions as espoused in *No Logos?* How would you respond to her propositions? Do you agree or disagree about her beliefs on the growth of corporate power?

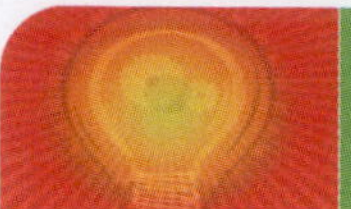

BRAND FOCUS 2.0

The Marketing Advantages of Strong Brands

Customer-based brand equity occurs when consumer response to marketing activity differs when consumers know the brand and when they do not. How that response differs will depend on the level of brand awareness and how favorably and uniquely consumers evaluate brand associations, as well as the particular marketing activity under consideration. A number of benefits can result from a strong brand, both in terms of greater revenue and lower costs.[62] For example, Ian Lewis from Time-Life categorizes the factors creating financial value for strong brands into two categories: factors related to growth (a brand's ability to attract new customers, resist competitive activity, introduce line extensions, and cross international borders) and factors related to profitability (brand loyalty, premium pricing, lower price elasticity, lower advertising/sales ratios, and trade leverage).[63]

This appendix considers in detail some of the benefits to the firm of having brands with a high level of awareness and a positive brand image.

Greater Loyalty and Less Vulnerability to Competitive Marketing Actions and Crises

Research shows that different types of brand associations—if favorable—can affect consumer product evaluations, perceptions of quality, and purchase rates.[64] This influence may be especially apparent with difficult-to-assess "experience" goods[65] and as the uniqueness of brand associations increases.[66] In addition, familiarity with a brand has been shown to increase consumer confidence, attitude toward the brand, and purchase intention,[67] and to mitigate the negative impact of a poor trial experience.[68]

For these and other reasons, one characteristic of brands with a great deal of equity is that consumers feel great loyalty to them. Some top brands have been market leaders for years despite significant changes in both consumer attitudes and competitive activity over time. Through it all, consumers have valued these brands enough to stick with them and reject the overtures of competitors, creating a steady stream of revenues for the firm. Research also shows that brands with large market shares are more likely to have more loyal customers than brands with small market shares, a phenomenon called *double jeopardy*.[69] One study found that brand equity was strongly correlated (.75) with subsequent market share and profitability.[70]

Brand loyalty is closely related to brand equity but is a distinct concept. We often measure brand loyalty as a behavior—say, the number of repeat purchases. Yet, a consumer may continually purchase without really thinking much about why, if the brand is prominently displayed or frequently promoted. When confronted by a new or resurgent competitor providing compelling reasons to switch, consumers' ties to the brand may be tested for the first time.

The bottom line is that repeat buying is a necessary but not sufficient condition for being a brand-loyal buyer: Someone can repeat buy but not be brand loyal. Brand loyalty is one of the many advantages of creating a positive brand image and of having brand equity. Thus, brand loyalty is related to, but distinct from, brand equity.

Returning to the benefits of brand equity, a brand with a positive brand image also is more likely to successfully weather a brand crisis or downturn in the brand's fortunes.[71] Perhaps the most compelling example is Johnson & Johnson's (J&J) Tylenol brand. Brand Focus 11.0 describes how J&J contended with a tragic product-tampering episode in the early 1980s. Despite seeing its market share drop from 37 percent to almost zero overnight and fearing Tylenol would be written off as a brand with no future, J&J was able to regain virtually all lost market share for the brand through its skillful handling of the crisis and a good deal of brand equity.

The lesson is that effective handling of a marketing crisis requires swift and sincere action, an immediate admission that something has gone wrong, and assurance that an effective remedy will be put in place. The greater the brand equity, the more likely that these statements will be credible enough to keep customers understanding and patient as the firm sets out to solve the crisis. Without some underlying brand equity, however, even the best-laid plans for recovery may fall short with a suspicious or uninformed public.[72] Finally, even absent a crisis, a strong brand offers protection in a marketing downturn or when the brand's fortunes fall.

Larger Margins

Brands with positive customer-based brand equity can command a price premium.[73] Moreover, consumers should also have a fairly inelastic response to price increases and elastic responses to price decreases or discounts for the brand over time.[74] Consistent with this reasoning, research has shown that consumers loyal to a brand are less likely to switch in the face of price increases and more likely to increase the quantity of the brand purchased in the face of price decreases.[75] In a competitive sense, brand leaders draw a disproportionate amount of share from smaller-share competitors.[76] At the same time, market leaders are relatively immune to price competition from these small-share brands.[77]

In an analysis of consumer goods manufacturers from the extensive PIMS database, Boulding, Lee, and Staelin found that by providing unique and positive messages, a firm could insulate itself from future price competition and enjoy less negative future price elasticities and therefore greater brand loyalty from consumers. Conversely, they also found that nonunique messages could decrease future differentiation.[78]

Intelliquest explored the role of brand name and price in the decision purchase of business computer buyers.[79] Survey respondents were asked, "What is the incremental dollar value you would be willing to pay over a 'no-name' clone computer brand?" IBM commanded the greatest price premium, followed by Compaq and Hewlett-Packard. Some brands had negative brand equity; they actually received negative numbers. Clearly, according to this study, brands had specific meaning in the personal computer market that consumers valued and were willing to pay for.

Greater Trade Cooperation and Support

Wholesalers, retailers, and other middlemen in the distribution channel play an important role in the selling of many products. Their activities can thus facilitate or inhibit the success of the brand.

If a brand has a positive image, retailers and other middlemen are more likely to respond to the wishes of consumers and actively promote and sell the brand.[80] Channel members are also less likely to require any marketing push from the manufacturer and will be more receptive to manufacturers' suggestions to stock, reorder, and display the brand,[81] as well as to pass through trade promotions, demand smaller slotting allowances, give more favorable shelf space or position, and so on. Given that many consumer decisions are made in the store, the possibility of additional marketing push by retailers is important.

Increased Marketing Communication Effectiveness

A host of advertising and communication benefits may result from creating awareness of and a positive image for a brand. One well-established view of consumer response to marketing communications is the hierarchy of effects models. These models assume that consumers move through a series of stages or mental states on the basis of marketing communications—for example, exposure to, attention to, comprehension of, yielding to, retention of, and behaving on the basis of a marketing communication.

A brand with a great deal of equity already has created some knowledge structures in consumers' minds, increasing the likelihood that consumers will pass through various stages of the hierarchy. For example, consider the effects of a positive brand image on the persuasive ability of advertising: Consumers may be more likely to notice an ad, may more easily learn about the brand and form favorable opinions, and may retain and act on these beliefs over time.

Familiar, well-liked brands are less susceptible to "interference" and confusion from competitive ads,[82] are more responsive to creative strategies such as humor appeals,[83] and are less vulnerable to negative reactions due to concentrated repetition schedules.[84] In addition, panel diary members who were highly loyal to a brand increased purchases when advertising for the brand increased.[85] Other advantages associated with more advertising include increased likelihood of being the focus of attention and increased "brand interest."[86]

Because strong brand associations exist, lower levels of repetition may be necessary. For example, in a classic study of advertising weights, Anheuser-Busch ran a carefully conducted field experiment in which it varied the amount of Budweiser advertising shown to consumers in different matched test markets.[87] Seven different advertising expenditure levels were tested, representing increases and decreases from the previous advertising expenditure levels: minus 100 percent (no advertising), minus 50 percent, 0 percent (same level), plus 50 percent, plus 100 percent (double the level of advertising), plus 150 percent, and plus 200 percent. These expenditure levels were run for one year and revealed that the "no advertising" level resulted in the same amount of sales as the current program. In fact, the 50 percent cut in advertising expenditures actually resulted in an increase in sales, consistent with the notion that strong brands such as Budweiser do not require the same advertising levels, at least over a short period of time, as a less well-known or well-liked brand.[88]

Similarly, because of existing brand knowledge structures, consumers may be more likely to notice sales promotions, direct mail offerings, or other sales-oriented marketing communications and respond favorably. For example, several studies have shown that promotion effectiveness is asymmetric in favor of a higher-quality brand.[89]

Possible Licensing Opportunities

A strong brand often has associations that may be desirable in other product categories. To capitalize on this value, a firm may choose to license its name, logo, or other trademark item to another company for use on its products and merchandise. Traditionally, licensing has been associated with characters such as Garfield the cat, Barney the dinosaur, and Disney's Mickey Mouse, or celebrities and designers such as Martha Stewart, Ralph Lauren, and Tommy Hilfiger. Recently, more conventional brands such as Caterpillar, Harley-Davidson, Coca-Cola, and others have licensed their brands.

The rationale for the licensee (the company obtaining the rights to use the trademark) is that consumers will pay more for a product because of the recognition and image lent by the trademark. One marketing research study showed that consumers would pay $60 for cookware licensed under the Julia Child name as opposed to only $40 for the identical cookware bearing the Sears name.[90]

The rationale for the licensor (the company behind the trademark) is increased profits, promotion, and legal protection. In terms of profits, a firm can expect an average royalty of about 5 percent of the wholesale price of each product, ranging from 2 percent to 10 percent depending on the circumstances involved. Because there are no manufacturing or marketing costs, these revenues translate directly to profits. Licensing is also a means to enhance the awareness and image of the brand. Linking the trademarks to other products may broaden its exposure and increase the strength, favorability, and uniqueness of brand associations. Finally, licensing may provide legal protection for trademarks. Licensing the brand for use in certain product categories prevents other firms or potential competitors from legally using the brand name to enter those categories. For example, Coca-Cola entered licensing agreements in a number of product areas, including radios, glassware, toy trucks, and clothes, in part as legal protection. As it turns out, its licensing program has been so successful the company has introduced a catalog sent directly to consumers that offers a variety of products bearing the Coca-Cola name.

Licensing certainly carries risks, too. A trademark can become overexposed if marketers adopt a saturation policy. Consumers do not necessarily know the motivation or marketing arrangements behind a product and can become confused or even angry if the brand is licensed to a product that seemingly bears no relation. Moreover, if the product fails to live up to consumer expectations, the brand name could become tarnished.

Additional Brand Extension Opportunities

A ***brand extension*** occurs when a firm uses an established brand name to enter a new market. A ***line extension*** uses a current brand name to enter a new market segment in the existing product class, say with new varieties, new flavors, or new sizes. For example, Colgate has introduced a number of different varieties of toothpaste that come in different flavors (Winterfresh Gel), have different ingredients (Colgate with Baking Soda), or provide a specific benefit (Tartar Control Colgate). In a ***category extension,*** the marketer uses the current brand name to enter a different product class. For example, Swiss Army Brands capitalized on the success and precision image of its knives to introduce watches, sunglasses, writing instruments, travel gear, and cutlery.

A product extension for a brand with a positive image allows the firm to capitalize on consumer knowledge of the parent brand to raise awareness of and suggest possible associations for the extension. Thus, extensions can provide the following benefits in a new-product introduction: reducing the risk perceived by customers and distributors, decreasing the cost of gaining distribution and trial, increasing the efficiency of promotional expenditures, avoiding the cost (and risk) of developing new names, allowing for packaging and labeling efficiencies, and creating product variety.

Extensions can also provide feedback benefits to the parent brand and the company as a whole. They can enhance the parent brand image by improving the strength, favorability, and uniqueness of brand associations, and by improving perceptions of company credibility, expertise, trustworthiness, or likability. Extensions may also help to convey the broader meaning of the brand to consumers, clarifying the company's core benefit proposition and business definition. Finally, extensions may also bring new customers into the brand franchise and increase market coverage.

Academic research has validated many of these assumptions. Studies have shown that well-known and well-regarded brands can extend more successfully and into more diverse categories than other brands.[91] In addition, the amount of brand equity has been shown to be correlated with the highest- or lowest-quality member in the product line for vertical product extensions.[92] Research has also shown that positive symbolic associations may be the basis of these evaluations, even if overall brand attitude itself is not necessarily high.[93]

Brands with varied product category associations through past extensions have been shown to be especially extendable.[94] As a result, introductory marketing programs for extensions from an established brand may be more efficient than others.[95] Several studies have indicated that extension activity has aided (or at least did not dilute) brand equity for the parent brand. For instance, brand extensions strengthened parent brand associations, and "flagship brands" were highly resistant to dilution or other potential negative effects caused by negative experiences with an extension.[96] Research has also found evidence of an ownership effect, whereby current owners generally had more favorable responses to brand line extensions.[97] Finally, extensions of brands that have both high familiarity and positive attitudes have been shown to receive higher initial stock market reactions than other brands.[98]

Other Benefits

Brands with positive customer-based brand equity may provide other advantages to the firm not directly related to the products themselves, such as helping the firm to attract better employees, generate greater interest from investors, and garner more support from shareholders. In terms of the latter, several research studies have shown that brand equity can be directly related to corporate stock price.[99]

Notes

1. Kevin Lane Keller, "Conceptualizing, Measuring, and Managing Customer-Based Brand Equity," *Journal of Marketing* (January 1993): 1–29.
2. Richard Jones, "Finding Sources of Brand Value: Developing a Stakeholder Model of Brand Equity," *Journal of Brand Management,* 13, no. 1 (October 2005): 10–32.
3. John R. Anderson, *The Architecture of Cognition* (Cambridge, MA: Harvard University Press, 1983); Robert S. Wyer, Jr. and Thomas K. Srull, "Person Memory and Judgment," *Psychological Review* 96, no. 1 (1989): 58–83.
4. John R. Rossiter and Larry Percy, *Advertising and Promotion Management* (New York: McGraw-Hill, 1987).
5. Burleigh B. Gardner and Sidney J. Levy, "The Product and the Brand," *Harvard Business Review* (March–April 1955): 33–39.
6. Dawn Dobni and George M. Zinkhan, "In Search of Brand Image: A Foundation Analysis," in *Advances in Consumer Research,* Vol. 17, eds. Marvin E. Goldberg, Gerald Gorn, and Richard W. Pollay (Provo, UT: Association for Consumer Research, 1990), 110–119.
7. H. Herzog, "Behavioral Science Concepts for Analyzing the Consumer," in *Marketing and the Behavioral Sciences,* ed. Perry Bliss (Boston: Allyn and Bacon, 1963), 76–86; Joseph W. Newman, "New Insight, New Progress for Marketing," *Harvard Business Review* (November–December, 1957): 95–102.
8. James R. Bettman, *An Information Processing Theory of Consumer Choice* (Reading, MA: Addison-Wesley, 1979); Rossiter and Percy, *Advertising and Promotion Management.*
9. William Baker, J. Wesley Hutchinson, Danny Moore, and Prakash Nedungadi, "Brand Familiarity and Advertising: Effects on the Evoked Set and Brand Preference," in *Advances in Consumer Research,* Vol. 13, ed. Richard J. Lutz (Provo, UT: Association for Consumer Research, 1986), 637–642; Prakash Nedungadi, "Recall and Consumer Consideration Sets: Influencing Choice without Altering Brand Evaluations," *Journal of Consumer Research* 17 (December 1990): 263–276.
10. For example, see Henry L. Roediger, "Inhibition in Recall from Cuing with Recall Targets," *Journal of Verbal Learning and Verbal Behavior* 12 (1973): 644–657; and Raymond S. Nickerson, "Retrieval Inhibition from Part-Set Cuing: A Persisting Enigma in Memory Research," *Memory and Cognition* 12 (November 1984): 531–552.
11. In an interesting twist, it is also the case that consumers would be more likely to recall closely related brands in the category, for example, Wendy's. See Prakash Nedungadi, "Recall and Consumer Consideration Sets."
12. Rashmi Adaval, "How Good Gets Better and Bad Gets Worse: Understanding the Impact of Affect on Evaluations of Known Brands," *Journal of Consumer Research* 30 (December 2003): 352–367.
13. Jacob Jacoby, George J. Syzabillo, and Jacqeline Busato-Schach, "Information Acquisition Behavior in Brand Choice Situations," *Journal of Consumer Research* 3 (1977): 209–216; Ted Roselius, "Consumer Ranking of Risk Reduction Methods," *Journal of Marketing* 35 (January 1977): 56–61.
14. James R. Bettman and C. Whan Park, "Effects of Prior Knowledge and Experience and Phase of the Choice Process on Consumer Decision Processes: A Protocol Analysis," *Journal of Consumer Research* 7 (December 1980): 234–248; Wayne D. Hoyer and Steven P. Brown, "Effects of Brand Awareness on Choice for a Common, Repeat-Purchase Product," *Journal of Consumer Research* 17 (September 1990): 141–148; C. W. Park and V. Parker Lessig, "Familiarity and Its Impact on Consumer Biases and Heuristics," *Journal of Consumer Research* 8 (September 1981): 223–230.
15. Richard E. Petty and John T. Cacioppo, *Communication and Persuasion* (New York: Springer-Verlag, 1986).
16. "Advertisers Often Take Bizarre Approaches," *Newsday.*
17. Joseph W. Alba and J. Wesley Hutchinson, "Dimensions of Consumer Expertise," *Journal of Consumer Research* 13 (March 1987): 411–453.
18. David A. Aaker, "Positioning Your Brand," *Business Horizons* 25 (May/June 1982): 56–62; Al Ries and Jack Trout, *Positioning: The Battle for Your Mind* (New York: McGraw-Hill, 1979); Yoram Wind, *Product Policy: Concepts, Methods, and Strategy* (Reading, MA: Addison-Wesley, 1982).

19. Dipankar Chakravarti, Deborah J. MacInnis, and Kent Nakamoto, "Product Category Perceptions, Elaborative Processing and Brand Name Extension Strategies," in *Advances in Consumer Research* 17, eds. M. Goldberg, G. Gorn, and R. Pollay (Ann Arbor, MI: Association for Consumer Research, 1990): 910–916; Mita Sujan and James R. Bettman, "The Effects of Brand Positioning Strategies on Consumers' Brand and Category Perceptions: Some Insights from Schema Research," *Journal of Marketing Research* 26 (November 1989): 454–467.
20. James R. Bettman and Mita Sujan, "Effects of Framing on Evaluation of Comparable and Noncomparable Alternatives by Expert and Novice Consumers," *Journal of Consumer Research* 14 (September 1987): 141–154; Michael D. Johnson, "Consumer Choice Strategies for Comparing Noncomparable Alternatives," *Journal of Consumer Research* 11 (December 1984): 741–753; C. Whan Park and Daniel C. Smith, "Product Level Choice: A Top-Down or Bottom-Up Process?" *Journal of Consumer Research* 16 (December 1989): 289–299.
21. Joel B. Cohen and Kanul Basu, "Alternative Models of Categorization: Towards a Contingent Processing Framework," *Journal of Consumer Research* 13 (March 1987): 455–472; Prakash Nedungadi and J. Wesley Hutchinson, "The Prototypicality of Brands: Relationships with Brand Awareness, Preference, and Usage," in *Advances in Consumer Research,* Vol. 12, eds. Elizabeth C. Hirschman and Morris B. Holbrook (Provo, UT: Association for Consumer Research, 1985), 489–503; Eleanor Rosch and Carolyn B. Mervis, "Family Resemblance: Studies in the Internal Structure of Categories," *Cognitive Psychology* 7 (October 1975): 573–605; James Ward and Barbara Loken, "The Quintessential Snack Food: Measurement of Prototypes," in *Advances in Consumer Research,* Vol. 13, ed. Richard J. Lutz (Provo, UT: Association for Consumer Research, 1986), 126–131.
22. Nedungadi and Hutchinson, "The Prototypicality of Brands"; Ward and Loken, "The Quintessential Snack Food."
23. George S. Day, Allan D. Shocker, and Rajendra K. Srivastava, "Customer-Oriented Approaches to Identifying Products-Markets," *Journal of Marketing* 43 (Fall 1979): 8–19.
24. K. E. Miller and J. L. Ginter, "An Investigation of Situational Variation in Brand Choice Behavior and Attitude," *Journal of Marketing Research* 16 (February 1979): 111–123.
25. Elizabeth Cowley and Andrew A. Mitchell, "The Moderating Effect of Product Knowledge on the Learning and Organization of Product Information," *Journal of Consumer Research* 30 (December 2003), 443–454.
26. Mita Sujan and Christine Dekleva, "Product Categorization and Inference Making: Some Implications for Comparative Advertising," *Journal of Consumer Research* 14 (December 1987): 372–378.
27. Thomas A. Fogarty, "A Company for All Seasons," *USA Today,* 13 January 2000, B3.
28. Stephanie Thompson, "Campbell Tries to Stir Soup Sales with $95 Million," *Advertising Age,* 11 October 1999; "TV Host Gordon Elliott Knocks on Doors to Urge 'Make It Campbell's Instead'," *Business Wire,* 26 August 2003.
29. David Garvin, "Product Quality: An Important Strategic Weapon," *Business Horizons* 27 (May–June): 40–43; Philip Kotler and Kevin Lane Keller, *Marketing Management,* 12th ed. (Upper Saddle River, NJ: Prentice Hall, 2000).
30. Robert C. Blattberg and Kenneth J. Wisniewski, "Price-Induced Patterns of Competition," *Marketing Science* 8 (Fall 1989): 291–309.
31. Joseph T. Plummer, "How Personality Makes a Difference," *Journal of Advertising Research* 24 (December 1984/January 1985): 27–31.
32. See Jennifer Aaker, "Dimensions of Brand Personality," *Journal of Marketing Research* 34 (August 1997): 347–357.
33. Aaker, "Dimensions of Brand Personality"; Susan Fournier, "Consumers and Their Brands: Developing Relationship Theory in Consumer Research," *Journal of Consumer Research* 24, no. 3 (1997): 343–373.
34. Gita Venkataramani Johar, Jaideep Sengupta, and Jennifer L. Aaker, "Two Roads to Updating Brand Personality Impressions: Trait Versus Evaluative Inferencing," *Journal of Marketing Research* 42 (November 2005), 458–469.
35. M. Joseph Sirgy, "Self Concept in Consumer Behavior: A Critical Review," *Journal of Consumer Research* 9 (December 1982): 287–300; Lan Nguyen Chaplin and Deborah Roedder John, "The Development of Self-Brand Connections in Children and Adolescents," *Journal of Consumer Research* 32 (June 2005), 119–129.
36. Timothy R. Graeff, "Consumption Situations and the Effects of Brand Image on Consumers' Brand Evaluations," *Psychology & Marketing* 14, no. 1 (1997): 49–70; Timothy R. Graeff, "Image Congruence Effects on Product Evaluations: The Role of Self-Monitoring and Public/ Private Consumption," *Psychology & Marketing* 13, no. 5 (1996): 481–499.
37. Jennifer L. Aaker, "The Malleable Self: The Role of Self-Expression in Persuasion," *Journal of Marketing Research* 36, no. 2 (1999): 45–57.
38. Douglas B. Holt, *How Brands Become Icons* (Cambridge, MA: Harvard Business School Press), 2004.
39. Douglas B. Holt, "What Becomes an Icon Most," *Harvard Business Review* (March 2003), 43.

40. William L. Wilkie, *Consumer Behavior,* 3rd ed. (New York: John Wiley & Sons, 1994).
41. www.harrisinteractive.com/productsandservices/equitrend.asp.
42. William D. Wells, "How Advertising Works," unpublished paper, 1980; Christopher P. Puto and William D. Wells, "Informational and Transformational Advertising: The Differential Effects of Time," in *Advances in Consumer Research,* Vol. 11, ed. Thomas C. Kinnear (Ann Arbor, MI: Association for Consumer Research, 1983), 638–643; Stephen J. Hoch and John Deighton, "Managing What Consumers Learn from Experience," *Journal of Marketing* 53 (April 1989): 1–20.
43. Lynn R. Kahle, Basil Poulos, and Ajay Sukhdial, "Changes in Social Values in the United States During the Past Decade," *Journal of Advertising Research* (February/March 1988): 35–41.
44. Greg Farrell, "Marketers Put a Price on Your Life," *USA Today,* 7 July 1999, 3B.
45. Arjun Chaudhuri and Morris B. Holbrook, "The Chain of Effects from Brand Trust and Brand Affect to Brand Performance: The Role of Brand Loyalty," *Journal of Marketing* 65 (April 2001): 81–93.
46. Thomas A. Stewart, "A Satisfied Customer Is Not Enough," *Fortune,* 21 July 1997, 112–113.
47. Thomas O. Jones and W. Earl Sasser Jr. "Why Satisfied Customers Defect," *Harvard Business Review* (November–December 1995): 88–99.
48. Fredrick Reichheld, *The Loyalty Effect: The Hidden Force Behind Growth, Profits, and Lasting Value* (Boston: Harvard Business School Press, 1996).
49. James H. McAlexander, John W. Schouten, and Harold F. Koenig, "Building Brand Community," *Journal of Marketing* 66 (January 2002): 38–54; Albert Muniz and Thomas O'Guinn, "Brand Community," *Journal of Consumer Research* 27 (March 2001): 412–432.
50. Gil McWilliam, "Building Stronger Brands Through Online Communities," *MIT Sloan Management Review* 41, no. 3 (Spring 2000), 43–54.
51. Rene Algesheimer, Utpal M. Dholakia and Andreas Hermann, "The Social Influence of Brand Community: Evidence from European Car Clubs," *Journal of Marketing* 69 (July 2005), 19–34.
52. Brian Sternberg, "Chewing-Gum Ads Sport New Flavor," *Wall Street Journal,* 31 December 2004.
53. Nikki Hopewell, "Generating Brand Passion," *Marketing News,* 15 May 2005, 10.
54. Diana Ransom, "The Brand Called Glue," *Fast Company* (May 2005), 35.
55. Joseph B. White and Stephen Power, "VW Chief Confronts Corporate Culture," *Wall Street Journal,* 19 September 2005, B2.
56. Larry Yu, "Successful Customer Relationship Management," *MIT Sloan Management Review,* 1 July 2001. See also Kevin Ferguson, "Closer Than Ever: CRM Software Keeps You and Your Customer Ultra-Cozy," *Business Week,* 12 May 2001. For a detailed discussion, see William Boulding, Richard Staelin, Michael Ehret, and Wesley J. Jonston, "A Customer Relationship Management Roadmap: What Is Known, Potential Pitfalls, and Where to Go," *Journal of Marketing* 69 (October 2005), 155–166, as well other articles and essays in that special issue.
57. Roland T. Rust, Valarie A. Zeithamal, and Katherine Lemon, "Customer-Centered Brand Management," *Harvard Business Review* (September 2004), 110–118.
58. Robert C. Blattberg and John Deighton, "Manage Marketing by the Customer Equity Test," *Harvard Business Review* (July–August 1996). See also Robert C. Blattberg, Gary Getz, and Jacquelyn S. Thomas, *Customer Equity: Building and Managing Relationships as Valuable Assets* (Boston, MA: Harvard Business School Press, 2001); Robert Blattberg and Jacquelyn Thomas, "Valuing, Analyzing, and Managing the Marketing Function Using Customer Equity Principles," in *Kellogg on Marketing,* ed. Dawn Iacobucci (New York, John Wiley & Sons, 2001).
59. Roland T. Rust, Valarie A. Zeithaml, and Katherine Lemon, *Driving Customer Equity* (New York: Free Press, 2000); Roland T. Rust, Valarie A. Zeithaml, and Katherine Lemon, "Customer-Centered Brand Management," *Harvard Business Review* (September 2004), 110–118.
60. W. Reinartz, J. Thomas, and V. Kumar "Balancing Acquisition and Retention Resources to Maximize Profitability," *Journal of Marketing* 69 (January 2005): 63–79; R. Venkatesan and V. Kumar, "A Customer Lifetime Value Framework for Customer Selections and Resource Allocation Strategy," *Journal of Marketing* 68, no. 4 (October 2004): 106–125; V. Kumar, G. Ramani, and T. Bohling, "Customer Lifetime Value Approaches and Best Practice Applications," *Journal of Interactive Marketing* 18, no. 3 (Summer 2004): 60–72; J. Thomas, W. Reinartz, and V. Kumar, "Getting the Most Out of All Your Customers," *Harvard Business Review* (July–August 2004): 116–123; W. Reinartz and V. Kumar, "The Impact of Customer Relationship Characteristics on Profitable Lifetime Duration," *Journal of Marketing* 67, no. 1 (2003): 77–99.
61. Roland T. Rust, Valarie A. Zeithamal, and Katherine Lemon, "Customer-Centered Brand Management," *Harvard Business Review* (September 2004), 110–118.
62. Brand Focus 2-0 is based in part on Steven Hoeffler and Kevin Lane Keller, "The Marketing Advantages of Strong Brands," *Journal of Brand Management* 10, no. 6 (2003): 421–445.

63. Ian M. Lewis, "Brand Equity or Why the Board of Directors Needs Marketing Research," paper presented at the ARF Fifth Annual Advertising and Promotion Workshop, 1 February 1993.
64. Peter A. Dacin and Daniel C. Smith, "The Effect of Brand Portfolio Characteristics on Consumer Evaluations of Brand Extensions," *Journal of Marketing Research* 31 (May 1994): 229–242; George S. Day and Terry Deutscher, "Attitudinal Predictions of Choices of Major Appliance Brands," *Journal of Marketing Research* 19 (May 1982), 192–198; W. B. Dodds, K. B. Monroe, and D. Grewal, "Effects of Price, Brand, and Store Information on Buyers' Product Evaluations," *Journal of Marketing Research* 28 (August 1991): 307–319; France Leclerc, Bernd H. Schmitt, and Laurette Dube, "Foreign Branding and Its Effects on Product Perceptions and Attitudes," *Journal of Marketing Research* 31, no. 5 (1994): 263–270; Akshay R. Rao and K. B. Monroe, "The Effects of Price, Brand Name, and Store Name on Buyers' Perceptions of Product Quality: An Integrative Review," *Journal of Marketing Research* 26 (August 1989): 351–357.
65. B. Wernerfelt, "Umbrella Branding as a Signal of New Product Quality: An Example of Signaling by Posting a Bond," *Rand Journal of Economics* 19, no. 3 (1988): 458–466; Tullin Erdem, "An Empirical Analysis of Umbrella Branding," *Journal of Marketing Research* 35, no. 8 (1998): 339–351.
66. Fred M. Feinberg, Barbara E. Kahn, and Leigh McAllister, "Market Share Response When Consumers Seek Variety," *Journal of Marketing Research* 29 (May 1992): 227–237.
67. Michel Laroche, Chankon Kim, and Lianxi Zhou, "Brand Familiarity and Confidence as Determinants of Purchase Intention: An Empirical Test in a Multiple Brand Context," *Journal of Business Research* 37 (1996): 115–120.
68. Robert E. Smith, "Integrating Information from Advertising and Trial," *Journal of Marketing Research* 30 (May 1993): 204–219.
69. Andrew S. C. Ehrenberg, Gerard J. Goodhardt, and Patrick T. Barwise, "Double Jeopardy Revisited," *Journal of Marketing* 54 (July 1990): 82–91.
70. Ipsos-ASI, January 30, 2003.
71. Rohini Ahluwalia, Robert E. Burnkrant, and H. Rao Unnava, "Consumer Response to Negative Publicity: The Moderating Role of Commitment," *Journal of Marketing Research* 37 (May 2000): 203–214; Narij Dawar and Madam M. Pillutla, "Impact of Product-Harm Crises on Brand Equity: The Moderating Role of Consumer Expectations," *Journal of Marketing Research* 37 (May 2000): 215–226.
72. Susan Caminit, "The Payoff from a Good Corporate Reputation," *Fortune,* 10 February 1992, 74–77.
73. Deepak Agrawal, "Effects of Brand Loyalty on Advertising and Trade Promotions: A Game Theoretic Analysis with Empirical Evidence," *Marketing Science* 15, no. 1 (1996): 86–108; Chan Su Park and V. Srinivasan, "A Survey-Based Method for Measuring and Understanding Brand Equity and Its Extendability," *Journal of Marketing Research* 31 (May 1994): 271–288; Raj Sethuraman, "A Model of How Discounting High-Priced Brands Affects the Sales of Low-Priced Brands," *Journal of Marketing Research* 33 (November 1996): 399–409.
74. Hermann Simon, "Dynamics of Price Elasticity and Brand Life Cycles: An Empirical Study," *Journal of Marketing Research* 16 (November 1979): 439–452; K. Sivakumar and S. P. Raj, "Quality Tier Competition: How Price Change Influences Brand Choice and Category Choice," *Journal of Marketing* 61 (July 1997): 71–84.
75. Lakshman Krishnamurthi and S. P. Raj, "An Empirical Analysis of the Relationship Between Brand Loyalty and Consumer Price Elasticity," *Marketing Science* 10, no. 2 (Spring 1991): 172–183.
76. Greg M. Allenby and Peter E. Rossi, "Quality Perceptions and Asymmetric Switching Between Brands," *Marketing Science* 10 (Summer 1991): 185–204; Rajiv Grover and V. Srinivasan, "Evaluating the Multiple Effects of Retail Promotions on Brand Loyal and Brand Switching Segments," *Journal of Marketing Research* 29 (February 1992): 76–89; Gary J. Russell and Wagner A. Kamakura, "Understanding Brand Competition Using Micro and Macro Scanner Data," *Journal of Marketing Research* 31 (May 1994): 289–303.
77. Albert C. Bemmaor and Dominique Mouchoux, "Measuring the Short-Term Effect of In-Store Promotion and Retail Advertising on Brand Sales: A Factorial Experiment," *Journal of Marketing Research* 28 (May 1991): 202–214; Robert C. Blattberg and Kenneth J. Wisniewski, "Price-Induced Patterns of Competition," *Marketing Science* 8 (Fall 1989): 291–309; Randolph E. Bucklin, Sunil Gupta, and Sangman Han, "A Brand's Eye View of Response Segmentation in Consumer Brand Choice Behavior," *Journal of Marketing Research* 32 (February 1995): 66–74; Sivakumar and Raj, "Quality Tier Competition."
78. William Boulding, Eunkyu Lee, and Richard Staelin, "Mastering the Mix: Do Advertising, Promotion, and Sales Force Activities Lead to Differentiation?" *Journal of Marketing Research* 31 (May 1994): 159–172. See also Vinay Kanetkar, Charles B. Weinberg, and Doyle L. Weiss, "Price Sensitivity and Television Advertising Exposures: Some Empirical Findings," *Marketing Science* 11 (Fall 1992): 359–371.
79. Kyle Pope, "Computers: They're No Commodity," *Wall Street Journal,* 15 October 1993, B1.

80. Peter S. Fader and David C. Schmittlein, "Excess Behavioral Loyalty for High-Share Brands: Deviations from the Dirichlet Model for Repeat Purchasing," *Journal of Marketing Research* 30, no. 11 (1993): 478–493; Rajiv Lal and Chakravarthi Narasimhan, "The Inverse Relationship Between Manufacturer and Retailer Margins: A Theory," *Marketing Science* 15, no. 2 (1996): 132–151.
81. David B. Montgomery, "New Product Distribution: An Analysis of Supermarket Buyer Decisions," *Journal of Marketing Research* 12, no. 3 (1978): 255–264.
82. Robert J. Kent and Chris T. Allen, "Competitive Interference Effects in Consumer Memory for Advertising: The Role of Brand Familiarity," *Journal of Marketing* 58 (July 1994): 97–105.
83. Amitava Chattopadyay and Kunal Basu, "Humor in Advertising: The Moderating Role of Prior Brand Evaluation," *Journal of Marketing Research* 27 (November 1990): 466–476; D. W. Stewart and David H. Furse, *Effective Television Advertising: A Study of 1000 Commercials* (Lexington, MA: D.C. Heath, 1986); M. G. Weinburger and C. Gulas, "The Impact of Humor in Advertising: A Review," *Journal of Advertising* 21, no. 4 (1992): 35–60.
84. Margaret Campbell and Kevin Lane Keller, "Brand Familiarity and Ad Repetition Effects," *Journal of Consumer Research* 30, no. 2 (September 2003), 292–304.
85. S. P. Raj, "The Effects of Advertising on High and Low Loyalty Consumer Segments," *Journal of Consumer Research* 9 (June 1982): 77–89.
86. Ravi Dhar and Itamar Simonson, "The Effect of the Focus of Comparison on Consumer Preferences," *Journal of Marketing Research* 29 (November 1992): 430–440; Karen A. Machleit, Chris T. Allen, and Thomas J. Madden, "The Mature Brand and Brand Interest: An Alternative Consequence of Ad-Evoked Affect," *Journal of Marketing* 57 (October 1993): 72–82; Itamar Simonson, Joel Huber, and John Payne, "The Relationship Between Prior Brand Knowledge and Information Acquisition Order," *Journal of Consumer Research* 14 (March 1988): 566–578.
87. Russell L. Ackoff and James R. Emshoff, "Advertising Research at Anheuser-Busch, Inc. (1963–1968)," *Sloan Management Review* (Winter 1975): 1–15.
88. These results should be interpreted carefully, however, as they do not suggest that large advertising expenditures did not play an important role in creating equity for the brand in the past, or that advertising expenditures could be cut severely without some adverse sales consequences at some point in the future.
89. See Robert C. Blattberg, Richard Briesch, and Edward J. Fox, "How Promotions Work," *Marketing Science* 14 (1995): G122–G132. See also Bart J. Bronnenberg and Luc Wathieu, "Asymmetric Promotion Effects and Brand Positioning," *Marketing Science* 15, no. 4 (1996): 379–394. This study shows how the relative promotion effectiveness of high- and low-quality brands depends on their positioning along both price and quality dimensions.
90. Frank E. James, "I'll Wear the Coke Pants Tonight; They Go Well with My Harley-Davidson Ring," *Wall Street Journal,* 6 June 1985.
91. David A. Aaker and Kevin Lane Keller, "Consumer Evaluations of Brand Extensions," *Journal of Marketing* 54, no. 1 (1990): 27–41; Kevin Lane Keller and David A. Aaker, "The Effects of Sequential Introduction of Brand Extensions," *Journal of Marketing Research* 29 (February 1992): 35–50; A. Rangaswamy, R. R. Burke, and T. A. Oliva, "Brand Equity and the Extendibility of Brand Names," *International Journal of Research in Marketing* 10, no. 3 (1993): 61–75.
92. Taylor Randall, Karl Ulrich, and David Reibstein, "Brand Equity and Vertical Product Line Extent," *Marketing Science* 17, no. 4 (1998): 356–379.
93. Srinivas K. Reddy, Susan Holak, and Subodh Bhat, "To Extend or Not to Extend: Success Determinants of Line Extensions," *Journal of Marketing Research* 31, no. 5 (1994): 243–262; C. Whan Park, Sandra Milberg, and Robert Lawson, "Evaluation of Brand Extensions: The Role of Product Feature Similarity and Brand Concept Consistency," *Journal of Consumer Research* 18, no. 9 (1991): 185–193; Susan M. Broniarcysyk and Joseph W. Alba, "The Importance of the Brand in Brand Extension," *Journal of Marketing Research* 31, no. 5 (1994): 214–228.
94. Peter A. Dacin and Daniel C. Smith, "The Effect of Brand Portfolio Characteristics on Consumer Evaluations of Brand Extensions," *Journal of Marketing Research* 31 (May 1994): 229–242; Keller and Aaker, "The Effects of Sequential Introduction of Brand Extensions"; Daniel A. Sheinin and Bernd H. Schmitt, "Extending Brands with New Product Concepts: The Role of Category Attribute Congruity, Brand Affect, and Brand Breadth," *Journal of Business Research* 31 (1994): 1–10.
95. Roger A. Kerin, Gurumurthy Kalyanaram, and Daniel J. Howard, "Product Hierarchy and Brand Strategy Influences on the Order of Entry Effect for Consumer Packaged Goods," *Journal of Product Innovation Management* 13 (1996): 21–34.
96. Maureen Morrin, "The Impact of Brand Extensions on Parent Brand Memory Structures and Retrieval Processes," *Journal of Marketing Research* 36 (November 1999): 517–525; John Roedder, Barbara Loken, and Christopher Joiner, "The Negative Impact of Extensions: Can Flagship Products Be Diluted?" *Journal of Marketing* 62 (January 1998): 19–32; Daniel A. Sheinin, "The Effects of Experience with Brand Extensions on Parent Brand

Knowledge," *Journal of Business Research* 49 (2000): 47–55.

97. Amna Kirmani, Sanjay Sood, and Sheri Bridges, "The Ownership Effect in Consumer Responses to Brand Line Stretches," *Journal of Marketing* 63 (January 1999): 88–101.
98. Vicki R. Lane and Robert Jacobson, "Stock Market Reactions to Brand Extension Announcements: The Effects of Brand Attitude and Familiarity," *Journal of Marketing* 59, no. 1 (1995): 63–77.
99. D. A. Aaker and R. Jacobson, "The Financial Information Content of Perceived Quality," *Journal of Marketing Research* 31, no. 5 (1994): 191–201; D. A. Aaker and R. Jacobson, "The Value Relevance of Brand Attitude in High-Technology Markets," *Journal of Marketing Research* 38 (November 2001): 485–493; M. E. Barth, M. Clement, G. Foster, and R. Kasznik, "Brand Values and Capital Market Valuation," *Review of Accounting Studies* 3 (1998): 41–68.

BRAND POSITIONING

Preview

We've shown that customer-based brand equity is the differential effect brand knowledge has on customer response to the marketing of that brand. This makes consumers' brand knowledge central to the creation and management of brand equity.

We've also seen that the customer-based brand equity (CBBE) model lays out a series of steps for building a strong brand: (1) Establish the proper brand identity, (2) create the appropriate brand meaning, (3) elicit positive brand responses, and (4) forge strong brand relationships with customers. Six building blocks—brand salience, brand performance, brand imagery, brand judgments, brand feelings, and brand resonance—provide the foundation for successful brand development.

This chapter, then, builds on Chapter 2 to consider how to define desired or ideal brand knowledge structures in the process of positioning a brand. ***Positioning*** means identifying and establishing points of parity and points of difference to establish the right brand identity and brand image.[1]

Unique, meaningful *points of difference* provide a competitive advantage and "reason why" consumers should buy the brand. On the other hand, some brand associations can be roughly as favorable as those of competing brands, so they function as *points of parity* in consumers' minds—and negate potential points of difference for competitors. In other words, these associations are designed to provide "no reason why not" for consumers to choose the brand.

The chapter reviews how to identify and establish core brand associations and a brand mantra, and how to conduct brand audits using a research approach to help formulate brand positioning. Brand Focus 3.0 provides an example of a sample brand audit for Rolex.

Identifying and Establishing Brand Positioning

The CBBE model provides a blueprint for the steps in building a strong brand. To put the model into action, marketers must make several strategic decisions about the specific nature of the brand building blocks they will use. To guide those decisions, we'll first describe brand positioning, and then brand mantras.

Basic Concepts

The CBBE model describes the general process by which marketers should build brand knowledge structures to create brand equity. Here we'll look at how marketers might determine *desired* brand meaning or positioning, that is, what they would like consumers to know about the brand as opposed to what they might currently know. Determining the desired brand knowledge structures means positioning the brand.

Brand positioning is at the heart of marketing strategy. It is the "act of designing the company's offer and image so that it occupies a distinct and valued place in the target customer's minds."[2] As the name implies, positioning means finding the proper "location" in the minds of a group of consumers or market segment, so that they think about a product or service in the "right" or desired way to maximize potential benefit to the firm. Good brand positioning helps to guide marketing strategy by clarifying what a brand is all about, how it is unique and how it is similar to competitive brands, and why consumers should purchase and use it.

According to the CBBE model, deciding on a positioning requires determining a frame of reference (by identifying the target market and the nature of competition) and the ideal points of parity and points of difference brand associations. In other words, marketers need to know (1) who the target consumer is, (2) who the main competitors are, (3) how the brand is similar to these competitors, and (4) how the brand is different from them. We'll talk about each of these. Branding Brief 3-1 describes some of the positioning problems that the cola companies have had in finding good positions for their diet soft drinks.

Target Market

Identifying the consumer target is important because different consumers may have different brand knowledge structures and thus different perceptions and preferences for the brand. Without this understanding, it may be difficult for marketers to say which brand associations should be strongly held, favorable, and unique. Let's look at defining and segmenting a market and choosing target market segments.

A ***market*** is the set of all actual and potential buyers who have sufficient interest in, income for, and access to a product. ***Market segmentation*** divides the market into distinct groups of homogeneous consumers who have similar needs and consumer behavior, and who thus require similar marketing mixes. Market segmentation requires making tradeoffs between costs and benefits. The more finely segmented the market, the more likely that the firm will be able to implement marketing programs that meet the needs of consumers in any one segment. That advantage, however, can be offset by the greater costs of reduced standardization.

Segmentation Bases. Figures 3-1 and 3-2 display some possible segmentation bases for consumer and industrial markets, respectively. We can classify these bases as descriptive or customer-oriented (related to what kind of person or organization the customer is), or as behavioral or product-oriented (related to how the customer thinks of or uses the brand or product).

Behavioral
User status
Usage rate
Usage occasion
Brand loyalty
Benefits sought

Demographic
Income
Age
Sex
Race
Family

Psychographic
Values, opinions, and attitudes
Activities and lifestyle

Geographic
International
Regional

FIGURE 3-1

Consumer Segmentation Bases

BRANDING BRIEF 3-1

Trying to Find Some Homes for New Diet Colas

With consumers turning to healthier options like water and sports drinks, U.S. soft drinks sales have been flat. Diet soda has been one of the few bright spots and, unlike regular soda, is still a growing market segment. Soft drink companies are therefore looking for new ways to appeal to calorie-conscious consumers, especially men who are turned off by the taste of traditional diet sodas or perceive a stigma attached to the word "diet." And new sweeteners, like Splenda, which appeals to low-carb dieters, create even more options.

The drive to appeal to the health-conscious crowd, however, is making soft drinks a crowded category, and success has not come easily for the cola giants. In recent years, Coca-Cola has tried to add Diet Coke with Splenda, Coke Zero, and C2 to its diet cola portfolio as companions to the hugely successful Diet Coke brand. In the process, it has been going head-to-head with Pepsi, which has a newly formulated Pepsi One, as well as Diet Pepsi and Pepsi EDGE.

Although these new line extension entries are intended to boost sales, some critics point out that they can also backfire if new versions cannibalize sales of the company's existing beverages. Even worse, many feel that Coke and Pepsi run the risk of confusing consumers with endless variants in both diet and regular versions. Despite millions spent on advertising by both firms, experts say customers don't always understand the differences between all the alternatives.

Introduced in 1998, Pepsi One has, appropriately, one calorie. Pepsi waited for Food and Drug Administration approval of sweetener acesulfame potassium (Ace-K) and spent more than $100 million on marketing the year following the launch. The firm positioned Pepsi One as a full-flavored yet healthy alternative to regular colas and targeted 20-to-30-year-old men who did not like the taste of diet colas. Unfortunately, initial advertising, featuring actor Cuba Gooding, Jr., failed to describe exactly what Pepsi One was and how it was different from Diet Pepsi. Subsequent ad campaigns came and went, and when Pepsi One failed to garner the market share the company hoped for, it was reformulated with Splenda.

With the launch of Coke Zero and Diet Coke with Splenda in 2005, consumers faced a growing array of low or no-calorie Coke options, including Diet Coke with Lime, Diet Coke with Lemon, Diet Cherry Coke, Diet Vanilla Coke, and Caffeine Free Diet Coke. Coke Zero, named for its zero calories, was designed to taste more like regular Coke than Diet Coke. Coke Zero began with the cola formula of Coke Classic and used aspartame and acesulfame potassium as sweeteners instead of sugar. Because the company was trying to stay away from the diet label, the words "diet" and "calories" were not mentioned in the initial marketing campaign. But as a result, consumers didn't really know what Coke Zero was, and the company eventually switched to ads emphasizing its "Real Coca-Cola taste, zero calories, no compromise."

Coke and Pepsi also introduced new options with half the calories of regular soft drinks that were marketed as "mid-calorie" colas. With 50 calories, Pepsi EDGE had 50 percent less sugar, carbohydrates, and calories than regular colas. Pepsi EDGE was geared toward calorie-conscious customers who vacillated between regular and diet colas, but preferred the sweeter version. But after failing to find a lucrative niche in the market, Pepsi phased out Pepsi EDGE by the end of 2005.

Coca Cola's mid-calorie drink, C2, also experienced slower sales than expected after its 2004 launch. Some experts maintain that both these brands were caught in "no man's land," offering an unsatisfactory compromise between taste and calories. In other words, people either want the taste and calories of a cola or they don't—there is not much middle ground.

Sources: Marilynn Marter, "Zero a Hero to Pop Makers, Drinkers," *The Philadelphia Inquirer,* 6 July 2005; Kenneth Hein, "Positioning: Desperately Seeking Men with Extra Pounds to Shed," *Brandweek,* 22 August 2005; Caroline Wilber, "Coke Zero Had Identity Crisis," *The Atlanta Journal-Constitution,* 12 August 2005; www.coke.com; www.pepsi.com; Chad Terhune, "Do Real Men Drink Diet Cola? Pepsi and Coke Duke It Out," *Wall Street Journal,* 2 July 2004, B1, B4; Heather Todd and Jeff Cioletti, "A Balanced Diet," *BeverageWorld,* June 2005, 24–28.

Nature of Good
Kind
Where used
Type of buy

Buying Condition
Purchase location
Who buys
Type of buy

Demographic
SIC code
Number of employees
Number of production workers
Annual sales volume
Number of establishments

FIGURE 3-2

Business-to-Business Segmentation Bases

Behavioral segmentation bases are often most valuable in understanding branding issues because they have clearer strategic implications. For example, defining a benefit segment makes it clear what should be the ideal point of difference or desired benefit with which to establish the positioning. Take the toothpaste market. One research study uncovered four main segments:[3]

1. *The Sensory Segment:* Seeking flavor and product appearance
2. *The Sociables:* Seeking brightness of teeth
3. *The Worriers:* Seeking decay prevention
4. *The Independent Segment:* Seeking low price

Given this market segmentation scheme, marketing programs could be put into place to attract one or more segments. For example, Close-Up initially targeted the first two segments, whereas Crest primarily concentrated on the third. Taking no chances, Beecham's Aquafresh went after all three segments, designing its toothpaste with three stripes to dramatize each of the three product benefits. With the success of multipurpose toothpastes such as Colgate Total, virtually all brands now offer products that emphasize multiple performance benefits. Branding Brief 3-2 describes a benefit segmentation plan for gasoline buyers devised by Mobil.

Other segmentation approaches build on brand loyalty in some way. For example, the conversion model measures the strength of the psychological commitment between brands and consumers, and consumers' openness to change.[4] To determine the ease with which a consumer can be converted to another choice, the model assesses commitment based on factors such as consumer attitudes toward and satisfaction with current brand choices in a category, and the importance of the decision to select a brand in that category.

The model segments users of a brand into four groups based on strength of commitment, from low to high, as follows:

1. *Convertible:* On the threshold of change; highly likely to switch brands
2. *Shallow:* Not ready to switch, but may be considering alternatives
3. *Average:* Comfortable with their choice; unlikely to switch in the future
4. *Entrenched:* Staunchly loyal; unlikely to change in the foreseeable future

The model also classifies nonusers of a brand into four other groups based on their openness to trying the brand, from low to high, as follows:

1. *Strongly Unavailable:* Strongly prefer their current brand
2. *Weakly Unavailable:* Prefer their current brand, although not strongly
3. *Ambivalent:* As attracted to the "other" brand as to their current choice
4. *Available:* Prefer the "other" brand but have not yet switched

Another loyalty perspective, the "funnel" model, traces consumer behavior in terms of initial awareness through brand most often used. Figure 3-3 shows a hypothetical pattern of results. For the purposes of brand building, marketers want to understand both (1) the percentage of target market that is present at each stage and (2) factors facilitating or inhibiting the transition from one stage to the next. In the hypothetical example, a key bottleneck appears to be converting never tried consumers to those who recently tried, as less than half "convert." To convince more consumers to consider the brand, marketers may need to raise brand salience or make the brand more acceptable in the target consumer's repertoire.

Marketers often segment consumers by their behavior. For example, a firm may target a certain age group, but the underlying reason is that they are particularly heavy users of the product, are unusually brand loyal, or are most likely to seek the benefit the product is best able to deliver. In some cases, however, broad demographic descriptors may mask important underlying differences.[5] A fairly specific target market of "women aged 40 to 49" may contain a number of very different segments who require totally different marketing mixes (think Amy Grant vs. Courtney Love).

The main advantage of demographic segmentation bases is that the demographics of traditional media vehicles are generally well known from consumer research; as a result, it has been easier to buy media on that basis. With the growing importance of nontraditional media and other forms of communication, as well as the capability to build databases to profile customers on a behavioral and media usage basis, however, this advantage has become less important. For example, online Web sites can now target such previously hard-to-reach markets as African Americans (NetNoir.com), Hispanics (Quepasa.com), Asian Americans (AsianAvenue.com), college students (Collegeclub.com), and gays (PlanetOut.com).

Criteria. A number of criteria have been offered to guide segmentation and target market decisions, such as the following:[6,7]

- *Identifiability:* Can we easily identify the segment?
- *Size:* Is there adequate sales potential in the segment?
- *Accessibility:* Are specialized distribution outlets and communication media available to reach the segment?
- *Responsiveness:* How favorably will the segment respond to a tailored marketing program?

The obvious overriding consideration in defining market segments is profitability. In many cases, profitability can be related to behavioral considerations. For example, one

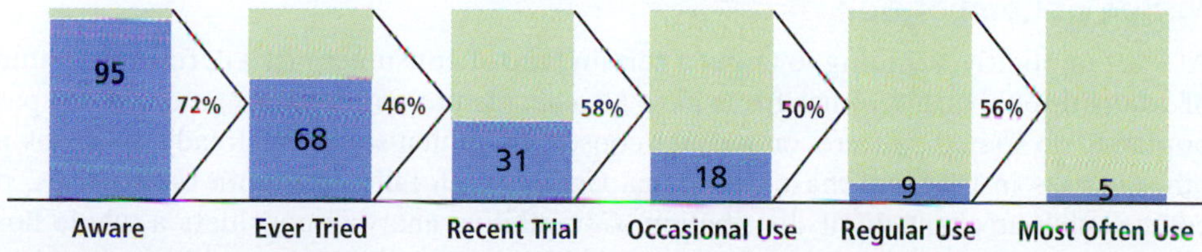

FIGURE 3-3

Hypothetical Example of Funnel Stages and Transitions

BRANDING BRIEF 3-2

Dividing Up Gasoline Buyers

In the 1950s, oil companies offered trading stamps, glasses, windshield washing services, and other incentives to differentiate their brands. In more recent years, however, gasoline marketing has been based primarily on attracting customers with low prices. In an attempt to break out of the sometimes vicious and unprofitable price wars that resulted, Mobil interviewed 2,000 customers to gain new insights into what gasoline customers wanted. According to their study, only 20 percent of Mobil's customers bought gasoline based solely on price. The surveys led the company to conclude that many motorists would forsake gasoline discounters in favor of a "quality buying experience."

Mobil segmented its market to find the best consumers to target.

Specifically, Mobil's research turned up five primary purchasing groups, labeled the Road Warriors, True Blues, Generation F3 Drivers (for fuel, food, and fast), Homebodies, and Price Driven. Different groups exhibited different needs and spending habits: The Price Driven group spent no more than $700 annually, whereas the biggest spenders, the Road Warriors and True Blues, averaged at least $1,200 a year (see the accompanying table). Mobil decided to target these big spenders, as well as Generation F3 Drivers (because Mobil felt many of them were destined to become Road Warriors).

With a 10 percent share of the U.S. market, Mobil overtook Shell in 1995 to become the leading gasoline seller. In 1996, Mobil introduced "Friendly Serve," a program that harked back to the days when gas stations provided full service at no extra cost. Mobil instructed its gas station attendants to approach customers and offer to pump gas and wash windows free of charge. The program, designed to improve customer loyalty, enabled Mobil to increase

brand loyalty segmentation scheme has four segments dubbed "Loyals," "Rotators," "Deal Selectives," and "Price Drivens."

Nature of Competition

At least implicitly, deciding to target a certain type of consumer often defines the nature of competition, because other firms have also decided to target that segment in the past or plan to do so in the future, or because consumers in that segment already may look to other brands in their purchase decisions. Competition takes place on other bases, of course, such as channels of distribution. Competitive analysis considers a whole host of factors—including the resources, capabilities, and likely intentions of various

MOBIL GASOLINE BUYER SEGMENTATION PLAN

Taxonomy at the Pump: Mobil's Five Types of Gasoline Buyers

Road Warriors:	True Blues:	Generation F3:	Homebodies:	Price Driven:
Generally higher-income middle-aged men who drive 25,000 to 50,000 miles a year . . . buy premium with a credit card . . . purchase sandwiches and drinks from the convenience store . . . will sometimes wash their cars at the car wash.	Usually men and women with moderate to high incomes who are loyal to a brand and sometimes to a particular station . . . frequently buy premium gasoline and pay in cash.	(for fuel, food, and fast): Upwardly mobile men and women—half under 25 years of age—who are constantly on the go . . . drive a lot and snack heavily from the convenience store.	Usually housewives who shuttle their children around during the day and use whatever gasoline station is based in town or along their route of travel.	Generally aren't loyal to either a brand or a particular station and rarely buy the premium line . . . frequently on tight budgets . . . efforts to woo them have been the basis of marketing strategies for years.

prices. Today's high price environment for gasoline has probably put even more pressure on oil companies to find ways to differentiate themselves besides costs.

Mobil provided another convenience for consumers when it introduced the Mobil Speedpass technology in 1997. Speedpass picked up where credit card payments at pumps left off by enabling customers to pay electronically by waving a transponder, which drivers attach to their keychains, in front of the pump. Speedpass could also be used to pay for items from mini-marts at Mobil stations.

Sources: Allanna Sullivan, "Mobil Bets Drivers Pick Cappuccino Over Low Prices," *Wall Street Journal,* 1 January 1995, B1; Leah Rickard, "Mobil Pumps Up Image for Friendlier Service," *Advertising Age,* 6 February 1995, 8; Peter Fritsch, "Mobil Aims to Turn Its Gasoline Pumps into Express Lanes," *Wall Street Journal,* 19 February 1997.

other firms—in order for marketers to choose markets where consumers can be profitably served.[8]

One lesson stressed by many marketing strategists is not to define competition too narrowly. Often, competition can occur at the benefit level rather than the attribute level. Thus, a luxury good with a strong hedonic benefit like stereo equipment may compete as much with a vacation as with other durable goods like furniture.

Unfortunately, many firms narrowly define competition and fail to recognize the most compelling threats and opportunities. For example, sales in the apparel industry have been stagnant in recent years as consumers have decided to spend on home furnishings, electronics, and other products that better suit their lifestyle.[9] Leading clothing makers may be better off considering the points of differences of their offerings not so much against other

BRANDING BRIEF 3-3

Digital Convergence Changing the Consumer Electronics Industry

The competition to dominate the consumer electronics market, an area with huge sales growth and profit potential, is heated and wide open. DVD films, downloaded music, digital photos, and the devices that connect and manipulate them are changing the playing field and the rules for the industry. Pressures to grow revenues and to keep customers have prompted mergers of products and services. For example, cable and phone companies are offering joint packages of voice, video, and Internet services. And industry executives are salivating over the increased revenue that comes with the opportunity to control multiple services.

New innovations such as flat screen TVs are keeping the consumer electronics market hot.

U.S. shipments of consumer electronics rose 11 percent in 2004 to $113.5 billion. Digital music players flew off the shelves to the tune of $1.2 billion in revenue and liquid crystal display TVs logged $2 billion in sales. Technology combinations and the power to transfer video content to cell phones, computers, and other devices are becoming popular, even though some consumers are still waiting for fast Internet connections.

Some industry leaders in the consumer electronics arena come from unexpected places. Japanese companies still lead the pack in high-end televisions, digital cameras, and other major categories. But now more than half of DVD players are made in China. Cell phone leaders are Nokia from Finland, Samsung from South Korea, and Motorola from the United States. And Apple's iPod leads the portable music category.

clothing labels as against other discretionary purchases. Branding Brief 3-3 describes some of the competitive developments in the consumer electronics industry.

We've seen that products are often organized in consumers' minds in a hierarchical fashion, meaning that marketers can define competition at a number of different levels. Take Fresca (a grapefruit-flavored soft drink) as an example: At the product type level, it competes with noncola flavored soft drinks; at the product category level, it competes with all soft drinks; and at the product class level, it competes with all beverages. The target and competitive frame of reference chosen will dictate the breadth of brand awareness and the situations and types of cues that should become closely related to the brand. Recognizing the nature of different levels of competition has important implications for the desired brand associations, as we describe next.

And companies that have been successful in one area are eager to compete in new categories. For example, computer maker Gateway is a top seller of plasma TVs in the United States, even selling more than 2,500 flat-panel plasma models to the Wynn Las Vegas for the hotel's guest rooms. Gateway purchases its consumer electronics products from manufacturers in Taiwan, China, or Southeast Asia and then couples those products with the distribution system it created for its PCs. The combination helps Gateway get new products to market quickly and price them lower than the Japanese competition.

Since PC sales are relatively flat, Microsoft and Intel are trying to carve out slices of the consumer electronics market. Both companies maintain that their experience creating connected digital devices gives them an advantage over traditional consumer electronics leaders like Sony. They face competition from new open-source companies that produce hardware inexpensively.

Consumers are becoming more willing to pay for things like online music services, satellite radio, video on demand, and wireless networking. But there are many disagreements that need to be settled before the consumer electronics boom takes off, including which appliance will be the hub of the digital revolution. PC companies claim it will be the PC, while other companies argue it will be the TV.

One reason why convergence of the consumer electronics and computer industries is slow is that quite a bit of wiring is needed to connect home video, audio, Internet, and game devices. Many start-ups, as well as major companies, are tinkering with technology to connect home appliances wirelessly. But that goal requires clearing several major hurdles, including creating uniform standards among telecommunications, computer, and appliance companies.

In March 2005, the Federal Communications Commission took a step toward setting a standard for a new wireless technology by approving ultra-wideband, or UWB. UWB uses computing power to send pulses over the radio spectrum. Unlike previous technologies that used only specific frequencies, UWB can send large quantities of information quickly and is less vulnerable to interference. Many experts say UWB will eventually replace the current Wi-Fi standard in wireless networking technology. For now, though, no one company is taking the lead in integrating the different systems found in homes.

Sources: Peter Lewis, "Who Will Own Your Living Room?" *Fortune,* 9 February 2004; Don Clark, "A New Tech Battle for the Home," *Wall Street Journal,* 1 January 2005; Matt Tichtel, "A Device Supports One-on-One Talk Among Appliances," *New York Times,* 5 October 2005; John Markoff, "A Bandwidth Breakthrough Hints at a Future Beyond Wi-Fi," *New York Times,* 4 May 2005.

Points of Parity and Points of Difference

Once marketers have fixed the appropriate competitive frame of reference for positioning by defining the customer target market and the nature of competition, they can define the basis of the positioning itself. Arriving at the proper positioning requires establishing the correct points of difference and points of parity associations.[10]

Points of Difference Associations. ***Points of difference*** (PODs) are attributes or benefits that consumers strongly associate with a brand, positively evaluate, and believe that they could not find to the same extent with a competitive brand.[11] Although myriad different types of brand associations are possible, according to the CBBE model we can classify candidates as either functional, performance-related considerations, or abstract, imagery-related considerations.

The concept of PODs has much in common with several other well-known marketing concepts. For example, it is similar to the notion of ***unique selling proposition*** (USP), pioneered by Rosser Reeves and the Ted Bates advertising agency in the 1950s. The original idea behind USP was that advertising should give consumers a compelling reason to buy a product that competitors could not match. Ads were designed to communicate a distinctive, unique product benefit and not necessarily to be creative. In other words, USP emphasized *what* was said in an ad as opposed to *how* it was said.

Another positioning concept is ***sustainable competitive advantage*** (SCA), which relates, in part, to a firm's ability to achieve an advantage in delivering superior value in the marketplace for a prolonged period of time.[12] Although the SCA concept is somewhat broader than points of difference—SCAs could be based on business practices such as human resource policies—it also emphasizes the importance of differentiating products in some fashion. Thus, the concept of points of difference is closely related to unique selling proposition and sustainable competitive advantage and maintains that a brand must have some strong, favorable, and unique associations to differentiate itself from other brands.

Consumers' actual brand choices often depend on the perceived uniqueness of brand associations. Swedish retailer Ikea took a luxury product—home furnishings and furniture—and made it a reasonably priced alternative for the mass market. Ikea supports its low prices by having customers serve themselves and deliver and assemble their own purchases. Ikea also gains a point of difference through its product offerings. As one commentator noted, "Ikea built their reputation on the notion that Sweden produces good, safe, well-built things for the masses. They have some of the most innovative designs at the lowest cost out there."[13] As another example, consider Subaru.

Subaru's success in the U.S. was partly fueled by a switch to AWD.

SUBARU

By 1993, Subaru was selling only 104,000 cars annually in the United States, down 60 percent from its earlier peak. Cumulative U.S. losses approached $1 billion. Advertised as "Inexpensive and Built to Stay That Way," Subaru was seen as a me-too car that was undifferentiated from Toyota, Honda, and all their followers. To provide a clear, distinct image, Subaru decided to sell only all-wheel-drive in its passenger cars. After upgrading its luxury image—and increasing its price—Subaru sold over 187,000 cars by 2004. The following year it launched an ad campaign in the United States that reflected its global brand positioning and further broadened its brand meaning. The ad slogan, "Think. Feel. Drive," was also used in other parts of the world such as Japan and the United Kingdom.

Points of difference may rely on performance attributes (Hyundai provides six front and back seat "side-curtain" airbags as standard equipment on all its models for increased safety) or performance benefits (Magnavox's electronic products have "consumer friendly" technological features, such as television sets with "Smart Sound" to keep volume levels constant while flipping through channels and commercial breaks and "Smart Picture" to automatically adjust picture settings to optimal levels). In other cases, PODs come from imagery associations (the luxury and status imagery of Louis Vuitton or the fact that British Airways is advertised as the "world's favourite airline"). Many top brands attempt to create a point of difference on "overall superior quality," whereas other firms become the "low-cost provider" of a product or service. Thus, a host of different types of PODs are possible.

Points of Parity Associations. ***Points of parity associations*** (POPs), on the other hand, are not necessarily unique to the brand but may in fact be shared with other brands. There are two types: category and competitive. ***Category points of parity*** represent necessary—but not necessarily sufficient—conditions for brand choice. They exist minimally at the generic product level and are most likely at the expected product level. Thus, consumers might not consider a bank truly a "bank" unless it offered a range of checking and savings plans; provided safety deposit boxes, travelers checks, and other such services; and had convenient hours and automated teller machines. Category POPs may change over time because of technological advances, legal developments, and consumer trends, but these attributes and benefits are like "greens fees" to play the marketing game.

Note that category POPs become especially critical when a brand launches a brand extension into a new category. In fact, the more dissimilar the extension category, the more important it is to make sure that category POPs are sufficiently well established. Consumers might have a clear understanding of the extension's intended point of difference because it uses an existing brand name. Where consumers often need reassurance, however, and what should often be the focus of the marketing program, is whether the extension also has the necessary points of parity.

NIVEA

Nivea became a leader in the skin cream category by creating strong points of difference on the benefits of "gentle," "protective," and "caring." As it leveraged its brand equity into categories such as deodorants, shampoos, and cosmetics, Nivea found it necessary to establish category points of parity before it could promote its brands' points of difference. These were of little value unless consumers believed that its deodorant was strong enough, its shampoo would produce beautiful enough hair, and its cosmetics would be colorful enough. Once points of parity were established, Nivea's heritage and other associations could be introduced as compelling points of difference.

Nivea has carefully positioned its extension products.

Competitive points of parity are those associations designed to negate competitors' points of difference. In other words, if a brand can "break even" in those areas where its competitors are trying to find an advantage and can achieve advantages in some other areas, the brand should be in a strong—and perhaps unbeatable—competitive position. For example, consider the introduction of Miller Lite beer.[14]

MILLER LITE

When Philip Morris bought Miller Brewing, its flagship High Life brand was not competing particularly well, leading the company to decide to introduce a light beer. The initial advertising strategy for Miller Lite was to assure parity with a necessary and important consideration in the category by stating that it "tastes great," while at the same time creating a point of difference with the fact that it contained one-third less calories (96 calories versus 150 calories for conventional 12-ounce full-strength beer) and was thus "less filling." As is often the case, the point of parity and point of difference were somewhat conflicting, as consumers tend to equate taste with calories.

To overcome potential consumer resistance to this notion, Miller employed credible spokespeople, primarily popular former professional athletes who would presumably not drink a beer unless it tasted good. These ex-jocks were placed in amusing situations in ads where they debated which of the two product benefits—"tastes great" or "less filling"—was more descriptive of the beer, creating valuable points of parity and points of difference. The ads ended with the clever tag line "Everything you've always wanted in a beer . . . and less."[15]

Points of Parity versus Points of Difference. For the brand to achieve a point of parity on a particular attribute or benefit, a sufficient number of consumers must believe that the brand is "good enough" on that dimension. There is a "zone" or "range of tolerance or acceptance" with POPs. The brand does not have to be seen as *literally* equal to competitors, but consumers must feel that it does sufficiently well on that particular attribute or benefit so that they do not consider it to be a negative or a problem. Assuming consumers feel that way, they may then be willing to base their evaluations and decisions on other factors potentially more favorable to the brand. Points of parity are thus easier to achieve than points of difference, where the brand must demonstrate clear superiority. Often, the key to positioning is not so much achieving a point of difference as achieving necessary or competitive points of parity.

Positioning Guidelines

The concepts of points of difference and points of parity can be invaluable tools to guide positioning. Two key issues in arriving at the optimal competitive brand positioning are (1) defining and communicating the competitive frame of reference and (2) choosing and establishing points of parity and points of difference.[16]

Defining and Communicating the Competitive Frame of Reference

A starting point in defining a competitive frame of reference for a brand positioning is to determine category membership. With which products or sets of products does the brand compete? Choosing to compete in different categories often results in different competitive frames of reference and thus different POPs and PODs (see Branding Brief 3-4).

The product's category membership tells consumers about the goals they might achieve by using a product or service. For highly established products and services, category membership is not a focal issue. Customers are aware that Coca-Cola is a leading brand of soft drink, Kellogg's Corn Flakes is a leading brand of cereal, McKinsey is a leading strategy consulting firm, and so on.

There are many situations, however, in which it is important to inform consumers of a brand's category membership. Perhaps the most obvious is the introduction of new products, where the category membership is not always apparent, especially for high-tech products.

Personal Digital Assistants

When personal digital assistants (PDAs) were first introduced, they could have been positioned as either a computer accessory or as a replacement for an appointment book. Motorola Envoy's failure could be attributed in part to the lack of a clearly defined competitive set. By contrast, Palm Pilot, a product that performed many of the same tasks as Envoy, achieved considerable success by claiming membership in the electronic organizer category. More recently, BlackBerry extended the category to encompass e-mail, an MP3 player, and cellular phone service, while offering a more traditional keyboard. As these handheld devices continue to offer these new features and services, their competitive frames of reference will continue to evolve.

Sometimes consumers know a brand's category membership but may not be convinced the brand is a true, valid member of the category. For example, consumers may be aware that Sony produces computers, but they may not be certain whether Sony computers are in the same "class" as Dell, HP, and Lenovo. In this instance, it might be useful to reinforce category membership.

Brands are sometimes affiliated with categories in which they do not hold membership rather than with the one in which they do. This approach is a viable way to highlight a brand's point of difference from competitors, provided that consumers know the brand's actual membership. For example, Bristol-Myers Squibb ran commercials for its Excedrin aspirin acknowledging Tylenol's perceived consumer acceptance for aches and pains, but touting the Excedrin brand as "The Headache Medicine." With this approach, however, it is important that consumers understand what the brand is, and not just what it is *not,* as evidenced by the following experience.

Zima

Zima was launched in 1994 by Adolph Coors Company in the midst of the New Age beverage craze. Zima was defined almost entirely by what it was not: not a beer and not a wine cooler. The colorless beverage was supported by an introductory ad campaign in which a mysterious pitchman in a white suit and black hat described the product as, "It'z a secret. It'z zomething different." Although the ads created some mystique, they never made it clear what Zima actually was. As one former executive of the company noted, "You couldn't tell whether you should be pounding it down or sipping it over ice." Compounding the problem was a quirky taste that many consumers did not like. Repeat sales stalled, and Coors management came to the realization that Zima was perhaps destined to be a niche brand. They subsequently launched the ad campaign "A Few Degrees Cooler" to reinforce Zima's product uniqueness.[17]

The preferred approach to positioning is to inform consumers of a brand's membership before stating its point of difference in relationship to other category members. Presumably, consumers need to know what a product is and what function it serves before they can decide whether it dominates the brands against which it competes. For new products, separate marketing programs are generally needed to inform consumers of membership and to educate them about a brand's point of difference. For brands with limited resources, this implies the development of a marketing strategy that establishes category membership prior to one that states a point of difference. Brands with greater resources can develop concurrent marketing programs, one of which features membership and the other the point of difference. Efforts to inform consumers of membership and points of difference in the same ad, however, are often not effective.

Occasionally, a company will undertake to straddle two frames of reference.

BRANDING BRIEF 3-4

Competitive Frames of Reference for FedEx

Consider the possible positioning options for FedEx, the U.S. market pioneer in the overnight delivery service (ONDS) category. Within the ONDS category, FedEx created strong, favorable, and unique associations to the consumer benefits of being the fastest and most dependable delivery service around (as reinforced by the firm's introductory slogan, "When it absolutely, positively has to be there overnight"). This association provided a key point of difference to traditional mail deliveries by the U.S. Postal Service (which would typically take two or more days depending on the destination involved), as well as other ONDS carriers who found it difficult, at least initially, to match FedEx's high level of service quality.

If FedEx were to define its competition as other brands in the ONDS category, then it might continue to design marketing programs to enhance its associations with speed and reliability. But what other forms of competition does FedEx face? We could argue that as a market leader it competes to a large extent with other types of products that can satisfy similar needs. For example, consider fax machines or e-mail. Many documents that would have been sent by

BMW

When BMW first made a strong competitive push into the U.S. market in the early 1980s, it positioned the brand as being the only automobile that offered both luxury and performance. At that time, American luxury cars were seen by many as lacking performance, and American performance cars were seen as lacking luxury. By relying on the design of its cars, its German heritage, and other aspects of a well-designed marketing program, BMW was able to simultaneously achieve (1) a point of difference on performance and a point of parity on luxury with respect to luxury cars and (2) a point of difference on luxury and a point of parity on performance with respect to performance cars. The clever slogan, "The Ultimate Driving Machine," effectively captured the newly created umbrella category—luxury performance cars.

Although a positioning that straddles two categories often is attractive as a means of reconciling potentially conflicting consumer goals, it carries an extra burden. If the points of parity and points of difference with respect to both categories are not credible, consumers may not view the brand as a legitimate player in *either* category. Many early PDAs that unsuccessfully tried to straddle categories ranging from pagers to laptop computers provide a vivid illustration of this risk.

There are three main ways to convey a brand's category membership: communicating category benefits, comparing to exemplars, and relying on the product descriptor.

To reassure consumers that a brand will deliver on the fundamental reason for using a category, marketers frequently use benefits to announce category membership. Thus, industrial motors might claim to have power, and analgesics might announce their efficacy. These benefits are presented in a manner that does not imply brand superiority but merely notes that the brand possesses them as a means to establish category POPs. Performance

overnight delivery—and most likely by FedEx—a few years ago can now be sent more quickly and easily via a fax machine or as an e-mail attachment.

On the other hand, the confidence and risk reduction of sending a document by FedEx may still be relevant when competing with fax delivery. FedEx may decide to emphasize security and confidentiality as advantages over fax machines and e-mails. Along those lines, note that the company's heavily promoted tracking capabilities may actually help it to compete with both other ONDS carriers and alternate delivery forms such as fax machines and e-mail.

Finally, perhaps FedEx's greatest growth opportunity is with Internet commerce and shipping for online retailers. However, at least initially, UPS has been able to gain more of that market due to its aggressive pricing and improved delivery capabilities.

Source: David Field, "FedEx Not Ready to Abandon Shipping," *USA Today,* 20 October 1999, B3; Dean Foust, "The Ground War at FedEx," *BusinessWeek,* 28 November 2005.

and imagery associations can provide supporting evidence. A cake mix might attain membership in the cake category by claiming the benefit of great taste and might support this benefit claim by possessing high-quality ingredients (performance) or by showing users delighting in its consumption (imagery).

Exemplars—well-known, noteworthy brands in a category—can also be used to specify a brand's category membership. When Tommy Hilfiger was an unknown designer, advertising announced his membership as a great American designer by associating him with Geoffrey Beene, Stanley Blacker, Calvin Klein, and Perry Ellis, who were recognized members of that category.

The product descriptor that follows the brand name is often a very compact means of conveying category origin. For example, USAir changed its name to USAirways, according to CEO Stephen Wolf, as part of the airline's attempted transformation from a regional carrier with a poor reputation to a strong national or even international brand. The argument was that other major airlines had the word *airlines* or *airways* in their names rather than *air,* which was felt to be typically associated with smaller, regional carriers.[18] Consider the following examples.

- A number of new models of cars have been introduced in recent years that combine the attributes of an SUV, a minivan, and a station wagon, including the Ford Escape, Honda CR-V, and BMW 530xi. To communicate this unique position, the vehicles have been designated "sports wagons."[19]
- When Campbell's launched its V-8 Splash beverage line, it deliberately avoided including the word "carrot" in the brand name despite the fact that carrot was the main ingredient. The name was chosen to convey healthful benefits but to avoid the negative perception of carrots.[20]

- California's prune growers and marketers have attempted to establish an alternative name for their product, "dried plums," because prunes were seen by the target market of 35- to 50-year-old women as "a laxative for old people."[21]

The product descriptor is often critical with new technology products. When IBM rebranded its multibillion-dollar server product line as the eSeries, it created four different sets of brands and products within the line. Although three of the series had clear designations—zSeries mainframe servers, pSeries Unix servers, and xSeries Intel servers—some critics felt the designation for the iSeries integrated application servers (formerly the highly successful AS/400) did not necessarily provide clear category membership, either within the IBM product line or with respect to its server competitors.

Establishing a brand's category membership is usually not sufficient for effective brand positioning. If many firms engage in category-building tactics, the result may be consumer confusion. For example, at the peak of the dot-com boom, Ameritrade, E*TRADE, Datek, and others advertised lower commission rates on stock trades than conventional brokerage firms; Pets.com, Petopia, and other pet food supply companies promoted their vast array of pet supplies; and so on. A sound positioning strategy requires marketers to specify not only the category but also how the brand dominates other members of its category. Developing compelling points of difference is thus critical to effective brand positioning.

Choosing Points of Difference

The two most important considerations in choosing PODs are that consumers find the POD desirable and that they believe the firm has the capabilities to deliver on it. If both these considerations are satisfied, the POD has the potential to become a strong, favorable, and unique brand association. Each of these considerations, desirability and deliverability, has a number of specific criteria, which we look at next.

Desirability Criteria. We've seen that there are three key desirability criteria for PODs—relevance, distinctiveness, and believability—that marketers must assess from a consumer perspective. Only by satisfying these three will the POD serve as a viable positioning alternative.

- *Relevance:* Target consumers must find the POD personally relevant and important. The test of relevance considerations can be easily overlooked. For example, in the early 1990s, a number of brands in different product categories (colas, dishwashing soaps, beer, deodorants, gasoline, etc.) introduced clear versions of their products to better differentiate themselves. Although "clear" perhaps signaled natural, pure, and lightness to consumers initially, a proliferation of clear versions of products that did not reinforce these other associations blurred its meaning. The "clear" association has not seemed to be of enduring value or to be sustainable as a point of difference. In many cases, these brands have experienced declining market share or disappeared altogether.
- *Distinctiveness:* Target consumers must find the POD distinctive and superior. When marketers are entering a category in which there are established brands, the challenge is to find a viable basis for differentiation. Sometimes the point of difference is one on which a brand dominates its competition but that is not important to consumers. Several analgesic brands, including Aleve, have found limited response to the claim that their brand was long lasting or required infrequent dosing. Most consumers place more importance on fast relief than long-lasting relief. Indeed, long lasting may imply slow acting—just the opposite of what most people want.

- *Believability:* A brand must offer a compelling and credible reason for choosing it over the other options. Perhaps the simplest approach is to point to a unique attribute of the product. Thus, Mountain Dew may argue that it is more energizing than other soft drinks and support this claim by noting that it has a higher level of caffeine. On the other hand, when the point of difference is abstract or image based, support for the claim may reside in more general associations to the company that have been developed over time. Thus, Chanel No. 5 perfume may claim to be the quintessential elegant, French perfume and support this claim by noting the long association between Chanel and haute couture.

Deliverability Criteria. If the three key deliverability criteria of feasibility, communicability, and sustainability are satisfied, the positioning has the potential to be enduring.

- *Feasibility:* Can the firm actually create the POD? The product and marketing must be designed in a way to support the desired association. It is obviously easier to convince consumers of some fact about the brand that they were unaware of or may have overlooked than to make changes in the product and convince consumers of the value of these changes.
- *Communicability:* The key issue in communicability is consumers' perceptions of the brand and the resulting brand associations. It is very difficult to create an association that is not consistent with existing consumer knowledge, or that consumers, for whatever reason, have trouble believing in. What factual, verifiable evidence or "proof points" can marketers communicate as support, so that consumers will actually believe in the brand and its desired associations?
- *Sustainability:* Is the positioning preemptive, defensible, and difficult to attack? Can the brand association be reinforced and strengthened over time? If these are the case, the positioning is likely to last for years. Sustainability depends on internal commitment and use of resources as well as external market forces. Applebee's strategy for leadership in the casual dining restaurant business, in part, is to enter smaller markets where a second major competitor might be unlikely to enter—hello Hays, Kansas! Although there are downsides to the strategy—potentially smaller volume and lethal word-of-mouth from any service snafus—competitive threats are minimal.[22]

Needless to say, the positioning must also be highly differentiated in order to be effective. These three considerations for developing an optimal positioning align with the three perspectives on which any brand must be evaluated, namely the consumer, the company, and the competition. Desirability is determined from the consumer's point of view, deliverability is based on a company's inherent capabilities, and differentiation is determined relative to the competitors.

Establishing Points of Parity and Points of Difference

One challenge for marketers is that many of the attributes or benefits that make up the POPs or PODs are negatively correlated. For example, it might be difficult to position a brand as "inexpensive" and at the same time assert that it is "of the highest quality." Figure 3-4 displays some other examples of negatively correlated attributes and benefits. Moreover, individual attributes and benefits often have both positive and negative aspects. A long heritage could be seen as a positive attribute because it can suggest experience, wisdom, and expertise. On the other hand, it could be a negative attribute because it might imply being old-fashioned and not contemporary and cutting-edge.

Low price vs. high quality
Taste vs. low calories
Nutritious vs. good tasting
Efficacious vs. mild
Powerful vs. safe
Strong vs. refined
Ubiquitous vs. exclusive
Varied vs. simple

FIGURE 3-4

Examples of Negatively Correlated Attributes and Benefits

Unfortunately, consumers typically want to maximize both the negatively correlated attributes and benefits. The challenge is that competitors often are trying to achieve their point of difference on an attribute that is negatively correlated with the point of difference of the target brand. Much of the art and science of marketing is knowing how to deal with tradeoffs, and positioning is no different. The best approach clearly is to develop a product or service that performs well on both dimensions. Thus, BMW's ability to establish its positioning image straddling luxury and performance was due in large part to product design and the fact that the car was considered both luxurious and high-performance. Similarly, Gore-Tex was able to overcome the seemingly conflicting product image of "breathable" and "waterproof" through technological advances.

Several additional ways exist to address the problem of negatively correlated POPs and PODs. The following three approaches are listed in increasing order of effectiveness—but also increasing order of difficulty.

Separate the Attributes. An expensive but sometimes effective approach is to launch two different marketing campaigns, each devoted to a different brand attribute or benefit. These campaigns may run concurrently or sequentially. For example, Head & Shoulders met success in Europe with a dual campaign in which one ad emphasized its dandruff removal efficacy while another ad emphasized the appearance and beauty of hair after its use. The hope is that consumers will be less critical when judging the POP and POD benefits in isolation, because the negative correlation might be less apparent. The downside is that two strong campaigns have to be developed—not just one. Moreover, if the marketer does not address the negative correlation head-on, consumers may not develop as positive an association as desired.

Leverage Equity of Another Entity. In the Miller Lite example discussed earlier, the brand "borrowed" or leveraged the equity of well-known and well-liked celebrities to lend credibility to one of the negatively correlated benefits. Brands can link themselves to any kind of entity that possesses the right kind of equity—a person, other brand, event, and so forth—as a means to establish an attribute or benefit as a POP or POD. Self-branded ingredients may also lend some credibility to a questionable attribute in consumers' minds. Borrowing equity, however, is neither costless nor riskless. Chapter 7 reviews these considerations in detail and outlines the pros and cons of leveraging equity.

Redefine the Relationship. Finally, another potentially powerful but often difficult way to address the negative relationship between attributes and benefits in the minds of consumers is to convince them that in fact the relationship is positive. Marketers can achieve this by providing consumers a different perspective and suggesting that they may be overlooking or ignoring certain factors or other considerations.

Apple sells products that combine ease of use and power and performance.

Apple Computers

When Apple Computers launched the Macintosh, its key point of difference was "user friendly." Although many consumers valued ease of use—especially those who bought personal computers for the home—one drawback with the association was that customers who bought personal computers for business applications inferred that if a personal computer was easy to use, then it also must not be very powerful—a key choice consideration in that market. Recognizing this potential problem, Apple ran a clever ad campaign with the tag line "The power to be your best," in an attempt to redefine what a powerful computer meant. The message behind the ads was that because Apple was easy to use, people in fact did just that—they used them!—a simple but important indication of "power." In other words, the most powerful computers were ones that people actually used.

Although difficult to achieve, such a strategy can be powerful because the two associations can become mutually reinforcing. The challenge is to develop a credible story with which consumers can agree.

Updating Positioning over Time

The previous section described some positioning guidelines that are especially useful for launching a new brand. With established brands, competitive forces often dictate shifts in positioning strategy over time. Branding Brief 3-5 describes how the two major U.S. political parties have applied branding principles and changed their positioning over time. The credit card wars provide another illustration.

Visa and American Express

In the 1990's, Visa's POD in the credit card category was that it was the most widely available card, which underscored the category's main benefit of convenience. American Express, on the other hand, had built the equity of its brand by highlighting the prestige associated with the use of its card. Having established their PODs, Visa and American Express then competed by attempting to blunt each other's advantage to create POPs. Along these lines, Visa offered gold and platinum cards to enhance the prestige of its brand and advertised "It's Everywhere You Want to Be" in aspirational settings that reinforced exclusivity and acceptability. American Express substantially increased the number of vendors that accepted American Express cards and created other value enhancements through its "Do More" campaign and

BRANDING BRIEF 3-5

Positioning Politicians

The importance of marketing has not been lost on politicians, and, although there are a number of different ways to interpret their words and actions, one way to interpret campaign strategies is from a brand equity perspective. For example, consultants to political candidates stress the importance of having "high name ID" or, in other words, a high level of brand awareness. In major races, at least 90 percent awareness is desired. Consultants also emphasize "positives-negatives"—voters' responses when asked whether they think positively or negatively of a candidate. A 3:1 ratio is desired (and 4:1 is even better). This measure corresponds to brand attitude in marketing terms.

Look at George Bush's textbook presidential campaign of 1988. Bush had been vice president for eight years under Ronald Reagan and was perceived by many as a moderate Republican. His Democratic opponent, the governor of Massachusetts, Michael Dukakis, was seen by many as being a traditional Democrat. The goal of Bush's campaign was to move Bush to the center of the political spectrum and make him a "safe" choice, a person who combined compassion with toughness and who was experienced and presidential in stature. The Republican campaign objective with Dukakis, on the other hand, was to make him seem liberal and move him to the left, emphasizing the risk of change. In terms of actual policies, the Republicans' strategy could be viewed as a classic application of positioning principles. Their goal was to create a point of difference on traditional Republican issues such as defense, the economy (and taxes), and crime and create a point of parity—thus negating their opponent's point of difference—on traditional Democratic issues such as the environment, education, and abortion rights.

The actual Bush campaign was a fully integrated modern communications program, skillfully blending public relations and media news coverage with paid advertising. As a result of this well-designed and well-executed campaign, by the time of the election, Bush's ratio of positives to negatives had dramatically shifted to 60 percent to 20 percent. Equally important, on those key Democratic issues that were to be their points of difference, the Republicans were able to break even. For example, when voters were asked in exit polls which presidential candidate would be better for the environment, they were almost equally split between the

later its "Make Life Rewarding" and "A World of Service" campaigns to try to reduce Visa's advantage on this dimension. Visa's 2006 launch of their "Life Takes Visa" ad campaign represented the next step in the evolution of that brand's positioning.

Updating positioning raises two main issues. The first is how to deepen the meaning of the brand to tap into core brand associations or other, more abstract considerations—***laddering***. The second is how to respond to competitive challenges that threaten an existing positioning—***reacting***.

Laddering. Although identifying PODs to dominate competition on benefits that are important to consumers provides a sound way to build an initial position, once the target market attains a basic understanding of how the brand relates to alternatives in the same

two candidates. Having successfully achieved these points of parity and points of difference in the minds of the voters, Bush won in a landslide.

Although the Republicans ran a nearly flawless campaign in 1988, that was not the case in 1992. The new Democratic candidate, Bill Clinton, was a fierce campaigner who ran a very focused campaign designed to create a key point of difference on one main issue—the economy. Rather than attempting to achieve a point of parity on this issue, Bush, who was running for reelection, campaigned on other issues such as family values. By conceding a key point of difference to the Democrats and failing to create a compelling one of their own, Bush and the Republicans were defeated handily. Failing to learn from their mistakes, the Republicans ran a meandering campaign in 1996 that failed to achieve points of parity or points of difference. Not surprisingly, their presidential candidate, Bob Dole, lost decisively to the incumbent Bill Clinton.

The closeness of the 2000 election between Al Gore and George W. Bush reflected the failure of either candidate to create a strong point of difference with the electorate. In an interesting study during the middle of the race, brand consultant Landor examined the images of the candidates and compared them to various companies. Bush was seen as tougher, more straightforward, and even glamorous, whereas Gore came across as kinder. Within the Republican faithful, Bush was seen to have much in common with IBM, Xerox, and Hewlett-Packard, whereas Gore's Democratic followers found him more closely aligned with Yahoo!, Alta Vista, and Lycos. Landor head Allen Adamson concluded that both men were like "classic brands that need to reinvent themselves . . . . Bush is like a line extension of a brand, former President Bush. . . and so much of Gore's success in the marketplace comes from the Clinton brand . . . he's got to totally re-launch himself."

There was a similarly tight election in 2004 because neither George W. Bush nor John Kerry was successful at carving out a strong position in voters' minds.

Source: "Gore and Bush Are Like Classic Brands," *New York Times,* 25 July 2000, B8.

category, it may be necessary to deepen the meanings associated with the brand positioning. It is often useful to explore underlying consumer motivations in a product category to uncover the relevant associations. For example, Maslow's hierarchy maintains that consumers have different priorities and levels of needs.[23] From lowest to highest priority, they are as follows:

1. Physiological needs (food, water, air, shelter, sex)
2. Safety and security needs (protection, order, stability)
3. Social needs (affection, friendship, belonging)
4. Ego needs (prestige, status, self-respect)
5. Self-actualization (self-fulfillment).

According to Maslow, higher-level needs become relevant once lower-level needs have been satisfied.

Marketers have also recognized the importance of higher-level needs. For example, ***means-end chains*** have been devised as a way of understanding higher-level meanings of brand characteristics.[24] A means-end chain takes the following structure: Attributes (descriptive features that characterize a product) lead to benefits (the personal value and meaning attached to product attributes), which, in turn, lead to values (stable and enduring personal goals or motivations).[25] In other words, a consumer chooses a product that delivers an attribute (A) that provides benefits or has certain consequences (B/C) that satisfy values (V). For example, in a study of salty snacks, one respondent noted that a flavored chip (A) with a strong taste (A) would mean that she would eat less (B/C), not get fat (B/C), and have a better figure (B/C), all of which would enhance her self-esteem (V).

Laddering thus progresses from attributes to benefits to more abstract values or motivations. In effect, laddering repeatedly asks what the implication of an attribute or benefit is for the consumer. Failure to move up the ladder may reduce the strategic alternatives available to a brand.[26] For example, P&G introduced low-sudsing Dash detergent to attract consumers who used front-loading washing machines. Many years of advertising Dash in this manner made this position impenetrable by other brands. Dash was so associated with front-loaders, however, that when this type of machine went out of fashion, so did Dash, despite the fact that it was among P&G's most effective detergents, and despite significant efforts to reposition the brand.

Some attributes and benefits may lend themselves to laddering more easily than others. For example, the Betty Crocker brand appears on a number of different baking products and is characterized by the physical warmth associated with baking. Such an association makes it relatively easy to talk about emotional warmth and the joy of baking or the good feelings that might arise from baking for others.

Thus, some of the strongest brands deepen their points of difference to create benefit and value associations, for example, Volvo and Michelin (safety and peace of mind), Intel (performance and compatibility), Marlboro (western imagery), Coke (Americana and refreshment), Disney (fun, magic, family entertainment), Nike (innovative products and peak athletic performance), and BMW (styling and driving performance). As a brand becomes associated with more and more products and moves up the product hierarchy, the brand's meaning will become more abstract. At the same time, it is important that the proper category membership and POPs and PODs exist in the minds of consumers for the particular products sold.

Reacting. Competitive actions are often directed at eliminating points of difference to make them points of parity or to strengthen or establish new points of difference. Often competitive advantages exist for only a short period of time before competitors attempt to match them. For example, when Goodyear introduced Run-Flat tires (which allowed tires to keep going for up to 50 miles at a speed of 55 mph after a tire puncture or blowout), Michelin quickly responded with the Zero Pressure tire, which offered the same consumer benefit.

When a competitor challenges an existing POD or attempts to overcome a POP, there are essentially three main options for the target brand—from no reaction to moderate to significant reactions.

- *Do nothing.* If the competitive actions seem unlikely to recapture a POD or create a new POD, then the best reaction is probably to just stay the course and continue brand-building efforts.
- *Go on the defensive.* If the competitive actions appear to have the potential to disrupt the market some, then it may be necessary to take a defensive stance. One way to defend the positioning is to add some reassurance in the product or advertising to strengthen POPs and PODs.

- *Go on the offensive.* If the competitive actions seem potentially quite damaging, then it might be necessary to take a more aggressive stance and reposition the brand to address the threat. One approach might be to launch a product extension or ad campaign that fundamentally changes the meaning of the brand.

A brand audit can help marketers assess the severity of the competitive threat and the appropriate competitive stance, as described in the section "Brand Audits."

Defining and Establishing Brand Mantras

Brand positioning describes how a brand can effectively compete against a specified set of competitors in a particular market. In many cases, however, brands span multiple product categories and therefore may have multiple distinct—yet related—positionings. As brands evolve and expand across categories, marketers will want to define a set of core brand associations to capture the important dimensions of the brand meaning and what the brand represents. They may also synthesize the core brand associations to a core brand promise or brand mantra that reflects the essential "heart and soul" of the brand. We'll talk about both core brand associations and brand mantras next.

Core Brand Associations

Core brand associations are those abstract associations (attributes and benefits) that characterize the 5 to 10 most important aspects or dimensions of a brand. They can serve as the basis of brand positioning in terms of how they create points of parity and points of difference.

How do marketers identify core brand associations? The first step in this structured process is to ask consumers to create a detailed mental map of the brand. A ***mental map*** accurately portrays in detail all salient brand associations and responses for a particular target market. One of the simplest means to get consumers to create a mental map is to ask them for their top-of-mind brand associations ("When you think of this brand, what comes to mind?"). The CBBE brand pyramid from Chapter 2 helps to highlight some of the types of associations and responses that may emerge from the creation of a mental map.

Next, marketers group brand associations into related categories with descriptive labels. For example, in response to a Nike brand probe, consumers may list LeBron James, Michael Jordan, Tiger Woods, Roger Federer, or Lance Armstrong, whom we could call "top athletes." The challenge is to include all relevant associations while making sure each is as distinct as possible. Figure 3-5 displays a hypothetical mental map and core brand associations for MTV.

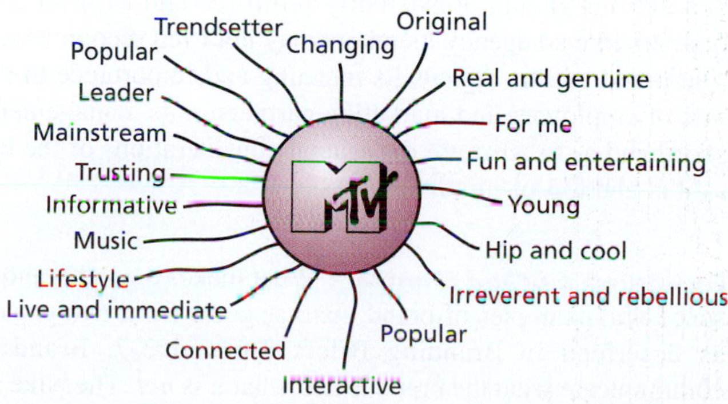

FIGURE 3-5a

MTV Mental Map

Music What's hot and what's new	**Community** Shared experience (literally and talk value)
Credibility Expert, trusting, reality	**Modern** Hip, Cool
Personality Irreverent, hip, cool	**Spontaneity** Up-to the-minute, Immediate
Accessibility Relevant, for everyone	**Originality** Genuine, creative
Interactivity Connected and participatory	**Fluidity** Always changing and evolving

FIGURE 3-5b

MTV Core Brand Associations

Brand Mantras

To find out even more about what a brand represents, marketers will often define a brand mantra.[27] A ***brand mantra*** is an articulation of the "heart and soul" of the brand, a short, three- to five-word phrase that captures the irrefutable essence or spirit of the brand positioning. It's similar to "brand essence" or "core brand promise," and its purpose is to ensure that all employees and external marketing partners understand what the brand most fundamentally is to represent to consumers, so they can adjust their actions accordingly. For example, McDonald's brand philosophy of "Food, Folks, and Fun" nicely captures its brand essence and core brand promise.

Brand mantras are powerful devices. They can provide guidance about what products to introduce under the brand, what ad campaigns to run, and where and how the brand should be sold. They may even guide the most seemingly unrelated or mundane decisions, such as the look of a reception area and the way employees answer the phone. In effect, brand mantras create a mental filter to screen out brand-inappropriate marketing activities or actions of any type that may have a negative bearing on customers' impressions of a brand.

Brand mantras help the brand present a consistent image. Any time a consumer or customer encounters a brand—in any way, shape, or form—his or her knowledge about that brand may change and affect the equity of the brand. Given that a vast number of employees come into contact with consumers, either directly or indirectly, their words and actions should consistently reinforce and support the brand meaning. Marketing partners like ad agency members may not even recognize their role in influencing equity. The brand mantra signals its meaning and importance to the firm, as well as the crucial role of employees and marketing partners in its management. It also provides memorable shorthand as to what are the crucial considerations of the brand that should be kept most salient and top-of-mind.

Designing a Brand Mantra. What makes a good brand mantra? Two high-profile and successful examples of brand mantras come from two powerful brands, Nike and Disney, as described in Branding Briefs 3-6 and 3-7. Brand mantras must economically communicate what the brand is and what it is *not*. The Nike and Disney examples show the power and utility of a well-designed brand mantra. They also help to suggest what might characterize a good brand mantra. Both examples are essentially structured the same way, with three terms, as follows:

	Emotional Modifier	Descriptive Modifier	Brand Function
Nike	Authentic	Athletic	Performance
Disney	Fun	Family	Entertainment

The ***brand functions*** term describes the nature of the product or service or the type of experiences or benefits the brand provides. It can range from concrete language that reflects the product category itself, to more abstract notions (like Nike's and Disney's), where the term relates to higher-order experiences or benefits that a variety of different products could deliver. The ***descriptive modifier*** further clarifies its nature. Thus, Nike's performance is not just any kind (not artistic performance, for instance) but only *athletic* performance; Disney's entertainment is not just any kind (not adult-oriented) but only *family* entertainment (and arguably an additional modifier, "magical" could add even more distinctiveness). Combined, the brand function term and descriptive modifier help to delineate the brand boundaries. Finally, the ***emotional modifier*** provides another qualifier—how exactly does the brand provide benefits and in what ways?

Brand mantras don't necessarily have to follow this exact structure, but they should clearly delineate what the brand is supposed to represent and therefore, at least implicitly, what it is not. Several additional points are worth noting.

First, brand mantras derive their power and usefulness from their collective meaning. Other brands may be strong on one, or perhaps even a few, of the brand associations making up the brand mantra. For the brand mantra to be effective, no other brand should singularly excel on all dimensions. Part of the key to both Nike's and Disney's success is that for years, no other competitor could really deliver on the promise suggested by their brand mantras as well as they did.

Second, brand mantras typically are designed to capture the brand's points of difference, that is, what is unique about the brand. Other aspects of the brand positioning—especially the brand's points of parity—may also be important and may need to be reinforced in other ways. Finally, for brands facing rapid growth, a brand functions term can provide critical guidance as to appropriate and inappropriate categories into which to extend. For brands in more stable categories, the brand mantra may focus more on points of difference as expressed by the functional and emotional modifiers, perhaps not even including a brand functions term.

Implementing a Brand Mantra. Brand mantras should be developed at the same time as the brand positioning. As we've seen, brand positioning typically is a result of an in-depth examination of the brand through some form of brand audit or other activities (as described in Brand Focus 3.0). Brand mantras may benefit from the learning gained from those activities but, at the same time, require more internal examination and involve input from a wider range of company employees and marketing staff. Part of this internal exercise is actually to determine the different means by which each and every employee currently affects brand equity, and how he or she can contribute in a positive way to a brand's destiny.

Marketers can often summarize the brand positioning in a few sentences or a short paragraph that suggests the ideal core brand associations consumers should hold. Based on

BRANDING BRIEF 3-6

Nike Brand Mantra

A brand with a keen sense of what it represents to consumers is Nike. Nike has a rich set of associations with consumers, revolving around such considerations as its innovative product designs, its sponsorships of top athletes, its award-winning advertising, its competitive drive, and its irreverent attitude. Internally, Nike marketers adopted a three-word brand mantra of "authentic athletic performance" to guide their marketing efforts. Thus, in Nike's eyes, its entire marketing program—its products and how they are sold—must reflect the key brand values conveyed by the brand mantra.

Nike's brand mantra is "authentic athletic performance."

Nike's brand mantra has had profound implications for its marketing. In the words of ex-Nike marketing gurus Scott Bedbury and Jerome Conlon, the brand mantra provided the "intellectual guard rails" to keep the brand moving in the right direction and to make sure it did not get off track somehow. Nike's brand mantra has even affected product development. Over the years, Nike has expanded its brand meaning from "running shoes" to "athletic shoes" to "athletic shoes and apparel" to "all things associated with athletics (including equipment)." Each step of the way, however, it has been guided by its "authentic athletic performance" brand mantra. For example, as Nike rolled out its successful apparel line, one important hurdle for the products was that they should be innovative enough through material, cut, or design to truly benefit top athletes. At the same time, the company has been careful to avoid using the Nike name to brand products that did not fit with the brand mantra, like casual "brown" shoes.

When Nike has experienced problems with its marketing program, they have often been a result of its failure to figure out how to translate its brand mantra to the marketing challenge at hand. For example, in going to Europe, Nike experienced several false starts until realizing that "authentic athletic performance" has a different meaning over there and, in particular, has to involve soccer in a major way. Similarly, Nike stumbled in developing its All Conditions Gear (ACG) outdoors shoes and clothing sub-brand, which attempted to translate its brand mantra into a less competitive arena.

these core brand associations, a brainstorming session can attempt to identify different brand mantra candidates. In the final brand mantra, the following considerations should come into play.

- *Communicate:* A good brand mantra should both define the category (or categories) of business to set the brand boundaries and clarify what is unique about the brand.
- *Simplify:* An effective brand mantra should be memorable. That means it should be short, crisp, and vivid. A three-word mantra is ideal because it is the most economical way to convey the brand positioning.
- *Inspire:* Ideally, the brand mantra should also stake out ground that is personally meaningful and relevant to as many employees as possible. Brand mantras can do more than inform and guide; they can also inspire, if the brand values tap into higher-level meaning with employees as well as consumers.

Regardless of how many words make up the mantra, however, *there will always be a level of meaning beneath the brand mantra itself that will need to be articulated.* Virtually any word may have many interpretations. For example, the words *fun, family,* and *entertainment* in Disney's brand mantra can each take on multiple meanings, leading Disney to drill deeper to provide a stronger foundation for the mantra. Two or three short phrases were therefore added later to clarify each of the three words.

Internal Branding

Brand mantras point out the importance of *internal branding*—making sure that members of the organization are properly aligned with the brand and what it represents. Much of the branding literature has taken an *external* perspective, focusing on strategies and tactics that firms should take to build or manage brand equity with customers.[28] Without question, at the heart of all marketing activity is the positioning of a brand and the essence of its meaning with consumers.

Equally important, however, is positioning the brand *internally.*[29] For service companies especially, it's critical that all employees have an up-to-date and deep understanding of the brand. Recently, a number of companies have put forth initiatives to improve their internal branding.

PEDIGREE

As part of a $200 million global marketing push for its Pedigree dog food in 2005, Mars Inc.'s Masterfoods USA allocated a chunk of its budget for an internal campaign to turn its 35,000 employees into better ambassadors for the brand. Management believed a seamless internal brand environment, aligned with external marketing efforts for the brand, could spur even higher levels than the $3 billion in annual global retail sales that Pedigree generated. The employee-led initiative aimed to make the office more "dog-friendly" and introduced new business cards, employee identification tags, and office murals that featured employees' dogs. As Masterfoods devised the program, the company enlisted the aid of its research and development, human resources, and marketing departments, as well as its ad agency, TBWA, and other marketing firms.[30]

Companies need to engage in continual open dialogue with their employees. Branding should be perceived as participatory. Some firms have pushed B2E (business-to-employee) programs through corporate intranets and other means. For example, after Ford Motor

BRANDING BRIEF 3-7

Disney Brand Mantra

Disney developed its brand mantra in response to its incredible growth through licensing and product development during the mid-1980s. In the late 1980s, Disney became concerned that some of its characters, like Mickey Mouse and Donald Duck, were being used inappropriately and becoming overexposed. To investigate the severity of the problem, Disney undertook an extensive brand audit. As part of a brand inventory, it first compiled a list of all Disney products that were available (licensed and company manufactured) and all third-party promotions (complete with point-of-purchase displays and relevant merchandising) from stores across the country and all over the world. At the same time, Disney launched a major consumer research study—a brand exploratory—to investigate how consumers felt about the Disney brand.

Disney's brand mantra is "fun family entertainment."

The results of the brand inventory revealed some potentially serious problems: The Disney characters were on so many products and marketed in so many ways that in some cases it was difficult to discern the rationale behind the deal to start with. The consumer study only heightened Disney's concerns. Because of the broad exposure of the characters in the marketplace, many consumers had begun to feel that Disney was exploiting its name. In some cases, consumers felt that the

Company offered its U.S. employees free personal computers to help them get online, it initiated a regular communication program with employees, now called "True Blue." Disney is seen as so successful at internal branding that its Disney Institute holds seminars on the "Disney Style" of creativity, service, and loyalty for employees from other companies.

In some cases, internal branding can both motivate employees and attract external customers. For example, to help create an expectation of trust with its customers, Midas ran an ad campaign showcasing its own employees as heros. Awareness of the Midas corporate brand rose 25 percent as a result.[31] In short, internal branding is a critical management priority.

Brand Audits

To learn what consumers know about brands and products so that the company can make informed strategic positioning decisions, marketers should first conduct a brand audit to profile consumer knowledge structures. A ***brand audit*** is a comprehensive examination of a brand to discover its sources of brand equity. In accounting, an audit is a systematic inspection by an outside firm of accounting records including analyses, tests, and confirmations.[32] The outcome is an assessment of the firm's financial health in the form of a report.

characters added little value to products and, worse yet, involved children in purchase decisions that they would typically ignore.

Because of its aggressive marketing efforts, Disney had written contracts with many of the "park participants" for co-promotions or licensing arrangements. Disney characters were selling everything from diapers to cars to McDonald's hamburgers. Disney learned in the consumer study, however, that consumers did not differentiate between all the product endorsements. "Disney was Disney" to consumers, whether they saw the characters in films, records, theme parks, or consumer products. Consequently, *all* products and services that used the Disney name or characters had an impact on Disney's brand equity. Consumers reported that they resented some of these endorsements because they felt that they had a special, personal relationship with the characters and with Disney that should not be handled so carelessly.

As a result of the brand audit, Disney moved quickly to establish a brand equity team to better manage the brand franchise and more carefully evaluate licensing and other third-party promotional opportunities. One of the mandates of this team was to ensure that a consistent image for Disney—reinforcing its key brand associations—was conveyed by all third-party products and services. To facilitate this supervision, Disney adopted an internal brand mantra of "fun family entertainment" to serve as a screening device for proposed ventures. Opportunities that were not consistent with the brand mantra—no matter how appealing—were rejected. For example, Disney was approached to co-brand a mutual fund in Europe that was designed as a way for parents to save for the college expenses of their children. The opportunity was declined despite the consistent "family" association, because Disney believed that a connection with the financial community or banking suggested other associations that were inconsistent with its brand image (mutual funds are rarely intended to be entertaining).

A similar concept has been suggested for marketing. A ***marketing audit*** is a "comprehensive, systematic, independent, and periodic examination of a company's—or business unit's—marketing environment, objectives, strategies, and activities with a view of determining problem areas and opportunities and recommending a plan of action to improve the company's marketing performance."[33] The process is a three-step procedure in which the first step is agreement on objectives, scope, and approach; the second is data collection; and the third and final step is report preparation and presentation. This is an internally, company-focused exercise to make sure that marketing operations are efficient and effective.

A brand audit, on the other hand, is a more externally, consumer-focused exercise to assess the health of the brand, uncover its sources of brand equity, and suggest ways to improve and leverage its equity. A brand audit requires understanding the sources of brand equity from the perspective of both the firm and the consumer. From the perspective of the firm, what products and services are currently being offered to consumers, and how they are being marketed and branded? From the perspective of the consumer, what deeply held perceptions and beliefs create the true meaning of brands and products?

The brand audit can set strategic direction for the brand, and management should conduct one whenever important shifts in strategic direction are likely.[34] Are the current sources of brand equity satisfactory? Do certain brand associations need to be strengthened? Does the brand lack uniqueness? What brand opportunities exist and what potential challenges exist for brand equity? As a result of this strategic analysis, management can put a marketing program into place to maximize long-term brand equity.

Conducting brand audits on a regular basis such as annually allows marketers to keep their fingers on the pulse of their brands so they can more proactively and responsively manage them. Brand audits are thus particularly useful background for managers as they set up their marketing plans.

Brand audits can have profound implications on the strategic direction for brands and their resulting performance. As a result of a brand audit, luxury goods marketer Alfred Dunhill refined its classic "English" appeal—which has been especially valuable in Asia—to take on more of a dynamic, international flavor. In Europe, the results of a brand audit led Polaroid to try to change its conventional photography image to emphasize the "fun side" of its cameras. Polaroid learned from research that its cameras could act as a social stimulant and catalyst, provoking fun moments in people's lives, a theme that was picked up in advertising and suggested the creation of new distribution strategies.

The brand audit consists of two steps: the brand inventory and the brand exploratory. We'll discuss each in turn. Brand Focus 3.0 illustrates a sample brand audit using the Rolex brand as an example.

Brand Inventory

The purpose of the ***brand inventory*** is to provide a current, comprehensive profile of how all the products and services sold by a company are marketed and branded. Profiling each product or service requires marketers to catalogue the following in both visual and written form for each product or service sold: the names, logos, symbols, characters, packaging, slogans, or other trademarks used; the inherent product attributes or characteristics of the brand; the pricing, communications, and distribution policies; and any other relevant marketing activity related to the brand.

The outcome should be an accurate, comprehensive, and up-to-date profile of how all the products and services are branded in terms of which brand elements are employed and how, and the nature of the supporting marketing program. Marketers should also profile competitive brands in as much detail as possible to determine points of parity and points of difference.

Rationale. The brand inventory is a valuable first step for several reasons. First, it helps to suggest what consumers' current perceptions may be based on. Consumer associations are typically rooted in the *intended* meaning of the brand elements attached to them—but not always. The brand inventory therefore provides useful information for interpreting follow-up research such as the brand exploratory we discuss next.

Although the brand inventory is primarily a descriptive exercise, it can supply some useful analysis too, and initial insights into how brand equity may be better managed. For example, marketers can assess the consistency of all the different products or services sharing a brand name. Are the different brand elements used on a consistent basis, or are there many different versions of the brand name, logo, and so forth for the same product—perhaps for no obvious reason—depending on which geographic market it is being sold in, which market segment it is being targeted to, and so forth? Similarly, are the supporting marketing programs logical and consistent across related brands? As firms expand their products geographically and extend them into other categories, deviations—sometimes significant in nature—commonly emerge in brand appearance and marketing. A thorough brand inventory should be able to reveal the extent of brand consistency.

At the same time, a brand inventory can reveal a lack of perceived differences among different products sharing the brand name—for example, as a result of line extensions—that are designed to differ on one or more key dimensions. Creating sub-brands with distinct positions is often a marketing priority, and a brand inventory may help to uncover undesirable redundancy and overlap that could lead to consumer confusion or retailer resistance.

Brand Exploratory

Although the supply-side view revealed by the brand inventory is useful, actual consumer perceptions, of course, may not necessarily reflect those the marketer intended. Thus, the second step of the brand audit is to provide detailed information about what consumers think of the brand by means of the ***brand exploratory***. The brand exploratory is research directed to understanding what consumers think and feel about the brand and its corresponding product category in order to identify sources of brand equity.

Preliminary Activities. Several preliminary activities are useful for the brand exploratory. First, in many cases, a number of prior research studies may exist and be relevant. It is important to dig through company archives to uncover reports that may have been buried, and perhaps even long forgotten, but that contain insights and answers to a number of important questions or suggest new questions that may still need to be posed.

Second, it is also useful to interview internal personnel to gain an understanding of their beliefs about consumer perceptions for the brand and competitive brands. Past and current marketing managers may be able to share some wisdom not necessarily captured in prior research reports.

The diversity of opinion that typically emerges from these internal interviews serves several functions, increasing the likelihood that useful insights or ideas will be generated, as well as pointing out any inconsistencies or misconceptions that may exist internally for the brand. Still, additional research is often required to better understand how customers shop for and use products and services and what they think of various brands. To allow marketers to cover a broad range of issues and to pursue some in greater depth, the brand exploratory often employs qualitative research techniques, as summarized in Figure 3-6.

Interpreting Qualitative Research. In choosing the range of possible qualitative research techniques to include in the brand exploratory, Gardner and Levy note:

> The emphasis in such research must necessarily be given to skill in interpretation and to reaching a coherent picture of the brand. The researchers must allow their

Free association	Day/Behavior reconstruction
Adjective ratings and checklists	Photo/Written journal
Confessional interviews	Participatory design
Projective techniques	Consumer-led problem solving
Photo sorts	Real-life experimenting
Archetypal research	Collaging and drawing
Bubble drawings	Consumer shadowing
Store telling	Consumer–product interaction
Personification exercises	Video observation
Role playing	
Metaphor elicitation*	

*ZMET trademark

FIGURE 3-6

Summary of Qualitative Techniques

> respondents sufficient self-expression so that the data are rich in complex evaluations of the brand. In this way, the consumer's thoughts and feelings are given precedence rather than the preconceptions of the researchers, although these are present too in hypotheses and questions.[35]

Levy identifies three criteria by which we can classify and judge a qualitative research program: direction, depth, and diversity.[36] For example, any projective technique varies in terms of the nature of the stimulus information (is it related to the person or the brand?), the extent to which responses are superficial and concrete as opposed to deeper and more abstract (and thus requiring more interpretation), and the way the information relates to information gathered by other projective techniques.

In Figure 3-6, the tasks at the top of the left-hand list ask very specific questions whose answers may be easier to interpret. The tasks on the bottom of the list ask questions that are much richer but also harder to interpret. Tasks on the top of the right-hand list are elaborate exercises that consumers undertake themselves and that may be either specific or broadly directed. Tasks at the bottom of the right-hand list consist of direct observation of consumers as they engage in various behavior.

According to Levy, the more specific the question, the narrower the range of information given by the respondent. When the stimulus information in the question is open-ended and responses are freer or less constrained, the respondent tends to give more information. The more abstract and symbolic the research technique, however, the more important it is to follow up with probes and other questions that explicitly reveal the motivation and reasons behind consumers' responses.

Ideally, qualitative research conducted as part of the brand exploratory should vary in direction and depth as well as in technique. The challenge is to provide accurate interpretation—going beyond what consumers explicitly state to determine what they implicitly mean.

Conducting Quantitative Research. Qualitative research is suggestive, but a more definitive assessment of the depth and breadth of brand awareness and the strength, favorability, and uniqueness of brand associations often requires a quantitative phase of research.

The guidelines for the quantitative phase of the exploratory are relatively straightforward. Marketers should assess all potentially salient associations identified by the qualitative research phase according to their strength, favorability, and uniqueness. They should examine both specific brand beliefs and overall attitudes and behaviors to reveal potential sources and outcomes of brand equity. And they should assess the depth and breadth of brand awareness by employing various cues. Typically, marketers will also need to conduct similar types of research for competitors to better understand their sources of brand equity and how they compare with the target brand.

Much of the above discussion of qualitative and quantitative measures has concentrated on associations to the brand name—for example, what do consumers think about the brand when given its name as a probe? Marketers should study other brand elements in the brand exploratory as well, because they may trigger other meanings and facets of the brand. For instance, we can ask consumers what inferences they make about the brand on the basis of the product packaging, logo, or other attribute alone, such as, "What would you think about the brand just on the basis of its packaging?" We can explore specific aspects of the brand elements—for example, the label on the package or the shape of the package itself—to uncover their role in creating brand associations and thus sources of brand equity. We should also determine which of these elements most effectively represents and symbolizes the brand as a whole.

Brand Positioning and the Supporting Marketing Program

The brand exploratory should uncover the current knowledge structures for the core brand and its competitors, as well as determining the desired brand awareness and brand image and points of parity and points of difference. Moving from the current brand image to the desired brand image typically means adding new associations, strengthening existing ones, or weakening or eliminating undesirable ones in the minds of consumers. John Roberts, a leading marketing academic in Australia, sees the challenge in achieving the ideal positioning for a brand as being able to achieve congruence among what customers currently believe about the brand (and thus find credible), what customers will value in the brand, what the firm is currently saying about the brand, and where the firm would like to take the brand.

A number of different internal management personnel can be part of the planning and positioning process, including brand, marketing research, and production managers, as can relevant outside marketing partners like ad agency representatives. Once marketers have a good understanding from the brand audit of current brand knowledge structures for their target consumers and have decided on the desired brand knowledge structures for optimal positioning, they may still want to do additional research testing alternative tactical programs to achieve that positioning.

Review

According to the customer-based brand equity model, deciding on a positioning requires determining a frame of reference (by identifying the target market and the nature of competition) and the ideal points of parity and points of difference brand associations. Marketers need to understand consumer behavior and the consideration sets that consumers adopt in making brand choices.

Points of difference are those associations that are unique to the brand, strongly held, and favorably evaluated by consumers. Marketers should find points of difference associations that are strong, favorable, and unique based on desirability and deliverability considerations, as well as the resulting anticipated levels of sales and costs that might be expected with achieving those points of difference. Points of parity, on the other hand, are those associations that are not necessarily unique to the brand but may in fact be shared with other brands. Category points of parity associations are necessary to being a legitimate and credible product offering within a certain category. Competitive points of parity associations negate competitors' points of differences. The choice of these four ingredients determines the brand positioning and the desired brand knowledge structures.

A broader set of considerations is also useful for positioning, especially for a more developed brand that spans multiple categories. A mental map accurately portrays in detail all salient brand associations and responses for a particular target market. Core brand associations are those sets of abstract associations that characterize the 5 to 10 most important aspects or dimensions of a brand. Core brand associations can serve as the basis of brand positioning as they can represent points of parity and points of difference. Finally, a brand mantra is an articulation of the "heart and soul" of the brand, a three- to five-word phrase that captures the irrefutable essence or spirit of the brand positioning and brand values. Its purpose is to ensure that all employees and all external marketing partners understand what the brand is, most fundamentally, in order to represent it with consumers

A brand audit is a consumer-focused exercise to assess the health of the brand, uncover its sources of brand equity, and suggest ways to improve and leverage its equity. It requires understanding brand equity from the perspective of both the firm and the consumer.

The brand audit consists of two steps: the brand inventory and the brand exploratory. The purpose of the brand inventory is to provide a complete, up-to-date profile of how all the products and services sold by a company are marketed and branded. Profiling each product or service requires us to identify the associated brand elements as well as the supporting marketing program. The brand exploratory is research activity directed to understanding what consumers think and feel about the brand to identify sources of brand equity.

Once marketers have determined the brand positioning strategy, they can put into place the actual marketing program to create, strengthen, or maintain brand associations. Chapters 4 through 7 in Part III of the text describe some of the important marketing mix issues in designing supporting marketing programs.

Discussion Questions

1. Apply the categorization model to a product category other than beverages. How do consumers make decisions whether or not to buy the product, and how do they arrive at their final brand decision? What are the implications for brand equity management for the brands in the category? How does it affect positioning, for example?
2. Pick a brand. Describe its breadth and depth of awareness.
3. Pick a category basically dominated by two main brands. Evaluate the positioning of each brand. Who are their target markets? What are their main points of parity and points of difference? Have they defined their positioning correctly? How might it be improved?
4. Can you think of any negatively correlated attributes and benefits other than those listed in Figure 3-4? Can you think of any other strategies to deal with negatively correlated attributes and benefits?
5. Think of one of your favorite brands. Can you come up with a brand mantra to capture its positioning?

BRAND FOCUS 3.0

Rolex Brand Audit

Brand Inventory

"The name of Rolex is synonymous with quality. Rolex—with its rigorous series of tests that intervene at every stage—has redefined the meaning of quality."

—Rolex.com

History

Rolex began when German-born Hans Wilsdorf and his brother-in-law, William Davis, founded the London-based company Wilsdorf & Davis in 1905. Wilsdorf registered the brand, Rolex, in Switzerland in 1908 and in 1910 created a timepiece that was small enough to be worn on the wrist. Rolex obtained the first official chronometer certification for a wristwatch that same year.

In 1912, Rolex moved its headquarters to Geneva, Switzerland, where it remains today. In 1914, a Rolex wristwatch obtained the first Kew "A" certificate after passing the world's toughest timing test. Twelve years later, Wilsdorf developed and patented the now famous Oyster waterproof case and screw crown. This mechanism revolutionized the watch industry as the first true protection against water, dust, and dirt.[37]

The Oyster was put to the test on October 7, 1927, when Mercedes Gleitze swam the English Channel wearing an Oyster. She emerged 15 hours later with the watch functioning perfectly, much to the amazement of all. Gleitze became the first of a long list of "ambassadors" Rolex uses to promote their wristwatches.

In 1931, Rolex pushed innovation in watches one step further by creating the Perpetual self-winding rotor mechanism. This rotor keeps the watch at an optimal tension and activates with the slightest movement of the wrist, therefore eliminating the need to wind the watch.

Private Ownership

Rolex is a privately owned company and has been controlled by only three people in its 100-year history. This has enabled the company to maintain a consistent focus on its core business. Andre Heiniger, managing chairman of Rolex through the 1980s, stated, "Rolex's strategy is oriented to marketing, maintaining quality, and staying out of fields where we are not prepared to compete effectively."

Product-Related Attributes

Throughout the years, Rolex timepieces have maintained the highest quality, durability, and prestige on which they originally were founded. Each Rolex consists of 10 unique features that the company states as its "10 Golden Rules:"[38]

1. Waterproof case
2. Perpetual rotor
3. The case back
4. The Oyster case
5. The winding crown
6. The finest and purest materials
7. Quality control
8. Rolex self-winding movement
9. Testing from the independent Controle Official Suisse des Chronometres
10. Rolex testing

Rolex Brand Portfolio

Rolex includes three family brands of wristwatches, called "collections," each with a subset of brands (see Figure 3-7).

- The Oyster Perpetual Collection includes the "traditional" Rolex wristwatch and has eight subbrands that are differentiated by features and design.

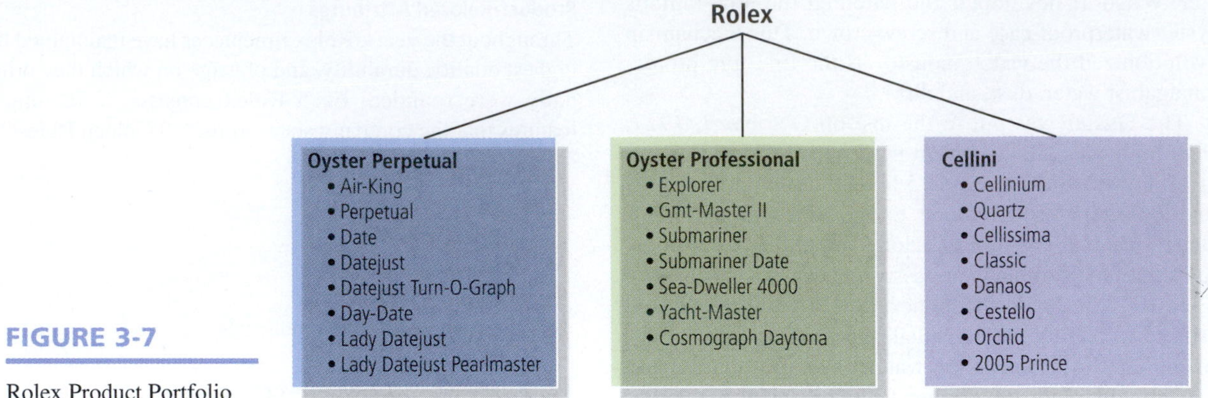

FIGURE 3-7

Rolex Product Portfolio

The Perpetual Collection targets affluent men and women.

- The Oyster Professional Collection targets specific athletic and adventurer user groups through its specific features and imagery. The Oyster Professional Collection includes seven sub-brands.
- The Cellini Collection focuses on formal occasions through its elegant designs and encompasses seven sub-brands. The Cellini Collection incorporates fashion and style features like colored leather bands and extensive use of diamonds.

Tudor. Rolex has many competitors in the $43.6 billion watch and jewelry industry; however, only a few brands compete in the very high-end market.[39] Nevertheless, Rolex developed its Tudor brand in 1946 as a "fighter brand" to stave off competition from mid-range watches such as Tag Heuer, Citizen, and Rado. Like Rolex, Tudor has a range of family brands or collections, namely Prince, Princess, Monarch, and Sport, each of which encompass a number of sub-brands. Tudor watches are sold at own-brand specialty stores and also sold through the network of exclusive Rolex dealers.

Communications, Pricing, and Distribution

Rolex's brand image has been maintained through communications focused on the product's high quality and its associations with top artists, athletes, and explorers. Rolex's image is also enhanced by its exclusivity, with premium pricing and limited distribution.

Rolex traditionally advertises its products in magazines. In 2003, Rolex spent $32.4 million in magazine ads, ranked seventh overall in the world in terms of magazine ad spending.[40] In addition to product imagery, Rolex magazine ads serve to maintain the brand's status by featuring its ambassadors, the sporting and cultural events it sponsors, and the philanthropic programs it supports.

Rolex also distinguishes itself through its premium pricing strategy. Prices start around $2,500 for the basic Oyster Perpetual and can reach as high as $200,000. Within each style, prices can vary by $2,000–$12,000 depending on the specific materials used such as steel or white gold. Rolex does not merchandise any of its watches online and only sells through "Official Rolex Dealers," of which there are approximately 60,000 worldwide.

Brand Exploratory

Customer Knowledge

Rolex has successfully leveraged its history and tradition of excellence along with innovation to become the most powerful and recognized watchmaker in the world. Typical consumer brand associations for Rolex might be "sophisticated," "prestigious," "exclusive," "powerful," "elegant," "snobby," "flashy," "high quality." Figure 3-8 displays a hypothetical Rolex mental map.

Sources of Brand Equity

The Rolex name, one of the most recognized luxury brands in the world, is inarguably the company's most important source of brand equity. Its crown logo is also a key source of equity. Equity is contributed by the functional benefits Rolex provides the user, namely the quality, craftsmanship, and innovation that go into making its watches as mandated by the "10 Golden Rules." An additional source of equity for Rolex is its image as an exclusive status symbol, which confers emotional and self-expressive benefits to the user and is reinforced by its premium pricing and limited distribution. Three other key sources of Rolex brand equity are Ambassadors, Sports & Culture, and Philanthropy.

Ambassadors. Ambassadors is the term Rolex uses to describe its celebrity endorsers. They fall into four categories: Artists, Athletes, Explorers, and Yachtsmen (see Figure 3-9). Rolex ambassadors have scaled Mt. Everest, broken the speed of sound, reached the depths of the ocean, and walked on the moon.

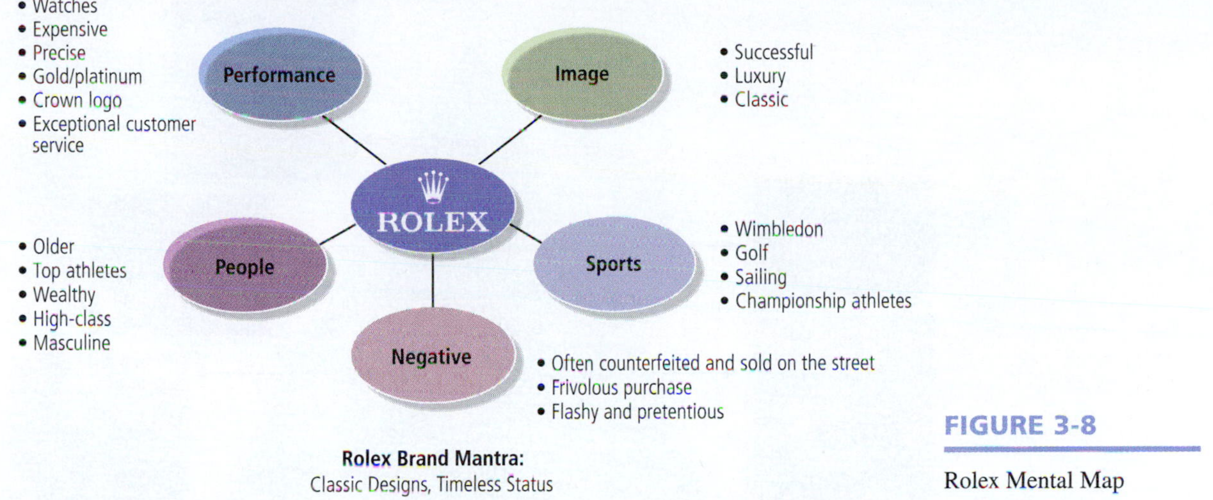

FIGURE 3-8

Rolex Mental Map

Sports & Culture. Rolex sponsors a variety of elite athletic and cultural events, thus targeting very specific consumers. Some of these events include Wimbledon, Rolex Trans-Atlantic Challenge, U.S. PGA, U.S. Open Championship, Ryder Cup, Rolex 24 Daytona, and Grand American Rolex Sports Car Series.

Philanthropy. Rolex has established two philanthropic programs:

1. The "Awards for Enterprise" is awarded every two years and recognizes innovative work in preserving the world's natural and cultural heritage.[41]
2. "The "Rolex Mentor and Protégé Arts Initiative" seeks out extraordinarily gifted young artists around the world and pairs them with established masters.[42]

The Customer-Based Brand Equity Pyramid (CBBE)

The Rolex customer-based brand equity pyramid is equally strong on the left-hand and right-hand sides. It is also strong from bottom to top, enjoying the highest brand awareness of any luxury brand as well as high repeat purchase rates and high customer loyalty. Rolex has successfully focused on both the superior product attributes and the imagery associated with owning and wearing a Rolex. Figure 3-10 highlights the key aspects of the Rolex CBBE pyramid.

Counterfeiting: Threat to Equity

Counterfeiting Rolex watches has become a sophisticated industry with sales exceeding $1.8 billion per year. Counterfeits damage the company's brand equity and present

Artists
- Emanuel Ax
- Cecilia Bartoli
- Eric Clapton
- Placido Domingo
- Renee Fleming
- Angela Gheorghiu
- Sylvie Guillem
- Carla Maria Izzo
- Dame Kiri Te Kanawa
- Diana Krall
- Marielle and Katia Labeque
- Yo-Yo Ma
- Lorin Maazel
- Sophie Mautner
- Yuan-Yuan Tan

Equestrians
- Nadine Capellmann
- Pippa Funnell
- Steve Guerdat
- Rodrigo Pessoa

Explorers
- David Doubilet
- Sylvia Earle
- Henri-Germain Delauze
- Sir Edmund Hillary
- Alain Hubert
- Christine Janin
- Erling Kagge
- George Schaller
- Jean Troillet
- Ed Viesturs
- Chuck Yeager

Golfers
- Retief Goosen
- Charles Howell
- Trevor Immelman
- Carin Koch
- Bernhard Langer
- Paula Marti
- Phil Mickelson
- Jack Nicklaus
- Lorena Ochoa
- Arnold Palmer
- Grace Park
- Gary Player
- Justin Rose
- Adam Scott
- Annika Sorenstam
- Sam Torrance

Racing Driver
- Sir Jackie Stewart

Tennis Players
- Vijay Amritraj
- Juan Carlos Ferrero
- Justine Henin-Hardenne
- Andy Roddick
- Marat Safin

Yachtsmen
- Paul Cayard

FIGURE 3-9

2005 Rolex Ambassadors

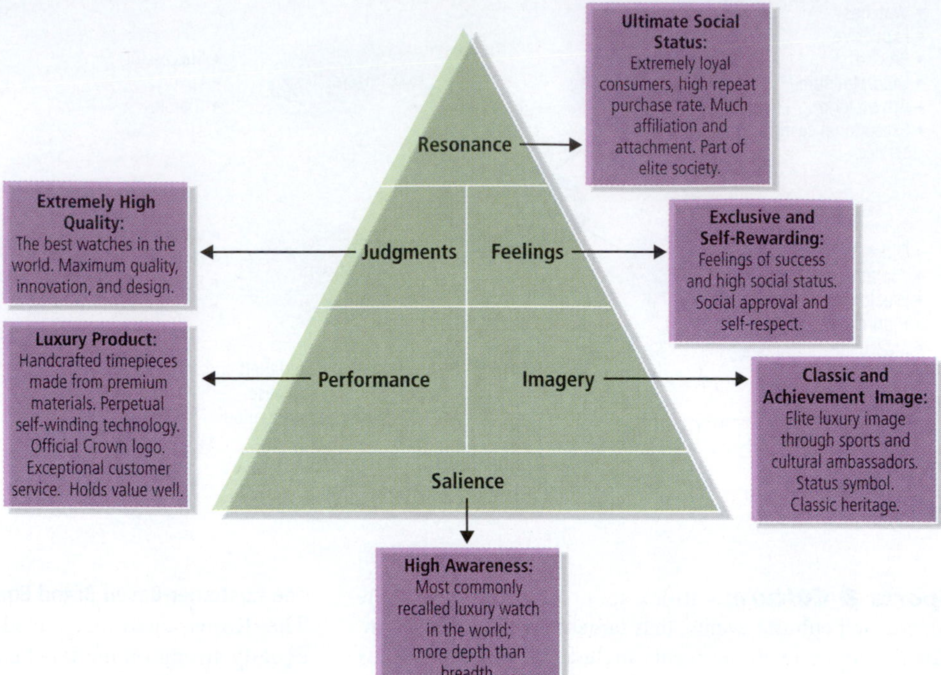

FIGURE 3-10

Rolex CBBE Pyramid

a huge risk to the brand. In fact, Rolex dedicates extensive resources to fight the illegal use of the brand, including sponsoring the International Anti-Counterfeiting Coalition and suing companies that allow the sale of counterfeit Rolexes.

Recommendations

The Rolex brand audit reveals a very strong brand with significant equity. However, there are five main areas of opportunity:

Introduce new designs

- Research shows that there is a trend toward more jeweled watches. Only 7 of Rolex's 22 sub-brands feature diamond watches. Rolex could increase this ratio slightly in order to capitalize on the trend without compromising the classic and timeless qualities it is known for.
- Luxury handbag maker Louis Vuitton benefited in terms of both PR and sales when it hired Japanese designer Takashi Murakami to design a limited edition line of bags. Rolex may consider partnering with an established designer for a limited edition watch that freshens the brand and creates a buzz while remaining consistent with its image and values.

Connect with the female consumer

- Women make the majority of jewelry and watch purchases. Rolex's image campaign, however, emphasizes males to a greater extent. Of its 70 official ambassadors, only 20 are female. Rolex may want to consider more female ambassadors of elite status, such as successful athletes like Serena Williams, artists like Norah Jones, or explorers like Ann Bancroft.
- Along the same lines, Rolex should enhance its sponsorship of female-attended sporting events. Whether it is ice skating, golf, or equestrian, Rolex should consider raising its profile with female sports enthusiasts and fans.
- Rolex's watch styles are predominantly aimed at male consumers as well. Of the 22 sub-brands contained in its 3 family brands, only 6 feature watches geared specifically for women. Rolex may want to consider increasing this number, or perhaps introducing a family of female-only watches.

Attack the online counterfeit industry

- The boom in e-commerce has taken counterfeit Rolexes from the street corner to the Internet, where fakes can reach far more consumers. Consequently, the age-old problem of counterfeiting is a bigger threat than ever before. To maintain its limited distribution, Rolex does not authorize any of its watches to be sold on the Internet. In order to combat the online sale of counterfeits, however, Rolex may consider building an exclusive online store, or an exclusive distribution site from which all official e-retailers must link.

Understand how younger consumers relate to luxury

- It is unlikely that young consumers' attitudes toward luxury goods will evolve in the same manner as did their parents'. As a result, Rolex should be researching the questions: How will prestige be defined in the 21st century? Will the same formula "work" for the millennial generation as they age and move into the Rolex target market?
- In addition to researching how their tastes will evolve, Rolex should research the current tastes of the many younger consumers who are already in the market for Rolex watches. Its marketers should consider tailoring campaigns and watch designs to these consumers, who generally part with their disposable income more freely than the older set.

Communicate long-term value

- Rolex competes with a host of other types of goods for a share of the luxury buyer's wallet, such as clothes, shoes, and handbags. Many are less durable over time than a Rolex watch and are susceptible to falling out of fashion. Rolex should leverage its superior value retention—both in resale value and in its "heirloom" quality—in order to better compete for luxury spending with brands outside its category.
- Swiss luxury watch competitor Patek Philippe used print advertising to communicate the "heirloom" quality of its watches, with copy stating "You never actually own a Patek Philippe. You merely take care of it for the next generation." Rolex could pursue a similar approach, perhaps using its more visible ambassadors, to communicate its own "heirloom" quality.
- Rolex watches retain their value better than almost any other type of good. Used Rolexes sell at or near their original retail price, and some rare vintage Rolexes are quite valuable. Rolex could make a subtle, sophisticated reference to its resale value through advertising and PR, being careful not to overtly drive consumers to the secondary market for used Rolexes.

Points of Parity	Points of Difference
• Swiss watchmaker • Durable • Fine materials • Quality craftsmanship • Accurate • Attractive	• History and heritage • Crown • Exclusive imagery • Premium price • Innovation • Distribution

FIGURE 3-11

POP vs. POD

Notes

1. Much of this chapter is based on Kevin Lane Keller, Brian Sternthal, and Alice Tybout, "Three Questions You Need to Ask About Your Brand," *Harvard Business Review* 80, no. 9 (September 2002): 80–89.
2. Phillip Kotler and Kevin Lane Keller, *Marketing Management,* 12th ed. (Upper Saddle River, NJ: Prentice-Hall, 2006).
3. Russell I. Haley, "Benefit Segmentation: A Decision-Oriented Research Tool," *Journal of Marketing,* 32 (July 1968), pp. 30–35.
4. Chip Walker, "How Strong Is Your Brand?" *Marketing Tools* (January/February 1995): 46–53.
5. Russell I. Haley, "Benefit Segmentation: A Decision-Oriented Research Tool," *Journal of Marketing* 32 (July 1968): 30–35.
6. Also, it may be the case that the actual demographic specifications given do not fully reflect consumers' underlying perceptions. For example, when the Ford Mustang was introduced, the intended market segment was much younger than the ages of the customers who actually bought the car. Evidently, these consumers felt or wanted to feel younger psychologically than they really were.
7. Ronald Frank, William Massey, and Yoram Wind, *Market Segmentation* (Englewood Cliffs, NJ: Prentice-Hall, 1972).
8. A complete treatment of this material is beyond the scope of this chapter. Useful reviews can be found in any good marketing strategy text. For example, see David A. Aaker, *Strategic Market Management,* 7th ed. (New York: John Wiley & Sons, 2005) or Donald R. Lehmann

and Russell S. Winer, *Product Management,* 4th ed. (New York: McGraw-Hill/Irwin, 2005).

9. Teri Agins, "As Consumers Find Other Ways to Splurge, Apparel Hits a Snag," *Wall Street Journal,* 4 February 2005, A1, A6.
10. Stacy Kravetz, "Baskin-Robbins Scoops Up a New Look," *Wall Street Journal,* 4 September 1977, B1.
11. Patrick Barwise and Sean Meehan, *Simply Better: Winning and Keeping Customers by Delivering What Matters Most,* (Cambridge, MA: Harvard Business School Press, 2004).
12. The concept of "points of parity" and "points of difference" and many of the other ideas and examples in this section were first developed by Northwestern University's Brian Sternthal and further refined in collaboration with Northwestern University's Alice Tybout.
13. John Czepiel, *Competitive Marketing Strategy* (Englewood Cliffs, NJ: Prentice Hall, 1992).
14. Richard Heller, "Folk Fortune," *Forbes,* 4 September 2000, 66–69.
15. Brian Sternthal, "Miller Lite Case," Kellogg Graduate School of Management, Northwestern University.
16. Interestingly, when Miller Lite was first introduced, the assumption was that the relevant motivation underlying the benefit of "less filling" for consumers was that they could drink more beer. Consequently, Miller targeted heavy users of beer with a sizable introductory ad campaign concentrated on mass-market sports programs. As it turned out, the initial research showed that the market segment they attracted was more the moderate user—older and upscale. Why? The brand promise of "less filling" is actually fairly ambiguous. To this group of consumers, "less filling" meant that they could drink beer and stay mentally and physically agile (sin with no penalty!). From Miller's standpoint, attracting this target market was an unexpected but happy outcome because it meant that there would be less cannibalization with their more mass-market High Life brand. To better match the motivations of this group, there were some changes in the types of athletes in the ads, such as using ex-bullfighters to better represent mental and physical agility.
17. Brian Sternthal, Alice Tybout, and D. Iacobucci, eds., *Kellogg on Marketing* (Chichester, NY: Wiley, 2001).
18. Richard A. Melcher, "Why Zima Faded So Fast," *Business Week,* 10 March 1997, 110–114.
19. David Field, "Airline Tries Loftier Name," *USA Today,* 10 March 1997, B7.
20. Keith Naughton, "Ford's 'Perfect Storm,'" Newsweek, 17 September 2001, 48–50.
21. Elizabeth Jensen, "Campbell's Juice Scheme: Stealth Health," *Wall Street Journal,* 18 April 1997, B6.
22. Steven Gray, "How Applebee's Is Making It Big in Small Towns," *Wall Street Journal,* 2 August 2004, B1, B4.
23. Shelly Branch, "Irradiated Food by Any Other Name Might Just Win Over Consumers," *Wall Street Journal,* 14 August 2001, B1.
24. Abraham Maslow, *Motivation and Personality,* 2nd ed. (New York: Harper & Row, 1970).
25. Thomas J. Reynolds and Jonathan Gutman, "Laddering Theory: Method, Analysis, and Interpretation," *Journal of Advertising Research* (February/March 1988): 11–31. Thomas J. Reynolds and David B. Whitlark, "Applying Laddering Data to Communications Strategy and Advertising Practice," *Journal of Advertising Research* (July/August 1995): 9–17.
26. Brian Wansink, "Using Laddering to Understand and Leverage a Brand's Equity," *Qualitative Market Research* 6, no. 2 (2003): 111–118.
27. Marco Vriens and Frenkel Ter Hofstede, "Linking Attributes, Benefits, and Consumer Values," *Marketing Research* (Fall 2000): 3–8.
28. For some notable exceptions, see Hamish Pringle and William Gordon, *Brand Manners: How to Create the Self-Confident Organization to Live the Brand* (New York: John Wiley & Sons, 2001); Thomas Gad, *4-D Branding: Cracking the Corporate Code of the Network Economy* (London: Financial Times Prentice Hall, 2000); Nicholas Ind, *Living the Brand: How to Transform Every Member of Your Organization into a Brand Champion,* 2nd ed. (London, UK: Kogan Page, 2004); Scott M. Davis and Kenneth Dunn, *Building the Brand-Driven Business: Operationalize Your Brand to Drive Profitable Growth* (San Francisco: Jossey-Bass, 2002).
29. Kevin Lane Keller, "Brand Mantras: Rationale, Criteria, and Examples," *Journal of Marketing Management* 15 (1999): 43–51.
30. Brian Sternberg, "House Training: Now, Employees Get Brand Boost," *Wall Street Journal,* 18 January 2005, B1, B4.
31. Nikki Hopewell, "Generating Brand Passion," *Marketing News,* 15 May 2005, 10.
32. Sidney Davidson, James Schindler, Clyde P. Stickney, and Roman Weil, *Financial Accounting: An Introduction to Concepts, Methods, and Uses* (Hinsdale, IL: Dryden Press, 1976).
33. Phillip Kotler, William Gregor, and William Rogers, "The Marketing Audit Comes of Age," *Sloan Management Review* 18, no. 2 (Winter 1977): 25–43.
34. Laurel Wentz, "Brand Audits Reshaping Images," *Ad Age International* (September 1996): 38–41.
35. Burleigh B. Gardner and Sidney J. Levy, "The Product and the Brand," *Harvard Business Review* (March–April 1955): 33–39.
36. Sidney J. Levy, "Dreams, Fairy Tales, Animals, and Cars," *Psychology and Marketing* 2, no. 2 (Summer 1985): 67–81.
37. www.brittons-watches.co.uk.
38. www.rolex.com.
39. *Women's Wear Daily,* July 2005.
40. *Adweek,* 28 October 2004.
41. *Watch World,* December 2004.
42. www.rolex.com.

4

CHOOSING BRAND ELEMENTS TO BUILD BRAND EQUITY

Preview

Brand elements, sometimes called brand identities, are those trademarkable devices that serve to identify and differentiate the brand. The main ones are brand names, URLs, logos, symbols, characters, spokespeople, slogans, jingles, packages, and signage. The customer-based brand equity model suggests that marketers should choose brand elements to enhance brand awareness; facilitate the formation of strong, favorable, and unique brand associations; or elicit positive brand judgments and feelings. The test of the brand-building ability of brand elements is what consumers would think or feel about the product if they knew only its brand name, associated logo, and other characteristics. A brand element that provides a positive contribution to brand equity conveys or implies certain valued associations or responses.

This chapter considers how marketers choose brand elements to build brand equity. After describing the general criteria for choosing brand elements, we consider specific tactical issues for each of the different types of brand elements and finish by discussing how to choose the best brand elements to build brand equity. Brand Focus 4.0 at the end of the chapter highlights some legal issues for branding.

Criteria for Choosing Brand Elements

In general, there are six criteria for brand elements (with more specific subchoices for each, as shown in Figure 4-1):

1. Memorability
2. Meaningfulness
3. Likability
4. Transferability
5. Adaptability
6. Protectability

The first three criteria—memorability, meaningfulness, and likability—are the marketer's offensive strategy and build brand equity. The latter three, however, play a defensive role for leveraging and maintaining brand equity in the face of different opportunities and constraints. Let's consider each of these general criteria.

Memorability

A necessary condition for building brand equity is achieving a high level of brand awareness. Brand elements that promote that goal are inherently memorable and attention-getting and therefore facilitate recall or recognition in purchase or consumption settings. For example, a brand of propane gas cylinders named Blue Rhino featuring a powder-blue animal mascot with a distinctive yellow flame is likely to stick in the minds of consumers.

1. **Memorable**
   Easily recognized
   Easily recalled
2. **Meaningful**
   Descriptive
   Persuasive
3. **Likable**
   Fun and interesting
   Rich visual and verbal imagery
   Aesthetically pleasing
4. **Transferable**
   Within and across product categories
   Across geographic boundaries and cultures
5. **Adaptable**
   Flexible
   Updatable
6. **Protectable**
   Legally
   Competitively

FIGURE 4-1

Criteria for Choosing Brand Elements

Meaningfulness

Brand elements may take on all kinds of meaning, with either descriptive or persuasive content. We saw in Chapter 1 that brand names can be based on people, places, animals or birds, or other things or objects. Two particularly important criteria are how well the brand element conveys the following:

- *General information about the nature of the product category:* Does the brand element have descriptive meaning and suggest something about the product category? How likely is it that a consumer could correctly identify the product category for the brand based on any one brand element? Does the brand element seem credible in the product category?
- *Specific information about particular attributes and benefits of the brand:* Does the brand element have persuasive meaning and suggest something about the particular kind of product, or its key attributes or benefits? Does it suggest something about a product ingredient or the type of person who might use the brand?

The first dimension is an important determinant of brand awareness and salience; the second, of brand image and positioning.

THE SCIENCE OF BRANDING 4-1

Brand Design and Aesthetics

Schmitt and Simonson explore the importance and applications of "marketing aesthetics," a concept with many branding implications. They refer to ***marketing aesthetics*** as "the marketing of sensory experiences in corporate or brand output that contributes to the organization's or brand's identity." They approach marketing aesthetics from three perspectives: product design, communications research, and spatial design. They argue that aesthetics offers tangible value to organizations by creating loyalty, allowing for premium pricing, cutting through information clutter, affording protection from competitive attacks, and saving costs and increasing productivity. The following provides a brief overview to this line of thinking.

Aesthetics strategy is "the strategic planning and implementation of identity elements that provide sensory experiences and aesthetic gratification to the organization's multiple constituents." Schmitt and Simonson describe the basic rationale for this approach as follows:

> Customers do not have direct access to an organization's or a brand's culture, missions, strategies, values, to the "private self" of the organization or the brand. They see the public face of the organization or brand—its expressions—projected through multiple identity elements with various aesthetic styles and themes. They never see these all at once but integrate various perceptions into their overall impressions.

Thus, according to Schmitt and Simonson's approach, the styles and themes of design elements are the means by which corporate expressions affect customer impressions, as follows.

Style refers to a distinctive quality or form, a manner of expression. Style is composed of primary elements, including sight (color, shape, line, pattern, and typeface), sound (loudness,

Likability

Independent of its memorability and meaningfulness, do customers find the brand element aesthetically appealing? Is it likable visually, verbally, and in other ways? Brand elements can be rich in imagery and inherently fun and interesting, even if not always directly related to the product. The Science of Branding 4-1 outlines how we can apply marketing aesthetics to brand elements and branding in general.

A memorable, meaningful, and likable set of brand elements offers many advantages because consumers often do not examine much information in making product decisions. Descriptive and persuasive elements reduce the burden on marketing communications to build awareness and link brand associations and equity, especially when few other product-related associations exist. Often, the less concrete the possible product benefits are, the more important is the creative potential of the brand name and other brand elements to capture intangible characteristics of a brand. Branding Brief 4-1 describes how PepsiCo introduced Mountain Dew Code Red soft drink.

Transferability

Transferability measures the extent to which the brand element adds to the brand equity of new products for the brand. In other words, how useful is the brand element for line or category extensions? In general, the less specific the name, the more easily it can be transferred across categories. For example, Amazon connotes a massive South American river and therefore as a brand can be appropriate for a variety of different types of products, whereas Books "R" Us obviously would not have afforded the same flexibility.

pitch, and meter), touch (material and texture), taste, and smell. Key strategic issues in style creation are whether to juxtapose design elements, and when to adapt or abandon styles. Four perceptual dimensions distinguish corporate or brand identity–related styles: complexity (minimalism vs. ornamentalism), representation (realism vs. abstraction), perceived movement (dynamic vs. static), and potency (loud/strong vs. soft/weak). Different international deluxe hotel brands (Ritz-Carlton, Four Seasons, Mandarin Oriental, and W) are positioned differently on these dimensions, for instance.

The authors argue that to be effective, styles must be combined with themes that express an organization's or brand's private self succinctly and directly. ***Themes*** refer to the content, meaning, and projected image of an identity that provide customers with mental anchors and reference points to put an organization in a wider context and to distinguish its position. They are expressed most pointedly if (1) they are used as prototypical expressions of an organization's core values or mission or of a brand's character, and (2) they are repeated and adapted over time, and (3) they are developed into a system of interrelated ideas. Marketers can express themes in a variety of ways: as corporate brand names, symbols, narratives, slogans or jingles, concepts, or combinations of elements and must choose between one theme and multiple themes, between theme variation and isolation, and whether to integrate verbal and visual information, as well as when to adapt or abandon themes.

Source: Bernd H. Schmitt and Alex Simonson, *Marketing Aesthetics: The Strategic Management of Brands, Identity, and Image* (New York: Free Press, 1997).

Second, to what extent does the brand element add to brand equity across geographic boundaries and market segments? To a large extent this depends on the cultural content and linguistic qualities of the brand element. One of the main advantages of nonmeaningful names like Exxon is that they transfer well into other languages. The mistakes that even top companies have made in translating their brand names, slogans, and packages into other languages and cultures over the years have become legendary. Figure 4-2 lists some well-known global branding mishaps. Companies must review all their brand elements for cultural meaning before introducing the brand into a new market.

Adaptability

The fifth consideration for brand elements is their adaptability over time. Because of changes in consumer values and opinions, or simply because of a need to remain contemporary, most brand elements must be updated (Branding Brief 4-3 describes how the Betty Crocker brand stays up-to-date). The more adaptable and flexible the brand element, the easier it is to update it. For example, logos and characters can be given a new look or a new design to make them appear more modern and relevant.

Protectability

The sixth and final general consideration is the extent to which the brand element is protectable—both in a legal and a competitive sense. Marketers should (1) choose brand elements that can be legally protected internationally, (2) formally register them with the

BRANDING BRIEF 4-1

Pepsi has embraced youth culture to sell its Mountain Dew soft drink.

Branding a New Soft Drink

When Pepsi-Cola's total volume increased a mere tenth of a percent in 2000, the company quickly sought to boost sales by launching the first line extension of its popular Mountain Dew drink since Diet Mountain Dew debuted in 1988. A cross-functional team composed of 35 people from seven Pepsi departments worked on developing the new product. The team considered several possibilities: Dew H2O bottled water, Dew Unplugged decaf Mountain Dew, a Mountain Dew sports drink, and a new Dew flavor. The company settled on creating a new flavor, and within 10 months, instead of the usual 2 years it takes Pepsi to develop a new product, it launched a bright red cherry-flavored beverage called Mountain Dew Code Red.

For the launch, Pepsi used radio and outdoor advertising, as well as sampling and in-store merchandising. To build buzz for Code Red, the company sent free samples to 4,000 select consumers, such as hip-hop producer Jermaine Dupri and radio DJ Funkmaster Flex. The drink was also heavily sampled at marquee sporting events such as the NCAA Final Four and ESPN's 2001 Winter X Games. Pepsi developed a special Web

appropriate legal bodies, and (3) vigorously defend trademarks from unauthorized competitive infringement. The necessity of legally protecting the brand is dramatized by the billions of dollars in losses in the United States alone from unauthorized use of patents, trademarks, and copyrights, as described in The Science of Branding 4-2.

Another consideration is whether the brand is competitively protectable. If a name, package, or other attribute is too easily copied, much of the uniqueness of the brand may disappear. For example, consider the once-hot ice-beer category. Although Molson Ice was one of the early entries in the category, it quickly lost its pioneering advantage when Miller Ice and what later became Bud Ice were introduced. Marketers need to reduce the likelihood that competitors can create a derivative based on the product's own elements.

Options and Tactics for Brand Elements

Consider the advantages of "Apple" as the name of a personal computer. Apple was a simple but well-known word that was distinctive in the product category—which helped develop brand awareness. The meaning of the name also gave the company a "friendly shine" and warm brand personality. It could also be reinforced visually with a logo that would transfer easily across geographic and cultural boundaries. Finally, the name could serve as a platform for sub-brands like the Macintosh, aiding the introduction of brand extensions. As Apple illustrates, a well-chosen brand name can make an appreciable contribution to the creation of brand equity.

site for the brand that featured an interactive game called "Mission: Code Red 2." And Pepsi marketed Code Red to urban consumers. When research revealed that urban and ethnic focus groups preferred the name Code Red to Wild Cherry Mountain Dew, Pepsi stuck with the former. The company also developed an ad campaign titled "Crack the Code" that used graffiti-art design elements and an urban setting.

Code Red attracted a rabid fan base. According to A.C. Nielsen, Code Red tested in the top 5 percent of all new product concepts ever tested among teens. The drink was also popular in the high-tech community. Two programmers who discovered a computer virus that eventually infected more than 700,000 computers named it "Code Red" after the beverage they used to survive the late hours in front of their monitors. Pepsi sent the pair five cases of Code Red in appreciation of the free publicity.

Within two months of its May 2000 launch, Code Red was the fifth-best-selling soft drink sold at convenience stores and gas stations (Mountain Dew is number one). This signaled tremendous success, considering that the drink came in only two single-serve sizes and the muted marketing campaign at the time did not yet include television spots. Though the drink was launched midway through the second quarter of 2000, Pepsi credited Code Red with helping to boost net sales 20 percent to $962 million that quarter. One bottler exclaimed, "It's flown off the shelves for us."

Sources: www.mountaindew.com; Hillary Chura, "Pepsi-Cola's Code Red Is White Hot," *Advertising Age,* 27 August 2001; Maureen Tkacik and Betsy McKay, "Code Red: PepsiCo's Guerilla Conquest," *Wall Street Journal,* 17 August 2001; Abigail Klingbeil, "The Making of a Brand," Gannett News Service, 29 June 2001.

What would an ideal brand element be like? Consider brand names—perhaps the most central of all brand elements. Ideally, a brand name would be easily remembered, highly suggestive of both the product class and the particular benefits that served as the basis of its positioning, inherently fun or interesting, rich with creative potential, transferable to a wide variety of product and geographic settings, enduring in meaning and relevant over time, and strongly protectable both legally and competitively.

Unfortunately, it is difficult to choose a brand name—or any brand element, for that matter—that satisfies all these criteria. The more meaningful the brand name, for example, the more difficult it is to transfer or translate it to other cultures. This is one reason why it's preferable to have multiple brand elements. Let's look at the major considerations for each type of brand element.

Brand Names

The brand name is a fundamentally important choice because it often captures the central theme or key associations of a product in a very compact and economical fashion. Brand names can be an extremely effective shorthand means of communication.[1] Whereas an advertisement lasts half a minute and a sales call could run to hours, customers can notice the brand name and register its meaning or activate it in memory in just a few seconds.

Because it is so closely tied to the product in the minds of consumers, however, the brand name is also the most difficult element for marketers to change. So they systematically

1. When Braniff translated a slogan touting its upholstery, "Fly in leather," it came out in Spanish as "Fly naked."
2. Coors put its slogan, "Turn it loose," into Spanish, where it was read as "Suffer from diarrhea."
3. Chicken magnate Frank Perdue's line, "It takes a tough man to make a tender chicken," sounds much more interesting in Spanish: "It takes a sexually stimulated man to make a chicken affectionate."
4. Why Chevy Nova never sold well in Spanish-speaking countries: *No va* means "it doesn't go" in Spanish.
5. When Pepsi started marketing its products in China, they translated their slogan, "Pepsi Brings You Back to Life," pretty literally. The slogan in Chinese really meant "Pepsi Brings Your Ancestors Back from the Grave."
6. When Coca-Cola first shipped to China, they named the product something that when pronounced sounded like "Coca-Cola." The only problem was that the characters used meant "Bite the wax tadpole." They later changed to a set of characters that mean "Happiness in the mouth."
7. A hair products company, Clairol, introduced the "Mist Stick," a curling iron, into Germany only to find out that *mist* is slang for manure in German.
8. When Gerber first started selling baby food in Africa, they used the same packaging as in the United States, with the cute baby on the label. Later they found out that in Africa, companies routinely put pictures on the label of what's inside because most people can't read.
9. Japan's Mitsubishi Motors had to rename its Pajero model in Spanish-speaking countries because the term related to masturbation.
10. Toyota Motor's MR2 model dropped the number in France because the combination sounded like a French swearword.

FIGURE 4-2

Ten Global Branding Mishaps

research them before making a choice. The days when Henry Ford II could name his new automobile the "Edsel" after the name of a family member seem to be long gone.

Is it difficult to come up with a brand name? Ira Bachrach, a well-known branding consultant, notes that although there are 140,000 words in the English vocabulary, the average American recognizes only 20,000; his consulting company, NameLab, sticks to the 7,000 words that make up the vocabulary of most TV programs and commercials. Although that may seem to allow a lot of choices, each year tens of thousands of new brands are registered as legal trademarks. In fact, arriving at a satisfactory brand name for a new product can be a painfully difficult and prolonged process. After realizing that most of the desirable brand names are already legally registered, many a frustrated executive has lamented that "all the good ones are taken."

In some ways, this difficulty should not be surprising. Any parent can probably sympathize with how hard it can be to choose a name for a child, as evidenced by the thousand of babies born without names each year because their parents have not decided on—or perhaps not agreed upon—a name yet. It is rare that naming a product can be as easy as it was for Ford when it introduced the Taurus automobile. "Taurus" was the code name given to the car during its design stage because the chief engineer's and product manager's wives were both born under that astrological sign. As luck would have it, upon closer examination, the name turned out to have a number of desirable characteristics. When it

I.Descriptive
Describes function literally; generally unregisterable
Examples: Singapore Airlines, Global Crossing

II.Suggestive
Suggestive of a benefit or function
Examples: marchFIRST, Agilent Technologies

III.Compounds
Combination of two or more, often unexpected, words
Example: redhat

IV.Classical
Based on Latin, Greek, or Sanskrit.
Example: Meritor

V.Arbitrary
Real words with no obvious tie-in to company
Example: Apple

VI.Fanciful
Coined words with no obvious meaning
Example: avanade

FIGURE 4-3

Landor's Brand Name Taxonomy

was chosen as the actual name for the car, Ford saved thousands of dollars in additional research and consulting expenses.

Naming Guidelines. Selecting a brand name for a new product is certainly an art and a science. Figure 4-3 displays the different types of possible brand names according to identity experts Landor Associates. Like any brand element, brand names must be chosen with the six general criteria of memorability, meaningfulness, likability, transferability, adaptability, and protectability in mind.

BRAND AWARENESS Brand names that are simple and easy to pronounce or spell, familiar and meaningful, and different, distinctive, and unusual can obviously improve brand awareness.[2]

Simplicity and Ease of Pronounciation and Spelling. Simplicity reduces the effort consumers have to make to comprehend and process the brand name. Short names often facilitate recall because they are easy to encode and store in memory—consider Aim toothpaste, Raid pest spray, Bold laundry detergent, Suave shampoo, Off insect repellent, Jif peanut butter, Ban deodorant, and Bic pens. Marketers can shorten longer names to make them easier to recall. For example, over the years Chevrolet cars have also become known as "Chevy," Budweiser beer has become "Bud," and Coca-Cola is also "Coke."

To encourage word-of-mouth exposure that helps to build strong memory links, marketers should also make brand names easy to pronounce. Also keep in mind that rather than risk the embarrassment of mispronouncing a difficult name like Hyundai automobiles, Fruzen Gladje ice cream, or Façonnable clothing, consumers may just avoid pronouncing it altogether.

Brands with difficult-to-pronounce names have an uphill battle to fight because the firm has to devote so much of the initial marketing effort to teaching consumers how to

THE SCIENCE OF BRANDING 4-2

Counterfeit Business Is Booming

As these destroyed counterfeit Louis Vuitton bags show, marketers must vigorously defend their trademarks.

From Calloway golf clubs to Louis Vuitton handbags, counterfeit versions of well-known brands are everywhere. The fakes are soaking up profits faster than multinationals can squash counterfeiting operations, and they're getting tougher and tougher to distinguish from the real thing. The difference can be as subtle as lesser-quality leather in a purse or fake batteries inside a cell phone. And counterfeiters can produce fakes cheaply by cutting corners on safety and quality without paying for marketing, R&D, or advertising.

Fakes have long thrived in Hong Kong, Rio de Janeiro, and Moscow, but counterfeiting has become increasingly sophisticated and pervasive. The World Customs Organization estimates counterfeit products account for 5 percent to 7 percent of global merchandise trade, equivalent to lost sales of as much as $512 billion. U.S. Customs seizures of fakes grew by 46 percent in 2004, partly because counterfeiters upped exports to Western markets.

And it's not just luxury items and consumer electronics that are being copied. The World Health Organization says up to 10 percent of medicines worldwide are counterfeited. Those drugs not only purloin pharmaceutical industry profits but also present a danger to anyone who takes them because they are manufactured under inadequate safety controls.

About two-thirds of counterfeit goods are produced in China. Other counterfeit hot spots include the Philippines, Vietnam, Russia, Ukraine, Brazil, Pakistan, and Paraguay. The operations are financed by such varied sources as Middle East businessmen who invest in facilities in Asian countries

pronounce the name. Wyborowa Polish vodka (pronounced VEE-ba-ro-va) was supported by a print ad to help consumers pronounce the brand name—a key factor for success in the distilled spirits category, where little self-service exists and consumers usually need to ask for the brand in the store.

Ideally, the brand name should have a clear, understandable, and unambiguous pronunciation and meaning. However, the way a brand is pronounced can affect its meaning, so consumers may take away different perceptions if ambiguous pronunciation results in different meanings. One research study showed that certain hypothetical products with brand names that were acceptable in both English and French, such as Vaner, Randal, and Massin, were perceived as more "hedonic" (providing pleasure) and were better liked when pronounced in French than in English.[3]

Pronunciation problems may arise from not conforming to linguistic rules. Although Honda chose the name "Acura" because it was associated with words connoting precision in several languages, it initially had some trouble with consumer pronunciation of the

for export, local Chinese entrepreneurs, and criminal networks. And some legitimate licensees make fakes on the side. Those authorized licensees can then use legitimate channels to get the products to retail outlets. Some counterfeiters mix real products with fake ones and others ship containers filled with fakes through so many ports it becomes impossible to tell where the product originated.

The replication process has also speeded up as counterfeiters have honed their engineering skills and increased their speed. Chinese factories can now copy a new model of a golf club in less than a week. And executives at a variety of companies say counterfeiters have no trouble copying holograms and other security devices intended to distinguish real products from fakes.

Experts say China is the key to stemming the counterfeiting tide. Producing counterfeit goods is as profitable as trading illegal drugs but does not carry the same risk. In many countries, convicted counterfeiters get off with a fine of a few thousand dollars. Chinese authorities have ignored the problem for years, mostly because it did not hurt Chinese industries. But as the country's corporate interests grow and Chinese companies are hurt by the counterfeit industry, experts say the Chinese government will be more cooperative.

Japanese company Nichia Corp. spent three years fighting court battles all over Asia to curb piracy of its white-light-emitting diode. The invention brings in $2 billion annually, but counterfeiters copied the design and have cut Nichia's market share and forced prices down. Nichia had little success in the Asian courts and decided instead to go after American companies purchasing the Asian knockoffs.

Other companies have also decided to target the end users of knockoff products, hoping that manufacturers will eventually be forced to get a license and pay royalties. And some patent holders are beginning to get creative and target anyone on the supply chain who knowingly ignores counterfeit businesses. Louis Vuitton has partnered with New York City landlords to prevent the sale of counterfeit Louis Vuitton goods by tenants on notorious knockoff hot spot Canal Street. But because the business of counterfeiting thrives on globalization, experts say all many companies can do for now is hope to slow, not stop, the counterfeiters.

Sources: Frederik Balfour, "Fakes," *Business Week,* 7 February 2005; Thomas Kellner, "Hit 'Em Where It Hurts," *Forbes,* 20 June 2005; Julia Boorstin, "Louis Vuitton Tests a New Way to Fight the Faux," *Fortune,* 16 May 2005.

name (AK-yur-a) in the American market, perhaps in part because the company chose not to use the phonetically simpler English spelling of Accura (with a double *c*).

To improve pronounceability and recallability, many marketers seek a desirable cadence and pleasant sound in their brand names.[4] For example, brand names may use alliteration (repetition of consonants, such as in Coleco), assonance (repetition of vowel sounds, such as in Ramada Inn), consonance (repetition of consonants with intervening vowel change, such as in Hamburger Helper), or rhythm (repetition of pattern of syllable stress, such as in Better Business Bureau). Some words employ onomatopoeia—words composed of syllables that when pronounced generate a sound strongly suggestive of the word's meaning, like Sizzler steak house, Cap'n Crunch cereal, Ping golf clubs, and Schweppes carbonated beverages.

Familiarity and Meaningfulness. The brand name should be familiar and meaningful so it can tap into existing knowledge structures. It can be concrete or abstract in meaning. Because the names of people, objects, birds, animals, and inanimate objects already exist in memory, consumers have to do less learning to understand their meanings as brand names.[5] Links form more easily, increasing memorability.[6]

Thus, when a consumer sees an ad for the first time for a car called "Neon," the fact that the consumer already has the word stored in memory should make it easier to encode the product name and thus improve its recallability. In fact, Chrysler chose that name for its new Dodge car because it also connoted "young, youthful, and vibrant," the desired image for the product.

To help create strong brand-category links and aid brand recall, the brand name may also suggest the product or service category, as do JuicyJuice 100 percent fruit juices, Ticketron ticket selling service, and *Newsweek* weekly news magazine. Brand elements that are highly descriptive of the product category or its attribute and benefits can be quite restrictive, however.[7] For example, it may be difficult to introduce a soft drink extension for a brand called JuicyJuice!

Differentiated, Distinctive, and Unique. Although choosing a simple, easy to pronounce, familiar, and meaningful brand name can improve recallability, to improve brand recognition, on the other hand, brand names should be different, distinctive, and unusual. As Chapter 2 noted, recognition depends on consumers' ability to discriminate between brands, and more complex brand names are more easily distinguished. Distinctive brand names can also make it easier for consumers to learn intrinsic product information.[8]

A brand name can be distinctive because it is inherently unique, or because it is unique in the context of other brands in the category.[9] Distinctive words may be seldom-used or atypical words for the product category like Apple computers, unusual combinations of real words like Toys "R" Us, or completely made-up words like Xerox or Exxon. Even made-up brand names, however, have to satisfy prevailing linguistic rules and conventions—for example, try to pronounce names without vowels such as Blfft, Xgpr, or Msdy!

Here too there are tradeoffs. Even if a distinctive brand name is advantageous for brand recognition, it also has to be credible and desirable in the product category. A notable exception is Smuckers jelly, which has tried to turn the handicap of its distinctive—but potentially dislikable—name into a positive through its slogan, "With a Name Like Smuckers, It Has to Be Good!"

BRAND ASSOCIATIONS Because the brand name is a compact form of communication, the explicit and implicit meanings consumers extract from it are important. In particular, the brand name can reinforce an important attribute or benefit association that makes up its product positioning (see Figure 4-4).

PowerBook

In 1989, Apple had just introduced a heavy, ineffective portable computer that had failed in the marketplace. Needing a name for its new line of portables, the company turned to name consultant Lexicon. Using focus groups of users of competitive products, Lexicon began working with the terms *laptop* and *notebook.* PowerBook became the winner because it combined two things that are very common but not typically used together: "book," a small product that holds a lot of information, and "power." Lexicon's linguists even liked the sound of the brand name and the way it would relate to the product positioning, asserting that the *p* in *power* would bring to mind compactness and speed, and the *b* in *book* would suggest dependability.[10]

Besides performance-related considerations, brand names can also communicate more abstract considerations as do names like Joy dishwashing liquid, Caress soap, and Obsession perfume.

ColorStay lipsticks
Head & Shoulders shampoo
Close-Up toothpaste
SnackWell reduced fat snacks
DieHard auto batteries
Mop & Glo floor wax
Lean Cuisine low-calorie frozen entrees
Shake'n Bake chicken seasoning
Sub-Zero refrigerators and freezers
Cling-Free static buildup remover

FIGURE 4-4
Sample Suggestive Brand Names

A descriptive brand name should make it easier to link the reinforced attribute or benefit.[11] Consumers will find it easier to believe that a laundry detergent "adds fresh scent" to clothes if it has a name like "Blossom" than if it's called something neutral like "Circle."[12] However, brand names that reinforce the initial positioning of a brand may make it harder to link new associations to the brand if it later has to be repositioned.[13] For example, if a laundry detergent named Blossom is positioned as "adding fresh scent," it may be more difficult to later reposition the product, if necessary, and add a new brand association that it "fights tough stains." Consumers may find it more difficult to accept or just too easy to forget the new positioning when the brand name continues to remind them of other product considerations.

With sufficient time and the proper marketing programs, however, this difficulty can sometimes be overcome. Southwest Airlines no longer stands for airline service in Texas and the southwestern United States. When two former Texas Instruments engineers were considering a name for their new line of portable personal computers, they chose "Compaq" because it suggested a small computer. Through subsequent introductions of "bigger" personal computers, advertising campaigns, and other marketing activity, Compaq has been able to transcend the initial positioning suggested by its name.

Such marketing maneuvers can be a long and expensive process, however. Imagine the difficulty of repositioning brands such as "I Can't Believe It's Not Butter!" or "Gee, Your Hair Smells Terrific!" Thus, it is important when choosing a meaningful name to consider the possiblity of later repositioning and the necessity of linking other associations.

Meaningful names are not restricted to real words. Consumers can extract meaning, if they so desire, even from made-up or fanciful brand names. For example, one study of computer-generated brand names containing random combinations of syllables found that "whumies" and "quax" reminded consumers of a breakfast cereal and that "dehax" reminded them of a laundry detergent.[14] Thus, consumers were able to extract at least some product meaning from these essentially arbitrary names when instructed to do so. Nevertheless, consumers are likely to extract meaning from highly abstract names only when they are motivated to do so.

Marketers generally devise made-up brand names systematically, basing words on combinations of morphemes. A ***morpheme*** is the smallest linguistic unit having meaning. There are 6,000 morphemes in the English language, including real words like "man" and prefixes, suffixes, or roots. For example, Nissan's Sentra automobile is a combination of two morphemes suggesting "central" and "sentry."[15] By combining carefully chosen morphemes, marketers can construct brand names that actually have some relatively easily inferred or implicit meaning.

Brand names raise a number of interesting linguistic issues.[16] Figure 4-5 contains an overview of different categories of linguistic characteristics, with definitions and examples. Even individual letters can contain meaning that may be useful in developing a new

Characteristics	Definitions and/or Examples
Phonetic Devices	
Alliteration	Consonant repetition (Coca-Cola)
Assonance	Vowel repetition (Kal Kan)
Consonance	Consonant repetition with intervening vowel changes (Weight Watchers)
Masculine rhyme	Rhyme with end-of-syllable stress (Max Pax)
Feminine rhyme	Unaccented syllable followed by accented syllable (American Airlines)
Weak/imperfect/slant rhyme	Vowels differ or consonants similar, not identical (Black & Decker)
Onomatopoeia	Use of syllable phonetics to resemble the object itself (Wisk)
Clipping	Product names attenuated (Chevy)
Blending	Morphemic combination, usually with elision (Aspergum, Duracell)
Initial plosives	*/b/, /c-hard/, /d/, /g-hard/, /k/, /p/, /q/, /t/* (Bic)
Orthographic Devices	
Unusual or incorrect spellings	Kool-Aid
Abbreviations	7 UP for Seven Up
Acronyms	Amoco
Morphologic Devices	
Affixation	Jell-O
Compounding	Janitor-in-a-Drum
Semantic Devices	
Metaphor	Representing something as if it were something else (Arrid); simile is included with metaphor when a name describes a likeness and not an equality (AquaFresh)
Metonymy	Application of one object or quality for another (Midas)
Synecdoche	Substitution of a part for the whole (Red Lobster)
Personification/pathetic fallacy	Humanizing the nonhuman, or ascription of human emotions to the inanimate (Betty Crocker)
Oxymoron	Conjunction of opposites (Easy-Off)
Paranomasia	Pun and word plays (Hawaiian Punch)
Semantic appositeness	Fit of name with object (Bufferin)

FIGURE 4-5

Brand Name Linguistic Characteristics

brand name. The letter *X* has become much more common in recent years (ESPN's X Games, Nissan's Xterra SUV, and the WWF's short-lived XFL) because *X* represents "extreme," "on-the-edge," and "youth"—"what's alternative, what's next, and what's new."[17] Research has shown that in some instances, consumers prefer products with brand names bearing some of the letters from their own name (Jonathan may exhibit a greater-than-expected preference for a product named Jonoki).[18]

The sounds of letters can take on meaning as well. For example, some words begin with phonemic elements called ***plosives,*** like the letters *b, c, d, g, k, p,* and *t,* whereas others use ***sibilants,*** which are sounds like *s* and soft *c.* Plosives escape from the mouth more quickly than sibilants and are harsher and more direct. Consequently, they are thought to make names more specific and less abstract, and to be more easily recognized and recalled.[19] On the other hand, because sibilants have a softer sound, they tend to conjure up romantic, serene images and are often found in the names of products such as perfumes—think of Cie, Chanel, and Cerissa.[20] One study found a relationship between certain characteristics of the letters of brand names and product features: As consonant hardness and vowel pitch increased in hypothetical brand names for toilet paper and household cleansers, consumer perception of the harshness of the product also increased.[21]

Brands are not restricted to letters alone.[22] Alphanumeric names may include a mixture of letters and digits (WD-40), a mixture of words and digits (Formula 409), or mixtures of letters or words and numbers in written form (Saks Fifth Avenue). They can also designate generations or relationships in a product line like BMW's 3, 5, and 7 series.

Naming Procedures. A number of different procedures or systems have been suggested for naming new products. Most adopt a procedure something along the following lines. Figure 4-6 displays some common naming mistakes according to leading brand name consultancy Interbrand.[23]

1. *Define objectives.* First, define the branding objectives in terms of the six general criteria we noted earlier, and in particular define the ideal meaning the brand should convey. Recognize the role of the brand within the corporate branding hierarchy and how it should relate to other brands and products (which we'll discuss in Chapter 11). In many cases, existing brand names may serve, at least in part. Finally, understand the role of the brand within the entire marketing program and the target market.
2. *Generate names.* With the branding strategy in place, next generate as many names and concepts as possible. Any potential sources of names are valid: company management and employees; existing or potential customers (including retailers or suppliers if relevant); ad agencies, professional name consultants, and specialized computer-based naming companies. Tens, hundreds, or even thousands of names may result from this step.
3. *Screen initial candidates.* Screen all the names against the branding objectives and marketing considerations identified in step 1, as well as applying the test of common

1. Treating naming as an afterthought
2. Ignoring complex trademark and URL issues
3. Keeping a brand name that is no longer relevant
4. Ignoring that naming is not only creative, but strategic
5. Falling into the subjectivity trap
6. Overlooking the global implications of names
7. Failing to effectively communicate the name internally
8. Ending verbal communication of a brand with its name
9. Naming when it's not very necessary
10. Believing that naming is an easy process

Source: Used with permission of Interbrand.

FIGURE 4-6

Top 10 Naming Mistakes

sense, to produce a more manageable list. For example, General Mills starts by eliminating the following:

- Names that have unintentional double meaning
- Names that are unpronounceable, already in use, or too close to an existing name
- Names that have obvious legal complications
- Names that represent an obvious contradiction of the positioning

Next General Mills runs in-depth evaluation sessions with management personnel and marketing partners to narrow the list to a handful of names, often conducting a quick-and-dirty legal search to help screen out possible problems.

4. *Study candidate names.* Collect more extensive information about each of the final 5 to 10 names. Before spending large amounts of money on consumer research, it is usually advisable to do an extensive international legal search. Because this step is expensive, marketers often search on a sequential basis, testing in each country only those names that survived the legal screening from the previous country.
5. *Research the final candidates.* Next, conduct consumer research to confirm management expectations about the memorability and meaningfulness of the remaining names. Consumer testing can take all forms. Many firms attempt to simulate the actual marketing program and consumers' likely purchase experiences as much as possible.[24] Thus, they may show consumers the product and its packaging, price, or promotion so that they understand the rationale for the brand name and how it will be used. Other aids in this kind of research are realistic three-dimensional packages and concept boards or low-cost animatic advertising using digital techniques. Marketers may survey many consumers to capture differences in regional or ethnic appeal. They should also factor in the effects of repeated exposure to the brand name and what happens when the name is spoken versus written.
6. *Select the final name.* Based on all the information collected from the previous step, management should choose the name that maximizes the firm's branding and marketing objectives and then formally register it.

Some segment of consumers or another will always have at least some potentially negative associations with the new brand name. In most cases, however, assuming they are not severe, these associations will disappear after the initial marketing launch. Some consumers will dislike a new brand name because it's unfamiliar or represents a deviation from the norm. Marketers should remember to separate these temporal considerations from more enduring effects. Here is how a new airline arrived at its name.[25]

JetBlue

Traditionally, airlines use descriptive names that evoke specific geographic origins like American, or broad geographic reach like United. In launching a new airline with a fresh concept—stylish travel for the budget-minded flier—JetBlue decided it needed an evocative name, but not one that sounded like an airline. Working with its ad agency, Merkley & Partners, and brand consultant, Landor, the company generated a list of candidate names—Fresh Air, Taxi, Egg, and It. The name Blue, suggesting peaceful clear skies, quickly became a favorite, but trademark lawyers noted that it would be impossible to protect the name without a distinctive qualifier. The first candidate, TrueBlue, went by the wayside when it was found to also be the name of a car rental agency. JetBlue emerged as the best substitute and the brand was born.

URLs

URLs (Uniform Resource Locators) specify locations of pages on the Web and are also commonly referred to as ***domain names***. Anyone wishing to own a specific URL must register and pay for the name with a service such as Register.com. In recent years, as companies clamored for space on the Web, the number of registered URLs increased dramatically. Every three-letter combination and virtually all words in a typical English dictionary have been registered. The sheer volume of registered URLs often makes it necessary for companies to use coined words for new brands if they wish to have a Web site for the brand. For example, when Andersen Consulting selected a new name, it chose the coined word "Accenture," in part because the URL www.accenture.com had not been registered.

Another issue facing companies with regard to URLs is protecting their brands from unauthorized use in other domain names.[26] A company can either sue the current owner of the URL for copyright infringement, buy the name from the current owner, or register all conceivable variations of its brand as domain names ahead of time. According to Gartner Inc., the average Global 2000 company had at least 300 registered URLs in 2001. Large companies are now carefully monitoring the Web for unauthorized use of their brands.

Caterpillar

Heavy-machinery manufacturer Caterpillar assigned its trademark counsel, Gene Bolmarcich, the task of protecting the company's brand online. Caterpillar has 600 registered URLs, and Bolmarcich estimates that he spends 95 percent of his time on this task. During the spring of 2000, the company reclaimed some 50 URLs by firing off cease-and-desist letters to companies registering names such as CAT that infringed on Caterpillar's copyright. Caterpillar also guards against infringement overseas by registering its name in 10 countries. But, Bolmarcich says, "You can't ever fully defend yourself."

Caterpillar found itself having to protect its URL name from trademark infringement.

Brand recall is critical for URLs because, at least initially, consumers must remember the URL to be able to get to the site. At the peak of the Internet boom, investors paid $7.5 million for Business.com, $2.2 million for Autos.com, and $1.1 million for Bingo.com. Many of these "common noun" sites failed, however, and were criticized, among other things, as being too generic in name. Many firms adopted names that started with a lowercase *e* or *i* and ended in "net," "systems," or, especially, "com." Most of these names became liabilities after the Internet bubble burst, forcing firms such as Internet.com to revert to a more conventional name, INTMedia Group. Yahoo, however, was able to create a memorable brand and URL.

Yahoo!

Jerry Yang and David Filo named their Internet portal (created as a Stanford University thesis project) "Yahoo!" after thumbing through the dictionary for words that began with "ya," the universal computing acronym for "yet another." Filo stumbled upon *yahoo,* which brought back fond childhood memories of his father calling him "little yahoo." Liking the name, they created a more complete acronym: "Yet another hierarchical officious oracle."[27]

Typically, for an existing brand, the main URL is a straightforward and maybe even literal translation of the brand name, like www.shell.com, although there are some exceptions and variations such as www.purplepill.com for the Nexium acid-reflux medication Web site.

Logos and Symbols

Although the brand name typically is the central element of the brand, visual elements typically also play a critical role in building brand equity and especially brand awareness. ***Logos*** have a long history as a means to indicate origin, ownership, or association. For example, families and countries have used logos for centuries to visually represent their names (think of the Hapsburg eagle of the Austro-Hungarian Empire).

Logos range from corporate names or trademarks (word marks with text only) written in a distinctive form, to entirely abstract designs that may be completely unrelated to the word mark, corporate name, or corporate activities.[28] Examples of brands with strong word marks and no accompanying logo separate from the name include Coca-Cola, Dunhill, and Kit Kat. Examples of abstract logos include the Mercedes star, Rolex crown, CBS eye, Nike swoosh, and Olympic rings. These non–word mark logos are also often called ***symbols***.

Many logos fall between these two extremes. Some are literal representations of the brand name, enhancing brand meaning and awareness, such as the Arm and Hammer, American Red Cross, and Apple logos. Logos can be quite concrete or pictorial in nature like the American Express centurion, the Land o' Lakes Native American, the Morton salt girl with umbrella, and Ralph Lauren's polo player. Certain physical elements of the product or company can become a symbol, as did the Goodyear blimp, McDonald's golden arches, and the Playboy bunny.

A recent study asked 150 consumers their impressions of companies based on their names alone, and then again when their logos were present. As Figure 4-7 shows, the results could differ fairly dramatically depending on the company. Clearly, logos have meanings and associations that change consumer perceptions of the company.[29]

Like names, abstract logos can be quite distinctive and thus recognizable. Nevertheless, because abstract logos may lack the inherent meaning present with a more concrete logo, one danger is that consumers may not understand what the logo is intended to represent without a significant marketing initiative to explain its meaning. Consumers can evaluate even fairly abstract logos differently depending on the shape.

Benefits. Logos and symbols are often easily recognized and can be a valuable way to identify products, although consumers may recognize them but be unable to link them to any specific product or brand.

Another branding advantage of logos is their versatility: Because they are often nonverbal, logos transfer well across cultures and over a range of product categories. For example, corporate brands often develop logos in order to confer their identity on a wide range of products and to endorse different sub-brands.

Abstract logos offer advantages when the full brand name is difficult to use for any reason. In the United Kingdom, for example, National Westminster Bank created a triangular device as a logo because the name itself was long and cumbersome and the logo could more easily appear as an identification device on checkbooks, literature, signage, and promotional material.[30] The logo also uses the shortened version of the company name, NatWest. Many insurance firms use symbols of strength (the Rock of Gibraltar for Prudential and the stag for Hartford), security (the "good hands" of Allstate and the hard hat of Fireman's Fund), or some combination of the two (the castle for Fortis).

Finally, unlike brand names, logos can be easily adapted over time to achieve a more contemporary look. For example, John Deere revamped its deer trademark for the first time in 32 years in 2000, making the animal appear to be leaping up rather than landing. The change was intended to "convey a message of strength and agility with a technology edge."[31]

In updating, however, marketers should make gradual changes and not lose sight of the inherent advantages of the logo. In the 1980s, the trend for many firms was to create more abstract, stylized versions of their logos. In the process, some of the meaning residing in these logos, and thus some equity, was lost. Recognizing the logo's potential contribution to brand equity, some firms in the 1990s reverted to a more traditional look for their symbols. Prudential's Rock of Gibraltar logo was changed back from black-and-white slanted lines to a more faithful rendition. To harken back to its historic past and reflect its engineering and design prowess, Chrysler used a winged badge to replace the Pentastar five-pointed star design as a symbol of the brand. The

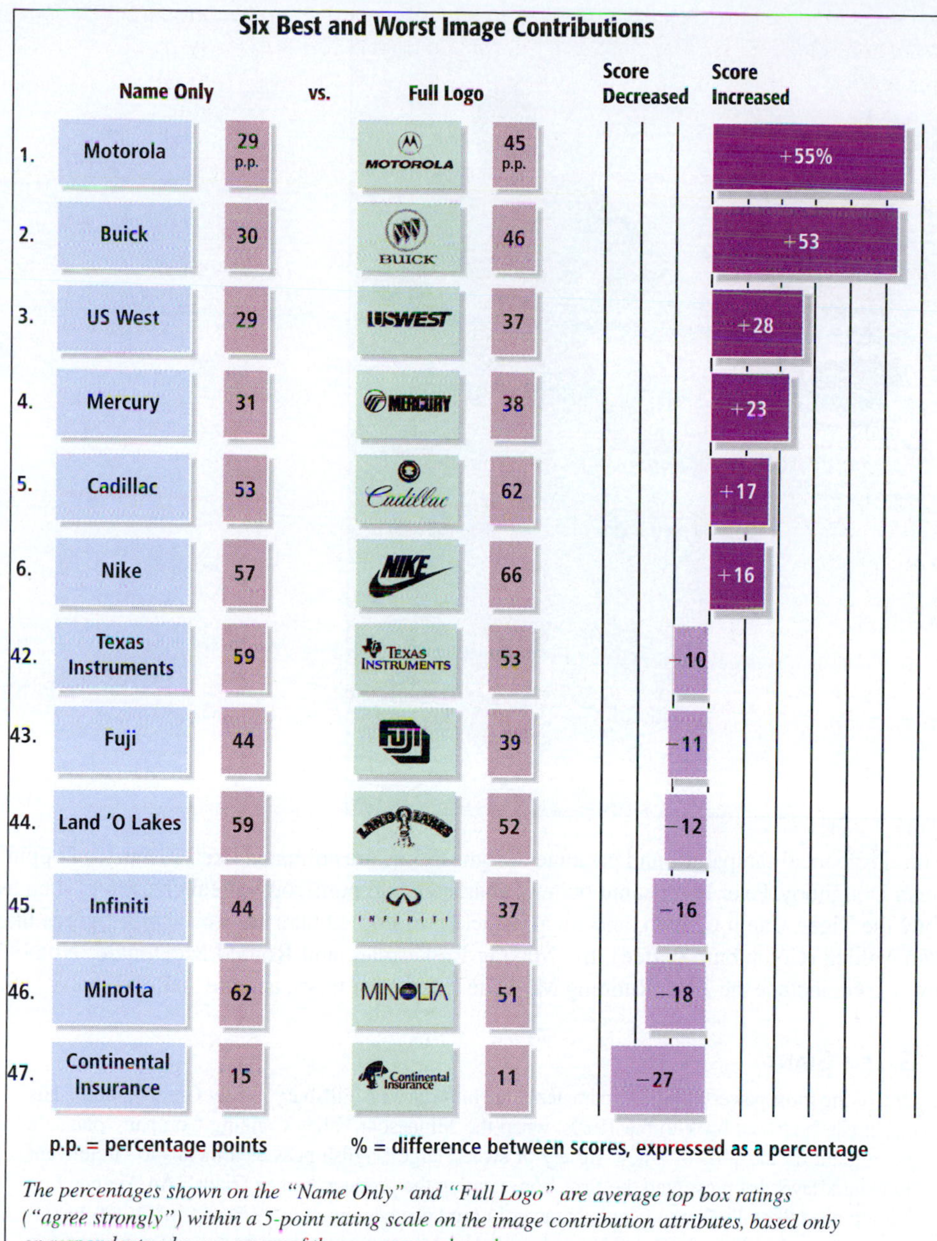

p.p. = percentage points **% = difference between scores, expressed as a percentage**

The percentages shown on the "Name Only" and "Full Logo" are average top box ratings ("agree strongly") within a 5-point rating scale on the image contribution attributes, based only on respondents who are aware of the company or brand.

Source: Alvin H. Schechter, "Measuring the Value of Corporate and Brand Logos," Design Management Journal, Winter, 1993.

FIGURE 4-7

Brand Evaluations with and without Logos

wings, intended to symbolize freedom and flying, were found on the first Chrysler manufactured in 1924.

Regardless of the reason for doing it, changing a logo is not cheap. According to Allen Adamson, managing director of the brand consultancy Landor Associates, creating a symbol or remaking an old one for a big brand "usually costs $1 million."[32]

Characters

Characters represent a special type of brand symbol—one that takes on human or real-life characteristics. Brand characters typically are introduced through advertising and can play a

The Jolly Green Giant is one of the most famous and successful brand characters in marketing.

central role in ad campaigns and package designs. Some are animated like Pillsbury's Poppin' Fresh Doughboy, Peter Pan peanut butter's character, and numerous cereal characters such as Tony the Tiger, Cap'n Crunch, and Snap, Crackle, & Pop. Others are live-action figures like Juan Valdez (Colombian coffee), the Maytag Repairman, and Ronald McDonald. Notable newcomers include the AOL Running Man, the Budweiser frogs, and the AFLAC duck.

Green Giant

One of the most powerful brand characters ever introduced is Pillsbury's Jolly Green Giant.[33] His origin can be traced back to the 1920s, when the Minnesota Valley Canning Company placed a green giant on the label of a new variety of sweet, large English peas as a means to circumvent trademark laws that prevented the firm from naming the product "Green Giant." Ad Agency Leo Burnett used the Jolly Green Giant character in print ads beginning in 1930 and in TV ads beginning in the early 1960s. At first, TV ads featured an actor wearing green body make-up and a suit of leaves. Later, the ads moved to full animation. Creatively, the ads have been very consistent. The Green Giant is always in the background, with his features obscure, and he says only "Ho-Ho-Ho." He moves very little, doesn't walk, and never leaves the valley. The Green Giant has been introduced into international markets, following the same basic set of rules. The Little Sprout character was introduced in 1973 to bring a new look to the brand and allow for more flexibility. Unlike the Green Giant, the Little Sprout is a chatterbox, often imparting valuable product information. The Green Giant brand has enormous equity to Pillsbury, and using the name and character on a new product has been an effective signal to consumers that the product is "wholesome" and "healthy."

Benefits. Because they are often colorful and rich in imagery, brand characters tend to be attention getting and quite useful for creating brand awareness. Branding Brief 4-2 describes how the GEICO gecko came to be. Brand characters can help brands break through marketplace clutter as well as help to communicate a key product benefit. For example, Maytag's Lonely Repairman has helped to reinforce the company's key "reliability" product association.

The human element of brand characters can enhance likeability and help to create perceptions of the brand as fun and interesting. A consumer may more easily form a relationship with a brand when the brand literally has a human or other character. Popular characters also often become valuable licensing properties, providing direct revenue and additional brand exposure.

Finally, because brand characters do not typically have direct product meaning, they may also be transferred relatively easily across product categories. For example, Aaker notes that "the Keebler's elf identity (which combines a sense of home-style baking with a touch of magic and fun) gives the brand latitude to extend into other baked goods—and perhaps even into other types of food where homemade magic and fun might be perceived as a benefit."[34]

Cautions. There are some cautions and drawbacks to using brand characters. Brand characters can be so attention getting and well liked that they dominate other brand elements and actually *dampen* brand awareness.

EVEREADY

When Ralston Purina introduced its drumming pink bunny that "kept going . . . and going . . . and going" in ads for the Eveready Energizer battery, many consumers were so captivated by the character that they paid little attention to the name of the advertised brand. As a result, they often mistakenly believed that the ad was for Eveready's chief competitor, Duracell. Eveready had to add the pink bunny to its packages, promotions, and other marketing communications to create stronger brand links.

Characters often must be updated over time so that their image and personality remain relevant to the target market. Recently, Michelin launched a newer, slimmer version of the famous tubby Michelin Man (whose real name is Bibendum) to mark his hundredth year. A company press release notes, "Thinner and smiling, Bibendum will look like the leader he is, with an open and reassuring manner." In general, the more realistic the brand character, the more important it is to keep it up-to-date. One advantage of fictitious or animated characters is that their appeal can be more enduring and timeless than that of real people. Branding Brief 4-3 describes the efforts by General Mills to evolve the Betty Crocker character over time. Finally, some characters are so culturally specific that they do not travel well to other countries. The Science of Branding 4-3 describes some guidelines from a leading consultant.

Slogans

Slogans are short phrases that communicate descriptive or persuasive information about the brand. They often appear in advertising but can play an important role on packaging and in other aspects of the marketing program. For example, Snickers' "Hungry? Grab a Snickers" slogan has appeared in ads and on the candy bar wrapper itself.

Slogans are powerful branding devices because, like brand names, they are an extremely efficient, shorthand means to build brand equity. They can function as useful "hooks" or "handles" to help consumers grasp the meaning of a brand—what it is and what makes it special. They are an indispensable means of summarizing and translating the intent of a marketing program in a few short words or phrases. For example, State Farm Insurance's "Like a Good Neighbor, State Farm Is There" has been used for decades to represent the brand's dependability and aura of friendship.

Benefits. Some slogans help to build brand awareness by playing off the brand name in some way, as in "The Citi Never Sleeps" or "You Can Do It If You B&Q It." Others build

BRANDING BRIEF 4-2

GEICO
geico.com
I FEEL LIKE I HAND OUT MONEY FOR A LIVING.

The GEICO Gecko has played a key role in building that brand.

GEICO Gecko Becomes Advertising Icon

Car insurance is a product aimed at consumers of all types. If you drive a car, GEICO wants your business. To reach as many market segments as possible, the company has always produced a wide variety of advertising that will appeal to many different people. Some ads are straightforward and tame (aimed at older drivers), and some are more whimsical. The company has tried to inject fun into a product that many consumers resent having to buy and associate with miserable moments.

GEICO's gecko made his debut during the 1999–2000 television season. A computer-generated six-inch, green lizard, the gecko grew out of the common mispronunciation of the name "GEICO."

In early commercials, phone callers confused the Gecko's phone book listing with the listing for GEICO, a Berkshire-Hathaway–owned insurance company. Speaking in a British accent, the Gecko (originally voiced by actor Kelsey Grammer)

brand awareness even more explicitly by making strong links between the brand and the corresponding product category, like "Lifetime. Television for Women." Most important, slogans can help to reinforce the brand positioning and desired point of difference, as in "Life Takes Visa," "Staples – That Was Easy," and "With Samsung, It's Not That Hard to Imagine." For market leaders, slogans often employ "puffery" in which the brand is praised with subjective opinions, superlatives, and exaggerations, like "It's Not TV. It's HBO" and Gillette's "The Best a Man Can Get."

Slogans often become closely tied to advertising campaigns and serve as tag lines to summarize the descriptive or persuasive information conveyed in the ads. For example, DeBeers' "A Diamond Is Forever" tag line communicates that diamonds bring eternal love and romance and never lose value. Slogans can be more expansive and more enduring than just ad tag lines, though campaign-specific tag lines may help reinforce the message of a particular campaign instead of the brand slogan for a certain period of time. For example, through the years, Nike has used ad tag lines such as "What Are You Getting Ready For?" "Why Sport?" and "I Can" for ad campaigns instead of the well-known brand slogan, "Just Do It." Such substitutions can emphasize that the ad campaign represents a departure of some kind from the message conveyed by the brand slogan, or just a means to give the brand slogan a rest so that it remains fresh.

Designing Slogans. Some of the most powerful slogans contribute to brand equity in multiple ways. They can play off the brand name to build both awareness *and* image, such

would answer the phone and end up irritated with callers looking for cheaper insurance. But he always kept his cool and his very proper English manners. Since he couldn't stop the GEICO phone calls, the gecko eventually "decided" to join the company as its official mascot.

The gecko has become so popular that he now makes special appearances at community events around the country and has become an advertising icon. He was one of two advertising characters named to the Madison Avenue Walk of Fame by consumers as part of Advertising Week 2005. Although GEICO now uses a variety of non-gecko commercials, the character is still featured on its Web site, where he even has his own blog, and the company periodically rolls out new initiatives that seek to capitalize on his fame.

Sources: Claudia H. Deutch, "Juan Valdez and the Gecko are Consumer Favorites," *New York Times*, 28 September 2005; www.geico.com.

I tell people: "You could save $500 by switching to GEICO."
WITH GEICO, IT'S EASY TO SAVE.
People say to me, I don't have time to look for car insurance. And I say to them, have you ever made $500 in 15 minutes? Go to geico.com. Do it at work or home, wherever. Answer some quick questions and you get an accurate rate quote. You buy right then, or if you want, call 1-800-947-AUTO to buy over the phone. Either way, you could save 15% or more.
VALUE. IT'S SAVINGS AND SERVICE.
People know they could save hundreds. But what about GEICO's service? I tell people, GEICO isn't just about saving hundreds. There's also the 24/7 service with real live people. They're on the phones at all hours answering your questions. And you can always get the help you need at geico.com. GEICO is about value. And that means savings and service.
CLAIMS MADE EASY.
A friend gets into a small accident. Everyone was OK. When he gets home he goes to geico.com, reports the claim and schedules an appointment. Later he goes back to the website, prints out his estimate and views photos of the damage. He picks up his car at a GEICO-approved shop and his claim repairs are guaranteed for as long he owns his car. Now that's what I call service.
DEPENDABILITY. IT'S THE GEICO WAY.
I get asked, how dependable is GEICO? They've been around for 70 years. The A.M. Best Company rates GEICO A++ (Superior) for financial stability and operating efficiency. That sounds dependable to me.
PROTECT LOTS OF THINGS WITH GEICO.
Sure, GEICO does cars. Everyone knows that. But, you could also save big when GEICO insures your motorcycle or ATV. Homeowner's and renter's insurance? GEICO can help you with those, and boats and PWCs, too.
LOOK, IT ALL MAKES A LOT OF SENSE.
It's easy to switch, so go to GEICO and you could save a lot of money. You'll get the GEICO value and claim service all my mates love.
15 MINUTES COULD SAVE YOU 15% OR MORE.

GEICO
geico.com
1-800-947-AUTO
or call your local office.

as "Be Certain with Certs" for Certs breath mints; "Maybe She's Born with It, Maybe It's Maybelline" for Maybelline cosmetics; or "The Big Q Stands for Quality" for Quaker State motor oil. Slogans also can contain product-related and other meanings. Consider the Champion sportswear slogan, "It Takes a Little More to Make a Champion." The slogan could be interpreted in terms of product performance, as meaning that Champion sportswear is made with a little extra care or with extra-special materials, but it could mean that Champion sportswear is associated with top athletes. This combination of superior product performance and aspirational user imagery is a powerful platform on which to build brand image and equity. Benetton has had an equally strong slogan on which to build brand equity ("United Colors of Benetton") but, as Branding Brief 4-4 describes, the company has not always taken full advantage of it.

Updating Slogans. Some slogans become so strongly linked to the brand that it becomes difficult to introduce new ones (take the slogan quiz in Figure 4-8 and check the accompanying footnote to see how many slogans you can correctly identify). Timex watches finally gave up trying to replace its classic "Takes a Licking and Keeps on Ticking" and returned to the tag line in its advertising, eventually evolving it to "Life Is Ticking." Marketers of 7UP tried a number of different successors to the popular "Uncola" slogan—including "Freedom of Choice," "Crisp and Clean and No Caffeine," "Don't You Feel Good About 7UP," and "Feels So Good Coming Down,"the somewhat edgy "Make 7UP Yours,and "The Only Way to Go Is Up" in 2004 before arriving at a "100% Natural" positioning.

THE SCIENCE OF BRANDING 4-3

Balance Creative and Strategic Thinking to Create Great Characters

Great characters, the Pillsbury Doughboy, for example, can embody a brand's story and spark enthusiasm for it. But bringing a character to life through advertising requires navigating a host of pitfalls. Character, a Portland, Oregon-based company, helps create new corporate brand characters and revitalize old ones.

During three-day "Character" camps, a team from a client company learns to flesh out a new or current brand character through improvisational acting, discussion, and reflection. According to Character president David Altschul, brand characters are unique in that they straddle the worlds of marketing and entertainment. Their function is to represent a brand, but they compete for attention with other characters to which consumers are exposed through television, movies, video games, and novels. Altschul emphasizes maintaining consistency across all communications and familiarizing all employees with the story behind the brand. The results of Character Camps are intended to equip creative directors with background and insights into the company's character that can spur new ideas and approaches.

These are some tips for brand characters presented at Character Camps.

1. ***Don't be a shill.*** Human traits are appealing. M&M's were successful in giving the brand more appeal once the M&M characters were given more human traits.
2. ***Create a life.*** Create a full backstory to fill out the character. This ensures that the character can evolve over time and continue to connect with consumers.
3. ***Make characters vulnerable.*** Even superheroes have flaws. Maytag launched a new character, the Apprentice, to complement its famous lonely repairman.
4. ***Imagine the long run.*** Characters like General Mills' Jolly Green Giant have been around for decades. Don't get rid of older characters just to make room for new ones. Consumers can get very attached to longtime characters.
5. ***Don't ask too much.*** Characters with a simple task or purpose work best. Using characters for new lines or other purposes can dilute their effectiveness.

Thus, a slogan that becomes so strongly identified with a brand can box it in. Or successful slogans can take on lives of their own and become public catch phrases (like Wendy's "Where's the Beef?" in the 1980s and Budweiser's "Whassup?!" in the 1990s), but there can also be a down side to this kind of success: The slogan can quickly become overexposed and lose specific brand or product meaning.

Once a slogan achieves such a high level of recognition and acceptance, it may still contribute to brand equity, but probably as more of a reminder of the brand. Consumers are unlikely to consider what the slogan means in a thoughtful way after seeing or hearing it too many times. At the same time, a potential difficulty arises if the slogan continues to convey some product meaning that the brand no longer needs to reinforce. In this case, by not facilitating the linkage of new, desired brand associations, the slogan can become restrictive and fail to allow the brand to be updated as much as desired or necessary.

To be truly effective, brand characters have to be engaging in their own right while staying true to the brand. Most characters though, are conceived as short-term solutions to solve specific problems. If the audience likes a character, companies face the challenge of turning it into an asset. At this point some companies try to freeze all the character's attributes and preserve them. But Altschul cautions against this strategy, saying static characters can lose their appeal and fail to emotionally connect with consumers. On the other hand, characters that are mass-marketed too heavily can also crash and burn. The California Raisins met such a fate when their licensing program pushed them into every possible type of paraphernalia without much thought about their backstory.

Altschul maintains that viewers connect with characters whose struggles are familiar. He says the way to ensure that a brand character adds value for the long run is to address strategic questions such as: "What is this story about?" "What are the flaws, vulnerabilities, and sources of conflict that connect the character to the brand in a deep, intrinsic way?" "What human truth is revealed through the story that audiences can relate to?"

Altschul's company helps clients find this intersection between story and marketing by defining the essence of a brand and the character and then clarifying the connection between the two. The brand character is profiled to bring out the personality traits, behavior, and mission that may be used for future storylines. And the participants talk about how the character should look, act, and interact with others to most effectively communicate the essence of the brand. The goal is to create guidelines for how the character may evolve and suggests ways the character could be used beyond traditional advertising media. Altschul suggests that companies also establish principles for the brand to stay "in character," including ways the character can serve as conscience for the brand when making decisions such as line extensions, alliances, and competitive responses.

Sources: Fara Warner, "Brands with Character," *Fast Company,* May 2004; David Altschul, "The Balancing Act of Building Character," *Advertising Age,* 4 July 2005; www.characterweb.com.

Because slogans are perhaps the easiest brand element to change over time, marketers have more flexibility in managing them. In changing slogans, however, they must do the following:

1. Recognize how the slogan is contributing to brand equity, if at all, through enhanced awareness or image.
2. Decide how much of this equity enhancement, if any, is still needed.
3. Retain the needed or desired equities still residing in the slogan as much as possible while providing whatever new twists of meaning are necessary to contribute to equity in other ways.

Sometimes modifying an existing slogan is more fruitful than introducing a new slogan with a completely new set of meanings. For example, Dockers switched its slogan from the well-received "Nice Pants" to "One Leg at a Time" in the late 1990s before reverting to the previous slogan when recognizing it had given up too much built-up equity.

BRANDING BRIEF 4-3

Updating Betty Crocker

In 1921, Washburn Crosby Company, makers of Gold Medal flour, launched a picture puzzle contest. The contest was a huge success—the company received 30,000 entries—and several hundred contestants sent along requests for recipes and advice about baking. To handle those requests, the company decided to create a spokesperson. Managers chose the name Betty Crocker because "Betty" was a popular, friendly sounding name and "Crocker" was a reference to William G. Crocker, a well-liked, recently retired executive. The company merged with General Mills in 1928, and the newly merged company introduced the *Betty Crocker Cooking School of the Air* as a national radio program. During this time, Betty was given a voice and her signature began to appear on nearly every product the company produced.

In 1936, the Betty Crocker portrait was drawn by artist Neysa McMein as a composite of some

BETTY CROCKER MAKEOVER

1936

1955

1965

1968

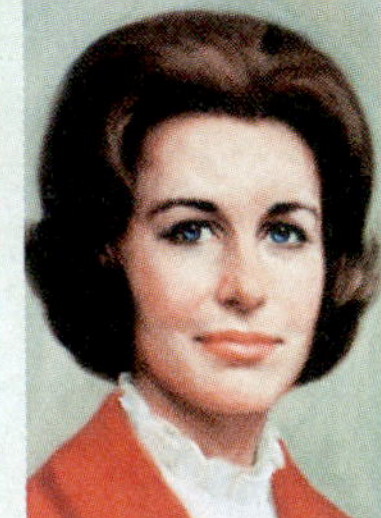

1972

1980

1986

1996

Betty Crocker has updated her image through the years.

Jingles

Jingles are musical messages written around the brand. Typically composed by professional songwriters, they often have enough catchy hooks and choruses to become almost permanently registered in the minds of listeners—sometimes whether they want them to or not! During the first half of the twentieth century, when broadcast advertising was confined primarily to radio, jingles were important branding devices. Figure 4-9 displays a list of famous brand jingles according to a leading advertising trade publication.

We can think of jingles as extended musical slogans and in that sense classify them as a brand element. Because of their musical nature, however, jingles are not nearly as transferable as other brand elements. They can communicate brand benefits, but they often convey product meaning in a nondirect and fairly abstract fashion. Thus the potential associations they might create for the brand are most likely to relate to feelings and personality and other intangibles.

Jingles are perhaps most valuable in enhancing brand awareness. Often, they repeat the brand name in clever and amusing ways that allow consumers multiple encoding

of the home economists at the company. Prim and proper, Betty was shown with pursed lips, a hard stare, and graying hair. Her appearance has been updated a number of times over the years (see the accompanying figure) and has become more friendly, although she has never lost her reserved look. Prior to a makeover in 1986, Betty Crocker was seen as honest and dependable, friendly and concerned about customers, and a specialist in baked goods, but also out-of-date, old and traditional, a manufacturer of "old standby products," and not particularly contemporary or innovative. The challenge was to give Betty a look that would attract younger consumers but not alienate older ones who remembered her as the stern homemaker of the past. There needed to be a certain fashionableness about her—not too dowdy and not too trendy, since the new look would need to last for 5 to 10 years. Her look also needed to be relevant to working women. Finally, for the first time, Betty Crocker's look was also designed to appeal to men, given the results of a General Mills study that showed that 30 percent of American men sometimes cooked for themselves.

A few years later, Betty Crocker received an Information Age update. This ultramodern Betty Crocker, the current model, is the work of a committee that selected images of 75 women of many different races to create a computerized composite. This seventh makeover seems to have taken—although Betty Crocker is now close to 75, she doesn't look a day over 35! Although the Betty Crocker name is on 200 or so products, her visual image has been largely replaced by the red spoon symbol and signature on package fronts, and she appears only on cookbooks and in advertising.

Sources: Charles Panati, *Panati's Extraordinary Origins of Everyday Things* (NewYork: Harper & Row,1989); Milton Moskowitz, Robert Levering, and Michael Katz, *Everybody's Business: A Field Guide to the 400 Leading Companies in America* (New York: Doubleday/Currency, 1990); "FYI Have You Seen This Person?" *Minneapolis–St. Paul Star Tribune*, 11 October 2000; Susan Marks, *Finding Betty Crocker: The Secret Life of America's First Lady of Food* (New York: Simon & Schuster, 2005).

opportunities. Consumers are also likely to mentally rehearse or repeat catchy jingles after the ad is over, providing even more encoding opportunities and increasing memorability.

A well-known jingle can serve as an advertising foundation for years. The familiar "Give Me a Break" jingle for Kit Kat candy bars has been sung in ads since 1988 and has helped make the brand the sixth best-selling chocolate candy bar in the United States. There was an uproar when after two decades the U.S. Army switched from its familiar "Be All That You Can Be" to "Army of One." Finally, the distinctive four-note signature to Intel's ads echoes the company's slogan "In-tel In-side." Although the jingle seems simple, the first note alone is a mix of 16 sounds, including a tambourine and a hammer striking a brass pipe.[35]

Packaging

Packaging is the activities of designing and producing containers or wrappers for a product. Like other brand elements, packages have a long history. Early humans used leaves and animal skin to cover and carry food and water. Glass containers first appeared in Egypt as early as

1.____________________ Reach Out and Touch Someone

2.____________________ Have It Your Way

3.____________________ Just Do It

4.____________________ When It Absolutely, Positively Has to Be There Overnight

5.____________________ Drivers Wanted

6.____________________ Don't Leave Home Without It

7.____________________ Like a Rock

8.____________________ Because I'm Worth It

9.____________________ The Ultimate Driving Machine

10.____________________ When You Care Enough to Send the Very Best

11.____________________ Capitalist Tool

12.____________________ The Wonder Drug That Works Wonders

13.____________________ No More Tears

14.____________________ Melts in Your Mouth, Not in Your Hands

15.____________________ We Try Harder

16.____________________ The Antidote for Civilization

17.____________________ Where Do You Want to Go Today?

18.____________________ Let Your Fingers Do the Walking

19.____________________ Breakfast of Champions

20.____________________ Fly the Friendly Skies

Answers: (1) Bell Telephone; (2) Burger King; (3) Nike; (4) Federal Express; (5) Volkswagen; (6) American Express; (7) Chevrolet; (8) L'Oreal; (9) BMW; (10) Hallmark; (11) Forbes magazine; (12) Bayer aspirin; (13) Johnson's Baby Shampoo; (14) M&M's (15) Avis; (16) Club Med; (17) Microsoft; (18) Yellow Pages; (19) Wheaties; and (20) United Airlines.

FIGURE 4-8

Famous Slogans Quiz

2000 B.C. Later, the French emperor Napoleon awarded 12,000 francs to the winner of a contest to find a better way to preserve food, leading to the first crude method of vacuum-packing.[36]

From the perspective of both the firm and consumers, packaging must achieve a number of objectives:[37]

- Identify the brand.
- Convey descriptive and persuasive information.
- Facilitate product transportation and protection.
- Assist at-home storage.
- Aid product consumption.

1. You Deserve a Break Today (McDonald's)
2. Be All That You Can Be (U.S. Army)
3. Pepsi-Cola Hits the Spot (Pepsi Cola)
4. M'm, M'm Good (Campbell's)
5. See the USA in Your Chevrolet (GM)
6. I Wish I Was an Oscar Meyer Wiener (Oscar Meyer)
7. Double Your Pleasure, Double Your Fun (Wrigley's Doublemint Gum)
8. Winston Tastes Good Like a Cigarette Should (Winston)
9. It's the Real Thing (Coca-Cola)
10. A Little Dab'll Do Ya (Brylcreem)

Source: www.adage.com. Reprinted with permission. Copyright Crain Communications Inc.

FIGURE 4-9

Advertising Age Top 10 Jingles of the 20th Century

Marketers must choose the aesthetic and functional components of packaging correctly to achieve marketing objectives and meet consumers' needs. Aesthetic considerations govern a package's size and shape, material, color, text, and graphics. Innovations in printing processes now permit eye-catching and appealing graphics that convey elaborate and colorful messages on the package at the "moment of truth"—the point of purchase.[38]

Functionally, structural design is crucial. For example, innovations over the years have resulted in food packages that are resealable, tamperproof, and more convenient to use—easy to hold, easy to open, or squeezable. Changes in canning processes have made vegetables crunchier, and special wraps have extended the life of refrigerated food.[39] Opportunities to produce innovative packaging remain, however, because consumers still report many problems with in-home use or storage. In a recent survey, they complained about food packages that stick, rip, or don't protect their contents. In frustration, some consumers were actually doing their own repackaging at home.[40]

Benefits. Often, one of the strongest associations consumers have with a brand is inspired by the look of its packaging. For example, if you ask the average consumer

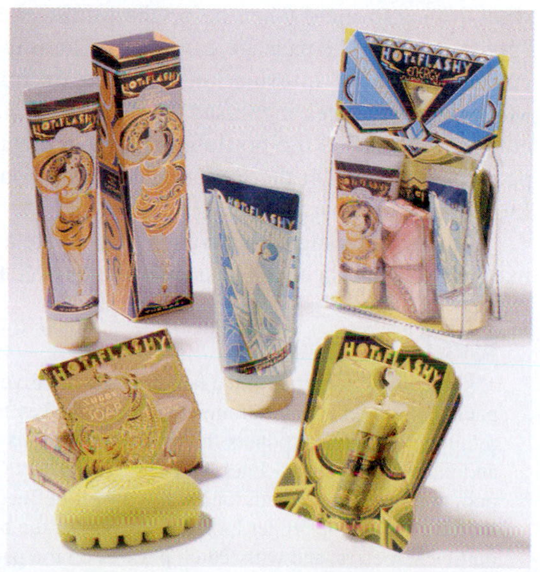

Blue Q's unique design and packaging has captured consumers' imaginations.

BRANDING BRIEF 4-4

Benetton's Brand Equity Management

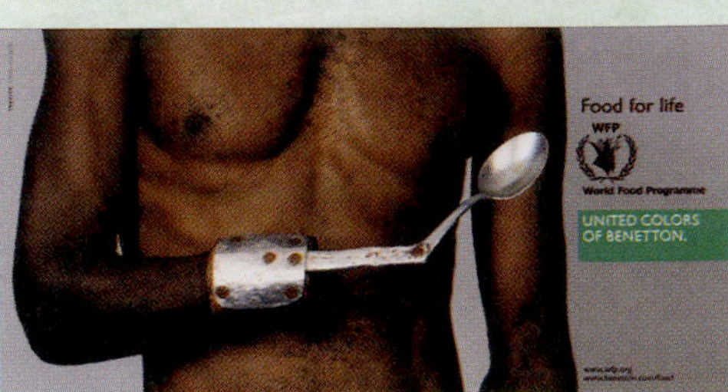

Benetton has employed edgy, controversial advertising.

One of the world's top clothing manufacturers (with global sales of $2.4 billion), Benetton has experienced some ups and downs in managing its brand equity. Benetton built a powerful brand by creating a broad range of basic and colorful clothes that appealed to a wide range of consumers. Their corporate slogan, "United Colors of Benetton," would seem to almost perfectly capture their desired image and positioning. It embraces both product considerations (the colorful character of the clothes) and user considerations (the diversity of the people who wore the clothes), providing a strong platform for the brand. Benetton's ad campaigns reinforced this positioning by showing people from a variety of different racial backgrounds wearing a range of different-colored clothes and products.

Benetton's ad campaigns switched directions, however, in the 1980s by addressing controversial social issues. Created in-house by famed designer Oliverio Toscani, Benetton print ads and posters featured such unusual and sometimes disturbing images as a white child wearing angel's wings alongside a black child sporting devil's horns; a priest kissing a nun; an AIDS patient and his family in the hospital moments before his death; and, in an ad run only once, 56 close-up photos of male and female genitalia. In 1994, Benetton launched a $15 million ad campaign in newspapers and billboards in 110 countries featuring the torn and bloodied uniform of a dead Bosnian soldier. In 2000, a campaign titled "We, on Death Row" showcased American death row inmates with pictures of the prisoners and details about their crimes and length of incarceration.

what comes to mind when he or she thinks of Heineken beer, a common response is "green bottle." The package can become an important means of brand recognition and convey or imply information to build or reinforce valuable brand associations. Molson's beer sales increased by 40 percent in the United States in 2004 after the company modified the bottle's back labels to include cheeky "ice-breakers" for bar patrons such as "On the Rebound," "Sure, You Can Have My Number," and "Fairly Intimidated by Your Beauty."[41]

Structural packaging innovations can create a point of difference that permits a higher margin. New packages can also expand a market and capture new market segments.

BLUE Q

Taking simple toiletries and a handful of other diverse products (such as air fresheners) and packaging them as entertainment has been the key to success for Blue Q. Sold by over 3,000 retailers, Blue Q's products marry unique designs with clever, quirky packaging to amuse and pamper customers. Each brand, such as Dirty Girl bath products, Vibrant Mullet shampoo, and Miso Pretty bath tonics, has a well-defined, distinctive personality. Designers have latitude to find the proper look and design for the brand. The eye-catching graphics, charismatic characters, and witty catch phrases on the packages have helped to drive sales.[42]

Critics labeled these various campaigns gimmicky "shock" advertising and accused Benetton of exploiting sensitive social issues to sell sweaters. One fact is evident. Although the campaigns may have succeeded with a certain market segment, they were certainly more "exclusive" in nature—distancing the brand from many other consumers—than the early Benetton ad campaigns, which were strikingly inviting to consumers and "inclusive" in nature. Not surprisingly, the new ads were not always well received by its retailers and franchise owners.

The ad displaying the dead Bosnian soldier received an especially hostile reaction throughout Europe. In the United States, some of Benetton's more controversial ads have been rejected by the media, and Benetton's U.S. retailers commissioned their own campaign from TBWA/Chiat/Day ad agency in an attempt to create a more sophisticated image for the brand. After the death row ads debuted, Sears pulled the brand from shelves of its 400 stores. Response from U.S. consumers was equally negative: U.S. sales of Benetton products shrank by 50 percent to $52 million between 1993 and 2000. By 2001, the number of Benetton stores in the United States dropped to 150 from 600 in 1987.

From 2001, Benetton's advertisements started featuring conventional images—teenagers in colorful Benetton clothing. Benetton, however, maintained that the company would maintain its "socially responsible" status by focusing on non-controversial themes like racial discrimination, poverty, child labor, AIDS awareness, and so forth. To that end, in early 2003 in association with the UN's World Food Programme, Benetton launched a year-long $16 million communication campaign called Food for Life.

Sources: Leigh Gallagher, "About Face," *Forbes,* 19 March 2001; Michael McCarthy, "Benetton in Spotlight," *USA Today,* 16 February 2002, B3; George E. Belch and Michael A. Belch, "Benetton Group: Evolution of Communication Strategy," *Advertising & Promotion: An Integrated Marketing Communications Perspective,* 7th ed. (Boston: McGraw-Hill, 2007).

Packaging changes can have immediate impact on sales. For example, sales of the Heath candy bar increased 25 percent after its wrapper was redone. Similarly, Rice-A-Roni's sales increased 20 percent in the first year after a packaging revitalization. One of the major packaging trends of recent years is to make both bigger and smaller packaged versions of products (as well as portions) to appeal to new market segments.[43] Jumbo sizes have been successfully introduced for hot dogs, pizzas, English muffins, frozen dinners, and beer. Pillsbury's Grand biscuits—40 percent larger than existing offerings—were the most successful new product in the company's 126-year history.

Packaging at the Point of Purchase. Packaging can create strong appeal on the store shelf and stand out from the clutter, critical when you realize that the average supermarket shopper can be exposed to 20,000 or more products in a shopping visit that may last less than 30 minutes and include many unplanned purchases. Many consumers may first encounter a new brand on the supermarket shelf or in the store. Because few product differences exist in some categories, packaging innovations can provide at least a temporary edge on competition.

For these reasons, packaging is a particularly cost-effective way to build brand equity.[44] It is sometimes called the "last five seconds of marketing" as well as "permanent media" or "the last salesman." Wal-Mart looks at packaging critically and tests whether consumers understand the brand promise behind the package within 3 seconds and up to 15 feet from the shelf. Note that consumer exposure to packaging is not restricted to the point of purchase and moments of consumption, because brand packages often can play a starring role in advertising.[45]

Packaging Innovations. In mature markets especially, package innovations can provide a short-term sales boost. For example, the 2-liter jug bottle and the 12-pack carton helped soft drink makers experience steady 5 percent to 7 percent growth in the 1980s. With the rate of growth of the soft drink industry slowing down to 2 percent to 3 percent in the 1990s, soft drink makers again sought packaging innovations to fuel additional growth. Pepsi-Cola introduced the 24-pack Cube, 12-ounce resealable bottles, 8-ounce Pepsi Mini cans, and the wide-mouth, 1-liter Big Slam bottle. Even the traditional look of Pepsi's packaging, which had not been changed since 1973, was updated in a $500 million global redesign, eventually arriving at space-age blue packaging with updated graphics.

The beverage industry in general has been characterized by a number of packaging innovations. Following the lead of Snapple's widemouth glass bottle, Arizona iced teas and fruit drinks in oversize (24-ounce), pastel-colored cans with a Southwestern motif became a $300 million brand in a few years with no marketing support beyond point-of-purchase and rudimentary outdoor ads, designed in-house.[46] More recently, a number of new beer and wine brands are appearing in aluminum bottles to be more appealing and convenient to drink.[47]

Package Design. An integral part of product development and launch, package design has become a more sophisticated process. In the past, it was often an afterthought, and colors, materials, and so forth were often chosen fairly arbitrarily. For example, legend has it that Campbell's famous soup is red and white because one executive at the company liked the uniforms of Cornell University's football team!

These days, specialized package designers bring artistic techniques and scientific skills to package design in an attempt to meet the marketing objectives for a brand. These consultants conduct detailed analyses to break down the package into a number of different elements. They decide on the optimal look and content of each element and choose which elements should be dominant in any one package—whether the brand name, illustration, or some other graphical element—and how the elements should relate to each other. Designers can also decide which elements should be shared across packages and which should differ (and how). The Science of Branding 4-4 describes the activities of Landor Associates, one of the leading package design and image management firms in the world.

Designers often refer to the "shelf impact" of a package—the visual effect the package has at the point of the purchase when consumers see it in the context of other packages in the category. For example, "bigger and brighter" packages are not always better when competitors' packages are also factored in.[48]

Although packaging is subject to some legal requirements, such as nutrition information on food products, there is plenty of scope for improving brand awareness and forming brand associations. Perhaps one of the most important visual design elements for a package is its color.[49] Some package designers believe that consumers have a "color vocabulary" when it comes to products and expect certain types of products to have a particular look. For example, it would be difficult to sell milk in anything but a white carton, club soda in anything but a blue package, and so forth. At the same time, certain brands are thought to have "color ownership" such that it would be difficult for other brands to use a similar look. One leading design executive outlined the following brand color palate:[50]

Red: Ritz crackers, Folgers coffee, Colgate toothpaste, and Coca-Cola soft drinks

Orange: Tide laundry detergent, Wheaties cereal, and Stouffer's frozen dinners

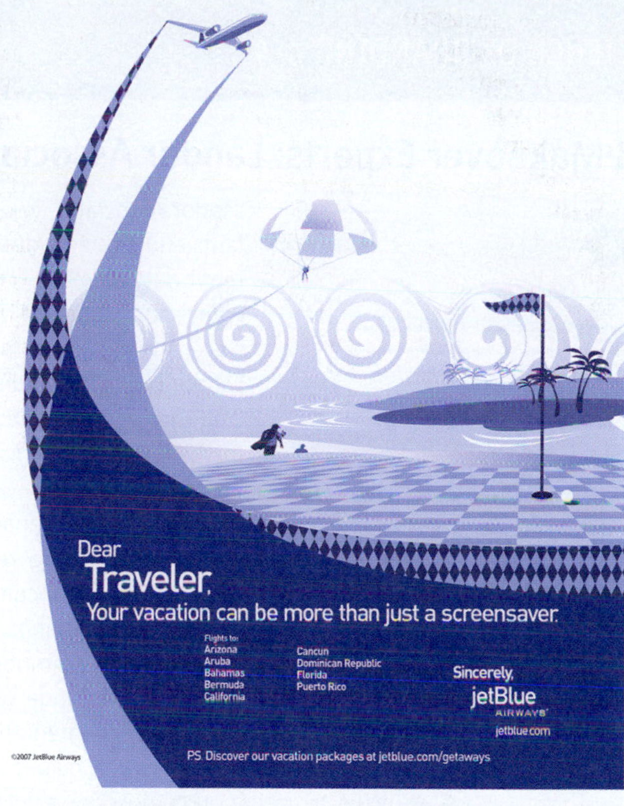

Jet Blue tapped into a popular color when designing its brand.

Yellow: Kodak film, Juicy Fruit chewing gum, Cheerios cereal, Lipton tea, and Bisquick biscuit mix

Green: Del Monte canned vegetables, Green Giant frozen vegetables, and 7UP lemon-lime soft drink

Blue: IBM computers, Windex cleaner, Downy fabric softener, and Pepsi-Cola soft drinks

Packaging color can affect consumers' perceptions of the product itself.[51] For example, the darker the orange shade of the can or bottle, the sweeter consumers believe the drink inside to be.

Color is thus a critical element of packaging. Recent years have seen a rise in the use of blue as the look or even the name of companies, including Blue Martini, JetBlue, and Bluefly, perhaps because blue "suggests stature and professionalism" and "is cool, hip, and relevant to technology" and therefore a "safe choice."[52] Purple also came on strong as a "funky alternative" and was embraced by many new-economy firms. Like other packaging design elements, color should be consistent with information conveyed by other aspects of the marketing program.

Packaging Changes. Although packaging changes can be expensive, they can be cost-effective compared with other marketing communication costs. Firms change their packaging for a number of reasons.[53] They may upgrade it to signal a higher price, or to more effectively sell products through new or shifting distribution channels. For instance, Kendall Oil redid its package to make it more appealing to do-it-yourselfers when it found more of its sales coming from supermarkets and hardware stores rather than service stations. Packaging will change when there is a significant product line expansion that would benefit from a common look, as with Planter's nuts, Weight Watchers foods, and

THE SCIENCE OF BRANDING 4-4

Brand Makeover Experts: Landor Associates

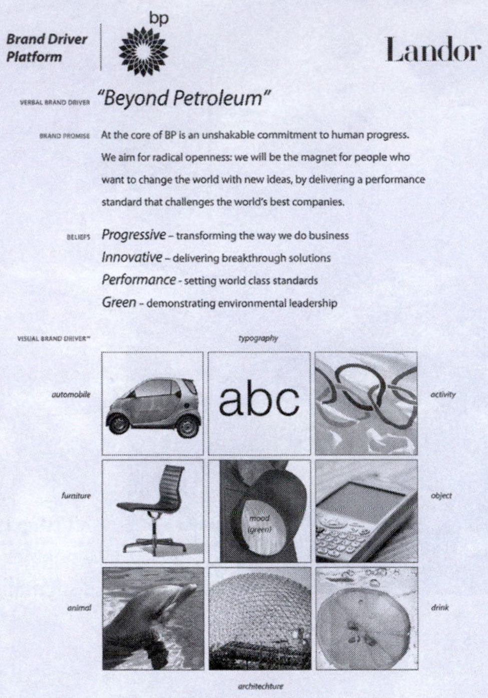

Landor Associates, one of the premier image consultants and strategic designers in the world, called the ferryboat *Kalmath,* anchored on Pier 5 in San Francisco, home for years. Although the firm has since moved into more spacious headquarters, Landor has retained the ferryboat as a symbol of the creativity and innovation that it feels it brings to its marketing assignments. Landor has provided a varied list of clients with a wide range of services including corporate image management; naming systems; corporate, brand, and retail identity systems design; identity systems documentation; consumer research; retail space planning; brand value analysis; product positioning; communication strategies; corporate positioning; signage systems development; and corporate culture integration.

Landor has helped build and revitalize some of the world's most powerful brands, including Pepsi, FedEx, GE, Delta, Frito-Lay, Hyatt, Levi's, Japan Airlines, Lucent, Procter & Gamble, Microsoft, Cathay Pacific, and LG Group. The firm has provided the name and graphic identity for Touchstone Pictures, Saturn automobiles, and Dollar Rent A Car; devised packaging for Miller Genuine Draft; created the Cotton Mark—making cotton the first commodity product to add value through strategic branding; redone packages for brands such as Coca-Cola,

Stouffer's frozen foods. Package redesign may also accompany a new product innovation to signal changes to consumers. For example, when Procter & Gamble introduced Liquid Tide laundry detergent, the company felt the brand achieved its 10 percent market share thanks to the addition of a drip-proof spout and bottle cap design.[54]

Perhaps the most common reason for package redesign is that the old package just looks outdated. Under these circumstances, marketers must not lose the key package equities that have been built up. In 1997, British Airways hoped for a more international look by adding Delft pottery, Chinese calligraphy, and other ethnic designs on the tail fins of many of its planes. A hostile public response from British passengers accustomed to seeing the Union Jack on the planes forced the company to repaint the fleet in 2001 with the Chatham Dockyard Union Flag, a design first used on the Concorde.[55]

MOTT'S JUICES

In 2004, Mott's redesigned its entire portfolio of apple sauces and juices—about 150 SKUs—to unify the brand and remind consumers of its healthy equity. Because the logo of the 162-year-old brand had 90 percent recognition among consumers, management retained its basic look.

Maxwell House, V-8, Hawaiian Punch, Jergens soaps and lotions, and Oral-B; created a branding and packaging system for 3M, Birds Eye, Lean Cuisine, and Black & Decker; and defined corporate identity for numerous airlines, including British Airways.

One recent client was BP, which Landor helped in its transformation from a mid-ranking oil company to a leading global brand. When BP acquired Amoco (1998), Castrol (2000), and Arco (2000), the brand became the means for unifying clashing cultures and rallying around a new vision for the future. The new brand captured BP's strategy, represented by the slogan "beyond petroleum," and four beliefs: performance, progressive, innovation, and green. Launched in July of 2000, BP's Brand Driver Platform became the foundation for a comprehensive brand strategy that extended from a new positioning to a new logo, redesigned service stations, and everything in between—advertisements, brochures, Web site, tanker trucks, kiosks, employee training, and rewards programs. Landor also spent time with BP employees, engaging them with the brand and shifting their focus from products to customers.

Moving the brand to the center of its business, BP has used it to guide strategic decisions—such as investing in renewable energy sources—and direct the daily activities of employees. By 2001, BP's sales increased 23 percent worldwide. By 2002, 65 percent of employees reported understanding how to apply brand to their job (an increase of 41 percent), and *Fortune* magazine named BP a "Most Admired Company." From 2001–2005, a period when most oil and petroleum companies were losing public favor, BP's brand strength increased by 27 percent. The value of its intangible assets, including brand, grew by more than $7 billion (a 30 percent increase). BP's ability to outperform its competitors and transcend the petroleum category led it to be named one of 10 "breakaway brands" by a *Fortune* magazine/Brand Economics study (31 October 2005).

Source: Internal company correspondence used with permission of Landor Associates.

Research revealed that consumers had fond, warm, fuzzy feelings about the brand, so it was given a softer, friendlier look with the logo encased in an oval instead of a rectangle. A bright green leaf to signify the apostrophe in "Mott's," more realistic images of fruits, and other adapted imagery reinforced Mott's core brand associations of "nurturing," "quality," and "taste."[56]

Packaging changes have accelerated in recent years as marketers have sought to gain an advantage wherever possible. As one Coca-Cola ad executive noted, "There's no question the crowded marketplace has inspired companies to change their boxes more often, and there's greater use of promotional packages to give the appearance that things are changing." In making a packaging change, marketers need to recognize its effect on the original or current customer franchise for the brand.[57] To identify or confirm key package equities, consumer research is usually helpful (see Branding Brief 4-5). If packaging recognition is a critical consumer success factor for the brand, however, marketers must be especially careful. It would be a mistake to change the packaging so significantly that consumers don't recognize it in the store.

Some marketing observers consider packaging important enough to be the "fifth P" of the marketing mix. Packaging can play an important role in building brand equity directly,

BRANDING BRIEF 4-5

Inside a Packaging Makeover

Betty Crocker carefully gives its packages makeovers through the years to improve their appeal.

Betty Crocker's parent company, General Mills, spent more than $1 million and one year making over its cake, cookie, and muffin boxes. A fleet of packaging consultants, food photographers, graphic artists, marketers, and consumers were consulted. Here's how it unfolded.

- In 2002, Betty Crocker conducted focus groups to find out whether customers agreed with internal suspicions that the company's inconsistent packaging designs were sorely in need of a facelift. When focus group participants said that the box failed to stand out, its purple background was "anti-Betty," and the cake "looked fake," the company sprang into action.
- The Betty Crocker team then got to work trying to nail down what Betty, a fictional homemaker, would like in a package. The company's design consultants, Lipson

through points of difference created by functional or aesthetic elements of the packaging, or indirectly through the reinforcement of brand awareness and image. Figure 4-10 contains the recommendations of one expert on how to create packaging with high impact, and The Science of Branding 4-5 reviews some insightful academic research.[58]

Putting It All Together

Each brand element can play a different role in building brand equity, so marketers "mix and match" to maximize brand equity. For example, meaningful brand names that are visually represented through logos are easier to remember with than without such reinforcement.[59]

The entire set of brand elements makes up the ***brand identity,*** the contribution of all brand elements to awareness and image. The cohesiveness of the brand identity depends on the extent to which the brand elements are consistent. Ideally, marketers choose each elements to support the others, and all can be easily incorporated into other aspects of the brand and the marketing program.

Some strong brands have a number of valuable brand elements that directly reinforce each other. For example, consider Charmin toilet tissue. Phonetically, the name itself conveys softness. The brand character, Mr. Whipple, and the brand slogan, "Please Don't Squeeze the Charmin," also help to reinforce the key point of difference for the brand of "softness."

Alport Glass and Associates, created more than 100 versions of Betty's red spoon logo, and handwriting analysts deconstructed dozens of versions of her signatures to go on the boxes. A team of 20 people at the consulting firm worked full-time on the redesign project in a war room papered with sketches.

- The firm finalized a design for the red spoon as well as colors, fonts, and logos to make sure the packaging would stay consistent and be striking. As one consultant noted, the goal was to "get that classic warm-and-homey feeling, with a soft, sunny background, evoking a kitchen." A red box border was created for uniformity, but a wavy band was included to "evoke the stirring of batter."
- A team including a photographer, art director, and four food stylists worked for weeks on the bakery photos that would appear on the cake box covers. Cakes were baked, sliced, and photographed by the dozen. Every angle, every size was discussed.
- With all the pieces in place, the new packaging was launched. How did it turn out? In 2003, a consumer survey showed four of five shoppers preferred the new boxes. And more than half those surveyed said they would be more likely to buy the product based on the new designs versus the old. The Betty Crocker management team was thrilled. As one marketing director commented, "It's like seeing your best friend get a makeover. You hope it'll be fabulous, and when it is, you want to applaud."

Sources: Michele Meyer, "Recipe for Success?" *USA Weekend Magazine,* 20 July 2003; Kate Bertrand, "Stylish Packaging Acts as Home Décor," *BrandPackaging,* September 2004; Ted Mininni, "True Brand Differentiation: Not New or Improved," *BrandPackaging,* April 2005.

Brand names characterized by rich, concrete visual imagery often can yield powerful logos or symbols. Wells Fargo, a large California-based bank, has a brand name rich in Western heritage that can be exploited throughout its marketing program. Wells Fargo has adopted a stagecoach as a symbol and has named individual services to be thematically consistent, for example, creating investment funds under the Stagecoach Funds brand umbrella.

1. *Know your consumer.* Get inside your consumer's head and heart to learn about what motivates the purchase.
2. *Take the big-picture approach.* Packages that are most effective borrow ideas from a wide range of other product categories. They look at all forms of packaging and put the best ideas together in unique ways.
3. *Understand that package aesthetics and function are both critical.* The package has to grab consumers' attention in a sea of competing messages—but it also has to work well so that consumers will buy again.
4. *Know your distribution channels.* How do retailers view your package? How are channels changing? Which retailers like which package configurations?
5. *Educate management.* Make sure senior management recognizes the importance of packaging.

FIGURE 4-10

Guidelines for Creating High-Impact Packaging

THE SCIENCE OF BRANDING 4-5

The Psychology of Packaging

Cornell University's Brian Wansink has conducted a series of research studies into the consumer psychology of packaging. Here is how he approaches the topic and views some of his findings:

> Packaging can be such an important brand-building tool that it is sometimes called the "5th P." Since it is estimated that the majority of brand choice decisions are made at the point-of-purchase, the right package can instantly catch a consumer's eye, communicate value, reinforce a brand's equity, and provide key comparison information. The bright red and yellow colors of a Tide box can attract attention, while the black and white boxes of an Apple iPod can reinforce an exclusive, "think different" image. The slender shape of one shampoo bottle emphasizes elegance, while the squat shape of another holding the same volume leads people to think it contains less shampoo.

Many managers think the package's main purpose is to encourage purchase. For many consumer packaged goods, the package keeps on marketing the brand and influencing consumers long after it is purchased. After it is home it can influence how a person perceives its taste and value, how much a person uses at a time, and even how he or she uses it.

Packaging Can Influence Taste

Our sense of taste and touch is very suggestible, and what we see on a package can lead us to taste what we think we are going to taste. In one study, 181 people were sent home with nutrition bars that claimed to contain either "10 grams of protein" or "10 grams of soy protein." In reality, both nutrition bars were identical, and neither contained any soy. Nevertheless, because many people believe soy to have an unappetizing taste, they rated the bars with "soy" on the package as "grainy," "unappealing," and "tasteless." The right words and image on a package can have a big influence on these expectations.

Packaging Can Influence Value

Long after we have bought a product, a package can still lead us to believe we bought it for a good value. First, most people believe the bigger the package, the better the price per ounce. Yet even the shape of a package can influence what we think. One study found that people believe tall, narrow packages hold more of a product than short, wide packages.

Packaging Can Influence Consumption

Studies of 48 different types of foods and personal care products have shown that people pour and consume 18–32 percent more of a product as the size of the container doubles. A big part of the

Review

Brand elements are those trademarkable devices that identify and differentiate the brand. The main ones are brand names, URLs, logos, symbols, characters, slogans, jingles, and packages. Brand elements can both enhance brand awareness and facilitate the formation of strong, favorable, and unique brand associations.

reason is that larger sizes subtly suggest a higher "consumption norm." One study gave Chicago moviegoers free medium-size or large-size popcorn buckets and showed that those given the larger buckets ate 45 percent more! Even when the popcorn was 14 days old, people still ate 32 percent more, though they said they hated it. The same thing happens at parties. MBA students at a Champaign, IL Super Bowl party were offered Chex Mix from either huge gallon-size bowls or from twice as many half-gallon bowls. Those dishing from the gallon-size bowls took and ate 53 percent more.

Packaging Can Influence How a Person Uses a Product

One strategy to increase use of mature products has been to encourage people to use the brand in new situations, like soup for breakfast, or for new uses, like baking soda as a refrigerator deodorizer. An analysis of 26 products and 402 consumers showed that twice as many people learned about the new use from the package than from television ads. Part of the reason such on-package suggestions are effective is that they are guaranteed to reach a person who is already favorable to the brand.

Sources: Peter H. Bloch, "Seeking the Ideal Form—Product Design and Consumer Response," *Journal of Marketing* 59, no. 3 (1995): 16–29; Peter H. Bloch, Frederick F. Brunel, and T. J. Arnold, "Individual Differences in the Centrality of Visual Product Aesthetics: Concept and Measurement," *Journal of Consumer Research* 29, no. 4 (2003): 551–565; Brian Wansink and Se-Bum Park, "Sensory Suggestiveness and Labeling: Do Soy Labels Bias Taste?" *Journal of Sensory Studies* 17, no. 5 (November 2002): 483–491; Valerie Folkes and Shashi Matta, "The Effects of Package Shape on Consumers' Judgment of Product Volume: Attention as Mental Containment," *Journal of Consumer Research* 31 (September 2004): 390–401; Priya Raghubir and Aradna Krishna, "Vital Dimensions in Volume Perception: Can the Eye Fool the Stomach?" *Journal of Marketing Research* 36 (August 1999): 313–326; Valerie Folkes, Ingrid Martin, and Kamal Gupta, "When to Say When: Effects of Supply on Usage," *Journal of Consumer Research* 20 (December 1993): 467–477; Brian Wansink, "Can Package Size Accelerate Usage Volume?" *Journal of Marketing* 60 (July 1996): 1–14; Brian Wansink, "Environmental Factors That Increase the Food Intake and Consumption Volume of Unknowing Consumers," *Annual Review of Nutrition* 24 (2004): 455–479; Brian Wansink and Se-Bum Park, "At the Movies: How External Cues and Perceived Taste Impact Consumption Volume," *Food Quality and Preference* 12, no. 1 (January 2001): 69–74; Brian Wansink and Junyong Kim, "Bad Popcorn in Big Buckets: Portion Size Can Influence Intake as Much as Taste, "*Journal of Nutrition Education and Behavior* 37 (Sept–Oct 2005): 242–245; Brian Wansink and Matthew M. Cheney, "Super Bowls: Serving Bowl Size and Food Consumption," *JAMA—Journal of the American Medical Association* 293, no. 14 (2005): 1727–1728; Brian Wansink and Jennifer M. Gilmore, "New Uses That Revitalize Old Brands," *Journal of Advertising Research* 39, no. 2 (April/May 1999): 90–98.

Six criteria are particularly important (see Figure 4-11). First, brand elements should be inherently memorable, easy to recognize and easy to recall. Second, they should be inherently meaningful to convey information about the nature of the product category, the particular attributes and benefits of a brand, or both. The brand element may even reflect brand personality, user or usage imagery, or feelings for the brand. Third, the information conveyed by brand elements does not necessarily have to relate to the product alone and

	Brand Element				
Criterion	Brand Names and URLs	Logos and Symbols	Characters	Slogans and Jingles	Packaging and Signage
Memorability	Can be chosen to enhance brand recall and recognition	Generally more useful for brand recognition	Generally more useful for brand recognition	Can be chosen to enhance brand recall and recognition	Generally more useful for brand recognition
Meaningfulness	Can reinforce almost any type of association, although sometimes only indirectly	Can reinforce almost any type of association, although sometimes only indirectly	Generally more useful for non-product-related imagery and brand personality	Can convey almost any type of association explicitly	Can convey almost any type of association explicitly
Likability	Can evoke much verbal imagery	Can provoke visual appeal	Can generate human qualities	Can evoke much verbal imagery	Can combine visual and verbal appeal
Transferability	Can be somewhat limited	Excellent	Can be somewhat limited	Can be somewhat limited	Good
Adaptability	Difficult	Can typically be redesigned	Can sometimes be redesigned	Can be modified	Can typically be redesigned
Protectability	Generally good, but with limits	Excellent	Excellent	Excellent	Can be closely copied

FIGURE 4-11

Critique of Brand Element Options

may simply be inherently appealing or likable. Fourth, brand elements can be transferable within and across product categories to support line and brand extensions, and across geographic and cultural boundaries and market segments. Fifth, brand elements should be adaptable and flexible over time. Finally, they should be legally protectable and, as much as possible, competitively defensible. Brand Focus 4.0 outlines some of the key legal considerations in protecting the brand.

Because different brand elements have different strengths and weaknesses, marketers "mix and match" to maximize their collective contribution to brand equity.

Discussion Questions

1. Pick a brand. Identify all its brand elements and assess their ability to contribute to brand equity according to the choice criteria identified in this chapter.
2. What are your favorite brand characters? Do you think they contribute to brand equity in any way? How? Can you relate their effects to the customer-based brand equity model?
3. What are some other examples of slogans not listed in the chapter that make strong contributions to brand equity? Why? Can you think of any "bad" slogans? Why do you consider them to be so?
4. Choose a package of any supermarket product. Assess its contribution to brand equity. Justify your decisions.
5. Can you think of some general guidelines to help marketers mix and match brand elements? Can you ever have "too many" brand elements? Which brand do you think does the best job of mixing and matching brand elements?

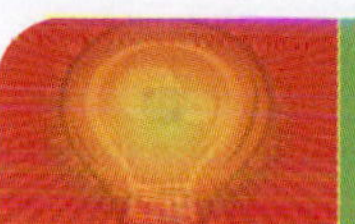

BRAND FOCUS 4.0

Legal Branding Considerations

According to Dorothy Cohen, under common law, "a 'technical' trademark is defined as any fanciful arbitrary, distinctive, and nondescriptive mark, word, letter, number, design, or picture that denominates and is affixed to goods; it is an inherently distinctive trade symbol that identifies a product."[60] She maintains that ***trademark strategy*** involves proper trademark planning, implementation, and control, as follows.

- ***Trademark planning*** requires selecting a valid trademark, adopting and using the trademark, and engaging in search and clearance processes.
- ***Trademark implementation*** requires effectively using the trademark in enacting marketing decisions, especially with respect to promotional and distributional strategies.
- ***Trademark control*** requires a program of aggressive policing of a trademark to ensure its efficient usage in marketing activities, including efforts to reduce trademark counterfeiting and to prevent the trademark from becoming generic, as well as instituting suits for infringement of the trademark.

This appendix highlights a few key legal branding considerations. For more comprehensive treatments, it is necessary to consider other sources.[61]

Counterfeit and Imitator Brands

Why is trademark protection of brand elements such as brand names, logos, and symbols such an important brand management priority? Counterfeiting alone costs U.S. companies an astounding $200 billion a year, and an estimated 5 percent of products sold worldwide are phony. Virtually any product is fair game for illegal counterfeiting or questionable copycat mimicking—from Nike apparel to Windows software, and from Similac baby formula to ACDelco auto parts.[62] Pirated products from China, Vietnam, and Russia, in particular, have flooded global markets. In China alone, copyright infringement costs Western businesses an estimated $16 billion in sales annually. Some 20 percent of Western brand name products sold in China are counterfeit. Procter & Gamble claims that counterfeiters sold $150 million worth—or 15 percent of its total 2000 Chinese sales—of products bearing P&G logos. Volkswagen discovered that almost two-thirds of the car parts sold to VW owners are fake. In China, 94 percent of all software units are believed to be counterfeit, compared with 24 percent in the United States.

In addition, some products attempt to gain market share by imitating successful brands. These copycat brands may mimic any one of the possible brand elements, such as brand names or packaging. For example, Calvin Klein's popular Obsession perfume and cologne has had to withstand imitators such as Compulsion, Enamoured, and Confess, whose package slogan proclaimed, "If you like Obsession, you'll love Confess." Many copycat brands are put forth by retailers as store brands, putting national brands in the dilemma of protecting their trade dress by cracking down on some of their best customers. Complicating matters is the fact that if challenged, many private labels contend, with some justification, that they should be permitted to continue labeling and packaging practices that have come to identify entire categories of products rather than a single national brand.[63] In other words, certain packaging looks may become a necessary point of parity in a product category.

A common victim of brand cloning, Contac cold medication underwent its first packaging overhaul in 33 years to better prevent knockoffs as well as update its image. Many national brand manufacturers are also responding through legal action. For national brands, the key is proving that brand clones are misleading consumers, who may think that they are buying national brands. The burden of proof is to establish that an appreciable number of reasonably acting consumers are confused and mistaken in their purchases.[64] In such cases, many factors might be considered by courts in determining likelihood of confusion, such as the strength of the national brand's mark, the relatedness of the national brand and brand clone products, the similarity of the marks, evidence of actual confusion, the similarity of marketing channels used, the likely degree of buyer care, the brand clone's intent in selecting the mark, and the likelihood of expansion of the product lines.

Simonson provides an in-depth discussion of these issues and methods to assess the likelihood of confusion and "genericness" of a trademark. He stresses the importance of recognizing that consumers may vary in their level or degree of confusion and that it is difficult as a result to identify a precise threshold level above which confusion occurs. He also notes how survey research methods must accurately reflect the consumers' state of mind when engaged in marketplace activities.[65]

Historical and Legal Precedence

Simonson and Holbrook have made some provocative observations about and connections between appropriation and dilution, making the following points.[66] They begin by noting that legally, a brand name is a "conditional-type property"—protected only after it has been used in commerce to identify products (goods or services) and only in relation to those products or to closely related offerings. To preserve a brand name's role in identifying products, the authors note, federal law protects brands from actions of others that may tend to cause confusion concerning proper source identification.

By contrast with the case of confusion, Simonson and Holbrook identify ***trademark appropriation*** as a developing area of state law that can severely curtail even those brand strategies that do not "confuse" consumers. They define appropriation in terms of enhancing the image of a new offering via the use of some property aspect of an existing brand. That is, appropriation resembles theft of an intangible property right. They note that the typical argument to prevent imitations is that even in the absence of confusion, a weaker brand will tend to benefit by imitating an existing brand name. Jerre Swann similarly argues that "the owner of a strong, unique brand should thus be entitled, incipiently, to prevent impairment of the brand's communicative clarity by its substantial association with another brand, particularly where there is an element of misappropriation."[67]

Simonson and Holbrook also summarize the legal concept of ***trademark dilution***:

> Protection from "dilution"—a weakening or reduction in the ability of a mark to clearly and unmistakably distinguish the source—arose in 1927 when a legal ruling declared that "once a mark has come to indicate to the public a constant and uniform source of satisfaction, its owner should be allowed the broadest scope possible for the 'natural expansion of his trade' to other lines or fields of enterprise."

They observe that two brand-related rights followed: (1) the right to preempt and preserve areas for brand extensions and (2) the right to stop the introduction of similar or identical brand names even in the absence of consumer confusion so as to protect a brand's image and distinctiveness from being diluted.

Dilution can occur in three ways: blurring, tarnishment, and cybersquatting.[68] ***Blurring*** happens when the use of an existing mark by a different company in a different category alters the "unique and distinctive significance" of that mark. ***Tarnishment*** is when a different company employs the mark in order to degrade its quality, such as in the context of a parody or satire. ***Cybersquatting*** occurs when an unaffiliated party purchases an Internet "domain name consisting of the mark or name of a company for the purpose of relinquishing the right to that domain name to the legitimate owner for a price."[69]

New American laws register trademarks for only 10 years (instead of 20); to renew trademarks, firms must prove they are using the name and not just holding it in reserve. The Trademark Law Revision Act of 1988 allowed entities to apply for a trademark based on their "intent to use" it within 36 months, eliminating the need to have an actual product in the works. To determine legal status, marketers must search trademark registrations, brand name directories, phone books, trade journals and advertisements, and so forth. As a result, the pool of potentially available trademarks has shrunk. In 1996, 200,000 trademark applications were filed with the U.S. Patent and Trademark Office, including a large number filed by foreign companies from Canada, Germany, Britain, and Japan.[70]

The remainder of this case describes some of the particular issues involved with two important brand elements: brand names and packaging.

Trademark Issues Concerning Names

Without adequate trademark protection, brand names can become legally declared generic, as was the case with *vaseline, victrola, cellophane, escalator, and thermos.* For example, when Bayer set out to trademark the "wonder drug" acetylsalicyclic acid, they failed to provide a "generic" term or common descriptor for the product and provided only a trademark, Aspirin. Without any other option available in the language, the trademark became the common name for the product. In 1921, a U.S. District Court ruled that Bayer had lost all its rights in the trademark. Other brand names have struggled to retain their legal trademark status, for example, Band Aids, Kleenex, Scotch Tape, Q-Tips, and Jello. Xerox spends $100,000 a year explaining that you don't "Xerox" a document, you photocopy it.[71]

Legally, the courts have created a hierarchy for determining eligibility for registration. In descending order of protection, these categories are as follows (with concepts and examples in parentheses):

1. Fanciful (made-up word with no inherent meaning, e.g., Kodak)
2. Arbitrary (actual word but not associated with product, e.g., Camel)
3. Suggestive (actual word evocative of product feature or benefit, e.g., Eveready)
4. Descriptive (common word protected only with secondary meaning, e.g., Ivory)
5. Generic (word synonymous with the product category, e.g., Aspirin)

Thus, fanciful names are the most easily protected, but at the same time are less suggestive or descriptive of the product itself, suggesting the type of tradeoff involved in choosing brand elements. Generic terms are never protectable. Marks that are difficult to protect include those that are surnames, descriptive terms, or geographic names or those that relate to a functional product feature. Marks that are not inherently distinctive and thus are not immediately protectable may attain trademark protection if they acquire secondary meaning.

Secondary meaning refers to a mark gaining a meaning other than the older (primary) meaning. The secondary meaning must be the meaning the public usually attaches to the mark and that indicates the association between the mark and goods from a single source. Secondary meaning is usually proven through extensive advertising, distribution, availability, sales volume, length and manner of use, and market share.[72] Secondary meaning is necessary to establish trademark protection for descriptive marks, geographic terms, and personal names.

Trademark Issues Concerning Packaging

In general, names and graphic designs are more legally defensible than shapes and colors. The issue of legal protection of the color of packaging for a brand is a complicated one. One federal appeals court in San Francisco ruled that companies cannot get trademark protection for a product's color alone.[73] The court ruled against a small Chicago manufacturer that makes green-gold padding used by dry cleaners and garment makers on machines that press clothes; the manufacturer had filed suit against a competitor that had started selling padding of the same hue. In rejecting protection for the color alone, the court said manufacturers with distinctively colored products can rely on existing law that protects "trade dress" related to the overall appearance of the product: "Adequate protection is available when color is combined in distinctive patterns or designs or combined in distinctive logos."

Color is one factor, but not a determinative one, under a trade dress analysis. This ruling differed from a landmark ruling in 1985 arising from a suit by Owens-Corning Fiberglas Corporation, which sought to protect the pink color of its insulation. A Washington court ruled in the corporation's favor. Other courts have made similar rulings, but at least two other appeals courts in other regions of the country have subsequently ruled that colors cannot be trademarked. Note that these trademark rulings apply only when color is not an integral part of the product. However, given the lack of uniform trademark protection across the United States, companies planning a national campaign may have to rely on the harder-to-prove trade dress arguments.

Notes

1. For a stimulating treatment of brand naming, see Alex Frankel, *Word Craft* (New York: Crown, 2004).
2. An excellent overview of the topic, some of which this section draws on, can be found in Kim R. Robertson, "Strategically Desirable Brand Name Characteristics," *Journal of Consumer Marketing* 6, no. 4 (1989): 61–71.
3. Frances Leclerc, Bernd H. Schmitt, and Laurette Dube, "Foreign Branding and Its Effects on Product Perceptions and Attitudes," *Journal of Marketing Research* 31 (May 1994): 263–270. See also M. V. Thakor and B. G. Pacheco, "Foreign Branding and Its Effect on Product Perceptions and Attitudes: A Replication and Extension in a Multicultural Setting," *Journal of Marketing Theory and Practice* (Winter 1997): 15–30.
4. Eric Yorkston and Geeta Menon, "A Sound Idea: Phonetic Effects of Brand Names on Consumer Judgments," *Journal of Consumer Research* 31 (June 2004): 43–51; Richard R. Klink, "Creating Brand Names with Meaning: The Use of Sound Symbolism," *Marketing Letters* 11, no. 1 (2000): 5–20.
5. Kim R. Robertson, "Recall and Recognition Effects of Brand Name Imagery," *Psychology and Marketing* 4 (1987): 3–15.
6. Robert N. Kanungo, "Effects of Fittingness, Meaningfulness, and Product Utility," *Journal of Applied Psychology* 52 (1968): 290–295.
7. Kevin Lane Keller, Susan Heckler, and Michael J. Houston, "The Effects of Brand Name Suggestiveness on Advertising Recall," *Journal of Marketing* 62 (January 1998): 48–57.
8. Luk Warlop, S. Ratneshwar, and Stijn M. J. van Osselaer, "Distinctive Brand Cues and Memory for Product Consumption Experiences," *International Journal of Research in Marketing* 22 (2005): 27–44.
9. Daniel J. Howard, Roger A. Kerin, and Charles Gengler, "The Effects of Brand Name Similarity on Brand Source Confusion: Implications for Trademark Infringement," *Journal of Public Policy & Marketing* 19 (Fall 2000): 250–264.
10. Alex Frankel, "Name-o-rama," *Wired*, June 1997, 94.
11. William L. Moore and Donald R. Lehmann, "Effects of Usage and Name on Perceptions of New Products," *Marketing Science* 1, no. 4 (1982): 351–370.
12. Keller, Heckler, and Houston, "Effects of Brand Name Suggestiveness on Advertising Recall."

13. Keller, Heckler, and Houston, "Effects of Brand Name Suggestiveness on Advertising Recall."
14. Robert A. Peterson and Ivan Ross, "How to Name New Brands," *Journal of Advertising Research* 12, no. 6 (December 1972): 29–34.
15. Robert A. Mamis, "Name Calling," *Inc.,* July 1984.
16. Tina M. Lowrey, L. J. Shrum, and Tony M. Dubitsky, "The Relationship Between Brand-Name Linguistic Characteristics and Brand-Name Memory," *Journal of Advertising* 32, no. 3 (2003,): 7–17.
17. Michael McCarthy, "Xterra Discovers Extra Success," *USA Today,* 26 February 2001, 4B.
18. C. Miguel Brendl, Amitava Chattopadyhay, Brett W. Pelham, and Mauricio Carvallo, "Name Letter Branding: Valence Transfers When Product Specific Needs Are Active," *Journal of Consumer Research* 32 (December (2005): 405–415.
19. Bruce G. Vanden Bergh, Janay Collins, Myrna Schultz, and Keith Adler, "Sound Advice on Brand Names," *Journalism Quarterly* 61, no. 4 (1984): 835–840; Bruce G. Vanden Bergh, Keith E. Adler, and Lauren Oliver, "Use of Linguistic Characteristics with Various Brand-Name Styles," *Journalism Quarterly* 65 (1987): 464–468.
20. Daniel L. Doeden, "How to Select a Brand Name," *Marketing Communications* (November 1981): 58–61.
21. Timothy B. Heath, Subimal Chatterjee, and Karen Russo, "Using the Phonemes of Brand Names to Symbolize Brand Attributes," in *The AMA Educator's Proceedings: Enhancing Knowledge Development in Marketing,* eds. William Bearden and A. Parasuraman (Chicago: American Marketing Association, August 1990).
22. Much of this passage is based on Teresa M. Paiva and Janeen Arnold Costa, "The Winning Number: Consumer Perceptions of Alpha-Numeric Brand Names," *Journal of Marketing* 57 (July 1993): 85–98.
23. Beth Snyder Bulik, "Tech Sector Ponders: What's in a Name?" *Advertising Age,* 9 May 2005, 24.
24. John Murphy, *Brand Strategy* (Upper Saddle River, NJ: Prentice Hall, 1990), 79.
25. Alex Frankel, "The New Science of Naming," *Business 2.0,* December 2004, 53–55.
26. Matt Hicks, "Order out of Chaos," *eWeek,* 1 July 2001.
27. Rachel Konrad, "Companies Resurrect Abandoned Names, Ditch '.com,'" CNET News.com, 13 November 2000.
28. Murphy, *Brand Strategy.*
29. Pamela W. Henderson and Jospeh A. Cote, "Guidelines for Selecting or Modifying Logos," *Journal of Marketing* 62, no. 2 (1998): 14–30.
30. Murphy, *Brand Strategy.*
31. Michael McCarthy, "More Firms Flash New Badge," *USA Today,* 4 October 2000, B3.
32. McCarthy, "More Firms Flash New Badge."
33. Cyndee Miller, "The Green Giant: An Enduring Figure Lives Happily Ever After," *Marketing News,* 15 April 1991, 2.
34. David A. Aaker, *Building Strong Brands* (New York: Free Press, 1996), 203.
35. Dirk Smillie, "Now Hear This," *Forbes,* 25 December 2000, 234.
36. Nancy Croft, "Wrapping Up Sales," *Nation's Business* (October 1985): 41–42.
37. Susan B. Bassin, "Value-Added Packaging Cuts Through Store Clutter," *Marketing News,* 26 September 1988, 21.
38. Raymond Serafin, "Packaging Becomes an Art," *Advertising Age,* 12 August 1985, 66.
39. Trish Hall, "New Packaging May Soon Lead to Food That Tastes Better and Is More Convenient," *Wall Street Journal,* 21 April 1986, 25.
40. "Food Packages Rile Consumers," *Wall Street Journal,* 11 November 1987.
41. Nate Nickerson, "How About This Beer Label: 'I'm in Advertising!'" *Fast Company,* March 2004, p. 43.
42. Elizabeth Esfahani, "Packaging as Entertainment," *Business 2.0,* June 2005, 73.; www.blueq.com/.
43. Eben Shapiro, "Portions and Packages Grow Bigger and Bigger," *Wall Street Journal,* 12 October 1993, B1.
44. Alecia Swasy, "Sales Lost Their Vim? Try Repackaging," *Wall Street Journal,* 11 October 1989, B1.
45. "Packaging Plays Starring Role in TV Commercials," *Marketing News,* 30 January 1987.
46. Gerry Khermouch, "John Ferolito, Don Vultaggio," *Brandweek,* 14 November 1995, 57.
47. Paul Glader and Christopher Lawton, "Beer and Wine Makers Use Fancy Cans to Court New Fans," *Wall Street Journal,* 24 August 2004, B1–B2.
48. For interesting discussion, see Margaret C. Campbell and Ronald C. Goodstein, "The Moderating Effect of Perceived Risk on Consumers' Evaluations of Product Incongruity: Preference for the Norm," *Journal of Consumer Research* 28 (December 2001): 439–449.
49. For an interesting application of color to brand names, see Elizabeth G. Miller and Barbara E. Kahn, "Shades of Meaning: The Effect of Color and Flavor Names on Consumer Choice," *Journal of Consumer Research* 32 (June 2005): 86–92.
50. Michael Purvis, president of Sidjakov, Berman, and Gomez, as quoted in Carla Marinucci, "Advertising on the Store Shelves," *San Francisco Examiner,* 20 October 1986, C1–C2.
51. Lawrence L. Garber Jr., Raymond R. Burke, and J. Morgan Jones, "The Role of Package Color in Consumer Purchase Consideration and Choice," MSI Report 00–104 (Cambridge, MA: Marketing Science Institute, 2000); Ronald Alsop, "Color Grows More Important in Catching Consumers' Eyes," *Wall Street Journal,* 29 November 1984, 37.
52. Susan Carey, "American Companies Are Blue and It's Not Just the Stock Market," *Wall Street Journal,* 30 August 2001, A1.

53. Bill Abrams and David P. Garino, "Package Design Gains Stature as Visual Competition Grows," *Wall Street Journal,* 14 March 1979, 48.
54. Amy Dunkin, "Want to Wake Up a Tired Old Package? Repackage It," *Business Week,* 15 July 1985, 130–134.
55. Melanie Wells, "Face-Lift Fever," *Forbes,* 15 November 1999, 58.
56. Sonia Reyes, "Mott's Juices Marketing in Portfolio Refreshening," *Brandweek,* 12 January 2004, 14.
57. Garber, Burke, and Jones, "Role of Package Color."
58. James W. Peters, "Five Steps to Packaging That Sells," *Brand Packaging* 3, no. 4 (July/August 1999): 3.
59. Terry L. Childers and Michael J. Houston, "Conditions for a Picture Superiority Effect on Consumer Memory," *Journal of Consumer Research* 11 (September 1984): 551–563; Kathy A. Lutz and Richard J. Lutz, "Effects of Interactive Imagery on Learning: Application to Advertising," *Journal of Applied Psychology* 62, no. 4 (1977): 493–498.
60. Dorothy Cohen, "Trademark Strategy," *Journal of Marketing* 50 (January 1986): 61–74; Dorothy Cohen, "Trademark Strategy Revisited," *Journal of Marketing* 55 (July 1991): 46–59.
61. For example, see Judy Zaichowsky, *Defending Your Brand Against Imitation* (Westpoint, CO: Quorom Books, 1995); Jerre B. Swann, Sr., David Aaker, and Matt Reback, "Trademarks and Marketing," *The Trademark Reporter* 91 (July–August 2001): 787.
62. David Stipp, "Farewell, My Logo," *Fortune,* 27 May 1996, 128–140.
63. Paul F. Kilmer, "Tips for Protecting Brand from Private Label Lawyer," *Advertising Age,* 5 December 1994, 29.
64. Greg Erickson, "Seeing Double," *Brandweek,* 17 October 1994, 31–35.
65. Itamar Simonson, "Trademark Infringement from the Buyer Perspective: Conceptual Analysis and Measurement Implications," *Journal of Public Policy & Marketing* 13, no. 2 (Fall 1994): 181–199.
66. Alex Simonson and Morris Holbrook, "Evaluating the Impact of Brand-Name Replications on Product Evaluations," working paper, Marketing Department, Seton Hall University, 1994.
67. Jerre B. Swann, "Dilution Redefined for the Year 2000," *Houston Law Review* 37 (2000): 729.
68. For a recent discussion of dilution, see Jerre B. Swann, "Dilution Redefined for the Year 2002," *The Trademark Reporter* 92 (May/June 2002): 585–613. See also Maureen Morrin and Jacob Jacoby, "Trademark Dilution: Empirical Measures for an Elusive Concept," *Journal of Public Policy & Marketing* 19, no. 2 (Fall 2000): 265–276; and Chris Pullig, Carolyn J. Simmons, and Richard G. Netemeyer, "Brand Dilution: When Do New Brands Hurt Existing Brands?" *Journal of Marketing* 70 (April 2006): 52–66.
69. J. Thomas McCarthy, *McCarthy on Trademarks and Unfair Competition,* 4th ed. (Deerfield, IL: Clark Boardman Callaghan, 1996).
70. Alex Frankel, "Name-o-rama," *Wired,* June 1997, 94.
71. Constance E. Bagley, *Managers and the Legal Environment: Strategies for the 21st Century,* 2nd ed. (Minneapolis, MN: West, 1995).
72. Garry Schuman, "Trademark Protection of Container and Package Configurations—A Primer," *Chicago Kent Law Review* 59 (1982): 779–815.
73. Junda Woo, "Product's Color Alone Can't Get Trademark Protection," *Wall Street Journal,* 5 January 1994, B8.

DESIGNING MARKETING PROGRAMS TO BUILD BRAND EQUITY

Preview

This chapter considers how marketing activities in general—and product, pricing, and distribution strategies in particular—build brand equity. How can marketers integrate these activities to enhance brand awareness, improve the brand image, elicit positive brand responses, and increase brand resonance?

Our focus is on designing marketing activities from a branding perspective. We'll consider how the brand itself can be effectively integrated into the marketing program to create brand equity. Of necessity we leave a broader perspective on marketing activities to basic marketing management texts.[1]

We begin by considering some new developments in designing marketing programs. After reviewing product, pricing, and channel strategies, we conclude by considering private labels in Brand Focus 5.0.

New Perspectives on Marketing

The strategy and tactics behind marketing programs have changed dramatically in recent years as firms have dealt with enormous shifts in their external marketing environments. As outlined in Chapter 1, changes in the economic, technological, political-legal, sociocultural, and competitive environments have forced marketers to embrace new approaches and philosophies. Four major drivers of this new economy are:[2]

- Digitization and connectivity (through Internet, intranet, and mobile devices)
- Disintermediation and reintermediation (via new middlemen of various sorts)
- Customization and customerization (through tailored products and ingredients provided to customers to make products themselves)
- Industry convergence (through the blurring of industry boundaries)

These drivers, and others such as privatization and regulation, have combined to give customers and companies new capabilities (see Figure 5-1). These new capabilities have a

Consumers

Can wield substantially more customer power.

Can purchase a greater variety of available goods and services.

Can obtain a great amount of information about practically anything.

Can more easily interact with marketers in placing and receiving orders.

Can interact with other consumers and compare notes on products and services.

Companies

Can operate a powerful new information and sales channel with augmented geographic reach to inform and promote their company and its products.

Can collect fuller and richer information about their markets, customers, prospects, and competitors.

Can facilitate two-way communication with their customers and prospects, and facilitate transaction efficiency.

Can send ads, coupons, promotion, and information by e-mail to customers and prospects who give them permission.

Can customize their offerings and services to individual customers.

Can improve their purchasing, recruiting, training, and internal and external communication.

FIGURE 5-1

The New Capabilities of the New Economy

Marketing can be crucial to the commercial success of Broadway shows such as Mary Poppins.

number of implications for the practice of brand management. Marketers are increasingly abandoning the mass-market strategies that built brand powerhouses in the 1950s, 1960s, and 1970s to implement new approaches.[3] Even marketers in staid, traditional industries are rethinking their practices and not doing business as usual.

BROADWAY MUSICALS

Broadway producer Jeffrey Seller made a name for himself by successfully marketing unconventional musicals such as *Rent* and *Avenue Q*. His tactics, unusual at the time, included giving out a limited number of $20 front row tickets to attract a younger audience, incorporating ads into sets, and marketing one of his plays with e-mails and ads proclaiming: "Warning: Full Puppet Nudity." Seller and his partner invested in an aggressive marketing campaign to win Tony awards, a common approach in Hollywood, but a dramatic departure for Broadway. They advertised on ethnic radio stations, distributed fliers for their shows in bars and nightclubs, and employed airline-style yield pricing to help keep theater seats filled during slow months. Their rationale? With a plethora of entertainment options, many people are reluctant to shell out $100 to see a show. The old formula of marketing live theater via radio spots, newspaper ads, and posters, which most theatrical producers still employed, left attendance at Broadway theaters stagnating for almost a decade. Eighty percent of Broadway shows have been estimated to lose money. No wonder Seller feels comfortable saying, "We like breaking the rules and being loud about it."[4]

The new marketing environment of the 21st century has forced marketers to fundamentally change how they develop their marketing progams. Integration and personalization have become increasingly crucial factors in building and maintaining strong brands, as companies use a broad set of tightly focused activities that are personally meaningful to their target customers.

Integrating Marketing Programs and Activities

In today's marketplace, there are many different means by which products and services and their corresponding marketing programs can build brand equity. Channel strategies, communication strategies, pricing strategies, and other marketing activities can all enhance or detract from brand equity. The customer-based brand equity model provides some useful guidance to interpret these effects. One implication of the conceptualization of customer-based brand equity is that the *manner* in which brand associations are formed does not matter—only the resulting awareness and strength, favorability, and uniqueness of brand associations.

In other words, if a consumer has an equally strong and favorable brand association from Rolaids antacids to the concept "relief" because of past product experiences, a *Consumer Reports* article, exposure to a "problem-solution" television ad that concludes with the tag line "Rolaids spells relief," *or* knowledge that Rolaids sponsors the "Rolaids Relief Pitcher of the Year" award for major league and minor league baseball, the impact in terms of customer-based brand equity should be identical unless additional associations such as "advertised on television" are created, or existing associations such as "speed or potency of effects" are affected in some way.

Thus, marketers should evaluate *all* possible means to create knowledge, considering not just efficiency and cost but also effectiveness. At the center of all brand-building efforts is the actual product or service. Marketing activities surrounding that product, however, can be critical, as is the way marketers integrate the brand into them.

Consistent with this view, Schultz, Tannenbaum, and Lauterborn conceptualize one aspect of integrated marketing, integrated marketing communications, in terms of contacts.[5] They define a ***contact*** as any information-bearing experience that a customer or prospect has with the brand, the product category, or the market that relates to the marketer's product or service. According to these authors, a person can come in contact with a brand in numerous ways:[6]

> For example, a contact can include friends' and neighbors' comments, packaging, newspaper, magazine, and television information, ways the customer or prospect is treated in the retail store, where the product is shelved in the store, and the type of signage that appears in retail establishments. And the contacts do not stop with the purchase. Contacts also consist of what friends, relatives, and bosses say about a person who is using the product. Contacts include the type of customer service given with returns or inquiries, or even the types of letters the company writes to resolve problems or to solicit additional business. All of these are customer contacts with the brand. These bits and pieces of information, experiences, and relationships, created over time, influence the potential relationship among the customer, the brand, and the marketer.

The bottom line is that there are many different ways to build brand equity. Unfortunately, there are also many different firms attempting to build their brand equity in the marketplace. Creative and original thinking is necessary to create fresh new marketing programs that break through the noise in the marketplace to connect with customers. Marketers are increasingly trying a host of unconventional means of building brand equity. As just one example, consider the existence of pop-up stores—temporary stores that blend retail and event marketing.

VACANT

Cutting-edge retailer Vacant has exclusive retail concept and exhibition stores that choose to open for only one month in empty spaces in major international cities. Vacant outlets have ranged from a Hummer parked in Miami's Design District to a boutique in Marshall Field's in Chicago. They showcase a range of one-off, hard-to-find, and strictly limited edition products from established brands such Reebok and Puma as well as emerging designers. Limited quantities are available, and not all products on display can be purchased. New store locations are announced by e-mail to Vacant Club members only moments before opening.[7]

Ultimately, however, creativity must not sacrifice a brand-building goal, and marketers must orchestrate programs to provide seamlessly integrated solutions and experiences for customers that create awareness, spur demand, and cultivate loyalty.

Personalizing Marketing

The rapid expansion of the Internet and continued fragmentation of mass media has brought the need for personalized marketing into sharp focus. Many maintain that the new economy celebrates the power of the individual consumer.[8] According to one writer, "the worry for big brand owners is that this [individualism] is leading to a fragmentation of brands as people try to express their individuality by moving away from the mass market."[9]

To adapt to the increased consumer desire for personalization, marketers have embraced concepts such as experiential marketing, one-to-one marketing, and permission marketing.

Experiential Marketing. ***Experiential marketing*** promotes a product by not only communicating a product's features and benefits but also connecting it with unique and interesting experiences. One marketing commentator describes experiential marketing this way: "The idea is not to sell something, but to demonstrate how a brand can enrich a customer's life."[10] Consider how American Express won the grand prize in *Adweek* Magazine's 2005 Buzz Awards for branded entertainment.

AMERICAN EXPRESS

A long-time sponsor of the U.S. Open tennis tournament in New York City, American Express decided to expand its sponsorship in 2004 beyond the actual tennis center grounds to the heart of Manhattan. As one company spokesperson noted, "American Express is always looking for ways to provide special experiences and access to our cardmembers." Rockefeller Center from 49th Street to 51st Street was converted into a tennis mecca with stadium seating for a 25-foot Jumbotron screen showing live match coverage. The site included concession stands, U.S. Open merchandise, a replica tennis court for exhibitions and participation, and a host of other activities and special events featuring past and current tennis notables. Many perks were reserved exclusively for American Express cardholders, including a daily drawing for court-side seats to the next evening's matches with limousine transportation. The major objective of the event, which drew 337,000 people, was to enhance the perception of American Express as an experience enhancer, not just a method of payment.[11]

American Express has maximized the value of its U.S. Open tennis tournament sponsorship.

Pine and Gilmore, pioneers on the topic, argue that we are on the threshold of the "Experience Economy," a new economic era in which all businesses must orchestrate memorable events for their customers.[12] They make the following assertions:

- If you charge for stuff, then you are in the *commodity business.*
- If you charge for tangible things, then you are in the *goods business.*
- If you charge for the activities you perform, then you are in the *service business.*
- If you charge for the time customers spend with you, then and only then are you in the *experience business.*

Citing a range of examples from Disney to AOL, they maintain that saleable experiences come in four varieties: entertainment, education, aesthetic, and escapist.

Columbia University's Bernd Schmitt underscores the importance of experiential marketing: "The degree to which a company is able to deliver a desirable customer experience—and to use information technology, brands, and integrated marketing communication and entertainment to do so—will largely determine its success in the global marketplace of the new millennium."[13]

Schmitt details five different types of experiences—sense, feel, think, act, and relate—that are becoming increasingly vital to consumers' perceptions of brands. He also describes how various "experience providers" (such as communications, visual/verbal identity and signage, product presence, co-branding, spatial environments, electronic media, and salespeople) can become part of a marketing campaign to create these experiences. In describing the increasingly more demanding consumer, Schmitt writes, "Customers want to be entertained, stimulated, emotionally affected and creatively challenged." Figure 5-2 lists Schmitt's 10 rules for successful experiential marketing. The Science of Branding 5-1 describes how some marketers are thinking more carefully about brand scents.

Large corporations are catching on to the experiential marketing trend.[14] In 2004, Bank of America used experiential marketing in introducing its brand to the Boston and

1. Experiences don't just happen; they need to be planned. In that planning process, be creative; use surprise, intrigue, and, at times, provocation. Shake things up.
2. Think about the customer experience first—and then about the functional features and benefits of your brand.
3. Be obsessive about the details of the experience. Traditional satisfaction models are missing the sensory, gut-feel, brain blasting, all-body, all-feeling, all-mind "EJ" experience. (EJ = *Exultate Jubilate*.) Let the customer delight in exultant jubilation!
4. Find the "duck" for your brand. More than five years ago, I stayed for the first time in the Conrad Hotel in Hong Kong. In the bathroom on the rim of the bathtub they had placed a bright yellow rubber duck with a red mouth. I fell in love with the idea (and the duck) immediately. It's the one thing that I always remember when I think about the hotel—and it becomes the starting point of remembering the entire hotel experience. Every company needs to have a duck for its brand. That is, a little element that triggers, frames, summarizes, stylizes the experience.
5. Think consumption situation, not product, e.g., "grooming in the bathroom" not "razor"; "casual meal" not "hot dog"; and "travel" not "transportation." Move along the sociocultural dimension.
6. Strive for "holistic experiences" that dazzle the senses, appeal to the heart, challenge the intellect, are relevant to people's lifestyles, and provide relational, i.e., social identity, appeal.
7. Profile and track experiential impact with the "Experiential Grid." Profile different types of experiences (Sense, Feel, Think, Act, and Relate) across experience providers (logos, ads, packaging, advertising, Web sites, etc.).
8. Use methodologies eclectically. Some methods may be quantitative (questionnaire analyses or logit); others qualitative (a day in the life of the customer). Some may be verbal (focus group); others visual (digital camera techniques). Some may be conducted in artificial lab settings; others in pubs or cafes. Anything goes! Be explorative and creative, and worry about reliability, validity, and methodological sophistication later.
9. Consider how the experience changes when extending the brand—into new categories, onto the Web, around the globe. Ask yourself how the brand could be leveraged in a new category, in an electronic medium, in a different culture through experiential strategies.
10. Add dynamism and "Dionysianism" to your company and brand. Most organization and brand owners are too timid, too slow, and too bureaucratic. The term "Dionysian" is associated with the ecstatic, the passionate, the creative. Let this spirit breathe in your organization, and watch how things change.

Source: Adapted with permission from Bernd H. Schmitt, *Experiential Marketing: How to Get Customers to Sense, Feel, Act, and Relate to Your Company and Brands* (New York: Free Press, 1999).

FIGURE 5-2

Guidelines for Experiential Marketing

THE SCIENCE OF BRANDING 5-1

Making Sense out of Brand Scents

The smell of a new car is distinctive. When Rolls-Royce customers complained in the 1990s that the new cars weren't as good as the old models, researched tracked the problem to a surprising source: the car's smell. The company then recreated the aroma of a 1965 Rolls and now sprays it in all the new models. So can scent be used to entice customers or to make a place a little more memorable?

Las Vegas casinos have long infused scents into gaming areas to encourage gamblers to stay a little longer. Now the connection between scent and shopping experience is being explored in more venues than ever. More and more companies looking for an edge are tinkering with scent as a way to distinguish their brand or store. The ever-growing barrage of advertising consumers take in is heavily weighted toward visuals. Although distinctive ring tones and other sounds are used to build brand awareness, most communication appeals to only one of the five human senses: sight.

Along with research institute Millward Brown, brand expert Martin Lindstrom conducted an international study to examine consumer reaction to color, smell, and taste. The study concluded that after sight, smell is the most important sense. In his analysis, Lindstrom found that 83 percent of all communication appeals to sight. Lindstrom maintains that all five senses are important to consider when building a brand. He urges companies to employ each of the five senses to amplify the company's recognition in the market. He says only 10 percent of the top 200 brands worldwide use all five senses.

In one test conducted as part of the study, identical pairs of Nike running shoes were placed in separate rooms. One room was infused with a pleasant floral scent and one wasn't. Test subjects preferred the Nikes in the scented room by a margin of 84 percent and even estimated the value of the shoes in the scented room to be higher than for the ones in the unscented room.

New York markets.[15] Roving brand ambassadors wearing Bank of America branded attire were part of a street-team marketing program to promote the bank and draw new checking account customers. In addition to promoting the bank's major league baseball sponsorship by engaging prospects in high-traffic locations with the opportunity to win World Series tickets, street teams also reinforced the advertising campaign message of "Higher Standards" in their personal interactions.

One-to-One Marketing. Don Peppers and Martha Rogers popularized the concept of ***one-to-one marketing.***[16] The basic rationale is that consumers help to add value by providing information to marketers; marketers add value, in turn, by taking that information and generating rewarding experiences for consumers. The firm is then able to create switching costs, reduce transaction costs, and maximize utility for consumers, all of which help to build strong, profitable relationships. One-to-one marketing is thus based on several fundamental strategies:

- Focus on individual consumers through consumer databases—"We single out consumers."
- Respond to consumer dialogue via interactivity—"The consumer talks to us."
- Customize products and services—"We make something unique for him or her."

On the heels of research like this, companies are looking to capitalize on scent as a way to lure customers into their stores and into lingering longer than they otherwise might. Victoria's Secret has long used vanilla scents in its stores, but now retailers like the Samsung Experience concept store are starting to get in on the action as a way to distinguish themselves from competitors. But experts caution that scents aren't guaranteed to boost sales. The best scents are unobtrusive. Anything overwhelming can be a negative. And smells should appeal to the same gender the product is trying to appeal to.

Westin Hotels carefully developed a new fragrance, White Tea, to infuse into the hotels' public spaces. The scent is designed to have international appeal and contribute to a subtle, relaxing vibe in the lobbies. Travelers also encounter a unique scent on Singapore Airlines through the scented towels handed out during all flights. The theory is that passengers will associate the subtle scent with a positive, relaxing experience.

Some brands have a built-in sensory marketing advantage. Crayola Crayons were not originally designed to have a signature scent, but the manufacturing process left them with a recognizable odor. Many adults connect the smell of Crayons with childhood, leaving Crayola with an incidental brand element that can be very valuable. When Crayola's parent company was recently considering ways to stand out among the generic competition in new markets, it decided to trademark the smell.

Sources: Martin Lindstrom, "Follow Your Nose to Marketing Evolution," *Advertising Age,* 23 May 2005; Linda Tischler, "Smells Like Brand Spirit," *Fast Company,* August 2005; Martin Lindstrom, "Smelling a Branding Opportunity," *Brandweek,* 14 March 2005; Lucas Conley, "Brand Sense," *Fast Company,* March 2005; Maureen Morrin and S. Ratneshwar, "Does It Make Sense to Use Scents to Enhance Brand Memory?" *Journal of Marketing Research* 40 (February 2003): 10–25.

Another tenet of one-to-one marketing is treating different consumers differently because of their different needs, and their different current and future value to the firm. In particular, Peppers and Rogers stress the importance of devoting more marketing effort to the most valuable consumers.

Peppers and Rogers identify several examples of brands that practice one-to-one marketing, such as Avon, Owens-Corning, Amway, and Nike.[17] They note how Ritz-Carlton hotels use databases to store consumer preferences, so that if a customer makes a special request in one of its hotels, it is already known when he or she stays in another. For example, if a customer requests "a glass of white wine with an ice cube" from room service while staying at the Ritz in San Francisco, room service at the Ritz in New York City would know to add an ice cube if the customer requested a glass of white wine there too.

Peppers and Rogers also provide an example of a localized version of one-to-one marketing. After having ordered flowers at a local florist for his or her mother, a customer might receive a postcard "reminding him that he had sent roses and star lilies last year and that a phone call would put a beautiful arrangement on her doorstep again for her birthday this year." Although such reminders can be helpful, marketers must not assume that customers always want to repeat their behaviors. For example, what if the flowers were a doomed, last-chance attempt to salvage a failing relationship—a reminder under such circumstances may not be so welcome! An example of a successful relationship marketing program comes from Tesco, the United Kingdom's largest grocer.[18]

Tesco has launched a highly successful loyalty program in the U.K.

TESCO

Launched in 1995, Tesco Clubcard is the world's most successful retail loyalty scheme. Each customer in the program has a unique "DNA profile" based on the products he or she buys. Products themselves are classified on up to 40 dimensions, such as package size, healthy, own label, eco-friendly, ready-to-eat, and so on, to faciltate this customer categorization. Based on the profile, customers receive their quarterly clubcard statement in one of literally 4 million different variations. Tracking customers purchases in the program helps to uncover price elasticities and set promotional schedules, resulting in savings to Tesco of over £300 million. The range of products, the nature of merchandising, and even the location of their convenience stores all benefit from the use of this customer data to develop tailored solutions.

Permission Marketing. ***Permission marketing,*** the practice of marketing to consumers only after gaining their express permission, is another tool with which companies can break through the clutter and build customer loyalty. A pioneer on the topic, Seth Godin, maintains that marketers can no longer employ "interruption marketing" or mass media campaigns featuring magazines, direct mail, billboards, radio and television commercials, and the like, because consumers have come to expect—but not necessarily appreciate—these interruptions.[19] By contrast, Godin asserts, consumers appreciate receiving marketing messages they gave permission for: "The worse the clutter gets, the more profitable your permission marketing efforts become."

Given the large number of marketing communications that bombard consumers every day, Godin argues that if marketers want to attract a consumer's attention, they first need to get his or her permission with some kind of inducement—a free sample, a sales promotion or discount, a contest, and so on. By eliciting consumer cooperation in this manner, marketers *might* develop stronger relationships with consumers so that they desire to receive further communications in the future. Those relationships will only develop, however, if marketers respect consumers' wishes, and if consumers express a willingness to become more involved with the brand.[20]

Permission marketing is capturing marketers' interest because of the powerful technology that now exists. With the help of large databases and advanced software, companies

1. Does every single marketing effort you create encourage a learning relationship with your customers? Does it invite customers to "raise their hands" and start communicating?
2. Do you have a permission database? Do you track the number of people who have given you permission to communicate with them?
3. If consumers gave you permission to talk to them, would you have anything to say? Have you developed a marketing curriculum to teach people about your products?
4. Once people become customers, do you work to deepen your permission to communicate with those people?

Source: Adapted with permission from Seth Godin, *Permission Marketing: Turning Strangers into Friends, and Friends into Customers* (New York: Simon & Schuster, 1999).

FIGURE 5-3

Four Tests for Permission Marketing

can store gigabytes of customer data and process this information in order to send targeted, personalized marketing messages to customers.

Godin identifies five steps to effective permission marketing:

1. Offer the prospect an incentive to volunteer.
2. Offer the interested prospect a curriculum over time, teaching the consumer about the product or service being marketed.
3. Reinforce the incentive to guarantee that the prospect maintains his or her permission.
4. Offer additional incentives to get more permission from the consumer.
5. Over time, leverage the permission to change consumer behavior toward profits.

Godin also offers four tests of permission marketing (see Figure 5-3). According to Godin, effective permission marketing works because it is "anticipated, personal, and relevant." For example, Columbia House—a classic permission marketer—sends its club members a monthly music selection, something the members anticipate and that is relevant to them. The selection is personal because it represents a category of music that the member has specified as a preference. If the member chooses not to keep the selection, he or she simply returns it. Amazon.com is a good example of permission marketing on the Web.

AMAZON.COM

With customer permission, Amazon uses database software to track its customers' purchase habits and send them personalized marketing messages. Each time a customer purchases something from Amazon.com, he or she can receive a follow-up e-mail containing information about other products that might interest him or her based on that purchase. For example, if a customer buys a book, Amazon might send an e-mail containing a list of titles by the same author, or of titles also purchased by customers who bought the original title. With just one click, the customer can get more detailed information. Amazon also sends periodic e-mails to customers informing them of new products, special offers, and sales. Each message is tailored to the individual customer based on past purchases and specified preferences, according to customer wishes. Amazon keeps an exhaustive list of past purchases for each customer and makes extensive recommendations.

Permission marketing is a way of developing the "consumer dialogue" component of one-to-one marketing in more detail. One drawback to permission marketing, however, is that it presumes that consumers know what they want to some extent. In many cases, consumers have undefined, ambiguous, or conflicting preferences that might be difficult for them to express. Thus, marketers must recognize that consumers may need to be given guidance and assistance in forming and conveying their preferences. In that regard, "participatory marketing" may be a more appropriate term and concept to employ, because marketers and consumers need to work together to find out how the firm can best satisfy consumer goals.[21]

Reconciling the New Marketing Approaches

These various new approaches to personlization and others help to reinforce a number of important marketing concepts and techniques. From a branding point of view, they are particularly useful means of both eliciting positive brand responses and creating brand resonance to build customer-based brand equity. One-to-one, permission, and experiential marketing are all potentially effective means of getting consumers more actively involved with a brand.

According to the CBBE model, however, the different approaches emphasize different aspects of brand equity. For example, one-to-one and permission marketing might be particularly effective at creating stronger behavioral loyalty and attitudinal attachment. Experiential marketing, on the other hand, would seem to be particularly effective at establishing brand imagery and tapping into a variety of different feelings as well as helping to build brand communities. Despite potentially different areas of emphasis, all three approaches can build stronger consumer–brand bonds.

Marketing strategies must transcend the actual product or service to create stronger bonds with consumers and maximize brand resonance. This broader set of activities is sometimes called ***relationship marketing***.[22] Relationship marketing attempts to provide a more holistic, personalized brand experience to create stronger consumer ties. It expands both the depth and the breadth of brand-building marketing programs. The new approaches to marketing we reviewed earlier are all relationship marketing activities.

One implication of these new approaches is that the traditional "marketing mix" concept and the notion of the "4 Ps" of marketing—product, price, place (or distribution), and promotion (or marketing communications)—may not fully describe modern marketing programs, or the many activities that do not necessarily fit neatly into one of those designations. Nevertheless, firms still have to make decisions about what exactly they are going to sell, how (and where) they are going to sell it, and at what price. In other words, firms must still devise product, pricing, and distribution strategies as part of their marketing programs. The specifics of how they set those strategies, however, have changed considerably. We turn next to these topics and some of the newer developments.

Product Strategy

The product itself is the primary influence on what consumers experience with a brand, what they hear about a brand from others, and what the firm can tell customers about the brand. In other words, at the heart of a great brand is invariably a great product.

Designing and delivering a product or service that fully satisfies consumer needs and wants is a prerequisite for successful marketing, regardless of whether the product is a tangible good, service, or organization. For brand loyalty to exist, consumers' experiences with the product must at least meet, if not actually surpass, their expectations.

This section considers two topics: how consumers form their opinions of the quality and value of a product, and how marketers can use the relationship marketing perspective in formulating product strategy and offerings.

Perceived Quality and Value

Perceived quality is customers' perception of the overall quality or superiority of a product or service compared to alternatives and with respect to its intended purpose. Achieving a satisfactory level of perceived quality has become more difficult as continual product improvements over the years have led to heightened consumer expectations.[23]

Much research has tried to understand how consumers form their opinions about quality. The specific attributes of product quality can vary from category to category. Nevertheless, consistent with the CBBE model from Chapter 2, research has identified the following general dimensions.[24]

- *Performance:* Levels at which the primary characteristics of the product operate (low, medium, high, or very high)
- *Features:* Secondary elements of a product that complement the primary characteristics
- *Conformance quality:* Degree to which the product meets specifications and is free of defects
- *Reliability:* Consistency of performance over time and from purchase to purchase
- *Durability:* Expected economic life of the product
- *Serviceability:* Ease of servicing the product
- *Style and design:* Appearance or feel of quality

Consumer beliefs about these characteristics often define quality and, in turn, influence attitudes and behavior toward a brand.

Brand Intangibles. Product quality depends not only on functional product performance but on broader performance considerations as well, like speed, accuracy, and care of product delivery and installation; the promptness, courtesy, and helpfulness of customer service and training; and the quality of repair service.

Brand attitudes may also depend on more abstract product imagery, such as the symbolism or personality reflected in the brand. These "augmented" aspects of a product are often crucial to its equity. Finally, consumer evaluations may not correspond to the perceived quality of the product and may be formed by less thoughtful decision making, such as simple heuristics and decision rules based on brand reputation or product characteristics such as color or scent.

Marketers thus must take a broad, holistic approach to building brand equity. Consistent with this observation, McKinsey Consulting has put forth an approach to marketing that it has dubbed ***3-D marketing***.[25] 3-D marketing emphasizes three product or service benefit dimensions:

1. *Functional benefits:* Product and performance attributes; value; quality
2. *Process benefits:* Ease of access to product information; broad product selection; simplified/ assisted decision making; convenient transactions; automatic product replenishment
3. *Relationship benefits:* Value based on personalized service; strong emotional relevance; information sharing that creates value exchange; differentiated loyalty rewards

McKinsey argues that whereas traditional marketing typically communicates functional benefits, in an increasingly crowded marketplace, marketers must employ experiential marketing tactics and differentiate their products or services by communicating benefits from among the other two dimensions: "By improving the fuller customer experience, companies can keep consumers happier and hold on to them longer."

Value Chain. Consumers often combine quality perceptions with cost perceptions to arrive at an assessment of the value of a product. Costs here are not restricted to the actual monetary price but may reflect opportunity costs of time, energy, and any psychological involvement in the decision that consumers might have.[26]

From a firm's perspective, it is therefore necessary to take a broad view of value creation. Harvard's Michael Porter has proposed the ***value chain*** as a strategic tool for identifying ways to create more customer value.[27] He views firms as a collection of activities that are performed to design, produce, market, deliver, and support products. The value chain identifies five primary value-creating activities (inbound logistics, operations, outbound logistics, marketing and sales, and service) and four support activities that occur throughout these primary activities (firm infrastructure, human resources management, technology development, and procurement). According to Porter, firms can achieve competitive advantages by improving performance and reducing costs in any or all of these value-creating activities. He also emphasizes the importance of effectively managing core business processes and cross-functional integration and cooperation.

Porter notes how firms can create competitive advantages by partnering with other members of the value chain (suppliers as well as distributors) to improve the performance of the customer value-delivery system. For example, Procter & Gamble works closely with retailers such as Wal-Mart to ensure that P&G brands can be quickly and efficiently distributed to stores. P&G created a well-staffed office in Bentonville, Arkansas—site of Wal-Mart's headquarters—to better coordinate these efforts. These activities are a means of creating strong, favorable, and unique brand associations that can serve as sources of brand equity.

Relationship Marketing

Relationship marketing is based on the premise that current customers are the key to long-term brand success.[28] Here are some of the benefits it provides:[29]

- Acquiring new customers can cost five times as much as satisfying and retaining current customers.
- The average company loses 10 percent of its customers each year.
- A 5 percent reduction in the customer defection rate can increase profits by 25 to 85 percent, depending on the industry.
- The customer profit rate tends to increase over the life of the retained customer.

Let's look at three important relationship marketing issues: mass customization, aftermarketing, and loyalty programs.

Mass Customization. The concept behind mass customization, namely, making products to fit the customer's exact specifications, is an old one, but the advent of digital-age technology enables companies to offer customized products on a previously unheard-of scale. Via the Internet, customers can communicate their preferences directly to the manufacturer, who, by using a sophisticated production line, can assemble the product for a price comparable to that of a noncustomized item. Dell Computers is now a classic example of the power of mass customization. Dell's built-to-order computers, sold directly by the company on the Internet or over the phone, helped make it the most successful computer manufacturer of the 1990s.

In an age defined by the pervasiveness of mass-market goods, mass customization enables consumers to distinguish themselves with even basic purchases. "Customization addresses the need for individuality," said an analyst with Fallon McElligott advertising. "We seek experiences and products that have our stamp, our seal as part of the look." For example, Nike enables customers to put their own personalized message on a pair of shoes with the NIKEiD program. At the NIKEiD Web site, visitors can make a customized shoe by selecting the size, width, and color scheme and affixing an eight-character personal ID to their creation. Land's End also allows customization of certain styles of pants and shirts on its Web site to allow for a better fit.

Mass customization can offer supply-side benefits too. Retailers can reduce inventory, saving warehouse space and the expense of keeping track of everything and discounting leftover merchandise.[30] Mass customization has its limitations, however, because not every product is easily customized and not every product demands customization. But even makers of expensive and production-intensive goods are looking for ways to employ mass customization. John Deere used complexity theory from mathematics to provide customized tractors for commercial farmers.[31]

Mass customization can be especially powerful when applied to Internet commerce.[32] From 10 to 15 percent of respondent samples reported themselves interested in customizing products online, ranging from greeting cards to consumer electronics, apparel, and jewelry.[33]

Mass customization is not restricted to products Many service organizations such as banks are developing customer-specific services and trying to improve the personal nature of their service experience with more service options, more customer-contact personnel, and longer service hours. In support of these activities, academic researchers Rust, Moorman, and Dickson provide evidence suggesting that to increase revenue, service firms should, on average, allocate *fewer* resources to traditional quality programs, productivity programs, and efficiency programs and allocate *more* to service-oriented initiatives such as customer satisfaction programs, customer retention and loyalty programs, customer relationship management (CRM) programs, and customer equity programs.[34]

Aftermarketing. To achieve the desired brand image, product strategies should focus on both purchase *and* consumption. Much marketing activity is devoted to finding ways to encourage trial and repeat purchases by consumers. Perhaps the strongest and potentially most favorable associations, however, result from actual product experience—what Procter & Gamble calls the "second moment of truth" (the first occurs at purchase).

Unfortunately, too little marketing attention is devoted to finding new ways for consumers to truly appreciate the advantages and capabilities of products. Perhaps in response to this oversight, one notable trend in marketing is the growing role of ***aftermarketing,*** that is, those marketing activities that occur after customer purchase. Innovative design, thorough testing, quality production, and effective communication—through mass customization or any other means—are without question the most important considerations in enhancing product consumption experiences that build brand equity. In many cases, however, they may only be necessary and not sufficient conditions for brand success, and marketers may need to use other means to enhance consumption experiences.

For example, instruction manuals for many products are too often an afterthought, put together by engineers who use overly technical terms and convoluted language.[35] As a result, consumers' initial product experiences may be frustrating or, even worse, unsuccessful. In many cases, even if consumers are able to figure out how to make the product perform its basic functions, they may not appreciate many more advanced features—highly desirable and potentially unique to the brand.

To enhance consumers' consumption experiences, marketers must develop user manuals that clearly and comprehensively describe both what the product can do for consumers and how consumers can realize these product benefits. With increasing globalization, writing easy-to-use instructions has become even more important because they often require translation into multiple languages.[36] Manufacturers are spending more time designing and testing instructions to make them as user friendly as possible.

1. Establishing and maintaining a customer information file (tracking all current, potential, inactive, and past customers)
2. "Blueprinting" customer contacts (identifying and characterizing points of interaction with customers in search of "moments of truth")
3. Analyzing customer feedback (explore the nature of satisfaction and dissatisfaction)
4. Conducting customer satisfaction surveys (to also signal interest in customer's reactions)
5. Formulating and managing communication programs (sending customers proprietary magazine or newsletters)
6. Hosting special customer events or programs (celebrating relationships with the brand)
7. Identifying and reclaiming lost customers (one of the best sources for new customers)

Source: Reprinted from Terry Vavra, *Aftermarketing: How to Keep Customers for Life through Relationship Marketing* (Chicago: Irwin Professional Publishers, 1995).

FIGURE 5-4

Seven Aftermarketing Activities

User manuals increasingly may need to appear in multimedia formats like DVDs or CDs to most effectively demonstrate product functions and benefits. Intuit, makers of the Quicken personal finance management software package, routinely sends researchers home with first-time buyers to check that its software is easy to install and to identify any sources of problems that might arise. Corel software adopts a similar "Follow Me Home" strategy and also has "pizza parties" at the company where marketing, engineering, and quality assurance teams analyze the market research together, so that marketing does not just hand down conclusions to other departments.[37]

Aftermarketing, however, is more than the design and communication of product instructions. As one expert in the area notes, "The term 'aftermarketing' describes a necessary new mind-set that reminds businesses of the importance of building a lasting relationship with customers, to extend their lifetimes. It also points to the crucial need to better balance the allocation of marketing funds between conquest activities (like advertising) and retention activities (like customer communication programs)."[38] Creating stronger ties with consumers can be as simple as creating a well-designed customer service department, easily accessible by a toll-free phone number or via the Web. Examples of seven specific activities to nurture loyalty and build relationships with customers are summarized in Figure 5-4.

Aftermarketing can include the sale of complementary products that help to make up a system or in any other way enhance the value of the core product. Printer manufacturers such as Hewlett-Packard derive much of their revenue from high-margin postpurchase items such as ink-jet cartridges, laser toner cartridges, and paper specially designed for PC printers. The average owner of a home PC printer spends much more on consumables over the lifetime of the machine than on the machine itself.[39]

Loyalty Programs. ***Loyalty*** or ***frequency programs*** have become one popular means by which marketers can create stronger ties to customers.[40] Their purpose is "identifying, maintaining, and increasing the yield from a firm's 'best' customers through long-term, interactive, value-added relationships."[41] Firms in all kinds of industries—most notably the airlines—have established loyalty programs through different mixtures of specialized services, newsletters, premiums, and incentives. Often these programs include extensive co-branding arrangements or brand alliances.

American Airlines

In 1981, American Airlines founded the first airline loyalty program, called AAdvantage. This frequent-flier program rewarded the airline's top customers with free trips and upgrades based on mileage flown. By recognizing customers for their patronage and giving them incentives to bring their business to American Airlines, the airline hoped to increase loyalty among its passengers. The program was an instant success, and other airlines quickly followed suit. These days, members can earn miles at more than 1,500 participating companies, which include over 35 hotel chains representing more than 75 brands, more than 20 airlines, eight car rental companies, and approximately 25 major retail/financial companies. In addition, members can earn miles when making purchases with one of more than 60 affinity card products in 30 countries. Today, more than 100 frequent-traveler programs exist, but American Airlines still has the largest, with membership of over 50 million by 2005.[42]

Many businesses besides airlines introduced loyalty programs in the intervening years. In 1991, American Express started its Membership Rewards program, which gives cardholders points based on the amount they charge. The points can be redeemed for a variety of items, including airline tickets, jewelry, and electronics. Also in 1991, Safeway, the third-largest grocer in the United States, started the Safeway Savings Club, which earned its members discounts on certain marked items in stores. Within a year of its debut, the Safeway Savings Club had 1.2 million members. Starwood Hotels launched an aggressive frequent guest program backed by a $50 million ad campaign in 1999.[43]

Loyalty programs have been adopted by a wide range of industries because they often yield results.[44] As one marketing executive said, "Loyalty programs reduce defection rates and increase retention. You can win more of a customer's purchasing share." The value created by the loyalty program creates switching costs for consumers, reducing price competition among brands. Some tips for building effective loyalty programs follow:[45]

- *Know your audience:* Most loyalty marketers employ sophisticated databases and software to determine which customer segment to target with a given program. Target customers whose purchasing behavior can be changed by the program.
- *Change is good:* Marketers must constantly update the program to attract new customers and prevent other companies in their category from developing "me-too" programs. "Any loyalty program that stays static will die," said one executive.
- *Listen to your best customers:* Suggestions and complaints from top customers deserve careful consideration, because they can lead to improvements in the program. Because they typically represent a large percentage of business, top customers must also receive better service and more attention.
- *Engage people:* Make customers want to join the program. Make the program easy to use and offer immediate rewards when customers sign up. Once they become members, make customers "feel special," for example, by sending them birthday greetings, special offers, or invitations to special events.

Summary

The product is at the heart of brand equity. Marketers must design, manufacture, market, sell, deliver, and service products in a way that creates a positive brand image with strong, favorable, and unique brand associations; elicits favorable judgments and feelings about the brand; and fosters greater degrees of brand resonance. Product strategy entails choosing both tangible and intangible benefits the product will embody, and marketing activities that consumers desire and the marketing program can deliver. A range of possible associations can become linked to the brand—some functional and performance-related, and some abstract and imagery-related. Perceived quality and perceived value are particularly important brand associations that often drive consumer decisions.

Because of the importance of loyal customers, relationship marketing has become a branding priority. Consequently, consumers' actual product experiences and aftermarketing activities have taken on increased importance in building customer-based brand equity. Those marketers who will be most successful at building CBBE will take the necessary steps to make sure they fully understand their customers and how they can deliver superior value before, during, and after purchase.

Pricing Strategy

Price is the one revenue-generating element of the traditional marketing mix, and price premiums are among the most important brand equity benefits of building a strong brand. This section considers the different kinds of price perceptions that consumers might form, and different pricing strategies that the firm might adopt to build brand equity.

Consumer Price Perceptions

The pricing strategy can dictate how consumers categorize the price of the brand (as low, medium, or high), and how firm or how flexible they think the price is, based on how deeply or how frequently it is discounted.

Consumers often rank brands according to price tiers in a category.[46] For example, Figure 5-5 shows the price tiers that resulted from a study of the ice cream market.[47] In that market, as the figure shows, there is also a relationship between price and quality. Within any price tier, there is a range of acceptable prices, called ***price bands,*** that indicate the flexibility and breadth marketers can adopt in pricing their brands within a tier. Some companies sell multiple brands to better compete in multiple categories. Figure 5-6 displays clothing offerings from Phillips Van Huesen that cover a wide range of prices and corresponding retail outlets.[48]

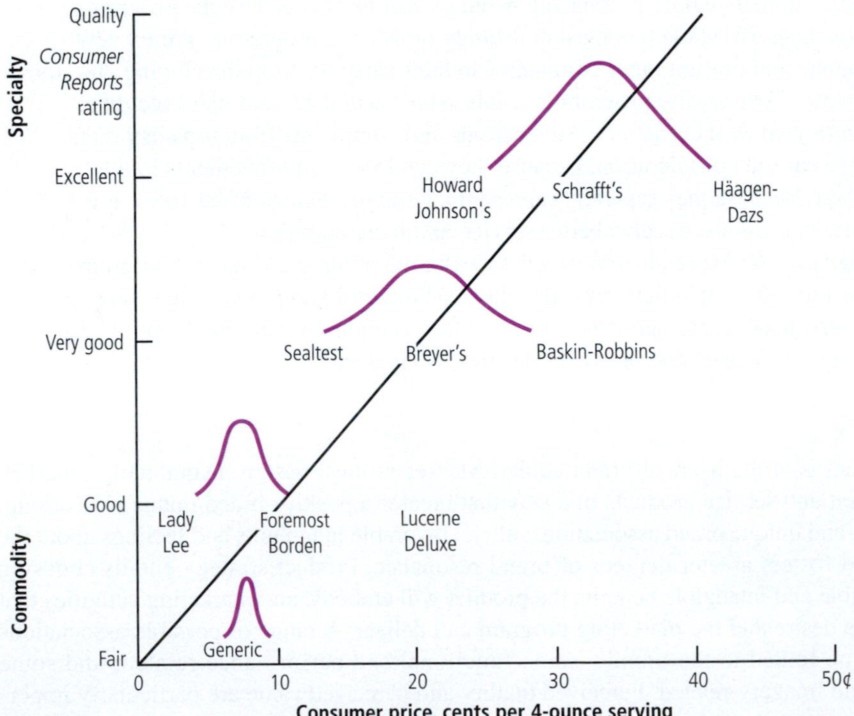

FIGURE 5-5

Price Tiers in the Ice Cream Market

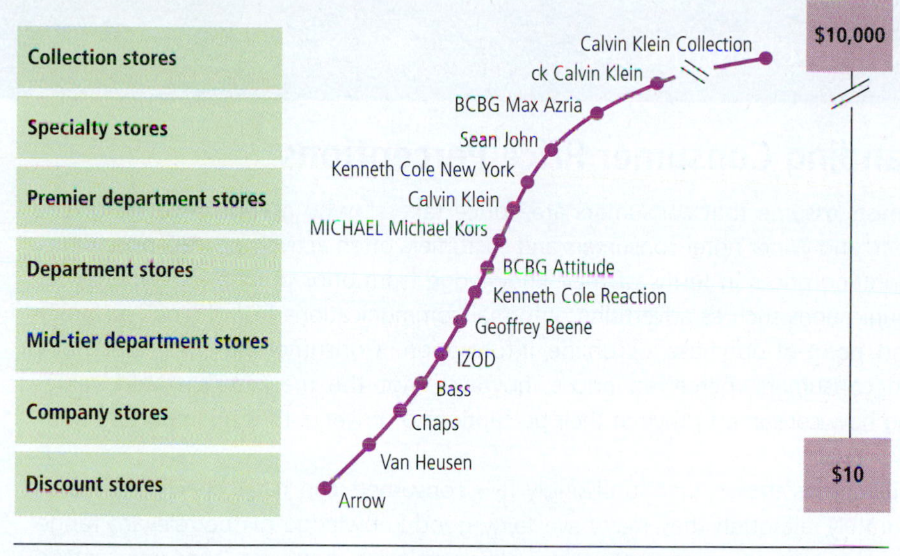

FIGURE 5-6

Phillips Van-Heusen Brand Price Tiers

Besides these descriptive "mean and variance" price perceptions, consumers may have price perceptions that have more inherent product meaning. In particular, in many categories, they may infer the quality of a product on the basis of its price and use perceived quality and price to arrive at an assessment of perceived value. Consumer associations of perceived value are often an important factor in purchase decisions. Thus many marketers have adopted ***value-based pricing strategies***—attempting to sell the right product at the right price—to better meet consumer wishes, as described in the next section.

Consumers' perceptions of value should obviously exceed the cost to the company of making and selling the product. As Chapter 2 pointed out, consumers are willing to pay a premium for certain brands based on tangible or intangible considerations. For example, at one time, Hitachi and General Electric (GE) jointly owned a factory in England that made identical televisions for the two companies. The only difference was the brand name on the television. Nevertheless, the Hitachi televisions sold for a $75 premium over the GE televisions. Moreover, Hitachi sold twice as many sets as GE despite the higher price.[49]

In short, price has complex meaning and can play multiple roles to consumers. The Science of Branding 5-2 provides insight into how consumers perceive and process prices as part of their shopping behavior. Marketers need to understand all price perceptions that consumers have for a brand, to uncover quality and value inferences, and to discover any price premiums that exist.

Setting Prices to Build Brand Equity

Choosing a pricing strategy to build brand equity means determining the following:

- A method for setting current prices
- A policy for choosing the depth and duration of promotions and discounts

There are many different approaches to setting prices, and the choice depends on a number of considerations. This section highlights a few of the most important issues as they relate to brand equity.[50]

THE SCIENCE OF BRANDING 5-2

Understanding Consumer Price Perceptions

Many economists assume that consumers are "price takers" who accept prices as given. However, as Ofir and Winer note, consumers and customers often actively process price information, interpreting prices in terms of their knowledge from prior purchasing experience, formal communications such as advertising, informal communications from friends or family members, and point-of-purchase or online information. Consumer purchase decisions are based on consumers' perceived prices, however, not the marketer's stated value. Understanding how consumers arrive at their perceptions of prices is thus an important marketing priority.

Much research has shown that surprisingly few consumers can recall specific prices of products accurately, although they may have fairly good knowledge of the relevant range of prices. When examining or considering an observed price, however, consumers often compare it with internal frames of reference (prices they remember) or external frames of reference (a posted "regular retail price"). Internal reference prices occur in many forms, such as the following:

- "Fair price" (what product should cost)
- Typical price
- Last price paid
- Upper-bound price (most consumer would pay)
- Lower-bound price (least consumer would pay)
- Competitive prices
- Expected future price
- Usual discounted price

When consumers evoke one or more of these frames of reference, their perceived price can vary from the stated price. Most research on reference prices has found that "unpleasant surprises," such as a stated price higher than the perceived price, have a greater impact on purchase likelihood than pleasant surprises.

Factors related to the costs of making and selling products and the relative prices of competitive products are important determinants in pricing strategy. Increasingly, however, firms are placing greater importance on consumer perceptions and preferences. Many firms now are employing a value-pricing approach to setting prices, and an everyday-low-pricing (EDLP) approach to determining their discount pricing policy over time. Let's look at both.

Value Pricing The objective of ***value pricing*** is to uncover the right blend of product quality, product costs, and product prices that fully satisfies the needs and wants of consumers and the profit targets of the firm. Marketers have employed value pricing in various ways for years. Its increasing popularity as a pricing strategy, however, is a result of an increased level of competition among brands and more demanding customers. With a debt-burdened and cost-conscious consumer base, many firms have met with resistance to higher prices—often for the first time in their history.[51] They have learned the hard way that consumers will not pay price premiums that exceed their perceptions of the value of

Consumer perceptions of prices are also affected by alternative pricing strategies. For example, research has shown that a relatively expensive item can seem less expensive if the price is broken down into smaller units (a $500 annual membership seems pricier than "less than $50 a month"). One reason prices often end with the number nine (as in, say, $49.99) is that consumers process prices in a left-to-right manner rather than holistically or by rounding. This effect is more pronounced when competing products' prices are numercially and psychologically closer together.

Even the competitive environment has been shown to affect consumer price judgments: Deep discounts (like everyday low pricing or EDLP) can lead to lower perceived prices over time than frequent, shallow discounts (high-low pricing), even if the average prices are the same in both cases.

Clearly, consumer perceptions of price are complex and depend on the pricing context involved.

Sources: Chezy Ofir and Russell S. Winer, "Pricing: Economic and Behavioral Models," in *Handbook of Marketing,* eds. Bart Weitz and Robin Wensley (New York: Sage Publications, 2002): 5–86; Peter R. Dickson and Alan G. Sawyer, "The Price Knowledge and Search of Supermarket Shoppers," *Journal of Marketing* (July 1990): 42–53; Gurumurthy Kalyanaram and Russell S. Winer, "Empirical Generalizations from Reference Price Research," *Marketing Science* (Fall 1995): 161–169; John T. Gourville, "Pennies-a-Day: The Effect of Temporal Reframing on Transaction Evaluation," *Journal of Consumer Research* (March 1998): 395–408; Mark Stiving and Russell S. Winer, "An Empirical Analysis of Price Endings with Scanner Data," *Journal of Consumer Research* (June 1997): 57–68; Joseph W. Alba, Carl F. Mela, Terence A. Shimp, and Joel E. Urbany, "The Effect of Discount Frequency and Depth on Consumer Price Judgments," *Journal of Consumer Research* (September 1999): 99–114; Manoj Thomas and Vicki Morwitz, "Penny Wise and Pound Foolish: The Left-Digit Effect in Price Cognition," *Journal of Consumer Research* 26 (June 2005): 54–64; Eric Anderson and Duncan Simester, "Mind Your Pricing Cues," *Harvard Business Review* 81, no. 9 (September 2003): 96–103; Tridib Mazumdar, S. P. Raj, and Indrajit Sinha, "Reference Price Research: Review and Propositions," *Journal of Marketing* 69 (October 2005), pp. 84–102.

a brand. Perhaps the most vivid illustration was the price cut for Philip Morris's leading cigarette brand, Marlboro, described in Branding Brief 5-1.[52]

Two important lessons emerged from the Marlboro episode. First, strong brands can command price premiums. Once Marlboro's price entered a more acceptable range, consumers were willing to pay the still-higher price, and sales of the brand started to increase. Second, strong brands cannot command an excessive price premium. The clear signal sent to marketers everywhere by Philip Morris's experience with Marlboro is that price hikes without corresponding investments in the value of the brand may increase the vulnerability of the brand to lower-priced competition. In these cases, consumers may be willing to "trade down" because they no longer can justify to themselves that the higher-priced brand is worth it. Although the Marlboro price discounts led to short-term profitability declines, they also led to regained market share that put the brand on a stronger footing over the longer haul.

In this challenging new climate, several firms have been successful by adopting a value-pricing strategy. For example, Wal-Mart's slogan, "We Sell for Less," describes the pricing strategy that has allowed it to become the world's largest retailer. Southwest

BRANDING BRIEF 5-1

Marlboro's Price Drop

On April 2, 1993, or "Marlboro Friday," Philip Morris dropped a bombshell in the form of a three-page announcement: "Philip Morris USA. . . announced a major shift in business strategy designed to increase market share and grow long-term profitability in a highly price sensitive market environment." Quoting tobacco unit president and CEO William I. Campbell, the statement continued, "We have determined that in the current market environment caused by prolonged economic softness and depressed consumer confidence, we should take those steps necessary to grow our market share rather than pursue rapid income growth rates that might erode our leading marketplace position."

Philip Morris announced four major steps, the fourth of which caught the eye of marketers and Wall Street alike: A major promotional cut in the price of Marlboro (roughly 40 to 50 cents a pack), which was expected to decrease earnings in Philip Morris's most profitable unit by 40 percent. The action was justified by the results of a month-long test in Portland, Oregon, the previous December in which a 40-cent decrease in pack price had increased market share by 4 points.

The stock market reaction to the announcement was swift. By day's end, Philip Morris's stock price had declined from $64.12 to $49.37, a 23 percent drop that represented a one-day loss of $13 billion in shareholder equity! There was a ripple effect in the stock market, with significant stock price declines for other consumer goods companies with major brands like Sara Lee, Kellogg's, General Mills, and Procter & Gamble. A company that took one of the biggest hits was Coca-Cola, whose shareholders lost $5 billion in paper earnings in the days following "Black Friday."

Airlines combined low fares with no-frills—but friendly—service to become a powerful force in the airline industry. Taco Bell reduced operating costs enough to lower prices for many items on the menu to under $1, sparking an industry-wide trend in fast foods. The success of these and other firms has dramatized the potential benefits of implementing a value-pricing strategy. Another recent convert is General Motors, although it faces a tougher test.

General Motors

GM launched its employee-pricing plan in June 2005 to clear out inventories of 2005 vehicles ahead of the new model year. The promotion was a wild success, racking up huge sales gains in the summer months. At the time, GM executives said the plan's simplicity—everyone got the same low price that company employees received—would help the automaker shift to a new pricing strategy aimed at switching consumers' focus to vehicle values instead of the size of the discounts. Although the plan was extended beyond the summer, the auto maker announced in September a transition toward "Total Value Promise" pricing, under which GM would try to offer prices on 2006 models that, in comparison with its traditional prices, would be closer to what GM believed were the prices customers actually paid once incentives were included. The prices, however, generally would be higher than the employee prices being advertised. One GM executive noted that employee pricing was never meant to be a long-term

A number of factors probably led Marlboro to cut prices so dramatically. The economy certainly was still sluggish, coming out of a recession. Private label or store brand cigarettes had been increasing in quality and were receiving more attention from customers and retailers.

A prime consideration suggested by many was related to Philip Morris's hefty price increases. These had often occurred two to three times a year, so that the retail price of a pack of Marlboros more than tripled between 1980 and 1992. The 80 cents to $1 difference between premium brands and discount brands that prevailed at that time was thought to have resulted in steady sales increases for the discount brands at the expense of Marlboro's market share, which had dropped to 22 percent and was projected to decline further to 18 percent if Philip Morris made no changes.

Although much of the popular press attempted to exploit Marlboro's actions to proclaim that "brands were dead," nothing could have been further from the truth. In fact, a more accurate interpretation of the whole episode is that it showed that new brands were entering the scene, as evidenced by the ability of discount brands to create their own brand equity on the basis of strong consumer associations to "value."

At the same time, existing brands, if properly managed, can command loyalty, enjoy price premiums, and still be extremely profitable. By cutting the difference between discount cigarettes and Marlboro to roughly 40 cents, Philip Morris was able to woo back many customers. Within nine months after the price drop, its market share increased to almost 27 percent, eventually rising to almost 30 percent.

Sources: Laura Zinn, "The Smoke Clears at Marlboro," *Business Week,* 31 January 1994, 76–77; Al Silk and Bruce Isaacson, "Philip Morris: Marlboro Friday (A)," Harvard Business School Case 9-596-001.

promotion. "Like any promotion, it has a life span," he said. "But what we learned is: The customer is smart. They recognize a really good value when they see one and they really appreciate transparent prices." Some industry analysts, however, felt it would be difficult for GM to wean consumers off employee pricing.[53]

As might be expected, there are a number of opinions regarding the keys for success in adopting a value-based pricing approach. In general, an effective value-pricing strategy should strike the proper balance among the following:

- Product design and delivery
- Product costs
- Product prices

In other words, as we've seen before, the right kind of product has to be made the right way and sold at the right price. Next we look at each of these three elements. The Science of Branding 5-3 describes an eight-step process for making better pricing decisions.

PRODUCT DESIGN AND DELIVERY. The first key is the proper design and delivery of the product. Product value can be enhanced through many types of well-conceived and well-executed marketing programs, such as those covered in this and other chapters of the

THE SCIENCE OF BRANDING 5-3

Eight Steps to Better Pricing

Robert J. Dolan, a well-known academic pricing expert, describes pricing as "managers' biggest marketing headache." To relieve this headache, Dolan recommends that managers focus on the process of pricing rather than the results. He suggests that managers can make improvements to the pricing process by following these eight steps:

1. ***Assess what value your customers place on a product or service.*** Rather than basing pricing decisions on product cost, companies should determine the product's value to the customer.
2. ***Look for variation in the way customers value the product.*** Customers often vary in how and why they use the product, leading different customers to value the product differently. Companies can customize prices to take advantage of these different values.
3. ***Assess customers' price sensitivity.*** Companies should determine the price elasticity (percent change in quantity sold given a 1 percent change in price) for its products in three areas: customer economics, customer search and usage, and the competitive situation.
4. ***Identify an optimal pricing structure.*** Rather than a fixed price, companies can decide to offer discounts based on quantity purchased or use bundle pricing to sell a combination of products. The different pricing structures can be analyzed to determine the optimal one.
5. ***Consider competitors' reactions.*** In order to avoid costly price wars, companies must consider the long-term effects of price decisions in terms of the competition.
6. ***Monitor prices realized at the transaction level.*** Though a product may have a single list price, it may have many possible final prices due to discounts and rebates. Additionally, the real net revenue from a product is affected by factors such as customer returns and damage claims. The real price of a product must account for these elements.
7. ***Assess customers' emotional response.*** A customer's emotional response to a price can have long-term effects that outweigh the short-term economic impact of a sale.
8. ***Analyze whether the returns are worth the cost to serve.*** High cost-to-serve customers do not necessarily pay high prices, just as customers who spend little do not always receive low-cost service. Where possible, companies should aim to get customers to spend in accordance with the cost of serving them.

Source: Robert J. Dolan, "How Do You Know When the Price Is Right?" *Harvard Business Review* (September–October 1995) Translated and reprinted by permission of *Harvard Business Review*.

book. Proponents of value pricing point out that the concept does not mean selling stripped-down versions of products at lower prices. Consumers are willing to pay premiums when they perceive added value in products and services. Branding Brief 5-2 describes how Louis Vuitton Moet Hennessey (LVMH) is able to command luxury prices.

Some companies actually have been able to *increase* prices by introducing new or improved "value-added" products. Some marketers have coupled product innovations and improvements with higher prices that strike an acceptable balance to at least some market segments. Examples of such additions range from new flavors and bottle designs for iced teas to newly designed toothbrushes with special features such as rippled bristles and handles with tiny shock absorbers to lavishly packaged facial tissues with aroma and lotion.

When Gillette introduced the Mach3 in 1998, it priced the cartridges at a 50 percent premium over its then-priciest blade, SensorExcel, despite the prevailing deflationary climate. The price increase did not deter customers, and Gillette reached its highest market share, 71 percent, since 1962. The major Mach3 extension, M3 Power, was launched in 2004 with similar premium pricing, and quickly achieved market leadership in many countries. Many products have been able to combine product improvements that provide consumers greater convenience with higher prices. For example, Hefty One-Zip sandwich, freezer, and food-storage bags, featuring more convenient "sliding tab" technology, were able to command a 15 percent premium over the older "tongue in groove" technology.[54]

With the advent of the Internet, many critics predicted that customers' ability to perform extensive, assisted online searches would result in only low-cost providers surviving. In reality the advantages of creating strong brand differentiation have led to price premiums when brands are sold online just as much as when sold off-line. For example, although undersold by numerous book and music sellers online, Amazon.com was able to maintain market leadership, eventually forcing low-priced competitors such as Books.com and others out of business.[55]

PRODUCT COSTS. The second key to a successful value-pricing strategy is to lower costs as much as possible. Meeting cost targets invariably requires finding additional cost savings through productivity gains, outsourcing, material substitution (less expensive or less wasteful materials), product reformulations, and process changes like automation or other factory improvements.[56] As one marketing executive put it:

> The customer is only going to pay you for what he perceives as real value-added. When you look at your overhead, you've got to ask yourself if the customer is really willing to pay for that. If the answer is no, you've got to figure out how to get rid of it or you're not going to make money.[57]

By investing in efficient manufacturing technology, Sara Lee was able to maintain adequate margins for years on its L'eggs women's hosiery with minimal price increases. The combination of low prices and the strong L'eggs brand image resulted in an almost 50 percent market share.[58] At the same time, cost reductions cannot sacrifice quality, effectiveness, or efficiency.

SEARS

When Sears downsized its apparel buyers by 30 percent after it acquired Land's End, the remaining personnel lacked the necessary merchandising experience with Sears stores. Overcompensating for the fact that they had ordered too much for the spring season during 2003, they underordered for 2004. As a result, Sears stores found themselves with the wrong merchandise at the wrong time. While other retailers reported vibrant apparel sales gains after the spring selling season, Sears reported an unexpected modest sales decline.[59]

BRANDING BRIEF 5-2

Selling Luxury at Louis Vuitton Moet Hennessey

Luxury leather goods maker Louis Vuitton was established in Paris in 1855. For more than a century and a half, the company made quality hand-crafted luggage and other leather goods. It remained a small, family-controlled company until the 1970s, when French businessman Henry Racamier married a Vuitton heiress and rapidly expanded and diversified the business. When Racamier took over in 1977, the company had only two shops in France and had combined sales of less than $50 million. By the mid-1980s, the company had 95 stores across the globe and reached revenues topping $500 million.

In 1987, the merger of Louis Vuitton with famed French spirits, champagne, and perfume group Moet-Hennessey marked a new era of consolidation in the luxury-goods industry. The newly formed Louis Vuitton Moet Hennessey (LVMH) instantly became the world's largest luxury-goods company, raking in $4 billion in revenues in 1991. The company's more notable brands included Christian Dior, Givenchy, Moet & Chandon, and Dom Perignon. The company continued to grow in the 1990s by acquiring a number of other luxury-goods companies, including fashion label Christian Lacroix and shoe designer Berluti in 1993, TAG Heuer watchmaker in 1999, and the Donna Karan brand in 2000. Today, LVMH has a portfolio of 60 luxury brands and is the number one worldwide seller of champagne, cognac, and fashion and leather goods, and the number three worldwide seller of perfumes and cosmetics. The company's revenues topped $13.5 billion in 2003.

LVMH has consistently pursued a luxury pricing strategy, which means high markups, limited availability, and few if any markdowns. Louis Vuitton sells its products only through a global network of company-owned stores. This keeps margins high and allows the company to

PRODUCT PRICES. The final key to a successful value-pricing strategy is to understand exactly how much value consumers perceive in the brand and thus to what extent they will pay a premium over product costs.[60] A number of techniques are available to estimate these consumer value perceptions. Perhaps the most straightforward approach is to directly ask consumers their perceptions of price and value in different ways.

The price suggested by estimating perceived value can often be a starting point for marketers in determining actual marketplace prices, adjusting by cost and competitive considerations as necessary. For example, to halt a precipitous slide in market share for its flagship 9-Lives brand, the pet products division of H.J. Heinz took a new tack in its pricing strategy. The company found from research that consumers wanted to be able to buy cat food at the price of "four cans for a dollar," despite the fact that its cat food cost between 29 and 35 cents per can. As a result, Heinz reshaped its product packaging and redesigned its manufacturing processes to be able to hit the necessary cost, price, and margin targets. Despite lower prices, profits for the brand doubled. Consumer-driven pricing strategies can thus lead to better marketing solutions.

Premium Ice Cream

Facing rising costs for raw ingredients like cream, cocoa, and vanilla, premium ice cream manufacturers found a subtle way to raise prices. Makers of brands such as Friendly's, Edy's,

maintain control of its products through every step in the channel. Bernard Arnault explained, "If you control your factory, you control your quality; if you control your distribution, you control your image." Today, LVMH maintains a global network of 1,286 stores, a 28 percent increase over 1999. Its 284 Louis Vuitton stores and 461 Sephora locations comprise over half the stores in this network.

Because maintaining an upscale image is vital to a luxury brand, LVMH devotes over 10 percent of annual sales to promotion and advertising. The company advertises its brands primarily in fashion and lifestyle publications. Some of the leading brands sponsor major international events with luxury cachet, as Louis Vuitton does by sponsoring the America's Cup. Because image is an essential part of marketing luxury goods, LVMH is careful to evaluate every advertising and promotional opportunity for consistency with the image of its brands. As a result, the company manages a portfolio of luxury brands unparalleled in both size and sales.

But managing a portfolio of luxury brands with a slowing global economy can be challenging. In recent years, LVMH found itself placing more attention on its highly profitable Vuitton brand (especially in Japan) and other top brands, such as Celine women's wear, Pucci fashion, Ruinart champagne, and Zenith watches, that were seen to have the most potential, and selling others, such as the Lacroix couture fashion house, that were struggling.

Sources: William Echikson, "Luxury Steals Back," *Fortune,* 16 January 1995; Lisa Marsh, "LVMH Thinks of Vuitton Globally, Acts on 5 Ave," *New York Post,* 5 December 2000; Joshua Levine, "Liberté, Fraternité—But to Hell with Égalité!" *Forbes,* 2 June 1997; Janet Guyon, "The Magic Touch," *Fortune,* 6 September 2004, 229–236; Alessandra Galloni, "Its Closets Full, LVMH Decides to Return to Basics," *Wall Street Journal,* 8 October 2004, A1, A10.

and Turkey Hill quietly shrank the size of their popular 64-ounce half-gallon containers by 8 ounces (about 2 servings) but kept the price steady, resulting in a per-ounce price about 14 percent higher than before. The rationale for the move was that consumers paid far more attention to prices than to weights, and at least some diet-oriented consumers preferred smaller quantities anyway. The new packages were the same height and width as the old packages (just thinner), making it harder for consumers to detect differences on the shelves. Concerns that consumers would feel cheated, however, caused some manufacturers to hold the line on their package sizes.[61]

SUMMARY. From a brand equity perspective, consumers must find the price of the brand appropriate and reasonable given the benefits they feel they receive. There is always tension between lowering prices on the one hand and increasing consumer perceptions of product quality on the other hand. Academic researchers Lehmann and Winer believe that although marketers commonly use price reductions to improve perceived value, in reality discounts are often a more expensive way to add value than brand-building marketing activities.[62] Their argument is that the lost revenue from a lower margin on each item sold is often much greater than the additional cost of value-added activities, primarily because many of these costs are fixed and spread over *all* the units sold, as opposed to the per unit reductions that result from lower prices.

At the same time, different consumers may have different value perceptions and therefore could—and most likely should—receive different prices. Price segmentation sets and adjusts prices for appropriate market segments. In part because of wider adoption of the Internet, firms are increasingly employing yield management principles, such as those adopted by airlines to vary their prices for different market segments according to their different demand and value perceptions.[63]

ALLSTATE

Allstate Insurance embarked on a yield management pricing program, looking at drivers' credit history, demographic profile, and other factors to better match automobile policy premiums to customer risk profiles. From three main pricing categories, the company moved to 1,500 electronically generated price levels. "Safe bets" now pay up to 20 percent less than they did under the old system; high-risk drivers are penalized, however, and pay up to 20 percent more. The new pricing system, plus a drop in number of claims filed, helped to drive operating income 16 percent higher in 2004 to $3.1 billion.[64]

Everyday Low Pricing. ***Everyday low pricing (EDLP)*** has received increased attention as a means of determining price discounts and promotions over time. EDLP avoids the sawtooth, whiplash pattern of alternating price increases and decreases or discounts in favor of a more consistent set of "everyday" base prices on products. In many cases, these EDLP prices are based on the value-pricing considerations we've noted above.

In the early 1990s, Procter & Gamble made a well-publicized conversion to EDLP (see Branding Brief 5-3). By reducing list prices on half its brands and eliminating many temporary discounts, P&G reported that it saved $175 million in 1991, or 10 percent of its previous year's profits. Advocates of EDLP argue that maintaining consistently low prices on major items every day helps build brand loyalty, fend off private label inroads, and reduce manufacturing and inventory costs.[65]

Even strict adherents of EDLP, however, see the need for some types of price discounts over time. Well-conceived, timely sales promotions can provide important financial incentives to consumers and induce sales. As part of revenue-management systems or yield-management systems, many firms have been using sophisticated models and software to determine the optimal schedule for markdowns and discounts.[66]

Why then do firms seek greater price stability? Manufacturers can be hurt by an overreliance on trade and consumer promotions and the resulting fluctuations in prices for several reasons.

It has been well documented that trade discounts rose considerably in past years in both breadth and depth. For example, the percentage of the total marketing communications expenditures devoted to trade promotions increased dramatically in the last several decades, from one-third to almost one-half the budget total, and the extent of the average price discount, previously 4 percent, rose to between 10 and 15 percent.

Unfortunately, these trade promotion dollars are not always passed along as savings to consumers.[67] For example, although trade promotions are only supposed to result in discounts on products for a certain length of time and in a certain geographic region, that is not always the case. With ***forward buying,*** retailers order more product than they plan to sell during the promotional period so that they can later obtain a bigger margin by selling the remaining goods at the regular price after the promotional period has expired. With ***diverting,*** retailers pass along or sell the discounted products to retailers outside the designated selling area.

Although these practices may seem to provide some financial benefits to the retailer, critics argue that they can produce a false economy. Often overlooked are the extra expenses of additional warehouse facilities, shipping costs, and overhead costs. In justifying its switch to EDLP, Procter & Gamble argued that only 30 percent of its trade promotion dollars actually reached consumers in the form of lower prices—35 percent was thought to be lost in the form of higher retailer costs, while another 35 percent was thought to be taken as direct profits by the retailers. By reducing both the number of trade discounts and wholesale list prices, P&G attempted to leave retailers in approximately the same net profitability position but to restore the price integrity of its brands in the process.

From the manufacturer's perspective, these retailer practices created production complications: Factories had to run overtime because of excess demand during the promotion period but had slack capacity when the promotion period ended, costing manufacturers millions. On top of it all, on the demand side, many marketers felt that the see-saw of high and low prices on products actually trained consumers to wait to buy the brand until it was discounted or on special, thus eroding its perceived value. Creating a brand association to "discount" or "don't pay full price" diminished brand equity.

Summary

To build brand equity, marketers must determine strategies for setting prices and adjusting them, if at all, over the short and long run. Increasingly, these decisions will reflect consumer perceptions of value. The benefits delivered by the product and its relative advantages with respect to competitive offerings, among other factors, will determine what consumers see as a fair price. Value pricing strikes a balance among product design, product costs, and product prices. Everyday low pricing is a complementary pricing approach to determine the nature of price discounts and promotions over time that maintains consistently low, value-based prices on major items on a day-to-day basis.

Channel Strategy

The manner by which a product is sold or distributed can have a profound impact on the resulting equity and ultimate sales success of a brand. ***Marketing channels*** are defined as "sets of interdependent organizations involved in the process of making a product or service available for use or consumption."[68] Channel strategy includes the design and management of intermediaries such as wholesalers, distributors, brokers, and retailers. Let's look at how channel strategy can contribute to brand equity.[69]

Channel Design

A number of possible channel types and arrangements exist, broadly classified into direct and indirect channels. ***Direct channels*** mean selling through personal contacts from the company to prospective customers by mail, phone, electronic means, in-person visits, and so forth. ***Indirect channels*** sell through third-party intermediaries such as agents or broker representatives, wholesalers or distributors, and retailers or dealers.

Increasingly, winning channel strategies will be those that can develop "integrated shopping experiences" that combine physical stores, Internet, telephone, and catalogs. For example, consider the wide variety of direct and indirect channels by which Nike sells its shoes, apparel, and equipment products:

- *Retail:* Nike products are sold in retail locations such as shoe stores, sporting goods stores, department stores, and clothing stores.
- *Branded Nike Town stores:* Nike Town stores, located in prime shopping avenues in metropolitan centers around the globe, offer a complete range of Nike products and serve as showcases for the latest fashions.

BRANDING BRIEF 5-3

Procter & Gamble Launches EDLP Value Pricing

In 1991, Procter & Gamble shifted from a discount- and promotion-driven pricing strategy to an everyday-low-pricing (EDLP) strategy. There were a number of problems with the old pricing system. First, many retailers didn't pass the discounts on to customers. Some retailers engaged in forward buying and diverting tactics—stocking up on huge quantities and selling them after the discount expired or in regions that were not even "on deal." Second, consumers became conditioned to buying brands only when they were discounted or on special. Even worse, consumers were looking to private label substitutes to obtain even lower prices. In order to stimulate sales, the frequency and depth of discounts kept increasing until at one point, 17 percent of all products sold by P&G, on average, were on deal. Escalating discounts and deals with the trade created cost whiplashes, and the company was making 55 daily prices on 80 or so brands, which necessitated reworking every third order.

P&G's solution to these problems was to implement its EDLP value-pricing strategy, although it faced several challenges in making the strategy successful. First, P&G could not deliver everyday low prices without incurring everyday costs. To reduce costs, the company cut overhead according to four simple guidelines: Change the work, do more with less, eliminate work, and reduce costs that cannot be passed on to consumers. P&G simplified the distribution chain to make restocking more efficient through continuous product replenishment. The company also scaled back its product portfolio by eliminating 25 percent of its stock-keeping units.

Over the course of about six years, P&G reduced its coupon expenditures by over 50 percent and trade promotions by 20 percent. With its EDLP policy, list prices were reduced by 12 to 24

- *Niketown.com:* Nike's e-commerce site allows consumers to place Internet orders for a range of products.
- *Catalog retailers:* Nike's products appear in numerous shoe, sporting goods, and clothing catalogs.
- *Outlet stores:* Outlet stores feature discounted Nike merchandise.
- *Specialty stores:* Nike equipment from product lines such as Nike Golf and Nike Hockey is often sold through specialty stores such as golf pro shops or hockey equipment suppliers.

Much research has considered the pros and cons of selling through various channels. Although the decision ultimately depends on the relative profitability of the different options, some more specific guidelines have been proposed. For example, one study for industrial products suggests that direct channels may be preferable when the following are true:[70]

- Product information needs are high.
- Product customization is high.
- Product quality assurance is important.
- Purchase lot size is important.
- Logistics are important.

On the other hand, this study suggests that indirect channels may be preferable when

percent on nearly all its U.S. brands. In their place, P&G put greater emphasis on brand-building advertising and marketing communications (increasing it by 20 percent). P&G also spent more than ever on research and development (over $1 billion in 1994) and halved the time to market for new products on a global basis. Moreover, P&G also improved its relationships with retailers and was rated in a national survey of retailers as the consumer goods company most helpful in making retailers more efficient.

What were the results? One award-winning academic study suggested that overall P&G's market share decreased 16 percent. The revenue from higher prices was somewhat offset by the increased cost of heavier advertising. According to the authors, the cuts in sales promotions decreased trial and penetration, as would be expected, but did not necessarily translate into greater behavioral loyalty from customers. When P&G encountered some difficulties in the late 1990s, it altered its value-pricing strategy in some segments and reinstated selected price promotions.

Sources: Alecia Swasy, "In a Fast-Paced World, Procter & Gamble Sets Its Store in Old Values," *Wall Street Journal,* 21 September 1989, A1; Zachary Schiller, "The Marketing Revolution at Procter & Gamble," *Business Week,* 25 July 1988, 72; Bill Saporito, "Behind the Tumult at P&G," *Fortune,* 7 March 1994, 74–82; Zachary Schiller, "Procter & Gamble Hits Back," *Business Week,* 19 July 1993, 20–22; Zachary Schiller, "Ed Artzt's Elbow Grease Has P&G Shining," *Business Week,* 10 October 1994, 84–86; Zachary Schiller, "Make It Simple," *Business Week,* 9 September 1996, 96–104; "Executive Update: Value Pricing Plan Helps Push Products," *Investor's Business Daily,* 30 August 1995. For an interesting analysis, see Kusum L. Ailawadi, Donald R. Lehmann, and Scott A. Neslin, "Market Response to a Major Policy Change in the Marketing Mix: Learning from P&G's Value Pricing Strategy," *Journal of Marketing* 65, no. 1 (2001): 71–89.

- A broad assortment is essential.
- Availability is critical.
- After-sales service is important.

Exceptions to these generalities exist, especially depending on the market segments involved.

It is rare that a manufacturer will use only a single type of channel. More likely, the firm will choose a hybrid channel design with multiple channel types.[71] Marketers must manage these channels carefully, as Tupperware found out.[72]

Tupperware has had to carefully consider how to expand its distribution beyond its classic living room selling parties.

Tupperware

In the 1950s Tupperware pioneered the plastic food storage container business and the means by which the containers were sold. With many mothers staying at home and growth in the suburbs exploding, Tupperware parties with a local neighborhood host became a successful avenue for selling. Unfortunately, with more women entering the workforce and heightened competition from brands such as Rubbermaid, Tupperware experienced a 15-year decline in sales to close out the twentieth century. Sales only turned around with some new approaches to selling, including booths at shopping malls and a move to the Internet. The decision to place products in all 1,148 Target stores, however, was a complete disaster. In-store selling was difficult given the very different retail environment. Moreover, because the product was made more widely available, interest in the in-home parties plummeted. Frustrated, many salespeople dropped out and fewer new ones were recruited. Although the products were yanked from the stores, the damage was done and profit plunged almost 50 percent in 2003. As one key distributor commented, "We just bit off more than we could chew."

The risk in designing a hybrid channel system is having too many channels (leading to conflict among channel members or a lack of support), or too few channels (resulting in market opportunities being overlooked). The goal is to maximize channel coverage and effectiveness while minimizing channel cost and conflict. John Deere, famed for its tractors as well as residential and commercial use products such as mowers, ATVs, and saws, was able to expand beyond its mainly rural network of more than 2,500 dealers and gain access to an additional 100,000 customers by beginning to sell through Home Depot. In doing so, Deere avoided conflict by assigning dealers to handle the service for purchases made from the mass channel, ensuring that the dealers gained immediate revenue and an opportunity for future sales.[73]

Because marketers use both direct and indirect channels, let's consider the brand equity implications of the two major channel design types.

Indirect Channels

Indirect channels can consist of a number of different types of intermediaries, but we will concentrate on retailers. Retailers tend to have the most visible and direct contact with customers and therefore have the greatest opportunity to affect brand equity. Consumers may have associations to any one retailer on the basis of product assortment, pricing and credit policy, and quality of service, among other factors. Through the products and brands they stock and the means by which they sell, retailers strive to create their own brand equity by establishing awareness and strong, favorable, and unique associations.

At the same time, retailers can have a profound influence on the equity of the brands they sell, especially in terms of the brand-related services they can support or help to create. Moreover, the interplay between a store's image and the brand images of the products it sells is an important one. Consumers make assumptions such as "this store only sells good-quality, high-value merchandise, so this particular product must also be good quality and high value."

Push and Pull Strategies. Beside the indirect avenue of image transfer, retailers can directly affect the equity of the brands they sell. Their methods of stocking, displaying, and selling products can enhance or detract from brand equity, suggesting that manufacturers must take an active role in helping retailers add value to their brands.

Yet, at the same time, a battle has emerged in recent years between manufacturers and retailers making up their channels of distribution. Because of greater competition for shelf space among what many retailers feel are increasingly undifferentiated brands, retailers have gained in power and are now in a better position to set the terms of trade with manufacturers. Increased power means that retailers can command more frequent and lucrative trade promotions.

Increasingly, supermarket retailers are demanding compensation to stock a new brand, in the form of cash payments for the shelf space itself (slotting allowances), introductory deals ("one free with three"), postponed billing or extended credit (dating), and payment for retailer advertising or promotion in support of the new brand.[74] Even after stocking the brands, retailers can later require generous trade promotions to keep them on the shelf. Outside the supermarket, department stores are requiring that suppliers guarantee their stores' profit margin and insist on cash rebates if the guarantee is not met.[75] For all these reasons, manufacturers are vulnerable to retailers' actions.

Retailers have thus increased their power over manufacturers. One way for manufacturers to regain some of their lost power is by creating strong brands through some of the brand-building tactics described in this book, for example, by selling innovative and unique products—properly priced and advertised—that consumers demand. In this way, consumers may ask or even pressure retailers to stock and promote manufacturers' products. By devoting marketing efforts to the end consumer, a manufacturer is said to employ a ***pull strategy***, since consumers use their buying power and influence on retailers to "pull" the product through the channel. Alternatively, marketers can devote their selling efforts to the channel members themselves, providing direct incentives for them to stock and sell products to the end consumer. This approach is called a ***push strategy,*** because the manufacturer is attempting to reach the consumer by "pushing" the product through each step of the distribution chain.

Although certain brands seem to emphasize one strategy more than another (push strategies are usually associated with more selective distribution, and pull strategies with broader, more intensive distribution), the most successful branding programs often skillfully blend push and pull strategies. For example, when Goodyear Tire & Rubber introduced its Aquatred tire, an all-season radial designed to provide better traction on wet roads, it was priced 10 percent higher than Goodyear's previous top-of-the-line mass-market tire. Nevertheless, Goodyear was able to sell 2 million Aquatreds in the first two years of its introduction by combining strong merchandising support to tire dealers and a persuasive advertising campaign directed to consumers.[76]

Channel Support. A number of different services provided by channel members can enhance the value to consumers of purchasing and consuming a brand name product (see Figure 5-7). Although firms are increasingly providing some of the services themselves through toll-free numbers and Web sites, establishing a "marketing partnership" with retailers may nevertheless be critical to ensuring proper channel support and the execution of these various services. Two such partnership strategies are retail segmentation activities and cooperative advertising programs.

Marketing research	Gathering information necessary for planning and facilitating interactions with customers
Communications	Developing and executing communications about the product and service
Contact	Seeking out and interacting with prospective customers
Matching	Shaping and fitting the product/service to the customer's requirements
Negotiations	Reaching final agreement on price and other terms of trade
Physical distribution	Transporting and storing goods (inventory)
Financing	Providing credit or funds to facilitate the transaction
Risk-taking	Assuming risks associated with getting the product or service from firm to customer
Service	Developing and executing ongoing relationships with customers, including maintenance and repair

Source: Reprinted from Donald Lehmann and Russell Winer, *Product Management* (Burr Ridge, IL: Irwin, 1994).

FIGURE 5-7

Services Provided by Channel Members

Retail Segmentation. Retailers are "customers" too. Because of their different marketing capabilities and needs, retailers may need to be divided into segments or even treated individually so they will provide the necessary brand support.[77] Consider how the following packaged goods companies have customized their marketing efforts to particular retailers:[78]

- Frito-Lay developed a tailored supply chain system for its corn chip and potato chip markets, enabling fast and broad distribution, fewer stock-outs, and better-turning store displays for its various retail customers.
- SC Johnson has leveraged customized market research insights to develop unique category management solutions to its strategic retail customers.
- Scotts Miracle-Gro customizes its product lines, marketing events, and supply chain for "big box," club, and hardware co-op channels.

Different retailers may need different product mixes, special delivery systems, customized promotions, or even their own branded version of the products.

For example, Shugan refers to ***branded variants*** as branded items in a diverse set of durable and semidurable goods categories that are not directly comparable to other items carrying the same brand name.[79] Manufacturers create branded variants in many ways, including making changes in color, design, flavor, options, style, stain, motif, features, and layout. For example, portable stereos from brands like Sony, Panasonic, and Toshiba come in a broad assortment of variants, varying in speaker size, total weight, number of audio controls, recording features, and SKU number. Branded variants are a means to reduce retail price competition because they make direct price comparisons by consumers difficult. Thus, different retailers may be given different items or models of the same brand to sell. Shugan and his colleagues show that as the manufacturer of a product offers more branded variants, a greater number of retail stores carry the product, and these stores offer higher levels of retail service for these products.[80]

Cooperative Advertising. One relatively neglected means of increasing channel support is well-designed cooperative advertising programs. Traditionally, in co-op advertising, a manufacturer pays for a portion of the advertising that a retailer runs to promote the manufacturer's product and its availability in the retailer's place of business.To be eligible to receive co-op funds, the retailer usually must follow the manufacturer's stipulations as to the nature of brand exposure in the ad. Manufacturers generally share the cost of the advertising on a percentage basis (usually 50–50), up to a certain limit. The total amount of cooperative advertising funds the manufacturer provides to the retailer is usually based on a percentage of dollar purchases made by the retailer from the manufacturer.[81]

The rationale behind cooperative advertising for manufacturers is that it concentrates some of the communication efforts at a local level where they may have more relevance and selling impact with consumers. Unfortunately, the brand image communicated through co-op ads is not as tightly controlled as when the manufacturer runs its own ads, and there is a danger that the emphasis in a co-op ad may be on the store or on a particular sale it is running rather than on the brand. Perhaps even worse, there is also a danger that a co-op ad may communicate a message about the brand that runs counter to its desired image.

Some manufacturers are attempting to gain better control over their cooperative advertising by providing greater assistance to retailers. For example, Goodrich created an image ad for its tires that could be recut to plug various local dealerships at the same time. Rubbermaid has collaborated with big retailers such as Wal-Mart and Home Depot to find ad approaches that achieve the best of both worlds—allowing Rubbermaid to create more awareness and loyalty for its brand while creating sales momentum for the retailer in the same ad.[82]

An ideal situation is to achieve synergy between the manufacturer's own ad campaigns for a brand and its corresponding co-op ad campaigns with retailers. The challenge in designing effective co-op ads will continue to be striking a balance between pushing the brand and the store at the same time. In that sense, cooperative advertising will have to live up to its name, and manufacturers will have to get involved in the design and execution of retailers' campaigns rather than just handing over money or supplying generic, uninspired ads.

Summary. In eliciting channel support, manufacturers must be creative in the way they develop marketing and merchandising programs aimed at the trade or any other channel members. They should consider how channel activity can encourage trial purchase and communicate or demonstrate product information, to build brand awareness and image and to elicit positive brand responses.

Direct Channels

For some of the reasons we've already noted, manufacturers may choose to sell directly to consumers. Let's examine some of the brand equity issues of selling through direct channels.

Company-Owned Stores. To gain control over the selling process and build stronger relationships with customers, some manufacturers are introducing their own retail outlets, as well as selling their product directly to customers through various means. These channels can take many forms, the most involved of which, from a manufacturer's perspective, is company-owned stores. Hallmark, Goodyear, and others have sold their own products in their own stores for years. Recently, a number of firms—including some of the biggest marketers around—have set up their own stores:

- In December 1994, after the Federal Trade Commission amended a 16-year ban on the jeans maker selling its own wares, Levi Strauss began to open up Original Levi's Stores in the United States and abroad, located mostly in downtown areas and upscale suburban malls.[83]
- Nike Town stores stock essentially all the products Nike sells. Each store consists of a number of individual shops or pavilions that feature shoes, clothes, and equipment for a different sport (tennis, jogging, biking, or water sports) or different lines within a sport (there might be three basketball shops and two tennis shops). Each shop develops its own concepts with lights, music, temperature, and multimedia displays.

A number of other brands have created their own stores, such as Bang & Olufsen audio equipment, OshKosh B'Gosh children's wear, and Warner Bros. entertainment. Even Dr. Martens—best known for its thick-soled lace-up boots—opened a five-story 13,957-square-foot store in London, trying to transform the brand into a lifestyle brand.

Company stores provide many benefits.[84] Primarily, they are a means to showcase the brand and all its different product varieties in a manner not easily achieved through normal retail channels. For example, Nike might find its products spread all through department stores and athletic specialty stores. These products may not be displayed in a logical, coordinated fashion, and certain product lines may not even be stocked. By opening its own stores, Nike can effectively put its best foot forward by showing the depth, breadth, and variety of its branded products. These stores can provide the added benefit of functioning as a test market to gauge consumer response to alternative product designs, presentations, and prices, allowing firms to keep their fingers on the pulse of consumers' shopping habits.

A disadvantage of company stores is that some companies lack either the skills, resources, or contacts to operate effectively as a retailer. For example, The Disney Store, started in 1987, sold exclusive Disney branded merchandise, ranging from toys and videos to collectibles and clothing, priced from $3 to $3,000. Disney viewed the stores as an extension of the "Disney experience," referring to customers as "guests" and employees as "cast members," just as it did in its theme parks. The company struggled, however, to find the right retail formula, and after experiencing slumping sales, the chain of stores in Japan and later North America were sold to The Children's Place.

Another issue with company stores, of course, is potential conflict with existing retail channels and distributors. In many cases, however, company stores can be a means of bolstering brand image and building brand equity rather than as direct sales devices. For example, Nike views its stores as essentially advertisements and tourist attractions. The company reports that research studies have confirmed that Nike Town stores enhanced the Nike brand image by presenting the full scope of its sports and fitness lines to customers and "educating them" on the value, quality, and benefits of Nike products. The research also revealed that although only about 25 percent of visitors actually made a purchase at a Nike Town store, 40 percent of those who did not buy during their visit eventually purchased Nike products from some other retailer.

These manufacturer-owned stores can also be seen as a means of hedging bets with retailers who continue to push their own labels. With one of its main suppliers, JCPenney, pushing its own Arizona brand of jeans, Levi's can protect its brand franchise to some extent by establishing its own distribution channel. Nevertheless, many retailers and manufacturers are dancing around the turf issue, avoiding head-on clashes in establishing competitive distribution channels. Manufacturers in particular have been careful to stress that their stores are not a competitive threat to their retailers but rather "showcases" that can help sell merchandise for any retailer carrying their brand.[85] Branding Brief 5-4 describes some of Goodyear's channel conflict issues.

Other Means. Besides creating their own stores, some marketers—such as Nike, Polo, and Levi Strauss (with Dockers)—are attempting to create their own shops within major department stores. Procter & Gamble has created informational and promotional electronic kiosks for Oil of Olay; and Diageo, seller of Smirnoff vodka and Bell's whiskey, has created in-house drink zones in Sainsbury and Tesco in the United Kingdom. These approaches can offer the dual benefits of appeasing retailers—and perhaps even benefiting from the retailer's brand image—while at the same time allowing the firm to retain control over the design and implementation of the product presentation at the point of purchase.

Finally, another channel option is to sell directly to consumers via phone, mail, or electronic means. Retailers have sold their goods through catalogs for years. Many mass marketers, especially those that also sell through their own retail stores, are increasingly using direct selling, a long-successful strategy for brands such as Mary Kay and Avon. These vehicles not only help to sell products but also contribute to brand equity by increasing consumer awareness of the range of products associated with a brand and increasing consumer understanding of the key benefits of those products. Marketers can execute direct marketing efforts in many ways such as catalogs, videos, or physical sites, all of which are opportunities to engage in a dialogue and establish a relationship with consumers.

Web Strategies

One lesson from the dot-com boom and bust is the advantage of having both a physical "brick and mortar" channel and a virtual, online retail channel. In some cases, consumers are ordering from companies online and picking up the physical products at their local

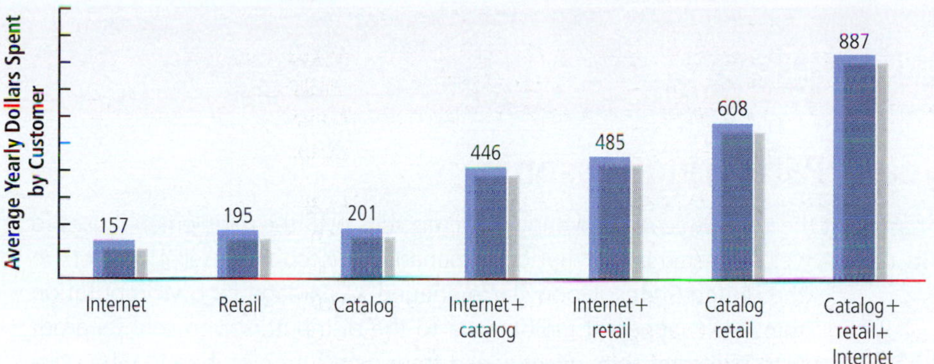

Source: Customer Value Analysis, Doubleclick (2004). Courtesy of Abacus Direct, LLC.

FIGURE 5-8

JCPenney Customer Channel Value Analysis

store rather than having it shipped.[86] The Boston Consulting Group concluded that multichannel retailers were able to acquire customers at half the cost of Internet-only retailers, citing a number of advantages for the multichannel retailers:[87]

- They have market clout with suppliers.
- They have established distribution and fulfillment systems (L.L. Bean and Land's End).
- They can cross-sell between Web sites and stores (The Gap and Barnes & Noble).

Many of these same advantages are realized by multichannel product manufacturers. Recognizing the power of integrated channels, many Internet-based companies are engaging in "physical world" activities to boost their brand. For example, Yahoo! opened a promotional store in New York's Rockefeller Center, and eTrade.com opened a flagship own-brand financial center on New York's Madison Avenue as well as mini-centers and kiosks in Target stores. Integrated channels allow consumers to shop when and how they want. For example, one research study suggested that nearly 50 percent of the most sophisticated shoppers found items they wanted online but purchased them in stores.[88] Figure 5-8 shows an analysis of JC Penney's channel mix, which reveals that its most profitable customers were those that shopped multiple channels.

Summary

Channels are the means by which firms distribute their products to consumers. Channel strategy to build brand equity includes designing and managing direct and indirect channels to build brand awareness and improve the brand image. Direct channels can enhance brand equity by allowing consumers to better understand the depth, breadth, and variety of the products associated with the brand as well as any distinguishing characteristics. Indirect channels can influence brand equity through the actions and support of intermediaries such as retailers, and the transfer of any associations that these intermediaries might have to the brand.

Direct and indirect channels offer varying advantages and disadvantages that marketers must thoughtfully combine, both to sell products in the short run, and maintain and enhance brand equity in the long run. As is often the case with branding, the key is to mix and match channel options so that they collectively realize these goals. Thus, it is important to assess each possible channel option in terms of its direct effect on product sales and brand equity, as well as its indirect effect through interactions with other channel options.

BRANDING BRIEF 5-4

Goodyear's Partnering Lessons

Goodyear has spent the last few years recovering from missteps with the middlemen it uses to distribute its tires. A well-respected brand that once managed the top tire reseller network in the United States, Goodyear managed to damage its own reputation through its apparent indifference to the distributors who sold its products. The company's prices varied from month to month, and when distributors would order tires, often only 50 percent of their order would be filled. Distributors nationwide said it was just getting hard to do business with Goodyear and many began hawking other brands instead.

Goodyear has learned many lessons in how to manage its channels.

Goodyear earned dealer loyalty in the 1970s and '80s through competitive pricing, on-time deliveries, and very visible marketing in the form of the Goodyear blimp. In 1992, Goodyear announced a distribution deal with Sears, even though the company had previously promised dealers that it would not sell tires through discount retailers. Then it made similar deals with Wal-Mart and Sam's Club. To increase sales, the company began to offer the big retailers bulk discounts. As a result, smaller individually owned dealers had to pay as much for their tires as customers could pay at other retailers.

Shortly after Firestone had to recall 6.5 million tires in 2000, Goodyear dealers—instead of taking advantage of its competitor's legal and image problems—annoyed many of its distributors. Goodyear dealership owners complained of pressure to buy more tires than they needed, uneven pricing, and poor quality.

Review

Marketing activities and programs are the primary means that firms build brand equity. Brand-building product, pricing, channel, and communication strategies must be put into place. In terms of product strategies, both tangible and intangible aspects of the brand will matter. Successful brands often create strong, favorable, and unique brand associations to both functional and symbolic benefits. Although perceived quality is often at the heart of brand equity, there is a wide range of associations that consumers may make to the brand.

Relationship marketing includes marketing activities that deepen and broaden the way consumers think and act toward the brand. Experiential, one-to-one, and permission marketing are all means of getting consumers more actively involved with the product or service. Mass customization, aftermarketing, and loyalty programs are also ways to help create holistic, personalized buying experiences.

In terms of pricing strategies, marketers should fully understand consumer perceptions of value. Increasingly, firms are adopting value-based pricing strategies to set prices and everyday-low-pricing strategies to guide their discount pricing policy over time. Value-based pricing strategies attempt to properly balance product design and delivery,

Goodyear has 5,300 authorized dealers, about the same number it has had since 1994. While overall U.S. tire sales have grown, Goodyear's replacement tire sales have slumped 14 percent. That represents a loss of about $550 million in sales.

Experts say there are a few things manufacturers can do to keep distributors happy and prevent breaks in the supply chain. Resellers often sink significant amounts of money into maintaining their facilities and paying sales staffs. To compensate them, manufacturers can offer dealers exclusive access to new products. Goodyear followed this advice in trying to win back its dealers. It originally sold its popular Assurance tires exclusively through authorized dealers.

Experts also advise that manufacturers stick to fixed prices when they offer products directly to consumers. If they do offer big discounts, they should offer them at outlet malls, where they won't confuse customers. And manufacturers can back up distributors by educating them about the products so the retail partners can shape an effective sales force. When makeup giant Mary Kay began selling its cosmetics online in 1997, it also helped the members of its direct sales force set up their own online stores. Sharing product information and also doing good advertising contributes to distributors' success. Ultimately, companies have to share the power to make decisions with their distributors and recognize that dealers' success benefits them too. In the tire business, dealers have captured more and more of the retail tire sales market, and so manufacturers must keep them happy and profitable if they want the benefits of a smooth supply chain.

Sources: Kevin Kelleher, "Giving Dealers a Raw Deal," *Business 2.0,* December 2004; Nirmalya Kumar, "Living with Channel Conflict," *CMO Magazine,* October 2004.

product costs, and product prices. Everyday-low-pricing strategies establish a stable set of "everyday" prices and introduce price discounts very selectively.

In terms of channel strategies, marketers need to appropriately match brand and store images to maximize the leverage of secondary associations; integrate push strategies for retailers with pull strategies for consumers; and consider a range of direct and indirect distribution options.

In the next chapter we consider how to develop integrated marketing communication programs to build brand equity.

Discussion Questions

1. Have you had any experience with a brand that has done a great job with relationship marketing, permission marketing, experiential marketing, or one-to-one marketing? What did the brand do? Why was it effective? Could others learn from that?
2. Think about the products you own. Assess their product design. Critique their aftermarketing efforts. Are you aware of all of the products' capabilities?

Identify a product whose benefits you feel you are not fully capitalizing on. How might you suggest improvements?

3. Choose a product category. Profile all the brands in the category in terms of pricing strategies and perceived value. If possible, review the brands' pricing histories. Have these brands set and adjusted prices properly? What would you do differently?
4. Take a trip to a department store. Evaluate the in-store marketing effort. Which categories or brands seem to be receiving the biggest in-store push? What unique in-store merchandising efforts do you see?
5. Take a trip to a supermarket. Observe the extent of private label brands. In which categories do you think private labels might be successful? Why?

BRAND FOCUS 5.0

Private Label Strategies and Responses

This appendix considers the issue of private labels or store brands. After portraying private label branding strategies, it describes how major manufacturers' brands have responded to their threat.

Private Labels

Although different terms and definitions are possible, ***private labels*** can be defined as products marketed by retailers and other members of the distribution chain. Private labels can be called ***store brands*** when they actually adopt the name of the store itself in some way (e.g., Safeway Select). Private labels should not be confused with ***generics,*** whose simple black and white packaging typically provides no information as to who made the product.

Private label brands typically cost less to make and sell than the national or manufacturer brands with which they compete. Thus, the appeal to consumers of buying private labels and store brands often is the cost savings involved; the appeal to retailers of selling private labels and store brands is that their gross margin is often 25 percent to 30 percent—nearly twice that of national brands.

The history of private labels is one of many ups and downs. The first private label grocery products in the United States were sold by the Great Atlantic and Pacific Tea Company (later known as A&P), which was founded in 1863. During the first half of the twentieth century, a number of store brands were successfully introduced. Under competitive pressure from the sophisticated mass marketing practices adopted by large packaged-goods companies in the 1950s, private labels fell out of favor with consumers.

Because the appeal of private labels to consumers has traditionally been their lower cost, the sales of private labels generally have been highly correlated with personal disposable income. The recession of the 1970s saw the successful introduction of low-cost, basic-quality, and minimally packaged generic products that appealed to bargain-seeking consumers. During the subsequent economic upswing, though, the lack of perceived quality eventually hampered sales of generics, and many consumers returned to national or manufacturers' brands.

To better compete in today's marketplace, private label makers have begun improving quality and expanding the variety of their private label offerings to include premium products. In recognition of the power of bold graphics, supermarket retailers have been careful to design attractive, upscale packages for their own premium branded products. Because of these and other actions, private label sales have recently made some major inroads in new markets. Retailers value private labels for their profit margins and their means of differentation to drive customer loyalty. Retailer Target has introduced a steady stream of exclusives, such as with their stylish Mossimo and Isaac Mizrahi apparel brands.[89]

Private Label Status

In the United States, private label goods have accounted for roughly 16 percent of total supermarket dollar volume. In other countries, these percentages are often quite higher. For example, Western Europe dominates the market for private labels in the supermarket, with the biggest being Switzerland at 45 percent, Germany at 30 percent, Spain at 26 percent, and Belgium at 25 percent.[90]

Private labels in the United Kingdom make up over a third of sales at grocery stores, in part because the grocery industry is more concentrated there. The five largest grocery chains make up almost two-thirds of sales in the United Kingdom (but only two-fifths of sales in the United States). Two of the large U.K. grocery chains are Tesco and Sainsbury.

- Tesco, with the brand slogan "Every Little Helps," has a number of its own private label brands, ranging from Value to Finest, and has its own lifestyle brands, such as Organic, Free Form, and Healthy Living, positioned as "Making Life Taste Better."
- Sainsbury has used its name to introduce 500 lines across fruit, vegetables, grocery, and household products. Sainsbury's own brand products are categorized into one of three quality tiers; for example, the lasagne range is comprised of the Basics sub-brand for "good," the core own label line for "better," and the premium Taste the Difference line for "best." Clothing and housewares were added to Sainsbury's own brand product ranges in late 2004.

Private label appeal is widespread. In supermarkets, private label sales have always been strong in product categories such as dairy goods, vegetables, and beverages. More recently, private labels have been successful in previously "untouchable" categories such as cigarettes, disposable diapers, and cold remedies. One study indicated that although the 17 percent of households who shop primarily on the basis of price and are classified as "heavy" private label buyers account for 42 percent of total private label sales, nearly one-third of all consumers now regularly buy some private label goods. Sixty-eight percent of consumers interviewed by ACNielsen either slightly or strongly agreed with the statement: "Private label brands are a good alternative to other brands."[91]

Nevertheless, some categories have not seen a strong private label presence. Many shoppers, for example, still seem unwilling to trust their hair, complexion, or dental care to store brands. Private labels also have been relatively unsuccessful in categories such as cookies, candy, cereal, pet foods, baby food, and beer.

One implication that can be drawn from this pattern of product purchases is that consumers are being more selective in what they buy, no longer choosing to buy only national brands. For less important products in particular, consumers seem to feel "that top-of-the-line is unnecessary and good is good enough."[92] Categories that are particularly vulnerable to private label advances are those in which there is little perceived quality differences among brands in the eyes of a sizable group of consumers, for example, over-the-counter pain relievers, bottled water, plastic bags, paper towels, and dairy products.

Private Label Branding Strategy

Although the growth of private labels has been interpreted by some as a sign of the decline of brands, the opposite conclusion may in fact be more valid: Private label growth could be seen in some ways as a consequence of cleverly designed branding strategies. In terms of building brand equity, the key point of difference for private labels in consumers' eyes has always been "good value," a desirable and transferable association across many product categories. As a result, private labels can be extremely broad, and their name can be applied across many diverse products.

As with national brands, implementing a value-pricing strategy for private labels requires determining the right price and product offering. For example, one reported rule of thumb is that the typical "no-name" product has to sell for at least 15 percent less than a national brand, on average, to be successful. The challenge for private labels has been to determine the appropriate product offering.

Specifically, to achieve the necessary points of parity, or even to create their own points of difference, private labels have been improving quality, and as a result are now aggressively positioning against even national brands. *Consumer Reports'* analysis of 65 store brand and national brand products in six categories—facial tissues, paper towels, plastic bags, canned peaches, french fries, and yogurt—revealed that many store brands were at least as good as national brands and consumers could cut their costs by as much as half by switching to a store brand.[93]

Many supermarket chains have introduced their own premium store brands, such as Safeway Select, Von's Royal Request, and Ralph's Private Selection. For example, A&P positioned their premium Master Choice brand to fill the void between the mass-market national brands and the upscale specialty brands that they sell. They have used the brand across a wide range of products, such as teas, pastas, sauces, and salad dressings. Trader Joe's offers 2,000 private label products—only 10 percent of what would be found in a typical supermarket—but creates a fun, roomy atmosphere for bargain seekers wanting the best in gourmet-style foods, health food supplements, and wines.[94]

Sellers of private labels are also adopting more extensive marketing communication programs to spread the word about their brands. For example, A&P produces a glossy Master Choice insert and uses Act Media shopping carts, freezer vision, instant coupon machines, and a television advertising campaign in selling its America's Choice brand. Consider how Loblaws has been successful at creating its own brands.

LOBLAWS

Loblaws is Canada's largest food distributor. In 1978, Loblaws was the first store in Canada to introduce generics, reflecting a carefully crafted strategy to build an image of quality and high value in six areas. By 1983, Loblaws carried over 500 generic products that accounted for 10 percent of store sales. This success was due to innovative marketing, low costs, and a large network of suppliers. In 1984 Loblaws chose to introduce a private label brand, President's Choice, that was designed to offer unique value through exceptional quality and moderate prices. These categories ranged from basic supermarket categories such as chocolate chip cookies, colas, and cereals to more exotic categories such as Devonshire custard from England and gourmet Russian mustard. These products also used distinctive and attractive packaging with modern lettering and colorful labels and names ("decadent" cookies, "ultimate" frozen pizza, "and "too good to be true" peanut butter). In terms of marketing communications, Loblaws put into place a strong promotional program with much in-store merchandising. Loblaws also introduced its *Insider's Report,* a quarterly publication featuring its own store brands and offering consumers shopping tips.[95]

Major Brand Response to Private Labels

Procter & Gamble's value-pricing program was one strategy to combat competitive inroads from private labels and other brands. Other major national brands also have been successful at fending off private labels.

Heinz customized product packaging helps to differentiate its ketchup from store brands.

HEINZ KETCHUP

H.J. Heinz has basically retained more than 50 percent market share in the ketchup category for years. Heinz's ingredients for success include a distinctive, slightly sweet-tasting product; a carefully monitored price gap with competitors; and aggressive packaging, product development, and promotional efforts. For example, since 1998, they have introduced EZ Squirt Bottles, spicy flavors, a "trap cap" that eliminates watery ooze, and colored (Blastin' Green) ketchup. "Hipper" advertising has been used to announce the innovations, and the price gap with private labels has been kept at under 20 percent.

As suggested by this example, the general approach adopted by Heinz and others to stay a step ahead of private label and other competitors is to emphasize both innovation and relevance throughout their marketing program (see Chapter 13).

To compete with private labels, a number of different tactics have been adopted by marketers of major national or manufacturer brands (see Figure 5-9). First, marketers of major brands have attempted to decrease costs and reduce price to negate the primary point of difference of private labels and achieve a critical point of parity. In many categories, prices of major brands had crept up to a point at which price premiums over private labels were 30 percent to 50 percent, or even 100 percent. In those categories in which consumers make frequent purchases, the cost savings of "trading down" to a private label brand were therefore quite substantial. For example, before Marlboro dropped its prices, a smoker who purchased, on average, 10 packs of cigarettes a week could have saved over $500 a year by switching from a premium brand such as Marlboro that cost $2 a pack to a private label brand that only cost $1 a pack.

In instances in which major brands and private labels are on a more equal footing with regard to price, major brands often compete well because of other favorable brand perceptions that consumers might have. For example, when StarKist cut prices on its tuna to only five cents higher than private labels, it was able to slice the private label share in the category in half (from 20 percent to 10 percent) because of the positive image its brand had with consumers.

Marketers of major brands have cut prices on older brands to make them more appealing. Procter & Gamble cut prices on a number of old standbys (e.g., Joy dishwashing detergent, Era laundry detergent, Luvs disposable diapers, and Camay beauty soap) by 12 percent to 33 percent, shifting them into the mid-tier level of pricing. Similarly, Miller Brewing Company dropped prices on its one-time flagship Miller High Life brand by 20 percent.

Decrease costs.

Cut prices.

Increase R&D expenditures to improve products and identify new product innovations.

Increase advertising and promotion budgets.

Eliminate stagnant brands and extensions and concentrate efforts on smaller number of brands.

Introduce discount "fighter" brands.

Supply private label makers.

Track store brands' growth and compete market-by-market.

FIGURE 5-9

Major Brand Response to Private Labels

It should be noted that one problem faced by marketers of major brands is that it can be difficult to actually lower prices even if they so desire. Supermarkets may not pass along the wholesale price cuts they are given. Moreover, marketers of major brands may not want to alienate retailers by attacking their store brands too forcefully, especially in zero-sum categories in which their brands could be easily replaced. For example, for their Luvs brand of diapers, P&G eliminated jumbo packs, streamlined package designs, simplified printing, and trimmed promotions, increasing retail margins from 3.3 percent to 8.6 percent as a result. Nevertheless, faced with margins on store brand diapers of 8 percent to 12 percent, the Safeway supermarket chain still chose to drop the Luvs brand altogether.

Besides these various pricing moves to achieve points of parity, marketers of major brands have used other tactics to achieve additional points of difference to combat the threat of private labels. They have increased R&D expenditures to improve products and identify new product innovations. They have increased advertising and promotion budgets. They have also tracked store brand growth more closely than in the past and are competing on a market-by-market basis. Marketers of major brands have also adjusted their brand portfolios. They have eliminated stagnant brands and extensions and concentrated their efforts on smaller numbers of brands. They have introduced discount "fighter" brands that are specially designed and promoted to compete with private labels.

Marketers have also been more aggressive legally protecting their brands. In 2005, Unilever filed suit against global supermarket giant Ahold alleging trademark and trade dress infringement across four of its European margarine brands as well as Lipton iced tea and Bertolli olive oil. Unilever maintains that their packaging looked too similar to its own brands.[96]

One controversial move by some marketers of major brands is to actually supply private label makers. For example, *Consumer Reports* reported that behind the scenes, Sara Lee, Del Monte, and Birds Eye all supplied products—sometimes lower in quality—to be used for private labels.[97] Other marketers, however, criticize this "if you can't beat 'em, join 'em" strategy, maintaining that these actions, if revealed, may create confusion or even reinforce a perception by consumers that all brands in a category are essentially the same.

Future Developments

Many marketers feel that the brands most endangered by the rise of private labels are second-tier brands that have not been as successful at establishing a clear identity as market leaders have. For example, in the laundry detergent category, the success of a private label brand such as Wal-Mart's Ultra Clean is more likely to come at the expense of brands such as Oxydol, All, or Fab rather than market leader Tide. In Britain, the average share of 52 leading brands measured fell only from 34.2 percent to 32.6 percent between 1975 and 1999—the "losers" were the smaller "trade dependent" brands that invest less in marketing and attempt to compete on price with private labels.[98] Highly priced, poorly differentiated and under-supported brands thus are especially vulnerable to private label competition.

At the same time, retailers will need the quality and image that go along with well-researched, efficiently manufactured, and professionally marketed major brands, if nothing else because of the wishes of consumers. When A&P let store brands soar to 35 percent of their dry grocery sales mix in the 1960s, many shoppers defected, and they were forced to drop the percentage to under 20 percent as a result. Similarly, Federated Department Stores, owners of private label wizard Macy's chain, vows to keep their percentage of revenue from private labels at under 20 percent.

Notes

1. Philip Kotler and Kevin Lane Keller, *Marketing Management,* 12th ed. (Upper Saddle River, NJ: Prentice Hall, 2006).
2. Ibid.
3. Greg Farrell, "Marketers Get Personal," *USA Today,* 19 July 1999, B9.
4. Brookes Raines, "To Push Musicals, Producer Shakes Up Broadway Tactics," *Wall Street Journal,* 10 March 2005, A1, A12.
5. Don E. Schultz, Stanley I. Tannenbaum, and Robert F. Lauterborn, *Integrated Marketing Communications* (Lincolnwood, IL: NTC Business Books, 1993).
6. For a description of a methodology to help identify and prioritize brand contact points, see Amitava Chattopadhyay and Jean-Louis Laborie, "Managing Brand Experience: The Market Contact Audit," *Journal of Advertising Research* (March 2005): 9–16.
7. Bridget Finn, "Why Pop-Up Shops Are Hot," *Business 2.0,* 17 November 2004; trendwatching.com
8. Christopher Locke, Rick Levine, Doc Searls, and David Weinberger, *The Cluetrain Manifesto: The End of Business as Usual* (Cambridge, MA: Perseus Press, 2000).
9. Richard Tomkins, "Fallen Icons," *Financial Times,* 1 February 2000.
10. Peter Post, "Beyond Brand—The Power of Experience Branding," *ANA/The Advertiser,* October/November 2000.
11. www.adweek.com/buzz.
12. B. Joseph Pine and James H. Gilmore, *The Experience Economy: Work Is Theatre and Every Business a Stage* (Cambridge, MA: Harvard University Press, 1999).
13. Bernd H. Schmitt, *Experiential Marketing: How to Get Customers to Sense, Feel, Think, Act, and Relate to Your Company and Brands* (New York: Free Press, 1999).
14. Dan Hanover, "Are You Experienced?" *Promo,* 28 February 2001.
15. Chris Reidy, "A Creator of Memorable Experiences," *Boston Globe,* June 19, 2005.
16. Don Peppers and Martha Rogers, *The One to One Future: Building Relationships One Customer at a Time* (New York: Doubleday, 1997); Don Peppers and Martha Rogers, *Enterprise One to One: Tools for Competing in the Interactive Age* (New York: Doubleday, 1999); Don Peppers and Martha Rogers, *The One to One Fieldbook: The Complete Toolkit for Implementing a 1 to 1 Marketing Program* (New York: Doubleday, 1999). For some more recent discussion from these authors, see Don Peppers and Martha Rogers, *Return on Customer: Creating Maximum Value from Your Scarcest Resource* (Currency, 2005). See also Sunil Gupta and Donald R. Lehmann, *Managing Customers as Investments: The Strategic Value of Customers in the Long Run* (Cambridge, MA: Harvard Business School Press, 2005).
17. Don Peppers and Martha Rogers, "Welcome to the 1:1 Future," *Marketing Tools,* 1 April 1994.
18. Clive Humby, "Leveraging Returns from a $100M Investment in Customer Rewards, through Communications, Price and Promotions," paper presented at Marketing Science Institute Conference, *Does Marketing Measure Up? Performance Metrics: Practices and Impacts,* 21–22 June 2004, London, United Kingdom.
19. Seth Godin, *Permission Marketing: Turning Strangers into Friends, and Friends into Customers* (New York: Simon & Schuster, 1999).
20. Susan Fournier, Susan Dobscha, and David Mick, "Preventing the Premature Death of Relationship Marketing," *Harvard Business Review* (January–February 1998): 42–51. See also Erwin Danneels, "Tight-Loose Coupling with Customers: The Enactment of Customer Orientation," *Strategic Management Journal* 24 (2003): 559–576.
21. Neeli Bendapudi and Robert P. Leone, "Psychological Implications of Customer Participation in Co-Production," *Journal of Marketing* 67 (January 2003): 14–28.
22. Jennifer Aaker, Susan Fournier, and S. Adam Brasel, "When Good Brands Do Bad," *Journal of Consumer Research* 31 (June 2004): 1–16; Pankaj Aggarwal, "The Effects of Brand Relationship Norms on Consumer Attitudes and Behavior," *Journal of Consumer Research* 31 (June 2004): 87–101; Pankaj Aggarwal and Sharmistha Law, "Role of Relationship Norms in Processing Brand Information," *Journal of Consumer Research* 32 (December 2005): 453–464.
23. Stratford Sherman, "How to Prosper in the Value Decade," *Fortune,* 30 November 1992, 91.
24. David Garvin, "Product Quality: An Important Strategic Weapon," *Business Horizons* 27 (May–June 1985): 40–43; Philip Kotler, *Marketing Management,* 10th ed. (Upper Saddle River, NJ: Prentice Hall, 2000).
25. David Court, Tom French, Tim McGuire, and Michael Partington, *Marketing in Three Dimensions: The New Challenge for Marketers* (White Paper: McKinsey & Company, 1999).
26. Kotler and Keller, *Marketing Management.*
27. Michael E. Porter, *Competitive Advantage* (New York: Free Press, 1985).
28. Robert M. Morgan and Shelby D. Hunt, "The Commitment-Trust Theory of Relationship Marketing," *Journal of Marketing* 58, no. 2 (1994): 20–38.
29. Frederick F. Reichheld, *The Loyalty Effect* (Boston: Harvard Business School Press, 1996).

30. Chris Woodyard, "Mass Production Gives Way to Mass Customization," *USA Today,* 16 February 1998, 3B.
31. Paul Roberts, "John Deere Runs on Chaos," *Fast Company,* November 1998, 164–173.
32. Evantheia Schibsted, "What Your Breakfast Reveals About You," *Business 2.0,* 20 March 2001, 80.
33. Christopher M. Kelley, "Do Your Shoppers Want Custom Products?" Forrester Research, 21 May 2003.
34. Roland T. Rust, Christine Moorman, and Peter R. Dickson, "Getting Returns from Service Quality: Is the Conventional Wisdom Wrong?" *MSI Report 00–120* (Cambridge, MA: Marketing Science Institute, 2000).
35. Lourdes Lee Valeriano, "Loved the Present! Hated the Manual!" *Wall Street Journal,* 15 December 1994, B1.
36. Jessica Mintz, "Using Hand, Grab Hair. Pull," *Wall Street Journal,* 23 December 2004, B1, B5.
37. Jacqueline Martense, "Get Close to Your Customers," *Fast Company,* August 2005, 37.
38. Terry Vavra, *Aftermarketing: How to Keep Customers for Life Through Relationship Marketing* (Chicago: Irwin Professional Publishers, 1995).
39. Lee Gomes, "Computer-Printer Price Drop Isn't Starving Makers," *Wall Street Journal,* 16 August 1996.
40. "Loyal, My Brand, to Thee," *Promo,* 1 October 1997; Arthur Middleton Hughes, "How Safeway Built Loyalty—Especially Among Second-Tier Customers," *Target Marketing,* 1 March 1999; Laura Bly, "Frequent Fliers Fuel a Global Currency," *USA Today,* 27 April 2001.
41. www.frequencymarketing.com
42. www.aa.com.
43. Christina Binkley, "Hotels Raise the Ante in Business-Travel Game," *Wall Street Journal,* 2 February 1999, B1.
44. James L. Heskett, W. Earl Sasser Jr., and Leonard A. Schlesinger, *The Service Profit Chain* (New York: Simon & Schuster, 1997).
45. Grahame R. Dowling and Mark Uncles, "Do Customer Loyalty Programs Really Work?" *Sloan Management Review* (Summer 1997): 71–82. See also Steven M. Shugan, "Brand Loyalty Programs: Are They Shams?" *Marketing Science* 24 (Spring 2005): 185–193.
46. Robert C. Blattberg and Kenneth Wisniewski, "Price-Induced Patterns of Competition," *Marketing Science* 8 (Fall 1989): 291–309.
47. Elliot B. Ross, "Making Money with Proactive Pricing," *Harvard Business Review* (November–December 1984): 145–155.
48. www.pvh.com/annual_pdfs/pdf_2004/corp_strategy.pdf. All brands in the figure are registered trademarks of Phillips-Van Heusen or its licensors.
49. Norman Berry, "Revitalizing Brands," *Journal of Consumer Marketing* 5, no. 3 (1988): 15–20.
50. For a more detailed and comprehensive treatment of pricing strategy, see Thomas T. Nagle and Reed K. Holden, *The Strategy and Tactics of Pricing: A Guide to Profitable Decision-Making,* 3rd ed. (Upper Saddle River, NJ: Prentice Hall, 2002); Kent B. Monroe, *Pricing: Making Profitable Decisions,* 3rd ed. (New York: McGraw-Hill/Irwin, 2002); and Robert J. Dolan and Hermann Simon, *Power Pricing* (New York: Free Press, 1997).
51. Yumiko Ono, "Companies Find That Consumers Continue to Resist Price Boosts," *Wall Street Journal,* 8 March 1994, B8.
52. Ira Teinowitz, "Marlboro Friday: Still Smoking," *Advertising Age,* 28 March 1994, 24.
53. Lee Hawkins Jr., "GM to End Employee-Pricing Plan," *Wall Street Journal,* 9 September 2005, A8; Christine Tierney, "GM Extends Employee Discount," *Detroit News,* 26 August 2005.
54. Dean Starkman, "Hefty's Plastic Zipper Bag Is Rapping Rivals," *Wall Street Journal,* 2 February 1999, B1.
55. Peter Coy, "The Power of Smart Pricing," *Business Week,* 10 April 2000, 600–164.
56. Allan J. Magrath, "Eight Timeless Truths About Pricing," *Sales & Marketing Management* (October 1989): 78–84.
57. Thomas J. Malott, CEO of Siemens, which makes heavy electrical equipment and motors, quoted in Stratford Sherman, "How to Prosper in the Value Decade," *Fortune,* 30 November 1992, 90–103.
58. Christopher Power, "Value Marketing," *Business Week,* 11 November 1991, 132–140.
59. Sandra Jones, "How Sears Came Down with Seasonal Disorder," *Business 2.0,* July 2004, 66–67.
60. For a discussion of the pros and cons of customer value mapping (CVM) and economic value mapping (EVM), see Gerald E. Smith and Thomas T. Nagle, "Pricing the Differential," *Marketing Management,* May/June 2005, 28–32.
61. Bruce Mohl, "Downsizing Ice Cream," *Boston Globe,* April 18, 2004.
62. Donald Lehmann and Russell Winer, *Product Management* (Burr Ridge, IL: Irwin, 1994).
63. Amy Cortese, "Goodbye to Fixed Pricing?" *Business Week,* 4 May 1998, 71–84.
64. Adrienne Carter, "Telling the Risky from the Reliable," *BusinessWeek,* 1 August 2005, 57–58.
65. Richard Gibson, "Broad Grocery Price Cuts May Not Pay," *Wall Street Journal,* 7 May 1993, B1.
66. Amy Merrick, "Retailers Try to Get Leg Up on Markdowns with New Software," *Wall Street Journal,* 7 August 2001, A1, A6
67. Zachary Schiller, "Not Everyone Loves a Supermarket Special," *Business Week,* 17 February 1992, 64–66.
68. Kotler and Keller, *Marketing Management.*
69. For a more detailed and comprehensive treatment of channel strategy, see Anne T. Coughlan, Erin Anderson, Louis W. Stern, and Adel I. El-Ansary, *Marketing Channels,* 6th ed. (Upper Saddle River, NJ: Prentice Hall, 2001).

70. V. Kasturi Rangan, Melvyn A. J. Menezes, and E. P. Maier, "Channel Selection for New Industrial Products: A Framework, Method, and Applications," *Journal of Marketing* 56 (July 1992): 69–82.
71. Rowland T. Moriarty and Ursula Moran, "Managing Hybrid Marketing Systems," *Harvard Business Review* 68 (1990): 146–155.
72. Rick Brooks, "A Deal with Target Put Lid on Revival at Tupperware," *Wall Street Journal,* 18 February 2004, A1, A9.
73. Mya Frazier, "John Deere Cultivates Its Image," *Advertising Age,* 25 July 2005, 6.
74. William M. Weilbacher, *Brand Marketing* (Lincolnwood, IL: NTC Business Books, 1993), 53.
75. Laura Bird and Wendy Bounds, "Stores' Demands Squeeze Apparel Companies," *Wall Street Journal,* 15 July 1997, B1.
76. Christopher Farrell, "Stuck! How Companies Cope When They Can't Raise Prices," *Business Week,* 15 November 1993, 146–150.
77. For a discussion of CRM issues with multichannel retailers, see Jacquelyn S. Thomas and Ursula Y. Sullivan, "Managing Marketing Communications," *Journal of Marketing* 69 (October 2005): 239–251.
78. Matthew Egol, Karla Martin, and Leslie Moeller, "One Size Fits All," *Point,* September 2005, 21–24.
79. Steven M. Shugan, "Branded Variants," *Research in Marketing,* AMA Educators' Proceedings, Series no. 55 (Chicago: American Marketing Association, 1989), 33–38. Shugan cites alarm clocks, answering machines, appliances, baby items, binoculars, dishwashers, luggage, mattresses, microwaves, sports equipment, stereos, televisions, tools, and watches as examples.
80. Mark Bergen, Shantanu Dutta, and Steven M. Shugan, "Branded Variants: A Retail Perspective," *Journal of Marketing Research* (February 1995): 9.
81. George E. Belch and Michael A. Belch, *Introduction to Advertising and Promotion* (Chicago: Irwin, 1995).
82. Raju Narisetti, "Joint Marketing with Retailers Spreads," *Wall Street Journal,* 24 October 1996.
83. Bill Richards, "Levi-Strauss Plans to Open 200 Stores in 5 Years, with Ending of FTC Ban," *Wall Street Journal,* 22 December 1994, A2.
84. Mary Kuntz, "These Ads Have Windows and Walls," *Business Week,* 27 February 1995, 74.
85. Elaine Underwood, "Store Brands," *Brandweek,* 9 January 1995, 22–27.
86. "Clicks, Bricks, and Bargains," *The Economist,* 3 December 2005, 57–58.
87. "The Real Internet Revolution," *The Economist,* 21 August 1999, 53–54.
88. Don Peppers and Martha Rogers, "The 'Store' Is Everywhere," *Business 2.0,* 6 February 2001, 72.
89. Lorrie Grant, "Retailers Private Label Brands See Sales Growth Boom," *USAToday,* April 15, 2004.
90. George Anderson, "Private Labels: The Global View," www.retailwire.com.
91. Anderson, "Private Labels," www.retailwire.com.
92. Chip Walker, "What's in a Name," *American Demographics,* February 1991, 54.
93. "Battle of the Brands," *Consumer Reports,* August 2005, 12–15.
94. Irwin Speizer, "The Grocery Store That Shouldn't Be," *Fast Company,* February 2004, p. 31.
95. Mary L. Shelman and Ray A. Goldberg, "Loblaw Companies Limited," Case 9–588–039 (Boston: Harvard Business School, 1994); Gordon H. G. McDougall and Douglas Snetsinger, "Loblaws," in *Marketing Challenges,* 3rd ed., eds. Christopher H. Lovelock and Charles B. Weinberg (New York: McGraw-Hill, 1993), 169–185; "President's Choice Continues Brisk Pace," *Frozen Food Age,* March 1998.
96. Jack Neff, "Marketers Put Down Foot on Private-Label Issue," *Advertising Age,* 4 April 2005, 14.
97. "Battle of the Brands."
98. Chris Hoyt, "Kraft's Private Label Lesson," *Reveries,* February 2004.

INTEGRATING MARKETING COMMUNICATIONS TO BUILD BRAND EQUITY

Preview

The preceding chapter described how various marketing activities and product, price, and distribution strategies can contribute to brand equity. This chapter considers the final and perhaps most flexible element of marketing programs. ***Marketing communications*** are the means by which firms attempt to inform, persuade, and remind consumers—directly or indirectly—about the brands they sell. In a sense, marketing communications represent the voice of the brand and are a means by which the brand can establish a dialogue and build relationships with consumers. Although advertising is often a central element of a marketing communications program, it is usually not the only element—or even the most important one—for building brand equity. Figure 6-1 displays some of the common marketing communication options for the consumer market.

Although advertising and other communication options can play different roles in the marketing program, one important purpose they all serve is to contribute to brand equity. According to the customer-based brand equity model, marketing communications can contribute to brand equity by creating awareness of the brand; linking points-of-parity and points-of-difference associations to the brand in consumers' memory; eliciting positive brand judgments or feelings; and facilitating a stronger consumer–brand connection and brand resonance. In addition to forming the desired brand knowledge structures, marketing communication programs can provide incentives eliciting the differential response that makes up customer-based brand equity.

The flexibility of marketing communications comes in part from the number of different ways they can contribute to brand equity. At the same time, brand equity helps

Media advertising
TV
Radio
Newspaper
Magazines

Direct response advertising
Mail
Telephone
Broadcast media
Print media
Computer-related
Media-related

Online advertising
Web sites
Interactive ads and e-mails

Place advertising
Billboards and posters
Movies, airlines, and lounges
Product placement
Point of purchase

Point-of-purchase advertising
Shelf talkers
Aisle markers
Shopping cart ads
In-store radio or TV

Trade promotions
Trade deals and buying allowances
Point-of-purchase display allowances
Push money
Contests and dealer incentives
Training programs
Trade shows
Cooperative advertising

Consumer promotions
Samples
Coupons
Premiums
Refunds and rebates
Contests and sweepstakes
Bonus packs
Price-offs

Event marketing and sponsorship
Sports
Arts
Entertainment
Fairs and festivals
Cause-related

Publicity and public relations

Personal selling

FIGURE 6-1

Marketing Communications Options

marketers determine how to design and implement different marketing communication options. In this chapter we consider how to develop marketing communication programs to build brand equity. We will assume the other elements of the marketing program have been properly put into place. Thus, the optimal brand positioning has been defined—especially in terms of the desired target market—and product, pricing, and distribution and other marketing program decisions have been made.

Designing marketing communication programs is a complex task. We begin by describing the new realities in marketing communications and the changing media landscape. To provide necessary background, we next evaluate how the major communication options contribute to brand equity and some of their main costs and benefits. We conclude by considering how to mix and match communication options—that is, how to employ a range of communication options in a coordinated or integrated fashion—to build brand equity. For the sake of brevity, we will not consider specific marketing communication issues such as media scheduling, budget estimation techniques, and research approaches.[1]

The New Media Environment

The media environment has changed dramatically in recent years. Traditional advertising media such as TV, radio, magazines, and newspapers seem to be losing their grip on consumers. After the dot-com crash and subsequent hangover in the early 2000s, marketers returned to the Web with a vengeance, pouring $18 billion into Internet advertising in 2005.[2] Although Web advertising jumped 20 percent during this time, spending for TV ads remained flat.

The prognosis for TV advertising going forward is not necessarily good. With more cable companies building TiVo-like digital video recorders (DVRs) into their digital set boxes, household penetration of DVRs in the United States was expected to jump to 33 percent by 2008.[3] One survey found that almost three-quarters of users of DVRs frequently or always skip over ads when watching recorded programs. Increased fragmentation from the proliferation of satellite and cable channels has only exacerbated the problem.

Although media rates have continued to climb, viewership and readership for some key demographics such as teenagers continue to slide. The results of a Forrester Research survey of online 12–17-year-olds revealed that 94 percent owned a game console of some kind, two-thirds considered themselves to be active gamers, and more than 50 percent of males said they would rather play video games than watch TV.

Paid search services from Yahoo! and Google have exploded to become a $3 billion industry. Consumers are actively creating and sharing content online as consumer communities and blogs have been created on virtually all topics. Seventy-two percent of teens exchange instant messages (IMs) each day and 64 million Americans use some type of IM application. Cell phones are becoming a critical device for far more than phone conversations.

This changing media landscape has forced marketers to reevaluate how they should best communicate with consumers. Consider how Mazda defied convention in launching a new vehicle.[4]

Mazda

Mazda, a unit of Ford Motor Co., broke its first-ever global ad campaign to launch the MX-5 Miata—formerly known as just the Miata—in September 2005. In an attempt to reverse the course of what had become an increasingly pronounced gender skew toward female purchasers since the Miata's introduction in 1989, two executions of a spot for the MX-5 targeted male drivers. Finished spots for its SUV alternative Mazda5, however, were shelved in the United States, where the automaker decided it could—for the first time in its history—launch a mass-appeal model without TV spots, even though the plan might result in a slower rollout and market penetration.

Mazda uses conventional and unconventional communications to launch its vehicles.

Thus the launch of the Mazda5—popular in Europe, but unseen at the time in the United States—bypassed TV to rely on event-marketing alliances and Web promotions, such as Quiksilver surfing contests and painted-and-wrapped vehicles; streetball tournaments; *American Baby* magazine photo contests; and Daily Candy e-blasts written in the female-oriented site's style.

Challenges in Designing Brand-Building Communications

The new media environment has further complicated marketers' perennial challenge to build effective and efficient marketing communication programs. Skillfully designed and implemented marketing communications programs require careful planning and a creative knack. Let's first consider a few useful tools to provide some perspective.

Perhaps the simplest—but most useful—way to judge advertising or any other communication option is by its ability to contribute to brand equity. For example, how well does a proposed ad campaign contribute to brand awareness or to creating, maintaining, or strengthening certain brand associations? Does a sponsorship cause consumers to have more favorable brand judgments and feelings? To what extent does a promotion encourage consumers to buy more of a product? At what price premium? Figure 6-2 displays a simple three-step model for judging the effectiveness of advertising or any communication option to build brand equity.

Information Processing Model of Communications. To provide some perspective, let's consider in more depth the process by which marketing communications might affect consumers. A number of different models have been put forth over the years to explain communications and the steps in the persuasion process—recall the discussion on the hierarchy of effects model from Brand Focus 2.0. For example, for a person to be

1. What is your current brand knowledge? Have you created a detailed mental map?
2. What is your desired brand knowledge? Have you defined optimal points of parity and points of difference and a brand mantra?
3. How does the communication option help the brand get from current to desired knowledge with consumers? Have you clarified the specific effects on knowledge engendered by communications?

FIGURE 6-2

Simple Test for Marketing Communication Effectiveness

persuaded by any form of communication (a TV advertisement, newspaper editorial, classroom lecture), the following six steps must occur:[5]

1. *Exposure:* A person must see or hear the communication.
2. *Attention:* A person must notice the communication.
3. *Comprehension:* A person must understand the intended message or arguments of the communication.
4. *Yielding:* A person must respond favorably to the intended message or arguments of the communication.
5. *Intentions:* A person must plan to act in the desired manner of the communication.
6. *Behavior:* A person must actually act in the desired manner of the communication.

You can appreciate the challenge of creating a successful marketing communication program when you realize that each of the six steps must occur for a consumer to be persuaded. If there is a breakdown or failure in any step along the way, then successful communication will not result. For example, consider the potential pitfalls in launching a new advertising campaign:

1. A consumer may not be exposed to an ad because the media plan missed the mark.
2. A consumer may not notice an ad because of a boring and uninspired creative strategy.
3. A consumer may not understand an ad because of a lack of product category knowledge or technical sophistication, or because of a lack of awareness and familiarity about the brand itself.
4. A consumer may fail to respond favorably and form a positive attitude because of irrelevant or unconvincing product claims.
5. A consumer may fail to form a purchase intention because of a lack of an immediate perceived need.
6. A consumer may fail to actually buy the product because he or she doesn't remember anything from the ad when confronted with the available brands in the store.

To show how fragile the whole communication process is, assume that the probability of *each* of the six steps being successfully accomplished is 50 percent—most likely an extremely generous assumption. The laws of probability suggest that the likelihood of all six steps successfully occurring, assuming they are independent events, would be $0.5 \times 0.5 \times 0.5 \times 0.5 \times 0.5 \times 0.5$, which equals 1.5625 percent. If the probability of each step occurring, on average, was a more pessimistic 10 percent, then the joint probability of all six events occurring would be .000001. In other words, only 1 in 1,000,000! No wonder advertisers sometimes lament the limited power of advertising.

One implication of the information processing model is that to increase the odds for a successful marketing communications campaign, marketers must attempt to increase the likelihood that *each* step occurs. For example, from an advertising standpoint, the ideal ad campaign would ensure that:

1. The right consumer is exposed to the right message at the right place and at the right time.
2. The creative strategy for the advertising causes the consumer to notice and attend to the ad but does not distract from the intended message.
3. The ad properly reflects the consumer's level of understanding about the product and the brand.
4. The ad correctly positions the brand in terms of desirable and deliverable points of difference and points of parity.
5. The ad motivates consumers to consider purchase of the brand.
6. The ad creates strong brand associations to all of these stored communication effects so that they can have an effect when consumers are considering making a purchase.

Clearly, marketers need to design and execute marketing communication programs carefully if they are to have the desired effects on consumers.

Role of Multiple Communications

How much and what kinds of marketing communications are necessary? Economic theory suggests placing dollars into a marketing communication budget and across communication options according to marginal revenue and cost. For example, the communication mix would be optimally distributed when the last dollar spent on each communication option generated the same return. Because such information may be difficult to obtain, however, other models of budget allocation emphasize more observable factors such as stage of brand life cycle, objectives and budget of the firm, product characteristics, size of budget, and media strategy of competitors. These factors are typically contrasted with the different characteristics of the media.

For example, marketing communication budgets tend to be higher when there is low channel support, much change in the marketing program over time, many hard-to-reach customers, more complex customer decision making, differentiated products and nonhomogeneous customer needs, and frequent product purchases in small quantities.[6] Personal selling tends to become a more dominant element in the communication mix when the brand has a high unit value, is technical in nature, requires demonstration, must be tailored to the specific needs of customers, and is purchased infrequently or involves a trade-in; when the firm has a limited communications budget; and when customers are easily identified.[7]

Besides these efficiency considerations, different communication options also may target different market segments. For example, advertising may attempt to bring new customers into the market or attract competitors' customers to the brand, whereas promotions might attempt to reward loyal users of the brand.

Invariably, marketers will employ multiple communications to achieve their goals. In doing so, they must understand how each communication option works and how to assemble and integrate the best set of choices. The following section presents an overview and critique of the major marketing communication options from a brand-building perspective: broadcast, print, direct response, online, and place advertising media; consumer and trade promotions; event marketing and sponsorship; publicity and public relations; and personal selling. Later in the chapter, we will consider how to combine these different options to build strong brands.

Overview of Marketing Communication Options

Advertising

Advertising is any paid form of nonpersonal presentation and promotion of ideas, goods, or services by an identified sponsor. Although it is a powerful means of creating strong, favorable, and unique brand associations and eliciting positive judgments and feelings, advertising is controversial because its specific effects are often difficult to quantify and predict. Nevertheless, a number of studies using very different approaches have shown the potential power of advertising on brand sales.

For example, the American Association of Advertising Agencies has compiled a list of some of the studies demonstrating the productivity of advertising expenditures. Analyses of advertising effects using the PIMS (Profit Impact of Marketing Strategy) database of 750 consumer businesses in a variety of industries showed that firms that increased advertising during a recessionary period gained one-half to a full market share point coming out of a recession, whereas firms that cut their advertising budget gained only two-tenths of a share point.[8]

Other comprehensive studies also document the power of advertising. For example, an analysis of the effects of advertising on sales using Nielsen's single-source database of 142 packaged-goods brands from 1991 to 1992 revealed that advertising worked around half the time. Specifically, 70 percent of the ad campaigns in the sample boosted sales immediately, although the effect was only strong in 30 percent of the cases. Forty-six percent of campaigns appeared to yield a long-term sales boost. Additional analyses revealed other interesting study findings:[9]

- Increased sales could come from a single advertisement.
- "Blitz campaigns" with concentrated exposure schedules could suffer from diminished returns, such that ads shown less frequently over a longer period of time were more effective.
- Advertising was more likely to increase both sales and profits than "money-off" sales promotions, which almost always lost money.

Another comprehensive study of advertising effectiveness, using a different database and conducted by a major research supplier, Information Resources Inc., reinforces these findings and provides several additional observations (see The Science of Branding 6-1).[10] Finally, one meta-analysis found that advertising effectiveness has remained stable through the years, although results are more pronounced for new products than for established products.[11]

Besides these broad-based empirical studies, numerous case studies point to the power of advertising, even during difficult economic times. For example, during the summer of 2001, Home Depot found sales surging 16 percent in the face of a sluggish economy when the firm invested in a heavy product push with advertising featuring paint, appliances, and energy-savers such as thermostats.[12] Coca-Cola, Red Lobster, Heinz, and Gillette also chose to step up their ad spending during this time and similarly experienced sales increases. These results echoed earlier experiences of other brands that chose to invest in advertising during an economic recession or downturn. For example, during the 1989–1991 recession, brands such as Jif peanut butter, Bud Light beer, and L'Oreal all increased advertising expenditures and thus their market share as a result.

Given the complexity of designing advertising—the number of strategic roles it might play, the sheer number of specific decisions to make, and its complicated effect on consumers—it is difficult to provide a comprehensive set of detailed managerial guidelines. Different advertising media clearly have different strengths, however, and therefore are best suited to play certain roles in a communication program. Figure 6-3 provides a breakdown of national advertising spending by major advertising media, and Figure 6-4

Advertising and Marketing Communications Forecast

2005-2007

UPDATED 11/1/06

ADVERTISING	2005			2006			2007		
	% Growth	$	% Share	% Growth	$	% Share	% Growth	$	%Share
Newspapers	3.4% $	47,874	23.0	0.2% $	47,970	21.6	21.8% $	47,106	20.4
Broadcast Network Television	2.6% $	17,851	8.6	4.0% $	18,565	8.3	23.0% $	18,008	7.8
Cable Network Television	8.5% $	15,905	7.6	6.0% $	16,859	7.6	4.0% $	17,534	7.6
Broadcast Syndication	2.5% $	2,980	1.4	2.0% $	3,040	1.4	1.0% $	3,070	1.3
Local & National Spot TV	24.0% $	25,451	12.2	9.0% $	27,741	12.5	25.0% $	26,354	11.4
Local/Regional Cable TV	9.0% $	5,341	2.6	9.0% $	5,822	2.6	9.0% $	6,346	2.8
Branded Entertainment/ Product Placement	22.7% $	4,245	2.0	28.0% $	5,433	2.4	35.0% $	7,335	3.2
Videogame Advertising	67.0% $	200	0.1	50.0% $	301	0.1	90.0% $	571	0.2
Cinema Advertising	20.0% $	526	0.3	21.0% $	636	0.3	15.0% $	731	0.3
Terrestial Radio	2.6% $	20,686	9.9	2.0% $	21,099	9.5	1.5% $	21,416	9.3
Satellite Radio	100.0% $	45	0.0	160.0% $	117	0.1	120.0% $	257	0.1
Consumer Magazines	5.8% $	13,225	6.3	4.5% $	13,820	6.2	4.2% $	14,401	6.2
Business-to-Business Magazines	3.5% $	8,694	4.2	3.5% $	8,998	4.0	3.0% $	9,268	4.0
Custom Publishing	9.0% $	15,260	7.3	20.0% $	18,312	8.2	14.0% $	20,876	9.0
Online / Internet	30.0% $	11,050	5.3	26.0% $	13,923	6.3	20.0% $	16,708	7.2
Out-of-Home	4.8% $	5,935	2.8	8.2$%	6,422	2.9	7.0%	6,872	3.0
Mobile Advertising	200.0% $	200	0.1	80.0% $	360	0.2	100.0% $	720	0.3
Yellow Pages-Print	2.7% $	12,838	6.2	1.8% $	13,069	5.9	0.5%$	13,134	5.7
			100%			100%			100%
MARKETING COMMUNICATIONS									
Total Advertising	5.0% $	208,305	30.2	6.8% $	222,487	30.7	3.7% $	230,706	30.6
Direct Mail / Marketing	6.5%	$149,100	21.6	6.6%	$158,941	21.9	6.0%	$168,477	22.4
Trade Promotion/Slotting Allowances	6.0%	$161,756	23.5	3.7%	$167,741	23.1	3.5%	$173,612	23.0
Consumer Sales Promotion/ Incentives	8.0%	$127,116	18.4	4.0%	$132,201	18.2	3.5%	$136,828	18.2
Event Marketing	10.0%	$13,200	1.9	12.0%	$14,784	2.0	15.0%	$17,002	2.3
Public Relations	10.0%	$3,850	0.6	3.5%	$3,985	0.5	7.5%	$4,284	0.6
Other	2.0%	$25,908	3.8	25.0%	$24,613	3.4	27.5%	$22,767	3.0
Total Advertising & Marketing	6.1%	$689,235	100.0	5.2%	$724,750	100.0	4.0%	$753,674	100.0

Source: Jack Myers Media Business Report © copyright 2006/2007 Myers Publishing LLC.

FIGURE 6-3

Jack Myers Media Business Report

summarizes the advantages and disadvantages of the main advertising media. Now we'll highlight some key issues about each type of advertising medium in turn.

Television. Television is a powerful advertising medium because it allows for sight, sound, and motion and reaches a broad spectrum of consumers. Virtually all U.S. households have televisions, and the amount of time that television sets are on each day, on average, is a staggering seven hours. The wide reach of TV advertising translates to low cost per exposure. From a brand equity perspective, TV advertising has two particularly important strengths. First, it can be an effective means of vividly demonstrating product attributes and persuasively explaining their corresponding consumer benefits. Second, TV advertising can be a compelling means for dramatically portraying user and usage imagery, brand personality, and other brand intangibles.

On the other hand, television advertising has its drawbacks. Because of the fleeting nature of the message and the potentially distracting creative elements often found in a TV ad, consumers can overlook product-related messages and the brand itself. Moreover, the

Medium	Advantages	Disadvantages
Television	Mass coverage High reach Impact of sight, sound, and motion. High prestige Low cost per exposure Attention getting Favorable image	Low selectivity Short message life High absolute cost High production costs Clutter
Radio	Local coverage Low cost High frequency Flexible Low production costs Well-segmented audiences	Audio only Clutter Low attention-getting capabilities Fleeting message
Magazines	Segmentation potential Quality reproduction High information content Longevity Multiple readers	Long lead time for ad placement Visual only Lack of flexibility
Newspapers	High coverage Low cost Short lead time for placing ads Ads can be placed in interest sections Timely (current ads) Reader controls exposure Can be used for coupons	Short life Clutter Low attention-getting capabilities Poor reproduction quality Selective reader exposure
Direct response	High selectivity Reader controls exposure High information content Opportunities for repeat exposures	High cost per contact Poor image (junk mail) Clutter
Interactive	Customized and personalized In-depth information Can be engaging	Nonobtrusive Often lacks emotionality
Outdoor	Location specific High repetition Easily noticed	Short exposure time requires short ad Poor image Local restrictions

Source: Reprinted from George E. Belch and Michael A. Belch, Introduction to Advertising and Promotion, 3rd ed. (Homewood, IL: Irwin, 1995).

FIGURE 6-4

Advertising Media Characteristics

large number of ads and nonprogramming material on television creates clutter that makes it easy for consumers to ignore or forget ads. The large number of channels creates fragmentation, and the existence of digital video recorders gives viewers the means to skip commercials (see Branding Brief 6-1). Another important disadvantage of TV ads is the high cost of production and placement. A 30-second spot on a popular primetime television show during the 2006-2007 season cost as much as $300,000 (*Survivor: Cook Islands, Extreme Makeover Home Edition, Lost,* or *Grey's Anatomy*) or even $400,000 and up (*American Idol* or *Desperate Housewives*). Even though the price of TV advertising has skyrocketed, the share of the prime time audience for the major networks has steadily declined.

By any number of measures, the effectiveness of any one ad, on average, has diminished. For example, Video Storyboards reported that the number of viewers who reported they paid attention to TV ads dropped significantly in the last decade. As a result, some

THE SCIENCE OF BRANDING 6-1

Understanding the Effects of Advertising

Information Resources Inc. (IRI) provides a unique, in-depth examination into how advertising works. IRI uses a single-source testing service called BehaviorScan. Single-source research suppliers track behavior of individual households from TV sets to checkout counters in supermarkets in test markets across the United States. Consumers in test markets who sign up to be members of IRI's "Shoppers Hotline" panel agree to have microcomputers record when their TV set is on and to which station it is tuned, to have electronic scanners record UPC codes of their household purchases at supermarkets, and to use a handheld scanner at home to record purchases they make at other retailers. IRI has the capability to send different commercials to different preselected homes to test the effects of advertising copy and weights. BehaviorScan can also test the effects of store features, displays, coupons, and so forth.

In 1989, IRI reviewed the results of 389 research studies conducted over the previous seven years and offered the following general principles concerning advertising and promotion effectiveness:

- ***TV advertising weight alone is not enough.*** Only roughly half of heavy TV advertising plans have a measurable effect on sales, although when they do have an effect it is often large. The success rate is higher for new products or line extensions than for established brands.
- ***TV advertising is more likely to work when there are changes in copy or media strategy.*** Examples are a new copy strategy or an expanded target market.
- ***When advertising is successful in increasing sales, its impact lasts beyond the period of peak spending.*** Recent evidence shows that the long-term positive effects of advertising last up to two years after peak spending. Moreover, the long-term incremental sales generated are approximately double the incremental sales observed in the first year of an advertising spending increase.

marketers are rethinking their media plans. Consider how Ford chose to market its new midsize Fusion model in 2005.

Ford Fusion

Having seen its once-competitive Taurus relegated to mostly rental car lots, Ford decided to come out swinging in an attempt to regain a foothold in the critical midsize car market in the United States. The stylish Ford Fusion's clear purpose was to take share from the highly successful Toyota Camry and Honda Accord models. With a distinctive three-bar chrome grill, the Fusion, base priced under $18,000, was seen as less conservative than its Ford midsize sibling, the Five Hundred, and was targeted at "moveups", aged 25 to 39 who were "reaching milestones in their lives both professionally and personally." Ford sought to connect with its audience in their environment and on their terms. Lifestyle advertising became the focus, launching with a music initiative called "Fusion Flash Concerts" where a spectrum of A list bands popped up in 11 cities nationwide. Online, e-mail, and text messaging also played a key role in the launch of the car, building awareness and consideration while providing a source for vehicle information. Finally, contextually relevant print, television, and collateral were utilized to further establish the brand. All mediums supported the camapgin messaging and ideals: "Life in Drive."[13]

- ***About 20 percent of advertising plans pay out in the short term.*** However, when we consider the long-term effect, most advertising plans that show a significant effect in a split cable experiment would most likely pay out.
- ***Promotions almost always have a measurable impact on sales.*** However, the effect is usually purely short term.
- ***Payout statistics on promotions are dismal.*** Roughly 16 percent of trade promotions are profitable. Furthermore, promotions' effects are often purely short term, except for new products.
- ***These statistics on advertising and promotion payouts show that many brands are overspending on marketing support.*** Many classes of spending can be reduced at an increase in profits.
- ***Allocating marketing funds requires a continuous search for marketing programs that offer the highest return on the marketing dollar.*** Tradeoffs between advertising, trade promotions, and consumer promotions can be highly profitable when based on reliable evaluation systems that measure this productivity at any point in time.
- ***The current trend toward promotion spending is not sound from a marketing productivity standpoint.*** When we include the strategic disadvantages of promotions (that is, losing control to the trade and training consumers to buy only on deal), then the case is compelling for a reevaluation of current practices and the incentive systems responsible for this trend.

Sources: Leonard M. Lodish, Magid Abraham, Stuart Kalmenson, Jeanne Livelsberger, et al., "How T.V. Advertising Works: A Meta Analysis of 389 Real World Split Cable T.V. Advertising Experiments," *Journal of Marketing Research* (May 1995): 125–239; Magid Abraham and Leonard Lodish, "Advertising Works," *Information Resources,* Inc. (1989).

Nevertheless, properly designed and executed TV ads can affect sales and profits. For example, over the years, one of the most consistently successful TV advertisers has been Apple. The "1984" ad for the introduction of its Macintosh personal computer—portraying a stark Orwellian future with a feature film look—ran only once on TV but is one of the best-known ads ever. In the years that followed, Apple advertising successfully created awareness and image for a series of products, more recently with the acclaimed Silhouettes iPod ad campaign. Each year, the American Marketing Association awards "EFFIEs" to those brands whose advertising campaigns have had a demonstrable impact on sales and profits. Branding Brief 6-2 discusses how Apple earned that honor with its iPod campaign.

GUIDELINES. In designing and evaluating an ad campaign, marketers should distinguish the ***message strategy*** or positioning of an ad (what the ad attempts to convey about the brand) from its ***creative strategy*** (the way the ad expresses the brand claims). Designing effective advertising campaigns is both an art and a science: The artistic aspects relate to the creative strategy of the ad and its execution; the scientific aspects relate to the message strategy and the brand claim information the ad contains. Thus, as

Ford adopted a new marketing approach to launch Fusion.

BRANDING BRIEF 6-1

Have It Your Way in the DVR Market

Digital video recorders have changed the way people watch television, enabling them to pause live TV, "time-shift" by recording hours of their favorite television shows at the touch of a button, and fast-forward through commercials. TiVo pioneered the category of digital video recorders (DVRs) in 1999. TiVo users purchased the TiVo box and then paid $12.95 a month for the device to record and store programming. TiVo succeeded in creating a niche for something completely new, reaching one of the ultimate benchmarks of cultural acceptance—it became a verb! To "TiVo" something now extends to the whole genre of DVRs.

Though TiVo established the DVR category, the company began losing ground to competitors as other brands such as Panasonic, Samsung, and Sony moved into the market. By 2005, TiVo had only 2.3 million subscribers, well short of targets. To curry favor with advertisers, TiVo announced in late 2004 that it would allow advertisers to put logos over their ads so the logos would be visible when viewers fast-forwarded through the ads. This tactic, some industry watchers say, contradicted TiVo's "TV your way" philosophy. In 2005, TiVo had to deal with the departures of the company's CEO and president, rumors of an Apple takeover, and the demise of its exclusive deal with DirecTV.

After these setbacks, TiVo finalized a seven-year deal with Comcast that allowed the cable operator to use TiVo technology for its cable boxes. Other cable companies recognized that DVRs were gaining popularity among consumers, and Cox, Comcast, Time Warner, and

Figure 6-5 describes, the two main concerns in devising an advertising strategy are as follows:

- Defining the proper positioning to maximize brand equity
- Identifying the best creative strategy to communicate or convey the desired positioning

Chapter 3 described a number of issues with respect to positioning strategies to maximize brand equity. Creative strategies can be either informational and elaborate on a specific product-related attribute or benefit, or transformational, portraying a specific non-product-related benefit or image.[14] These two general categories each encompass several different specific creative approaches. Regardless of which general creative approach marketers take, however, certain motivational or "borrowed interest" devices can attract consumers' attention and raise their involvement with an ad. These devices include cute babies, frisky puppies, popular music, well-liked celebrities, amusing situations, provocative sex appeals, or fear-inducing threats. Many believe such techniques are necessary in the tough new media environment characterized by low-involvement consumer processing and much competing ad and programming clutter.

Unfortunately, these attention-getting tactics are often *too* effective and distract from the brand or its product claims. Thus, the challenge in arriving at the best creative strategy is figuring out how to break through the clutter to attract the attention of consumers but still deliver the intended message. Consider how Virgin chose to introduce its new credit card in Australia.[15]

EchoStar, among other cable and satellite providers, soon began including DVRs in their cable boxes for a small additional fee. Forrester Research reported that DVR penetration in the United States should reach nearly 50 percent in 2009.

Advertisers have had to come up with new formats that work with DVRs. Some advertisers have created mini-programs, similar to movie trailers, and other long-form advertisements that viewers can access on their DVRs. Several new companies already offer technology to help satellite and cable operators target viewers with customized ads. Companies such as Honda and Miramax Films have already used interactive commercials with DVD-like menus to give viewers options.

The challenge is that advertisers initially cannot predict how many people will go into the interactive ads and how far into the ad they will venture. But experimentation with interactive ads is growing, and some view them as a potential venue for educational programming. One problem is that the ads take a long time to produce. Ultimately ad executives are hoping interactive ads will be more appealing than traditional ads because viewers control them and decide when they want to watch them.

Sources: Megan Larson, "Fast Forward," *Adweek*, 4 April 2005; Allen P. Adamson, "I Love You, TiVo, Now Change," *Advertising Age*, 17 January 2005; Tony Case, "Sizing up DVRs," *Brandweek*, 20 September 2004; Diane Anderson, "Second Act," *Adweek*, 4 April 2005.

DEFINE POSITIONING TO ESTABLISH BRAND EQUITY

Competitive frame of reference

Nature of competition

Target market

Point-of-parity attributes or benefits

Necessary

Competitive

Point-of-difference attributes or benefits

Desirable

Deliverable

IDENTIFY CREATIVE STRATEGY TO COMMUNICATE POSITIONING CONCEPT

Informational (benefit elaboration)

Problem-solution

Demonstration

Product comparison

Testimonial (celebrity or unknown consumer)

Transformational (imagery portrayal)

Typical or aspirational usage situation

Typical or aspirational user of product

Brand personality and values

Motivational ("borrowed interest" techniques)

Humor

Warmth

Sex appeal

Music

Fear

Special effects

Source: Based in part on an insightful framework put forth in John R. Rossiter and Larry Percy, *Advertising and Promotion Management*, 2nd ed. (New York: McGraw-Hill, 1997).

FIGURE 6-5

Factors in Designing Effective Advertising Campaigns

Virgin Credit Card

When the Virgin credit card was launched in the Australian market, 80 percent of the market was dominated by the four big banks, and the rest of the market was crowded with 300 different credit cards. Australians had low expectations with regard to their credit cards. Most cards charged an annual fee of at least $100, with interest rates of 16–18 percent, and rewards were taking longer to earn. The campaign for Virgin credit cards, entitled "Plastic Surgery," was based on showcasing the discounts and rewards available when using the card, and the 12.4 percent rate of interest and zero annual fee. The television ad featured extra costs being snipped off the card. Virgin also used press advertisements, online banner ads, radio, and direct marketing. Within a week of launching the card, Virgin had 50,000 applications. After 17 months it had 400,000 customers, or 4 percent of the total market.

What makes an effective TV ad? Fundamentally, a TV ad should contribute to brand equity in some demonstrable way, for example, by enhancing awareness, strengthening a key association or adding a new association, or eliciting a positive consumer response. We identified six broad information-processing factors as affecting the success of advertising: consumer targeting, the ad creative, consumer understanding, brand positioning, consumer motivation, and ad memorability. The EFFIE awards for advertising effectiveness are based on the following subjective criteria: Background/Strategy (marketing challenge, target insight, campaign objective), Creative (idea, link to strategy, and quality of execution), and Media (link to market strategy, link to creative strategy), which together account for 70 percent of an ad campaign's score. Proof of Results accounts for 30 percent.[16]

Although managerial judgment using criteria such as these can and should be employed in evaluating advertising, research also can play a productive role. Advertising strategy research is often invaluable in clarifying communication objectives, target markets, and positioning alternatives. To evaluate the effectiveness of message and creative strategies, ***copy testing*** is often conducted, in which a sample of consumers is exposed to candidate ads and their reactions are gauged in some manner.

Unfortunately, copy-testing results vary considerably depending on exactly how they are conducted. Consequently, the results of an ad copy test must be interpreted as only one possible data point that should be combined with managerial judgment and other information in evaluating the merits of an ad. Copy testing is perhaps most useful when managerial judgment reveals some fairly clear positive and negative aspects to an ad and is therefore somewhat inconclusive. In this case, copy-testing research may shed some light on how these various conflicting aspects "net out" and collectively affect consumer processing.

Regardless, copy-testing results should not be seen as a means of making a "go" or "no go" decision; ideally, they should play a diagnostic role in helping to understand *how* an ad works. As an example of the potential fallibility of pretesting, consider NBC's experiences with the popular TV series *Seinfeld*.

SEINFELD

In October 1989, *The Seinfeld Chronicles,* as it was called then, was shown to several groups of viewers in order to gauge the show's potential, like most television pilot projects awaiting final network approval. The show tested badly—very badly. The summary research report noted that "no segment of the audience was eager to watch the show again." The reaction to Seinfeld himself was "lukewarm" because his character was seen as "powerless, dense, and naïve." The test report also concluded that "none of the supports were particularly liked and viewers felt that Jerry needed a better back-up ensemble." Despite the weak reaction, NBC decided to go ahead with what became one of the most successful television shows of the 1990s. Although they later also changed their testing methods, NBC's experience reinforces the limitations of testing and the dangers of relying on single numbers.[17]

If NBC executives had followed its pilot research results, they would have never launched the popular TV series, Seinfeld.

FUTURE PROSPECTS. In the new computer era, the future of television and traditional mass marketing advertising is uncertain. In 2004, Procter & Gamble CMO Jim Stengel gave a sobering status report to the advertising industry.[18] Stengel pointed out that although new media were now abundant, marketers and agencies were not using or measuring them sufficiently. He noted how 90 percent of P&G's global ad spending was on TV in 1994, but one of its most successful brand launches in history, for Prilosec OTC in 2003, allocated only about one-quarter of its spending to TV.

Other advertisers have stated they will eventually bypass ad agencies via interactive shopping channels, CD-ROM catalogs, multimedia kiosks, and online services.[19] Nevertheless, at least for some, the power of TV ads remains. As one advertising executive put it, "Nothing competes with prime time television when it comes to communicating with a mass audience. Other mediums can't entertain and inform in the same captivating way."

BRANDING BRIEF 6-2

iPod Silhouettes Campaign Captures Music Lovers

Apple Computer and its ad agency, TBWA/Chiat/Day Los Angeles won a Grand EFFIE in June 2005 for the iPod "Silhouettes" advertising campaign. The EFFIE awards are given annually by the New York American Marketing Association in recognition of the year's most effective advertising campaigns.

Apple began selling the iPod MP3 player, a compact music player with a streamlined style, in 2001. The new device was a hit with celebrities and technical writers, but many consumers were under the impression that it was a sophisticated device for tech fans, rather than the average music lover. The ad agency and Apple set a goal to "create a campaign that extended iPod's relevance to more music lovers and told the world this wasn't just a tech-gadget available to few, but was the icon that stood for a new experience with music."

The marketing effort was designed to appeal to Mac fans as well as people who had not used Apple products in the past. The Silhouettes campaign ran all over the world, so the message had to be simple enough to work across cultures. The ads also had to portray the iPod as cool, but not so cool as to be beyond the reach of anyone who enjoyed music.

Apple wanted to establish the iPod as a universal icon of digital music. The company set a goal of increasing sales by 50 percent in the United States and 25 percent in other markets. The idea behind the campaign was that the iPod was a passport to enjoying music whenever and wherever a consumer wanted. Text within the ads, such as "*iPod. Welcome to the digital music*

Radio. Radio is a pervasive medium: 96 percent of all Americans 12 years and older listen to the radio daily and, on average, over 20 hours a week. Perhaps the main advantage to radio is flexibility—stations are highly targeted, ads are relatively inexpensive to produce and place, and short closings allow for quick responses. For example, AT&T uses radio to target African American consumers.[20] African Americans spend an average of 4 hours every day listening to the radio, far more time than the national average of 2.8 hours. As the centerpiece of its 2000 multimedia campaign, AT&T sponsored a live radio broadcast of a Destiny's Child concert that included a promotion through which listeners could win a trip to New Orleans.

Radio is a particularly effective medium in the morning and can effectively complement or reinforce TV ads. Radio also enables companies to achieve a balance between broad and localized market coverage. Obvious disadvantages of radio, however, are the lack of visual image and the relatively passive nature of consumer processing that results. Several brands, however, have effectively built brand equity with radio ads.[21]

Motel 6 has one of the most successful radio campaigns around.

MOTEL 6

One notable radio ad campaign is for Motel 6, the nation's largest budget motel chain, which was founded in 1962 when the "6" stood for $6 a night. After finding its business fortunes hitting bottom in 1986 with an occupancy rate of only 66.7 percent, Motel 6 made a number of marketing changes, including the launch of a radio campaign of humorous 60-second ads featuring folksy contractor-turned-writer Tom Bodett. Containing the clever tag line "We'll leave the light on for you," the ad campaign is credited with a rise in occupancy and a revitalization of the brand that continues to this day.

revolution. 10,000 songs in your pocket. Mac or PC," told the story of the iPod's capabilities in a simple, appealing way. And the concept of 10,000 songs was designed to appeal to consumers in markets like Japan, where other mini-disk players with less capacity crowded the market.

The top markets for digital music were picked based on their role as influencers for youth culture in their regions. Apple's campaign strategically targeted a handful of big cities such as San Francisco and Shanghai and used them as the focus for all media spending in that market. Those cities were flooded with iPod billboards, bus posters, print ads, and TV commercials that were intended to spread the message "iPod is everywhere."

Silhouettes television commercials featured people in silhouette listening to iPods and dancing in front of neon backgrounds. Songs in the ads included U2's "Vertigo" and Eminem's "Lose Yourself." Similar images of people dancing were used for the print ads, billboards, and posters.

Three months after the start of the "Silhouettes" campaign, iPod sales were up 50 percent over sales from the quarter before the campaign launched. In the United States, the iPod grabbed the biggest market share of all MP3 players. Duke University began giving iPods to all incoming freshmen, and school districts started experimenting with the devices as tools for teaching language skills. The campaign ran or is still running in 16 countries.

Sources: Jay Parsons, "A Is for Apple on iPod," *Dallas Morning News,* 6 October 2005; www.apple.com; www.effie.org, "Apple Computer: iPod Silhouettes," New York Marketing Association.

What makes an effective radio ad?[22] Radio has been less studied than other media. Because of its low-involvement nature and limited sensory options, advertising on radio often must be fairly focused. For example, the advertising pioneer David Ogilvy believes four factors are critical:[23]

1. Identify your brand early in the commercial.
2. Identify it often.
3. Promise the listener a benefit early in the commercial.
4. Repeat it often.

Nevertheless, radio ads can be extremely creative. Some see the lack of visual images as a plus because they feel the clever use of music, sounds, humor, and other creative devices can tap into the listener's imagination in a way that creates powerfully relevant and liked images.

Print. Print media offer a stark contrast to broadcast media. Most important, because they are self-paced, magazines and newspapers can provide detailed product information. At the same time, the static nature of the visual images in print media makes it difficult to provide dynamic presentations or demonstrations. Another disadvantage of print advertising is that it can be a fairly passive medium.

The two main print media—magazines and newspapers—have many of the same advantages and disadvantages. Magazines are particularly effective at building user and usage imagery. Magazines can also be highly engaging: One study showed that consumers are more likely to view magazine ads as less intrusive, more truthful, and more relevant than ads in other media and are less likely to multitask while reading.[24] Newspapers, however, are more timely and pervasive. Daily newspapers are read by over half of the population (with almost two-thirds reading the Sunday edition) and tend to be used a lot for local (especially retailer) advertising. On the other hand, although advertisers have some flexibility in designing and placing newspaper ads, poor reproduction quality and short shelf life can diminish some of the possible impact of newspaper advertising. These are disadvantages that magazine advertising usually doesn't share.

Although print advertising is particularly well suited to communicate product information, it can also effectively communicate user and usage imagery. Brands such as Calvin Klein, Tommy Hilfiger, and Guess have also created strong nonproduct associations through print advertising. Some brands attempt to communicate both product benefits and user or usage imagery in their print advertising, for example, car makers such as Ford, Lexus, and Volvo or cosmetics makers such as Maybelline and Revlon.

One of the longest running and perhaps most successful print ad campaigns ever is for Absolut vodka.

Absolut

In 1980, Absolut was a tiny brand, selling 100,000, 9-liter cases that year. Research conducted at that time had pointed out a number of liabilities for the brand: The name was seen as too gimmicky, the bottle shape was ugly and bartenders found it hard to pour, shelf prominence was limited, and there was no credibility for a vodka brand made in Sweden. Michel Roux, president

Absolut's print campaign is one of the most famous in magazine history.

Source: ABSOLUT COUNTRY OF SWEDEN VODKA & LOGO, ABSOLUT BOTTLE

of Carillon (Absolut's importer), and TBWA (Absolut's New York ad agency) decided to use the oddities of the brand—its quirky name and bottle shape—to create brand personality and communicate quality and style in a series of creative print ads. Each ad in the campaign visually depicted the product in an unusual fashion and verbally reinforced the image with a simple, two-word headline using the brand name and some other word in a clever play on words. For example, the first ad showed the bottle prominently displayed, crowned by an angel's halo, with the headline "Absolut Perfection" appearing at the bottom of the page. Follow-up ads explored various themes (seasonal, geographic, celebrity artists) but always attempted to put forth a fashionable, sophisticated, and contemporary image. By 2001, Absolut had become the leading imported vodka in the United States, and by 2006, the brand had become the third largest premium spirits brand in the world, with sales of 9.8 million 9 liter cases.

GUIDELINES. What makes an effective print ad? The evaluation criteria we noted earlier for television advertising apply, but print advertising has some special requirements and rules. For example, research on print ads in magazines reveals that it is not uncommon for two-thirds of a magazine audience to not even notice any one particular print ad, or for only 10 percent or so of the audience to read much of the copy of any one ad. Many readers only glance at the most visible elements of a print ad, making it critical that an ad communicate clearly, directly, and consistently in the ad illustration and headline. Figure 6-6 contains some important creative guidelines for print ads. We can sum them up in three simple criteria: clarity, consistency, and branding.[25]

Direct Response. In contrast to advertising in traditional broadcast and print media, which typically communicates to consumers in a nonspecific and nondirective manner, ***direct response*** uses mail, telephone, Internet, and other nonpersonal contact tools to communicate with or solicit a response from specific customers and prospects. Direct response can take many forms and is not restricted to solicitations by mail, telephone, or even within traditional broadcast and print media.[26]

One increasingly popular means of direct marketing is infomercials.[27] In a marketing sense, an infomercial attempts to combine the sell of commercials with the draw of

In judging the effectiveness of a print ad, in addition to considering the communication strategy (target market, communication objectives, and message strategy), marketers should be able to answer yes to the following questions about the execution:

1. Is the message clear at a glance? Can you quickly tell what the advertisement is all about?
2. Is the benefit in the headline?
3. Does the illustration support the headline?
4. Does the first line of the copy support or explain the headline and illustration?
5. Is the ad easy to read and follow?
6. Is the product easily identified?
7. Is the brand or sponsor clearly identified?

Source: Philip Ward Burton and Scott C. Purvis, *Which Ad Pulled Best?* 9th ed. (Lincolnwood, IL: NTC Business Books, 2002). Used with permission of McGraw-Hill.

FIGURE 6-6

Print Ad Evaluation Criteria

educational information and entertainment. As such, infomercials can be thought of as a cross between a sales call and a television ad. Infomercials can vary in length but are often 30-minute video programs that are made at the cost of $250,000 to $500,000. A number of individuals have become famous with late-night channel switchers for pitching various wares. Increasingly, companies selling products that are complicated, technologically advanced, or simply require a great deal of explanation are turning to infomercials, such as Callaway Golf, Carnival Cruises, Mercedes, Microsoft, Philips Electronics, Universal Studios, and even the online job search site Monster.com.[28]

GUIDELINES. Direct marketing has consistently outgrown every media spending category since 1986. This steady growth is a function of technological advances like the ease of setting up toll-free numbers, changes in consumer behavior such as the increased demand for convenience, and the needs of marketers, who want to avoid wasteful communications to nontarget customers or customer groups. The advantage of direct response is that it makes it easier for marketers to establish relationships with consumers.

Direct communications through newsletters, catalogs, electronic home pages, and so forth allow marketers to explain new developments with their brands to consumers on an ongoing basis, as well as allow consumers to provide feedback to marketers about their likes and dislikes and specific needs and wants. By learning more about customers, marketers can fine-tune marketing programs to offer the right products to the right customers at the right time. In fact, direct marketing is often seen as a key component of relationship marketing—an important marketing trend we reviewed in Chapter 5.

As the name suggests, the goal of direct response is to elicit some type of behavior from consumers; given that, it is easy to measure the effects of direct marketing efforts—people either respond or they do not. The disadvantages to direct response, however, are intrusiveness and clutter. To implement an effective direct marketing program, marketers need the three critical ingredients of (1) developing an up-to-date and informative list of current and potential future customers, (2) putting forth the right offer in the right manner, and (3) tracking the effectiveness of the marketing program.

To improve the effectiveness of direct marketing programs, many marketers are embracing database marketing. Regardless of the particular means of direct marketing, database marketing can help create targeted communication and marketing programs tailored to the needs and wants of specific consumers. Database marketers collect consumers' names and information about their attitudes and behavior, which they compile in a comprehensive database. They obtain this information from consumers when they place orders, send in a coupon, fill out a warranty card, or enter a sweepstakes.

Database marketing is generally more effective at helping firms retain existing customers than in attracting new ones. Many marketers believe that database marketing makes more sense the higher the price of the product and the more often consumers buy it. Database marketing pioneers include a number of financial services firms and airlines. Even packaged-goods companies, however, are exploring the possible benefits of database marketing. For example, Procter & Gamble created a database to market Pampers disposable diapers, allowing P&G to send out "individualized" birthday cards for babies and reminder letters to parents to move their child up to the next size.[29] Database management tools will become a priority to marketers as they attempt to track the lifetime value of customers.

Interactive. The end of the twentieth century was the dawn of interactive, online marketing communications. With the growth of the Internet, marketers scrambled to build a presence in cyberspace. The approaches that companies adopted vary widely. Reviewing all the guidelines for online marketing communications is beyond the scope of this text.[30] Here we'll concentrate on two crucial online brand-building tools: Web sites and interactive ads.

WEB SITES. The main advantages to marketing on the Web are the low cost, and the level of detail and degree of customization it offers. By capitalizing on its interactive nature, marketers can construct Web sites that allow any consumer to choose the brand information relevant to his or her needs or desires. Interactive marketing can thus pave the way for solid relationship building. In creating online information sources for consumers at company Web sites, marketers will want to deliver timely and reliable information. Web sites must be updated frequently and offer as much customized information as possible, especially for existing customers.

Because consumers often go online to seek information rather than be entertained, some of the more successful Web sites are those that are able to convey expertise in a consumer-relevant area. For example, Web sites such as P&G's Pampers.com and General Mills' Cheerios.com offer baby and parenting advice. Web sites can store company and product information, press releases, advertising and promotional information, as well as links to partners and key vendors. Many Web marketers collect names and addresses for a database and conduct e-mail surveys and online focus groups.

Designing Web sites requires creating eye-catching pages that can sustain browsers' interest, employing the latest technology and effectively communicating the corporate message. One top designer notes that it is important for users to feel as if they have just entered a new, cohesive world, requiring that different pages and content areas within a site have consistent design elements, colors, and placement. Web site design is crucial because if consumers do not have a positive experience, it may be very difficult to entice them back in the highly competitive and cluttered online world.

To spread the word about their Web sites, advertisers adopt a number of approaches. Marketing on the Web will clearly change dramatically as its technology changes. Improved audio and video capabilities will allow for advertising with more impact, and advances in software that ensure secure transactions will drive more online sales. Traditional print and broadcast ads, however, may not translate well to a high-tech media form. The challenge will be to entertain people but still communicate desired information.

ONLINE ADS. A number of potential advantages exist for Web advertising: It is accountable, because software can track which ads went to which sales; it is nondisruptive, so it doesn't interrupt consumers; and it can target consumers so that only the most promising prospects are contacted, who can then seek as much or as little information as they desire.[31]

Unfortunately, there are also many disadvantages. Many consumers find it easy to ignore banner ads. From 1995 to 2001, the click-through rate for banner ads slipped from 40 percent to 0.5 percent. Too many ads were uninspired as advertisers struggled to learn how to use the medium. Efforts to create more attention through pop-up or pop-under ads that generate mini-windows, however, often infuriated consumers.

Increasingly, Web ads are becoming closer to traditional forms of advertising, like streaming Web ads. BMW created a series of made-for-the-Web movies using well-known directors such as Guy Ritchie and actors such as Madonna. Ford and General Motors both created online videogames to promote their cars. For example, Ford's game for its Escape small sport utility vehicle allowed players to steer the vehicle through a race course on the moon. Users could then e-mail the game to friends and issue a challenge to beat their score.[32]

As a manifestation of permission marketing, e-mail ads in general—often including advanced features such as personalized audio messages, color photos, and streaming video—have increased in popularity. E-mail ads often receive response rates of 20 percent to 30 percent at a cost less than that of banner ads. Tracking these response rates, marketers can fine-tune their messages. The key, as with direct advertising, is to create a good customer list.

Another alternative to banner ads that advertisers employ is search advertising, in which users are presented with sponsored links relevant to their search words alongside unsponsored search results. Since these links are tied to specific keywords, marketers can

BRANDING BRIEF 6-3

More Revenue, Interest Pour into Online Ads

Online video ads are grabbing more of the advertising action and providing advertisers with an increasingly appealing avenue for reaching consumers. Some online ads with embedded hyperlinks and pop-up windows now allow customers to interact with images instead of just watching ads. Spending on online advertising is on the rise as the technology improves and more households acquire high-speed Internet connections.

Mitsubishi's 2004 Super Bowl advertising was one of the first successful uses of online video ads. The commercials closed with a dramatic, ambiguous scene and announced that the ending could be viewed online. The Mitsubishi site received a million visitors, more than 70 percent of whom watched the ad more than once. A significant benefit of such ads is that because traffic on the Internet is easily tracked, companies know how long visitors stay on their Web site and what they view. The Mitsubishi effort yielded a big spike in sales of the sedan featured in the ads.

Innovative campaigns like Mitsubishi's also draw viewers in a valuable demographic: 18- to 34-year-olds. Young adults are spending more and more time on the Web, and online ads are being created as interactive entertainment to capture them as they troll their favorite Web sites. Access to that demographic is prompting big companies like McDonald's, Coke, and Cadillac to create their own video ads. In 2001, McDonald's spent 80 percent of its ad budget on prime-time television. In 2005, it allocated less than half its ad budget to prime-time. McDonald's airs some of its television ads online and also offers customized videos featuring stars like Beyonce Knowles.

target them more effectively than banner ads and thus generate higher response rates. Google pioneered search advertising, and helped make it a cost-effective option for online advertisers, by offering "cost-per-click" pricing, wherein advertisers were charged based on the number of times a sponsored link was actually clicked. Other sites such as Yahoo! and Ask.com also began offering search advertising, making it a $5-billion-per-year market by 2005.[33] Branding Brief 6-3 describes the growth of online ads.

MOBILE MARKETING.[34] Personal digital assistants and cell phones are playing an increasingly important role in consumers' lives, and more marketers are taking notice. Because many consumers use the gadgets for information and entertainment as well as communication, investment in mobile marketing from a range of sectors looking to tap a new revenue stream is expected to grow rapidly during the next few years.

Mobile content owners are expected to concentrate on communicating with their customers, promoting personalization options like logos, ringtones, and wallpapers. Broadcast media owners and publishers are looking to build interactivity into their programming to establish closer relationships with audiences. Packaged goods, travel, fashion, and financial services are interested in mobile marketing as a cost-effective channel for customer communications. And more companies will offer "infotainment" content services such as news, sports, and games.

Cell phones present a unique opportunity for marketers because they can be in consumers' hands at the point of sale or consumption. A campaign for Hershey's chocolate milk at 15,000 convenience stores featured a sticker on store refrigerators instructing the purchaser to text the bar code on the milk container to enter a contest. That interaction,

Video ads are far outpacing other forms of Internet advertising and are expected to keep growing. One obstacle to the growth of the ads, though, is that because many Web sites are not configured to support video ads, there are a limited number of slots for the videos. Many companies believe that the more time a consumer spends on their site, the better. For American Express, one of the attractions of using the Web in this way is that the Internet fosters a sense of community, a feeling that works well for a company promoting the benefits of membership. American Express is experimenting with advertising content in other places as well, gradually shifting its budget to new places, including the reality television series *The Restaurant,* where it can connect with consumers.

Video advertising is also finding a new niche on cell phones, iPods, and BlackBerries. Nestle Purina PetCare Co. decided to explore this venue in 2005 with sound files for downloading onto music players and tips for pet owners that can be sent to mobile devices. Purina, looking to differentiate itself in the highly competitive pet food business, strategized that it would be best to reach consumers via the devices they spend the most time with. Efforts like Purina's are becoming more and more common as digital video recorders allow television viewers to skip commercials.

Sources: Ann M. Mack, "Buddy Movies," *Brandweek,* 22 November 2004; Matthew Maier, "What's Next," *Business 2.0,* May 2005; Ronald Grover, "Mad Ave Is Starry-Eyed over Net Video," *BusinessWeek,* 23 May 2005; Mei Fong, "Don't Tell the Kids: Computer Games Can Make You Rich," *Wall Street Journal,* 21 May 2004; Janet Whitman, "Even Fido Is Going Wireless," *Dow Jones,* 29 June 2005.

besides promoting the brand, also provides data about advertising campaigns and distribution strategies. A marketer can put different short-code key words into calls to text the various print and electronic media, and then determine which ad medium is most effective in driving consumer awareness and interaction.

Most of these efforts requires consumer permission and opt-in; therefore, they reach only subscribers willing to participate. But many consumers will also receive messages from their network operator or handset without opting in. A key question is, how can marketers get cell phone users to opt in? Spam is already a problem for some cell phone users, because in the U. S., users pay for incoming calls and messages. Network operators may need to initiate controls to assure consumers that they will not be inundated with mobile marketing messages. Some experts believe the answer lies in quality content, which could range from weather updates to downloadable coupons, and ensuring messages become more sophisticated and appealing as new and better data formats are adopted.

Vibes Media

Vibes Media creates text message–based marketing programs and has developed software that allows marketers to communicate with customers in new ways. The company has used its live Text-2-Screen and Pix-2-Screen platforms to allow users to submit text and images that go directly to a screen behind a band or on a Jumbotron at a venue. Vibes Media used this technology for a Motorola promotion in Times Square on New Year's Eve and for the band Green Day's concert tour. It also runs programs in bars for clients such as Bed Light, where customers can type text into their phones and the message will be flashed on a big screen. And song requests can be texted to radio stations, letting listeners avoid the busy signal they would usually encounter on the phone.

Several years ago, the idea of mobile marketing was met with fear that marketers would alienate customers with annoying product pitches. But creative messages that pull consumers into dialogue with the brand have evolved into an appealing way to increase brand awareness, especially when it is part of a larger campaign in other media.

Place. The last category of advertising is also often called "nontraditional," "alternative," or "support" advertising, because it has arisen in recent years as a means to complement more traditional advertising media. ***Place advertising***, also called ***out-of-home advertising***, is a broadly defined category that captures advertising outside traditional media. Increasingly, ads and commercials are showing up in unusual spots, sometimes as parts of experiential marketing programs. The rationale is often that because traditional advertising media—especially television advertising—are becoming less effective, marketers are better off reaching people in other environments, such as where they work, play, and, of course, shop. Some of the options available include billboards; movies, airlines, and lounges; product placement; and point-of-purchase advertising.

BILLBOARDS AND POSTERS. In 1925, Burma-Shave placed a set of four billboards in sequence along roads nationwide with the following jingle:

Shave the modern way.
Fine for the skin.
Druggists have it.
Burma-Shave.

The success of Burma-Shave billboards convinced marketers that consumers would notice and remember simple messages conveyed in "unexpected" places. Billboards have been transformed over the years and now employ colorful, digitally produced graphics, backlighting, sounds, movement, and unusual—even three-dimensional—images to attract attention. Billboards do not even necessarily have to stay in one place. Marketers can buy ad space on billboard-laden trucks that are driven around all day in marketer-selected areas. For example, Oscar Mayer sends six "Wienermobiles" traveling across the country.

Billboard-type poster ads are now showing up everywhere in the United States each year to increase brand exposure and goodwill. Transit ads on buses, subways, and commuter trains—around for years—have now become a valuable means to reach working women. Street furniture (bus shelters, kiosks, and public areas) has become a fast-growing area. Goodyear, whose brand-emblazoned blimp enjoyed clear skies for over 50 years, has been joined by Fuji, Met Life, Monster.com, Blockbuster Video, and others who sponsor a blimp.

Advertisers now can buy space in stadiums and arenas and on garbage cans, bicycle racks, parking meters, airport luggage carousels, elevators, gasoline pumps, the bottom of golf cups, airline snacks, and supermarket produce in the form of tiny labels on apples and bananas. Leaving no stone unturned, advertisers can even buy space in toilet stalls and above urinals, which, according to research studies, office workers visit an average of three to four times a day for roughly four minutes per visit.[35] Figure 6-7 displays some of the most successful outdoor advertisers.

MOVIES, AIRLINES, LOUNGES, AND OTHER PLACES. Increasingly, advertisers are placing traditional TV and print ads in unconventional places.[36] Companies such as Whittle Communication and Turner Broadcasting have tried placing TV and commercial programming in classrooms, airport lounges, and other public places. Airlines now offer media-sponsored audio and video programming that accepts advertising (*USA Today Sky Radio* and *National Geographic Explorer*) and include catalogs in seat pockets for leading mail-order companies (High Street Emporium). Movie theater chains such as Loews Cineplex now run 30-, 60-, or 90-second ads on 2,000-plus screens. Although the same ads that appear on TV or in magazines often appear in these unconventional places, many

U.S. Army posters (1992)
Volkswagen and Burma-Shave (1993)
Nike (1994)
San Diego Zoo (1995)
Nissan (1996)
Coca-Cola (1997)
Levi's (1998)
Budweiser (1999)
Ford (2000)
Chevrolet (2001)
Target (2002)
McDonald's (2003)
Bank of America (2004)
Apple Computer (2005)

Year of induction is listed in parentheses.

FIGURE 6-7

Obie Hall of Fame Winners (as selected by the Outdoor Advertising Association of America)

advertisers believe it is important to create specially designed ads for these out-of-home exposures to better meet consumer expectations.

PRODUCT PLACEMENT. Many major marketers pay fees of $50,000 to $100,000 and even higher so that their products can make cameo appearances in movies and on television, with the exact fee depending on the amount and nature of the brand exposure. This practice got a boost in 1982 when—after Mars declined an offer for use of its M&M's brand—sales of Reese's Pieces increased 65 percent after the candy appeared prominently in the blockbuster movie *E.T.: The Extraterrestrial*.[37] Placement is not restricted to movies. Branding Brief 6-4 provides more detail on product placement.

Marketers combine product placements with special promotions to publicize a brand's entertainment tie-ins and create "branded entertainment." For example, BMW complemented product placement in the James Bond film *Goldeneye* with an extensive direct mail and advertising campaign to help launch its Z3 roadster. Some firms benefit from product placement at no cost by supplying their product to the movie company in return for exposure (Nike does not pay to be in movies but often supplies shoes, jackets, and bags), or simply because of the creative demands of the storyline (the central character in the film *Castaway,* played by Tom Hanks, was a FedEx pilot; as a result, the brand played a prominent role in the plot development without having to pay a cent).[38] To test the effects of product placement, marketing research companies such as CinemaScore conduct viewer exit surveys to determine which brands actually were noticed during movie showings.

POINT OF PURCHASE. Myriad possibilities have emerged in recent years as ways to communicate with consumers at the point of purchase. In-store advertising includes ads on shopping carts, cart straps, aisles, or shelves, as well as promotion options such as in-store demonstrations, live sampling, and instant coupon machines. Point-of-purchase radio provides FM-style programming and commercial messages to 6,500 food stores and 7,900 drugstores nationwide. Programming includes a store-selected music format,

BRANDING BRIEF 6-4

Product Placement Becomes More Creative, More Lucrative

As product placement during prime time grows steadily, advertisers have begun to employ the approach in other arenas as well. In video games, in the booming category of reality television, and in TV programming abroad, product placement is viewed as an effective way to reach an increasingly fragmented audience.

Many different brands employ product placement, as here with Apple and "24".

Media research firm PQ Media found that product placement has increased an average of 16 percent per year since 1999 and projected that spending on the practice would reach $4.25 billion in 2005. Advertisers are embracing product placement because they are discouraged by the returns on traditional commercials, and they are wary of viewers with digital video recorders skipping right over commercials. Also, product placement enjoys a reputation as a more subtle consumer overture than traditional commercials. Some experts warn; however, that viewers will reach a limit when it comes to accepting product placements. Too many products, especially if they are not woven smoothly into the content, will be a turn-off.

Formulas for structuring product-placement deals vary. When Oprah Winfrey wanted to give new cars to all members of her studio audience in 2004, General Motors agreed to provide more than 275 cars, worth a total of $7 million, in hopes that Oprah's reputation for good taste and quality would rub off on the new Pontiac G6 models. In 2005, nine

consumer tips, and commercials. Wal-Mart TV is installed in over 2,800 stores and is a mixture of information content and advertising.

The appeal of point-of-purchase advertising lies in the fact that, as numerous studies have shown, consumers in many product categories make the bulk of their final brand decisions in the store. For example, according to a study by ActMedia, which places ads in 7,000 supermarkets nationwide, 70 percent of all buying decisions are made in the store. In-store media are designed to increase the number and nature of spontaneous and planned buying decisions.

GUIDELINES. Nontraditional or place media present some interesting options for marketers to reach consumers in new ways. Ads now can appear virtually anyplace where consumers have a few spare minutes or even seconds and thus enough time to notice them. The main advantage of nontraditional media is that they can reach a very precise and captive audience in

brands supported Warner Bros.' teen movie *The Sisterhood of the Traveling Pants* with print campaigns, contests, and e-mails to customers in exchange for exposure in the film. And little-known bands have watched their record sales shoot up following appearances on television shows such as Fox's *The O.C.* and HBO'S *Six Feet Under.*

Usually those partnerships are the results of calculated negotiations. Sometimes, though, companies just get lucky. During the April 2005 Masters tournament, Tiger Woods sunk a spectacular chip shot that happened to put Nike's new One Platinum ball in perfect camera position. Viewers saw the Nike Swoosh inch toward the hole and then hover for a full second before dropping in. Experts say Nike couldn't have choreographed a better product placement.

Product placement deals tend to be creative, and they tend to be more experimental than traditional advertising. For the 2003–2004 season premiere of the TV show *24,* Ford reached a deal with Fox to feature a Ford-150 truck in the show and created long ads that mirrored the plot lines of the show to air at the beginning and the end of the episode. As deals like this have become more common, advertisers have gained the clout to dictate how their products are portrayed. Set designers and prop masters rely on free product placements to meet their budgets and are therefore more willing to let advertisers weigh in on when and how their products appear.

In China, some television stations are airing shows produced entirely by advertisers as product placement vehicles, much as American networks did at the dawn of the TV age. The arrangement is a boon to the advertisers, who spend much less on producing brand-centered shows than on creating pricey Chinese TV ads, and to the broadcasters, who get free programming out of the deal.

Interactive, exciting, and largely untapped by advertisers, video games are another relatively new entrée to consumers. Videogames have charged onto the advertising scene, representing a chance to reach a valuable demographic: young males. The ad industry is excited by the potential for live, in-game product placements and ads delivered to gamers who play while connected to the Internet. Nielson is working on creating new metrics to measure game-play behavior so that advertisers will have more data about ad viewership.

Sources: Marc Graser, "Product-Placement Spending Poised to Hit $4.25 Billion in '05," *Advertising Age,* 4 April 2005; Geoffrey A. Fowler, "New Star on Chinese TV: Product Placements," *Wall Street Journal,* 2 June 2004; Ethan Smith, "Ticket out of Obscurity," *Wall Street Journal,* 2 August 2004.

a cost-effective manner. Because the audience must process out-of-home ads quickly, however, the message must be simple and direct. In fact, outdoor advertising is often called the "15-second sell." Thus, strategically, out-of-home advertising is often more effective at enhancing awareness or reinforcing existing brand associations than at creating new ones.

The challenge with nontraditional media is demonstrating their reach and effectiveness through credible, independent research. Another danger of nontraditional media is consumer backlash against overcommercialization. Perhaps because of the sheer pervasiveness of advertising, however, consumers seem to be less bothered by nontraditional media now than in the past. For example, unlike Europeans, Americans resisted the notion of on-screen advertising in movie theaters and videos.[39] Yet, almost half of all theaters now run ads, albeit often bigger and more cinematic than their small-screen companions.

Consumers must be favorably affected in some way to justify the marketing expenditures for nontraditional media, and some firms offering ad placement in supermarket checkout lines, fast-food restaurants, physicians' waiting rooms, health clubs, and truck stops have suspended business at least in part because of lack of consumer interest. The bottom line, however, is that there will always be room for creative means of placing the brand in front of consumers. The possibilities are endless. For example, who could have guessed that RJR Nabisco would distribute sandals with the word *Camel* carved onto the bottom of their soles so that beachgoers could leave "Camel tracks" in the sand to help promote its cigarette![40]

Promotion

Sales promotions are short-term incentives to encourage trial or usage of a product or service.[41] Marketers can target sales promotions at either the trade or end consumers. Like advertising, sales promotions come in all forms. Whereas advertising typically provides consumers a *reason* to buy, sales promotions offer consumers an *incentive* to buy. Thus, sales promotions are designed to do the following:

- Change the behavior of the trade so that they carry the brand and actively support it
- Change the behavior of consumers so that they buy a brand for the first time, buy more of the brand, or buy the brand earlier or more often

Analysts maintain that the use of sales promotions grew in the 1980s and 1990s for a number of reasons. Brand management systems with quarterly evaluations were thought to encourage short-term solutions, and an increased need for accountability seemed to favor communication tools like promotions, whose behavioral effects are more quickly and easily observed than the often "softer" perceptual effects of advertising. Economic forces worked against advertising effectiveness as ad rates rose steadily despite what marketers saw as an increasingly cluttered media environment and fragmented audience. Consumers were thought to be making more in-store decisions, and to be less brand loyal and more immune to advertising than in the past. Many mature brands were less easily differentiated. On top of it all, retailers became more powerful.

For all these reasons, some marketers saw consumer and trade promotions as a more effective means than advertising to influence the sales of a brand. They favored trade promotions especially, because a product has to secure distribution before consumers can even have the opportunity to buy the brand if they so choose.

There clearly are advantages to sales promotions. Consumer sales promotions permit manufacturers to price discriminate by effectively charging different prices to groups of consumers who vary in their price sensitivity. Besides conveying a sense of urgency to consumers, carefully designed promotions can build brand equity through information or actual product experience that helps to create strong, favorable, and unique associations. Sales promotions can encourage the trade to maintain full stocks and actively support the manufacturer's merchandising efforts.

On the other hand, from a consumer behavior perspective, there are a number of disadvantages of sales promotions, such as decreased brand loyalty and increased brand switching, decreased quality perceptions, and increased price sensitivity. Besides inhibiting the use of franchise-building advertising or other communications, diverting marketing funds into coupons or other sales promotion sometimes has led to reductions in research and development budgets and staff. Perhaps most important, the widespread discounting arising from trade promotions may have led to the increased importance of price as a factor in consumer decisions, breaking down traditional brand loyalty patterns.

Another disadvantage of sales promotions is that in some cases they may merely subsidize buyers who would have bought the brand anyway. Moreover, new consumers attracted to the brand may attribute their purchase to the promotion and not to the merits of

1. *Type:* What type of promotion should be used?
   Immediate vs. delayed value
   Price cut vs. added value
2. *Product scope:* To what pack sizes or models should the promotion apply?
   Multiple or selective
   More or less popular
   In-line or out-of-line
3. *Market scope:* In which geographic markets should the promotion be offered?
   National or regional
4. *Timing:* When should the promotion be offered and for how long?
   When to promote (in- or off-season)
   When to announce (early or later)
   Duration (long or short)
   Frequency (high or low)
5. *Discount rate:* What explicit or implicit discount should the promotion include?
   Deep or shallow
6. *Terms:* What terms of sale should be attached to the promotion?
   Tight or loose

Source: Adapted from John A. Quelch, "Note on Sales Promotion Design," Teaching Note N-589-021 (Boston: Harvard Business School, 1988).

FIGURE 6-8

Issues in Designing Sales Promotions

the brand per se and, as a result, may not repeat their purchase when the promotional offer is withdrawn. Finally, retailers have come to expect and now demand trade discounts. The trade may not actually provide the agreed-upon merchandising and may engage in nonproductive activities such as forward buying and diversion (see Chapter 5). Because of these perceived drawbacks with sales promotions, recent years have seen some shift back to other forms of communication.[42]

Promotions have a number of possible objectives.[43] With consumers, objectives may target new category users, existing category users, and/or existing brand users. With the trade, objectives may center on distribution, support, inventories, or goodwill. Harvard's John Quelch proposes that marketers should address six issues in designing a sales promotion (see Figure 6-8). He argues that their actual choices in each area will depend on a number of factors, such as the level of consumer involvement, inventory risk, and franchise strength of the brand. Next, we consider some specific issues related to consumer and trade promotions.

Consumer Promotions. Consumer promotions are designed to change the choices, quantity, or timing of consumers' product purchases. Although they come in all forms, we distinguish between customer franchise building promotions like samples, demonstrations, and educational material, and noncustomer franchise building promotions such as price-off packs, premiums, sweepstakes, and refund offers.[44] Customer franchise building promotions can enhance the attitudes and loyalty of consumers toward a brand—in other words, affect brand equity.

For example, sampling is a means of creating strong, relevant brand associations while also perhaps kick-starting word of mouth among consumers. Marketers are increasingly using sampling at the point of use, growing more precise about where and how they deliver samples to maximize brand equity. As part of a sampling program, aerobics instructors at Bally's Fitness Clubs handed out Dove body wash, deodorant, and face cloths to students at the end of their classes before they showered.[45]

BRANDING BRIEF 6-5

Samsung DigitAll Matrix Promotional Campaign

Samsung's DigitAll Matrix campaign, linked with the Hollywood blockbuster *The Matrix,* marked the first time the manufacturer launched a global promotional/advertising campaign linked to a massive Hollywood film. The breakthrough visual effects and prestige of the film resonated with Samsung's core audience of high-tech enthusiasts—trendsetting, stylish consumers aged 17 to 39, eager to own the latest and greatest gadgets. Samsung's creative focus centered on the marriage of state-of-the-art technology with high fashion and enhanced experiences—traits shared by the film and the manufacturer.

The initial component of the Matrix campaign was Samsung's development of a limited-edition Matrix-themed wireless telephone, a reproduction of the prop created by the producers and production designer for in-film use by the lead characters. Samsung received logo exposure on the phone in the video releases of *The Matrix Reloaded* and also the "Enter the Matrix" video game. Samsung's development, manufacture, and launch of this custom product were achieved in fewer than 12 months.

Samsung's ad creative showcased the film's stars with 10 Samsung electronics products from a variety of brand groups. Broadcast spots mirrored the look and action of the movie and utilized talent from the film. The film's assistant director, James McTeigue, was retained to film

Thus, marketers increasingly judge sales promotions by their ability to contribute to brand equity as well as generate sales. The Promotion Marketing Association (PMA) bestows Reggie awards to recognize "superior promotional thinking, creativity, and execution across the full spectrum of promotional marketing." Branding Brief 6-5 describes a Reggie award–winning promotion that Samsung executed in 2004. As this example shows, creativity is as critical to promotions as it is to advertising or any other form of marketing communications.

Promotion strategy must reflect the attitudes and behavior of consumers. The percentage of coupons consumers redeem has dropped steadily in the last decade: The redemption rate was 3.5 percent in 1983, but only 0.94 percent in 2004.[46] Although there are a number of possible explanations, certainly one contributing factor is the large amount of coupon clutter. In 2004, marketers distributed 342 billion coupons, about 82 percent of which were in free-standing inserts (FSIs) in Sunday newspapers. As a result, one area of promotional growth is in-store coupons, which marketers have increasingly turned to as redemption rates of traditional out-of-store coupons slip.

Trade Promotions. Trade promotions are often financial incentives or discounts given to retailers, distributors, and other members of the trade to stock, display, and in other ways facilitate the sale of a product through slotting allowances, point-of-purchase displays, contests and dealer incentives, training programs, trade shows, and cooperative advertising. Trade promotions are typically designed either to secure shelf space and distribution for a new brand, or to achieve more prominence on the shelf and in the store. Shelf and aisle positions in the store are important because they affect the ability of the brand to catch the eye of the consumer—placing a brand on a shelf at eye level may double sales over placing it on the bottom shelf.[47]

Because of the large amount of money spent on trade promotions, there is increasing pressure to make trade promotion programs more effective, as suggested by the following commentary:

the TV spots, which featured five different products. The appearance and parameters of the campaign were carefully reinforced across all Samsung communications channels.

Globally, participating territories were encouraged to develop relevant holistic campaigns on a regional basis, utilizing some or all of the following elements: advertising media, Samsung's online microsite, POP displays, banners and signage, corporate film screenings, wireless marketing tie-ins (such as the Samsung Fun Club), PR and buzz marketing, and guerilla marketing (moving vehicle advertising, building wraps, public transportation).

Corporate screenings in London, Brazil, and Singapore surrounding the premiere helped bring Samsung employees and consumers further into the Matrix moment. Samsung received additional branding at these events via building signage, press coverage, on-site displays and product sampling, bandit marketing, popcorn bags, and other similar elements.

In total, Samsung spent $100 million on media and promotions globally, generating more than 1 billion advertising impressions received, and Samsung.com Web site page viewers increased 65 percent after the Samsung.com/Matrix microsite was opened. This traffic surpassed Samsung's previously most-popular microsite (the Olympics) by 500,000 impressions.

Sources: www.pmalink.org; www.samsung.com/my/presscenter/pressrelease/pressrelease_20030424_0000017602.asp.

> Increasingly the answer that glues the two into a workable partnership is account-specific promotions, tailored to each retailer, with budgets carved up to suit each market's demands. Manufacturers are decentralizing promotions, giving more responsibility for trade budgets to field salesmen. Big companies are setting up internal departments to implement and track these myriad local promotions; mid-size and smaller companies who can't afford the infrastructure are turning to outside services.[48]

As we noted in Chapter 5, some firms are attempting to substitute consumer-oriented promotions and advertising that can build the brand in a way to satisfy retailers and manufacturers. For example, since 1992, Procter & Gamble has run brand-specific TV and direct mail advertising customized for Wal-Mart, Kmart, Target, and other retailers.

Event Marketing and Sponsorship

Event marketing is public sponsorship of events or activities related to sports, art, entertainment, or social causes. Although the origin of event marketing can be traced back to philanthropic activities over a century ago, many observers identify mega-events in the mid-1980s, such as the 1984 Summer Olympics, Statue of Liberty Centennial, and Live Aid concert, as arousing marketers' interest in sponsorship in the United States.[49] According to the International Events Group, event sponsorship has grown rapidly in recent years, to total $33.7 billion globally in 2006. As Figure 6-9 shows, the vast majority of event expenditures occur in the world of sports. Once employed mostly by cigarette, beer, and auto companies, sports marketing is now being embraced by virtually every type of company. Moreover, virtually every sport—from dogsled racing to fishing tournaments and from tractor pulls to professional beach volleyball—now receives corporate backing of some kind.[50] Branding Brief 6-6 describes auto-racing sponsorship with NASCAR. Chapter 7 examines the issues of event marketing and sponsorship in terms of the secondary associations that they bring to the brand.

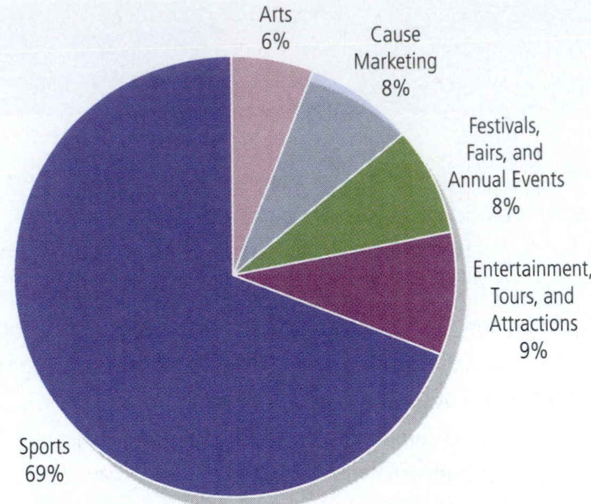

FIGURE 6-9

North American Sponsorship Spending by Property Type

BRANDING BRIEF 6-6

Building Sponsorship Resonance with Nascar

The National Association for Stock Car Auto Racing (NASCAR), founded in 1947 by stock-car promoter Bill France, descended from amateur dirt-track car racing in the South. Modern-day NASCAR races, with 200,000-capacity stadiums, 200 mph speeds, Fortune 500 sponsors, and nationally televised coverage, bear little resemblance to the races during NASCAR's first official season, when former bootleggers driving hot rods vied for $1,000 purses. NASCAR eventually outgrew its provincial roots in the South by holding races in northern cities like Detroit and significantly improving racetrack facilities, but not until the sport reached a national television audience with a CBS broadcast of the entire Daytona 500 in 1979 did NASCAR racing truly become a big-ticket event. The broadcast exceeded all expectations and earned a 10.5 rating, which corresponded with 15 million viewers.

NASCAR has attracted a wide range of sponsors.

The NASCAR audience continued to grow from that point. By 2004, NASCAR had become the second highest rated regular season sport on American TV, with 75 million fans or one-third of the U.S. adult population. As audience interest grew, corporations became increasingly interested in affiliating themselves with NASCAR. In 1971, R.J. Reynolds ushered in the era of corporate sponsorship when it paid $100,000 to sponsor the Winston Cup Series because tobacco companies were prohibited from advertising on television. In 2004, major corporations paid between $5 million and $10 million to sponsor a racing team, and more Fortune 500 companies participate in NASCAR than any other sport. Sponsoring companies include DuPont, Home Depot, and Nextel; sponsoring brands include Mountain Dew, Miller Lite, and Viagra.

Rationale. Event sponsorship provides a different kind of communication option for marketers. By becoming part of a special and personally relevant moment in consumers' lives, sponsors can broaden and deepen their relationship with their target market. Marketers report a number of reasons why they sponsor events:

- *To identify with a particular target market or lifestyle:* Marketers can link their brands to events popular with either a select or broad group of consumers. They can target customers geographically, demographically, psychographically, or behaviorally according to the sponsored events. In particular, marketers can choose events based on attendees' attitudes and usage of certain products or brands. Lexus sponsors tennis tournaments such as the U.S. Open because of a belief that tennis players are prime customers for its product. Similarly, Subaru believed there was a match between skiing events and potential buyers of its four-wheel-drive vehicles.
- *To increase awareness of the company or product name:* Sponsorship often offers sustained exposure to a brand, a necessary condition to building brand recognition. By skillfully choosing sponsorship events or activities, marketers can enhance identification with a product and thus also brand recall. For example, Dutch Boy has sponsored an "In the Paint" graphic in televised NBA coverage to update key game statistics (as hoop fans know, the area within the foul lines on a basketball court is referred to as "the paint").

Perhaps the main appeal to NASCAR sponsors is the large amount of exposure time for their brands, because the cars, visible for much of the event, are typically emblazoned with the brand logo. Moreover, NASCAR fans are an attractive audience to corporate sponsors because they tend to support NASCAR sponsors, more than fans of other sports do. Seventy-six percent of NASCAR fans know which company sponsors which drivers, and NASCAR fans are three times more likely to purchase the products and services of sponsors. According to Joyce Julius & Associates' Sponsors Report, NASCAR sponsors received nearly $5 billion in on-air exposure from televised events in 2001.

Today's NASCAR audience is also appealing to corporate sponsors because of its considerable demographic and economic diversity: 42 percent of fans have annual income exceeding $50,000, 32 percent of fans are between the ages of 18 and 34, and 40 percent of the audience is female. NASCAR races are becoming prized programming among television networks. In 2005, NASCAR agreed to a staggering 8-year, $4.48 billion television deal that split its schedule among five networks.

The strength of the NASCAR brand is that it combines thrilling and exciting entertainment with a sense of belonging and tradition. NASCAR generated $2.1 billion in licensed sales in 2003. In recent years, NASCAR has expanded its reach beyond the racetrack with an interactive Web site (www.nascar.com), a $20 million entertainment complex and museum called Daytona USA, the NASCAR Thunder chain of retail stores, and a restaurant called the NASCAR Café.

Sources: Robert G. Hagstrom, *The NASCAR Way* (New York: John Wiley & Sons, 1998); Keith Dunnavant, "NASCAR: Unsafe at This Speed?" *Business Week*, 1 November 1999; Brian O'Keefe, "America's Fastest Growing Sport, *Fortune*, September 5, 2005.

- *To create or reinforce consumer perceptions of key brand image associations:* Events themselves have associations that help to create or reinforce brand associations. For example, 24 Hour Total Fitness became the sponsor of NBC's surprise 2004 reality hit TV show, *The Biggest Loser,* about contestants competing to lose weight. In some cases, the product itself may be used at an event, providing demonstration of its abilities. For example, Seiko has been the official timer of the Olympics and other major sporting events for years.
- *To enhance corporate image dimensions:* Sponsorship is a soft sell and a means to improve perceptions that the company is likable, prestigious, and so forth. Marketers hope consumers will credit the company for its sponsorship and favor it in later product choices.
- *To create experiences and evoke feelings:* Events can be part of an experiential marketing program. The feelings engendered by an exciting or rewarding event may indirectly link to the brand. Marketers can also use the Web to provide further event support and additional experiences. American Express launched its Blue card through an outdoor concert in New York's Central Park featuring Sheryl Crow, among others.
- *To express commitment to the community or on social issues:* Often called cause-related marketing, sponsorships dedicated to the community or to promoting social issues create corporate tie-ins with nonprofit organizations and charities (see Chapter 11). An early pioneer in this area, American Express supported more than 70 causes in 18 countries with $8.6 million in donations from 1981 to 1986, ranging from the preservation of the national bird of Norway to the protection of the Italian coastline. As another example, for years Colgate-Palmolive has sponsored the Starlight Foundation, which grants wishes to young people who are critically ill.
- *To entertain key clients or reward key employees:* Many events have lavish hospitality tents and other special services or activities that are available only for sponsors and their guests. Involving clients with the event in these and other ways can engender goodwill and establish valuable business contacts. From an employee perspective, events can build participation and morale or create an incentive. For example, when John Hancock, as part of its Winter Olympic sponsorship in 1994, offered trips to Lillehammer, Norway, as a reward for agents who generated $100,000 in commissions, twice the number of agents qualified as in years past.
- *To permit merchandising or promotional opportunities:* Many marketers tie in contests or sweepstakes, in-store merchandising, and direct response or other marketing activities with their event. When Sprint sponsored the World Cup in 1994, its related activities included long-distance calling cards picturing soccer stars, a geography program for Latin American schools tied to game results, and discounts on long-distance calls for soccer-related businesses and local soccer groups.[51]

Despite these potential advantages, there are a number of potential disadvantages to sponsorship. The success of an event can be unpredictable and out of the sponsor's control. There can be much clutter in sponsorship. Finally, although many consumers will credit sponsors for providing necessary financial assistance to make an event possible, some consumers may still resent the commercialization of events through sponsorship.

Guidelines. Developing successful event sponsorship means choosing the appropriate events, designing the optimal sponsorship program, and measuring the effects of sponsorship on brand equity.[52]

CHOOSING SPONSORSHIP OPPORTUNITIES. Because of the huge amount of money involved and the number of event opportunities, many marketers are thinking more strategically about the events with which they will get involved and the manner by which they will do so. As it is, the sophistication in marketing events in the United States lags behind that of many countries in Europe and elsewhere, where restricted media options have spawned greater sponsorship activity over the years.

There are a number of potential guidelines for choosing events. First, the event must meet the marketing objectives and communication strategy defined for the brand. That is, the audience delivered by the event must match the target market of the brand. Moreover, the event must have sufficient awareness, possess the desired image, and be capable of creating the desired effects with that target market. Of particular concern is whether consumers make favorable attributions to the sponsor for its participation. An "ideal event" might be one whose audience closely matches the ideal target market, that generates much favorable attention, that is unique but not encumbered with many sponsors, that lends itself to ancillary marketing activities, and that reflects or even enhances the brand or corporate image of the sponsor.

Of course, rather than linking themselves to an event, some sponsors create their own. The cable sports network ESPN created the X Games to capture youth-oriented activities like road-luge racing, in-line skating, skateboarding, bungee jumping, and sky surfing that appealed to a market segment not as easily attracted to traditional sports. More and more firms are also using their names to sponsor the arenas, stadiums, and other venues that actually hold the events. Staples paid $100 million over 20 years to name the downtown Los Angeles arena where the NBA Lakers and Clippers and the NHL Kings play, and where concerts and other events are also held. Although stadium naming rights can command high fees, its direct contribution to building brand equity is primarily in creating brand recognition—not brand recall—and marketers can expect it to do little for brand image except perhaps to convey a certain level of scope and size.

DESIGNING SPONSORSHIP PROGRAMS. Many marketers believe that the marketing program accompanying a sponsorship is what ultimately determines its success. A sponsor can strategically identify itself at an event in a number of ways, including banners, signs, and programs. For more significant and broader impact, however, sponsors typically supplement such activities with samples, prizes, advertising, retail promotions, publicity, and so forth. Marketers often note that the budget for related marketing activities should be at least two to three times the amount of the sponsorship expenditure.

David D'Allesandro, former CEO of John Hancock, believes the key to successful sponsorship is leveraging the event so that it goes beyond simple calculations such as cost-per-thousand TV advertising exposures. John Hancock used sponsorships to entertain big clients, attract new customers, inspire current salespeople, recruit new salespeople, and raise employee morale. For Hancock, D'Allesandro believed the best events were either very big in scope, like the Olympics, or very localized, like a youth hockey clinic with an Olympian.

MEASURING SPONSORSHIP ACTIVITIES. There are two basic approaches to measuring the effects of sponsorship activities: The ***supply-side method*** focuses on potential exposure to the brand by assessing the extent of media coverage, and the ***demand-side method*** focuses on reported exposure from consumers.

Supply-side methods attempt to approximate the amount of time or space devoted to the brand in media coverage of an event. For example, we can estimate the number of seconds the brand is clearly visible on a television screen, or the column inches of press clippings covering an event that mention the brand. Then we can translate this measure of potential impressions delivered by an event sponsorship into an equivalent value in advertising dollars, according to the fees associated with actually advertising in the particular media vehicle.

JOHN HANCOCK

In 1991, John Hancock calculated that the value of press coverage of the college football bowl it sponsored—which included 7,829 stories and some TV reports—was worth $1.1 million.

John Hanock has sponsored many different things, including the prestigious Roberto Clemente award, which Albert Pujols receives here with his family.

Broadcast of the game by the CBS network included approximately 60 minutes of exposure to the brand in the four-hour telecast, which, when combined with the company's pregame promotions, added another $4 million in value. All told, Hancock believed the financial benefit of the sponsorship, based on the amount of coverage and what Hancock would have to pay for the same amount of ad space in print or commercial time on TV, was $5.1 million. Given that the total cost of the sponsorship was $1.6 million (which included $1 million sponsorship fees, $500,000 in TV rights fees, 10.5 minutes of paid commercial time during the TV broadcast, and $100,000 for various charity scholarships and a game banquet in the host city of El Paso), John Hancock believed the sponsorship was effective.[53]

Although supply-side exposure methods provide quantifiable measures, equating media coverage with advertising exposure ignores the content of the respective communications that consumers receive. The advertiser uses media space and time to communicate a strategically designed message. Media coverage and telecasts only expose the brand and don't necessarily embellish its meaning in any direct way. Although some public relations professionals maintain that positive editorial coverage can be worth 5 to 10 times the advertising equivalency value, it is rare that sponsorship affords the brand such favorable treatment. As one group of critics noted:

> Equating incidental visual and audio exposures with paid advertising time is, we feel, questionable at best. A commercial is a carefully crafted persuasive declaration of a product's virtues. It doesn't compete for attention with the actual on-camera action of a game or race. A 30-second exposure of a billboard in the background can't match the value of 30 seconds in which the product is the only star.[54]

An alternative measurement approach is the demand-side method, which attempts to identify the effects that sponsorship has on consumers' brand knowledge structures. Thus, tracking or custom surveys can explore the ability of the event sponsorship to affect awareness, attitudes, or even sales.

We can identify and survey event spectators after the event to measure recall of the event's sponsor, as well as attitudes and intentions toward the sponsor as a result of the event. For example, a survey by DDB Needham in 1992 indicated that 22 of 37 Olympic sponsors created no connection in consumer minds with the event.[55] A random survey of viewers who watched 10 or so hours of television coverage of the 1993 U.S. Open tennis tournament found that only 7 percent knew who sponsored the men's singles title (Nissan Motor Corporation's Infiniti brand), and only 14 percent knew who sponsored the women's singles title (Bristol-Meyer's Clairol brand).

Public Relations and Publicity

Public relations and publicity relate to a variety of programs and are designed to promote or protect a company's image or its individual products. ***Publicity*** is nonpersonal communications such as press releases, media interviews, press conferences, feature articles, newsletters, photographs, films, and tapes. ***Public relations*** may also include annual reports, fund-raising and membership drives, lobbying, special event management, and public affairs.

The marketing value of public relations got a big boost in 1983 when public relations firm Burson-Marsteller's skillful handling of Johnson & Johnson's Tylenol product tampering incident was credited with helping to save the brand. Brand Focus 11.0 provides a comprehensive account of that landmark campaign. Around that time, politicians also discovered the power of campaign sound bites that were picked up by the press as a means of broad, cost-efficient candidate exposure.

Marketers now recognize that although public relations is invaluable during a marketing crisis, it also needs to be a routine part of any marketing communications program. Even companies that primarily use advertising and promotions can benefit from well-conceived and well-executed publicity. For example, when Heinz launched its new EZ Squirt kids' condiments, an extensive PR effort resulted in 4,000 news stories and a 5 percent increase in market share before advertising even hit the airwaves.

Buzz Marketing. Occasionally, a product enters the market with little fanfare yet is still able to attract a strong customer base. Something about the product attracts a core group of consumers, who are eager to spread word of the product among their peers. News travels in this fashion until enough tongues are wagging to constitute a "buzz" about the brand. Increasingly, companies are attempting to create consumer word of mouth through various techniques often called ***buzz marketing***.[56]

Established companies do not have the luxury of time, so they often attempt to catalyze the buzz marketing effect for new product introductions. One popular method is to allow consumers who are likely to influence other consumers to "discover" the product in the hopes that they will pass a positive endorsement on to their peers. To improve its image with teenage boys, Lee jeans identified 200,000 "influentials" from online communities devoted to video games and sent them a series of short films from unknown characters who turned out to be protagonists in a video game developed by Lee. On average, these films were forwarded to about six people each.[57] Back in the real world, Piaggio USA hired a street team of models to drive its Vespa scooters around Los Angeles and talk up the brand. Procter & Gamble has created a program specifically designed to enhance buzz.

TREMOR

Procter & Gamble's proprietary word-of-mouth technology, Tremor, has enlisted over 250,000 teen girls who quality as "connectors." A connector is a person with a social network five to six times larger than the average person's, and with a deep propensity to talk about ideas with that network. To identify a connector, a questionnaire weeds out 90 percent of potential respondents. Connectors, who are not paid, are attracted to the idea of hearing things first and being able to communicate directly back to the company. P&G has used Tremor for its own products, such as Noxzema and Pringles, and leased it to other companies, including Coca-Cola and Dreamworks (which used Tremor subjects to name the 2004 teen film compedy, *Eurotrip*). Steve Knox, CEO of the P&G unit, claims the real key to success is creating messaging that creates word of mouth. "The way we phrase this to people is there's a message that the consumer wants to hear and then there's a message they want to share with their friends and those are two different messages." He claims the biggest mistake made with word of mouth is to say "Here's my marketing message. Make them talk about this." P&G signed up 500,000 mothers for a new version of Tremor for 2006.[58]

Buzz marketing works well when the marketing message appears to originate with an independent source and not with the brand. Because consumers are becoming increasingly skeptical and wary of traditional advertising, buzz marketers seek to expose consumers to their brands in a unique and innocuous fashion.[59] One approach is to enlist genuine consumers able to give authentic-seeming endorsements of the brand. An ad executive with Bates USA explained the goal of this strategy: "Ultimately, the brand benefits because an accepted member of the social circle will always be more credible than any communication that could ever come directly from the brand."[60]

Some criticize buzz marketing as "a form of cultural corruption" in which marketers are actually creating the culture at a fundamental level. Critics claim that buzz marketing's interference in consumers' lives is insidious because participants cannot always detect the pitch. Another potential problem with buzz marketing is that it requires a buzz-worthy product. As one marketing expert said, "The bad news is that [buzz marketing] only works in high-interest product categories." In spite of these drawbacks, experts predicted that buzz marketing would retain its appeal for marketers. Said one ad executive, "The biggest problem with buzz marketing in the next 24 months will be the glut of people trying to do it."[61]

Author and former Silicon Valley marketing executive Emanuel Rosen developed the following guidelines to help marketers avoid buzz marketing pitfalls in their advertising:[62]

- *Keep it simple.* Simple messages spread across social networks more easily.
- *Tell us what's new.* The message must be relevant and newsworthy for people to want to tell others about it.
- *Don't make claims you can't support.* Making false claims will kill buzz or, worse, lead to negative buzz.
- *Ask your customers to articulate what's special about your product or service.* If customers can explain why they like the product or service, they can then communicate this to others.
- *Start measuring buzz.* This can help determine which strategies generate the most buzz.
- *Listen to the buzz.* Monitoring consumer reaction can yield insights such as how to improve the product or service.

Personal Selling

Personal selling is face-to-face interaction with one or more prospective purchasers for the purpose of making sales. It represents a communication option with pros and cons almost exactly the opposite of those of advertising. Specifically, the main advantages to personal selling are that it can send a detailed, customized message to customers and that marketers can gather feedback to help close the sale. Marketers can identify prospective customers and tailor solutions to their needs. And they can demonstrate products, often with customer involvement as part of the sales pitch for the brand. Personal selling can also be beneficial after the sale to handle customer problems and ensure customer satisfaction. Its main disadvantages are its high cost and lack of breadth. For many mass-market products, personal selling would be cost prohibitive.[63]

Personal selling practices have changed in recent years in recognition of the importance of achieving competitive parity or even superiority with sales and customer service. According to a *Business Week* cover story, "smart selling" means focusing the entire company on its customers, including changing the way salespeople are hired, trained, and paid.[64] These commentators believe that the keys to better selling are to

- *Rethink training.* Forget high-pressure, slam-dunk selling. Sales reps need new skills: They must learn to become customer advocates whose detailed knowledge of their customers' businesses helps them spot sales opportunities and service problems.
- *Get everyone involved.* Salespeople should no longer act solo. Everyone in a company, from product designers to plant managers and financial officers, must be a part of selling to and serving customers.
- *Inspire from the top.* Chief executives and top managers must frequently and visibly lead the smart-selling charge in their companies. Having the boss call regularly on customers and lead sales training sessions is a must.
- *Change the motivation.* Salespeople need constant recognition—but not in the form of the old-fashioned commission. That can be an incentive to scoring a quick sales hit. Instead, include measures of long-term customer satisfaction in calculating compensation.
- *Forge electronic links.* Use computerized marketing and distribution technology to track relationships with customers, make sure the right products get to the right stores at the right times, and make order-taking easy. It all adds up to high-tech intimacy.
- *Talk to your customers.* Make frequent phone calls, assign a company employee to a customer's plant, or drop notes to frequent shoppers. Customers like the attention, and the added communication makes for better intelligence gathering.

Developing Integrated Marketing Communication Programs

We've examined in depth the various communication options available to marketers. Now we consider how to develop an integrated marketing communication (IMC) program, choose the best options, and manage the relationships between them.[65] Our main theme is that marketers should "mix and match" communication options to build brand equity—that is, choose a variety of different communication options that share common meaning and content but also offer different, complementary advantages so that the whole is greater than the sum of the parts.[66] This description of the communications challenge for the Saturn automobile, as seen by the company's ad agency, Goodby, Silverstein & Partners, highlights the need to integrate communications.

> In being assigned the Saturn automobile account in 2002 by General Motors, ad agency Goodby, Silverstein & Partners began deciding that the key brand truth to communicate was that Saturn thought differently from other car companies and truly put "people first"—a phrase that became their new tagline. A critical part of the Saturn account was then integrating the brand voice and philosophy across all media, including TV, print, outdoor advertising, brochures, auto show handouts, retail displays, direct mail, over 66 retail broadcast spots and 1,500 retail newspaper ads per year, as well as the Internet site at saturn.com. The success in integration was seen in increased and sustained sales for Saturn vehicles from 2002–2004.[67]

This broad view of brand-building activities is especially relevant when designing marketing communications to improve brand awareness. As we noted in Chapter 2, brand awareness is closely related to brand familiarity, and we can view it as a function of the number of brand-related exposures and experiences the consumer has accumulated.[68] Thus, *anything* that causes the consumer to notice and pay attention to the brand can increase brand awareness, at least in terms of brand recognition. Obviously, the visibility of the brand in many marketing communications—such as sponsorship—suggests that these activities may be especially valuable for enhancing brand recognition.

To enhance brand recall, however, marketers might need to inspire more intense and elaborate processing of the brand so that consumers form stronger brand links to the product category to improve memory performance. Similarly, because brand associations can be abstract in many different ways, consider a wide variety of possible marketing communications to create the desired brand image and knowledge structures.

Criteria for IMC Programs

In assessing the collective impact of an IMC program, the marketer's overriding goal is to create the most effective and efficient communication program possible. Here are six relevant criteria:[69]

1. Coverage
2. Contribution
3. Commonality
4. Complementarity
5. Versatility
6. Cost

After considering the concept of coverage and how it relates to the other five criteria, let's look quickly at each in turn.

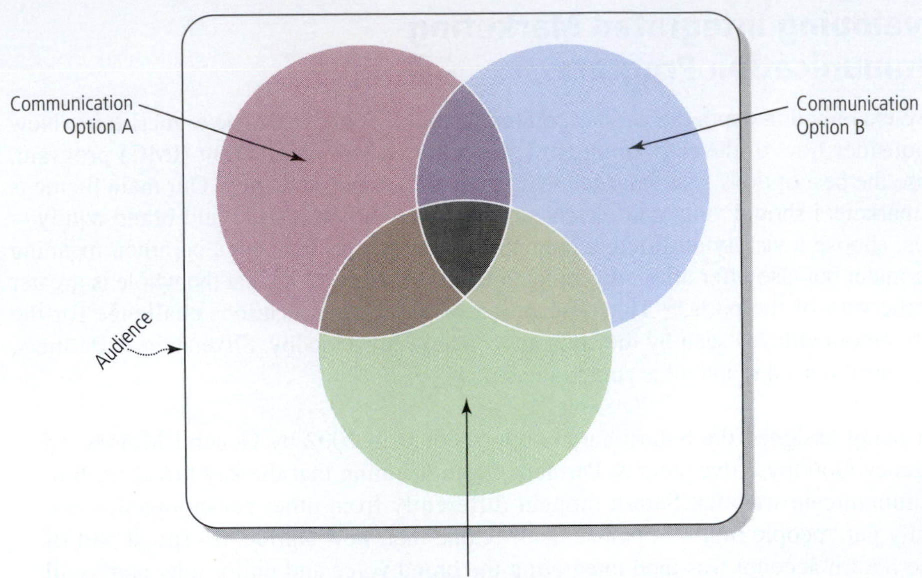

FIGURE 6-10

IMC Audience Communication Option Overlap

Coverage. Coverage is the proportion of the audience reached by each communication option, as well as how much overlap exists among communication options. In other words, to what extent do different communication options reach the designated target market, and the same or different consumers making up that market? As Figure 6-10 shows, the unique aspects of coverage relate to the direct main effects of any communication; the common aspects relate to the interaction or multiplicative effects of two communication options working together.

The unique aspect of coverage is the inherent communication ability of a marketing communication option, as suggested by the second criterion, contribution. If there is some overlap in communication options, however, marketers must decide how to design their communication program to reflect the fact that consumers may already have some communication effects in memory prior to exposure to any particular communication option. A communication option can either reinforce associations and strengthen linkages that are also the focus of other communication options, or it can address other associations and linkages, as suggested by the third and fourth criteria, commonality and complementarity. Moreover, if less than perfect overlap exists—which is almost always the case—marketers can design a communication option to reflect the fact that consumers may or may not have seen other communication options, as suggested by the fifth criterion, versatility. Finally, all of these considerations must be offset by their cost, as suggested by the sixth criterion.

Contribution. Contribution is the inherent ability of a marketing communication to create the desired response and communication effects from consumers *in the absence of exposure to any other communication option.* In other words, contribution describes the main effects of a marketing communication option in terms of how it affects consumers' processing of a communication and the resulting outcomes. As we noted earlier, marketing communications can play many different roles, like building awareness, enhancing image, eliciting responses, and inducing sales, and the contribution of any marketing communication option will depend on how well it plays that role. Also as we noted earlier, much prior research has considered this aspect of communications, generating conceptual guidelines and evaluation criteria in the process. Given that overlap with communication options exists, however, marketers must consider other factors, as follows.

Commonality. Regardless of which communication options marketers choose, they should coordinate the entire marketing communication program to create a consistent and cohesive brand image in which brand associations share content and meaning. The consistency and cohesiveness of the brand image is important because the image determines how easily consumers can recall existing associations and responses and how easily they can link additional associations and responses to the brand in memory.

Commonality is the extent to which *common* information conveyed by different communication options shares meaning across communication options. Most definitions of IMC emphasize only this criterion. For example, Burnett and Moriarty define integrated marketing communications as the "practice of unifying all marketing communication tools—from advertising to packaging—to send target audiences a consistent, persuasive message that promotes company goals."[70]

In general, we learn and recall information that is consistent in meaning more easily than unrelated information—though the unexpectedness of inconsistent information sometimes can lead to more elaborate processing and stronger associations than consistent information.[71] Nevertheless, with inconsistent associations and a diffuse brand image, consumers may overlook some associations or, because they are confused about the meaning of the brand, form less strong and less favorable new associations.

Therefore, in the long run, marketers should design different communication elements and combine them so that they work effectively together to create a consistent and cohesive brand image. As branding expert Larry Light states: "The total brand experience must be a result of an integrated, focused, strategically sound, differentiated, consistent, branded marketing program. Inconsistency, instead of integration, leads to uncertainty. Yet, uncertainty and inconsistency do seem to be the result of a lot of today's marketing practices."[72]

Note also that there may actually be memory advantages to using multiple communication options to create positive brand images. The ***encoding variability principle*** in psychology argues that presenting information in varied contexts causes information to be encoded in slightly different ways. As a result, consumers form multiple retrieval routes in memory, each of which converges on the information to be recalled, thereby enhancing recall. Thus, the encoding variability principle suggests that an IMC program, by employing multiple communication elements, may be an effective way to create, maintain, or strengthen brand associations in memory.

The more abstract the association to be created or reinforced by marketing communications, the more likely it would seem that we could effectively reinforce it in different ways across heterogeneous communication options.[73] For example, if the association we desire is "contemporary," then there may be a number of different ways we can make a brand seem modern and relevant. On the other hand, if our desired association is a concrete attribute, say, "rich chocolate taste," then it may be difficult to convey it in communication options that do not permit explicit product statements, such as sponsorship.

Finally, another commonality issue is the extent of executional consistency across communication options—that is, the extent to which we convey non-product-related information in different communication options. The more coordinated executional information is, the more likely it is that this information can serve as a retrieval cue to other communication effects.[74] In other words, if a symbol is established in one communication option, like a feather in a TV ad for a deodorant to convey mildness and softness, then marketers can use it in other communications to help trigger the knowledge, thoughts, feelings, and images stored in memory from exposure to a previous communication.

Complementarity. Communication options are often more effective when used in tandem. *Complementarity* describes the extent to which *different* associations and linkages are emphasized across communication options. For example, research has shown that promotions can be more effective when combined with advertising.[75] In both cases, the awareness and attitudes created by advertising campaigns can improve the success of more direct sales pitches. Thus, the ideal marketing communication program would ensure that the communication options chosen are mutually compensatory and reinforcing to create desired consumer knowledge structures.

Marketers might most effectively establish different brand associations by capitalizing on those marketing communication options best suited to eliciting a particular consumer response or establishing a particular type of brand association. For example, some media, like sample and other forms of sales promotion, are demonstrably better at generating trial than engendering long-term loyalty. As part of the highly successful "Drivers Wanted" campaign, VW used television to introduce a story line that it continued and embellished on its Web site. Research with some industrial distributors has shown that follow-up sales efforts generate higher sales productivity when firms have already exposed customers to its products at a trade show.[76] Brand Focus 6.0 describes how communication options may need to be explicitly tied together to capitalize on complementarity to build brand equity.

Versatility. Versatility refers to the extent that a marketing communication option is robust and effective for different groups of consumers. There are two types of versatility: communication and consumer. The reality of any IMC program is that when consumers are exposed to a particular marketing communication, some consumers will have already been exposed to other marketing communications for the brand, and others will not. The ability of a marketing communication to work at two levels—effectively communicating to both groups—is critically important. Some communications will be ineffective unless consumers have already been exposed to other communications. For example, mass advertising or some type of awareness-creating communication is often seen as a necessary condition for personal selling. We consider a marketing communication option robust when it achieves its desired effect *regardless* of consumers' past communication history.

Besides this communication versatility, we can also judge communication options in terms of their broader consumer versatility, that is, how well do they inform or persuade consumers who vary on dimensions other than communication history? Communications directed at primarily creating brand awareness, like sponsorship, may be more robust by virtue of their simplicity.

There seem to be two possible means of achieving this dual communication ability:

1. *Multiple information provision strategy:* Provide different information within a communication option to appeal to the different types of consumers. An important issue here is how information designed to appeal to one target market of consumers will be processed by other consumers and target markets. Issues of information overload, confusion, and annoyance may come into play if communications become burdened with a great deal of detail.
2. *Broad information provision strategy:* Provide information that is rich or ambiguous enough to work regardless of prior consumer knowledge. The important issue here is how potent or successful marketers can make that information. If they attempt to appeal to the lowest common denominator, the information may lack precision and sufficient detail to have any meaningful impact on consumers. Consumers with disparate backgrounds will have to find information in the communication sufficiently relevant to satisfy their goals, given their product or brand knowledge or communications history.

Cost. Finally, evaluations of marketing communications on all of the preceding criteria must be weighed against their cost to arrive at the most effective *and* efficient communication program.

Using IMC Choice Criteria

The IMC choice criteria can provide some guidance for designing and implementing integrated marketing communication programs. Three steps are evaluating communication options, establishing priorities and tradeoffs, and executing the final design and implementation.

Evaluating Communication Options. We can judge marketing communication options or communication types according to the response and communication effects they can create, as well as how they rate on the IMC choice criteria (see Figure 6-11 for a subjective macro appraisal). Different communication types and options have different strengths and weaknesses and raise different issues. Several points about the IMC choice criteria ratings are worth noting. First, there are not necessarily any inherent differences across communication types for contribution and complementarity, because each communication type, if properly designed, can play a critical and unique role in achieving communication objectives. Similarly, all marketing communications appear expensive, although some differences in cost per thousands can prevail. Communication types vary, however, in their breadth and depth of audience coverage, and in terms of commonality and versatility according to the number of modalities they employ: The more modalities available with a communication type, the greater its potential commonality and versatility.

Arriving at a final mix requires making decisions on priorities and tradeoffs among the IMC choice criteria, discussed next.

	TV	Print	Sales Promotions	Sponsorship	Interactive
Coverage					
Breadth	+++	+	++	+++	+
Depth	+	++	++	++	+++
Contribution	+++	+++	+++	+++	+++
Commonality	+++	++	++	+	+++
Complementary	+++	+++	+++	+++	+++
Versatility	+	++	+	+	+++
Cost	+++	+++	+++	+++	+++

FIGURE 6-11

Macro Perspectives

Establishing Priorities and Tradeoffs. The IMC program a marketer adopts, after profiling the various options, will depend in part on how he or she ranks the choice criteria. Because the IMC choice criteria themselves are related, the marketer must also make tradeoffs. The objectives of the marketing communication program, and whether they are short run or long run, will set priorities along with a host of factors beyond the scope of this chapter. We look at a number of possible tradeoffs with the IMC choice criteria, primarily dealing with the three factors that are concerned with overlaps in coverage.

- Commonality and complementarity will often be inversely related. The more various marketing communication options emphasize the same brand attribute or benefit, all else being equal, the less they can effectively emphasize other attributes and benefits.
- Versatility and complementarity will also often be inversely related. The more a communication program accounts for differences in consumers across communication options, the less necessary it is that any one communication be designed to appeal to many different groups.
- Commonality and versatility, on the other hand, do not share an obvious relationship. It may be possible, for example, to develop a sufficiently abstract message, like "Brand X is contemporary," to effectively reinforce the brand across multiple communication types including advertising, interactive, sponsorship, and promotions.

Executing Final Design and Implementation. Once the broad strategic guidelines are in place, the marketer determines in detail how to execute each communication option and puts into place the specific parameters of the media plan. Communications should be as creative as possible to ensure they achieve their desired objectives. *Concentration* refers to the amount of communications that consumers receive. Consumers may be exposed to a varying amount of the same or different communications. *Continuity* refers to the distribution of those exposures, in terms of how massed or diffused they are.

Review

This chapter provided conceptual frameworks and managerial guidelines for how marketing communications can be integrated to enhance brand equity. The chapter addressed this issue from the perspective of customer-based brand equity, which maintains that brand equity is fundamentally determined by the brand knowledge created in consumers' minds by the supporting marketing program. A number of basic communication options were reviewed (broadcast, print, direct response, online, and place advertising media; consumer and trade promotions; event marketing and sponsorship; publicity and public relations; and personal selling) in terms of basic characteristics as well as success factors for effectiveness. The chapter also provided criteria as to how different communication options should be combined to maximally build brand equity.

Two key implications emerge from this discussion. First, from the perspective of customer-based brand equity, all possible communication options should be evaluated in terms of their ability to affect brand equity. In particular, the CBBE concept provides a common denominator by which the effects of different communication options can be evaluated: Each communication option can be judged in terms of the effectiveness and efficiency by which it affects brand awareness and by which it creates, maintains, or strengthens favorable and unique brand associations. Different communication options have different strengths and can accomplish different objectives. Thus, it is important to employ a mix of different communication options, each playing a specific role in building or maintaining brand equity.

1. ***Be analytical:*** Use frameworks of consumer behavior and managerial decision making to develop well-reasoned communication programs.
2. ***Be curious:*** Better understand customers by using all forms of research, and always be thinking of how you can create added value for consumers.
3. ***Be single-minded:*** Focus your message on well-defined target markets (less can be more).
4. ***Be integrative:*** Reinforce your message through consistency and cuing across all communication options and media.
5. ***Be creative:*** State your message in a unique fashion; use alternative promotions and media to create favorable, strong, and unique brand associations.
6. ***Be observant:*** Keep track of competition, customers, channel members, and employees through monitoring and tracking studies.
7. ***Be patient:*** Take a long-term view of communication effectiveness to build and manage brand equity.
8. ***Be realistic:*** Understand the complexities involved in marketing communications.

FIGURE 6-12

General Marketing Communication Guidelines

The second important insight that emerges from the conceptual framework is that the marketing communication program should be put together in a way such that the whole is greater than the sum of the parts. In other words, as much as possible, there should be a match among certain communication options so that the effects of any one communication option are enhanced by the presence of another option.

In closing, the basic message of this chapter is simple: Advertisers need to evaluate marketing communication options strategically to determine how they can contribute to brand equity. To do so, advertisers need some theoretical and managerial guidelines by which they can determine the effectiveness and efficiency of various communication options both singularly and in combination with other communication options. Figure 6-12 provides the author's philosophy concerning the design, implementation, and interpretation of marketing communication strategies.

Discussion Questions

1. Pick a brand and gather all its marketing communication materials. How effectively has the brand mixed and matched marketing communications? Has it capitalized on the strengths of different media and compensated for their weaknesses at the same time? How explicitly has it integrated its communication program?
2. What do you see as the role of the Internet for building brands? How would you evaluate the Web site for a major brand, for example, Nike, Disney, or Levi's?
3. From a current issue of *Newsweek* or *Time* magazine, decide which print ad you feel is the best and which ad you feel is the worst based on the criteria described in this chapter.
4. Pick up a Sunday newspaper and look at the coupon supplements. How are they building brand equity, if at all? Try to find a good example and a poor example of brand-building promotions.
5. Choose a popular event. Who sponsors it? How are they building brand equity with their sponsorship? Are they integrating the sponsorship with other marketing communications?

BRAND FOCUS 6.0

Coordinating Media to Build Brand Equity

In developing effective integrated marketing communications programs, marketing communications must sometimes be explicitly tied together to create or enhance brand equity. This appendix, after reviewing the nature of the problem, proposes alternative strategies as solutions.

Factors Creating Weak Brand Links

For brand equity to be built, it is critical that the communication effects created by advertising be linked to the brand. Often, such links are difficult to create. For example, TV ads often do not "brand" well; that is, weak links may exist from the communication effects created by a TV ad to knowledge about the brand in memory. The three main reasons for this are competitive clutter, ad content and structure, and lack of consumer involvement. The following sections examine these factors.

Competitive Clutter

Competing ads in the product category can create interference and consumer confusion as to which ad goes with which brand.[77] Chapter 4 described the ad campaign for Energizer batteries that featured a pink toy bunny that kept on "going . . . and going . . . and going." Unfortunately, consumer research by Video Storyboard discovered that of the people in their annual survey who named this popular commercial as their favorite of the year, 40 percent mistakenly attributed it to Eveready's main competitor, Duracell—only 60 percent correctly identified it as an Energizer ad! To exacerbate this interference problem, it is often the case that competing ads appear in the same media vehicle because they typically target the same consumers. For example, an analysis of one week of prime time television advertising found that of the 57 commercials that ran in an average hour, 24, or 42 percent, faced at least one competitor running an ad during that same time period.[78]

Ad Content and Structure

Factors related to the content and structure of the ad itself can result in weak links from the brand to communication effects created by ad exposure. For example, advertisers have a vast range of creative strategies and techniques at their disposal to improve consumer motivation and lead to greater involvement and enhanced ad processing on their part. Although these "borrowed interest" tactics may effectively grab consumers' attention for an ad, the resulting focus of attention and processing may be directed in a manner that does *not* create strong brand associations. For example, when the popular actor James Garner was advertising for Polaroid, marketing research surveys routinely noted that many interview respondents mistakenly attributed his promotion to Kodak, its chief competitor. Moreover, when these attention-getting creative tactics are employed, the position and prominence of the brand in the ad are often downplayed. Delaying brand identification or providing few brand mentions in an ad may also raise processing intensity but result in attention directed away from the brand. Furthermore, limited brand exposure time in the ad allows little opportunity for elaboration of existing brand knowledge, also contributing to weak brand links.[79]

Consumer Involvement

In certain circumstances, consumers may not have any inherent interest in the product or service category or may lack knowledge of the specific brand (e.g., in the case of a low-share brand or a new market entry). The resulting decrease in consumer motivation and ability to process translates to weaker brand links. Similarly, a change in advertising strategy to target a new market segment or add a new attribute, benefit, or usage association to the brand image may also fail to produce strong brand links because consumers lack the ability to easily relate this new advertising information to existing brand knowledge.[80]

Strategies to Strengthen Communication Effects

Thus, for a variety of reasons, consumers may fail to correctly identify advertising with the advertised brand or, even worse, incorrectly attribute advertising to a competing brand. In these cases, advertising worked in the sense that communication effects—ad claims and executional information, as well as cognitive and affective responses by consumers to that information—were stored in memory. Yet advertising failed in the sense that these communication effects were not accessible when critical brand-related decisions were made.

To address this problem, one common tactic marketers employ to achieve ad and point-of-purchase congruence and improve ad recall is to make the brand name and package information prominent in the ad. Unfortunately, this increase in brand emphasis means that communication effects and brand associations that can potentially affect brand evaluations are less likely to be able to be created by the ad and stored in consumer memory. In other words, although consumers are better able to recall the advertised brand with this tactic, there is *less* other information about the brand to actually recall. Three potentially more effective strategies are brand signatures, ad retrieval cues, and media interactions, as follows.

Brand Signatures

Perhaps the easiest way to increase the strength of brand links to communication effects is to create a more powerful and compelling brand signature. The ***brand signature*** is the manner by which the brand is identified at the conclusion of a TV or radio ad or displayed within a print ad. The brand signature must creatively engage the consumer and cause him or her to pay more attention to the brand itself and, as a consequence, increase the strength of brand associations created by the ad. An effective brand signature often dynamically and stylistically provides a seamless connection to the ad as a whole. For example, the famous "Got Milk?" campaign always displayed that tag line or slogan in a manner fitting the ad (e.g., in flames for the "yuppie in hell" ad or in primary school print for the "school lunchroom bully" ad). As another example, the introductory Intel Inside ad campaign always ended with a swirling image from which the Intel Inside logo dramatically appeared, in effect stamping the end of the ad with Intel Inside in an "in your face" manner.

Ad Retrieval Cues

An effective tactic to improve consumers' motivation and ability to retrieve communication effects when making a brand-related decision is to use advertising retrieval cues. An ***advertising retrieval cue*** is visual or verbal information uniquely identified with an ad that is evident when consumers are making a product or service decision. The purpose is to maximize the probability that consumers who have seen or heard the cued ad will retrieve from long-term memory the communication effects that were stored from earlier processing of that ad. Ad retrieval cues may consist of a key visual, a catchy slogan, or any unique advertising element that serves as an effective reminder to consumers. For example, in an attempt to remedy the problem they had with mistaken attributions, Quaker Oats placed a photograph of the "Mikey" character from the popular Life cereal ad on the front of the package. More recently, Eveready featured a picture of their pink bunny character on the packages for their Energizer batteries to reduce consumer confusion with Duracell.

Ad retrieval cues can be placed in the store (e.g., on the package or as part of a shelf talker or some other point-of-purchase device), combined with a promotion (e.g., with a free-standing insert coupon), included as part of a Yellow Pages directory listing, or embedded in any marketing communication option where recall of communication effects can be advantageous to marketers. By using ad retrieval cues, greater emphasis can be placed in the ad on supplying persuasive information and creating positive associations so that consumers have a reason *why* they should purchase the brand. Ad retrieval cues allow for creative freedom in ad execution because the brand and package need not be the centerpiece of the ad. The effectiveness of ad retrieval cues depends on how many communication effects are potentially retrievable and how likely these communication effects are to be retrieved from memory with only the brand as a cue, as compared with the executional information making up the ad retrieval cue. An ad retrieval cue is most effective when many communication effects are stored in memory but are only weakly associated to the brand because of one or more of the various factors noted previously.

Media Interactions

Other strategies besides ad retrieval cues may be employed to maximize the brand equity arising from TV advertising. Print and radio reinforcement of TV ads (in which the video and audio components of a TV ad serve as the basis for the respective type of ads) can be an effective means to leverage existing communication effects from TV ad exposure and more strongly link them to the brand. Cueing a TV ad with an explicitly linked radio or print ad can create similar or even enhanced processing outcomes that can substitute for additional TV ad exposures. Moreover, a potentially useful, although rarely employed, media strategy is to run explicitly linked print or radio ads *prior* to the accompanying TV ad. The print and radio ads in this case function as teasers and increase consumer motivation to process the more complete TV ad consisting of both audio and video components.

As another strategy, different combinations of TV ad excerpts within a campaign (e.g., 15-second spots consisting of highlights from longer 30- or 60-second spots for those campaigns characterized by only one dominant ad, or umbrella ads consisting of highlights from a pool of ads for those campaigns consisting of multiple ad executions) and across campaigns over time (e.g., including key elements from past ad campaigns that are strongly identified with the brand as part of the current ad campaign) may be particularly helpful for strengthening dormant associations and facilitating the formation of consumer evaluations of and reactions to the ads and their linkage to the brand.

TV Ads Over Time

The basic rationale for these different strategies is that TV ads should not be considered as discrete units that are created for a particular ad campaign and therefore run for a certain length of time before being replaced by a new ad campaign. Rather, TV ads should be thought of more broadly as consisting of different ingredients or pieces of information that advertisers might choose to combine in different ways over time to improve their brand-building abilities. The most important ingredients are those identifiable visual scenes, characters, symbols, and verbal phrases or slogans that can serve as cues or reminders of communication effects created by a single TV ad, an ad campaign with multiple TV ads, or a previous ad campaign.

Combining these ingredients to leverage communication effects over time offers several potential benefits. First, it can help to maintain the strength of unique and favorable brand associations. In particular, without such reminders, the heritage of a brand and its original associations may become weakened because the ad campaign is not being currently aired or a new ad campaign is using different appeals or creative strategies to reposition or modernize the brand. Second, it can facilitate the formation of favorable attitudes by consumers toward the advertising and brand. In other words, consumers may be likely to say, "I like the ads for that brand." As noted previously, these attitudes toward the ad can favorably affect brand evaluations, especially for low-involvement consumer decisions.

Note that an implicit issue in this discussion is the optimal continuity to have with advertising and communication campaigns over time. Congruity theory would suggest that a moderate amount of change is appropriate.[81] Too little change may not be noticed by consumers and thus have no effect. On the other hand, more dramatic changes in brand positioning may confuse consumers and result in them still continuing to think of the brand in the "old way." Because of strong associations already in memory, consumers may either fail to incorporate new ad information into their brand knowledge structures or fail to retrieve new ad information when making later product or service decisions. In many cases, a moderate change in creative (e.g., retaining the current positioning but communicating it with a new creative) may be the most effective way to maintain or enhance the strength of brand associations. If the favorability or uniqueness of brand associations are deficient in some way, however, then a more severe change in positioning emphasizing different points of parity or points of difference may be necessary.

Notes

1. To obtain a broader perspective, it is necessary to consult good advertising texts such as George E. Belch and Michael A. Belch, *Advertising and Promotion: An Integrated Marketing Communications Perspective,* 6th ed. (Homewood, IL: McGraw-Hill/Irwin, 2004); Thomas C. O'Guinn, Richard J. Seminik, and Chris T. Allen, *Advertising and Integrated Brand Promotion,* 4th ed. (Cincinnati, OH: South-Western, 2006); or John R. Rossiter and Larry Percy, *Advertising and Promotion Management,* 2nd ed. (New York: McGraw-Hill/Irwin, 1997).
2. Matthew Swibel, "You've Got Ads," *Forbes,* 5 September 2005, 63–67.
3. Paul Keegan, "The Man Who Can Save Advertising," *Business 2.0,* November 2004, 119–128.
4. Gregory Solman, "Mazda Goes Global for the 1st Time with MX-5 Launch," *Brandweek,* 22 August 2005.
5. William J. McGuire, "The Nature of Attitudes and Attitude Change," in *The Handbook of Social Psychology,* Vol. 3, 2nd ed., eds. G. Lindzey and E. Aronson (Reading, MA: Addison-Wesley, 1969):136–314.
6. Thomas C. Kinnear, Kenneth L. Bernhardt, and Kathleen A. Krentler, *Principles of Marketing,* 4th ed. (New York: HarperCollins, 1995).
7. Philip L. Kotler and Kevin Lane Keller, *Marketing Management,* 12th ed. (Upper Saddle River, NJ: Prentice Hall, 2006).
8. Alexander L. Biel, "Converting Image into Equity," in *Brand Equity and Advertising,* eds. David A. Aaker and Alexander L. Biel (Hillsdale, NJ: Lawrence Erlbaum Associates, 1993), 67–82.
9. "How to Turn Junk Mail into a Goldmine—Or Perhaps Not," *The Economist,* 1 April 1995, 51–52.
10. Leonard M. Lodish, Magid Abraham, Stuart Kalmenson, Jeanne Livelsberger, et al., "How T.V. Advertising Works: A Meta Analysis of 389 Real World Split Cable T.V. Advertising Experiments," *Journal of Marketing Research* 32 (May 1995): 125–139; Magid Abraham and Leonard Lodish, *Advertising Works: A Study of Advertising Effectiveness and the Resulting Strategies and Tactical Implications* (Chicago: Information Resources Inc., 1989).
11. Greg Allenby and Dominique Hanssens, "Advertising Response," *MSI Special Reports,* No. 05-200, 1–8.
12. Lorrie Grant, "Home Depot Sales Soar 16%," *USA Today,* 15 August 2001, B1.
13. Poornima Gupta, "Ford Woos Young Car Buyers," *Reuters,* September 4, 2005. Eric Mayne, "Ford Puts Focus on Fusion," *Detroit News,* July 3, 2005.

14. Rossiter and Percy, *Advertising and Promotion Management.*
15. Amanda Swinburn, "Virgin Money Scoops Top Marketing Award," *B&T,* 29 October 2004.
16. www.effie.org.
17. Max Robins, "Seinfeld Aces Ultimate Test," *TV Guide,* 81.
18. Jack Neff and Lisa Sanders, "It's Broken," *Advertising Age,* 16 February 2004, 1, 30.
19. John Flinn, "Advertising's New Age," *San Francisco Chronicle,* 23 October 1994, B14.
20. Radio Advertising Bureau, "Radio Is Everyone [advertising supplement]" (Irving, TX: Radio Avertising Bureau).
21. Ibid.
22. For a comprehensive overview, see Bob Schulberg, *Radio Advertising: The Authoritative Handbook* (Lincolnwood, IL: NTC Business Books, 1990).
23. David Ogilvy, *Ogilvy on Advertising* (New York: Vintage Books, 1983).
24. Magazine Publishers of America, "How Do You Measure a Smile?" *Advertising Age,* 26 September 2005, M6.
25. For more discussion on these guidelines, see Philip Ward Burton and Scott C. Purvis, eds., *Which Ad Pulled Best?* 9th ed. (New York: McGraw-Hill/Irwin, 2003).
26. Julia Reed, "Ads Where You Least Expect Them," *U.S. News and World Report,* 9 March 1987, 46.
27. Kevin Goldman, "P&G Experiments with an Infomercial," *Wall Street Journal,* 8 July 1994, B9.
28. Jim Edwards, "The Art of the Infomercial," *Brandweek,* 3 September 2001, 14–19.
29. "How to Turn Junk Mail into a Goldmine"; Gary Levin, "Going Direct Route," *Advertising Age,* 11 November 1991, 37.
30. See Jakki J. Mohr, Sanjit Sengupta, and Stanley J. Slater, *Marketing of High-Technology Products and Innovations,* 2nd ed. (Upper Saddle River, NJ: Prentice Hall, 2005); Ward Hanson, *Principles of Internet Marketing* (Cincinnati, OH: South-Western, 1999); and Eloise Coupey, *Marketing and the Internet* (Upper Saddle River, NJ: Prentice Hall, 2001).
31. "Banner-Ad Blues," *The Economist,* 24 February 2001, 63–64.
32. Suzanne Vranica, "GM Is Joining Online Videogame Wave," *Wall Street Journal,* 26 July 2001, B11.
33. Fred Vogelstein and Kate Bonamici, "Yahoo!'s Brilliant Solution," *Fortune,* 8 August 2005, 42.
34. This section is based on material from "To Boldly Go Fully Mobile," *Marketing Week,* 27 September 2005; Adam Woods, "Brands Wait for 3G Opportunity," *Revolution,* 21 June 2005; www.vibes.com.
35. Jeff Pelline, "New Commercial Twist in Corporate Restrooms," *San Francisco Chronicle,* 6 October 1986.
36. Chuck Stogel, "Quest for the Captive Audience," *Superbrands 1992,* 106–107.
37. David T. Friendly, "Selling It at the Movies," *Newsweek,* 4 July 1983, 46.
38. Joanne Lipman, "Product Placement Can Be Free Lunch," *Wall Street Journal,* 25 November 1991; John Lippman and Rick Brooks, "Hot Holiday Flick Pairs FedEx, Hanks," *Wall Street Journal,* 11 December 2001, B1.
39. Scott Hume and Marcy Magiera, "What Do Moviegoers Think of Ads?" *Advertising Age,* 23 April 1990, 4.
40. *Consumer Reports,* December 1982, 752–755.
41. For an excellent summary of issues related to the type, scope, and tactics of sales promotions design, see John A. Quelch, "Note on Sales Promotion Design," Teaching Note N-589-021 (Boston: Harvard Business School, 1988).
42. Andrew Ehrenberg, and Kathy Hammond, "The Case Against Price-Related Promotions," *Admap,* June 2001.
43. Quelch, "Note on Sales Promotion Design."
44. Michael L. Ray, *Advertising and Communication Management* (Upper Saddle River, NJ: Prentice Hall, 1982).
45. Geoffrey Fowler, "When Free Samples Become Saviors," *Wall Street Journal,* 14 August 2001, B1.
46. "Coupon Trend Reports," www.santella.com/Trends.htm.
47. Rossiter and Percy, *Advertising and Promotion Management.*
48. Eric Hollreiser, "Trading Up from Tactics to Strategy in the Trade Game," *Brandweek,* 3 October 1994, 26–33.
49. See Peggy Cunningham, Shirley Taylor, and Carolyn Reeder, "Event Marketing: The Evolution of Sponsorship from Philanthropy to Strategic Promotion," Conference on Historical Analysis & Research in Marketing, 1993, 407–425.
50. Michael Oneal and Peter Finch, "Nothing Sells Like Sports," *Business Week,* 31 August 1987, 48–53.
51. Chris Roush, "A Sports Marketer with a Mean Curve," *Business Week,* 12 September 1994, 96.
52. The Association of National Advertisers has a useful source, *Event Marketing: A Management Guide,* 2nd ed., which is available at www.ana.net.
53. Michael J. McCarthy, "Keeping Careful Score on Sports Tie-Ins," *Wall Street Journal,* 24 April 1991, B1.
54. William L. Shankin and John Kuzma, "Buying That Sporting Image," *Marketing Management* (Spring 1992): 65.
55. Jim Crimmins, "Most Sponsorships Waste Money," *Advertising Age,* 21 June 1993, S-2.
56. Gerry Khermouch, "Buzz Marketing," *Business Week,* 30 July 2001; Catherine Valenti, "Some Brands Thrive Without Advertising," ABCNews.com, 23 August 2001.
57. Gerry Kermouch, "Buzz Marketing: Suddenly This Stealth Strategy Is Hot – But It's Still Fraught with Risk," *Business Week,* 30 July 2001, 50. As cited in David Godes and Dina Mayzlin, "Firm-Created Word-of-Mouth Communication: A Field-Based Quasi-Experiment," working paper, Yale University. These researchers show how effective word of mouth can be created by nonloyal customers, as well as offering a scale of the breadth of a person's social network.

58. Todd Wasserman, "P&G Buzz Program Tremor Moving On to Mothers," *Brandweek,* 26 September 2006, 15; Robert Berner, "I Sold It Through the Grapevine," *BusinessWeek,* 29 May 2006; www.tremor.com.
59. Mark Hughes, *Buzzmarketing* (New York: Penguin/Portfolio, 2005).
60. Gerry Khermouch, "Buzz Marketing: Suddenly This Stealth Strategy Is Hot," *Business Week,* 30 July 2001, 50.
61. Ibid.
62. Emanuel Rosen, *The Anatomy of Buzz* (New York: Currency, 2000).
63. John Quelch, "Communications Policy," Teaching Note 5–585–021 (Boston: Harvard Business School, 1984).
64. Christopher Power, "Smart Selling," *Business Week,* 3 August 1992, 46–52.
65. For a review of some academic and practitioner issues with IMC, see Prasad A. Naik, "Integrated Marketing Communications: Provenance, Practice and Principles," in *Handbook of Advertising,* eds. Gerard J. Tellis and Tim Ambler, Sage Publications, forthcoming; and Tom Duncan and Frank Mulhern, eds., "A White Paper on the Status, Scope, and Future of IMC," March 2004, Daniels College of Business at the University of Denver.
66. Prasad A. Naik, Kalyan Raman, and Russ Winer, "Planning Marketing-Mix Strategies in the Presence of Interactions," *Marketing Science* 24, no. 10 (2005): 25–34.
67. www.goodbysilverstein.com. For another example of IMC principles applied to automotive marketing, see Rex Briggs, R. Krishnan, and Norm Borin, "Integrated Multichannel Communication Strategies: Evaluating the Return on Marketing Objectives—The Case of the 2004 Ford F-150 Launch," *Journal of Interactive Marketing* 19, no. 3 (2005): 81–90.
68. Joseph W. Alba and J. Wesley Hutchinson, "Dimensions of Consumer Expertise," *Journal of Consumer Research* 13 (March 1987): 411–453.
69. This discussion assumes that the marketer has already thoroughly researched the target market and fully understands who they are—their perceptions, attitudes, and behaviors—and therefore knows exactly what needs to be done with them in terms of communication objectives.
70. John Burnett and Sandra Moriarty, *Introduction to Marketing Communications: An Integrated Approach* (Upper Saddle River, NJ: Prentice Hall, 1998).
71. Susan E. Heckler and Terry L. Childers, "The Role of Expectancy and Relevancy in Memory for Verbal and Visual Information: What Is Incongruency?" *Journal of Consumer Research* 18 (March 1992): 475–492; Michael J. Houston, Terry L. Childers, and Susan E. Heckler, "Picture-Word Consistency and the Elaborative Processing of Advertisements," *Journal of Marketing Research* 24 (November 1987): 359–369; Thomas K. Srull and Robert S. Wyer, "Person Memory and Judgment," *Psychological Review* 96, no. 1 (1989): 58–83.
72. Larry Light, "Bringing Research to the Brand Equity Process," paper presented at the ARF Brand Equity Workshop, February 15–16, 1994.
73. Michael D. Johnson, "Consumer Choice Strategies for Comparing Noncomparable Alternatives," *Journal of Consumer Research* 11 (December 1984): 741–753.
74. Julie A. Edell and Kevin Lane Keller, "The Information Processing of Coordinated Media Campaigns," *Journal of Marketing Research,* 26 (May 1989): 149–163; Julie Edell and Kevin Lane Keller, "Analyzing Media Interactions: The Effects of Coordinated Print-TV Advertising Campaigns," Marketing Science Institute Report No. 99–120.
75. William T. Moran, "Insights from Pricing Research," in *Pricing Practices and Strategies,* ed. E. B. Bailey (New York: The Conference Board, 1978), 7–13.
76. Timothy M. Smith, Srinath Gopalakrishna, and Paul M. Smith, "The Complementary Effect of Trade Shows on Personal Selling," *International Journal of Research in Marketing* 21, no. 1 (2004): 61–76.
77. Raymond R. Burke and Thomas K. Srull, "Competitive Interference and Consumer Memory for Advertising," *Journal of Consumer Research* 15 (June 1988): 55–68; Kevin Lane Keller, "Memory Factors in Advertising: The Effect of Advertising Retrieval Cues on Brand Evaluations," *Journal of Consumer Research* 14 (December 1987): 316–333; Kevin Lane Keller, "Memory and Evaluations in Competitive Advertising Environments," *Journal of Consumer Research* 17 (March 1991): 463–476; Robert J. Kent and Chris T. Allen, "Competitive Interference Effects in Consumer Memory for Advertising: The Role of Brand Familiarity," *Journal of Marketing* 58 (July 1994): 97–105.
78. Joe Mandese, "Rivals' Ads Cluttering TV," *Advertising Age,* 14–20 October 1991.
79. David Walker and Michael J. von Gonten, "Explaining Related Recall Outcomes: New Answers from a Better Model," *Journal of Advertising Research* 29 (1989): 11–21.
80. Kevin Lane Keller, Susan Heckler, and Michael J. Houston, "The Effects of Brand Name Suggestiveness on Advertising Recall," *Journal of Marketing* 62 (January 1998): 48–57.
81. Joan Meyers-Levy and Alice M. Tybout, "Schema Congruity as a Basis for Product Evaluation," *Journal of Consumer Research* 16 (June 1989): 39–54.

LEVERAGING SECONDARY BRAND ASSOCIATIONS TO BUILD BRAND EQUITY

Preview

The preceding chapters described how we can build brand equity through the choice of brand elements (Chapter 4) or through marketing program activities and product, price, distribution, and marketing communication strategies (Chapters 5 and 6). This chapter considers the third means of building brand equity—namely, through the leverage of related or secondary brand associations.

Brands themselves may be linked to other entities that have their own knowledge structures in the minds of consumers. Because of these linkages, consumers may assume or infer that some of the associations or responses that characterize the other entities may also be true for the brand. In effect, the brand "borrows" some brand knowledge and, depending on the nature of those associations and responses, perhaps some brand equity from other entities. This indirect approach to building brand equity is ***leveraging secondary brand knowledge*** for the brand. Secondary brand knowledge may be quite important to creating strong, favorable, and unique associations or positive responses if existing brand associations or responses are deficient in some way. It can also be an effective way to reinforce existing associations and responses in a fresh and different way.

This chapter considers the different means by which we can create secondary brand knowledge by linking the brand to the following (see Figure 7-1):

1. Companies (through branding strategies)
2. Countries or other geographic areas (through identification of product origin)
3. Channels of distribution (through channel strategy)
4. Other brands (through co-branding)
5. Characters (through licensing)
6. Spokespersons (through endorsements)
7. Events (through sponsorship)
8. Other third-party sources (through awards or reviews)

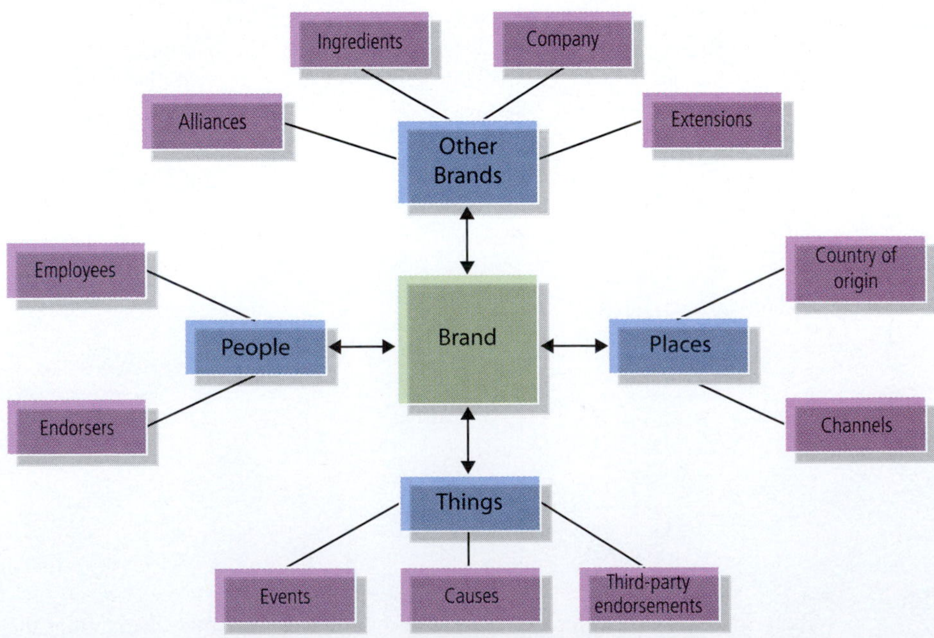

FIGURE 7-1

Secondary Sources of Brand Knowledge

The first three entities reflect source factors: who makes the product, where the product is made, and where it is purchased. The remaining entities deal with related people, places, or things.

As an example, suppose that Salomon—makers of alpine and cross-country ski bindings, ski boots, and skis—decided to introduce a new tennis racquet called "The Avenger." Although Salomon has been selling safety bindings for skis since 1947, much of its growth was fueled by its diversification into ski boots and the introduction of a revolutionary new type of ski called the monocoque. Salomon's innovative, stylish, and top-quality products have led to strong leadership positions. In creating the marketing program to support the new Avenger tennis racquet, Salomon could attempt to leverage secondary brand knowledge in a number of different ways.

- Salomon could leverage associations to the corporate brand by sub-branding the product—for example, by calling it "Avenger by Salomon." Consumers' evaluations of the new product extension would be influenced by the extent to which they held favorable associations about Salomon as a company or brand because of its skiing products, and how strongly they felt that such knowledge could predict the quality of a Salomon tennis racquet.
- Salomon could try to rely on its European origins (it is headquartered near Lake Annecy at the foot of the Alps), although such a location would not seem to have much relevance to tennis.
- Salomon could also try to sell through upscale, professional tennis shops and clubs in hopes that these retailers' credibility would rub off on the Avenger brand.
- Salomon could attempt to co-brand by identifying a strong ingredient brand for its grip, frame, or strings (as Wilson did by incorporating Goodyear tire rubber on the soles of its ProStaff Classic tennis shoes).
- Although it is doubtful that a licensed character could be effectively leveraged, Salomon obviously could attempt to find one or more top professional players to endorse the racquet or could choose to become a sponsor of tennis tournaments, or even the entire professional ATP men's or WTA women's tennis tour.
- Salomon could attempt to secure and publicize favorable ratings from third parties like *Tennis* magazine.

Thus, independent of the associations created by the racquet itself, its brand name, or any other aspects of the marketing program, Salomon may be able to build equity by linking the brand to other entities in various ways.

This chapter first considers the nature of brand knowledge that marketers can leverage or transfer from other entities, and the process for doing it. We then consider in detail each of the eight different means of leveraging secondary brand knowledge. The chapter concludes by considering the special topic of Olympic sponsorship in Brand Focus 7.0.

Conceptualizing the Leveraging Process

Linking the brand to some other entity—some source factor or related person, place, or thing—may create a new set of associations from the brand to the entity, as well as affecting existing brand associations. Let's look at both these outcomes.[1]

Creation of New Brand Associations

By making a connection between the brand and another entity, consumers may form a mental association from the brand to this other entity and, consequently, to any or all associations, judgments, feelings, and the like linked to that entity. In general, this secondary brand knowledge is most likely to affect evaluations of a new product when consumers lack either the motivation or the ability to judge product-related concerns. In other words, when consumers either don't care much about or don't feel that they possess the knowledge to choose the appropriate brand, they may be more likely to make brand decisions on the basis of secondary considerations such as what they think, feel, or know about the country from which the product came, the store in which it is sold, or some other characteristic.

Effects on Existing Brand Knowledge

Linking the brand to some other entity may not only create new brand associations to the entity but also affect existing brand associations. The basic mechanism is this. Consumers have some knowledge of an entity. When a brand is identified as linked to that entity, consumers may infer that some of the particular associations, judgments, or feelings that characterize the entity may also characterize the brand. A number of different theoretical mechanisms from psychology predict this type of inference. One is "cognitive consistency"—in other words, in the minds of consumers, what is true for the entity, must be true for the brand.

To describe the process more formally, here are three important factors in predicting the extent of leverage from linking the brand to another entity:

1. *Awareness and knowledge of the entity:* If consumers have no familiarity with or knowledge of the secondary entity, then obviously there is nothing they can transfer from it. Ideally, consumers would be aware of the entity; hold some strong, favorable, and perhaps even unique associations about it; and have positive judgments and feelings about it.
2. *Meaningfulness of the knowledge of the entity:* Given that the entity evokes some positive associations, judgments, or feelings, is this knowledge relevant and meaningful for the brand? The meaningfulness may vary depending on the brand and product context. Some associations, judgments, or feelings may seem relevant to and valuable for the brand, whereas others may seem to consumers to have little connection.
3. *Transferability of the knowledge of the entity:* Assuming that some potentially useful and meaningful associations, judgments, or feelings exist regarding the entity and could possibly transfer to the brand, how strongly will this knowledge actually become linked to the brand?

In other words, the basic questions we want to answer about transferring secondary knowledge from another entity are: What do consumers know about the other entity? and, Does any of this knowledge affect what they think about the brand when it becomes linked or associated in some fashion with this other entity?

Theoretically, consumers can infer any aspect of knowledge from other entities to the brand (see Figure 7-2), although some types of entities are more likely to inherently create or affect certain kinds of brand knowledge than others. For example, events may be especially conducive to the creation of experiences; people may be especially effective for the elicitation of feelings; other brands may be especially well suited for establishing particular attributes and benefits; and so on. At the same time, any one entity may be associated with multiple dimensions of knowledge, each of which may affect brand knowledge directly or indirectly.

For example, consider the effects on knowledge of linking the brand to a cause, like Avon's Breast Cancer Crusade. A cause marketing program could build brand awareness via recall and recognition; enhance brand image in terms of attributes such as brand personality or user imagery like kind and generous; evoke brand feelings like social approval and self-respect; establish brand attitudes such as trustworthy and likable; and create experiences through a sense of community and participation in cause-related activities.

Judgments or feelings may transfer more readily than more specific associations, which are likely to seem irrelevant or be too strongly linked to the original entity to

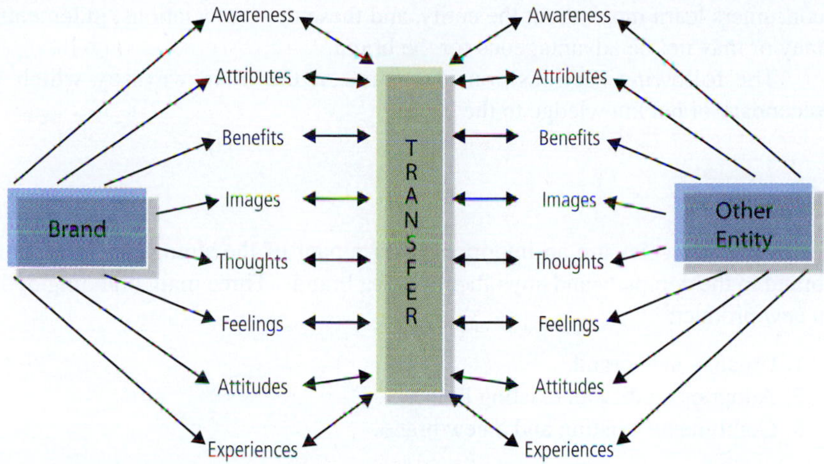

FIGURE 7-2

Understanding Transfer of Brand Knowledge

transfer. As we'll see in Chapter 12, the inferencing process depends largely on the strength of the linkage or connection in consumers' minds between the brand and the other entity. The more consumers see similarity between the entity and the brand, the more likely they will infer similar knowledge about the brand.

Guidelines

Leveraging secondary brand knowledge may allow marketers to create or reinforce an important point of difference versus competitors, or a necessary or competitive point of parity. When choosing to emphasize source factors or a particular person, place, or thing, marketers should take into account consumers' awareness of that entity, as well as how the associations, judgments, or feelings for it might become linked to the brand or affect existing brand associations.

Marketers can choose entities for which consumers have some or even a great deal of similar associations. A ***commonality*** leveraging strategy makes sense when consumers have associations to another entity that are congruent with desired brand associations. For example, consider a country such as New Zealand, which is known for having more sheep than people. A New Zealand sweater manufacturer that positioned its product on the basis of its "New Zealand wool" presumably could more easily establish strong and favorable brand associations because New Zealand may already mean "wool" to many people.

On the other hand, there may be times when entities are chosen that represent a departure for the brand because there are few if any common or similar associations. Such ***complementarity*** branding strategies can be strategically critical in terms of delivering the desired position. The marketer's challenge here is to ensure that the less congruent knowledge for the entity has either a direct or an indirect effect on existing brand knowledge. This may require skillfully designed marketing programs that overcome initial consumer confusion or skepticism. For example, when Buick signed Tiger Woods as an endorser, many questioned whether consumers would find a fit or consistency between the golfer and the car maker, and, if not, how much value the endorsement would add to the Buick brand.

Even if consumers buy into the association one way or another, leveraging secondary brand knowledge may be risky because the marketer gives up some control of the brand image. The source factors or related person, place, or thing will undoubtedly have a host of other associations, of which only some smaller set will be of interest to the marketer. Managing the transfer process so that only the relevant secondary knowledge becomes linked to the brand may be difficult. Moreover, this knowledge may change over time as consumers learn more about the entity, and these new associations, judgments, or feelings may or may not be advantageous for the brand.

The following sections consider some of the main ways by which we can link secondary brand knowledge to the brand.

Company

Branding strategies are an important determinant of the strength of association from the brand to the company and any other existing brands. Three main branding options exist for a new product:

1. Create a new brand.
2. Adopt or modify an existing brand.
3. Combine an existing and a new brand.

Existing brands may be related to the corporate brand, say Motorola, or a specific product brand like Motorola Razr V3 GSM mobile phone. If the brand is linked to an existing brand, as with options 2 and 3, then knowledge about the existing brand may also become linked to the brand. In particular, a corporate or family brand can be a source of much brand equity. For example, a corporate brand may evoke associations of common product attributes, benefits, or attitudes; people and relationships; programs and values; and corporate credibility. Branding Brief 7-1 describes the corporate image campaign for Hewlett-Packard.

BRANDING BRIEF 7-1

HP Brand Campaign Promotes Change

Hewlett-Packard's capabilities range from IT infrastructure to personal computers to imaging and printing devices. As it expanded in recent years, HP introduced several new advertising campaigns. Following a merger with Compaq in 2002, the Palo Alto, California-based company launched the +HP brand campaign to publicize the capabilities of the new Hewlett-Packard.

The campaign was divided into separate appeals to consumers and businesses. The consumer part of the campaign was called "You + HP." To publicize the company's digital photography technology, HP created a campaign that featured pieces of images freezing on screen and then becoming floating still pictures. The images floated to the tune of the Cure song, "Pictures of You." The marketing team also designed an interactive online photo gallery and a digital billboard in Times Square with 20 minutes of original content.

In 2004, HP began the +HP campaign for businesses called "Change + HP." The message was aimed at business and IT executives and was designed to communicate that HP could help them with one of the toughest aspects of their jobs: succeeding in an environment of constant change. As part of the campaign, HP put up a billboard in San Francisco with the phrase "Change happens." Over several weeks, more and more fake ivy was attached to the billboard until only the words were visible. Another ad was posted on sliding doors at airports, with the same "Change happens" message constantly sliding open and shut. *Adweek* named the HP effort its "Campaign of the Year" in 2004.

Leveraging a corporate brand may not always be useful, however. For example, Beatrice once attempted to create a corporate brand umbrella over some of the diverse products it sold at the time, such as Hunt Wesson foods, Stiffel lamps, and Orville Redenbacher popcorn. An expensive ad campaign uniting the products around the theme "You've Known Us All Along" failed to connect with consumers. In fact, in some cases, large companies have deliberately introduced new brands in an attempt to convey a "smaller" image.[2] For example, Gallo created two folksy farmers, Ed Bartles and Frank Jaymes, to sell their wine cooler product. Miller Brewing has used its Plank Road Brewery brand to introduce Icehouse and Red Dog beers.

Finally, brands and companies are often unavoidably linked to the category and industry in which they compete, sometimes with adverse consequences. Some industries are characterized by fairly divided opinions, but consider the challenges faced by a brand in the oil and gas industry, which consumers generally view in a negative light. By virtue of membership in the category in which it competes, an oil company may expect to face a potentially suspicious or skeptical public *regardless* of what it does.

Country of Origin and Other Geographic Areas

Besides the company that makes the product, the country or geographic location from which it originates may also become linked to the brand and generate secondary associations.[3] Many countries have become known for expertise in certain product categories or for conveying a particular type of image. The world is becoming a "cultural bazaar" where consumers can pick and choose brands originating in different countries, based on their beliefs about the quality of

In 2005, HP ads focused on the power of technology with the "Everything Is Possible" campaign, letting consumers know how HP was connected to some of their favorite businesses. The campaign featured HP customers such as DreamWorks, Federal Express, and National Gallery of London and illustrated the breadth and depth of HP products. Photos illustrating the various HP clients were framed by the plus sign and explained HP's partnership with the other business. For example, a photo of Amazon's warehouse was captioned, "The store never closes. HP helped Amazon design a Linux environment, one is that is exceptionally secure, stable, flexible, and economical. The site stays up and running, ensuring that, at 2 A.M., you can order the odd little item you simply can't do without." This tagline linked to the earlier work with copy explaining "[Amazon] + HP = everything is possible."

In 2006, HP introduced a several-hundred-million-dollar campaign for one of its core businesses, personal computers, themed "The Computer Is Personal Again." Print ads sought to reinforce the often personal connections consumers have to their computers by reminding consumers that "Your personal computer is your backup brain. It's your life and the life of your business. It's your astonishing strategy, your staggering proposal, dazzling calculation." TV ads featured the torso and hands—but not the heads—of celebrities such as Jay-Z, Mark Cuban, and snowboarder Shaun White showing all the different uses they have for their HP laptops.

Sources: Eleftheria Parpis, "Campaign of the Year: Hewlett-Packard," *Adweek,* 7 February 2005; "HP OKs First TV Ads to Target IT Types," *Brandweek,* 1 March 2004; www.hp.com.

BRANDING BRIEF 7-2

Selling Brands the New Zealand Way

In 1991, New Zealand set out to create "The New Zealand Way" (NZW) brand. The key objectives of the New Zealand Brand campaign were to build a strong national umbrella brand that added value to the marketing of New Zealand–origin products and services by differentiating them in international markets; to raise the awareness of New Zealand's unique values and personality; and to utilize the promotional activities of the New Zealand Tourism Board, Tradenz (a government trade development board), and manufacturers to heighten the profile of branded New Zealand products and services. The NZW brand was designed to position a broad range of the country's tourism and trade products and services at the forefront of world markets.

New Zealand has developed a new logo to help its branding efforts.

The focal point for communicating the personality and meaning of the NZW brand was to be the brand design and the campaign built around it. The three components of the NZW brand design were the brand logo, a descriptor word or short phrase such as *quality,* and the slogan, "The New Zealand Way." The descriptor words were to allow users of the NZW brand to customize it to suit their marketing program.

The campaign to launch and support the NZW brand included a range of promotional techniques, such as public relations, direct marketing, and events in key geographic markets. By 1998, more than 170 companies were licensed to use the New Zealand Way fern brand. Goods produced by these companies accounted for more than $4 billion, or 20 percent, of New Zealand's foreign exchange earnings that year.

certain types of products from certain countries or the image that these brands or products communicate. Thus, a consumer from anywhere in the world may choose to wear Italian suits, exercise in American athletic shoes, listen to a Japanese MP3 player, drive a German car, or drink English ale. Choosing brands with strong national ties may reflect a deliberate decision to maximize product utility and communicate self-image, based on what consumers believe about products from those countries.

Thus, a number of brands are able to create a strong point of difference, in part because of consumers' identification of and beliefs about the country of origin. For example, consider the following strongly linked brands and countries:

Levi's jeans—United States	Dewar's whiskey—Scotland
Chanel perfume—France	Kikkoman soy sauce—Japan
Foster's beer—Australia	Bertolli olive oil—Italy
Barilla pasta—Italy	Gucci shoes and purses—Italy
BMW—Germany	Mont Blanc pens—Switzerland

Other geographic associations besides country of origin are possible, such as states, regions, and cities. Marketers can establish a geographic or country-of-origin association

The year 2005 saw the launch of a new campaign for Brand New Zealand: "New Zealand New Thinking," which marketers motivated as follows:

"Brand New Zealand" aims to create a national brand that will differentiate New Zealand internationally, better support key sectors, and enhance New Zealand's established and emerging areas of competitive advantage.

New Zealand New Thinking is the new positioning that has been developed to provide an umbrella positioning for New Zealand from an economic development perspective.

The key goal is to ensure:

New Zealand is recognized globally for the value its businesses and people bring to the world—through creativity, innovation, and technology.

For many years, common perceptions of New Zealand have revolved around its landscape and accompanying clean, green image. These are important but we also need to convey a richer set of messages that create recognition for the broader characteristics that define our people, business, and country.

Raising global recognition of New Zealand's competitive edge through the New Zealand New Thinking programme will benefit every New Zealander by increasing opportunities for international trade and economic growth, securing foreign investment and enhancing New Zealand's attractiveness for skilled or business migrants.

Sources: http://business.newzealand.com/; Turi Park, "A New Brand for New Zealand or a New Zealand Visual Language?" www.nzedge.com/; Sue Warren, "Branding New Zealand," *Locum Destination Review,* Winter 2002, 54–56.

in different ways. They can embed the location in the brand name, such as Idaho potatoes, Irish Spring soap, or South African Airways, or combine it with a brand name in some way as in Bailey's Irish Cream. Or they can make the location the dominant theme in brand advertising, as has Foster's and Coors beer. Some countries have even created advertising campaigns to promote their products. For example, "Rums of Puerto Rico" advertise that they are the finest quality rums, leading to a 70 percent share of U.S. brand sales. Other countries have developed and advertised labels or seals for their products.[4] Branding Brief 7-2 describes New Zealand's attempt to create a brand, "The New Zealand Way."

Because it's typically a legal necessity for the country of origin to appear somewhere on the product or package, associations to the country of origin almost always have the potential to be created at the point of purchase and to affect brand decisions there. The question really is one of relative emphasis, and the role of country of origin or other geographic regions throughout the marketing program. Becoming strongly linked to a country of origin or specific geographic region is not without potential disadvantages. Events or actions associated with the country may color people's perceptions. For example, strong connections to a country may pose problems if the firm desires to move production elsewhere.

WATERFORD

Waterford Wedgwood PLC's famous, ornate crystal had been promoted as the ultimate in Irish handmade luxury for decades. Ads called Waterford "the ambassador of a nation" and attributed its brilliance to "deep, prismatic cutting that must be done entirely by skilled hands rather than machines." Because of cost considerations, Waterford had to confront the issue of shifting production out of Ireland and using machines to make some lines. In 2003, Wedgwood decided to close two factories and move production from Stoke-on-Trent to Asia. Waterford was encouraged to make such a move because of consumer research in the United States—home to more than 70 percent of Waterford's crystal sales—that indicated that what mattered to its customers there was the Waterford label and not where the crystal was made. Nevertheless, many retailers worried that such a move could destroy the precious brand image that Waterford had built.

Finally, consider the favorability of a country-of-origin association from both a domestic and a foreign perspective. In the domestic market, country-of-origin perceptions may stir consumers' patriotic notions or remind them of their past. As international trade grows, consumers may view certain brands as symbolically important of their own cultural heritage and identity. Some research found that domestic brands were more strongly favored in collectivistic countries such as Japan and other Asian countries that have strong group norms and ties to family and country. In individualistic societies such as the United States and other Western countries that are more guided by self-interest and personal goals, consumers demand stronger evidence of product superiority.[5]

Patriotic appeals have been the basis of marketing strategies all over the world. However, they can lack uniqueness and even be overused. For example, during the Reagan administration in the 1980s, a number of different U.S. brands in a diverse range of product categories including cars, beer, and clothing used pro-American themes in their advertising, perhaps diluting the efforts of all as a result. In recent years, the debate over outsourcing and offshoring and, tragically, the events of September 11, 2001, raised the visibility of patriotic appeals once again.

Channels of Distribution

Chapter 5 described how members of the channels of distribution can directly affect the equity of the brands they sell because of consumers' associations linked to the retail stores. Let's next consider how retail stores can indirectly affect brand equity through this "image transfer" process.

Because of associations to product assortment, pricing and credit policy, quality of service, and so on, retailers have their own brand images in consumers' minds. The Science of Branding 7-1 summarizes academic research into the dimension of retailer images. Retailers create these associations through the products and brands they stock and the means by which they sell them. To more directly shape their images, many retailers aggressively advertise and promote directly to customers. For example, a consumer may infer certain characteristics about a product on the basis of where it is sold. "If it's sold by Nordstrom, it must be good quality." Consumers may perceive the same brand differently depending on whether it is sold in a store seen as prestigious and exclusive, or in a store designed for bargain shoppers and having more mass appeal.

The transfer of store image associations can be either positive or negative for a brand. For many high-end brands, a natural growth strategy is to expand the customer base by tapping new channels of distribution. Such strategies can be dangerous, however, depending on how existing customers and retailers react. When Levi Strauss & Company decided to expand the distribution channels for its Levi's jeans in the early 1980s beyond department and specialty shops to include mass-market chains Sears and Penney's, RH Macy's decided to drop the brand because it felt the brand's image had been cheapened. A brand revitalization program in the mid-1980s brought the jeans back into the department store chain, and Levi's was careful to sub-brand its 2003 entry into discount retailers Target and Wal-Mart as Levi Strauss Signature.

Branding Brief 7-3 describes the fierce battle between Calvin Klein and Warnaco that revolved largely on the issue of the appropriateness of retail distribution for the Calvin Klein brand.

Co-Branding

We've noted that through a brand extension strategy, a new product can become linked to an existing corporate or family brand that has its own set of associations. An existing brand can also leverage associations by linking itself to other brands from the same or different company. ***Co-branding***—also called brand bundling or brand alliances—occurs when two or more existing brands are combined into a joint product or are marketed together in some fashion.[6] A special case of this strategy is ingredient branding, which we'll discuss in the next section.[7]

Co-branding has been around for years; for example, Betty Crocker paired with Sunkist Growers in 1961 to successfully market a lemon chiffon cake mix.[8] Interest in co-branding as a means of building brand equity has increased in recent years. For example, Hershey's Heath toffee candy bar has not only been extended into several new products—Heath Sensations (bite-sized candies) and Heath Bits and Bits of Brickle (chocolate-covered and plain toffee baking products)—but also has been licensed to a variety of vendors, such as Dairy Queen (with its Blizzard drink), Ben & Jerry's, and Blue Bunny (with its ice cream bar).[9]

Some other notable supermarket examples of co-branding are Kellogg's Pop-Tarts with Smuckers fruit filling, Yoplait Trix yogurt, and Smuckers Dove ice cream sauce. In the credit card market, co-branding often links three brands, as in the Shell MasterCard from Citi Cards. With airlines, brand alliances can unite a host of brands, such as Star Alliance, which includes 16 different airlines such as United Airlines, Lufthansa, and Singapore Airlines.

Figure 7-3 summarizes the advantages and disadvantages of co-branding and licensing. The main advantage to co-branding is that a product may be uniquely and

Advantages

- Borrow needed expertise
- Leverage equity you don't have
- Reduce cost of product introduction
- Expand brand meaning into related categories
  - Broaden meaning
  - Increase access points
- Source of additional revenue

Disadvantages

- Loss of control
- Risk of brand equity dilution
- Negative feedback effects
- Lack of brand focus and clarity
- Organizational distraction

FIGURE 7-3

Advantages and Disadvantages of Co-branding and Licensing

THE SCIENCE OF BRANDING 7-1

Understanding Retailers' Brand Image Dimensions

Like the brands they sell, retailers have brand images that influence consumers and must be carefully constructed and maintained. Academics have identified the following five dimensions of retailers' brand image:

Access

The location of a store and the distance that consumers must travel to shop are basic criteria in their store choice decisions. Access is a key component in consumers' assessment of total shopping costs, and is especially important for retailers who wish to get a substantial share of wallet from fill-in trips and small-basket shoppers.

Store Atmosphere

Different elements of a retailer's in-store environment, like color, music, and crowding, can influence consumers' perceptions of its atmosphere, whether or not they visit a store, how much time they spend in it, and how much money they spend there. A pleasing in-store atmosphere provides substantial hedonic utility to consumers and encourages them to visit more often, stay longer, and buy more. Although it improves consumers' perceptions of the quality of merchandise in the store, consumers also tend to associate it with higher prices. An appealing in-store atmosphere also offers much potential in terms of crafting a unique store image and establishing differentiation. Even if the products and brands stocked by a retailer are similar to those sold by others, the ability to create a strong in-store personality and rich experiences can play a crucial role in building retailer brand equity.

Price and Promotion

A retailer's price image is influenced by attributes like average level of prices, how much variation there is in prices over time, the frequency and depth of promotions, and whether the retailer positions itself on a continuum between EDLP (everyday low price) and HILO (high-low promotional) pricing. Consumers are more likely to develop a favorable price image when retailers offer frequent discounts on a large number of products than when they offer less frequent, but steeper discounts. Further, products that have high unit price

convincingly positioned by virtue of the multiple brands in the campaign. Co-branding can create more compelling points of difference or points of parity for the brand—or both—than otherwise might have been feasible. As a result, it can generate greater sales from the existing target market as well as open additional opportunities with new consumers and channels. Co-branding can reduce the cost of product introduction because it combines two well-known images, accelerating potential adoption. Co-branding also may

and are purchased more frequently are more salient in determining the retailer's price image. One pricing format does not dominate another, but research has shown that large-basket shoppers prefer EDLP stores while small-basket shoppers prefer HILO, and it is optimal for HILO stores to charge an average price that is higher than the EDLP. Finally, price promotions are associated with store switching, but the effect is indirect, altering consumers' category purchase decisions while they are in the store rather than their choice of which store to visit.

Cross-Category Assortment

Consumers' perception of the breadth of different products and services offered by a retailer under one roof significantly influence store image. A broad assortment can create customer value by offering convenience and ease of shopping. It is risky to extend too far too soon, but staying too tightly coupled to the current assortment and image may unnecessarily limit the retailer's range of experimentation. The logic and sequencing of a retailer's assortment policy are critical to its ability to successfully expand its meaning and appeal to consumers over time.

Within-Category Assortment

Consumers' perceptions of the depth of a retailer's assortment within a product category are an important dimension of store image and a key driver of store choice. As the perceived assortment of brands, flavors, and sizes increases, variety-seeking consumers will perceive greater utility, consumers with uncertain future preferences will believe they have more flexibility in their choices, and, in general, consumers are more likely to find the item they desire. A greater number of SKUs need not directly translate to better perceptions. Retailers often can reduce the number of SKUs substantially without adversely affecting consumer perceptions, as long as they pay attention to the most preferred brands, the organization of the assortment, and the availability of diverse product attributes.

Sources: Kusum L. Ailawadi and Kevin Lane Keller, "Understanding Retail Branding: Conceptual Insights and Research Priorities," *Journal of Retailing* 80 (2004): 331–342. Used with permission of Professor C. Samuel Craig. See also Dennis B. Arnett, Debra A. Laverie, and Amanda Meiers "Developing Parsimonious Retailer Equity Indexes Using Partial Least Squares Analysis: A Method and Applications," *Journal of Retailing* 79 (2003): 161–170.

be a valuable means to learn about consumers and how other companies approach them. In poorly differentiated categories especially, co-branding may be an important means of creating a distinctive product.[10]

The potential disadvantages of co-branding are the risks and lack of control that arise from becoming aligned with another brand in the minds of consumers. Consumer expectations about the level of involvement and commitment with co-brands

BRANDING BRIEF 7-3

Calvin Klein and Warnaco's Battle of the Brands

From a humble start as a designer of women's coats, Calvin Klein bred a fashion empire with the help of savvy, high-image, and often risqué marketing created by his in-house CRK Advertising team. Calvin Klein started the designer jeans craze in the late 1970s with ads that featured a teenaged Brooke Shields claiming that nothing came between her and her Calvins. Ads in 1985 for Obsession perfume depicted a provocative "pseudo-orgy," and the fragrance quickly became the number-two seller in the country. Klein touched off a scandal and an FBI investigation in 1995 when many of his jeans ads were labeled pornographic and exploitive because they contained revealing images of underage models. Through success and scandal, Calvin Klein remained one of the foremost names in American fashion.

Calvin Klein's business success was fueled in part by the licensing of his name for a variety of products other than the seasonal designer clothing that made the brand a household name. For every $3,000 dress sold at Saks Fifth Avenue, many more pairs of $50 jeans, $14 cotton briefs, and $40 bottles of perfume bearing the familiar CK logo pass through checkout lines at department stores across the globe. Calvin Klein and his team do the design work for their products, while licensees take care of the logistics of manufacturing, distribution, and retail contracts. Although licensing his name led to millions in profits, it also reduced the control Calvin Klein had over his brand.

In a move that set off a highly publicized legal dispute, Calvin Klein sued jeanswear licensee Warnaco in June 2000 for "improper sales" to discounters such as Costco and Sam's Club. Calvin Klein alleged that by "producing jeans and underwear expressly for downmarket discount stores," the licensee was "cheapening" the Calvin Klein brand. In particular, Klein found fault with Warnaco's decision to sell CK underwear to low-cost retailer JCPenney. Other

are likely to be high. Unsatisfactory performance thus could have negative repercussions for both (or all) brands.[11] If the other brand has entered into a number of co-branding arrangements, there also may be a risk of overexposure that would dilute the transfer of any association. It may also result in distraction and a lack of focus on existing brands.

Guidelines

The Science of Branding 7-2 provides some additional insight about how consumers evaluate co-branded products. To create a strong co-brand, both brands should have adequate brand awareness; sufficiently strong, favorable, and unique associations; and positive consumer judgments and feelings. Thus, a necessary but not sufficient condition for co-branding success is that the two brands *separately* have some brand equity. The most important requirement is a logical fit between the two brands, so that the combined

major Calvin Klein retail accounts, such as Dillard's and Federated Department stores, were angered by this decision and threatened to slow or halt future orders of CK underwear. The suit claimed that Warnaco had been pushing CK merchandise into other low-cost retailers without permission.

A month after Klein's filing, Warnaco countersued, charging Calvin Klein with violating the license agreement. Linda Wachner, CEO of Warnaco, defended her company's sales to discounters by saying, "[Calvin Klein] gets a full list every year of every account and every shipment, of every dollar." Warnaco's countersuit also accused Calvin Klein of trade libel and bad-faith dealing, claiming the designer had failed to attend a design meeting for over a year.

The two sides settled as the case was going to trial in 2001, and the license agreement remained intact. Warnaco agreed not to sell CK jeanswear and underwear to JCPenney but was allowed to continue selling to discount retailers Costco, Sam's Club, and B.J.'s. at "dramatically reduced volume." Other terms of the settlement effectively gave Calvin Klein more control over Warnaco's dealings with the brand.

Phillips-Van Heusen acquired Calvin Klein in 2003 for a deal worth $700 million that gave it the rights to the brand name, the collection business, and the brand's related licensing revenue. By then Wachner had been ousted as CEO, and relations between Warnaco and the new brand owners were subsequently seen to be positive.

Sources: Teri Agins, "Calvin Klein, Warnaco Settle Their Bitter Feud," *Wall Street Journal,* 23 January 2001; Teri Agins and Rebecca Quick, "Illegal Briefs?" *Wall Street Journal,* 1 June 2000; Lisa Marsh, "To Where from Eternity?" *Sunday Herald,* September 28, 2003.

brand or marketing activity maximizes the advantages of the individual brands while minimizing the disadvantages.

Swatch

Some eyebrows were raised when DaimlerChrysler AG's Mercedes Benz unit agreed to manufacture a "Swatchmobile," named after SMH's colorful and fashionable lines of Swatch watches.[12] Personally championed by SMH's charismatic chairman, Nicolas Hayek, the Smart Car, as it came to be known, was designed to be small (less than 10 feet long) and low cost (under $10,000). The car combined the three most important features of Swatch watches—affordability, durability, and stylishness—with an important feature of a Mercedes Benz automobile—safety and security in a crash. A number of critics believed the Mercedes Benz image could suffer if the car was unsuccessful, which was a very possible outcome given the fact that many products bearing the Swatch name (like clothes, bags, telephones, pagers, and sunglasses) saw disappointing sales

THE SCIENCE OF BRANDING 7-2

Understanding Brand Alliances

Brand alliances, which combine two brands in some way, come in all forms. Academic research has explored the effects of co-branding, ingredient branding strategies, and advertising alliances.

Co-Branding

Park, Jun, and Shocker compare co-brands to the notion of "conceptual combinations" in psychology. A conceptual combination ("apartment dog") consists of a modifying concept, or "modifier" *apartment*) and a modified concept, or "header" (*dog*). Experimentally, Park and his colleagues explored the different ways that Godiva (associated with expensive, high-calorie boxed chocolates) and Slim-Fast (associated with inexpensive, low-calorie diet food) could hypothetically introduce a chocolate cake mix separately or together through a co-brand.

They found that the co-branded version of the product was better accepted than if either brand attempted to extend individually into the cake mix category. They also found that consumers' impressions of the co-branded concept were driven by the header brand—Slim-Fast chocolate cake mix by Godiva was seen as lower calorie than if the product was called Godiva chocolate cake mix by Slim-Fast; the reverse was true for associations of richness and luxury. Similarly, consumers' impressions of Slim-Fast after exposure to the co-branded concept were more likely to change when it was the header brand than when it was the modifier brand. The findings show how carefully selected brands can be combined to overcome the potential problems of negatively correlated attributes (here, rich taste and low calories).

Simonin and Ruth found that consumers' attitudes toward a brand alliance could influence subsequent impressions of each partner's brands (spillover effects existed), but that these effects also depended on other factors such as product fit or compatibility and brand fit or image congruity. Brands less familiar than their partners contributed less to an alliance but experienced stronger spillover effects than their more familiar partners. Voss and Tansuhaj found that consumer evaluations of an unknown brand from another country were more positive when it was allied with a well-known domestic brand.

Levin and Levin explored the effects of dual branding, which they defined as a marketing strategy in which two brands, usually restaurants, share the same facilities while providing consumers with the opportunity to use either one or both brands. Kumar found that introducing a co-branded extension into a new product category made it less likely that a brand from the new category could turn around and introduce a counterextension into the original product category. LeBar and colleagues found that joint branding helped to increase a brand's perceived differentiation, but also sometimes decreased consumers' perceived esteem for the brand and knowledge about the brand.

Ingredient Branding

Desai and Keller conducted a laboratory experiment to consider how ingredient branding affected consumer acceptance of an initial line extension, as well as the ability of the brand to introduce future category extensions. They studied two particular types of line extensions, defined as brand expansions: (1) ***slot filler expansions,*** in which the level of one existing product attribute changed (a new type of scent in Tide detergent), and (2) ***new attribute expansions,*** in which an entirely new attribute or characteristic was added to the product (cough relief liquid added to LifeSavers candy). They examined two types of ingredient branding strategies by branding the target attribute ingredient for the brand expansion with either a new name as a ***self-branded ingredient*** (Tide with its own EverFresh scented bath soap) or an established, well-respected name as a ***co-branded ingredient*** (Tide with Irish Spring scented bath soap).

The results indicated that with slot filler expansions, although a co-branded ingredient eased initial acceptance of the expansion, a self-branded ingredient led to more favorable later extension evaluations. With more dissimilar new attribute expansions, however, a co-branded ingredient led to more favorable evaluations of both the initial expansion and the subsequent extension.

Venkatesh and Mahajan derived an analytical model based on bundling and reservation price notions to help formulate optimal pricing and partner selection decisions for branded components. In an experimental application in the context of a university computer store selling 486-class laptop computers, they showed that at the bundle level, an all-brand Compaq PC with Intel 486 commanded a clear price premium over other alternatives. The relative brand strength of the Intel brand, however, was shown to be stronger in some senses than that of the Compaq brand.

Advertising Alliances

Samu, Krishnan, and Smith showed that the effectiveness of advertising alliances for new product introductions depended on the interactive effects of three factors: the degree of complementarity between the featured products, the type of differentiation strategy (common versus unique advertised attributes with respect to the product category), and the type of ad processing (top-down or bottom-up) that an ad evoked (such as by the explicitness of the ad headline).

Sources: Akshay R. Rao, "Strategic Brand Alliances," *Journal of Brand Management* 5, no. 2 (1997): 111–119; Akshay R. Rao, L. Qu, and Robert W. Ruekert, "Signaling Unobservable Product Quality through a Brand Ally," *Journal of Marketing Research* (May 1999): 258–268; Allen D. Shocker, Raj K. Srivastava, and Robert W. Ruekert, "Challenges and Opportunities Facing Brand Management: An Introduction to the Special Issue," *Journal of Marketing Research* 31, no. 5 (1994): 149–158; Tom Blackett and Bob Boad, *Co-Branding—The Science of Alliance* (London: Palgrave MacMillan, 1999); C. Whan Park, Sung Youl Jun, and Allan D. Shocker, "Composite Branding Alliances: An Investigation of Extension and Feedback Effects," *Journal of Marketing Research* (November 1996): 453–467; Bernard L. Simonin and Julie A. Ruth, "Is a Company Known by the Company It Keeps? Assessing the Spillover Effects of Brand Alliances on Consumer Brand Attitudes," *Journal of Marketing Research* 35, no. 2 (1998): 30–42; Kevin E. Voss and P. Tansuhaj, "A Consumer Perspective on Foreign Market Entry: Building Brands through Brand Alliances," *Journal of International Consumer Marketing* 11, no. 2 (1999): 39–58; Irwin P. Levin and Aron M. Levin, "Modeling the Role of Brand Alliances in the Assimilation of Product Evaluations," *Journal of Consumer Psychology* 9, no. 1 (2000): 43–52; Piyush Kumar, "The Impact of Cobranding on Customer Evaluation of Brand Counterextensions," *Journal of Marketing* 69 (July 2005): 1–18; Ed Lebar, Phil Buehler, Kevin Lane Keller, Monika Sawicka, et al., "Brand Equity Implications of Joint Branding Programs," *Journal of Advertising Research* 45, no. 4 (2005): 413–425; Kalpesh Desai and Kevin Lane Keller, "The Effects of Brand Expansions and Ingredient Branding Strategies on Host Brand Extendibility," *Journal of Marketing* 66 (January 2002): 73–93; R. Venkatesh and Vijay Mahajan, "Products with Branded Components: An Approach for Premium Pricing and Partner Selection," *Marketing Science* 16, no. 2 (1997): 146–165; Sridhar Samu, H. Shanker Krishnan, and Robert E. Smith, "Using Advertising Alliances for New Product Introduction: Interactions between Product Complementarity and Promotional Strategies," *Journal of Marketing* 63, no. 1 (1999): 57–74.

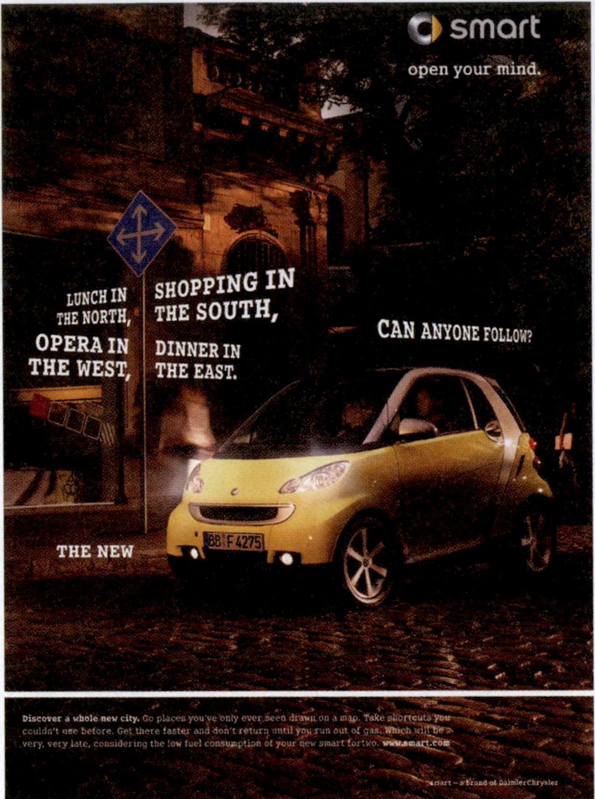

The Smart Car experienced greater success after its sale from Swatch.

or were dropped altogether. Swatch sold its share of the Smart Car business to DaimlerChrysler in 1998. The Smart Car became very popular in Europe, however, selling over 130,000 units in 2004.

Besides these strategic considerations, marketers must enter into and execute co-branding ventures carefully. They must ensure the right kind of fit in values, capabilities, and goals in addition to an appropriate balance of brand equity. When it comes to execution, marketers need detailed plans to legalize contracts, make financial arrangements, and coordinate marketing programs. As one executive at Nabisco put it, "Giving away your brand is a lot like giving away your child—you want to make sure everything is perfect." The financial arrangement between brands may vary, although one common approach involves a licensing fee and royalty from the brand that is more involved in the production process. The aim is for the licensor and the licensee to benefit from these agreements as a result of the shared equity, increased awareness for the licensor, and greater sales for the licensee. Branding Brief 7-4 describes some of General Mills's co-branding and licensing experiences.

More generally, brand alliances, such as co-branding, require marketers to ask themselves a number of questions, such as:

- What capabilities do we *not* have?
- What resource constraints do we face (people, time, money)?
- What growth goals or revenue needs do we have?

BRANDING BRIEF 7-4

Co-Branding and Licensing at General Mills

General Mills, a consumer-goods giant that began as a single flour mill in 1877, has traditionally forged licensing and co-branding partnerships as part of its marketing program. General Mills partners with other leading brands to create new co-branded products, as it did with Pac-Man in the 1980s, or forges licensing agreements with other marketers, as when Honey Nut Cheerios, in the early 1990s, included Topps trading cards featuring members of the TV show *Beverly Hills 90210*.

General Mills has expanded and licensed brands such as Cheerios into many areas.

General Mills also licenses its own brands to other companies for use with a diverse range of products, carefully selecting each license opportunity to ensure that it fits with the overall brand image of the company. Since 1987, General Mills has licensed the Betty Crocker name and likeness for use with cookbooks, cookware, and other products related to food preparation. More recently, the company has licensed some of its other brand names, such as Wheaties and Cheerios. General Mills partnered with publisher Simon & Schuster to produce a series of Cheerios books aimed at young readers. The books, which include interactive counting games that encourage the use of actual Cheerios, are among the top sellers in the Little Simon imprint of Simon & Schuster. The company also forged an agreement with toy company Hasbro to develop plastic Cheerios dispensers molded in shapes such as cell phones. Other Cheerios licensed products include a toy tractor-trailer and a line of children's place settings. General Mills also licensed its Wheaties brand to sports memorabilia marketer Asset Marketing Services for a series of collectible miniature Wheaties boxes bearing classic "Wheaties Champions." The company is developing plans for other licensing deals involving products such as Lucky Charms and Cocoa Puffs. General Mills' 2001 acquisition of Pillsbury from parent Diageo PLC gave it an additional licensing tool, the Pillsbury Doughboy.

Sources: Jennifer Franklin, "Big G Builds Brands by Books and Baseball," *Minneapolis-St. Paul CityBusiness*, 17 March 2000; "Cheerios Getting Zip from '90210,'" *Entertainment Marketing Letter*, 1 January 1993.

In assessing a joint branding opportunity, marketers will ask themselves:

- Is it a profitable business venture?
- How does it help to maintain or strengthen brand equity?
- Is there any possible risk of dilution of brand equity?
- Does it offer any extrinsic advantages such as learning opportunities?

One of the highest-profile brand alliances is that of Disney and McDonald's, which had the exclusive global rights from 1996–2006 in the fast-food industry to promote everything from Disney movies and videos to TV shows and theme parks. McDonald's has brand partnerships with a number of brands, including Fisher-Price toys for its Happy Meals.

Ingredient Branding

A special case of co-branding is ***ingredient branding***, which creates brand equity for materials, components, or parts that are necessarily contained within other branded products. Some successful ingredient brands include Dolby noise reduction, Gore-Tex water-resistant fibers, Teflon nonstick coatings, Stainmaster stain-resistant fibers, and Scotchgard fabrics. Some popular ingredient-branded products are Betty Crocker baking mixes with Hershey's chocolate syrup, Lunchables lunch combinations with Taco Bell tacos, and Lay's potato chips made with KC Masterpiece barbecue sauce. Ingredient brands attempt to create enough awareness and preference for their product that consumers will not buy a host product that does not contain the ingredient.

From a consumer behavior perspective, branded ingredients are often a signal of quality. In a provocative study, Carpenter, Glazer, and Nakamoto found that the inclusion of a branded attribute ("Alpine Class" fill for a down jacket) significantly affected consumer choices even when consumers were explicitly told that the attribute was not relevant to their decision.[13] Clearly, consumers inferred certain quality characteristics as a result of the branded ingredient.

The uniformity and predictability of ingredient brands can reduce risk and reassure consumers. As a result, ingredient brands can become industry standards and consumers will not want to buy a product that does not contain the ingredient. In other words, ingredient brands can become, in effect, a category point of parity. Consumers do not necessarily have to know exactly how the ingredient works—just that it adds value.

Ingredient branding has become more prevalent as mature brands seek cost-effective means to differentiate themselves on the one hand, and potential ingredient products seek means to expand their sales opportunities on the other hand. To illustrate the range of alternatives in ingredient branding, consider the copy from a Singapore Airlines magazine ad, which prominently featured both co-branded and self-branded ingredients in promoting one of their service offerings:

Singapore Airlines New Raffles Class: Business in a Class of its Own

Singapore Airlines has searched the world to bring you the finest business class in the sky. Top French design house *Givenchy* has created a cabin of contemporary elegance. And, for the ultimate in comfort, our new *Ultimo* seats from Italy are electrically controlled, offering luxurious legroom as well as personal privacy screens—a world first. In-seat laptop power is on hand for those who need to work; whereas those who prefer to relax can enjoy *KrisWorld,* your in-flight entertainment system, with over 60 entertainment options. And for the first time in the sky, you can enjoy blockbuster movies with *Dolby Headphone* surround sound. In addition our *World Gourmet Cuisine*—created by an international panel of acclaimed chefs—brings you a dining experience reminiscent of fine earth-bound restaurants, complemented by in-flight service even other airlines talk about.

Thus, as in this example, one product may contain a number of different branded ingredients. Ingredient brands are not restricted to products and services. For example, electronics specialty retailer RadioShack has established strategic alliances with Compaq, Microsoft, RCA, Sprint, Verizon Wireless, and others that let the manufacturers set up kiosks within many of RadioShack's 7,000 stores in the United States.

Singapore Airlines has many ingredient brands that help to improve passengers in-flight experiences.

Advantages and Disadvantages. The pros and cons of ingredient branding are similar to those of co-branding.[14] From the perspective of the firm making and supplying the ingredient, the benefit of branding its products as ingredients is that by creating consumer pull, the firm can generate greater sales at a higher margin. There may also be more stable and broader customer demand and better long-term supplier-buyer relationships. Enhanced revenues may accrue from having two revenue streams—the direct revenue from the cost of the supplied ingredients, as well as possible extra revenue from the royalty rights paid to display the ingredient brand.

From the standpoint of the manufacturer of the host product, the benefit is in leveraging the equity from the ingredient brand to enhance its own brand equity. On the demand side, the host product brands may achieve access to new product categories, different market segments, and more distribution channels than they otherwise could have expected. On the supply side, the host product brands may be able to share some production and development costs with the ingredient supplier.

Ingredient branding is not without its risks and costs. The costs of a supporting marketing communication program can be high—advertising to sales ratios for consumer products often surpass 5 percent—and many suppliers are relatively inexperienced at designing mass media communications that may have to contend with inattentive consumers and noncooperative middlemen. As with co-branding, there is a loss of control, because marketing programs for the supplier and manufacturer may have different objectives and thus may send different signals to consumers. Some manufacturers may be reluctant to become supplier dependent or may not believe that the branded ingredient adds value, resulting in a loss of possible accounts. Manufacturers may resent any consumer confusion about what is the "real brand" if the branded ingredient gains too much equity. Finally, the sustainability of the competitive advantage may be somewhat uncertain, because brands that follow may benefit from consumers' increased understanding of the role of the ingredient. As a result, follower brands may have to communicate not so much the importance of the ingredient as why their particular ingredient brand is better than the pioneer or other brands.

BRANDING BRIEF 7-5

Ingredient Branding the DuPont Way

Perhaps one of the most successful ingredient brand marketers of all times is DuPont, which was founded in Delaware as a black-powder manufacturer in 1802 by Frenchman E. I. duPont de Nemours. Over the years, the company introduced a number of innovative products for use in markets ranging from apparel to aerospace. Many of the company's innovations, such as Lycra and Stainmaster fabrics, Teflon coating, and Kevlar fiber, became household names as ingredient brands in consumer products manufactured by many other companies.

Early on, DuPont learned an important branding lesson the hard way. Because the company did not protect the name of its first organic chemical fiber, nylon, it was not trademarkable and became generic. The brands created by DuPont through the years have been components in a wide variety of products that are marketed to make everyday life better, safer, and healthier. By 2004, DuPont sold over 30,000 products across 1,500 different product lines, and used 2,000 unique brands and 15,000 different brand registrations to support these products.

These innovations were the result of the company's massive R&D program ($1.33 billion spent in 2004). DuPont has over 75 R&D facilities globally, including 35 outside the United States. These sites are staffed by nearly 2,000 scientists and researchers—including 600 with Ph.D.s—who work to pursue science-based solutions for global markets. When the company began to focus on revitalizing its R&D in early 2000, 40 percent of its technology resources and assets were dedicated to growth; the rest supported existing products and operations. By 2005, 65 percent of the company's research was focused on growth.

Several recent ingredient brands include Supro isolated soy proteins, used in food products, and RiboPrinter genetic fingerprinting technology. A key question that DuPont constantly confronts is whether to brand a product as an ingredient brand. To address this question, the firm typically applies several criteria, both quantitative and qualitative.

Guidelines. Ingredient branding programs build brand equity in many of the same ways that conventional branding programs do. Branding Brief 7-5 describes ingredient branding efforts at DuPont, which has successfully introduced a number of such brands. What are some specific requirements for successful ingredient branding? In general, ingredient branding must accomplish four tasks:

1. Consumers must first perceive that the ingredient matters to the performance and success of the end product. Ideally, this intrinsic value is visible or easily experienced.
2. Consumers must then be convinced that not all ingredient brands are the same and that the ingredient is superior. Ideally, the ingredient would have an innovation or some other substantial advantage over existing alternatives.
3. A distinctive symbol or logo must be designed to clearly signal to consumers that the host product contains the ingredient. Ideally, the symbol or logo would function essentially as a "seal" and would be simple and versatile—it could appear virtually anywhere—and credibly communicate quality and confidence to consumers.

- On the quantitative side, DuPont has a model that estimates the return on investment of promoting a product as an ingredient brand. Inputs to the model include brand resource allocations such as advertising and trade support; outputs relate to favorability ratings and potential sales. The goal of the model is to determine whether branding an ingredient can be financially justified, especially in industrial markets.
- On the qualitative side, DuPont assesses how an ingredient brand can help a product's positioning. If competitive and consumer analyses reveal that conveying certain associations would boost sales, DuPont is more likely to brand the ingredient. For example, one reason that DuPont launched its stain-resistant carpet fiber under the ingredient brand Stainmaster was that the company felt a "tough" association would be highly valued in the market.

DuPont maintains that an appropriate, effective ingredient branding strategy leads to a number of competitive advantages, such as higher price premiums (often as much as 20 percent), enhanced brand loyalty, and increased bargaining power with other members of the value chain. DuPont employs both push and pull strategies to create its ingredient brands. Consumer advertising creates consumer pull by generating interest in the brand and a willingness to specifically request it. Extensive trade support in the form of co-op advertising, training, and trade promotions creates push by fostering a strong sense of loyalty to DuPont from other members of the value chain. This loyalty helps DuPont negotiate favorable terms from distributors and leads to increased cooperation when new products are introduced.

Sources: Sasha Planting, DuPont Company Overview, www.financialmail.co.za, 17 June 2005; Monica Roman, "How DuPont Keeps 'Em Coming Back for More," *Business Week,* 20 August 1990, 68.

4. Finally, a coordinated push and pull program must be put into place such that consumers understand the importance and advantages of the branded ingredient. Often this will include consumer advertising and promotions and, sometimes in collaboration with manufacturers, retail merchandising and promotion programs. As part of the push strategy, some communication efforts may also need to be devoted to gaining the cooperation and support of manufacturers or other channel members

Licensing

Licensing creates contractual arrangements whereby firms can use the names, logos, characters, and so forth of other brands to market their own brands for some fixed fee. Essentially, a firm is "renting" another brand to contribute to the brand equity of its own product. Because it can be a shortcut means of building brand equity, licensing has gained in popularity in recent years—North American retail sales of licensed products jumped from $4 billion in 1977 to $72 billion in 2005.[15]

Entertainment licensing has also become big business in recent years. Successful licensors include movie titles and logos like *Harry Potter, Star Wars,* and *Spider-Man;*

BRANDING BRIEF 7-6

Licensing the Disney Way

The Walt Disney Company is recognized as having one of the strongest brands in the world. Much of its success lies in its flourishing television, movie, theme park, and other entertainment ventures. These different vehicles have created a host of well-loved characters and a reputation for quality entertainment. Disney Consumer Products is designed to keep the Disney name and characters fresh in the consumer's mind through six business areas in the following ways:

Disney actively and successfully licenses its brands across many products.

1. *Merchandising licensing:* Selectively authorizing the use of Disney characters on high-quality merchandise
2. *Publishing:* Telling the Disney story in books, magazines, comics, and art
3. *Music and audio:* Playing favorite Disney songs and stories on tape and compact disc
4. *Computer software:* Programming Disney "fun" into home computers and computer game systems
5. *Educational production:* Casting the characters in award-winning films for schools and libraries
6. *Catalog marketing:* Offering Disney and Disney-quality products via top catalogs

The pervasiveness of these product offerings is staggering: All in all, children receive over 3 billion entertainment-based impressions of Mickey Mouse every year, equivalent to 10 million impressions a day.

Disney believes its characters' appearances on quality merchandise for years have added greatly to their popularity. The first hand-made Mickey Mouse doll appeared in 1930. Disney

comic strip characters such as *Garfield* and *Peanuts* characters; and television and cartoon characters from *Sesame Street, The Simpsons, SpongBob SquarePants* and others. Every summer, marketers spend millions of dollars in movie tie-ins as marketers look for the next blockbuster franchise. Even athletes participate in the action. In 1999, retired boxer George Foreman signed an astounding $27.5-million-a-year licensing deal with housewares company Salton to use his name on food preparation products such as the popular Lean Mean Low Fat Grilling Machine. Perhaps the champion of licensing is Walt Disney. Branding Brief 7-6 describes some of its licensing practices and strategies.

Licensing can be quite lucrative for the licensor. It has long been an important business strategy for designer apparel and accessories, for example. Designers such as Donna Karan, Calvin Klein, Pierre Cardin, and others command large royalties for the right to use their name on a variety of merchandise such as clothing, belts, ties, and luggage. Over the course of three decades, Ralph Lauren became the world's most successful designer, creating a $5-billion-dollar business licensing his Ralph Lauren, Double RL, and Polo brands to many different kinds of products. Everyone seems to get into the act with

started licensing its characters for toys made by Mattel in the 1950s. Disney Licensing is now responsible for some 3,000 contracts for 16,000 products with top manufacturers worldwide. Disney licenses its standard characters like Mickey, Minnie, Donald, Goofy, and Pluto; filmed entertainment including *Finding Nemo, The Lion King,* and the *Toy Story* franchise; and TV properties such as *Kim Possible* and *Lilo & Stitch: The Series.* Disney continues to reign as the world's largest licensor with global retail sales of $15 billion from licensing in 2004.

Artists in Disney Licensing's Creative Resources department work closely with manufacturers on all aspects of product marketing, including design, prototyping, manufacturing, packaging, and advertising. At each step, they take care to ensure that the products are faithful to the look and personality of the characters. To protect and enhance the value of its brands, Disney issues a thick notebook of standards and guidelines for licensed brand identities. Disney maintains a team of employees who strictly interpret these guidelines, fiercely guarding the image of the characters.

One of Disney's most successful licensed characters is Winnie the Pooh. Disney has three separate Winnie the Pooh product lines: the familiar "red shirt" Pooh from Disney movies; the 100 Acre Collection, a more upscale line comprising products that typically sell in department stores; and the Classic Pooh line based on the original illustrations from A. A. Milne's *Winnie the Pooh* books. Pooh products, which have existed since Disney's 1966 animated short *Winnie the Pooh and the Honey Tree,* have recently become a virtual goldmine. Between 1995 and 2004, the total licensing market for Winnie the Pooh grew from $390 million to $5.6 billion in retail sales for Disney, and *Forbes* ranks it as the second most valuable character for licensing. By comparison, Disney's other core characters—Mickey, Minnie, Goofy, Donald Duck, and Pluto—grew only 20 percent over the same period. In 2001, Disney bought the rights to Winnie the Pooh and all the related characters for $340 million and no longer has to pay licensing fees to the group of former rights holders.

Sources: Bruce Orwall, "Disney's Magic Transformation?" *Wall Street Journal,* 4 October 2000; Michael McCarthy, "Judge Pooh-Poohs Lawsuit over Disney Licensing Fees," *USA Today,* March 29, 2004; Sonia Reyes, "Disney Tries Magic in Kroger Markets," *Brandweek,* 24 July 2006.

licensing. Sports licensing of clothing apparel and other products has grown considerably to become a multibillion-dollar business.

Guidelines

One danger in licensing is that manufacturers can get caught up in licensing a brand that might be popular at the moment but is really only a fad and produces short-lived sales. Because of multiple licensing arrangements, licensed entities easily can become overexposed and wear out quickly as a result. Licensed merchandise sales of Barney products hit a $500 million jackpot in 1993 but faded significantly the following year before making a later comeback. Sales of Izod Lacoste, with its familiar alligator crest, peaked at $450 million in 1982 but dwindled to an estimated $150 million in shirt sales in 1990 after the brand became overexposed and discount priced.[16] Subsequently purchased by Phillips-Van Heusen, the brand made a comeback as the result of more careful marketing.

Teenage Mutant Ninja Turtles

First introduced in 1988, Teenage Mutant Ninja Turtles products were licensed for better or worse to more than a hundred businesses, riding the wave of three live-action films that grossed a cumulative total of more than $256 million domestically. An estimated $1 billion in sales was generated in 1991 for products bearing the Turtle name, ranging from conventional souvenirs and T-shirts to more exotic alternatives such as vanilla-flavored pizza candy and even pork rinds! After this high-water mark, however, sales of licensed Teenage Mutant Ninja Turtles merchandise dropped to $100 million in 1993. In 2003, the Turtles returned to television after a five-year hiatus, appearing on Cartoon Network and 4Kids TV on Fox in the United States and on major TV channels around the world. A new live action feature film created as part of the entertainment re-launch of the Teenage Mutant Ninja Turtles generated hundreds of millions of dollars of worldwide retail sales of new licensed products, including an entirely new range of toys from longtime licensee Playmates Toys.

Firms are taking a number of steps to protect themselves in their licensing agreements, especially those firms that have little brand equity of their own and rely on the image of their licensor.[17] For example, firms are obtaining licensing rights to a broad range of licensed entities—some of which are more durable—to diversify their risk. Licensees are developing unique new products and sales and marketing approaches so that their sales are not merely a function of the popularity of other brands. Some firms conduct marketing research to ensure the proper match of product and licensed entity or to provide more precise sales forecasts for effective inventory management.

Corporate trademark licensing—one of the fastest-growing segments of the licensing industry—is the licensing of company names, logos, or brands for use on various, often unrelated products.[18] For example, in the depths of a financial crisis a number of years ago, Harley-Davidson chose to license its name—synonymous with motorcycles and a certain lifestyle—to a polo shirt, a gold ring, and even a wine cooler. Other seemingly narrowly focused brands such as Jeep, Caterpillar, Deere, and Jack Daniels have also entered a broad portfolio of licensing arrangements. Standard & Poor's and Dow Jones now license their trademarks to manufacturers of financial products and to the exchanges where the products trade.

In licensing their corporate trademarks, firms may have different motivations, including generating extra revenues and profits, protecting their trademarks, increasing their brand exposure, or enhancing their brand image. The profit appeal can be enticing because there are no inventory expenses, accounts receivables, or manufacturing expenses. In an average deal, a licensee pays a corporation a royalty of about 5 percent of the wholesale price of each product, although the actual percentage can vary from 2 percent to 10 percent. As noted in Chapter 5, some firms now sell licensed merchandise through their own catalogs.

As with any co-branded arrangement, however, the risk is that the product will not live up to the reputation established by the brand. Inappropriate licensing can dilute brand meaning with consumers and marketing focus within the organization. When Eddie Bauer, in the midst of a retailing slump in November 2000, announced a two-year licensing deal with Compaq for special-edition Compaq Presario 1400 notebook computers sporting a distinctive trim, one industry analyst complained, "Their business has been terribly disappointing—their entire focus should be unrelentingly on their merchandise assortment."[19]

Celebrity Endorsement

Using well-known and admired people to promote products is a widespread phenomenon with a long marketing history. Even the late U.S. president Ronald Reagan was a celebrity endorser, pitching several different products, including cigarettes, during his acting days. Some American actors or actresses who refuse to endorse products in the United States are willing to do so in Japan, including Meg Ryan for Dingo autos, Leonardo DiCaprio for Suzuki Wagon R, Jodie Foster for Morinaga Caffe Latte, and Harrison Ford for Honda Legend. Brad Pitt and Bruce Willis have actually done a series of commercials overseas for a number of different brands.

The rationale behind these strategies is that a famous person can draw attention to a brand and shape the perceptions of the brand, by virtue of the inferences that consumers make based on the knowledge they have about the famous person. The celebrity must be well enough known to improve awareness, image, and responses for the brand.

In particular, a celebrity endorser should have a high level of visibility and a rich set of potentially useful associations, judgments, and feelings.[20] Ideally, he or she would be credible in terms of expertise, trustworthiness, and likability or attractiveness, as well as having specific associations that carry potential product relevance.

Q Scores

Marketing Evaluations/TvQ Inc. conducts surveys to determine "Q Scores" for a broad range of entertainers and other public figures like TV performers, news and sports anchors and reporters, athletes, and models. Each performer is rated on the following scale: "One of My Favorites," "Very Good," "Good," "Fair," "Poor," and "Never Seen or Heard of Before." The sum of the "Favorite" through "Poor" ratings is "Total Familiar." The "One of My Favorites" rating is an absolute measure of appeal or popularity, since it is based on 100 percent. Because some performers are not very well known and would have a low "Favorite" rating, the Q Score is a ratio of the "Favorite" rating to the "Familiar" score. It addresses the question, How appealing is this figure among those who do know him or her? Q Scores reflect the potential of lesser-known personalities and provide an equivalent basis for comparison with more established personalities. As of 2004, Negative Q Scores (the ratio of the "Fair" plus "Poor" ratings to the "Familiar" score) are being published as well, in order to reflect the proportion of the population that dislikes a particular personality. Figure 7-4 displays some of Marketing Evaluation's recent familiarity scores, Q scores, and negative Q scores for popular entertainers.

A number of different brands have created strong associations to celebrities that have served as sources of brand equity. For example, down-to-earth sportscaster John Madden has been a long-time pitchman for Ace Hardware. NFL football players such as Donovan McNabb and their real-life mothers have been a winning combination in ads for Campbell's Chunky Soup—sales increased from $200 million in 1998 when the ad campaign began to $500 million by 2005.

Dave Thomas and Wendy's

Founder and chairman Dave Thomas was an effective pitchman for his Wendy's restaurant chain because of his down-home, unpretentious, folksy style and strong product focus. Recognized by over 90 percent of adult consumers, he appeared in hundreds of commercials over a 12-year period. A heart attack scare in 1997 forced Wendy's executives to contemplate "life after Dave"—a scary prospect given their belief that "nothing else builds traffic and moves product as well," and a reality they had to face with his death early in 2002. Their follow-up campaign created a fictitious character, Mr. Wendy, who served as "unofficial spokesperson." Seen as largely ineffective, it was replaced by an ad campaign in 2005 that focused on more prominently positioning Wendy's food and heritage of quality.[21]

Dave Thomas was a highly successful spokesperson for the Wendy's brand, which was made dramatically clear after his death.

Potential Problems

There are a number of potential problems with linking a celebrity endorser to a brand. First, celebrity endorsers can endorse so many products that they lack any specific product meaning or are seen as opportunistic or insincere. Anna Kournikova leveraged her good looks off the tennis court to sign endorsements worth millions of dollars with a wide variety of

Rank	Performer	Percentage of Total Familiar	Q-Score	Negative Q-Score
1.	Tom Hanks	93	57	5
2.	Mel Gibson	90	52	5
3.	Bill Cosby	94	49	11
4.	William Petersen	43	46	8
5.	Sean Connery	87	45	8
6.	Eddie Murphy	91	40	10
7.	Julia Roberts	86	39	14
8.	Robert De Niro	86	39	10
9.	Harrison Ford	87	38	8
10.	Will Smith	86	38	10
11.	Jack Nicholson	82	38	11
12.	Maurice Benard	18	37	23
13.	Steve Martin	87	36	13
14.	Jerry Orbach	44	36	8
15.	Jorja Fox	39	36	9
16.	Jim Carrey	92	35	16
17.	George Eads	42	35	10
18.	Mariska Hargitay	41	35	7
19.	Anthony LaPaglia	34	35	11
20.	Adam Sandler	82	34	20
21.	Danny Glover	81	34	9
22.	Doris Roberts	66	34	11
23.	Toby Keith	59	34	19
24.	Christopher Meloni	38	34	9
25.	John M. Jackson	28	34	13

Source: Marketing Evaluations/TvQ, Inc., Winter 2004 Performer Q Study. Courtesy of TVQ, Inc. Marketing Evaluations, Inc.

FIGURE 7-4

Q Ranking of Performers (Among Population Aged 6 Years and Older)

brands, including Adidas, Berlei lingerie, Charles Schwab, Lycos, Microsoft's XSN Sports, Multiway Sports Bra, Omega watches, Pegasus cell phones, and Yonex racquets.

It could be argued that Michael Jordan, as talented a basketball player and as likable a person as he might be, lost effectiveness as an endorser when he was associated with so many brands and products, starring in ads for Nike athletic shoes, Gatorade sports drink, Bijan fragrances, Hanes underwear, McDonald's restaurants, Ball Park Franks, Rayovac batteries, Wheaties cereal, and MCI WorldCom long-distance telecommunications. He even supported his own brand in the form of Michael Jordan men's cologne and, later, the Nike subsidiary Jordan brand.

Second, there must be a reasonable match between the celebrity and the product.[22] Many past endorsements would seem to fail this test. A classic mismatch occurred when the CEO of Bristol-Myers insisted on using his favorite Western actor, rugged John Wayne, as the spokesperson for Datril pain reliever. Oddly, tennis star John McEnroe was an early spokesperson for Bic disposable razors despite his trademark two-day stubble. George C. Scott, an Oscar winner for his patriotic movie portrayal of Patton, seemed to be a curious choice to endorse the French Renault car. Some better matches in recent years include actor Paul Hogan of *Crocodile Dundee* fame for Subaru's line of Outback sports utility vehicles and Lance Armstrong for Bristol-Myers Squibb's cancer medicines.

Third, celebrity endorsers can get in trouble or lose popularity, diminishing their marketing value to the brand, or just fail to live up to expectations. In 2005, American Express decided to focus its U.S. Open tennis advertising and promotion campaign on top American star Andy Roddick. The ad theme of "Have You Seen Andy's Mojo?" took on new meaning, however, when Roddick tumbled out of the tournament in the first round in straight sets. Thus, linking the brand to a celebrity results in a certain lack of control. A number of spokespeople over the years have run into legal difficulties, personal problems, or controversies of some form that diminished their marketing value such as O.J. Simpson, Martha Stewart, and Michael Jackson.

Fourth, many consumers feel that celebrities are only doing the endorsement for the money and do not necessarily believe in or even use the endorsed brand. Even worse, some consumers feel that the fees celebrities earn to appear in commercials add a significant and unnecessary cost to the brand. In reality, celebrities often do not come cheap and can demand literally millions of dollars to endorse a brand. Celebrities also can be difficult to work with and may not willingly follow the marketing direction of the brand. Tennis player Andre Agassi tried Nike's patience when—at the same time he was advertising for Nike—he appeared in commercials for the Canon Rebel camera. In these ads, he looked into the camera and proclaimed "Image Is Everything"—the antithesis of the "authentic athletic performance" positioning that is the foundation of the Nike brand equity.

Finally, as noted in Chapter 6, celebrities may distract attention from the brand in ads so that consumers notice the stars but have trouble remembering the advertised brand. Pepsi decided to drop singers Beyoncé Knowles and Britney Spears from high-profile ad campaigns when they felt the Pepsi brand did not get the same promotion from the campaign that the stars were getting. Pepsi decided to put the spotlight back on the product with its endorsement-free follow-up, "Pepsi. It's the Cola." After signing Celine Dion for a three-year, $14 million deal, Chrysler dumped her in the first year when commercials featuring Dion driving a Pacifica produced great sales for the singer, but not the car!

Guidelines

To overcome these problems, marketers should strategically evaluate, select, and use celebrity spokespeople. First, choose a well-known and well-defined celebrity whose associations are relevant to the brand and likely to be transferable. NASCAR driver Jeff Gordon has been an effective pitchman for a variety of brands, including Pepsi, Ray-Ban sunglasses, Close-Up toothpaste, and Edy's ice cream, because his good looks and self-effacing manner appeal to a wide segment of consumers who buy his endorsed products in support.

Then, there must be a logical fit between the brand and person.[23] To reduce confusion or dilution, the celebrity ideally would not be linked to a number of other brands or be overexposed. After winning Olympic gold in 1984, Mary Lou Retton appeared in commercials for so many brands that one marketing critic wearily complained, "I've seen more of her in the past year than I have of my mother—and I love my mother more!" [24] To broaden the appeal and reduce the risks of linking to one celebrity, some marketers have employed several different celebrities.

Third, the advertising and communication program should use the celebrity in a creative fashion that highlights the relevant associations and encourages their transfer. For example, comedian Jerry Seinfeld's popular commercials for American Express used the same unflappable charm and knack for finding himself in unusual situations that Seinfeld displayed on his popular TV show. Finally, marketing research must help identify potential endorser candidates and facilitate the development of the proper marketing program, as well as track their effectiveness.

Sporting, Cultural, or Other Events

As Chapter 6 described, events have their own set of associations that may become linked to a sponsoring brand under certain conditions. Sponsored events can contribute to brand equity by becoming associated to the brand and improving brand awareness, adding new

BRANDING BRIEF 7-7

Celebrity Endorsers Connect Brands with Fans

Celebrities routinely lend their famous faces and personas to brands in exchange for lucrative endorsement contracts. Companies hire famous athletes and actors in hopes that the celebrities' fans will also become fans of their products or services. The superstar endorsers can leverage their own popularity to create positive associations for brands in the minds of consumers.

NBA star Yao Ming has joined a select group of athletes—among them Michael Jordan, Tiger Woods, and Pele—whose international appeal makes him a one-man brand bonanza. Yao, a 7-ft., 6-in. center for the Houston Rockets, makes marketers salivate because he represents an entrée to China's 1.3 billion potential consumers. A Shanghai native, Yao is hugely popular all over China. Among Yao's endorsements are multiyear deals with Pepsico, Gatorade, Reebok, Disney, and McDonald's, all of whom are seeking to boost their brands in the burgeoning Chinese market.

The best brand ambassadors are not only top performers in their fields but also winners with the average folks whom marketers are trying to reach. Yao is extremely likeable, having earned a reputation as a soft-spoken, polite guy with a shy smile. That likeability has translated into big earnings for the businesses with which he is associated. Sponsorship revenue for the Rockets has jumped 30 percent since Yao joined the team. A Gatorade commercial featuring Yao, shortstop Derek Jeter, and quarterback Payton Manning received the highest likeability rating in the sports drink's history.

Golfer Michelle Wie turned pro a few days before her sixteenth birthday in October 2005 and immediately inked endorsement deals with Nike and Sony said to be worth $10 million a year. Born in Hawaii to Korean parents, Wie speaks Korean and Japanese and has been touted as the next to join Yao and Tiger Woods as a worldwide ambassador for her sport as well as the brands that

associations, or improving the strength, favorability, and uniqueness of existing associations. The main means by which an event can transfer associations is credibility. A brand may seem more likable or perhaps even trustworthy or expert by virtue of becoming linked to an event. The extent to which this transfer takes place will depend on which events are selected and how the sponsorship program is designed and integrated into the entire marketing program to build brand equity. For example, Branding Brief 7-8 describes how event sponsorship has played an important role in building brand equity for Visa credit cards.[25] Brand Focus 7.0 discusses sponsorship strategies for the Olympic Games.

Third-Party Sources

Finally, marketers can create secondary associations in a number of different ways by linking the brand to various third-party sources. For example, the *Good Housekeeping* seal has been seen as a mark of quality for decades, offering product replacement or refunds for defective products for up to two years from purchase. Endorsements from leading magazines like *PC* magazine, organizations like the American Dental Association, and experts including film critic Roger Ebert can obviously improve perceptions of and attitudes toward brands.

Third-party sources can be especially credible sources. As a result, marketers often feature them in advertising campaigns and selling efforts. J.D. Power and Associates'

sponsor her. As an amateur, Wie was the youngest ever winner of the Women's Amateur Public Links Championship. In 2004, she was the first female player to qualify for the Men's U.S. Amateur Public Links Championship, earning a shot at competing in the Masters—where no woman has played before. Wie enjoyed early popularity among golf fans: *Golf for Women* reported that the magazine had an increase in sales when she appeared on the July 2004 cover. Both Wie and Yao are under pressure to win championships to maintain their status as superstar endorsers.

Celebrity endorsers can carry big risks for companies, which often hire famous people as much for their clean-cut images as their professional accomplishments. Most companies conduct background checks before signing celebs, but that doesn't guard against bad behavior in the future. In 1988, Anheuser-Busch built a campaign for Michelob beer around singer Eric Clapton's version of "After Midnight" shortly before Clapton revealed that he was battling alcoholism. NBA star Kobe Bryant lost millions in endorsements with McDonald's, Sprite, and Nutella after he was charged with sexual assault in 2001. And in September 2005, supermodel Kate Moss was photographed using cocaine and was promptly dropped as an endorser by H&M, Chanel, and Burberry. It is possible for celebrities to reestablish their images and regain endorsement appeal, however, as Kate Moss' experience shows. Just six months after her public fall from grace, Moss was rehired by Burberry and signed a new deal with Calvin Klein that brought her total earnings to almost double what she was making before the scandal.

Sources: Eugenia Levenson, "Risky Business," *Fortune,* 17 October 2005; Tom Lowry, "For U.S. Brands Selling in China, NBA Sensation Yao Ming Is One Hot Ticket," *BusinessWeek,* 25 October 2004; Katrina Brooker, "(Michelle) Wie Will Rock You," *Fortune,* 17 October 2005; Andrew Johnson and Anthony Barnes, "New Deal for Kate Mo$$," *The Independent,* February 26, 2006.

well-publicized Customer Satisfaction Index helped to cultivate an image of quality for Japanese automakers in the 1980s, with a corresponding adverse impact on the quality image of their U.S. rivals. In the 1990s, they began to rank quality in other industries, such as airlines, credit cards, rental cars, and phone service, and top-rated brands in these categories began to feature their awards in ad campaigns. Grey Goose vodka cleverly employed a third-party endorsement to drive sales.

Grey Goose

Sidney Frank first found success in the liquor industry with a little known German liqueur, Jagermeister, which he began to market in the United States in the mid-1980s and drove to 700,000 cases in sales and market leadership by 2001. Turning his sights to the high-margin superpremium market, Frank decided to create a French vodka that would use water from the Cognac region and be distilled by the makers of Cardin brandy. Branded as "Grey Goose," the product had distinctive packaging—a must in the category—with a bottle taller than competitors that combined clear and frosted glass with a cutaway of geese in flight and the French flag. But perhaps the most important factor in the brand's eventual success was a taste test result from the Beverage Testing Institute that ranked Grey Goose as the number-one imported vodka. Fueled by exhaustive advertising that trumpeted its big win, Grey Goose became a top seller. Frank eventually sold Grey Goose Vodka brand to Bacardi in 2004 for a stunning $2 billion.

BRANDING BRIEF 7-8

Event Sponsorship at Visa

Back in 1985, Visa and MasterCard were seen as essentially identical products that faced stiff competition from other brands, particularly American Express, which had a strong and desirable prestige image with consumers. Visa set out to create a differentiating and enduring perception of its brand as the best payment system for all types of purchases. Visa was positioned as the brand with superior acceptance by virtue of hard-hitting comparative ads with American Express. The "It's Everywhere You Want to Be" campaign featured interesting, unique, and prestigious locations where consumers might expect American Express to be accepted but were told to "bring your Visa card, because they don't take American Express." In event marketing, Visa aligned itself with high-profile sporting events, concert tours, and the like that did not take American Express, and it backed up its sponsorships with additional comparative advertising campaigns.

Starting in 1988, the Olympics became Visa's biggest event association. Visa's Olympic connection has helped to reinforce its desired positioning as a high-quality, globally accepted product. Its sponsorship has made the brand the Exclusive Payment Card and the Official Payment Service for the Olympics. Ads for the 1992 Olympic Games focused on how tough the competition would be at the Games, "but not as tough as the sellers at the ticket window if you don't have your Visa card."

To support Olympic fund-raising, cardholder transactions were tied to Visa donations to certain Olympic teams in several countries. Visa also provided direct financial support to certain Olympic athletes and teams. Since 1994, Visa's "Olympics of the Imagination" has brought schoolchildren from all over the world to the Olympics as part of an art competition tied into the Winter and Summer games. The sponsorship also allows Visa's 21,000-member financial institutions to tie in exclusive marketing and merchandising campaigns around the Olympic Games, promoting Visa products and services to cardholders and merchants on a worldwide basis.

The effects of these sponsorship and other communication efforts have been dramatic. The Athens 2004 Olympic Games and Paralympic Games generated an 87 percent consumer awareness of Visa as a sponsor, the highest level of all sponsors in key markets. More importantly, research has shown that Visa is now perceived as more widely accepted than other cards and, as a result, as the card of choice for personal and family shopping, personal travel and entertainment, and even international travel, a former American Express stronghold.

Sources: http://sponsorships.visa.com/olympic/, "So You Want to Be an Olympic Sponsor," *Brandweek,* 7 November 2005; Alex Blyhte, "Sponsorship: The Gold Standard," www.redmandarin.com, 1 August 2004.

Review

This chapter considered the process by which other entities can be leveraged to create secondary associations. These other entities include source factors such as the company that makes a product, where the product is made, and where it is purchased, as well as related people, places, or things. When they link the brand to other entities with their own set of associations, consumers may expect that some of these same associations also characterize the brand. Thus, independent of how a product is branded, the nature of the product itself, and its supporting marketing program, marketers can create brand equity by "borrowing" it from other sources. Creating secondary associations in this fashion may be quite important if the corresponding brand associations are deficient in some way. Secondary associations may be especially valuable as a means to link favorable brand associations that can serve as points of parity or to create unique brand associations that can serve as points of difference in positioning a brand.

Eight different ways to leverage secondary associations to build brand equity are linking the brand to (1) the company making the product, (2) the country or some other geographic location in which the product originates, (3) retailers or other channel members that sell the product, (4) other brands, including ingredient brands, (5) licensed characters, (6) famous spokespeople or endorsers, (7) events, and (8) third-party sources. In general, the extent to which any of these entities can be leveraged as a source of equity depends on consumer knowledge of the entity and how easily the appropriate associations or responses to the entity transfer to the brand. In general, global credibility or attitudinal dimensions may be more likely to transfer than specific attribute and benefit associations, although the latter can be transferred, too. Linking the brand to other entities, however, is not without risk. Marketers give up some control, and managing the transfer process so that only the relevant secondary associations become linked to the brand may be difficult.

Discussion Questions

1. The Boeing Company makes a number of different types of aircraft for the commercial airline industry, for example, the 727, 747, 757, 767, 777, and now the 787 jet models. Is there any way for Boeing to adopt an ingredient branding strategy with its jets? How? What would be the pros and cons?
2. After winning major championships, star players often complain about their lack of endorsement offers. Similarly, after every Olympics, a number of medal-winning athletes lament their lack of commercial recognition. From a branding perspective, how would you respond to the complaints of these athletes?
3. Think of the country in which you live. What image might it have with consumers in other countries? Are there certain brands or products that are highly effective in leveraging that image in global markets?
4. Which retailers have the strongest image and equity in your mind? Think about the brands they sell. Do they contribute to the equity of the retailer? Conversely, how does that retailer's image help the image of the brands it sells?
5. Pick a brand. Evaluate how it leverages secondary associations. Can you think of any ways that the brand could more effectively leverage secondary brand knowledge?

BRAND FOCUS 7.0

Going for Corporate Gold at the Olympics

Competition at the Olympics is not restricted to just the athletes. A number of corporate sponsors also vie to maximize the return on their sponsorship dollars.[26] Corporate sponsorship is a significant part of the business side of the Olympics and contributed 32 percent of the revenue of the 2004 Athens Games. Some of the world's largest and most visible companies, including McDonald's, Coca-Cola, Visa, and Kodak, spent as much as $50 million to sponsor the 2002 and 2004 Olympics. In 2005 Coca-Cola extended its Olympic sponsorship through 2020.

Corporate sponsorship of the Olympics exploded with the commercial success of the 1984 Summer Games in Los Angeles. Many international sponsors, like Fuji, realized positive image building and increased market share. In Atlanta in 1996, top-tier "Worldwide" corporate sponsors spent $40 million for the rights to display all Olympic logos, exclusive rights to the five-ring logo in their ads and on their packaging, and prime access to tickets, hotel rooms, athletes, cultural events, and the hospitality village. Besides direct expenditures, firms spent hundreds of millions more on related marketing efforts. Coca-Cola's total Olympic-related expenditure reportedly topped $500 million and included funding for the torch relay and a mega-retail promotion, Coke's Red Hot Olympic Summer.

The marketing impact of Olympic sponsorship is widely debated. For example, despite the fact that Hilton was the official hotel of the 1992 Summer Games, only 8 percent of consumers were aware of the sponsorship just weeks after the Olympics ended. Even worse, 9 percent thought the sponsor was Holiday Inn. Similarly, Kellogg also was a 1992 sponsor, but only 20 percent of consumers named Kellogg's Corn Flakes as a brand sponsor while 35 percent named Wheaties. In 1996, licensees fell short of their goal of $1 billion in total sales.

In some cases, sponsorship confusion may be due to ***ambush marketing***, in which advertisers attempt to give consumers the false impression they are Olympic sponsors by, for instance, running Olympic-themed ads that publicize other forms of sponsorship like sponsoring a national team, by identifying the brand as an official supplier, or by using current or former Olympians as endorsers. To retaliate against Visa's ads stressing its exclusive Olympic acceptability, American Express ran ads that focused on the card's presence in Olympic host cities. To improve the marketing effectiveness of sponsorship, the Olympic Committee has vowed to fight ambush marketing and reduce the number of sponsors to avoid clutter.

Following the scandal surrounding Salt Lake City's bid for the 2002 Winter Olympics, when it was revealed that organizers gave cash and gifts to some 30 International Olympic Committee (IOC) members, many criticized the Games for being overcommercialized. The scandal generated feelings of disillusionment from fans and compounded image problems resulting from drug use and poor sportsmanship in past Olympics. A survey conducted soon after the scandal broke revealed that 39 percent of people felt more negatively about the Games than in the past.

To counteract the negative perceptions, the IOC launched an image campaign to promote the 2000 Games. The ads, which ran in 200 countries, reflected the "core values of the Olympic movement" by featuring footage of former Olympic champions such as Jesse Owens, as well as unsung heroes. The $150 million campaign featured Internet advertising, six television spots, six radio spots, and four different print ads, one of which detailed how corporate sponsors contribute to the Games.

The scandal caused some corporations to reconsider their role in the games. An executive for Miller Brewing—which has not been a sponsor of the Games—said, "The Olympics, quite frankly, have never been more overpriced or overvalued." Sponsorship remained a big part of the 2000 Sydney Games, but some major sponsors toned down their Olympic ad blitz in order to seem less opportunistic and commercial. Instead of purchasing space on 50 billboards, as the company did for the 1996 Atlanta Games, Kodak dressed 35 actors like rolls of film and had them walk around the venue. Goodyear changed the logo on its blimp to display the Australian greeting "G'Day" on one side and "Good Luck" on the other. Even the typically brash marketer Nike adopted a more subtle approach to advertising at the Sydney Games. When the company wrapped a highly visible 30-story downtown building with images of Australian athletes, it used an undersized swoosh only a few stories high.

In 2001, the U.S. Olympic Committee (USOC) developed an advertising campaign to convey a "wholesome" image of the Olympics to Americans. The USOC hired Goodby Silverstein & Partners to create ads that targeted younger viewers and emphasized the Olympic ideals of fair play, honesty, and passion for sport. In another attempt to generate excitement for the Games among America's youth, the USOC developed a line of apparel such as baseball caps, fleece vests, and jackets.

The 2008 Summer Games in Beijing held special appeal for some advertisers because the Games represented a connection to the burgeoning Chinese market. General Electric began its first global campaign revolving around the Beijing Games in 2005. GE chose the Olympics to position the company as global and innovative to Chinese consumers. UPS also chose the Beijing games to strengthen its brand presence in China. UPS was a global Olympic sponsor in 1996, 1998, and 2000, but then dropped out of the Games after 2000, saying its brand awareness goals had been achieved. But in 2005, UPS announced it would rejoin the Olympics for 2008, this time in a limited deal that allowed the company to use the Olympic logo for marketing in China only—not in the United States. International and local sponsors were expected to spend a total of $1 billion on the Beijing Olympics, aided partly by the nationalist spirit that drives some Chinese companies to sponsor the Games.

Nevertheless, Olympic sponsorship remains highly controversial. Many corporate sponsors continue to believe that their Olympic sponsorship yields many significant benefits, creating an image of goodwill for their brand, serving as a platform to enhance awareness and communicate messages, and affording numerous opportunities to reward employees and entertain clients. Other still view the Games as overly commercialized, despite the measures undertaken by the IOC and USOC to portray the Olympics as wholesome. In any case, the success of Olympic sponsorship—like any sports sponsorship—depends in large part on how well the sponsorship is executed and incorporated into the entire marketing plan.

Notes

1. Kevin Lane Keller, "Brand Synthesis: The Multi-Dimensionality of Brand Knowledge," *Journal of Consumer Research* 29, no. 4 (2003): 595–600.
2. Suen L. Hwang, "Philip Morris Makes Dave's—but Sh! Don't Tell," *Wall Street Journal,* 2 March 1995, B1.
3. Wai-Kwan Li and Robert S. Wyer Jr., "The Role of Country of Origin in Product Evaluations: Informational and Standard-of-Comparison Effects," *Journal of Consumer Psychology* 3, no. 2 (1994): 187–212.
4. For a broader discussion of "nation branding," see Philip Kotler, Somkid Jatusriptak, and Suvit Maesincee, *The Marketing of Nations: A Strategic Approach to Building National Wealth* (New York: Free Press, 1997); Wally Olins, "Branding the Nation—The Historical Context," *Journal of Brand Management* 9 (April 2002): 241–248; and for an interesting analysis in the context of Iceland, see Hlynur Gudjonsson, "Nation Branding," *Place Branding* 1, no. 3)(2005): 283–298.
5. Zeynep Gurhan-Canli and Durairaj Maheswaran, "Cultural Variations in Country of Origin Effects," *Journal of Marketing Research* 37 (August 2000): 309–317.
6. Akshay R. Rao and Robert W. Ruekert, "Brand Alliances as Signals of Product Quality," *Sloan Management Review* (Fall 1994): 87–97; Akshay R. Rao, Lu Qu, and Robert W. Ruekert, "Signalling Unobservable Product Quality through Brand Ally," *Journal of Marketing Research* 36, no. 2 (May 1999): 258–268.
7. Robin L. Danziger, "Cross Branding with Branded Ingredients: The New Frontier," paper presented at the ARF Fourth Annual Advertising and Promotion Workshop, February 1992.
8. Kim Cleland, "Multimarketer Melange an Increasingly Tasty Option on the Store Shelf," *Advertising Age,* 2 May 1994, S-10.
9. Teresa Gubbins, "Spinoffs Carry Popular Products All Over the Store," *Dallas Morning News.*
10. Ed Lebar, Phil Buehler, Kevin Lane Keller, Monika Sawicka, et al., "Brand Equity Implications of Joint Branding Programs," *Journal of Advertising Research* 45, no. 4 (2005).
11. Nicole L. Votolato and H. Rao Unnava, "Spillover of Negative Information on Brand Alliances," *Journal of Consumer Psychology* 16, no. 2 (2006): 196–202.
12. www.swatch.com; Kevin Helliker, "Can Wristwatch Whiz Switch Swatch Cachet to an Automobile?" *Wall Street Journal,* 4 March 1994, A1; Audrey Choi and Margaret Studer, "Daimler-Benz's Mercedes Unit to Build a Car with Maker of Swatch Watches," *Wall Street Journal,* 23 February 1994, A14; Beth Demain Reigber, "DaimlerChrysler Smarts as BMW Mini Looms," *Dow Jones Newswire,* 20 June 2001.
13. Gregory S. Carpenter, Rashi Glazer, and Kent Nakamoto, "Meaningful Brands from Meaningless Differentiation: The Dependence on Irrelevant Attributes," *Journal of Marketing Research* (August 1994): 339–350. See also Susan M. Broniarczyk and Andrew D. Gershoff, "The Reciprocal Effects of Brand Equity and Trivial Attributes," *Journal of Marketing Research* 41 (2003): 161–175.
14. Donald G. Norris, "Ingredient Branding: A Strategy Option with Multiple Beneficiaries," *Journal of Consumer Marketing* 9, no. 3 (1992): 19–31.

15. *The Licensing Letter,* epmcom.com.
16. Teri Agins, "Izod Lacoste Gets Restyled and Repriced," *Wall Street Journal,* 22 July 1991, B1.
17. Udayan Gupta, "Licensees Learn What's in a Pop-Culture Name: Risk," *Wall Street Journal,* 8 August 1991, B2.
18. Frank E. James, "I'll Wear the Coke Pants Tonight; They Go Well with My Harley-Davidson Ring," *Wall Street Journal,* 6 June 1985, 31.
19. Robert Berner, "The Name of the Game Is—The Name," *Business Week,* 27 November 2000, 12.
20. Grant McCracken, "Who Is the Celebrity Endorsor? Cultural Foundations of the Endorsement Process," *Journal of Consumer Research* 16 (December 1989): 310–321.
21. John Grossman, "Dave Thomas' Recipe for Success," *Sky,* November 2000, 103–107; Bruce Horvitz, "Wendy's Icon Back at Work," *USA Today,* 31 March 1997, B1-B2.
22. Shekhar Misra and Sharon E. Beatty, "Celebrity Spokesperson and Brand Congruence," *Journal of Business Research* 21 (1990): 159–173.
23. Misra and Beatty, "Celebrity Spokesperson and Brand Congruence."
24. Roderick Townley, "Is That Winning Smile Losing Its Charm?" *TV Guide,* 28 June 1986, 41–42.
25. Janet Soderstrom, "Brand Equity. It's Everywhere You Want to Be," talk given at Branding Conference, San Francisco, California, 26 October 1995.
26. "Wait in Wings as Olympic Sponsors Waffle," *USA Today,* 15 March 1999; Michael McCarthy, "Olympic Ads to Stress 'Core Values,'" *USA Today,* 20 December 1999; Bruce Horowitz, "Sponsors Scale Back Ad Blitz," *USA Today,* 26 September 2000; Bruce Horowitz, "Sponsors Warm Up a Year Before Games," *USA Today,* 19 July 1995, 1B–2B; Olympic Partnership, *Sports Illustrated* special advertising section.

8

DEVELOPING A BRAND EQUITY MEASUREMENT AND MANAGEMENT SYSTEM

Preview

The previous six chapters, which made up Parts II and III of the text, described various strategies and approaches to building brand equity. In the next three chapters, which make up Part IV, we take a detailed look at what consumers know and feel about and act toward brands and how marketers can develop measurement procedures to assess how well their brands are doing.

The CBBE model provides guidance about how we can measure brand equity. Given that customer-based brand equity is the differential effect that knowledge about the brand has on customer response to the marketing of that brand, two basic approaches to measuring brand equity present themselves. An ***indirect approach*** can assess potential sources of customer-based brand equity by identifying and tracking consumers' brand knowledge—all the thoughts, feelings, images, perceptions, and beliefs linked to the brand. A ***direct approach,*** on the other hand, can assess the actual impact of brand knowledge on consumer response to different aspects of the marketing program.

The two approaches are complementary, and marketers can and should use both. In other words, for brand equity to provide a useful strategic function and guide marketing decisions, marketers must fully understand the sources of brand equity, how they affect outcomes of interest such as sales, and how these sources and outcomes change, if at all, over time. Chapter 2 provided a framework for conceptualizing consumers' brand knowledge structures. Chapter 9 uses this information and reviews research methods to measure sources of brand equity and the customer mind-set. Chapter 10 reviews research methods to measure outcomes of brand equity (e.g., the various benefits that potentially may result from creating these sources of brand equity).

Before we get into specifics of measurement, this chapter offers some big-picture perspectives of how to think about brand equity measurement and management. Specifically, we'll consider how to develop and implement a brand equity measurement system. A ***brand equity measurement system*** is a set of research procedures designed to provide marketers with timely, accurate, and actionable information on brands so they can make the best possible tactical decisions in the short run and strategic decisions in the long run. The goal is to achieve a full understanding of the sources and outcomes of brand equity and to be able to relate the two as much as possible.

The ideal brand equity measurement system would provide complete, up-to-date, and relevant information on the brand and all its competitors, to the right decision makers at the right time within the organization. We'll look in detail at two steps toward achieving that ideal—designing brand tracking studies and establishing a brand equity management system.

Crucial, however, is understanding how brand equity or value gets created. So we'll first present a model of brand equity or value creation. The ***brand value chain*** is a means by which marketers can trace the value creation process for their brands to better understand the financial impact of their marketing expenditures and investments. Based in part on the CBBE model developed in Chapter 2, it offers a holistic, integrated approach to understanding how brands create value.

The New Accountability

Although senior managers at many firms have embraced the marketing concept and the importance of brands, they often struggle with questions such as: How strong is our brand? How can we ensure that our marketing activities create value? How do we measure that value?

Virtually every marketing dollar spent today must be justified as both effective and efficient in terms of ***return of marketing investment*** (ROMI).[1] This increased accountability has forced marketers to address tough challenges and develop new measurement approaches.[2] But progress has been slow: A 2003 ARF-APQC study revealed that only one in five "ROMI-achieving" companies had experienced a substantial change in the speed of decision making due to marketing analytics, while none of the "ROMI-aspiring" firms had done so.[3]

Complicating matters is that, depending on the particular industry or category, some observers believe that up to 70 percent (or even more) of marketing expenditures may be devoted to programs and activities that cannot be linked to short-term incremental profits, but yet can be seen as improving brand equity.[4] Measuring the long-term value of marketing in terms of its full short-term and long-term impact on consumers is thus crucial for assessing return on investment.

Jonathan Knowles argues that for marketers to secure a seat in the corporate boardroom, they must go beyond ROI measurement to address whether brands truly are assets that enable the business to generate superior returns over time. He offers the following advice to support his contention:[5]

1. To qualify a brand as an asset in financial terms, marketers need to measure it in terms of its ability to generate future cash flows.
2. Marketers can create value only by changing customer behavior—changes in attitude don't generate cash flow.
3. Marketers should measure brand equity in a way that captures the source and scale of the emotional component the brand adds to the functionality of the product.

Clearly marketers need new tools and procedures that clarify and justify the value of their expenditures, beyond ROMI measures tied to short-term changes in sales. In the remainder of this chaper, we offer several concepts and perspectives to help in that pursuit, beginning with the brand value chain.

The Brand Value Chain

To understand how to design and implement a brand equity measurement and management system, we'll take a broader perspective than just the CBBE model. The ***brand value chain*** is a structured approach to assessing the sources and outcomes of brand equity and the manner by which marketing activities create brand value.[6] It recognizes that many different people within an organization can affect brand equity and need to be aware of relevant branding effects. The brand value chain thus provides insights to support brand managers, chief marketing officers, managing directors, and chief executive officers, all of whom may need different types of information.

The brand value chain has several basic premises. Fundamentally, it assumes that the value of a brand ultimately resides with customers. Based on this insight, the model next assumes that the brand value creation process begins when the firm invests in a marketing program targeting actual or potential customers (stage 1). The associated marketing activity then affects the customer mind-set—what customers know and feel about the brand (stage 2). This mind-set, across a broad group of customers, produces the brand's performance in the marketplace—how much and when customers purchase, the price that they pay, and so forth (stage 3). Finally, the investment community considers this market performance—and other factors such as replacement cost and purchase price in acquisitions—to arrive at an assessment of shareholder value in general and a value of the brand in particular (stage 4).

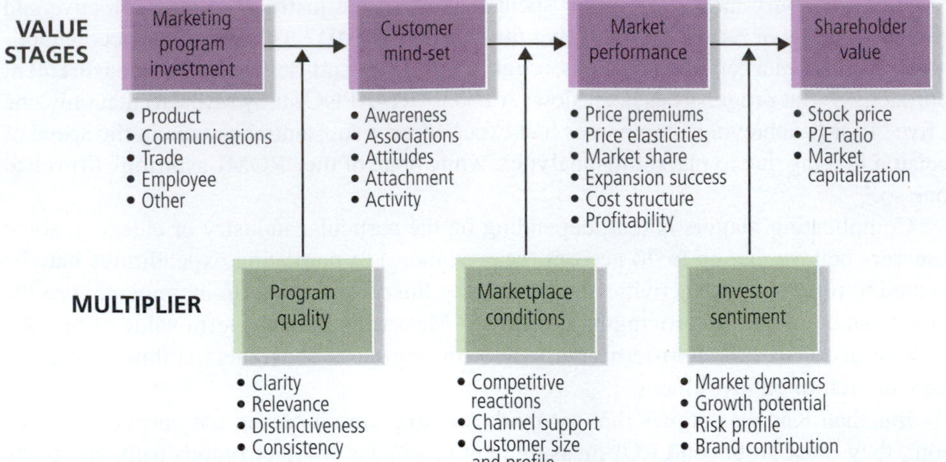

FIGURE 8-1

The Brand Value Chain

The model also assumes that a number of linking factors intervene between these stages. These linking factors determine the extent to which value created at one stage transfers or "multiplies" to the next stage. Three sets of multipliers moderate the transfer between the marketing program and the three value stages: the program quality multiplier, the marketplace conditions multiplier, and the investor sentiment multiplier. The brand value chain model is summarized in Figure 8-1. Next we describe the value stages and multiplying factors in more detail and look at examples of both positive and negative multiplier effects.

Value Stages

Brand value creation begins with marketing activity by the firm.

Marketing Program Investment. Any marketing program investment that can contribute to brand value development, intentionally or not, falls into this first value stage. Chapters 4 to 7 outlined many such marketing activities, like product research, development, and design; trade or intermediary support; marketing communications including advertising, promotion, sponsorship, direct and interactive marketing, personal selling, publicity, and public relations; and employee training. A big investment of course does not guarantee success. In the 1990s, Miller Brewing spent over $2.5 billion in measured advertising in an effort to reestablish its brand portfolio, but it launched questionable and ultimately ineffective campaigns. Anheuser-Busch, Heineken, and Corona were therefore able to steal key market positions and become the leading growth brands during that time, dominating the beer category as a result. The ability of a marketing program investment to transfer or multiply farther down the chain depends on *qualitative* aspects of the marketing program and the program quality multiplier.

Program Quality Multiplier. The ability of the marketing program to affect the customer mind-set will depend on its quality. In earlier chapters we reviewed a number of different means to judge the quality of a marketing program. Four particularly important ones are:

1. *Clarity:* How understandable is the brand marketing program? Do consumers properly interpret and evaluate its meaning?
2. *Relevance:* How meaningful is the marketing program to customers? Do consumers feel the brand is one they should seriously consider?

3. *Distinctiveness:* How unique is the marketing program? How creative or differentiating is it?
4. *Consistency:* How cohesive and well integrated is the marketing program? Do all aspects combine to create the biggest impact with customers? Does the marketing program relate effectively to past marketing programs and properly balance continuity and change, evolving the brand in the right direction?

Not surprisingly, a well-integrated marketing program, carefully designed and implemented to be highly relevant and unique, is likely to achieve a greater return on investment from marketing program expenditures. For example, despite being outspent by such beverage brand giants as Coca-Cola, Pepsi, and Budweiser, the California Milk Processor Board was able to reverse a decades-long decline in consumption of milk in California through the well-designed and executed "Got Milk?" campaign. On the other hand, numerous marketers have found that expensive marketing programs do not necessarily produce sales unless they are well conceived. For example, brands such as Michelob, Minute Maid, 7UP, and others have seen their sales slide in recent years despite sizable marketing expenditures because of poorly targeted and delivered marketing campaigns.

Customer Mind-Set. In what ways have customers been changed as a result of the marketing program? How have those changes manifested themselves in the customer mind-set?

Remember, the customer mind-set includes everything that exists in the minds of customers with respect to a brand: thoughts, feelings, experiences, images, perceptions, beliefs, and attitudes. Understanding customer mind-set can have important implications for marketing programs. Branding Brief 8-1 describes how CVS redesigned its stores on the basis of insights from consumer research.

Five dimensions have emerged from prior research (and are highlighted in the CBBE model) as particularly important measures of the customer mind-set:

1. *Brand awareness:* The extent and ease with which customers recall and recognize the brand and can identify the products and services with which it is associated.
2. *Brand associations:* The strength, favorability, and uniqueness of perceived attributes and benefits for the brand. Brand associations often represent key sources of brand value, because they are the means by which consumers feel brands satisfy their needs.
3. *Brand attitudes:* Overall evaluations of the brand in terms of its quality and the satisfaction it generates.
4. *Brand attachment:* The degree of loyalty the customer feels toward the brand. A strong form of attachment, ***adherence,*** is the consumer's resistance to change and the ability of a brand to withstand bad news like a product or service failure. In the extreme, attachment can even become ***addiction.***
5. *Brand activity:* The extent to which customers use the brand, talk to others about the brand, seek out brand information, promotions, and events, and so on.

An obvious hierarchy exists in the dimensions of value: Awareness supports associations, which drive attitudes that lead to attachment and activity. Brand value is created at this stage when customers have (1) deep, broad brand awareness; (2) appropriately strong, favorable, and unique points of parity and points of difference; (3) positive brand judgments and feelings; (4) intense brand attachment and loyalty; and (5) a high degree of brand activity.

Creating the right customer mind-set can be critical in terms of building brand equity and value. AMD and Cyrix found that achieving performance parity with Intel's microprocessors did not return benefits in 1998, when original equipment manufacturers were reluctant to adopt the new chips because of their lack of a strong brand image with consumers. Moreover,

BRANDING BRIEF 8-1

Consumer Insights Creates New Look for CVS

The first CVS drugstore opened in 1963 and the Woonsocket, Rhode Island chain has grown steadily since then. In 2004, CVS bought JC Penney's Eckerd drugstore chain and became the largest U.S. drugstore retailer, with more than 5,400 stores.

CVS used consumer insights to redesign its drugstores.

CVS began adding pharmacies to its stores in the late 1960s and pharmacy operations eventually grew to about 70 percent of sales. In recent years, lower margins on prescription drugs have meant drugstores have needed to boost sales outside the pharmacy. Adding to the pressure, competition between CVS and rivals Walgreens and Rite Aid has ramped up as each chain has expanded into the others' territories.

As legwork for a print and television campaign, CVS analyzed data gathered from its loyalty card program, which offers rebates and also allows the company to gather information about its customers. The company analyzed data from 45 million customers and talked to focus groups about their impressions of CVS. Participants were quizzed on their shopping habits and asked to envision the ideal store layout. Eighty percent of CVS customers were women, and the research highlighted fitness, nutrition, and beauty as important themes for them. CVS then evaluated its product categories to identify which were growing and most profitable.

CVS then used the shopper data to create three generic customer profiles: a married 30-year-old woman with a newborn who tends to buy diapers and cosmetics, a married 42-year-old mother of three who buys items like school supplies, and a married, female empty nester who shops CVS primarily for greeting cards, prescriptions and vitamins.

success with consumers may not translate to success in the marketplace unless other conditions also prevail. The ability of this customer mind-set to create value at the next stage depends on external factors we call the marketplace conditions multiplier, as follows.

Marketplace Conditions Multiplier. The extent to which value created in the minds of customers affects market performance depends on factors beyond the individual customer. Three such factors are:

1. *Competitive superiority:* How effective are the marketing investments of competing brands?
2. *Channel and other intermediary support:* How much brand reinforcement and selling effort is being put forth by various marketing partners?
3. *Customer size and profile:* How many and what types of customers are attracted to the brand? Are they profitable?

The value created in the minds of customers will translate to favorable market performance when competitors fail to provide a significant threat, when channel members and other

CVS then found real customers who fit each category and shadowed them to study their shopping habits.

The research and customer input yielded a comprehensive store redesign. CVS pursued the modifications to distinguish its store from other drugstores as well as to align the look of its stores with its mission to cater to all aspects of wellness. A major element of the redesign was adding a clear path from the entrance of the store to the pharmacy. Because the research showed that many customers valued convenient and efficient pharmacy services, the company wanted to make sure they did not have to navigate a maze of aisles to find it.

The redesign was incorporated into all new stores and gradually implemented in more and more existing stores. It included streamlined aisles with less clutter and more sophisticated-looking signage. The new color-coded signs, a mix of cheery blues, greens, and yellows, were designed to evoke feelings of wellness and rejuvenation as well as help customers navigate sections such as stationery, cosmetics, and grocery. A self-service digital photo center was also added to new stores. The company installed new shelves that were five feet high, instead of the old six feet, so women of average height (5 feet, 4 inches) could more easily see over the tops to other sections of the store.

The redesign also included a new beauty counter staffed by a cosmetics consultant trained to analyze women's skin and recommend one of the three European skin-care lines CVS carries. This move was designed to attract women who wanted the same service found at department-store beauty counters and products at lower prices. The emphasis on cosmetics signaled CVS's hope that sales of these beauty products, which are more expensive than traditional drugstore offerings, would boost overall sales.

Sources: Gene G. Marcel, "CVS' Ever-Expanding Aisles," *Business Week,* 19 September 2005; Naomi Aoki, "CVS Gives Itself a Full Makeover," *Boston Globe,* 2 May 2004; "World Class Retailer—American Remedies," *Retail Week,* 5 December 2003.

intermediaries provide strong support, and when a sizable number of profitable customers are attracted to the brand.

The competitive context faced by a brand can have a profound effect on its fortunes. For example, Nike and McDonald's have benefited in the past from the prolonged marketing woes of their main rivals, Reebok and Burger King, which both have suffered from numerous repositionings and management changes. On the other hand, MasterCard has had to contend for the past decade with two strong, well-marketed brands in Visa and American Express and consequently has faced an uphill battle gaining market share despite its well-received "Priceless" ad campaign. As another example, Clorox found its initially successful entry into the detergent market thwarted by competitive responses once major threats such as P&G introduced products like Tide with Bleach. Arm & Hammer's brand extension program also met major resistance in categories such as deodorants when existing competitors fought back.

Market Performance. We saw in Chapter 2 that the customer mind-set affects how customers react in the marketplace in six main ways. The first two relate to price premiums and price elasticities. How much extra are customers willing to pay for a comparable product because of its brand? And how much does their demand increase or decrease when the price rises or falls? A third outcome is market share, which measures the success of the marketing program in driving brand sales. Taken together, the first three outcomes determine the direct revenue stream attributable to the brand over time. Brand value is created with higher market shares, greater price premiums, and more elastic responses to price decreases and inelastic responses to price increases.

The fourth outcome is brand expansion, the success of the brand in supporting line and category extensions and new-product launches into related categories. This dimension captures the brand's ability to add enhancements to the revenue stream. The fifth outcome is cost structure or, more specifically, reduced marketing program expenditures thanks to the prevailing customer mind-set. When customers already have favorable opinions and knowledge about a brand, any aspect of the marketing program is likely to be more effective for the same expenditure level; alternatively, the same level of effectiveness can be achieved at a lower cost because ads are more memorable, sales calls more productive, and so on. When combined, these five outcomes lead to brand profitability, the sixth outcome.

The ability of the brand value created at this stage to reach the final stage in terms of stock market valuation again depends on external factors, this time according to the investor sentiment multiplier.

Investor Sentiment Multiplier. Financial analysts and investors consider a host of factors in arriving at their brand valuations and investment decisions. Among them are the following:

- *Market dynamics:* What are the dynamics of the financial markets as a whole (interest rates, investor sentiment, supply of capital)?
- *Growth potential:* What are the growth potential or prospects for the brand and the industry in which it operates? For example, how helpful are the facilitating factors and how inhibiting are the hindering external factors that make up the firm's economic, social, physical, and legal environment?
- *Risk profile:* What is the risk profile for the brand? How vulnerable is the brand to those facilitating and inhibiting factors?
- *Brand contribution:* How important is the brand to the firm's brand portfolio?

The value the brand creates in the marketplace is most likely fully reflected in shareholder value when the firm is operating in a healthy industry without serious environmental hindrances or barriers, and when the brand contributes a significant portion of the firm's revenues and appears to have bright prospects. The obvious examples of brands that benefited from a strong market multiplier—at least for a while—were the numerous dot-com brands, such as Pets.com, eToys, Boo.com, and Webvan. The huge premium placed on their (actually negative) market performance, however, quickly disappeared—and in some cases so did the whole company!

On the other hand, many firms have lamented what they perceive as undervaluation by the market. For example, repositioned companies such as Corning have found it difficult to realize what they viewed as their true market value due to lingering investor perceptions from their past (Corning's heritage was in dishes and cookware; its more recent emphasis is on telecommunications, flat panel displays, and the environmental, life sciences, and semiconductor industries).

Shareholder Value. Based on all available current and forecasted information about a brand, as well as many other considerations, the financial marketplace formulates opinions and assessments that have very direct financial implications for the brand value. Three particularly important indicators are the stock price, the price/earnings multiple, and overall market capitalization for the firm. Research has shown that not only can strong brands deliver greater returns to stockholders, they can do so with less risk.[7]

An Illustrative Example: Starbucks. Figure 8-2 shows how Starbucks created value in its corporate brand during the period from 1993 to 2003. Although Starbucks increased its advertising budget somewhat during this time, its main marketing investment was in market expansion and an increase in the number of outlets—and thus potential consumption opportunities for consumers. As one marketing observer noted, "Despite its lack of national advertising, Starbucks has become a household word by turning coffee into a ubiquitous attitude product . . . and by expanding the brand beyond its traditional roots—strategically placed, extremely fragrant coffee shops—into airplanes, restaurants, hotels, supermarkets and other venues."[8] Another commentary noted, "Starbucks' growth has come with virtually no use of traditional media advertising; the chain has relied on in-store marketing initiatives and word of mouth to develop brand cachet."[9] Founder Howard Schultz noted, "The marketing of Starbucks is not only what people see on the outside. The cost of internal marketing is quite high, but it is the key to our success."[10] Because of Starbucks's superior product and service delivery, the expansion investment enhanced the customer mind-set.

Figure 8.2 also displays Young & Rubicam's BrandAsset Valuator (BAV) ratings of brand strength (brand relevance and differentiation) and stature (brand esteem and knowledge) as perceived by consumers (described in Brand Focus 9.0). Brand strength and stature bear a strong relationship to the five dimensions of the customer mind-set identified earlier. Starbucks experienced a steady improvement in consumer perceptions during this period. This increasingly favorable customer mind-set led to greater sales and a higher stock price and market capitalization.

Thus, Starbucks's marketing investment appeared to pay clear financial dividends. Starbucks was able to create so much brand value in part because of the positive multipliers it evidentily experienced. Starbucks's program multiplier was positive because of the relevance and distinctiveness of its product offerings. The company also maintained great consistency during this period of time. Its customer multiplier was positive because of the lack of any strong competitive reactions, the strong channel support it provided itself due to

	1993	1997	1999	2001	2003
I. Marketing Program Investment					
Advertising (LNA millions)	3.73	13.48	12.24	N/A	N/A
Number of outlets	272	1,412	2,498	4,709	8,569
II. Customer Mind-set					
BAV strength	0.6	1.5	1.8	2.4	2.2
BAV stature	2.4	6.7	10.1	13.4	13.6
III. Market Performance					
Sales (revenue) (millions—net)	—	$975	$1,680	$2,600	$3,500
IV. Shareholder Value					
Stock price	2.78	4.80	6.06	9.53	16.40
Market capitalization (millions)	$621	3,034	4,445	8,400	9,700

LNA—Leading National Advertisers; BAV—BrandAsset Valuator.

FIGURE 8-2

Brand Value Chain Analysis for Starbucks

its retail presence, and its single-minded customer focus on coffee lovers during this time. As one research analyst said during this period, "It's a foregone conclusion that Starbucks owns the specialty coffee market nationally. . . . No one wants to take them head on."[11] Another analyst noted, "Local competition among coffee stores is intense, but Starbucks is the only one out there that has a national level of recognition and awareness."[12] Finally, the market multiplier was equally positive due to Starbucks's corporate branding strategy and favorable financial market conditions.

Implications

According to the brand value chain, marketers create value first by making shrewd investments in their marketing program and then by maximizing, as much as possible, the program, customer, and market multipliers that translate that investment into bottom-line financial benefits. The brand value chain thus provides a structured means for managers to understand where and how value is created and where to look to improve that process. Certain stages will be of greater interest to different members of the organization.

Brand and category marketing managers are likely to be interested in the customer mind-set and the impact of the marketing program on customers. Chief marketing officers (CMOs), on the other hand, are likely to be more interested in market performance and the impact of customer mind-set on actual market behaviors. Finally, a managing director or CEO is likely to focus on shareholder value and the impact of market performance on investment decisions.

The brand value chain has a number of implications. First, value creation begins with the marketing program investment. Therefore, a necessary—but not sufficient—condition for value creation is a well-funded, well-designed, and well-implemented marketing program. It is rare that marketers can get something for nothing.

Second, value creation requires more than the initial marketing investment. Each of the three multipliers can increase or decrease market value as it moves from stage to stage. In other words, value creation also means ensuring that value transfers from stage to stage. Unfortunately, many factors that can inhibit value creation may be largely out of the marketer's hands, like investors' industry sentiment. Recognizing the uncontrollable nature of these factors is important to help put in perspective the relative success or failure of a marketing program to create brand value. Just as sports coaches cannot be held accountable for unforeseen circumstances such as injuries to key players and financial hardships that make it difficult to attract top talent, so marketers cannot necessarily be held accountable for certain market forces and dynamics.

Third, as we'll outline in the following two chapters, the brand value chain provides a detailed road map for tracking value creation that can make marketing research and intelligence efforts easier. Each of the stages and multipliers has a set of measures by which we can assess it. In general, there are three main sources of information, and each taps into one value stage and one multiplier. The first stage, the marketing program investment, is straightforward and can come from the marketing plan and budget. We can assess both customer mind-set and the program quality multiplier with quantitative and qualitative customer research. Market performance and the marketplace conditions multiplier appear in market scans and internal accounting records. Finally, we can estimate shareholder value and the investor sentiment multiplier through investor analysis and interviews.

Modifications to the brand value chain can expand its relevance and applicability. First, there are a number of feedback loops. For example, stock prices can have an important effect on employee morale and motivation. Second, in some cases, the value creation may not occur sequentially. For example, stock analysts may react to an ad campaign for the brand—either personally or in recognition of public acceptance—and factor those reactions directly into their investment assessments. Third, some marketing activities may have only very diffuse effects that manifest over the long term. For example, cause–related or social responsibility marketing activity might affect customer or investor sentiment slowly over time. Fourth, both the mean and the variance of some brand value chain measures could matter. For example, a niche brand may receive very high marks but only across a very narrow range of customers.

Designing Brand Tracking Studies

In Chapter 3 we described the concept of brand audits, a means to provide in-depth information and insights essential for setting long-term strategic direction for the brand. But to gather information for short-term tactical decisions, marketers will collect less detailed brand-related information through ongoing ***tracking studies.***

Tracking studies collect information from consumers on a routine basis over time, typically through quantitative measures of brand performance on a number of key dimensions marketers can identify in the brand audit or other means. They apply the brand value chain to understanding where, how much, and in what ways brand value is being created, thus offering invaluable information about how well the brand has achieved its positioning. As more marketing activity surrounds the brand—as the firm introduces brand extensions or incorporates an increasing variety of communication options in support of the brand—it becomes difficult and expensive to research each one. Regardless of how few or how many changes are made in the marketing program over time, however, marketers need to monitor the health of the brand and its equity so they can make adjustments if necessary. Tracking studies thus play an important role by providing consistent baseline information to facilitate day-to-day decision making. A good tracking system can help marketers better understand a host of important considerations such as category dynamics, consumer behavior, competitive vulnerabilities and opportunities, and marketing effectiveness and efficiency.

What to Track

Chapter 2 provided a detailed list of potential measures that correspond to the customer-based brand equity model, all of which are candidates for tracking. It is usually necessary to customize tracking surveys to address the specific issues faced by the brand or brands in question. To a great extent, each brand faces a unique situation that the different types of questions in its tracking survey should reflect.

Product–Brand Tracking. Tracking an individual branded product requires measuring brand awareness and image, using both recall and recognition measures and moving from more general to more specific questions. Thus, it may make sense to first ask consumers what brands come to mind in certain situations, to next ask for recall of brands on the basis of various product category cues, and to then finish with tests of brand recognition (if necessary).

Moving from general to more specific measures is also a good idea in brand tracking surveys to measure brand image, especially specific perceptions like what consumers think characterizes the brand, and evaluations such as what the brand means to consumers. A number of specific brand associations typically exist for the brand, depending on the richness of consumer knowledge structures, that marketers can track over time.

Given that brands often compete at the augmented product level (see Chapter 1), it is important to measure all associations that may distinguish competing brands. Thus, measures of specific, "lower-level" brand associations should include all potential sources of brand equity such as performance and imagery attributes and benefits. Benefit associations often represent key points of parity or points of difference, so it is particularly important to track them as well. To better understand any changes in benefit beliefs for a brand, however, marketers may also want to measure the attribute beliefs that underlie those benefits. In other words, changes in descriptive attribute beliefs may help to explain changes in more evaluative benefit beliefs for a brand.

Marketers should assess those key brand associations that make up the potential sources of brand equity on the basis of strength, favorability, and uniqueness *in that order.* Unless associations are strong enough for consumers to recall them, their favorability does not matter, and unless they are favorable enough to influence consumers' decisions, their uniqueness does not matter. Ideally, marketers will collect measures of all three dimensions, but perhaps for only certain associations and only some of the time; for example, favorability and uniqueness may be measured only once a year for three to five key associations.

At the same time, marketers will track more general, "higher-level" judgments, feelings, and other outcome-related measures. After soliciting their overall opinions, ask consumers whether they have changed their attitudes, intentions, or behavior in recent weeks or months and, if so, why.

Benefit associations are often important determinants of behavior. Patrick LaPointe advocates four key measures that he believes are largely predictive of future behavior of prospects and customers in many markets:[13]

1. Functional performance of the underlying product or service
2. Convenience and ease of accessing the product or service
3. Brand personality
4. Pricing and value component

Branding Brief 8-2 provides an illustrative example of a simple tracking survey for McDonald's.

Corporate or Family Brand Tracking. Marketers may also want to track the corporate or family brand separately or concurrently (or both) with individual products. Besides the measures of corporate credibility we identified in Chapter 2, you can consider other measures of corporate brand associations including the following (illustrated with the GE corporate brand):

- How well managed is GE?
- How easy is it to do business with GE?
- How concerned is GE with its customers?
- How approachable is GE?
- How accessible is GE?
- How much do you like doing business with GE?

The actual questions should reflect the level and nature of experience that your respondents are likely to have had with the company.

A number of firms track corporate image. For example, at one time DuPont tracked the following broad measures of corporate image:[14]

- Outstanding American companies (unaided)
- Outstanding companies on 11 different attributes (unaided)
- Rating on those attributes
- Outstanding companies in eight different industries (unaided)
- Association with those industries
- Ratings in associated industries
- Familiarity with products and services
- Likelihood of investing in stock
- Feeling about friend accepting employment

When a brand is identified with multiple products, as in a corporate or family branding strategy, one important issue is which particular products the brand reminds consumers of. Marketers also want to know which particular products are most influential in affecting consumer perceptions about the brand. To identify them, ask consumers which products they associate with the brand on an unaided basis ("What products come to mind when you think of the Nike brand?") or an aided basis by listing sub-brand names ("Are you aware of Nike Air Force basketball shoes? Nike Sphere React tennis apparel? Nike Air Max running shoes?"). To better understand the dynamics between the brand and its corresponding products, also ask consumers about their relationship between them ("There are many different products associated with Nike. Which ones are most important to you in formulating your opinion about the brand?").

Global Tracking. If your tracking covers diverse geographic markets—especially in both developing and developed countries—then you may need a broader set of background measures to put the brand development in those markets in the right perspective. You would not need to collect them frequently, but they could provide useful explanatory information (see Figure 8-3 for some representative measures).

Economic Indicators
Gross domestic product
Interest rates
Unemployment
Average wage
Disposable income
Home ownership and housing debt
Exchange rates, share markets, and balance of payments

Retail
Total spent in supermarkets
Change year to year
Growth in house brand

Technology
Computer at home
DVR
Access to and use of Internet
Phones
PDA
Microwaves
Television

Personal Attitudes and Values
Confidence
Security
Family
Environment
Traditional values
Foreigners vs. sovereignty

Media Indicators
Media consumption: total time spent watching TV, consuming other media
Advertising expenditure: total, by media and by product category

Demographic Profile
Population profile: age, sex, income, household size
Geographic distribution
Ethnic and cultural profile

Other Products and Services
Transport: own car—how many
Best description of car
Motorbike
Home ownership or renting
Domestic trips overnight in last year
International trips in last two years

Attitude to Brands and Shopping
Buy on price
Like to buy new things
Country of origin or manufacture
Prefer to buy things that have been advertised
Importance of familiar brands

FIGURE 8-3

Brand Context Measures

BRANDING BRIEF 8-2

Sample Brand Tracking Survey

Assume that McDonald's is interested in designing a short tracking survey to be conducted over the phone. How might you set it up? Although there are a number of different types of questions, your tracking survey might take the following form.

Interviewer: We're conducting a short phone interview to gather consumer opinions about quick-service or "fast-food" restaurant chains.

Brand Awareness and Usage

a. What brands of quick-service restaurant chains are you aware of?
b. At which brands of quick-service restaurant chains would you consider eating?
c. Have you eaten in a quick-service restaurant chain in the last week? Which ones?
d. If you were to eat in a quick-service restaurant tomorrow for lunch, which one would you go to?
e. What if instead it were for dinner? Where would you go?
f. Finally, what if instead it were for breakfast? Where would you go?
g. Which are your favorite quick-service restaurant chains?

We want to ask you some general questions about a particular quick-service restaurant chain, McDonald's.

Have you heard of this restaurant? [Establish familiarity.]

Have you eaten at this restaurant? [Establish trial.]

When I say McDonald's, what are the first associations that come to your mind? Anything else? [List all.]

Brand Judgments

We're interested in your overall opinion of McDonald's.

a. How favorable is your attitude toward McDonald's?
b. How well does McDonald's satisfy your needs?
c. How likely would you be to recommend McDonald's to others?
d. How good a value is McDonald's?
e. Is McDonald's worth a premium price?
f. What do you like best about McDonald's?
g. What is most unique about McDonald's?
h. To what extent does McDonald's offer advantages that other brands cannot?
i. To what extent is McDonald's superior to other brands in the quick-service restaurant category?
j. Compared to other brands in the quick-service restaurant category, how well does McDonald's satisfy your basic needs?

We now want to ask you some questions about McDonald's as a company. Please indicate your agreement with the following statements.

McDonald's is . . .

a. Innovative
b. Knowledgeable
c. Trustworthy
d. Likable
e. Concerned about their customers
f. Concerned about society as a whole
g. Likable
h. Admirable

Brand Performance

We now would like to ask some specific questions about McDonald's. Please indicate your agreement with the following statements.

McDonald's . . .

a. Is convenient to eat at
b. Provides quick, efficient service
c. Has clean facilities
d. Is for the whole family
e. Has delicious food
f. Has healthy food
g. Has a varied menu
h. Has friendly, courteous staff
i. Offers fun promotions
j. Has a stylish and attractive look
k. Has high-quality food

Brand Imagery

a. To what extent do people you admire and respect eat at McDonald's?
b. How much do you like people who eat at McDonald's?
c. How well do each of the following words describe McDonald's?
Down-to-earth, honest, daring, up-to-date, reliable, successful, upper class, charming, outdoorsy
d. Is McDonald's a restaurant that you can use in a lot of different situations?
e. To what extent does thinking of McDonald's bring back pleasant memories?
f. To what extent do you feel that you grew up with McDonald's?

(*Continued*)

(Continued)

Brand Feelings

Does McDonald's give you a feeling of . . .

a. Warmth?
b. Fun?
c. Excitement?
d. Sense of security or confidence?
e. Social approval?
f. Self-respect?

Brand Resonance

a. I consider myself loyal to McDonald's.
b. I buy McDonald's whenever I can.
c. I would go out of my way to eat at McDonald's.
d. I really love McDonald's.
e. I would really miss McDonald's if it went away.
f. McDonald's is special to me.
g. McDonald's is more than a product to me.
h. I really identify with people who eat at McDonald's.
i. I feel a deep connection with others who eat at McDonald's.
j. I really like to talk about McDonald's to others.
k. I am always interested in learning more about McDonald's.
l. I would be interested in merchandise with the McDonald's name on it.
m. I am proud to have others know I eat at McDonald's.
n. I like to visit the Web site for McDonald's.
o. Compared to other people, I follow news about McDonald's closely.

How to Conduct Tracking Studies

Which elements of the brand should you use in tracking studies? In general, marketers use the brand name, but it may also make sense to use a logo or symbol in probing brand structures, especially if these elements can play a visible and important role in the decision process.

You also need to decide whom to track, as well as when and where to track.

Whom to Track. Tracking often concentrates on current customers, but it can also be rewarding to monitor nonusers of the brand or even of the product category as a whole, for example, to suggest potential segmentation strategies. Marketers can track those customers loyal to the brand against those loyal to other brands, or against those who switch brands. Among current customers, marketers can distinguish between heavy and light users of the brand. Dividing up the market typically requires writing different questionnaires (or at least sections of a basic questionnaire) to better capture the specific issues of each segment.

ALKA SELTZER

Miles Laboratory collects much data on the image of its flagship product, Alka Seltzer. The data have revealed marked differences in the product image among users and nonusers. For example, users regard effervescence as a highly convenient feature of the Alka Seltzer brand, while nonusers regard it as highly inconvenient. Desired benefits for Alka Seltzer also vary by type of user. Heavy users claim "efficacy" and "speed of relief" as the most valued attributes. Light users, on the other hand, value "gentleness" and "no side effects" more highly. Recognizing that effervescence is a key source of the brand equity for Alka Seltzer, Miles' marketers track it closely. Because of the strategic importance of this association, the company deliberated carefully before introducing a liquid-gel version of the product and keenly watched subsequent consumer reaction, eventually restricting it to only its more distinct Alka Seltzer Plus cold and flu medicine.

It's often useful to closely track other types of customers, too, such as channel members and other intermediaries, to understand their perceptions and actions toward the brand. Of particular interest is their image of the brand and how they feel they can help or hurt its equity. Retailers can answer direct questions such as, "Do you feel that products in your store sell faster if they have [the brand name] on them? Why or why not?" Marketers might also want to track employees such as salespeople, to better understand their beliefs about the brand and how they feel they're contributing to its equity now or could do so in the future. Such tracking may be especially important with service organizations, where employees play profound roles in affecting brand equity.

When and Where to Track. How often should you collect tracking information? One useful approach for monitoring brand associations is continuous tracking studies, which collect information from consumers continually over time. The advantage of continuous tracking is that it smoothes out aberrations or unusual marketing activities or events like a splashy new ad campaign or an unlikely occurrence in the marketing environment to provide a more representative set of baseline measures.

The frequency of such tracking studies, in general, depends on the frequency of product purchase (marketers typically track durable goods less frequently because they are purchased less often), and on the consumer behavior and marketing activity in the product category. Many companies conduct a certain number of interviews of different consumers every week—or even every day—and assemble the results on a rolling or moving average basis for monthly or quarterly reports.

MILLWARD BROWN

Marketing research tracking pioneer Millward Brown usually interviews 50 to 100 people a week and looks at the data with moving averages trended over time in its Advanced Tracking Program. Typically, the interviews are short (10 to 20 minutes in length, on the phone or Web), covering the client brand and competitive set. The company collects data on a variety of topics as dictated by the client needs. Modules include: brand loyalty, brand positioning, value perceptions, awareness and response to marketing communications and in-store promotions, consumer profiles, and so on. A 12-minute interview for a typical consumer product administered over the phone to 50 nationally representative consumers weekly can cost roughly $250,000 annually, depending on modality.[15]

When the brand has more stable and enduring associations, tracking on a less frequent basis can be enough. Nevertheless, even if the marketing of a brand does not appreciably change over time, competitive entries can change consumer perceptions of the dynamics within the market, making tracking critical. Finally, the stage of the product or brand life cycle will affect your decision about the frequency of tracking: Opinions of consumers in mature markets may not change much, whereas emerging markets may shift quickly and perhaps unpredictably.

How to Interpret Tracking Studies

To yield actionable insights and recommendations, tracking measures must be as reliable and sensitive as possible. One problem with many traditional measures of marketing phenomena is that they don't change much over time. Although this stability may mean the data haven't changed much, it may also be that one or more brand dimensions have changed to some extent but the measures themselves are not sensitive enough to detect subtle shifts. To develop sensitive tracking measures, marketers might need to phrase questions in a comparative way—"compared to other brands, how much . . ." or in terms of time periods—"compared to one month or one year ago, how much . . ."

Another challenge in interpreting tracking studies is deciding on appropriate benchmarks. For example, what is a sufficiently high level of brand awareness? When are brand associations sufficiently strong, favorable, and unique? How positive should brand judgments and feelings be? What are reasonable expectations for the amount of brand resonance? The cut-offs must not be unreasonable and must properly reflect the interests of the intended internal management audience. Appropriately defined and tested targets can help management benchmark against competitors and assess the productivity of brand marketing teams.

Marketers may also have to design these targets with allowance for competitive considerations and the nature of the category. In some low-involvement categories like, say, lightbulbs, it may be difficult to carve out a distinct image, unlike the case for higher-involvement products like cars or computers. Marketers must allow for and monitor the number of respondents who indicate they "don't know" or have "no response" to the brand tracking measures: The more of these types of answers collected, the less consumers would seem to care.

AC Nielsen's Alastair Gordon highlights some of the reasons brand equity or health metrics have not always been helpful:[16]

1. Too much focus on "top-level" boxes or scores and indices (often too general and not prescriptive enough)
2. Targets that are not set at all, are unattainable, or are inappropriate for the management level they are given to
3. Metrics treated as an independent research study and not integrated with other information such as category trends
4. Too much focus on consumer attitudes and emotional connections without a link to behaviors

Gordon advocates that brand health measures become more multidimensional, more directly address why consumers decide between brands, and take a clear "report card" approach to understanding opportunities and setting appropriate targets.

One of the most important tasks in conducting brand tracking studies is to identify the determinants of brand equity.[17] Which brand associations actually influence consumer attitudes and behavior and create value for the brand? Marketers must identify the real value drivers for a brand—that is, those tangible and intangible points of difference that influence and determine consumers' product and brand choices. Similarly, marketers must identify the marketing activities that have the most effective impact on brand knowledge, especially consumer exposure to advertising and other communication mix elements. Carefully monitoring and relating key sources and outcome measures of brand equity should help to address these issues. The CBBE model and brand value chain suggest many possible links and paths to explore for their impact on brand equity. (Chapters 9 and 10 discuss several measures in more detail.)

Establishing a Brand Equity Management System

Brand tracking studies, as well as brand audits, can provide a huge reservoir of information about how best to build and measure brand equity. To get the most value from these research efforts, firms need proper internal structures and procedures to capitalize on the usefulness of the brand equity concept and the information they collect about it. Although a brand equity measurement system does not ensure that managers will always make "good" decisions about the brand, it should increase the likelihood they do and, if nothing else, decrease the likelihood of "bad" decisions.

Embracing the concept of branding and brand equity, many firms constantly review how they can best factor it into the organization. Interestingly, perhaps one of the biggest threats to brand equity comes from within the organization, and the fact that too many marketing managers remain on the job for only a limited period of time. As a result of these short-term assignments, marketing managers may adopt a short-term perspective, leading to an overreliance on quick-fix sales-generating tactics such as line and category extensions, sales promotions, and so forth. Because these managers lack an understanding and appreciation of the brand equity concept, some critics maintain, they are essentially running the brand "without a license."

To counteract these and other potential forces within an organization that may lead to ineffective long-term management of brands, many firms have made internal branding a top priority, as we noted in Chapter 3. As part of these efforts, they must put a brand equity management system into place. A ***brand equity management system*** is a set of organizational processes designed to improve the understanding and use of the brand equity concept within a firm. As one set of commentators noted:[18]

> Implementing a brand equity management system is critical to managing one of the company's most valuable assets. It will give the company a better way to inform how to position its brands, become a living bible of what matters most for brands to succeed, enable charting brand progress toward goals, and become a tool for diagnosing and fixing a weakness that might be emerging.

Three major steps help to implement a brand equity management system: creating brand equity charters, assembling brand equity reports, and defining brand equity responsibilities. The following subsections discuss each of these in turn. Branding Brief 8-3 describes how the Mayo Clinic has developed a brand equity measurement and management system.

Brand Equity Charter

The first step in establishing a brand equity management system is to formalize the company view of brand equity into a document, the ***brand equity charter,*** that provides relevant guidelines to marketing managers within the company as well as to key marketing partners outside the company such as ad agency staff. This document should do the following:

- Define the firm's view of the brand equity concept and explain why it is important.
- Describe the scope of key brands in terms of associated products and the manner by which they have been branded and marketed (as revealed by historical company records as well as the most recent brand inventory).

BRANDING BRIEF 8-3

Understanding and Managing the Mayo Clinic Brand

Mayo Clinic was founded in the late 1800s by Dr. William Worral Mayo and his two sons, who later pioneered the "group practice of medicine" by inviting other physicians to work with them in Rochester, Minnesota. The Mayos believed that "two heads are better than one and three are even better." From this beginning on the frontier, Mayo Clinic grew to be a worldwide leader in patient care, research, and education and became renowned for its world-class specialty care and medical research. In addition to the original facilities in Rochester, Mayo later built clinics in Jacksonville, Florida and Scottsdale, Arizona during the 1980s. More than 500,000 patients are cared for in Mayo's inpatient and outpatient practice annually.

The Mayo Clinic has developed a brand equity measurement and management system.

In 1996, Mayo undertook its first brand equity study and conducted both quantitative and qualitative studies. Mayo repeated the qualitative research in 2005, including 15 focus groups in five cities. The focus groups identified seven key brand attributes or values, including: (1) integration, (2) integrity, (3) longevity, (4) exclusivity, (5) leadership, (6) wisdom, and (7) dedication. Although some of these values also characterize other high-quality medical centers, integration and integrity are more nearly unique to Mayo. In terms of integration, respondents described Mayo as bringing together a wealth of resources to provide the best possible care. They perceived Mayo to be efficient, organized, harmonious, and creating a sense of participation and partnership. For example, one person described Mayo as: "A well conducted symphony . . . works harmoniously . . . One person can't do it alone . . . Teamwork, cooperation, compatibility." For integrity, respondents placed great value on the fact that Mayo is noncommercial and committed to health and healing over profit. One participant said, "The business element is taken out of Mayo . . . Their ethics are higher . . . which gives me greater faith in their diagnosis."

- Specify what the actual and desired equity is for a brand at all relevant levels of the brand hierarchy, for example, at both the corporate and the individual product level (as outlined in Chapter 11). The charter should define a range of relevant associations, including those that constitute points of parity and points of difference, as well as core brand associations and the brand mantra.
- Explain how brand equity is measured in terms of the tracking study and the resulting brand equity report (described shortly).
- Suggest how marketers should manage brand equity with some general strategic guidelines, such as stressing clarity, relevance, distinctiveness, innovativeness, and consistency in marketing programs over time.

Although none of Mayo Clinic's brand attributes are solely negative, perceptions of exclusivity pose some specific challenges. This attribute was sometimes described positively, in perceptions that Mayo offers the highest quality care and elite doctors, but inaccurate beliefs that it serves only the rich and famous and the sickest of the sick were emotionally distancing and made Mayo seem inaccessible.

In a more recent quantitative study, overall awareness of the Mayo Clinic in the United States was 90.2 percent, and a remarkable one-third know at least one Mayo patient. One of the key questions in the survey asked, "Suppose your health plan or personal finances permitted you to go anywhere in the U.S. for a serious medical condition which required highly specialized care, to which one institution would you prefer to go?" Mayo Clinic was the most popular choice, earning 18.6 percent of the responses, compared with 5.0 percent for the next most frequently mentioned medical center. Word of mouth has the most influence on these preferences for highly specialized medical care.

From its research, Mayo Clinic concluded that its brand "is precious and powerful." Mayo realized that while it had an overwhelmingly positive image, it was vital to develop guidelines to protect the brand. In 1999, the clinic created a brand management infrastructure to be the "institutional clearinghouse for ongoing knowledge about external perceptions of Mayo Clinic and its related activities." Mayo Clinic also established guidelines for applying the brand to products and services. Its brand management measures work to ensure that the clinic preserves its brand equity, as well as allowing Mayo to continue to accomplish its mission:

> *Mayo Clinic will provide the best care to every patient every day through integrated clinical practice, education, and research.*

Sources: Thanks to Mayo's John La Forgia, Kent Seltman, and Scott Swanson for assistance and cooperation. www.mayoclinic.org; "Mayo Clinic Brand Management," internal document, 1999. See also Leonard L. Berry and Neeli Bendapudi, "Clueing in Customers," *Harvard Business Review,* February 2003, 100–106; Paul Roberts, "The Agenda—Total Teamwork," *Fast Company,* April 1999, 148.

- Outline how to devise marketing programs along specific tactical guidelines, including criteria for ad evaluation and brand name choice.
- Specify the proper treatment of the brand in terms of trademark usage, packaging, and communications.

Although parts of the brand equity charter may not change from year to year, the firm should nevertheless update it on an annual basis to provide decision makers with a current brand profile and to identify new opportunities and potential risks for the brand. As marketers introduce new products, change brand programs, and conduct other marketing initiatives, they should reflect these adequately in the brand equity charter. Many of the in-depth insights that emerge from brand audits also belong in the charter.

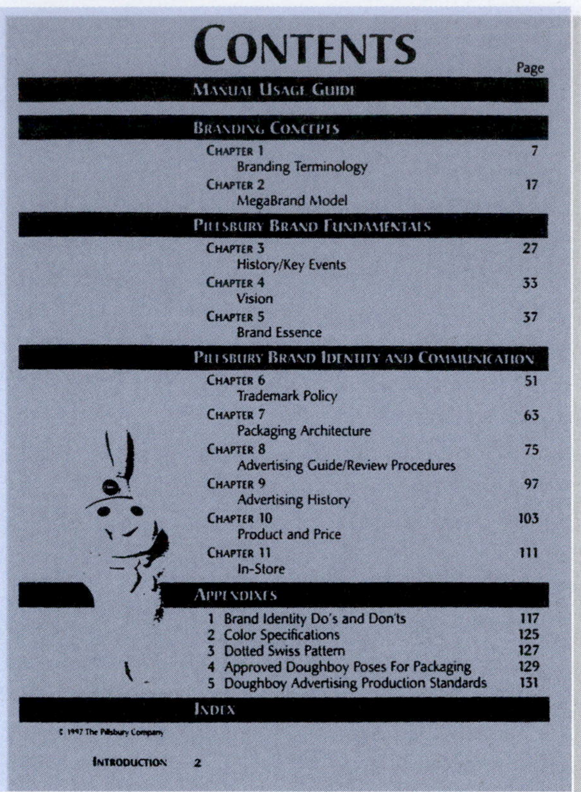

CONTENTS

INTRODUCTION 2

FIGURE 8-4

Pillsbury Brand Manual: Table of Contents
Source: Used with permission of General Mills, Inc.

Figure 8-4 displays the table of contents for the Pillsbury brand manual. A brand with a creative brand charter is Burger King.

BURGER KING

As part of its brand revitalization in 2004, Burger King completely overhauled its marketing, inside and out. In addition to introducing quirky advertising for the brand, Burger King's ad agency, Crispin Porter + Bogusky, also transformed many internal aspects of the brand, from the off-beat instrumental telephone "hold" music to its *Go Forward* employee handbook. Burger King made sure that the handbook was written to be accessible in tone and language, embracing the qualities of corporate culture the firm was trying to adopt.

Brand Equity Report

The second step in establishing a successful brand equity management system is to assemble the results of the tracking survey and other relevant performance measures for the brand into a brand equity report or scorecard to be distributed to management on a regular basis (monthly, quarterly, or annually). Much of the information relevant to the report may already exist within the organization. Yet it may have been presented to management in disjointed chunks so that no one has a holistic understanding of it. The brand equity report attempts to effectively integrate all these different measures.[19]

The brand equity report should describe *what* is happening with the brand as well as *why* it is happening. It should include all relevant internal and external measures of

Burger King has gone under a brand transformation, including quirky ads and co-promotions, to help revitalize sales.

The combined print and TV "Got Milk?" campaign has helped to stem the decline in milk sales.

brand performance and sources and outcomes of brand equity.[20] In particular, one section of the report should summarize consumers' perceptions of key attribute or benefit associations, preferences, and reported behavior as revealed by the tracking study. Another section of the report should include more descriptive market-level information such as the following:

- Product shipments and movement through channels of distribution
- Retail category trends
- Relevant cost breakdowns
- Price and discount schedules where appropriate
- Sales and market share information broken down by relevant factors (such as geographic region, type of retail account, or customer)
- Profit assessments

Robert Malcolm from Diageo notes that his firm measures both input and outcome metrics and applies a complementary approach based on the GAME plan:[21]

1. *Goal:* Identify key brands for the next fiscal period.
2. *Activity:* Locate current status on a baseline, compared with brands owned by the firm or competition.
3. *Measurement:* Allocate inputs with specific objectives like changing consumer behavior and increasing purchase intensity.
4. *Evaluation:* Assess the outputs.

These measures can provide insight into the market performance component of the brand value chain. Management can compare them to various frames of reference—performance last month/quarter/year—and color code them green, yellow, or red, depending on whether the trends are positive, neutral, or negative, respectively.

To provide feedback on marketing peformance to boards of directors, Harvard Business School's Gail McGovern and John Quelch advocate quarterly tracking reports of the three or four marketing or customer-related metrics that truly drive and predict the company's business performance—the behavioral measures that are specific to a company's business model.[22] As an example, they note how the board of casino operator Harrah's focuses on three metrics: share of its customer's gaming dollars (share of wallet); loyalty program updates (an indicator of increased concentration of a customer's gaming at Harrah's); and percent of revenue from customers visiting more than one of Harrah's 30 casinos (an indicator of cross-selling). To support its tracking, Harrah's spends $50 million annually on a customer information system.

Similarly, Ambler and Clark offer three recommendations.[23] First, marketers must work with their CFO to develop marketing dashboards and to shift metrics and forecasting responsibilities to the finance department. Second, marketers should develop with each agency a detailed brief with measurable objectives and a results-driven compensation (for agencies) component. Finally, marketers need to dedicate extra time to securing buy-in from colleagues on their business model, strategy, and metrics.

THE SCIENCE OF BRANDING 8-1

Maximizing Internal Branding

Branding expert Scott Davis offers a number of insights into what it takes to make a brand-driven organization.

According to Davis, for employees to become passionate brand advocates, they must understand what a brand is, how it is built, what their organization's brand stands for, and what their role is in delivering on the brand promise. Formally, he sees the process of helping an organization's employees assimilate the brand as three stages:

1. "*Hear It*": How do we best get it into their hands?
2. "*Believe It*": How do we best get it into their heads?
3. "*Live It*": How do we best get it into their hearts?

Davis also argues that six key principles should guide the brand assimilation process within an organization, offering the following examples.

1. *Make the brand relevant.* Each employee must understand and embrace the brand meaning. For example, Nordstrom, whose brand relies on top-notch customer service, empowers sales associates to approve exchanges without manager approval.
2. *Make the brand accessible.* Employees must know where they can get brand knowledge and answers to their brand-related questions. For example, Ernst & Young launched "The Branding Zone" on its intranet to provide employees easy access to information about its branding, marketing, and advertising programs.

With advances in computer technology, it will be increasingly easy for firms to place the information that makes up the brand equity report online, so that managers can access it through the firm's intranet or some other means. For example, NFO MarketMind has developed a brand management database system that integrates continuous consumer tracking survey data, media weight (or cost) data, warehouse sales and retail scan data, and PR and editorial content.

Brand Equity Responsibilities

To develop a brand equity management system that will maximize long-term brand equity, managers must clearly define organizational responsibilities and processes with respect to the brand. Brands need constant, consistent nurturing to grow. Weak brands often suffer from a lack of discipline, commitment, and investment in brand building. In this section we consider internal issues of assigning responsibilities and duties for properly managing brand equity, as well as external issues related to the proper roles of marketing partners. The Science of Branding 8-1 describes some important principles in building a brand-driven organization.

Overseeing Brand Equity. To provide central coordination, the firm should establish a position entitled vice president or director of strategic brand management or brand equity management. This person is responsible for overseeing the implementation of the brand

3. *Reinforce the brand continuously.* Management must reinforce the brand meaning with employees beyond the initial rollout of an internal branding program. For example, Southwest Airlines continually reinforces its brand promise of "a symbol of freedom" through ongoing programs and activities with a freedom theme.
4. *Make brand education an ongoing program.* Provide new employees with inspiring and informative training. For example, Ritz-Carlton ensures that each employee participates in an intensive orientation called "The Gold Standard" that includes principles to improve service delivery and maximize guest satisfaction.
5. *Reward on-brand behaviors.* An incentive system to reward employees for exceptional support of the brand strategy should coincide with the roll-out of an internal branding program. For example, Continental Airlines rewards employees with cash bonuses each month that the airline ranks in the top five of on-time airlines.
6. *Align hiring practices.* HR and marketing must work together to develop criteria and screening procedures to ensure that new hires are good fits for the company's brand culture. For example, Pret A Manger sandwich shops has such a carefully honed screener that only 20 percent of applicants end up being hired.

Davis also emphasizes the role of senior management in driving internal branding, noting that the CEO ultimately sets the tone and compliance with a brand-based culture and determines whether proper resources and procedures are put into place.

Source: Scott Davis, "Building a Brand-Driven Organization," in *Kellogg on Branding,* eds. Alice M. Tybout and Tim Calkins (Hoboken, NJ: John Wiley & Sons, 2005).

equity charter and brand equity reports, to ensure that product and marketing actions across divisions and geographic boundaries reflect their spirit as closely as possible and maximize the long-term equity of the brand. A natural place to house such oversight duties and responsibilities is in a corporate marketing group that has a senior management reporting relationship.

Scott Bedbury, who helped direct the Nike and Starbucks brands during some of their most successful years, is emphatic about the need for "top-down brand leadership."[24] He advocates the addition of a chief brand officer (CBO) who reports directly to the CEO of the company and who:

- ***Is an omnipresent conscience whose job is to champion and protect the brand—the way it looks and feels—both inside and outside the company.*** The CBO recognizes that the brand is the sum total of everything a company does and strives to ensure that all employees understand the brand and its values, creating "brand disciples" in the process.
- ***Is an architect and not only helps build the brand but also plans, anticipates, researches, probes, listens, and informs.*** Working with senior leadership, the CBO helps envision not just what works best for the brand today but also what can help drive it forward in the future.
- ***Determines and protects the voice of the brand over time by taking a long-term (two to three years) perspective.*** The CBO can be accountable for brand-critical and corporate-wide activities such as advertising, positioning, corporate design, corporate communications, and consumer or market insights.

Even strong brands need careful watching to prevent managers from assuming it's acceptable to "make one little mistake" with brand equity or to "let it slide." A number of top companies like Colgate-Palmolive, Canada Dry, Quaker Oats, Pillsbury, Coca-Cola, and Nestlé Foods have created brand equity gatekeepers for some or all their brands at one time.[25]

IBM

IBM assigned a team to determine specifically what customers were looking for from IT services providers. The team's first important insight was to shift the dialogue from the existing attribute-focused view to a customer-defined benefit view. The team began by developing an understanding of the benefits customers sought and then how they evaluated the provider's perceived ability to deliver those benefits. Using a structural equation model, the team was able to identify which brand elements had the largest impact on customer share of wallet. IBM could then prioritize activities to focus on and develop programs and associated metrics to improve the overall customer experience. This group has since had input into a wide variety of areas—including overall communications strategy and the general "look and feel" of products—to ensure that the products reinforced the brand equity as much as possible. The team also has had responsibility for communicating the brand equity message throughout IBM's many divisions and arbitrating any disputes that might arise among groups concerning brand equity.[26]

Bedbury also advocates periodic brand development reviews (full-day meetings quarterly, or even half-day meetings monthly) for brands in difficult circumstances. As part of a brand development review, he suggests the following topics and activities:[27]

- *Review brand-sensitive material:* For example, review brand strength monitors or tracking studies, brand audits, and focus groups, as well as less formal personal observations or "gut feelings."

IBM has carefully managed its brand image as it has put more emphasis on its service offerings.

- *Review the status of key brand initiatives:* Because brand initiatives include strategic thrusts to either strengthen a weakness in the brand or exploit an opportunity to grow the brand in a new direction, customer perceptions may change and marketers therefore need to assess them.
- *Review brand-sensitive projects:* For example, evaluate advertising campaigns, corporate communications, sales meeting agendas, and important human resources programs (recruitment, training, and retention that profoundly affect the organization's ability to embrace and project brand values).
- *Review new product and distribution strategies with respect to core brand values:* For example, evaluate licensing the brand to penetrate new markets, forming joint ventures to develop new products or brands, and expanding distribution to nontraditional platforms such as large-scale discount retailers.
- *Resolve brand positioning conflicts:* Identify and resolve any inconsistencies in positioning across channels, business units, or markets.

Branding Brief 8-4 contains a checklist by which firms can assess their marketing skills and performance.

One of senior management's important roles is to determine marketing budgets and decide where and how to allocate company resources within the organization. The brand equity management system must be able to inform and provide input to decision makers so that they can recognize the short-term and long-term ramifications of their decisions for brand equity. Decisions about which brands to invest in, and whether to implement

BRANDING BRIEF 8-4

How Good Is Your Marketing? Rating a Firm's Marketing Assessment System

Famed London Business School professor Tim Ambler has a wealth of experience in working with companies. He notes that in his interactions, "most companies do not have a clear picture of their own marketing performance which may be why they cannot assess it." To help companies evaluate if their marketing assessment system is good enough, he suggests that they ask the following 10 questions—the higher the score, the better the assessment system.

1. Does the senior executive team regularly and formally assess marketing performance?
   - a. Yearly—10
   - b. Six-monthly—10
   - c. Quarterly—5
   - d. More often—0
   - e. Rarely—0
   - f. Never—0

2. What does the senior executive team understand by "customer value"?
   - a. Don't know. We are not clear about this—0
   - b. Value of the customer to the business (as in "customer lifetime value")—5
   - c. Value of what the company provides from the customers' point of view—10
   - d. Sometimes one, sometimes the other—10

3. How much time does the senior executive team give to marketing issues?
   - a. >30%—10
   - b. 20–30%—6
   - c. 10–20%—4;
   - d. < 10%—0

4. Does the business/marketing plan show the nonfinancial corporate goals and link them to market goals?
   - a. No/no plan—0
   - b. Corporate no, market yes—5
   - c. Yes to both—10

brand-building marketing programs or leverage brand equity through brand extensions instead, should reflect the current and desired state of the brand as revealed through brand tracking and other measures.

Organizational Design and Structures. The firm should organize its marketing function to optimize brand equity. Several trends have emerged in organizational design and structure that reflect the growing recognition of the importance of the brand and the challenges of managing brand equity carefully. For example, an increasing number of firms are embracing brand management. Firms from more and more industries—such as

5. **Does the plan show the comparison of your marketing performance with competitors or the market as a whole?**
   a. No/no plan—0
   b. Yes, clearly—10
   c. In between—5
6. **What is your main marketing asset called?**
   a. Brand equity—10
   b. Reputation—10
   c. Other term—5
   d. We have no term—0
7. **Does the senior executive team's performance review involve a quantified view of the main marketing asset and how it has changed?**
   a. Yes to both—10
   b. Yes but only financially (brand valuation)—5
   c. Not really—0
8. **Has the senior executive team quantified what "success" would look like five or ten years from now?**
   a. No—0
   b. Yes—10
   c. Don't know—0
9. **Does your strategy have quantified milestones to indicate progress toward that success?**
   a. No—0
   b. Yes—10
   c. What strategy?—0
10. **Are the marketing performance indicators seen by the senior executive team aligned with these milestones?**
    a. No—0
    b. Yes, external (customers and competitors)—7
    c. Yes, internal (employees and innovativeness)—5
    d. Yes, both—10

Sources: Adapted from Tim Ambler, *Marketing and the Bottom Line*, 2nd ed. (London: FT Prentice Hall, 2004).

the automobile, health care, pharmaceutical, and computer software and hardware industries—are introducing brand managers into their organizations. Often, they have hired managers from top packaged-goods companies, adopting some of the same brand marketing practices as a result.

Interestingly, packaged-goods companies, such as Procter & Gamble, continue to evolve the brand management system (see Branding Brief 8-5). With category management, manufacturers offer retailers advice about how to best stock their shelves. An increasing number of retailers are also adopting category management principles. For example, Borders asks HarperCollins to help it select which cookbooks to carry—and not

BRANDING BRIEF 8-5

Category Management at Procter & Gamble

Procter & Gamble, pioneers of the brand management system, and several other top firms made a significant shift a number of years back to incorporate category management. Previously, senior management at P&G included a handful of divisional marketing vice presidents, who were responsible for 3 to 6 product categories and 12 to 18 brands. With the company's new category emphasis, starting in the late 1980s, a general manager was assigned to each of the 40 or so product categories in which P&G competed (laundry detergents, dishwashing detergents, and specialty products; see the accompanying photo) and given direct profit responsibility. The duties of individual brand managers, however, were essentially unchanged.

P&G uses category management principles to handle all its different brands.

Although in some ways P&G's new organizational structure is counter to management trends toward downsizing the organization and reducing management levels, the company cites a number of advantages. By fostering internal competition among brand managers, the traditional brand management system created strong incentives to excel. These inducements came at the cost of internal coordination, however, because brand managers sometimes contested corporate resources like ad spending dollars or manufacturing capacity and failed to synchronize their programs. Whereas a smaller-share category might have been relatively neglected before—say, in product categories such as

just the ones HarperCollins publishes but those published by competitors as well.[28] One survey found that retailers reported 14 percent sales growth from adopting category management, and manufacturers reported an 8% hike.[29] Although manufacturers functioning as category captains can improve sales, experts caution retailers to exercise their own insights and values to retain their distinctiveness in the marketplace.

In considering the future of brand management, Hulbert, Berthon, and Pitt make several observations and forecasts:[30]

- It is incumbent upon the whole organization to commit to a focus on the customer, and brands will increasingly become a means to that end.
- Marketing must become far more active in initiating and driving innovation.
- Information technology will increasingly become a tool for allowing and maintaining large-scale customer and consumer interaction and conversation.
- The onus for ownership and management of change in brands and the brand management system will increasingly shift to senior management.

Many firms are thus attempting to redesign their marketing organizations to better reflect the challenges faced by their brands. At the same time, because of changing job requirements and duties, the traditional marketing department is disappearing from a number of companies that are exploring other ways to conduct their marketing functions through business groups, multidisciplinary teams, and so on.[31] The goal in these new

"hard surface cleaners"—the new scheme was designed to ensure that all categories would receive adequate resources. Thus, category management became a means to provide better management of brand portfolios to increase the similarity, where appropriate, as well as the differences among brands in categories.

Another often-cited rationale for placing more emphasis on category management is the increasing power of the trade. Because the retail trade has tended to think in terms of product categories and the profitability derived from different departments and sections of their stores, P&G felt it only made sense to deal with the trade along similar lines. Retailers such as Wal-Mart and regional grocery chains such as Dominick's have embraced category management themselves as a means to define a particular product category's strategic role within the store (in terms of its ability to generate store traffic or help provide a particular consumer image) and to address such operating issues as logistics, the role of private label products, and the tradeoffs between offering product variety and avoiding inefficient duplication.

Sources; Zachary Schiller, "The Marketing Revolution at Procter & Gamble," *Business Week,* 25 July 1988, 72–76. Laurie Freeman, "P&G Widens Power Base: Adds Category Managers," *Advertising Age,* 12 October 1987; John Byrne, "The Horizontal Corporation," *Business Week,* 20 December 1993, 76–81; As academic validation, Zenor provides a game theoretic analysis and empirical demonstration of the profit advantages of coordinating prices and other marketing activity for a firm's different products and brands through category management: Michael J. Zenor, "The Profit Benefits of Category Management," *Journal of Marketing Research* 31 (May 1994): 202–213; Gerry Khermouch, "Brands Overboard," *Brandweek,* 22 August 1994, 25–39.

organizational schemes is to improve internal coordination and efficiencies as well as external focus on retailers and consumers. Although these are laudable goals, clearly one of the challenges with these new designs is to ensure that brand equity is preserved and nurtured, and not neglected due to a lack of oversight. Branding Brief 8-6 describes General Motors's struggles to better manage the equity of its brands.

With a multiple-product, multiple-market organization, the difficulty often lies in making sure that both place and product are in balance. As one commentator noted:

> As companies grow more global, they keep running into the same basic management dilemma. . . . Is it better to be organized by product line or geography? NCR Corp., Ford Motor Co., Procter & Gamble Co., and several others have spent fortunes transforming themselves from one to the other. But taken too far, either model can spark fresh headaches. In the product model, businesses can reap efficiencies by standardizing manufacturing, introducing products around the world faster, coordinating prices better, and eliminating overlapping plants. Yet, companies typically find that tilting too far away from a geographic model slows their decision making, reduces their pricing flexibility, and can impair their ability to tailor products to the needs of specific customers.[32]

As in many marketing and branding activities, achieving the proper balance is the goal, in order to maximize the advantages and minimize the disadvantages of both approaches.

BRANDING BRIEF 8-6

General Motors's Branding Challenges

GM's U.S. market share dropped from 46 percent to 32 percent between 1980 and 1996. To combat this erosion of market share, General Motors adopted a brand management

GM has struggled to adopt the right approach to brand management for its portfolio of brands.

approach, called Brandscape, whereby each of 65 different GM car models received separate and distinct branding efforts under the direction of a different brand manager. In this brand management system, the brand manager was responsible for vehicle style and personality, advertising, pricing, promotion, and other marketing decisions. The brand management program enabled each model to target a specific consumer segment. For example, the Buick LeSabre was designed for "people seeking security, comfort, safety, and peace of mind." GM indicated that the shift to brand management would enable the company to "chase the needs of the customer" rather than "chase the competition."

The brand management program also involved establishing separate identities for each of GM's six car divisions: Buick, Cadillac, Chevrolet, Oldsmobile, Pontiac-GMC, and Saturn. Under the old corporate structure, divisions often competed against each other for the same customers. As a result, the distinction between divisions grew less obvious, particularly in the case of Buick, Oldsmobile, and Pontiac. Brand management aimed to sharpen the contrast between divisions and reduce sales cannibalization. Between 2000 and 2006, GM planned to release a new or "refreshed" product every 28 days, on average. The result, claimed the company, would be greater differentiation among brands.

Some criticized GM for adopting the brand management model, which was initially developed at packaged-goods giant Procter & Gamble. "You can't sell cars like a box of soap," said one industry expert. Another industry executive criticized the tag line for the Pontiac Bonneville by saying, "'Luxury with Attitude' sounds an awful lot like 'Tide with Bleach.'" Still, executives at GM insisted the packaged-goods model worked with cars. "There's a high degree of overlap between a packaged-goods company and General Motors," said Jeffrey Cohen, brand manager at GMC Jimmy.

The switch to brand management was not altogether uniform. The Oldsmobile line was intended as a brand management test piece. GM aimed to target younger consumers in order to reduce Oldsmobile's average buyer's age, which was 62 in 1996. The switch to brand management yielded models like the Oldsmobile Intrigue, a sleek sedan introduced in the 1997 model year and backed by a $50 million campaign. GM significantly downplayed the presence of the Oldsmobile name on the Intrigue by affixing it to the car in only one location: on the dashboard. As a result, claimed an auto industry analyst, despite the fact that "the Intrigue is one of the best cars on the road . . . no one knows where to buy it." Unable to attract younger buyers and drifting away from their traditional older customer base, sales at Oldsmobile fell toward 300,000 vehicles per year, down from over 1 million annually in the 1980s, and eventually the line was discontinued.

In the case of some other GM models, the brand management concept seemed to lack enforcement. One writer cited the Cadillac Escalade as an example of "brand management without backbone." In 1998, Cadillac introduced the Escalade, a ritzier version of the GMC Yukon Denali. Up to that point, however, GMC had been GM's luxury truck division and Cadillac had never made a truck. Robert Zarella, GM's North American president and champion of the brand management program until he was relieved of his position in 2001, admitted that the Escalade introduction was not representative of brand management, but rather about "doing something fast and making a lot of money."

The immediate results of GM's brand management program were not promising: Market share fell to 29.5 percent in 2000. One automotive-marketing executive summarized the results of the program by stating the company "made almost no progress . . . in terms of changing the perception of GM brands." Following Robert Zarella's departure, GM began to move away from the brand management concept of separate and distinct models. In 2001, both Cadillac and Chevrolet developed advertising campaigns that focused on their umbrella brands. Additionally, GM allocated a greater percentage of its $2.8 billion annual advertising budget for overall brand marketing. "The lesson is that divisional positioning has to be king," said John G. Middlebrook, GM's general manager for brand marketing and corporate advertising. This means that individual models and advertising will reinforce each division's positioning, such as "American Value" for Chevrolet and "Art and Science" for Cadillac.

Sources: John McElroy, "GM's Brand Management Might Work," Automotive Industries, 1 September 1996; Charles Child, "GM Brand Management Talk Is Cheap," *Automotive News,* 8 March 1999; David Welch, "Consumers to GM: You Talking to Me?" *Business Week,* 19 June 2000; Lawrence Ulrich, "With His Departure, General Motors' Chief Leaves Behind Brand-Management Style," *Detroit Free Press,* 14 November 2001; David Welch and Dan Beucke, "Why GM's Plan Won't Work," *Business Week*, 9 May 2005.

Managing Marketing Partners. Because the performance of a brand also depends on the actions taken by outside suppliers and marketing partners, firms must manage these relationships carefully. Increasingly, firms have been consolidating their marketing partnerships and reducing the number of their outside suppliers. This trend has been especially apparent with global advertising accounts, where a number of firms have placed most, if not all, their business with one agency. For example, Colgate-Palmolive works solely with Young & Rubicam, and American Express and IBM with Ogilvy & Mather. Factors like cost efficiencies, organizational leverage, and creative diversification affect the number of outside suppliers the firm will hire in any one area. From a branding perspective, one advantage of dealing with a single major supplier such as an ad agency is the greater consistency in understanding and treatment of a brand that can result.

Other marketing partners can also play an important role. For example, Chapter 5 described the importance of channel members and retailers in enhancing brand equity and the need for cleverly designed push programs.

Review

The brand value chain is a means to trace the value creation process for brands to better understand the financial impact of brand marketing expenditures and investments. Taking the customer's perspective of the value of a brand, the brand value chain assumes that the brand value creation process begins when the firm invests in a marketing program targeting actual or potential customers. Any marketing program investment that potentially can be attributed to brand value development falls into this category, for example, product research, development, and design; trade or intermediary support; and marketing communications.

The marketing activity associated with the program then affects the customer mind-set with respect to the brand—what customers know and feel about the brand. The customer mind-set includes everything that exists in the minds of customers with respect to a brand: thoughts, feelings, experiences, images, perceptions, beliefs, attitudes, and so forth. Consistent with the customer-based brand equity model, five key dimensions that are particularly important measures of the customer mind-set are brand awareness, brand associations, brand attitudes, brand attachment, and brand activity or experience.

The customer mind-set affects how customers react or respond in the marketplace in a variety of ways. Six key outcomes of that response are price premiums, price elasticities, market share, brand expansion, cost structure, and brand profitability. Based on all available current and forecasted information about a brand, as well as many other considerations, the financial marketplace then formulates opinions and makes various assessments that have direct financial implications for the value of the brand. Three particularly important indicators are the stock price, the price/earnings multiple, and overall market capitalization for the firm.

The model also assumes that a number of linking factors intervene between these stages. These linking factors determine the extent to which value created at one stage transfers or "multiplies" to the next stage. Thus, there are three sets of multipliers that moderate the transfer between the marketing program and the subsequent three value stages: the program multiplier, the customer multiplier, and the market multiplier.

A brand equity measurement system is defined as a set of research procedures designed to provide timely, accurate, and actionable information for marketers regarding brands so that they can make the best possible tactical decisions in the short run as well as strategic decisions in the long run. Implementing a brand equity measurement system involves two steps: designing brand tracking studies and establishing a brand equity management system.

Brand audits can be used to set the strategic direction for the brand (see Brand Focus 3.0). As a result of this strategic analysis, a marketing program can be put into place to maximize long-term brand equity. Tracking studies employing quantitative measures can then be conducted to provide marketers with current information as to how their brands are performing on the basis of a number of key dimensions identified by the brand audit. Tracking studies involve information collected from consumers on a routine basis over time and provide valuable tactical insights into the short-term effectiveness of marketing programs and activities. Whereas brand audits measure "where the brand has been," tracking studies measure "where the brand is now" and whether marketing programs are having their intended effects.

Three major steps must occur as part of a brand equity management system. First, the company view of brand equity should be formalized into a document, the brand equity charter. This document serves a number of purposes: It chronicles the company's general philosophy with respect to brand equity; summarizes the activity and outcomes related to brand audits, brand tracking, and so forth; outlines guidelines for brand strategies and tactics; and documents proper treatment of the brand. The charter should be updated annually to identify new opportunities and risks and to fully reflect information gathered by the brand inventory and brand exploratory as part of any brand audits. Second, the results of the tracking surveys and other relevant outcome measures should be assembled into a brand equity report that is distributed to management on a regular basis (monthly, quarterly, or annually). The brand equity report should provide descriptive information as to *what* is happening to a brand as well as diagnostic information as to *why* it is happening. Finally, senior management must be assigned to oversee how brand equity is treated within the organization. The people in that position would be responsible for overseeing the implementation of the brand equity charter and brand equity reports to make sure that, as much as possible, product and marketing actions across divisions and geographic boundaries are performed in a way that reflects the spirit of the charter and the substance of the report so as to maximize the long-term equity of the brand.

An alternative—albeit complementary—view of how firms should incorporate the brand equity concept into their marketing research and planning is described in Brand Focus 8.0, which examines how one of the world's best ad agencies, Ogilvy & Mather, incorporates branding issues in the services they provide their clients.

Discussion Questions

1. Pick a brand. Try to do an informal brand value chain analysis. Can you trace how the brand value is created and transferred? What are the roles of the multipliers?
2. Update and supplement the brand value chain analysis for Starbucks presented in this chapter. What does the analysis suggest about the brand's fortunes in recent years?
3. A few years ago, Disney entered into a long-term agreement with McDonald's that included, among other things, joint promotions. From Disney's perspective and what you know about the two brands, was this the right decision? Is there any downside? Would you have wanted to conduct any research to inform the decision? What kind?
4. Consider the McDonald's tracking survey presented in Branding Brief 8.2. What might you do differently? What questions would you change or drop? What questions might you add? How might this tracking survey differ from those used for other products?
5. Can you develop a tracking survey for the Mayo Clinic? How might it differ from the McDonald's tracking survey?

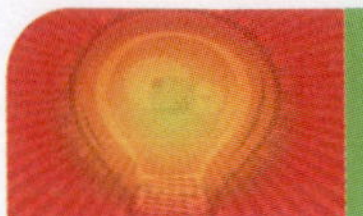

BRAND FOCUS 8.0

Managing Brands at Ogilvy & Mather

Ogilvy & Mather (O&M), one of the world's largest marketing communications networks, is in the forefront of bringing branding issues and perspectives to the development of advertising and other communications. O&M manages its clients' brands by a three-step process called 360 Degree Brand Stewardship ®. The steps are (1) discovery, (2) strategy and planning, and (3) execution, each of which asks a number of key questions.

Phase 01: Discovery

What is the essence of the brand? Ogilvy first attempts to get to the core of the brand via a brand audit to assess what consumers think and feel about it. During this process, the goal is to have consumers tell stories and share personal histories about their experiences with the brand. Ogilvy emphasizes brand-probing questions like, "How does using the brand make you feel about yourself?", "What's the first thing that comes to mind when you think of this brand?", "What unique contribution does the brand make to your life?", and "What personal recollections does the brand bring to mind?"

The rich personal accounts that emerge help the agency put into words the actual role of a brand in the life of a user—what it calls the BrandPrint™—which is the starting point for all further brand-building activities.

What is the brand voice and personality? With the BrandPrint in hand, Ogilvy can make sure the brand speaks and acts consistently—how the brand both "talks and walks" in all communications.

What is the product behind the brand and who's buying it? Ogilvy also learns about the product or service itself by asking questions such as: What does the brand do? What does it look like? What are its other physical characteristics? What are its ingredients or component parts? What is its history? Is the brand sensitive to price changes? Ogilvy also collects information on consumers themselves. Who's using the product? What do they watch on TV? What do they read? What do they do for a living? What separates heavy users from light ones? Who are our loyalists and why? Are there distinct communities of users united by specific affinities other than usage?

What is the company behind the brand? Ogilvy also strives to fully know the company behind the brand (history, values, milestones, corporate infrastructure) by interviewing key executives and employees and studying the company closely.

What is the environment in which the brand operates? Ogilvy recognizes that they must fully understand the market and all the different dimensions in which a brand competes.

What is the brand vision? Ogilvy believes great brands have a road map for the future, a galvanizing principle or course of action that everyone can get behind for the brand's growth and prosperity. For example, Ogilvy maintains that IBM's vision of the technological future — e-business — has provided clear direction and inspiration for all who work for the brand.

Phase 02: Strategy and Planning

With discovery complete, Ogilvy assesses what the brand needs to do from a strategic and tactical standpoint. Where a brand stands in its life cycle—the type of challenges and opportunities facing it—determines what type of creative is done, what audiences are spoken to, which media vehicles are chosen.

Who are the brand's audiences? And what is their understanding of the brand? Since a brand has many audiences or constituents that shape its image, Ogilvy studies them and how well they understand the brand; internal audiences, for example, need to know clearly what the brand is about if they are to deliver products and services that enhance the brand, rather than detract from it; industry analysts and trade reporters need to know where the brand is and where it is going if they are to write about it accurately; and dealers and distributors need to treat customers in a way that is true to the brand so that the actual sale and post-sale experiences deliver on the brand's promise. Audience assessment is often essential to the communication recommendations Ogilvy makes to its clients as it often uncovers an unexpected weak spot that requires special programs and/or funding to correct.

Where does the brand touch consumers? At this point, Ogilvy seeks to uncover all consumer touch points and evaluate how much impact each has in molding images and perceptions of the brand—the who, what, when, where, and how of the brand experience.

Which of these touch points are "moments of truth?" Ogilvy believes that some consumer touch points with the brand are more powerful than others and provide make it or break it moments for the brand or "moments of truth." These moments of truth vary by brand, category, and geography. Ogilvy's conviction is that at these moments of truth, consistency of brand promise and brand behavior is absolutely essential, and energies must be focused to make sure that the brand delights, not disappoints consumers.

Phase 03: Execution

Turning insight and strategy into work is where the "rubber meets the road" for Ogilvy. Although they feel that there is no blueprint for creativity, they do use several basic questions that drive the process and need to be answered.

What is the idea? Unless 360 Degree Branding® efforts are based on a "big idea," Ogilvy claims that they will "pass like a ship in the night." Besides getting to the core of the consumer/brand relationship, Ogilvy feels there is nothing more important than coming up with the big brand idea that both anchors and drives brand-building campaigns. Ogilvy notes that it's difficult to predict where the big idea will come from. Any member of the brand team—creative, account, planning, media, etc.—can spark the thought that drives a campaign.

How does the idea inform all creative efforts? All communications Ogilvy recommends (whether a commercial, a Web site, a postcard, or a telemarketing script) must reflect and reinforce the big idea, although that does not mean that all communications must look exactly alike. Ogilvy asserts that 360 Degree communications are linked by the brand essence, brand voice, the idea, and how they work together to affect attitudes and behaviors.

Where is this idea going to play out? In an ideal world, the brand idea would play out at relevant brand touch points, particularly at and around moments of truth (focusing on whom we need to talk to, in what manner, and what vehicle is most relevant to their needs and most likely to get their attention and drive action). In reality, Ogilvy recognizes that it's a matter of budget and objectives and timing. Sometimes the company uses all of the communication and experiential vehicles at its disposal to help a brand; other times, it uses a few or just one.

How is success measured? Success in the long term is measured by the growth and vitality of the brand. In the short term, however, there are many markers of success for Ogilvy, depending upon the objectives of the effort. Success metrics can be one or more of the following: market share, awareness and attitude levels, depth of brand bonding, response rates, click-through rates, pages viewed, return on marketing investment, customer lifetime value, and others.

Ogilvy & Mather, internal handbook, "360 Degree Brand Stewardship®". 2002 Ogilvy & Mather Worldwide.Used with permission.

Notes

1. Frederick E. Webster, Jr., Alan J. Malter, and Shankar Ganesan, "Can Marketing Regain Its Seat at the Table?" Marketing Science Institute Report No. 03–113, Cambridge, MA, 2003. See also Frederick E. Webster Jr., Alan J. Malter, and Shankar Ganesan, "The Decline and Dispersion of Marketing Competence," *MIT Sloan Management Review* 46, no. 4 (Summer 2005): 35–43.
2. See Don E. Schultz and Heidi F. Schultz, "Measuring Brand Value," in *Kellogg on Branding,* eds. Alice M. Tybout and Timothy Calkins (Hoboken, NJ: John Wiley & Sons, 2005).
3. William A. Cook and Vijay S. Talluri, "How the Pursuit of ROMI is Changing Marketing Management," *Journal of Advertising Research* 44, no. 3 (January 2004): 244–254.
4. Patrick LaPointe, *Marketing by the Dashboard Light—How to Get More Insight, Foresight, and Accountability from Your Marketing Investment* (New York: Association of National Advertisers, 2005).
5. Jonathan Knowles, "In Search of a Reliable Measure of Brand Equity," *MarketingNPV* 2, no. 3 (July 2005).
6. Kevin Lane Keller and Don Lehmann, "How Do Brands Create Value?" *Marketing Management* (May/June 2003): 26–31. See also R. K. Srivastava, T. A. Shervani, and L. Fahey, "Market-Based Assets and Shareholder Value," *Journal of Marketing* 62, no. 1 (1998): 2–18; and M. J. Epstein and R. A. Westbrook, "Linking Actions to Profits in Strategic Decision Making," *MIT Sloan Management Review* (Spring 2001): 39–49. In terms of related empirical insights, see Manoj K. Agrawal and Vithala Rao, "An Empirical Comparison of Consumer-Based Measures of Brand Equity," *Marketing Letters* 7, no. 3 (1996): 237–247; and Walfried Lassar, Banwari Mittal, and Arun Sharma, "Measuring Customer-Based Brand Equity," *Journal of Consumer Marketing* 12, no. 4 (1995): 11–19.
7. Thomas J. Madden, Frank Fehle, and Susan Fournier, "Brands Matter: An Empirical Demonstration of the Creation of Shareholder Value Through Branding" *Journal of the Academy of Marketing Science,* 2006.
8. Adrienne W. Fawcett, "The Marketing 100: Starbucks: Scott Bedbury," *Advertising Age,* 30 June 1997, S18.
9. Louise Kramer, "Brand Man Bedbury Departing Starbucks," *Advertising Age,* 18 May 1998, 1.
10. Alice Z. Cuneo, "Starbucks' Word-of-Mouth Wonder," *Advertising Age,* 7 March 1994.
11. Kim Murphy, "More Than Coffee: A Way of Life," *Los Angeles Times Magazine,* 22 September 1996, 8.

12. Seana Browder, "Starbucks Does Not Live by Coffee Alone," *Business Week,* 5 August 1996, 76.
13. LaPointe, *Marketing by the Dashboard Light.*
14. John B. Frey, "Measuring Corporate Reputation and Its Value," paper presented at the Marketing Science Conference at Duke University, 17 March 1989.
15. Nigel Hollis, personal correspondence, 2005
16. Alastair Gordon, "Managing by Metrics: Practical Issues & Guidelines," talk at MSI Asian Marketing Conference, July 2005, Singapore.
17. Na Woon Bong, Roger Marshall, and Kevin Lane Keller, "Measuring Brand Power: Validating a Model for Optimizing Brand Equity," *Journal of Product and Brand Management* 8, no. 3 (1999): 170–184.
18. Joel Rubinson and Markus Pfeiffer, "Brand Performance Indicators as a Force for Brand Equity Management," *Journal of Advertising Research* (June 2005): 187–197.
19. Joel Rubinson, "Brand Strength Means More Than Market Share," paper presented at the ARF Fourth Annual Advertising and Promotion Workshop, New York, 1992.
20. Tim Ambler, *Marketing and the Bottom Line,* 2nd ed. (London: FT Prentice Hall, 2004).
21. Rob Malcolm, "Getting the Right Measure for Drinks," paper presented at Marketing Science Institute Conference, *Does Marketing Measure Up? Performance Metrics: Practices and Impacts,* 21–22 June 2004, London, United Kingdom.
22. Gail McGovern and John Quelch, "Sarbox Still Putting the Squeeze on Marketing," *Advertising Age,* 19 September 2005, 28.
23. Tim Ambler and Bruce Clark, "What Will Matter Most to Marketers Three Years from Now?" paper presented at Marketing Science Institute Conference, *Does Marketing Measure Up? Performance Metrics: Practices and Impacts,* 21–22 June 2004, London, United Kingdom. See also Bruce H. Clark and Tim Ambler, "Marketing Performance Measurement: Evolution of Research and Practice," *International Journal of Business Performance Management* 3, nos. 2/3/4 (2001): 231–244; and Bruce H. Clark, Andrew Abela, and Tim Ambler, "Organizational Motivation, Opportunity and Ability to Measure Marketing Performance," *Journal of Strategic Marketing* 13, no. 4 (December 2005): 241–259.
24. Scott Bedbury, *A New Brand World* (New York: Viking Press, 2002).
25. Betsy Spethman, "Companies Post Equity Gatekeepers," *Brandweek,* 2 May 1994, 5.
26. David Harkleroad, private correspondence.
27. Bedbury, *A New Brand World.*
28. "Stock Tips: The Growing Trend of Category Management," *Daily News,* 22 January 2003 (www.nacsonline.com).
29. www.cannondaleassoc.com/.
30. J. M. Hulbert, P. Berthon, and L. F. Pitt, "Brand Management Prognostications," *Sloan Management Review* (Winter 1998): 53–65.
31. "The Death of the Brand Manager," *The Economist,* 9 April 1994, 67–68.
32. Joann S. Lubin, "Place versus Product: It's Tough to Choose a Management Model," *Wall Street Journal.*

MEASURING SOURCES OF BRAND EQUITY

CAPTURING CUSTOMER MIND-SET

Preview

Understanding the current and desired brand knowledge structures of consumers is vital to effectively building and managing brand equity. As Gardner and Levy note in a classic marketing article:

> The image of a product associated with the brand may be clear-cut or relatively vague; it may be varied or simple; it may be intense or innocuous. Sometimes the notions people have about a brand do not seem very sensible or relevant to those who know what the product is "really" like. But they all contribute to the customer's deciding whether or not the brand is "for me." These sets of ideas, feelings, and attitudes that consumers have about brands are crucial to them in picking and sticking to ones that seem most appropriate.[1]

Ideally, marketers would be able to construct detailed "mental maps" of consumers to understand exactly what exists in their minds—all their thoughts, feelings, perceptions, images, beliefs, and attitudes toward different brands. These mental blueprints would then provide managers with strategic and tactical guidance to help them make brand decisions. Unfortunately, these brand knowledge structures are not easily measured because they reside only in consumers' minds.

Nevertheless, effective brand management requires us to thoroughly understand the consumer. Often a simple insight into how consumers think of or use products and the particular brands in a category can help create a profitable change in the marketing program. That's why many large companies conduct exhaustive research studies (or brand audits, as described in Chapter 3) to learn as much as possible about consumers. A number of detailed, sophisticated research techniques and methods now exist to help marketers better understand consumer knowledge structures. Branding Brief 9-1 describes the lengths to which marketers have gone in the past to learn about consumers. This chapter highlights some of the important considerations critical to the measurement of brand equity.[2] Figure 9-1 outlines some general considerations in understanding consumer behavior.

According to the brand value chain, sources of brand equity arise from the customer mind-set. In general, measuring sources of brand equity requires that the brand manager fully understand how customers shop for and use products and services and, most important, what customers know, think, and feel about various brands. In particular, measuring sources of customer-based brand equity requires us to measure various aspects of brand awareness and brand image that can lead to the differential customer response making up brand equity. Consumers may have a holistic view of brands that is difficult to divide into component parts. But many times we can, in fact, isolate perceptions and assess them in greater detail. The remainder of this chapter describes qualitative and quantitative approaches to identifying potential sources of brand equity, that is, capturing the customer mind-set.

Qualitative Research Techniques

As Chapter 3 noted, a number of different types of associations can become linked to a brand. The Science of Branding 9-1 describes some of the basic ideas behind and applications of the associative network model of memory, which, as Chapter 2 noted, is a useful theoretical means of representing these associations.

There are also many different ways to uncover the types of associations linked to the brand and their corresponding strength, favorability, and uniqueness. ***Qualitative research techniques*** often identify possible brand associations and sources of brand equity. Qualitative research techniques are relatively unstructured measurement approaches that

Who buys our product or service?
Who makes the decision to buy the product?
Who influences the decision to buy the product?
How is the purchase decision made? Who assumes what role?
What does the customer buy? What needs must be satisfied?
Why do customers buy a particular brand?
Where do they go or look to buy the product or service?
When do they buy? Any seasonality factors?
What are customers' attitudes toward our product?
What social factors might influence the purchase decision?
Does the customers' lifestyle influence their decisions?
How is our product perceived by customers?
How do demographic factors influence the purchase decision?

Source: Based on a list from George Belch and Michael Belch, *Advertising and Communication Management*, 3rd ed. (Homewood, IL: Irwin, 1995).

FIGURE 9-1

Understanding Consumer Behavior

permit a range of possible consumer responses. Because of the freedom afforded both researchers in their probes and consumers in their responses, qualitative research can often be a useful first step in exploring consumer brand and product perceptions.

Qualitative research has a long history in marketing. Ernest Dichter, one of the early pioneers in consumer psychoanalytic research, first applied these research principles in a study for Plymouth automobiles in the 1930s.[3] His research revealed the important—but previously overlooked—role that women played in the automobile purchase decision. Based on his consumer analysis, Plymouth adopted a new print ad strategy that highlighted a young couple gazing admiringly at a Plymouth automobile under the headline "Imagine Us in a Car Like That." Dichter's subsequent work had an important impact on a number of different ad campaigns.[4]

Some of Dichter's assertions were fairly controversial. Based on his research, Dichter argued that women used Ivory soap to wash away their sins before a date. He also equated convertibles with mistresses and suggested "Putting a Tiger in the Tank" for Exxon, resulting in a long-running and successful ad campaign.

This section next reviews a number of qualitative research techniques for identifying sources of brand equity such as brand awareness, brand attitudes, and brand attachment. These techniques also can identify outcomes of brand equity such as price elasticities and brand choice and preference. Branding Brief 9-2 examines some practical issues in conducting focus groups.

Free Association

The simplest and often the most powerful way to profile brand associations is free association tasks, in which subjects are asked what comes to mind when they think of the brand, without any more specific probe or cue than perhaps the associated product category ("What does the Rolex name mean to you?" or "Tell me what comes to mind when you think of Rolex watches."). Marketers can use the resulting associations to form a rough mental map for the brand (see Figure 9-2 for a sample mental map for State Farm insurance).

Marketers use free association tasks mainly to identify the range of possible brand associations in consumers' minds, but free association may also provide some rough indication of the relative strength, favorability, and uniqueness of brand associations.[5] Coding free association responses in terms of the order of elicitation—early or late in the sequence—at least gives us a rough measure of their strength.[6] For example, if many

BRANDING BRIEF 9-1

Digging Beneath the Surface to Understand Consumer Behavior

Most consumer research relies on surveys to obtain consumers' reported beliefs, attitudes, and behavior. However, useful marketing insights sometimes emerge from unobtrusively observing consumer behavior rather than talking to consumers. In many instances, consumer behavior that we observe differs from the behavior that consumers report in surveys. For example, Hoover became suspicious when people claimed in surveys that they vacuumed their houses for an hour each week. To check, the company installed timers in certain models and exchanged them for the same models in consumers' homes. The timers showed that people actually spent only a little over *half* an hour vacuuming each week. One researcher analyzed household trash to determine the types and quantities of food people consumed, finding that people really don't have a very good idea of how much and what types of food they eat and tend to overestimate. Similarly, much research has shown that people report they eat healthier food than would appear to be case if you opened their cabinets!

DuPont commissioned marketing studies to uncover personal pillow behavior for its Dacron Polyester unit, which supplies filling to pillow makers and sells its own Comforel brand. One challenge: People don't give up their old pillows. Thirty-seven percent of one sample described their relationship with their pillow as like "an old married couple," and an additional 13 percent characterized their pillow like a "childhood friend." The researchers found that people fell into distinct groups in terms of pillow behavior: stackers (23 percent),

consumers mention "fast and convenient" as one of their first associations when given "McDonald's restaurants" as a probe, then the association is probably a relatively strong one and likely able to affect consumer decisions. Associations later in the list may be weaker and thus more likely to be overlooked during consumer decision making. Comparing associations with those elicited for competitive brands can also tell us about their relative uniqueness. Finally, we can discern even favorability, to some extent, on the basis of how consumers phrase their associations.

Answers to free-association questions help marketers clarify the range of possible associations and assemble a brand profile.[7] To better understand the favorability of associations, we can ask consumers follow-up questions about the favorability of associations they listed or, more generally, what they like best about the brand. Similarly, we can ask them follow-up questions about the uniqueness of associations they listed or, more generally, about what they find unique about the brand. Useful questions include the following:

1. What do you like best about the brand? What are its positive aspects?
2. What do you dislike? What are its disadvantages?
3. What do you find unique about the brand? How is it different from other brands? In what ways is it the same?

Archetype research is one technique for eliciting deeply held consumer attitudes and feelings. According to medical anthropologist G. C. Rapaille, consumers often make purchase decisions based on factors of which they are only subconsciously aware.

plumpers (20 percent), rollers or folders (16 percent), cuddlers (16 percent), and smashers, who pound their pillows into a more comfy shape (10 percent). Women were more likely to plump while men were more likely to fold. The prevalence of stackers led the company to sell more pillows packaged as pairs, as well as to market different levels of softness or firmness.

Much of this type of research has its roots in *ethnography,* the anthropological term for the study of cultures in their natural surroundings. The intent behind these in-depth, observational studies is for consumers to drop their guard and provide a more realistic portrayal of whom they are rather than whom they would like to be. On the basis of ethnographic research that uncovered consumers' true feelings, ad campaigns have been created for a Swiss chocolate maker with the theme "The True Confessions of a Chocaholic" (because chocolate lovers often hid stashes all though the house), for Tampax tampons with the theme "More Women Trust Their Bodies to Tampax" (because teen users wanted the freedom to wear body-conscious clothes), and for Crisco shortening with the theme "Recipe for Success" (because people often baked pies and cookies in a celebratory fashion).

Sources: Jennifer Chang Coupland, "Invisible Brands: An Ethnography of Households and the Brands in Their Kitchen Pantries," *Journal of Consumer Research* 32 (June 2005): 106–118; John Koten, "You Aren't Paranoid If You Feel Someone Eyes You Constantly," *Wall Street Journal,* 2 March 1985; Susan Warren, "Pillow Talk: Stackers Outnumber Plumpers; Don't Mention Drool," *Wall Street Journal,* 8 January 1998, B1.

Conventional market research typically does not uncover these motivations, so Rapaille employs the archetype research technique to find them.[8]

Rapaille believes that children experience a significant initial exposure to an element of their world called the "imprinting moment." The pattern that emerges when we generalize these imprinting moments for the entire population is the ***archetype,*** a fundamental psychological association, shared by the members of the culture, with a given cultural object. Different cultures have dramatically different archetypes for the same objects. In France, the archetype for cheese is "alive" because age is its most important trait. By contrast, the American archetype for cheese is "dead"; it is wrapped in plastic ("a body-bag"), put in the refrigerator ("a morgue"), and pasteurized ("scientifically dead").

Rapaille uses relaxation exercises and visualization with consumers to find the imprinting moments appropriate to the product he is researching. For example, at a focus group he will dim the lights, play soothing music, and coax the subjects into a meditative state. He will then elicit stories about the product from the subjects, and analyze these stories to illuminate the archetype.

These simple, direct measures can be extremely valuable for determining core aspects of a brand image. To elicit more structure and guidance, ask consumers further follow-up questions about what the brand means to them in terms of "who, what, when, where, why, and how":

1. Who uses the brand? What kind of person?
2. When and where do they use the brand? What types of situations?
3. Why do people use the brand? What do they get out of using it?
4. How do they use the brand? What do they use it for?

THE SCIENCE OF BRANDING 9-1

Understanding Consumer Memory

The associative network memory model views memory as a network of nodes and connecting links. According to this model, recall or retrieval of information occurs through a concept called ***spreading activation***. At any point in time, an information node may be a source of activation because it is either presented with external information (when a person reads or hears a word or phrase) or it retrieves internal information currently being processed (when a person thinks about some concept). A particular node in memory is activated, and activation spreads from that node to other nodes connected to it in memory. When the activation of a particular node exceeds a threshold level, the person recalls the contents of that node. The spread of activation depends on the number and strength of the links connected to the activated node: Concepts whose linkages have the greatest strength will receive the most activation.

As a result of spreading activation, the strength and organization of brand associations are important in determining what the person recalls about the brand that can influence his or her response and brand-related decisions. Research in psychology provides useful insights into some factors affecting association strength. In general, the strength of an association depends on how consumers initially process information as it enters memory and where it is actually located as a result. Psychologists refer to these two processes as memory ***encoding*** and ***storage***. We can characterize encoding processes according to the amount, or *quantity,* of processing the information receives (how much a person thinks about the information) and the nature, or *quality,* of the processing (the manner in which the person thinks about the information). The quantity and quality of processing are both important determinants of the strength of an association. Research has shown that a number of factors affect the quantity and quality of encoding processes, the accessibility of information from memory, and the ability of consumers to recall or retrieve brand associations. We'll briefly highlight some of those factors here.

Encoding Brand Associations

In terms of qualitative considerations, the more attention a person places on the meaning of information during encoding, the stronger the resulting associations in memory will be. Thus, when a consumer actively thinks about and elaborates on the significance of product or service information, stronger associations are created in memory. Another key determinant of the strength of a newly formed association is the content, organization, and strength of existing brand associations. All else being equal, it will be easier for consumers to create an association to new information when extensive, relevant knowledge structures already exist in memory. One reason that personal experiences create such strong brand associations is that information about the product is likely to be related to existing knowledge.

The ease with which we integrate new information into established knowledge structures clearly depends on the nature of that information, such as its inherent simplicity, vividness, and concreteness.

In terms of quantitative considerations, repeated exposure to information provides greater opportunity for processing and thus the potential for stronger associations. Recent advertising research in a field setting, however, suggests that high levels of repetition for an uninvolving, unpersuasive ad are unlikely to have as much sales impact as lower levels of repetition for an involving, persuasive ad.

Recall of Brand Associations

According to the associative network memory model, the strength of a brand association increases both the likelihood that that information will be accessible and the ease with which it can be recalled by spreading activation. Accessible, recalled information is important because it can create the differential response that makes up customer-based brand equity. Consumers' successful recall of brand information does not depend only on the initial associative strength of that information in memory, however, but also on other considerations. Three are particularly important.

First, the presence of *other* product information in memory can produce interference effects and may cause the target information to be either overlooked or mistaken for this other information. Second, the time between exposure and encoding affects the strength of a new association: The longer the time delay, the weaker the association. However, cognitive psychologists believe that memory is extremely durable, so that once we store information in memory, its strength of association decays very slowly. Third, the number and type of external retrieval cues affect memory accessibility. That is, information may be available in memory, but consumers may not be able to access it without the proper retrieval cues or reminders. Thus, the particular associations for a brand that are salient and come to mind depend on the context in which the brand is considered. The more cues linked to a piece of information, however, the greater the likelihood that we can recall the information.

Sources: John R. Anderson, *The Architecture of Cognition* (Cambridge, MA: Harvard University Press, 1983); John G. Lynch, Jr. and Thomas K. Srull, "Memory and Attentional Factors in Consumer Choice: Concepts and Research Methods," *Journal of Consumer Research* 9 (June 1982): 18–36; Joseph W. Alba, J. Wesley Hutchinson, and John G. Lynch Jr., "Memory and Decision Making," in *Handbook of Consumer Theory and Research,* eds. Harold H. Kassarjian and Thomas S. Robertson (Englewood Cliffs, NJ: Prentice Hall, 1992), 1–49; Fergus I. M. Craik and Robert S. Lockhart, "Levels of Processing: A Framework for Memory Research," *Journal of Verbal Learning and Verbal Behavior* 11 (1972): 671–684; Fergus I. M. Craik and Endel Tulving, "Depth of Processing and the Retention of Words in Episodic Memory," *Journal of Experimental Psychology* 104, no. 3 (1975): 268–294; Robert S. Lockhart, Fergus I. M. Craik, and Larry Jacoby, "Depth of Processing, Recognition, and Recall," in *Recall and Recognition,* ed. John Brown (New York: John Wiley & Sons, 1976); Magid Abraham and Leonard Lodish, *Advertising Works: A Study of Advertising Effectiveness and the Resulting Strategies and Tactical Implications* (Chicago: Information Resources Inc., 1989); Elizabeth F. Loftus and Gregory R. Loftus, "On the Permanence of Stored Information in the Human Brain," *American Psychologist* 35 (May 1980): 409–420.

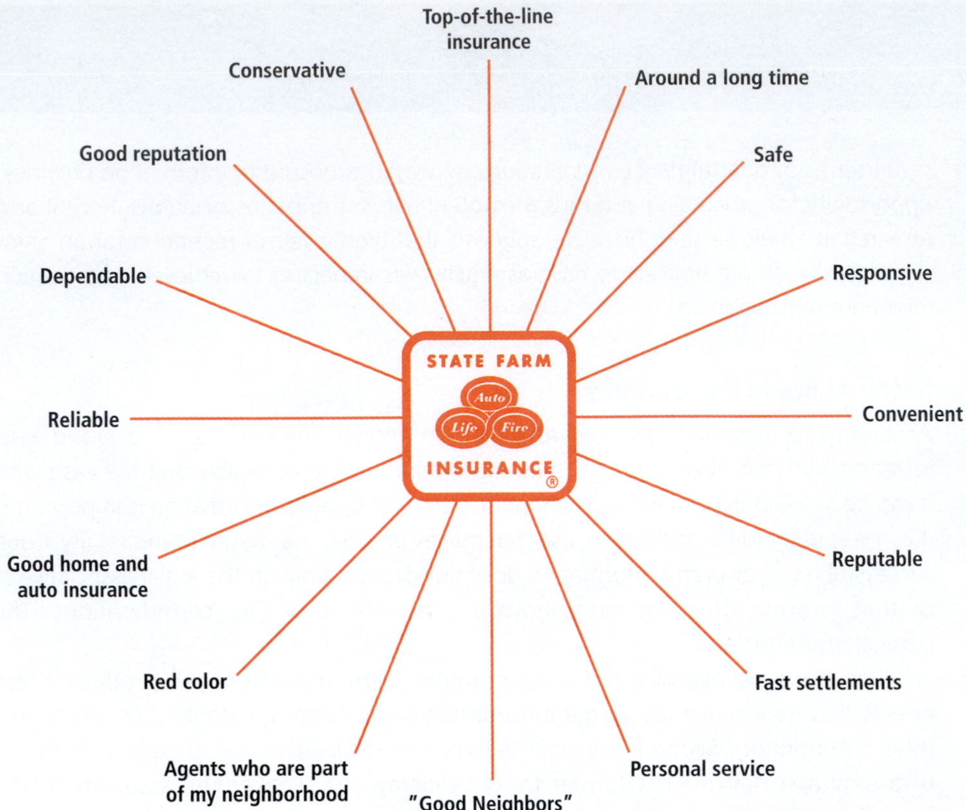

FIGURE 9-2

Sample State Farm Mental Map

Source: Used with permission of State Farm Insurance.

Guidelines. The two main issues to consider in conducting free association tasks are what types of probes to give to subjects, and how to code and interpret the resulting data. In order not to bias results, it is best to move from general considerations to more specific considerations, as we illustrated earlier. Thus, ask consumers first what they think of the brand as a whole without reference to any particular category, followed by specific questions about particular products and aspects of the brand image.

Consumers' responses to open-ended probes can be either oral or written. The advantage of oral responses is that subjects may be less deliberate and more spontaneous in their reporting. Figure 9-3 lists one researcher's broad set of guidelines for eliciting brand associations from consumers.

In terms of coding the data, divide the protocols each consumer provides into phrases and aggregate them across consumers in categories. Because of their more focused nature, responses to specific probes and follow-up questions are naturally easier to code.

Projective Techniques

For marketers to succceed in uncovering the sources of brand equity, they must profile consumers' brand knowledge structures as accurately and completely as possible. Unfortunately, under certain situations, consumers may feel that it would be socially unacceptable or undesirable to express their true feelings—especially to an interviewer whom they don't even know! As a result, they may find it easier to fall back on stereotypical, pat answers that they believe would be acceptable or perhaps even expected by the interviewer.

Consumers may be particularly unwilling or unable to reveal their true feelings when marketers ask about brands characterized by a preponderance of imagery associations.

1. Include at least one visual technique (e.g., moodboard technique of selecting pictures from magazines or newspapers).
2. Include at least one object-projective technique (e.g., describing brand as a car, animal, fabric, vegetable, celebrity, etc.).
3. Probe for secondary associations (e.g., use primary associations as stimulus words for subsequent probing, such as "What do you associate with quality?").
4. Probe for relevant situations in which individuals have experienced the brand or drawn on knowledge about the brand.
5. Address sensory associations directly (e.g., evoke product-related associations of appearance, sound, taste, smell, or feel).
6. Use real stimuli when practically possible (e.g., let consumers sample products or be exposed to a broad set of brand elements).
7. Use established scales for emotional and personality associations.
8. Instruct respondents to take their time and create acceptance for pauses.
9. Assure confidential treatment of responses.
10. Use person-projective techniques (e.g., to mitigate censoring effects, have respondents report associations on behalf of some person or figure belonging to the same group as the respondent).
11. Validate minority associations on a subset of the majority (ensure that responses from verbal respondents are also valid for less verbal respondents by follow-up interview).
12. Criteria of salience and frequency should not be used uncritically (recognize that some words or phrases are easier to report and come to mind more quickly and that this may not always reflect the strength of brand associations).
13. Use a follow-up survey or other methods to determine relationships between strength, favorability, and uniqueness of associations.
14. Elicit associations from different types of customers and from the advertising people (e.g., heavy users, average users, light users, and nonusers).
15. Divide the sample into two and include both users and nonusers (i.e., avoid respondent fatigue and potential "halo" effects).
16. Start with thorough instructions and visual techniques (verbalizations may disrupt visualizations).
17. Adapt to individual differences in response styles and response attitudes (i.e., make sure that the measures fit the sample appropriately).

Source: Magne J. Supphellen, "Understanding Core Brand Equity: Guidelines for In-Depth Elicitation of Brand Associations," *International Journal of Market Research* 42, no. 3 (2001): 319–337. Used with permission of International Journal of Market Research.

FIGURE 9-3

Tapping into Consumers: Free Association and Projective Techniques

For example, it may be difficult for consumers to admit that a certain brand name product has prestige and enhances their self-image. They may instead refer to some particular product feature as the reason they like or dislike the brand. Or they may simply find it difficult to identify and express their true feelings when asked directly, *even if they attempt to do so.* For either of these reasons, it might be impossible to obtain an accurate portrayal of brand knowledge structures without some rather unconventional research methods.

BRANDING BRIEF 9-2

Focus Group Guidelines

When conducting qualitative research, marketers may collect consumer responses either in small groups called focus groups or individually, depending on the depth and nature of the task. ***Focus groups*** are a data collection tool that gathers the opinions of 6 to 10 people who are carefully selected based on certain demographic, psychographic, or other considerations and brought together to freely discuss various topics of interest at length. A professional research moderator provides questions and probes based on a discussion guide or agenda prepared by the responsible marketing managers to ensure that the right material gets covered. However, moderators lead the discussion at times, to track down some potentially useful insight as they attempt to discern the real motivations of consumers and why they are saying and doing certain things. The sessions are typically taped in some fashion, and marketing managers often remain behind one-way mirrors in the room.

Many useful insights can emerge from thoughtfully run focus groups, but, like any research technique, they can be abused if not conducted carefully. The key for marketers is to *listen.* Consumer responses are subject to interpretation, so marketers should eliminate their own personal biases in assessing these responses as much as possible. There are also questions about the validity of focus groups, especially in today's marketing environment. Some researchers believe that consumers have been so bombarded with ads that they unconsciously (or perhaps cynically) parrot what they have already heard rather than what they really think. There is also always a concern that participants are just trying to maintain their self-image and public persona or have a need to identify with the other members of the group. Participants may not be willing to admit in public—or may not even recognize—their behavior patterns and motivations. For all these reasons, participants must feel as relaxed and at ease as possible and feel a strong obligation to speak the truth.

Projective techniques are diagnostic tools to uncover the true opinions and feelings of consumers when they are unwilling or otherwise unable to express themselves on these matters. Marketers present consumers with an incomplete stimulus and ask them to complete it, or they give consumers an ambiguous stimulus and ask them to make sense of it. The idea is that in the process consumers will reveal some of their true beliefs and feelings. Thus, projective techniques can be especially useful when deeply rooted personal motivations or personally or socially sensitive subjects are at issue.

In psychology, the most famous example of a projective technique is the ***Rorschach test,*** in which experimenters present ink blots to subjects and ask them what the ink blots remind them of. In responding, subjects may reveal certain facets of their own, perhaps subconscious, personality. Projective techniques have a long history in marketing, beginning with the motivation research of the late 1940s and 1950s.[9] A classic example is an experiment exploring hidden feelings toward instant coffee conducted by Mason Haire in the late 1940s, summarized in Branding Brief 9-3.[10] Although projective techniques don't always yield results as powerful as in that example, they often provide useful insights that help to assemble us a more complete picture of consumers and their relationships with brands. Many kinds of projective techniques are possible. We'll highlight a few here.[11]

Researchers at one ad agency knew they had a problem when a fight broke out between participants at one of their sessions. As one executive noted, "We wondered why people always seemed grumpy and negative—people were resistant to any idea we showed them." The problem was the room itself: cramped, stifling, forbidding. "It was a cross between a hospital room and a police interrogation." To fix the problem, the agency employed the ancient Chinese practice of feng shui.

There is always the "loudmouth" problem as well—when one highly opinionated person drowns out the rest of the group. Moreover, it can be expensive to recruit qualified subjects ($3,000 to $5,000 per group). And, even when marketers use multiple focus groups, it can be difficult to generalize the results to a broader population. For example, within the United States, focus group findings often vary from region to region. One New York firm specializing in focus group research claimed that the best city in which to conduct focus groups was Minneapolis, because one could get a fairly well-educated sample of people who were honest and forthcoming about their opinions. The firm maintained, however, that other cities could be more useful for special purposes; for example, focus group participants in Houston provided valuable information on underarm deodorants because they were used to having to contend with the relentless heat and humidity of that city. Many marketers interpret focus groups in New York and other Northeastern cities carefully because the people in this area tend to be highly critical and generally do not report that they like much.

Sources: Sarah Stiansen, "How Focus Groups Can Go Astray," *Adweek,* 5 December 1988, FK 4–6; Jeffrey Kasner, "Fistfights and Feng Shui," *Boston Globe,* 21 July 2001, C1–C2; Leslie Kaufman, "Enough Talk," *Newsweek,* 18 August 1997, 48–49.

Completion and Interpretation Tasks. Classic projective techniques use incomplete or ambiguous stimuli to elicit consumer thoughts and feelings. One approach is "bubble exercises" which depict different people buying or using certain products or services. Empty bubbles, as in cartoons, are placed in the scenes to represent the thoughts, words, or actions of one or more of the participants. Marketers then ask consumers to "fill in the bubble" by indicating what they believe is happening or being said in the scene. The stories and conversations told through bubble exercises and picture interpretations can be especially useful for assessing user and usage imagery for a brand.

Comparison Tasks. Another useful technique is comparison tasks, in which we ask consumers to convey their impressions by comparing brands to people, countries, animals, activities, fabrics, occupations, cars, magazines, vegetables, nationalities, or even other brands.[12] For example, we might ask consumers, "If Dannon yogurt were a car, which one would it be? If it were an animal, which one might it be? Looking at the people depicted in these pictures, which ones do you think would be most likely to eat Dannon yogurt?" In each case, we would ask a follow-up question about why subjects made the comparison they did. The objects people choose to represent the brand and their reasons can provide glimpses into the psyche of the consumer with respect to a brand, particularly useful in understanding imagery associations.

BRANDING BRIEF 9-3

Once Upon a Time . . . You Were What You Cooked

One of the most famous applications of psychographic techniques was made by Mason Haire in the 1940s. The purpose of the experiment was to uncover consumers' true beliefs and feelings toward Nescafé instant coffee.

The impetus for the experiment was a survey conducted to determine why the initial sales of Nescafé instant coffee were so disappointing. The majority of the people who reported they didn't like the product stated that the reason was they didn't like the flavor. On the basis of consumer taste tests, however, Nescafé's management knew that consumers found the taste of instant coffee acceptable when they didn't know what type of coffee they were drinking. Suspecting that consumers were not expressing their true feelings, Haire designed a clever experiment to discover what was really going on.

Haire set up two shopping lists containing the same six items. Shopping List 1 specified Maxwell House drip ground coffee, whereas Shopping List 2 specified Nescafé instant coffee, as follows:

Shopping List 1	**Shopping List 2**
Pound and a half of hamburger	Pound and a half of hamburger
2 loaves Wonder bread	2 loaves Wonder bread
Bunch of carrots	Bunch of carrots
1 can Rumford's Baking Powder	1 can Rumford's Baking Powder
Maxwell House coffee (drip ground)	Nescafé instant coffee
2 cans Del Monte peaches	2 cans Del Monte peaches
5 lbs. potatoes	5 lbs. potatoes

Two groups of matched subjects were each given one of the lists and asked to "Read the shopping list. . . . Try to project yourself into the situation as far as possible until you can more or less characterize the woman who bought the groceries." Subjects then wrote a brief description of the personality and character of that person.

For example, during the 2004 U.S. presidential election, a random sample of undecided voters offered the following comparisons of the Republican candidate, President George W. Bush, and the Democratic candidate, Senator John Kerry, to various popular brands.

ASSOCIATION	BUSH	KERRY
Coffee	Dunkin' Donuts	Starbucks
Technology	IBM	Apple
Auto	Ford	BMW
Retail	Kmart	Target
Fast Food	McDonald's	Subway

After coding the responses into frequently mentioned categories, Haire found that two starkly different profiles emerged:

	List 1 (Maxwell House)	**List 2 (Nescafé)**
Lazy	4%	48%
Fails to plan household purchases and schedules well	12%	48%
Thrifty	16%	4%
Not a good wife	0%	16%

Haire interpreted these results as indicating that instant coffee represented a departure from homemade coffee and traditions with respect to caring for one's family. In other words, at that time, the "labor-saving" aspect of instant coffee, rather than being an asset, was a liability in that it violated consumer traditions. Consumers were evidently reluctant to admit this fact when asked directly but were better able to express their true feelings when asked to project to another person.

The strategic implications of this new research finding were clear. Based on the original survey results, the obvious positioning for instant coffee with respect to regular coffee would have been to establish a point of difference on "convenience" and a point of parity on the basis of "taste." Based on the projective test findings, however, it was obvious that there also needed to be a point of parity on the basis of user imagery. As a result, a successful ad campaign was launched that promoted Nescafé coffee as a way for housewives to free up time so they could devote additional time to more important household activities.

Sources: Mason Haire, "Projective Techniques in Marketing Research," *Journal of Marketing* (April 1950): 649–652; J. Arndt, "Haire's Shopping List Revisited," *Journal of Advertising Research* 13 (1973): 57–61; G. S. Lane and G. L. Watson, "A Canadian Replication of Mason Haire's 'Shopping List' Study," *Journal of the Academy of Marketing Science* 3 (1975): 48–59; William L. Wilkie, *Consumer Behavior,* 3rd ed. (New York: John Wiley and Sons, 1994).

By examining the answers to probes, researchers may be better able to assemble a rich image for the brand, for example, identifying key brand personality associations. Branding Brief 9-4 outlines how hotel chain Joie de Vivre uses magazine imagery to clarify its brand positions.

Zaltman Metaphor Elicitation Technique

One interesting new approach to better understand how consumers view brands is the Zaltman Metaphor Elicitation Technique (ZMET).[13] ZMET is based on a belief that consumers often have subconscious motives for their purchasing behavior. "A lot goes on in our minds that we're not aware of," said former Harvard Business School professor Gerald Zaltman. "Most of what influences what we say and do occurs below the level of awareness. That's why we need new techniques to get at hidden knowledge—to get at what people don't know they know."

BRANDING BRIEF 9-4

Finding the Good Life at Joie de Vivre

Joie de Vivre Hospitality Inc. operates a chain of boutique hotels, restaurants, and resorts in the San Francisco area. Chip Conley founded the company in 1987 when he purchased a rundown motel in a seedy area of San Francisco and converted it into the Phoenix, a fashionable destination popular among entertainment celebrities. In establishing Joie de Vivre, Conley's goal was "to create a company with hip hotel concepts that appealed to a younger consumer base."

Joie de Vivre uses magazine and media imagery to inspire its boutique hotel designs. Hotel Bijou is inspired by Hollywood movies.

Since launching the Phoenix, the company has grown to a total of 28 hotels, the largest group of boutique hotels in Northern California. "Each hotel is a specific world of style and service catering to the needs and wishes of like-minded travelers." Each property's unique décor, quirky amenities, and thematic style are loosely based on popular magazines. Conley explains the design choices for the hotels and resorts as follows:

> *What we've learned over time is that people choose their hotels based on the brand as a mirror. So every time we create a new hotel, spa, or resort, we imagine a magazine that defines the hotel. We choose five words that define the magazine, and by doing that, we get the psychographic fit.*

For example, the Phoenix is represented by *Rolling Stone*. The five words used by Conley to describe the magazine are "adventurous, hip, irreverent, funky, and young at heart." The Hotel del Sol—a converted motel bearing a yellow exterior and surrounded by palm trees wrapped with festive lights—is described as "kind of *Martha Stewart Living* meets *Islands* magazine." Costanoa, a luxury camping resort that features a lodge, cabins, and tent bungalows as well as room service, is characterized by "*Outside* magazine meets *Metropolitan Home*."

To access this hidden knowledge, he developed the Zaltman Metaphor Elicitation Technique. As described in its U.S. patent, ZMET is "a technique for eliciting interconnected constructs that influence thought and behavior." The word *construct* refers to "an abstraction created by the researcher to capture common ideas, concepts, or themes expressed by customers." For example, the construct "ease of use" might capture the statements "simple to operate," "works without hassle," and "you don't really have to do anything."

ZMET stems from knowledge and research from varied fields such as "cognitive neuroscience, neurobiology, art critique, literary criticism, visual anthropology, visual sociology, semiotics, . . . art therapy, and psycholinguistics." The technique is based on the idea that "most social communication is nonverbal" and as a result approximately two-thirds of all stimuli received by the brain are visual. Using ZMET, Zaltman teases out consumers' hidden thoughts and feelings about a particular topic, which often can be

Joie de Vivre hotels strive to combine style and flavor with comfort and service. The boutique concept enables the hotels to offer personal touches for its clients, such as vitamins in place of chocolates on pillows, a standard at the Lambourne on Nob Hill. Other complimentary amenities at different Joie de Vivre hotels include CD/DVD players in rooms, billiards tables, and afternoon tea service. The Rex Hotel has a library and a literary flavor. The newest offering, the Hotel Vitale, showcases yoga classes in the rooftop penthouse of its Financial District building. It is described as *Real Simple* magazine meets *Dwell* magazine; the five words that define it are "nurturing, fresh, modern, urbane, and revitalizing."

In addition to providing comfort considerations, Joie de Vivre creates loyalty among its customers with a dedication to customer service. The company condenses all pertinent service information onto a small laminated card that all employees carry with them while they work. By way of introducing the staff to the guests, the company displays "Host Profiles" at the check-in desk that give useful and interesting information about the employees. Various hotel staff contributed to a set of 20 free guides to San Francisco that guests can use to find out about the city from a local's perspective. Joie de Vivre also developed a loyalty program, called Experience Rewards Club, whereby frequent guests earn redeemable points based on what they spend during each stay at one of the company's properties.

The personal touches and unique personality offered by Joie de Vivre hotels have helped the company build a loyal customer base (see the accompanying photo). One repeat customer referred to the company's Hotel Rex as "a home-away-from-home." To help first-time visitors choose the right hotel for them, the company's Web site includes a Hotel Matchmaker personality test offered by a fictional character, "Yvette," that offers recommendations based on answers to five key questions.

Sources: Neal Templin, "Boutique-Hotel Group Thrives on Quirks," *Wall Street Journal,* 18 March 1999; Clifford Carlsen, "Joie de Vivre Resorts to New Hospitality Strategy," *San Francisco Business Times,* 18 June 1999; Chip Conley, *The Rebel Rules* (New York: Fireside, 2001); "On the Record," *San Francisco Chronicle,* 7 August 2005, www.jdvhospitality.com.

expressed best using visual metaphors. Zaltman defines a metaphor as "a definition of one thing in terms of another, [which] people can use. . . to represent thoughts that are tacit, implicit, and unspoken."

A ZMET study starts with a group of participants who are asked in advance to think about the research topic at hand and select a minimum of 12 images from their own sources (e.g., magazines, catalogs, and family photo albums) that represent their thoughts and feelings about the research topic. The participants bring these images with them for a personal one-on-one two-hour interview with a study administrator who uses advanced interview techniques to explore the images with the participant and reveal hidden meanings through a "guided conversation." Finally, the participants use a computer program to create a collage with these images that communicates their subconscious thoughts and feelings about the topic. Researchers compile the findings in an interactive multimedia computer application. The guided conversation consists of a series of steps that includes some or all of the following:

1. *Story telling:* Participants describe the content of each picture.
2. *Missed images:* Participants describe the picture or pictures that they were unable to obtain and explain their relevance.
3. *Sorting task:* Participants sort pictures into meaningful groups and provide a label or description for each group.
4. *Construct elicitation:* Participants reveal basic constructs and their interconnections using images as stimuli through the Kelly repertory grid and laddering techniques (described in Chapter 3).
5. *The most representative picture:* Participants indicate which picture is most representative.
6. *Opposite images:* Participants indicate pictures that describe the opposite of the brand or the task they were given.
7. *Sensory images:* Participants indicate what does and does not describe the concept in terms of color, emotion, sound, smell, taste, and touch.
8. *Mental map:* After reviewing all the constructs discussed and asking participants whether the constructs are accurate representations of what they meant and whether any important ideas are missing, researchers ask them to create a map or causal model connecting the constructs.
9. *Summary image:* Participants create a summary image or montage using their own images (sometimes augmented by images from an image bank) to express important issues. Digital imaging techniques may be employed to facilitate the creation of the image.
10. *Vignette:* Participants put together a vignette or short video to help communicate important issues.

Once the participants' interviews have been completed, researchers identify key themes or constructs, code the data, and assemble a consensus map of the most important constructs. Quantitative analyses of the data can provide information for advertising, promotions, and other marketing mix decisions. ZMET has been applied in a variety of different ways, including as a means to help understand consumers' images of brands, products, and companies. Marketers can employ ZMET for a variety of consumer-insight research topics. Zaltman lists several of these:

> ZMET is useful in understanding consumers' images of brands, products, companies, brand equity, product concepts and designs, product usage and purchase experiences, life experiences, consumption context, and attitudes toward business.

For example, DuPont enlisted Zaltman to research women's attitudes toward hosiery. Conventional research yielded the conclusion that "women mostly hated wearing pantyhose," but DuPont market researchers were not convinced that this conclusion provided a complete picture. Zaltman used ZMET with 20 subjects in order to uncover deeper answers to the question: "What are your thoughts and feelings about buying and wearing pantyhose?" He discovered that women had a "like-hate" relationship with pantyhose; they disliked the discomfort and run-proneness of pantyhose but liked the feel of elegance and sexiness they got from wearing it. This discovery prompted a number of hosiery manufacturers to include more sexy and alluring imagery in their advertising. Figure 9-4 displays a consensus map that emerged from a study of intimate apparel.

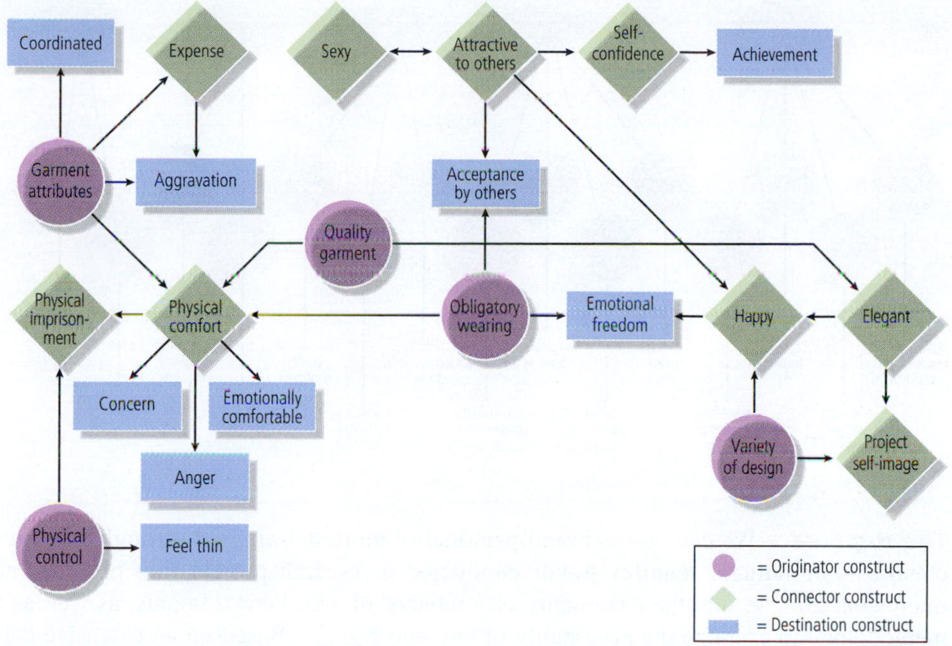

FIGURE 9-4

Application of ZMET to Intimate Apparel Market

Brand Personality and Values

As defined in Chapter 2, brand personality is the human characteristics or traits that consumers can attribute to a brand.[14] We can measure it in different ways. Perhaps the simplest and most direct way is to solicit open-ended responses to a probe such as the following:

> If the brand were to come alive as a person, what would it be like? What would it do? Where would it live? What would it wear? Who would it talk to if it went to a party (and what would it talk about)?

If consumers have difficulty getting started in their descriptions, an easily understood example or prompt serves as a guide. For example, if Campbell's soup were to be described as a person, one possible response might be as follows:[15]

> Mrs. Campbell is a rosy-cheeked and plump grandmother who lives in a warm, cozy house and wears an apron as she cooks wonderful things for her grandchildren.

Other means are possible to capture consumers' points of view. For example, marketers can give consumers a variety of pictures or a stack of magazines and ask them to assemble a profile of the brand. Ad agencies often conduct "picture sorting" studies to clarify who are typical users of a brand. As Chapter 3 noted, brand personality and user imagery may not always agree. When *USA Today* was first introduced, a research study exploring consumer opinions of the newspaper indicated that the benefits readers and nonreaders perceived were highly consistent. Perceptions of the *USA Today* brand personality—as colorful, friendly, and simple—were also highly related. User imagery, however, differed dramatically: Nonreaders viewed a typical *USA Today* reader as a shallow "air head"; readers, on the other hand, saw a typical *USA Today* reader as a well-rounded person interested in a variety of issues. Based on these findings, an advertising campaign was introduced to appeal to nonreaders that showed how prominent people endorsed the newspaper.[16]

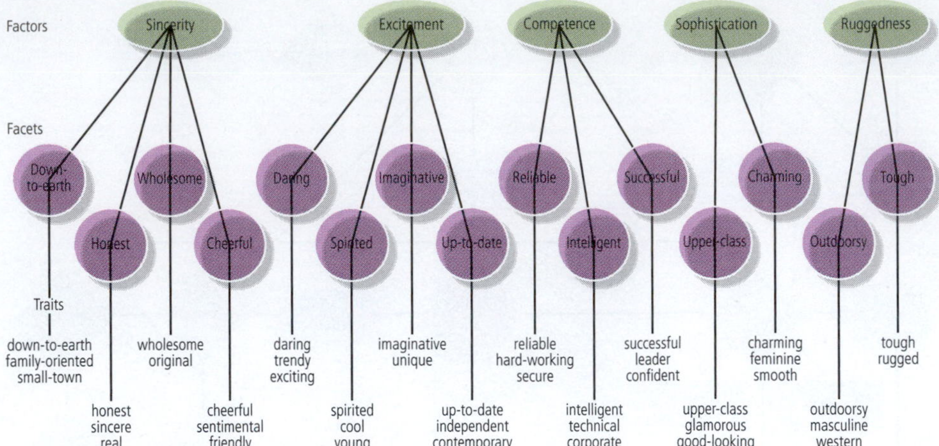

FIGURE 9-5

Brand Personality Scale Measures

The Big Five. We can assess brand personality more definitively through adjective checklists or ratings. Jennifer Aaker conducted a research project that provides an interesting glimpse into the personality of a number of well-known brands, as well as a methodology to examine the personality of any one brand.[17] Based on an extensive data collection of ratings of 114 personality traits on 37 brands in various product categories by over 600 individuals representative of the U.S. population, she created a brand personality scale that reflected the following five factors (with underlying facets) of brand personality:

1. Sincerity (down-to-earth, honest, wholesome, and cheerful)
2. Excitement (daring, spirited, imaginative, and up-to-date)
3. Competence (reliable, intelligent, and successful)
4. Sophistication (upper class and charming)
5. Ruggedness (outdoorsy and tough)

Figure 9-5 depicts the specific trait items that make up the Aaker brand personality scale. Respondents in her study rated how descriptive each personality trait was for each brand according to a 7-point scale (1 = not at all descriptive; 7 = extremely descriptive); Aaker averaged responses to provide summary measures. Figure 9-6 contains the actual ratings of the 37 brands from the study on the five factors. Note that certain brands tended to be strong on one particular factor (Hallmark on "sincerity," Porsche on "excitement," AT&T on "competence," Lexus on "sophistication," and Levi's on "ruggedness"). Other brands, like Nike, were high on more than one factor. Some brands, like MCI, scored poorly on all factors. A cross-cultural study exploring the generalizability of this scale outside the United States found that three of the five factors applied in Japan and Spain, but that a "peacefulness" dimension replaced "ruggedness" both in Japan and Spain, and a "passion" dimension emerged in Spain instead of "competency."[18] Research on brand personality in Korea revealed that two culture-specific factors emerge (passive likeableness and ascendancy), reflecting the importance of Confucian values in Korea's social and economic systems.[19]

Experiential Methods

More than ever, researchers are working to improve the effectiveness of their qualitative approaches, as well as go beyond traditional qualitative techniques to research consumers in their natural environment.[20] The rationale is that no matter how clever the research design, consumers may not be able to fully express their true selves as part of a formalized research study. By tapping more directly into their actual home, work, or shopping

	AT&T	Advil	AMEX	Apple	Avon	Campbell's	Charlie	Cheerios
Sincerity	1.06	.92	.83	.92	1.08	1.25	.83	1.14
Excitement	.91	.72	.83	.95	1.03	.87	.96	.77
Competence	1.15	.95	.99	1.07	1.01	1.01	.77	.88
Sophistication	.85	.75	.87	.86	1.22	.89	1.13	.76
Ruggedness	.94	.90	.83	.92	.92	.93	.77	.84

	CNN	Crest	Diet Coke	ESPN	Guess?	Hallmark	Hershey	IBM
Sincerity	.99	1.09	.94	.99	.88	1.27	1.11	.89
Excitement	1.02	.84	.93	1.10	1.15	1.21	.88	.91
Competence	1.18	.99	.85	1.04	.90	1.12	.89	1.10
Sophistication	.93	.87	.90	.89	1.24	1.31	.96	.84
Ruggedness	1.01	.94	.89	1.23	1.03	.95	.85	.91

	K-Mart	Kodak	LEGO	Lee	Levi's	Lexus	Mattel	McDonald's
Sincerity	1.07	1.10	1.11	1.14	1.20	.87	1.13	1.14
Excitement	.85	.99	1.10	1.00	1.11	1.12	1.10	.97
Competence	.97	1.08	1.01	.99	1.05	1.07	1.04	1.02
Sophistication	.78	.96	.87	1.09	1.13	1.27	.90	1.02
Ruggedness	.91	1.02	1.10	1.34	1.43	1.03	1.13	.90

	MCI	Mercedes	Michelin	MTV	Nike	Oil of Olay	Pepsi	Porsche
Sincerity	.81	.84	.96	.70	.98	1.00	1.02	.71
Excitement	.82	1.07	.86	1.27	1.17	.85	1.04	1.26
Competence	.90	1.06	1.03	.82	1.03	.94	.89	.95
Sophistication	.73	1.31	.82	1.02	1.05	1.17	.95	1.37
Ruggedness	.75	.99	1.20	.93	1.36	.76	.99	1.07

	Reebok	Revlon	Saturn	Sony	Visa
Sincerity	.94	.96	.96	.87	.90
Excitement	1.12	1.06	1.05	.94	.87
Competence	.97	.98	.99	1.02	1.02
Sophistication	1.00	1.31	1.08	.89	.87
Ruggedness	1.30	.85	1.00	.90	.87

FIGURE 9-6

Personality Ratings of Selected Brands

behaviors, researchers might be able to elicit more meaningful responses from consumers.[21] As markets become more competitive and many brand differences are threatened, any insight that helps to support a stronger brand positioning or create a stronger link to consumers is valuable (see Branding Brief 9-5).

Advocates of the experiential approach have sent researchers to consumers' homes in the morning to see how they approach their days, given business travelers Polaroid cameras and diaries to capture their feelings when in hotel rooms, and conducted "beeper studies" in which participants are instructed to write down what they're doing when they are paged.[22]

Ogilvy & Mather has sent researchers into homes with hand-held cameras to get an up-close picture of how people live. Hours of footage are then condensed into documentary-like 30-minute videos to help marketers and the agency see how people communicate and interact in different real-life situations.[23] The idea is to unobtrusively as possible observe consumers as they shop or as they consume products to capture every nuance of their behavior.

Marketers such as Procter & Gamble seek consumers' permission to spend time with them in their homes to see how they actually use and experience products. Business-to-business firms can also benefit from company visits that help to cement relationships and supplement research efforts. Technology firms such as Hewlett-Packard use cross-functional customer visits as a market research tool to gain a competitive advantage. One expert on the subject, Ed McQuarrie, offers the following advice about best practices for an outbound or inbound customer visit:[24]

1. Leverage the visits you already make by coordinating them via perennial questions and logging and reviewing customer profiles.
2. Take every opportunity to ask questions (for instance, formally set aside an hour to solicit feedback).

BRANDING BRIEF 9-5

Making the Most of Consumer Insights

Consumer research plays a significant role in uncovering information valuable to consumer-focused companies. David Taylor, founder of the Brand Gym consultancy, cautions that not all findings from consumer research can be considered insights. He defines an insight as "a penetrating, discerning understanding that unlocks an opportunity." An insight holds far more potential than a finding. Using Microsoft as an example, Taylor draws the contrast between the finding that "people need to process more and more information and data" and the insight that "information is the key to power and freedom." This insight might help Microsoft develop products that appeal to a larger consumer base than if the company relied solely on the finding.

Taylor developed a set of criteria to evaluate insights:

- *Fresh:* An insight might be obvious and, in fact, be overlooked or forgotten as a result. Check again.
- *Relevant:* An insight when played back to other target consumers should strike a chord.
- *Enduring:* By building on a deep understanding of consumers' beliefs and needs, a true consumer insight should have potential to remain relevant over time.
- *Inspiring:* All the team should be excited by the insight and see different but consistent applications.

Insights can come from consumer research such as focus groups, but also from using what Taylor describes as the "core insight drills." A sample of these drills follows:

- How could the brand/category do more to help improve people's lives?
- What do people really value in the category, and what would they not miss?
- What conflicting needs do people have? How can these tradeoffs be solved?
- What bigger market is the brand really competing in from a consumer viewpoint? What could the brand do more of to better meet these "higher-order" needs?
- What assumptions do people make about the market that could be challenged?
- How do people think the product works, and how does it work in reality?
- How is the product used in reality? What other products are used instead of the brand, where the brand could do a better job?

These "drills" can help companies unearth consumer insights that lead to better products and services, and ultimately to stronger brands.

Source: David Taylor, "Drilling for Nuggets: How to Use Insight to Inspire Innovation," *Brand Strategy,* March 2000. Used with permission of Brand Strategy, www.brandstrategy.co.uk.

3. Get engineers in front of customers, not just marketers.
4. Conduct programmatic visits.
5. Visit different kinds of customers.
6. Get out of the conference room.

Yahoo! has moved to "immersion groups," where a select group of 4–5 people talk informally with the company's product developers and even interact in work sessions to actually design products.[25]

WARNER-LAMBERT

To find out what customers thought of Fresh Burst Listerine, a new mint-flavored product designed to compete with Scope, Warner-Lambert had 37 families set up cameras in their bathrooms to film their routines around the sink. Users of both brands said they rinsed with mouthwash to make their breath smell good, but they treated the products very differently. Scope users gave the product a quick swish and spit it out. Users of the new Listerine, on the other hand, felt obliged to keep the wash in their mouth for a lot longer. Warner-Lambert interpreted the evidence to suggest that Listerine still hadn't shaken its medicinal image.[26]

Red Lobster no longer relies exclusively on focus groups and management approval for new recipes: Chefs now also go into restaurants for up to a month, test new dishes on real customers, and get feedback from the people who cook and serve the meals (Asian-style lobster rolls were introduced as a result of one such study).[27] Other companies using observational or ethnographic research to study consumers include 3Com (to uncover hidden needs that might be served by an electronic home organizer), Best Western (to learn how seniors decide when and where to shop), and Moen (to observe over an extended time how customers really use their shower devices).[28]

Of special importance to many companies are lead or leading users. Many firms ask online groups of consumers to give feedback via instant-messages or chat-rooms. One company with close ties to leading-edge users is Burton Snowboards.

Burton Snowboards stays close to top snowboarders such as Hannah Teter to remain at the top of the sport.

BURTON SNOWBOARDS

The best-known snowboard brand, Burton Snowboards, saw its market share increase from 30 percent to 40 percent by focusing on one objective—providing the best equipment to the largest number of snowboarders. To accomplish this goal, Burton's research approach is to focus on the 300 professional riders worldwide, 39 of whom are on its sponsored team. Staff members talk to the riders—on the slopes or on the phone—almost every day, and riders help to design virtually every Burton product. Company researchers immerse themselves in the riders' lives, watching where they shop, what they buy, and what they think about the sport and the equipment. To make sure it doesn't lose touch with its rank-and-file consumers, however, the company makes sure at least 10 of its 22 U.S. sales representatives hit the slopes on the weekend to interact with amateur snowboarders. Moreover, at any given time, two 35-foot trailers are traveling in North America, six buses are criss-crossing Japan, and four trucks are rumbling through Europe, all with the purpose of testing gear on consumers. Burton also has the eTeam—an online community of 25,000 kids who provide real-time feedback in exchange for free product trials.[29]

Summary

Qualitative research techniques are a creative means of ascertaining consumer perceptions that may otherwise be difficult to uncover. The range of possible qualitative research techniques is limited only by the creativity of the marketing researcher.

Qualitative research also has drawbacks. The in-depth insights that emerge have to be tempered by the realization that the samples are often very small and may not necessarily generalize to broader populations. Moreover, given the qualitative nature of the data, there may be questions of interpretation. Different researchers examining the same results from a qualitative research study may draw different conclusions.

Quantitative Research Techniques

Although qualitative measures are useful to identify the range of possible associations to a brand and their characteristics in terms of strength, favorability, and uniqueness, marketers often want a more definitive portrait of the brand to allow them to make more confident and defensible strategic and tactical recommendations. Whereas qualitative research typically elicits some type of verbal response from consumers, ***quantitative research*** typically employs various types of scale questions from which researchers can draw numerical representations and summaries. Quantitative measures of brand knowledge can help to better assess the depth and breadth of brand awareness; the strength, favorability, and uniqueness of brand associations; the valence of brand judgments and feelings; and the extent and nature of brand relationships. Quantitative measures are often the primary ingredient in tracking studies that monitor brand knowledge structures of consumers over time, as we discussed in Chapter 8. Quantitative measures are increasingly being collected online, as described in Branding Brief 9-6.

Brand Awareness

Recall that brand awareness is related to the strength of the brand in memory, as reflected by consumers' ability to identify various brand elements like the brand name, logo, symbol, character, packaging, and slogan under different conditions. Brand awareness describes the likelihood that a brand will come to mind in different situations and the ease with which it does so given different types of cues.

Marketers use several measures of awareness of brand elements.[30] Choosing the right one is a matter of knowing the relative importance of brand awareness forconsumer behavior in the category and the role it plays in the success of the marketing program, as we discussed in Chapter 2. Let's look at some of these awareness issues.

Recognition. Brand recognition requires consumers to identify the brand under a variety of circumstances and can rest on the identification of any of the brand elements. The most basic recognition test gives consumers a set of individual items visually or orally and asks them if they think they've previously seen or heard of these items. To provide a more sensitive test, it is often useful to include decoys or lures—items that consumers could not possibly have seen. In addition to "yes" or "no" responses, consumers can also rate how confident they are in their recognition of an item.

Other, somewhat more subtle, recognition measures test "perceptually degraded" versions of the brand, which are masked or distorted in some way or shown for extremely brief duration. For example, we can test brand name recognition with missing letters. Figure 9-8 tests your ability to recognize brand names with less than full information. These more subtle measures may be particularly important for brands that have a high level of recognition, in order to provide more sensitive assessments.

Brand recognition is especially important for packaging, and some marketing researchers have used creative means to assess the visibility of package design. As a starting point, they consider the benchmark or "best case" of the visibility of a package when a consumer (1) with 20–20 vision (2) is face-to-face with a package (3) at a distance of less than five feet (4) under ideal lighting conditions.

A key question then is whether the package design is robust enough to be still recognizable if one or more of these four conditions are not present. Because shopping is often not conducted under "ideal" conditions, such insights are important. For example, some consumers who wear eyeglasses may not wear them when shopping in a supermarket.[31] Is the package still able to effectively communicate to consumers under such conditions?

Research methods using tachistoscopes (T-scopes) and eye tracking techniques exist to test the effectiveness of alternative package designs according to a number of specific criteria:

- Degree of shelf impact
- Impact and recall of specific design elements
- Distance at which the package can first be identified
- Angle at which the package can first be identified
- Speed with which the package can be identified
- Perceived package size
- Copy visibility and legibility

These additional measures can provide more sensitive measures of recognition than simple "yes" or "no" tasks. By applying these direct and indirect measures of brand recognition, marketers can determine which brand elements exist in memory and, to some extent, the strength of their association. One advantage brand recognition measures have over recall measures is the chance to use visual recognition measures. It may be difficult for consumers to describe a logo or symbol in a recall task; it's much easier for them to assess the same elements visually in a recognition task.

Nevertheless, brand recognition measures provide only an approximation of *potential* recallability. To determine whether consumers will actually recall the brand elements under various circumstances, we need measures of brand recall.

Recall. To demonstrate brand recall, consumers must retrieve the actual brand element from memory when given some related probe or cue. Thus, brand recall is a more demanding memory task than brand recognition because consumers are not just given a brand element and asked to say whether they've seen it before.

Different measures of brand recall are possible depending on the type of cues provided to consumers. ***Unaided recall*** on the basis of "all brands" provided as a cue is likely to identify only the very strongest brands. ***Aided recall*** uses various types of cues to help consumer recall. One possible sequence of aided recall might use progressively narrower cues—such as product class, product category, and product type labels—to provide insight into the organization of consumers' brand knowledge structures. For example, if recall of the Porsche Boxster (a high-performance German sports car) in non-German markets were of interest, the recall probes could begin with "all cars" and move to more and more narrowly defined categories such as "sports cars," "foreign sports cars," or even "high-performance German sports cars." For example, marketers could ask consumers: "When you think of foreign sports cars, which brands come to mind?"

Other types of cues can help measure brand recall. For example, marketers can ask about product attributes ("When you think of chocolate, which brands come to mind?) or usage goals ("If you were thinking of having a healthy snack, which brands come to mind?"). Often, to capture the breadth of brand recall and to assess brand salience, we might need to examine the context of the purchase decision or consumption situation, such as different times and places. The stronger the brand associations to these nonproduct considerations, the more likely it is that consumers will recall them when

BRANDING BRIEF 9-6

Online Market Research on the Rise

Online market research is gaining credibility as a way to test advertising, conduct focus groups, and gather opinions. Soliciting and collecting consumer data online can be less expensive and easier to oversee than traditional market research. Record Web penetration—about 68 percent of Americans have online access—and decreasing telecommunication costs have driven companies to devote more energy to online research. The migration of market research to the Internet began with companies asking Web users specifically about Internet sites but quickly expanded into other areas. In some situations, however, online research cannot be as effective as face-to-face interviews or focus groups. Nevertheless, in 2005 companies spent more than $1.1 billion on online market research, a 16 percent increase over 2004, according to *Inside Research.*

The online approach to market research has many positives. Projects are unrestricted by geography, so marketers can manage multi-country research from one location. This method avoids interviewer bias and ensures that data is analyzed uniformly, rather than sourced to different researchers. Proponents say online surveys are convenient, far less intrusive than a telephone call during dinnertime or a sidewalk interview by a researcher with a clipboard. Respondents may be more comfortable sitting down with surveys in their homes and therefore offer more thoughtful and honest answers, especially on sensitive issues. Online research results come back quickly and marketers can analyze them in real time rather than waiting weeks to process paper surveys. Administration and analysis costs plummet with online surveys, and the costs are scalable.

Recruitment is essential to conducting useful online marketing research. In some instances, invitations to participate in an online survey are e-mailed to a large group and recipients click on a link if they are willing to take the survey. Other marketers rely on pop-up links to questionnaires and commission online panels of consumers who agree to participate in a series of surveys. The best online panels make respondents feel they belong to a club where their input is valuable. Toymaker Lego brought together 10,000 customers online who responded to an e-mail invitation to participate in a new product contest. The online brainstorming bonanza led to the creation of the 3,100-piece Star Wars Imperial Destroyer, the company's largest and most expensive set ever. It sold out in five weeks.

Online market research is not a perfect research tool. Programming costs for online research are higher than for regular questionnaires. If online surveys are too long, customers can easily opt not to finish. Also, the absence of an interviewer makes it harder to gauge whether a respondent is being honest, especially since online surveys can attract Internet junkies who crank out questionnaires by the dozen. Participants may be tempted to rush through Internet surveys, where there is no interviewer to prod them with a follow-up

given those situational cues. Combined, measures of recall based on product attribute or category cues and situational or usage cues give an indication of breadth and depth of recall.

We can further distinguish brand recall according to the order as well as the latency or speed of recall. In many cases, people will recognize a brand when it is shown to them and

Online Survey Guidelines

- Don't take advantage of respondents' willingness to participate. Diversity in respondents is essential to generating solid data.
- Recruit consumers and profile them when they first join a panel and then match them to projects, rather than letting them self-select for certain projects.
- Engage consumer participants in ongoing conversations. For example, Bose created the Bose Information Exchange to encourage fans to discuss its technology.
- Keep questions focused. Experts say respondents will not want to spend more than five minutes answering questions. Offer incentives if respondents need to be willing to offer in-depth answers or answer questions on a regular basis.
- If surveying children, obtain parental consent.
- E-mail invitations are effective for a well-defined audience and Web links are a good way to tease out general feedback from Website visitors. It is more difficult to target particular respondent profiles using Web links.
- Include the purpose of the survey and how long it should take to complete.
- Utilize open-ended questions.

Source: Richard Kottler, "Eight Tips Offer Best Practices for Online MR," *Marketing News*, 1 April 2005. Courtesy of American Marketing Association.

FIGURE 9-7

On-line Survey Guidelines

question. Another concern is whether online users differ from the general population, because online surveys obviously leave out non-Internet users who may have a different perspective on products like digital cameras.

An area where online research fails to measure up to traditional focus groups is in situations where marketers want to closely document reaction to new products. Although Web cameras can link virtual focus groups, many researchers prefer in-person interaction for the opportunity to watch a consumer's face as he or she interacts with a new product. For some research goals, such as testing the smell or feel of a product, off-line research is more effective. Figure 9-7 has some guidelines outlining best practices for conducting surveys via the Internet.

Sources: Allison Fass, "Collective Opinion," *Forbes,* 28 November 2005; Robin T. Peterson and Zhilin Yang, "Web Product Reviews Help Strategy," *Marketing News,* 1 April 2004; "Marketing Research Association Executive Director Predicts Dramatic Growth for Online Marketing Research in 2006 and Beyond," *Business Wire,* 18 January 2006.

will recall it if they are given a sufficient number of cues. Thus, potential recallability is high. The more important issue is the salience of the brand: Do consumers think of the brand under the right circumstances, for example, when they could be either buying or using the product? How quickly do they think of the brand? Is it automatically or easily recalled? Is it the first brand they recall?

FIGURE 9-8

Don't Tell Me, It's on the Tip of My Tongue

A brand name with a high level of awareness will be recognized under less than ideal conditions. Consider the following list of incomplete names (i.e., word fragments). Which ones do you recognize? Compare your answers to the answer key in the footnote to see how well you did.

1. D _ _ N E _
2. K O _ _ K
3. D U _ A C _ _ _
4. H Y _ T _
5. A D _ _ L
6. M _ T _ E L
7. D _ L T _
8. N _ Q U _ L
9. G _ L L _ T _ _
10. H _ _ S H _ Y
11. H _ L L _ _ R K
12. M _ C H _ _ I N
13. T _ P P _ R W _ _ E
14. L _ G _
15. N _ K _

Answers: (1) Disney; (2) Kodak; (3) Duracell; (4) Hyatt; (5) Advil; (6) Mattel; (7) Delta; (8) NyQuil; (9) Gillette; (10) Hershey; (11) Hallmark; (12) Michelin; (13) Tupperware; (14) Lego; (15) Nike.

Corrections for Guessing. Any research measure must consider the issue of consumers making up responses or guessing. That problem may be especially evident with certain types of aided awareness or recognition measures for the brand. Spurious awareness occurs when consumers erroneously claim they recall something that they really don't and that maybe doesn't even exist. For example, one market research firm, Oxtoby-Smith, conducted a benchmark study of awareness of health and beauty products.[32] In the study, they asked consumers questions like this:

> "The following is a list of denture adhesive brand names. Please answer yes if you've heard the name before and no if you haven't. Okay? Orafix? Fasteeth? Dentu-tight? Fixodent?"

Although 16 percent of the sample reported that they had heard of Dentu-Tight, there was one problem: It didn't really exist! Similarly high levels of reported recall were reported for plausible-sounding but fictitious brands such as Four O'Clock Tea (8 percent), Leone Pasta (16 percent), and Mrs. Smith's Cake Mix (31 percent). On the basis of this study, Oxtoby-Smith found that spurious awareness was around 8 percent for new health and beauty products and even higher in some other product categories. In one case, a proposed line extension was mistakenly thought to already exist by about 50 percent of the sample (a finding that no doubt sent a message to the company that they should go ahead and introduce the product!).

From a marketing perspective, the problem with spurious awareness is that it may send misleading signals about the proper strategic direction for a brand. For example, Oxtoby-Smith reported that one of its clients was struggling with a 5 percent market share despite the fact that 50 percent of survey respondents reported they were aware of the brand. On the surface, it would seem a good idea to improve the image of the brand and attitudes toward it in some way. Upon further examination, marketers determined that spurious awareness accounted for *almost half* the survey respondents who reported brand awareness, suggesting that a more appropriate solution to the true problem would be to first build awareness to a greater degree. Marketers should be sensitive to the possibilities of misleading signals because of spurious brand awareness, especially with new brands or ones with plausible-sounding names.

Strategic Implications. The advantage of aided recall measures is that they yield insight into how brand knowledge is organized in memory and what kind of cues or reminders may be necessary for consumers to be able to retrieve the brand from memory. Understanding recall when we use different levels of product category specificity as cues is important, because it has implications for how consumers form consideration sets and make product decisions.

For example, again take the case of the Porsche Boxster. Assume that consumer recall of this particular car model was fairly low when all cars were considered but very high when foreign sports cars were considered. In other words, consumers strongly categorized the Porsche Boxster as a prototypical sports car but tended to think of it in only that way. If that were the case, for more consumers to entertain the possibility of buying a Porsche Boxster, it might be necessary to broaden the meaning of Porsche so that it had a stronger association to cars in general. Of course, such a strategy would run the risk of alienating existing customers who had been initially attracted by the "purity" and strong identification of the Porsche Boxster as a sports car. The choice of appropriate strategy would depend on the relative costs and benefits of targeting the two different segments.

The important point to note is that the category structure that exists in consumers' minds—as reflected by brand recall performance—can have profound implications for consumer choice and marketing strategy, as demonstrated by The Science of Branding 9-2. The insights gleaned from measuring brand recall are also valuable for developing brand identity and integrated marketing communication programs, as we showed in Chapters 4 and 6. For example, we can examine brand recall for each brand element to explore the extent to which any one brand element (the name, symbol, logo) suggests another. Are consumers aware of all the different brand elements and how they relate?

We also need a complete understanding of brand image, as covered in the following section.

Brand Image

One vitally important aspect of the brand is its image, as reflected by the associations that consumers hold for it. It is useful for marketers to make a distinction between lower-level considerations, related to consumer perceptions of specific performance and imagery attributes and benefits, and higher-level considerations related to overall judgments, feelings, and relationships. There is an obvious connection between the two levels, because consumers' overall responses and relationship with a brand typically depend on perceptions of specific attributes and benefits of that brand. This section considers some issues in measuring lower-level brand performance and imagery associations.

Beliefs are descriptive thoughts that a person holds about something (for instance, that a particular software package has many helpful features and menus and is easy to use).[33] Brand association beliefs are those specific attributes and benefits linked to the brand and its competitors. For example, consumers may have brand association beliefs for Sony Playstation home video games such as "fun and exciting," "cool and hip," "colorful," "good graphic quality," "advanced technology," "variety of software titles," and "sometimes violent." They may also have associations to the brand logo and the slogan, "Live in Your World. Play in Ours." Playstation user imagery may be "used by a teenager or 20-something male who is serious about playing video games, especially sports games."

THE SCIENCE OF BRANDING 9-2

Understanding Categorical Brand Recall

An experiment by Prakash Nedungadi provides a compelling demonstration of the importance of understanding the category structure that exists in consumer memory, as well as the value of strategies for increasing the recallability or accessibility of brands during choice situations. As a preliminary step in his research study, Nedungadi first examined the category structure for fast-food restaurants that existed in consumers' minds. He found that a "major subcategory" was "hamburger chains" and a "minor subcategory" was "sandwich shops." He also found, on the basis of usage and linking surveys, that within the major subcategory of national hamburger chains, a major brand was McDonald's and a minor brand was Wendy's, and within the minor subcategory of local sandwich shops, a major brand was Joe's Deli (a brand in his survey area) and a minor brand was Subway. Consistent with this reasoning, in an unaided recall and choice task, consumers were more likely to remember and select a brand from a major subcategory than from a minor subcategory and, within a subcategory, a major brand rather than a minor brand.

Nedungadi next looked at the effects of different brand "primes" on subsequent choices among the four fast-food restaurants. Brands were primed by having subjects in the experiment first answer a series of seemingly unrelated questions—including some questions about the brand to be primed—before making their brand selections. Because of this initial exposure, a target brand was "primed" in memory and therefore potentially more accessible during the choice task. Two key findings emerged. First, a major brand that was primed was more likely to

In Chapter 2 we provided a structured set of measures to tap into performance and imagery associations. The qualitative research approaches we described earlier are useful in uncovering the different types of specific brand associations making up the brand image. To better understand their potential contribution to brand equity, we can assess belief associations on the basis of one or more of the three key dimensions—strength, favorability, and uniqueness—making up the sources of brand equity.

As a first cut, we can use open-ended measures that tap into the strength, favorability, and uniqueness of brand associations, as follows:

1. What are the strongest associations you have to the brand? What comes to mind when you think of the brand? (Strength)
2. What is good about the brand? What do you like about the brand? What is bad about the brand? What do you dislike about the brand? (Favorability)
3. What is unique about the brand? What characteristics or features does the brand share with other brands? (Uniqueness)

To gain more specific insights, we could rate these belief associations according to strength, favorability, and uniqueness, as Figure 9-9 illustrates with Lipton iced tea.

We will want to measure any potentially relevant association, including performance-related attributes and benefits—such as (where appropriate) primary characteristics and supplementary features; product reliability and durability; service effectiveness, efficiency, and empathy; style and design; and price—as well as imagery-related attributes and benefits related to user profiles; purchase and usage situations; brand personality and values;

be selected in the later choice task even though the attitudes toward the brand were no different from those of a control group. In other words, merely making the brand more accessible in memory increased the likelihood that it would be chosen *independent of any differences in brand attitude.* Second, priming a minor brand in a minor subcategory actually benefited the *major* brand in that subcategory more. In other words, by drawing attention to the minor subcategory of sandwich shops—which could easily be overlooked—the minor brand, Subway, indirectly primed the major brand, Joe's Deli, in the subcategory. The implications of his research are that marketers must understand how consumers' memory is organized and, as much as possible, ensure that the proper cues and primes are evident to prompt brand recall.

In sum, brand recall provides insight into category structure and brand positioning in consumers' minds. Brands tend to be recalled in categorical clusters when consumers are given a general probe. Certain brands are grouped together in memory because they share certain associations and are thus likely to cue and remind consumers of each other if one is recalled.

Sources: Prakash Nedungadi, "Recall and Consumer Consideration Sets: Influencing Choice without Altering Brand Evaluations," *Journal of Consumer Research* 17 (December 1990): 263–276; Joseph W. Alba and J. Wesley Hutchinson, "Dimensions of Consumer Expertise," *Journal of Consumer Research* 13 (March 1987): 411–454; Kalpesh Kaushik Desai and Wayne D. Hoyer, "Descriptive Characteristics of Memory-Based Consideration Sets: Influence of Usage Occasion Frequency and Usage Location Familiarity," *Journal of Consumer Research* 27 (2000): 309–323.

and history, heritage, and experiences. Indirect tests also can assess the derived importance and favorability of these brand associations (through multivariate regression techniques).

A recently proposed methodology, brand concept maps (BCM), elicits brand association networks (brand maps) from consumers and aggregates individual maps into a consensus map.[34] This approach structures the brand elicitation stage of identifying brand associations by providing survey respondents with a set of brand associations used in the mapping stage. The mapping stage is also structured and has respondents use the provided set of brand associations to build an individual brand map that shows how brand associations are linked to each other and to the brand, as well as how strong these linkages are. Finally, the aggregation stage is also structured and analyzes individual brand maps step by step, uncovering the common thinking involved. Figure 9-10 displays a brand concept map for the Mayo Clinic (the subject of Branding Brief 8.3) provided by a sample of patients.

Other Approaches. A more complicated quantitative technique to assess overall brand uniqueness is multidimensional scaling, or perceptual maps. ***Multidimensional scaling*** (MDS) is a procedure for determining the perceived relative images of a set of objects, such as products or brands. MDS transforms consumer judgments of similarity or preference into distances represented in perceptual space. For example, if brands A and B are judged by respondents to be the most similar of a set of brands, the MDS algorithm will position brands A and B so that the distance between them in multidimensional space is smaller than the distance between any other two pairs of brands. Respondents may base their similarity between brands on any basis—tangible or intangible.[35]

1. To what extent do you feel the following product characteristics are descriptive of Lipton iced tea (where 1 = strongly disagree and 7 = strongly agree)?

   ________ convenient
   ________ refreshing and thirst quenching
   ________ real and natural
   ________ good-tasting
   ________ contemporary and relevant
   ________ used by young professionals

2. How good or bad is it for iced tea to have the following product characteristics (where 1 = very bad and 7 = very good)?

   ________ convenient
   ________ refreshing and thirst quenching
   ________ real and natural
   ________ good-tasting
   ________ contemporary and relevant
   ________ used by young professionals

3. How unique is Lipton iced tea in terms of the following product characteristics (where 1 = not at all unique and 7 = highly unique)?

   ________ convenient
   ________ refreshing and thirst quenching
   ________ real and natural
   ________ good-tasting
   ________ contemporary and relevant
   ________ used by young professionals

FIGURE 9-9

Example of Brand Association Ratings in Terms of Strength, Favorability, and Uniqueness

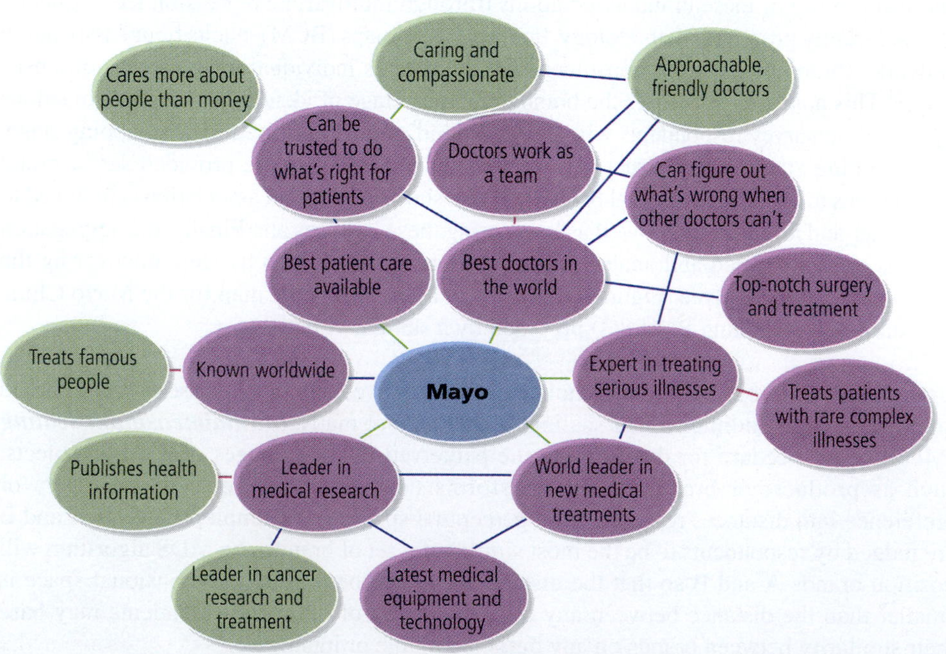

FIGURE 9-10

Sample Mayo Clinic Brand Concept Map

Direct Questions

Forced choice between two items

1. For PRODUCT . . .
"I prefer to buy a well known brand" or
"I don't mind buying the store brand"

Four Likert items

2. "When I buy a PRODUCT, I look at the brand."
3. "I do not choose a PRODUCT according to the brand."
4. "For a PRODUCT, the brand name is not that important."
5. "When I buy a PRODUCT, I take account of the brand."

Indirect Measures

6. A dollarmetric measure involving three well-known brands: the last brand purchased by consumer in the product category and the first other two brands mentioned in a spontaneous brand awareness question. Would the consumer maintain his/her choice if the price differential increased by 10 percent, 25 percent, 50 percent between the chosen brand and the other two competitors?
7. A dollarmetric measure between the last brand bought by consumer and a private label or store brand in the product category.
8. A mini-information display board choice task. Five brands and five product attributes (including brand name and price) were included in a grid and consumers were asked to choose a brand. Brand sensitivity was indicated by usage of the brand name attribute in making the choice.

FIGURE 9-11

Kapferer and Laurent's Brand Sensitivity Measure

European academic branding experts Kapferer and Laurent have proposed a related scale to measure the brand sensitivity of a product class as a whole.[36] They characterize brand sensitivity in terms of the relationship among brands for a given consumer in a given product class, particularly with respect to comparisons between national brands versus unbranded products or private labels in that product class. The types of items in their scale are displayed in Figure 9-11. According to their approach, the strength of a brand is reflected by the number of its customers who are brand sensitive. Brand sensitivity can be seen as a potential proxy for or measure of brand uniqueness. In other words, if consumers are not brand sensitive for a category as a whole, it is unlikely that any one specific brand will be unique.

Brand Responses

The purpose of measuring more general, higher-level considerations is to find out how consumers combine all the more specific, lower-level considerations about the brand in their minds to form different types of brand responses and evaluations. Chapter 2 provided examples of measures of key brand judgments and feelings. The Science of Branding 9-3 provides additional insight into brand attitudes and judgment. Reynolds and Phillips advocate a "share tiering" approach to measuring brand equity with a combination of four key brand response constructs: (1) relative barrier or brand price, (2) brand quality perceptions, (3) brand purchase loyalty, and (4) self-report future brand purchase trend.[37]

Purchase Intentions. Another set of possible measures closely related to brand attitudes and consideration is purchase intentions.[38] Intention measures could focus on the

THE SCIENCE OF BRANDING 9-3

Understanding Brand Attitudes

Here we highlight two ways to conceptualize or model attitudes. One view takes the position that consumers form attitudes because they provide a function of some kind for a person. Daniel Katz, a social psychologist, developed a functional theory of attitudes to account for the different types of roles that attitudes can play. He identified four main functions:

1. The *utilitarian function* deals with attitudes formed on the basis of rewards and punishments.
2. The *value-expressive function* deals with attitudes formed to express an individual's central value or self-concept.
3. The *ego-defensive function* deals with attitudes formed to protect an individual from either external threats or internal feelings of insecurity.
4. The *knowledge function* deals with attitudes formed to satisfy an individual's need for order, structure, and meaning.

Consumers thus form attitudes toward brands to provide the function they are seeking. In this way, they might like and use certain brands because they satisfy their needs (utilitarian function), allow themselves to express their personality (value-expressive function), bolster a perceived weakness they have (ego-defensive function), or simplify decision making (knowledge function).

Perhaps the most widely accepted approach to actually modeling attitudes is based on a multi-attribute formulation, in which we assume brand attitudes are a function of the associated attributes and benefits that are salient for the brand. Fishbein and Ajzen have proposed what has been probably the most influential multi-attribute model.[2] As applied to marketing, this ***expectancy-value model*** views brand attitudes as a multiplicative function of (1) the salient beliefs that a consumer has about the brand (the extent to which consumers think the brand possesses certain attributes or benefits) and (2) the evaluative judgment regarding those beliefs (how good or bad it is that the brand possesses those attributes or benefits). Thus, overall brand attitudes depend on the strength of association between the brand and salient attributes or benefits and the favorability of those beliefs.

According to the multi-attribute model, we can measure belief strength by having consumers rate the probability that the brand possesses each of the salient attributes or benefits, as follows.

How likely is it that Colgate toothpaste fights tooth decay?

Extremely Unlikely 1 2 3 4 5 6 7 Extremely Likely

Similarly, we can measure belief evaluations by having consumers rate the favorability of the salient attributes or benefits.

How good or bad is it that Colgate toothpaste fights tooth decay?

Very Bad −3 −2 −1 0 1 2 3 Very Good

Overall brand attitudes are then the sum of each attribute belief strength multiplied by its favorability. Fishbein and Ajzen also developed the theory of reasoned action to extend the multi-attribute model to include interpersonal, social effects. According to the theory, attitudes toward brands can also depend on consumers' beliefs about other people's opinions as well as consumers' motivation to comply with these other people's wishes.

Brand attitudes and judgments can vary in their strength. Attitude strength has been measured in psychology by the reaction time to evaluative queries about the attitude object: Individuals who can evaluate an attitude object quickly are assumed to have a highly accessible attitude. Research has shown that attitudes formed from direct behavior or experience are more accessible than attitudes based on information or other indirect forms of behavior. Highly accessible brand attitudes are more likely to be activated spontaneously upon exposure to the brand and to guide subsequent brand choices.

Because of the embedded meaning they contain, abstract associations such as attitudes, or even benefits to some extent, tend to be inherently more evaluative than attributes. More abstract associations can thus be more durable and accessible in memory than the underlying attribute information. Moreover, consumers may store and retrieve brand attitudes separately from the underlying attribute information. In fact, Claremont's Peter Farquhar believes that one key element of brand equity is attitude accessibility. Attitude accessibility can be measured on a microcomputer by seeing how long it takes a consumer to indicate his or her brand evaluation ratings. Although these differences may be in microseconds, they may still be significant managerially.

Sources: Daniel Katz, "The Functional Approach to the Study of Attitudes," *Public Opinion Quarterly* 24 (1960): 163–204; Martin Fishbein and Icek Ajzen, *Belief, Attitude, Intention, and Behavior: An Introduction to Theory and Research* (Reading, MA: Addison-Wesley, 1975); Icek Ajzen and Martin Fishbein, *Understanding Attitudes and Predicting Social Behavior* (Englewood Cliffs, NJ: Prentice Hall, 1980); Russell H. Fazio, David M. Sanbonmatsu, Martha C. Powell, and Frank R. Kardes, "On the Automatic Activation of Attitudes," *Journal of Personality and Social Psychology* 50 (February 1986): 229–238; Russell H. Fazio and Mark Zanna, "Direct Experiences and Attitude Behavior Consistency," in *Advances in Experimental Social Psychology,* Vol. 14, ed. Leonard Berkowitz (New York: Academic Press, 1981), 161–202; Ida E. Berger and Andrew A. Mitchell, "The Effect of Advertising on Attitude Accessibility," *Journal of Consumer Research* 16 (December 1989): 280–288; Russell H. Fazio, Martha C. Powell, and Carol J. Williams, "The Role of Attitude Accessibility in the Attitude and Behavior Process," *Journal of Consumer Research* 16 (December 1989): 288–316; Amitava Chattopadhyay and Joseph W. Alba, "The Situational Importance of Recall and Inference in Consumer Decision Making," *Journal of Consumer Research* 15 (June 1988): 1–12; John G. Lynch Jr., Howard Mamorstein, and Michael Weigold, "Choices from Sets Including Remembered Brands: Use of Recalled Attributes and Prior Overall Evaluations," *Journal of Consumer Research* 15 (September 1988): 169–184; Peter H. Farquhar, "Managing Brand Equity," *Marketing Research* 1 (September 1989): 24–33.

likelihood of buying the brand or of switching to another brand. Research in psychology suggests that purchase intentions are most likely to be predictive of actual purchase when there is correspondence between the two in the following categories:[39]

- Action (buying for own use or to give as a gift)
- Target (specific type of product and brand)
- Context (in what type of store based on what prices and other conditions)
- Time (within a week, month, or year)

In other words, when asking consumers to forecast their likely purchase of a product or a brand, we want to specify *exactly* the circumstances—the purpose of the purchase, the location of the purchase, the time of the purchase, and so forth. For example, we could ask consumers:

> "Assume your refrigerator broke down over the next weekend and could not be inexpensively repaired. If you went to your favorite appliance store and found all the different brands competitively priced, how likely would you be to buy a General Electric refrigerator?"

Consumers could indicate their purchase intention on a 11-point probability scale that ranges from 0 (definitely would not buy) to 10 (definitely would buy).

Brand Relationships

Chapter 2 characterized brand relationships in terms of brand resonance and offered possible measures for each of the four key dimensions: behavioral loyalty, attitudinal attachment, sense of community, and active engagement. This section considers several additional considerations with respect to those dimensions.

Behavioral Loyalty. To capture reported brand usage and behavioral loyalty, we could ask consumers several questions directly. Or we could ask them what percentage of their last purchases in the category went to the brand (past purchase history) and what percentage of their planned next purchases will go the brand (intended future purchases). For example, the marketers or brand managers of Duracell batteries might ask the following questions:

- Which brand of batteries do you usually buy?
- Which brand of batteries did you buy last time?
- Do you have any batteries on hand? Which brand?
- Which brands of batteries did you consider buying?
- Which brand of batteries will you buy next time?

These types of questions can provide information about brand attitudes and usage for Duracell, including potential gaps with competitors and which other brands might be in the consideration set at the time of purchase.

Marketers can make their measures open ended, dichotomous (forcing consumers to choose a brand), or offer multiple choice or rating scales. They can compare the answers with actual measures of consumer behavior to assess whether consumers are accurate in their predictions. For example, if 30 percent of consumers reported, on average, that they thought they would take pictures in the next two weeks, but only 15 percent of consumers reported two weeks later that they actually had taken pictures during that period, then Fuji film brand managers might need to devise strategies to better convert intentions to actual behavior.

Brand Substitutability. Industry consultants Longman and Moran have developed a measure of substitutability related to brand behaviors that they see as a key source of brand equity.[40] Their measure is based on a scale produced by the answers to two questions:

1. Which brand did you buy last time?
2. If the brand had not been available, what would you have done (waited, gone to another store, or bought another brand—and, if another brand, which one)?

Based on the responses, they place consumers into one of six segments, of decreasing value for the brand:

1. People who bought your brand last time and who would have waited or gone to another store to buy your brand
2. People who bought your brand last time but would have accepted any other brand as a substitute
3. People who bought your brand last time but specified a particular other brand as a substitute
4. People who bought another brand last time but named your brand as a possible substitute
5. People who bought another brand last time and did not name your brand as a substitute
6. People who bought another brand last time and would have waited or gone to another store to buy that brand

Longman and Moran view repeat rate—how many of the people who bought a particular brand last time would buy it again this time—as a key indicator of brand equity: The higher the repeat rate, the greater the brand equity and the greater the marketing profitability; the less people are willing to accept substitute brands, the more they are likely to repeat buy.

In a business-to-business setting, Narayandas advocates analyzing sales records, talking to sales teams, and conducting surveys to assess where customers stand on a "loyalty ladder." Successively higher levels of loyalty are associated with (in ascending order):[41]

1. Wants to grow the relationship
2. Endorses products
3. Resists competitor's blandishments
4. Is willing to pay premiums, seeks to collaborate on new product development
5. Is willing to invest in partner firms

Other Brand Resonance Dimensions. Although attitudinal attachment may require a fairly straightforward set of questions, both sense of community and active engagement could call for more varied measures because of their more diverse set of issues. For example, in terms of engagement, measures could explore word-of-mouth behavior, online behavior, and so forth in depth. For online behavior, measures could explore the extent of customer-initiated versus firm-initiated interactions, the extent of learning and teaching by the customer versus by the firm, the extent of customers teaching other customers, and so on.[42] The key to such metrics is the qualitative nature of the interaction and how it reflects intensity of feelings. One mistake many Internet firms made was to put too much emphasis on "eyeballs" and "stickiness"—the number and duration of page views at a Web site, respectively. The depth of the underlying brand relationships of the customers making those visits, however, and the manner in which those relationships manifest themselves in brand-beneficial actions, will typically be more important.

Fournier's Brand Relationship Research. Boston University's Susan Fournier has reframed brand personality in relationship terms.[43] Fournier views brand personality not as a set of interpersonal attributes, but as the relationship role enacted by the brand in its partnership with the consumer. She has proposed a number of interesting ideas concerning brand equity by developing a framework for conceptualizing and understanding the relationships that consumers form with the brands they know and use.

Fournier argues that brands can and do serve as viable relationship partners, and suggests a reconceptualization of the notion of brand personality within this framework. Specifically, Fournier suggests that the everyday execution of marketing mix decisions constitutes a set of behaviors enacted on the part of the brand. These actions trigger a series of inferences regarding the implicit *contract* that appears to guide the engagement of the consumer and brand and, hence, the type of relationship that is formed. Brand personality as conceptualized within this framework concerns the *relationship role* enacted by the brand in its partnership capacity. For example, if the brand expresses behaviors that signal commitment to the consumer, and further if it sends gifts as symbols of affection, the consumer may infer a courtship or marriage type of engagement with the brand.

Fournier identifies a typology of 15 different relationship types characterizing consumers' engagement with brands (see Figure 9-12). Fournier argues that this relationship role view of brand personality provides more actionable guidance to managers who wish to create and manage their brand personalities in line with marketing actions than does the trait-based view, which identifies general personality tendencies that might or might not be connected to marketing strategies and goals.

Fournier has conducted fascinating research that reframes the conceptualization and measurement of brand strength strictly in relationship terms. It defines a brand's strength in terms of the strength, depth, and durability of the consumer-brand relational bond using the multifaceted concept of ***brand relationship quality***, or BRQ. Extensive validation work supported a multifaceted hierarchical structure for the BRQ construct that includes six main dimensions of relationship strength, many with important subfacets. The main facets are (1) interdependence, (2) self-concept connection, (3) commitment, (4) love/passion, (5) intimacy, and (6) brand partner quality.

Fournier argues that these facets and their subfacets (such as trust within the partner quality facet or consumer-to-firm and firm-to-consumer intimacy) have superior diagnostic value over competing strength measures, and she suggests they have greater managerial utility in their application. In her experience, BRQ measures have been successfully incorporated in brand tracking studies, where they provide profiles of brand strength versus competitors, useful ties to marketplace performance indicators, and specific guidance for the enhancement and dilution of brand equity through managerial actions in the marketplace. Although brand relationship quality shares some characteristics with brand resonance, it provides valuable additional perspectives and insights.

The six main facets of brand relationship quality are as follows.

- *Interdependence:* The degree to which the brand is ingrained in the consumer's daily course of living, both behaviorally (in terms of frequency, scope, and strength of interactions) and cognitively (in terms of longing for and preoccupation with anticipated brand interactions). Interdependence is often revealed through the presence of routinized behavioral rituals surrounding brand purchase and use, and through separation anxiety experienced during periods of product deprivation. At its extremes, interdependence becomes dependency and addiction.
- *Self-concept connection:* The degree to which the brand delivers on important identity concerns, tasks, or themes, thereby expressing a significant part of the self-concept, both past (including nostalgic references and brand memories) and present,

Relationship Form	Case Examples
Arranged marriage: Nonvoluntary union imposed by preferences of third party. Intended for long-term, exclusive commitment.	Karen's husband's preferred brands (e.g., Mop'n Glo, Palmolive, Hellman's); Karen's Esteé Lauder, imposed through gift-giving; Jean's use of Murphy's Oil Soap as per manufacturer recommendation.
Casual friend/buddy: Friendship low in affect and intimacy, characterized by infrequent or sporadic engagement and few expectations of reciprocity or reward.	Karen and her household cleaning brands.
Marriage of convenience: Long-term, committed relationship precipitated by environmental influence rather than deliberate choice, and governed by satisfying rules.	Vicki's switch to regional Friend's Baked Beans brand from favored B&M brand left behind; Jean's loyalty to DeMoulas salad dressing brand left behind by client at the bar.
Committed partnership: Long-term, voluntarily imposed, socially supported union high in love, intimacy, trust, and commitment to stay together despite adverse circumstances. Adherence to exclusivity rules expected.	Jean and virtually all her cooking, cleaning, and household appliance brands; Karen and Gatorade.
Best friendship: Voluntary union based on reciprocity principle, the endurance of which is ensured through continued provision of positive rewards. Characterized by revelation of true self, honesty, and intimacy. Congruity in partner images and personal interests common.	Karen and Reebok running shoes.; Vicki and Crest or Ivory.
Compartmentalized friendship: Highly specialized, situationally confined, enduring friendship characterized by lower intimacy than other friendship forms but higher socio-emotional rewards and interdependence. Easy entry and exit.	Vicki and her stable of shampoos, perfumes, and lingerie brands.
Kinship: Nonvoluntary union with lineage ties.	Vicki's preferences for Tetley tea or Karen's for Ban, Joy, and Miracle Whip, all of which were inherited through their mothers.
Rebound relationship: Union precipitated by desire to replace prior partner, as opposed to attraction to replacement partner.	Karen's use of Comet, Gateway, and Success Rice.
Childhood friendship: Infrequently engaged, affective relation reminiscent of childhood times. Yields comfort and security of past self.	Jean and Jell-O pudding.
Courtship: Interim relationship state on the road to committed partnership contract.	Vicki and her Musk scent brands.
Dependency: Obsessive, highly emotional, selfish attractions cemented by feeling that the other is irreplaceable. Separation from other yields anxiety. High tolerance of other's transgressions results.	Karen and Mary Kay; Vicki and Soft 'n Dry.
Fling: Short-term, time-bounded engagement of high emotional reward. Devoid entirely of commitment and reciprocity demands.	Vicki's trial-size shampoo brands.
Enmity: Intensely involving relationship characterized by negative affect and desire to inflict pain or revenge on the other.	Karen and her husband's brands, postdivorce; Jean and her other-recommended-but-rejected brands (e.g., ham, peanut butter, sinks).
Enslavement: Nonvoluntary relationship union governed entirely by desires of the relationship partner.	Karen and Southern Bell, Cable Vision. Vicki and Playtex, a bra for large-breasted women.
Secret affair: Highly emotive, privately held relationship considered risky if exposed to others.	Karen and the Tootsie Pops she sneaks at work.

FIGURE 9-12

A Typology of Consumer-Brand Relationships

and personal as well as social. Grounding of the self provides feelings of comfort, connectedness, control, and security. In its extreme form, self-connection reflects integration of concepts of brand and self.

- *Commitment:* Dedication to continued brand association and betterment of the relationship, despite circumstances foreseen and unforeseen. Commitment includes professed faithfulness and loyalty to the other, often formalized through stated pledges and publicized intentions. Commitment is not defined solely by sunk costs and irretrievable investments that pose barriers to exit.
- *Love/passion:* Affinity toward and adoration of the brand, particularly with respect to other available alternatives. The intensity of the emotional bonds joining relationship partners may range from feelings of warmth, caring, and affection to those of true passion. Love includes the belief that the brand is irreplaceable and uniquely qualified as a relationship partner.
- *Intimacy:* A sense of deep familiarity with and understanding of both the essence of the brand as a partner in the relationship and the nature of the consumer-brand relationship itself. Intimacy is revealed in the presence of a strong consumer-brand relationship culture, the sharing of little-known personal details of the self, and an elaborate brand memory containing significant experiences or associations. Intimacy is a two-dimensional concept: The consumer develops intimate knowledge of the brand, and also feels a sense of intimacy exhibited on the part of the brand toward the individual as a consumer.
- *Partner quality:* Perceived partner quality involves a summary judgment of the caliber of the role enactments performed by the brand in its partnership role. Partner quality includes three central components: (1) an empathic orientation toward the other (ability of the partner to make the other feel wanted, cared for, respected, noticed, and important; responsiveness to needs); (2) a character of reliability, dependability, and predictability in the brand; and (3) trust or faith in the belief that the brand will adhere to established relationship rules and be held accountable for its actions.

Comprehensive Models of Consumer-Based Brand Equity

The customer-based brand equity model presented in this text provides a comprehensive, cohesive overview of brand building and brand equity. Other researchers and consultants have also put forth consumer-based brand equity models that share some of the same principles and philosophy as the CBBE model, although developed in a different way. Brand Focus 9.0 presents a detailed account of arguably the most successful and influential industry branding model, Young and Rubicam's BrandAsset Valuator. Several other firms have also introduced well-received models of brand building that provide insight into how to measure brand equity.[44]

Brand Dynamics

Marketing research supplier Millward Brown's Brand Dynamics model offers a graphical model to represent the strength of relationship consumers have with a brand. As Figure 9-13 displays, the Brand Dynamics model adopts a hierarchical approach to determine the strength of relationship a consumer has with a brand. The five levels of the model, in ascending order of an increasingly intense relationship, are presence, relevance, performance, advantage, and bonding. Consumers are placed into one of the five levels depending on their brand responses. By comparing the pattern across brands, it is easy to uncover

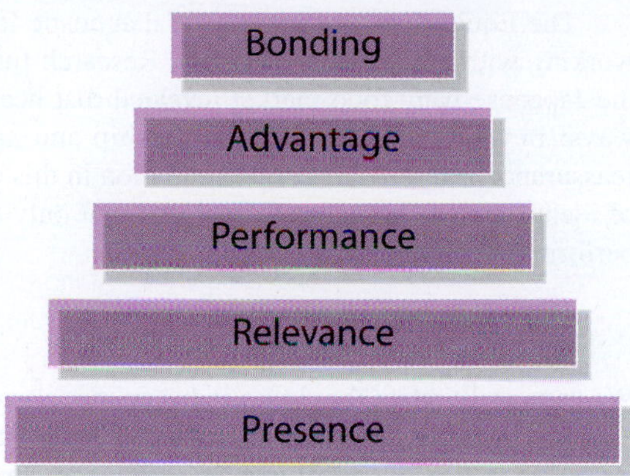

FIGURE 9-13

BrandDynamics™ from Millward Brown

relative strengths and weaknesess and where brands can focus their efforts to improve their loyalty relationships.

Equity Engine

Another marketing research supplier, Research International, has also developed a comprehensive model of brand equity, Equity Engine (see Figure 9-14).[45] This model deliniates three key dimensions of brand affinity—the emotional and intangible benefits of a brand—as follows:

- *Authority:* The reputation of a brand, whether as a long-standing leader or as a pioneer in innovation
- *Identification:* The closeness customers feel for a brand and how well they feel the brand matches their personal needs
- *Approval:* The way a brand fits into the wider social matrix and the intangible status it holds for experts and friends

The model combines the affinity measures with measures of a brand's perceived functional performance to provide an assessment of overall equity. Finally, the equity measure is combined with price to provide a closer marketplace approximation of how consumers combine brand associations to make decisions.

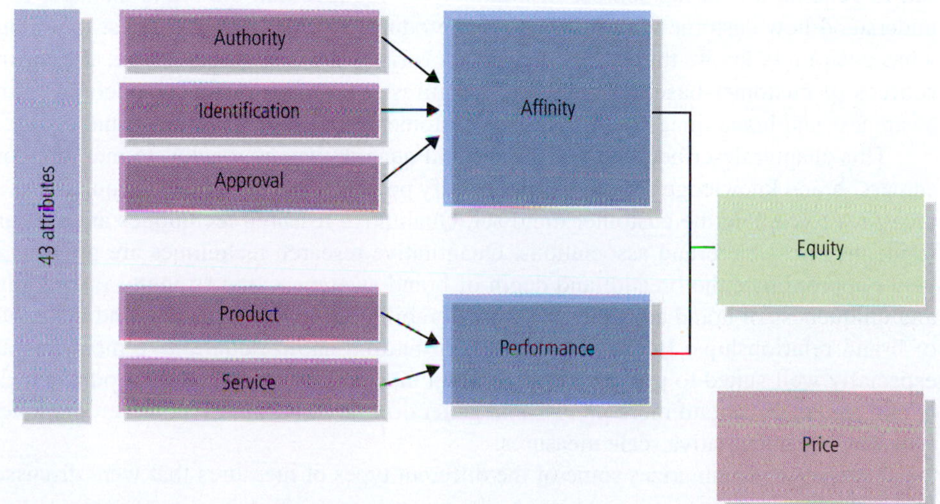

FIGURE 9-14

Equity Engine™ from Research International

The Equity Engine can provide diagnostic information as to what is working or not working with a brand. For example, Research International describes how an analysis of the Japanese baby food market revealed that health and nutrition were important in two ways: in terms of category membership and as a point of parity but also to provide reassurance and trust. True differentiation in this category was related to emotional issues of identification and peer acceptability, but only once the image of acceptable functional performance was firmly in place.[46]

Relationship to the CBBE Model

We can easily relate these two industry models of brand equity to the CBBE model. For example, the five sequenced stages of Millward Brown's Brand Dynamics model—presence, relevance, performance, advantage, and bonding—relate to the four ascending steps of the CBBE model (identity, meaning, responses, and relationships) and specific CBBE model concepts (e.g., salience, consideration, performance or quality, superiority, and resonance). Similarly, each of the dimensions and sub-dimensions of Research International's Equity Engine model also directly relate to components of the CBBE model, namely authority (credibility), identification (consideration), approval (brand imagery), which lead to affinity (resonance), and the functional aspects of a product or service contribute to performance (brand performance). With its inclusion of a price measure, the Equity Engine also relates to the market performance stage of the brand value chain.

Thus, the CBBE model synthesizes the concepts and measures from these leading industry models and at the same time provides much additional substance and insight. Several particularly noteworthy aspects of the CBBE model are: (1) its emphasis on brand salience and breadth and depth of brand awareness as the foundation of brand building; (2) its recognition of the dual nature of brands and the significance of both rational and emotional considerations in brand building; and (3) the importance it places on brand resonance as the culmination of brand building and a more meaningful way to view brand loyalty.

Review

According to the brand value chain, sources of brand equity arise from the customer mind-set. In general, measuring sources of brand equity requires that the brand manager fully understand how customers shop for and use products and services and, most important, what customers know, think, and feel about various brands. In particular, measuring sources of customer-based brand equity requires measuring various aspects of brand awareness and brand image that lead to the customer response that creates brand equity.

This chapter described both qualitative and quantitative approaches to measure consumers' brand knowledge structures and identify potential sources of brand equity, that is, measures to capture the customer mind-set. Qualitative research techniques are a means to identify possible brand associations. Quantitative research techniques are a means to better approximate the breadth and depth of brand awareness; the strength, favorability, and uniqueness of brand associations; the favorability of brand responses; and the nature of brand relationships. Because of their unstructured nature, qualitative measures are especially well suited to provide an in-depth glimpse of what brands and products mean to consumers. To obtain more precise and generalizable information, however, marketers typically use quantitative scale measures.

Figure 9-15 summarizes some of the different types of measures that were discussed in the chapter.

I. Qualitative Research Techniques
Free association
Adjective ratings and checklists
Projective techniques
Photo sorts
Bubble drawings
Story telling
Personification exercises
Role playing
Experiential methods

II. Quantitative Research Techniques
A. Brand Awareness
Direct and indirect measures of brand recognition
Aided and unaided measures of brand recall
B. Brand Image
Open-ended and scale measures of specific brand attributes and benefits
Strength
Favorability
Uniqueness
Overall judgments and feelings
Overall relationship measures
Intensity
Activity

FIGURE 9-15

Summary of Qualitative and Quantitative Measures

Discussion Questions

1. Pick a brand. Employ projective techniques to attempt to identify sources of its brand equity. Which measures work best? Why?
2. Run an experiment to see if you can replicate the Mason Haire instant coffee experiment (see Branding Brief 9.3). Do the same attributions still hold? If not, can you replace coffee with a brand combination from another product category that would produce pronounced differences?
3. Pick a product category. Can you profile the brand personalities of the leading brands in the category using Aaker's brand personality inventory?
4. Pick a brand. How would you best profile consumers' brand knowledge structures? How would you use quantitative measures?
5. Think of your brand relationships. Can you find examples of brands that fit into Fournier's different categories?

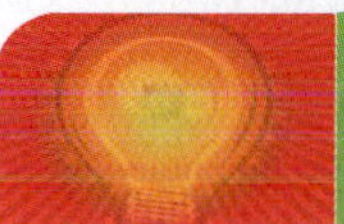

BRAND FOCUS 9.0

Young & Rubicam's BrandAsset Valuator

This feature summarizes Young & Rubicam's development of its BrandAsset Valuator (BAV), the world's largest database of consumer-derived information on brands.[47] BAV measures brands on five fundamental measures of equity value and in terms of a broad array of perceptual dimensions. BAV provides comparative measures of the equity value of thousands of brands across hundreds of different categories, as well as a set of strategic brand management tools for planning brand extensions, joint branding ventures, and other strategies designed to maintain and grow brand value. BAV has now also been linked to a unique set of financial analytics, which allows determining a brand's contribution to a company's intangible value.

Since 1993 BAV has carried out research with almost 400,000 consumers in 44 countries. Consumers' perceptions of approximately 20,000 brands have been collected across the same set of 72 dimensions. BAV represents a unique brand equity research tool. Unlike most conventional brand image surveys, respondents evaluate brands from many different categories rather than just those within a narrowly defined category. BAV is thus able to follow truly global brand trends and to draw the broadest possible conclusions about how consumer-level brand equity is created and built—or lost. In the United States, data are now collected in quarterly waves, which allows short-term trends in branding to be followed.

In addition to the original measures, recent BAV surveys have included greater emphasis on brand usage and future usage intent, and have also built in a specially developed set of measures of brand loyalty.

Five Pillars

There are five key components of brand health in BAV—the five pillars. Each pillar is derived from various measures that relate to different aspects of consumers' brand perceptions and that together trace the progression of a brand's development.

- *Differentiation* measures the degree to which a brand is seen as different from others. This is a necessary condition for profitable brand building.
- *Energy* measures the brand's ability to meet future consumer needs and attract new customers. It reveals the strength of momentum that a brand has and accounts for changes in financial performance.
- *Relevance* measures the breadth of a brand's appeal (the overall size of a brand's franchise), but not necessarily its profitability.
- *Esteem* measures how well the brand is regarded and respected—in short, how well it's liked.
- *Knowledge* measures how familiar and intimate consumers are with the brand. Interestingly, high knowledge is inversely related to a brand's potential.

Leading Indicators of Brand Health: Brand Energy

Differentiation (the extent to which a brand has a distinctive meaning for the consumer and is able to gain consumer choice, preference, and loyalty), energy (which reflects how dynamic the brand is), and relevance (which correlates with household penetration) combine to determine brand energy. These three pillars point to the brand's future value, rather than just reflecting its past.

Lagging Indicators of Brand Health: Brand Stature

Esteem and knowledge together create brand stature, which is a "report card" on a brand's past performance.

Pillar Patterns

The examination of the relationships between these five dimensions—a brand's "pillar pattern"—reveals much about a brand's current and future status. New brands, just after they are launched, show low levels on all five pillars. Strong new brands tend to show higher levels of differentiation and energy than relevance; both esteem and knowledge are lower still. "Leadership" brands show high levels on all five pillars. Finally, declining brands show high knowledge—evidence of past performance—relative to a lower level of esteem, and even lower relevance, energy, and differentiation.

Comparison of pillar patterns between brands—in the same or different categories—permits the diagnosis of brands' relative strengths and weaknesses, whereas tracking changes in pillar patterns for the same brand over time traces the progress of the brand's consumer equity value.

The PowerGrid

Young & Rubicam has integrated the two macrodimensions of brand strength (differentiation, energy, and relevance) and brand stature (esteem and knowledge) into a visual analytical device known as the PowerGrid, illustrated in Figure 9-16. The PowerGrid depicts the stages in the cycle of brand development—each with its characteristic pillar patterns—in successive quadrants.

Brands generally begin their life in the lower left quadrant, where they first need to develop relevant differentiation and establish their reason for being.

Most often, the movement from there is "up" into the top left quadrant. Increased differentiation, followed by relevance, initiates a growth in brand strength. These developments occur before the brand has acquired esteem or is widely known. This quadrant represents two types of brands: For brands destined for a mass target, this is the stage of emerging potential, in which the brand's growing strength must be translated into stature. Specialist or narrowly targeted brands, however, tend to remain in this quadrant (when viewed from the perspective of a mass audience) and can use their strength to occupy a profitable niche. From the point of view of brand leaders, new potential competitors will emerge from this quadrant.

The upper right quadrant, the leadership quadrant, is populated by brand leaders—those that have both high

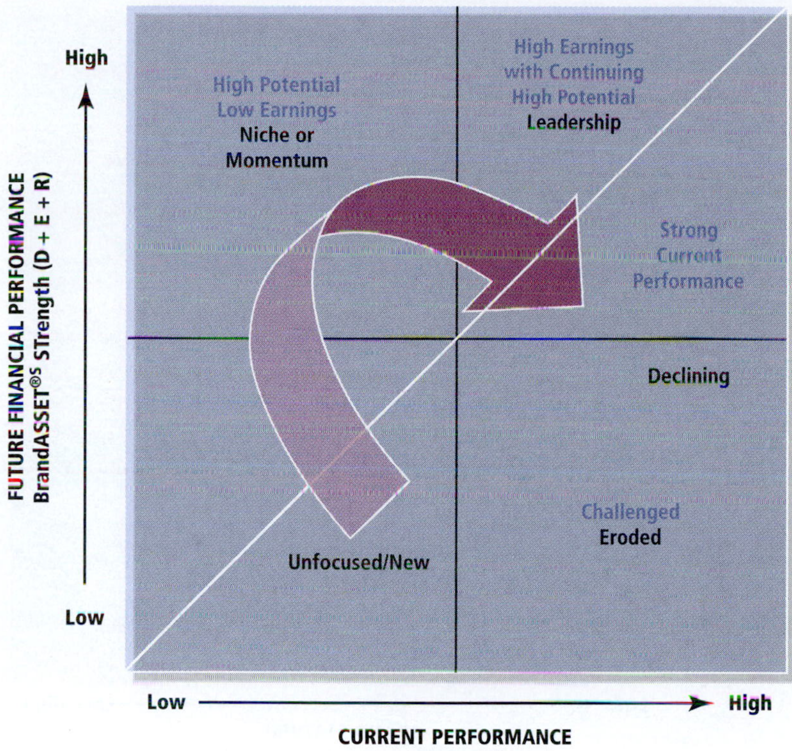

FIGURE 9-16

The BAV PowerGrid

levels of brand strength and brand stature. Both older and relatively new brands can be in this quadrant, meaning that brand leadership is truly a function of the pillar measures, not just of longevity, and that, when properly managed, a brand can build and maintain a leadership position indefinitely. Although declining brand equity is not inevitable, brands whose strength has declined (usually driven by declining differentiation) can also be seen in this same quadrant. Brands whose strength has started to dip below the level of their stature display the first signs of weakness, which may well be masked by their still-buoyant sales and wide penetration.

Brands that fail to maintain their brand strength—their relevant differentiation—begin to fade and move "down" into the bottom right quadrant. These brands become vulnerable not just to existing competitors, but also to the depredations of discount price brands, and they frequently end up being drawn into heavy and continuous price promotion in order to defend their consumer franchise and market share. This process, if allowed to continue, takes its toll on brand stature, which also starts to decline. Figure 9-17 shows brand examples in all four quadrants, and Figure 9-18 shows how brand development may vary by different markets; for example, Coca-Cola has a much more uniform global image than, say, Apple Computer, Esteé Lauder, or American Express.

Brand Image Associations

In addition to the pillar measures, BAV measures brands on a series of 48 brand image and brand personality attributes. Brand imagery can be analyzed in terms of all the single attributes or in terms of a reduced number of factor groupings. Because, like all BAV measures, the image attributes have been selected for their applicability to all categories, it is possible to compare the images of brands in widely differing categories. One very useful technique when trying to understand a brand's positioning is to determine which other brands its image is closest to. For example, for an Internet commerce site or computer brand, it is very helpful to know whether the brand's image has more in common with the Gap or with Macy's.

Drivers of Brand Energy and Stature

By analyzing the relationships between a brand's imagery on attributes and its position in the PowerGrid, it is possible to obtain a very precise understanding of the type of imagery that drives brand strength and brand stature.

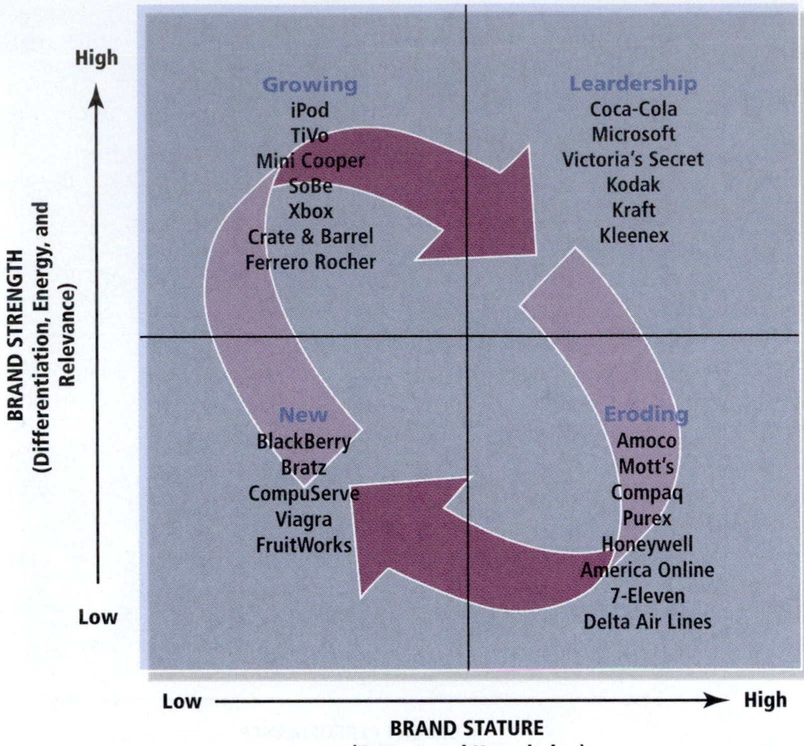

FIGURE 9-17

BAV Power Grid Brand Examples

Base: USA, Adults, 2004.

Brand Elasticity. Because the BAV covers so many different categories, one of the key uses of the brand image component of the BAV is to examine brand elasticity—the ease with which a brand can be "stretched" into a new category. According to the BAV, the probability of success of such brand extensions depends on two criteria:

- Brand profile similarity: How similar—across all 48 attributes—is the image of the brand to the image of the brands in the target category? Does the brand have "permission to play"? Does its image match the lowest common denominator of the target category, the imagery shared by all brands in the category and which thus represents the minimum cost of entry?
- Does the brand have what it takes to stand out, to create differentiation in the new category? Although the image of the brand may have given it strong differentiation in its original category, this same imagery may not serve it so well in the new category. Does it also have necessary points of parity that would allow this differentiation to matter?

As shown in Figure 9-19, cross-analysis of these two criteria, according to Young & Rubicam, provides a clear prescription for alternative brand extension strategies. If the brand's imagery satisfies the cost of entry for the category and also has the ability to drive differentiation, this is the clearest green light for pushing ahead with the brand extension.

When a brand's imagery has what it takes to create differentiation in the new category but lacks the cost-of-entry image characteristics, then entry into that category will not be easy, but the brand may be able to achieve an "ambush" entry. If its differentiating characteristics are sufficient to overcome the barriers and gain it credibility, they will then propel it to a position of strength in the new category.

When the brand's image profile is dissimilar to the new category and its current imagery would not differentiate it in the new category, then the chances of a successful extension are low, and an entry into the category would be better accomplished via the acquisition either of an existing brand already in the category or of one whose imagery makes it more suitable for the job.

If a brand's imagery meets the cost-of-entry level for the new category but is lacking in drivers of differentiation, then it is clear that a successful entry can be achieved, but only with considerable investment. In this case, an alternative solution is to seek an alliance with another brand in the category: The two brands may be able to reinforce each other's strengths and jointly create a stronger presence there.

Brand Alliances. In a recent addition to the BAV, the effect on individual brands of different types of brand alliances—from sweepstakes promotions through Web site links between brands—has been directly measured. The effects are various and unpredictable. For example:

- Alliances between Levi's and Wal-Mart produced an improvement of the brand strength of Wal-Mart, but left Levi's virtually unchanged.
- In contrast, Levi's did benefit from an alliance with Yahoo, growing in differentiation and brand strength.

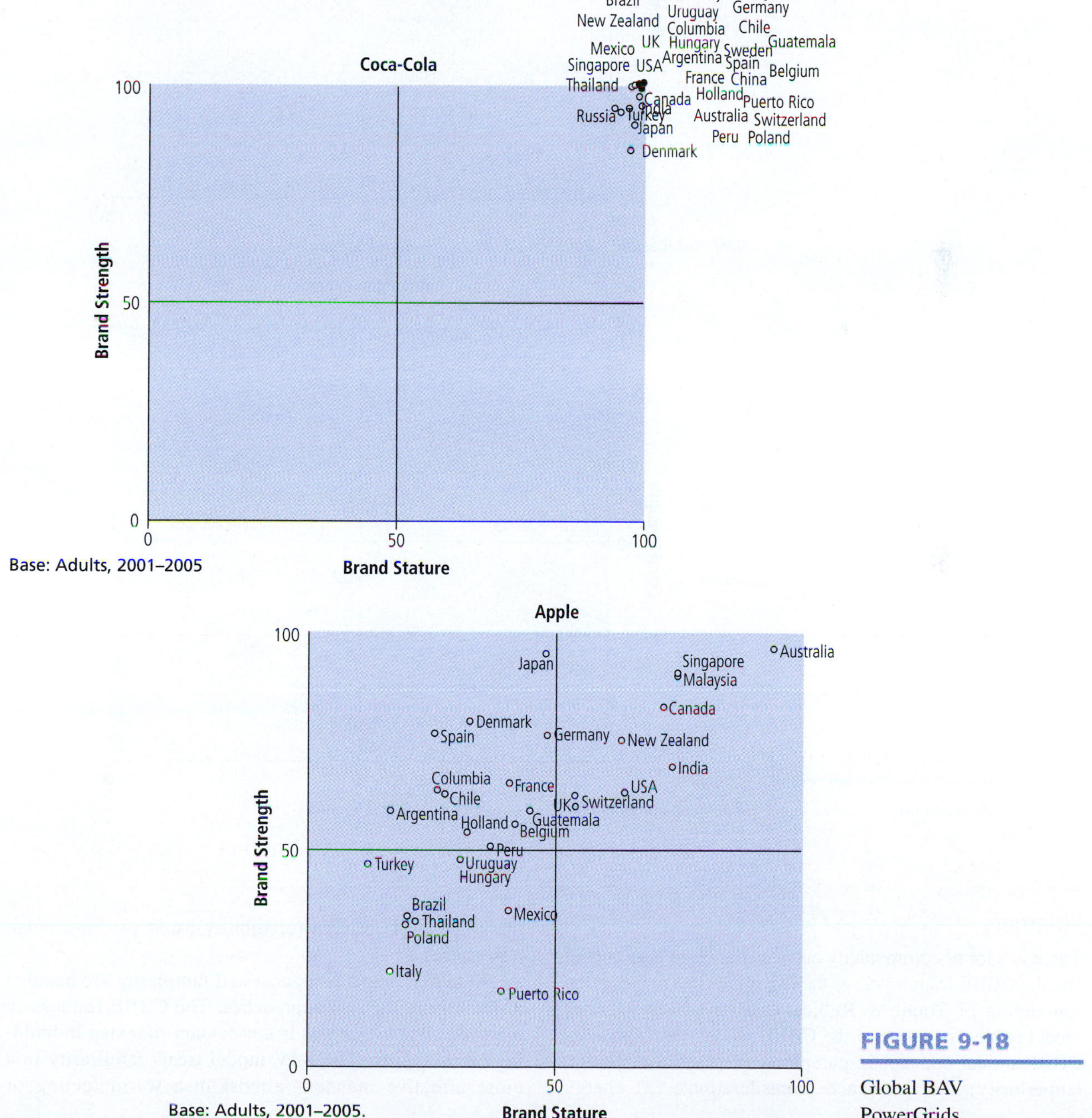

FIGURE 9-18
Global BAV PowerGrids

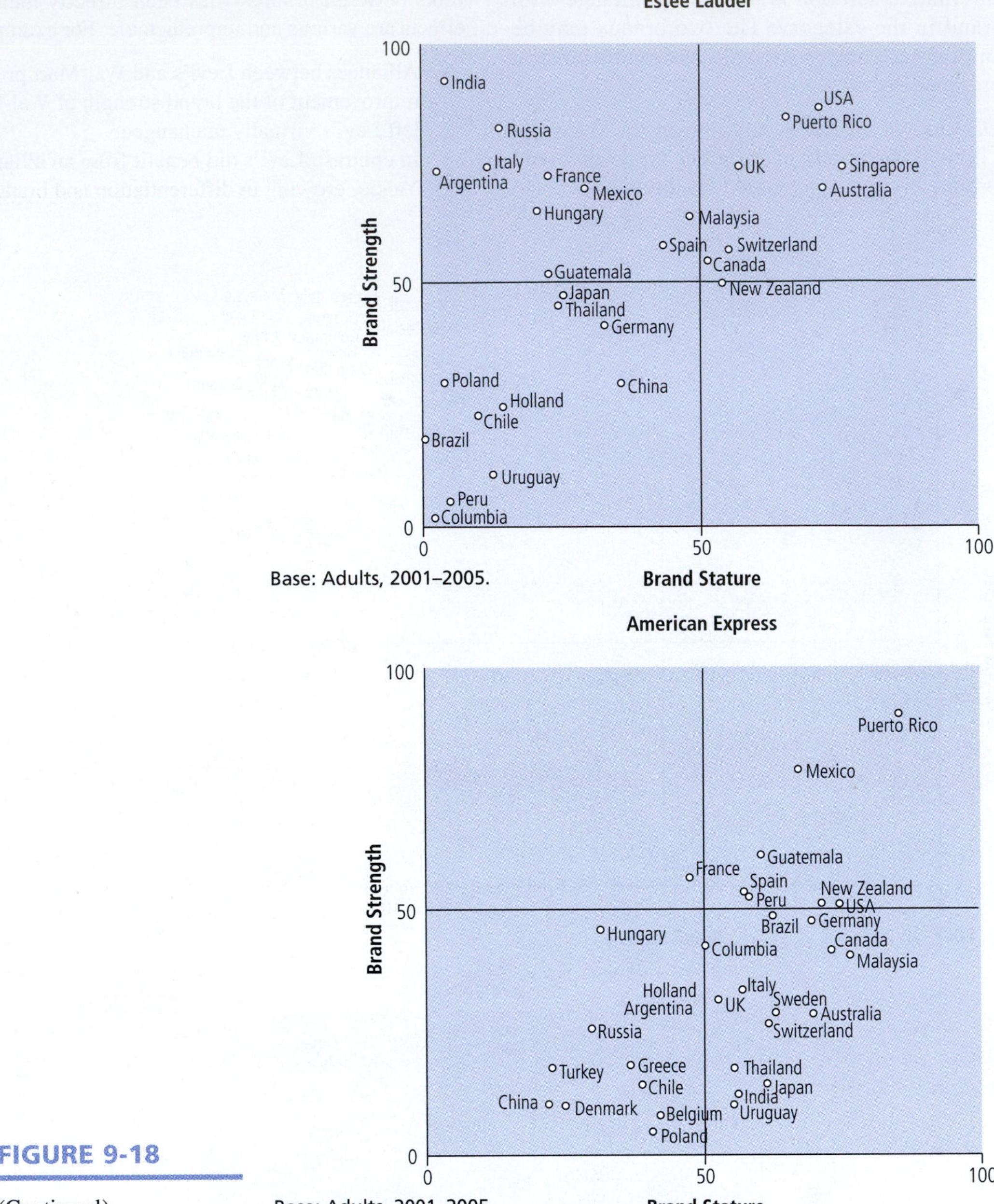

FIGURE 9-18

(Continued)

Summary

There is a lot of commonality between the basic BAV model and the CBBE framework, as the five pillars that make up the foundation of Young & Rubicam's BrandAsset Valuator model relate to aspects of the CBBE model (corresponding CBBE model concept in parentheses): (1) differentiation (superiority); (2) relevance (consideration); (3) energy (judgment); (4) esteem (credibility); and (5) knowledge (resonance).

Note that brand awareness and familiarity are handled differently in the two approaches. The CBBE framework maintains that awareness is a necessary *first* step in building brand equity. The BAV model treats familiarity in a more affective manner—almost in a warm feeling or

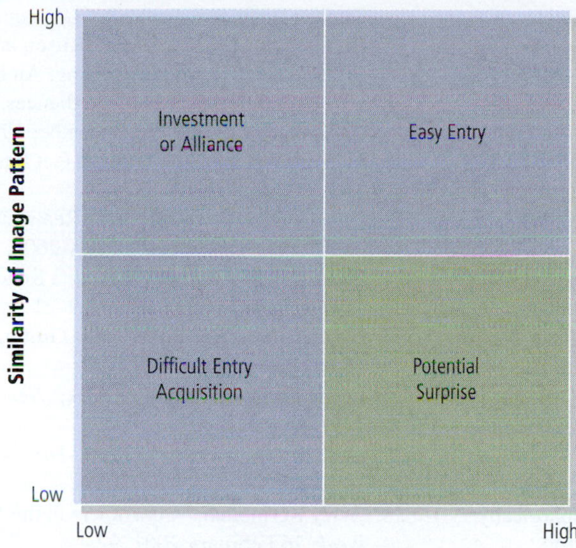

FIGURE 9-19

Brand Elasticity

friendship sense—and thus sees it as the *last* step in building brand equity, more akin to the CBBE concept of resonance, as noted above.

The main advantage of the BAV model is that it provides rich descriptions and profiles of a number of brands. It also provides focus on four key branding dimensions. It provides a brand landscape in which marketers can see where their brands are located relative to other prominent brands or with respect to different markets. The descriptive nature of the BAV model does mean, however, that there is potentially less insight as to exactly *how* a brand could rate highly on those factors. Because the measures underlying the four factors have to be relevant across a very disparate range of product categories, the measures (and thus the factors) tend to be abstract in nature and not related directly to product attributes or benefits and more specific marketing concerns. Nevertheless, the BAV model represents a landmark study in terms of marketers' ability to better understand what drives top brands and where their brands fit in with other brands.

Notes

1. Burleigh B. Gardner and Sidney J. Levy, "The Product and the Brand," *Harvard Business Review* (March–April 1955): 35.
2. Some leading textbooks in this area are J. Paul Peter and Jerry C. Olson, *Consumer Behavior and Marketing Strategy,* 7th ed. (Homewood, IL: Irwin, 2005); Wayne D. Hoyer and Deborah J. MacInnis, *Consumer Behavior,* 3rd ed. (Boston: Houghton Mifflin College, 2004); and Michael R. Solomon, *Consumer Behavior: Buying, Having, and Being,* 7th ed. (Upper Saddle River, NJ: Prentice Hall, 2007).
3. John Motavalli, "Probing Consumer Minds," *Adweek,* 7 December 1987, 4–8.
4. Ernest Dichter, *Handbook of Consumer Motivations* (New York: McGraw-Hill, 1964).
5. H. Shanker Krishnan, "Characteristics of Memory Associations: A Consumer-Based Brand Equity Perspective," *International Journal of Research in Marketing* (October 1996): 389–405.
6. J. Wesley Hutchinson, "Expertise and the Structure of Free Recall," in *Advances in Consumer Research,* Vol. 10, eds. Richard P. Bagozzi and Alice M. Tybout (Ann Arbor, MI: Association of Consumer Research, 1983), 585–589.
7. Yvan Boivin, "A Free Response Approach to the Measurement of Brand Perceptions," *International Journal of Research in Marketing* 3 (1986): 11–17.
8. Alexandra Harrington, "G. C. Rapaille: Finding the Keys in the Cultural Unconscious," *Response TV,* 1 September 2001; Jeffrey Ball, "'But How Does It Make You Feel?'" *Wall Street Journal,* 3 May 1999; Jack Hitt, "Does the Smell of Coffee Brewing Remind You of Your Mother?" *New York Times Magazine,* 7 May 2000.
9. Sydney J. Levy, "Dreams, Fairy Tales, Animals, and Cars," *Psychology and Marketing* 2, no. 2 (1985): 67–81.

10. Mason Haire, "Projective Techniques in Marketing Research, *Journal of Marketing* (April 1950): 649–656. Interestingly, a follow-up study conducted several decades later suggested that instant coffee users were no longer perceived as psychologically different from drip grind users. See Frederick E. Webster Jr. and Frederick Von Pechmann, "A Replication of the 'Shopping List' Study," *Journal of Marketing* 34 (April 1970): 61–63.
11. Levy, "Dreams, Fairy Tales."
12. Jeffrey Durgee and Robert Stuart, "Advertising Symbols and Brand Names That Best Represent Key Product Meanings," *Journal of Consumer Marketing* 4, no. 3 (1987): 15–24.
13. Gerald Zaltman and Robin Higie, "Seeing the Voice of the Customer: Metaphor-Based Advertising Research," *Journal of Advertising Research* (July/August 1995): 35–51; Daniel H. Pink, "Metaphor Marketing," *Fast Company,* April 1998; Gerald Zaltman, "Metaphorically Speaking," *Marketing Research* (Summer 1996); www.olsonzaltman.com; Gerald Zaltman, "How Customers Think: Essential Insights into the Mind of the Market," *Harvard Business School Press,* 2003; Wendy Melillo, "Inside the Consumer Mind: What Neuroscience Can Tell Us About Marketing," *Adweek,* 16 January 2006.
14. For an approach to brand personality based on narrative thought processes, see Jerry Olson and Doug Allen, "Building Bonds between the Brand and the Customer by Creating and Managing Brand Personality," paper presented at Marketing Science Institute Conference on Brand Equity and the Marketing Mix: Creating Customer Value, Tucson, AZ, 2–3 March 1995.
15. Jennifer Aaker, "Dimensions of Brand Personality," *Journal of Marketing Research* 34, no. 8 (1997): 347–356.
16. Jay Dean, "A Practitioner's Perspective on Brand Equity," in *Proceedings of the Society for Consumer Psychology,* eds. Wes Hutchinson and Kevin Lane Keller (Clemson, SC: CtC Press, 1994), 56–62.
17. Aaker, " Dimensions of Brand Personality." See also Jennifer Aaker, "The Malleable Self: The Role of Self-Expression in Persuasion," *Journal of Marketing Research* 36, no. 2 (1999): 45–57.
18. Jennifer L. Aaker, Veronica Benet-Martinez, and Jordi Garolera, "Consumption Symbols as Carriers of Culture: A Study of Japanese and Spanish Brand Personality Constructs," *Journal of Personality and Social Psychology* 81, no. 3 (2001): 492–508.
19. Yongjun Sung and Spencer F. Tinkham, "Brand Personality Structures in the United States and Korea: Common and Culture-Specific Factors," *Journal of Consumer Psychology* 15, no. 4 (2005): 334–350.
20. Gil Ereaut and Mike Imms, " 'Bricolage': Qualitative Market Research Redefined," *Admap,* December 2002, 16–18.
21. Jennifer Chang Coupland, "Invisible Brands: An Ethnography of Households and the Brands in Their Kitchen Pantries," *Journal of Consumer Research* 32 (June 2005): 106–118; Mark Ritson and Richard Elliott, "The Social Uses of Advertising: An Ethnographic Study of Adolescent Advertising Audiences," *Journal of Consumer Research* 26 (December 1999): 260–277.
22. Melanie Wells, "New Ways to Get Into Our Heads," *USA Today,* 2 March 1999, B1–B2.
23. David Goetzel, "O&M Turns Reality TV into Research Tool," *Advertising Age,* 10 July 2000, 6.
24. Edward F. McQuarrie, "Taking a Road Trip," *Marketing Management* 3, no. 4 (1995): 9–21.
25. David Kiley, "Shoot the Focus Group," *Business Week,* 14 November 2005, 120–121.
26. Leslie Kaufman, "Enough Talk," *Newsweek,* 18 August 1997, 48–49.
27. Luisa Kroll, "Crawling Back," *Forbes,* 26 July 1999, 80.
28. Gerry Kermouch, "Consumers in the Mist," *Business Week,* 26 February 2001, 92–94.
29. Rekha Balu, "Listen Up! (It Might Be Your Customer Talking)," *Fast Company,* May 2000, 304–316.
30. Thomas K. Srull, "Methodological Techniques for the Study of Person Memory and Social Cognition," in *Handbook of Social Cognition,* Vol. 2, eds. Robert S. Wyer and Thomas K. Srull (Hillsdale, NJ: Lawrence Erlbaum, 1984), 1–72.
31. Bill Abrams and David P. Garino, "Package Design Gains Stature as Visual Competition Grows," *Wall Street Journal,* 6 August 1981, 25.
32. Raymond Gordon, "Phantom Products," *Forbes,* 21 May 1984, 202–204.
33. Philip Kotler, *Marketing Management: Analysis, Planning, Implementation, and Control,* 12th ed. (Upper Saddle River, NJ: Prentice Hall, 2006).
34. Deborah Roeddder John, Barbara Loken, Kyeong-Heui Kim, and Alokparna Basu Monga, "Brand Concept Maps: A Methodology for Identifying Brand Association Networks," Marketing Science Institute Report No. 05–112.
35. Joseph F. Hair Jr., Rolph E. Anderson, Ronald Tatham, and William C. Black, *Multivariate Data Analysis,* 4th ed. (Englewood Cliffs, NJ: Prentice Hall, 1995).
36. Jean-Noel Kapferer and Gilles Laurent, "Consumers' Brand Sensitivity: A New Concept for Brand Management," paper presented at the Annual Conference of the European Marketing Academy, 1985; Jean-Noel Kapferer and Gilles Laurent, "Consumer Brand Sensitivity: A Key to Measuring and Managing Brand Equity," presentation at Marketing Science Institute Conference on Defining, Measuring, and Managing Brand Equity, Austin, TX, 1–3 March 1988.
37. Thomas J. Reynolds and Carol B. Phillips, "In Search of True Brand Equity Metrics: All Market Share Ain't Created Equal," *Journal of Advertising Research* (June 2005): 171–186.

38. J. Scott Armstrong, Vicki G. Morwitz and V. Kumar, "Sales Forecasts for Existing Consumer Products and Services: Do Purchase Intentions Contribute to Accuracy?" *International Journal of Forecasting* 16 (2000): 383–397.
39. Icek Ajzen and Martin Fishbein, *Understanding Attitudes and Predicting Social Behavior* (Englewood Cliffs, NJ: Prentice Hall, 1980).
40. "Longman-Moran Analytics," unpublished internal company document.
41. Das Narayandas, "Building Loyalty in Business Markets," *Harvard Business Review* (September 2005): 131–138.
42. Vikas Mittal and Mohanbir S. Sawhney, "Managing Customer Retention in the Attention Economy," working paper, University of Pittsburgh, 2001.
43. Susan M. Fournier, "Consumers and Their Brands: Developing Relationship Theory in Consumer Research," *Journal of Consumer Research* 24, no. 3 (1998): 343–373; Susan M. Fournier, "Dimensioning Brand Relationships Using Brand Relationship Quality" paper presented at the Association for Consumer Research Annual Conference, Salt Lake City, UT, October 2000; Susan M. Fournier, Susan Dobscha, and David G. Mick, "Preventing the Premature Death of Relationship Marketing," *Harvard Business Review* (January–February): 42–51; Susan M. Fournier and Julie L. Yao, "Reviving Brand Loyalty: A Reconceptualization within the Framework of Consumer-Brand Relationships," *International Journal of Research in Marketing* 14 (1997): 451–472.
44. For a helpful review of different perspectives, see Jonathan Knowles, "In Search of a Reliable Measure of Brand Equity," *MarketingNPV* 2, no. 3 (July 2005).
45. www.research-int.com.
46. Phil Sutcliffe, "Fact or Fallacy—Branding Realities or Myths?" Research International white paper, 20 July 2000.
47. This case study benefited from contributions by Ed Lebar, Phil Buehler, Monika Sawicka, and Ryan Barker.

MEASURING OUTCOMES OF BRAND EQUITY

CAPTURING MARKET PERFORMANCE

Preview

Ideally, to measure brand equity, we would create a "brand equity index"-one easily calculated number that would summarize the health of the brand and completely capture its brand equity. But just as a thermometer measuring body temperature provides only one indication of how healthy a person is, so does any one measure of brand equity provide only one indication of the health of a brand. Brand equity is a multidimensional concept, and complex enough to require many different types of measures. Multiple measures increase the diagnostic power of marketing research and the likelihood that managers will better understand what is happening to their brands and, perhaps more important, why.[1]

In arguing that researchers should employ multiple measures of brand equity, marketing executive Richard Chay drew an interesting comparison between measuring brand equity and determining the performance of an aircraft in flight:

> The pilot of the plane has to consider a number of indicators and gauges as the plane is flown. There is the fuel gauge, the altimeter, and a number of other important status indicators. All of these dials and meters tell the pilot different things about the health of the plane. There is no one gauge that summarizes everything about the plane. The plane needs the altimeter, compass, radar, and the fuel gauge. As the pilot looks at the instrument cluster, he has to take all of these critical indicators into account as he flies.[2]

Chay concludes by noting that the gauges on the plane, which together measure its health in flight, are analogous to the multiple measures of brand equity necessary to assess the health of a brand.

The preceding chapter described different approaches to measuring brand knowledge structures and the customer mind-set that marketers can use to identify and quantify potential sources of brand equity. By applying these measurement techniques, we should gain a good understanding of the depth and breadth of brand awareness; the strength, favorability, and uniqueness of brand associations; the valence of brand responses; and the nature of brand relationships for their brands. As we described in Chapter 2, a product with positive brand equity can enjoy the following seven important customer-related benefits:

1. Be perceived differently and produce different interpretations of product performance
2. Enjoy greater loyalty and be less vulnerable to competitive marketing actions
3. Command larger margins and have more inelastic responses to price increases and elastic responses to price decreases
4. Receive greater trade cooperation and support
5. Increase marketing communication effectiveness
6. Yield licensing opportunities
7. Support brand extensions

The customer-based brand equity model maintains that these benefits, and thus the ultimate value of a brand, depend on the underlying components of brand knowledge and sources of brand equity. As Chapter 9 described, we can measure these individual components; however, to provide more direct estimates, we still must assess their resulting value in some way. This chapter examines measurement procedures to assess the effects of brand knowledge structures on these and other measures that capture market performance for the brand. The Science of Branding 10-1 describes how academic researchers have explored the way branding affects basic consumer behavior processes.

First we review comparative methods, which are means to better assess the effects of consumer perceptions and preferences on consumer response to the marketing program and the specific benefits of brand equity. Next, we look at holistic methods, which attempt to estimate the overall or summary value of a brand.[3] Some of the interplay between branding and financial considerations is included in Brand Focus 10.0.

Comparative Methods

Comparative methods are research studies or experiments that examine consumer attitudes and behavior toward a brand to directly estimate the benefits arising from having a high level of awareness and strong, favorable, and unique brand associations. There are two types of comparative methods. ***Brand-based comparative approaches*** use experiments in which one group of consumers responds to an element of the marketing program or some marketing activity when it is attributed to the target brand, and another group responds to that same element or activity when it is attributed to a competitive or fictitiously named brand. ***Marketing-based comparative approaches*** use experiments in which consumers respond to changes in elements of the marketing program or marketing activity for the target brand or competitive brands.

The brand-based approach holds the marketing program fixed and examines consumer response based on changes in brand identification, whereas the marketing-based approach holds the brand fixed and examines consumer response based on changes in the marketing program. We'll look at each of these two approaches in turn and then describe conjoint analysis as a technique that, in effect, combines the two.

Brand-Based Comparative Approaches

Competitive brands can be useful benchmarks in brand-based comparative approaches. Although consumers may interpret marketing activity for a fictitiously named or unnamed version of the product or service in terms of their general product category knowledge, they may also have a particular brand, or ***exemplar,*** in mind. This exemplar may be the category leader or some other brand that consumers feel is representative of the category, like their most preferred brand. Consumers may make inferences to supply any missing information based on their knowledge of this particular brand. Thus, it may be instructive to examine how consumers evaluate a proposed new ad campaign, new promotion offering, or new product when it is also attributed to one or more major competitors.

Applications. The classic example of the brand-based comparative approach is "blind testing" research studies in which consumers examine or use a product with or without brand identification. For example, recall the beer taste test results from Chapter 2, which showed how dramatically consumer perceptions differed depending on the presence or absence of brand identification. One natural application of the brand-based comparative approach is product purchase or consumption research for new or existing products, as long as the brand identification can be hidden in some way for the "unbranded" control group. Brand-based comparative approaches are also useful to determine brand equity benefits related to price margins and premiums.

T-Mobile

Deutsche Telecom has invested much time and money in recent years in building its T-Mobile mobile communication brand. In the United Kingdom, however, the company leases its network lines to competitor Virgin Mobile. As a result, the audio quality of the signal that a T-Mobile customer receives in making a call should be virtually identical to the audio quality of the signal for a Virgin Mobile USA customer. After all, the same network is being used to send the signal. Despite that fact, research has shown that Virgin Mobile customers rate their signal quality significantly higher than do T-Mobile customers. The strong Virgin brand image appears to cast a halo over its different service offerings, literally causing consumers to change their impressions of product performance.

Critique. The main advantage of a brand-based comparative approach is that because it holds all aspects of the marketing program fixed for the brand, it isolates the value of a brand in a very real sense. Understanding exactly how knowledge of the brand affects consumer responses to prices, advertising, and so forth is extremely useful in developing strategies in these different areas. At the same time, we could study an almost infinite variety of marketing activities, so what we learn is limited only by the number of different applications we examine.

Brand-based comparative methods are particularly applicable when the marketing activity under consideration represents a change from past marketing of the brand, for example, a new sales or trade promotion, ad campaign, or proposed brand extension. If the marketing activity under consideration is already strongly identified with the brand—like an ad campaign that has been running for years—it may be difficult to attribute some aspect of the marketing program to a fictitiously named or unnamed version of the product or service in a believable fashion.

Thus, a crucial consideration with the brand-based comparative approach is the realism we can achieve in the experiment. We usually have to sacrifice some realism in order to gain sufficient control to isolate the effects of brand knowledge. When it is too difficult for consumers to examine or experience some element of the marketing program without being aware of the brand, we can use detailed concept statements of that element instead. For example, we can ask consumers to judge a proposed new product when it is either introduced by the firm as a brand extension or introduced by an unnamed firm in that product market. Similarly, we can ask about acceptable price ranges and store locations for the brand name product or a hypothetical unnamed version.

One concern with brand-based comparative approaches is that the simulations and concept statements may highlight the particular product characteristics enough to make them more salient than they would otherwise be, distorting the results.

Marketing-Based Comparative Approaches

Marketing-based comparative approaches hold the brand fixed and examine consumer response based on changes in the marketing program.

Applications. There is a long academic and industry tradition of exploring price premiums using marketing-based comparative approaches. In the mid-1950s, Edgar Pessemier developed a dollarmetric measure of brand commitment that relied on a step-by-step increase of the price difference between the brand normally purchased and an alternative brand.[4] To reveal brand-switching and loyalty patterns, Pessemier plotted the percentage of consumers who switched from their regular brand as a function of the brand

THE SCIENCE OF BRANDING 10-1

Understanding How Brands Affect Consumer Behavior

Academic researchers have identified a number of different theoretical mechanisms, based on consumer behavior, to explain why strong brands for which consumers have high brand knowledge receive a differential response. We can classify the mechanisms in three different stages of consumers' creation and use of brand knowledge: (1) *attention and learning,* that is, the building of brand knowledge structures; (2) *interpretation and evaluation* of marketing information or brand alternatives, that is, the use of brand knowledge; and (3) mechanisms that affect the *actual choice process,* that is, the application of brand knowledge. All through these three different stages of consumer behavior, research has documented advantages for strong brands.

Attention and Learning

Strong brands can have an advantage over unknown or weak brands because consumers familiar with the brand have better encoding ability and better-developed procedural knowledge. They can develop a greater number of stronger links for familiar brands.

Moreover, because strong brands have better-developed brand knowledge structures in the minds of consumers, consumers are more likely to uniquely associate these links with the brand. When consumers have less developed knowledge structures, on the other hand, associations may end up being stored under the product category and not the specific brand. Learning can even decrease for brands that are late to enter a market, because consumers see them as having fewer or less novel features.

Consideration

Another advantage related to brand strength is that strong brands with more associations are more likely to be in consumers' consideration sets. Strong brands also receive an advantage when consumers begin their search with well-known and well-regarded brands that they see as more likely to satisfy their needs.

Selective Attention

Consumers may automatically encode frequency information as they are exposed to brand names, symbols, slogans, and logos through various marketing activities. Nonverbal information may be more potent than verbal cues. Consumers might also give strong or well-known brands more attention, comprehension, and retention.

In short, it appears that consumers more easily notice information about strong brands, and the frequency of advertising may create favorable associations even in the absence of voluntary processing of brand information.

price increases. A number of marketing research suppliers have adopted variations of this approach to derive similar types of demand curves, and many firms now try to assess price sensitivity and thresholds for different brands. For example, Intel routinely surveys computer shoppers to find out how much of a discount they would require before switching to a personal computer that did not have an Intel microprocessor in it or,

Interpretation and Evaluation

There is evidence that both direct and indirect mechanisms create differences in the way consumers interpret and evaluate brands and related marketing information.

Direct effects occur when brand-related information is input directly into the decision process. For instance, in ***loss aversion,*** the losses of switching from a known brand loom larger than the potential gains from using a lesser-known brand (say, in response to a price reduction). Thus, the possibility of a potential loss leads to an advantage for strong brands. The halo effects related to positive feelings about a strong brand can positively bias the way consumers evaluate brand advertising. Similarly, consumer confidence increases when consumers get more familiar in a domain and may lead them to use more favorable associations when making a decision.

Indirect effects are perhaps more common than direct effects and are driven by uncertainty or ambiguity in the decision process. After they acquire brand information, consumers may interpret or evaluate it, which can be especially critical if the information is ambiguous. The primary factor that determines our decisions under ambiguity is our prior attitudes. If they're positive, we are usually more receptive and less critical. Ambiguity generally favors the incumbent or stronger brand through, for example, confirmation biases.

Finally, consumers may use brand names as a signal of the credibility of product claims. Thus, evaluation advantages—through more elaboration—may help strong brands to *indirectly* create even stronger and more favorable associations.

Choice

Perhaps the most frequently cited advantage for strong brands at the choice stage is the notion of brand recognition or familiarity as a choice heuristic. Essentially, when consumers have limited prior knowledge in a product category, the brand name may be the most accessible cue available. In addition, using a familiar brand name as a diagnostic cue is thought to be a consumer strategy for dealing with risk and uncertainty, especially when consumers have limited prior experience. The presence of a known brand can limit consumers' ability to detect differences in product quality across brands, even when they sample other brands. Clearly, one of the most effective mechanisms that provide advantages to strong brands is their inherent familiarity.

Source: This summary is based on Steven Hoeffler and Kevin Lane Keller, "The Marketing Advantages of Strong Brands," *Journal of Brand Management* 10, no. 6 (2003): 421–445. Specific refereences to academic research supporting all these assertions can be found in that article.

conversely, what premium they would be willing to pay to buy a personal computer with an Intel microprocessor in it.

We can apply marketing-based comparative approaches in other ways, assessing consumer response to different advertising strategies, executions, or media plans through multiple test markets. For example, IRI's electronic test markets (see The Science of

Average Scale Rating[a]	Proposed Extensions
10	Peanuts
9	Snack mixes, nuts for baking
8	—
7	Pretzels, chocolate nut candy, caramel corn
6	Snack crackers, potato chips, nutritional granola bars
5	Tortilla chips, toppings (ice cream/dessert)
4	Lunchables/lunch snack packs, dessert mixes (cookie/cake/brownie)
3	Ice cream/ice cream bars, toppings (salad/vegetable)
2	Cereal, toaster pastries, Asian entrees/sauces, stuffing mix, refrigerated dough, jams/jellies
1	Yogurt

[a]Consumers rated proposed extensions on an 11-point scale anchored by 0 (definitely would *not* expect Planter's to sell it) and 10 (definitely would expect Planter's to sell it).

FIGURE 10-1

Reactions to Proposed Planter's Extensions

Branding 6.1) and similar research methodologies can permit tests of different advertising weights or repetition schedules as well as ad copy tests. By controlling for other factors, we can isolate the effects of the brand and product. Recall from Chapter 2 how Anheuser-Busch conducted an extensive series of test markets that revealed that Budweiser beer had such a strong image with consumers that advertising could be cut, at least in the short run, without hurting sales performance.

Marketers can also explore potential brand extensions by collecting consumer evaluations of a range of concept statements describing brand extension candidates. For example, Figure 10-1 displays the results of a consumer survey examining reactions to possible extensions of the Planter's nuts brand. Contrasting those extensions provides some indication of the equity of the brand. In this example, the survey results suggest that consumers expected any Planter's brand extension to be "nut-related." Appropriate product characteristics for a possible Planter's brand extension seem to be "crunchy," "sweet," "salty," "spicy," and "buttery." In terms of where in the store consumers would expect to find new Planter's products, the snack and candy sections seem most likely. On the other hand, consumers do not seem to expect to find new Planter's products in the breakfast food aisle, bakery product section, refrigerated section, or frozen food section. Consistent with these survey results, besides selling peanuts, mixed nuts, cashews, almonds, and baking nuts, Planters now sells trail mix, peanut bars, and chocolate-covered nuts.

Critique. The main advantage of the marketing-based comparative approach is ease of implementation. We can compare virtually any proposed set of marketing actions for the brand. At the same time, the main drawback is that it may be difficult to discern whether consumer responses to changes in the marketing stimuli are being caused by brand knowledge or by more generic product knowledge. In other words, it may be that for *any* brand in the product category, consumers would be willing to pay certain prices, accept a particular brand extension, and so forth. One way to determine whether consumer response is specific to the brand is to conduct similar tests of consumer response with competitive brands. A statistical technique well suited to do just that is described next.

Conjoint Analysis

Conjoint analysis is a survey-based multivariate technique that enables marketers to profile the consumer decision process with respect to products and brands.[5] Specifically, by asking consumers to express preferences or choose among a number of carefully designed product profiles, researchers can determine the tradeoffs consumers are making between various brand attributes, and thus the importance they are attaching to them.[6] Each profile consumers see is made up of a set of attribute levels chosen on the basis of experimental design principles to satisfy certain mathematical properties. The value consumers attach to each attribute level, as statistically derived by the conjoint formula, is called a ***part worth***. We can use the part worths in various ways to estimate how consumers would value a new combination of the attribute levels. For example, one attribute is the brand name. The part worth for the "brand name" attribute reflects its value.

One classic study of conjoint analysis, reported by Green and Wind,[7] examined consumer evaluations of a spot-remover product on five attributes: package design, brand name, price, *Good Housekeeping seal,* and money-back guarantee. Figure 10-2 contains the 18 profiles that made up the experimental design. Figure 10-3 shows the results of the statistical analyses to determine the part worths.

Applications. Conjoint analysis has a number of possible applications. Ogilvy & Mather ad agency has used a brand/price tradeoff methodology as a means of assessing advertising effectiveness and brand value.[8] Brand/price tradeoff is a simplified version of conjoint measurement with just two variables—brand and price. Consumers make a series of simulated purchase choices between different combinations of brands and prices. Each choice triggers an increase in the price of the selected brand, forcing the consumer to choose between buying a preferred brand and paying less. In this way, consumers reveal how much their brand loyalty is worth and, conversely, which brands they would relinquish for a lower price.

Academic researchers with an interest in brand image and equity have used other variations and applications of conjoint analysis.[9] For example, Rangaswamy, Burke, and Oliva use conjoint analysis to explore how brand names interact with physical product features to affect the extendability of brand names to new product categories.[10] Barich and Srinivasan apply conjoint analysis to corporate image programs, to show how it can determine the company attributes relevant to customers, rank the importance of those attributes, estimate the costs of making improvements (or correcting customer perceptions), and prioritize image goals to obtain the maximum benefit, in terms of improved perceptions, for the resources spent.[11]

Critique. The main advantage of the conjoint-based approach is that it allows us to study different brands and different aspects of the product or marketing program (product composition, price, distribution outlets, and so on) simultaneously. Thus, we can uncover information about consumers' responses to different marketing activities for both the focal and competing brands.

One of the disadvantages of conjoint analysis is that marketing profiles may violate consumers' expectations based on what they already know about brands. Thus, we must take care that consumers do not evaluate unrealistic product profiles or scenarios. It can also be difficult to specify and interpret brand attribute levels, although some useful guidelines have been put forth to more effectively apply conjoint analysis to brand positioning.[12]

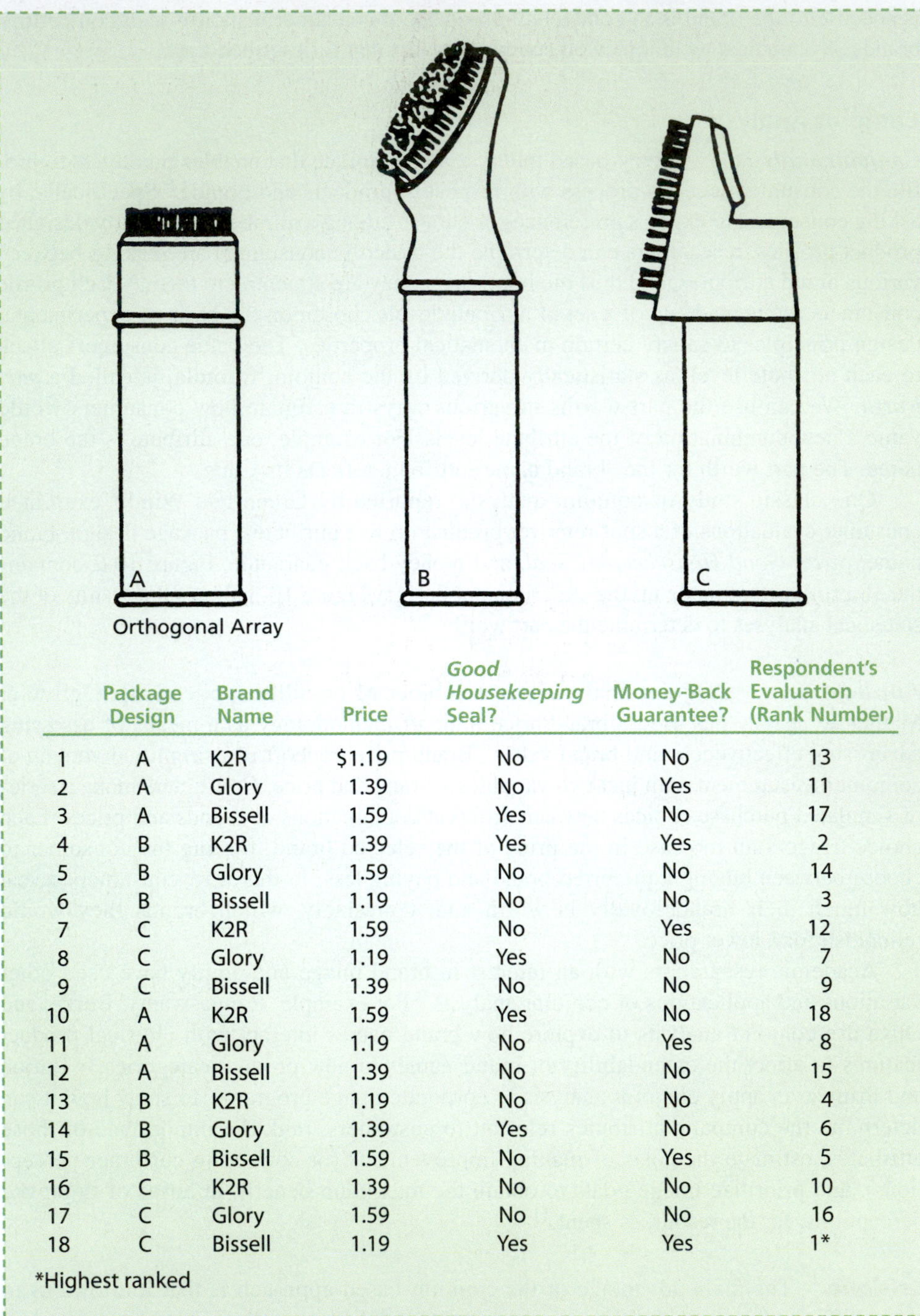

Orthogonal Array

	Package Design	Brand Name	Price	*Good Housekeeping* Seal?	Money-Back Guarantee?	Respondent's Evaluation (Rank Number)
1	A	K2R	$1.19	No	No	13
2	A	Glory	1.39	No	Yes	11
3	A	Bissell	1.59	Yes	No	17
4	B	K2R	1.39	Yes	Yes	2
5	B	Glory	1.59	No	No	14
6	B	Bissell	1.19	No	No	3
7	C	K2R	1.59	No	Yes	12
8	C	Glory	1.19	Yes	No	7
9	C	Bissell	1.39	No	No	9
10	A	K2R	1.59	Yes	No	18
11	A	Glory	1.19	No	Yes	8
12	A	Bissell	1.39	No	No	15
13	B	K2R	1.19	No	No	4
14	B	Glory	1.39	Yes	No	6
15	B	Bissell	1.59	No	Yes	5
16	C	K2R	1.39	No	No	10
17	C	Glory	1.59	No	No	16
18	C	Bissell	1.19	Yes	Yes	1*

*Highest ranked

FIGURE 10-2

Product Profiles for Conjoint Analysis Application

Holistic Methods

We use comparative methods to approximate specific benefits of brand equity. ***Holistic methods*** place an overall value on the brand in either abstract utility terms or concrete financial terms. Thus, holistic methods attempt to "net out" various considerations to determine the unique contribution of the brand. The ***residual approach*** examines the value of the brand by subtracting consumers' preferences for the brand—based on physical

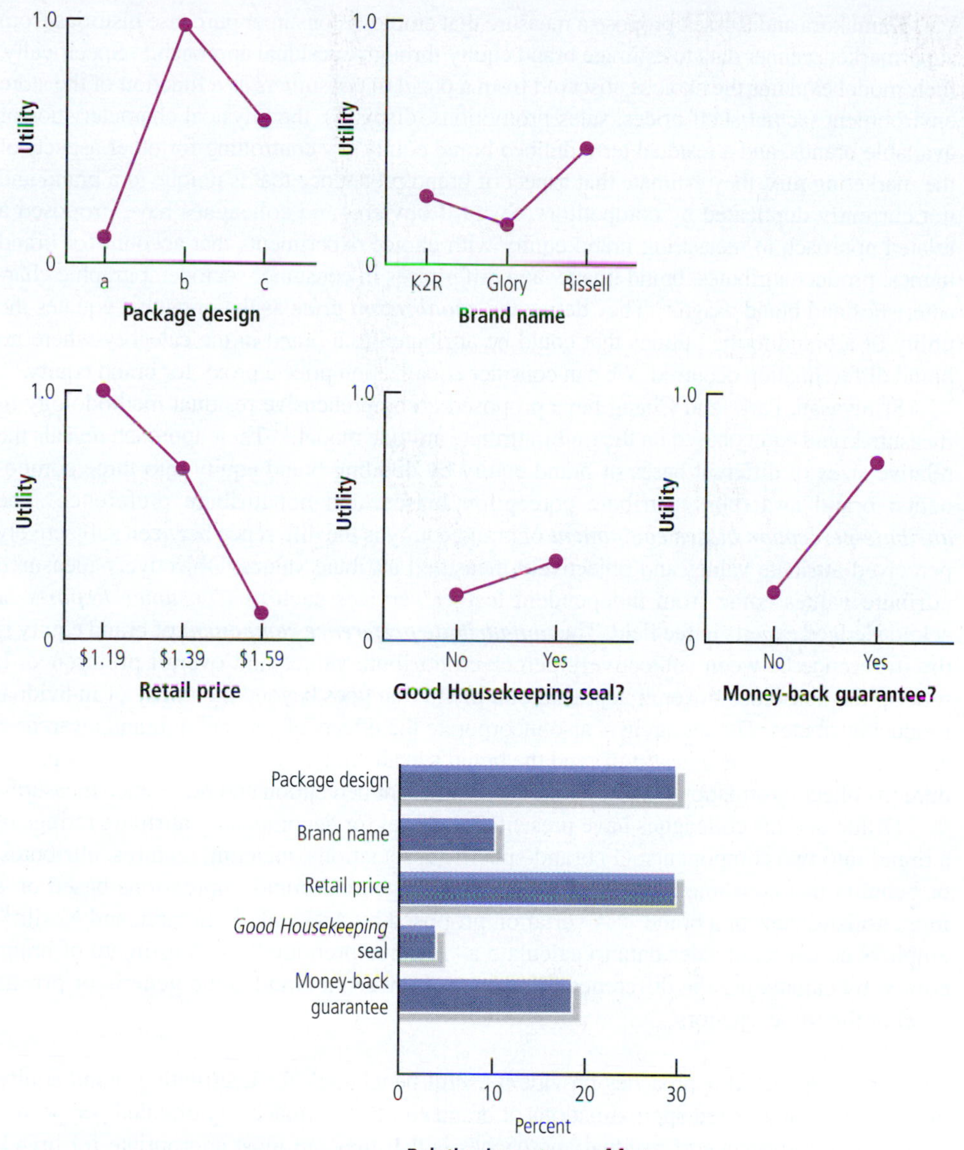

FIGURE 10-3

Part-Worth Results for Conjoint Analysis Application

product attributes alone—from their overall brand preferences. The ***valuation approach*** places a financial value on brand equity for accounting purposes, mergers and acquisitions, or other such reasons. We'll look at each of these approaches.

Residual Approaches

The rationale behind residual approaches is the view that brand equity is what remains of consumer preferences and choices after we subtract physical product effects. The idea is that we can infer the relative valuation of brands by observing consumer preferences and choices *if* we take into account as many sources of measured attribute values as possible. Several researchers have defined brand equity as the incremental preference over and above that which would result for the product without brand identification. In this view, we can calculate brand equity by subtracting preferences for objective characteristics of the physical product from overall preference.[13]

Kamakura and Russell propose a measure that employs consumer purchase histories from supermarket scanner data to estimate brand equity through a residual approach.[14] Specifically, their model explains the choices observed from a panel of consumers as a function of the store environment (actual shelf prices, sales promotions, displays), the physical characteristics of available brands, and a residual term dubbed brand equity. By controlling for other aspects of the marketing mix, they estimate that aspect of brand preference that is unique to a brand and not currently duplicated by competitors. Swait, Louviere, and colleagues have proposed a related approach to measuring brand equity with choice experiments that account for brand names, product attributes, brand image, and differences in consumer sociodemographic characteristics and brand usage.[15] They define the ***equalization price*** as the price that equates the utility of a brand to the utilities that could be attributed to a brand in the category where no brand differentiation occurred. We can consider equalization price a proxy for brand equity.[16]

Srinivasan, Park, and Chang have proposed a comprehensive residual methodology to measure brand equity based on the multi-attribute attitude model.[17] Their approach reveals the relative sizes of different bases of brand equity by dividing brand equity into three components: brand awareness, attribute perception biases, and nonattribute preference. The ***attribute-perception biased component*** of brand equity is the difference between subjectively perceived attribute values and objectively measured attribute values. Objectively measured attribute values come from independent testing services such as *Consumer Reports* or acknowledged experts in the field. The ***nonattribute preference component*** of brand equity is the difference between subjectively perceived attribute values and overall preference. It reflects the consumer's overall appraisal of a brand that goes beyond the utility of individual product attributes. The researchers also incorporate the effects of enhancing brand awareness and preference on consumer "pull" and the brand's availability. They propose a survey procedure to collect information for estimating these different perception and preference measures.

Dillon and his colleagues have presented a model for decomposing attribute ratings of a brand into two components: (1) brand-specific associations, meaning features, attributes, or benefits that consumers link to a brand, and (2) general brand impressions based on a more holistic view of a brand.[18] A variation proposed by Ailawadi, Lehmann, and Neslin[19] employs actual retail sales data to calculate a "revenue premium" as an estimate of brand equity, by calculating the difference in revenues between a brand and a generic or private label in the same category.

Critique. Residual approaches provide a useful benchmark for interpreting brand equity, especially when we need approximations of brand equity or a financially oriented perspective on it. The disadvantage of residual approaches is that they are most appropriate for brands with a lot of product-related attribute associations, because they are unable to distinguish between different types of non-product-related attribute associations. Consequently, the residual approach's diagnostic value for strategic decision making in other cases is limited.

More generally, residual approaches take a fairly static view of brand equity by focusing on consumer *preferences*. This contrasts sharply with the process view advocated by the customer-based brand equity framework. The brand-based and marketing-based comparative approaches stress looking at consumer *response* to the marketing of a brand and attempting to uncover the extent to which that response is affected by brand knowledge.

This distinction is also relevant for the issue of "separability" in brand valuation that various researchers have raised. For example, Barwise and his colleagues note that marketing efforts to create an extended or augmented product, say, with extra features or service plus other means to enhance brand value, "raise serious problems of separating the value of the brand name and trademark from the many other elements of the 'augmented' product."[20] According to customer-based brand equity, those efforts could affect the favorability, strength, and uniqueness of various brand associations, which would, in turn, affect consumer response to *future* marketing activities. For example, imagine that a brand becomes known for providing extraordinary customer service because of certain policies and favorable advertising, publicity, or word of mouth (like Nordstrom department stores or Singapore Airlines). These favorable perceptions of customer service and the attitudes they engender could create customer-based brand equity by affecting consumer response to a price policy (consumers would be willing to pay higher prices), a new ad campaign (consumers would accept an ad illustrating customer satisfaction), or a brand extension (customers would become interested in trying a new type of retail outlet).

Valuation Approaches

The bulk of corporate value for many companies is wrapped up in the brand. For example, *Forbes* magazine noted that although PepsiCo has a net tangible book value of only $6.5 billion, it now has a market value or cap of over $90 billion, with brands estimated to make up 70 percent of its intangible assets or more than $50 billion.[21] The ability to put a specific price tag on a brand's value may be useful for a number of reasons:

- *Mergers and acquisitions:* Both to evaluate possible purchases as well as to facilitate disposal
- *Brand licensing:* Internally for tax reasons and to third parties
- *Fund raising:* As collateral on loans or for sale or leaseback arrangements
- *Brand management decisions:* To allocate resources, develop brand strategy, or prepare financial reports

For example, many companies appear to be attractive acquisition candidates because of the strong competitive positions of their brands and their reputation with consumers. Unfortunately, the value of the brand assets in many cases is largely excluded from the company's balance sheet and is therefore of little use in determining overall value. As one commentator put it:

> The worth of a strong brand is rarely represented fully in a company's stock price. It doesn't appear on a balance sheet. But it's the motor behind the numbers, the fuel that drives consumers to the marketplace and helps them make choices.[22]

It has been argued that adjusting the balance sheet to reflect the true value of a company's brands permits us to take a more realistic view and assess the purchase premium to book value that might be earned from the brands after acquisition. Such a calculation, however, would require estimates of capital required by brands and the expected after-acquisition return on investment (ROI) of a company.

Separating out the percentage of revenue or profits attributable to brand equity is a difficult task.[23] In the United States, there is no conventional accounting method for doing so. Thus, despite the fact that expert analysts estimate the value of the Coca-Cola name as approaching $67 billion, it appears in the owner's books as only $25 *million*. Based on accounting rules, Coca-Cola's assets in 2004 had a book value of $31.3 billion, with various intangible assets assessed at $3.8 billion and a market cap of $100 billion. Clearly, market-based estimates of value can differ dramatically from those based on U.S. accounting conventions.[24] Other countries, however, are trying to capture that value. How do you calculate the financial value of a brand? This section, after providing some accounting background and historical perspective, describes the leading brand valuation approach.[25]

Accounting Background. The assets of a firm can be either tangible or intangible. ***Tangible assets*** include property, plant, and equipment; current assets (inventories, marketable securities, and cash); and investments in stocks and bonds. We can estimate the value of tangible assets using accounting book values and reported estimates of replacement costs. ***Intangible assets,*** on the other hand, are any factors of production or specialized resources that permit the company to earn cash flows in excess of the return on tangible assets. In other words, intangible assets augment the earning power of a firm's physical assets. They are typically lumped under the heading of ***goodwill*** and include things such as patents, trademarks, and licensing agreements, as well as "softer" considerations such as the skill of the management and customer relations.

In an acquisition, the goodwill item often includes a premium paid to gain control, which, in certain instances, may even exceed the value of tangible and intangible assets. In Britain and certain other countries, it has been common to write off the goodwill element of an acquisition against reserves; tangible assets, on the other hand, are transferred straight to the acquiring company's balance sheet.

Historical Perspectives. Brand valuation's more recent past started with Rupert Murdoch's News Corporation, which included a valuation of some of its magazines on its balance sheets in 1984, as permitted by Australian accounting standards. The rationale was that the goodwill element of publishing acquisitions—the difference in value between net assets and the price paid—was often enormous and negatively affecting the balance sheet. News Corporation used the recognition that the titles themselves contained much of the value of the acquisition to justify placing them on the balance sheet, improving the debt/equity ratio and allowing the company to get some much needed cash to finance acquisition of some foreign media companies.

In the United Kingdom, Grand Metropolitan was one of the first British companies to place a monetary value on the brands it owned and to put that value on its balance sheet. When Grand Met acquired Heublein distributors, Pearle eye care, and Sambuca Romana liqueur in 1987, it placed the value of some of its brands—principally Smirnoff—on the balance sheet for roughly $1 billion. In doing so, Grand Met used two different methods. If a company consisted of primarily one brand, it figured that the value of the brand was 75 percent of the purchase price, whereas if the company had many brands, it used a multiple of an income figure.

British firms used brand values primarily to boost their balance sheets. By recording their brand assets, the firms maintained, they were attempting to bring their shareholder funds nearer to the market capitalization of the firm. In the United Kingdom, Rank Hovis McDougal (RHM) succeeded in putting the worth of the company's existing brands as a figure on the balance sheet to fight a hostile takeover bid in 1988. With the brand value information provided by Interbrand (via a method described later in this chapter), the RHM board was able to go back to investors and argue that the bid was too low, and eventually to repel it.

Accounting firms in favor of valuing brands argue that it is a way to strengthen the presentation of a company's accounts, to record hidden assets so they are disclosed to company's shareholders, to enhance a company's shareholders' funds to improve its earnings ratios, to provide a realistic basis for management and investors to measure a company's performance, and to reveal detailed information on brand strengths so that management can formulate appropriate brand strategies. In practical terms, however, recording brand value as an intangible asset from the firm's perspective is a means to increase the asset value of the firm.

Actual practices have varied from country to country. Brand valuations have been accepted for inclusion in the balance sheets of companies in countries such as the United Kingdom, Australia, New Zealand, France, Sweden, Singapore, and Spain. When Grand Met acquired Pillsbury for $5.5 billion in January 1989, it revalued Pillsbury's intangible assets to add $2.4 billion to its intangible assets. Unlike a U.S. company, Grand Met did not intend to write down those intangible assets (unless permanently impaired). Grand Met also adjusted its goodwill account (separate from intangible assets) by a substantial amount as a result of the Pillsbury acquisition.[26]

In the United Kingdom, Martin Sorrell improved the balance sheet of WPP by attaching brand value to its primary assets, including J. Walter Thompson Company, Ogilvy & Mather, and Hill & Knowlton, stating in the annual report that:

> Intangible fixed assets comprise certain acquired separable corporate brand names. These are shown at a valuation of the incremental earnings expected to arise from the ownership of brands. The valuations have been based on the present value of notional royalty savings arising from [ownership] and on estimates of profits attributable to brand loyalty.[27]

In the United States, generally accepted accounting principles (blanket amortization principles) mean that placing a brand on the balance sheet would require amortization of that asset for up to 40 years. Such a charge would severely hamper firm profitability; as a result, firms avoid such accounting maneuvers. On the other hand, certain other countries (including Canada, Germany, and Japan) have gone beyond tax deductibility of brand equity to permit some or all of the goodwill arising from an acquisition to be deducted for tax purposes.

General Approaches. In determining the value of a brand in an acquisition or merger, firms can choose from three main approaches: the cost, market, and income approaches.[28]

The cost approach maintains that brand equity is the amount of money that would be required to reproduce or replace the brand (including all costs for research and development, test marketing, advertising, and so on). One common criticism of approaches relying on historic or replacement cost is that they reward past performance in a way that may bear little relation to future profitability—for example, many brands with expensive introductions have been unsuccessful. On the other hand, for brands that have been around for decades (such as Heinz, Kellogg's, and Chanel), it would be virtually impossible to find out what the investment in brand development was—and largely irrelevant as well. Finally, it obviously is easier to estimate costs of tangible assets than intangible assets, but the latter often may lie at the heart of brand equity. Similar problems exist with a replacement cost approach; for example, the cost of replacing a brand depends a great deal on how quickly the process would take and what competitive, legal, and logistical obstacles might be encountered.

According to the market approach, we can think of brand equity as the present value of the future economic benefits to be derived by the owner of the asset. In other words, it is the amount an active market would allow so that the asset would exchange between a willing buyer and willing seller. The main problems with this approach are the lack of open market transactions for brand name assets, and the fact that the uniqueness of brands makes extrapolating from one market transaction to another problematic. Brand Focus 10.0 reviews some considerations in the relationship of brand equity to the stock market.

The third approach to determining the value of a brand, the income approach, argues that brand equity is the discounted future cash flow from the future earnings stream for the brand. Three such income approaches are as follows:

1. Capitalizing royalty earnings from a brand name (when these can be defined)
2. Capitalizing the premium profits that are earned by a branded product (by comparing its performance with that of an unbranded product)
3. Capitalizing the actual profitability of a brand after allowing for the costs of maintaining it and the effects of taxation

As a very rough rule of thumb, Chevron's Lew Winters reports that accountants are inclined to price a brand at four to six times the annual profit realized from the sale of the product bearing the brand name to be acquired. The methodology described in the next section is largely based on an income approach. The Science of Branding 10-2 describes another income-based valuation approach.[29]

THE SCIENCE OF BRANDING 10-2

What Is a Brand Worth?

BrandMetrics is a "no-frills" valuation methodology that arose from academic work in South Africa (see Figure 10-4 for an overview). The model is based on the premise that the definition of an asset given by accountants—resources under the control of an enterprise that will generate future economic benefits for the enterprise—applies to brands. The BrandMetrics model was conceived to bring two concepts together: the accounting definition of an asset and the marketing presumption that brands generate future economic benefits.

Conceptualizing brand equity as the "incremental cash flows that accrue to a branded as compared with a nonbranded product," the researchers set out to distinguish the financial structure of the brand that belongs to the nonbranded and branded portions by using the concept of economic profit. Economic profit is understood today to be the amount of after-tax operating profit a company earns that exceeds the cost of the capital the company has employed in operating the business.

The BrandMetrics approach therefore starts with a calculation of the economic profit on the basis that a normal company (or unbranded product) would earn no more than the cost of capital. The excess profit over and above the cost of capital is attributable to resources that must be identified. Among these are the brand and its customers. A BrandMetrics valuation requires income statement and balance sheet data for each brand being valued. Because this is not always available, various accounting techniques of allocation have been adopted for the process.

The researchers then borrowed a technique from actuarial science to figure out what proportion of the economic profit we can ascribe to the brand. Resource recognition procedure (RRP) is based on the Delphi forecasting technique. A gathering of experts from within the company representing all the major functions attend a three-hour session controlled by a trained facilitator. Using Excel spreadsheets to capture and analyze the data as it comes in, the group moves through at least four rounds of analysis.

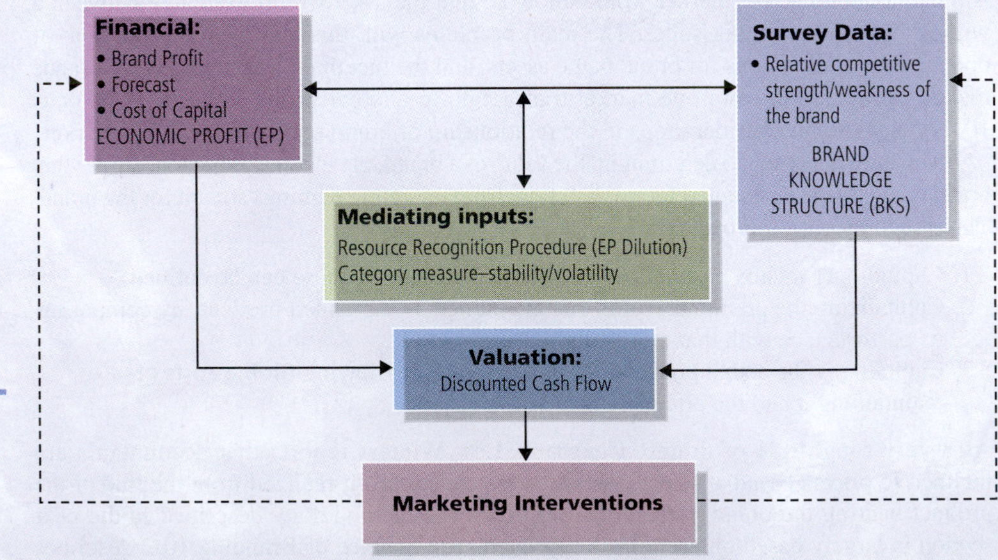

FIGURE 10-4

The Valuation Flowchart

Source: Used with permission of Canadian Marketing Association.

In the first round, the group generates an exhaustive list of possible resources that might drive economic profit and projects them on the screen. Through an iterative process during which group members vote, rank, and rate the resources, they gradually reduce the list. Typically there will be consensus on a final five to eight items. Each member then allocates 100 percent across the final resources and the scores are averaged to give a weighting to each.

Finally, each member allocates a score from a scale anchored at its poles on 0 and 10, to indicate the extent to which brand equity influences each resource. The mean, weighted scores are summed to produce a percentage that, when applied to the economic profit, produces the brand premium profit (BPP) or the portion attributable to the brand.

BrandMetrics does not limit the projection of the brand profits to a set number of years. Due to the algorithms that support the model, each brand is uniquely modeled to represent its relative strength in numbers of years of economic expected life. Two devices are used to calculate this:

- *Category Expected Life analysis:* Because the ability of a brand to sustain economic profits is a function of the category in which it trades, BrandMetrics evaluates profits according to four variables: longevity (category maturity); leadership (market share stability or volatility); barriers and churn (competitive activity); and vulnerability (external forces). The model examines each in detail and scores it on a 5-point scale. When multiplied, the set values behind each score produce numbers of years out of 40 for a notional dominant brand; and out of 10 for a notional marginal brand. Thus, each category is defined by a number of years of economic expected life.
- *Brand Knowledge Structure (BKS) analysis:* Consistent with the customer-based brand equity model, BKS is a function of both awareness and associations. Market research is used to establish levels of awareness and brand associations for each brand in the category. These are reduced to a single score out of 100 percent. The highest scores and the lowest scores achieved by any brand in the category are computed to represent the notional dominant and marginal brands and these scores are mathematically transformed into the years of economic expected life described above. Scores for the brands being valued are then converted by the same method, thus producing the unique number of years for the brand being measured.

Each brand has a franchise run (the years closest to the base year of the valuation), and a decay phase or theoretical period of decline. Thus the marketing task is to ensure that the total number of years never decreases, and the marketing objectives should be to increase the number of years in the franchise run, thus improving the overall brand value.

The BPP is projected into the future using the budget data for the brand and a conservative growth rate for years further into the future. These are eventually stepped down to a reasonable growth rate based on consensus for the country's GDP and inflation.

The brand value is the capitalized present value of this projection, using the weighted average cost of capital (WACC) as the discount rate calculated according to corporate finance principles. It comprises a risk-free rate, a cost of debt extracted from the annual accounts; a cost of equity calculated according to the capital asset pricing model (CAPM), which uses market betas and a risk premium estimated with reference to stock market data. These are weighted according to the balance between debt and equity funding.

Simon and Sullivan's Brand Equity Value. Simon and Sullivan have developed a technique for estimating a firm's brand equity derived from financial market estimates of brand-related profits.[30] They define brand equity as the incremental cash flows that accrue to branded products over and above the cash flows that would result from the sale of unbranded products. To implement their approach, they begin by estimating the current market value of the firm. They assume the market value of the firm's securities to provide an unbiased estimate of the future cash flows attributable to all the firm's assets. Their methodology attempts to extract the value of a firm's brand equity from the value of the firm's other assets. The result is an estimate of brand equity based on the financial market valuation of the firm's future cash flows.

Their rationale is as follows. They assume that the financial market value of a firm is based on the aggregate earning power of both tangible and intangible assets. They also make the "efficient-market" assumption that in a well-functioning capital market, securities prices provide the best available unbiased estimate of the value of a company's assets. In other words, the financial market's valuation of the firm incorporates the expected value of future cash flows and returns.

From these basic premises, Simon and Sullivan derive their methodology to extract the value of brand equity from the financial market value of the firm. The total asset value of the firm is the sum of the market value of common stock, preferred stock, long-term debt, and short-term debt. The value of intangible assets is captured in the ratio of the market value of the firm to the replacement cost of its tangible assets. There are three categories of intangible assets: brand equity, nonbrand factors that reduce the firm's costs relative to competitors like R&D and patents, and industrywide factors that permit monopoly profits, such as regulation. By considering factors such as the age of the brand, order of entry in the category, and current and past advertising share, Simon and Sullivan then provide estimates of brand equity.

Figure 10-5 displays their estimates of brand equity for some selected food companies. According to this analysis, the high estimated brand equity of Tootsie Roll suggests that even though it may be relatively easy to develop a "me-too" candy product, a considerable amount of the profits ascribed to Tootsie Roll accrue directly from its strong brand name. Simon and Sullivan conducted an in-depth analysis tracing the brand equity of Coca-Cola and Pepsi over three major events in the soft drink industry from 1982 to 1986—for example, showing how the introduction of Diet Coke increased the equity of Coca-Cola and decreased the equity of Pepsi.

Interbrand's Brand Valuation Methodology. Interbrand, probably the premier brand valuation firm, evaluated a number of different approaches in developing its brand valuation methodology. Its goal was to identify an approach that incorporated marketing, financial, and legal aspects; followed fundamental accounting concepts; allowed for regular revaluation on a consistent basis; and was suitable for acquired and home-grown brands.

Interbrand decided to approach the problem of brand valuation by assuming that the value of a brand, like the value of any other economic asset, was the present worth of the benefits of future ownership.[31] In other words, according to Interbrand, brand valuation is based on an assessment of what the value is today of the earnings or cash flow that the brand can be expected to generate in the future.[32]

Interbrand follows a methodology largely based on an income approach.[33] To capture the complex value creation of a brand, Interbrand recommends the following five valuation steps (see Figure 10-6):[34]

1. *Market segmentation:* Split the consumer market for the brand into non-overlapping and homogenous groups of consumers according to applicable criteria such as product or service, distribution channels, consumption patterns, purchase sophistication,

Company	Brand Equity (% of replacement value)
Anheuser-Busch	35
Brown-Foreman	82
Cadbury Schweppes	44
Campbell	31
Dreyer's Ice Cream	151
General Mills	52
Heinz	62
Kellogg	61
Pillsbury	30
Quaker	59
Ralston Purina	40
Sara Lee	57
Seagram	73
Smucker	126
Tootsie Roll	148

FIGURE 10-5

Simon and Sullivan's Measured Brand Equity for Food Product Companies (as a percentage of firm replacement value)

geography, existing and new customers. Value the brand in each segment; the sum of the segment valuations constitutes the total value of the brand.

2. *Financial (role of branding) analysis:* Identify and forecast revenues and "earnings from intangibles" generated by the brand for each of the distinct segments determined in step 1. Intangible earnings are defined as: branded revenues less operating costs, applicable taxes, and a charge for the capital employed. The concept is similar to the notion of economic profit.
3. *Demand (brand strength) analysis:* Assess the role the brand plays in driving demand for products and services in the markets in which it operates. Measure the proportion of intangible earnings attributable to the brand by an indicator referred to as the role of branding index (RBI), by first identifying the various drivers of demand for the branded business, then determining the degree to which each driver is directly influenced by the brand. The role of branding represents the percentage of intangible earnings generated by the brand. Derive brand earnings by multiplying the role of branding by intangible earnings.

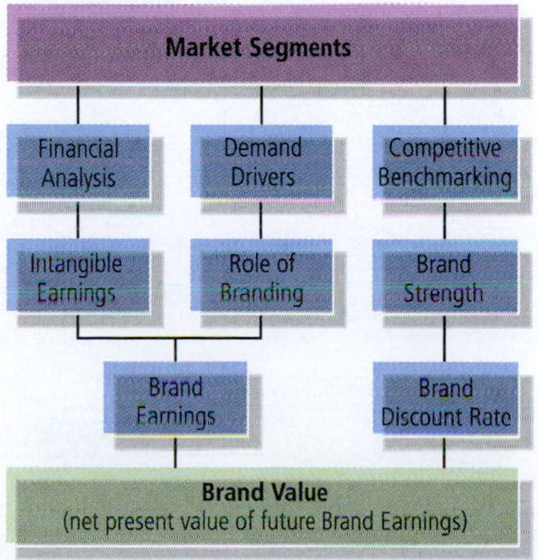

FIGURE 10-6

Brand Valuation Model

4. *Competitive benchmarking:* Determine the competitive strengths and weaknesses of the brand, deriving a specific brand discount rate that reflects the risk profile of its expected future earnings via a brand strength score (see Figure 10-7). This measure relies on extensive competitive benchmarking and a structured evaluation of the brand's market, stability, leadership position, growth trend, support, geographic footprint, and legal protectability. The ideal brand would be a risk-free asset (or government bond yield).
5. *Brand value calculation:* Calculate the brand value as the net present value (NPV) of the forecast brand earnings, discounted by the brand discount rate. The NPV calculation comprises both the forecast period and the period beyond, reflecting the ability of brands to continue generating future earnings.

According to Interbrand, the RBI index can vary considerable, on average, by industry, from a low of 10 percent for bulk chemicals to over 80 percent for soft drinks and even 90 percent for perfumes. Other observed RBI indices are hotels (30 percent), financial services (40 percent), household appliances (55 percent), and consumer electronics (70 percent). Figure 10-8 shows the calculation of the RBI index for a hypothetical beer brand.

Summary. Brand valuation and the "brands on the balance sheet" debate are controversial subjects.[35] The advantage of the Interbrand valuation approach is that it is very generalizable and can be applied to virtually any type of brand or product. Yet even Interbrand recognizes the complexities involved:

> The valuation of brands is still a relatively new concept. There is no active market in brands, as there is with stocks and shares or real estate. Brand valuation is without question partly art and partly science. Judgment is involved just as it is for any other valuation method for any other asset, tangible or intangible. Specialized knowledge of marketing, accounting, and trademark law is required to ensure that the correct

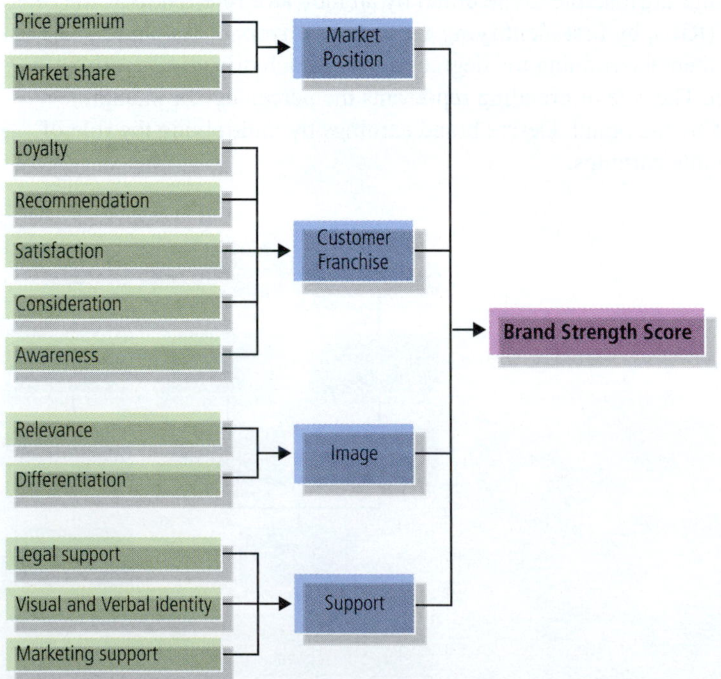

FIGURE 10-7
Brand Strength Assessment

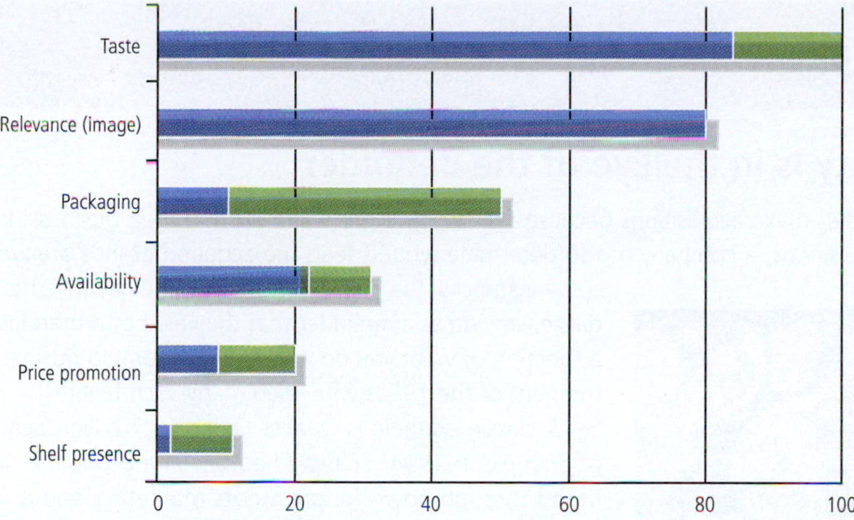

FIGURE 10-8
Example of Role of Branding in the Beer Segment

> blend of professional skills is present. Any brand valuation method has to take into account a wide variety of data, both factual and qualitative. Skilled professional judgment is needed to arrive at the right conclusions on the role of the brand, its strength, and the underlying stream of cash flow it generates. All of the conclusions reached need to be supported as far as possible by independent research studies.[36]

Many marketing experts, however, feel it is impossible to reduce the richness of a brand to a single, meaningful number, and that any formula that tries to do so is an abstraction and arbitrary. Thus, the primary disadvantage of valuation approaches is that they make a host of potentially oversimplified assumptions to arrive at one measure of brand equity. For example, Sir Michael Perry, chairman of Unilever, objects for philosophical reasons:

> The seemingly miraculous conjuring up of intangible asset values, as if from nowhere, only serves to reinforce the view of the consumer skeptics, that brands are just high prices and consumer exploitation. At Unilever, we have consistently rejected this approach.[37]

Wharton's Peter Fader points out a number of limitations of valuation approaches: They require much judgmental data and thus contain much subjectivity; intangible assets are not always synonymous with brand equity; the methods sometimes defy common sense and lack "face validity" (IBM's brand equity bounced around from number 3 or 4 to as low as number 282 over just a few years, according to *Financial World*); the financial measures generally ignore or downplay current investments in future equity like advertising or R&D; and the strength of the brand measures may be confounded with the strength of the company.[38]

At the heart of much of the criticism is the issue of separability we identified earlier. An Economist editorial put it this way: "Brands can be awkward to separate as assets. With Cadbury's Dairy Milk, how much value comes from the name Cadbury? How much from Dairy Milk? How much merely from the product's (replicable) contents or design?"[39] To draw a sports analogy, extracting brand value may be as difficult as determining the value of the coach to a team's performance. And the way a brand is managed can have a large effect, positive or negative, on its value. Branding Brief 10-1 describes several brand acquisitions that turned out unsuccessfully for firms.

BRANDING BRIEF 10-1

Beauty Is in the Eye of the Beholder

Companies make acquisitions because they wish to grow and expand their business. In making acquisitions, a company has to determine what it feels the acquired brands are worth. In some instances, the hoped-for brand value has failed to materialize, serving as a reminder that the value of a brand is partly a function of what you do with it. The booming business environment of the 1990s witnessed many such failures.

Bruegger's Bagels survived a disastrous acquisition to later find success.

A classic example is Quaker Oats's $1.7 billion acquisition of Snapple in 1994. Snapple had become a popular national brand through powerful grassroots marketing and a willingness to distribute to small outlets and convenience stores. Quaker changed Snapple's ad campaign—abandoning the rotund and immensely popular Snapple Lady—and revamped its distribution system. Quaker also changed the packaging by updating the label and putting Snapple in 64-ounce bottles, moves that did not sit well with loyal customers. The results were disastrous: Snapple began losing money and market share, allowing a host of competitors to move in. Unable to revive the foundering brand, Quaker sold the company in 1997 for $300 million to Triarc, which owned other beverages such as Royal Crown Cola and Diet Rite.

Another unsuccessful acquisition occurred when Quality Dining bought Bruegger's Bagels in 1996 with $142 million in stock. Within one year, Quality Dining agreed to sell the bagel chain back to its original owners for $50 million after taking a $203 million charge on the acquisition. Experts blamed an overly ambitious expansion strategy. Quality Dining planned to

As a result of these criticisms, the climate regarding brand valuation has changed. Many experts insist that other measures beyond brand value are vital for assessing brand equity. Figure 10-9 displays "The Brand Equity Ten"—a set of crucial brand equity and tracking measures according to leading branding guru David Aaker.[40] In 1989, Britain's Accounting Standards Committee ruled that companies could value brands only if they were acquired in a takeover and only if they were then depreciated over 20 years against profits—adopting the more conservative American practice of gradually writing off goodwill (brands and all). The International Accounting Standards Committee is also grappling with the issue. See Brand Focus 10.0 for more on how accounting standards have changed to accommodate the concept of brand value.

Review

This chapter considered the two main ways to measure the benefits or outcomes of brand equity: comparative methods (a means to better assess the effects of consumer perceptions and preferences on aspects of the marketing program) and holistic methods (attempts to

expand to 2,000 stores within four years, despite the fact that before the acquisition, Bruegger's posted two consecutive annual losses due to its expansion to 339 stores. The new ownership also set the lofty goal of entering the top 60 domestic markets, which limited the amount of advertising and promotional support each market received. As Bruegger's fortunes turned, competitor Einstein/Noah Bagel overtook the company as the market leader in the United States. One franchisee commented, "[Quality Dining] would have had to stay up pretty late at night to screw up anything more than they did."

In 1996, Wells Fargo acquired competitor First Interstate Bancorp for $12.9 billion. The acquisition failed largely because the two banks had differing business styles. Wells Fargo focused on providing convenience for its customers, whereas First Interstate concentrated on offering customer service and support through its network of neighborhood branches. Following the merger, however, Wells Fargo alienated many First Interstate customers by failing to deliver on its promise that "it will be business as usual" for those customers. The bigger bank lost customers' deposits, bounced good checks, made balance errors, and answered customer complaints slowly or not at all. Many customers closed their accounts with Wells Fargo, causing non-California accounts to fall between 1 percent and 1.5 percent per month during 1997. The chairman and president of Wells Fargo apologized to bank customers in the 1997 annual report and admitted that "Overall, it was a sorry experience for far too many of our customers." Unfortunately for Wells Fargo, the customer exodus had a negative effect on earnings, and the bank was acquired in 1998 by Minneapolis-based Norwest.

Sources: "Cadbury Is Paying Triarc $1.45 Billion for Snapple Unit," *Baltimore Sun,* 19 September 2000; Thomas M. Burton, "The Profit Center of the Bagel Business Has Quite a Big Hole," *Wall Street Journal,* 6 October 1997; Jim Carlton, "Wells Fargo Discovers Getting Together Is Hard to Do," *Wall Street Journal,* 21 July 1997; David Olive, "Merger Track Record Spotty," *Financial Post,* 15 December 1998.

come up with an estimate of the overall value of the brand). Figure 10-10 summarizes the different but complementary approaches. In fact, understanding the particular range of benefits for a brand on the basis of comparative methods may be useful as an input in estimating the overall value of a brand by holistic methods.

Combining these outcome measures with the measures of sources of brand equity from Chapter 9 as part of the brand value chain can provide insight into the effectiveness of marketing actions. Nevertheless, assessing the ROI of marketing activities remains a challenge.[41] Here are four general guidelines for creating and detecting ROI from brand marketing activities:

1. ***Spend wisely—focus and be creative.*** To be able to measure ROI, we need to be earning a return to begin with! Investing in distinctive and well-designed marketing activities increases the chance for a more positive and discernible ROI.
2. ***Look for benchmarks—examine competitive spending levels and historical* company norms.** It is important to get the lay of the land in a market or category in order to understand what we may expect.

3. ***Be strategic—apply brand equity models.*** Use models such as the CBBE model and the brand value chain to provide discipline and a structured approach to planning, implementing, and interpreting marketing activity.
4. ***Be observant—track both formally and informally.*** Qualitative and quantitative insights can help us understand brand performance.

Perhaps the dominant theme of this and the previous chapter on measuring sources of brand equity is the importance of using multiple measures and research methods to capture the richness and complexity of brand equity. No matter how carefully we apply them, single measures of brand equity run the risk of missing important dimensions of

Loyalty

1. Price Premium
   - For a 17-ounce package of chocolate chip cookies, Nabisco is priced at $2.16. How much extra would you be willing to pay to obtain Pepperidge Farm instead of Nabisco?
   - Brand Y would have to cost _____ percent less than Brand X before I would switch brands.
   - For a 16-ounce package of chocolate chip cookies, would you prefer Nabisco at $2.16 or Pepperidge Farm at $2.29?
2. Satisfaction/Loyalty (among those who have used the brand)
   - Considering my recent use experience, I would say I was (dissatisfied, satisfied, delighted).
   - The brand met my expectations during the last use experience.
   - Would you buy the brand on the next opportunity?
   - Would you recommend the product or service to others?
   - The brand is (the only, one of two, one of three, one of more than three) brand(s) that I buy and use.

Perceived Quality and Leadership

3. Perceived Quality
   In comparison with alternative brands, this brand is . . .
   - Very high quality
   - Consistently high quality
   - (The best, one of the best, one of the worst, the worst)
4. Leadership/Popularity
   In comparison with alternative brands, this brand is . . .
   - Growing in popularity
   - A leading brand in the category
   - Respected for innovation

Esteem

In comparison with alternative brands, I
   - Hold this brand in high esteem
   - Highly respect this brand

Associations and Differentiation

5. Perceived Value
   - The brand is good value for the money.
   - There is a reason to buy this brand over others.
6. Personality
   - This brand has a personality.
   - This brand is interesting.
   - I have a clear image of the type of person who would use the brand.
   - This brand has a rich history.

FIGURE 10-9

Aaker's Measures of Brand Equity across Products and Markets

7. Organization
    - This is a brand I would trust.
    - I admire the Brand X organization.
    - I would be proud to do business with the Brand X organization.

Differentiation
- This brand is different from other brands.
- This brand is basically the same as the other brands.

Awareness

8. Brand Awareness
    - Name the brands in this product class.
    - Have you heard of this brand?
    - Do you have an opinion about this brand?
    - Are you familiar with this brand?

Market Behavior

9. Market Share
    - Market share based on market surveys of usage or syndicated data
10. Price and Distribution Indices
    - Relative market price—the average price at which the brand was sold during the month, divided by the average price at which all brands were sold
    - The percentage of stores carrying the brand
    - The percentage of people who have access to the brand

FIGURE 10-9

(Continued)

Comparative methods: Use experiments that examine consumer attitudes and behavior toward a brand, to more directly assess the benefits arising from having a high level of awareness and strong, favorable, and unique brand associations.

- ***Brand-based comparative approaches:*** Experiments in which one group of consumers responds to an element of the marketing program when it is attributed to the brand and another group responds to that same element when it is attributed to a competitive or fictitiously named brand.
- ***Marketing-based comparative approaches:*** Experiments in which consumers respond to changes in elements of the marketing program for the brand or competitive brands.
- ***Conjoint analysis:*** A survey-based multivariate technique that enables marketers to profile the consumer buying decision process with respect to products and brands.

Holistic methods: Attempt to place an overall value on the brand in either abstract utility terms or concrete financial terms. Thus, holistic methods attempt to "net out" various considerations to determine the unique contribution of the brand.

- ***Residual approach:*** Examines the value of the brand by subtracting out from overall brand preferences consumers' preferences for the brand based on physical product attributes alone.
- ***Valuation approach:*** Places a financial value on the brand for accounting purposes, mergers and acquisitions, or other such reasons.

FIGURE 10-10

Measures of Outcomes of Brand Equity

brand equity. Recall the problems encountered by Coca-Cola from its overreliance on blind taste tests, described in Branding Brief 1.1. In explaining the New Coke debacle, marketing consultant Randy Scruggs makes an interesting analogy concerning the effects of Coca-Cola's focus on a single measure to assess consumer response, likening it to the interpretation that someone might give when viewing a pencil head-on from the end with the eraser.[42] From that perspective, a pencil might look like a circle. If we were to look through a magnifying glass—Coke's 190,000 taste tests—we would be even more convinced that we were looking at a circle! Only if we were to look at the pencil from other angles and perspectives would we see that the object was multidimensional and had shape. A single measure provides at best a one- or two-dimensional view of a brand. To extend Scruggs's analogy, measuring the volume of a pencil may reveal something about its size but would say nothing about how well the pencil writes, how comfortable it would be to hold, and so forth. Thus, any one measure of a multidimensional concept such as brand equity necessarily overlooks or distorts important information.

Consistent with this view and according to the definition of customer-based brand equity, no single number or measure fully captures brand equity.[43] Rather, we should think of brand equity as a multidimensional concept that depends on what knowledge structures are present in the minds of consumers, and what actions a firm takes to capitalize on the potential offered by these knowledge structures. Thus, there are many different sources of brand equity and many different possible outcomes of brand equity, depending on the skill and ingenuity of the marketers involved. Different firms may be more or less able to maximize the potential value of a brand according to the type and nature of their marketing activities. As Wharton's Peter Fader says:

> The actual value of a brand depends on its fit with buyer's corporate structure and other assets. If the acquiring company has manufacturing or distribution capabilities that are synergistic with the brand, then it might be worth paying a lot of money for it. Paul Feldwick, a British executive, makes the analogy between brands and properties on the Monopoly game board. You're willing to pay a lot more for Marvin Gardens if you already own Atlantic and Ventnor Avenues![44]

The customer-based brand equity framework therefore emphasizes employing a range of research measures and methods to fully capture the multiple potential sources and outcomes of brand equity, as the next two chapters will consider.

Discussion Questions

1. Choose a product. Conduct a branded and unbranded experiment. What do you learn about the equity of the brands in that product class?
2. Can you identify any other advantages or disadvantages of the comparative methods?
3. Pick a brand and conduct an analysis similar to that done with the Planter's brand. What do you learn about its extendability as a result?
4. What do you think of the Interbrand methodology? What do you see as its main advantages and disadvantages?
5. How do you think Young & Rubicam's BrandAsset Valuator relates to the Interbrand methodology (see Brand Focus 9.0)? What do you see as its main advantages and disadvantages?

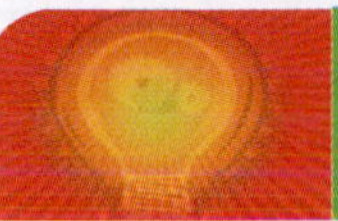

BRAND FOCUS 10.0

Branding and Finance

Marketers increasingly must be able to quantify their actitivities directly or indirectly in financial terms. One important topic that has received increasing academic interest is the relationship between brand equity valuations and stock market information and performance. Another important topic is the accounting implications of branding. We review issues around these topics in this appendix.

Stock Market Reactions

Several researchers have studied how the stock market reacts to the brand equity for companies and products. For example, David Aaker and Robert Jacobson examined the association between yearly stock return and yearly brand changes (as measured by EquiTrend's perceived quality rating of brand equity) for 34 companies during the years 1989 to 1992.[45] They also compared the accompanying changes in current-term return on investment (ROI). They found that, as expected, stock market return was positively related to changes in ROI. Interestingly, they also uncovered a strong positive relationship between brand equity and stock return. Firms that experienced the largest gains in brand equity saw their stock return average 30 percent. Conversely, those firms with the largest losses in brand equity saw stock return average a negative 10 percent. The researchers concluded that investors can and do learn about changes in brand equity—not necessarily through EquiTrend studies (which may have little exposure to the financial community) but by learning about a company's plans and programs.

More recently, using data for firms in the computer industry in the 1990s, Aaker and Jacobson found that changes in brand attitude were associated contemporaneously with stock return and led accounting financial performance.[46] They also found five factors (new products, product problems, competitor actions, changes in top management, and legal actions) that were associated with significant changes in brand attitudes. Awareness that did not translate into more positive attitudes, however, did little to the stock price (Ameritrade, Juno, and Priceline). The authors conclude, "So it's not the brands customers know, but the brands customers respect, that are ultimately successful." Similarly, using *Financial World* estimates of brand equity, another comprehensive study found that brand equity was positively related to stock return and that this effect was incremental to other accounting variables such as the firm's net income.[47]

Adopting an event study methodology, Lane and Jacobson were able to show that stock market participants' response to brand extension announcements, consistent with the tradeoffs inherent in brand leveraging, depend interactively and nonmonotonically on brand attitude and familiarity.[48] Specifically, the stock market responded most favorably to extensions of high-esteem, high-familiarity brands (Hershey, Coke, Norton/Symantec) and to low-esteem, low-familiarity brands (in the latter case, presumably because there was little to risk and much to gain with extensions). The stock market reaction was less favorable (and sometimes even negative!) for extensions of brands for which consumer familiarity was disproportionately high compared with consumer regard and to extensions of brands for which consumer regard was disproportionately high compared with familiarity. Mizik and Jacobson found that the stock market reacted favorably when a firm increased its emphasis on value appropriation (extracting profits in the marketplace) over value creation (innovating, producing, and delievering products to the market), although certain qualifying conditions prevailed.[49]

In another event study of 58 firms that changed their names in the 1980s, Horsky and Swyngedouw found that for most of the firms, name changes were associated with improved performance; the greatest improvement tended to occur in firms that produced industrial goods and whose performance prior to the change was relatively poor.[50] Not all changes, however, were successful. The researchers interpreted the act of a name change as a signal that other measures to improve performance (changes in product offerings and organizational changes) will be seriously and successfully undertaken.

Rao and his colleagues analyzed financial performance of 113 firms over a five-year period and found that corporate branding strategies were associated with higher values of Tobin's Q.[51] Tobin's Q is a forward-looking measure of intangible assets and a firm's future profit potential calculated as the ratio of the market value of the firm to the replacement cost of the firm's assets. A mixed branding strategy (where a firm used corporate names for some products and individual names for others) was associated with lower values of Tobin's Q. The researchers also concluded that most firms would have been able to improve their Tobin's Q had they adopted a branding strategy different from the one suggested by examining their brand portfolios. Madden, Fehle, and Fournier found that strong brands not only delivered greater returns to stockholders versus a relevant market benchmark, they did so with less risk.[52] Fornell and his colleagues find similar benefits of higher returns and lower risk for saisfied, loyal customers.[53]

Accounting Perspectives on Brands[54]

Accountants have adopted generally accepted accounting practices (GAAP) and a series of accounting standards to allow comparability in financial information. Two organizations inform these standards: the Financial Accounting Standards Board (FASB) for the United States and the London-based International Accounting Standards Board (IASB) for much of the rest of the world. FASB and IASB have a close working arrangement and their standards are increasingly similar. Over 90 countries use the IASB standards and those that do not (e.g., Japan, Hong Kong, Canada, and Australia, each of whom have their own standard-setting bodies) work closely with the IASB to ensure that their financial reporting is not out of step.

Producing accounting standards or even modifying existing ones is a slow process. Suggestions are received from a variety of sources and once they are on the agenda as a project, they are subject to open forum discussions and research by FASB and IASB staff. Each series of changes or development has to be published in exposure drafts (ED), discussion papers, and working drafts. Comments are received, assessed, and accommodated until the final standard is deemed ready for issue. The final standard is issued by FASB under the title Statement of Financial Accounting Standards (SFAS), and by IASB as International Financial Reporting Standards (IFRS).

Intangible assets have been a focus of attention by both bodies since the events of the 1980s. Events of the first five years of the new century have signalled substantial change in the restricted role previously given to brands as intangible assets. The rationale?

> (Investors need) better information about intangible assets because those assets are an increasingly important economic resource for many entities and are an increasing proportion of the assets acquired in many business combinations.[55]

FASB issued the revised SFAS 141 in June 2001. IASB followed suit with very similar amendments to IFRS 3 in January 2005. With these new directives, when company A buys company B, the difference between the purchase price and net asset value (if it exists) may no longer be ascribed solely to goodwill. The new standards require the accountants to account for the costs of the intangibles that make up the goodwill portion. In other words they have to work out why the premium over net asset value was paid. What was bought for that price? The task of the accountants, after the event, is to identify and value as many of these intangibles as the standard will permit them to recognize.

The standard provides detailed guidance as to which intangibles will and are likely to meet the recognition criteria. In particular, they recognize trademarks, trade names, service marks, collective marks, and certification marks. Thus, brands are now recognized as intangible assets and must be valued at their fair value at the time of the purchase, where fair value is defined as:

> the price that would be received for an asset . . . in a current transaction between marketplace participants in the reference market.[56]

Fair value is the market value of the asset, not its book value. Because the concept of fair value is new, both FASB and IASB have issued standards on fair value measurement. Notably, the measurement of fair value (1) reflects the market estimate of the future discounted inflows associated with the asset, and (2) is based on a premise that the asset is valued "in-use." In other words, the buyer of the asset would continue to use it as it had previously been used and would operate it in conjunction with other assets in the business.

The statement limits the accountant's choice to three main valuation types: market, cost, and income, as described above. The statement recommends that accountants maximize the use of inputs from the market rather from the entity itself, reducing the extent to which the company's own, probably subjective views are incorporated. The standard also suggests that risk be accommodated through the use of a discount rate in which a risk premium is added to the risk-free rate.

So if a company is acquired, the acquired company brand will be valued and appear in the acquiring company's balance sheet as an acquired intangible asset. The acquiring company's brand, however, will still not be listed in the balance sheet as an asset because it is internally generated and the accounting standards do not accommodate internally generated brands. Undoubtedly, the accounting boards will address this anomaly in the future with further statements.

Notes

1. C. B. Bhattacharya and Leonard M. Lodish, "Towards a System for Monitoring Brand Health," *Marketing Science Institute Working Paper Series* (00-111) (July 2000).
2. Richard F. Chay, "How Marketing Researchers Can Harness the Power of Brand Equity," *Marketing Research 3,* no. 2 (1991): 10–30.
3. Peter Farquhar and Yuji Ijiri make several other distinctions in classifying brand equity measurement procedures. Peter H. Farquhar, Julia W. Han, and Yuji Ijiri, "Recognizing and Measuring Brand Assets," *Marketing Science Institute Report* (1991): 91–119. They describe two broad classes of measurement approaches to brand equity: Separation approaches and integration approaches. Separation approaches view brand equity as the value added to a product. Farquhar and Ijiri categorize separation approaches into residual methods and comparative methods. Residual methods determine brand equity by what remains after subtracting physical product effects. Comparative methods determine brand equity by comparing the branded product with an unbranded product or an equivalent benchmark.

   Integration approaches, on the other hand, typically define brand equity as a composition of basic elements. Farquhar and Ijiri categorize integration approaches into association and valuation methods. Valuation methods measure brand equity by its cost or value as an intangible asset for a particular owner and intended use. Association methods measure brand equity in terms of the favorableness of brand evaluations, the accessibility of brand attitudes, and the consistency of brand image with consumers.

   The previous chapter described techniques that could be considered association methods. This chapter considers techniques related to the other three categories of methods.
4. Edgar Pessemier, "A New Way to Determine Buying Decisions," *Journal of Marketing* 24 (1959): 41–46.
5. Paul E. Green and V. Srinivasan, "Conjoint Analysis in Consumer Research: Issues and outlook," *Journal of Consumer Research* 5 (1978): 103–123; Paul E. Green and V. Srinivasan, "Conjoint Analysis in Marketing: New Developments with Implications for Research and Practice," *Journal of Marketing* 54 (1990): 3–19.
6. For more details see Betsy Sharkey, "The People's Choice," *Adweek,* 27 November 1989, MRC 8.
7. Paul E. Green and Yoram Wind, "New Ways to Measure Consumers' Judgments," *Harvard Business Review* 53 (July–August 1975): 107–111.
8. Max Blackstone, "Price Trade-Offs as a Measure of Brand Value," *Journal of Advertising Research* (August/September 1990): RC3-RC6.
9. For some discussion, see Jordan Louviere and Richard Johnson, "Measuring Brand Image with Conjoint Analysis and Choice Models," in *Defining, Measuring, and Managing Brand Equity: A Conference Summary,* ed. Lance Leuthesser, MSI Report 88–104 (Cambridge, MA: Marketing Science Institute, 1988).
10. Arvind Rangaswamy, Raymond R. Burke, and Terence A. Oliva, "Brand Equity and the Extendibility of Brand Names," *International Journal of Research in Marketing* 10 (March 1993): 61–75. See also Moonkyu Lee, Jonathan Lee, and Wagner A. Kamakura, "Consumer Evaluations of Line Extensions: A Conjoint Approach," in *Advances in Consumer Research*, Vol. 23 (Ann Arbor, MI: Association of Consumer Research, 1996), 289–295.
11. Howard Barich and V. Srinivasan, "Prioritizing Marketing Image Goals under Resource Constraints," *Sloan Management Review* (Summer 1993): 69–76.
12. Marco Vriens and Curtis Frazier, "The Hard Impact of the Soft Touch: How to Use Brand Positioning Attributes in Conjoint," *Marketing Research* (Summer 2003): 23–27.
13. V. Srinivasan, "Network Models for Estimating Brand-Specific Effects in Multi-Attribute Marketing Models," *Management Science* 25 (January 1979): 11–21.
14. Wagner A. Kamakura and Gary J. Russell, "Measuring Brand Value with Scanner Data," *International Journal of Research in Marketing* 10 (1993): 9–22.
15. Joffre Swait, Tulin Erdem, Jordan Louviere, and Chris Dubelar, "The Equalization Price: A Measure of Consumer-Perceived Brand Equity," *International Journal of Research in Marketing* 10 (1993): 23–45.
16. See also Eric L. Almquist, Ian H. Turvill, and Kenneth J. Roberts, "Combining Economic Analysis for Breakthrough Brand Management," *Journal of Brand Management* 5, no. 4 (1998): 272–282.
17. V. Srinivasan, Chan Su Park, and Dae Ryun Chang, "An Approach to the Measurement, Analysis, and Prediction of Brand Equity and Its Sources," *Management Science* 51, no. 9 (September 2005): 1433–1448. See also Chan Su Park and V. Srinivasan, "A Survey-Based Method for Measuring and Understanding Brand Equity and Its Extendability," *Journal of Marketing Research* 31 (May 1994): 271–288. See also Na Woon Bong, Roger Marshall, and Kevin Lane Keller, "Measuring Brand Power: Validating a Model for Optimizing Brand Equity," *Journal of Product and Brand Management 8,* no. 3 (1999): 170–184.
18. William R. Dillon, Thomas J. Madden, Amna Kirmani, and Soumen Mukherjee, "Understanding What's in a Brand Rating: A Model for Assessing Brand and Attribute Effects and Their Relationship to Brand Equity," *Journal of Marketing Research* 38 (November 2001): 415–429.
19. Kusum Ailawadi, Donald R. Lehmann, and Scott A. Neslin, "Revenue Premium as an Outcome Measure of

Brand Equity," *Journal of Marketing* 67, no. 4 (2003): 1-17. See also Avi Goldfarb, Qiamg Lu, and Sridhar Moorthy, "Measuring Brand Equity in an Equilibrium Framework: A Structural Approach," working paper, University of Toronto, 2005.

20. Patrick Barwise (with Christopher Higson, Andrew Likierman, and Paul Marsh), "Brands as 'Separable Assets,'" *Business Strategy Review* (Summer 1990): 49.
21. Oliver Hupp and Ken Powaga, "Using Consumer Attitudes to Value Brands: Evaluation of the Financial Value of Brands," *Journal of Advertising Research* (September 2004): 225–231.
22. Sharkey, "The People's Choice."
23. Joanne Lipman, "British Companies Value U.S. Brand Names—Literally," *Wall Street Journal,* 9 February 1989, B6; Laurel Wentz, "WPP Considers Brand Valuation," *Advertising Age,* 16 January 1989, 24.
24. Bernard Condon, "Gaps in GAAP," *Forbes,* 25 January 1999, 76–80.
25. For an excellent summary of key issues, see Jeffrey Parkhurst, "Leveraging Brand to Generate Value," Chapter 18, in *From Ideas to Assets,* ed. Bruce Berman (New York: John Wiley & Sons, 2002).
26. David M. Fredricks, "Branded Assets: The Issue of Measurement," paper presented at the ARF Fourth Annual Advertising and Promotion Workshop, 12–13 February 1992.
27. Quoted in "What's a Brand Worth? [editorial]," *Advertising Age,* 18 July 1994.
28. Lew Winters, "Brand Equity Measures: Some Recent Advances," *Marketing Research* (December 1991): 70–73; Gordon V. Smith, *Corporate Valuation: A Business and Professional Guide* (New York: John Wiley & Sons, 1988).
29. The Science of Branding 10.2 is based on the research and writings of Roger Sinclair whose considerable input is gratefully acknowledged. For more information, visit www.brandmetrics.com. Note that in the discussion of Category Expected Life analysis, the 40-year limit was chosen because it was the number of years used by the American accounting profession for the amortization of goodwill. The 10 years was broadly based on estimates of product failure rates.
30. Carol J. Simon and Mary W. Sullivan, "Measurement and Determinants of Brand Equity: A Financial Approach," *Marketing Science* 12, no. 1 (Winter 1993): 28–52.
31. Michael Birkin, "Assessing Brand Value," in *Brand Power,* ed. Paul Stobart (Washington Square, NY: New York University Press, 1994).
32. Simon Mottram, "The Power of the Brand," paper presented at the ARF Brand Equity Conference, 15–16 February 1994.
33. Raymond Perrier, *Brand Valuation,* 3rd ed. (Interbrand London, Premier Books, 1997). For some additional perspectives, see Jeffrey Parkhurst, "Leveraging Brand to Generate Value," Chapter 18, in *From Ideas to Assets,* ed. Bruce Berman (New York: John Wiley & Sons, 2002).
34. Jan Lindemann, "Brand Valuation," *Pool* 24 (Autumn 2003).
35. For some stimulating points of view, see the special issue on brand valuation of the *Journal of Brand Management* (Vol. 5, no. 4, 1998).
36. Susannah Hart and John Murphy, *Brands: The New Health Creators* (New York: New York University Press, 1998).
37. Diane Summers, "IBM Plunges in Year to Foot of Brand Name Value League," *Financial Times,* 11 July 1994.
38. Peter Fader, Course notes, Wharton Business School, University of Pennsylvania, 1998.
39. "On the Brandwagon," *The Economist,* 20 January 1990.
40. David A. Aaker, *Building Strong Brands* (New York: Free Press, 1996).
41. Scott Davis and Jeff Smith, "Do You Know Your Brand ROBI?" Management Review (October 1998): 55–57.
42. Randy Scruggs, personal communication, 1996.
43. For an interesting empirical application, see Manoj K. Agarwal and Vithala Rao, "An Empirical Comparison of Consumer-Based Measures of Brand Equity," *Marketing Letters* 7, no. 3 (1996): 237–247.
44. Fader, course notes.
45. David A. Aaker and Robert Jacobson, "The Financial Information Content of Perceived Quality," *Journal of Marketing Research* 31 (May 1994): 191–201.
46. David A. Aaker and Robert Jacobson, "The Value Relevance of Brand Attitude in High-Technology Markets," *Journal of Marketing Research* 38 (November 2001): 485–493.
47. M. E. Barth, M. Clement, G. Foster, and R. Kasznik, "Brand Values and Capital Market Valuation," *Review of Accounting Studies 3* (1998): 41–68.
48. Vicki Lane and Robert Jacobson, "Stock Market Reactions to Brand Extension Announcements: The Effects of Brand Attitude and Familiarity," *Journal of Marketing* 59 (January 1995): 63–77.
49. Natalie Mizik and Robert Jacobson, "Trading Off between Value Creation and Value Appropriation: The Financial Implications of Shifts in Strategic Emphasis," *Journal of Marketing* 67 (January 2003): 63–76.
50. Dan Horsky and Patrick Swyngedouw, "Does It Pay to Change Your Company's Name? A Stock Market Perspective," *Marketing Science* (Fall 1987): 320–335.
51. Vithala R. Rao, Manoj K. Agrawal, and Denise Dahlhoff. "How is Manifested Branding Strategy Related to the Intangible Value of a Corporation?" *Journal of Marketing* 68 (October 2004): 126–141.
52. Thomas J. Madden, Frank Fehle, and Susan M. Fournier, "Brands Matter: An Empirical Demonstration of the Creation of Shareholder Value through Brands," Harvard Business School working paper no. 02–098.

53. Clas Fornell, Sunil Mithas, Forrest V. Morgeson III, and M. S. Krishnan, "Customer Satisfaction and Stock Prices: High Returns, Low Risk," *Journal of Marketing* 70 (January 2006): 3–14.
54. This section is largely based on a white paper, "The Final Barrier: Marketing and Accounting Converge at the Corporate Finance Interface," by Roger Sinclair (www.brandmetrics.com).
55. FAS 141. *Business Combinations.* FASB in June 2001.
56. *Statement of Accounting Standards No. 15X. Fair Value Measurement.* FASB, 21 October 2005, i.

11 DESIGNING AND IMPLEMENTING BRANDING STRATEGIES

Preview

Parts II, III, and IV of this book examined strategies for building and measuring brand equity. Part V takes a broader perspective and considers how to create, maintain, and enhance brand equity under various situations and circumstances.

In this chapter, we consider issues related to branding strategies, and how to maximize brand equity across all the different brands and products the firm might sell. The branding strategy of a firm determines which brand elements a firm chooses to apply across the products it offers for sale. Many firms employ complex branding strategies. For example, brand names may consist of multiple brand name elements (Toyota Camry V6 XLE) and may be applied across a range of products (Toyota cars and trucks). What is the best way to characterize a firm's branding strategy under such instances? What guidelines exist to choose the right combinations of brand names and other brand elements to best manage brand equity across the entire range of a firm's products? Branding strategy is critical because it is the means by which the firm can help consumers understand its products and services and organize them in their minds.

We begin by describing two important strategic tools. The ***brand–product matrix*** and the ***brand hierarchy*** help to characterize and formulate branding strategies by defining various relationships among brands and products. The chapter next suggests some guidelines for designing branding strategies. Finally, we conclude by considering a number of different issues in implementing branding strategies, including designing the brand hierarchy and the supporting marketing program. We offer guidelines for the number of levels of the hierarchy to use, how to combine brands from different levels of the hierarchy for any particular product, and how to link any one brand to multiple products. Brand Focus 11.0 devotes special attention to the topic of cause marketing.

Brand Architecture

The ***branding strategy***, or ***brand architecture***, for a firm tells marketers which brand names, logos, symbols, and so forth to apply to which new and existing products. We often distinguish branding strategies by whether a firm is or should be employing an umbrella corporate or family brand for all its products (as a "branded house"), or a collection of individual brands all with different names (as a "house of brands").

Brand architecure defines both brand boundaries and brand complexity. Which different products should share the same brand name? How many variations of that brand name should we employ? The role of defining branding strategies and brand architecture is twofold:

- *Clarify—Brand Awareness:* Improve consumer understanding and communicate similarity and differences between individual products.
- *Motivate—Brand Image:* Maximize transfer of equity to/from the brand to individual products to improve trial and repeat purchase.

The Brand–Product Matrix

To characterize the product and branding strategy of a firm, one useful tool is the ***brand–product matrix***, a graphical representation of all the brands and products sold by the firm. The matrix (or grid) has the brands of a firm as rows and the corresponding products as columns (see Figure 11-1).

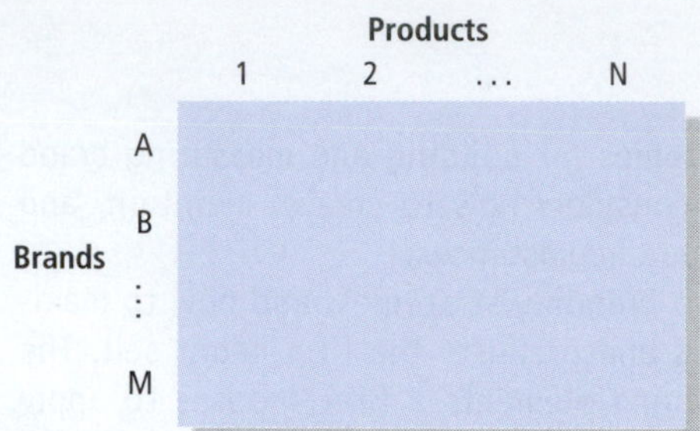

FIGURE 11-1
Brand-Product Matrix

The rows of the matrix represent ***brand–product relationships*** and capture the brand extension strategy of the firm in terms of the number and nature of products sold under the firm's different brands. A ***brand line*** consists of all products—original as well as line and category extensions—sold under a particular brand. Thus, a brand line is one row of the matrix. We want to judge a potential new product extension for a brand on how effectively it leverages existing brand equity from the parent brand to the new product, as well as how effectively the extension, in turn, contributes to the equity of the parent brand.

The columns of the matrix represent ***product–brand relationships*** and capture the brand portfolio strategy in terms of the number and nature of brands to be marketed in each category. The ***brand portfolio*** is the set of all brands and brand lines that a particular firm offers for sale to buyers in a particular category. Thus, a brand portfolio is one particular column of the matrix. Marketers can of course design and market different brands to appeal to different market segments.

We judge a brand portfolio on its ability to maximize brand equity: Any one brand in the portfolio should not harm or decrease the equity of the others. In the optimal brand portfolio, each brand maximizes equity in combination with all other brands in the portfolio. Branding Brief 11-1 describes the design of the Gap's brand portfolio.

One final set of definitions is useful.[1] A ***product line*** is a group of products within a product category that are closely related because they function in a similar manner, are sold to the same customer groups, are marketed through the same type of outlets, or fall within given price ranges. A product line may include different brands, or a single family brand or individual brand that has been line extended. A ***product mix*** (or product assortment) is the set of all product lines and items that a particular seller makes available to buyers. Thus, product lines represent different sets of columns in the brand–product matrix that, in total, make up the product mix. A ***brand mix*** (or brand assortment) is the set of all brand lines that a particular seller makes available to buyers.

We can characterize a firm's branding strategy according to its *breadth* (in terms of brand–product relationships and brand extension strategy) and its *depth* (in terms of product–brand relationships and the brand portfolio or mix). For example, a branding strategy is both deep and broad if the firm has a large number of brands, many of which have been extended into various product categories. This chapter only briefly considers some basic issues concerning the breadth of a branding strategy and brand extensions; Chapter 12 is devoted to these topics. Following this brief discussion, the remainder of this section outlines some of the key issues associated with the depth of a branding strategy and the topic of brand portfolios.

Breadth of a Branding Strategy

The breadth of a branding strategy describes the number and nature of different products linked to the brands sold by a firm. The firm has to make strategic decisions about how many different product lines it should carry (the breadth of the product mix), as well as how many variants to offer in each product line (the depth of the product mix).

Breadth of Product Mix. Lehmann and Winer provide an in-depth consideration of factors affecting product category attractiveness.[2] They note that three main sets of factors determine the inherent attractiveness of a product category, as follows (see Figure 11-2).

1. *Aggregate market factors:* Descriptive characteristics of the market itself. All else being equal, a category is attractive if it is relatively large (measured in both units and dollars); fast-growing (in current and projected terms) and in the growth stage of the product life cycle; noncyclical and nonseasonal in sales patterns; and characterized by relatively high, steady profit margins.
2. *Category factors:* Underlying structural factors affecting the category. In general, a category is attractive if the threat of new entrants is low (due to barriers of entry from economies of scale, product differentiation, capital requirements, switching costs, or distribution systems); bargaining power of buyers is low (when the product is a small percentage of buyers' costs or is sharply differentiated, or when buyers are earning high profits, lack information about competitive offerings, or are unable to integrate backward); current category rivalry is low (when there are few or an imbalance of competitors in fast-growing markets); few close product substitutes exist in the eyes of consumers; and the market is operating at or near capacity.
3. *Environmental factors:* External forces unrelated to the product's customers and competitors that affect marketing strategies. A host of technological, political, economic, regulatory, and social factors will affect the future prospects of a category.

Aggregate Market Factors
Market size
Market growth
Stage in product life cycle
Sales cyclicity
Seasonality
Profits

Category Factors
Threat of new entrants
Bargaining power of buyers
Bargaining power of suppliers
Current category rivalry
Pressures from substitutes
Category capacity

Environmental Factors
Technological
Political
Economic
Regulatory
Social

FIGURE 11-2
Category Attractiveness Criteria

BRANDING BRIEF 11-1

Bridging the Gap Brand

Donald Fisher founded the Gap in San Francisco in 1969 and named the store after the "generation gap." Fisher targeted baby boomers who had embraced jeans in general—and Levi's in particular—as the uniform of their generation. As the popularity of Gap stores increased, Fisher broadened the merchandising assortment by adding a limited number of Gap brand products and as many as 15 other national brands. To avoid shrinking margins and to tap into a more affluent market than students, Fisher decided to upgrade the Gap image starting in 1983.

The Gap has experienced many highs and lows.

The Gap also expanded beyond its flagship stores through acquisitions and extensions. GapKids is a highly successful extension introduced in 1986. Riding the wave of the baby boom "echo" to successfully open more than 350 stores by 1995, GapKids accounted for approximately 16 percent of Gap's annual earnings that year. The Gap bought Banana Republic and its unique travel- and safari-themed stores and catalogs in 1983 and reformulated the clothing to reflect more urban tastes. In March 1994, Gap introduced Old Navy Clothing stores to sell Gap-like men's, women's, and children's apparel at lower prices in large warehouse-style outlets. Old Navy rapidly became popular with consumers, and the brand's contribution to Gap sales grew from 3 percent ($120 million) in 1994 to more than 30 percent ($4.3 billion) in 2000. Old Navy encountered a drop-off in business, however, following its half-decade of success. Adults began avoiding Old Navy because its styles catered to teens. The company planned to broaden its stylistic palette because, as then-CEO Mickey Drexler said, "This business is too big to focus on a narrow consumer segment."

Old Navy's woes, however, were not as serious as those of the Gap, which also saw customers abandon it in droves when it changed its styles to match the teen trends. In

All these factors relate in some way to consumers, competition, and the marketing environment. Marketers must assess them to determine the inherent attractiveness of a product category or market, as well as taking into account its own core competencies and strategic objectives and goals. The actual names for the products to enter these different markets will depend on the branding strategy.

Xerox

Xerox chose to brand its first computers with the Xerox name. Because of the near-generic qualities of the name—virtually synonymous with photocopying—it is perhaps not surprising that consumers balked. Print ads announcing that "Here's a Xerox that does not even make

November 2001, the Gap recorded the nineteenth consecutive month of declines in same-store sales. CEO Mickey Drexler admitted, "We changed too much, too quickly, in ways that weren't consistent with our brands." A fashion industry consultant had stronger criticism: "Today there's no compelling reason to visit the Gap for fashion. It has fallen flat on its face."

Between 2000 and 2002, Gap's stock fell by two-thirds to $10 per share, as the company endured 29 months of same-store sales declines. A new CEO, Paul Pressler, was brought in from Disney to improve the company's fortunes. When consumer insights achieved through extensive market research revealed that the Gap's three brands were "sitting on top of each other," Pressler sought to push the brands further apart by focusing Old Navy on basic items sold at a discount, while Banana Republic increased prices and offered runway-inspired designs and the Gap remained in the middle. In the short term, the strategy worked as same-store sales and cash flow increased, enabling the Gap to pay off $2.9 billion in debt. Gap management elected to build on this success by pushing the brands even further apart, which alienated core customers who had come to expect a certain look for each brand. Same-store sales at each location remained flat or declined in 2005, and Gap's three brands endured disappointing sales declines during the all-important holiday season that year.

The Gap responded by repositioning its brands again—the Gap offered high-quality basics with style; Banana Republic focused on fashionable classics but avoided the cutting edge; Old Navy "rededicate[d] itself to disposably priced trendy items." An additional brand, Forth & Towne, a new chain store for women 35 and over, was launched. Forth & Towne, which represented in Gap's view an "untapped market," sold clothing and accessories under four labels: Allegory, Vocabulary, Prize, and Gap Edition. Unlike with Old Navy, Forth & Towne did not prosper and was closed down in 2007. After continued sales troubles, Paul Pressler exited the company in January 2007.

Sources: Julia Boorstin, "Fashion Victim: Can a Numbers Guy from Disney Correct Gap's Style Missteps?" *Fortune,* 17 April 2006, 160; Amy Merrick, "CEO Concedes Gap Made Errors, Promises Senior-Level Oversight," *Wall Street Journal,* 10 September 2001; Julie Creswell, "Confessions of a Fashion Victim," *Fortune,* 10 December 2001, 48–50.

a copy" may have raised questions in consumers' minds about how—or even whether—the computer worked. Xerox ultimately exited the personal computer business, though it still manufactures computer monitors.

Depth of Product Mix. Once marketers have made their broad decisions concerning appropriate product categories and markets in which to compete, they need to choose the optimal product line strategy. Product line analysis requires a clear understanding of the market and the cost interdependencies between products.[3] This requires examining the percentage of sales and profits contributed by each item in the product line, and its ability to withstand competition and address consumer needs. A product line is too short if the manager can increase long-term profits by adding items; the line is too long if the manager can increase profits by dropping items.[4] Increasing the length of the product line by adding new variants or items typically expands market coverage and therefore market share but also increases costs. From a branding perspective, longer product lines may decrease the consistency of the associated brand image if all items use the same brand.

Laura Ashley

Although a raging success in the 1980s, Laura Ashley found its sales wilting in the 1990s. The brand meant different things to different people, and, unfortunately, many of these people worked at Laura Ashley! Stores in the United States and Europe offered vastly different product lines. Designers and buyers were scattered all over the world and introduced hundreds of clothing styles, many of which clashed with the English country styles and flowery fashions for which Laura Ashley had become famous. The chain's vast range of product lines—which included adult clothes, children's clothes, and home furnishings—was filled with weak sellers and duplicate styles. Eighty-two percent of the company's sales came from just 22 percent of the merchandise. New management pared down the brands, eliminating 30 percent of the clothing styles and 20 percent of the home furnishing lines. They also consolidated design, buying, and merchandise and took steps to create a more common store design and format.[5] Having lost momentum, however, Laura Ashley found itself struggling in the marketplace as a succession of 10 CEOs in 13 years attempted to reenergize the brand. In 2005, a new CEO shifted the company's core focus from fashion to home furnishings, and sales began to rise.

Given appropriate product categories and product lines, marketers next decide which products to attach to any one brand as well as how many brands to support in any one product category. The former decision concerns brand extensions and we discuss it in detail in the next chapter; the latter decision concerns brand portfolios, which we address next.

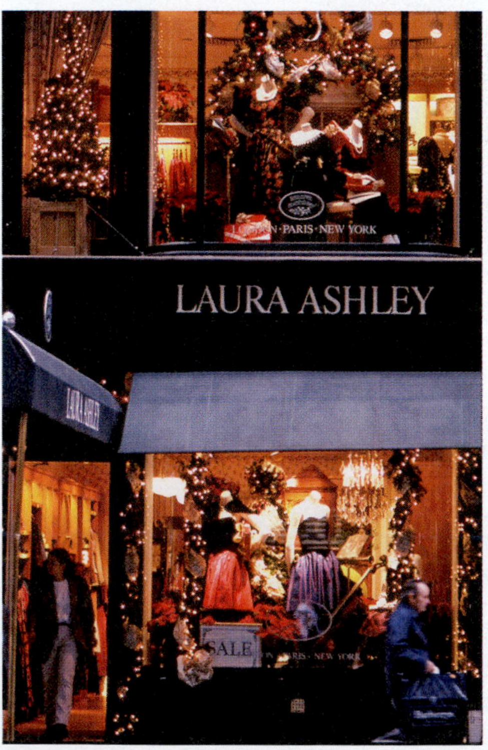

The Laura Ashley brand has experienced some ups and downs through the years.

Branding Brief 11-2 describes VF's experiences in stretching its brand name and business through strategic acquisitions.

Depth of a Branding Strategy

The depth of a branding strategy is the number and nature of different brands marketed in the product class sold by a firm. Why might a firm have multiple brands in the same product category? The primary reason is market coverage. Although multiple branding was originally pioneered by General Motors, Procter & Gamble is widely recognized as popularizing the practice. P&G became a proponent of multiple brands after introducing its Cheer detergent brand as an alternative to its already successful Tide detergent, resulting in higher combined product category sales.

The main reason to adopt multiple brands is to pursue different price segments, different channels of distribution, different geographic boundaries, and so forth.[6] For example, as part of a plan to upgrade Holiday Inn Worldwide, the hotel chain broke its domestic hotels into five separate chains to tap into five different benefit segments: the upscale Crowne Plaza, the traditional Holiday Inn, the budget Holiday Inn Express, and the business-oriented Holiday Inn Select and Holiday Inn Suites & Rooms.[7] Different branded chains received different marketing programs and emphasis; for example, Holiday Inn Express has been advertised with the humorous "Stay Smart" advertising campaign showing the brilliant feats that ordinary people can attempt after staying at the chain. Posing as scientists, doctors, and even members of the rock group Kiss, these people always utter the same line when their identity and credentials are questioned, "No, but I did stay at a Holiday Inn Express." Marriott adopted a very similar brand portfolio strategy at an earlier date, and other hotel chains have followed suit.

Many firms have to introduce multiple brands because no one brand is viewed equally favorably by all the different market segments the firm would like to target. Branding Brief 11-3 outlines Ford's brand portfolio strategy. Some other reasons for introducing multiple brands in a category include the following:[8]

- To increase shelf presence and retailer dependence in the store
- To attract consumers seeking variety who may otherwise switch to another brand
- To increase internal competition within the firm
- To yield economies of scale in advertising, sales, merchandising, and physical distribution

In designing the optimal brand portfolio, marketers generally need to trade off market coverage and these other considerations with costs and profitability. Like a product line, a portfolio is too big if profits can be increased by dropping brands; it is not big enough if profits can be increased by adding brands. Brand lines with poorly differentiated brands are likely to be characterized by much cannibalization and require appropriate pruning.[9] The Science of Branding 11-1 describes an academic approach to brand portfolio management.

The basic principle in designing a brand portfolio is to *maximize market coverage* so that no potential customers are being ignored, but *minimize brand overlap* so that brands aren't competing among themselves to gain the same customer's approval. Each brand should have a distinct target market and positioning.[10] For example, beginning in 2000, Procter & Gamble sought to maximize market coverage and minimize brand overlap by pursuing organic growth from existing core brands, rather than introducing so many new brands. The company focused its innovation efforts on core brands, which led to numerous successful market-leading brand extensions such as Crest whitening products, Pamper's training diapers, and Mr. Clean Magic Eraser products.[11]

BRANDING BRIEF 11-2

Stretching the VF Brand

The largest clothing maker in the world, VF was founded in 1899 as Reading Glove & Mitten Co., but in 1919 it was renamed Vanity Fair Silk Mills after its focus shifted to women's underwear. In the 1970s it expanded into jeanswear and workwear by acquiring H. D. Lee, manufacturer of Lee jeans. During the next three decades, VF acquired a number of other jeanswear and intimates brands. This narrowly focused growth strategy served the company well for some time, but VF sales flattened by 2000 as further expansion in the jeanswear and intimates category became difficult. As one commentator noted, "There's only so much growth you can squeeze from dungarees and bras." To spur further growth, VF sought to stretch its brand by acquiring clothing companies in other categories.

VF acquired Nautica from its founder, David Chu.

Beginning in 2000 with its $135 million acquisition of the well-known (but then loss-making) North Face brand of outdoor apparel and equipment, VF has made a series of successful acquisitions of popular brands in the outdoor apparel category. In 2004, VF acquired skateboard and surf footwear label Vans, surf footwear company Reef, outfitter Napapijri, and lifestyle backpack brand Kipling for more than $400 million combined. It also expanded into sportswear with its $631 million acquisition of the men's sportswear brand Nautica, which also included the designer label John Varvatos. VF's scale advantages and its long-standing expertise in the apparel industry enabled it to quickly revamp the sourcing, distribution, and financial operations of each of these acquired brands in order to make them more profitable. For example, The North Face posted a net loss of $100 million the year before it was purchased by VF; five years later sales nearly doubled to $500 million and operating profit margins rose from –35 percent to 13 percent.

Besides these considerations, brands can play a number of specific roles as part of a brand portfolio. Figure 11-3 summarizes some of them.

Flankers. An increasingly important role for certain brands is as protective flanker or "fighter" brands. The purpose of flanker brands typically is to create stronger points of parity with competitors' brands so that more important (and more profitable) flagship brands can retain their desired positioning. In particular, as we noted in Chapter 5, many firms are introducing discount brands as flankers to better compete with store brands and private labels and protect their higher-priced brand companions. In some cases, firms

Owned Brands

Jeanswear: Lee, Wrangler, Timber Creek by Wrangler, Hero by Wrangler, Riders, Rustler, Brittania, Chic, Gitano, 20X, Maverick, H.I.S., Old Axe,

Intimates: Vanity Fair, Vassarette, Bestform, Lily of France, Curvation, Gemma, Lou, Bolero, Intima Cherry, Variance, Belcor

Imagewear: Red Kap, Bulwark, Penn State Textile, Horace Small, Lee Sport, CSA, Chase Authentics, VF Solutions, E. Magrath

Outdoor: The North Face, JanSport, Eastpak, Napapijri, Kipling, Vans, Reef

Sportswear: Nautica, John Varvatos

Licensed Brands

Tommy Hilfiger intimates, NFL Red and NFL White imagewear

VF's brand expansion has been a significant contributor to its recent success. As stated on its Web site, two key points of VF's core strategy are to:

- Build a portfolio of strong brands that deliver great value to consumers.
- Target our brands to reach a variety of consumer segments across all retail channels.

These strategic moves enabled VF to achieve sales exceeding $6.2 billion—more than any other apparel maker—and over $500 million in net profit during 2006, while maintaining industry-leading operating margins. As one analyst noted, "VF has outperformed the competition because when the performance of one brand goes a little bit south, there are others that pick up the slack."

Sources: www.vfc.com; Michael V. Copeland, "Stitching Together an Apparel Powerhouse," *Business 2.0,* April 2005, 52.

are repositioning existing brands in their portfolio to play that role. For example, the one-time "champagne of bottled beer" Miller High Life beer was relegated in the 1990s to being a discount brand to protect the more premium-priced Miller Genuine Draft and Miller Lite. Similarly, P&G repositioned its one-time top-tier Luvs diaper brand to serve as a price fighter against private labels and store brands to protect the premium-positioned Pampers brand.

In designing fighter brands, marketers must walk a fine line. Fighter brands must not be so attractive that they take sales away from their higher-priced comparison brands or referents. At the same time, if fighter brands are connected to other brands in the portfolio

BRANDING BRIEF 11-3

Ford's Brand Portfolio

Ford Motor Company, traditionally known for its American-made brands Ford, Lincoln, and Mercury, expanded in the past two decades with a string of foreign automaker acquisitions, beginning with the 1987 purchase of British luxury automaker Aston Martin. Over the next decade, Ford purchased Land Rover, Volvo, and Jaguar. These moves transformed Ford Motor Company into the world's number-two seller by volume of luxury cars. All told, Ford invested more than $12 billion in acquiring luxury brands in the 1980s and 1990s.

In 2000, Ford's Premier Automotive Group (PAG)—Jaguar, Volvo, Land Rover, Aston Martin, and Lincoln—sold just under one million units worldwide. In contrast to competitors Lexus, BMW, and Mercedes, which sell a range of cars under a single brand, Ford's portfolio of luxury brands catered to different types of buyer. For example, Volvo attracts buyers interested in safety, Land Rover appeals to four-wheel-drive connoisseurs, and Jaguar represents tradition and British elegance. Victor H. Doolan, executive director for the premium auto group, explained the benefit of the portfolio: "We don't have to stretch our brands beyond their core values."

Ford's purchase of luxury automaker Jaguar has not yet met with great success.

FIGURE 11-3

Possible Special Roles of Brands in the Brand Portfolio

1. To attract a particular market segment not currently being covered by other brands of the firm
2. To serve as a flanker and protect flagship brands
3. To serve as a cash cow and be milked for profits
4. To serve as a low-end entry-level product to attract new customers to the brand franchise
5. To serve as a high-end prestige product to add prestige and credibility to the entire brand portfolio
6. To increase shelf presence and retailer dependence in the store
7. To attract consumers seeking variety who may otherwise have switched to another brand
8. To increase internal competition within the firm
9. To yield economies of scale in advertising, sales, merchandising, and physical distribution

Initially, the luxury division planned to earn profits by ramping up production of high-margin luxury vehicles and leveraging economies of scale by using the same basic car platforms across models. This dual strategy proved problematic, as Ford found it difficult to convince entry-level luxury buyers that the Jaguar X-Type sedan, for example, was worth purchasing if consumers learned that it was based on the same platform as the low-priced Ford Mondeo. Additionally, producing higher numbers of entry-level X-types was damaging to the exclusive image of the brand. After losing $800 million in 2002, Ford restructured the PAG division by reassigning Lincoln to the North American cars division and brought in new management to refocus PAG with lower sales targets. The luxury division posted a $164 million profit in 2003. But despite the success at Volvo, troubles with the Jaguar brand continued and the PAG recorded combined $840 million in losses in 2004 and 2005.

The struggles of Ford's luxury brands were mirrored by poor results in its North American division, which posted a pretax loss of $1.6 billion in 2005 due to high labor costs and declining demand for Ford, Lincoln, and Mercury cars. To improve performance in its North American division, in 2006 Ford announced its "Way Forward" plan, which in addition to a number of cost-cutting initiatives included efforts to strengthen the Ford, Lincoln, and Mercury brands. A new ad campaign for Ford was launched that year, themed "Bold Moves," designed to signal a new, positive direction for the brand.

Sources: www.ford.com; Kathleen Kerwin, "Ford Learns the Lessons of Luxury," *Business Week,* 1 March 2004, 116; Sarah A. Webster, "More Pain Ahead: Ford Lays Out Deep Cuts, But Details Unclear," *Detroit Free Press,* 24 January 2006, 1.

in any way (say, through a common branding strategy), they must not be designed so cheaply that they reflect poorly on these other brands.

Cash Cows. Some brands may be kept around despite dwindling sales because they still manage to hold on to a sufficient number of customers and maintain their profitability with virtually no marketing support. Marketers can effectively milk these "cash cows" by capitalizing on their reservoir of existing brand equity. For example, despite the fact that technological advances have moved much of the market to its newer Mach3 brand of razors, Gillette still sells its older Trac II, Atra, and Sensor brands. Because withdrawing these brands may not necessarily result in customers switching to another Gillette brand, it may be more profitable for Gillette to keep them in its brand portfolio than to discontinue them.

Low-End Entry-Level or High-End Prestige Brands. Many brands introduce line extensions or brand variants in a certain product category that vary in price and quality. These sub-brands leverage associations from other brands while distinguishing themselves on the basis of their price and quality dimensions. In this case, the end points of the brand line often play a specialized role.

THE SCIENCE OF BRANDING 11-1

Achieving the Ideal Brand Portfolio

As brand portfolios evolve and grow, they require more precise management focus. Periodic efforts to analyze and streamline expanding portfolios play an important role in brand management. Firms need a structured, clear-cut method for evaluating and refining their brand inventories to maximize how well they fit together and enhance each other's strength, not just to ensure they are strong independently. This approach prevents small, niche brands that still bring value to the company from stagnating due to underinvestment.

Hill, Ettenson, and Tyson detail five steps to help managers decide how to allocate their branding budgets across a portfolio of brands. The authors recommend periodic portfolio planning, which is an analysis of the entire brand roster that complements ongoing brand management efforts. Their portfolio planning framework allows managers to compare brands directly and offers direction both for the individual brands and the entire portfolio.

Step 1: Understanding the Portfolio

This step first requires taking an inventory of all brands owned by the company. Hill, Ettenson, and Tyson suggest compiling a list of all the company's owned trademarks and adding to it any partner brands closely associated with the company. The list should not include just the most prominent brands on a company's roster, because often the older, underutilized, or struggling brands need the most attention. Management then updates the final list by deleting obsolete trademarks and checking against the company's communications materials.

Step 2: Assessing Brand Contribution

The second step requires analyzing the contribution of each brand in the inventory to the overall portfolio. The analysis accounts for revenues, marketing expenses, and senior management time per brand, and the brand's importance relative to others in the portfolio. The authors note that brands can have hidden benefits, such as providing leverage with trade partners or a serving as a platform for a product line extension. Managers then evaluate all these variables to rank the brands in triads according to profit and overhead.

Step 3: Assessing Market Position

The authors assert that brands are like vectors: they have force and direction. The next step of portfolio analysis is gauging these two variables to get a sense of the overall health of the brand. Traction is a measure of the current strength of the brand. Marketers determine it from market research data as well as feedback from customers, suppliers, and employees. Traction captures loyalty to the brand and the brand's overall fit within the company.

The momentum variable shows managers where the brand is headed. The purpose of measuring momentum is to identify problems with brands before they appear as declines in volume and market share. To determine a brand's momentum, managers need to interview internal and external stakeholders and ask them incisive questions to understand previously unspoken thoughts and feelings about the brand and its place relative to competitors.

The researchers suggest managers take note of subtleties like body language to accurately capture responses.

Step 4: Addressing Problems and Identifying Opportunities

The researchers maintain that most brands fall into eight categories determined by their contribution to the company, current market performance, and future prospects. These are the categories:

1. *Power:* A brand that needs to be defended ferociously and deployed judiciously
2. *Sleeper:* A brand that with a little fast tracking can grow into a power brand
3. *Slider:* A valuable brand that has lost momentum, is slipping backwards, and needs immediate intervention to prevent meltdown
4. *Soldier:* A solid brand that contributes quietly without the need for much management attention
5. *Black hole:* A brand that sucks up resources and may not ever pay out
6. *Rocket:* A brand on its way to power-brand status
7. *Wallflower:* A small, underappreciated brand with very loyal customers, often under-priced and under-marketed
8. *Discard:* A brand that should have been retired years ago

The authors contend that the most difficult brands to categorize and manage are those with low traction and contribution but high momentum. They can be either black holes or rockets and are tough to distinguish because they are often newer brands that have yet to reach their full potential. Many companies fail to funnel enough resources to power, sleeper, soldier, and wallflower brands because they are spending so much time and attention on brands that should be discontinued. Soldier brands often form 60–80 percent of a brand portfolio. Managers should be careful to boost these brands with periodic infusions of resources.

Step 5: Developing a Plan for the Portfolio

Managers face the challenge of maximizing the entire brand portfolio. They must allocate funds to each of the brands, knowing that in the zero-sum game of portfolio planning, giving resources to one brand takes opportunity away from another. The available options include selling, repositioning, promoting, and consolidating brands. Hill, Ettenson, and Tyson argue that knowing when and where to invest in a brand is critical. They recommend creating a list of brands to watch closely and establishing deadlines for making decisions on the futures of those brands. This analysis should provide guidance for streamlining the portfolio and following up with brands that require attention. One of the most valuable aspects of the process is the investment of management time, which requires managers to engage with the brands and think strategically about the future of the portfolio.

Source: Sam Hill, Richard Ettenson, and Dane Tyson, "Achieving the Ideal Brand Portfolio," *MIT Sloan Management Review* (Winter 2005).

The role of a relatively low-priced brand in the brand portfolio often may be to attract customers to the brand franchise. Retailers like to feature these traffic builders because they often are able to "trade up" customers to a higher-priced brand. For example, BMW introduced certain models into its 3-series automobiles in part as a means of bringing new customers into its brand franchise with the hope of later moving them up to higher-priced models when they traded their cars in. BMW then took this approach one step further in 2004 by introducing the 1-series, which started at $23,800 and was built on the same production line as the 3-series.

On the other hand, the role of a relatively high-priced brand in the brand family often is to add prestige and credibility to the entire brand portfolio. For example, one analyst argued that the real value to Chevrolet of its Corvette high-performance sports car was in "its ability to lure curious customers into showrooms and at the same time help improve the image of other Chevrolet cars. It does not mean a hell of a lot for GM profitability, but there is no question that it is a traffic builder."[12] Corvette's technological image and prestige cast a halo over the entire Chevrolet line.

Summary. In short, brands can expand coverage, provide protection, extend an image, or fulfill a variety of other roles for the firm. In all brand portfolio decisions, the basic criteria are simple, even though their application can be quite complicated: To minimize overlap and get the most from the portfolio, each brand-name product must have (1) a well-defined role to fulfill for the firm and, thus, (2) a well-defined positioning indicating the benefits or promises it offers consumers. Many firms are finding that due to product proliferation through the years, they now can cut the number of brands and product variants they offer and still profitably satisfy consumers.[13]

Brand Hierarchy

The brand–product matrix helps to highlight the range of products and brands sold by a firm. For example, a Dell Inspiron XPS notebook computer consists of three different brand name elements, "Dell," "Inspiron," and "XPS." Some of these may be shared by many different products; others are limited. Dell uses its corporate name to brand many of its products, but Inspiron designates a certain type of computer (portable), and XPS identifies a particular model of Inspiron (designed to maximize gaming performance).

A ***brand hierarchy*** is a useful means of graphically portraying a firm's branding strategy by displaying the number and nature of common and distinctive brand elements across the firm's products, revealing the explicit ordering of brand elements. It's based on the realization that we can brand a product in different ways depending on how many new and existing brand elements we use and how we combine them for any one product. We can construct a hierarchy to represent how (if at all) products are nested with other products because of their common brand elements. Figure 11-4 displays a simple characterization of ESPN's brand hierarchy at one time.

There are different ways to define brand elements and levels of the hierarchy. Perhaps the simplest representation of brand elements and levels of a brand hierarchy—from top to bottom—might be:

1. Corporate or company brand (General Motors)
2. Family brand (Buick)
3. Individual brand (Park Avenue)
4. Modifier (designating item or model) (Ultra)

The highest level of the hierarchy technically always consists of one brand—the ***corporate or company brand***. For legal reasons, the company or corporate brand is almost always present somewhere on the product or package, although the name of a company

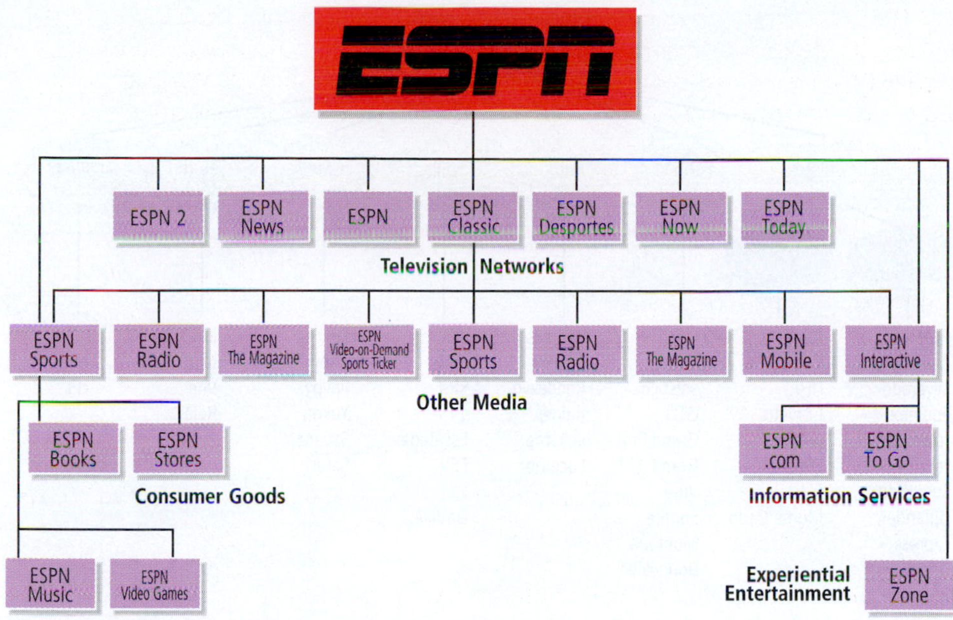

Source: 2006 Tuck Brand Audit Project.

FIGURE 11-4

ESPN Brand Hierarchy

subsidiary may appear instead of the corporate name. For example, Fortune Brands owns many different companies, such as Titleist golf balls and clubs, Footjoy golf shoes and gloves, Jim Beam whiskey, Courvoisier cognac, Master Lock locks, and Moen faucets, but it does not use its corporate name on any of its lines of business. For some firms like General Electric and Hewlett-Packard, the corporate brand is virtually the only brand. Some firms combine their corporate brand name with family brands or individual brands (conglomerate Siemens's varied electrical engineering and electronics business units are branded with descriptive modifiers, such as Siemens Transportation Systems). Finally, in some other cases, the company name is virtually invisible and, although technically part of the hierarchy, receives virtually no attention in the marketing program (Black & Decker does not use its name on its high-end DeWalt professional power tools).

At the next-lower level, a ***family brand*** is used in more than one product category but is not necessarily the name of the company or corporation. For example, ConAgra's Healthy Choice family brand appears on a wide spectrum of food products, including packaged meats, soups, pasta sauces, breads, popcorn, and ice cream. Other examples of family brands boasting over a billion dollars in annual sales include Seagram's Tropicana juices, PepsiCo's Gatorade sports drink, and Anheuser-Busch's Budweiser beer. Most firms typically support only a handful of family brands. If the corporate brand is applied to a range of products, then it functions as a family brand too, and the two levels collapse to one for those products.

An ***individual brand*** is a brand restricted to essentially one product category, although it may be used for several different product types within the category. For example, in the "salty snack" product class, Frito-Lay offers Fritos corn chips, Doritos tortilla chips, Lays and Ruffles potato chips, and Rold Gold pretzels. Each brand has a dominant position in its respective product category within the broader salty snack product class. A ***modifier*** is a means to designate a specific item or model type or a particular version or configuration of the product. Land O'Lakes offers "whipped," "unsalted," and "regular" versions of its butter. Yoplait yogurt comes as "light," "custard style," or "original" flavors.

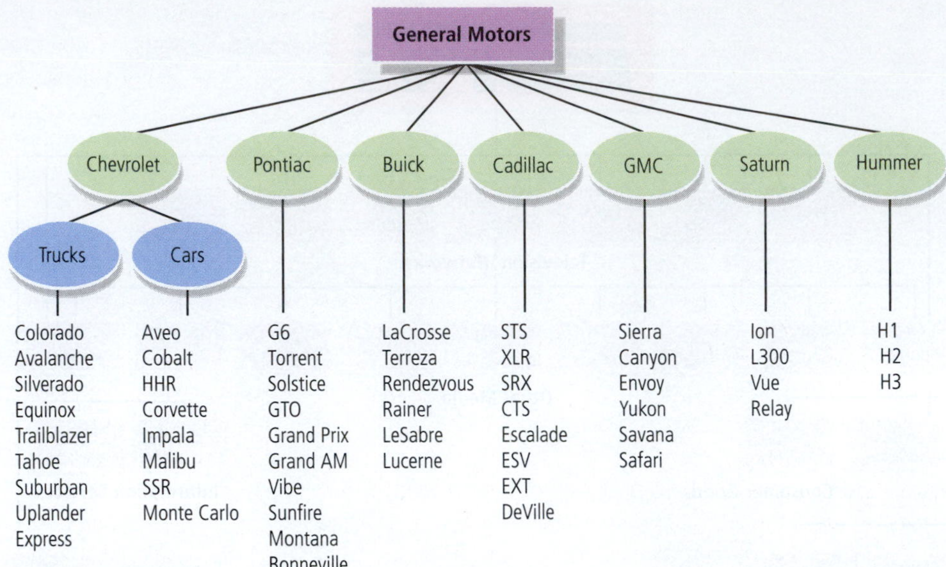

FIGURE 11-5

General Motors's Brand Hierarchy

Figure 11-5 displays an abridged version of a brand hierarchy that shows General Motors's branding strategy in 2005. As this example suggests, different levels of the hierarchy may receive different emphasis in developing a branding strategy. For example, General Motors traditionally chose to downplay its corporate name in branding its cars, although the name recently has played a more important role in its supporting marketing activities. Such shifts in emphasis are an attempt to harness the positive and mitigate against the negative associations of different brands in different contexts, and there are a number of ways to place more or less emphasis on the different elements that combine to make up the brand.

AKZO NOBEL

A Netherlands-based maker of health care products, coatings, chemicals, and fibers, Akzo Nobel uses a four-tier brand hierarchy based on the following rationale:[14]

1. Use of the *corporate brand* only in some industrial markets for chemicals, coatings, and fibers where the company name establishes the product's reputation
2. Use of the *corporate brand plus a product brand* in some industrial markets for chemicals, coatings, and fibers to add value or help position the product in relationship to other brands
3. Use of a *prominent product brand endorsed by the corporate brand* in some industrial markets for coating materials where the product brand is especially strong but can still be helped by a corporate endorsement
4. Use of *only a product brand* in pharmaceuticals and some coating products where marketing strategy makes this approach most desirable (but the corporate name might still appear on company stationery and signage)

Building Equity at Different Hierarchy Levels

Before considering how the brand hierarchy can help to formulate branding strategies, let's first examine some of the specific issues in building brand knowledge structures—and thus brand equity—at each of the different levels of the brand hierarchy.

Corporate or Company Brand Level. For simplicity, this chapter refers to corporate and company brands interchangeably, recognizing that consumers may not necessarily draw a distinction between the two or know that corporations may subsume multiple companies. We can think of a corporate image as the consumer associations to the company or corporation making the product or providing the service. Corporate image is particularly relevant when the corporate or company brand plays a prominent role in the branding strategy.

Some marketing experts believe that a factor increasing in importance in purchase decisions is consumer perceptions of a firm's role in society, for example, how a firm treats its employees, shareholders, local neighbors, and others. As the head of a large ad agency put it: "The only sustainable competitive advantage any business has is its reputation."[15] Consistent with this reasoning, a large global survey of financial analysts and others in the investment community indicated that 91 percent of the sample agreed a company that fails to look after its reputation will endure financial difficulties. Moreover, 96 percent of the analysts responded that the CEO's reputation was fairly, very, or extremely important in influencing their ratings.[16] Similarly, the annual Reputation Quotient (RQ) survey of nearly 20,000 Americans by Harris Interactive concluded that a strong statistical correlation exists between an excellent corporate reputation and consumers' intentions to buy a company's products and services, recommend them to other people, buy a company's stock, and recommend the stock to other investors.[17] Interbrand found that a strong corporate brand could improve a company's stock price from 5 percent to 7 percent in a bull market and mitigate losses in a bear market.[18] Not coincidentally, a survey of CEOs conducted by *PR Week* magazine found that almost 75 percent of the CEO respondents stated they were worried about threats to their organization's corporate reputation.[19] In justifying their marketing investments, executives at Accenture maintain that a strong corporate image can also be an effective means to attract and motivate employees.

The realization that consumers and others may be interested in issues beyond product characteristics and associations has prompted much marketing activity to establish the proper corporate image. A corporate image will depend on a number of factors, such as the products a company makes, the actions it takes, and the manner in which it communicates to consumers. Barich and Kotler identify a host of specific determinants of company image (see Figure 11-6).[20] As the CEO at Johnson & Johnson once observed, "Reputations reflect behavior you exhibit day in and day out through a hundred small things. The way you manage your reputation is by always thinking and trying to do the right thing every day."[21] Brand Focus 11-0 details how Johnson & Johnson managed to preserve both the reputation of the Tylenol product line and its own corporate reputation by responding appropriately to a serious product-safety crisis.

Corporate brand equity is the differential response by consumers, customers, employees, other firms, or any relevant constituency to the words, actions, communications, products, or services provided by an identified corporate brand entity. In other words, positive corporate brand equity occurs when a relevant constituency responds more favorably to a corporate ad campaign, a corporate-branded product or service, a corporate-issued PR release, and so on than if the same offering were attributed to an unknown or fictitious company. A corporate brand can be a powerful means for firms to express themselves in a way that isn't tied to their specific products or services. The Science of Branding 11-2 describes one approach to defining corporate brand personality.

A corporate brand is distinct from a product brand in that it can encompass a much wider range of associations. For example, a corporate brand name may be more likely to evoke associations of common products and their shared attributes or benefits; people and relationships; programs and values; and corporate credibility. These associations can have an important effect on the brand equity and market performance of individual products. For example, one research study revealed that consumers with a more favorable corporate image of DuPont were more likely to respond favorably to the claims made in an ad for Stainmaster carpet and therefore actually buy the product.[22]

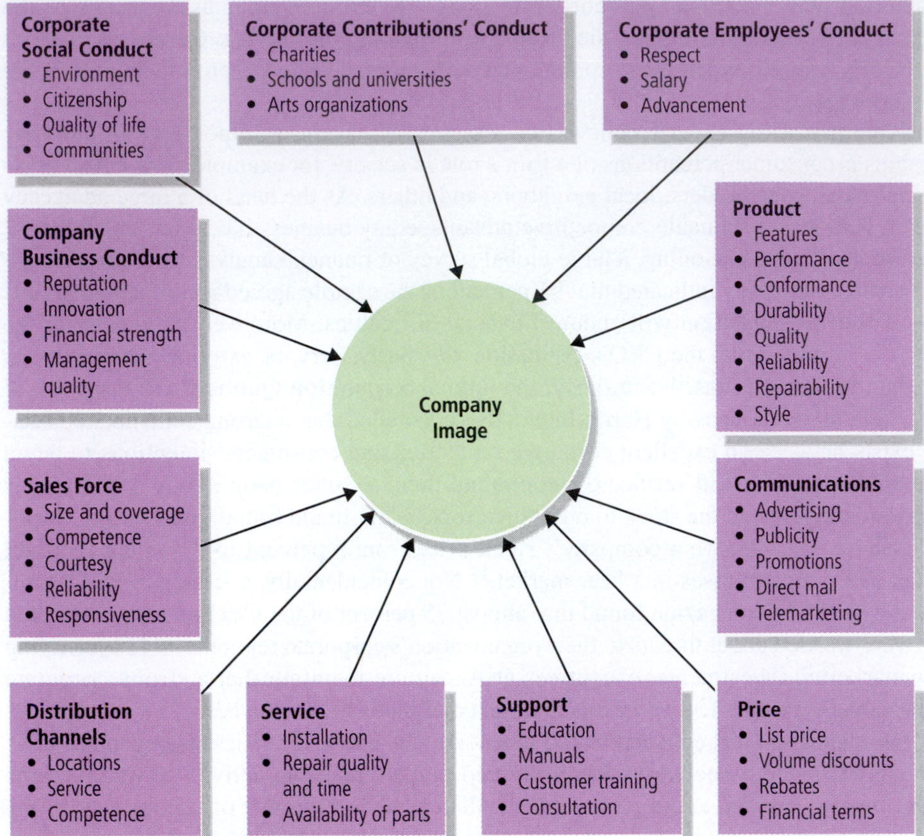

FIGURE 11-6

Determinants of Corporate Image

Building and managing a strong corporate brand has additional requirements. It necessitates that the firm keep a high public profile, especially in terms of influencing and shaping some of the more abstract types of associations. The CEO or managing director, if associated with a corporate brand, must be willing to maintain a more public profile to help to communicate news and information, as well as perhaps provide a symbol of current marketing activities. At the same time, by virtue of having a more visible public profile, a firm must also be willing to subject itself to more scrutiny and be more transparent in its values, activities, and programs. Corporate brands thus have to be comfortable with a high level of openness.

A corporate brand offers a host of potential marketing advantages, but only if corporate brand equity is carefully built and nurtured—a challenging task. Many marketing winners in the coming years will therefore be those firms that properly build and manage corporate brand equity. Branding Brief 11-4 describes a closely related concept—corporate reputation—and how we can look at it from the perspective of consumers and other firms.[23] This chapter next considers brand image issues at the other three levels of the brand hierarchy.

Family Brand Level. Family brands, like corporate or company brands, are brands applied across a range of product categories. The main difference is that because a family brand may be distinct from the corporate or company brand, company-level associations may be less salient. Other authors sometimes refer to these types of brands as ***range brands*** or ***umbrella brands.***

Marketers may apply family brands instead of corporate brands for several reasons. As products become more dissimilar, it may be harder for the corporate brand to retain any product meaning or to effectively link the disparate products. We saw in Chapter 7 that Beatrice Inc. was unable to create a meaningful corporate brand around its heterogeneous collection of products. Distinct family brands, on the other hand, can evoke a specific set of associations across a group of related products.[24] As with corporate brands, these associations may relate to common product attributes, benefits, and attitudes, and, perhaps to a lesser extent, to people and relationships, programs and values, and corporate credibility.

Family brands thus can be an efficient means to link common associations to multiple, but distinct, products. The cost of introducing a related new product can be lower and the likelihood of acceptance can be higher when marketers apply an existing family brand to a new product. On the other hand, if the products linked to the family brand and their supporting marketing programs are not carefully considered and designed, the associations to the family brand may become weaker and less favorable. Moreover, the failure of one product may have adverse ramifications on other products sold by the firm under the same brand by virtue of the common brand identification. These pros and cons will help determine whether a "branded house" or "house of brands" is the more appropriate strategy.

Individual Brand Level. Individual brands are restricted to essentially one product category, although multiple product types may differ on the basis of model, package size, flavor, and so forth. The main advantage of creating individual brands is that we can customize the brand and all its supporting marketing activity to meet the needs of a specific customer group. Thus, the name, logo, and other brand elements, as well as product design, marketing communication programs, and pricing and distribution strategies, can all focus on a certain target market. Moreover, if the brand runs into difficulty or fails, the risk to other brands and the company itself is minimal. The disadvantages of creating individual brands, however, are the difficulty, complexity, and expense of developing separate marketing programs to build sufficient levels of brand equity.

Modifier Level. Regardless of whether marketers choose corporate, family, or individual brands, they must often further distinguish brands according to the different types of items or models. Adding a modifier often can signal refinements or differences in brands related to factors such as quality levels (Johnnie Walker Red Label, Black Label, Gold Label, and Blue Label Scotch whiskey), attributes (Wrigley's Spearmint, Doublemint, and Juicy Fruit flavors of chewing gum), functions (Kodak's 100-, 200-, and 400-speed 35 mm and APS film), and so forth.[25] Brand modifiers communicate how different products within a category that share the same brand name differ on one or more significant attribute or benefit dimensions. Thus, one of their uses is to show how one brand variation relates to others in the same brand family. Modifiers help to make products more understandable and relevant to consumers or even the trade. Farquhar, Herr, and their colleagues note how modifiers can even become strong trademarks if they are able to develop a unique association with the parent brand, citing as examples the fact that only Uncle Ben has "Converted Rice" and only Orville Redenbacher sells "Gourmet Popping Corn."[26]

Product Descriptor. Although not considered a brand element per se, the product descriptor for the branded product may be an important ingredient of branding strategy. The product descriptor helps consumers understand what the product is and does and also helps to define the relevant competition in consumers' minds. In some cases, it may be hard to describe succinctly what the product is, especially in the case of a new product with unusual functions.

THE SCIENCE OF BRANDING 11-2

Corporate Brand Personality

In an article in the *Journal of Brand Management,* Kevin Lane Keller and Keith Richey outline and define three core dimensions that the successful 21st-century corporation's brand personality needs to reflect: namely, the Heart, Mind, and Body. These three core dimensions are composed of two personality traits each—Passionate and Compassionate (Heart); Creative and Disciplined (Mind); and Agile and Collaborative (Body).

The authors define corporate personality as "a form of brand personality specific to a corporate brand" and "the human characteristics or traits that can be attributed to a brand." They note that despite the fact that brand personality refers to both product brands and corporate brands, corporate brands are designed to encompass a wider range of associations than the product brands that might fall under them. Keller and Richey define the three core dimensions of corporate personality as follows:

- The "heart" of the company is made up of two traits: *passionate* and *compassionate.* The company must be passionate about serving its customers and competing in the market and must have compassion for employees, stakeholders, and members of the communities in which it operates.
- The "mind" of the company contains two traits: *creative* and *disciplined.* A successful company must be creative in its approach to serving its customers and winning in the market, while also adopting a disciplined approach that ensures appropriate and consistent actions across the organization.
- The "body" of the company is *agile* and *collaborative.* The successful company must possess the agility to profitably react to changes in the market and also employ a collaborative approach that ensures it works well together inside and outside the company toward common goals.

The authors point out that a tradeoff exists between the two traits within the "mind" dimension. They note that "while it is necessary to encourage and maintain creativity in the organization, this creativity must be focused to a certain degree." In order to be successful, a

MySpace.com

One of the branding challenges at News Corporation, now the owner of the highly successful MySpace.com Web site, is saying exactly what MySpace is. Although accurate, the label "social networking Web site" may not be a product category descriptor with which consumers have much familiarity. Fortunately for MySpace, young Web surfers seemed to have an intuitive sense for the utility of such a product and were flocking to the site at the rate of 160,000 new registered users per day in 2006.[27]

Introducing a truly new product with a familiar product name may facilitate basic familiarity and comprehension, but perhaps at the expense of a richer understanding of how the new product is different from closely related products that already exist.

firm must leverage its core capabilities and focus on its core business, instead of pursuing every new business opportunity that arises. This tradeoff can be managed by "setting appropriate priorities that provide clear direction to all members of the organization as to what its business goals are and how they can be met." One company that has succesfully blended creativity and discipline is 3M, which requires its scientists to spend 15 percent of their work time researching topics of interest to them beyond their specific research role. Thus the company encourages innovative research and thinking, but ensures that this research augments its core business rather than distracting from it.

According to the article, these three core dimensions of corporate personality have an multiplicative, not merely an additive, effect. That is, "the effects of these three pairs of corporate personality traits are enhanced by each other." For example, passion can drive creativity in an organization. In turn, creativity spurs agility, as more creative firms are able to rapidly find solutions to problems or recognize new opportunities. Discipline engenders better collaborative efforts, as employees more readily establish and follow guidelines and partnership principles.

The authors contend that these dimensions of corporate personality traits are important to build in a brand, because the corporation competing in the 21st century will be defined "as much by *who* it is as *what* it does." This contrasts with the historical case for corporations, in which a company drew its identity primarily from products and services it sold and its actions in the market. A company's employees are, in many cases, the outward face of the company that consumers see, and they define "who" a corporation is. It is therefore necessary, the authors assert, that employees embody the personality traits the company has established. If all employees act with a "heart," "mind," and "body," then the company will be better positioned to achieve success in the 21st-century business environment.

Source: Kevin Lane Keller and Keith Richey (2006), "The Importance of Corporate Brand Personality Traits to a Successful 21st Century Business, *Journal of Brand Management,* 14 (September-November), pp. 74–81.

Corporate Image Dimensions

Before considering some of the decisions needed to set up a brand hierarchy, let's consider in more detail the types of associations that may exist at the corporate or company brand level—or perhaps even at the family brand level. This section highlights some of the different types of associations that are likely to be linked to a corporate brand and can potentially affect brand equity (see Figure 11-7).[28] The Science of Branding 11-2 describes some academic research into corporate branding.

Common Product Attributes, Benefits, or Attitudes. Like individual brands, a corporate or company brand may evoke in consumers a strong association to a product attribute (Hershey with "chocolate"), type of user (BMW with "yuppies"), usage situation (Club Med with "fun times"), or overall judgment (Sony with "quality").

BRANDING BRIEF 11-4

Corporate Reputations: America's Most Admired Companies

Every year, *Fortune* magazine conducts a comprehensive survey of business perceptions of the companies with the best corporate reputations. The 2006 survey included the 1,000 largest U.S. companies (ranked by revenue) and the 25 largest U.S. subsidiaries of foreign-owned companies in 70 industry groups. More than 10,000 senior executives, outside directors, and financial analysts were asked to select the five companies they admired most, regardless of industry. To create industry lists, respondents rated companies in their industry by eight attributes: (1) quality of management; (2) quality of products or services; (3) innovativeness; (4) long-term investment value; (5) financial soundness; (6) ability to attract, develop, and keep talented people; (7) responsibility to the community and the environment; and (8) wise use of corporate assets.

Many of the same companies make the list year after year; for example, General Electric has been number 1 in six of the last eight years. *Fortune*'s Top Ten Most Admired companies in 2006 and their rankings are as follows:

Rank	Company	Rank	Company
1	General Electric	6	Johnson & Johnson
2	FedEx	7	Berkshire Hathaway
3	Southwest Airlines	8	Dell
4	Procter & Gamble	9	Toyota Motor
5	Starbucks	10	Microsoft

The results of the RQ 2005 study of corporate reputations conducted each year since 1999 by Harris Interactive and the Reputation Institute demonstrate both the enduring character of

Common Product Attributes, Benefits, or Attitudes
Quality
Innovativeness

People and Relationships
Customer orientation

Values and Programs
Concern with environment
Social responsibility

Corporate Credibility
Expertise
Trustworthiness
Likability

FIGURE 11-7

Some Important Corporate Image Associations

corporate reputations and their ability to change quickly. According to Dr. Charles Fombrun, executive director of the Reputation Institute and co-creator of the annual RQ study, "Corporate reputations are Janus-faced. Companies like Johnson & Johnson and Coca-Cola have consistently dominated our public rankings, whereas oil, tobacco, and scandal-plagued companies have anchored the bottom of the distribution. At the same time, reputations can change quickly, with autos and pharmaceuticals taking a big hit in 2005, but technology companies like Google skyrocketing to the top of the list."

Researchers determine the rated companies on the basis of a preliminary sampling of over 6,000 respondents who are asked to name two companies with the best corporate reputations in the United States and two companies with the worst reputations. They sum the open-ended nominations to create a list of the 60 "most visible companies." Some 20,000 people then rate these companies on the 20 attributes of the Harris-Fombrun Reputation Quotient, a scientifically developed instrument designed to measure corporate reputations in six key areas: emotional appeal, product/service quality, financial performance, social responsibility, vision and leadership, and workplace environment. The 2006 results are as follows:

Rank	**Company**	**Rank**	**Company**
1	Microsoft	6	General Mills
2	Johnson & Johnson	7	UPS
3	3M	8	Sony
4	Google	9	Toyota
5	Coca-Cola	10	Procter & Gamble

Sources: "America's Most Admired Companies," *Fortune,* 22 February 2006; "Microsoft Jumps to No. 1 in National Corporate Reputation Survey," press release, Harris Interactive, 1 February 2007.

If a corporate brand is linked to products across diverse categories, then some of its strongest associations are likely to be those intangible attributes, abstract benefits, or attitudes that span each of the different product categories. For example, companies may be associated with products or services that solve particular problems (Black & Decker), bring excitement and fun to certain activities (Nintendo), are built with the highest quality standards (Motorola), contain advanced or innovative features (Rubbermaid), or represent market leadership (Hertz). Two specific product-related corporate image associations—high quality and innovation—deserve special attention.

A ***high-quality corporate image association*** creates consumer perceptions that a company makes products of the highest quality. A number of different organizations like J.D. Power, *Consumer Reports,* and various trade publications for automobiles rate products, and the Malcolm Baldrige award is one of many that distinguishes companies on the basis of quality. Quality is one of the most important, if not *the* most important, decision factors for consumers.

An ***innovative corporate image association*** creates consumer perceptions of a company as developing new and unique marketing programs, especially with respect to product introductions or improvements. Keller and Aaker experimentally showed how different corporate image strategies—being innovative, environmentally concerned, or community involved—could differentially affect corporate credibility and strategically benefit the firm by increasing the acceptance of brand extensions as a result.[29] Specifically, they showed how corporate images of being environmentally concerned and community involved affected consumer perceptions of corporate trustworthiness and likability but not corporate expertise. Interestingly, consumers saw a company with an innovative corporate image as not only expert but also as trustworthy and likable.

Being innovative is seen in part as being modern and up-to-date, investing in research and development, employing the most advanced manufacturing capabilities, and introducing the newest product features. An image priority for many Japanese companies—from consumer product companies such as Kao to more technically oriented companies such as Canon—is to be perceived as innovative.[30] Perceived innovativeness is also a key

BRANDING BRIEF 11-5

3M is well-respected as a highly innovative and creative organization.

Corporate Innovation at 3M

3M has fostered a culture of innovation and improvisation evident in its very beginnings. In 1904, the company's directors were faced with a failed mining operation, but they turned the leftover grit and wastage into a revolutionary new product: sandpaper. Today 3M makes more than 50,000 products, including sandpaper, adhesives, contact lenses, and optical films. Each year 3M launches scores of new products, and the company generates significant revenues from products introduced within the past five years. It regularly ranks among the top 10 U.S. companies each year in patents received. 3M has an annual R&D budget of $1 billion, which is a healthy portion of its annual $22.9 billion in sales.

3M has a long history of innovation and has developed numerous products in its 99-year history that were the first of their kind. Here's a brief timeline:

1925: Scotch® masking tape
1930: Scotch® transparent tape
1939: First reflective traffic sign
1956: Scotchgard™ fabric protector
1962: Tartan Track, first synthetic running track
1979: Thinsulate™ thermal insulation
1980: Post-it® Notes
1985: First refastening diaper tape

competitive weapon and priority for firms in other countries. Michelin ("A Better Way Forward") describes how its commitment to the environment, security, value, and driving pleasure has been driving innovation. Branding Brief 11-5 describes how 3M has developed an innovative culture and image.

People and Relationships. Corporate image associations may reflect characteristics of the employees of the company. Although this is a natural positioning strategy for service firms including airlines like Southwest, rental cars like Avis, hotels such as Ritz-Carlton, and retailers like Wal-Mart, in fact manufacturing firms such as GE and others have also focused attention on their employees in communication programs in the past. Their rationale is that the traits exhibited by employees will directly or indirectly have implications for consumers about the products the firm makes or the services it provides.

1995: First nonchlorofluorocarbon aerosol inhaler

2000: First laminating products that do not require heat

2001: 3M™ Novec™ fire protection fluid, first alternative to halon for fire suppression

2003: First aluminum composite conductor that can transport up to three times more electricity than conventional overhead conductors

3M is able to consistently produce innovations in part because it promotes a corporate environment that facilitates new discoveries. Here are some tactics the company uses to ensure its culture remains focused on innovation:

- 3M encourages everyone, not just engineers, to become "product champions." The company's "15 percent time" allows all employees to spend up to 15 percent of their time working on projects of personal interest. Products such as Post-it Notes, masking tape, and the company's microreplication technology developed as a result of 15-percent time activities.
- Each promising new idea is assigned to a multidisciplinary venture team headed by an "executive champion."
- 3M expects some failures and uses failed products as opportunities to learn how to make products that work.
- 3M hands out its Golden Step awards each year to the venture teams whose new products earned more than $2 million in U.S. sales or $4 million in worldwide sales within three years of commercial introduction.

In the late 1990s, 3M struggled some as sales stalled and profits fell. The company restructured, shed several proprietary noncore businesses, and cut its workforce. As a result of these moves, 3M saw record sales and income in 2000. When 3M named former GE executive James McNerney as its new chairman and CEO that year, McNerney vowed he would continue to improve the company's bottom line while keeping its culture of innovation intact. When replaced by George Buckley in 2006, greater emphasis was placed on driving fast growth.

Sources: www.3m.com; 3M 2006 annual report.

GM has applied a different kind of marketing for Saturn.

SATURN

General Motors created an entire car division, Saturn, that advertises itself as a "Different Kind of Car Company" in an attempt to build unique relationships with consumers. According to then GM chairman John Smale, Saturn's brand promise (and point of difference) was that it was the car to buy for consumers who "want a car built, sold, and serviced by people who really care—people whose No. 1 priority is to satisfy you and build and preserve a relationship with you, no matter what it takes." The entire marketing program created associations to Saturn as coming from a "dedicated and caring" car company.[31]

Retail stores also derive much brand equity from employees within the organization. For example, growing from its origins as a small shoe store, Seattle-based Nordstrom became one of the nation's leading fashion specialty stores through a commitment to quality, value, selection, and, especially, service. Legendary for its "personalized touch" and willingness to go to extraordinary lengths to satisfy its customers, Nordstrom creates brand equity in large part through the efforts of its salespeople and the relationships they develop with consumers.

Thus, a ***customer-focused corporate image association*** creates consumer perceptions of a company as responsive to and caring about its customers. Consumers believe their voice will be heard and that the company has their best interests in mind. Often this philosophy is reflected throughout the marketing program and communicated through advertising.

Values and Programs. Corporate image associations may reflect values and programs of the company that do not always directly relate to the products it sells. Branding Brief 11-6 describes how Clif Bar has remained consistent with its values in an increasingly competitive energy-bar category. Firms can run corporate image ad campaigns to describe to consumers, employees, and others their philosophy and actions with respect to organizational, social, political, or economic issues.

For example, a focus of many recent corporate advertising campaigns has been company programs and activities designed to address environmental issues and communicate social responsibility. A ***socially responsible corporate image association*** creates consumer perceptions of a company as contributing to community programs, supporting artistic and social activities, and generally attempting to improve the welfare of society as a whole. An ***environmentally concerned corporate image association*** creates consumer perceptions of a company as developing marketing programs to protect or improve the environment and make more effective use of scarce natural resources. Later in the chapter, we consider the broader issue of cause marketing in more detail.

British Airways: Change For Good

British Airways partnered with UNICEF and developed a cause marketing campaign called Change For Good, in which travelers on British Airways flights are encouraged to donate leftover foreign currency from their travels. Because coins in particular are difficult to exchange at banks and currency exchanges, the program targets this loose change. The scheme is simple: Passengers deposit their surplus currency in envelopes provided by British Airways, which collects the deposits and donates them directly to UNICEF. British Airways advertises its program during an in-flight video, on the backs of seat cards, and with in-flight announcements. The company also developed a television advertisement that featured a child thanking British Airways for its contribution to UNICEF. The success of the program has resulted in all the international carriers of the oneworld Alliance to participate.

Other airlines such as Cathay Pacific Airways have joined British Airways in supporting the Change for Good program.

Corporate Credibility. Besides all the associations already noted, consumers may form more abstract judgments or even feelings about the company, such as perceptions of the personality of a corporate brand. For example, one major public utility company was described by customers as "male, 35–40 years old, middle class, married with children, wearing a flannel shirt and khaki pants, who would be reliable, competent, professional, intelligent, honest, ethical, and business-oriented." On the downside, the company was also described by these same customers as "distant, impersonal, and self-focused," suggesting an important area for improvement in its corporate brand image.

A particularly important set of abstract associations to a corporate brand is corporate credibility. As defined in Chapter 2, ***corporate credibility*** measures the extent to which consumers believe a firm can design and deliver products and services that satisfy customer needs and wants. It is the reputation the firm has achieved in the marketplace. Corporate credibility depends on three factors:

1. *Corporate expertise:* The extent to which consumers see the company as able to competently make and sell its products or conduct its services
2. *Corporate trustworthiness:* The extent to which consumers believe the company is motivated to be honest, dependable, and sensitive to customer needs
3. *Corporate likability:* The extent to which consumers see the company as likable, attractive, prestigious, dynamic, and so forth

We can identify a number of other characteristics as consequences of these three dimensions, for example, success and leadership. Perceived brand credibility increases the likelihood of consumer consideration and choice.[32] Creating a firm with a strong and credible reputation may offer benefits beyond the consumer response in the marketplace.

BRANDING BRIEF 11-6

Corporate Values Take Center Stage at Clif Bar

Clif Bar & Co. is a leader in coupling sustainability and healthy living with operating a successful company. Gary Erickson founded the Berkeley, California-based business in 1990 after what he calls "the epiphany." Erickson was in the middle of a 175-mile bike ride and couldn't stand another bite of the bland energy bars he had brought along. He decided that he could make a better bar himself. Erickson developed his own recipe and named his company after his father Clif. The company has grown to $100 million in sales and has been profitable every year since its launch.

Clif Bar has a strong corporate brand image and values.

Clif Bar's focus on health extends from products aimed toward consumers with an active lifestyle to its work environment. Corporate headquarters houses a gym with personal trainers, loaner bikes so employees can pedal to errands during lunchtime, and a climbing wall. The company's employees have the option to work longer hours and take off every other Friday. They are encouraged to use company time to volunteer for service projects such as Habitat for Humanity. Additionally, Clif Bar invested in a South Dakota wind farm that creates clean energy to offset the carbon dioxide generated by the company's manufacturing, offices, and employee commutes.

As the energy bar market matured, Clif Bar began to compete against food conglomerates with big advertising budgets. In 2000, Kraft bought competitor Balance Bar and Nestlé scooped

L.L.Bean

A brand seen by its customers as highly credible, outdoors product retailer L.L.Bean attempts to earn consumers' trust every step of the way—providing prepurchase advice, secure transactions, best-in-class delivery, and easy returns and exchanges. Founded in 1912, L.L.Bean backs its efforts with a 100-percent satisfaction guarantee as well as its Golden Rule: "Sell good merchandise at a reasonable profit, treat your customers like human beings, and they will always come back for more." Now a billion-dollar brand in sales, the company still retains its original image of being passionate about the outdoors with a profound belief in honesty, product quality, and customer service.

A highly credible company may be treated more favorably by other external constituencies, such as government or legal officials. It also may be able to attract better-qualified employees and motivate existing employees to be more productive and loyal. As one Shell Oil employee remarked as part of some internal corporate identity research, "If you're really

up PowerBar. The same year, Erickson turned down a buyout offer from a large food conglomerate, reasoning that a corporate owner would destroy the culture he had worked so hard to create. The decision to remain private has worked so far; profits have been rising since 1998.

In the late 1990s, Clif Bar sponsored Lance Armstrong and the U.S. Postal Service team in the Tour de France. But when Armstrong became more of a celebrity, Clif Bar lost the sponsorship. But Erickson and Sheryl O'Loughlin, a former marketing manager at Kraft and Quaker Oats who later became CEO, realized they needed to rely on more grassroots promotion. They designed a program recognizing the support riders who help cyclists win, which drove thousands of cycling enthusiasts to the Clif Bar Web site.

Clif Bar prefers direct methods of interacting with consumers in person, as opposed to TV ads. One of the company's primary methods is sampling in grocery stores, at marathon finish lines, and at other events such as the opening of "eco-friendly" hotel rooms in San Francisco. Clif Bar wrappers tell the story of the company's founding and promote the causes it supports.

In 2003 Clif Bar & Co. made a bold move and converted the Clif Bar brand to 70% organic. The switch required finding many new suppliers. Although costs rose, Erickson chose not to raise retail prices, a decision that a corporate parent might not have approved. But Erickson felt the move was the right one, considering sales of all organic products had been growing, and Clif Bar sales subsequently rose in natural-food stores.

The rising popularity of organic products helped offset the sales slowdown endured in the energy bar category as a result of the low-carb craze. Brand extensions such as the Luna bar designed especially for women and the Clif Nectar with five or fewer ingredients have also helped spur growth. By remaining committed to making healthy products and demonstrating respect for employees, consumers, and the environment, Clif Bar has remained successful even as competition in the energy bar category intensified.

Sources: Melanie Warner, "Clif Bar's Solo Climb," *Business 2.0,* December 2004; Julie Schmit, "Raising the Bar on How Business Gets Done," *USA Today,* 14 March 2005; Gary Erickson, "Bottom Line Is Where You Draw It," *Seattle Post Intelligencer,* 28 October 2005; www.clifbar.com.

proud of where you work, I think you put a little more thought into what you did to help get them there." A strong corporate reputation can help a firm survive a brand crisis and avert public outrage that could potentially depress sales, encourage unionism, or block expansion plans. As Harvard's Steve Greyser notes, "Corporate reputation . . . can serve as a capital account of favorable attitudes to help buffer corporate trouble." Brand Focus 11-0 considers some marketing communication issues for handling a marketing crisis.

Summary. Many types of associations may become linked to a corporate brand that transcend physical product characteristics.[33] These intangible associations may provide valuable sources of brand equity and serve as critical points of parity or points of difference. Companies have a number of means—indirect or direct—of creating these associations. In doing so, they must "talk the talk" and "walk the walk" by communicating to consumers as well as backing up their claims with concrete programs that consumers can easily understand or even experience.

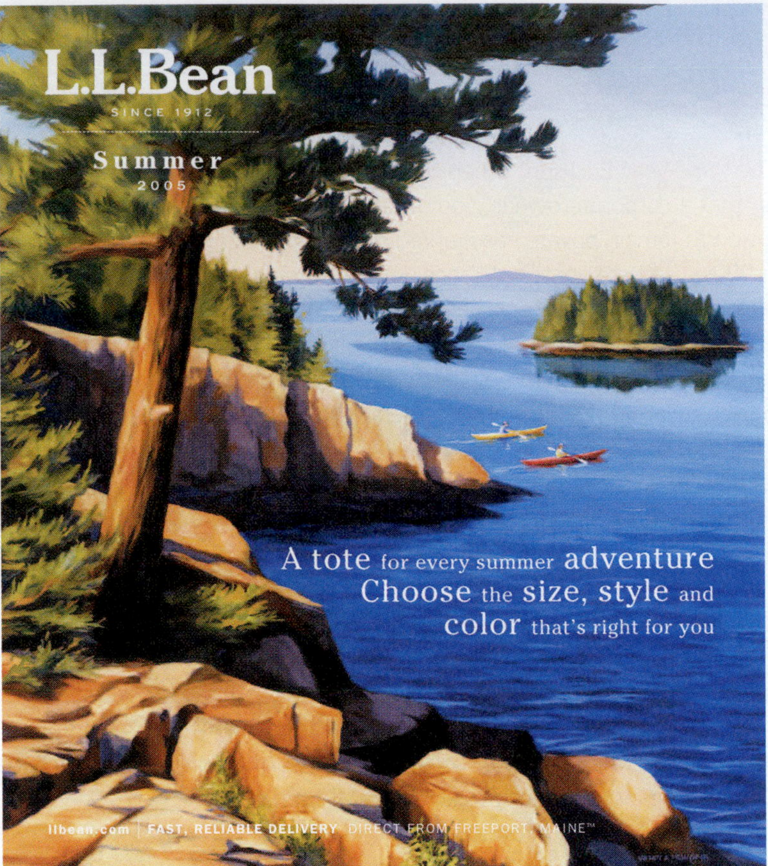

L.L.Bean is seen as a highly credible, trustworthy retailer.

Designing a Branding Strategy

Given the different possible levels of a branding hierarchy, a firm has a number of branding options available to it, depending on how it employs each level. There is no uniform agreement on the one type of branding strategy that all firms should adopt for all products. LaForet and Saunders conducted a content analysis of the branding strategies adopted by 20 key brands sold by 20 of the biggest suppliers of grocery products to Tesco and Sainsbury, Britain's two leading grocery chains.[34] They categorized the brand strategy adopted by each brand into a classification scheme (Figure 11-8) that is essentially a refinement of the four-level brand hierarchy we described earlier in this chapter. The authors note how different companies within the same market could adopt sharply contrasting strategies, offering the following example:

> For a long time Cadbury, Mars, and Nestlé have competed in the confectionery market. They often match each other brand for brand but their branding strategies are quite different. While Cadbury led with the Cadbury name and colors across virtually all their products, such as Cadbury's Dairy Milk, Cadbury's Milk Tray, Cadbury's Flake, etc., Mars led with their brands such as Mars Bars, Snickers, and Twix with no corporate endorsement. Until recently, Nestlé Rowntree pursued a branded approach like Mars, but now the Nestlé name has started to appear upon the once independently branded products.[35]

Branding Strategy	Percentage of Occurrence
Corporate Dominant	
Corporate brands: Corporate name used	5
House brands: Subsidiary name used	11
Mixed Brands	
Dual brands: Two or more names given equal prominence	38.5
Endorsed brands: Brand endorsed by corporate or house identity	13.5
Brand Dominant	
Mono brands: Single brand name used	19
Furtive brands: Single brand name used and corporate identity undisclosed	13

Source: Sylvie LaForet and John Saunders, "Managing Brand Portfolios: How the Leaders Do It," *Journal of Advertising Research* (September/October 1994): 64–76. Used with permission of International Journal of Market Research.

FIGURE 11-8

Breakdown of Brand Types

Even within any one firm, marketers may adopt different branding strategies for different products. For example, although Miller has used its name across its different types of beer over the years with various sub-brands like Miller High Life, Miller Lite, and Miller Genuine Draft, it carefully branded its no-alcohol beer substitute as Sharp's, its ice beer as Icehouse, and its low-priced beer as Milwaukee's Best, with no overt Miller identification. The assumption was that the corporate family brand name would not be relevant to or valued by the target market in question. Following its 2002 merger with South Africa Breweries to form SAB Miller, the company chose not to apply the Miller brand to any others of the more than 150 international and regional brands it now owned.

Thus, *the brand hierarchy may not be symmetric.* Corporate objectives, consumer behavior, or competitive activity may sometimes dictate significant deviations in branding strategy and the way the brand hierarchy is organized for different products or for different markets. Brand elements may receive more or less emphasis, or not be present at all, depending on the particular products and markets. For example, in an organizational market segment where the DuPont brand name may be more valuable, that element might receive more emphasis than associated sub-brands. In appealing to a consumer market segment, a sub-brand such as Dacron may be more meaningful and thus receive relatively more emphasis. (See Figure 11-9.)

How does a firm use different levels of the brand hierarchy to build brand equity? Brand elements at each level of the hierarchy may contribute to brand equity through their

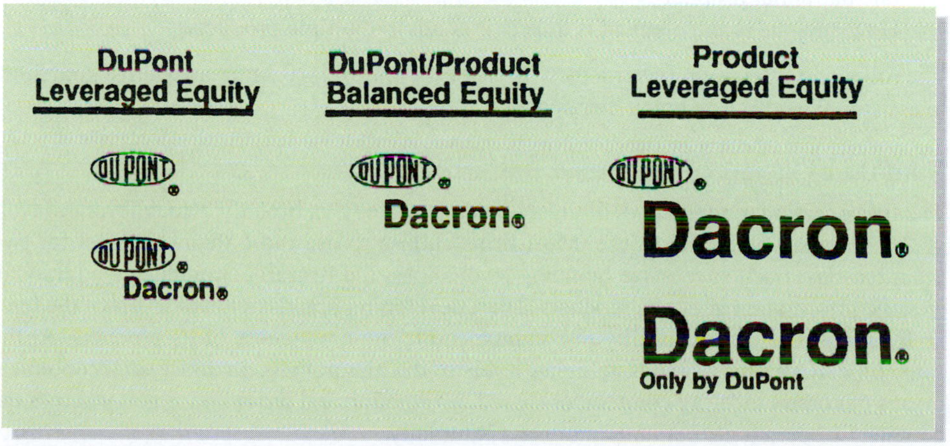

FIGURE 11-9

DuPont "Product-Endorsed" Business Strategy

1. **Decide on the number of levels.**
   - *Principle of simplicity:* Employ as few levels as possible.
   - *Principle of clarity:* Logic and relationship of all brand elements employed must be obvious and transparent.
2. **Decide on the levels of awareness and types of associations to be created at each level.**
   - *Principle of relevance:* Create abstract associations that are relevant across as many individual items as possible.
   - *Principle of differentiation:* Differentiate individual items and brands.
3. **Decide on which products are to be introduced.**
   - *Principle of growth:* Invest in market penetration or expansion vs. product development according to ROI opportunities.
   - *Principle of survival:* Brand extensions must achieve brand equity in their categories.
   - *Principle of synergy:* Brand extensions should enhance the equity of the parent brand.
4. **Decide on how to link brands from different levels for a product.**
   - *Principle of prominence:* The relative prominence of brand elements affects perceptions of product distance and the type of image created for new products.
5. **Decide on how to link a brand across products.**
   - *Principle of commonality:* The more common elements products share, the stronger the linkages.

FIGURE 11-10

Guidelines for Brand Hierarchy Decisions

ability to create awareness as well as foster strong, favorable, and unique brand associations and positive responses. Therefore, the challenge in setting up the brand hierarchy and arriving at a branding strategy is to (1) design the proper brand hierarchy with the right number and nature of brand elements to use at each level, and (2) design the optimal supporting marketing program to create the desired amount of brand awareness and type of brand associations at each level. Specifically, marketers must decide:

1. The number of levels of the hierarchy to use in general
2. The desired brand awareness and image at each level
3. Combinations of brand elements from different levels of the hierarchy, if any, for any one particular product
4. How any one brand element is linked, if at all, to multiple products

The following discussion reviews these decisions. Figure 11-10 summarizes five guidelines to assist in the design of brand hierarchies.

Number of Levels of the Brand Hierarchy

The first decision to make in defining a branding strategy is, broadly, which level or levels of the branding hierarchy to use. Most firms choose to use more than one level for two main reasons. Each successive branding level allows the firm to communicate additional, specific information about its products. Thus, developing brands at lower levels of the hierarchy allows the firm flexibility in communicating the uniqueness of its products. At the same time, developing brands at higher levels of the hierarchy is obviously an economical means of communicating common or shared information and providing synergy across the company's operations, both internally and externally.

The practice of combining an existing brand with a new brand is called ***sub-branding*** because the subordinate brand is a means of modifying the superordinate brand. ThinkPad was a sub-brand to the IBM name, and T42 was a second-level sub-brand to further modify the meaning of the product. A sub-brand, or hybrid branding, strategy can also allow for the creation of specific brand beliefs. This benefit enabled Chinese computer manufacturer Lenovo, when it purchased IBM's PC division and began selling laptops under the Lenovo brand, to retain the brand strength that had been built at the ThinkPad sub-brand level.

Hershey's Kisses

Hershey's chocolate has a traditional, homespun image, as reflected by its 20-plus-year-old advertising slogan, "Hershey's. The Great American Candy Bar." As a result of a clever ad campaign that transforms the teardrop-shaped, foil-wrapped Hershey's Kisses into animate objects and places them in amusing, product-relevant situations, however, the Kisses sub-brand has a much more playful and fun brand image than the company brand. The successful Hershey's Kisses sub-brand led to a further extension, Hershey's Hugs (a Hershey's Kiss with an outside layer of white chocolate). Additional flavor extensions included caramel, peanut butter, and dark chocolate fillings.

Sub-branding thus creates a stronger connection to the company or family brand and all the associations that come along with that. Consider the cereal category, in which Kellogg has adopted a sub-branding strategy while other manufacturers like Post have adopted an endorsement strategy. These different strategies should have profound implications on consumers' identification of and associations with certain cereal brands. Through its sub-branding strategy and marketing activities, Kellogg should be more effective than Post in connecting its corporate name to its products and, as a result, creating favorable associations to its corporate name.

At the same time, developing sub-brands allows for the creation of brand-specific beliefs. This more detailed information can help customers better understand how products vary and which particular product may be the right one for them. Sub-brands also help to organize selling efforts so that salespeople and retailers have a clear picture of how the product line is organized and how best to sell it. For example, one of the main advantages to Nike of continually creating sub-brands in its basketball line with Air Jordan, Air Flight, Air Force, and others has been to generate retail interest and enthusiasm.

The ***principle of simplicity*** is based on the need to provide the right amount of branding information to consumers—no more and no less. The desired number of levels of the brand hierarchy depends on the complexity of the product line or product mix and thus on the combination of shared and separate brand associations the company would like to link to any one product in its product line or mix.

With relatively simple, low-involvement products—such as lightbulbs, batteries, and chewing gum—the branding strategy often consists of an individual or perhaps a family brand combined with modifiers that describe differences in product features. For example, GE has two main brands of lightbulbs (Soft White and Enrich) combined with designations for functionality (3-way, Super, and Miser) and performance (40, 60, and 100 watts).

A company with a strong corporate brand, such as Sony or Philips, can more easily use nondescriptive alphanumeric product names because consumers strongly identify with the parent brand. Thus, Sony has family brand names such as CyberShot for its cameras, Wega for TVs, and Handycams for its camcorders.[36]

A complex set of products—such as cars, computers, or other durable goods—requires more levels of the hierarchy. It's difficult to brand a product with more than three levels of brand names without overwhelming or confusing consumers. A better approach might be to introduce multiple brands at the same level (multiple family brands) and expand the depth of the branding strategy.

Desired Awareness and Image at Each Hierarchy Level

How much awareness and what types of associations should marketers create for brand elements at each level? Achieving the desired level of awareness and strength, favorability, and uniqueness of brand associations may take some time and call for a considerable change in consumer perceptions. Assuming marketers use some type of sub-branding strategy for two or more brand levels, two general principles—relevance and differentiation—should guide the brand knowledge creation process at each level.

The ***principle of relevance*** is based on the advantages of efficiency and economy. Marketers should create associations that are relevant to as many brands nested at the level below as possible, especially at the corporate or family brand level. The more an association has some value in the marketing of products sold by the firm, the more efficient and economical it is to consolidate this meaning into one brand linked to all these products.[37] For example, Nike's slogan ("Just Do It") reinforces a key point of difference for the brand—performance—that is relevant to virtually all the products it sells.

The more abstract the association, in general, the more likely it is to be relevant in different product settings. Thus, benefit associations are likely to be extremely advantageous associations because they can cut across many product categories. Brands with strong product category and attribute associations, however, can find it difficult to create a robust enough brand image to permit successful extensions into new categories. For example, Blockbuster attempted to broaden its meaning from "a place to rent videos" to "your neighborhood entertainment center" to create a broader brand umbrella with greater relevance to more products.

The ***principle of differentiation*** is based on the disadvantages of redundancy. Marketers should distinguish brands at the same level as much as possible. If marketers cannot easily distinguish two brands, it may be difficult for retailers or other channel members to justify supporting both, and for consumers to choose between them. Consider the following three Microsoft products: Media Extender, Media Connect, and Windows Connect Now. On the basis of the names alone, there would seem to be the potential for consumer confusion about what the products mean. Although the names are similar, the products are in fact completely different, and are, respectively, a device to make Xbox function as a media center, a device to deliver PC-stored content to your stereo or TV, and an architecture to simplify wireless home networking.[38]

Although new products and brand extensions are critical to keeping a brand innovative and relevant, marketers must introduce them thoughtfully. Without restraint, brand variations can easily get out of control.[39] The typical grocery store now stocks 40,000 items, twice as many as a few years ago, which raises the question: Do consumers really need nine kinds of Kleenex tissues, Eggo waffles in 16 flavors, and 72 varieties of Pantene shampoo, all of which are potentially available at one point in time? To better control its inventory and avoid brand proliferation, Colgate-Palmolive has begun to discontinue one item for each product it introduces.

Although the principle of differentiation is especially important at the individual brand or modifier levels, it's also valid at the family brand level. For example, one of the criticisms of marketing at General Motors is that the company has failed to adequately distinguish its family brands of automobiles (recall Branding Brief 8-6). The principle of differentiation also implies that not all products should receive the same emphasis at any level of the hierarchy. A key issue in designing a brand hierarchy is thus choosing the relative emphasis to place on different products making up the brand hierarchy. If a corporate or family brand is associated with multiple products, which product should be the core or flagship product? What should represent "the brand" to consumers? Which product do consumers think best represents or embodies the brand? Understanding these brand drivers is important in identifying sources of brand equity and determining how to best fortify and leverage the brand.

Combining Brand Elements from Different Levels

If we combine multiple brand elements from different levels of the brand hierarchy to brand new products, we must decide how much emphasis to give each. For example, if we adopt a sub-brand strategy, how much prominence should we give individual brands at the expense of the corporate or family brand?

The ***prominence*** of a brand element is its relative visibility compared with other brand elements. For example, the prominence of a brand name element depends on several factors, such as its order, size, and appearance, as well as its semantic associations. A name is generally more prominent when it appears first, is larger, and looks more distinctive. Assume PepsiCo has adopted a sub-branding strategy to introduce a new vitamin-fortified cola, combining its corporate family brand name with a new individual brand name (say, "Vitacola"). We could make the Pepsi name more prominent by placing it first and making it bigger: PEPSI *Vitacola.* Or we could make the individual brand more prominent by placing it first and making it bigger: Vitacola BY PEPSI.

Along these lines, Gray and Smeltzer define ***corporate/product relationships*** as the approach a firm follows in communicating the relationship of its products to one another and to the corporate entity. They identified five possible categories (with illustrative examples):[40]

1. *Single entity:* The company offers one product line or set of services such that the image of the company and the product tend to be one and the same (Federal Express).
2. *Brand dominance:*The company makes a strategic decision not to relate brand and corporate names (Philip Morris makes little connection to Marlboro, Merit, and its other cigarettes).
3. *Equal dominance:* The company maintains separate images for products but also associates each with the corporation. Neither the corporate nor the individual brand name dominates (at the company level, General Motors with its different car divisions and individual brands—Buick LeSabre, Buick Electra, Buick Riviera, and so forth).
4. *Mixed dominance:* Sometimes the individual product brands are dominant and sometimes the corporate name is dominant, and in some cases, they appear together with equal emphasis (the German firm Bosch uses its corporate name on some of the products it manufactures but not on others, such as Blaupunkt radios).
5. *Corporate dominance:*The corporate name is supreme and applies across a range of product lines, and communications tend to reinforce the corporate image (Xerox).

The ***principle of prominence*** states that the relative prominence of the brand elements determines which element or elements become the primary one(s) and which become the secondary one(s). Primary brand elements should convey the main product positioning and points of difference. Secondary brand elements convey a more restricted set of supporting associations such as points of parity or perhaps an additional point of difference. A secondary brand element may also facilitate awareness. Thus, with the Motorola Razr cellular phone handset, the primary brand element—reinforced through the slender, hinged design—is the Razr name, which connotes the sleek, cutting-edge style that makes up the desired user and usage imagery for the phone. The Motorola name, on the other hand, is a secondary brand element that ideally conveys credibility, quality, and professionalism.

The relative prominence of the individual and the corporate brand should affect perceptions of product distance and the type of image created for the new product. If the corporate or family brand is made more prominent, then its associations are more likely to dominate. If the individual brand is made more prominent, on the other hand, then it should be easier to create a more distinctive brand image. In this case, the corporate or family brand is signaling to consumers that the new product is not as closely related to its other products that share that name. As a result, consumers should be less likely to transfer corporate or family brand associations. At the same time, because of the greater perceived distance, the success or failure of the new product should be less likely to affect the image of the corporate or family brand. With a more prominent corporate or family brand, however, feedback effects are probably more likely to be evident.

To illustrate how relative prominence can affect the resulting image of a product, assume that in the Pepsi Vitacola example, Pepsi is the more prominent brand element. If we make the corporate and family brand prominent, the new product will take on many of the associations common to other Pepsi-branded products like cola. If the Vitacola brand were more prominent, however, then the new product would most likely take on a more distinct positioning. In this case, the Pepsi name would function more for awareness and perhaps only transfer broader, more abstract associations, such as perceived quality or brand personality.

Finally, in some cases, the brand elements may not be explicitly linked at all. A ***brand endorsement strategy*** is in operation when a brand element appears on the package, signage, or product appearance in some way but is not directly included as part of the brand name. Often this distinct brand element is the corporate brand name or logo. For example, General Mills places its "Big G" logo on its cereal packages but retains distinct brand names such as Cheerios, Wheaties, and so forth. As noted earlier, Kellogg, on the other hand, adopts a sub-brand strategy with its cereals that combines the corporate name with individual brands, e.g., Kellogg's Corn Flakes, Kellogg's Special K, and so on. The brand endorsement strategy presumably establishes the maximum distance between the corporate or family brand and the individual brands, suggesting that it would yield the smallest transfer of brand associations to the new product but, at the same time, minimize the likelihood of any negative feedback effects.

Linking Brand Elements to Multiple Products

So far we've highlighted how to apply different brand elements to a particular product—the "vertical" aspects of the brand hierarchy. Next, we consider how to link any one brand element to multiple products—the "horizontal" aspects of the brand hierarchy. The ***principle of commonality*** states that the more common brand elements products share, the stronger the linkages between the products.

The simplest way to link products is to use the brand element "as is" across the different products involved. Adapting the brand, or some part of it, to make the connection offers additional possibilities. For example, Hewlett-Packard capitalized on its highly successful LaserJet computer printers to introduce a number of new products using the "Jet" suffix, for example, the DeskJet, PaintJet, ThinkJet, and OfficeJet printers. Sony has given its portable audio equipment a "man" suffix: Walkman personal stereos and Discman portable CD players. McDonald's has used its "Mc" prefix to introduce a number of products, such as Chicken McNuggets, Egg McMuffin, and the McRib sandwich. Donna Karan's DKNY brand, Calvin Klein's CK brand, and Ralph Lauren's Double RL brand rely on initials.

We can also create a relationship between a brand and multiple products with common symbols. For example, corporate brands like Nabisco often place their corporate logo more prominently on their products than their name, creating a strong brand endorsement strategy.

Nestlé

At one time, Nestlé ran advertising that attempted to create greater awareness and understanding of its corporate brand. The ads contained the slogan "makes the very best"—a subtle variation of its well-known "Nestlé's makes the very best chocolate" slogan—and prominently displayed a logo of a nest with a mother and two baby birds. Although the founder's name, Nestlé, in fact means "little nest," the company's hope in using the symbol was to communicate abstract associations of warmth, family, and shelter. The symbol is still used on Nestlé packaging as a means to unite a diversified set of products with vastly different names.

Finally, it's often a good idea to logically order brands in a product line, to communicate how they are related and to simplify consumer decision making. We can communicate the order though colors (American Express offers Red, Blue, Green, Gold, Platinum, and "Black" or Centurion cards), numbers (BMW offers its 3-, 5-, and 7-series cars), or other means. Branding Brief 11-7 describes how Acura attempted to rename its product line to create more structure. This strategy is especially important in developing brand migration pathways for customers to switch among the brands offered by the company.

Developing a Brand Architecture

In developing the optimal brand strategies, marketers must first define the relevant customer segments. How much overlap exists across segments, and how much can products be cross-sold? Second, marketers must have well-defined brand positioning and equity in terms of points of parity and points of difference. The brand mantra can be crucial to help establish product boundaries or brand "guard rails." A good brand mantra should offer rational and emotional benefit underpinning and be sufficiently robust to permit growth, relevant enough to drive consumer and retailer interest, and differentiated enough to sustain longevity. Finally, marketers must assess the brand equity implications of the brand architecture in terms of the transfer (both positive and negative) from the parent brands to individual products, as well as the feedback from the individual products to the parent brands in return.

Keep the following brand architecture guidelines in mind:

1. Adopt a strong customer focus.
2. Avoid overbranding.
3. Establish rules and conventions and be disciplined.
4. Create broad, robust brand platforms.
5. Selectively employ sub-brands as a means of complementing and strengthening brands.
6. Selectively extend brands to establish new brand equity and enhance existing brand equity.

In evaluating an existing brand architecture, carefully evaluate the brand portfolio and hierarchy. For the brand portfolio, do all brands have defined roles? Do brands collectively maximize coverage and minimize overlap? For the brand hierarchy, does the brand have extension potential? Within the category? Outside the category? Is the brand overextended?

Adjustments to the Marketing Program

When a firm moves away from a simple "single brand–single product" branding strategy to adopt more complex branding strategies—perhaps involving multiple brand extensions, multiple brands, or multiple levels of the hierarchy used to brand any one product—it might need to make certain adjustments in the supporting marketing program. For example, different brands can play different roles and therefore require quite different marketing mixes. Consequently, product design, pricing policies, distribution plans, and marketing communication campaigns may differ significantly depending on the role of the brand and its interdependencies with other brands. In general, many of the principles discussed in Chapters 5 to 7 for developing supporting marketing programs to build brand equity still apply. This section highlights some of the marketing communication adjustments that may be necessary in the supporting marketing program as a result of having interrelated brands and products.

If the firm is using multiple levels of a branding hierarchy, it may desire different levels of awareness and image at each level. In particular, in the case of a sub-brand strategy, it may make sense to create a marketing communication campaign at the corporate, company, or family brand levels to complement more product-specific or individual brand marketing

BRANDING BRIEF 11-7

Renaming the Acura Brand Portfolio

Honda grew from humble origins as a motorcycle manufacturer to become a top automobile import competitor in the United States. Recognizing that future sales growth would come from more upscale customers, Honda set out in the early 1980s to compete with European luxury cars. Deciding that the Honda image of dependable, functional, and economical cars did not have the cachet to appeal to luxury car buyers, Honda set up the new Acura division. Matching the quality, performance, and luxury of the European imports but costing thousands less, the $10,000 Acura Integra and the $20,000 Acura Legend were introduced in 1986. By the time Lexus and Infiniti (luxury brands from Toyota and Nissan, respectively) entered the market in 1989, Acura was selling 142,000 cars annually and receiving top marks in customer satisfaction.

Acura rebranded its product line with alphanumeric names, such as this Acura RL, to improve its brand equity.

Rapidly rising sticker prices—due in part to a strengthening yen—and increased competition eroded sales until Acura sales in the United States barely topped 100,000 cars in 1993. With its market leadership threatened and its customer base splintering (the average Integra buyer made $57,000 annually, or half of what the average Legend owner earned), Honda felt it needed a dramatic marketing move. Research indicated that its Legend, Integra, and Vigor

communication campaigns. As part of this higher-level campaign, companies may employ the full range of marketing communication options, including advertising, public relations, promotions, and sponsorship. We next discuss two potentially useful marketing communication strategies to build brand equity at the corporate brand or family brand level.

Corporate Image Campaigns. ***Corporate image campaigns*** are designed to create associations to the corporate brand as a whole and, consequently, tend to ignore or downplay individual products or sub-brands in the process.[41] As we would expect, some of the biggest spenders on these kinds of campaigns are those well-known firms that prominently use their company or corporate name in their branding strategies, such as GE, Toyota, British Telecom, IBM, Novartis, Microsoft, Deutsche Bank, Siemens, and Hewlett-Packard. More firms are now running these types of non-product-specific ads—especially retail and service brands that commonly use their corporate name—in part because so many products have become linked to their family or corporate brands over time.

sub-brand names did not communicate luxury and order in the product line as well as the alphanumeric branding scheme of competitors BMW, Mercedes, Lexus, and Infiniti. Honda decided that the strength of the brand should lie in the Acura name. Thus, despite the fact that nearly $600 million had been spent on advertising those Acura sub-brands over the past eight years to build their equity, Honda announced a new alphanumeric branding scheme in the winter of 1995. The accompanying $100 million advertising campaign retained the upscale theme, "Some Things Are Worth the Price."

The new 2.5 TL and 3.2 TL (for Touring Luxury) sedan series, designed to replace the Vigor, was the first rebranded model available in 1995. The following year, Acura rolled out the 3.5 RL, a replacement for its top-of-the-line Legend model. At that time, Acura also introduced two new cars, called the 2.2 CL and 3.0 CL, priced in the mid-$20,000 range. The CL line was positioned below the TL but above the Integra, which had been renamed the RSX. In 1997, Honda estimated that up to 21 percent of Acura owners were switching to other brands that offered SUVs, so Acura introduced the SLX (later renamed the MDX) sport utility vehicle. The NSX sports car retained its name.

Acura spokesperson Mike Spencer said, "It used to be that people said they owned or drove a Legend. . . . Now they say they drive an Acura, and that's what we wanted." Acura's name awareness in 2001 was 25 percent higher than in 1996. With almost everything included as standard equipment for competitive base prices, overall Acura sales rose from 142,681 in 1996 to almost 200,000 cars by 2004.

Sources: David Kiley, "I'd Like to Buy a Vowel, Drivers Say," *USA Today,* 9 August 2000; Mark Rechtin, "Honda Hopes New CR-V Will Win Back Defectors," *Automotive News,* 3 February 1997; Stewart Toy, "The Selling of Acura—A Honda That's Not a Honda," *Business Week,* 17 March 1986, 93; Fara Werner, "Remaking of a Legend," *Brandweek,* 25 April 1994, 23–28; Neal Templin, "Japanese Luxury-Car Makers Unveiling Cheaper Models in Bid to Attract Buyers," *Wall Street Journal,* 9 February 1995; T. L. Stanley and Kathy Tryer, "Acura Plays Numbers Game to Fortify Future," *Brandweek,* 20 February 1995, 3; T. L. Stanley, "Acura Rolls TL, New Nameplate Position with $40M in Ad Fuel," *Brandweek,* 20 March 1995, 4.

Some have criticized corporate image campaigns in the past as an ego-stroking waste of time. It can be easy for consumers to ignore these marketing activities. However, a strong corporate brand can provide invaluable marketing and financial benefits by allowing the firm to express itself and embellish the meaning of and associations for its individual products. To maximize the probability of success, however, marketers must clearly define the objectives of a corporate image campaign *and* carefully measure results against these objectives.[42] A number of different objectives are possible in a corporate brand campaign:[43]

- Build awareness of the company and the nature of its business.
- Create favorable attitudes and perceptions of company credibility.
- Link beliefs that can be leveraged by product-specific marketing.
- Make a favorable impression on the financial community.
- Motivate present employees and attract better recruits.
- Influence public opinion on issues.

In terms of building customer-based brand equity, the first three objectives are particularly critical. A corporate image campaign can enhance awareness and create a more positive image of the corporate brand that will influence consumer evaluations and increase the equity associated with individual products and any related sub-brands. In certain cases, however, the latter three objectives can take on greater importance.[44] Notable examples of the first three objectives—the ones most directly related to building customer-based brand equity—are highlighted in the following paragraphs.

- *Building awareness of the company and the nature of its business:* Cingular Wireless launched a teaser corporate campaign to build brand recognition during the 2001 Super Bowl. Later, it launched a $75 million ad campaign emphasizing self-expression as a means of differentiating itself from other wireless marketers.[45] In 2004, following its merger with AT&T wireless, Cingular introduced a new tagline, "Raising the Bar," that highlighted the company's extensive national network coverage. Although clearly a mature brand, HP ran a corporate brand campaign themed "Expanding Possibilities" before switching to one themed "Invent" as a means to emphasize its technological leadership, vision, and broad capabilities.
- *Building company trustworthiness and credibility:* Johnson & Johnson ran an ad campaign to promote the trustworthiness of the corporate brand. The commercials featured many "warm and fuzzy" shots of families. Johnson & Johnson products were not emphasized, although its baby powder, Band-Aids, and Reach toothbrush products were shown in passing. The ad concluded with the words: "Over the years, Johnson & Johnson has taken care of more families than anyone else." Similarly, to create an image that transcended its products, Kraft ran a corporate brand campaign featuring its Kool-Aid, Philadelphia cream cheese, Post cereal, and Tombstone frozen pizza brands in a single TV spot or Sunday circular. The intent was to show that Kraft "got the importance of family values and made the kind of food that families with values ate."[46]
- *Creating corporate image associations that can be leveraged by product-specific marketing:* To reposition itself as a more consumer-friendly brand, Philips Consumer Electronics launched a global corporate advertising campaign in 2004. Centered on the company's new tagline, "Sense and Simplicity," which replaced the nine-year-old tagline, "Let's Make Things Better," the ads showcase innovative Philips products fitting in effortlessly with users' sophisticated lifestyles. The campaign featured existing Philips flagship products, such as FlatTV with Ambilight, the HDRW720 DVD recorder with built-in hard disk, and the Sonicare Elite toothbrush. Philips president and CEO Gerard Kleisterlee described the rationale for the repositioning campaign by saying, "Our route to innovation isn't about complexity—it's about simplicity, which we believe will be the new cool."[47]

Thus, corporate image campaigns focus on characteristics or aspects of the brand as a whole. They can also work at the family brand level.

Brand Line Campaigns. A second marketing communication strategy to build brand equity at the corporate brand or family brand level is a brand line campaign. ***Brand line campaigns*** emphasize the breadth of products associated with the brand. Unlike a corporate image campaign that presents the brand in abstract terms with few, if any, references to specific products, brand line campaigns refer to the range of products associated with a brand line. By showing consumers the different uses or benefits of the multiple products offered by a brand, brand line ads may be particularly useful in building brand awareness, clarifying brand meaning, and suggesting additional usage applications. Brand line promotions can achieve similar goals.

Even when they use individual brands, umbrella ads that encompass multiple brands may serve a purpose. For example, in 2004 General Mills elected to make all its cereals with 100 percent whole grains and promoted the health benefits of 100 percent whole grain cereal on all product packaging and with an advertising campaign. The benefits of whole grains included lowering the risk of chronic diseases such as heart disease, certain cancers, and diabetes. Because 9 out of 10 Americans were not getting sufficient levels of whole grain in their diet, these benefits are a point of difference (compared with non–whole grain competitors) shared by all General Mills brands in the category.

Using Cause Marketing to Build Brand Equity

The 1980s saw the advent of cause marketing. Formally, ***cause-related* (or *cause*) *marketing*** has been defined as "the process of formulating and implementing marketing activities that are characterized by an offer from the firm to contribute a specified amount to a designated cause when customers engage in revenue-providing exchanges that satisfy organizational and individual objectives."[48] As Varadarajan and Menon note, the distinctive feature of cause marketing is the link between the firm's contribution to a designated cause and customers' engaging in revenue-producing transactions with the firm.

Many observers credit American Express for raising awareness of the mutual benefits of cause marketing through its 1983 campaign to help restore the Statue of Liberty. Donating a penny for every credit card transaction and a dollar for each new card issued, American Express gave $1.7 million to the Statue of Liberty—Ellis Island Foundation. In the process, transactions for American Express rose 30 percent, and the issuance of new cards increased by 15 percent during this period. In the next five years, American Express supported more than 70 different causes in 18 countries, ranging from the preservation of the national bird of Norway to the protection of the Italian coastline.

During this time, American Express's competitors followed suit: Visa created a transaction-based donation program to support the 1988 Olympics (see Chapter 7), and MasterCard tied the use of its credit card to donations to six charitable organizations with its "Make a Difference" campaign. Other companies sponsor charitable activities such as the Special Olympics, Live Aid, and Hands Across America. Despite some drop in interest during tighter economic times in the early 1990s, companies again have begun to look to cause marketing as a means of differentiating themselves. For example, in its first national media campaign for a philanthropic cause since its Statue of Liberty campaign, American Express initiated the "Charge Against Hunger" campaign in 1993. The campaign, which raised $5 million in its first year, contributed three cents to feed the hungry every time members used their American Express cards during the months of November and December.[49] American Express also supports the arts at the local community level, publicizing its efforts with ads praising the charitable cause while underscoring the convenience of using the card. In 2006, the company partnered with Bono—lead singer of the band U2—and his AIDS organization Project RED to introduce the American Express RED card, through which American Express contributes 1 percent of charges made with the card to fight AIDS in Africa.

Advantages of Cause Marketing

One reason for the rise in cause marketing is the positive response it elicits from consumers.[50] Cone Communications, a firm that advises companies on cause-related marketing, revealed in the results of the 2004 Cone Corporate Citizenship Study that 80 percent of Americans have a more positive image of companies that support a cause they care about, 86 percent report they would be likely to switch brands to one associated with a good cause, and almost three-quarters approve of cause programs as a business practice. Prior reports also documented the positive impact on employees: 90 percent of employees felt proud of their companies' values when the companies had a cause program, and 87 percent of employees felt a strong sense of loyalty toward companies with cause programs.

Cause or corporate societal marketing (CSM) programs offer many potential benefits to a firm:

- *Building brand awareness:* Because of the nature of the brand exposure, CSM programs can be a means of improving recognition for a brand, although not necessarily recall. Like sponsorship and other indirect forms of brand-building communications, most CSM programs may be better suited to increasing exposure to the brand and less suited to tying the brand to specific consumption or usage situations, because it can be difficult or inappropriate to include product-related information. At the same time, repeated or prominent exposure to the brand as a result of the CSM program can facilitate brand recognition.
- *Enhancing brand image:* Because most CSM programs do not include much product-related information, we would not expect them to have much impact on more functional, performance-related considerations. On the other hand, we can link two types of abstract or imagery-related associations to a brand via CSM: user profiles—CSM may allow consumers to develop a positive image of brand users to which they also may aspire in terms of being kind, generous, and doing good things; and personality and values—CSM could clearly bolster the sincerity dimension of a brand's personality such that consumers would think of the people behind the brand as caring and genuine.
- *Establishing brand credibility:* CSM could affect all three dimensions of credibility, because consumers may think of a firm willing to invest in CSM as caring more about customers and being more dependable than other firms, at least in a broad sense, as well as being likable for "doing the right things."
- *Evoking brand feelings:* Two categories of brand feelings that seem particularly applicable to CSM are social approval and self-respect. In other words, CSM may help consumers to justify their self-worth to others or to themselves. CSM programs may need to provide consumers with external symbols to explicitly advertise or signal their affiliation to others—for example, bumper stickers, ribbons, buttons, and T-shirts. They can also give people the notion that they are doing the right thing and they should feel good about themselves for having done so. External symbols in this case may not be as important as the creation of "moments of internal reflection" during which consumers are able to experience these feelings. Communications that reinforce the positive outcomes associated with the cause program—and how consumer involvement contributed to that success—could help to trigger these types of experiences. To highlight the consumer contribution, it may be necessary to recommend certain actions or outcomes such as having consumers donate a certain percentage of income or a designated amount.
- *Creating a sense of brand community:* CSM and a well-chosen cause can serve as a rallying point for brand users and a means for them to connect to or share experiences with other consumers or employees of the company itself. One place where communities of like-minded users exist is online. Marketers may be able to tap into the many close-knit online groups that have sprung up around cause-related issues (for instance, medical concerns such as Alzheimer's, cancer, and autism). The brand might even serve as the focal point or ally for these online efforts to be seen in a more positive light.

- *Eliciting brand engagement:* Participating in a cause-related activity as part of a CSM program for a brand is certainly one means of eliciting active engagement. As part of any of these activities, customers themselves may become brand evangelists and ambassadors and help to communicate about the brand and strengthen the brand ties of others. A CSM program of "strategic volunteerism," whereby corporate personnel volunteer their time to help administer the nonprofit program, could actively engage consumers with both the cause and the brand.

Perhaps the most important benefit of cause-related marketing is that by humanizing the firm, it may help consumers develop a strong, unique bond with the firm that transcends normal marketplace transactions. A dramatic illustration is McDonald's, whose franchises have long been required to stay close to local communities and whose 206 Ronald McDonald Houses for sick children in 19 countries concretely symbolize the firm's "do-good" efforts. When whole blocks of businesses were burned and looted in the south-central Los Angeles riots in 1992, one McDonald's executive observed, "We literally had people standing in front of some restaurants saying, 'No, don't throw rocks through this window—these are the good guys.'" When the dust cleared, all 60 McDonald's restaurants in the area had been spared.

Designing Cause Marketing Programs

Cause marketing comes in many forms.[51] Although often associated with advertising and promotional activities, it may also be part of product development. For example, Dannon launched a new line of yogurts that tied in with the National Wildlife Federation, and Johnson & Johnson provides the World Wildlife Fund with a cut from sales of a special line of children's toiletries.

Some firms have used cause marketing very strategically to gain a marketing advantage.[52] Branding Brief 11-8 describes how the Body Shop adopted cause-related marketing as the essence of its brand positioning. Ben & Jerry's is another firm that has created a strong association as a "do-gooder" through various programs and products (such as its Rain Forest Crunch ice cream) and its donation of 7.5 percent of its pretax profits to various causes. Toyota ran an extensive print ad campaign with the slogan "Investing in the Things We All Care About" to show how it has invested in local U.S. communities. For Toyota, this campaign may go beyond cause marketing to become a means to help the brand create a vital point of parity with respect to domestic car companies on "country of origin."

A danger is that the promotional efforts behind a cause marketing program could backfire if cynical consumers question the link between the product and the cause and see the firm as being self-serving and exploitative as a result. The hope is that cause marketing strikes a chord with consumers and employees, improving the image of the company and energizing these constituents to act. With near-parity products, some marketers feel that a strongly held point of difference on the basis of community involvement and concern may in some cases be the best way—and perhaps the only way—to uniquely position a product.

To realize brand equity benefits, firms must brand their cause marketing efforts in the right manner. In particular, consumers must be able to make some kind of connection from the cause to the brand. Perhaps the classic example is again McDonald's, which has effectively leveraged its Ronald McDonald character and its identification with children. Ronald McDonald House Charities provides comfort and care to children and their families by supporting Ronald McDonald Houses in communities around the world and by making grants to other not-for-profit organizations whose programs help children in need.

BRANDING BRIEF 11-8

Image Management the Body Shop Way

In 1976, Anita Roddick opened the first Body Shop in Brighton, a little village on the south coast of England. In her first store, Anita offered some 25 natural body products. Now, the Body Shop has over 1,900 outlets in 50 countries, many of them franchised. The company offers over 400 naturally based body care products, over 550 sundry items, and customized care. Its colorful, fragrant products are based on natural ingredients, particularly fruits, vegetables, flowers, and herbs.

Since its early days, the Body Shop tried to avoid packaging excesses for its products. In the beginning, Roddick asked her customers to bring bottles back for refilling because the company didn't have a large bottle inventory. Today, the Body Shop has made refilling and recycling of bottles an integral part of the company's overall environmental stewardship program. The bottles, which were originally chosen for their simplicity and low cost, are still the primary packaging form. In addition, the Body Shop has a number of sub-brands, almost all of which are identified with new labeling and some new package forms as well.

The Body Shop has attempted to avoid the "narrow images" of "flawless beauty" portrayed in traditional cosmetic advertising. It has followed a strategy of avoiding direct advertising and relying heavily on in-store promotion, word of mouth, and public relations or third-party reporting. In-store promotion is abundant. Bright, colorful posters announcing holidays, supporting AIDS protection, or promoting particular product lines are in all the display windows. All over the world the Body Shop stores look and feel the same. The typical outside look is a dark-green wooden facade with large floor-to-ceiling display windows accented with bright, colorful, catchy campaign or promotional posters. The look inside is also consistent across all stores

The Body Shop became not only a successful natural body products company, but also an organization that has attempted to make a difference in the lives of humans and animals and

This well-branded cause program enhances McDonald's reputation as caring and concerned for customers. Two other noteworthy programs are:

- *The Avon Breast Cancer Crusade:* Founded in 1993, the Avon Breast Cancer Crusade is a U.S. initiative of Avon Products, Inc. Its mission has been to provide women, particularly those who are medically underserved, with direct access to breast cancer education and early detection screening services such as mammograms and clinical breast exams. In the United States, Avon is the largest corporate supporter of the breast cancer cause, with some $100 million generated since 1993. The Crusade raises funds to accomplish this mission in two ways: through the sale of special Crusade fund-raising (pink ribbon) products by Avon's nearly 500,000 independent sales representatives, and through the Avon Breast Cancer 3-Days, a series of three-day, 60-mile fund-raising walks.[53]
- *Liz Claiborne's Women's Work campaign against domestic violence:* In 1991, at a time when domestic violence was often a taboo or hot-potato issue, Liz Claiborne developed its Women's Work campaign against domestic violence. Prior to starting the campaign, the company had conducted research that revealed that 96 percent of its customers believed that domestic violence was a problem and 91 percent of those

the protection of the environment. In addition to the traditional "4 Ps" marketing mix, the Body Shop has a "Fifth P" in its marketing mix to build brand equity—its corporate philosophy of "Profits with Principles," also known as "Doing Good by Doing Well." To this end, the Body Shop is against animal testing, actively attempts to minimize the company's impact on the environment, engages in fair trading relationships, and encourages education, awareness, and community involvement among its staff.

Although initially quite successful, the Body Shop has struggled in recent years. Look-alike products from retailers like Bath and Body Works and Boots, and from supermarkets like Tesco and Sainsbury, have chipped away at its market share, and its messages on social causes don't seem to arouse the same passion from customers. Body Shop stores became overstocked and cluttered with a poor product mix, and advertising efforts often missed the mark.

In response to its troubles, Roddick chose to step down as head in 1998, and the firm underwent a radical makeover of its operations and management structure in a bid to cut costs and freshen its image. The firm embraced a "masstige" positioning (mass-market combined with prestige), with relatively low-priced products sold under the banner of its prestigious brand name. Although this approach met with some success, Dame Roddick stepped down as co-chair of the board in 2002 but remained as a consultant to the company. Eventually, the company agreed in early 2006 to be taken over by French cosmetics giant L'Oreal in a deal worth £652m. L'Oreal stated that it would allow the Body Shop to be run as a stand-alone business with Roddick continuing to provide advice.

Sources: This brief is based on published sources and a brand audit conducted as part of a Stanford Business School class project by Janet Kraus, Kathy Apruzzese, Maria Nunez, and Karen Reaudin.

same customers would have a positive opinion of a company that started an awareness campaign about the issue. The major fund-raising event has been an annual charity shopping day every October at Liz Claiborne stores across the United States. The company donates 10 percent of sales to local organizations fighting domestic violence. Liz Claiborne also contributes proceeds from the sale of T-shirts, jewelry, and other products related to the campaign; pays for public service campaigns that appear on television, radio, billboards, and bus shelters; and distributes awareness posters, brochures, and mailings. Over the years, Liz Claiborne has also sponsored workshops, surveys, celebrity-endorsed awareness campaigns, and other events.[54]

Green Marketing

A special case of cause marketing is ***green marketing.*** Concern for the environment is a growing social trend reflected in the attitudes and behavior of both consumers and corporations. For example, one survey found that 83 percent of American consumers said they prefer buying environmentally safe products.[55] Another survey found that 23 percent of American consumers now claim to make purchases based on environmental considerations.[56]

Although environmental issues have long affected marketing practices, especially in Europe, their salience has increased in recent years. The well-publicized Earth Day activities in the United States in April 1990 led to an explosion of "environmentally friendly" products and marketing programs. The green marketing movement was born, and firm after firm tried to capitalize on consumers' perceived increased sensitivity to environmental issues. On the corporate side, a host of marketing initiatives have been undertaken with environmental overtones. For example, Chevron's highly visible "People Do" ad campaign attempted to transform consumers' negative perceptions of oil companies and their effect on the environment by describing specific Chevron programs designed to save wildlife and preserve seashores.

McDonald's has introduced a number of well-publicized environmental initiatives through the years, such as moving to unbleached paper carry-out bags and replacing polystyrene foam sandwich clamshells with paper wraps and lightweight recyclable boxes. The company received the EPA WasteWise Partner of the Year award for its waste reduction efforts, which conserved 3,200 tons of paper and cardboard by eliminating sandwich containers and replacing them with single-layer flexible sandwich wraps; eliminating 1,100 tons of cardboard materials that would have been used for shipping by switching to light drink cups; and spending $355 million on recycled content products. Branding Brief 11-9 describes other green marketing initiatives by large corporations.

BRANDING BRIEF 11-9

Marketing Goes Green

Companies are increasingly recognizing that the environment is an important issue to their customers and shareholders and, therefore, their bottom lines. Research shows the environment is one of the top five issues that youth care most about. Renewable energy power systems are already growing rapidly in Europe and China. Additionally, rising oil and gas prices contribute to the need and enthusiasm for fuel-saving technologies. The following examples show how companies have capitalized on these trends by leading the way in their industries with green marketing efforts.

Despite its industrial past, GE views eco-friendly products as a high-growth business. Spurred by environmental concerns voiced by its customers, in 2005 GE launched Ecomagination, a play on its ongoing ad campaign "Imagination at Work." The initiative includes $1.5 billion in annual investment in research and technology into cleaner technologies and is intended to double GE revenue from sales of products and services that provide environmental advantages and a reduction in greenhouse gas emissions to $20 billion in 2010. The company built an advertising campaign around Ecomagination that targeted the company's business-to-business customers, investors, employees, and consumers. GE even designed a children's magazine to introduce Ecomagination to the children of employees.

The auto industry is responding to the duel motivators of concerned consumers and rising oil prices by introducing gas-saving and emission-reducing hybrid models. The Toyota Prius, the biggest hybrid hit to date, accounts for about half of all hybrid sales. Toyota followed up its initial success with a second-generation Prius, which it marketed in a joint campaign with the Sierra Club. Although sales of hybrids have increased in the United States, they amount to only 1.2 percent of the total auto market. To attract more consumers, automakers are introducing new hybrid powertrains and hydrogen fuel cells that deliver cleaner emissions and better mileage without compromising power. Toyota is developing an improved third generation of its hybrid,

From a branding perspective, however, green marketing programs have not been entirely successful.[57] Despite reported public interest in greater environmental responsibility, many of these new products and programs were unsuccessful. What obstacles did the green marketing movement encounter?

Overexposure and Lack of Credibility So many companies made environmental claims that the public became skeptical of their validity. Government investigations into some "green" claims like the degradability of trash bags and media reports of the spotty environmental track records behind others only increased consumers' doubts. This backlash led many consumers to consider environmental claims to be marketing gimmicks.

Consumer Behavior Like many well-publicized social trends, corporate environmental awareness is often fairly complex in reality and does not always fully match public perceptions. Several studies help to put consumer attitudes toward the environment in perspective.

and a consortium of BMW, DaimlerChrysler, and General Motors engineers have developed a two-mode hybrid, which can use electric motors more efficiently than other hybrid engines.

Along with new opportunities, environmental awareness has created sometimes uneasy partnerships between companies and activist groups, as an example from Home Depot demonstrates. The company is the largest seller of lumber in the world and buys almost 10 percent of Chile's wood exports, mostly from tree farms. Beginning in 1997, environmentalists protested its wood-buying practices outside hundreds of Home Depot stores. In response, the company announced it would not buy wood that came from endangered forests and created an environmental global project manager position to oversee contracts with its suppliers. In 2003 the company facilitated a deal between Chile's environmentalists and the logging industry to protect Chilean forests. Home Depot found that working with environmental organizations was an inexpensive way to win support from customers and counter negative publicity.

Pressure from activists has forced other companies to look carefully at environmental risks before investing in projects like gas pipelines in ecologically vulnerable places. Activism has prompted creativity within big companies looking for growth opportunities. Wal-Mart is experimenting with a new prototype store that is 25–30 percent more efficient and will produce up to 30 percent fewer greenhouse gas emissions. The new design includes more than two dozen energy-saving and renewable-materials experiments. Experiments like these are garnering favorable consumer reviews, as well as effecting environmental results.

Sources: Karl Greenberg, "Green Is Good," *Brandweek,* 3 January 2005; Matthew Creamer, "GE Sets Aside Big Bucks to Show Off Some Green," *Advertising Age,* 9 May 2005; Daren Fonda, "GE's Green Awakening," *Time,* August 2005; Jim Carlton, "Once Targeted by Protesters, Home Depot Plays Green Role," *Wall Street Journal,* August 2004; Beth Daley, "Eco-Products in Demand, but Labels Can Be Murky," *Boston Globe,* 9 February 2005; Theresa Howard, "Being Eco-Friendly Can Pay Economically," *USA Today,* 15 August 2005; www.bp.com; Lindsay Brooke, "Challenging Toyota's Hybrid Hegemony," *New York Times,* 30 April 2006.

One study found that the average price increases consumers were willing to pay for otherwise identical products in six categories (gasoline, paper, plastics, aerosols, detergents, and autos) in order to buy products that would cause one-third less pollution was 6.6 percent. One-third of the sample was not willing to pay *anything* more. The study concluded that the products needed to achieve points of parity on quality and price and credible environmental claims for green marketing to work. A Syracuse University study also found that the proper price and quality were key to successful green marketing strategies. Two-thirds of the Syracuse sample believed that the badge of "environmental correctness" should not result in higher prices—for example, "environmentally safe products shouldn't have to cost more because they use natural ingredients." The study revealed that environmental appeals were more likely to be effective for certain market segments such as 31- to 45-year-old women and in certain product categories like cleaners, detergents, fabric softeners, diapers, aerosol sprays, paints, and canned tuna.[58]

The main conclusion from these and other studies is that consumers as a whole may not be willing to pay a premium for environmental benefits, although certain market segments will. Most consumers appear unwilling to give up the benefits of other options to choose green products. For example, some consumers dislike the performance, appearance, or texture of recycled paper and household products. Similarly, some consumers are unwilling to give up the convenience of disposable products, such as diapers.

Poor Implementation In jumping on the green marketing bandwagon, many firms did a poor job implementing their marketing programs. Products were poorly designed in terms of their environmental worthiness, overpriced, and inappropriately promoted. Starch, a well-known research supplier, surveyed thousands of magazine readers to study 300 "green" ads that appeared in 186 magazines since 1991. The analysis revealed that the main mistake with those ads that tested as "unpersuasive" was that they forgot to emphasize "what's in it for me" to the consumer—they failed to make the connection between what the company was doing for the environment and how it affected individual consumers. Starch's study conclusion was that firms should be specific about product benefits in their ads.[59]

Possible Solutions The environmental movement in Europe and Japan has a longer history and firmer footing than that in the United States. In Europe, many of Procter & Gamble's basic household items, including cleaners and detergents, are available in refills that come in throw-away pouches. P&G says U.S. customers probably would not take to the pouches. In the United States, firms continue to strive to meet the wishes of consumers concerning the environmental benefits of their products, while maintaining necessary profitability. One expert in the field offers the following recommendations:[60]

- Green your product before forced to.
- Communicate environmental aspects of products, especially recycled content.
- Deliver on performance and price.
- Dramatize environmental benefits.
- Stress direct, tangible benefits.
- Be consistent and thorough.

Review

A key aspect of managing brand equity is the proper branding strategy. Brand names of products typically consist of a combination of different names and other brand elements. A ***branding strategy*** for a firm identifies which brand elements a firm chooses to apply across the various products it sells. Combining the brand–product matrix and the brand hierarchy with customer, company, and competitive considerations can help a marketing manager formulate the optimal branding strategy.

The brand–product matrix is a graphical representation of all the brands and products sold by the firm. The matrix or grid has the brands for a firm as rows and the corresponding products as columns. The rows of the matrix represent brand–product relationships and capture the firm's brand extension strategy. Marketers should judge potential extensions by how effectively they leverage existing brand equity to a new product, as well as how effectively the extension, in turn, contributes to the equity of the existing parent brand. The columns of the matrix represent product–brand relationships and capture the brand portfolio strategy in terms of the number and nature of brands to be marketed in each category.

We characterize a branding strategy according to its breadth in terms of brand–product relationships and brand extension strategy, and its depth in terms of product–brand relationships and the brand portfolio or mix. The breadth of the branding strategy describes the product mix and which products the firm should manufacture or sell. We considered how many different product lines the company should carry (the breadth of the product mix), as well as how many variants it should offer in each product line (the depth of the product mix). The depth of the branding strategy deals with the brand portfolio and the set of all brands and brand lines that a particular seller offers to buyers. A firm may offer multiple brands in a category to attract different—and potentially mutually exclusive—market segments. Brands also can take on very specialized roles in the portfolio: as flanker brands to protect more valuable brands, as low-end entry-level brands to expand the customer franchise, as high-end prestige brands to enhance the worth of the entire brand line, or as cash cows to milk all potentially realizable profits. Companies must be careful to understand exactly what each brand should do for the firm and, more important, what they want it to do for the customer.

A brand hierarchy reveals an explicit ordering of all brand names by displaying the number and nature of common and distinctive brand name elements across the firm's products. By capturing the potential branding relationships among the different products sold by the firm, a brand hierarchy graphically portrays a firm's branding strategy. One simple representation of possible brand elements and thus of potential levels of a brand hierarchy is (from top to bottom): corporate (or company) brand, family brand, individual brand, and modifier.

A number of specific issues arise in designing the brand hierarchy. Brand elements at each level of the hierarchy may contribute to brand equity through their ability to create awareness and foster strong, favorable, and unique brand associations. The challenge in setting up the brand hierarchy and arriving at a branding strategy is (1) to design the proper brand hierarchy in terms of the number and nature of brand elements to use at each level, and (2) to design the optimal supporting marketing program in terms of creating the desired amount of brand awareness and type of brand associations at each level.

In designing a brand hierarchy, marketers should define the number of different levels of brands (generally two or three) and the relative emphasis that brands at different levels will receive when combined to brand any one product. One common strategy to brand a new product is to create a sub-brand, combining an existing company or family brand with a new individual brand. When marketers use multiple brand names, as with a sub-brand, the relative visibility of each brand element determines its prominence. Brand visibility and prominence will depend on factors such as the order, size, color, and other aspects of the brand's physical appearance. To provide structure and content to the brand hierarchy, marketers must make clear to consumers the specific means by which a brand applies across different products and, if different brands are used for different products, the relationships among them.

In designing the supporting marketing program in the context of a brand hierarchy, marketers must define the desired awareness and image at each level of the brand hierarchy for each product. In a sub-branding situation, the desired awareness of a brand at any level will dictate the relative prominence of the brand and the extent to which associations linked to the brand will transfer to the product. In terms of building brand equity, we should link associations at any one level based on principles of relevance and differentiation. In general, we want to create associations relevant to as many brands nested at the level below as possible and to distinguish any brands at the same level. Corporate or family brands can establish a number of valuable associations to differentiate the brand, such as common product attributes, benefits, or attitudes; people and relationships; programs and values; and corporate credibility. A corporate image will depend on a number of factors, such as the products a company makes, the actions it takes, and the manner in which it communicates to consumers. Communications may focus on the corporate brand in the abstract or on the different products making up the brand line.

Discussion Questions

1. Pick a company. As completely as possible, characterize its brand portfolio and brand hierarchy. How would you improve the company's branding strategies?
2. Do you think the Nestlé corporate image campaign described in this chapter will be successful? Why or why not? What do you see as key success factors for a corporate image campaign?
3. Contrast the branding strategies and brand portfolios of market leaders in two different industries. For example, contrast the approach by Anheuser-Busch and its Budweiser brand with that of Kellogg in the ready-to-eat cereal category.
4. What are some of the product strategies and communication strategies that General Motors could use to further enhance the level of perceived differentiation between its divisions?
5. Consider the companies listed in Branding Brief 11-4 as having strong corporate reputations. By examining their Web sites, can you determine why they have such strong corporate reputations?

BRAND FOCUS 11.0

Weathering a Brand Crisis: The Tylenol Experience

Building the Tylenol Brand

Tylenol has been a true marketing success story.[61] Originally introduced by McNeil Laboratories as a liquid alternative to aspirin for children, Tylenol achieved nonprescription status when McNeil was bought by Johnson & Johnson (J&J) in 1959. J&J's initial marketing plan promoted a tablet form of the product for physicians to prescribe as a substitute for aspirin when allergic reactions occurred. Tylenol consists of acetaminophen, a drug as effective as aspirin in the relief of pain and fever but without the stomach irritation that often accompanies aspirin. Backed by this selective physician push, sales for the brand grew slowly but steadily over the course of the next 15 years. By 1974, sales reached $50 million, or 10 percent of the analgesic market. In defending its turf from the competitive entry of Bristol-Myers' low-priced, but heavily promoted, competitor Datril, J&J recognized the value of advertising Tylenol directly to consumers.

Thanks also to the successful introduction of a line extension, Extra-Strength Tylenol in tablet and capsule form, the brand's market share had risen to 37 percent of the pain reliever market by 1982. As the largest single brand in the history of health and beauty aids, Tylenol was used by 100 million Americans. It contributed 8 percent to J&J's sales but almost twice that percentage in net profits. Advertising support for the brand was heavy. A $40 million media campaign for 1982 used two different messages. The "hospital campaign" employed testimonials from people who had been given Tylenol in the hospital and reported that they had grown to trust it. The ad concluded with the tag line, "Trust Tylenol—hospitals do." The "hidden camera" campaign showed subjects who had been unobtrusively filmed while describing the symptoms of their headache, trying Extra-Strength Tylenol as a solution, and vowing to use it again based on its effectiveness. These ads concluded with the tag line, "Tylenol . . . the most potent pain reliever you can buy without a prescription."

The Tylenol Crisis

All this success came crashing to the ground with the news in the first week of October 1982 that seven people had died in the Chicago area after taking Extra-Strength Tylenol capsules that turned out to contain cyanide poison. Although it quickly became evident that the problem was restricted to that area of the country and had almost certainly been the work of some deranged person outside the company, consumer confidence was severely shaken. Most marketing experts believed that the damage to the reputation of the Tylenol brand was irreparable and that it would never fully recover. For example, well-known advertising guru Jerry Della Femina was quoted in the *New York Times* as saying, "On one day, every single human being in the country thought that Tylenol might kill them. I don't think there are enough advertising dollars, enough marketing men, to change that. . . . You'll not see the name Tylenol in any form within a year." Tylenol's comeback from these seemingly insurmountable odds has become a classic example of how best to handle a marketing crisis.

The Tylenol Recovery

Within the first week of the crisis, J&J issued a worldwide alert to the medical community, set up a 24-hour toll-free telephone number, recalled and analyzed sample batches of the product, briefed the Food and Drug Administration, and offered a $100,000 reward to apprehend the culprit of the tampering. During the week of October 5, J&J began a voluntary withdrawal of the brand by repurchasing 31 million bottles with a retail value of $100 million. The company stopped advertising, and all communications with the public were in the form of press releases. To monitor consumer response to the crisis, J&J started to conduct weekly tracking surveys with 1,000 consumer respondents. Ultimately, the company spent a total of $1.5 million for marketing re-search in the fourth quarter of 1982. The following week of October 12, it introduced a capsule exchange offer, promoted in half-page press announcements in 150 major markets across the country, inviting the public to mail in bottles of capsules to receive tablets in exchange. Although well intentioned, this offer met with poor consumer response.

During the week of October 24, J&J made its return to TV advertising with the goals of convincing Tylenol users that they could continue to trust the safety of Tylenol products as well as encouraging the use of the tablet form until tamper-resistant packaging was available. The spokesperson for the ad was Dr. Thomas N. Gates, the company's medical director, whose deep, reassuring voice exuded confidence and control. Looking calmly straight into the camera, he stated:

> You're all aware of the recent tragic events in which Extra-Strength Tylenol capsules were criminally tampered with in limited areas after they left our factories. This act damages all of us—you the American public because you have made Tylenol a trusted part of your healthcare and we who make Tylenol because we've worked hard to earn that trust. We will now work even harder to keep it. We have voluntarily withdrawn all Tylenol capsules from the shelf. We will reintroduce capsules in tamper-resistant containers as quickly as possible. Until then, we urge all Tylenol capsule users to use the tablet form and we have offered to replace your capsules with tablets. Tylenol has had the trust of the medical profession and 100 million Americans for over 20 years. We value that trust too much to let any individual tamper with it. We want you to continue to trust Tylenol.

The heavy media schedule for this ad ensured that 85 percent of the market viewed the ad at least four times during this week.

On November 11, 1982, six weeks after the poisonings and after intense behind-the-scenes activity, the chairman of J&J held a live teleconference with 600 news reporters throughout the United States to announce the return of Tylenol capsules to the market in a new, triple-seal package that was regarded as virtually tamperproof. To get consumers to try the new packaging, the company undertook the largest program of couponing in commercial history. On November 28, 1982, 60 million coupons offering a free Tylenol product (valued up to $2.50) were distributed in Sunday newspapers nationwide. Twenty million more coupons were distributed the following Sunday. By the end of December, 30 percent of the coupons had been redeemed. J&J also engaged in a number of activities to enlist the support of retailers in the form of trade promotions, sales calls, and so forth.

Convinced that market conditions were now stable enough to commence regular advertising, J&J's ad agency developed three ad executions using the testimony of loyal Tylenol users with the goal of convincing consumers that they could continue to use Tylenol with confidence. The first ad execution contained excerpts of consumers' reaction to the tampering incident, the second ad brought back a Tylenol supporter from an ad campaign run before the tampering incident to reassert her trust in Tylenol, and the third ad used the testimony of a Tylenol user who reasoned that she could still trust the product because hospitals still used it. The recall scores for two of the commercials were among the highest ever recorded by ASI, a well-known marketing research firm that conducted the ad testing for J&J. The return to advertising was accompanied by additional coupon promotional offers to consumers.

Incredibly, by February 1983, sales for Tylenol had almost fully returned to the lofty pretampering sales levels the brand had enjoyed six months earlier. Figure 11-11 displays Tylenol's sales growth with respect to management actions during this period. Decades later, the brand is virtually a $1 billion brand, with extensions into cough and cold remedies. The next largest pain reliever competitor has only half the market share of Tylenol. Clearly, J&J's skillful handling of an extremely difficult situation was a major factor in the brand's comeback. Another important factor, however, was the equity of the brand and its strong and valuable "trust" association built up over the years prior to the incident. The feelings of trust engendered by the brand helped to speed the brand recovery, a fact certainly evident to J&J (note the number of times the word *trust* appears in the initial Gates ad—five times).

Crisis Marketing Guidelines

Not all brands have handled their crises as well. Although Exxon spent millions of dollars advertising its gasoline and crafting its brand image over the years, it had essentially ignored the need to market its corporate identity and image. This decision came back to haunt the company in the weeks following March 24, 1989. That morning, the tanker *Exxon Valdez* hit a reef in Prince William Sound,

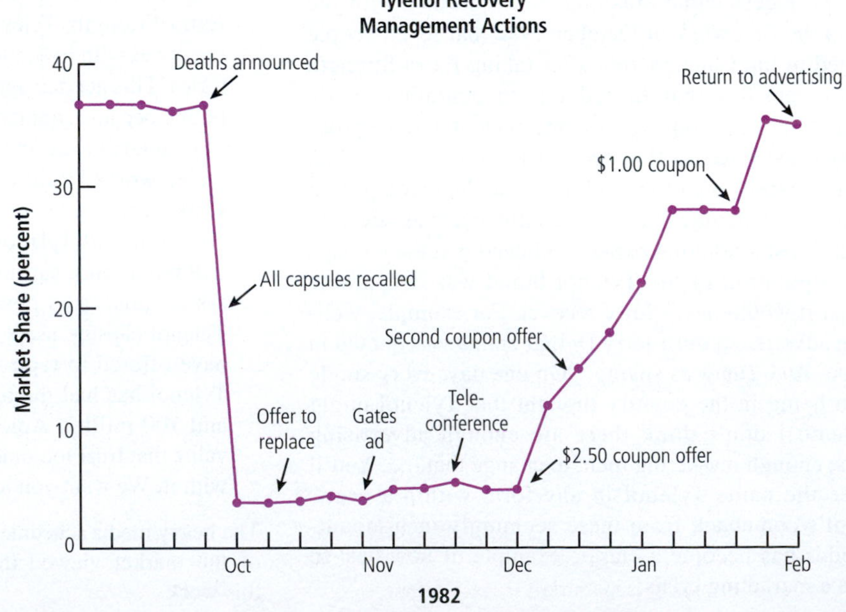

FIGURE 11-11

Tylenol Sales Growth

Alaska, spilling some 11,000,000 gallons of oil into the waters off the Alaska shoreline. The oil spill wreaked devastation on the fish and wildlife of some 1,300 square miles of the previously unspoiled area. Top Exxon officials declined to comment publicly for almost a week after the incident, and the public statements that were eventually made sometimes appeared to contradict information from other sources involved in the situation (for instance, regarding the severity of the spill) or assigned blame for the slow clean-up efforts to other parties, such as the U.S. Coast Guard. Exxon received withering negative press and was the source of countless jokes on late-night talk shows. In frustration and anger, some of Exxon's consumers began to cut up their Exxon credit cards. On April 3, 10 days after the accident, Exxon's chairman ran an open letter to the public in the form of a full-page message expressing the company's concern and justifying its actions to address the situation.[62]

Marketing managers must assume that at some point in time, some kind of brand crisis will arise. Diverse brands such as Wendy's restaurants, Firestone tires, Tyco diversified holdings, and Vioxx painkiller have all experienced a serious, potentially crippling brand crisis. In general, the more that brand equity and a strong corporate image have been established—especially with respect to corporate credibility and trustworthiness—the more likely it is that the firm can weather the storm. Careful preparation and a well-managed crisis management program, however, are also critical. Most experts would agree that the Exxon incident is a good example of how *not* to handle a brand crisis. As Johnson & Johnson's nearly flawless handling of the Tylenol product tampering incident suggests, the two keys to effectively managing a crisis are that the firm's response should be swift *and* that it should be sincere.

Swiftness

The longer it takes a firm to respond to a marketing crisis, the more likely it is that consumers can form negative impressions as a result of unfavorable media coverage or word of mouth. Perhaps even worse, consumers may find out that they do not really like the brand that much after all and permanently switch to alternative brands or products. For example, Perrier was forced to halt production worldwide and recall all existing bottles in February 1994 when traces of benzene, a known carcinogen, were found in excessive quantities in the bottled water. Over the course of the next few weeks, several explanations were offered as to how the contamination occurred, creating confusion and skepticism. Perhaps even more damaging, the product itself was off the shelves until May 1994. Despite an expensive relaunch featuring ads and promotions, the brand struggled to regain lost market share, and a full year later found its sales less than half what they once had been. Part of the problem was that during the time the product was unavailable, consumers and retailers found satisfactory substitutes such as Saratoga and San Pellegrino. With its key "purity" association tarnished (the brand had been advertised as the "Earth's First Soft Drink" and "It's Perfect. It's Perrier."), the brand had no other compelling points of difference over these competitors.[63] Finally, compounding the problems arising from the marketing crisis, the brand was gaining an increasingly stodgy image and was seen as much more appealing to the over-45 consumer market and much less appealing to those consumers under 25 years old. Eventually, the company was taken over by Nestlé SA.

Sincerity

Swift actions must also come across to consumers as sincere. The more sincere the response by the firm—in terms of public acknowledgment of the severity of the impact on consumers and the firm's willingness to take whatever steps are necessary and feasible to solve the crisis—the less likely it is that consumers will form negative attributions regarding the firm's behavior. For example, although Gerber had established a strong image of trust with consumers, baby food is a product category characterized by an extremely high level of involvement and need for reassurance. When consumers reported finding shards of glass in some jars of its baby food, Gerber tried to reassure the public that there were no problems in its manufacturing plants but adamantly refused to have its baby food withdrawn from grocery stores. Some consumers clearly found Gerber's response unsatisfactory because the brand's market share slumped from 66 percent to 52 percent within a couple of months. As one company official admits, "Not pulling our baby food off the shelf gave the appearance that we aren't a caring company."[64]

Brand crises are difficult to manage because, despite a firm's best efforts, it is difficult to be in control of the situation. To some extent, the firm is at the mercy of public sentiment and media coverage, which it can attempt to direct and influence but which sometimes can take on a life of their own. Swift and sincere words and actions, however, often can go a long way toward defusing the situation. As one commentator notes:

> No one strategy works in every crisis. There are too many variables—the news play, the marketplace, public sympathy or antipathy, whether the company cleans house as well as its image . . . Reality still counts. But simple honesty—"We've got a problem and we're doing X, Y, and Z about it"—is inevitably the last resort.[65]

Notes

1. Philip Kotler and Kevin Lane Keller, *Marketing Management,* 12th ed. (Upper Saddle River, NJ: Prentice Hall, 2006).
2. Donald R. Lehmann and Russell S. Winer, "Category Attractiveness Analysis" (Chapter 4) and "Market Potential and Forecasting" (Chapter 7), in *Product Management* (Burr Ridge, IL: Irwin, 1994).
3. Glen L. Urban and Steven H. Star, *Advanced Marketing Strategy: Phenomena, Analysis, and Decisions* (Englewood Cliffs, NJ: Prentice Hall, 1991).
4. Kotler and Keller, *Marketing Management.*
5. Tara Parker-Pope, "Laura Ashley's Chief Tries to Spruce Up Company That Isn't Dressing for Success," *Wall Street Journal,* 22 September 1995, B1.
6. Neil A. Morgan and Lopo Leotte do Rego, "Brand Portfolio Strategy and Firm Performance," Marketing Science Institute Working Paper 06–101, 2006.
7. David Greising, "Major Reservations," *Business Week,* 26 September 1994, 66.
8. Kotler and Keller, *Marketing Management;* Patrick Barwise and Thomas Robertson, "Brand Portfolios," *European Management Journal* 10, no. 3 (September 1992): 277–285.
9. For a methodological approach for assessing the extent and nature of cannibalization, see Charlotte H. Mason and George R. Milne, "An Approach for Identifying Cannibalization within Product Line Extensions and Multi-brand Strategies," *Journal of Business Research* 31 (1994): 163–170.
10. Jack Trout, *Differentiate or Die: Survival in Our Era of Killer Competition* (New York: Wiley, 2000).
11. Patricia Sellers, "P&G: Teaching an Old Dog New Tricks," *Fortune,* 31 May 2004, 166–172.
12. Paul W. Farris, "The Chevrolet Corvette," Case UVA-M-320 (Charlottesville, VA: Darden Graduate Business School Foundation, University of Virginia, 1995).
13. Laurens M. Sloot , Dennis Fok, and Peter C. Verhoef, "The Short- and Long-term Impact of an Assortment Reduction on Category Sales," Marketing Science Institute Working Paper 06–116, 2006; Jie Zhang and Aradhna Krishna, "Brand Level Effects of SKU Reductions," working paper, University of Michigan, 2006.
14. Kathryn Troy, "Managing the Corporate Brand," Research Report 1214–98-RR (New York: The Conference Board, 1998).
15. Laurel Cutler, vice-chairman of FCB/Leber Katz Partners, a New York City advertising agency, quoted in Susan Caminit, "The Payoff from a Good Reputation," *Fortune,* 6 March 1995, 74.
16. Hill & Knowlton, Return on Reputation Study, March 2006.
17. Harris Interactive, Reputation Quotient Survey, 2005; Ronald Alsop, "A Good Corporate Reputation Draws Consumers and Investors," *Wall Street Journal Books,* November 2005.
18. Jeffrey Parkhurst, "Leveraging Brand to Generate Value," in *From Ideas to Assets,* ed. Bruce Berman (New York: John Wiley & Sons, 2002).
19. Louis Capozzi, "Corporate Reputation: Our Role in Sustaining and Building a Valuable Asset." *Journal of Advertising Research* (September 2005): 290–293.
20. Howard Barich and Philip Kotler, "A Framework for Image Management," *Sloan Management Review* (Winter 1991): 94–104.
21. Kate Ballen, "America's Most Admired Corporations," *Fortune,* 10 February 1992, 40.
22. "DuPont: Corporate Advertising," Case 9–593–023 (Boston: Harvard Business School, 1992); John B. Frey, "Measuring Corporate Reputation and Its Value," presentation given at Marketing Science Conference, Duke University, 17 March 1989.
23. Charles J. Fombrun, *Reputation* (Boston: Harvard Business School Press, 1996).
24. Zeynep Gurhan-Canli, "The Effect of Expected Variability of Product Quality and Attribute Uniqueness on Family Brand Evaluations," *Journal of Consumer Research* 30 (June 2003): 105–114.
25. Much of this section—including examples—is based on an excellent article by Peter H. Farquhar, Julia Y. Han, Paul M. Herr, and Yuji Ijiri, "Strategies for Leveraging Master Brands," *Marketing Research* (September 1992): 32–43.
26. Farquhar, Han, Herr, and Ijiri, "Strategies for Leveraging Master Brands."
27. Natalie Pace, "Q&A: MySpace Founders Chris DeWolfe and Tom Anderson," Forbes.com, 4 January 2006.
28. Several excellent reviews of corporate images are available. See, for example, Grahame R. Dowling, *Corporate Reputations* (Melbourne, Australia: Longman Professional, 1994); and James R. Gregory, *Marketing Corporate Image* (Lincolnwood, IL: NTC Business Books, 1991).
29. Kevin Lane Keller and David A. Aaker, "The Effects of Sequential Introduction of Brand Extensions," *Journal of Marketing Research* 29 (February 1992): 35–50. See also Thomas J. Brown and Peter Dacin, "The Company and the Product: Corporate Associations and Consumer Product Responses," *Journal of Marketing* 61 (January 1997): 68–84.
30. Masashi Kuga, "Kao's Strategy and Marketing Intelligence System," *Journal of Advertising Research* 30 (April/May 1990): 20–25.
31. John Smale, "Smale on Saturn—Don't Change What's Working," *Advertising Age,* 28 March 1994, S24.
32. Tulun Erdem and Joffre Swait, "Brand Credibility, Brand Consideration and Choice," *Journal of Consumer*

Research 31 (June 2004): 191–198; Marvin E. Goldberg and Jon Hartwick, "The Effects of Advertiser Reputation and Extremity of Advertising Claim on Advertising Effectiveness," *Journal of Consumer Research* 17 (September 1990): 172–179.

33. Majken Schultz, Mary Jo Hatch, and Mogens Holten Larsen, eds., *The Expressive Organization: Linking Identity, Reputation, and the Corporate Brand* (New York: Oxford University Press, 2000); Mary Jo Hatch and Majken Schultz, "Are the Strategic Stars Aligned for Your Corporate Brand?" *Harvard Business Review* (February 2001): 129–134; James Gregory, *Leveraging the Corporate Brand* (Chicago: NTC Press, 1997); Lynn B. Upshaw and Earl L. Taylor, *The Masterbrand Mandate* (New York: John Wiley & Sons, 2000).
34. Sylvie LaForet and John Saunders, "Managing Brand Portfolios: How the Leaders Do It," *Journal of Advertising Research* (September/ October 1994): 64–76. See also Sylvie LaForet and John Saunders, "Managing Brand Portfolios: Why Leaders Do What They Do," *Journal of Advertising Research* (January/February 1999): 51–65.
35. LaForet and Saunders, "Managing Brand Portfolios: How the Leaders Do It."
36. Beth Snyder Bulik, "Tech Sector Ponders: What's in a Name?" *Advertising Age,* 9 May 2005, 24.
37. Tulin Erdem and Baohung Sun, "An Empirical Investigation of the Spillover Effects of Advertising and Sales Promotions in Umbrella Branding," *Journal of Marketing Research* 39 (November 2002)): 408–420.
38. Bulik, "Tech Sector Ponders: What's in a Name?"
39. Emily Nelson, "Too Many Choices," *Wall Street Journal,* 20 April 2001, B1, B4.
40. Edmund Gray and Larry R. Smeltzer, "Corporate Image—An Integral Part of Strategy," *Sloan Management Review* (Summer 1985): 73–78.
41. For a review of current and past practices, see David W. Schumann, Jan M. Hathcote, and Susan West, "Corporate Advertising in America: A Review of Published Studies on Use, Measurement, and Effectiveness," *Journal of Advertising* 20, no. 3 (September 1991): 35–56.
42. David M. Bender, Peter Farquhar, and Sanford C. Schulert, "Growing from the Top: Corporate Advertising Nourishes the Brand Equity from Which Profits Sprout," *Marketing Management* 4, no. 4 (1996): 10–19; Nicholas Ind, "An Integrated Approach to Corporate Branding," *Journal of Brand Management* 5, no. 5 (1998): 323–329; Cees B. M. Van Riel, Natasha E. Stroker, and Onno J. M. Maathuis, "Measuring Corporate Images," *Corporate Reputation Review* 1, no. 4 (1998): 313–326.
43. Gabriel J. Biehal and Daniel A. Shenin, "Managing the Brand in a Corporate Advertising Environment," *Journal of Advertising* 28, no. 2 (1998): 99–110.
44. Mary C. Gilly and Mary Wolfinbarger, "Advertising's Internal Audience," *Journal of Marketing* 62 (January 1998): 69–88.
45. Suzanne Vranica, "Cingular Ads Shift to Clear from Cryptic," *Wall Street Journal,* 27 August 2001, B7.
46. Vanessa O'Connell, "Kraft Foods Plans 'Umbrella' Campaign," *Wall Street Journal,* 15 June 1998, B8.
47. "Sense and Simplicity: Philips is Spending 80 Million [Euro] on a Rebranding Strategy That Will Emphasize Simplicity and Give Consumers What They Want," *ERT Weekly,* 23 September 2004,
48. P. Rajan Varadarajan and Anil Menon, "Cause-Related Marketing: A Coalignment of Marketing Strategy and Corporate Philanthropy," *Journal of Marketing* 52 (July 1988): 58–74.
49. Greg Goldin, "Cause-Related Marketing Grows Up," *Adweek,* 17 November 1987, 20–22; Ronald Alsop, "More Firms Push Promotion Aimed at Consumers' Hearts," *Wall Street Journal,* 29 August 1985, 23.
50. Sankar Sen and C. B. Bhattacharya, "Does Doing Good Always Lead to Doing Better? Consumer Reactions to Corporate Social Responsibility," *Journal of Marketing Research* 38 (May 2001): 225–243.
51. Yumiko Ono, "Do-Good Ads Aim for Sales That Do Better," *Wall Street Journal,* 2 September 1994, B8.
52. M. Drumwright, "Company Advertising with a Social Dimension: The Role of Noneconomic Criteria," *Journal of Marketing* 60 (October 1996): 71–87; A. Menon and A. Menon, "Enviropreneurial Marketing Strategy: The Emergence of Corporate Environmentalism as Market Strategy," *Journal of Marketing* 61 (January 1997): 51–67.
53. Hamish Pringle and Marjorie Thompson, *Brand Spirit: How Cause Related Marketing Builds Brands* (Chichester, NY: Wiley, 1999).
54. Ibid.
55. Judann Dagnoli, "Consciously Green," *Advertising Age,* 19 September 1991, 14.
56. Lawrence E. Joseph, "The Greening of American Business," *Vis a Vis,* May 1991, 32.
57. Joanne Lipman, "Environmental Theme Hits Sour Notes," *Wall Street Journal,* 3 May 1990, B6.
58. Leah Rickard, "Natural Products Score Big on Image," *Advertising Age,* 8 August 1994, 26; Kevin Goldman, "Survey Asks Which 'Green' Ads Are for Real," *Wall Street Journal;* Lorne Manly, "It Doesn't Pay to Go Green When Consumers Are Seeing Red," *Adweek,* 23 March 1992, 32–33.
59. Rickard, "Natural Products Score Big on Image"; Goldman, "Survey Asks Which 'Green' Ads Are for Real."
60. Jacquelyn A. Otman, "When It Comes to Green Marketing, Companies Are Finally Getting It Right," *Brandweek,* 17 April 1995.

61. John A. Deighton, "Features of Good Integration: Two Cases and Some Generalizations," in *Integrated Communications: The Search for Synergy in Communication Voices,* ed. J. Moore and E. Thorsen (Hillsdale, NJ: Lawrence Erlbaum Associations, 1996).
62. Nancy Langford and Steven A. Greyser, "Exxon: Communications after Valdez," Case 9-593-014 (Boston: Harvard Business School, 1995).
63. Stephen A. Greyser and Norman Klein, "The Perrier Recall: A Source of Trouble," Case 9-590-104 (Boston: Harvard Business School, 1990); Stephen A. Greyser and Norman Klein, "The Perrier Relaunch," Case Supplement 9–590–130 (Boston: Harvard Business School, 1990).
64. Ronald Alsop, "Enduring Brands Hold Their Allure by Sticking Close to Their Roots," *Wall Street Journal Centennial Edition,* 1989.
65. Leslie Savan, "Selling a Sullied Product," *San Francisco Chronicle,* 17 August 1986, 5.

INTRODUCING AND NAMING NEW PRODUCTS AND BRAND EXTENSIONS

Preview

Chapter 11 introduced two useful brand architecture tools: the brand–product matrix—a graphical means of representing the products and brands marketed by a firm—and the brand hierarchy—a visual means to portray relationships among various brand elements. This chapter considers in more detail the role of product strategy in creating, maintaining, and enhancing brand equity. Specifically, we'll develop guidelines to facilitate the introduction and naming of new products and brand extensions.

Let's start with a little historical perspective. For years firms tended to follow the lead of Procter & Gamble, Coca-Cola, and other major consumer goods marketers that essentially avoided introducing any new products using an existing brand name. Over time, tight economic conditions, a need for growth, and other factors forced firms to rethink their "one brand–one product" policies. Recognizing that one of their most valuable assets is their brands, many firms have since decided to leverage that asset by introducing a host of new products under some of their strongest brand names.

More and more firms are seeking to build "power" or "mega" brands that establish a broad market footprint, appealing to multiple customer segments with multiple products all underneath the brand umbrella. Unilever's Dove brand has made successful forays from its roots in soap into a range of skin care and body care products, backed by its "Campaign for Real Beauty" media campaign. At the same time, marketers are also realizing that too many product variations can be counterproductive, and ill-advised brand proliferation may actually repel consumers.

We've learned much about the best-practice management of brand extensions. This chapter begins by describing some basic issues about brand extensions and outlining their advantages and disadvantages. Then we present a simple model of how consumers evaluate brand extensions and offer managerial guidelines for introducing and naming new products and brand extensions. We conclude with a thorough summary of academic research findings on brand extensions. Brand Focus 12.0 addresses some important issues for line extensions.

New Products and Brand Extensions

As background, first consider the sources of growth for a firm. One useful perspective is Ansoff's product/market expansion grid. As shown in Figure 12-1, we can categorize growth strategies according to whether they rely on existing or new products, and whether

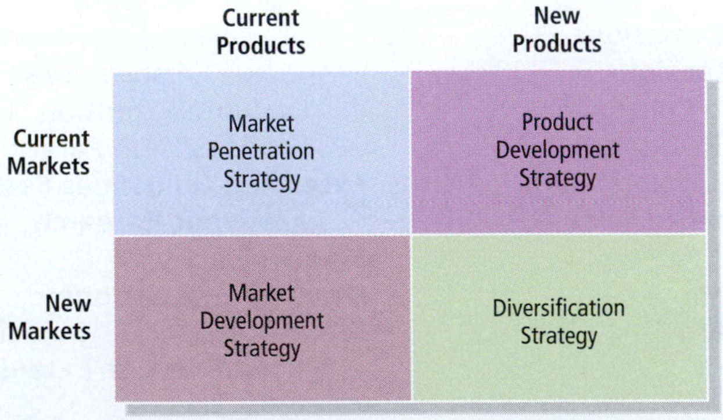

	Current Products	New Products
Current Markets	Market Penetration Strategy	Product Development Strategy
New Markets	Market Development Strategy	Diversification Strategy

FIGURE 12-1

Ansoff's Growth Share Matrix

they target existing or new customers or markets. Branding Brief 12-1 describes McDonald's growth strategies along these lines. Although existing products can further penetrate existing customer markets or push into additional ones (the focus of Chapter 13), new product introductions are often vital to the long-run success of a firm.

The experience of Segway, as summarized in Branding Brief 12-2, is a clear demonstration of how difficult it is to introduce new products and how carefully designed *and* marketed they must be. A discussion of all the issues in effectively managing the development and introduction of new products is beyond the scope of this chapter. Here we'll simply addresses some brand equity implications of new products.[1]

First we'll establish some terminology. When a firm introduces a new product, it has three choices for branding it:

1. It can develop a new brand, individually chosen for the new product.
2. It can apply, in some way, one of its existing brands.
3. It can use a combination of a new brand and an existing brand.

A ***brand extension*** occurs when a firm uses an established brand name to introduce a new product (approaches 2 or 3). When a new brand is combined with an existing brand (approach 3), the brand extension can also be a ***sub-brand.*** An existing brand that gives birth to a brand extension is the ***parent brand.*** If the parent brand is already associated with multiple products through brand extensions, then it may also be called a ***family brand.***

Brand extensions fall into two general categories:[2]

- *Line extension:* Marketers apply the parent brand to a new product that targets a new market segment within a product category the parent brand currently serves. A line extension often adds a different flavor or ingredient variety, a different form or size, or a different application for the brand (like Head & Shoulders Dry Scalp shampoo).
- *Category extension:* Marketers apply the parent brand to enter a different product category from the one it currently serves (like Swiss Army watches).

Typically 80 percent to 90 percent of new products in any one year are line extensions. Moreover, many of the most successful new products are extensions, like Mr. Clean windshield wash, Apple's iPod digital music player, Starbucks coffee liqueur, and Iams pet insurance. Nevertheless, many new products are introduced each year as new brands, like Vitamin Water beverages, the YouTube video hosting Web site, and Zometa, a cancer drug.

Brand extensions can come in all forms. One well-known branding expert, Edward Tauber, identifies the following seven general strategies for establishing a category—or what he calls a franchise—extension:[3]

1. *Introduce the same product in a different form.* Examples: Ocean Spray Cranberry Juice Cocktail and Jell-O Pudding Pops
2. *Introduce products that contain the brand's distinctive taste, ingredient, or component.* Examples: Philadelphia cream cheese salad dressing and Häagen-Dazs cream liqueur
3. *Introduce companion products for the brand.* Examples: Coleman camping equipment and Duracell Durabeam flashlights
4. *Introduce products relevant to the customer franchise of the brand.* Examples: Gerber insurance and Visa traveler's checks
5. *Introduce products that capitalize on the firm's perceived expertise.* Examples: Honda lawn mowers and Canon photocopy machines

BRANDING BRIEF 12-1

Growing the McDonald's Brand

In the 2000s, McDonald's faced a challenging environment. Market saturation and global health concerns provided obstacles to its growth. To generate growth, the company employed a number of different growth strategies in the pursuit of global brand leadership that illustrate the quadrants of the Ansoff growth matrix.

McDonald's has grown in part through market development and overseas success.

Market Penetration

McDonald's found its popularity in its core markets under threat following international concern about the role of fast food in poor health and obesity, highlighted by the negative publicity that came from the 2001 book *Fast Food Nation* and the 2004 movie *Super Size Me.* The company posted its first quarterly loss in 2002 and, as a consequence, "needed to look at why its customers weren't buying and recognize that they wanted better choices and healthier options." McDonald's responded by adding many new, healthier products (see the "Product Development" section) and launched a "Bag a McMeal" Web site that enabled users to calculate the nutritional content of any combination of McDonald's menu items. It also launched a global advertising campaign, based on the "I'm Lovin' It" tagline, which it translated into a number of languages. This global campaign replaced some 20 different ad platforms that had been running in different regions. In 2004, McDonald's CMO, Larry Light, lauded the campaign's success, stating, "The global common brand approach has been successful beyond our expectations. Since September 2003 we've had incremental visits to our stores of 2.3 million customer visits per day and that's continuing to grow."

Market Development

Although McDonald's was forced to close restaurants in some markets such as the United Kingdom and Japan as demand slowed, it still pursued growth via overseas expansion, opening more than 1,200 new restaurants in 2003, bringing the total to more than 30,000 restaurants in 119 countries. Roughly 65 percent of McDonald's revenues in 2004 came from outside the United States, and its fastest growing market in the mid-2000s was China, where the company hoped to have 1,000 locations by the 2008 Beijing Olympics. The company sought to highlight its expansive global presence with a 2006 global "reality packaging" promotion tied to the "I'm Lovin' It" campaign, whereby customers from all over the world were encouraged to participate in a "global casting call" by submitting online a personal story and digital photo representing what they love.

In 2007, 25 finalists were featured on cups and bags at McDonald's restaurants around the globe. McDonald's also sought to develop a new market domestically by attracting twenty- and thirty-something females to the brand, with premium salads served with Newman's Own dressing and other lighter menu options and targeted marketing as part of the "I'm Lovin' It" campaign.

Product Development

McDonald's extended its brand in 2001 with the opening of its first domestic McCafé, a gourmet coffee shop inspired by the success of Starbucks that debuted in Portugal and Austria. Another extension is McTreat, an ice cream and dessert shop. Additionally, McDonald's began offering specialized menu items in different countries, such as the Teriyaki Burger in Japan, and Vegetable McNuggets in England.

The biggest new product developments, however, were necessitated by the health concerns surrounding fast food. McDonald's overhauled its menu, removing "Super Size" options and adding healthier options such as a number of fresh salads, adult versions of its Happy Meals that included salad, bottled water, and a pedometer to encourage exercise, and healthier versions of its children's Happy Meals. McDonald's rapidly became the number-one salad brand in the United States. The revamp of its menu was coupled with a number of other health initiatives, including its Balanced Lifestyles platform for children that promoted healthy food choices, education, and physical activity and its Go Active! campaign to promote active lifestyles, which were both endorsed by Bob Greene, Oprah Winfrey's personal trainer. This shift in focus toward healthy eating and physical activity was emphasized by McDonald's recasting of Ronald McDonald as its "Chief Happiness Officer," a sports enthusiast, who donned a more athletic version of his traditional yellow and red suit and snowboarded, skateboarded, and juggled fruit in a new TV spot.

The company also tapped into the growing premium-coffee trend in the United States by launching McDonald's Premium Roast coffee, which retails for about 35 percent less than a cup of Starbucks coffee. Another popular new product was the McGriddle breakfast sandwich.

Diversification

McDonald's diversifies its product offerings according to regional tastes when it enters new markets. For example, when McDonald's entered India—where beef is not consumed because cows are sacred—it introduced the Maharaja Mac made from mutton. The company also developed spicy sauces such as McMasala and McImli.

As a result of McDonald's growth strategies, the company's financial fortunes rebounded. Furthermore, the brand was credited with a "halo effect" that was "driving growth for the entire quick-service restaurant category."

Sources: "McDonald's to Spend $1.5 Billion to Expand in Asia-Pacific Region," *Wall Street Journal,* 10 April 1998; Richard Gibson and Matt Moffett, "Why You Won't Find Any Egg McMuffins for Breakfast in Brazil," *Wall Street Journal,* 23 October 1997; Joanna Doonar, "Life in the Fast Lane," *Brand Strategy,* 6 October 2004, 20; Gina Piccolo, "Fries with That Fruit?" *Los Angeles Times,* 18 July 2005, F1; Pallavi Gogoi and Michael Arndt, "Hamburger Hell," *Business Week,* 3 March 2003, 104; Kate MacArthur, "Big Mac's Back," *Advertising Age,* 13 December 2004, S1; Normandy Madden, "In China, Golf and American Fare," *Advertising Age,* 25 July 2005, S6.

BRANDING BRIEF 12-2

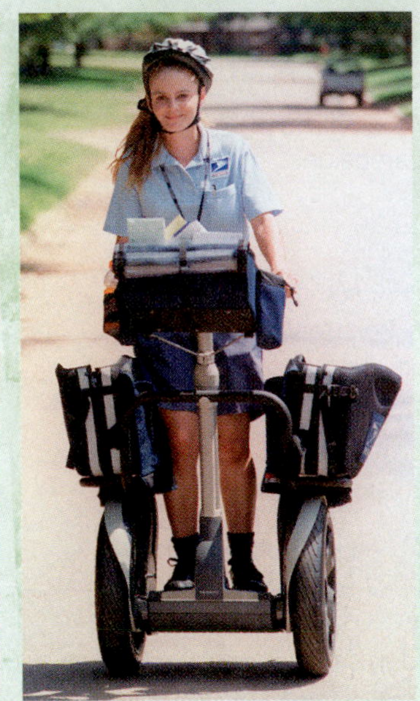

Segway Scooters is an example of how difficult it is to introduce radically new products.

Segway Scooter

Famed inventor Dean Kamen, who boasts a roster of successful inventions that include a mobile dialysis unit, a portable insulin pump for diabetics, and an all-terrain wheelchair called the iBot, developed a "revolutionary" new mode of transportation called the Segway HT (HT stands for "Human Transporter"). The motorized scooter used a gyroscopic rotor device that allowed users to stand upright while rolling on it and to turn it by leaning in the desired direction of the turn. The electrically powered Segway, which achieves a top speed of 12 miles per hour, was lauded as an energy-efficient replacement for other forms of urban motorized personal transport.

The Segway remained in "secret" development for years until its official demonstration in December 2001. Prior to the unveiling, a number of rumors and leaks about the Segway helped build anticipation for the machine, which cost about $4,000. Segway LLC, the company formed to manufacture and market the scooters, anticipated sales of 50,000 to 100,000 units in the first year of availability. Venture capitalist and Segway board member John Doerr, whose firm Kleiner Perkins Caufield & Byers invested in the Segway, predicted that the company would reach $1 billion in sales faster than any other start-up in history.

Despite attracting a core base of loyal users, the Segway never caught on with the wider population. Far from achieving its 50,000 to 100,000 unit

6. *Introduce products that reflect the brand's distinctive benefit, attribute, or feature.* Examples: Lysol's "deodorizing" household cleaning products and Ivory's "mild" cleaning products
7. *Introduce products that capitalize on the distinctive image or prestige of the brand.* Examples: Calvin Klein clothes and accessories and Porsche sunglasses

Next, we'll outline some of the main advantages and disadvantages of brand extensions.

Advantages of Extensions

For most firms, the question is not *whether* to extend the brand, but when, where, and how to extend it. Well-planned and well-implemented extensions offer a number of advantages to marketers that we can broadly categorize as those that facilitate new product acceptance and those that provide feedback benefits to the parent brand or company as whole (see Figure 12-2).

Facilitate New Product Acceptance

The high failure rate of new products has been well documented. Marketing analysts estimate that only 2 of 10 new products will be successful, or maybe even as few as 1 of 10. Robert McMath, who launched a collection of over 75,000 once-new consumer products

sales goal within one year, Segway managed to move only 6,000 units during the first 12 months. Then, the Consumer Products Safety Commission issued a recall of Segways due to a software glitch that in some cases caused riders to fall off their scooters. Negative publicity continued to accumulate when President Bush was pictured falling off a Segway while on vacation at his family's Kennebunkport, Maine home. Sales in 2003 totalled only $25 million, and in 2004 the company installed Ronald A. Bills as its fourth chief executive in as many years.

The new management blamed part of Segway's troubles on limited distribution and planned to establish a network of licensed dealers. Initially, the Segway was available for purchase only on Amazon.com or through specialty retailer Brookstone and a limited number of dealers. "Imagine if Ford or Chevy had no dealerships," said CEO Bills. "Where would you buy them?" Another plan was to make financing available for Segway buyers, which would expand the addressable market beyond "wealthy individuals looking for a unique toy."

These moves helped to a degree. By 2006, Segway had more than 100 dealerships, and sales were increasing 50 percent annually. These numbers still fell far short of the firm's initial sales expectations. Critics blamed the Segway's lack of mass-market success on the fact that its high price was not justified by the incremental functionality it offered over other low-emission forms of transportation such as biking and walking.

Sources: David Armstrong, "Segway: A Bright Idea, but Business Model Wobbles," *Wall Street Journal,* 14 February 2004; Victor Godinez, "Segways Rolling into Texas," *Dallas Morning News,* 12 March 2006, 2D; Justin Menkes, "Hiring for Smarts," *Harvard Business Review,* November 2005, 100.

Facilitate New Product Acceptance

Improve brand image
Reduce risk perceived by customers
Increase the probability of gaining distribution and trial
Increase efficiency of promotional expenditures
Reduce costs of introductory and follow-up marketing programs
Avoid cost of developing a new brand
Allow for packaging and labeling efficiencies
Permit consumer variety-seeking

Provide Feedback Benefits to the Parent Brand and Company

Clarify brand meaning
Enhance the parent brand image
Bring new customers into brand franchise and increase market coverage
Revitalize the brand
Permit subsequent extensions

FIGURE 12-2

Advantages of Brand Extension

BRANDING BRIEF 12-3

Law & Order has been a television brand blockbuster.

Law & Order

Since its launch in 1990, NBC's *Law & Order* has grown into television's most valuable franchise, generating revenues exceeding $1 billion a year. This success is driven by the stable of four *Law & Order*–branded programs that air during prime time each week on NBC: the original *Law & Order, Law & Order: Special Victims Unit, Law & Order: Criminal Intent,* and *Law & Order: Trial by Jury.* Reruns of *Law & Order* and *Law & Order: Special Victims Unit* air on TNT and USA each night of the week. Across these three networks, *Law & Order* shows account for about 40 hours of programming each week. Its closest analogue, CBS' *CSI* franchise, airs around 25 hours of programming with three primetime shows and reruns.

Law & Order was developed by Dick Wolf, who formerly worked in advertising as a copywriter and broke into show business writing for *Hill Street Blues,* a gritty police drama on NBC

called the New Products Showcase and Learning Center in Ithaca, New York, identifies nine main reasons for product failure:[4]

1. The market was too small (insufficient demand for type of product).
2. The product was a poor match for the company.
3. The product was justified on inadequate or inaccurate marketing research, or the company ignored research results.
4. The company was too early or too late in researching the market (failure to capitalize on its marketing window).
5. The product provided insufficient return on investment (poor profit margins and high costs).
6. The product was not new or different (a poor idea that really offered nothing new).
7. The product did not go hand in hand with familiarity.
8. Credibility was not confirmed on delivery.
9. Consumers could not recognize the product.

Brand extensions can certainly suffer from some of the same shortcomings faced by any new product. Nevertheless, a new product introduced as a brand extension may be more likely to succeed, at least to some degree, because it offers the advantages described in the following subsections. Branding Brief 12-3 describes the successful extension strategy pursued by the *Law & Order* television program.

that Wolf's own show owes a debt to. He later wrote for *Miami Vice,* another popular 1980s police drama. These early writing experiences convinced Wolf that the secret to long-running success for a program was to make each episode self-contained—having no plot relationship to the shows that air before or after. This enables word of mouth to build an audience in the initial season, and also makes for more lucrative syndication fees because reruns work better if they do not need to be sequenced. Hence, viewers can tune into *Law & Order* shows at any point in the season. As Wolf says, "It doesn't matter if you haven't seen it in a day, a week, a month, or five years."

The extension strategy pursued by *Law & Order* producers enables the show to easily migrate audiences from one program to another, because viewers have familiarity with and a certain expectation of quality for the *Law & Order* franchise. The franchise approach also provides NBC with cost efficiencies in promotion: It costs less to launch and sustain a brand extension of a show than it does to launch a new show.

By extending its brand, *Law & Order* has achieved unparalleled success in television. In addition to domestic and international syndication fees, the brand generates revenues through DVD sales, books, a computer game, and apparel. The *Law & Order* franchise is expected to make up to $10 billion between 2005 and 2010 if all four versions remain on the air.

Sources: Marc Gunther, "Crime Pays," *Fortune,* 21 March 2005, 186–192; www.nbc.com/Law_&_Order/about/; James Poniewozik, "The Next Friday," *Time,* 30 January 2003.

Improve Brand Image. As Chapter 2 noted, one of the advantages of a well-known and well-liked brand is that consumers form expectations of its performance over time. Similarly, with a brand extension, consumers can make inferences and form expectations about the likely composition and performance of a new product, based on what they already know about the brand itself and the extent to which they feel this information is relevant to the new product.[5] These inferences may improve the strength, favorability, and uniqueness of the extension's brand associations. For example, when Sony introduced a new personal computer tailored for multimedia applications, Vaio, consumers may have been more likely to feel comfortable with its anticipated performance because of their experience with and knowledge of other Sony products than if the product had been branded by Sony as something completely new.

Reduce Risk Perceived by Customers. One research study found that the most important factor for predicting initial trial of a new product was the extent to which it connected to a known family brand.[6] Extensions from well-known corporate brands such as General Electric, Hewlett-Packard, Motorola, or others may communicate longevity and sustainability. Although corporate brands can lack specific product associations because of the breadth of products attached to their name, their established reputation for introducing high-quality products and standing behind them may be an important risk-reducer for consumers.[7] Thus, perceptions of corporate credibility—in terms of expertise and trustworthiness—can be valuable associations in introducing brand extensions.[8] Similarly, although widely extended supermarket family brands such as Betty Crocker, Green Giant, Del Monte, and Pepperidge Farm may lack specific product meaning, they may still stand for product quality in the minds of consumers and, by reducing perceived risk, facilitate the adoption of brand extensions.

Increase the Probability of Gaining Distribution and Trial. Because of potentially increased consumer demand for a new product introduced as an extension, it may be easier to convince retailers to stock and promote it. For example, one study indicated that brand reputation was a key screening criteria of gatekeepers making new-product decisions at supermarkets.[9]

Increase Efficiency of Promotional Expenditures. From a marketing communications perspective, one obvious advantage of introducing a new product as a brand extension is that the introductory campaign does not have to create awareness of both the brand and the new product but instead can concentrate on only the new product itself. In general, it should be easier to add a link to a new product from a brand already existing in memory than it is to first establish the brand in memory and then also link the new product to it.[10]

Several research studies document this extension benefit. One study of 98 consumer brands in 11 markets found that successful brand extensions spent less on advertising than did comparable new-name entries.[11] Another comprehensive study found similar results, indicating that the average advertising-to-sales ratio for brand extensions was 10 percent, compared with 19 percent for new brands. This study identified some underlying factors moderating this extension advantage. The difference in advertising efficiency between brand extensions and new brands was shown to increase as the fit with other products affiliated with the parent brand increased, as the new product's relative price compared with that of competitors increased, and as distribution intensity increased. On the other hand, the difference in advertising efficiency between brand extensions and new brands was shown to decrease when the new product was composed primarily of search attributes (when product quality could be judged through visual inspection), as the new product became established in the market, and as consumers' knowledge of the new product category increased.[12]

Reduce Costs of Introductory and Follow-Up Marketing Programs. Because of these push and pull considerations in distribution and promotion, it has been estimated that a firm can save 40 percent to 80 percent on the estimated $30 million to $50 million it can cost to launch a new supermarket product nationally in the United States. Other efficiencies can result after the launch. For example, when a brand becomes associated with multiple products, advertising can be more cost-effective for the family brand as a whole. In 2001, Apple introduced the iPod portable digital music player, which quickly became the market leader and one of the company's most successful products. In subsequent years, the iPod received the majority of Apple's marketing budget and was credited with a "halo effect" that boosted sales for the company's other products, particularly computers and software. In its first quarter results of 2007, Apple reported record revenue of $7.1 billion — its highest quarterly revenue in the company's history and record net quarterly profit of $1.0 billion. Although nearly half of Apple's revenue was generated from sales of iPods, their Macintosh computers also experienced sustained 30% growth in sales.[13]

Avoid Cost of Developing a New Brand. Developing new brand elements is an art and a science. To conduct the necessary consumer research and employ skilled personnel to design high-quality brand names, logos, symbols, packages, characters, and slogans can be quite expensive, and there is no assurance of success. As the number of available—and appealing—brand names keeps shrinking, legal conflicts are more likely to result. To avoid such a conflict, a global trademark search is a must for any major new brand launch or rebranding, and it can cost millions of dollars. Even after the marketer has completed a search, other costs can arise. PricewaterhouseCooper's consulting group spinoff Monday elected to pay a reported $6.5 million to acquire the worldwide rights to the public relations firm OneMonday's trademark and domain name.[14] Monday's money was perhaps not well spent; the consulting unit was acquired and folded into the IBM brand one month after the name change.

Allow for Packaging and Labeling Efficiencies. Similar or virtually identical packages and labels for extensions can result in lower production costs and, if coordinated properly, more prominence in the retail store where they can create a "billboard" effect. For example, Stouffer's offers a variety of frozen entrees with identical orange packaging that increases their visibility when stocked together in the freezer. A similar effect is evident with other supermarket brands, such as Coca-Cola soft drinks and Pepperidge Farm cookies.

Permit Consumer Variety-Seeking. If offered a portfolio of brand variants within a product category, consumers who need a change—because of boredom, satiation, or whatever—can switch to a different product type if they so desire without having to leave the brand family. A complement of line extensions can also encourage customers to use the brand to a greater extent or in different ways. Moreover, to even compete effectively in some categories, marketers may need to have multiple items that together form a cohesive product line.

SUAVE

As an example of the benefits of expansive market coverage, consider the low-priced family brand Suave, sold by Helene Curtis. Suave includes a variety of personal care products, such as shampoos and conditioners, skin lotions and body washes, and antiperspirants and deodorants. Given the amount of brand switching and the large number of brands consumers use for personal care products in general and shampoos in particular, Suave's ability to offer a full product line is a competitive advantage. By continually line extending, Suave keeps up with any new market trend or shift in consumer demand.[15] Helene Curtis has adopted a "follower" strategy: Whenever a new type of product becomes successful, the company introduces a similar version under the Suave name designed to match it. Suave's advertising slogans have included "You Don't Have to Spend a Lot to Get a Lot" and "Say Yes to Beautiful Without Paying the Price." Suave's well-defined brand image and branding strategy have resulted in high degrees of consumer loyalty and market share for the brand.

Provide Feedback Benefits to the Parent Brand

Besides facilitating acceptance of new products, brand extensions can also provide positive feedback to the parent brand in a number of ways.

Clarify Brand Meaning. Extensions can help to clarify the meaning of a brand to consumers and define the kinds of markets in which it competes. Thus, through brand extensions, Hunt's means "tomato," Clairol means "hair coloring," Gerber means "baby care," Nabisco means "baked cookies and crackers," and ESPN means "sports" to consumers. Figure 12-3 shows how other brands that have introduced multiple brand extensions may have broadened their meaning with consumers.

FIGURE 12-3

Expanding Brand Meaning through Extensions

Brand	Original Product	Extension Products	New Brand Meaning
Weight Watchers	Fitness centers	Low-calorie foods	Weight loss and maintenance
Sunkist	Oranges	Vitamins, juices	Good health
Kellogg's	Cereal	Nutri-Grain bars, Special K bars	Healthy snacking
Aunt Jemima	Pancake mixes	Syrups, frozen waffles	Breakfast foods

Crayola has transcended its crayon product roots.

CRAYOLA

Crayola, known for its crayons, first sought to expand its brand meaning by making some obvious brand extensions into other drawing and coloring implements such as markers, pencils, paints, pens, brushes, and chalk. The company further expanded beyond coloring and drawing into arts and crafts with extensions such as Crayola Clay, Crayola Dough, Crayola Glitter Glue, and Crayola Scissors. These extensions established a new brand meaning for Crayola of "colorful crafts for kids." In 2005, the company attempted to expand its brand meaning once again with the introduction of children's personal care products, Squeeze & Squirt Foaming Hand Soap and Body Soap. The products were designed to recall the familiar crayon packaging and were emblazoned with a new brand character called "Tip" that leveraged the equity that research revealed resided in the Crayola tip. It was not immediately clear, however, whether the Crayola brand had "permission" from consumers to expand successfully into cleaning products.

Broader brand meaning often is necessary so that firms avoid "marketing myopia" and do not mistakenly draw narrow boundaries around their brand, either missing market opportunities or becoming vulnerable to well-planned competitive strategies. Thus, as Harvard's Ted Levitt pointed out in a pioneering article, railroads are not just in the "railroad" business but also the "transportation" business.[16] Thinking more broadly about product meaning can easily inspire different marketing programs and new product opportunities. For example, Steelcase's one-time slogan, "A Smarter Way to Work," reflected the fact that the company defines its business not as manufacturing desks, chairs, file cabinets, and credenzas but as "helping to enhance office productivity." For some brands, creating broader meaning is critical and may be the only way to expand sales.

OCEAN SPRAY

The growers' cooperative Ocean Spray Cranberries, Inc., found itself in a difficult position in the mid-2000s. With growth in carbonated beverages slowing, Coca-Cola and PepsiCo began to grow aggressively into noncarbonated drinks, including juices. Ocean Spray contemplated selling the brand to PepsiCo, but ultimately the growers' coop voted to remain independent. To remain competitive in the face of these larger players, Ocean Spray introduced a number of brand extensions in 2004 and 2005, including the Juice & Tea line, a line of chilled juices, variety packs of its popular Craisins dried cranberries, Craisins trail mix, a sparkling red and white cranberry beverage, and squeezeable cranberry sauce. The brand's meaning to consumers has thus expanded over time from "cranberry sauce" in the 1960s and 1970s to "good-tasting fruit juice drinks that are good for you" in the 1980s and 1990s to "good-tasting fruit juice drinks, snacks, and innovative products."[17]

In some cases, it is advantageous to establish a portfolio of related products that completely satisfy consumer needs in a certain area. For example, the $36 billion enterprise software market is characterized by a few mega-brands like Oracle and SAP that compete in multiple segments with multiple product offerings. Although at one time these different brands were limited to a few specific products, they have broadened their meaning through brand extensions and acquisitions to represent "complete business software solutions." Similarly, many specific-purpose cleaning products have broadened their meaning to be seen as multipurpose, including Lysol, Comet, and Mr Clean.

Enhance the Parent Brand Image. According to the customer-based brand equity model, one desirable outcome of a successful brand extension is that it may enhance the parent brand image by strengthening an existing brand association, improving the favorability of an existing brand association, adding a new brand association, or a combination of these.

One common way that a brand extension affects the parent brand image is by helping to clarify its core brand values and associations. Core brand associations, as we defined them in Chapter 3, are those attributes and benefits that come to characterize all the products in the brand line and, as a result, are those with which consumers often have the strongest associations. For example, Nike has expanded from running shoes to other athletic shoes, athletic clothing, and athletic equipment, strengthening its associations to "peak performance" and "sports" in the process.

Another type of association that successful brand extensions may improve is consumer perceptions of the credibility of the company behind the extension. For example, one research study showed that a successful corporate brand extension led to improved perceptions of the expertise, trustworthiness, and likability of the company.[18] In the late 1990s, several firms chose to introduce online versions of their services under a separate brand name (Bank One chose to launch its online bank as Wingspan). Besides increasing the difficulty and expense of launching a new brand, these companies also lost the opportunity to modernize the parent brand image and improve its technological credentials. In many cases, the new ventures failed and their capabilities were folded back into the parent organization.

Bring New Customers into the Brand Franchise and Increase Market Coverage. Line extensions can benefit the parent brand by expanding market coverage, such as by offering a product benefit whose absence may have prevented consumers from trying the brand. For example, when Tylenol introduced a capsule form of its acetaminophen pain reliever, it was able to attract consumers who had difficulty swallowing tablets and might have otherwise avoided the brand. Creating "news" and bringing attention to the parent brand may benefit the family brand as a whole. Snapple strove to renew its customers' interest and engagement in the brand, as well as attract new customers, with the 2004 introduction of its Snapple Lip Slicks fruit-flavored lip balm. The brand extension served to highlight "the wonderful attributes of Snapple—variety, flavor, smell—in a very creative, fun way."[19] Similarly, through the skillful introduction of extensions, Tide as a family brand has managed to maintain its market leadership from the 1950s to the present.

Revitalize the Brand. Sometimes brand extensions can be a means to renew interest in and liking for the brand.

Old Spice

Procter & Gamble's Old Spice had to wrestle with the problem of being seen by young males as "your father's aftershave." As one P&G marketing executive noted, "We recognize the need to change and bring in a new generation of young users. At the same time, we don't want to alienate the users we already have." To revitalize the brand, P&G launched a new campaign backed by heavy spending. The TV ads eliminated the trademark "whistling sailor" character to show—via rapid-fire editing—active, contemporary men. On the product side, P&G put heavy support behind its fast-selling and more youthfully positioned Old Spice High Endurance family of personal care products (deodorant, antperspirant, bar soap, body spray,

Old Spice has successfully balanced young and old in rejuvenating its Old Spice brand.

and shaving products) through a NASCAR sponsorship and driver Tony Stewart endorsement, as well as the Old Spice Red Zone family (deodorant, antperspirant, and body spray) which was launched with ads featuring All-Pro Chicago Bear linebacker Brian Urlacher.[20]

Permit Subsequent Extensions. One benefit of a successful extension is that it may serve as the basis for subsequent extensions. For example, Goodyear's successful introduction of its Aquatred tires sub-brand led to the introduction of Eagle Aquatred for performance vehicles with either wider wheels like the Ford Mustang or a luxury image like the Cadillac Seville.

Billabong, one of Australia's most successful brands, has grown beyond its surfing roots.

BILLABONG

The Billabong brand was established in 1973 by Gordon Merchant, who wanted to create a brand that had "functional products for surfers to help us better enjoy our sport." During the 1970s and 1980s, Billabong established its brand credibility with the young surfing community as a designer and producer of quality surf apparel. In the early 1980s, Billabong began to sell its products in Japan, Europe, and the United States through licensees. In the late 1980s and early 1990s, the brand extended into other youth-oriented areas, such as snowboarding and skateboarding, sticking to its core brand proposition: contemporary, relevant, innovative products of consistent high quality. In 2004, the company launched an entirely new brand called Honolua Surf Co. inspired by Hawaiian surf styles. As a result of its consistent growth, Billabong was ranked as the seventh most valuable brand in Australia, with an estimated value of $1.1 billion.

Disadvantages of Brand Extensions

Despite their potential advantages, brand extensions have a number of disadvantages (see Figure 12-4).

Can Confuse or Frustrate Consumers

Different varieties of line extensions may confuse and perhaps even frustrate consumers about which version of the product is the "right one" for them. With 16 varieties of Coke, 35 versions of Crest toothpaste, and so on, consumers can easily feel overwhelmed.[21]

Can confuse or frustrate consumers
Can encounter retailer resistance
Can fail and hurt parent brand image
Can succeed but cannibalize sales of parent brand
Can succeed but diminish identification with any one category
Can succeed but hurt the image of parent brand
Can dilute brand meaning
Can cause the company to forgo the chance to develop a new brand

FIGURE 12-4

Disadvantages of Brand Extension

For example, one study found that consumers were more likely to make a purchase after sampling a product (and being given a coupon) when there were 6 product flavors to sample than when there were 24.[22]

So, in some situations, greater product variety may induce shoppers to buy less. Consumers may reject new extensions for tried and true favorites or all-purpose versions that claim to supersede more specialized product versions. Moreover, because of the large number of new products and brands continually being introduced, many retailers do not have enough shelf or display space to stock them all. Some consumers may be disappointed when they're unable to find an advertised brand extension because a retailer is unable or unwilling to stock it. If a firm launches extensions that consumers deem inappropriate, they may question the integrity and competence of the brand.

Can Encounter Retailer Resistance

The number of consumer packaged-goods stock-keeping units (SKUs) outpaces the growth of retail space in year-on-year percentage growth. Additionally, own-brand or private-label goods rose from 15 percent to 20 percent of total grocery sales between 1994 and 2004.[23] Many brands now come in a multitude of different forms. For example, Crest toothpaste comes in 42 varieties, Head & Shoulders shampoo boasts more than 30 varieties, and American Express customers can choose from among 20 different card types. Campbell's has introduced a number of different lines of soup—including Condensed, Home Cookin', Chunky, Healthy Request, Select, Simply Home, Ready-to-Serve Classic, and portable Soup at Hand—and offers more than 100 flavors in all.

As a result, it has become virtually impossible for a grocery store or supermarket to offer all the different varieties available across all the different brands in any one product category. Moreover, retailers often feel that many line extensions are merely "me-too" products that duplicate existing brands in a product category and should not be stocked even if there were space. Wal-Mart, the biggest retailer in the United States, attempts to stock the items that sell best, dropping as many as 20 percent of slow-moving items from its shelves annually.[24]

Attacking brand proliferation, a year-long Food Marketing Institute (FMI) study showed that retailers could reduce their SKUs by 5 to 25 percent in certain product categories without hurting sales or consumer perceptions of the variety offered by their stores.[25] The FMI "product variety" study recommended that retailers systematically identify duplicated and slow-moving items and eliminate them to maximize profitability.[26] Many large packaged food brands took this advice to heart and began trimming their product lines in order to focus on the top-selling brands. Heinz culled 40 percent of its items between 2002 and 2004, a move that yielded an operating income increase of 18 percent in 2003. General Mills reduced the number of products it sells by 20 percent in 2004, while Hershey Foods made similar cuts.[27] The Science of Branding 12-1 summarizes one perspective on how to reduce brand proliferation and simplify marketing.

THE SCIENCE OF BRANDING 12-1

Fighting Feature Fatigue

Today, consumers face an unprecedented number of choices. Supermarkets contain more than 40,000 products, up from only 7,000 in the 1960s, and features on products continue to multiply. It is now possible to purchase a wireless device that also functions as a video game console, PDA, e-mail and Internet connection, digital camera, MP3 player, and GPS system. Consumers are often overwhelmed by this abundance of choice, and studies have shown that increased choice does not always yield ultimate satisfaction with the purchase decision. Even though a majority of participants in one study initially selected so-called "high feature" models of a given product, fewer than half actually preferred the high-feature products in actual usage situations. When consumers reach their threshold for comparing features, they often engage in what Yankelovich Partners calls "one-think shopping" by choosing familiar brands that function as "simplifiers" offering "the shortest, most efficient path to potential satisfaction and tension release." New or exciting features can initially help a brand stand out among the wealth of options and clarify a consumer's purchase decision. But as the product life cycle passes, competitors copy features or bring additional features to market, and consumer tastes evolve. As a consequence, "feature fatigue"—also referred to as "featuritis" and "feature creep"—sets in, and the brand loses its ability to differentiate.

Roland Rust, Debora Viana Thompson, and Rebecca Hamilton recommend several measures companies can take in order to fight feature fatigue. Their first recommendation is to seek an optimal number of features that will drive initial sales while delivering the ease of use that engenders long-term product loyalty. Too few features and the product will not make it into the consideration set; too many and frustrated consumers will seek alternatives. On this latter point, the authors' second recommendation is for companies to build simpler products with a greater degree of specialization for specific target segments. Third, the authors suggest giving consumers decision aids that make it easier to choose between specialized products or competing products. "Recommendation agents"—salespeople trained to question consumers about their preferences—and extended product trials are two such decision aids. Fourth, companies can design products that do one thing very well, rather than doing many things in a middling fashion. The authors cite Apple's iPod as an example of "how effectively a company can make sales and satisfy customers with a tightly focused solution." Finally, the authors recommend that companies use prototypes and in-use research when developing products. This solves the product-design dilemma that leads many consumers to prefer high-feature products when making a choice but not during actual use.

In proposing a different remedy for feature fatigue, Keith Goffin, Mike Northcott, and Rick Mitchell recommend that companies expand their focus beyond the technical aspects of product innovation and recognize the "importance of innovating across the whole product (pre- and post-sales) experience." The authors cite HP as a company that successfully innovated beyond product features when it became clear in 2002 that the speed and performance of its low-cost ink-jet printers were no longer differentiating to consumers. In response, HP developed product solutions that gave consumers something different and desirable: the ability to print photo-quality images onto a variety of surfaces. HP developed a marketing campaign that demonstrated how its digital imaging products fit into consumers' lives, and as a result it continues to enjoy market leadership in the ink-jet printer market.

More specifically, the authors adopt the Kano model (see Figure 12-A – it is below in box) to illustrate how a company can fight feature fatigue at the concept stage of product development. As the Kano model shows, from a consumer's point of view, features fall into three categories according to their effect on consumer satisfaction. "Basic" features (also called "hygiene factors") are those that are currently taken for granted and without which a product would fail to be considered for purchase, such as rechargeable laptop computer batteries. Providing additional performance on basic features will neither increase benefits to consumers nor raise their satisfaction. "Performance" features, such as processor speed or screen resolution on a laptop, provide real benefits to consumers, so adding additional Performance features increases consumer satisfaction. "Excitement" features (also called "Delighters") are differentiating features that "surprise and delight customers" by providing unexpected additional value. The authors give the example of navigation systems in cars as an Excitement feature, while warning that "overcomplicating products can be severely damaging to brands." A successful brand will have an optimal combination of all three types of features.

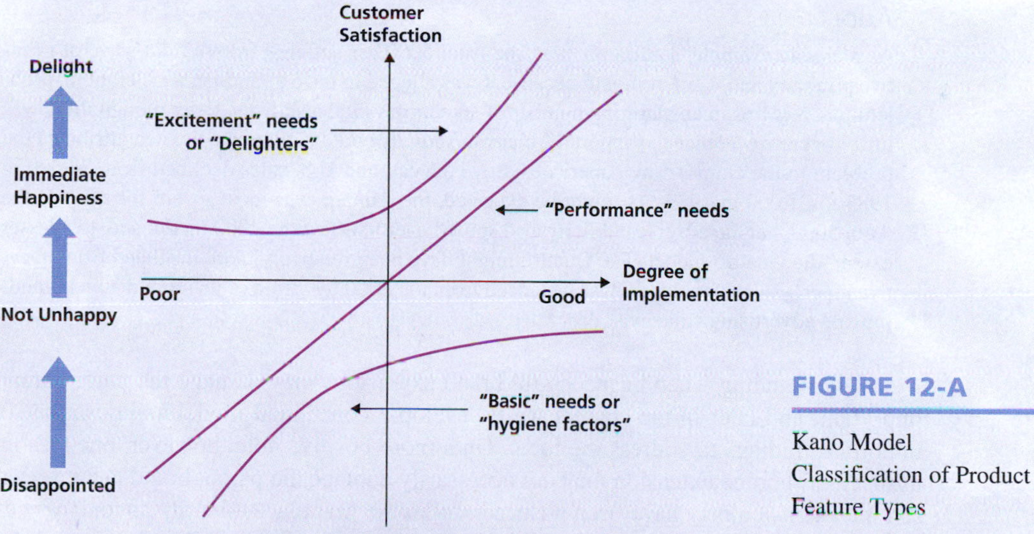

FIGURE 12-A

Kano Model Classification of Product Feature Types

Sources: Keith Goffin, et al., "New Product Strategy: Prevent Feature Fatigue!" *Critical Eye,* September–November 2005, 66; Steven M. Cristol and Peter Sealey, *Simplicity Marketing* (New York: Free Press, 2000); Sheena S. Iyengar and Barry Schwartz, "Doing Better but Feeling Worse: Looking for the 'Best' Job Undermines Satisfaction," *Psychological Science* 17, no. 2 (2006): 143–150; Roland T. Rust, Debora Viana Thompson, and Rebecca W. Hamilton, "Defeating Feature Fatigue," *Harvard Business Review,* February 2006, 98–107.

Can Fail and Hurt Parent Brand Image

The worst possible scenario for an extension is not only to fail, but to harm the parent brand image in the process. Unfortunately, these negative feedback effects can sometimes happen.

Consider General Motors' experience with the Cadillac Cimarron.[28] This model, introduced in the early 1980s, was a "relative" of models in other GM lines, such as the Pontiac 2000 and Chevrolet Cavalier. The target market was less affluent buyers seeking a small luxury car who wanted, but could not really afford, a full-size Cadillac. Not only was the Cadillac Cimarron unsuccessful at generating new sales with this market segment, but existing Cadillac owners hated it. They felt it was inconsistent with the large size and prestige image they expected from Cadillac. As a result, Cadillac sales dropped significantly in the mid-1980s. Looking back, one GM executive offered the following insights:

> The decision was made purely on the basis of short-sighted profit and financial analysis, with no accounting for its effect on long-run customer loyalty or, if you will, equity. A typical financial analysis would argue that the Cimarron will rarely steal sales from Cadillac's larger cars, so any sale would be one that we wouldn't have gotten otherwise. The people who were most concerned with such long-range issues raised serious objections but the bean counters said, "Oh no, we'll get this many dollars for every model sold." There was no thinking about brand equity. We paid for the Cimarron down the road. Everyone now realizes that using the model to extend the name was a horrible mistake.

Even if an extension initially succeeds, by linking the brand to multiple products, the firm increases the risk that an unexpected problem or even a tragedy with one product in the brand family can tarnish the image of some or all the remaining products.

Audi

As a classic example, starting in 1986 the Audi 5000 car suffered from a tidal wave of negative publicity and word of mouth because it was alleged to have a "sudden acceleration" problem that resulted in an alarming number of sometimes fatal accidents. Even though there was little concrete evidence to support the claims, Audi, in a public relations disaster, attributed the problem to the clumsy way Americans drove the car, and U.S. sales declined from 74,000 in 1985 to 21,000 in 1989. As might be expected, the damage was most severe for sales of the Audi 5000, but the adverse publicity also spilled over to affect the 4000 model and, to a lesser extent, the Quattro model. The Quattro might have been relatively more insulated from negative repercussions because it was distanced from the 5000 by virtue of its more distinct branding and advertising strategy.[29]

Understanding when unsuccessful brand extensions may damage the parent brand is important, and later in the chapter we'll develop a conceptual model and describe some important findings to address the topic. On a more positive note, however, one reason an unsuccessful brand extension may not necessarily damage the parent brand is the very reason the extension may have been unsuccessful in the first place—hardly anyone may even have heard of it! Thus, the silver lining when a brand extension fails to secure adequate distribution or to achieve sufficient brand awareness is that the parent brand is more likely to survive unscathed. But as we'll argue below, product failures in which the extension is found to be inadequate on the basis of performance are more likely to hurt perceptions of the parent brand than these "market" failures.

Can Succeed but Cannibalize Sales of Parent Brand

Even if sales of a brand extension are high and meet targets, this revenue may have resulted merely from consumers switching to the extension from existing product offerings of the parent brand—in effect cannibalizing the parent brand. Line extensions designed to establish points of parity with current offerings in the parent brand category particularly may result in cannibalization. Sometimes, however, such intrabrand shifts in sales are not undesirable; we can think of them as a form of "preemptive cannibalization." In other words, without the introduction of the line extension, consumers might have switched to a competing brand instead.

For example, Diet Coke's point of parity of "good taste" and point of difference of "low calories" undoubtedly took some sales from regular Coke drinkers. In fact, although U.S. sales of Coca-Cola's cola products have held steady since 1980, sales in 1980 came from Coke alone, whereas sales today include significant contributions from Diet Coke, Cherry Coke, and uncaffeinated and flavored forms of Coke. Without the introduction of those extensions, however, some of Coke's sales might have gone to competing Pepsi products or other soft drinks or beverages instead.

Can Succeed but Diminish Identification with Any One Category

One risk of linking multiple products to a single brand is that the brand may not be strongly identified with any one product. Thus, brand extensions may obscure the identification of the brand with its original categories, reducing brand awareness.[30] For example, when Cadbury became linked in the United Kingdom to mainstream food products such as Smash instant potatoes, marketers of the brand may have run the risk of weakening its association to fine chocolates. Pepperidge Farm is another brand that has been accused by marketing critics of having been extended so much (into pastries, bread, and snacks) that the brand has lost its original meaning of "delicious, high-quality cookies."

This potential drawback has been popularized by the vociferous business consultants Al Ries and Jack Trout, who in 1981 introduced the notion of the "line extension trap." They provide a number of examples of brands that, at the time, they believed had overextended.

Scott Paper

One such example was Scott Paper, which Ries and Trout believe became overextended when its name was expanded to encompass ScotTowels paper towels, ScotTissue bath tissue, Scotties facial tissues, Scotkins, and Baby Scot diapers.[31] Interestingly, in the mid-1990s, Scott decided to attempt to unify its product line by renaming ScotTowels as Scott Towels and ScotTissue as Scott Tissue, and adding a common look and logo (although some distinct colors) on both packages as well as their Scott Napkins. In perhaps a risky move, Scott also decided to phase out local brand names in 80 foreign countries where Scott garnered almost half its sales, including Andrex, its top-selling British bath tissue.[32] Scott's hope was that the advantages of brand consolidation and global branding would offset the disadvantages of losing local brand equity. Packaging was updated in 2005, keeping a unified look, and emphasis was continued on the shared "common sense" positioning theme, as exemplified by the "Common Sense on a Roll" slogan.

Some notable—and fascinating—counterexamples to these dilution effects exist, however, in firms that have branded a heterogeneous set of products and still achieved a reasonable level of perceived quality for each product in the minds of consumers. As we saw in Chapter 11, many Japanese firms have adopted a corporate branding strategy with a very broad product portfolio. For example, Yamaha developed a strong reputation selling an extremely diverse brand line that includes motorcycles, guitars, and pianos. Mitsubishi uses its name to brand a bank, cars, and aircraft. Canon has successfully marketed cameras, photocopiers, and office equipment. In a similar vein, the founder of Virgin Records, Richard Branson, has conducted an ambitious, and perhaps risky, brand extension program (see Branding Brief 12-4). In all these cases, it seems the brand has been able to secure a dominant association to quality in the minds of consumers without strong product identification that might otherwise limit it.

BRANDING BRIEF 12-4

Are There Any Boundaries to the Virgin Brand Name?

Perhaps the most extensive brand extension program in recent years has been undertaken by Richard Branson with his Virgin brand. Branson founded the Virgin record label at the age of 21, and in 1984 he launched Virgin Atlantic Airways. Later, he made millions on the sale of his record label, his Virgin record retail chain, and his Virgin computer games business. After licensing the use of the Virgin name to European startup airlines that were flying the London/Athens and London/Dublin routes, Branson decided to expand the range of products carrying the Virgin brand. He has since licensed the Virgin name for use on personal computers and set up joint ventures in 1994 to market Virgin Vodka and Virgin Cola. In 1997, he took over six of the United Kingdom's government rail lines and established Virgin Rail. In 1999, Branson launched Virgin Mobile, a wireless company that provides cellular service through a partnership with Deutsche Telecom. He branched into e-commerce that same year with the debut of Virgin.com, a portal where consumers can purchase every product or service offered by the Virgin brand.

The always outrageous Richard Branson dressed up as a bride at the 1996 launch of Virgin Bride in London.

Today the Virgin Group spans three continents and contains more than 200 companies marketing such diverse products as financial services, music, autos (online), cola, cosmetics, utilities, mobile phones, bridal wear, and a variety of e-commerce ventures. Virgin had 2004 revenues of an estimated $8.1 billion, and Branson's personal fortune was estimated at $6 billion in 2006.

Travel and Transport	Leisure and Entertainment	House and Home	Business and Finance
Virgin Atlantic	Virgin Active	Virgin Brides	Virgin Biz.net
Virgin Balloon Flights	Virgin Drinks	Virgin Cosmetics	Virgin Direct
Virgin Bikes	Virgin Megastores	Virgin Energy	Virgin Money
Virgin Blue	Virgin Mobile	Virgin Wines	Virgin Incentives
Virgin Books	V.Shop	Virgin Jewellery	Virgin Life Care
Virgin Cars	Virgin Galactic	Virgin Ware	

Can Succeed but Hurt the Image of the Parent Brand

If the brand extension has attribute or benefit associations that are seen as inconsistent or perhaps even as conflicting with the corresponding associations for the parent brand, consumers may change their perceptions of the parent brand as a result. For example, when Evian licensed its brand in 2004 to Johnson & Johnson for the Affinity brand of skin care products, it risked eroding the associations of "pure" and "refreshing" for its water, with associations more common to skin care, such as "cleaning," "chemical," and "cream."

Virgin Express	Virgin Student
Virgin Holidays	Virgin Wines
Virgin Limited Edition	V2 Music
Virgin.net	Radio Free Virgin
Virgin Trains	Virgin Vacations
Virgin Vacations	Virgin Digital
Virgin Limo	

Virgin's growth and expansion has sparked debate about Branson's seemingly undisciplined extension of the brand. One branding expert criticized Virgin's rapid expansion: "Virgin makes no sense; it's completely unfocused." When Virgin ventures are poorly received, as Virgin Cola, Virgin Vodka, Virgin PCs, Virgin Jeans, Virgin Brides, and Virgin Clothing were in recent years, experts worry about the cumulative negative effect of these unsuccessful brands on the company's overall equity. One marketing executive illustrated the risk of launching an unsuccessful brand by saying, "When I'm delayed on a Virgin train, I start wondering about Virgin Atlantic. Every experience of a brand counts, and negative experiences count even more."

Some critics believe that Virgin consumer products will do little more than generate publicity for Virgin airlines. They also caution of overexposure, even with the young, hip audience the Virgin brand has attracted. For example, one advertising agency executive remarked, "I would imagine the risk is that the Virgin brand name can come to mean everything to everybody, which in turn means it becomes nothing to nobody." In Branson's view, as long as a new brand adds value for the consumer, then it strengthens the Virgin image: "If the consumer benefits, I see no reason why we should be frightened about launching new products." Among the new products Branson hopes to launch in the future are a Virgin Sports cable channel in the United Kingdom and space tourism on rocket ships with Virgin Galactic. Yet Virgin has become more disciplined about its expansion in recent years: The company only pursues new businesses if they can be projected to generate more than $150 million in sales within three years.

Sources: Raymond Snoddy, "The Moon's the Limit," *The Independent,* 8 May 2006, 5; Alan Deutscham, "The Gonzo Way of Branding," *Fast Company,* October 2004, 91; www.virgin.com; Melanie Wells, "Red Baron," *Forbes,* 3 July 2000; Quentin Sommerville, "High-Flying Brand Isn't All It Appears," *Scotland on Sunday,* 24 December 2000; Roger Crowe, "Global—A Brand Too Far?" *GlobalVue,* 28 October 1998.

As another example, Miller Brewing has had much difficulty in creating a "hearty" association to its flagship Miller High Life beer brand, in part because of its clear bottle and its advertising heritage as the "champagne of bottled beer." It has often been argued that the early success of Miller Lite—its extension-market share soared from 9.5 percent in 1978 to 19 percent in 1986—only exacerbated the tendency of consumers to think of Miller High Life as "watery" tasting and not a full-bodied beer. These unfavorable perceptions were thought to have helped contribute to the sales decline of Miller High Life, whose market share slid from 21 percent to 12 percent during that same eight-year period.

Can Dilute Brand Meaning

The potential drawbacks of a brand extension's lack of identification with any one category and a weakened image may be especially evident with high-quality or prestige brands.

GUCCI

In its prime, the Gucci brand symbolized luxury, status, elegance, and quality. By the 1980s, however, the label had become tarnished by sloppy manufacturing, countless knock-offs, and even a family feud among the managing Gucci brothers. The product line consisted of 22,000 items, distributed extensively across all types of department stores. Not only were there too many items, but some items did not even fit the Gucci image—for example, a cheap canvas pocketbook with the double-G logo that was easily counterfeited and sold on the street for $35. Sales recovered only when Gucci refocused the brand, paring the product line to 7,000 high-end items and selling them through its own company-owned outlets. The strategy helped propel Gucci to the height of the fashion business. With sales of $3.2 billion in 2004, Gucci is now the world's third-biggest luxury goods company.[33]

To protect their brands from dilution, many fashion companies seeking to grow through brand extensions are now forging exclusive licensing partnerships with a single retailer, such as Target's exclusive deals with Todd Oldham, Mossimo, and Isaac Mizrahi. These exclusive licenses enable the licensor to better control the inventory, avoid discounts, and, most importantly, protect the brand. Nicole Miller, a fashion brand famous for cocktail gowns that can cost up to $2,500, selected Bed Bath & Beyond as the exclusive licensing partner for its line of upscale sheets and bedding.[34]

Can Cause the Company to Forgo the Chance to Develop a New Brand

One easily overlooked disadvantage to brand extensions is that by introducing a new product as a brand extension, the company forgoes the chance to create a *new* brand, with its own unique image and equity. For example, consider the advantages to Disney of having introduced Touchstone films, which attracted an audience interested in movies with more adult themes and situations than Disney's traditional family-oriented releases; to Levi's of having introduced Dockers pants, which attracted a customer segment interested in casual pants; to General

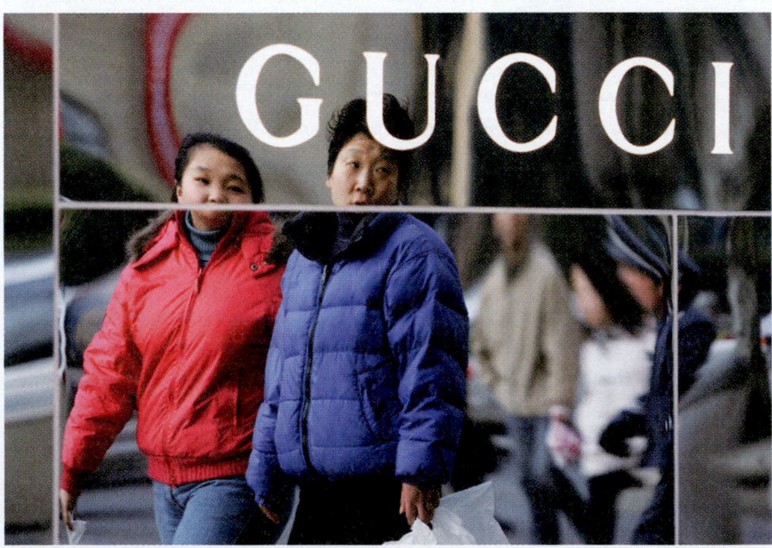

Gucci has become one of the world's most successful luxury brands.

Motors of having introduced Saturn, which attracted consumers weary of "the same old cars sold the same old way"; and to Black & Decker of having introduced DeWalt power tools.

Each of these brands created its own associations and image and tapped into markets completely different from those that currently existed for other brands sold by the company. Thus, introducing a new product as a brand extension can have significant and potentially hidden costs in terms of the lost opportunities of creating a new brand franchise. Moreover, there may be a loss of flexibility in the brand positioning for the extension, given that it has to live up to the parent brand's promise and image. The positioning of a new brand could be introduced and updated in the most competitively advantageous way possible.

Understanding How Consumers Evaluate Brand Extensions

What determines whether a brand extension is able to capitalize on these potential advantages and avoid, or at least minimize, potential disadvantages? Figure 12-5 displays some examples of successful and unsuccessful brand extensions through the years. Note how even leading marketing companies have sometimes failed, despite their best intentions, in launching a brand extension.

This section examines how consumers evaluate brand extensions. It develops some ideas to help a marketing manager better forecast and improve the odds for success of a brand extension.[35]

Managerial Assumptions

To analyze potential consumer response to a brand extension, let's start with a baseline case in which consumers are evaluating the brand extension based only on what they already know about the parent brand and the extension category, and before any advertising, promotion, or detailed product information is available. This baseline case provides the cleanest test of the extension concept itself, and it gives managers guidance about whether to proceed with an extension concept and, if so, what type of marketing program they might need.

Under these baseline conditions, we can expect consumers to use their existing brand knowledge, as well as what they know about the extension category, to try to infer what the

Successful Category Extensions	Unsuccessful Category Extensions
Dove shampoo and conditioner	Campbell's tomato sauce
Vaseline Intensive Care skin lotion	Life Savers chewing gum
Hershey chocolate milk	Cracker Jack cereal
Jell-O Pudding Pops	Harley-Davidson wine coolers
Visa traveler's checks	Hidden Valley Ranch frozen entrees
Sunkist orange soda	Bic perfumes
Colgate toothbrushes	Ben-Gay aspirin
Mars ice cream bars	Kleenex diapers
Arm & Hammer toothpaste	Clorox laundry detergent
Bic disposable lighters	Levi's Tailored Classics suits
Honda lawn mowers	Nautilus athletic shoes
Mr. Clean Auto Dry car wash system	Domino's fruit-flavored bubble gum
Fendi watches	Smucker's ketchup
Head golf clubs	Fruit of the Loom laundry detergent
Porsche coffee makers	Coors Rocky Mountain Spring Water
Jeep strollers	Cadbury Soap

FIGURE 12-5

Examples of Category Extensions

extension product might be like. In order for these inferences to result in favorable evaluations of an extension, four basic conditions must generally hold true:

1. ***Consumers have some awareness of and positive associations about the parent brand in memory.*** Unless beneficial consumer knowledge exists about the parent brand, it is difficult to expect consumers to form favorable expectations of an extension.
2. ***At least some of these positive associations will be evoked by the brand extension.*** A number of different factors will determine which parent brand associations are evoked, but in general, consumers are likely to infer associations similar in strength, favorability, and uniqueness to the parent brand when they see the brand extension as similar or close in fit to the parent.
3. ***Negative associations are not transferred from the parent brand.*** Ideally, any negative associations that do exist for the parent brand will be left behind and not play a prominent role in the evaluation of the extension. For example, in 2005 radio station conglomerate Clear Channel Communications restored the original names of the concert promotion companies it had acquired and folded into the Clear Channel brand, including Cellar Door, Electric Factory Concerts, and Bill Graham Presents, a move attributed to the potential loss of ticket sales stemming from some music fans' negative perceptions of the Clear Channel parent company.[36]
4. ***Negative associations are not created by the brand extension.*** Finally, any attributes or benefits that are viewed positively—or at least neutrally—by consumers with respect to the parent brand must not be seen as negative for the extension. Consumers must also not infer any new attribute or benefit associations that did not characterize the parent brand but which they see as a potential drawback to the extension.

The more these four assumptions hold true, the more likely it is that consumers will form favorable attitudes toward an extension. Now we'll examine some factors that influence the validity of these assumptions and consider in more detail how a brand extension, in turn, affects brand equity.

Brand Extensions and Brand Equity

The ultimate success of an extension will depend on its ability to both achieve some of its own brand equity in the new category and contribute to the equity of the parent brand.

Creating Extension Equity. For the brand extension to create equity, it must have a sufficiently high level of awareness and achieve necessary and desired points of parity and points of difference. Brand awareness will depend primarily on the marketing program and resources devoted to spreading the word about the extension. As Chapter 11 described, it will also obviously depend on the type of branding strategy adopted: The more prominently we use an existing brand that has already achieved a certain level of awareness and image to brand an extension, the easier it should be to create awareness of and an image for the extension in memory.

Initially, creating a positive image for an extension will depend primarily on three consumer-related factors:

1. How *salient* parent brand associations are in the minds of consumers in the extension context, that is, what information comes to mind about the parent brand when consumers think of the proposed extension and the strength of those associations
2. How *favorable* any inferred associations are in the extension context, that is, whether this information suggests the type of product or service that the brand

extension would be, and whether consumers view these associations as good or bad in the extension context
3. How *unique* any inferred associations are in the extension category, that is, how these perceptions compare with those about competitors

As with any brand, successful brand extensions must achieve desired points of parity and points of difference. Without powerful points of difference, the brand risks becoming an undistinguished "me-too" entry, vulnerable to well-positioned competitors.[37] Tauber refers to "competitive leverage" as the set of advantages that a brand conveys to an extended product in the new category, that is, "when the consumer, by simply knowing the brand, can think of important ways that they perceive that the new brand extension would be better than competing brands in the category."[38] This appeared to be the case with the U.K. launch of the Dettol Easy Mop disposable mop system, an extension of Reckitt Benckiser's Dettol household cleaner brand, which leveraged the familiar Dettol brand in outselling other entrants into the category.[39]

At the same time, marketers must also establish any required points of parity. The more dissimilar the extension product is to the parent brand, the more likely it is that points of parity will become a positioning priority. For example, when Johnson & Johnson test-marketed a brand of aspirin for babies, the product failed despite the fact that the Johnson & Johnson name is virtually synonymous with baby products. As it turned out, parents were just as concerned with getting fevers down quickly as they were with the safety and gentleness of an aspirin—Johnson & Johnson's key point of difference and core benefit association for their existing baby products. Thus, the lack of a necessary point of parity association doomed the product.

Contributing to Parent Brand Equity. To contribute to parent brand equity, an extension must strengthen or add favorable and unique associations to the parent brand and not diminish the strength, favorability, or uniqueness of any already existing associations for the parent brand. The effects of an extension on consumer brand knowledge will depend on four factors:

1. How *compelling* the evidence is about the corresponding attribute or benefit association in the extension context—that is, how attention getting and unambiguous or easily interpretable the information is about product performance or imagery for that association. Strong evidence is attention getting and unambiguous. Weak evidence—whether it is less attention getting or more ambiguous—may be ignored or discounted.
2. How *relevant* or diagnostic the extension evidence is for the attribute or benefit for the parent brand, that is, how much consumers see evidence on product performance or imagery in one category as predictive of product performance or imagery for the brand in other categories. Evidence will affect parent brand evaluations only if consumers feel that extension performance is indicative, in some way, of the parent brand.
3. How *consistent* the extension evidence is with the corresponding parent brand associations. Consistent extension evidence is less likely to change the evaluation of existing parent brand associations. Inconsistent extension evidence creates the potential for change, with the direction and extent of change depending on the relative strength and favorability of the evidence. Note, however, that consumers may discount or ignore highly inconsistent extension evidence if they don't view it as relevant.[40]
4. How *strongly* existing attribute or benefit associations are held in consumer memory for the parent brand, that is, how easy an association might be to change.

According to these factors, feedback effects that change brand knowledge are most likely when consumers view information about the extension as equally revealing about the parent brand, and when they hold only a weak and inconsistent association between the parent brand

Michelin has built an expansive brand on a foundation of safety and dependability.

and that information. The nature of the feedback effects will depend on the nature of the actual information: An unfavorable extension evaluation can lead to negative feedback effects, whereas a favorable extension evaluation can lead to positive feedback effects. Note that negative feedback effects are not restricted to product-related performance associations. As we noted earlier, if a brand has a favorable prestige image association, then consumers may disapprove or even resent a vertical extension (a new version of the product at a lower price).

Michelin

Michelin, which possesses favorable image associations of safety and dependability, began extending its brand into a broad variety of licensed merchandise that retails for far less than the average Michelin tire. The new products, developed by a new division called Michelin Lifestyle, fell into four distinct areas: (1) tire accessories, such as foot pumps, floor mats, and windshield wipers; (2) "high-specification lifestyle products," such as bicycle helmets, scuba suits, and soccer balls; (3) clothing and accessories featuring Michelin's brand mascot Bibendum; and (4) safety products developed in concert with other companies, including ear plugs, safety goggles, and gloves. Michelin intended these brand extensions to "enhance the value of our brand and add emotional-type values, not just functionality, and reach out to . . . a new generation that doesn't yet associate with us." Still, Michelin Lifestyle management was careful not to stretch the brand too far by moving into "fragrances and other things that have some legitimacy for a lifestyle brand. There still has to be an authentic Michelin reason for everything."[41]

Vertical Brand Extensions

We've seen that brand extensions can expand market coverage and bring new consumers into the brand franchise. Vertical brand extensions, where the brand is extended up into more premium market segments or down into more value-conscious segments, are a common means of attracting new groups of consumers. The central logic behind vertical extensions is that the equity of the parent brand can be transferred in either direction in order to appeal to consumers who otherwise would not consider the parent brand.

Vertical extensions can confer a number of the advantages of brand extensions. An upward extension can improve brand image, as a more premium version of a brand often brings with it positive associations. Extensions in either direction can permit consumer variety seeking, revitalize the parent brand, or permit subsequent extensions further in a given direction. Yet vertical extensions are also susceptible to many of the disadvantages of brand extensions that we previously discussed. A vertical extension to a new price point, either higher or lower, can confuse or frustrate consumers who have learned to expect a certain price range from a brand. There is always the possibility, particularly with an upward extension, that consumers will reject the extension and the parent brand's image will suffer. Even a successful downward extension has the possibility of harming the parent's brand image by introducing associations common to lower-priced brands, such as inferior quality or reduced service.

One of the biggest risk factors of a vertical extension is that it will succeed but cannibalize sales of a parent brand. Though the extension may bring new consumers to the brand franchise, it may bring a greater number of existing customers of the parent brand. This problem is common when brands attempt downmarket vertical extensions. For example, Philip Morris launched Marlboro Basic to compete with Monarch, a discount brand. This move led to massive cannibalization of the flagship Marlboro brand, and Philip Morris operating profit plummeted 46 percent while profitability fell across the tobacco industry. Similarly, at a time when it held 70 percent global market share with its Kodak Gold brand, Kodak launched the discount Kodak Funtime brand to compete with the threat of lower-priced Fuji film. Cannibalization of the Kodak Gold brand soon followed, and Kodak found itself in a price war with Fuji that ultimately led to a significant decline in Kodak Gold market share. While the parent brand name "gives you the credibility to quickly gain share in the lower-end market," cannibalization is a likely outcome because ''if you've already persuaded people that only the best products are sold under your brand, then they'll readily buy the least expensive item with that brand name."[42]

Despite the problems inherent in vertical extensions, many companies have succeeded in extending their brands to enter new markets across a range of price points. For example, Marriott hotels covers a range of options above and below the mid-range Marriott parent brand, from luxury hotels and resorts under the J.W. Marriott brand to smaller suburban hotels under Courtyard by Marriott to value hotels/motels under Fairfield Inn by Marriott. In fashion, the Armani brand has extended from high-end Giorgio Armani and Giorgio Armani Privé to mid-range luxury with Emporio Armani, to affordable luxury with Armani Jeans and Armani Exchange. In each of these cases, a clear differentiation exists between brands, minimizing the potential for brand overlap and accompanying consumer confusion and brand cannibalization. Each of these extensions also lived up to the core promise of the parent brand, thus reducing the possibility that any of them would hurt the parent's image.

In order to avoid the difficulties associated with vertical extensions, companies sometimes elect to use new and different brand names to expand vertically. Many examples of this strategy exist, including Toyota, which expanded upward into the luxury category with the Lexus brand after determining that the Toyota mark did not have the credibility to enter the luxury space. When it elected to move downmarket, Toyota developed the Scion brand in part to avoid reducing the strength of the Toyota image. The Gap pursued a similar expansion strategy, using the Banana Republic brand to command a 40 percent price premium that the Gap would likely never attain on its own, and it launched the Old Navy brand to offer 40 percent discounts. By developing unique brand names, companies pursuing vertical expansion can avoid a negative transfer of equity from a "lower" brand to a "higher" brand, but sacrifice to some extent the ability to transfer positive associations from existing brands to new ones. Yet when the parent brand makes no secret of its ownership of the vertical brands, as is the case with both the Gap and Toyota, some associations may be transferred because the parent acts as a "shadow endorser" of the new brand.[43]

Branding Brief 12-5 illustrates how Levi's has been able to expand its market coverage and attract new consumers through vertical extensions into both high-end and discount jeans.

BRANDING BRIEF 12-5

Levi's Extends Its Brand

Levi Strauss is an iconic American brand, best known for the distinctive red tab on the back pocket of its jeans. Founded in 1853 by Bavarian immigrant Levi Strauss, Levi Strauss & Co. grew to be one of the world's largest apparel companies with more than $6 billion in revenue and cachet as the cool jeans teens aspired to wear. During the late 1990s, though, Levi's faced declining sales and growing debt. The company's long history and tradition of producing durable jeans became a liability for its fashion image. The San Francisco–based company remained private despite pressure to take all or part of the company public to pay down debt.

Levi-Strauss licensed the image of the famous celebrity Andy Warhol to launch the $200 jeans, "Warhol Factory X Levi's."

For years market power had been shifting away from suppliers like Levi and toward retailers. Mass merchants were selling about one-third of all jeans in the United States, and their share of the market was growing. The advent of discount stores made many consumers more price-sensitive. In 1999, Levi Strauss brought in a new CEO, Philip Marineau, from PepsiCo. Marineau favored increased segmentation as a way to boost sales, so Levi's adopted a segmentation strategy to convince different types of retailers (department stores, specialty chains, upscale boutiques, and mass merchants) to carry Levi's products.

With the segmentation strategy, Levi's brands ranged from a relatively inexpensive discount line to $150-and-up vintage designs. Levi's had already sold to J.C. Penney Co. and Sears, Roebuck and Co., and those choices had alienated some major retail customers who preferred the brand remain exclusive and slightly more upscale. Despite concerns among management about potential reputation damage, Levi created the Levi Strauss Signature brand to sell at mass merchants and began selling to Wal-Mart in 2003.

The Levi Strauss Signature brand carried new labels and styles manufactured from less expensive fabric. The company positioned it as a premium mass brand. Gone were the red tab and traditional Levi pocket stitching and logo. The Signature brand featured the Levi's name in cursive. Levi priced Signature jeans at $23—more than other mass brands but below Levi's $29

Evaluating Brand Extension Opportunities

Academic research and industry experience have revealed a number of principles governing successful brand extensions. Marketers must consider their strategies carefully by systematically following the steps listed in Figure 12-6 and use managerial judgment and marketing research to help make *each* of these decisions.

regular brand. The new brand initially experienced some bumps. Wal-Mart's other jeans were priced at $15 to $18 and outsold the Signature brand. In response, Wal-Mart lowered the price of men's Levi Strauss Signature jeans from $23 to $19, squeezing Levi's profit margins. To improve margins, in 2005, the Signature line was expanded to include an Authentics collection, with more fashion-conscious fits and finishes, priced at about $25.

Initially, the segmentation strategy also created rough spots for other Levi's brands. As Levi's executives struggled to appease Wal-Mart and find the right price point for mass retailers, other parts of the business suffered. Orders from department stores slipped and sales of regular Levi's, which had finally steadied leading up to the launch of the Signature brand, resumed their decline. Furthermore, a new high-fashion line called Type 1 failed. In 2006, however, Wal-Mart's price-chopping move ultimately proved effective and the Signature jeans began to sell more quickly. The company also added lines of baby clothing, bags and wallets, and men's khaki pants under its Signature brand

Around the same time, the company's expansion into premium segments began to pay off as well. Levi's began selling its premium lines, such as Levi's Capital E, to Bloomingdales and Barney's New York, which had not carried the brand for years, and reported strong sales. In early 2006, Levi's launched a new style that integrated a special pocket and controls for an iPod music player and retailed for $200. The segmentation strategy seems to have worked to some extent. The company posted a profit in early 2006, ending an eight-year sales decline.

LEVI'S JEAN SEGMENTS

Brand	Price Range
Levi Strauss Signature	$19–$23
Levi Strauss Signature Authentics	$24–$25
Levi's Redtab	$25–$50
Levi's Silvertab	$25–$58
Levi's Red	$49–$68
Levi's Capital E	$70–$178
Levi's Vintage	$80–$325

Sources: www.levi.com; Sandra O'Loughlin, "Levi Strauss Seeing Green with Signature Blues," *Brandweek,* 25 July 2005; "In Bow to Retailer's New Clout, Levi Strauss Makes Alterations," *Wall Street Journal,* 17 June 2004; Robert Guy Matthews, "Levi Strauss Bowwows a Page from Shakespeare," *Wall Street Journal,* 14 January 2005; Sandra O'Loughlin, "Dockers Addresses Growth by Dropping 'Pants'," *Brandweek,* 12 September 2005; "The Original Denim Brand Kicks Off the Next Revolution in Digital Music Storage," *Business Wire,* 20 January 2006; Jacques Chevron, "Tacit Messages: A Lesson from Levi's," *Brandweek,* 6 February 2006; "Strauss & Co.; On the Record: Phil Marineau," *San Francisco Chronicle,* 6 March 2006.

1. Define actual and desired consumer knowledge about the brand (e.g., create mental map and identify key sources of equity).
2. Identify possible extension candidates on basis of parent brand associations and overall similarity or fit of extension to the parent brand.
3. Evaluate the potential of the extension candidate to create equity according to the three-factor model:
   - Salience of parent brand associations
   - Favorability of inferred extension associations
   - Uniqueness of inferred extension associations
4. Evaluate extension candidate feedback effects according to the four-factor model:
   - How compelling the extension evidence is
   - How relevant the extension evidence is
   - How consistent the extension evidence is
   - How strong the extension evidence is
5. Consider possible competitive advantages as perceived by consumers and possible reactions initiated by competitors.
6. Design marketing campaign to launch extension.
7. Evaluate extension success and effects on parent brand equity.

FIGURE 12-6

Steps in Successfully Introducing Brand Extensions

Define Actual and Desired Consumer Knowledge about the Brand

It's critical for marketers to fully understand the depth and breadth of awareness of the parent brand, and the strength, favorability, and uniqueness of its associations. Moreover, marketers must know what is to be the basis of positioning and core benefits satisfied by the brand. Profiling actual and desired knowledge structures helps to identify possible brand extensions as well as to guide decisions that contribute to their success. In evaluating an extension, a company must understand where it would like to take the brand in the long run. Because the introduction of an extension can change brand meaning, it can affect consumer response to all subsequent marketing activity as well (see Chapter 13).

Identify Possible Extension Candidates

Chapter 11 described a number of consumer, firm, and competitor criteria for choosing which products and markets a firm should enter. With respect to consumer factors, marketers should consider parent brand associations—especially as they relate to brand positioning and core benefits—and product categories that might seem to fit with that brand image in the minds of consumers.[44] Although consumers are generally better able to react to an extension concept than to suggest one, it still may be instructive to ask consumers what products the brand should consider offering if it were to introduce a new product. Brainstorming is another way to generate category extension candidates, along with consumer research.

One or more associations can often serve as the basis of fit. Figure 12-7 displays an analysis by Ed Tauber of possible extensions of the Vaseline Intensive Care brand that recognize the range of associations held by consumers. Consider how Lucozade was transformed in the United Kingdom through brand extensions.

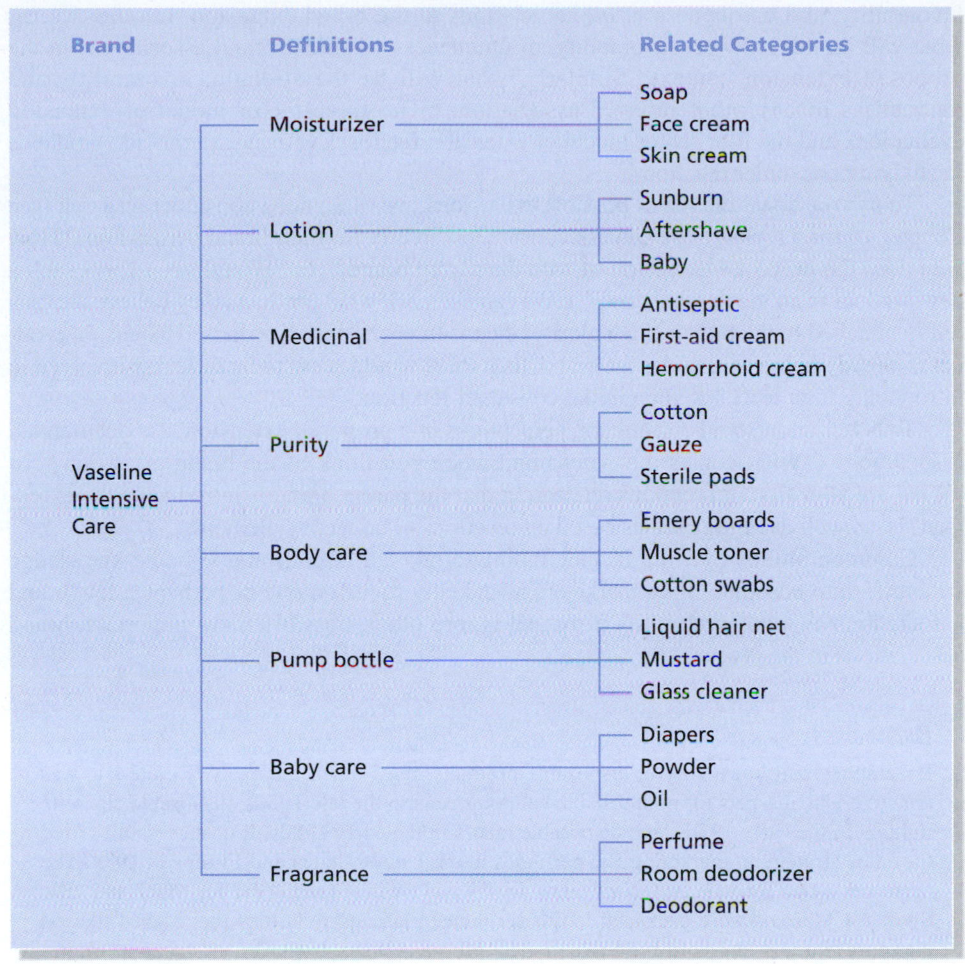

FIGURE 12-7

Possible Extensions of Vaseline Intensive Care Brand

LUCOZADE

Beecham marketed Lucozade in Britain for years as a glucose drink to combat dehydration and other maladies of sick children. By introducing new flavor formulas, packaging formats, and so forth, Beecham was able to capitalize on the association of the brand as a "fluid replenisher" to transform its meaning to "a healthy sports drink for people of all ages." Reinforced by ads featuring the famous British Olympic decathlete Daley Thompson, sales and profits for the brand increased dramatically. Thus, by recognizing that Lucozade did not have to be just a pharmaceutical product but could be repositioned through brand extensions and other marketing activity as a healthy and nutritious drink, Beecham was able to credibly transform the brand.[45]

Evaluate the Potential of the Extension Candidate

In forecasting the success of a proposed brand extension, marketers should assess—through judgment and research—the likelihood that the extension will realize the advantages and avoid the disadvantages of brand extensions as summarized in Figures 12-2 and 12-4. As with any new product, analysis of consumer, corporate, and competitive factors can be useful.

Consumer Factors. To evaluate the potential of a proposed brand extension, we assess its ability to achieve its own brand equity, as well as the likelihood that it can affect the existing brand equity of the parent brand. First, marketers must forecast the strength, favorability, and uniqueness of *all* associations to the brand extension. In other words, what will be the salience, favorability, or uniqueness of parent brand associations in the proposed extension context? Similarly, what will be the strength, favorability, and uniqueness of any other inferred associations? The three-factor model of extension evaluations and the four-factor model of extension feedback effects can provide guidance in studying consumer reactions.

To narrow down the list of possible extensions, we often need consumer research (see Chapter 10 for a review). We can ask consumers directly for their brand permission ("How well does the proposed extension fit with the parent brand?" or "Would you expect such a new product from the parent brand?"). We can even ask what products they believe are currently attached to the brand: If a majority of consumers believe a proposed extension product is already being sold under the brand, then there would seem to be little risk involved in introducing it, at least based on initial consumer reaction.

To better understand consumers' perceptions of a proposed extension, use open-ended associations ("What comes into your mind when you think of the brand extension?" or "What are your first impressions on hearing that the parent brand is introducing the extension?"), as well as ratings scales based on reactions to concept statements.

Common pitfalls to avoid include failing to take all of consumers' brand knowledge structures into account. Often marketers mistakenly focus on one or perhaps a few brand associations as a potential basis of fit and ignore other, possibly more important, brand associations in the process.

BIC

By emphasizing inexpensive, disposable products, the French company Société Bic was able to create markets for nonrefillable ballpoint pens in the late 1950s, disposable cigarette lighters in the early 1970s, and disposable razors in the early 1980s. It unsuccessfully tried the same strategy in marketing Bic perfumes in the United States and Europe in 1989. The perfumes—two for women ("Nuit" and "Jour") and two for men ("Bic for Men" and "Bic Sport for Men")—were packaged in quarter-ounce glass spray bottles that looked like fat cigarette lighters and sold for $5 each. The products were displayed on racks in plastic packages at checkout counters throughout Bic's extensive distribution channels, which included 100,000 or so drugstores, supermarkets, and other mass merchandisers. At the time, a Bic spokeswoman described the new products as extensions of the Bic heritage—"high quality at affordable prices, convenient to purchase, and convenient to use."[46] The brand extension was launched with a $20 million advertising and promotion campaign containing images of stylish people enjoying themselves with the perfume and using the tag line "Paris in Your Pocket." Nevertheless, Bic was unable to overcome its lack of cachet and negative image associations; by failing to achieve a critical point of parity, the extension was a failure.

Another major mistake in evaluating brand extensions is overlooking how literal consumers can be in evaluating brand extensions. Although consumers ultimately care about benefits, they often notice and evaluate attributes—especially concrete ones—in reacting to an extension. Brand managers, though, tend to focus on perceived benefits in predicting consumer reactions, and, as a result, they may overlook some potentially damaging attribute associations. For example, in 1992 Bausch & Lomb introduced Bausch & Lomb Clear Choice, a colorless, alcohol-free mouthwash. This brand extension was thought to fit with Bausch & Lomb's strategy of marketing care products for "above-the-shoulders" orifices—the eyes, ears, nose, and throat—but the Bausch & Lomb name, traditionally associated with contact lenses and eye care, was not easily transferred to mouthwash, and the product never gained significant market share before being discontinued in 1995.[47]

Corporate and Competitive Factors. Marketers must take not only a consumer perspective in evaluating a proposed brand extension, but also a broader corporate and competitive perspective. How effectively are the corporate assets leveraged in the extension setting? How relevant are existing marketing programs, perceived benefits, and target customers to the extension? What are the competitive advantages to the extension as consumers perceive them, and possible reactions initiated by competitors as a result?

Too many extension products and too strongly entrenched competition can put a strain on company resources. For example, Church & Dwight in the 1980s decided to extend its Arm & Hammer baking soda brand and its familiar yellow box into a variety of new product categories—toothpaste, carpet deodorizer, air freshener, antiperspirant, and so forth. Despite some early successes, the company had one of its worst years ever in 1994 as earnings fell 77 percent from the previous year. What happened? The market share of two of its more promising product introductions—toothpaste and laundry detergent—fell sharply when, after observing increased consumer acceptance of baking soda–based products, packaged-goods giants such as Procter & Gamble, Unilever, and Colgate-Palmolive aggressively introduced their own baking soda versions of these products. Priced higher and with less advertising support, Arm & Hammer's products lost market share. Church & Dwight management admitted that "it was too much for a company of our size to introduce so many new products in one year" and vowed to focus on existing products in the short run.

Design Marketing Programs to Launch Extension

Too often companies use extensions as a shortcut means of introducing a new product and pay insufficient attention to developing a branding and marketing strategy that will maximize the equity of the brand extension as well as enhance the equity of the parent brand. As is the case with a new brand, building brand equity for a brand extension requires choosing brand elements, designing the optimal marketing program to launch the extension, and leveraging secondary associations.

Choosing Brand Elements. By definition, a brand extension retains one or more elements from an existing brand. Marketers should realize that brand extensions do not necessarily have to leverage only a brand name but can use other brand elements too. For example, companies such as Heinz and Campbell Soup have implemented package designs that attempt to distinguish different line extensions or brand types but reveal their common origin at the same time.[48]

Sometimes packaging is such a critical component of equity for the brand that it is hard to imagine an extension without the same package design elements. Brand managers are in a real dilemma in such cases, because if they choose the same type of packaging, they run the risk that the extension will not be well distinguished. On the other hand, if they use a different type of packaging, a key source of brand equity may be left behind.

Kapferer describes the experiences of Kodak when it began marketing alkaline batteries under the Ultra Life brand name in 1985. Instead of the familiar yellow and red colors, the new battery had its own look and identity, with the Kodak name appearing in small type. After disappointing sales, Kodak changed the packaging to give more emphasis to the Kodak name and return to the more familiar Kodak look, with an immediate increase in sales.[49]

Thus, a brand extension can retain or modify one or more brand elements from the parent brand as well as adopt its own brand elements. In creating new brand elements for an extension, marketers should follow the same guidelines of memorability, meaningfulness, likeability, protectability, adaptability, and transferability that we described in Chapter 4 for the development of any brand. New brand elements are often necessary to help to distinguish the brand extension from the parent brand to build its awareness and image. As Chapter 11 noted, the relative prominence of existing parent brand elements and new extension brand elements will dictate the strength of transfer from the parent brand to the extension, as well as the feedback from the extension to the parent brand.

Designing Optimal Marketing Program. The marketing program for a brand extension must consider the same guidelines in building brand equity that we described in Chapters 5 and 6. Consumer perceptions of value must guide pricing decisions, distribution strategies must blend push and pull considerations, and the firm must integrate marketing communications by mixing and matching communication options.

When it comes to positioning, the less similar the extension is to the parent brand, the more important it typically is to establish necessary and competitive points of parity. The points of difference for a category extension in many cases directly follow from the points of difference for the parent brand, and consumers readily perceive them. Thus, when Nivea extended into shampoos and conditioners, deodorants, cosmetics and other beauty products, its key "gentleness" point of difference transferred relatively easily. With line extensions, on the other hand, marketers have to create a new association that can serve as an additional point of difference and help to distinguish the extension from the parent brand too.

For line extensions, consumers must also understand how the new product relates to existing products in order to minimize possible cannibalization or confusion. For example, in 2005 Anheuser-Busch launched Budweiser Select, a low-carb beer with no aftertaste positioned as an "upscale, white-collar brew." The emphasis on no aftertaste, however, drew an implicit comparison that cast other Anheuser-Busch products in a dim light and caused some consumers to abandon their usual Bud or Bud Light in favor of the new brand. As a result, nearly all of Bud Select's 1.3 percent share of supermarket sales earned in the month after its launch came at the expense of other Anheuser-Busch beers, which lost a share point during the same period.[50]

America Online, owned by Time Warner, ran into a similar problem when it extended the Netscape brand by using it to launch a low-cost dial-up-only Internet service provider (ISP) in 2004. At $9.95 per month, Netscape Internet service was priced well below $23.90 for standard AOL service and offered limited features. Ironically, the Netscape Internet service initially was bundled with Microsoft's Internet Explorer browser, not the latest version of the Netscape browser. For consumers who had known Netscape as an innovative pioneer of Internet browsers during the 1990s, seeing it emerge as a "cut-rate" ISP bundled with the arch-rival Internet Explorer browser was confusing and represented a "low point" for the brand.[51]

Leveraging Secondary Brand Associations. In general, brand extensions will often leverage the same secondary associations as the parent brand, although there may be instances in which competing in the extension category requires some additional fortification like linking to other entities. A brand extension differs in that, by definition, there is always some leveraging of another brand or company. The extent to which these other associations become linked to the extension, however, depends on the branding strategy the firm adopts and how it brands the extension. As we've seen, the more common the brand elements and the more prominence they receive, the more likely it is that parent brand associations will transfer.

Evaluate Extension Success and Effects on Parent Brand Equity

The final step in evaluating brand extension opportunities is to assess the extent to which an extension is able to achieve its own equity as well as contribute to the equity of the parent brand. To help measure its success, we can use brand tracking based on the

1. Does the parent brand have strong equity?
2. Is there sufficient equity transfer to the extension?
3. Is extension consistent with brand vision and essence?
4. Is it a logical fit that will make sense to target market(s)?
5. Will it create strong competitive positioning in new category?
6. Will it avoid creating negative associations in new category?
7. What implications will the extension have on brand equity?
8. Does it minimize downside risk and dilution?
9. Does it offer additional extension opportunities?
10. Will extension have necessary points of parity and points of difference?
11. How can the marketing program enhance extension equity?
12. Do the organizational skills and resources required to develop extension exist or can they be obtained?
13. How should extension feedback effects to the parent brand best be managed?

FIGURE 12-8
Brand Extension Checklist

customer-based brand equity model or other key measures of consumer response, centered on both the extension and the parent brand as a whole. Figure 12-8 contains a summary checklist of 13 important conceptual considerations in evaluating brand extensions. Brand Focus 12.0 describes a perceptive analysis of line extensions by Quelch and Kenny.

Extension Guidelines Based on Academic Research

Now we turn to some specific guidance about brand extensions. Fortunately, much academic research has focused on this strategy in recent years. We summarize some of the important conclusions in Figure 12-9 and describe them in detail in this section.

1. ***Successful brand extensions occur when the parent brand has favorable associations and consumers perceive a fit between the parent brand and the extension product.*** To better understand the process by which consumers evaluate a brand extension, many academic researchers have adopted a "categorization" perspective. Categorization research has its roots in psychological research that shows that people do not deliberately and individually evaluate each new stimulus to which they are exposed, but often evaluate a stimulus in terms of whether or not they can classify it as a member of a previously defined mental category, as illustrated by the following example.

    Assume you went to a party and found yourself in a conversation with an athletic-looking person who was casually dressed in sportswear and seemed to only want to talk about sports—what he or she read in the paper, saw on television, and was involved with as a participant. You might already have a mental category of a "sports fanatic" as someone who looked like a "jock" and read only the sports section of the newspaper, watched sports on television, and talked sports with friends and family. As a result of this knowledge, you might quickly categorize the person at the party as a "sports fanatic," and your evaluation of him or her would probably depend on how you felt about the category of sports fanatics in general. In contrast to this "categorical processing," assume that you went up to another person at the party. This extremely pale person was dressed in a very aggressive "punk" manner yet, at the same time, also seemed to only want to talk

1. Successful brand extensions occur when the parent brand is seen as having favorable associations and there is a perception of fit between the parent brand and the extension product.
2. There are many bases of fit: product-related attributes and benefits as well as non-product-related attributes and benefits related to common usage situations or user types.
3. Depending on consumer knowledge of the product categories, perceptions of fit may be based on technical or manufacturing commonalities or more surface considerations such as necessary or situational complementarity.
4. High-quality brands stretch farther than average-quality brands, although both types of brands have boundaries.
5. A brand that is seen as prototypical of a product category can be difficult to extend outside the category.
6. Concrete attribute associations tend to be more difficult to extend than abstract benefit associations.
7. Consumers may transfer associations that are positive in the original product class but become negative in the extension context.
8. Consumers may infer negative associations about an extension, perhaps even based on other inferred positive associations.
9. It can be difficult to extend into a product class that is seen as easy to make.
10. A successful extension can not only contribute to the parent brand image but also enable a brand to be extended even farther.
11. An unsuccessful extension hurts the parent brand only when there is a strong basis of fit between the two.
12. An unsuccessful extension does not prevent a firm from backtracking and introducing a more similar extension.
13. Vertical extensions can be difficult and often require sub-branding strategies.
14. The most effective advertising strategy for an extension is one that emphasizes information about the extension (rather than reminders about the parent brand).

FIGURE 12-9

Brand Extension Guidelines Based on Academic Research

about sports. Because of his or her appearance, this other person might not fit so neatly into your category of "sports fanatic," so you would have to form your evaluation in a more detailed fashion, that is, by "piecemeal processing" in which you constructed an attitude based on many different considerations.

We could argue that consumers use their categorical knowledge of brands and products to simplify, structure, and interpret their marketing environment.[52] For example, consumers may see brands as categories that over time have acquired a number of specific attributes based on the individual members of the brand category.[53] Nivea might be associated with "care," "mildness," "quality," and "beauty" as a result of its skin care, hair care, and cosmetic products.

In this categorization perspective, if consumers saw a brand extension as closely related or similar to the brand category, they could easily transfer their existing attitude about the parent brand to the extension. If they were not as sure about the similarity, they might evaluate the extension in a more detailed, piecemeal fashion. In this case, the favorability of any specific associations would determine how they viewed the extension.[54]

Thus, a categorization view considers consumers' evaluations of brand extensions to be a two-step process. First, consumers determine whether there is a match between what they know about the parent brand and what they believe to be true about the extension. Second, if the match is good, then consumers might transfer their existing brand attitudes to the extension. Otherwise, consumers might be more likely to evaluate the brand in a piecemeal fashion. Here, their evaluations would depend on the strength, favorability, and uniqueness of salient brand associations in the extension context.

Consistent with these notions, Aaker and Keller collected consumer reactions to 20 proposed extensions from six well-known brands and found that both a perception of fit between the original and extension product categories and a perception of high quality for the parent brand led to more favorable extension evaluations.[55] A number of subsequent studies have explored the generalizability of these findings to markets outside the United States. Based on a comprehensive analysis of 131 brand extensions from seven such replication studies around the world, Bottomly and Holden concluded that this basic model clearly generalized, although cross-cultural differences influenced the relative importance attached to the model components.[56]

Thus, in general, brand extensions are more likely to be favorably evaluated by consumers if they see some bases of fit or similarity between the proposed extension and parent brand.[57] A lack of fit may doom a potentially successful brand extension.[58]

2. ***There are many bases of fit: product-related attributes and benefits, as well as non-product-related attributes and benefits related to common usage situations or user types.*** Any association about the parent brand that consumers hold in memory may serve as a potential basis of fit. Most academic researchers assume that consumers' judgments of similarity are a function of salient shared associations between the parent brand and the extension product category. Specifically, the more common and fewer distinctive associations that exist, the greater the perception of overall similarity, whether based on product- or non-product-related attributes and benefits.[59] Consumers may also use attributes for a prototypical brand or a particular exemplar as the standard of reference for the extension category and form their perceptions of fit with the parent brand on that basis.

   To demonstrate how fit does not have to be based on product-related associations alone, Park, Milberg, and Lawson have distinguished between fit based on "product-feature similarity" (as described earlier) and "brand-concept consistency."[60] They define ***brand concepts*** as the brand-unique image associations that arise from a particular combination of attributes, benefits, and the marketing efforts used to translate these attributes into higher-order meanings (such as high status). ***Brand-concept consistency*** measures how well the brand concept accommodates the extension product. The important point these researchers make is that different types of brand concepts from the same original product category may extend into the same category with varying degrees of success, even when product-feature similarity is high.

   Park and his coauthors further distinguish between ***function-oriented brands,*** whose dominant associations relate to product performance (like Timex watches), and ***prestige-oriented brands,*** whose dominant associations relate to consumers' expression of self-concepts or images (like Rolex watches). Experimentally, they showed that the Rolex brand could more easily extend into categories such as grandfather clocks, bracelets, and rings than the Timex brand; however, Timex could more easily extend into categories such as stopwatches, batteries, and calculators than Rolex. In the former case, there was high brand-concept consistency for Rolex that overcame a lack of product-feature similarity; in the latter case, there was enough product-feature similarity to favor a function-oriented brand such as Timex.

Broniarczyk and Alba provide another compelling demonstration of the importance of recognizing salient brand associations. They show that a brand that may not even be as favorably evaluated as a competing brand in its category may be more successfully extended into certain categories, depending on the particular parent brand associations involved. For example, although Close-Up toothpaste was not as well liked by their sample as Crest toothpaste, a proposed Close-Up breath mint extension was evaluated more favorably than one from Crest. Alternatively, a proposed Crest toothbrush extension was evaluated more favorably than one from Close-Up. Figure 12-10 displays some of their experimental results from other categories.[61]

Broniarczyk and Alba also showed that a perceived lack of fit between the parent brand's product category and the proposed extension category could be overcome if key parent brand associations were salient and relevant in the extension category. For example, Froot Loops cereal—which has strong brand associations to "sweet," "flavor," and "kids"—was better able to extend to dissimilar product categories such as lollipops and popsicles than to similar product categories such as waffles and hot cereal, because of the relevance of its brand associations in the dissimilar extension category. The reverse was true for Cheerios cereal, however, which had a "healthy grain" association that was relevant only in similar extension product categories.

Thus, extension fit is more than just the number of common and distinctive brand associations between the parent brand and the extension product category.[62] These research studies and others demonstrate the importance of taking a broader perspective of categorization and fit. For example, Bridges, Keller, and Sood refer to "category coherence." Coherent categories are those whose members "hang together" and "make sense." According to these authors, to understand the rationale for a grouping of products in a brand line, a consumer needs "explanatory links" that tie the products together and summarize their relationship. For example, the physically dissimilar toy, bath care, and car seat products in the Fisher-Price product line can be united by the link "products for children."[63] Similarly, Schmitt and Dubé proposed that marketers view brand extensions as conceptual combinations.[64] A conceptual combination (such as "apartment dog") consists of a modifying concept, or "modifier" (apartment), and a modified concept, or "header" (dog). Thus, according to this view, a proposed brand extension such as McDonald's Theme Park would be

Product Category	Preferred Brand and Focal Brand	Corresponding Favorably Evaluated Extensions[a]
Cereal	Cheerios	Oatmeal; waffles
	Froot Loops	Lollipops
Soap	Camay	Moisturizer; cleansing cream
	Irish Spring	Deodorant
Computer	Apple	Video games
	IBM	Cellular phones
Beer	Coors	Wine coolers; bottled water
	Budweiser	Scotch

[a]The table should be interpreted as indicating that Cheerios was more successfully extended to oatmeal and waffles, whereas Froot Loops was more easily extended to lollipops, and so on.

FIGURE 12-10

Role of Brand-Specific Associations in Determining Fit

interpreted as the original brand or company name (McDonald's) acting on the "header concept" of the extension category (theme parks) as a "modifier."

Finally, researchers have explored other, more specific, aspects of fit. Boush provides experimental data as to the context sensitivity of fit judgments.[65] Similarity judgments between pairs of product categories were found to be asymmetrical, and brand name associations could reverse the direction of asymmetry. For example, more subjects agreed with the statement "*Time* magazine is like *Time* books" than with the statement, "*Time* books are like *Time* magazine," but without the brand names (just using "books" and "magazines"), the preferences were reversed. Smith and Andrews surveyed industrial goods marketers and found that the relationship between fit and new product evaluations was not direct but was mediated by customers' sense of certainty that a firm could provide a proposed new product.[66]

3. ***Depending on their knowledge of the product categories, consumers may perceive fit based on technical or manufacturing commonalities, or on surface considerations such as necessary or situational complementarity.*** Consumers can also base fit on considerations other than attributes or benefits. Taking a demand-side and supply-side perspective of consumer perceptions, Aaker and Keller showed that perceived fit between the parent brand and the extension product could be related to the economic notions of substitutability and complementarity in product use (from a demand-side perspective), as well as to the firm's perceived grasp of the skills and assets necessary to make the extension product (from a supply-side perspective). Thus, Honda's perceived expertise in making motors for lawn mowers and cars may help perceptions of fit for any other machinery with small motors that Honda might want to introduce. Similarly, expertise with small disposable products offers numerous opportunities for Bic. On the other hand, some extension examples have little manufacturing compatibility but greater usage complementarity, for example, Colgate's extension from toothpaste to toothbrushes or Duracell's extension from batteries to flashlights.

   These perceptions of fit, however, may depend on how much consumers know about the product categories. As demonstrated by Muthukrishnan and Weitz, knowledgeable "expert" consumers are more likely to use technical or manufacturing commonalities to judge fit, considering similarity in terms of technology, design and fabrication, and the materials and components used in the manufacturing process. Less knowledgeable "novice" consumers, on the other hand, are more likely to use superficial, perceptual considerations such as common package, shape, color, size, and usage.[67] Specifically, these researchers showed experimentally that less knowledgeable consumers were more likely to see a basis of fit between tennis racquets and tennis shoes than between tennis racquets and golf clubs, despite the fact that the latter actually share more manufacturing commonalities. The effects for more knowledgeable consumers were reversed because they recognized the technical synergies in manufacturing tennis racquets and golf clubs.

   Broniarczyk and Alba also showed that perceptions of fit on the basis of brand-specific associations were contingent on consumers having the necessary knowledge about the parent brand. Without such knowledge, consumers again tended to rely on more superficial considerations in forming extension evaluations, such as their level of awareness of or overall regard for the brand.[68]

4. ***High-quality brands stretch farther than average-quality brands, although both types have boundaries.*** Consumers often see high-quality brands as more credible, expert, and trustworthy. As a result, even though consumers may still believe a relatively distant extension does not really fit with the brand, they may be more willing to give a high-quality brand the benefit of the doubt. When they see a brand as more average in quality, however, they may be less willing to make such favorable source

attributions and more likely to question the company's ability or motives.[69] Thus, one important benefit of building a strong brand is that it can extend more easily into more diverse categories.[70]

Regardless, all brands have boundaries, as a number of observers have persuasively argued by pointing out ridiculous, and even comical, hypothetical brand extension possibilities. For example, as Tauber once noted, few consumers would want Jell-O shoelaces or Tide frozen entrees!

5. ***A brand that consumers see as prototypical for a product category can be difficult to extend outside the category.*** As a caveat to the previous conclusion, if consumers see a brand as exemplifying a category too strongly, it may be difficult for them to think of it in any other way. Numerous examples exist of category leaders that have failed in introducing brand extensions.[71] Bayer, a brand synonymous with aspirin, ran into a stumbling block introducing the Bayer Select line of specialized nonaspirin painkillers.[72] Chiquita was unsuccessful in its attempt to move beyond its strong "banana" association with a frozen juice bar extension.[73] Country Time could not overcome its "lemonade" association to introduce an apple cider. Perhaps the most extreme example are brands that lost their trademark distinctiveness and became a generic term for the category, such as Thermos and Kleenex.

   To illustrate the difficulty a prototypical brand may have in extending, consider Clorox, a well-known brand whose name is virtually synonymous with bleach. In 1988, Clorox took on consumer goods giants Procter & Gamble and Unilever by introducing the first bleach with detergent. After pouring $225 million into the development and distribution of its detergent products over three years, Clorox was able to achieve only a 3 percent market share. Despite being beaten to market, P&G subsequently introduced Tide with Bleach and was able to achieve a 17 percent market share. Reluctantly, Clorox chose to exit the market. Although a number of factors may have driven that decision, Clorox's failure can certainly be attributed in part to the fact that consumers could think of Clorox only in a very limited sense as a bleach product. On the other hand, Clorox has successfully extended its brand into household cleaning products like toilet bowl cleaners, where the bleach ingredient is seen as more relevant.

   Also note that Clorox's extension may have failed because in a combined "laundry detergent with bleach" product, consumers see laundry detergent as the primary ingredient and bleach as the secondary ingredient. As a result, we might expect a laundry detergent extension such as Tide with Bleach to have an advantage over a bleach extension such as Clorox when entering the combined laundry detergent with bleach category.[74] This reasoning might also explain why Aunt Jemima was successful in introducing a pancake syrup extension from its well-liked pancake mix product, but Log Cabin was less successful in introducing a pancake mix extension from its well-regarded pancake syrup product: Pancake mix is seen as a more dominant ingredient than pancake syrup in breakfast pancakes. The Science of Branding 12-2 describes an interesting approach to dealing with this extendability challenge.

6. ***Concrete attribute associations tend to be more difficult to extend than abstract benefit associations.*** The limits to market leaders' extension boundaries may be more rigid because many market leaders have strong concrete product attribute associations. These may even be reinforced by their names, like Liquid Paper, Cheez Whiz, and Shredded Wheat.[75] La-Z-Boy, for example, has struggled to expand outside the narrow product line of recliners and its strong usage imagery.

THE SCIENCE OF BRANDING 12-2

Understanding Master Brands

Farquhar, Herr, and their colleagues have developed an intriguing approach to generating brand extension possibilities for prototypical brands and market leaders. They define a ***master brand*** as an established brand so dominant in customers' minds that it "owns" a particular association: The mention of a product attribute or category, a usage situation, or a customer benefit instantly brings a master brand to mind. Examples of master brands, according to these researchers, include Arm & Hammer baking soda, Band-Aid adhesive bandages, Bacardi rum, Alka-Seltzer antacid, Jell-O gelatin, Campbell's soup, Crayola crayons, Morton salt, Lionel toy trains, Philadelphia cream cheese, and Vaseline petroleum jelly.

Recognizing that the exceptionally strong associations of a master brand often make it difficult to extend it directly to other product categories, they propose strategies to extend master brands *indirectly* by leveraging alternative master brand associations that come from different parts of the brand hierarchies. Specifically, they describe the brand-leveraging compass to illustrate four principal directions for leveraging master brands:

1. *Sub-branding* introduces a new element into the brand hierarchy below the level of the master brand to refine or modify its meaning (such as DuPont Stainmaster carpet).
2. *Super-branding* adds new elements to an existing brand hierarchy above the level of the master brand, typically to suggest some product improvement (such as Eveready Energizer batteries).
3. *Brand bundling,* or "cross branding," fortifies a master brand through associations with other brands, including cooperative or co-branding (for instance, Citibank AAdvantage Visa card).
4. *Brand bridging* uses the master brand to endorse a new brand as the company attempts to move to a more distant product category (T/Gel therapeutic shampoo was initially endorsed by Neutrogena).

These strategies, all of which we have discussed in prior chapters, can be different means to shield the parent or master brand by creating some distance to the extension, and to build brand equity for the extension by incorporating additional brands or brand elements. The authors note that marketing efforts can also "stay close to home" and fortify master brands by strengthening the brand's basic competencies, attracting new users, and developing new uses or expanding consumption among current users.

Source: Peter H. Farquhar, Julia Y. Han, Paul M. Herr, and Yuji Ijiri, "Strategies for Leveraging Master Brands," *Marketing Research* (September 1992): 32–43. Courtesy of American Marketing Association.

Concrete attribute associations may not transfer as broadly to extension categories as more abstract attribute associations. For example, the Aaker and Keller study showed that consumers dismissed a hypothetical Heineken popcorn extension as potentially tasting bad or like beer; a hypothetical Vidal Sassoon perfume extension as having an undesirably strong shampoo scent; and a hypothetical Crest chewing gum extension as tasting unappealing or like toothpaste. In each case, consumers inferred a concrete attribute association for an extension that was technically feasible, even though common sense might have suggested that a manufacturer logically would not be expected to introduce a product with such an attribute.

More abstract associations, on the other hand, may be more relevant across a wide set of categories because of their intangible nature. For example, the Aaker and Keller study also showed that the Vuarnet brand had a remarkable ability to be exported to a disparate set of product categories, such as sportswear, watches, wallets, and even skis. In these cases, complementarity may have led consumers to infer that the extension would have the "stylish" attribute associated with the Vuarnet name, and they valued such an association in the different extension contexts.

We should note several caveats, however, concerning the relative extendability of concrete and abstract associations. First, concrete attributes can transfer to some product categories.[76] For example, if the parent brand has a concrete attribute association that is highly valued in the extension category because it creates a distinctive taste, ingredient, or component, an extension on that basis can often be successful. According to Farquhar and Herr, examples of such extensions might include Philadelphia cream cheese salad dressing, Tylenol sinus medication, Häagen-Dazs cream liqueur, Oreo cookies and cream ice cream, and Arm & Hammer carpet deodorizer.[77]

Second, abstract associations may not always transfer easily. This second caveat emerged from a study conducted by Bridges, Keller, and Sood, who examined the relative transferability of product-related brand information when it was represented either as an abstract brand association or as a concrete brand association.[78] For example, one such comparison contrasted the relative transferability of a watch characterized by dominant concrete attribute associations such as "water-resistant quartz movements, a time-keeping mechanism encased in shockproof steel covers, and shatterproof crystal," with that of a watch characterized by dominant abstract attribute associations such as "durable." Although these authors expected the abstract brand representation to fare better, they found that, for several reasons, the two types of brand images extended equally well into a dissimilar product category (handbags). Perhaps the most important reason was that consumers did not believe the abstract benefit would have the same meaning in the extension category (durability does not necessarily "transfer" because durability for a watch is not the same as durability for a handbag).

Finally, Joiner and Loken, in a demonstration of the "inclusion effect" in a brand extension setting, showed that consumers often generalized possession of an attribute from a specific category (like Sony televisions) to a more general category (say, all Sony products) more readily than they generalized the attribute from the specific category (Sony televisions) to another specific category (Sony bicycles). The effect was greater the more the specific extension category was typical of the general category (Sony cameras are more typical than Sony bicycles).[79]

7. ***Consumers may transfer associations that are positive in the original product class but become negative in the extension context.*** Because they have different motivations

or use the product differently in the extension category, consumers may not value a brand association as highly as the original product. For example, when Campbell test-marketed a tomato sauce with the Campbell's name, it flopped. Apparently, Campbell's strong associations to soup signaled to consumers that the new product would be watery. To give the product more credibility, Campbell changed the name to the Italian-sounding "Prego," and the product has gone on to be a long-term success.

8. ***Consumers may infer negative associations about an extension, perhaps even based on other inferred positive associations.*** Even if consumers transfer positive associations from the parent brand to the extension, they may still infer other negative associations. For example, the Bridges, Keller, and Sood study showed that even if consumers thought a proposed handbag extension from a hypothetical maker of durable watches also would be durable, they often assumed that it would not be fashionable, helping to contribute to low extension evaluations.[80]

9. ***It can be difficult to extend into a product class that consumers see as easy to make.*** Consumers may dismiss some seemingly appropriate extensions if they see the product as comparatively easy to make and brand differences are hard to come by. Then a high-quality brand may seem incongruous; alternatively, consumers may feel that the brand extension will attempt to command an unreasonable price premium and be too expensive.

   For example, Aaker and Keller showed that hypothetical extensions such as Heineken popcorn, Vidal Sassoon perfume, Crest shaving cream, and Häagen-Dazs cottage cheese received relatively poor marks from experimental subjects in part because all brands in the extension category were seen as being about the same in quality, suggesting that the proposed brand extension was unlikely to be superior to existing products. The failure of designers such as Bill Blass and Gloria Vanderbilt to introduce certain products such as chocolates and perfume under their names may be in part a result of these perceptions of incongruity, lack of differentiation, and unwarranted price premiums.

   When consumers see the extension category as difficult to make, on the other hand, such that brands can vary a great deal in quality, a brand extension has a greater opportunity to differentiate itself, although consumers may also be less sure what the exact quality level of the extension will be.[81]

10. ***A successful extension can not only contribute to the parent brand image but also enable a brand to extend even farther.*** An extension can help the image of the parent brand by improving the strength, favorability, or uniqueness of its associations. For example, Keller and Aaker showed that when consumers did not already have strongly held attitudes, the successful introduction of a brand extension improved their evaluations of a parent brand that they originally perceived to be of only average quality. Finally, the associations that become linked to the parent brand by virtue of the extension product category may help clarify the basic core benefits for the brand. For example, one of Australia's leading cereal brands, Uncle Toby's, was able to broaden its meaning to a "healthy breakfast and snack food" by introducing muesli bars and other products.

    If an extension changes the image and meaning of the brand, then subsequent brand extensions that otherwise might not have seemed appropriate to consumers may make more sense and appear to be a better fit. For example, Keller and Aaker showed that by taking little steps, that is, by introducing a series of closely related but increasingly distant extensions, marketers may insert brands into product categories that would have been much more difficult, or perhaps even impossible, to enter directly.[82]

DUNHILL

The Dunhill brand provides an excellent example of gradually extending a brand to transform its meaning.[83] For all practical purposes, Dunhill started as a cigarette brand that was first extended into smoking accessories, including pipes, pouches, and lighters. After establishing itself there, the brand extend into other high-end men's accessories like belts, desktop items, cufflinks, rings, and clothing. Most recently, the company extended the brand yet again into male fragrances and mainstream fashion items. As a result of all this extension activity, the Dunhill brand now not only represents a leading cigarette brand but also "luxury products and accessories for both men and women." Said one commentator, "It used to be all about gold cigarette cases and lighters, but Dunhill has managed to become smart without being stuffy or boring."[84]

Boush and Loken found that consumers evaluated far extensions from a "broad" brand more favorably than from a "narrow" brand.[85] Dacin and Smith have shown that if the perceived quality levels of different members of a brand portfolio are more uniform, then consumers tend to make higher, more confident evaluations of a proposed new extension.[86] They also showed that a firm that had demonstrated little variance in quality across a diverse set of product categories was better able to overcome perceptions of lack of extension fit. In other words, it is as if consumers in this case think, "Whatever the company does, it tends to do well."

In an empirical study of 95 brands in 11 nondurable consumer goods categories, Sullivan found that, in terms of stages of the product category life cycle, early-entering brand extensions did not perform as well, on average, as either early-entering new-name products or late-entering brand extensions.[87] DeGraba and Sullivan provided an economic analysis to help interpret this observation.[88] They posited that the major source of uncertainty in introducing a new product is the inability to know whether it will be received by customers in a way that will allow it to be a commercial success. They further argued that this source of uncertainty could be mitigated by spending more time on the development process. Under such assumptions, they showed that the large spillover effects triggered by introducing a poorly received brand extension caused introducers of brand extensions to spend more time on the development process than did introducers of new-name products.

11. ***An unsuccessful extension hurts the parent brand only when there is a strong basis of fit between the two.*** The general rule of thumb emerging from academic research and industry experience is that an unsuccessful brand extension can damage the parent brand only when there is a high degree of similarity or fit—for example, in the case of a failed line extension in the same category. Roedder John and Loken found that perceptions of quality for a parent brand in the health and beauty aids area decreased with the hypothetical introduction of a lower-quality extension in a similar product category (shampoo). Quality perceptions of the parent brand were unaffected, however, when the proposed extension was in a dissimilar product category (facial tissue).[89] Similarly, Keller and Aaker as well as Romeo found that unsuccessful extensions in dissimilar product categories did not affect evaluations of the parent brand.[90] When the brand extension is farther removed, it seems easier for consumers to compartmentalize the brand's products and disregard its performance in what is seen as an unrelated product category.

    Additional research reinforces and amplifies this conclusion. Roedder John, Loken, and Joiner found that dilution effects were less likely to be present with flagship products and occurred with line extensions but were not always evident for more dissimilar category extensions.[91] Gürhan-Canli and Maheswaran extended the results of these studies by considering the moderating effect of consumer motivation and extension typicality.[92] In high-motivation conditions, they found that incongruent extensions were scrutinized in detail and led to the modification of family brand evaluations, regardless of the typicality of the extensions. In low-motivation conditions, however, brand evaluations were more extreme in the context of high (than low) typicality. Because consumers considered the less typical extension an exception, it had reduced impact. Consistent with these high-motivation findings, Milberg and colleagues found that negative feedback effects were present when (1) consumers perceived extensions as belonging to product categories dissimilar from those associated with the family brand, and (2) extension attribute information was inconsistent with image beliefs that consumers associated with the family brand.[93]

In terms of individual differences, Lane and Jacobson found some evidence of a negative reciprocal impact from brand extensions, especially for high-need-for-cognition subjects, but did not explore extension similarity differences.[94] Kirmani, Sood, and Bridges found dilution effects with owners of prestige-image automobiles when low-priced extensions were introduced, but not with owners of nonprestige automobiles or nonowners of either automobile.[95]

Finally, Morrin examined the impact of brand extensions on the strength of parent brand associations in memory. Two computer-based studies revealed that exposing consumers to brand extension information strengthened rather than weakened parent brand associations in memory, particularly for parent brands that were dominant in their original product category. Higher fit also resulted in greater facilitation, but only for nondominant parent brands. Moreover, improvements in memory for the parent brand due to the advertised introduction of an extension was not as great as when the same level of advertising directly promoted the parent brand.[96]

12. ***An unsuccessful extension does not prevent a firm from backtracking and introducing a more similar extension.*** The Keller and Aaker study also showed that unsuccessful extensions do not necessarily prevent a company from retrenching and later introducing a more similar extension. Consider the failure of Levi's Tailored Classics. In the early 1980s, Levi Strauss attempted to introduce a Tailored Classics line of men's suits. Levi's Tailored Classics was targeted to independent-thinking "clothes horses," dubbed by research "Classic Individualists." Although the suit was not supposed to need tailoring, to allow for the better fit necessary for these demanding consumers, Levi Strauss designed the suit slacks and coat to be sold as separates. It chose to price these wool suits quite competitively and to distribute them through its existing department store accounts, instead of the specialty stores where the classic individualist traditionally shopped. Despite a determined marketing effort, the product failed to achieve its desired sales goals. There were problems with the chosen target market, distribution channels, and product design, but perhaps the most fundamental problem was the lack of fit between the Levi's informal, rugged, outdoor image and the image the company sought from its suits.

    Despite the ultimate withdrawal of the product, Levi Strauss later was able to execute one of the most successful apparel launches ever—Dockers pants. As these experiences with brand extensions illustrate, failure does not doom a firm *never* to be able to introduce any extensions—certainly not for a brand with as much equity as Levi's. An unsuccessful extension does, however, create a "perceptual boundary" of sorts, in that it reveals the limits of the brand in the minds of consumers. It does not preclude a firm from later introducing an extension with a higher degree of fit, however, as Levi Strauss was able to discover.

13. ***Vertical extensions can be difficult and often require sub-branding strategies.*** For market reasons or competitive considerations, it may be desirable for the firm to introduce a lower-priced version of a product or stretch the brand downward by vertically extending. The danger with such an extension strategy, however, is that the parent brand image could be cheapened or tarnished in some way.

BRANDING BRIEF 12-6

Expanding the Marriott Brand

Marriott International grew to an international hospitality giant from humble roots as a single root beer stand started by John and Alice Marriott in Washington, D.C., during the 1920s. The Marriotts added hot food to their root beer stand and renamed their business the Hot Shoppe, which they incorporated in 1929 when they began building a regional chain of restaurants. As the number of Hot Shoppes in the Southeast grew, Marriott expanded into in-flight catering by serving food on Eastern, American, and Capital Airlines beginning in 1937. In 1939, Hot Shoppes began its food service management business when it opened a cafeteria in the U.S. Treasury building. The company expanded into another hospitality sector in 1957, when Hot Shoppes opened its first hotel in Arlington, Virginia. Hot Shoppes, which was renamed Marriott Corporation in 1967, grew nationally and internationally by way of strategic acquisitions and entering new service categories; by 1977, sales topped $1 billion.

Marriott has found success in developing a strong brand portfolio.

In the pursuit of continued growth, Marriott continued to diversify its business. Marriott's 1982 acquisition of Host International made it America's top operator of airport food and beverage facilities. Over the course of the following three years, Marriott added 1,000 food service accounts by purchasing three food service companies: Gladieux, Service Systems, and Saga Corporation. Determining that its high penetration in the traditional hotel market did not offer many opportunities for growth, the company initiated a segmented marketing strategy for its hotels by introducing the moderately priced Courtyard by Marriott hotels in 1983. Moderately priced hotels constituted the largest segment of the U.S. lodging industry, a segment filled with established competitors such as Holiday Inn, Ramada, and Quality Inn. Research conducted by Marriott registered the greatest consumer dissatisfaction in the moderately priced hotels, and Courtyard hotels were designed to offer travelers greater convenience and amenities, such as balconies and patios, large desks and sofas, and pools and spas.

As a result, firms often adopt sub-branding strategies as a means to distinguish their lower-priced entries. For example, Gillette introduced the Good News brand as a line of inexpensive personal care products such as disposable razors. US Airways introduced US Airways Shuttle as an inexpensive short-haul carrier to compete with no-frills Southwest Airlines in the lucrative Eastern corridor market. Courtyard by Marriott was a lower-priced version of the regular Marriott and upscale Marriott Marquis hotel chains (see Branding Brief 12-6). Such extension introductions clearly must be handled carefully; typically, the parent brand plays a secondary role.

Early success with Courtyard prompted Marriott to expand further. In 1984, Marriott entered the vacation timesharing business by acquiring American Resorts Group. The following year, the company purchased Howard Johnson Company, selling the hotels and retaining the restaurants and rest stops. In 1987, Marriott added three new market segments: Marriott Suites, full-service suite accommodations; Residence Inn, extended-stay rooms for business travelers; and Fairfield Inn, an economy hotel brand. A company spokesman explained this rapid expansion: "There is a lot of segmentation that's going on in the hotel business. Travelers are sophisticated and have many wants and needs. In addition to that, we saw there would be a finite . . . ability to grow the traditional business."

Marriott Corporation split into two in 1993, forming Host Marriott to own the hotel properties and Marriott International primarily to engage in the more lucrative practice of managing them and franchising its brands. In 1995, Marriott International bought a minority stake in the Ritz-Carlton luxury hotel group (Marriott purchased the remaining share in 1998). In 1997, it expanded again by acquiring the Renaissance Hotel Group and introducing TownePlace Suites, Fairfield Suites, and Marriott Executive Residences. Marriott added a new hotel brand in 1998 with the introduction of SpringHill Suites, which provide moderate-priced suites that are 25 percent larger than standard hotel rooms. The following year, the company acquired corporate housing specialist ExecuStay Corporation and formed ExecuStay by Marriott. Its size and breadth enabled Marriott to recover from the post-September 11 travel and tourism downturn, and by 2004 Marriott's net income per share was down only 3 percent from 2000 levels and its revenue per available room was $69 per night, $20 above the industry average.

The last Hot Shoppe restaurant, located in a shopping mall in Washington, D.C., closed on December 2, 1999. This closing was fitting, since the tiny restaurant in no way resembled the multinational hospitality leader it spawned. Today, Marriott International is the largest hotel and resort company in America; with 374,000 rooms in the United States, it controls up to one-third of available rooms in some markets. It is also one of the leading hospitality companies in the world, maintaining well over half a million rooms in 68 countries that brought in almost $12 billion in global revenues in 2005.

Sources: www.marriott.com; Kim Clark, "Lawyers Clash on Timing of Marriott's Plan to Split," *Baltimore Sun,* 27 September 1994; Neil Henderson, "Marriott Gambles on Low-Cost, Classy Suburban Motels," *Washington Post,* 18 June 1994; Neil Henderson, "Marriott Bares Courtyard Plans," *Washington Post,* 12 June 1984; Elizabeth Tucker, "Marriot's Recipe for Corporate Growth," *Washington Post,* 1 June 1987; Paul Farhi, "Marriott to Sell 800 Restaurants," *Washington Post,* 19 December 1989; Stephane Fitch, "Soft Pillows and Sharp Elbows," *Forbes,* 10 May 2004, 66.

An even more difficult vertical extension is an upward brand stretch.[97] In general, it is difficult to sufficiently change people's impressions of the brand to justify a significant upward extension.

GALLO

For years, Gallo stubbornly refused to put any other brand on the label of its better vintages than Gallo. Despite repeated ad campaigns that promised some new varietal would "change the way you think about Gallo" (as when the winery introduced White Grenache), many consumers continued to think of the brand as they did before—as a relatively inexpensive jug wine.[98] In 1995, recognizing the boundaries that exist with even strong brands, Gallo spent heavily to launch the more upscale Turning Leaf (priced at $7 to $8 a bottle), which contained no mention of the Gallo name. Several years later, it launched Gallo of Sonoma (priced at $10 to $30 a bottle) to better compete in the premium wine segment, using the founder's grandchildren as spokespeople in an intensive push and pull campaign. With a hip, young, and fun image, case sales volume tripled to 680,000 in 1999. The brand upgraded its image again in 2006, launching the Gallo Family Vineyards umbrella brand for its high-end wines like Gallo of Sonoma, which became a sub-brand known as Gallo Family Vineyards Sonoma Reserve. The new umbrella brand brought with it price increases of one to two dollars and "an overall upgrade in quality."[99]

Concern about the unwillingness of consumers to update their brand knowledge was what led Honda, Toyota, and Nissan to introduce their luxury car models as separate nameplates (Acura, Lexus, and Infiniti, respectively). As it turns out, product improvements to the upper ends of their brand lines since the introduction of these new car nameplates may have made it easier to bridge the gap into the luxury market with their brands.

At the same time, it is possible to use certain brand modifiers to signal a noticeable, although presumably not dramatic, quality improvement—for example, Ultra Dry Pampers, Extra Strength Tylenol, or PowerPro Dustbuster Plus. As noted earlier, Farquhar, Herr, and their colleagues state that this means of indirect extension, or "super-branding," may be less risky than direct extensions when moving a master brand up-market.[100] They recommend veiling the master brand from the customer's view. The idea would be for the new super-brand to draw attention to itself and the merits of the product and later unveil the super-brand's link to the "hidden master brand" to provide familiar reassurance to consumers. They caution that a premature connection with the master brand can generate skepticism and indecision, citing as supporting evidence Coleman's success at introducing up-market camping equipment first as Peak 1 and then only later making the Coleman connection.

Vertical extensions can be especially tricky for prestige brands. In such cases, firms must often maintain a balance between availability and scarcity such that people always aspire to be a customer and do not feel excluded. By launching ambitious marketing campaigns with such offerings as "How to Buy a Diamond" and "Pearl Authority," the tony retail chain Tiffany's has attempted to convince buyers of the quality of its products and the fact that they are attainable. With an average retail price of goods sold of around $250, Tiffany's has managed to maintain its lofty image while also drawing a wider array of customers.[101]

Comparatively little empirical academic research, however, has been conducted on this topic. In an empirical study of the U.S. mountain bicycle industry, Randall, Ulrich, and Reibstein found that brand price premium was significantly positively correlated with the quality of the lowest-quality model in the product line for the lower-quality segments of the market; for the upper-quality segments of the market, brand price premium was also significantly positively correlated with the quality of the highest-quality model in the product line. They concluded that these results suggest managers wishing to maximize the equity of their brands should offer only high-quality products, although overall profit maximization could dictate a different strategy.[102]

Kirmani, Sood, and Bridges examined the "ownership effect"—whereby owners have more favorable responses than nonowners to brand extensions—in the context of brand line stretches. They found that the ownership effect occurred for upward and downward stretches of nonprestige brands (like Acura) and for upward stretches of prestige brands (like Calvin Klein and BMW). For downward stretches of prestige brands, however, the ownership effect did not occur because of owners' desires to maintain brand exclusivity. In this situation, a sub-branding strategy protected owners' parent brand attitudes from dilution.[103]

14. ***The most effective advertising strategy for an extension is one that emphasizes information about the extension (rather than reminders about the parent brand).*** A number of studies have shown that the information provided about brand extensions, by triggering selective retrieval from memory, may frame the consumer decision process and affect extension evaluations. In general, the most effective strategy appears to be one that recognizes the type of information that is already salient for the brand in the minds of consumers when they first consider the proposed extension and highlights additional information that would otherwise be overlooked or misinterpreted.

For example, Aaker and Keller found that cueing or reminding consumers about the quality of a parent brand did not improve evaluations for poorly rated extensions. Because the brands they studied were well known and well liked, such reminders may have been unnecessary. Elaborating briefly on specific extension attributes about which consumers were uncertain or concerned, however, did lead to more favorable evaluations. Bridges, Keller, and Sood found that providing information could improve perceptions of fit in the following two cases when consumers perceived low fit between the brand and the extension.[104]

When the parent brand and the extension shared physical attributes but the parent brand image was non-product-related and based on abstract user characteristics, consumers tended to overlook an obvious explanatory link between the parent brand and extension on the basis of shared product features (a tennis shoe with a high-fashion image attempting to extend to work boots was not evaluated favorably). Information that raised the salience of the physical relationship relative to distracting non-product-related associations—a "relational" communication strategy—improved extension evaluations (when subjects were told the work boots would have leather uppers similar to those used in the tennis shoes).

When the parent brand and the extension shared only non-product-related associations and the parent brand image was product-related, consumers often made negative inferences on the basis of existing associations (a tennis shoe with an image for durability attempting to extend to swimsuits was seen as unfashionable). In this case, providing information that established an explanatory link on an entirely new, "reassuring" association—an "elaborational" communication strategy—improved extension evaluations (when subjects were told the swimsuits would be similar in fashionability to the tennis shoes).[105]

Lane found that repetition of an ad that evoked primarily benefit brand associations could overcome negative perceptions of a highly incongruent brand extension. Moreover, for moderately incongruent brand extensions, even ads that evoked peripheral brand associations (say, via brand packaging or character) could improve negative extension perceptions with sufficient repetition.[106] In a somewhat similar vein, Barone, Miniard, and Romeo experimentally demonstrated that positive mood primarily enhanced evaluations of extensions that consumers viewed as moderately similar (as opposed to very similar or dissimilar) to a favorably evaluated core brand.[107]

Research has also explored several other aspects of extension marketing programs. Keller and Sood found that "branding effects" in terms of inferences based on parent brand knowledge operated both in the absence and presence of product experience with an extension, although they were less pronounced or, in the case of an unambiguous negative experience, even nonexistent.[108] In considering the effects of retailer displays, Buchanan, Simmons, and Bickart found that evaluations of a "high-equity" brand could be diminished by an unfamiliar competitive brand when (1) a mixed display structure led consumers to believe that the competitive brand was diagnostic for judging the high-equity brand, (2) the precedence given to one brand over another in the display made expectations about brand differences or similarities accessible, and (3) the unfamiliar competitive brand disconfirmed these expectations.[109]

Review

This chapter examined the role of brand extensions in managing brand equity. Brand extensions occur when a firm uses an established brand name to introduce a new product. We can distinguish them by whether the new product is being introduced in a product category currently served by the parent brand (a line extension) or in a completely different product category (a category extension). Brand extensions can come in all forms. They offer many potential benefits but also can pose many problems.

The basic assumptions regarding brand extensions are that consumers have some awareness of and positive associations about the parent brand in memory and that the brand extension will evoke at least some of these. Moreover, marketers assume that negative associations will not be transferred from the parent brand or created by the brand extension. The ability of the extension to establish its own equity will depend on the salience of parent brand associations in the minds of consumers in the extension context and the resulting favorability and uniqueness of any inferred associations. The ability of the extension to contribute to parent brand equity will depend on how compelling the evidence is concerning the corresponding attribute or benefit association in the extension context, how relevant or diagnostic the extension evidence is concerning the attribute or benefit for the parent brand, and how strong existing attribute or benefit associations are held in consumer memory for the parent brand.

The chapter also outlined a process to evaluate brand extension opportunities. Marketers need to carefully consider brand extension strategies by applying managerial judgment and consumer research to the following steps: Define actual and desired consumer knowledge about the brand, identify possible extension candidates, evaluate the potential of extension candidates, design marketing programs to launch extensions, and evaluate extension success and effects on parent brand equity. Finally, a number of important research findings deal with factors affecting the acceptance of a brand extension as well as the nature of feedback to the parent brand.

Discussion Questions

1. Pick a brand extension. Use the models presented in the chapter to evaluate its ability to achieve its own equity as well as contribute to the equity of a parent brand. If you were the manager of that brand, what would you do differently?
2. Do you think a brand like Xerox will be able to transform its product meaning? What are the arguments for or against?
3. How successful do you predict these recently proposed extensions will be? Why?
   a. Mont Blanc (famous for pens) and fragrances and other accessories (watches, cufflinks, sunglasses, and pocket knives)
   b. Evian (famous for water) and high-end spas
   c. Starbucks (famous for coffee) and film production and promotion
   d. Trump (famous for hotels and casinos) and vodka and mortgage services

4. Consider the following brands, and discuss the extendability of each:[110]
   a. Harley-Davidson
   b. Red Bull
   c. Tommy Hilfiger
   d. Whole Foods
   e. Netflix
   f. U.S. Marines
   g. Grey Goose Vodka
   h. Victoria's Secret
   i. BlackBerry
   j. Las Vegas
   k. Kate Spade
5. There are four fake brand extensions among the following list; the other six were marketed at one point. Can you identify the four fakes?[111]
   a. Ben-Gay Aspirin: Pain Relief That Comes with a Warm Glow
   b. Burberry Baby Stroller: For Discriminating Newborns
   c. Smith & Wesson Mountain Bikes: Ride without Fear
   d. Atlantic City Playing Cards: Talcum-Coated for Easy Shuffling
   e. Pond's Toothpaste: Reduces the Appearance of Fine Wines
   f. Slim Jim Beef-Flavored Throat Lozenges: For Meat Lovers Who Like to Sing Karaoke
   g. Frito-Lay Lemonade: A Tangy, Crunchy Thirst Quencher
   h. Cosmo Yoghurt: Spoon It Up, Slim Down Those Thighs
   i. Richard Simmons Sneakers: Shake Your Cute Little Booty to the Oldies
   j. Madonna Condoms: For Men Who Are Packing

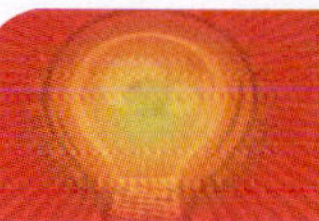

BRAND FOCUS 12.0

Guidelines for Profitable Line Extensions

In a perceptive and illuminating analysis, Quelch and Kenney persuasively argue that unchecked product-line expansion can weaken a brand's image, disturb trade relations, and disguise cost increases.[112] In describing the lure of line extensions, Quelch and Kenny began by noting seven factors that explain why so many companies have aggressively pursued such a strategy:

1. *Customer segmentation:* Line extensions are seen as a low-cost, low-risk way to meet the needs of target market segments, which can be increasingly refined due to sophisticated marketing research, advertising media, and direct marketing practices.
2. *Consumer desires:* More consumers than ever are switching brands and making in-store purchase decisions. A full brand line can offer "something for everyone" and attracts consumer attention.
3. *Pricing breadth:* Line extensions give marketers the opportunity to offer a broader range of price points in order to capture a wider audience.
4. *Excess capacity:* Many companies have added faster production lines without retiring older ones. These already existing manufacturing capabilities can often be easily modified to produce line extensions.
5. *Short-term gain:* Many managers believe line extensions offer immediate rewards with minimal risk. Similar to sales promotions, line extensions are seen as a dependable, quick fix to improve sales.
6. *Competitive intensity:* Many managers also believe that extensions can expand the retail shelf space for the category, or at least that amount devoted to the brand itself. Frequent line extensions are often used by major brands to raise the admission price to the

category for newly branded or private label competitors and to drain the limited resources of third- and fourth-place brands.

7. *Trade pressure:* The proliferation of different types of retail channels—often demanding their own special versions of the brand to suit their marketing needs or to reduce price-shopping by consumers—necessitates a more varied product line.

Quelch and Kenny continue by noting that although it is easy to understand why line extensions have been so widely embraced against such a backdrop, managers are also discovering problems and risks from brand proliferation.

- *Weaker line logic:* Because managers often extend a line without removing any existing items, the strategic role of each item becomes muddled. As a result, retailers may fail to stock the entire line or even appropriate items. A disorganized product line may result in consumers seeking out a simple, all-purpose product as a result.
- *Lower brand loyalty:* Although line extensions can help a single brand satisfy a consumer's diverse needs, they can also motivate customers to seek variety and hence indirectly encourage brand switching. If line extensions result in cannibalization, a suboptimal shift in marketing support, or a blurring in image, the long-term health of the brand franchise will be weakened.
- *Underexploited ideas:* Some important new products justify the creation of a new brand, and potential long-term profits may suffer if such products are introduced as an extension.
- *Stagnant category demand:* A review of several product categories (pet food, crackers and cookies, ketchup, coffee, shampoo and conditioner, cake mix and frosting, and spaghetti sauce) reveals that line extensions rarely expand total category demand.
- *Poorer trade relations:* An explosion of line extensions in virtually every product category has put a squeeze on available shelf space. As manufacturers' credibility has declined, retailers have allocated more shelf space to their own private label products. Competition among manufacturers for limited shelf space has escalated overall promotion expenditures and shifted margin to increasingly powerful retailers.
- *More competitor opportunities:* By spreading marketing efforts across a range of line extensions, some of the most popular entries in the brand line may be vulnerable to well-positioned and supported competitors.
- *Increased costs:* Although marketers can correctly anticipate many of the increased costs of extensions, other possible complications may be overlooked, such as fragmentation of the marketing effort and dilution of the brand image, increased production complexities resulting from shorter production runs and more frequent line changeovers, more errors in forecasting demand, increased logistics complexity, increased supplier costs, and distraction of the research and development group from new product development.
- *Hidden costs:* Although these increased costs may make it difficult for a line extension to increase demand enough or command a high enough margin to achieve profitability, they remain hidden for several reasons. Traditional cost accounting systems allocate overheads to items in proportion to their sales, which can overburden the high sellers and undercharge the slow movers. Moreover, because line extensions are added one at a time, it is easy to overlook broader cost considerations that may affect or be affected by the entire brand line.

Line extensions also carry inherent risks due to their contribution to the already overwhelming number of choices consumers face (see The Science of Branding 12-1). With 8 varieties of Budweiser and 35 versions of Crest already in the market, each successive line extensions threatens to drive choice-saturated consumers to competing brands with fewer varieties.[113]

Quelch and Kenny conclude their analysis by offering eight directives to help marketing managers improve their product-line strategies:

1. *Improve cost accounting:* Study, in detail, the absolute and incremental costs associated with the production and distribution of each stock-keeping unit (SKU) from the beginning to the end of the value chain, accounting for timing of demand. Target underperforming SKUs and consider the incremental sales, costs, and savings of adding a new SKU.
2. *Allocate resources to winners:* To avoid undersupporting new, up-and-coming SKUs and oversupporting long-established SKUs whose appeal may be weakening, use an accurate activity-based cost-accounting system combined with an annual zero-based appraisal of each SKU to ensure a focused product line that optimizes the company's use of manufacturing capacity, advertising and promotion dollars, salesforce time, and available retail space.
3. *Research consumer behavior:* Make an effort to learn how consumers perceive and use each SKU, especially in terms of loyalty and switching patterns among SKUs. Identify core items that have a long-standing appeal to loyal heavy users and other items

that reinforce and expand usage among existing customers. Consider a third set of SKUs to attract new customers or to persuade multibrand users to buy more from the same line more often.

4. *Apply the line logic test:* Ensure that everyone who may affect the success of the marketing program (e.g., salespeople) is able to state in one sentence the strategic role that a given SKU plays in the brand line. Similarly, ensure that the consumer is able to understand quickly which SKU fits his or her needs.
5. *Coordinate marketing across the line:* Adopt consistent and logical pricing and packaging to simplify understanding of the brand line by salespeople, trade partners, customers, and others.
6. *Work with channel partners:* To improve trade relations and new product acceptance, set up multifunctional teams to screen new product ideas and arrange in-store testing with leading trade customers in order to research, in advance, the sales and cost effects of adding new SKUs to the brand line.
7. *Expect product-line turnover:* Foster a climate in which product-line deletions are not only accepted but also encouraged.
8. *Manage deletions:* If items identified as unprofitable cannot be quickly and easily restored to profitability, develop a deletion plan that addresses customers' needs while managing costs.

In related research, Reddy, Holak, and Bhat studied the determinants of line extension success using data on 75 line extensions of 34 cigarette brands over a 20-year period.[114] The major findings from their study reinforce many of the Quelch and Kenney conclusions, indicating that:

- Line extensions of strong brands are more successful than extensions of weak brands.
- Line extensions of symbolic brands enjoy greater market success than those of less symbolic brands.
- Line extensions that receive strong advertising and promotional support are more successful than those extensions that receive meager support.
- Line extensions entering earlier into a product subcategory are more successful than extensions entering later, but only if they are extensions of strong brands.
- Firm size and marketing competencies also play a part in an extension's success.
- Earlier line extensions have helped in the market expansion of the parent brand.
- Incremental sales generated by line extensions may more than compensate for the loss in sales due to cannibalization.

Despite the pitfalls of line extensions and the many considerations necessary to properly manage extensions, the allure of line extensions for companies remains strong, primarily due to the cost and risk involved in launching an entirely new brand. One report showed that line extensions take half as long to develop, cost far less to market, and enjoy twice the success rate of major new brand launches (see Figure 12-11).[115] For these reasons, it comes as no surprise that of the 1,561 new consumer packaged goods products introduced in 2004, 94 percent were line extensions or brand extensions, up from an average of 87 percent since 1995.[116]

	Line Extensions	Substantially New Product
Annual sales	$24 million	$53 million
Average cost	$10 million	$25 million
Success rate	51%	26%
Average time to market	10 months	15 months
Average time to pay back Investment	12 months	20 months
	Cost of Major Product Launch	
Concept screening	$2.5 million	
Concept and use test	$1.0 million	
TV commercial production	$0.6 million	
In-market test	$1.2 million	
Slotting fees	$15.0 million	
Consumer promotion	$8.0 million	
Advertising	$40.0 million	
Total	**$68.3 million**	

FIGURE 12-11

Brand Launch Economics

Notes

1. For a more comprehensive treatment, see Glen Urban and John Hauser, *Design and Marketing of New Products,* 2nd ed. (Upper Saddle River, NJ: Prentice Hall, 1993).
2. Peter Farquhar, "Managing Brand Equity," *Marketing Research* 1 (September 1989): 24–33.
3. Edward M. Tauber, "Brand Leverage: Strategy for Growth in a Cost Controlled World," *Journal of Marketing Research* 28, (August/September 1988): 26–30.
4. Robert M. McMath, "The Vagaries of Brand Equity," paper presented at the ARF Fourth Annual Advertising and Promotion Workshop, 12–13 February, 1992).
5. Byung-Do Kim and Mary W. Sullivan, "The Effect of Brand Experience on Extension Choice Probabilities: An Empirical Analysis," working paper, University of Chicago Graduate School of Business, 1995.
6. Henry J. Claycamp and Lucien E. Liddy, "Prediction of New Product Performance: An Analytical Approach," *Journal of Marketing Research* (November 1969): 414–420.
7. Kevin Lane Keller and David A. Aaker, "The Effects of Sequential Introduction of Brand Extensions," *Journal of Marketing Research* 29 (February 1992): 35–50; John Milewicz and Paul Herbig, "Evaluating the Brand Extension Decision Using a Model of Reputation Building," *Journal of Product & Brand Management* 3, no. 1 (1994): 39–47.
8. See also Jonlee Andrews, "Rethinking the Effect of Perceived Fit on Customers' Evaluations of New Products," *Journal of the Academy of Marketing Science* 23, no. 1 (1995): 4–14.
9. David B. Montgomery, "New Product Distribution: An Analysis of Supermarket Buyer Decisions," *Journal of Marketing Research* 12, no. 3 (1978): 255–264.
10. David A. Aaker and Ziv Carmon, "The Effectiveness of Brand Name Strategies at Creating Brand Recall," working paper, University of California at Berkeley, 1992.
11. Mary W. Sullivan, "Brand Extensions: When to Use Them," *Management Science* 38, no. 6 (June 1992): 793–806.
12. Daniel C. Smith, "Brand Extension and Advertising Efficiency: What Can and Cannot Be Expected," *Journal of Advertising Research* (November/December 1992): 11–20. See also Daniel C. Smith and C. Whan Park, "The Effects of Brand Extensions on Market Share and Advertising Efficiency," *Journal of Marketing Research* 29 (August 1992): 296–313.
13. Al Reis, "Understanding Marketing Psychology and the Halo Effect," *Advertising Age,* 17 April 2006; Mike Musgrove, "At 30, Apple Is Mainstream—and a Target," *Washington Post,* 7 April 2006, F1.
14. Joff Wild, "A Trademark Minefield Out There," *Financial Times,* 22 July 2002, 15.
15. Laurie Freeman, "Helene Curtis Relies on Finesse," *Advertising Age,* 14 July 1986, 2.
16. Theodore Levitt, "Marketing Myopia," *Harvard Business Review* (July–August 1960): 45–46.
17. Naomi Aoki, "Beyond the Bag," *Boston Globe,* 26 September 2004, E1.
18. Keller and Aaker, "Effects of Sequential Introduction of Brand Extensions."
19. Jeff Cioletti, "It's Da Balm!" *Beverage World,* December 2004, 37.
20. Kevin Goldman, "Old Spice's Familiar Sailor Is Lost at Sea," *Wall Street Journal,* 10 September 1993, B2. Jane L. Levere, "A Guy's Guy Tired of Plain Old Soap? Old Spice Is Counting on It," *New York Times,* 1 August 2003.
21. Barry Schwartz, *The Paradox of Choice: Why More is Less* (New York: Ecco, 2004).
22. Laura Shanahan, "Designated Shopper," *Brandweek,* 26 March 2001, 46.
23. Robert Berner, "There Goes the Rainbow Nut Crunch," *BusinessWeek,* 19 July 2004, 38.
24. Ibid.
25. Ira Teinowitz and Jennifer Lawrence, "Brand Proliferation Attacked," *Advertising Age,* 10 May 1993, 1, 48. The product categories studied were spaghetti sauce, toilet tissue, pet food, salad dressing, cereal, and toothpaste.
26. For additional support, see Peter Boatwright and Joseph C. Nunes, "Reducing Assortment: An Attribute-Based Approach," *Journal of Marketing* 65 (July 2001): 50–63.
27. Berner, "There Goes the Rainbow Nut Crunch."
28. B. G. Yovovich, "Hit and Run: Cadillac's Costly Mistake," *Adweek's Marketing Week,* 8 August 1988, 24.
29. Mary W. Sullivan, "Measuring Image Spillovers in Umbrella-Branded Products," *Journal of Business* 63, no. 3 (1990): 309–329.
30. Maureen Morrin, "The Impact of Brand Extensions on Parent Brand Memory Structures and Retrieval Processes," *Journal of Marketing Research* 36, no. 4 (1999): 517–525.
31. Al Ries and Jack Trout, *Positioning: The Battle for Your Mind* (New York: McGraw-Hill, 1985).
32. Joseph Weber, "Scott Rolls Out a Risky Strategy," *Business Week,* 22 May 1995, 48.
33. Alessandra Galloni, "Inside Out: At Gucci, Mr. Polet's New Design Upends Rules for High Fashion," *Wall Street Journal,* 9 August 2005, A1.

34. Teri Agins, "Bringing Chic to Sheets," *Wall Street Journal,* 8 September 2004.
35. For a review of some of the early brand extension literature, see Elyette Roux and Frederic Lorange, "Brand Extension Research: A Typology," working paper DR 92033, CERESSEC (Centre d'Etudes et de Recherche de l'ESSEC), Cergy Pontoise Cedex, France, 1993.
36. Geoff Dougherty, "Clear Channel Changes Script, Lets Promoters from Past Reclaim Stage." *Chicago Tribune,* 27 March 2005.
37. Kalpesh Kaushik Desai, Wayne D. Hoyer, and Rajendra Srivastava, "Evaluation of Brand Extension Relative to the Extension Category Competition: The Role of Attribute Inheritance from Parent Brand and Extension Category," working paper, State University of New York at Buffalo, 1996.
38. Edward M. Tauber, "Brand Leverage: Strategy for Growth in a Cost-Control World," *Journal of Advertising Research* (August/September 1988): 26–30.
39. Adam Bass, "Brand Extensions: Marketing in Inner Space," brandchannel.com.
40. B. Loken and D. Roedder John, "Diluting Brand Beliefs. When Do Brand Extensions Have a Negative Impact?" *Journal of Marketing* 57, no. 7 (1993): 71–84.
41. Dale Buss, "Making Tracks Beyond Tires," *Brandweek,* 15 September 2003, 16.
42. Claudia H. Deutsch, "Name Brands Embrace Some Less-Well-Off Kinfolk," *New York Times,* 24 June 2005, C7.
43. David A. Aaker, "Should You Take Your Brand Where the Action Is?" *Harvard Business Review,* September–October 1997, 135.
44. Gillian Oakenfull, Edward Blair, Betsy Gelb, and Peter Dacin, "Measuring Brand Meaning," *Journal of Advertising Research,* September–October 2000, 43–53.
45. John M. Murphy, *Brand Strategy* (New York: Prentice Hall, 1990).
46. Andrea Rothman, "France's Bic Bets U.S. Consumers Will Go for Perfume on the Cheap," *Wall Street Journal,* 12 January 1989, B6.
47. Seema Nayyar, "In Your Face," *Brandweek,* 7 December 1992; Dave Kansas, "Mouthwash Makers See Sales Evaporate," *Wall Street Journal,* 1 December 1992; Jennifer Reingold, "Above the Neck," *FW,* 18 January 1994; "Oral Care Products: Mouthwashes," *OTC Update,* 1 September 1996.
48. Murphy, *Brand Strategy.*
49. Jean-Noel Kapferer, *Strategic Brand Management* (London: Kogan Page, 1992).
50. Jim Arndorfer, "Bud Select Cannibalizes Sales of Sibling Brands," *Advertising Age,* 11 April 2005, 3.
51. Rob Pegoraro, "Fast Forward," *Washington Post,* 29 May 2005, F6.
52. Mita Sujan, "Nature and Structure of Product Categories," working paper, Pennsylvania State University, 1990; Joan Myers-Levy and Alice M. Tybout, "Schema Congruity as a Basis for Product Evaluation," *Journal of Consumer Research* 16 (June 1989): 39–54.
53. Deborah Roedder John and Barbara Loken, "Diluting Brand Equity: The Impact of Brand Extensions," *Journal of Marketing* (July 1993): 71–84.
54. David Boush and Barbara Loken, "A Process Tracing Study of Brand Extension Evaluations," *Journal of Marketing Research* 28 (February 1991): 16–28; Cathy L. Hartman, Linda L. Price, and Calvin P. Duncan, "Consumer Evaluation of Franchise Extension Products: A Categorization Processing Perspective," *Advances in Consumer Research,* Vol. 17 (Provo, UT: Association for Consumer Research, 1990): 120–126.
55. David A. Aaker and Kevin Lane Keller, "Consumer Evaluations of Brand Extensions," *Journal of Marketing* 54 (January 1990): 27–41.
56. P. A. Bottomly and Stephen Holden, "The Formation of Attitudes towards Brand Extensions: Empirical Generalizations Based on Secondary Analysis of Eight Studies," *Journal of Marketing Research* (November 2001): 494.
57. David Boush, Shannon Shipp, Barbara Loken, Ezra Gencturk, et al., "Affect Generalization to Similar and Dissimilar Line Extensions," *Psychology and Marketing* 4 (Fall 1987): 225–241.
58. On the other hand, applying Mandler's congruity theory, Meyers-Levy and her colleagues showed that suggested products associated with moderately incongruent brand names could be preferred over ones that were associated with either congruent or extremely incongruent brand names. They interpreted this finding in terms of the ability of moderately incongruent brand extensions to elicit more processing from consumers that could be satisfactorily resolved (assuming consumers could identify a meaningful relationship between the brand name and the product). See J. Meyers-Levy, T. A. Louie, and M. T. Curren, "How Does the Congruity of Brand Names Affect Evaluations of Brand Name Extensions?" *Journal of Applied Psychology* 79, no. 1 (1994): 46–53.
59. Deborah MacInnis and Kent Nakamoto, "Cognitive Associations and Product Category Comparisons: The Role of Knowledge Structures and Context," working paper, University of Arizona, 1990.
60. C. Whan Park, Sandra Milberg, and Robert Lawson, "Evaluation of Brand Extensions: The Role of Product Level Similarity and Brand Concept Consistency," *Journal of Consumer Research* 18 (September 1991): 185–193.
61. Susan M. Broniarczyk and Joseph W. Alba, "The Importance of the Brand in Brand Extension," *Journal of Marketing Research* 31 (May 1994): 214–228. Incidentally, although a Crest toothbrush was not available at the time that this study was conducted, one was later in fact introduced as Crest Complete.

62. T. H. A. Bijmolt, M. Wedel, R. G. M. Pieters, and W. S. DeSarbo, "Judgments of Brand Similarity," *International Journal of Research in Marketing* 15 (1998): 249–268.
63. Sheri Bridges, Kevin Lane Keller, and Sanjay Sood, "Explanatory Links and the Perceived Fit of Brand Extensions: The Role of Dominant Parent Brand Associations and Communication Strategies," *Journal of Advertising* 29, no. 4 (2000): 1–11.
64. B. H. Schmitt and L. Dubé, "Contextualized Representations of Brand Extensions: Are Feature Lists or Frames the Basic Components of Consumer Cognition?" *Marketing Letters* 3, no. 2 (1992): 115–126.
65. D. M. Boush, "Brand Name Effects on Interproduct Similarity Judgments," *Marketing Letters* 8, no. 4 (1997): 419–427.
66. D. C. Smith and Jonlee Andrews, "Rethinking the Effect of Perceived Fit on Customers' Evaluations of New Products," *Journal of the Academy of Marketing Science* 23, no. 1 (1995): 4–14.
67. A. V. Muthukrishnan and Barton A. Weitz, "Role of Product Knowledge in Brand Extensions," in *Advances in Consumer Research,* Vol. 18, eds. Rebecca H. Holman and Michael R. Solomon (Provo, UT: Association for Consumer Research, 1990), 407–413.
68. Broniarczyk and Alba, "Importance of the Brand."
69. Keller and Aaker, "Effects of Sequential Introduction of Brand Extensions."
70. See also Arvind Rangaswamy, Raymond Burke, and Terence A. Oliva, "Brand Equity and the Extendibility of Brand Names," *International Journal of Research in Marketing* 10 (1993): 61–75.
71. See, for example, Peter H. Farquhar and Paul M. Herr, "The Dual Structure of Brand Associations," in *Brand Equity and Advertising: Advertising's Role in Building Strong Brands,* eds. David A. Aaker and Alexander L. Biel (Hillsdale, NJ: Lawrence Erlbaum Associates, 1993), 263–277.
72. Ian M. Lewis, "Brand Equity or Why the Board of Directors Needs Marketing Research," paper presented at the ARF Fifth Annual Advertising and Promotion Workshop, 1 February 1993.
73. Stephen Phillips, "Chiquita May Be a Little Too Ripe," *Business Week,* 30 April 1990, 100.
74. Robert D. Hof, "A Washout for Clorox?" *Business Week,* 9 July 1990, 32–33; Alicia Swasy, "P&G and Clorox Wade into Battle over the Bleaches," *Wall Street Journal,* 16 January 1989, 5; Maria Shao, "A Bright Idea That Clorox Wishes It Never Had," *Business Week,* 24 June 1991, 118–119.
75. Peter H. Farquhar, Julia Y. Han, Paul M. Herr, and Yuji Ijiri, "Strategies for Leveraging Master Brands," *Marketing Research* (September 1992): 32–43.
76. P. M. Herr, P. H. Farquhar, and R. H. Fazio, "Impact of Dominance and Relatedness on Brand Extensions," *Journal of Consumer Psychology* 5, no. 2 (1996): 135–159.
77. Farquhar, Han, Herr, and Ijiri, "Strategies for Leveraging Master Brands."
78. Bridges, Keller, and Sood, "Explanatory Links."
79. C. Joiner and B. Loken, "The Inclusion Effect and Category-Based Induction: Theory and Application to Brand Categories," *Journal of Consumer Psychology* 7, no. 2 (1998): 101–129.
80. Bridges, Keller, and Sood, "Explanatory Links and the Perceived Fit of Brand Extensions."
81. Frank Kardes and Chris Allen, "Perceived Variability and Inferences about Brand Extensions," in *Advances in Consumer Research,* Vol. 18, eds. Rebecca H. Holman and Michael R. Solomon (Provo, UT: Association for Consumer Research, 1990), 392–398.
82. See also Sandy D. Jap, "An Examination of the Effects of Multiple Brand Extensions on the Brand Concept," in *Advances in Consumer Research,* Vol. 20 (Provo, UT: Association for Consumer Research, 1993), 607–611.
83. Murphy, *Brand Strategy.*
84. Simon Brooke, "Spoiled Goods," *Marketing,* 22 June 2005, 32.
85. Boush and Loken, "Process Tracing Study."
86. Peter Dacin and Daniel C. Smith, "The Effect of Brand Portfolio Characteristics on Consumer Evaluations of Brand Extensions," *Journal of Marketing Research* 31 (May 1994): 229–242. See also Boush and Loken, "Process Tracing Study"; and Niraj Dawar, "Extensions of Broad Brands: The Role of Retrieval in Evaluations of Fit," *Journal of Consumer Psychology* 5, no. 2 (1996): 189–207.
87. M. W. Sullivan, "Brand Extensions: When to Use Them," *Management Science* 38, no. 6 (1992): 793–806.
88. P. DeGraba and M. W. Sullivan, "Spillover Effects, Cost Savings, R&D and the Use of Brand Extensions," *International Journal of Industrial Organization* 13 (1995): 229–248.
89. Deborah Roedder John and Barbara Loken, "Diluting Brand Beliefs: When Do Brand Extensions Have a Negative Impact?" *Journal of Marketing* 57 (Summer 1993): 71.
90. Jean B. Romeo, "The Effect of Negative Information on the Evaluation of Brand Extensions and the Family Brand," in *Advances in Consumer Research,* Vol. 18, eds. Rebecca H. Holman and Michael R. Solomon (Provo, UT: Association for Consumer Research, 1990), 399–406.
91. D. Roedder John, B. Loken, and C. Joiner, "The Negative Impact of Extensions: Can Flagship Products Be Diluted?" *Journal of Marketing* 62 (January 1998): 19–32.
92. Z. Gürhan-Canli and D. Maheswaran, "The Effects of Extensions on Brand Name Dilution and Enhancement,"

Journal of Marketing Research 35, no. 11 (1998): 464–473.

93. S. J. Milberg, C. W. Park, and M. S. McCarthy, "Managing Negative Feedback Effects Associated with Brand Extensions: The Impact of Alternative Branding Strategies," *Journal of Consumer Psychology* 6, no. 2 (1997): 119–140.
94. V. R. Lane and R. Jacobson, "Stock Market Reactions to Brand Extension Announcements: The Effects of Brand Attitude and Familiarity," *Journal of Marketing* 59, no. 1 (1995): 63–77.
95. A. Kirmani, S. Sood, and S. Bridges, "The Ownership Effect in Consumer Responses to Brand Line Stretches," *Journal of Marketing* 63, no. 1 (1999): 88–101.
96. Maureen Morrin, "The Impact of Brand Extensions on Parent Brand Memory Structures and Retrieval Processes," *Journal of Marketing Research* 36, no. 4 (1999): 517–525.
97. For related research, see Carol M. Motely and Srinivas K. Reddy, "Moving Up or Down: An Investigation of Repositioning Strategies," working paper 93–363, University of Georgia, Athens, 1993; and Carol M. Motely, "Vertical Extensions: Strategies for Changing Brand Prestige," working paper, University of Georgia, Athens, 1993.
98. Joshua Levine, "Pride Goeth Before a Fall," *Forbes,* 29 May 1989, 306.
99. Jerry Shriver, "Gallo, Kendall-Jackson Uncork Fresh Identities," *USA Today,* 17 March 2006, 8D.
100. Farquhar, Han, Herr, and Ijiri, "Strategies for Leveraging Master Brands."
101. Lori Bongiorno, "How Tiffany's Took the Tarnish Off," *Business Week,* 26 August 1996, 67–69.
102. T. Randall, K. Ulrich, and D. Reibstein, "Brand Equity and Vertical Product Line Extent," *Marketing Science* 17, no. 4 (1998): 356–379.
103. Kirmani, Sood, and Bridges, "The Ownership Effect."
104. Hyeong Min Kim, "Evaluations of Moderately Typical Products: the Role of Within- Versus Cross-manufacturer Comparisons," *Journal of Consumer Psychology* 16, no. 1 (2006): 70–78.
105. Bridges, Keller, and Sood, "Explanatory Links."
106. V. R. Lane, "The Impact of Ad Repetition and Ad Content on Consumer Perceptions of Incongruent Extensions," *Journal of Marketing* 64, no. 4 (2000): 80–91.
107. M. J. Barone, P. W. Miniard, and J. B. Romeo, "The Influence of Positive Mood on Brand Extension Evaluations," *Journal of Consumer Research* 26, no. 3 (2000): 386–400.
108. Kevin Lane Keller and Sanjay Sood, "The Effects of Product Experience and Branding Strategies on Brand Evaluations," working paper, University of California, Los Angeles, 2000.
109. L. Buchanan, C. J. Simmons, and B. A. Bickart, "Brand Equity Dilution: Retailer Display and Context Brand Effects," *Journal of Marketing Research* 36, no. 8 (1999): 345–355.
110. For additional insights into extendability of these brands, refer to Jeff Ousbourne, "Feel the Stretch," MBA Jungle, www.jungleonline.com.
111. The fakes are Burberry Baby Stroller, Atlantic City Playing Cards, Slim Jim Beef Jerky Throat Lozenges, Richard Simmons Sneakers. From Ousbourne, "Feel the Stretch."
112. John A. Quelch and David Kenny, "Extend Profits, Not Product Lines," *Harvard Business Review* (September–October 1994): 153–160. See also the commentary on this article and the issue of product line management in "The Logic of Line Extensions," *Harvard Business Review* (November–December 1994): 53–62.
113. "Line Extensions: Less Is More," *Advertising Age,* 28 February 2005, 26.
114. Srinivas K. Reddy, Susan L. Holak, and Sbodh Bhat, "To Extend or Not to Extend: Success Determinants of Line Extensions," *Journal of Marketing Research* 31 (May 1994): 243–262. For some conceptual discussion, see Kalpesh Kaushik Desai and Wayne D. Hoyer, "Line Extensions: A Categorization and an Information Processing Perspective," in *Advances in Consumer Research,* Vol. 20 (Provo, UT: Association for Consumer Research, 1993), 599–606.
115. Jack Neff, "Small Ball: Marketers Rely on Line Extensions," *Advertising Age,* April 11, 2005, p. 10.
116. Ibid.

MANAGING BRANDS OVER TIME

Preview

One of the obvious challenges in managing brands is the many changes in the marketing environment in recent years. Undoubtedly, the marketing environment will continue to evolve and change, often in very significant ways. Shifts in consumer behavior, competitive strategies, government regulations, and other aspects of the marketing environment can profoundly affect the fortunes of a brand. Besides these external forces, the firm itself may engage in a variety of activities and changes in strategic focus or direction that may necessitate minor or major adjustments in the way that its brands are being marketed. Effective brand management thus requires proactive strategies designed to at least maintain—if not actually enhance—customer-based brand equity in the face of all these different forces.

This chapter considers how to best manage brands over time. Any marketing action a firm takes can change consumers' brand awareness or brand image. These changes in consumer brand knowledge will have an indirect effect on the success of *future* marketing activities. Thus, from the perspective of customer-based brand equity, we want to know how they may help or hurt subsequent marketing decisions (see Figure 13-1). For example, the frequent use of temporary price decreases as sales promotions may create or strengthen a "discount" association to the brand, with potentially adverse implications on customer loyalty and responses to future price changes or non-price-oriented marketing communication efforts.

Unfortunately, marketers may have a particularly difficult time trying to anticipate future consumer response: If the new knowledge structures that will influence future consumer response don't exist until the short-term marketing actions actually occur, how can we realistically simulate future consumer response to permit accurate predictions?

The main assertion of this chapter is that marketers must actively manage brand equity over time by reinforcing the brand meaning and, if necessary, by making adjustments to the marketing program to identify new sources of brand equity. In considering these two topics, we'll look at a number of different issues, including the advantages of maintaining brand consistency, the importance of protecting sources of brand equity, tradeoffs between fortifying and leveraging brands, and different possible brand revitalization strategies. Brand Focus 13.0 considers how to change a corporate name.

Reinforcing Brands

How should we reinforce brand equity over time? How can marketers make sure that consumers have knowledge structures that support brand equity for their brands? Generally we reinforce brand equity by marketing actions that consistently convey the meaning of the brand to consumers in terms of brand awareness and brand image. Questions marketers should consider are as follows:

- *What products does the brand represent, what benefits does it supply, and what needs does it satisfy?* For example, Nutri-Grain has expanded from cereals into granola bars and other products, cementing its reputation as "makers of healthy breakfast and snack foods."
- *How does the brand make those products superior? What strong, favorable, and unique brand associations exist in the minds of consumers?* For example, through product development and the successful introduction of brand extensions, Black & Decker is now seen as offering "innovative designs" in its small appliance products.

Both these issues—brand meaning in terms of products, benefits, and needs as well as in terms of product differentiation—depend on the firm's general approach to product development,

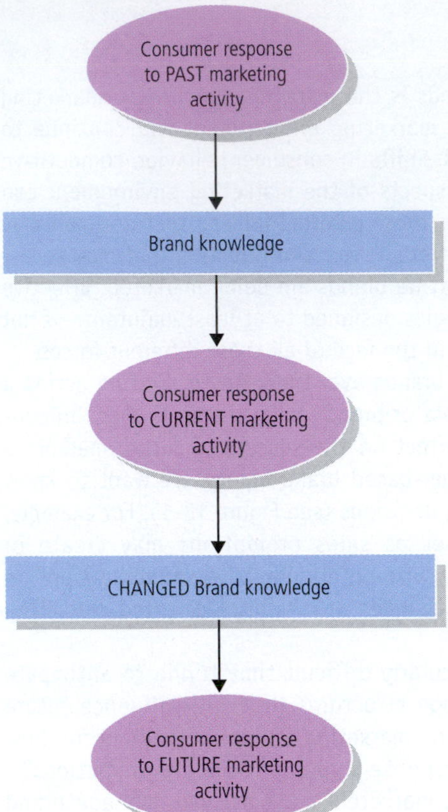

FIGURE 13-1

Understanding the Long-Term Effects of Marketing Actions on Brand Equity

branding strategies, and other strategic concerns, as we discussed in Chapters 11 and 12. This section reviews some other important considerations concerning brand reinforcement.

Maintaining Brand Consistency

Without question, the most important consideration in reinforcing brands is the consistency of the nature and amount of marketing support the brand receives. Brand consistency is critical to maintaining the strength and favorability of brand associations. Brands with shrinking research and development and marketing communication budgets run the risk of becoming technologically disadvantaged—or even obsolete—as well as out-of-date, irrelevant, or forgotten.

Market Leaders and Failures. Inadequate marketing support is an especially dangerous strategy when combined with price increases. An example of the consequences of failing to adequately support a brand occurred in the kitchen and bath fixtures market.

Delta

Delta Faucet, the first company to advertise faucets on television in the 1970s, was the market leader with more than 30 percent market share in the 1980s. Beginning in the 1990s, however, two major factors contributed to a decline in market share. First, whereas Delta had built a strong business model based on the loyalty of professional plumbers, the advent of hardware superstores and Internet shopping empowered consumers to make their own choices and repairs. Second, Delta's support for its brand through innovation and advertising diminished during this time. These factors combined to give rival Moen an opportunity to gain market share, and by 2005 each company held 25 percent of the U.S. faucet market. That same year, Delta countered by raising its advertising budget 60 percent and conducting thousands of interviews and other forms of consumer research to feed R&D efforts.[1]

Even a cursory examination of the brands that have maintained market leadership for the last 50 or 100 years or so testifies to the advantages of staying consistent. Brands such as Budweiser, Coca-Cola, Hershey, and others have been remarkably consistent in their strategies once they achieved a preeminent market leadership position.

Perhaps an even more compelling demonstration of the benefits of consistency is the fortunes of brands that have been inconsistent in their marketing programs—for example, by constantly repositioning or changing ad agencies.

GATEWAY

Like its rival Dell, Gateway Computer achieved success in the 1990s by selling computers directly to consumers. But Gateway's fortunes suffered seriously in the 2000s as the company endured four years of negative profitability between 2001 and 2004. In 2005 its stock traded below $3 per share, off from a peak of over $100 in 1999, and it fell off the Fortune 500 rankings. Analysts blamed Gateway's lack of execution on its core PC business as it pursued new growth areas with a succession of new strategies, such as the 1996 introduction of own-brand Gateway Country Stores, 1998's launch of an Internet access provider, a move into branded consumer electronics in 2002, and a 2004 merger with PC maker eMachines. Remarked one analyst, "I've been following the company since 2000, and it's had almost as many strategies as years."[2] Interim CEO Rick Snyder, appointed in 2006, admitted that Gateway "took a simple business and made it more complex than it needed to be." Although Snyder's turnaround strategy was a simpler approach involving marketing high- and mid-range PCs to sophisticated users and capturing corporate accounts with cost-effective models, it reflected yet another change of direction for Gateway.[3]

Consistency and Change. Being consistent does not mean, however, that marketers should avoid making any changes in the marketing program. On the contrary, managing brand equity with consistency may require making numerous tactical shifts and changes in order to maintain the strategic thrust and direction of the brand. The tactics that are most effective for a particular brand at any one time can certainly vary. Prices may move up or down, product features may be added or dropped, ad campaigns may employ different creative strategies and slogans, different brand extensions may be introduced or withdrawn, and so on over time in order to create the same desired knowledge structures in consumers' minds. Nevertheless, despite these different types of changes in marketing programs, the strategic positioning of many leading brands has remained remarkably consistent over time. A contributing factor to their success is that despite these tactical changes, certain key elements of the marketing program are always retained and brand meaning has remained consistent over time.

In fact, many brands have kept a key creative element in their marketing communication programs over the years and, as a result, have effectively created some "advertising equity." For example, Jack Daniels bourbon whiskey has stuck with rural scenes of its Tennessee home and the slogan "Charcoal Mellowed Drop by Drop" literally for decades. Demonstrating the latent value of past advertising is the return of such advertising icons as Colonel Sanders for KFC, who appears in new advertising and packaging focused on the restaurant's Southern roots, albeit with a thinner face and a red apron instead of the classic three-piece suit.[4] Dubbed ***retro-branding*** or ***retro-advertising*** by some marketing pundits, the tactic is a means to tie in with past advertising that was, and perhaps could still be, a key source of brand equity. Most important, it may activate and strengthen brand associations that would be virtually impossible to recreate with new advertising today.

From an awareness standpoint, such efforts obviously make sense. At the same time, marketers should be sure these old advertising elements have enduring meaning with older consumers and relevance to younger consumers. They should examine the entire marketing program to determine which elements are making a strong contribution to brand equity and therefore must be protected, as we discuss next.

Protecting Sources of Brand Equity

Consistency thus guides strategic direction and does not necessarily prescribe the particular tactics of the supporting marketing program for the brand at any one point in time. Unless some change in either consumers, competition, or the company makes the strategic positioning of the brand less powerful, there is likely little need to deviate from a successful positioning. Although brands should always look for potentially powerful new sources of brand equity, a top priority is to preserve and defend those sources of brand equity that already exist, as illustrated by the examples of Cascade and Intel.

While rolling out its value-pricing initiative, Procter & Gamble made a minor change in the formulation of its Cascade automatic dishwashing detergent, primarily for cost-savings reasons. As a result, the product was not quite as effective as it previously had been under certain, albeit somewhat atypical, water conditions. After discovering the fact, one of P&G's chief competitors, Lever Brothers, began running comparative ads for its Sunlight brand featuring side-by-side glasses that claimed, "Sunlight Fights Spots Better Than Cascade." Because the consumer benefit of "virtually spotless" is a key brand association and source of brand equity for Cascade, P&G reacted swiftly. It immediately returned Cascade to its original formula and contacted Lever Brothers to inform that company of the change, effectively forcing it to stop running the new Sunlight ads on legal grounds. As this episode clearly demonstrates, Procter & Gamble fiercely defends the equity of its brands, perhaps explaining why so many of P&G's brands have had such longevity.

As another example, consider the public relations problems encountered by Intel Corporation with the "floating decimal" problem in its Pentium microprocessors in December 1994. Although the flaw in the chip resulted in miscalculation problems in only extremely unusual and rare instances, Intel was probably at fault—as company executives now admit—for not identifying the problem and proposing remedies to consumers more quickly. Once the problem became public, Intel endured an agonizing six-week period as the focus of media scrutiny and criticism for its reluctance to publicize the problem and its failure to offer replacement chips. Two key sources of brand equity for Intel microprocessors like the Pentium—emphasized throughout the company's marketing program—are "power" and "safety." Although consumers primarily think of safety in terms of upgradability, the perceptions of financial risk or other problems that might result from a potentially flawed chip certainly should have created a sense of urgency within Intel to protect one of its prize sources of brand equity. Eventually, Intel capitulated and offered a replacement chip. Perhaps not surprisingly, only a very small percentage of consumers (an estimated 1 percent to 3 percent) actually requested it, suggesting that it was Intel's stubbornness to act and not the defect per se that rankled many consumers. Although it was a painful episode, Intel maintains it learned a lot about how to manage its brand in the process.

Ideally, the key sources of brand equity are of enduring value. Unfortunately, marketers can easily overlook that value as they attempt to expand the meaning of their brands and add new product-related or non-product-related brand associations. The next section considers these types of tradeoffs. Brand Focus 13.0 deals with the topic of corporate name changes.

Fortifying versus Leveraging

Chapters 4 to 7 described a number of different ways to raise brand awareness and create strong, favorable, and unique brand associations in consumer memory to build customer-based brand equity. In managing brand equity, marketers face tradeoffs between activities that fortify brand equity and those that leverage or capitalize on existing brand equity to reap some financial benefit.

Marketers can design marketing programs that mainly try to capitalize on or maximize brand awareness and image—for example, by reducing advertising expenses, seeking increasingly higher price premiums, or introducing numerous brand extensions. The more we pursue this strategy, however, the easier it is to neglect and perhaps diminish the brand and its sources of equity. Without its sources of brand equity, the brand itself may not continue to yield such valuable benefits.[5] Just as a failure to properly maintain a car eventually affects its performance, so too neglecting a brand, for whatever reason, can catch up with marketers.

Wonder Bread

With its familiar blue, red, and yellow packaging, Wonder Bread was introduced as America's first sliced bread in the 1930s and was a staple in many homes for decades since. After a series of ownership changes increased the company's focus on cost-cutting, however, Wonder Bread ceased advertising in the 1970s. Later, as consumer tastes shifted toward multi-grain breads, Wonder Bread's corporate owners balked at the expense and time required to produce that type of bread. Although a new owner resurrected the brand's advertising campaign in 1996, the brand had effectively lost "two generations [of customers]" and was unable to recover, eventually filing for bankruptcy in 2004.[6]

Fine-Tuning the Supporting Marketing Program

Although marketers are more likely to change the specific tactics and supporting marketing program for the brand than its basic positioning and strategic direction, marketers should change tactics only when it's clear they are no longer making the desired contributions to maintaining or strengthening brand equity.

The way brand meaning is reinforced may depend on the nature of brand associations. The Science of Branding 13-1 outlines one perspective on different ways to manage brand concepts. We next look at specific considerations in terms of product-related performance and non-product-related imagery associations.

Product-Related Performance Associations. For brands whose core associations are primarily product-related performance attributes or benefits, innovation in product design, manufacturing, and merchandising is especially critical to maintaining or enhancing brand equity. For example, after Timex watched brands such as Casio and Swatch gain significant market share by emphasizing digital technology and fashion (respectively) in their watches, it made a number of innovative marketing changes. Within a short period of time, Timex introduced Indiglo glow-in-the dark technology, showcased popular new models such as the Ironman in mass media advertising, and launched new Timex stores to showcase its products. Timex also bought the Guess and Monet watch brands to distribute through upscale department stores and expand its brand portfolio. These innovations in product design and merchandising have significantly revived the brand's fortunes.[7]

For companies in categories as diverse as toys and entertainment products, personal care products, and insurance, innovation is critical to success. For example, Progressive has become one of the most successful auto insurers, in part due to consistent innovations

THE SCIENCE OF BRANDING 13-1

Brand Concept Management

In an award-winning academic article, C. W. Park, Bernard Jaworski, and Deborah MacInnis present a normative framework termed ***brand concept management*** (BCM) for selecting, implementing, and controlling brand image over time to enhance market performance. The framework consists of a sequential process of selecting, introducing, elaborating, and fortifying a "brand concept." The brand concept guides positioning strategies, and hence the brand image, at each of these stages. The method for maintaining this concept-image linkage depends on whether the brand concept is functional, symbolic, or experiential.

Specifically, the authors define a brand concept in terms of firm-selected brand meaning derived from basic consumer needs. For example, the concept for Clorox Bleach is "whiter and brighter clothes." An important factor in influencing the selection of a brand concept is the different types of consumer needs that might prevail, as follows:

- *Functional needs:* Functional needs motivate the search for products that solve consumption-related problems, whether current or potential. These needs are often linked to fairly basic motivations (physiological and safety needs) and are met by products with functional benefits. For example, functional benefits of a shampoo might be that it eliminates dandruff, removes greasiness, makes hair and scalp healthy, and gives hair moisture and body. A brand with a ***functional concept*** is one designed to solve externally generated consumption needs.
- *Symbolic needs:* Symbolic needs are desires for products that fulfill internally generated needs for self-enhancement, role position, group membership, social approval, or ego identification. Thus, consumers may value the prestige, exclusivity, or fashionability of a brand because it relates to their self-concept. For example, a symbolic benefit of a shampoo might be the assurance that only "beautiful people" who appreciate the

in service. A pioneer in direct sales of insurance online, it was the first to offer prospective customers the ability to instantly compare price quotes from up to three other insurers. Other Progressive innovations include an accident "concierge service" where Progressive representatives handle all aspects of the claims and repair process for its customers, and online policy management where customers can make payments and change coverage at any time. See Branding Brief 13-1 for a summary of how Gillette has built equity in its razor and blades categories through innovation.

Failure to innovate can have dire consequences. Smith Corona, after struggling to sell its typewriters and word processors in a booming personal computer market, finally filed for bankruptcy. As one industry expert observed, "Smith Corona never realized they were in the document business, not the typewriter business. If they had understood that, they would have moved into software."[8] London Fog rainwear found its sales slipping away when it faced sleek competition from the likes of Ralph Lauren and Liz Claiborne. London Fog revamped its products and launched a bold ad campaign to attempt to avoid bankruptcy.[9] Maytag struggled when it focused on cost-cutting instead

"good things in life" use it. A brand with a ***symbolic concept*** is one designed to associate the individual with a desired group, role, or self-image.

- *Experiential needs:* Experiential needs are desires for products that provide sensory pleasure, variety, or cognitive stimulation. For example, experiential benefits of a shampoo might be its scent and lather, and the feelings of beauty and cleanliness from applying or using it. A brand with an ***experiential concept*** is designed to fulfill these internally generated needs for stimulation or variety.

Once a marketer selects a broad needs-based concept, according to these researchers, it can guide positioning decisions. For each of the three management stages, positioning strategies will enable consumers to understand a brand image (introduction), perceive its steadily increasing value (elaboration), and generalize it to other products produced by the firm (fortification). Specifically, the ***introductory stage*** of BCM is a set of activities designed to establish a brand image and position in the marketplace during the period of market entry. During the ***elaboration stage,*** positioning strategies focus on enhancing the value of the brand's image so that the firm can establish or sustain its perceived superiority to competitors. At the final stage of BCM, the ***fortification stage,*** the aim is to link an elaborated brand image to the image of the firm's other products in different product classes.

Sources: C. Whan Park, Bernard J. Jaworski, and Deborah J. MacInnis, "Strategic Brand Concept-Image Management," *Journal of Marketing* 50 (October 1986): 135–145; Abraham H. Maslow, *Motivation and Personality,* 2nd ed. (New York: Harper & Row, 1970); Geraldine Fennell, "Consumers' Perceptions of the Product-Use Situations," *Journal of Marketing* 42 (April 1978): 38–47; John R. Rossiter and Larry Percy, *Advertising and Promotion Management* (New York: McGraw-Hill, 1987); Michael R. Solomon, "The Role of Products as Social Stimuli: A Symbolic Interactionism Perspective," *Journal of Consumer Research* 10 (December 1983): 319–329.

of making sought-after new products, leading retailers such as Best Buy to stop carrying the brand.[10] General Motors' Oldsmobile brand seemed to suffer from a perpetual lack of innovation and relevance.

Oldsmobile

In 1988, Oldsmobile attempted to break from its recent past with a lavish, $100 million-plus ad campaign. Bearing the theme "This Is Not Your Father's Oldsmobile," each ad featured an icon from the 1960s—such as Star Trek's William Shatner, TV game-show host Monty Hall, the Beatle's Ringo Starr, astronaut Scott Carpenter, and actress Priscilla Presley—paired with their children. The ads showed the celebrity parent being driven away in an Oldsmobile by his or her child. With the average age of an Oldsmobile buyer being 51 years, the purpose of the ads was to redefine user and usage imagery and make the brand relevant for a new market. Although the ads were among the best remembered of the year—especially among the target consumers aged 35 to 44—sales continued to slide even after the campaign was introduced. Ultimately, it was withdrawn from the air. Critics faulted it for drawing attention to the dowdiness of the brand's image and the fact that Oldsmobile's models really hadn't changed all that much. Subsequent efforts to revive the brand similarly stuttered, and the brand was dropped from GM's portfolio in 2004.

BRANDING BRIEF 13-1

Razor-Sharp Branding at Gillette

One of the strongest brands in the world is Gillette. The company owns roughly two-thirds of the U.S. blade and razor market and even more in Europe and Latin America. In fact, more than 70 percent of sales and profits come from overseas operations in 200 countries. Moreover, its 10 percent profit margin is substantially higher than that at most packaged-goods companies. How has Gillette been so successful? The company's marketing and branding practices provide a number of useful lessons to marketers.

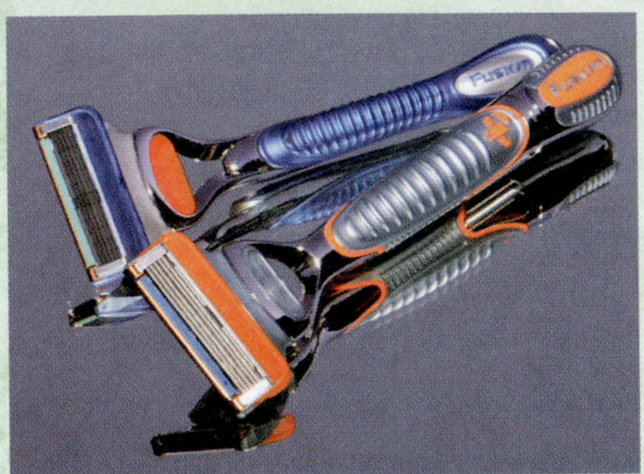

Gillette has thrived by emphasizing innovation and relevance with its razor blades, as with its Fusion razor.

Fundamentally, Gillette continually innovates to produce a demonstrably superior product. More than 40 percent of Gillette's sales in the first half of the 1990s came from new products. Gillette's credo is to "increase spending in 'growth drivers'—R&D, plants and equipment, and advertising—at least as fast as revenues go up." As Gillette's former CEO Alfred Zeien proclaimed, "Good products come out of market research. Great products come from R&D." Gillette spent more than 2 percent of its annual sales—or over $200 million—on R&D during the late 1990s, double the average for most consumer products companies. Gillette also backs its products with strong advertising and promotional support. TV ads in the past often used a montage of slow-motion scenes of men in different roles interspersed with product shots with upbeat background music and the now-familiar tag line "The Best a Man Can Get." Thus, Gillette's marketing creates both strong performance and imagery associations.

Here is a history of Gillette's product innovations during the last 30 years:

Trac II (1971): First twin-blade razor

Atra (1977): First twin-blade razor with a pivoting head

Good News (1976): Top-selling disposable twin-blade razor since introduction

Atra Plus (1985): Twin-blade razor with a lubricant strip

Sensor (1990): Individually mounted twin blades

Thus, product innovations are critical for performance-based brands whose sources of equity reside primarily in product-related associations. Branding Brief 13-2 describes the sales setbacks Mattel experienced after failing to innovate its Barbie doll to keep pace with trends. In some cases, product advances may include brand extensions based on a new or improved product ingredient or feature—for example, Hot & Spicy Spam, mini-Oreos, Ruffles potato chips with larger "Flavor Ridges," Tide Rapid Action Tablets, and Yoplait Go-Gurt.[11] In fact, in many categories, a strong family sub-brand has emerged from product innovations associated with brand extensions (such as Wilson Hammer wide-body tennis racquets). In other cases, product innovations may center on existing brands. For

Sensor for Women (1992): First razor designed specifically for women

Sensor Excel (1993): Fitted with microfins that stretch skin for closer shave

Mach3 (1998): First triple-blade razor

M3 Power (2004): First disposable razor to include battery-powered vibration

Fusion: (2006): First five-blade razor (included a single sixth blade on the top side of the cartridge)

Gillette considered the Mach3 to be the "most important new product" in its history, and invested more than $750 million in research and development and manufacturing expenses, securing 35 patents in the process. The major advancement of the Mach3 was the triple blade, each designed to shave progressively closer. The product was highly anticipated: Before the advertising campaign began, Mach3 generated more than 500 million media impressions. During the launch year for the Mach3, Gillette set a marketing budget of $300 million globally and $100 million in the United States. The Mach3, which cost 35 percent more than the Sensor Excel, captured a stunning 35 percent of the razor market within two weeks of its launch date and surpassed the $1 billion sales mark only 15 months after its debut. In 2001, Gillette released a women's version of the Mach3 called the Venus. Gillette spent $150 million on marketing for the worldwide Venus launch. In 2004, it upgraded the Mach3 by introducing the M3 Power, the first disposable razor to feature a battery-powered vibration option, which allowed for a closer shave. A Venus version, called Venus Vibrance, soon followed.

Acquired by Procter & Gamble in 2005, Gillette launched the six-bladed Fusion and Fusion Power razors the following year. Gillette had spent $1.2 billion on R&D since intoducing Mach3 and more than $1 billion to market the product to the world's 3.2 billion males. The payoff? A four-pack of Fusion cartridges cost double Mach3's original price.

Sources: Patricia Sellers, "Brands, It's Thrive or Die," *Fortune,* 23 August 1993, 52–56; Linda Grant, "Gillette Knows Shaving—and How to Turn Out Hot New Products," *Fortune,* 14 October 1996, 207–210; www.gillette.com; "Gillette to Launch Massive Atra Plus Advertising Campaign," *PR Newswire,* 14 December 1988; William C. Symonds, "Gillette's Edge," *Business Week,* 19 January 1998; Editorial, "Gillette Spends Smart on Fusion," *Advertising Age,* 26 September 2005, 24.

example, General Mills' "Big G" cereal division strives to improve at least a third of its nearly two dozen brand lines each year.[12] As another example, Bacardi recovered from a sales slide by introducing a variety of new products.

Bacardi

In the early 1990s, the increasing popularity of vodka combined with a lack of innovation in marketing for Bacardi's rum caused significant erosion among Bacardi's user base, and it suffered one of the worst sales drops in modern spirits history, losing over two million cases in sales during 1991 as sales dropped to 6.4 million cases. To stop the slide in sales, Bacardi introduced a series of new products, beginning with a new premixed drink called Bacardi Breezer that came

BRANDING BRIEF 13-2

A runaway success, Bratz dolls now challenge Mattel's legendary Barbie.

Barbie vs. Bratz

Mattel's Barbie doll first appeared on store shelves in 1959 and took on a life of her own, successfully going through countless makeovers to stay relevant to the core target of young girls. For many years, Barbie was the undisputed market leader, without peer among American dolls. But in 2001, Barbie's dominance was challenged by an upstart doll brand called Bratz, produced by MGA Entertainment. In only four years, Bratz became a billion-dollar brand, stealing market share from Barbie in the process.

Bratz dolls bore little resemblance to Barbies; they had cartoonishly large heads, came dressed in garish and revealing hip-hop styles, and wore considerable amounts of makeup. The Bratz tagline, "The ONLY Dolls with a Passion for Fashion," underscored this difference. The designer of the Bratz dolls, Carter Bryant, allegedly had the idea for Bratz when he worked on Barbie at Mattel, but took his idea to a rival when he realized such a reinterpretation of Barbie would not go over well at tradition-bound Mattel. Bratz rapidly captured the imagination of American girls, particularly

in 12-ounce bottles. The company also introduced a lemon-flavored rum (Bacardi Limon) in 1995 and a spiced rum (Bacardi Spice) in 1996. The company continued to develop innovative products, and between 2001 and 2005 it launched several flavored rums including orange-seasoned Bacardi O and raspberry-flavored Bacardi Razz, another line of premixed drinks called Bacardi Silver, a series of premixed cocktails called Bacardi Party Drinks, and a low-calorie rum called Bacardi Island Breeze. These products brought Bacardi's total revenues up to $3.5 billion and reenergized sales of the flagship rum, which grew to 8.75 million cases, in 2005.[13]

At the same time, it is important not to change products too much, especially if the brand meaning to consumers is wrapped up in the product design or makeup. Recall the strong consumer resistance encountered by New Coke described in Chapter 1. As another example, Revlon also underestimated how passionately consumers can feel about well-established brands and how much they can resent any tampering with the products themselves. To better appeal to younger women, Revlon reformulated the heavy floral scent of its 30-year-old Intimate fragrance to a lighter, less sweet scent. Longtime customers protested, forcing the company to reintroduce the old formulation as "Intimate the Original" while continuing to market the reformulated Intimate.

In making product changes to a brand, marketers want to reassure loyal consumers that it is a better product but not necessarily a *different* one. The timing of the announcement and the introduction of a product improvement are also important: If the brand improvement is announced too soon, consumers may stop buying existing products; if too late, competitors may already have taken advantage of the market opportunity with their own introductions.

tweens who had outgrown Barbie. One Mattel employee conceded that "Bratz reached older girls who had left the market." The company rapidly expanded its brand by striking deals for some 350 licensing products, including clothing, accessories, DVDs, and electronics. It tallied $2.5 billion in sales in 2004, within range of Barbie's $3 billion total that same year.

Meanwhile, Barbie had not changed meaningfully in some years. Some commentators described the brand as "stale," and consumers agreed. Between 2001 and early 2004, Barbie sales dropped 27 percent. To counter this slide, Mattel began generating scenarios to broaden Barbie's appeal to older girls, including having her "break up" with long-time boyfriend Ken in 2004, compete as a "contestant" on American Idol, and "hang out" with singer Hilary Duff in commercials promoting Barbie's doll clothing line, Fashion Fever. Mattel also introduced a Lindsay Lohan Barbie, which sought to capitalize on the tabloid-fixture actress's popularity among older girls. Mattel even introduced two sub-brands of Bratz-esque dolls to connect with tweens and early teens, "Flavas" and "My Scene," neither of which initially earned an enthusiastic response from consumers. Combined, these and other measures finally stopped Barbie's sales slide, as sales rose in 2006. It appeared, however, that Barbie finally had a worthy rival.

Source: Dorothy Pomerantz, "The Barbie Bust," *Forbes,* 28 March 2005, 64; Christopher Palmeri, "Hair-Pulling in the Dollhouse," *Business Week,* 2 May 2005; T. L. Stanley, "Barbie Hits the Skids," *Advertising Age,* 31 October 2005, 1.

Non-Product-Related Imagery Associations. For brands whose core associations are primarily non-product-related attributes and symbolic or experiential benefits, relevance in user and usage imagery is critical. Because of their intangible nature, non-product-related associations may be easier to change, for example, through a major new advertising campaign that communicates a different type of user or usage situation. Nevertheless, ill-conceived or too-frequent repositionings can blur the image of a brand and confuse or perhaps even alienate consumers.

In categories in which advertising plays a key role in building brand equity, imagery may be an important means of differentiation. For example, in the soft drinks category, marketers spend millions of dollars in advertising to craft an image for a brand. Pepsi-Cola's fresh, youthful appeal has been a key point of difference with Coca-Cola. Pepsi-Cola has also used a number of slogans over the years, from its original "Pepsi Generation," to "The Choice of a New Generation." Pepsi next launched a campaign with the slogan "Gotta Have It" during the 1992 Super Bowl. The ads, showing young and old Pepsi drinkers, was an attempt to expand the "Pepsi Generation" to include older age groups. With little indication of sales success, Pepsi returned to its more familiar and powerful positioning, introducing new ads with the snappy tag line "Be Young. Have Fun. Drink Pepsi."[14] After that, however, Pepsi again ran the risk of straying away from a key source of equity with the introduction of the broader-appealing ad theme "Nothing Else Is a Pepsi." More recently, it returned to the youth-focused "Generation Next" before arriving at "The Joy of Cola," which was changed slightly to "The Joy of Pepsi" in 2000. In 2003, Pepsi changed its slogan once more to the generic-sounding "It's the Cola," which represents a shift away from the youth-oriented themes of its recent past to stake more of a leadership claim. Finally, 2007 saw Pepsi revert back to a more emotional pitch, "More Happy."

It is particularly dangerous to flip-flop between product-related performance and non-product-related imagery associations, because of the fundamentally different marketing and advertising approaches each entails. Consider Heineken. Earlier ads showed simple scenes of the bottle or people peacefully drinking the beer, backed by the slogan "Just being the best is enough." Subsequent ads, in an attempt to make the brand more hip and contemporary, were much artier—featuring a bright red star logo—and had a more prominent lifestyle component. Perhaps because they were too much of a departure, the ads failed to really drive sales and Heineken lost its spot as the leading import beer in the United States to Corona. A new, edgy campaign from 1999, called "It's All about the Beer," was much more successful at communicating the quality message in a contemporary, humorous manner. The tagline continued into 2007 and it and the introduction of a Premium Light version contributed to the company's recapturing its U.S. market share.[15]

Significant repositionings may be dangerous for other reasons too. Brand images can be extremely sticky, and once consumers form strong associations, they may be difficult to change. Consumers may choose to ignore or simply be unable to remember the new positioning when strong, but different, brand associations already exist in memory.[16] Club Med has attempted for years to transcend its image as a vacation romp for swingers to attract a broader cross-section of people. Branding Brief 13-3 describes how Michelob's constant repositioning coincided with a steady sales decline.

For dramatic repositioning strategies to work, they must present convincing new brand claims in a compelling fashion. One brand that successfully shifted from a primarily non-product-related image to a primarily product-related image is BMW, uniformly decreed the quintessential "yuppie" vehicle of the 1980s. The brand's sales dropped almost in half from 1986 to 1991 as new Japanese competition emerged and a backlash to the "Greed Decade" set in. Convinced that high status was no longer a sufficiently desirable and sustainable position, marketers switched the focus to BMW's product developments and improvements, such as the responsive performance, distinctive styling, and leading-edge engineering. These efforts, showcased in well-designed ads, helped to diminish the "yuppie" association, and by 1995 sales had approached their earlier peak.[17]

Summary. Reinforcing brand equity requires consistency in the amount and nature of the supporting marketing program for the brand. Although the specific tactics may change, marketers should preserve and amplify the key sources of equity for the brand where appropriate. Product innovation and relevance are paramount in maintaining continuity and expanding the meaning of the brand. Branding Brief 13-4 describes how the British brand Burberry remade itself in the world of fashion. Next we consider situations in which more drastic brand actions are needed.

Revitalizing Brands

In virtually every product category, there are examples of once prominent and admired brands that have fallen on hard times or even completely disappeared. Nevertheless, a number of these brands have managed to make impressive comebacks in recent years as marketers have breathed new life into their customer franchises. Brands such as *Reader's Digest,* Boston Market, Coach, and Bally have all seen their brand fortunes successfully turn around to varying degrees. Branding Brief 13-5 describes how Lacoste and Pabst Blue Ribbon restored the status of their brands.

BRANDING BRIEF 13-3

Pick a Positioning! Brand Repositioning with Michelob

A brand that failed to turn around sales while enduring numerous repositionings is Michelob, which celebrated its 100th anniversary in 1996. Michelob has always been positioned as an upscale, superpremium beer. In the 1970s, it ran ads featuring successful young professionals that confidently proclaimed, "Where You're Going, It's Michelob." Moving away from the strong user imagery of that campaign, the next ad campaign trumpeted, "Weekends Were Made for Michelob." Later, to bolster sagging sales, the ad theme switched to "Put a Little Weekend in Your Week." In the mid-1980s, the firm launched yet another campaign—featuring laid-back rock music and stylish shots of beautiful people—that proclaimed "The Night Belongs to Michelob."

None of these campaigns could stop a sales slide to 2.3 million barrels in 1994, compared with a 1980 peak of 8.1 million. Finally, in 1994 another ad campaign, "Some Days Are Better Than Others," explained to consumers that "A Special Day Requires a Special Beer," which later became "Some Days Were Made for Michelob."

Pity the poor consumers! After so many different messages, they could hardly be blamed if they had no idea when they were supposed to drink the beer. Meanwhile, sales performance for Michelob continued to suffer.

In 2002, Michelob launched a brand extension to capitalize on the low-carb craze with a low-carb beer called Michelob Ultra. The brand was marketed to beer drinkers with active lifestyles and advertised with the functional benefit-specific tagline: "Lose The Carbs. Not The Taste." The sub-brand naming strategy closely tied the new beer to the parent brand Michelob, and given the high profile of the Ultra marketing campaign, it essentially repositioned the Michelob brand as a beer for young, active, health-conscious consumers. Michelob Ultra achieved early success, reaching shipments of 3.1 million barrels in 2003, but sales began to decline the following year as the low-carb trend waned. As a consequence, some commentors argued that Michelob Ultra needed a new positioning, and by extension, Michelob would be repositioned yet again. The brand received a packaging and communications make-over in 2007 to try to tap back into its heritage and roots.

Source: Kevin Goldman, "Michelob Tries to Rebottle Its Old Success," *Wall Street Journal,* 28 September 1995, B8; James B. Arndorfer, "Low-Carb Beer Buzz Starts to Lose Steam," *Advertising Age,* 23 August 2004, 6.

As these examples illustrate, brands sometimes have had to return to their roots to recapture lost sources of equity. In other cases, the meaning of the brand has had to fundamentally change for it to regain lost ground and recapture market leadership. Regardless of which approach marketers take, brands on the comeback trail have to make more "revolutionary" changes than the "evolutionary" changes to reinforce brand meaning that we described earlier in this chapter.

BRANDING BRIEF 13-4

Remaking Burberry's Image

Burberry, founded in 1856 by 21-year-old Thomas Burberry, was a veritable "fashion disaster" in the mid-1990s. It was known to many as a stodgy throwback brand making raincoats for the middle-aged. Burberry was, in the words of one commentator, "far off the radar screens of the fashion world." Yet within a span of several years, with the help of contemporary designs and updated marketing, the brand shrugged off its staid image and became fashionable again. The company instituted a new motto—"Never stop designing"—that encapsulated its new approach to establishing and maintaining relevance with the fickle fashion consumer.

One of Burberry's first moves to freshen its brand was to leverage its classic beige-check plaid in a series of accessories that quickly became best-sellers, including handbags, scarves, and headbands. Another move was rejuvenating the check itself by using different colors, patterns, sizes, and materials in designs. Burberry was careful to maintain a balance between the contemporary and the traditional, the latter of which still resonated with modern consumers. It also sought to leverage other iconic imagery such as the trench coat and Prorsum horse insignia. The use of these brand icons reflected the fact that Burberry management felt "the core ethos and aesthetics of the brand were relevant today because of Thomas Burberry's ingenuity and creativity."

Another key to Burberry's turnaround was refreshing its advertising. It hired famed fashion photographer Mario Testino to shoot a spread featuring edgy supermodels such as Kate Moss wearing the iconic Burberry raincoats. The ads were credited with bringing a "rebellious, streetwise image to the brand." The company gave its retail stores a makeover as well in order to match the contemporary feel of the new designs. Together, Burberry's efforts turned the company's fortunes around. Between 2000 and 2004, the company recorded five consecutive annual revenue increases, and net profit rose 75 percent in 2004 to $163 million. An efficiency push in 2005–2006 somewhat diminished the growth in profit, but improved the long-term prospects of the brand. One commentator summed up the keys to the company's turnaround, saying, "Burberry appeals to a very broad market, which is why it is doing so well. But the great advertising campaigns and cool models keep the Burberry label very high-end, appealing and desirable."

Sources: Sally Beatty, "Plotting Plaid's Future," *Wall Street Journal,* 9 September 2004, B1; Mark Tungate, "Fashion Statement," *Marketing,* 27 July 2005, 28; Sharon Wright, "The Tough New Yorker Who Transformed a UK Institution Gets Her Reward," *The Express,* 5 August 2004, 17.

BRANDING BRIEF 13-5

Two Brand Comeback Stories

Lacoste

Lacoste, founded in France in 1933, became a style icon for its tennis-themed sportswear and is credited with selling the first polo shirt, the famed "alligator shirt" featuring the animal—actually a crocodile—as the logo. During the 1980s, when it was owned by cereal maker General Mills, Lacoste failed to keep up with the prevailing fashion trends and saw its sales drop. In response, the company cut prices and sold to discounters like Wal-Mart and Kmart, which further damaged the brand's image. Lacoste continued to suffer from slow sales until 2002, when Robert Siegel, a former Levi's executive credited with creating Dockers, was brought in to oversee the relaunch of the brand in the United States. Under Siegel, Lacoste stopped selling to non-luxury retailers, prohibiting sales to places like T.J. Maxx and a number of Macy's department stores. The company also regenerated its fading fashion lines by introducing tighter-fitting shirts for women, a move that increased the contribution to Lacoste's U.S. revenues of women's wear from 7 percent to 33 percent. Lacoste went a step further and opened own-brand boutiques in fashionable shopping areas to showcase its new look. As a consequence of these measures, Lacoste's U.S. revenues rose more than 280 percent between 2003 and 2005.

Pabst Blue Ribbon

Pabst Blue Ribbon (PBR) was born in 1882 when the Pabst brewing company began tying silk ribbons to bottles of its "Select" beer. The company became one of the major beer brands in America and remained so through 1977, when sales peaked at 18 million barrels. As competition from Budweiser and Miller increased, the PBR brand suffered as a consequence of price cuts, quality problems, and ownership changes. After years of decline, sales of PBR suddenly spiked in the Portland, Oregon area in 2001. Management investigated, and discovered that young trend-setters were adopting the beer as a "blue-collar, Americana" alternative to the big brands and craft beers favored by their parents. Rather than using above-the-line advertising, which it had not done since the 1970s, Pabst sought to capitalize on this market through word of mouth, on-premise promotions, and event sponsorships, primarily of local bands and concerts, and licensed merchandise aimed at "hipsters." As a result, PBR saw 15 percent sales growth in both 2003 and 2004, following 5 percent growth in 2002.

Sources: Greg Lindsay, "The Alligator's New Look," *Business 2.0,* April 2006, 68–69; Georgina Safe, "Crocodile Rocks a Comeback," *The Australian,* 28 July 2006; www.pabstblueribbon.com; Jeremy Mullman, "Schlitz Tries to Revive '50s Heyday," *Advertising Age,* 17 April 2006, 8; Ann Cortissoz, "Not Your Father's Beer: Your Grandfather's," *Boston Globe,* 20 October 2004, F1.

Often, the first place to look in turning around the fortunes of a brand is the original sources of brand equity. As Ogilvy & Mather's Norman Berry once remarked:

> The brands most likely to respond to revitalization efforts are those that have clear and relevant values that have been left dormant for a long time, have not been well expressed in the marketing and communications recently, have been violated by product problems, cost reductions, and so on. *Where there is evidence that these values exist and that they were indeed a part of the brand's magnetism during healthier days, then chances of revitalization are good.* If you find that the brand really does not have any strong values, chances are that the product or business strength in the past was a function simply of performance and spending characteristics and that, in fact, according to our definition, it never really became a true brand. Bringing these brands back to life is more like starting from scratch. It really isn't revitalization.[18]

In profiling brand knowledge structures to guide repositioning, marketers need to accurately and completely characterize the breadth and depth of brand awareness; the strength,

BRANDING BRIEF 13-6

Harley-Davidson Motor Company

Harley-Davidson is one of the few companies in the world that can claim a legion of fans so dedicated to the brand that some of them get tattoos depicting the logo. Even more impressive is the fact that Harley-Davidson attracted such a loyal customer base with a minimum of advertising. Founded in 1903 in Milwaukee, Wisconsin, Harley-Davidson has twice narrowly escaped bankruptcy but is today one of the most recognized brands in the world, enjoying 55 percent unaided awareness. Customers are known to endure waiting lists in order to get their hands on a Harley.

Before the 1980s, the company relied almost exclusively on word-of-mouth endorsements and the image of its user group to sell its motorcycles. In 1983 the company established an owners' club, the Harley Owners Group (HOG), which sponsored bike rallies, charity rides, and other motorcycle events. Every Harley owner receives free admission into the group and can sign up at the www.hog.com Web site. In its first year, HOG had 33,000 members. By 2006, there were more than one million HOG members in more than 1,200 chapters throughout the world.

Harley-Davidson has always cultivated a somewhat rebellious image.

In the early 1980s, Harley-Davidson began a licensing program to protect its trademarks and promote the brand. Early efforts were primarily to support the riding experience such as t-shirts, jewelery, small leather goods and other products appealing to riders. Currently, the primary customer for Harley-Davidson licensed products is the Harley dealer network. Additionally, to attract new customers, Harley-Davidson has licensed children's

favorability, and uniqueness of brand associations and brand responses held in consumer memory; and the nature of consumer–brand relationships. A comprehensive brand equity measurement system as outlined in Chapter 8 should help reveal the current status of these sources of brand equity. If not, or to provide additional insight, a special brand audit may be necessary. Of particular importance is the extent to which key brand associations are still adequately functioning as points of difference or points of parity to properly position the brand. Are positive associations losing their strength or uniqueness? Have negative associations become linked to the brand, for example, because of some change in the marketing environment?

Marketers must next decide whether to retain the same positioning or to create a new one and, if the latter, which positioning to adopt. The positioning considerations outlined in Chapter 3 can provide useful insights as to the desirability and deliverability of different possible positions based on company, consumer, and competitive considerations. Sometimes the positioning is still appropriate, but the marketing program is the source of the problem because it is failing to deliver on it. In these instances, a "back to basics" strategy may make sense. Branding Brief 13-6 describes how Harley-Davidson rode a back-to-basics strategy

clothing, toys, games, and many other items aimed at children and sold beyond the dealer network. In the world of licensing, Harley-Davidson is considered an "evergreen" brand and earns the Motor Company tens of millions in revenue annually.

Motorcycle riding gear has been around almost as long as there have been motorcycles. As business grew for Harley-Davidson, the Company created Harley-Davidson MotorClothes to include traditional riding gear along with mens and womens casual sportswear and accessories to help reach an ever expanding and diverse customer base of both riders and non-riders. Harley MotorClothes are a key facet of the Company's General Merchandise division, whose revenues grew from $151 million in 2000 to $247 million in 2005.

Harley-Davidson continues to promote its brand with grassroots marketing efforts. For example, many employees and executives at the company own Harleys and often ride them with customers. This customer intimacy makes traditional advertising almost unnecessary. In 1996, Harley spent no money on advertising. In 1997, Harley's total marketing budget was $20 million, only $1 million of which went to advertising. As ever, Harley's highly visible contingent of riders provides invaluable promotions and endorsements free of cost. Many other marketers seek to borrow the Harley cachet and use the bikes in their ads, giving the company free product placement.

One of the newest areas of growth is women riders. The company designs its motorcycles to be a more comfortable ride for a variety of riders, and it encourages women to take its Rider's Edge Academy of Motorcycling classes with a poster showing a woman biker and the tagline "I am not a backrest." In 2004, about 40 percent of Rider's Edge participants were women. After making up small percentage of Harley owners in the 1980s, women represented about 11 percent in 2005. As it attracts new customers, the company continues to please customers and investors: In 2005, profits rose 8 percent to $960 million on sales of $5.3 billion, up 6.5 percent from the previous year, capping 21 consecutive years of record growth.

Sources: Bill Tucker, Terry Keenan, and Daryn Kagan, "In the Money," *CNNfn*, 20 January 2000; "Harley-Davidson Extends MDI Entertainment License for Lotteries' Hottest Brand," *Business Wire*, 1 May 2001; Glenn Rifkin, "How Harley-Davidson Revs Its Brand," *Strategy & Business*, Fourth Quarter 1997; Joseph Weber, "He Really Got Harley Roaring," *Business Week*, 21 March 2005, 70; Rick Barrett, "From the Executive Suite to the Saddle," *Chicago Tribune*, 1 August 2004, CN3.

BRANDING BRIEF 13-7

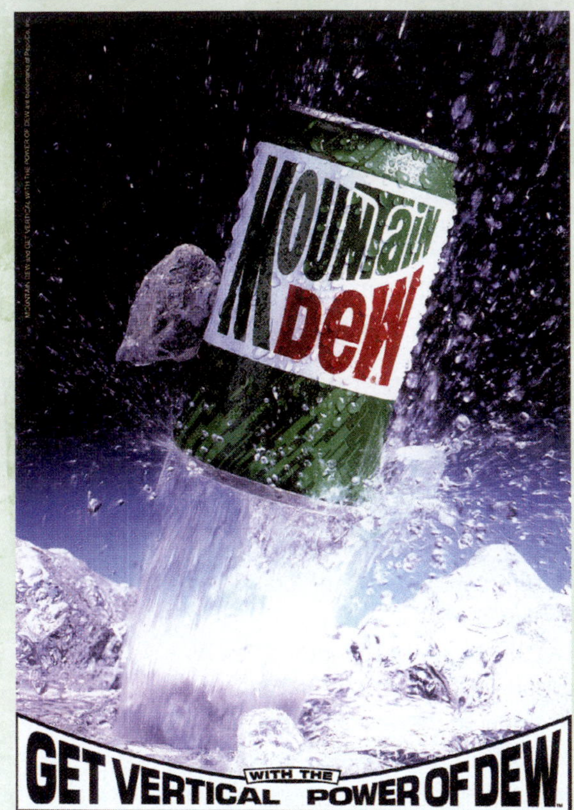

Mountain Dew has been completely repositioned with great success.

A New Morning for Mountain Dew

Mountain Dew was launched in 1969. PepsiCo initially marketed it with the countrified tag line "Yahoo Mountain Dew! It'll tickle your innards." Since then, the drink has outgrown its provincial roots. After an unsuccessful attempt in the early 1980s to bring urban teenage drinkers to the brand by advertising on MTV, the company switched its focus to using outdoors action scenes in its ads. In the late 1980s, Mountain Dew posted double-digit annual volume increases. This phenomenal growth continued through the 1990s, and Mountain Dew was the fastest-growing major soft drink in America for much of the decade. The brand's aggressive pursuit of young soda drinkers helped its market share rise from 2.7 percent in 1980 to 7.2 percent in 2000.

Mountain Dew updated its outdoors image in the 1990s by using extreme sports such as skydiving, skateboarding, and snowboarding. Early ads featured athletes participating in extreme sports while consuming Mountain Dew products, accompanied by the tag line "Do the Dew." A more recent ad featured a man on a mountain bike chasing a cheetah to retrieve a can of Dew, while another portrayed a man who butts heads with a ram in order to protect his Mountain Dew. To reach the urban demographic, which typically does not watch action sports competitions, Mountain Dew also developed a series of print, radio, and television ads featuring hip-hop superstar endorser Busta Rhymes.

to icon status. In other cases, however, the old positioning is just no longer viable and a "reinvention" strategy is necessary. Branding Brief 13-7 describes how Mountain Dew completely overhauled its brand image to become a soft drink powerhouse. As that example illustrates, it is often easiest to revive a brand that has simply been forgotten.

Revitalization strategies obviously run along a continuum, with pure "back to basics" at one end and pure "reinvention" at the other. Many campaigns combine elements of both strategies. Finally, note that *marketing* failures, in which insufficient consumers are attracted to a brand, are typically much less damaging than *product* failures, in which the brand fundamentally fails to live up to its consumer promise. In the latter case, strong, negative associations may be difficult to overcome. As an example of a market failure, Napster, the poster child for Internet file sharing, was litigated out of business in 2002 for providing more than 60 million users with access to illegally copied digital files of songs. Given that many music fans still had a fondness for the brand and there was nothing wrong

Mountain Dew balances its high-profile nationally televised campaigns with grassroots marketing efforts, such as sponsoring action-sports athletes and events like the ESPN X-Games, offering samples from its branded Dew Hummer trucks and subway cars, and staging promotions at local skate parks. Scott Moffitt, Mountain Dew's director of marketing, acknowledged the challenge of keeping Dew's marketing fresh, saying, "You can't preach to [our customers] or tell them what's cool."

Mountain Dew again proved the power of its marketing program in 2000 when it introduced Mountain Dew Code Red, its first line extension since Diet Mountain Dew debuted in 1988. The bright red cherry-flavored drink was supported by a national advertising campaign that employed grassroots marketing as well as high-profile media buys. The Code Red launch was an unqualified success (see Branding Brief 4.1).

Following that success, however, the Mountain Dew franchise suffered as consumption of soft drinks declined because consumers migrated toward water and juices. To reconnect with its core teen audience, Mountain Dew increased its grassroots activities by sponsoring the Mix Tape street basketball tour and the Dew Action Sports Tour. The company also launched the Dew U loyalty program, in which drinkers exchanged codes printed under bottle caps for a variety of goods available on the Dew U Internet site. In 2005, Mountain Dew launched another brand extension, a highly caffeinated energy drink called MDX aimed at the estimated 180 million video game players, by introducing it as the "official soft drink" of the E3 Electronics Entertainment Expo. Prior to the launch, the company invited gamers to "beta-test" the product in order to refine the recipe and name. These moves combined to reverse a four-year slide, growing sales volume 1.5 percent in 2004 and enabling Mountain Dew to remain the number-four carbonated beverage in America in terms of sales through 2006.

Sources: Theresa Howard, "Being True to Dew," *Brandweek,* 24 April 2000; Greg Johnson, "Mountain Dew Hits New Heights to Help Pepsi Grab a New Generation," *Los Angeles Times,* 6 October 1999; Michael J. McCarthy, "Mountain Dew Goes Urban to Revamp Country Image," *Wall Street Journal,* 19 April 1989; "Top-10 U.S. Soft Drink Companies and Brands for 2000," *Beverage Digest,* 15 February 2001; Kate MacArthur, "Mountain Dew Gives Gamers More Caffeine," *Advertising Age,* 26 September 2005, 6; Kate MacArthur, "Angelique Bellmer Krembs: Director—Consumer Marketing, Pepsi-Cola North America," *Advertising Age,* 30 May 2005, S6.

with the service performance per se, digital music company Roxio bought it in a bankruptcy auction for $5 million in 2002 and used it to rebrand its Pressplay music download subscription service. The new Napster enjoyed moderate success, generating revenues of $23 million in 2006, nearly double the 2005 figure.[19]

With an understanding of the current and desired brand knowledge structures in hand, we can again look to the customer-based brand equity framework for guidance about how to best refresh old sources of brand equity or create new ones to achieve the intended positioning. According to the model, we have two options:

1. Expand the depth or breadth of brand awareness, or both, by improving consumer recall and recognition of the brand during purchase or consumption settings.
2. Improve the strength, favorability, and uniqueness of brand associations making up the brand image. This may require programs directed at existing or new brand associations.

By enhancing brand salience and brand meaning in these ways, we can achieve more favorable responses and greater brand resonance. We can refurbish lost sources of brand equity and establish new ones in the same three ways we create sources of brand equity to start with: by changing brand elements, changing the supporting marketing program, or leveraging new secondary associations. In this section we consider several alternative strategies for leveraging awareness and image of an existing brand to refresh old sources or create new sources of brand equity.

Expanding Brand Awareness

With a fading brand, often *depth* of awareness is not the problem—consumers can still recognize or recall the brand under certain circumstances. Rather, the *breadth* of brand awareness is the stumbling block—consumers tend to think of the brand only in very narrow ways. As we suggested in Chapter 3, one powerful means of building brand equity is to increase the breadth of brand awareness, making sure consumers don't overlook the brand.

Let's consider strategies to increase usage of and find new uses for the brand. Assuming a brand has a reasonable level of consumer awareness and a positive brand image, perhaps the most appropriate starting point for creating new sources of brand equity is to increase usage. In many cases, this approach represents the path of least resistance because it does not require difficult and costly changes in brand image or positioning but rather relatively easy changes in brand salience and awareness.

We can increase usage either by increasing the level or the quantity of consumption (how *much* consumers use the brand) or by increasing the frequency of consumption (how *often* they use it).

It is probably easier to increase the number of times a consumer uses the product than to actually change the amount he or she uses at any one time. A possible exception is impulse-purchase products like soft drinks and snacks, whose usage increases when the product is more available.

Increasing frequency of use, on the other hand, requires either identifying new opportunities to use the brand in the same basic way, or identifying completely new and different ways to use the brand. Increasing frequency of use is a particularly attractive option for brands with large market share that are leaders in their product category. Let's look at both approaches.

Identifying Additional or New Usage Opportunities. To identify additional or new opportunities for consumers to use the brand more—albeit in the same basic way—marketers should design a marketing program to include both of the following:

- Communications about the appropriateness and advantages of using the brand more frequently in existing situations or in new situations
- Reminders to consumers to actually use the brand as close as possible in time to those situations for which it could be used

For many brands, increasing usage may be as simple as improving top-of-mind awareness through reminder advertising (as was the case with V-8 vegetable juice and its classic "Wow! I Could Have Had a V-8" ad campaign). In other cases, more creative types of retrieval cues may be necessary. These reminders may be critical because consumers often adopt "functional fixedness" with a brand, which makes it easy to ignore in nontraditional consumption settings.

For example, consumers see some brands as appropriate only for special occasions. An effective strategy here may be to redefine what it means for something to be "special." For example, at one time Chivas Regal ran a print ad campaign for its Blended Scotch with the theme "What are you saving the Chivas for?" The ads, showing different people in different scenes, included headlines such as "Sometimes life begins when the baby-sitter arrives," "Your Scotch and soda is only as good as your Scotch and soda," and "If you think people might think you order Chivas to show off, maybe you're thinking too much." For campaigns like this to work, however, the brand has to retain its "premium" brand association—a key source of equity—while consumers are convinced to adopt broader usage habits at the same time.

Another opportunity to increase frequency of use occurs when consumers' *perceptions* of their usage differ from the reality. For many products with relatively short life spans, consumers may fail to buy replacements soon enough or often enough.[20] One strategy to speed up product replacement is to tie the act of replacing the product to a certain holiday, event, or time of year. For example, several brands such as Oral-B toothbrushes have run promotions tied in with the springtime switch to daylight saving time. Another strategy is to provide consumers with better information about either (1) when they first used the product or need to replace it, or (2) the current level of product performance. For example, batteries offer built-in gauges that show how much power they have left, and toothbrushes have color indicators to indicate when they are too worn.

Finally, perhaps the simplest way to increase usage occurs when it is less than the optimal or recommended level. Here we want to persuade consumers of the merits of more regular usage and overcome any potential hurdles to increased usage, such as by making product designs and packaging more convenient and easier to use.

Identifying New and Completely Different Ways to Use the Brand. The second approach to increasing frequency of use for a brand is to identify completely new and different applications. For example, food product companies have long advertised new recipes that use their branded products in entirely different ways. After years of sales declines of 3 percent to 4 percent annually, sales of Cheez-Whiz rose 35 percent when the brand was backed by a new ad campaign promoting the product as a cheese sauce accompaniment to be used in the microwave oven.[21] Perhaps the classic example of finding creative new applications for a product is Arm & Hammer baking soda, whose deodorizing and cleaning properties have led to a number of new uses for the brand.

Other brands have taken a page from Arm & Hammer's book: Clorox has run ads stressing the many benefits of its bleach, such as how it eliminates kitchen odors; Wrigley's chewing gum has run ads touting its product as a substitute for smoking; and Tums has run ads for its antacid that promote its benefits as a calcium supplement. Coach managed to expand usage and increase frequency both for its brand and the category.

COACH

American women purchased an average of 2.4 handbags in 2000, up from 1.9 in 1988, and Coach played a prominent role in this rise. Coach's strategy for growth was to fill "usage voids"—situations where existing bag options were not appropriate—with a plethora of different bag options for almost every occasion, including evening bags, backpacks, satchels, totes, briefcases, coin purses, and duffels. Rather than owning a small number of bags suitable for a limited number of uses, women were encouraged by Coach to treat handbags as "the shoes of the 21st century: a way to frequently update wardrobes with different styles without shelling out for new clothes." One recent usage void the company identified was summer weekend use, so Coach filled it by introducing the Hamptons Weekend line, which featured durable, weatherproof materials mixed with high-quality leather. Coach retail stores educated consumers on the new usage by displaying the bags filled with beach towels and flip-flops. In the two years following its 2003 launch, the Hamptons Weekend bag sold almost 250,000 units for $40 million in sales.[22]

New usage applications may require more than just new ad campaigns or merchandising approaches. Often, new uses can arise from new packaging. For example, Arm & Hammer introduced a "Fridge-Freezer Pack" (with "freshflo vents") for its natural baking soda that was specially designed to better freshen and deodorize refrigerators and freezers. The Science of Branding 13-2 describes a number of ways to expand usage.

Improving Brand Image

Although changes in brand awareness are probably the easiest means of creating new sources of brand equity, more fundamental changes are often necessary. We may need to create a new marketing program to improve the strength, favorability, and uniqueness of brand associations making up the brand image. As part of this repositioning—or recommitment to the existing positioning—we may need to bolster any positive associations that have faded, neutralize any negative associations that have been created, and create additional positive associations.

Repositioning the Brand. In some cases, repositioning the brand requires us to establish more compelling points of difference. This may mean simply reminding consumers of the virtues of a brand that they have begun to take for granted. Recall how the New Coke debacle described in Chapter 1 accomplished just that, in a round-about way. Kellogg's Corn Flakes ran a successful ad campaign with the slogan "Try Them Again for the First Time." Disneyland similarly tried to walk consumers down memory lane in a series of 2005 ads celebrating the theme park's 50th anniversary. In some cases, a key point of difference may turn out to be nostalgia and heritage rather than any product-related difference.

Research has indicated that nostalgic advertising can positively influence consumers. One empirical study confirmed that intentionally nostalgic advertisements yielded favorable attitudes toward the advertisement and the brand.[23] Another study identified a potential source of nostalgic purchase behavior, called "intergenerational influence," or the influence of a parent's purchase behavior and brand attitudes on a child's behavior and attitudes.[24] This study found that intergenerational influences can function as a source of brand equity but are not felt uniformly by all mature brands. Rather, certain product categories and brands exhibit more of an "intergenerational effect"—in which parent and child share the same brand preference—than others. Categories (and corresponding brands) that exhibited the highest intergenerational effects include soup (Campbell's), ketchup (Heinz), facial tissue (Kleenex, Puffs), peanut butter (Peter Pan, Jif, Skippy), mayonnaise (Miracle Whip, Kraft, Hellman's) and pasta (Mueller, Ronzoni).

Other times we need to reposition a brand to establish a point of parity on some key image dimension. A common problem for marketers of established, mature brands is to make them more contemporary by creating relevant usage situations, a more contemporary user profile, or a more modern brand personality. Heritage brands that have been around for years may be seen as trustworthy but also boring, uninteresting, and not that likable. Updating a brand may require some combination of new products, new advertising, new promotions, new packaging, and so forth. For example, the 170-year-old regional beer Yuengling saw its sales virtually double when the firm introduced lighter and fuller-flavored versions; new labels that gave the beer an arty, nostalgic look; and new promotions that tapped into regional pride by focusing on the brewery's place in history. The new image permitted higher prices and allowed the brand to gain more high-end, on-premise accounts.[25]

Changing Brand Elements. Often we must change one or more brand elements to either convey new information or signal that the brand has taken on new meaning

THE SCIENCE OF BRANDING 13-2

Understanding Usage Expansion

Cornell University professor Brian Wansink has studied various marketing and branding issues associated with product consumption. He describes a number of different ways to identify and communicate new usage situations. An obvious starting point for generating potential expansion opportunities is brainstorming meetings or focus groups with loyal or heavy users and less loyal or light users. Contrasting the preferences and behaviors of the two groups can yield insights into potential barriers in perceptions and usage to overcome, as well as opportunities for further growth. Wansink also notes that marketers can uncover perceptions of potentially related products and situations through cluster analysis or other multivariate statistical approaches.

Wansink further argues that successful media strategies for expansion ad campaigns often rely on clever targeting and timing. Small-share brands can more affordably target users of their brands by advertising new uses on their packages and labels. For example, Trix cereal used a side panel to note complementary products like ice cream, yogurt, and trail mix on which Trix could be sprinkled. Murphy's Oil Soap printed a series of different usage ideas under peel-off stickers affixed to its spray bottles. Roy Rogers restaurants used its paper placemats to advertise eight situations—parties, picnics, meetings, and so forth—in which customers could eat its carry-out chicken. In terms of timing, Wansink notes that advertising exposure should coincide with situations in which consumers are most likely to make brand choices. For example, Campbell schedules radio ads for its soups to be broadcast just prior to lunch and dinner in order to be top-of-mind at the most opportune moment.

Wansink defines ***usage variant products*** as those that have elastic demand functions because they have a high degree of substitutability or because they are able to create their own demand when salient, such as food and household cleaning products. For these types of products, marketing strategies to increase consumer stockpiling, like promotions or changes in packaging, may increase the salience and thus the usage of the product. For example, larger package sizes and price discounts, by lowering the perceived unit cost of the product, have accelerated usage. Another way to increase the quantity used is to reduce the undesirable consequences of an increased usage level. For example, a shampoo designed to be gentle enough for daily use may alleviate concerns among consumers who believe that frequent hair washing is undesirable and thus eliminate their tendency to conserve the amount of product they use.

Sources: Brian Wansink, "Advertising Strategies to Increase Usage Frequency," *Journal of Marketing* 60, no. 1 (January 1996): 31–46; Brian Wansink and Jennifer Marie Gilmore, "New Uses That Revitalize Old Brands," *Journal of Advertising Research* (March–April 1999): 90–98; Brian Wansink, "Can Package Size Accelerate Usage Volume?" *Journal of Marketing* 60, no. 3 (July 1996): 1–14; David A. Aaker, *Managing Brand Equity* (New York: Free Press, 1991).

because the product or some other aspect of the marketing program has changed. The brand name is typically the most important brand element, and it's often the most difficult to change. Nevertheless, we can drop names or combine them into initials to reflect shifts in marketing strategy or to ease pronounceability and recall. Shortened names or initials also can disguise potentially negative product associations. For example, in an attempt to convey a healthier image, Kentucky Fried Chicken abbreviated its name to the initials KFC. The company also introduced a new logo incorporating the character of Colonel Sanders as a means to maintain tradition but also modernize its appeal. Brand names may change for other reasons. Federal Express chose to officially shorten its name to FedEx and introduce a new logo to acknowledge what consumers were actually calling the brand.[26]

It is easier to change other brand elements, and we may need to, especially if they play an important awareness or image function. Chapter 4 described how to modify and update packaging, logos, characters, and so forth over time. We noted there that changes generally should be moderate and evolutionary in nature, and marketers must take great care to preserve the most salient aspects of the brand elements. For example, when Ramada decided it wanted to communicate a fresh, upscale look to the public—but not lose the valuable equity it had accrued in its name—it chose to introduce a sleek new logo and signage that retained the Ramada name and bright red color, while phasing out the Ramada Inn and Ramada Limited brands from its portfolio and spending more than a year upgrading its properties.[27] Brand Focus 13.0 considers in more detail issues in changing corporate names.

Entering New Markets

Positioning decisions require us to specify the target market and the nature of the competition to set the competitive frame of reference. Market segments the firm currently serves with other products may represent potential growth targets for the brand. Effectively targeting these other segments, however, typically requires some changes or variations in the marketing program, especially in advertising and other communications, and the decision whether to do so ultimately depends on a cost-benefit analysis. Chapter 3 introduced some basic segmentation issues, and Chapter 14 considers some specific segmentation issues in the context of global brands as well as geographic and other factors. This section highlights a few key segmentation issues as they relate to brand revitalization.

To grow the brand franchise, many firms have reached out to new customer groups to build brand equity. Johnson & Johnson baby shampoo achieved greater success by promoting the gentleness and everyday applicability of its shampoo to an adult audience. Consider Brunswick.

BRUNSWICK

Seeking to boost sales of its high-margin pool tables, Brunswick Billiards targeted design-conscious women who might have previously rejected the purchase of a pool table on aesthetic grounds. Focus groups conducted by the company revealed that pool table purchases were predominantly "male-initiated, wife-approved," except that the wives often did not give their approval.[28] The company courted female consumers by sponsoring the Women's Professional Billiard Association, which attracts 15 percent female viewership when televised on ESPN. The company also introduced new eye-catching pool table designs, and encouraged retailers to install "pavilions" that showcased the tables with track lighting and hardwood floors. Brunswick also introduced a number of furniture accessories to fit with the pool tables in a game room, including a player's chair, standing bar, and foosball table. Between 1998 and 2003, Brunswick's profits rose 50 percent to $5.5 million.

The pool hall has been transformed by Brunswick who has actively pursued the female market.

Segmenting on the basis of demographic variables or other means and identifying neglected segments is thus one viable brand revitalization option. In some cases, just retaining existing customers who might eventually move away from the brand, or recapturing lost customers who no longer use the brand, can be a means to increase sales. Brands such as Kellogg's Frosted Flakes cereal, Oreo cookies, and Keds tennis shoes have run ad campaigns targeting adults who presumably stopped using the product long ago. Some of these ads use themes and appeals to nostalgia or heritage. Others attempt to make the case that the product's enduring appeal is still relevant for users today. The importance of retaining current customers can be seen by calculating their lifetime value. One study noted that a purchaser of automobiles would spend more than $500,000 on cars during her lifetime, but that it costs five times as much to sell an automobile to a new customer as it does to sell to a satisfied existing customer.[29]

Attracting a new market segment can be deceptively difficult. Gillette, Harley-Davidson, Wrangler, and ESPN have struggled for years to find the right blend of products and advertising to make their brands—which have more masculine-oriented images—appear relevant and appealing to women. Creating marketing programs to appeal to women has become a priority of makers of products from cars to computers. Marketers have also introduced new marketing programs targeted to different racial groups (African Americans, Asian Americans, and Hispanic Americans), age groups, and income groups. Attracting emerging new cultural market segments may require different messages, creative strategies, and media.[30]

Of course, one strategic option for revitalizing a fading brand is simply to more or less abandon the consumer group that supported the brand in the past to target a completely new market segment.

TOMMY HILFIGER

One of the hottest fashion brands in the 1990s, Tommy Hilfiger was struggling to stay relevant by the early 2000s. Other labels such as Phat Farm, FUBU, Sean John, and Ecko had drawn customers away by executing the young urban, hip-hop style on which Hilfiger had built its '90s success in more "authentic" ways. Bloomingdales reduced the number of Hilfiger boutiques to 1 from 23, and Hilfiger closed all but 7 of its 44 own-brand specialty shops in 2003. To recover, Hilfiger essentially cut all ties with the style that had made it

Hilfiger, like many other fashion brands, has experienced ups and downs.

popular—oversized apparel, even more oversized logos, and an edgy urban aura—even going so far as to remove the stylized American flag logo from many of its clothing products. Hilfiger struck out in a new direction with preppy styles inspired by the sun and surf, or as a competitor described a billboard advertising the new line, "Pacific Sunwear meets Ralph Lauren meets 'From Here to Eternity.'" One analyst questioned the logic of Hilfiger's embracing its preppy past, asking, "Why would he try to go back to being Ralph Lauren, when that market is already saturated?"[31]

Adjustments to the Brand Portfolio

Managing brand equity and the brand portfolio requires taking a long-term view and carefully considering over time the role of different brands in the portfolio and their relationships. In particular, a brand migration strategy should help consumers understand how various brands in the portfolio can satisfy their needs as they change over time, or as the products and brands themselves change over time. Managing brand transitions is especially important in rapidly changing, technologically intensive markets. Branding Brief 13-8 describes some branding issues faced by the AT&T brand portfolio as it navigated a series of spinoffs and mergers.

Migration Strategies

We noted in Chapter 11 that brands can play special roles to facilitate the migration of customers within the brand portfolio. For example, entry-level brands are often critical in bringing in new customers and introducing them to the brand offerings. Ideally, brands will be organized in consumers' minds so that they know at least implicitly how they can switch among brands within the portfolio as their needs or desires change. For example, a corporate or family branding strategy in which brands are ordered in a logical manner could provide the hierarchical structure in consumers' minds to facilitate

BRANDING BRIEF 13-8

AT&T: The Incredible Shrinking (and Growing) Portfolio

The American Telephone and Telegraph Company (AT&T), founded in 1885, is one of America's most enduring brands. Yet in 2005, the AT&T brand appeared to be headed for extinction following a succession of sell-offs to other companies. AT&T Broadband and AT&T Wireless had been sold in 2002 and 2004, respectively. When SBC Communications that year bought the last remaining piece of the AT&T portfolio—its long-distance business—for $16.5 billion and announced plans to eliminate the brand, the public assumed it was "lights out for AT&T." Just one year later, as it turned out, the brand got a new lease on life when SBC reversed its decision and decided to rebrand SBC as AT&T.

This news was the latest chapter in a bizarre 12-year mini-history that saw the AT&T portfolio go from broad to narrow and back to broad again. In 1994, AT&T began a period of expansion into different communication technologies with the launch of AT&T Wireless. Beginning in 1997, the company spent $116 billion buying cable systems, which became AT&T Broadband. The company also marketed dial-up and DSL Internet services under the AT&T Worldnet brand.

The bursting of the Internet bubble forced the AT&T portfolio into a period of contraction. In 2002, Comcast acquired AT&T Broadband, and AT&T Wireless was purchased by Cingular in 2004. Both Comcast and Cingular dropped the AT&T moniker following the acquisitions. The AT&T portfolio shrank even further following these acquisitions. Fresh on the heels of the sale of its wireless brand, AT&T launched a campaign aimed at driving sales of its remaining business, long distance, in both the B2B and consumer markets. Only months later, it elected to pursue only B2B customers, signaling an end to its consumer-facing brand. The apparent nail in the coffin for the AT&T brand came in the form of SBC's acquisition of this long-distance business.

In a move that stunned many, SBC announced six months after the merger that the AT&T brand would replace the three brands that SBC had spent $10.5 billion promoting for the previous five years: SBC, Cingular, and BellSouth. The move was not without justification, however, as recognition for the SBC brand was low outside its 13-state operating area. Further, promoting a single brand would yield cost savings of an estimated $500 million. Thus, in 2006 the AT&T brand was relaunched with a $1 billion ad campaign, the biggest in the company's history. It featured 12 new TV spots, 32 print ads, sponsorhip of the Masters golf tournament, and a flashy Times Square billboard, all suported by the tagline "Your World. Delivered" and theme song "All Around the World" by Oasis. The AT&T logo was updated with lowercase "at&t" to appear more casual. Still, for some commentators, the resurrection of the AT&T brand to encompass a broad portfolio was a "recipe for confusion."

Sources: Todd Wasserman, "AT&T: We're All About Business Now," *Brandweek,* 9 August 2004, 4; Tim Doyle, "A Battered Brand, Reborn," *Forbes,* 24 April 2006; Allan Sloan, "AT&T Hits Redial for an Old Strategy," *Newsweek,* 20 March 2006, 14.

Generation	Birth Dates	Size	Experiences and Attitudes
GI Generation	1901–1924	16 million	• Survivors of the Depression and two World Wars • Conservative spenders • Civic-minded
Silent Generation	1925–1945	35 million	• Much like GIs before them, lived with specter of Depression and war, but were born too late to be war heroes • Conformists; raised families at young age • The grandparents of the Millennials are now involved in civic life and extended families in a bid to recapture lost youth
Baby Boomers	1946–1964	76 million	• Great acquisitors, unapologetic consumers • Now often newly liberated parents with high disposable income • Value-driven despite indulgences • Fearful of words related to aging
Generation X	1961–1981	57 million	• Cynical and media-savvy • Once rebellious, now a big economic force • Alienated, alternative, sexy
Generation Y	1976–1981 (a subset of Generation X)	32 million	• Edgy, focused on urban style • Moved toward more positive, retro style: swing dancing, big band, outdoor life
Millennials	1982–2002	70 million	• Tech-savvy and educated • Multicultural • Bombarded by media messages; accustomed to sex, violence • Growing up in affluent society; big spending power

FIGURE 13-2

Advertising Age's Profiles of Generations

brand migration. Car companies are quite sensitive to this issue, and brands such as BMW with its 3-, 5- and 7-series numbering systems to denote increasingly higher levels of quality are good examples of such a strategy. Chrysler designated Plymouth as its "starter" car line and expected Plymouth owners to trade up in later years to higher-priced Chrysler models.

Acquiring New Customers

All firms face tradeoffs in their marketing efforts between attracting new customers and retaining existing ones. In mature markets, trial is generally less important than building loyalty and retaining existing customers. Nevertheless, some customers inevitably leave the brand franchise—even if only from natural causes. Consequently, firms must proactively develop strategies to attract new customers, especially younger ones. The marketing challenge in acquiring new customers, however, lies in making a brand seem relevant to vastly different generations and cohort groups or lifestyles (see Figure 13-2). This challenge is exacerbated when the brand has strong personality or user image associations that tie the brand to one particular consumer group. Branding Brief 13-9 describes Volkswagen's highly successful appeals to younger drivers.

Unfortunately, even as younger consumers age, there is no guarantee they will have the same attitudes and behaviors of the older consumers who preceded them. In 1996, the first wave of post–World War II baby boomers celebrated their 50th birthdays and officially entered the "senior market." Many experts forecast that this group will demand that companies embrace their own unique values in marketing their products and services. As one demographic expert says, "Nothing could be further from the truth than saying boomers will be like their parents." Because there can be no expectations that younger consumers will necessarily view brands and products in the same way as consumers who preceded them, marketers need proactive strategies both to acquire new customers and to retain existing ones.

The response to the challenge of marketing across generations and cohort groups has taken all forms. Some marketers have attempted to cut loose from the past, as Tommy Hilfiger did by renouncing the urban styles it had come to embody in the 1990s. Other brands have attempted to develop more inclusive marketing strategies to encompass both new and old customers.

Unilever has thoughtfully transformed Dove into a power or mega brand.

Dove

Unilever's Dove brand was known primarily for bar soap since its introduction in 1955. Originally launched in the United States, it became one of Unilever's biggest global brands. As the company sought to grow the franchise, it realized Dove needed to extend beyond soap to meet the changing personal care needs of its customers, which had become more concerned about total body care. Beginning in 1999, Dove introduced body wash, facial cleansers, deodorant, and, in 2003, shampoo. Dove kept its bar soap line intact, and each extension emphasized Dove's moisturizing properties, so the brand broadened its appeal without alienating its core customers. Its "Real Beauty" campaign has also struck a chord with its target market.[32]

Let's turn to some alternative approaches that broaden the marketing program and attract new customers as well as retain existing ones.

Multiple Marketing Communication Programs. One approach to attracting a new market segment and satisfying current ones is to create separate advertising campaigns and communication programs for each. For example, Dewars launched the "Authentic" and "Profiles" campaigns, each directed to a different market segment. The "Authentic" campaign focused on the brand heritage in terms of its product quality and Scottish roots and was focused on an older segment, including existing customers. The "Profiles" campaign took a completely different tack, literally profiling younger users of the brand to make the brand seem relevant and attractive to a younger audience. Different media buys then ensured that each market segment saw the appropriate campaign.

Beer companies have adopted similar approaches. The increased effectiveness of targeted media makes multiple targets more and more feasible. The obvious drawbacks are the expense and potential blurring of images if there is too much media overlap among target groups and if consumers see the respective ad positionings as incompatible.

Brand Extensions and Sub-Brands. Another approach to attracting new customers to a brand and keeping the brand modern and up-to-date is to introduce a line extension or establish a new sub-brand. These new product offerings for the brand can incorporate new technology, features, and other attributes to satisfy the needs of new customers as well as satisfy the changing desires of existing customers. For example, in 2005 Jeep introduced the Commander, a large SUV with a V-8 Hemi engine that featured three rows of seating, an increasingly popular feature, but a first for

BRANDING BRIEF 13-9

Volkswagen's Branding U-Turn

Volkswagen, the fifth-largest automaker in the world, was founded in 1937 and, with the help of creative and effective marketing, became a household name in America during the 1960s. Volkswagen's economy car—the classic Beetle—rapidly became a cult favorite, then a popular favorite, and eventually the number one–selling car in history with over 22 million units sold. Sales of VW cars in America peaked, however, at 569,000 units in 1970. Cutthroat competition among compacts, especially from Japanese manufacturers, hurt Volkswagen's sales during the 1970s. The 1980s were not much better for the company, as sales continued to decline.

By 1990, U.S. sales had slipped to a mere 1.3 percent of the American market from a high of 7 percent in 1970. In an attempt to revitalize its business, Volkswagen unveiled an advertising campaign centered on the word *Fahrvergnugen,* German for "driving pleasure." The hard-to-pronounce word became an instant pop-culture buzzword, but U.S. sales dropped under 50,000 units in 1993.

Volkswagen attempted to breath new life into its Jetta brand with an emphasis on safety.

The company clarified its brand message under the umbrella of the "Drivers Wanted" slogan in 1995, and U.S. sales rose 18 percent to 135,907 cars in 1996. The "Drivers Wanted" campaign was designed to revitalize the company by appealing not to the mass market but to core customers willing to spend a little extra on a Volkswagen because they liked the car's German engineering, sportier image, and versatility. The voiceover on the introductory television spot identified the target audience by saying, "On the road of life, there are passengers and there are drivers."

In 1998, Volkswagen released a modernized version of its iconic Beetle. Ads for the New Beetle contained irreverent humor, like "If you sold your soul in the '80s, here's your chance to buy it back." American buyers leaped at the chance to buy the classically influenced—but clearly modern—cars, often at well above sticker price. Waiting lists for the new cars,

Jeep. At the same time, Jeep announced plans to launch two smaller "crossover" vehicles that would appeal to fuel- and safety-conscious consumers reluctant to buy a full-size SUV.[33]

New Distribution Outlets. In some cases attracting a new market segment may be as simple as making the product more available to that group. For example, the sunglasses industry, which grew sales from $100 million in 1972 to $2.5 billion 15 years later, benefited from social and fashion trends but also from a shift in distribution strategies. Sunglasses used to be sold mostly by opticians, but in the 1970s Sunglass Hut and other companies moved into malls, sporting goods stores, and campuses. A leader in specialty niche retailing, Sunglass Hut uses a wide variety of over 2,000 high-traffic shopping and tourist destinations to reach new audiences.

which sold more than 55,000 units in 1998, were common. Volkswagen sold out its inventory immediately. Said one dealer, "The New Beetle is like a magnet that draws people back to us." By bringing consumers into Volkswagen showrooms, the New Beetle helped the company achieve 50 percent growth in sales volume between 1998 and 1999.

The company struggled to find an encore worthy of succeeding the Beetle, however. The company's "next big idea," a $70,000 luxury sedan called the Phaeton, failed to grab a foothold in the United States, selling fewer than 700 cars during its first 10 months of availability before being discontinued in early 2006. Core models Jetta, Passat, and Golf had gone years without updates and were plagued by quality problems, as Volkswagen ranked next to last on the 2005 J.D. Power survey of customer complaints one year from purchase. U.S. sales plummeted to 256,111 units in 2004, down 40 percent from 2001.

Seeking to make another U-turn, VW fired its longstanding agency of record, Arnold Worldwide, and brought in upstarts Crispin Porter + Bogusky to breathe some new life into the brand. The agency developed a series of attention-getting and sometimes bizarre new ads, including ones for the new Jetta that dramatically demonstrated the safety features of the car by showing drivers unexpectedly getting into serious accidents. Ads for the GTI featured spoofs of a German engineer and dominatrix, named Wolfgang and Helga, respectively. Perhaps the agency's biggest coup was convincing VW to resurrect the Rabbit brand for the 2006 U.S. debut of the new Golf, already two years old in Europe. VW hoped the new ads would generate the sort of enthusiasm and excitement about the brand that accompanied the New Beetle but had lately been missing.

Sources: Al Beeber, "Volkswagen Sets Stage for New Microbus," *Lethbridge Herald,* 14 June 2001; Rupert Spiegelberg, "If You Love Bug, Rejoice," *Houston Chronicle,* 29 June 1997; David Kiley, "VW Goes More Off Beat with 'Wanted' Ads," *Brandweek,* 28 April 1997; David Welch, "VW: Now That's How to Rebuild a Brand," *Business Week,* 19 June 2000; Keith Naughton, "Can You Say Fahrvergnugen?" *Detroit News,* 2 February 1990; Randall Rothenberg, "The Advertising Century," *Advertising Age,* 29 March 1999; "Volkswagen Sales Fall with Beetle's Demise," Reuters News Agency, 15 October 1982; David Kiley, "The Craziest Ad Guys in America," *BusinessWeek,* 22 May 2006, 72; Alex Taylor III, "Can America Fall in Love with VW Again?" *Fortune,* 16 May 2005, 129; David Kiley, "Can VW Find Its Beetle Juice?" *BusinessWeek,* 31 January 2005, 76.

Retiring Brands

Because of dramatic or adverse changes in the marketing environment, some brands are just not worth saving. Their sources of brand equity may have essentially dried up, or, even worse, damaging and difficult-to-change new associations may have been created. At some point, the size of the brand franchise—no matter how loyal—fails to justify the support of the brand. In the face of such adversity, decisive management actions are necessary to properly retire or milk the brand.

Several options are possible to deal with a fading brand. A first step in retrenching a fading brand is to reduce the number of its product types (package sizes or variations). Such actions reduce the cost of supporting the brand and allow the brand to put its best foot forward. Under these reduced levels of support, a brand may more easily hit profit targets. If a sufficiently large and loyal enough customer base exists, eliminating marketing support can be a means to milk or harvest brand profits from these cash cows. An ***orphan brand*** is a once-popular brand with diminished equity that a parent company allows to decline by withdrawing marketing support. Typically these orphan brands have a customer base too small to warrant advertising and promotional expenditures. The Polaroid camera is an example. After filing for bankruptcy in 2001, the brand was purchased by a private equity firm. A 2003 market research study indicated the brand name itself was still a powerful asset, so the Polaroid name soon appeared on electronic devices much more sophisticated than its outmoded instant camera, such as TVs and DVDs. These items, which achieved distribution in Wal-Mart and Target, generated a reported $300 million in annual sales, proving that the orphan Polaroid still had some life in it.[34]

In some cases, the brand is beyond repair and marketers have to take more drastic measures. One option for fading brands is to consolidate them into a stronger brand. For example, Procter & Gamble merged White Cloud and Charmin toilet paper, eliminating the White Cloud line in 1992. P&G also merged Solo and Bold detergents. With shelf

BRANDING BRIEF 13-10

Building a Business by Resurrecting Orphan Brands

With the right marketing approach, it is possible to bring a jettisoned brand back to life. For example, after P&G discontinued White Cloud toilet paper, Wal-Mart secured the rights to the White Cloud brand and used it to help successfully brand its own private label diapers, enabling it to drop P&G's Pampers from its shelves. Recently, companies have emerged that do nothing but take orphan brands and regenerate them, in effect becoming "orphan adopters."

Redox

Redox, a company headed by two former P&G executives, bought Oxydol for an estimated $7 million. P&G had marketed Oxydol since 1927, but the brand was stocked by only 15 percent of U.S. stores and was only available in grocery stores by the time Redox purchased it. Annual sales of Oxydol had fallen from $80 million in 1992 to a mere $5 million in 2000. While focus groups revealed that older consumers exhibited more brand loyalty and were unlikely to switch to Oxydol, consumers in their twenties were less loyal and in fact wanted to buy different detergent than their parents. Redox repositioned Oxydol as an "extreme clean," updated the packaging by enlarging the letter X and using a green container, and launched a Web site (www.the-extreme-clean.com) boasting, "We're proud that Oxydol kicks some mean bootie in the washing machine." By summer 2001, Oxydol was stocked in 70 percent of the retail outlets in the United States.

Following the success of Oxydol, Redox purchased Biz bleach, another orphan, from P&G. The two brands combined brought in an estimated $80 million in 2001. Soon space at a premium, brand consolidation will become increasingly necessary to create a stronger brand, cut costs, and focus marketing efforts.[35]

Finally, a more permanent solution may be to discontinue the product altogether. The marketplace is littered with brands that either failed to establish an adequate level of brand equity or saw their sources of brand equity disappear because of changes in the marketing environment. Companies sometimes spin off their orphan brands when sales drop too far. Campbell spun off a number of labels, including Vlasic pickles and Swanson frozen dinners in 1998. Similarly, American Home Products spun off Chef Boyardee, Bumble Bee tuna, and Pam cooking spray. Other companies sell the orphan, as Procter & Gamble did by selling its Oxydol laundry detergent to Redox Brands in 2000. Branding Brief 13-10 describes how the existence of orphan brands has spawned a new business model of "orphan adopters."

Harvard professor Nancy Koehn explains that old brands retain some value because consumers often remember them from childhood. "There's at least an unconscious link," says Koehn.[36] Perhaps this fact helps to explain why a Web site called www.hometownfavorites.com, which offers more than 400 exotic orphan brands such as Bre'r Rabbit Molasses and My-T-Fine Pudding, has revenue approaching $1 million.

thereafter, the private equity firm Allied Capital acquired a majority stake in the company for $22 million.

River West

River West, founded in 2002 by a former Kraft executive, has helped rescue seven brands from the trash heap: Nuprin pain reliever, Metrecal diet drink, Soho soft drinks, Silkience shampoo, Structure men's clothing, Underalls underwear, and Coleco videogames. The company does not actually buy brands, but collects a royalty from the manufacturer based on sales. River West took Coleco, which had not survived the 1980s, and relaunched it to a gaming audience of 20- and 30-somethings who remembered growing up with the brand. River West introduced new hand-held and head-to-head games for Coleco, and announced plans to relaunch Colecovision, an early 1980s precursor to the ultra-modern video game consoles Xbox and Playstation. The brand took in an estimated $50 million in 2005. To revive Nuprin, River West expanded the brand's range beyond just ibuoprofen into a full-line pain medication available only in CVS drug stores.

These examples demonstrates how the company's business model is predicated on finding a new story to tell with the brands. "We really don't see ourselves as a nostalgia company," said Paul Earle, founder and president of River West. "We can only target the heartstrings for only so long. That is not a sustainable business model."

Sources: Steve Watkins, "Investment Firm to Sell Redox Brands," *Cincinnati Business Courier,* 18 October 2004; Jim Hopkins, "Partners Turn Decrepit Detergent into Boffo Start-Up," *USA Today,* 20 June 2001; John Schmeltzer, "Reviving the Past," *Chicago Tribune,* 2 May 2006, 1.

As long as orphan brands remain popular with a core audience, it seems that companies are willing to sell them.[37]

Obsoleting Existing Products. How do you decide which brands to attempt to revitalize (or at least milk) and which ones to obsolete? Beecham chose to abandon such dying brands as 5-Day deodorant pads, Rose Milk skin care lotion, and Serutam laxative, but attempted to resurrect Aqua Velva aftershave, Geritol iron and vitamin supplement, and Brylcreem hair styling products. The decision to retire a brand depends on a number of factors. Aaker outlines strategic questions to ask when considering whether to invest in a fading brand (see Figure 13-3).[38]

Fundamentally, the issue is the existing and latent equity of the brand. As the head of consumer packaged-goods giant Unilever commented in explaining his company's decision to review about 75 percent of its brands and lines of businesses for possible sell-offs, "If businesses aren't creating value, we shouldn't be in them. It's like having a nice garden that gets weeds. You have to clean it up, so the light and air get in to the blooms which are likely to grow the best."[39] Branding Brief 13-11 describes how Unilever is attempting to clean up its brand portfolio.

BRANDING BRIEF 13-11

Brand Migration at Unilever

Unilever, which was formed in 1929 by the merger of Dutch-owned Margarine Unie and the British-based Lever Brothers soap concern, owned more than 1,600 distinct brands in 2000. They include Lipton tea, Snuggle fabric softener, Ragu pasta sauces, Birds Eye frozen foods, Close-Up toothpaste, Calvin Klein fragrances, and Dove personal care products. Unilever also had thousands of lesser-known brands that were not strong competitors in their markets. In an effort called "Path to Growth" designed to get the most value from its brand portfolio, the company announced in 1999 its intention of eliminating three-quarters of its brands by 2003.

Antony Burgmans, Unilever co-chairman, described the means of reducing the brand portfolio:

Some [brands] we will try and fold into a power brand. . . . Another way of doing it is just letting [a brand] fade away and see where it stops. And some may be disposed of.

The company intended to retain its global brands such as Lipton, as well as its regional brands and "local jewels" such as Persil, the leading detergent in the United Kingdom. Unilever sold brands such as Batchelors and Elizabeth Arden, delisted brands including Blueband and Krona margarine, and merged second-tier brands like Radion into leading brands like Surf. Additionally, Unilever planned to reduce headcount by 25,000, or 10 percent of its workforce, in five years. The company also planned to close 100 of its 380 manufacturing sites.

While Unilever was reducing its brand portfolio, it was also making several high-profile acquisitions and expanding into services. Between 1996 and 2000, the company spent more than $28 billion on acquisitions. In 2000, it acquired Slim-Fast Foods and Ben & Jerry's ice cream for a total of more than $2.6 billion. Since only 6 percent of Slim-Fast's sales came from outside North

Market Prospects

- Is the rate of decline orderly and predictable?
- Are there pockets of enduring demand?
- What are the reasons for the decline—is it temporary? Might it be reversed?

Competitive Intensity

- Are there dominant competitors with unique skills or assets?
- Are there many competitors unwilling to exit or contract gracefully?
- Are customers brand-loyal? Is there product differentiation?
- Are there price pressures?

Brand Strength and Organizational Capabilities

- Is the brand strong? Does it enjoy high recognition and positive, meaningful associations?
- What is the market share position and trend?
- Does the business have some key sustainable competitive advantages with respect to key segments?
- Can the business manage a milking strategy?
- Is there synergy with other businesses?
- Does the brand fit with the firm's current strategic thrust?
- What are the exit barriers?

FIGURE 13-3

Investment Decisions in a Declining Industry

America, Unilever expected to use its global distribution network to significantly expand the brand. Ben & Jerry's gave Unilever a superpremium ice cream to compete against Häagen-Dazs, owned by rival General Mills' Pillsbury unit. Unilever also added a host of services in the "health, hygiene, and indulgence sectors." The company launched MyHome, a home-cleaning service available in the United Kingdom, and opened a chain of tea houses under the name Cha.

By the end of the first quarter in 2001, Unilever had significantly reduced its portfolio to 900 brands, and had another 250 brands "marked for disposal." Unilever estimated it achieved $356 million in cost savings in 2001 from its brand reductions. Following this initial success, the company continued on its "Path to Growth," further lowering the number of brands it owned to 400 by 2005. The company still fell short of sales targets, in part because its heritage as a joint Anglo-Dutch company involved higher personnel and marketing costs, with many job functions and ad agencies overlapping. In 2003, Unilever posted $44.8 billion in sales, on par with rival Procter & Gamble. Because Unilever employed more than twice as many people as P&G, however, its net income for the year was 45 percent lower than P&G's. Unilever launched a parallel program, called "One Unilever," to remedy the duplication, streamline the agency buys, and eliminate many "contradictory local [marketing] projects."

Sources: John Willman, "Leaner, Cleaner, and Healthier Is the Stated Aim," *Financial Times,* 23 February 2000; John Thornhill, "A Bad Time to Be in Consumer Goods," *Financial Times,* 28 September 2000; "Unilever's Goal: 'Power Brands,'" *Advertising Age,* 3 January 2000; "Unilever Axes 25,000 Jobs," *CNNfn,* 22 February 2000; "Unilever Sees 395 Mln Eur Cost Savings This Yr from Brand Reduction," *AFX* (UK), 9 May 2001; "A Chat with Unilever's Niall FitzGerald," *Business Week Online,* 2 August 2001; Harriet Marsh, "Unilever a Year Down the 'Path,'" *Marketing,* 22 February 2001, 30; Deborah Ball, "Despite Revamp, Unwieldy Unilver Falls Behind Rivals," *Wall Street Journal,* 3 January 2005, A1.

Review

Effective brand management requires taking a long-term view of marketing decisions and recognizing that any changes in the supporting marketing program for a brand may, by changing consumer knowledge, affect the success of future marketing programs. A long-term view also dictates proactive strategies designed to maintain and enhance customer-based brand equity over time in the face of external changes in the marketing environment and internal changes in a firm's marketing goals and programs.

Marketers reinforce brand equity by marketing actions that consistently convey the meaning of the brand to consumers in terms of what products the brand represents, what core benefits it supplies, and what needs it satisfies, and in terms of how the brand makes those products superior and which strong, favorable, and unique brand associations should exist in the minds of consumers. The most important consideration in reinforcing brands is the consistency of the marketing support that the brand receives, both in the amount and nature of that support. Consistency does not mean that marketers should avoid making any changes in the marketing program; in fact, many tactical changes may be necessary to maintain the strategic thrust and direction of the brand. Unless there is some change in the marketing environment, however, there is little need to deviate from a successful positioning. In such cases, the critical points of parity and points of difference that represent sources of brand equity should be vigorously preserved and defended.

The strategy for reinforcing brand meaning depends on the nature of the brand association. For brands whose core associations are primarily product-related attributes and functional benefits, innovation in product design, manufacturing, and merchandising is especially critical to maintaining or enhancing brand equity. For brands whose core associations are primarily non-product-related attributes and symbolic or experiential benefits, relevance in user and usage imagery is especially critical to maintaining or enhancing brand equity.

In managing brand equity, managers have to make tradeoffs between those marketing activities that fortify the brand and reinforce its meaning, and those that attempt to leverage or borrow from its existing brand equity to reap some financial benefit. At some point, failure to fortify the brand will diminish brand awareness and weaken brand image. Without these sources of brand equity, the brand itself may not continue to yield valuable benefits. Figure 13-4 summarizes brand reinforcement strategies.

Revitalizing a brand requires marketers to either recapture lost sources of brand equity or establish new ones. According to the CBBE framework, two general approaches are possible: (1) Expand the depth or breadth (or both) of brand awareness by improving brand recall and recognition by consumers during purchase or consumption settings; and (2) improve the strength, favorability, and uniqueness of brand associations making up the brand image. This latter approach may involve programs directed at existing or new brand associations.

With a fading brand, the depth of brand awareness is often not as much of a problem as the breadth; that is, consumers tend to think of the brand in very narrow ways. Although changing brand awareness is probably the easiest means of creating new sources of brand equity, we may often have to create a new marketing program to improve the strength, favorability, and uniqueness of brand associations. As part of this repositioning, we may tap new markets. The challenge in all these efforts to modify the brand image is not to destroy the equity that already exists. Figure 13-5 summarizes brand revitalization strategies.

Managers must also consider the role of different brands in the portfolio and their relationships over time. In particular, a brand migration strategy should ensure that consumers understand how various brands in the portfolio can satisfy their needs as they change over time or as the products and brands themselves change over time. Strategies exist to retire those brands whose sources of brand equity have essentially dried up or that have acquired damaging and difficult-to-change associations.

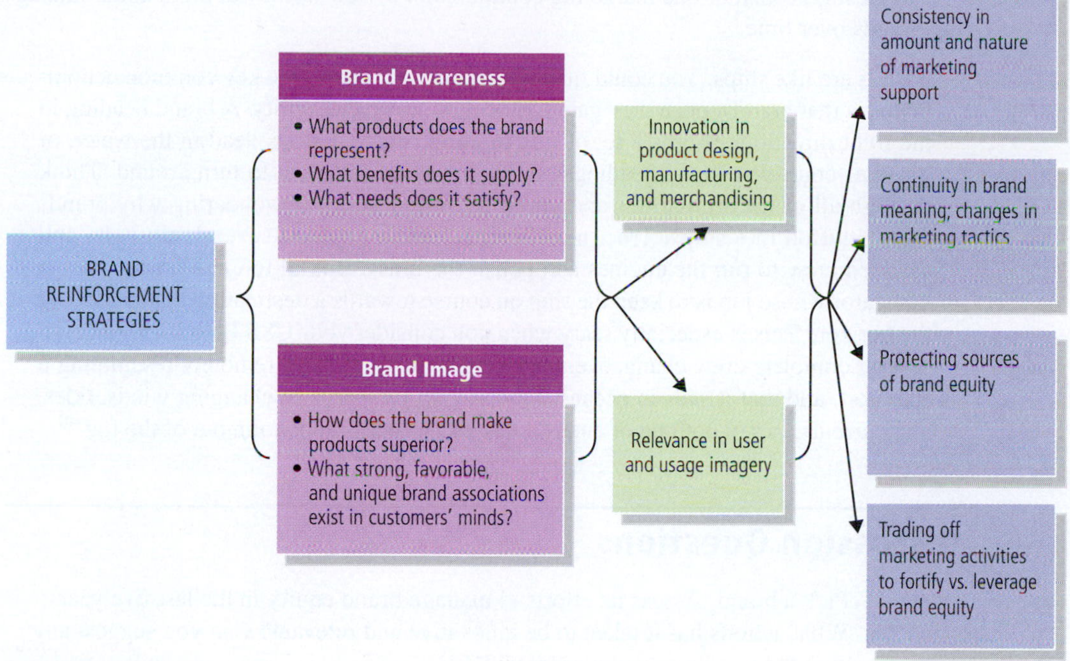

FIGURE 13-4

Brand Reinforcement Strategies

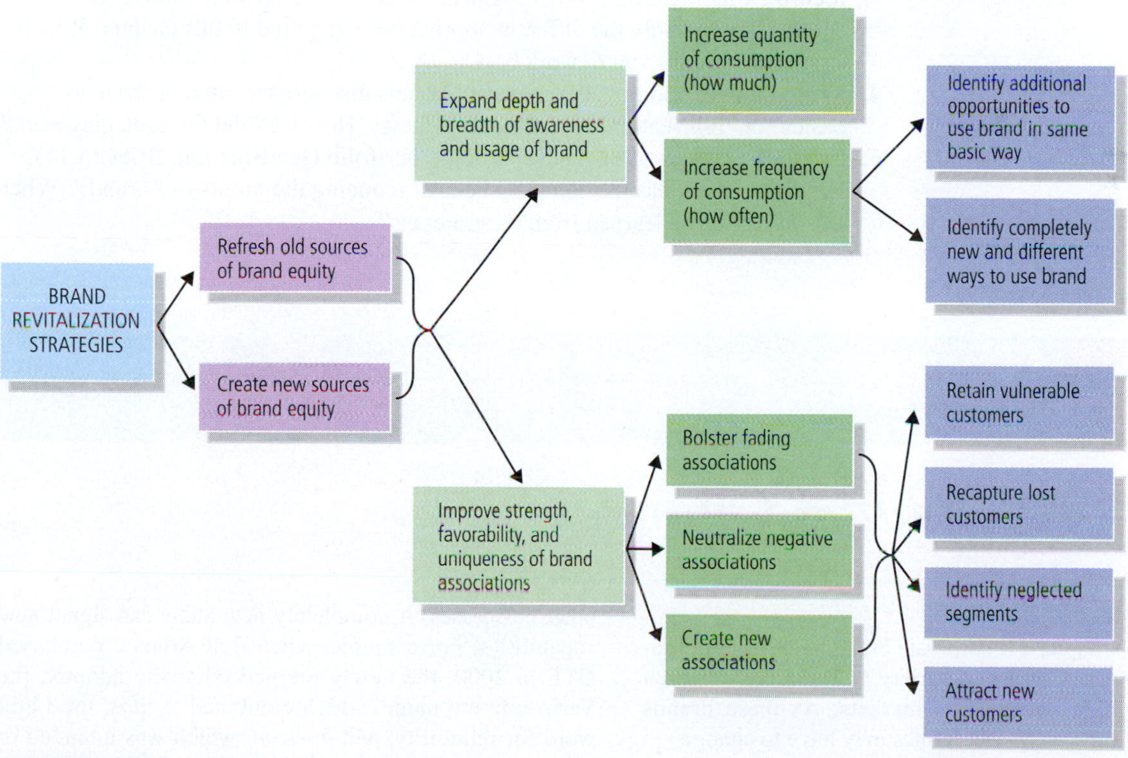

FIGURE 13-5

Brand Revitalization Strategies

In closing, consider one marketing commentator's view of how to think about managing brands over time:

> Brands are like ships. You could fill a book with analogies. One key common denominator is that brands, once they gain momentum, overtake agility. A brand heading in the right direction absorbs a lot of mishandling before it stops dead in the water, or goes off course. A brand heading south takes effort and time to turn around. Think through all of the similarities and you'll soon find yourself wondering why brands aren't staffed like ships. True, most brands have a captain, several admirals, and assorted crew to run the engines and polish the brass. But all too few brands have a navigator whose job is to keep the ship on course towards a destination that is far over the horizon. This is especially scary when you consider your USS Brand will undergo several complete crew changeovers before reaching anything remotely resembling a safe port, and that it sails in oceans studded with the perils of changing winds, tides, and currents, to say nothing of enemy subs and icebergs appearing out of the fog.[40]

Discussion Questions

1. Pick a brand. Assess its efforts to manage brand equity in the last five years. What actions has it taken to be innovative and relevant? Can you suggest any changes to its marketing program?
2. Pick a product category. Examine the histories of the leading brands in that category over the last decade. How would you characterize their efforts to reinforce or revitalize brand equity?
3. Identify a fading brand. What suggestions can you offer to revitalize its brand equity? Try to apply the different approaches suggested in this chapter. Which strategies would seem to work best?
4. Try to think of additional examples of brands that adopted either a "back to basics" or "reinvention" revitalization strategy. How well did the strategies work?
5. Conduct a review of the Unilever brand portfolio (see Branding Brief 13.11). How successful has the company been at reducing the number of brands? What lessons are to be learned from its strategies?

BRAND FOCUS 13.0

Corporate Name Changes

Rationale

As noted in Chapter 11, corporate brand names and corporate images can perform a variety of functions to reach multiple audiences or target markets. As these brands evolve over time, corporate names may have to change.

Hundreds of private and public companies change their names each year because of mergers and acquisitions with other businesses. A completely new name can signal new capabilities. For example, when Bell Atlantic purchased GTE in 2000, the newly merged company adopted the Verizon brand name, which combined *veritas,* the Latin word for reliability, and *horizon,* which was intended to signify a forward-looking attitude. In other cases, a new corporate name arising from a merger or acquisition may be based on some combination of the two existing corporate names. For example, when Glaxo Wellcome merged in 2000 with SmithKline Beecham, the new company became GlaxoSmithKline, and J.P. Morgan & Co. and Chase Manhattan Corporation became J.P. Morgan Chase after their 2000 merger. Finally, in some cases, the firm chooses the name with more inherent brand equity and relegates the other to a sub-brand role or eliminates it altogether. For example, when Citicorp merged with Travelers, the latter's name was dropped, although its familiar red umbrella symbol was retained as part of the new Citigroup brand look. Deciding which is the appropriate strategy is a matter of weighing the existing and potential brand equity of each brand in the context of the newly merged business.

Corporate names also change because of divestitures, leveraged buyouts, or the sale of assets. For example, when Andersen Consulting was allowed to separate from Arthur Andersen following an arbitrator's ruling in 2000, it was required to stop using the Anderson Consulting name by the end of the year. Following an extensive naming search and rebranding project, which included names solicited by Andersen Consulting employees, the firm was renamed "Accenture"—an employee suggestion meant to connote an "accent on the future." The move to a new name proved especially fortuitous when in 2002 Arthur Andersen was convicted of obstruction of justice in the wake of the Enron scandal and ceased to operate as a business. Some residual negative perceptions from Arthur Andersen would likely have transferred to the Andersen Consulting brand.

Corporate names can also chanage to correct public misperceptions about the nature of the company's business. For example, Europe's third-largest food company, BSN, renamed itself for its Danone brand—a hugely successful fresh dairy products subsidiary, second only to Coca-Cola in terms of branded sales in Europe—because many consumers didn't know what the old name stood for. Moreover, BSN was already used by other companies in other countries: a bank in Spain, a textile firm in the United States, and a television station in Japan.[41]

Significant shifts in corporate strategy may necessitate name changes. For example, US Steel changed its name to USX to downplay the importance of steel and metal in its product mix. Allegheny Airlines changed its name to USAir when it moved from a regional to a national carrier, and then later to USAirways when it wanted to be seen as an international carrier.

Finally, the desire to create distance from scandal can also motivate a name change. A new name cannot repair a company's damaged reputation, though, and experts advise against making a switch in the midst of bad publicity; otherwise the stigma and suspicion will follow the new name. Philip Morris Co. decided to change its name to get away from the association with tobacco and emphasize its range of companies, including Kraft Foods. In 2003, the company adopted the new name Altria Group Inc. ValuJet Airlines in 1997 merged with AirTran and the new company took the AirTran name to distance itself from the 1996 ValuJet crash.

Guidelines

Although name changes can yield growth opportunities, experts recommend a cautious approach to renaming. Name changes are typically complicated, time-consuming, and expensive, and firms should undertake them only when compelling marketing or financial considerations prevail and a proper supporting marketing program can be put into place. A new corporate name cannot hide product or other marketing deficiencies. Rebranding campaigns usually forfeit the brand recognition and loyalty that went along with the old name. And a new name requires extensive legal and URL vetting to make sure it is available and appropriate.

Once the firm has chosen the new name, the practical work of introducing it to clients, suppliers, and employees begins—often with the launch of a new marketing campaign and the opportunity to work with a blank canvas. A company with little consumer exposure may spend as much as $5 million on research, advertising, and other marketing costs (new signs, stationery, business cards, Web site, and so on) to change its identity, but a company with a high public profile may have to spend up to $100 million.[42] These factors combine to make corporate rebranding a time- and resource-intensive process demanding a company's total commitment in order to succeed.

Many of the same branding issues we discussed in Chapter 4 are relevant in choosing or changing a corporate name. Firms should evaluate candidate names in terms of memorability, meaningfulness, likability, protectability, adaptability, and transferability. The importance of the name will depend on the corporate branding strategy and the marketing objectives for different target markets. If the consumer market is the primary objective, the name may reflect or be suggestive of certain product characteristics, benefits, or values. Consolidated Foods Corporation switched to Sara Lee Corporation; Castle & Cooke, Inc., switched to Dole Food Company; and United Brands Company switched to Chiquita Brands International.

It takes a substantial effort to sell the new name to employees, customers, suppliers, investors, and the public at large.[43] Initial reaction is almost always negative simply because people resist change. Sometimes, however, an especially harsh reception will cause a firm to abandon a new name. One of the biggest name-change fizzles ever occurred with UAL, the parent company of United Airlines. In 1987, UAL was no longer just an airline but a

$9 billion business that owned Hertz car rental, as well as Westin and Hilton International hotels. The company decided a new name was necessary to convey the identity of a travel company that offered one-stop shopping. After extensive research, it chose the name "Allegis," a compound of "allegiance" and "aegis." Public reaction was decidedly negative. Critics maintained that the name was difficult to pronounce, sounded pretentious, and had little connection with travel services. Famed mogul Donald Trump, formerly a major UAL shareholder, said the new name was "better suited to the next world-class disease." After six weeks and $7 million in research and promotion expenditures, the company decided to shed its car rental and hotel businesses and rename the surviving company United Airlines Inc.[44]

Over time, though, if properly chosen and handled, new names gain familiarity and acceptance. Guidelines that encourage uniformity and consistency in the appearance and usage of the brand help make the implementation effective; these rules should be part of a revised brand charter (see Chapter 8).

Creating the UBS Brand

UBS was formed in 1998 when Union Bank of Switzerland and Swiss Bank Corporation merged. The bank struggled for recognition outside Switzerland, especially in the United States. After a period of acquiring better-known companies such as SG Warburg and PaineWebber, UBS reviewed its branding strategy. The results showed product overlap among UBS businesses, a weak branding culture, and a focus on individual employees rather than on the brand.[45]

The company worked with consultants and looked at research showing similarities between the needs of clients across different parts of the business. To better address these needs in a consistent manner and reduce overlap between sub-brands, in 2003 the company adopted the UBS brand for all its businesses. It decided to use only the UBS letters in its name, a challenging tactic because the name had no built-in personality.[46]

To build equity in the new brand, UBS launched a global brand-building effort. A new brand group was created to handle all advertising for the firm. The goal was to emphasize the bank's scope and resources, while also playing up its one-on-one client relationships. The "You and Us" campaign debuted in 2004, with global campaign expenditures above $100 million. It illustrated the traditional banker-client relationship as well as the international presence of the company by using wide shots of two people in sweeping mountain settings or in airy corporate spaces. "Could this be the world's most powerful two-person financial firm?" asks a voiceover or a tagline. "You and us: UBS." The goal was to assure customers that they could rely on the breadth and depth of the bank's offerings whatever their financial needs.

In terms of brand recognition, the effort worked. In 2004, UBS ranked 45th worldwide in its debut on *BusinessWeek*'s list of the Top 100 Global Brands. Awareness of the company in its target segments has also risen.

Notes

1. J. K. Wall, "Delta Opens Faucet on Marketing with New Ads," *USA Today,* 4 May 4 2005, 6B.
2. Robert Levine, "The Cow in Winter," *Fortune,* 17 April 2006, 55–56.
3. Ibid.
4. Bruce Horovitz, "Southern Finger-Lickin' Roots Help KFC Revamp," *USA Today,* 20 April 2005, 3B.
5. For an empirical examination of the power of sustained advertising, see Cathy J. Cobb-Walgren, Cynthia A. Ruble, and Naveen Donthu, "Brand Equity, Brand Preference, and Purchase Intent," *Journal of Advertising* 24, no. 3 (Fall 1995): 25–40.
6. Marj Charlier, "Coors Pours on Western Themes to Revive Flagship Beer's Cachet," *Wall Street Journal,* 2 August 1994, B6.
7. Chris Roush, "At Timex, They're Positively Glowing," *Business Week,* 12 July 1993, 141.
8. Jonathan Auerbach, "Smith Corona Seeks Protection of Chapter 11," *Wall Street Journal,* 6 July 1995, A4.
9. Melanie Wells, "Foggy Bottom," *Forbes,* 28 May 2001, 155.
10. Michael V. Copeland, "Stuck in the Spin Cycle," *Business 2.0,* May 2005, 74.
11. Peter H. Farquhar, "Managing Brand Equity," *Marketing Research* 1 (September 1989): 24–33.
12. Richard Gibson, "Classic Cheerios and Wheaties Reformulated," *Wall Street Journal,* 31 August 1994, B1.
13. Adapted from Suein L. Hwang, "As Rivals Innovate, Old-Line Bacardi Becomes a Chaser," *Wall Street Journal,* 6 July 1994, B4. See also Rich Brandes, "Liquor Holds Its Breath as Economy Teeters," *Beverage Industry,* 1 May 2001.
14. Michael J. McCarthy, "Pepsi Is Returning to Original Focus: Its Profitable Younger Generation," *Wall Street Journal,* 22 January 1993, B6.
15. "Glass Half Full," *Journal of Commerce,* 30 May 2005, 36A.

16. Susan Heckler, Kevin Lane Keller, and Michael J. Houston, "The Effects of Brand Name Suggestiveness on Advertising Recall," *Journal of Marketing* 62 (January 1998): 48–57.
17. Raymond Serafin, "BMW: From Yuppie-Mobile to Smart Car of the '90s," *Advertising Age,* 3 October 1994, S2.
18. Norman C. Berry, "Revitalizing Brands," *Journal of Consumer Marketing* 5, no. 3 (Summer 1988): 15–20.
19. Dawn C. Chmielewski, "Napster Posts Loss Despite Surge in Sales," *Los Angeles Times,* 9 February 2006, C1.
20. John D. Cripps, "Heuristics and Biases in Timing the Replacement of Durable Products," *Journal of Consumer Research* 21 (September 1994): 304–318.
21. Ronald Alsop, "Giving Fading Brands a Second Chance," *Wall Street Journal,* 24 January 1989, B1.
22. Ellen Byron, "How Coach Won a Rich Purse by Inventing New Uses for Bags," *Wall Street Journal,* 17 November 2004, A1.
23. Darrel D. Muehling and David E. Sprott, "The Power of Reflection: An Empirical Examination of Nostalgia Advertising Effects," *Journal of Advertising* 33, no. 3 (Fall 2004): 25.
24. Elizabeth S. Moore, William L. Wilkie, and Richard J. Lutz, "Passing the Torch: Intergenerational Influences as a Source of Brand Equity." *Journal of Marketing* 66, no. 2 (April 2002): 17.
25. Marj Charlier, "Yuengling's Success Defies Convention," *Wall Street Journal,* 26 August 1993, B1.
26. Tim Triplett, "Generic Fear to Xerox Is Brand Equity to FedEx," *Marketing News,* 15 August 1994, 12–13.
27. Mike Beirne, "New Logo, Upscale Image In at Revamped Ramada," *Brandweek,* November 8, 2004, p. 6.
28. Stephane Fitch, "Pocketing a New Market," *Forbes,* October 13, 2003, p. 125.
29. David W. Stewart, "Advertising in a Slow-Growth Economy," *American Demographics* (September 1994): 40–46.
30. Ibid.
31. Tracie Rozhon, "Reinventing Tommy: More Surf, Less Logo," *New York Times,* 16 March 2003, 1.
32. Deborah Ball and Sarah Ellison, "Two Shampoos Lather Up for Duel," *Wall Street Journal,* 28 January 2003, B7.
33. Kathleen Kerwin, "Can Jeep Bust Out of Its Rut?" *BusinessWeek,* 24 January 2005, 37.
34. Peter Lattman, "Rebound," *Forbes,* 28 March 2005, 58.
35. Jennifer Reingold, "Darwin Goes Shopping," *Financial World,* 1 September 1993, 44.
36. Nancy F. Koehn, *Brand New: How Enterpreneurs Earned Consumers' Trust from Wedgwood to Dell* (Boston: Harvard Business School Press, 2001).
37. Betsy McKay, "Why Coke Indulges (the Few) Fans of Tab," *Wall Street Journal,* 13 April 2001, B1; Devon Spurgeon, "Aurora Bet It Could Win by Fostering Neglected Foods," *Wall Street Journal,* 13 April 2001, B1; Jim Hopkins, "Partners Turn Decrepit Detergent into Boffo Start-Up," *USA Today,* 20 June 2001, 6B; Matthew Swibel, "Spin Cycle," *Forbes,* 2 April 2001, 118.
38. David A. Aaker, *Managing Brand Equity* (New York: Free Press, 1991).
39. Tara Parker-Pope, "Unilever Plans a Long-Overdue Pruning," *Wall Street Journal,* 3 September 1996, A13.
40. Brad Morgan, "Navigating Marketing Waters Is a Risky, Learning Process," *Brandweek,* 5 September 1994, 17.
41. "BSWho?" *The Economist,* 14 May 1994, 70.
42. Dottie Enrico, "Companies Play Name-Change Game," *USA Today,* 28 December 1994, 4B.
43. Amanda Bennett, "Firms Grapple to Find New Names as Images and Industries Change," *Wall Street Journal,* 17 November 1986, 36.
44. "Allegis: A $7 Million Name Is Grounded," *San Francisco Examiner,* 16 June 1987, C9.
45. Jestyn Thirkell-White, "UBS: Brand Building in a Global Market," *Admap,* July/August 2004.
46. Haig Simoniam, "Three Letters Gain a Personality," *Financial Times,* 18 April 2005.

14

MANAGING BRANDS OVER GEOGRAPHIC BOUNDARIES AND MARKET SEGMENTS

Preview

An important consideration in managing brand equity is recognizing and accounting for different types of consumers in developing brand marketing programs. In previous chapters we've considered how and why marketers may need to (1) create brand portfolios to satisfy different market segments and (2) develop brand migration strategies to attract new and retain existing customers through brand and family life cycles. This chapter examines in more detail the implications for managing brand equity given the existence of different types of market segments. We'll pay particular attention to international issues and global branding strategies, given their increased prevalence and importance.

Specifically, we begin by considering brand management issues over regional, demographic, and cultural market segments. Next, after reviewing the basic rationale for taking brands into new international markets, we consider the broader issues in developing a global brand strategy and look at some of the pros and cons of developing a standardized global marketing program.

In the remainder of the chapter we concentrate on specific strategic and tactical issues in building global customer-based brand equity, organized around the concept of the "Ten Commandments of Global Branding." To illustrate these guidelines, we'll rely on global brand pioneers such as Coca-Cola, Nestlé, and Procter & Gamble. Brand Focus 14.0 addresses branding issues in the exploding Chinese market.[1]

Regional Market Segments

Regionalization is an important recent trend that, perhaps on the surface, seems to run counter to globalization. Although marketers have developed different marketing programs for different geographic regions of a country for years, regional marketing received a boost in the United States with Campbell's well-publicized move to a regionalized marketing plan. Starting in the 1980s, Campbell began to tailor its soup products, advertising, promotion, and sales efforts to fit different regions of the country—and even to individual neighborhoods within cities. The company divided the United States into 22 regions; it gave a combined sales and marketing force marketing strategy and media buying information and an ad and trade promotion budget.[2] Some examples of tailored Campbell's programs during this time included a car giveaway in Pittsburgh tied to a local TV station, short film spots for Campbell's dip soups and its brand name mushrooms in two Sacramento cinemas, soup billboards atop a ski lift in upstate New York, and a Spanish radio and giveaway campaign for V-8 juice in Northern California.[3] In a similar spirit, Pepsi divided its U.S. operations into four regional companies to gear its marketing locally.

Around the same time, Joel Garreau published *The Nine Nations of North America,* which argued that North America was divided into nine different "nations," regions populated by people sharing distinct values, attitudes, and styles. Garreau found the differences between the nine areas manifested in market behavior. As one observer noted:

> [P]eople are different in different parts of the country. For example, Northeasterners and Midwesterners prefer chicken noodle and tomato soups, but in California, cream of mushroom is number one. Pepper pot soup sells primarily in the Philadelphia area, and cream of vegetable on the West Coast. People in the Southwest drive more pickup trucks, people in the Northeast more vans, and Californians like high-priced imported cars such as BMWs and Mercedes Benzes. Texans drive big cars, New Yorkers like smaller ones. New Hampshirites drink more beer per capita than

other Americans. The anxious denizens of Atlanta consume more aspirin and antacids a head, and sweet toothed Mormons of Salt Lake City eat more candy bars and marshmallows.[4]

Interest in regional marketing derives from a number of factors: the realization that mass markets are splintering, the availability of computerized sales data from supermarket scanners that reveal pockets of sales strengths and weaknesses in different parts of the country, and the opportunity to employ marketing communications that permit more focused targeting of consumer groups defined along virtually any lines. The shift from national advertising to sales promotions, in particular, necessitated more market-by-market planning.

Different battles are now being fought between brands in different regions of the country. Anheuser-Busch and Miller Brewing have waged a fierce battle in Texas for years, where nearly 1 in 10 beers sold in the United States is consumed. Anheuser-Busch has made sizable inroads in recent years through special ad campaigns, displays, and sales strategies. As one observer noted, "Texans believe it's a whole different country down here. They don't want you to just slap an armadillo in a TV spot."[5]

Regional marketing is not without its drawbacks.[6] Modifying products can lead to production headaches. For example, when Campbell set out to make a spicier version of its nacho cheese soup for the west and southwest United States, the jalapeno peppers added during manufacturing created a gas cloud that factory workers could not overcome! Marketing efficiency may suffer and costs may rise with regional marketing. Moreover, regional campaigns may force local producers to become more competitive or they may blur a brand's national identity.

Other Demographic and Cultural Segments

Any market segment—however we define it—may be a candidate for a specialized marketing and branding program. For example, demographic dimensions such as age, income, gender, and race—as well as psychographic considerations—often are related to more fundamental differences in shopping behaviors or attitudes about brands. These differences can often serve as the rationale for a separate branding and marketing program. The decision ultimately rests on the costs and benefits of customized marketing efforts versus those of a less targeted focus.

For example, Chapter 13 described how important it is for marketers to consider age segments, and how younger consumers can be brought into the consumer franchise. As another example, the 2000 census revealed that Asians and Hispanics accounted for 79 million of 281 million people in the United States and an estimated $1 trillion in annual purchasing power. Various firms have created specialized marketing programs with different products, advertising, promotions, and so on to better reach and persuade this market. For example, Sears Roebuck & Company's most profitable stores were the ones near Hispanic neighborhoods that carried clothing and cosmetics specially designed for Hispanics. Bank of America prospered by targeting Asians in San Francisco with separate TV campaigns aimed at Chinese, Korean, and Vietnamese customers. When Frito-Lay introduced line extensions in 1997 targeted primarily to the U.S. Hispanic market, with zesty flavors such as Salsa Verde and Flamin' Hot Sarositos, sales topped $100 million. General Mills approached the Hispanic market with a cereal line, Para su Familia ("For Your Family"), that featured bilingual packaging and a strong nutritional message.[7] Branding Brief 14-1 describes marketing efforts to build brand equity with African Americans.

Beyond the expense, other challenges exist in targeting cultural groups. Data on media habits, buying behavior, and so on are difficult to obtain. For example, although Mott's Inc. managed to build a following among Hispanics for its Mott's Juice, Hawaiian Punch, and

Clamato brands, the company admits that it had few numbers to use for guidance. Language problems can make surveys hard to conduct, especially in Asian households where a range of languages and dialects may prevail. One major concern raised by marketing critics about creating separate marketing campaigns for different demographic groups is that some consumers may not like being targeted because they are "different," because that only reinforces their image as outsiders or a minority. Moreover, consumers not in the targeted segment may feel more alienated or distanced from the company and brand as a result.[8]

Rationale for Going International

A number of well-known global brands have derived much of their sales and profits from nondomestic markets for years, for example, Coca-Cola, Shell, Bayer, Rolex, Marlboro, Pampers, and Mercedes-Benz, to name a few. Brands such as Apple computers, L'Oreal cosmetics, and Nescafé instant coffee have become fixtures on the global landscape (see Branding Brief 14-2). The successes of these brands have provided encouragement to many firms to market their brands internationally. A number of other forces have also contributed to the growing interest in global marketing, including the following:

- Perception of slow growth and increased competition in domestic markets
- Belief in enhanced overseas growth and profit opportunities
- Desire to reduce costs from economies of scale
- Need to diversify risk
- Recognition of global mobility of customers

In more and more product categories, the ability to establish a global profile is becoming virtually a prerequisite for success.[9] For example, in luxury goods such as jewelry, watches, and handbags where the addressable market is a relatively small percentage of the global market, a global profile is necessary to grow profitably.

Ideally, the marketing program for a global brand consists of one product formulation, one package design, one advertising program, one pricing schedule, one distribution plan, and so on that would turn out to be the most effective and efficient possible option for each and every country in which the brand was sold. Unfortunately, such a uniformly optimal strategy is rarely possible. Before we consider the decisions in developing a global marketing program for a brand, and the factors affecting the tradeoff between standardization and customization, let's first consider some of the main advantages and disadvantages of creating globally standardized marketing programs for brands.

Advantages of Global Marketing Programs

A number of potential advantages have been put forth for the development of a global marketing program (see Figure 14-1).[10] In general, the more standardized the marketing program—the less it varies from country to country—the more these different advantages will actually be realized.

Economies of scale in production and distribution
Lower marketing costs
Power and scope
Consistency in brand image
Ability to leverage good ideas quickly and efficiently
Uniformity of marketing practices

FIGURE 14-1

Advantages of Global Marketing Programs

BRANDING BRIEF 14-1

Marketing to African Americans

Census and marketing surveys have revealed the buying power of the African American community. Despite the fact that it represents approximately 13 percent of the population, with buying power approaching $800 billion, only $1.6 billion was spent to specifically target the African American market in 2003, or about 1 percent of total ad spending in the United States. Although much marketing has targeted baby boomers, the elderly, Hispanics, and other demographic and psychographic groups, many critics argue that firms have not effectively targeted the African American market.

Because almost all African Americans speak English as their first and primary language and watch much network television, many companies rely on their general marketing campaigns to reach these consumers. Black media executives such as Thomas Burrell, chairman of Burrell Advertising in Chicago, the largest black-owned agency in the United States, maintains that such an approach is a mistake: "Black people aren't dark-skinned white people. We have different preferences and customs, and we require special effort."

African Americans can be found in virtually every income, education, and geographic segment. At the same time, they often have unique attitudes and behaviors that distinguish them from other groups, and many observers note the important role for them of religion, church, and family. As a result of their historical experiences, African Americans are often thought to exhibit a strong togetherness and pride in their heritage. In terms of buying habits, they spend a disproportionate amount of their income on apparel, footwear, and home electronics. For example, recognizing that African Americans often prefer larger helpings of sugar, cream, or nondairy creamer in their coffee, CoffeeMate began marketing to African Americans more specifically through black radio, magazines, and billboards, with a corresponding increase in sales.

Alcohol and tobacco companies were some of the first firms to develop campaigns targeted specifically to African American consumers, in recognition of their different product preferences (they make a disproportionate amount of purchases of menthol cigarettes, certain types of hard liquors—brandy, scotch, cognac—and malt liquor beers). Given that African Americans are prone to certain health risks, food and drug advertising often also specifically targets African American consumers. Black adults carry higher risk for hypertension and cardiovascular disease, so ads for St. Joseph Aspirin highlighted the fact that the aspirin contains the dosage recommended by the Association of Black Cardiologists. Similarly, because black adults are more likely to suffer from diabetes, Kraft foods created a Diabetic & Delightful

Economies of Scale in Production and Distribution

From a supply-side or cost perspective, the primary advantages of a global marketing program are the manufacturing efficiencies and lower costs that derive from higher volumes in production and distribution. The more that strong experience curve effects exist—driving down the cost of making and marketing a product with increases in production—the more economies of scale in production and distribution from a standardized global marketing program will exist.

marketing program for its SnackWell cookies, sugar-free Jell-O, Cool Whip Free, and General Foods International Coffee.

In terms of building brand equity, the challenge is how to create relevant marketing programs and communication campaigns for African American consumers that accurately portray brand personality and user and usage imagery. The president of one black-owned agency asserted that the formula for marketing to blacks consists of relevance, recognition, and respect. Author Marlene Rossman offers several guidelines.

First, recognize the diversity of the African American market—just as in the mass market, there is great variety in lifestyle across different geographic and psychographic segments in the African American market. For example, in 2006 Infiniti introduced an ad campaign targeting Generation-X African American luxury car buyers that featured a jazz and hip-hop infused soundtrack. Gaining understanding clearly requires properly conducting and interpreting marketing research.

Second, design marketing campaigns relevant to the lifestyles of African Americans and reflecting their consumer sensibilities. One survey indicated that 60 percent of black consumers feel most television and print ads "are designed only for white people." What types of messages should marketers send? Rossman makes the following argument: "When marketing to African-Americans, keep in mind that they value self-image, style, and personal elegance . . . . African-Americans are trendsetters . . . . African-Americans often want to define their own style rather than follow what the establishment dictates."

Finally, explore media that specifically targets African Americans, such as cable's Black Entertainment Television (BET); *Ebony, Essence, Black Enterprise,* and other magazines and newspapers; and urban contemporary and other types of radio stations. Even general media should be bought differently. For example, through much of the 1990s, virtually none of the top 10 programs most watched by African Americans were on the list of the top 10 shows most watched by the general market.

The challenge is to target African Americans in a way that builds brand equity without fostering stereotypes, offending sensibilities, or lumping segments together. As with global brand programs, marketers should blend standardization and customization as appropriate.

Sources: Based on material from Marlene L. Rossman, *Multicultural Marketing: Selling to a Diverse America* (New York: AMACOM, 1994); and Barbara Lloyd, *Capitalizing on the American Dream: Marketing to America's Ethnic Minorities,* Stanford Business School independent study, 1990; "African American Marketing Profile," Magazine Publishers of America, 2004; Mike Beirne, "Has This Group Been Left Behind?" *Brandweek,* 14 March 2005.

Lower Marketing Costs

Another set of cost advantages arise from uniformity in packaging, advertising, promotion, and other marketing communication activities. In particular, the more uniform the branding strategy adopted across countries, the greater the potential cost savings that should be seen. A global corporate branding strategy such as Sony's is perhaps the most efficient means of spreading marketing costs across both products and countries.

BRANDING BRIEF 14-2

L'Oreal Colors the World

L'Oreal was founded in 1907 by French chemist Eugene Schueller, who developed a safe hair color formula named "Aureole." Today, L'Oreal is the largest cosmetics company in the world. It markets more than 500 brands and over 2,000 products in all sectors of the beauty business.

Recently, L'Oreal has pursued an aggressive global growth strategy, prompting one business writer to christen the company "the United Nations of beauty." L'Oreal has a number of global mega-brands that cast a broad net over the world's markets. For example, Maybelline is the best-selling brand in many Asian markets, while eastern Europeans prefer L'Oreal's French brands, and African immigrants in Europe go for the American brand Dark & Lovely. At the same time, the company ensures its business remains sound on a local level by establishing national divisions. Gilles Weil, L'Oreal's head of luxury products, said, "You have to be local and as strong as the best locals but backed by an international image and strategy."

One of L'Oreal's global success stories started with the acquisition of struggling American cosmetics company Maybelline in 1996. With the help of a series of innovative product introductions, L'Oreal turned Maybelline into the number-one makeup brand in the United States. Its star product was Wondercurl, a mascara and brush that curls and thickens eyelashes. Wondercurl took off again when L'Oreal took control of Maybelline Japan in 1999 and quickly introduced the product. Within three months, Wondercurl captured 18 percent of the market and became Japan's leading mascara. Unit sales of Maybelline Japan rose from 5 million to 12 million within one year of L'Oreal's takeover.

Within national markets, L'Oreal devotes attention to serving different customer segments. For example, in 2000 L'Oreal captured 20 percent of the $1.2 billion U.S. "ethnic hair care"

ExxonMobil

In 1999, ExxonMobil launched a $150 million marketing effort to promote its portfolio of brands (Exxon, Esso, Mobil, and General). To make sure the ads had the same look and feel regardless of the 100 or so countries in which they might appear, the company produced five hours of commercial footage to be used as a library by local markets. As many as six different casts acted out essentially the same story lines, and 25 different languages made up the voiceovers. ExxonMobil's ad agency, DDB Worldwide, noted that the campaign, which carried the tag line "We Are Drivers Too," was tweaked to account for cultural differences (making sure actors ate with their right hands in some shots, as is customary in some Muslim markets).[11] Management believed this approach helped to save the company millions.

Power and Scope

A global brand profile may communicate credibility.[12] Consumers may believe that selling in many diverse markets is an indication that a manufacturer has gained much expertise and acceptance. The fact that the brand is widely available may signal that the product is high quality and convenient to use. An admired global brand can also signal social status and prestige.[13] A prominent international profile may be especially important for certain

market, with separate acquisitions of Soft Sheen Products and Carson Products. The company considered the ethnic hair care market vital because African Americans account for 30 percent of total U.S. hair care expenditures, despite being only 13 percent of the population. These acquisitions figured to add to L'Oreal's 49 percent share of the $1.3 billion U.S. hair color market.

L'Oreal's next big focus for global growth was China, where in 2004 it purchased the country's most popular cosmetics brand, Yue Sai, and bought bargain brand Mininurse, which had an enviable distribution network of more than 250,000 small stores. L'Oreal also invested in a 32,000-square-foot laboratory in Pudong to develop products specific to the Chinese market, including products containing local ingredients such as ginkgo leaf and ginseng. One of the company's big challenges in China was educating consumers about the benefits of different cosmetic products. "In other countries women learn how to use cosmetics from the mom," said Paolo Gasparrini, president of L'Oreal China. "That's not the case in China. We have to substitute [for the] mom." Still, L'Oreal's Chinese sales in 2004 were up 58 percent from the previous year to $350 million.

In addition to China, L'Oreal was also experiencing growth in other developing markets. In 2005, revenues rose 42 percent in Russia, 22 percent in Taiwan, 15 percent in Thailand, 13 percent in Brazil and Mexico. L'Oreal's growth helped push revenues up 6 percent to $16.1 billion in 2005, ahead of all cosmetics competitors. As one analyst puts it, "L'Oreal is the only real global leader in every segment of the industry."

Sources: Richard C. Morais, "The Color of Beauty," *Forbes,* 27 November 2000, 170–176; Gail Edmondson, "L'Oreal: The Beauty of Global Branding," *Business Week,* 28 June 1999, 24; Sheridan Prasso, "Battle for the Face of China," *Fortune,* 12 December 2005, 156.

service brands. For example, Avis assures its customers that they can receive the same high-quality service renting its cars anywhere in the world, further reinforcing a key benefit promise embodied in its slogan, "We Try Harder."

Consistency in Brand Image

Maintaining a common marketing platform all over the world helps to maintain the consistency of brand and company image. This consideration becomes particularly important in those markets where there is much customer mobility or where media exposure transmits images across national boundaries. For example, Gillette sells "functional superiority" and "an appreciation of human character and aspirations" for its razors and blades brands worldwide. Services often desire to convey a uniform image due to consumer movements. For example, American Express communicates the prestige and utility of its card and the convenience and ease of replacement of its traveler's checks worldwide.

Ability to Leverage Good Ideas Quickly and Efficiently

One global marketer notes that globalization also can result in increased sustainability and "facilitate continued development of core competencies with the organization . . . in manufacturing, in R&D, in marketing and sales, and in less talked about areas such as competitive intelligence . . . all of which enhance the company's ability to compete."[14] Not having to develop strictly local versions speeds up a brand's market entry process. Marketers can leverage good ideas across markets as long as the right knowledge transfer systems are put into place. IBM has a Web-based communications tool that provides instant, multimedia interaction to connect marketers. MasterCard's corporate marketing group helps to facilitate information and best practices across the organization.[15]

OREO

In marketing its Oreo brand of cookies, General Mills chose to adopt a similar global positioning, "Milk's Favorite Cookie." Although not highly relevant in all countries (for example, China), it did reinforce generally desirable associations like nurturing, caring, and health. To help ensure global understanding, General Mills created a brand book with a CD in an Oreo-shaped box that summarized brand management fundamentals—what needed to be common across countries, what could be changed, and what could not. Addressing core needs and realizing brand synergies helped to drive profitability.

Uniformity of Marketing Practices

Finally, a standardized global marketing program may simplify coordination and provide greater control of the way the brand is being marketed in different countries. By keeping the core of the marketing program constant, greater attention can be paid to making refinements across markets and over time to improve its effectiveness.

MASTERCARD

MasterCard developed its successful "Priceless" campaign into a "worldwide platform."[16] By 1998, the tagline "The best things in life are free. For everything else, there's MasterCard" was in use in over 30 countries. Some ads' premises were universal enough that they worked as is, with only language translation, such as the "Zipper" ad where the priceless moment is a man realizing his zipper is down before anyone else does. In other cases, a locally relevant premise was used instead, with the same tagline. "Every culture has those meaningful moments, which is why we've been able to globalize the campaign," stated a creative director for McCann Erickson, which developed the campaign.[17] Sponsorships for sports with international appeal, such as World Cup soccer and Forumla 1 racing, increased the campaign's ability to connect with a worldwide audience. The campaign was credited with lifting brand awareness in a number of nations, driving card sales, and enabling MasterCard to take market share from Visa.

Disadvantages of Global Marketing Programs

There are also a number of potential disadvantages of standardized global marketing programs (see Figure 14-2). Perhaps the most compelling is that standardized global marketing programs often ignore fundamental differences of various kinds across countries

FIGURE 14-2

Disadvantages of Global Marketing Programs

- Differences in consumer needs, wants, and usage patterns for products
- Differences in consumer response to marketing mix elements
- Differences in brand and product development and the competitive environment
- Differences in the legal environment
- Differences in marketing institutions
- Differences in administrative procedures

and cultures. Critics claim that designing one marketing program for all possible markets results in unimaginative and ineffective strategies geared to the lowest common denominator. Possible differences across countries come in a host of forms, as we discuss next.

Differences in Consumer Needs, Wants, and Usage Patterns for Products

Because of differences in cultural values, economic development, and other factors across nationalities, consumer behavior with respect to many product categories is fundamentally different. For example, marketing research revealed that the per capita consumption of carbonated soft drinks, beer, and bottled water varies dramatically from country to country (see Figure 14-3). Product strategies that work in one country may not work in another. Tupperware, which makes more than 70 percent of its annual sales overseas, needed to adjust its products to satisfy different consumer behavior. In India, a plastic container paired with a spoon becomes a "masala keeper" for spices. In Korea, stain-resistant canisters are ideal for kimchi fermentation. Larger boxes work as safe, airtight "kimono keepers" in Japan.

Differences in Consumer Response to Marketing Mix Elements

Consumers in different parts of the world vary in their attitudes toward and opinions about marketing activity.[18] For example, U.S. consumers, in general, tend to be fairly cynical toward advertising, whereas Japanese view it much more positively. Research has also shown differences in advertising style between the two countries: Japanese ads tend to be softer and more abstract in tone, whereas U.S. ads tend to be richer in product information.

Price sensitivity, promotion responsiveness, sponsorship support, and other activities all may differ by country, and these differences can motivate differences in consumer behavior and decision making. For example, in a comparative study of brand purchase intentions for Korean and U.S. consumers, the purchase intentions of the latter were twice as likely to be affected by their product beliefs and attitudes toward the brand itself, whereas Koreans were eight times more likely to be influenced by social normative beliefs and what they felt others would think about the purchase.[19]

Country	Carbonated Soft Drinks	Beer	Bottled Water
Australia	111.8	93.0	25.3
Brazil	69.6	46.7	24.7
China	7.3	15.8	6.0
France	42.1	35.9	131.3
Germany	90.5	123.1	106.6
India	1.7	0.7	2.6
Ireland	155.2	150.8	24.1
Mexico	152.1	48.6	130.0
South Africa	53.5	55.8	1.9
United States	203.9	83.1	73.8

Source: "Drink Globally," *Beverage World*, May 2003, p.17. Used with permission of Beverage World.

FIGURE 14-3

Per Capita Beverage Consumption (in Liters)

Rank	United States (2005)	United Kingdom (2005)	Germany (2005)	Brazil (2005)	China (2005)	Japan (2004)	France (2005)
1	United States	United Kingdom	Germany	Coca-Cola	China (PRC)	Tokyo Disneyland	Arte
2	Disney	Cadbury Dairy Milk	Aldi	Jornal Nacional	Xin Wen Lian Bo	Studio Ghibli	France
3	Coca-Cola	Cadbury	IKEA	Jornal da Globo	CCTV	Doraemon	Nutella
4	The Wonderful World of Disney	England	Die Olympischen Spiele	Nescau	Beijing 2008 Olympics	Mickey Mouse	Coca-Cola
5	The Discovery Channel	Channel 4	Nivea	Nestlé	Coca-Cola	UNIQLO	Le TGV
6	M&M's	The Pound (£)	Ritter Sport	Fantástico	The Olympic Games	Disney	Levi's
7	Hallmark	Heinz	Günther Jauch	Ayrton Senna	Nokia	Nike	Häagen-Dazs
8	The History Channel	Coca-Cola	ARD	Globo Reporter	Pepsi-Cola	Muji	Perrier
9	Dr Pepper	Dyson	Nutella	Brasil	Shanghai	Sony	Tefal
10	Hershey's	Disney	Coca-Cola	Copa do Mundo	CCTV Movie	KFC/Kentucky Fried Chicken	IKEA
11	National Geographic	Cadbury Flake	adidas	Rede Globo	CCTV News	Universal Studios	Carte D'or
12	U.S. Marines	Galaxy (chocolate)	Milka	Carrefour	CCTV Sports	New York City	Canal +
13	Pringles	BBC	Maggi	O Boticário	Dove (Chocolate)	Mister Donuts	Ferrero Rocher
14	Subway	Maltesers	Haribo	Sonho de Valsa	Beijing (city)	Walt Disney Pictures	Evian
15	Oreo	BBC ONE	Tempo (Taschentücher)	Kibon	Jet Li	7-Eleven	M6
16	Pepsi-Cola	Cadbury Creme Egg	Mon Cheri	McDonald's	CCTV Drama	Toys R Us	Kinder
17	Microsoft Windows	Pringles	ADAC	Brastemp	Jackie Chan	Mosburger	Bounty
18	Reese's	The Olympic Games	Deutsches Rotes Kreuz	Bombeiros	Yao Ming	Honda	Haribo
19	Kraft Foods	ITV	Leibniz	Dove (sabonete)	Safeguard	McDonald's	Orangina
20	Levi's	Kellogg's Corn Flakes	Italy	Sadia	Liu Xiang	Nintendo	Hollywood (chewing gum)

FIGURE 14-4

Global Brand Rankings (includes products, people, and countries)

Differences in Brand and Product Development and the Competitive Environment

Products may be at different stages of their life cycle in different countries. Moreover, the perceptions and positions of particular brands may also differ considerably across countries. Figure 14-4 shows the results of a comprehensive study of leading brands (of all kinds, including people and country brands) in different parts of the world by Young & Rubicam with its BrandAsset Valuator (see Brand Focus 9.0). Relatively few brands appear on all the lists, suggesting that, if nothing else, consumer perceptions of even top brands can vary significantly by geographic region. The nature of competition may also differ. Europeans tend to see more competitors because shipping products across borders is easy. For example, Procter & Gamble competes in France against Italian, Swedish, and Danish companies in many categories.[20]

Differences in the Legal Environment

One of the challenges in developing a global ad campaign is the maze of constantly changing legal restrictions that exist from country to country. For example, at one time, laws in Venezuela, Canada, and Australia stipulated that commercials had to be physically produced in the native country. Canada banned prescription drug advertising on television. Poland required commercial lyrics to be sung in Polish. Sweden prohibited advertising to children. Malaysia did not allow lawyers or law firms to advertise. Advertising restrictions have been placed on the use of children in commercials in Austria, comparative ads in Singapore, and product placement on public television channels in Germany. Although some of these laws have been or are being relaxed, numerous legal differences still exist.

Differences in Marketing Institutions

Basic marketing infrastructure may differ from country to country, making implementation of the same marketing strategy difficult. For example, channels of distribution, retail practices, media availability, and media costs all may vary significantly. Foreign companies have struggled for years to break into Japan's rigid distribution system that locks out many foreign goods. The penetration of television sets, telephones, supermarkets, and so on may vary considerably, especially in developing countries.

Differences in Administrative Procedures

In practice, it may be difficult to achieve the control necessary to implement a standardized global marketing program. Local offices may resist having their autonomy threatened. Local managers may suffer from the "not invented here" syndrome and raise objections—rightly or wrongly—that the global marketing program misses some key dimension of the local market. Local managers who feel their autonomy has been reduced may lose motivation and feel doomed to failure.

Standardization versus Customization

As the preceding discussion suggests, although firms are increasingly adopting an international marketing perspective to capitalize on market opportunities, a number of possible pitfalls exist. Before providing some strategic and tactical guidelines as to how to build global customer-based brand equity, we'll examine standardization versus customization of brand marketing programs. In many ways, the most fundamental issue in developing a global marketing program is the extent to which the marketing program should be standardized across countries, because this decision has such a deep impact on marketing structure and processes.

Perhaps the biggest proponent of standardization is the legendary Harvard professor Ted Levitt. In a controversial 1983 article, Levitt argued that companies needed to learn to operate as if the world were one large market, ignoring superficial regional and national differences:

> A thousand suggestive ways attest to the ubiquity of the desire for the most advanced things that the world makes and sells—goods of the best quality and reliability at the lowest price. The world's needs and desires have been irrevocably homogenized. This makes the multinational corporation obsolete and the global corporation absolute . . .
>
> But although companies customize products for particular market segments, they know that success in a world with homogenized demand requires a search for sales opportunities in similar segments across the globe in order to achieve the economies of scale necessary to compete.[21]

According to Levitt, because the world is shrinking—due to leaps in technology, communication, and so forth—well-managed companies should shift their emphasis from customizing items to offering globally standardized products that are advanced, functional, reliable, and low-priced for all.

Levitt's strong position elicited an equally strong response. One ad executive commented, "There are about two products that lend themselves to global marketing—and one of them is Coca-Cola." Other critics pointed out that even Coca-Cola did not standardize its marketing and noted the lack of standardization in other leading global brands, such as McDonald's and Marlboro. The experiences of these top marketers have been shared by others who found out—in many cases, the hard way—that differences in consumer behavior still prevail across countries. Many firms have been forced to tailor products and marketing programs to different national markets as a result.

HEINZ

Heinz ketchup has a slightly sweet taste in the United States but is spicier in certain European countries, where it is available in hot, Mexican, and curry flavors. In the Philippines, Heinz offers a ketchup made from bananas that is dyed red. Ketchup usage varies by country too. In Greece, ketchup is poured on pasta, eggs, and cuts of meat. In Japan, it is promoted as an ingredient for Western-style foods such as omelets, sausages, and pasta. Heinz has downplayed its U.S. heritage in certain countries, for example in Sweden, where ketchup is used to accompany traditional meatballs and fishballs. In fact, Swedes thought the brand was German because of the name. In Germany, however, U.S. themes work well and have appeared in advertising.[22]

In summary, it's difficult to identify any one company applying the global marketing concept in the strict sense—by selling the same brand exactly the same way everywhere.

BRANDING BRIEF 14-3

Coca-Cola Becomes the Quintessential Global Brand

The most recognized brand name in the world got its start in an Atlanta pharmacy, where it sold for five cents a glass. The name Coca-Cola was registered as a trademark on January 31, 1893. The drink soon became a national phenomenon; by 1895, the company had established syrup plants in Chicago, Dallas, and Los Angeles.

In the 1920s, Coca-Cola pursued aggressive global branding, finding such creative placements for its logo as on dogsleds in Canada and on the walls of bullfighting arenas in Spain. Its popularity throughout the world was fueled by colorful and persuasive advertising that cemented its image as the "All-American" beverage. When the Vietnam War tarnished the American iconography, Coca-Cola developed more globally aware advertising. In 1971, it ran its legendary "I'd like to buy the world a Coke" television spot, in which a crowd of children sang the song from atop a hill in Italy. Coca-Cola's early moves into formerly restricted markets, such as China in 1978 and the Soviet Union in 1979, bolstered its image as a global company. By 1988, Coca-Cola was voted the best known and most admired brand in the world.

Despite—or perhaps as a result of—this immense scope, Coca-Cola did not institute a uniform marketing program in each of its global markets. Rather, the company often tailored the flavor, packaging, price, and advertising to match tastes in specific markets. For example, Coke's famous "Mean Joe" Green TV ad from the United States—in which the weary football star reluctantly accepts a Coke from an admiring young fan and then unexpectedly tosses the kid his jersey in appreciation—was replicated in a number of different regions using the same format but substituting famous athletes from those regions (ads in South America used the Argentine soccer star Maradona, while those in Asia used the Thai soccer star Niat). Local managers were assigned responsibility for sales and distribution programs of Coke products, to reflect the marked differences in consumer behavior across countries.

Perhaps the most consistently standardized element of Coca-Cola is its product appearance. Coke essentially keeps the same basic look and packaging of the product everywhere (except in countries where laws dictate use of the local language). The company simultaneously stresses that the brand be *relevant* and *well-positioned* against the competition. To keep it relevant, Coca-Cola uses different advertising agencies in different countries in order to make the brand feel local. For example, in Australia the advertising appeals to the same

Standardization *and* Customization

Increasingly, marketers are blending global objectives with local or regional concerns. In 1999, Coca-Cola's new global marketing mantra became "Think Local. Act Local"—an important twist on its old mantra, "Think Global. Act Local." Intended to get Coca-Cola back to the basics, the strategy meant hiring more local staff and allowing field managers to tailor marketing to their regions.[23] But after some "un-Coke-like" ads began to appear, and it became apparent that some localities were not ready to develop Coke's marketing entirely on their own, the company scrapped the "Think Local. Act Local" mantra in favor of a hybrid strategy, in which a global marketing network of local executives took direction from Coke's Atlanta headquarters, with some room for interpretation at the local level. Branding Brief 14-3 describes some of the history of Coca-Cola's global branding efforts.

"classic, original" ideals but in a very Australian fashion. Moreover, the marketing mix is designed in each country to stress that Coke is positioned positively on attributes relative to local competitive products. Hence, although Coke looks similar across the globe, its specific image may be very different, depending on what is considered "relevant" in each country.

The advantage of this approach is that Coke becomes entwined with the cultural fabric of the country, just as it has in the United States. Over time this yields an advantage with younger generations who don't even think of Coke as an imported brand. An example that Coca-Cola recounts is of a Japanese family visiting the United States for the first time. The young son, upon passing a vending machine, joyfully exclaimed to his parents, "Look, they have Coke here too!"

Today, Coca-Cola conducts business with more than 400 brands in over 200 countries. More than 70 percent of Coca-Cola's revenues come from outside the United States, a fact that inspired Douglas Daft, when he took over as chairman and CEO in 2000, to express his desire for Coca-Cola managers to adopt the new mantra: "Think Local. Act Local." The results of this hyper-local focus were missed sales targets and local advertising that, in some cases, did not fit with the carefully crafted Coke image, such as an Italian ad featuring skinny-dippers running along a beach. Local marketers actually requested more help from Coke headquarters in Atlanta, so in 2002 Coke formed a 100-person team there that became the centerpiece of the global marketing group, setting strategy, hiring agencies, developing talent, and sharing best practices among the local managers. Stephen Jones, Coke's then-chief marketing officer, was careful to point out that the moves did not signal that headquarters would dictate all the marketing programs and activities, instead noting that "the local markets are still accountable, but now they have guidance, process, and strategy." With this new hybrid strategy in place, Coke increased its spending on major global ad campaigns in 2004 while simultaneously "boost[ing] collaboration between regions to balance global and local efforts."

Sources: "The Story of Coca-Cola," www.coca-cola.com; Betsy McKay, "Coca-Cola Restructuring Effort Has Yet to Prove Effective," *Asian Wall Street Journal,* 2 March 2001; Andrew Marshall, "Focus: Can They Still Sell the World a Coke?" *The Independent,* 20 June 1999; Betsy McKay, "Coke Hunts for Talent to Re-Establish Its Marketing Might," *Wall Street Journal,* 6 March 2002, B4; Kate MacArthur, "Coke Commits $400M to Fix It," *Advertising Age,* 15 November 2004, 1.

Procter & Gamble's strategy is similar—to make global plans, replan for each region, and execute locally. Former P&G head of marketing Robert L. Wehling made the following comments concerning the company's global marketing efforts during the 1990s:

> To us, a global brand is one that has a clear and consistent equity—or identity—with consumers across geographies. It is generally positioned the same from one country to another. It has essentially the same product formulation, delivers the same benefits and uses a consistent advertising concept. That isn't to say there isn't room for local tailoring. In fact, there must be room to adapt to local needs. But where there's no justification for difference, the brand is the same in every part of the world.[24]

From these perspectives, transferring products across borders may mean consistent positioning for the brand, but not necessarily the same brand name and marketing program in each market. Similarly, packaging may have the same overall look but be tailored as required to fit the local populace and market needs. As brand consultant Robert Kahn notes, "Global branding does not mean having the same brand everywhere. It means having an overarching strategy that optimizes brand effectiveness in local, regional, and international markets." According to Kahn, one soap formula sold under different names can achieve global brand status as long as the marketing efforts are managed centrally.[25] As another example, Danone's kids' yogurts are sold under a variety of names—Danonino, Danonetje, Danimals, Petit Danone—in over 30 countries, while a general manager leads a central team that coordinates and oversees the local marketing efforts.[26]

In short, centralized marketing strategies that preserve local customs and traditions can be a boon for products sold in more than one country—even in diverse cultures. Fortunately, firms have improved their capabilities to tailor products and programs to local conditions: "[New technologies] have the important attribute of allowing customized or tailored product offerings reflecting local conditions at much lower costs. The need to standardize products worldwide is diminishing."[27] Flexible manufacturing technology has decreased the concentration of activities, and advances in information systems and telecommunications have allowed increased coordination.

Many good examples exist of companies that have successfully blended standardization and customization. For example, Domino's Pizza tries to maintain the same delivery system everywhere but has to adapt the model to local customs. In Britain, customers think anybody knocking on the door is rude; in Kuwait, the delivery is just as likely to be made to a limousine as it is to a house; and in Japan, houses are not numbered sequentially, making finding a particular address difficult. Consider how McDonald's has modified and adapted its successful formula of "food, fun, and families" in going overseas.

McDonald's

Although the Big Mac and Ronald McDonald appear worldwide, McDonald's customizes other aspects of its marketing program. It serves beer in Germany, wine in France, and coconut, mango, and tropical mint shakes in Hong Kong. Hamburgers are made with different meat and spices in Japan, and McSpaghetti is offered in the Philippines. McDonald's joint venture partners, who typically run the franchises abroad, take much of the responsibility for their own local marketing. Nevertheless, McDonald's fierce commitment to product and service standardization is one reason the retail outlets are also so similar all over the world. After such a rigorous qualification process, partners come to understand and appreciate McDonald's attention to detail. As a result, most partners strictly follow the operating manual, meticulously detailed and as thick as a phone book. The rules cover everything from how often to clean the bathrooms to the temperature of the grease to fry potatoes.

Although McDonald's famous service stays the same around the world, their menu often differs.

Other notable examples of brands with differentiated global marketing strategies are Heineken and Nescafé. Although Heineken is seen as an everyday brand in the Netherlands, it is considered a "top-shelf" brand almost everywhere else. For example, a case of Heineken costs almost twice as much in the United States as a case of the most popular American beer, Budweiser.[28] For a long time, Heineken's slogan in the United Kingdom and other countries—"Heineken Refreshes the Parts Other Beers Can't Reach"—was different from its U.S. positioning. Although advertising for Nescafé, the world's largest brand of coffee, generally stresses the taste, aroma, and warmth of shared moments, the brand was successfully positioned in Thailand as a way to escape from the pressures of daily life.[29]

Global Brand Strategy

With that background, let's turn to some basic strategic issues in global branding. The contention of this chapter is that in building brand equity, we often must create different marketing programs to satisfy different market segments. Therefore we must:

1. Identify differences in consumer behavior—how consumers purchase and use *products* and what they know and feel about *brands*—in each market.
2. Adjust the branding program accordingly through the choice of brand elements, the nature of the actual marketing program and activities, and the leveraging of secondary associations.

Heineken has a very different brand image in Europe than in North America.

THE SCIENCE OF BRANDING 14-1

American Brands in the Wake of War

The Iraq War, which began in March 2003, has compounded the United States' image problem abroad. Anti-American sentiment either worsened or emerged in many parts of the world following the start of the war. A global study conducted by the Pew Research Center for the People and the Press a year after the war began found the percentage of respondents in Europe who had a favorable view of the United States in precipitous decline. Between summer 2002 and March 2004, favorability ratings for the United States fell in France and Germany by more than 20 percent. Even in Great Britain, perhaps the country's strongest ally in the war, favorability fell from 75 percent to 58 percent in March 2004. Ratings in the Middle East, while starting from a lower point, still fell. In Jordan, for example, the U.S. favorability rating dropped to 5 percent from 25 percent during the same period. The image problem was severe enough for a group of private-sector marketers, academics, and corporations to join forces in 2004 to combat anti-Americanism abroad by creating the Business for Diplomatic Action council.

In spite of the prevalence of negative attitudes toward the U.S. government, consumer research conducted since the start of the war shows that the response abroad to U.S. brands has been far milder. Although there were isolated attacks targeting U.S. businesses, such as the burning of a KFC outlet in Pakistan that killed six employees in 2005, overall, U.S. brands have not suffered, in terms of image or sales, in the same fashion as the country's image abroad has.

A joint research project by Research International and the Harvard Business School investigated how consumers value global brands and revealed that the prevailing anti-U.S. sentiment did not influence purchase decisions about U.S.-based brands. One South African respondent showed it was possible to hold opposing views about the country and the brands it produces, saying, "I hate the country, but I love their products." In an interview separate from this study, a South Korean expressed similar sentiment, saying, "Calling for political independence from the U.S. is one thing, and liking American brands is another. Of course I like IBM, Dell, Microsoft, Starbucks, and Coke."

The annual survey of power brands by NOP World from 2004 evidenced a drop in trust and usage of U.S. brands overseas, but only by a few percentage points on average. Between 2003 and 2004, the total percentage of consumers from 30 countries who use 15 U.S. brands—

Note that the third way to build global brand equity, leveraging secondary brand associations, is probably the most likely to have to be changed across countries. Because the various entities that may be linked to a brand may take on very different meanings in different countries, secondary associations may have to be leveraged differently in different countries. For example, American companies such as Coca-Cola, Levi Strauss, and Nike traditionally gained an important source of equity in going overseas by virtue of their U.S. heritage, which is not as much of an issue or asset in their domestic market. Harley-Davidson has aggressively marketed its classic U.S. image—customized for different cultures—to generate a quarter of its sales from abroad. The Science of Branding 14-1 shows how, despite America's slipping image after the start of the Iraq War, brands of U.S. companies were largely unaffected.

Chapter 7 reviewed how marketers could leverage country of origin, as in these cases, to build brand equity. Thus, in developing global brands, consider how secondary associations

including McDonald's, Microsoft, Yahoo!, and Nike—fell from 30 percent to 27 percent. The percentage of respondents who said they trusted Coca-Cola, McDonald's, Nike, and Microsoft fell between 3 and 6 percent during the same period. Although these declines were "not good news for companies that want to grow," they did not mirror the simultaneous decline in attitudes toward the U.S. government.

In fact, in some areas where anti-U.S. sentiment was strongest, for example in France and the Middle East, U.S. brands experienced sales growth following the start of the war. In the consumer goods category, where boycotting was expected to have the most impact, sales in these regions rose. Coca-Cola sales in the Middle East rose by double digits following a small decline at the outset of the war, while sales in Europe rose between 5 and 8 percent during the first half of 2003. Same-store sales for McDonald's in Paris were up between 8 and 10 percent during the same period.

One possible explanation for the disparity between the levels of resentment for the country and its brands is the global image the brands project. Consumers buy global brands because, for example, they "make us feel like citizens of the world and . . . somehow give us an identity." Research by Roper has shown that consumers are more inclined to think of a brand as global, rather than as originating in a specific country. Another explanation is the fact that many of the biggest U.S. brands have large local operations that employ thousands and bring investment in local communities. For example, Coca-Cola employs 20,000 locals in its Middle Eastern operations, paying them 15 percent more on average than locally based competitors. Procter & Gamble spent $97 million in Egypt, building factories and schools and financing health education. Whatever the reason, U.S. brands have yet to experience an image decline equivalent to that of the United States itself.

Sources: "A Year after Iraq War," Pew Research Center for the People and the Press report, 16 March 2004; Clay Risen, "Re-Branding America," *Boston Globe,* 13 March 2005, D1; Douglas B. Holt, John A. Quelch, and Earl L. Taylor, "How Consumers Value Global Brands," Harvard Business School Working Knowledge, 20 September 2004; "Brands in an Age of Anti-Americanism," *BusinessWeek,* 4 August 2003, 69; Parija Bhatnagar, "U.S. Brands Losing Luster," *CNN Money,* 21 May 2004; Janet Guyon, "Brand America," *Fortune,* 27 October 2003, 179; "Regime Change: Brand Wars in the Middle East," *Economist,* 2 November 2002, 65.

may vary in their strength, favorability, and uniqueness and may therefore play a different role in building brand equity.

Global Customer-Based Brand Equity

As we explained in Chapter 2, to build customer-based brand equity, marketers must (1) establish breadth and depth of brand awareness; (2) create points of parity and points of difference; (3) elicit positive, accessible brand responses; and (4) forge intense, active brand relationships. Achieving these four steps, in turn, requires establishing six core brand building blocks: brand salience, brand performance, brand imagery, brand judgments, brand feelings, and brand resonance. In each and every market in which marketers sell the brand, they must consider how to achieve these steps and create these building blocks. Some of the issues that come into play are discussed in the following subsections.

Creating Brand Salience. One of the most challenging aspects of building global brand equity for a widely extended, multiple-product brand is the order of product introduction. It is rare that the product rollout for a brand in new markets will duplicate the order of product introduction in the home market. Often, product introductions in the domestic market are sequential, stretched out over a longer period of time than the nearly simultaneous introductions that occur in overseas markets.

Nivea

Nivea's flagship product in its European home market has been its category leader, Nivea Creme. Although the company had introduced other skin care and personal care products, Nivea Creme was the product with the most history and heritage and reflected many of the key Nivea core brand values. In Asia, however, for cultural and climate reasons, the creme product was less well received, and the facial skin care sub-brand, Nivea Visage, and creme line extension, Nivea Soft, were of greater strategic and market importance. Because these two product brands have slightly different images than the Creme brand, an important issue is what would be the impact on consumers' collective impressions of Nivea. A strong emphasis on Nivea for Men in North America raises similar questions.

Different orders of introduction can have a very profound impact on consumer perceptions about what products the brand offers, and the benefits supplied and needs satisfied. Thus, we need to examine the breadth and depth of recall to ensure that the proper brand salience and meaning exist along those lines.

Crafting Brand Image. If the product does not vary appreciably across markets, basic brand performance associations may not need to be that different. Brand imagery associations, on the other hand, may be quite different, and one challenge in global marketing is to meaningfully refine the brand image across diverse markets. For example, the brand's history and heritage, which may be rich and a strong competitive advantage in the home market, may be virtually nonexistent in a new market. A desirable brand personality in one market may be less desirable in another. Nike's competitive, aggressive user imagery turned out to be a detriment in its introduction into European markets in the early 1990s. The company achieved greater success when it dialed down its image somewhat and emphasized team concepts more.

Eliciting Brand Responses. Brand judgments must be positive in new markets—consumers must find the brand to be of good quality, credible, worthy of consideration, and superior. Crafting the right brand image will help to accomplish these outcomes. One of the challenges in global marketing, however, is creating the proper balance and type of emotional responses and brand feelings. Blending inner (enduring and private) and outer (immediate experiential) emotions can be difficult, given cultural differences across markets.

Cultivating Resonance. Finally, achieving brand resonance in new markets means that consumers must have sufficient opportunities and incentives to buy and use the product, interact with other consumers and the company itself, and actively learn and experience the brand and its marketing. Clearly, interactive, online marketing can be advantageous here, as long as it can be accessible and relevant anywhere in the world. Nevertheless, digital efforts cannot completely replace grassroots marketing efforts that help to connect the consumer with the brand. Simply exporting marketing programs, even with some adjustments, may be insufficient because consumers may be too much at "arm's length." As a result, they may not be able to develop the intense, active loyalty that characterizes brand resonance.

Global Brand Positioning

To best capture differences in consumer behavior, and to guide our efforts in revising the marketing program, we must revisit the brand positioning in each market. Recall that brand positioning means creating mental maps, defining core brand associations, identifying points of parity and points of difference, and crafting a band mantra. In developing a global brand positioning, we need to answer three key sets of questions:

1. How valid is the mental map in the new market? How appropriate is the positioning? What is the existing level of awareness? How valuable are the core brand associations, points of parity, and points of difference?
2. What changes should we make to the positioning? Do we need to create any new associations? Should we *not* recreate any existing associations? Should we modify any existing associations?
3. How should we create this new mental map? Can we still use the same marketing activities? What changes should we make? What new marketing activities are necessary?

Because the brand is often at an earlier stage of development when going abroad, we often must first establish awareness and key points of parity. Then we can consider additional competitive considerations. In effect, we need to define a hierarchy of brand associations in the global context that defines which associations we want consumers in all countries to hold, and which we want consumers only in certain countries to have. We have to determine how to create these associations in different markets to account for different consumer perceptions, tastes, and environments. Thus, we must be attuned to similarities and differences across markets. The remainder of this chapter provides a set of tactical guidelines to help fulfill these strategic imperatives.

Building Global Customer-Based Brand Equity

In designing and implementing a marketing program to create a strong global brand, marketers want to realize the advantages of a global marketing program while suffering as few of its disadvantages as possible.[30] This section explores in more detail exactly how to best build strong global brands, relying on the "Ten Commandments of Global Branding" (see Figure 14-5).

1. Understand similarities and differences in the global branding landscape.
2. Don't take shortcuts in brand building.
3. Establish marketing infrastructure.
4. Embrace integrated marketing communications.
5. Cultivate brand partnerships.
6. Balance standardization and customization.
7. Balance global and local control.
8. Establish operable guidelines.
9. Implement a global brand equity measurement system.
10. Leverage brand elements.

FIGURE 14-5

The Ten Commandments of Global Branding

1. Understand Similarities and Differences in the Global Branding Landscape

The first—and most fundamental—guideline is to recognize that international markets can vary in terms of brand development, consumer behavior, marketing infrastructure, competitive activity, legal restrictions, and so on. Virtually every top global brand and company adjusts its marketing program in some way across some markets but holds the parameters fixed in other markets.

Indeed, one key to global success is to recognize and take advantage of local consumer behavior. For example, when MTV made a major push for its cable channel overseas beginning in the 1990s, it initially kept much of the same programming that it played to U.S. audiences. In most markets, however, music, film, and other cultural tastes were almost completely different, and the channel quickly learned that it needed a much greater proportion of locally relevant programming in its mix. Now, MTV International channels such as MTV India program as much as 80 percent of their content in local languages, and viewership has risen significantly.[31]

The experience of mobile phone operator Vodafone illustrates an interesting juxtaposition that reflects just how important consumer behavior can be to the success or failure of any brand, even dominant brands, when entering new markets.

VODAFONE

When Vodafone acquired J-Phone, the third-biggest cell phone operator in Japan, known for its cutting-edge phones, in 2002, it hoped that the renamed Vodafone Japan would be a key component of its global brand strategy. Instead, Vodafone lost customers and revenues fell. The problem: "By focusing too much on building a globally oriented brand, Vodafone failed to give Japanese consumers what they want, chiefly a wide lineup of phones with fancy features."[32] Vodafone sought to leverage its image as a global company by offering phones that consumers could use anywhere, home or abroad. Yet the heaviest cellphone users, many of whom were young and not likely to go abroad, were more interested in phones with advanced features, such as video games, digital cameras, ring tones, and e-mail. Japanese users also favor a broad selection of phones that is constantly updated, but Vodafone offered only 15 models, compared with market leader DoCoMo's 38 models, and was often late to market with new technology. Vodafone was unable to recover from its early missteps and sold Vodafone Japan to Softbank in 2006, which announced plans to rename the brand Softbank Mobile.[33]

The best examples of global brands often retain a thematic consistency and alter specific elements of the marketing mix in accordance with consumer behavior and the competitive situation in each country. Unilever's Snuggle fabric softener offers an example of effectively custom-tailoring the marketing mix.

SNUGGLE

The fabric-softener product was initially launched in Germany in 1970 as an economy brand in a category dominated by Procter & Gamble. To counteract the negative quality inferences associated with low price, Unilever emphasized softness as the product's key point of difference. The softness association was communicated through the name, Kuschelweich, which meant "enfolded in softness," and through a picture of a teddy bear on the package. When the product was launched in France, Unilever kept the brand positioning of economy and softness but changed the name to Cajoline, meaning softness in French. In addition, the teddy bear that had been inactive in Germany took center stage in the French advertising as the brand symbol for softness and quality. Success in France led to global expansion, and in each case the brand name was changed to connote softness in the local language, while the advertising featuring the teddy bear remained virtually identical across global markets. By the 1990s, Unilever was marketing the fabric softener around the globe with over a dozen brand names including Coccolino in Italy and Mimosin in

Spain, all with the same product positioning and advertising support. More important, the fabric softener was generally the number-one or number-two brand in each market.[34] Unilever continued its global expansion of the Snuggle brand by launching it with that name in Mexico in 2003.[35]

The success of Snuggle reflects the importance of understanding similarities and differences in the branding landscape. Although marketers typically strive to keep the same brand name across markets, in this case the need for a common name was reduced since people generally don't buy fabric softener away from home. On the other hand, a common consumer desire for softness that transcended country boundaries could be effectively communicated by a teddy bear as the main character in a global ad campaign.

Developed versus Developing Markets. Perhaps the most basic distinction we make with global brands is between developing and developed markets (such as India and Germany, respectively). Typically, differences in consumer behavior, marketing infrastructure, competitive frame of reference, and so on are so profoundly different that we need distinct marketing programs for each type of market. With developing markets, often the product category itself may not be well developed, so that the marketing program must operate at a very fundamental level.

Changing Landscape for Global Brands. Finally, the landscape for global brands is dramatically changing, especially with respect to younger consumers. Because of increased consumer mobility, better communication capabilities, and expanding transnational entertainment options, lifestyles are fast becoming more similar *across* countries within sociodemographic segments, than they are *within* countries across sociodemographic segments. Because of the growth of global media such as MTV, a teenager in Paris may have more in common with a teenager in London, New York, Sydney, or almost any other major city in the world than with his or her own parents. This younger generation may be more easily influenced by trends and broad cultural movements fueled by worldwide exposure to movies, television, and other media than ever before. Certainly one result of this trend is that those brands that are able to tap into the global sensibilities of the youth market may be better able to adopt a standardized branding program and marketing strategy. Unilever uses a standard approach to market its Axe Body Spray globally based on sex appeal.

2. Don't Take Shortcuts in Brand Building

In terms of building global customer-based brand equity, many of the basic tactics we discussed in Part II of the text still apply. In particular, we must create brand awareness and a positive brand image in each country in which the brand is sold. The means may differ from country to country, or the actual sources of brand equity themselves may vary. Nevertheless, it is critically important to have sufficient levels of brand awareness and strong, favorable, and unique brand associations to provide sources of brand equity in each country.

The danger in entering new markets is that marketers will take shortcuts and fail to build the necessary sources of brand equity by inappropriately exporting marketing programs from other countries or markets in which the brand has already established a great deal of equity. Many companies have learned this lesson the hard way. For example, in 1990, Pepsi bought the rights to bottle and sell its soft drink to German retailers. Pepsi attempted to match Coke's high prices in the market without sufficient pull from brand-building activities and merchandising, and without sufficient push from a strong distribution network with the right kind of trucks, coolers, and so forth. Pepsi so alienated two major German retailers, Tengelmann and Asko, that it actually lost distribution in those stores for a couple of years. The brand languished with a market share under 5 percent as a result and has only recently started to bounce back.[36]

Building a brand in new markets must be done from the bottom up. Strategically, that means concentrating on building awareness first, before the brand image. Tactically, or operationally, it means determining how to best create sources of brand equity in new markets. The way a brand is built in one market, with distribution, communication, and pricing strategies, may not be appropriate in another market even if the same overall brand image is desired in both.

If the brand is at an earlier stage of development, rather than alter it or the advertising to conform to local tastes, marketers will try to influence local behavior so that it fits with the established uses of the brand. Consumer education then accompanies brand development efforts.

KELLOGG

When Kellogg first introduced its corn flakes into the Brazilian market in 1962, cereal was eaten as a dry snack —the way U.S. consumers eat potato chips—because many Brazilians did not eat breakfast at all. As a result, the ads there centered on the family and breakfast table—much more so than in the United States. As in other Latin American countries where big breakfasts have not been part of the meal tradition, Kellogg's task was to inform consumers of the "proper" way to eat cereal with cold milk in the morning.[37] Similarly, Kellogg had to educate French consumers that corn flakes were meant to be eaten with cold instead of warm milk. Initial advertising showed milk being poured from transparent glass pitchers that were used for cold milk, rather than opaque porcelain jugs that were used for warm milk. A challenge to Kellogg in increasing

BRANDING BRIEF 14-4

Building Brands in India

With a population of over a billion and a growing middle class of about 300 million, India has been an attractive market for global brands seeking new consumers since 1991, when the Indian government relaxed restrictions on foreign investment. Yet some of the most powerful global companies have found that the level of success they enjoy at home and in other international markets by no means guarantees success in India. Motorola and Coca-Cola are just two of the numerous Western brands for whom growth in India proved elusive at some point.

For Motorola, India's ranking as the second-fastest-growing mobile phone handset market, after China, makes it a vital place to do business. Yet in 2006, Motorola had only 6 percent of the market. Despite being priced lower than its Western competitors, Motorola did not often make it into the Indian consumer's consideration set, primarily because it had little brand awareness. Compounding this problem was the fact that the company had no distribution network in India, and was thus reliant on local wireless operators to push the phones to consumers, which the operators were reluctant to do due to Motorola's lack of profile. Motorola announced plans in 2006 to increase its advertising in India, admitting that "We have a long way to go, but there's definitely momentum."

Coca-Cola, which has a number of different brands in India that give it more than 50 percent market share in total, still struggled to achieve the same success it had enjoyed elsewhere with its flagship brand, Coke. Coca-Cola overestimated demand and came to market with prices too high and sizes too large for Indian consumers, who prefer to purchase in small quantities to save money. As a result it endured years of losses, culminating in a $400 million

the relatively low per capita consumption of ready-to-eat breakfast cereals in Asia was the low consumption of milk products and the positive distaste with which drinking milk was held in many Asian countries. Because cereal consumption and habits vary widely across countries, Kellogg has learned to build the brand from the bottom up in each market.

This guideline suggests having some patience with the potential need to backtrack on brand development, to engage in a set of marketing programs and activities that the brand has long since moved beyond in its original markets. Although the period needed to build the brand in new markets may be compressed, it will still take some time. The temptation—and often the mistake—is to export the current marketing program because it seems to "transfer" or "work." Although that may be the case, the fact that a marketing program can meet with acceptance or even some success doesn't mean it is the best way to build strong, sustainable global brand equity. An important key to success is to understand each consumer, recognize what he or she knows or could potentially value about the brand, and tailor marketing programs to his or her desires.

In short, one of the major pitfalls that global markers can fall into is a mistaken belief that their strong position in a domestic market can easily—or even automatically—translate into a strong position in a foreign market, especially with respect to the brand associations held by consumers. Marketers sometimes fail to realize that in their own country, they are building on a foundation of perhaps decades of carefully compiled associations in customers' minds. Branding Brief 14-4 describes some of the challenges encountered by

write-down on the value of its Indian bottling assets in 2000. In 2003, Coca-Cola's market share was 16.5 percent, making it only the third-largest cola. To boost sales, it reduced the price of a 10.1-ounce bottle from 24 cents to 17 cents, and introduced a 6.8-ounce bottle for 10 cents. A new ad campaign was also introduced featuring a Bollywood movie star, a break with tradition at Coca-Cola, which has not used celebrity spokespersons for some time. This move was indicative of the fact that "Coke had to break a lot of its rules for India," as one former employee put it.

Although these and other global brands have struggled, others have succeeded by better understanding the Indian consumers and tailoring their offerings accordingly. Hyundai became India's second-largest carmaker by offering small, affordable, and fuel-efficient cars such as the $7,000 Santro. Nokia earned 58 percent market share by selling models specially made for the Indian market, such as its 1100 phone that features a flashlight. Pepsi earned 24 percent market share in part because it was the first Western cola to feature Indian mega-celebrities as spokespeople, including cricketer Sachin Tendulkar and actor Shahrukh Khan. LG outpaced competitors Whirlpool and Haier to $1 billion in annual sales by offering refrigerators and air conditioners that stand up better to the temperature extremes and power surges that characterize rural India. As the Indian market continues to grow and mature, catering to local tastes will become even more important for global brands seeking to compete there.

Sources: Om Malik, "The New Land of Opportunity," *Business 2.0,* July 2004, 72; Cris Prystay, "Branding Gains Respect in Emerging Markets," *Wall Street Journal,* 3 January 2006; Manjeet Kripalani, "Finally, Coke Gets It Right," *BusinessWeek,* 10 February 2003, 47.

some global brands as they entered the emerging Indian market. Observing that many large companies simply diluted formulas to make less expensive products, Hindustan Lever, an Indian subsidiary of Unilever, made a substantial commitment to R&D and innovation to better serve the Indian market. These efforts resulted in completely new products that were both affordable and uniquely suited to India's rural poor, including a high-quality combination soap and shampoo, and that were backed by successful new sales and marketing tactics specifically developed to reach remote and highly dispersed populations.[38]

3. Establish Marketing Infrastructure

A critical success factor for many global brands has been their manufacturing, distribution, and logistical advantages. They have created the appropriate marketing infrastructure from scratch if necessary, as well as adapting to capitalize on the existing marketing infrastructure in other countries.

Because international markets vary greatly in their existing infrastructure, companies have gone to great lengths to ensure consistency in product quality. In some cases, they have to build distribution channels from scratch. For example, after 13 years of negotiations, Nestlé was finally invited into the Heilongjiang province of China in 1987 to boost milk production. Soon thereafter, Nestlé opened a powdered milk and baby cereal plant in China. The company deemed the overburdened local trains and roads undependable to collect milk and deliver finished goods. Nestlé chose to establish its own distribution network, known as "milk loads," between 27 villages in the region and factory collection points called "chilling centers," where farmers could push wheel barrows, pedal bicycles, or walk to have their milk weighed and analyzed. Production has exploded as a result.[39] Similarly, McDonald's gets over 90 percent of its raw materials from local suppliers and will even expend resources to create the necessary inputs if they are not locally available. Hence, investing to improve potato farms in Russia is standard practice because French fries are one of McDonald's core products and a key source of brand equity.

More often, however, companies have to adapt operations, invest in foreign partners, or both, in order to succeed abroad. In many cases, production and distribution are the keys to the success of a global marketing program. For example, General Motors' success in Brazil in the 1990s after years of mediocre performance came about in part because of its concerted efforts to develop a lean manufacturing program and a sound dealership strategy to create the proper marketing infrastructure.[40]

Companies often differ in their approach to distribution, and the results can be dramatic. For example, Coca-Cola's distribution strategy has been one key to its global success. Rather than leaving foreign operations in the control of fragmented local bottlers, Coca-Cola's anchor bottler model led it to either use only large bottlers like Norway's Ringnes or Australia's Amatil, or take an equity stake in smaller bottlers in order to gain control of local management. At a micro level, Coca-Cola's intensive deployment of vending machines in Japan was a key to success in that market. Overall, from 1981 to 1993 Coca-Cola invested over $3 billion internationally in infrastructure and marketing. PepsiCo, on the other hand, sold off some of its bottling investments during this time. Despite investing in expensive ad campaigns and diversifying into restaurants and snack foods, PepsiCo saw its global fortunes sag relative to Coca-Cola and has renewed its efforts in recent years. Figure 14-6 summarizes a set of guidelines to help multinational corporations maximize their control and learn from distribution partnerships in developing markets.

As in domestic markets, firms will often want to blend push and pull strategies internationally to build brand equity. This is certainly true in global markets and can present special challenges. Concerned about poor refrigeration in European stores, Häagen-Dazs ended up supplying thousands of free freezers to retailers across the continent.[41]

Seven Rules for International Distribution

1. Select distributors. Don't let them select you.
2. Look for distributors capable of developing markets, rather than those with a few obvious customer contacts.
3. Treat the local distributors as long-term partners, not temporary market-entry vehicles.
4. Support market entry by committing money, managers, and proven marketing ideas.
5. From the start, maintain control over marketing strategy.
6. Make sure distributors provide you with detailed market and financial performance data.
7. Build links among national distributors at the earliest opportunities.

Source: David Arnold, "Seven Rules of International Distribution," *Harvard Business Review* (November–December 2000): 131–137.

FIGURE 14-6

Seven Rules for International Distribution

Sometimes companies mistakenly adapt strategies that were critical factors to success, only to discover that they erode the brand's competitive advantage. For example, Dell Computer initially abandoned its direct distribution strategy in Europe and instead decided to establish a traditional retailer network through existing channels. The end result was a paltry 2.5 percent market share, and the company lost money for the first time ever in 1994. Ignoring critics who claimed that a direct distribution model would never work in Europe, Dell revamped its direct approach and relaunched its personal computer line with a new management team to execute the direct model the company had pioneered in the United States. Since then it has never looked back. Between 1999 and 2004, Dell's sales in Europe grew at an average rate of 19 percent annually, substantially outpacing other competitors in the industry. By 2005, Dell had a 13 percent share of the European PC market, and the company predicted it would double or even triple that figure in the coming years.[42]

4. Embrace Integrated Marketing Communications

A number of top global firms have introduced extensive integrated marketing communications programs. Overseas markets don't have the same advertising opportunities as the expansive, well-developed U.S. media market. As a result, U.S.-based marketers have had to embrace other forms of communication in those markets—such as sponsorship, promotions, public relations, merchandising activity, and so on—to a much greater extent.

Any nontraditional form of advertising should be consistent with the brand's overall positioning and heritage. Disney's theme parks are not only huge profit generators (Tokyo Disneyland has been an overwhelming success with over 75 percent repeat visitors) but also serve as advertising vehicles that help solidify Disney's association with "fun family entertainment." eBay adopted a grassroots approach in its entry into Europe, shunning advertising just as it had done in the United States. Besides costing less, eBay's approach seemed to produce better customers: Although chief competitor QXL had 50 percent more users than eBay, eBay users averaged 90 minutes a month on site compared with under 20 minutes for QXL.[43] By 2006, eBay's business in Germany, where over 20 million registered users purchased over $6 billion worth of merchandise, was second only to its U.S. market in size.

Non-U.S. companies often undertake smaller, local events that can also serve a brand-building purpose. For example, Guinness often partners with aspiring entrepreneurs to develop the Irish pub business concept in a variety of countries. In 1995, some of the best pubs in Ireland joined forces with some of the best pubs in Europe in what Guinness called the Twinning Initiative. These events had two-fold benefits in that they generated local publicity and interest as well as served to reinforce Guinness beer's Irish association.

To help make the quintessential Vermont brand Ben & Jerry's more locally relevant in Britain, the company ran a contest to create the "quintessential British ice cream flavor." Finalists covered the gamut of the British cultural spectrum and included references to royalty (Cream Victoria and Queen Yum Mum), rock and roll (John Lemon and Ruby Chewsday), literature (Grape Expectations and Agatha Crispie) and Scottish heritage (Nessie's Nectar and Choc Ness Monster). Other finalists included Minty Python, Cashew Grant, and James Bomb. The winning flavor, Cool Britannia, was a play on the popular British military anthem "Rule Britannia" and consisted of vanilla ice cream, English strawberries, and chocolate-covered Scottish shortbread.[44]

Although some companies have managed to execute their global marketing program entirely with nontraditional forms of advertising, as the Body Shop did, for example, traditional advertising still has a place.

Advertising. Although the brand positioning may be the same in different countries, creative strategies in advertising may have to differ. Red Bull uses the same basic template for marketing in any country it sells in, to reinforce its positioning as an energy drink: quirky, hand-drawn cartoon commercials extolling the fact that "Red Bull gives you wiiiiiings," sponsorship of action sports athletes and competitions, and availability at popular nightspots. Yet Red Bull adapts this template for local "market cells" by translating the ads into the local language, selecting locally relevant athletes and events to sponsor, and initially targeting the trendiest nightspots where "opinion leaders" are likely to congregate.

Different countries can be more or less receptive to different creative styles. For example, humor is more common in U.S. and U.K. ads than, say, in German ads. European countries such as France and Italy are more tolerant of sex appeal and nudity in advertising.[45]

CAMAY

Procter & Gamble found that although its U.S. ads for Camay soap could be effectively adapted for other countries, they turned out to be a disaster in Japan. Specifically, Camay traditionally has been advertised as a luxury soap that makes a woman's skin feel soft and smell sweet, allowing her to feel more attractive as a result. Ads in other countries showed a beautiful woman bathing blissfully in a bathtub of suds. In ads developed for France, Italy, and Venezuela, her husband came into the bathroom and talked to her while she was bathing. In Japan, the ads also featured a man entering the bathroom and gently touching the woman's skin and complimenting her while she bathed. Although these ads might perhaps be seen as sensual in other countries, such behavior could be considered rude and in bad taste in Japan—even the idea of a man being in the same bathroom with a woman can be taboo there. As a result of negative public reaction, the Japanese ad for Camay was changed to show a beautiful European-looking woman—alone—in a European-style bath.

Although commercial television time has been limited worldwide, the penetration of satellite and cable TV has expanded the broadcast media options available. As a result, it's now easier to simultaneously air the same TV commercial in many different countries. U.S. cable networks such as CNN, MTV, and the Cartoon Network, and other networks such as Sky TV in Commonwealth countries and Star TV in Asia, have increased advertisers' global reach. *Fortune, Time, Newsweek,* and other magazines have printed foreign editions in English for years. Increasingly, other publishers are starting or adding local-language editions, by licensing their trademarks to local companies, entering into joint ventures, or creating wholly owned subsidiaries. For example, *Rolling Stone* has 10 international editions outside the United States including one for mainland China; *Maxim* has 27 including Greek; and *Newsweek* appears in Arabic and five other languages.[46] *Elle* has 35 editions targeting the same demographic group but tailored to the country where each is published.

Each country has its own unique media challenges and opportunities. For example, when Colgate-Palmolive decided to further penetrate the market of the 630 million or so people who live in rural India, the company had to overcome the fact that more than half of all Indian villagers are illiterate and only one-third live in households with television sets. Its solution was to create half-hour infomercials carried through the countryside in video vans.[47] To sell Tampax tampons in Mexico, Procter & Gamble created in-home informational gatherings or "bonding sessions" akin to Tupperware parties led by company-designated counselors. Although about 70 percent of women in the United States, Canada, and Western Europe use tampons, just 2 percent of women in most of Latin America do so. To overcome cultural inhibitors, P&G developed its unorthodox approach.[48]

Promotion and Sponsorship. Sponsorship programs have a long tradition in many countries outside the United States because of a historical lack of advertising media there. Increasingly, marketers can execute sponsorship on a global basis. Entertainment and sports sponsorships can be an especially effective way to reach a younger audience. For example, Nestlé has run worldwide promotional tie-ins with Disney movies such as *Atlantis* and *Monsters, Inc.* Mars has become a worldwide sponsor of the World Cup and Olympics.

5. Cultivate Brand Partnerships

Most global brands have marketing partners of some form in their international markets, ranging from joint venture partners, licensees or franchisees, and distributors to ad agencies and other marketing support personnel.

One common reason for establishing brand partnerships is to gain access to distribution. For example, Guinness has very strategically used partnerships to develop markets or provide expertise it lacked. Joint venture partners, such as with Moet Hennessey, have provided access to distribution abroad that otherwise would have been hard to achieve within the same time constraints. These partnerships have been crucial for Guinness as it expands operations into developing markets (where almost half its profits are now derived). Similarly, Lipton increased its sales by 500 percent in the first four years of partnering with PepsiCo to distribute the product. Lipton adds the power of its brand to the ready-to-drink iced tea market, while PepsiCo adds its contacts in global distribution. On the other hand, AOL struggled in entering the European market due to its initial failure to link up with either a media or telecommunications company.

Barwise and Robertson identify three alternative ways to enter a new global market:[49]

1. By exporting existing brands of the firm into the new market (introducing a "geographic extension")
2. By acquiring existing brands already sold in the new market but not owned by the firm
3. By creating some form of brand alliance with another firm (joint ventures, partnerships, or licensing agreements)

They also identify three key criteria—speed, control, and investment—by which to judge the different entry strategies.

According to Barwise and Robertson, there are tradeoffs among the three criteria such that no strategy dominates (see Figure 14-7). For example, the major problem with geographic extensions is speed. Because most firms don't have the necessary financial resources and marketing experience to roll out products to a large number of countries simultaneously, global expansion can be a slow, market-by-market process. Brand acquisitions, on the other

FIGURE 14-7

Tradeoffs in Market Entry Strategies

Strategy	Criteria for Evaluation: Speed	Control	Investment
Geographic extension	Slow	High	Medium
Brand acquisition	Fast	Medium	High
Brand alliance	Moderate	Low	Low

hand, can be expensive and often more difficult to control than typically assumed. Brand alliances may offer even less control, although they are generally much less costly.

The choices among these different entry strategies depend in part on how the resources and objectives of the firm match up with each strategy's costs and benefits. For example, Procter & Gamble would enter new markets in categories in which it excels (diapers, detergents, and sanitary pads), building its infrastructure and then bringing in other categories such as personal care or health care. Heineken's sequential strategy has been slightly different. The company first enters a new market by exporting to build brand awareness and image. If the market response is deemed satisfactory, the company will then license its brands to a local brewer in hopes of expanding volume. If that relationship is successful, Heineken may then take an equity stake or forge a joint venture. In doing so, Heineken piggybacks sales of its high-priced Heineken brand with an established local brand.[50] As a result, Heineken now sells in more than 170 countries with a product portfolio of over 80 brands. With more than 110 breweries in over 50 countries and export activities all over the world, Heineken is the most international brewery group in the world

In some countries, companies are legally required to partner with a local company, as is the case in many Middle Eastern countries, or when entering certain markets, such as insurance and telecoms in India. In other cases, companies elect to establish a joint venture with a corporate partner, a common entry strategy often seen as a fast and convenient way to enter complex foreign markets. Fuji Xerox, initially formed to give Xerox a foothold in Japan, has been a highly successful joint venture that dominated the Japanese office equipment market for years and has even outperformed Xerox's U.S. parent company.

Joint ventures have been popular in Japan, where convoluted distribution systems, tightly knit supplier relationships, and close business–government cooperation have long encouraged foreign companies to link up with knowledgeable local partners.[51] Blockbuster entered Japan with a joint venture with one of that country's best-known retailers, Den Fujita, which also runs McDonald's (Japan) and has a stake in Toys'R'Us in Japan. Blockbuster also negotiated joint ventures in France, Germany, and Italy.[52] Pier 1 similarly expanded through joint ventures and licensing accords.[53] Pepsi has ownership positions via joint ventures and five outright acquisitions in 40 percent of its bottling networks outside North America.[54]

Finally, in some cases, mergers or acquisitions result from a desire to command a higher global profile. For example, U.S. baby food maker Gerber agreed to be acquired by Swiss drug maker Sandoz in part because it needed to establish a stronger presence in Europe and Asia, where Sandoz has a solid base.[55] Sandoz later merged with Ciba-Geigy and now is part of the Novartis group of companies.

As these examples illustrate, different entry strategies have been adopted by different firms, by the same firm in different countries, or even in combination by one firm in the same country. Branding Brief 14-5 describes how global brand powerhouse Nestlé enters new markets. These entry strategies also may evolve over time. For example, in Australia, Coca-Cola, through its licensee Coca-Cola Amatil, not only sells its global brands such as Coke, Fanta, and Sprite, but also sells local brands it has acquired such as Lift, Deep

BRANDING BRIEF 14-5

Managing Global Nestlé Brands

For a roughly 15-year period starting in 1984, Nestlé spent more than $30 billion on acquisitions in different countries, including such major brands as Carnation dairy (and other) products (United States), Perrier (France) and San Pellegrino (Italy) mineral water, Stouffer's frozen foods (United States), Rowntree confectionery (United Kingdom), Ralston Purina pet food (USA), and Buitoni-Perugina pasta and chocolate (Italy). Thus, major acquisitions yield valuable economies of scale to Nestlé in developed markets. In less-developed markets, however, they adopt a different strategy. The company's entry strategy there is to manipulate ingredients or processing technology for local conditions and then apply the appropriate brand name, for example, existing brands like Nescafé coffee in some cases or new brands, such as Bear brand condensed milk in Asia, in other cases. Nestlé strives to get into markets first and is patient—the company negotiated for more than a decade to enter China. To limit risks and simplify its efforts in new markets, Nestlé attacks with a handful of labels, selected from a set of 11 strategic brand groups. Nestlé then concentrates its advertising and marketing money on just two or three brands.

Nestlé attempts to balance global and local control in managing its brands. Some decisions, such as branding, follow strict corporate guidelines. The company has 10 *worldwide corporate* strategic brands, including Nestlé, Nescafé, Maggi, and Carnation. There are 45 different strategic *worldwide product* brands, including Kit Kat, Coffeemate, and Crunch. Twenty-five *regional corporate strategic* brands include Perugina, Findus, and Stouffer's. There are 100 *regional product* brands, including Eskimo, Taster's Choice, and Go-Cat. Finally, 700 *local strategic* brands are important to particular countries, including Brigadeiro in Brazil.

Nestlé had used a decentralized management approach, in which most decisions apart from the worldwide and corporate brands were primarily decided by the local managers. In 1997, following most of the acquisitions mentioned above, a new CEO determined that Nestlé needed more formal central and regional control. The company consolidated factory management by region and combined oversight of similar products into strategic business units. Still, local managers retained the decision-making power necessary to adapt products to local tastes. For example, Nestlé continues makes 200 different varieties of its Nescafé instant coffee, each tuned to local palates.

Nestlé's more centralized management approach enabled the company to focus on growing its core brands at each level. From 1999 to 2003, organic growth (excluding acquisitions) was 5.1 percent, almost double Unilever's organic growth rate of 2.7 percent.

Sources: Carla Rapoport, "Nestlé's Brand Building Machine," *Fortune,* 19 September 1994, 147–156; "Daring, Defying, to Grow," *Economist,* 7 August 2004, 55.

Spring, and Mount Franklin. One of Coca-Cola's objectives with these acquisitions is to slowly migrate demand from some of the local brands to global brands, thus capitalizing on economies of scale.

6. Balance Standardization and Customization

One implication of similarities and differences across international markets is that marketers need to blend local and global elements in their marketing programs. The challenge, of course, is to get the right balance—to know which elements to customize or adapt and which to standardize.

Some of the factors often suggested in favor of a more standardized global marketing program include the following:

- Common customer needs
- Global customers and channels
- Favorable trade policies and common regulations
- Compatible technical standards
- Transferable marketing skills

Similarly, one industry observer offered the following three criteria as essential for the development of a global brand:[56]

- Basic positioning and branding that can be applied globally
- Technology that can be applied globally, with local tailoring
- Capabilities for local implementation

Reinforcing these points, Ed Meyer, the long-time head of one of the world's largest ad agencies, Grey Advertising, asserted that there are two key considerations in implementing a global marketing program.[57] First, market development and the competitive environment must be at similar stages from country to country. New products thus often represent more promising candidates for standardization. Whereas mature products may have vastly different histories (or even positionings) in different markets, consumer knowledge for new products is generally the same everywhere because perceptions have yet to be formed. For example, the "Intel Inside" campaign has transferred relatively easily across geographic boundaries because personal computers have been relatively new to each market they enter.

The second key consideration according to Meyer is that consumer target markets should be alike, and consumers must share the same desires, needs, and uses for the product. Similarly, Harvard's Stephen Greyser claims, "The fulcrum of global marketing rests on whether the consumer or customer segment is similar across countries seeking the same values in physical performance or psychological satisfactions or both."[58] In other words, according to Greyser, brand image must be relevant to consumers in both a product-related and non-product-related sense.

What types of products are difficult to sell through standardized global marketing programs? Many experts note that foods and beverages that have years of tradition and entrenched preferences and tastes can be particularly difficult to sell in a standardized global fashion. For example, Unilever has found that standard preferences are more common across countries for cleaning products such as detergents and soaps than for food products. In addition, high-end products can also benefit from standardization because high quality or prestige often can be marketed similarly across countries. For example, Italian coffee maker Illycafé maintains a "one brand, one blend" strategy, offering only a single blend of espresso made of 100 percent Arabica beans across the globe. As Andrea Illy, CEO of his family's business since 1994, states, "Our marketing strategy focuses on building quality consumer perceptions—no promotions, just differentiating ourselves from the competition by offering top quality, consistency, and an image of excellence."

The following are likely candidates for global campaigns that retain a similar marketing strategy worldwide:

- *High-technology products with strong functional images:* Examples are televisions, VCRs, watches, computers, cameras, and automobiles. Such products tend to be universally understood and are not typically part of the cultural heritage.
- *High-image products with strong associations to fashionability, sensuality, wealth, or status:* Examples are cosmetics, clothes, jewelry, and liquor. Such products can appeal to the same type of market worldwide.
- *Services and business-to-business products that emphasize corporate images in their global marketing campaigns:* Examples are airlines and banks.
- *Retailers that sell to upper-class individuals or that specialize in a salient but unfulfilled need:* For example, by offering a wide variety of toys at affordable prices, Toys'R'Us transformed the European toy market by getting Europeans to buy toys for children any time of the year, not just Christmas, and forcing competitors to level prices across countries.
- *Brands positioned primarily on the basis of their country of origin:* An example is Australia's Foster's beer.[59]
- *Products that do not need customization or other special products to be able to function properly:* ITT found that stand-alone products such as heart pacemakers could be sold easily the same way worldwide, but that integrated products such as telecommunications equipment have to be tailored to function within local phone systems.[60]

We earlier outlined tradeoffs between standardization and customization and issues in communication and distribution strategies. Now let's consider product and pricing strategies.

Product Strategy. Many marketers believe that only certain products can be marketed similarly—in some places—and only after they have fully analyzed, understood, and incorporated into the marketing program variables such as marketing mix and culture. One reason so many companies ran into trouble initially going overseas is that they unknowingly—or perhaps even deliberately—overlooked differences in consumer behavior. Because of the relative expense and sometimes unsophisticated nature of the marketing research industry in smaller markets, many companies chose to forgo basic consumer research and put products on the shelf to see what would happen. As a result, they sometimes became aware of these consumer differences only after the fact. To better understand consumer preferences and avoid these types of mistakes, marketers may need to conduct research into local markets. For example, Japanese firms often hire local marketing experts to help design their products to better suit local tastes.[61]

In many cases, however, marketing research reveals that product differences are just not justified for certain countries. At one time, Palmolive soap was sold globally, although with 22 different fragrances, 17 different packages, 9 different shapes, and with numerous different positionings. After marketing analyses to reap the benefits of global marketing, the company now employs just 7 fragrances, 1 core packaging design, and 3 main shapes, all executed around two related positionings (one for developing markets and one for developed markets).[62] Branding Brief 14-6 describes how UPS has attempted to adapt its service for the European market.

From a corporate perspective, one obvious solution to the tradeoff between global and local brands is to sell both types of brands as part of the brand portfolio in a category. Even companies that have succeeded with global brands maintain that standardized international marketing programs work only with some products, in some places, and at some times, and will never totally replace brands and ads with local appeal.[63] For example, while Coca-Cola sells Coke to a growing group of consumers in Asia, it also sells local brands there, such as the hugely successful Georgia iced coffee in Japan, which actually outsells Coke, as well as

BRANDING BRIEF 14-6

UPS's European Express

Between 1987 and 1997, United Parcel Service of America spent $1 billion to buy 16 delivery businesses, put brown uniforms on 25,000 Europeans, and spray its brown paint on 10,000 delivery trucks in the process of becoming the largest delivery company in Europe. To achieve that goal, UPS had to overcome a number of obstacles along the way. French drivers were outraged that they could not have wine with lunch, British drivers protested when their dogs were banned from delivery trucks, Spaniards were dismayed when they realized the brown UPS trucks resembled the local hearses, and Germans were shocked when brown shirts were required for the first time since 1945. UPS ultimately allowed a degree of local intepretation while standing firm on some issues of company policy, such as brown trucks and uniforms and alcohol-free drivers.

UPS has worked hard to be a delivery force in Europe.

Although UPS operations were basically the same, the company faced problems that were less common or even nonexistent in the United States at that time: truck restrictions on weekends and holidays, low bridges and tunnels, widely varying weight regulations, terrible traffic, and, in some places, limited highway systems, primitive airports, and night curfews. Also, the standard of service in Europe in the 1990s was typically well below what U.S.

new drinks in Japan such as Nagomi green tea and the honey-and-grapefruit drink Hachimitsu. In China, the company introduced Tian Yu Di ("heaven and earth"), a fruit juice and tea, and Yangguang ("sunshine") lemon tea, plus other flavors. In India, Coca-Cola's biggest selling cola is Thums Up, an indigenous variant it bought in 1993. It also sells Maaza fruit-based drinks there. This combination of local and global brands enables Coca-Cola to exploit the benefits of global branding and global trends in tastes while tapping into traditional domestic markets at the same time.[64] Thus, despite the trend toward globalization, it seems that there will always be opportunities for good local brands.

Pricing Strategy. When it comes to designing a global pricing strategy, the value-pricing principle from Chapter 5 still generally applies. Thus, marketers need to understand in each country what consumer perceptions of the value of the brand are, their willingness to pay, and their elasticities with respect to price changes. Sometimes differences in these considerations permit differences in pricing strategies. For example, brands such as Levi's, Heineken, and Perrier have been able to command a much higher price outside their domestic market because they have a distinctly different brand image—and thus sources of brand equity—in other countries that consumers place more value on. In addition to these

consumers were accustomed to. Another issue was that express delivery was not yet as popular in Europe as it was in the States. As one industry analyst observed then, "Europeans are not as time-sensitive as the Americans are."

The spread of services and service-related jobs in Europe over the last few decades had been hampered by a reluctance there to part with traditional ways of doing business, such as state-owned monopolies and rigid work practices. Workers have resisted part-time work and had stronger employment protection and higher nonwage costs than workers in the United States. As a result, Manpower Inc. virtually created the temporary help business in Europe and was able to derive more than 40 percent of its worldwide revenues there.

To improve its share of European business, UPS spent an estimated $1.1 billion between 1995 and 2000 upgrading its European operations by purchasing vehicles, aircraft, buildings, and logistics systems. Consequently, export shipping in Europe via UPS rose at a compound annual rate of 22 percent between 1996 and 2002. UPS has continued to invest in their European business since then, acquiring package delivery companies Stolica and Lynx in Poland and the U.K., respectively, in 2005; building a modern new $135 million automated package sorting hub at Cologne/Bonn airport, doubling their processing capacity; and introducing three daily time-definite delivery options to provide the greatest shipping flexibility to customers.

All these investments have paid off. Now the world's largest package delivery company and a global leader in supply chain management, UPS serves 57 European countries and territories with a staff of 32,000 employees and has experienced nearly 10 years of strong export volume growth in Europe.

Sources: Adapted from Dana Milbank, "Can Europe Deliver?" *Wall Street Journal,* 30 September 1994, R15; Alan Saloman, "Delivering a Market Battle," *Advertising Age;* and William Echikson, "The Continent Is Still a Tough Neighborhood For UPS," *Business Week,* 29 September 1997; UPS Annual Report, 2002 and 2005; www.ups.com.

consumer differences across countries, differences in distribution structures, competitive positions, and tax and exchange rates all may justify differences in prices.

But setting drastically different prices across countries is becoming more difficult.[65] Pressures for international price alignment have arisen, in part, because of the increasing numbers of legitimate imports and exports and the ability of retailers and suppliers to exploit price differences through "gray imports" across borders. This problem is especially acute in Europe, where price differences are often large (prices of identical car models may vary by 30 percent to 40 percent) and ample opportunity exists to ship or shop across national boundaries.

Hermann Simon, a German expert on pricing, recommends creating an international "price corridor" that takes into account both the inherent differences between countries and alignment pressures. Specifically, the corridor is calculated by company headquarters and its country subsidiaries by considering market data for the individual countries, price elasticities in the countries, parallel imports resulting from price differentials, currency exchange rates, costs in countries and arbitrage costs between them, and data on competition and distribution. No country is then allowed to set its price outside the corridor: Countries with lower prices have to raise them, and countries with higher prices have to lower them. Another possible strategy suggested by Simon is to introduce different brands in high-price, high-income countries and in low-price, low-income countries, depending on the relative cost tradeoffs of standardization versus customization.

In Asia, many U.S. brands command hefty premiums over inferior home-grown competitors because consumers in these countries strongly associate the United States with high-quality consumer products.[66] In assessing the viability of Asian markets, marketers look at average income but also consider the distribution of incomes, because the consumer population is so large. For example, although the average annual income in India may be only $737, some 300 million people can still afford the same types of products that might be sold to middle-class Europeans. In China, Gillette recently introduced Oral-B toothbrushes at 90 cents, compared with locally produced toothbrushes sold at 19 cents. Gillette's reasoning was that even if it only gained 10 percent of the Chinese market, it still would sell more toothbrushes there than it is currently selling in the U.S. market.

7. Balance Global and Local Control

Building brand equity in a global context must be a carefully designed and implemented process. A key decision in developing a global marketing program is choosing the most appropriate organizational structure for managing global brands. In general, there are three main approaches to organizing for a global marketing effort:

1. Centralization at home office or headquarters
2. Decentralization of decision making to local foreign markets
3. Some combination of centralization and decentralization

In general, firms tend to adopt a combination of centralization and decentralization to better balance local adaptation and global standardization.

In many, if not most, markets, the cost savings of standardization may not outweigh the revenue potential from tailoring programs in some fashion to different groups of consumers.[67] Each aspect of the marketing program is a candidate for globalization. Which elements of the marketing program should we standardize, and to what degree?[68] Cost and revenue should be the primary considerations in deciding which elements of the marketing program that will be adapted for which country. Riesenbeck and Freeling advocate a mixed strategy, standardizing the "core aspects" of the brand (those that provide its main competitive edge) but allowing local adaptation of "secondary aspects." According to their approach, branding, positioning, and product formulation are more likely to be standardized, and advertising and pricing less so; distribution is most often localized.[69]

Many global companies divide their markets into five or so regions, for example, Europe, Asia, Latin America, North America, and Africa/Middle East. A key theme is the need to balance global and local control. Coca-Cola, for example, distinguishes between local marketing activities that would appear to dilute brand equity and those that are not as effective as desired. Headquarters would stop the first from occurring but would not stop the latter, leaving the activity's appropriateness to the local manager's judgment but also holding him or her responsible for its success. Similarly, Levi Strauss has balanced global and local control with a "thermometer" model. Marketing elements below the "freezing point" are fixed: "Brand soul" (described shortly) and logos are standardized worldwide. Above the freezing point, product quality, pricing, advertising, distribution, and promotions are all fluid, meaning each international division can handle the marketing mix elements in any way that it feels is appropriate for its region.

Firms often centralize advertising, consolidating their worldwide ad accounts and shifting most or all of their advertising billings to agencies with extensive global networks to reduce costs and increase efficiency and control. Nevertheless, Braun's and Levi Strauss's regional managers have been able to bar a global campaign from their area.

Unilever's regional managers who seek to substitute their own campaigns must produce research showing that the global plan is inappropriate. Coke and Procter & Gamble take the middle ground, developing a global communications program but testing and fine-tuning it in meetings with regional managers.[70]

8. Establish Operable Guidelines

Brand definitions and guidelines must be established, communicated, and properly enforced so that marketers in different regions have a good understanding of what they are and are not expected to do. The goal is for everyone within the organization to understand the brand's meaning and be able to translate it to satisfy local consumer preferences. Brand definition and communication often revolve around two related issues. First, some sort of document, such as a brand charter, should detail what the brand is and what it is not. Second, the product line should reflect only those products consistent with the brand definition.

Coca-Cola has a strategy document that clearly articulates the company's strategy and how the brand positioning is manifested in various aspects of the marketing mix elements. This document sets out the parameters for the brand and therefore determines how much is left to chance. Similarly, McDonald's operating manual imposes rigorous worldwide controls (for example, the 19 steps to cook and bag french fries). Nestlé ensures that branding decisions at least follow strict corporate guidelines.

COLGATE-PALMOLIVE

Colgate-Palmolive has been a highly successful global marketer for years because of its tight focus on marketing strategies and objectives.[71] Colgate's "bundle books" contain, down to the smallest details, everything that Colgate knows about any given brand—and that a country or regional manager needs to know. The books describe how to effectively market a particular product, including the product attributes, its formulas, ingredient sourcing information, market research, pricing positions, graphics, and even advertising, public relations, and point-of-sales materials. With a bundle book, a Colgate manager in any one of the more than 200 countries and territories where Colgate sells its products can project the Colgate brand exactly like every one of her or his counterparts. As one executive noted, "As the smallest among our major competitors, we are trying to make sure that we maximize our resources. By having tightly controlled brands, we can leverage across borders rapidly."

As an example of deriving product strategy from a brand definition, consider Disney. Everyone at Disney is exposed to the Disney brand mantra, "fun family entertainment" (see Branding Brief 3-7). To establish global guidelines, Disney's centralized marketing group worked with members of the consumer products group for months to assign virtually every possible product to one of three categories:

- Acceptable to license without permission (like T-shirts)
- Not permissible to ever license (such as toilet paper)
- Requires validation from headquarters to license (about 20 categories including air fresheners)

Internationally, Disney has noticed that the "gray areas" grow larger and more numerous. The company also has been trying to identify which product groups may be more amenable to localizing than others. For example, movies cannot be tailored for the European market because it is difficult to determine what will be attractive to those consumers. On the other hand, certain items may sell well in Germany but not in Japan.

Finally, for all this to work, there must be effective lines of communication. Coca-Cola stresses the importance of having people on the ground who can effectively manage the brand in concert with headquarters in Atlanta. To facilitate coordination, much training occurs in headquarters; a sophisticated e-mail and voicemail system is in place; and global databases are available. The goal of this heavily integrated information system is to facilitate the local manager's ability to tap into what constitutes "relevance" in any particular country and then communicate those ideals to headquarters.

9. Implement a Global Brand Equity Measurement System

As suggested by the guidelines in Chapter 8, a global brand equity measurement system would be a set of research procedures designed to provide timely, accurate, and actionable information for marketers on brands, so they can make the best possible tactical decisions in the short run and strategic decisions in the long run in all relevant markets. As part of this system, a global brand equity management system defines the brand equity charter in a global context, outlining how to interpret the brand positioning and resulting marketing program in different markets, as suggested by the previous commandment. With the global brand strategy template in place, brand tracking can assess progress, especially in terms of creating the desired positioning, eliciting the proper responses, and developing brand resonance.

Levi Strauss

Levi Strauss & Co. continually monitors its brand equity among consumers in most of its key markets around the world. The company developed "Brand Value Propositions" for each of its three brands. These are a set of enduring strategies that define each brand and differentiate them from competition. They succinctly list the brands global positioning (including frame of reference and point of difference), its global character, and its global "building blocks" or desired state regarding consumer wants and needs. The Brand Value Propositions drive all brand strategies and actions and provide a globally consistent platform for regionally relevant product and marketing execution. In tracking each brand's equity, via on-going consumer surveys, Levi Strauss & Co. monitors the consumer's perceptions and interactions with its brands; the impact its clothes, retail distribution, marketing and other touch points are having on consumers; and whether the results of its efforts are in line with its Brand Value Propositions. Through these efforts, Levi Strauss & Co. is able to tailor brand strategies to ensure each brand is meeting consumer needs while being true to its essence.

The challenge is that the marketing research infrastructure may be lacking in many countries. When DuPont set out to implement a global tracking system for its various brands, its efforts were hampered by the fact that the level of sophistication of local marketing research companies varied considerably for the 40 primary countries in which DuPont operated.

10. Leverage Brand Elements

Proper design and implementation of brand elements (the brand name and all related trademarked brand identifiers) can often be critical to the successful building of global brand equity. As Figure 4-3 showed, a number of brands have encountered resistance because of difficulty in translating their name, packaging, slogans, or other brand elements to another culture. The Science of Branding 14-2 describes some cultural differences in brand name memorability and recall.

In general, nonverbal brand elements such as logos, symbols, and characters are more likely to directly transfer effectively—at least as long as their meaning is visually clear—than verbal brand elements that may need to be translated into another language. Nonverbal brand elements are more likely to be helpful in creating brand awareness than brand image, however, which may require more explicit meaning and direct statements. If the meaning of a brand element is visually clear, it can be an invaluable source of brand equity worldwide. As the old saying goes, "A picture is worth a thousand words," so it is not surprising that choosing the right brand logo, symbol, or character can have a huge impact on global marketing effectiveness.

For example, the image of Ronald McDonald clearly communicates McDonald's association with kids without the need for words. Similarly, Mr. Peanut, the Apple logo, and the M&M characters need no translation. Other brand elements become synonymous with an association and also serve as effective communications tools without the use of words. Thus, brand logos and symbols also play an important role in global branding. The Nike swoosh connotes sports, Coke's contour bottle connotes refreshment, and the Mercedes star connotes status and prestige worldwide. Perhaps the most compelling example of the importance of brand symbols is the Marlboro man.

Marlboro

In repositioning the Marlboro brand, Philip Morris created the Marlboro man, a cowboy who is almost always depicted somewhere in the western United States among magnificent scenery deemed "Marlboro country." By 1975, Marlboro had become the best-selling cigarette in the United States. But the appeal of the Marlboro man extends far beyond the United States. Indeed, the cowboy imagery attracts consumers from all over the world, in part by capturing an image that is uniquely American. Today the Marlboro man appears in over 150 countries, and Marlboro is the biggest-selling brand in Germany, Mexico, Switzerland, Saudi Arabia, Hong Kong, Argentina, and 11 other major global markets. The Marlboro brand is consistently ranked as one of the world's most valuable brands, due in large part to the widespread appeal of its brand character and personality.

Even nonverbal elements, however, can encounter translation problems. For example, certain colors have strong cultural meaning. Marketing campaigns using various shades of green in advertising, packaging, and other marketing programs ran into trouble in Malaysia, where these colors symbolize death and disease.[72] In some cases, verbal elements can be translated into native languages without much appreciable loss in meaning. For example, Coke's "Can't Beat the Feeling" slogan was translated to the equivalent of "I Feel Coke" in Japan, "Unique Sensation" in Italy, and "The Feeling of Life" in Chile. Germany proved a problem—no translation really worked—so the slogan was kept in English because of the relatively large bilingual audience there.

Because of a desire to standardize globally, however, many firms have attempted to create more uniform brand elements. Pursuing a global branding strategy, Mars chose to replace its Treets and Bonitos brands with the M&M's brand worldwide and changed the name of its third-largest U.K. brand—Marathon—to the Snickers name used in the rest of Europe and the United States.[73] To create a stronger global brand, PepsiCo pulled together its dozens of company-owned brands of potato chips—previously sold under different names—and began to market them all abroad under a more uniform Lay's logo. The company also boosted advertising and improved quality to enhance the brand image at the same time.[74]

Review

Increasingly, marketers must properly define and implement a global branding strategy. A number of factors are encouraging firms to sell their products and services abroad. Some advantages of a global marketing program are economies of scale in production and distribution, lower marketing costs, communication of power and scope, consistency in brand image, an ability to leverage good ideas quickly and efficiently, and uniformity of marketing practices and thus greater competitiveness. The more standardized the marketing program, in general, the more the firm can actually realize these different advantages. At the same time, the primary disadvantages of a standardized global marketing program are that

THE SCIENCE OF BRANDING 14-2

Brand Recall and Language

Given the linguistic differences that exist between cultures whose languages do not share a common root, perhaps it is not surprising that differences exist in what types of brand names are more likely to be recalled in one culture versus another. A series of studies addressing this issue in the cases of Chinese- and English-speaking consumers found that significant differences existed in how they processed brand names. These studies have implications for companies looking to adapt or create brands in China.

In one study, Chinese speakers were more likely to recall brand names in visual, rather than spoken, recall, whereas English speakers were more likely to recall the names in spoken rather than visual recall, suggesting that mental representations of verbal information in Chinese are coded mainly visually, whereas verbal information in English is coded primarily in a phonological manner.

Another study showed that a match between peripheral features of a brand name ("script" aspects, such as the type of font employed, or "sound" aspects, such as the way the name is pronounced) and the associations or meaning of the brand resulted in more positive brand attitudes than a mismatch: Chinese native speakers were affected primarily by script matching, whereas English native speakers' attitudes were primarily affected by sound matching. These results were interpreted in terms of structural differences between logographic systems (such as Chinese, where characters stand for concepts and not sounds) and alphabetic systems (such as English, where the writing of a word is a close cue of its pronunciation) and their resulting visual and phonological representations in memory.

A related study investigated perceptions of brand names translated into Chinese. There are three possible types of translation for names. The first is phonetic: Chinese characters are used that sound most like the English word. The second is semantic: Chinese characters are chosen

it may ignore important differences across countries in consumer needs, wants, and usage patterns for products; consumer response to marketing mix elements; product development and the competitive environment; the legal environment; marketing institutions; and administrative procedures.

In developing a global marketing program, marketers attempt to obtain as many of these advantages as possible while minimizing any possible disadvantages. Building global customer-based brand equity means creating brand awareness and a positive brand image in each country in which the brand is sold. It is difficult to identify any one company applying the global marketing concept in the strictest sense. Increasingly, marketers are blending global objectives with local or regional concerns. The means by which brand equity is built may differ from country to country, or the actual sources of brand equity themselves may vary across countries in terms of specific attribute or benefit associations. Nevertheless, there must be sufficient levels of brand awareness and strong, favorable, and unique brand associations in each country in which the brand is sold to provide sources of brand equity. It is necessary to identify differences in consumer behavior (how consumers purchase and use products and what they know and feel about brands) and adjust the branding program accordingly (i.e., through the choice of brand elements, nature of the supporting marketing program, and leverage of secondary associations).

that approximate the meaning of the English word. The third is phono-semantic: A translation is formed that shares similarities in meaning and sound with the English original. It is common for products in China to use "bilingual" packaging that carries the brand name both in logographic form (Chinese characters) and in the English alphabet. Typically, a package will emphasize one name over the other by making it appear larger on the package. The study found that consumers preferred phonetic translations if a hypothetical product emphasized the English name, while they favored both phono-semantic and semantic translations equally regardless of which name was emphasized.

A different study demonstrated that "classifiers," a grammatical feature present in Chinese but not English, affected perceived similarity among objects and how words are clustered upon recall. Chinese speakers were more likely to cluster names according to classifiers than English speakers. This finding suggested that judicious selection of classifiers could influence the way consumers perceive a brand. The study also showed that for Chinese speakers, images in hypothetical advertisements that corresponded with a classifier present in the ad copy were preferable to images that had no correspondence.

Sources: Bernd H. Schmitt, Yigang Pan, and Nader T. Tavassoli, "Language and Consumer Memory: The Impact of Linguistic Differences between Chinese and English," *Journal of Consumer Research* 21, no. 12 (1994): 419–431; Nader T. Tavassoli and Yih Hwai Lee, "The Differential Effect of Auditory and Visual Advertising Elements with Chineses and English," *Journal of Marketing Research* 40 (November 2003): 468–480; Yigang Pan and Bernd H. Schmitt, "Language and Brand Attitudes: Impact of Script and Sound Matching in Chinese and English," *Journal of Consumer Psychology* 5, no. 3 (1996): 263–277; Shi Zhang, Bernd H. Schmitt, and Hillary Haley, "Language and Culture: Linguistic Effects on Consumer Behavior in International Marketing Research," in *Handbook of Research in International Marketing,* ed. Subhash C. Jain, 228–242 (Northampton, MA: Edward Elgar, 2003).

Figure 14-8 lists the "Ten Commandments of Global Branding" and a series of questions that can be asked to help guide effective global brand management.

Discussion Questions

1. Pick a brand marketed in more than one country. Assess the extent to which the brand is marketed on a standardized versus customized basis.
2. How aware are you of the country of origin of different products you own? For which products do you care about the country of origin? Why? For those imported brands that you view positively, find out and critique how they are marketed in their home country.
3. Pick a product category. Consider the strategies of market leaders in different countries. How are they the same and how are they different?
4. Pick a product category. How are different leading brands targeting different demographic market segments?
5. Contrast Coca-Cola's and McDonald's global branding strategies. How are they similar and how are they different? Why are they so well respected?

1. *Understand similarities and differences in the global branding landscape.*
   - Have you tried to find as many commonalities as possible across markets?
   - Have you identified what is unique about different markets?
   - Have you examined all aspects of the marketing environment (e.g., stages of brand development, consumer behavior, marketing infrastructure, competitive activity, legal restrictions)?
   - Have you reconciled these similarities and differences in the most cost-effective and brand-building manner possible?
2. *Don't take shortcuts in brand building.*
   - Have you ensured that the brand is being built from the bottom up strategically by creating brand awareness first before crafting the brand image?
   - Have you ensured that the brand is being built from the bottom up tactically by determining the appropriate marketing programs and activity for the brand in each market given the particular strategic goals?
3. *Establish marketing infrastructure.*
   - Have you created the appropriate marketing infrastructure—in terms of manufacturing, distribution, and logistics—from scratch if necessary?
   - Have you adapted to capitalize on the existing marketing infrastructure in other countries?
4. *Embrace integrated marketing communications.*
   - Have you considered nontraditional forms of communication that go beyond conventional advertising?
   - Have you ensured that all communications are integrated in each market and are consistent with the brand's desired positioning and heritage?
5. *Cultivate brand partnerships.*
   - Have you formed partnerships with global and local partners to improve possible deficiencies in your marketing programs?
   - Have you ensured that all partnerships avoid compromising the brand promise and do not harm brand equity in any way?
6. *Balance standardization and customization.*
   - Have you been careful to retain elements of marketing programs that are relevant and add value to the brand across all markets?
   - Have you sought to find local adaptations and additions that complement and supplement these global elements to achieve greater local appeal?
7. *Balance global and local control.*
   - Have you established clear managerial guidelines as to principles and actions that all global managers must adhere to?
   - Have you carefully delineated the areas in which local managers are given discretion and autonomy in their decision making?
8. *Establish operable guidelines.*
   - Have you explicated brand management guidelines in a clear and concise fashion in a document to be used by all global marketers?
   - Have you established means of seamless communication between headquarters and local and regional marketing organizations?
9. *Implement a global brand equity measurement system.*
   - Do you conduct brand audits when appropriate in overseas markets?
   - Have you devised a brand tracking system to provide timely, accurate, and actionable information on brands in relevant markets?
   - Have you established a global brand equity management system with brand equity charters, brand equity reports, and brand equity overseers?
10. *Leverage brand elements.*
    - Have you checked the relevance of brand elements in global markets?
    - Have you established visual brand identities that transfer across market boundaries?

FIGURE 14-8

Self Evaluation Ratings for the Ten Commandments of Global Branding

BRAND FOCUS 14.0

China's Global Brand Ambitions

Growth at Home

China, the world's most populous country with more than 1.3 billion people, was essentially closed to the West during the period between the Communist overthrow of the government in 1949 until gradual economic reforms began in 1978, culminating with China's admission into the World Trade Organization in 2001. Since reforms began, China has industrialized at a remarkable rate and is now the world's fourth-largest economy, a manufacturing giant boasting a record $100 billion trade surplus in 2005. The statistics of China's production are staggering: It is the world's largest garment exporter by a large margin, it is also the world's largest manufacturer of consumer electronics, and it manufactures 80 percent of the clocks sold in the world, 50 percent of all cameras, and 60 percent of all bicycles. The primary reason for China's manufacturing prowess is its remarkably cheap labor pool. Manufacturing wages in China average 60 cents an hour, 95 percent lower than U.S. averages.

China's economic boom has created a wealth of opportunity for the country's citizens and companies, as well as providing an attractive consumer base for foreign companies seeking growth. For each group, however, a number of mitigating factors prevented the pursuit of these opportunities from being entirely seamless. The following sections will illustrate the successes and difficulties that characterize modern China.

A Growing Consumer Class

Not surprisingly, China's rise to a global economic superpower enriched many of its citizens. By 2006, *BusinessWeek* estimated that 300,000 Chinese citizens were millionaires.[75] With this newfound wealth came a newfound interest in consuming conspicuously, which precipitated a windfall for foreign luxury-goods manufacturers. China went from consuming 1 percent of the world's luxury goods in 2001 to 12 percent in 2006, the third-highest tally in the world. Luxury brands flocked to the mainland to cash in. By 2006, Louis Vuitton had 12 boutiques spread across China, Ermenegildo Zegna had more than 50 shops in a dozen cities, Rolls Royce's Beijing outlet was one of the company's top-selling dealerships, and Cartier began targeting second- and third-tier cities in search of additional growth. The luxury market is expected to expand even more rapidly in the coming years. As China's middle class grows from 50 million in 2002 to a predicted 100 million by 2010, luxury goods brands will have a large audience for their more modestly priced items. China's vast population of only children—called "Little Emperors" for the way many of them are spoiled by their doting parents—made up 20 percent of the population under age 25 in 2004 and are expected to drive demand for luxury goods for years to come.[76]

Times were not always so good, however, for China's wealthy elite. *Forbes'* 1999 survey of China's wealthiest individuals became known as the "death list" after the government initiated a "tax crackdown" on many of the lists' members and even led to jail terms for some.[77] Attitudes have since changed, and as one wealthy film producer noted, "We are more accepted by the media, government, and society today."[78] Yet the fact that a fortunate few have experienced an exponential increase in personal wealth belies the vast numbers of urban and, especially, rural poor that have been left behind. Rural workers earn half the average salary of urban factory workers, which is often not enough for the rural dwellers to send their children to school. Consequently, rural Chinese are migrating to cities in search of better-paying jobs, increasing urban congestion and yielding higher unemployment rates. By 2010, a predicted 50 percent of the population will live in cities, aggravating these problems.

Despite the concerns generated by this wealth polarization, China's consumer class still harbors enough purchasing power to attract foreign brands, as the next section describes.

Foreign Interest

Ever since China began relaxing its trade policy in 1978, foreign companies have eagerly sought the Chinese consumer's *yuan* (Chinese for dollar). Coca-Cola was one of the first Western brands in China, entering the country in 1979. Through an investment of more than $1 billion in a series of joint venture bottling plants, Coke gradually expanded its presence there. Over the years, it became far more successful than Jianlibao, China's biggest domestic soft drinks player, which saw its market share fall from 15 percent in the early 1990s to five percent in 2002.

By 2003, Coca-Cola employed 20,000 people in China and had been profitable for eight years.[79] FedEx also made an early move into China by buying a regional cargo airline for almost a billion dollars in 1989, nearly 10 years before rivals moved into the Chinese market. By 2006, FedEx controlled 39 percent of the China-U.S. air express shipping market, more than any other foreign competitor.[80] Other foreign companies have also achieved considerable success in China. For example, beauty-conscious China is a $2 billion market for Procter & Gamble. China accounts for more than 30 percent of international profits for Yum Brands, which owns KFC and Pizza Hut. China is the second-largest film market for Kodak, which runs more than 8,000 photo stores there. China has 126 television sets for every 100 households.[81] Additionally, some faded foreign brands have managed to remake their images in China. For example, Howard Johnson operates four- and five-star hotels in China, complete with marble floors, that have enabled the company to successfully position itself there as an upscale chain.

Other foreign companies have targeted Chinese consumers by acquiring Chinese brands and keeping the original names intact. For Danone, 80 percent of its sales are generated by Chinese brands.[82] It bought a local milk and vitamin drink brand, Wahaha, in 1996 and increased sales from 800 million bottles to 4 billion bottles within two years. It then extended Wahaha into China's largest bottled water brand, making China Danone's largest water market. In China, Danone has higher profit margins than its global average and earns more than $1.2 billion in annual revenues.

Motorola is one of the most successful companies to enter the Chinese market, yet it found its market leadership besieged by a wave of local competition in the 2000s. With 300 million mobile phone users and 5 million more signing up each month in early 2004, China is by far the largest national market in the world.[83] Motorola, recognizing this potential early, entered in the late 1980s and worked extensively with government leaders to develop China's wireless telecommunications infrastructure and related skilled manufacturing, becoming the largest foreign investor in China's electronics industry. Unfortunately for Motorola, by 2004, the market was incredibly competitive: Consumers had over 800 models to choose from, and young urban users typically changed phones every 8 months. Furthermore, more than 40 percent of the handset market in China had been captured by local companies such as Ningbo Bird, Nanjing Panda Electronics, and TCL Mobile, many of which would not exist had it not been for Motorola's initial investment in China's mobile phone industry. Motorola's experience in the mobile phone market illustrates the problem of technology transfer to local companies, one of the means by which local Chinese brands grow strong locally. The next section highlights the growing number of local Chinese brands who are competing with, and at times beating, the foreign competition.

Emerging Local Leaders

The Chinese handset manufacturers mentioned above are just one of many examples where local brands take or keep share from foreign heavyweights. Many Chinese consumer electronics and consumer packaged goods brands are also the market leaders at home. Haier, China's number-one appliance maker, is a $10 billion manufacturing giant based in Qingdao. GOME is China's top electronics retailer with over 100 stores, $2 billion in sales, and "the kind of high-plateau brand recognition that Circuit City and Best Buy enjoy in the U.S."[84] Foreign brewers were forced to regroup after early forays into China were confounded by the cheaper and better-distributed market leader Tsingtao and a host of other, smaller local beers. The Internet is another area where Chinese brands often rule at home. With 94 million Internet users in 2005, China had the second-largest online population after the United States. In instant-messaging, AOL and MSN are also-rans: A local company, Tencent, was leader in 2005, with 70 percent of the market. eBay is a distant second in online auctions to TaoBao, which transacted 72 percent of the $1.7 billion of online auctions conducted in 2005.[85]

One of the reasons for the local brands' success is the superior distribution networks they possess. Many Chinese firms built local distribution from the ground up, enabling them to reach millions of consumers not served by the multinationals, who initially targeted only major Chinese cities. Many local brands are outspending their foreign rivals on advertising. Advertising is justifiably a major battleground: With 126 television sets for every 100 households, brands can reach many of China's billion-plus customers relatively efficiently with television. Of the top 10 advertisers in China in 2004, half were Chinese brands, spending a combined $1.5 billion.[86] Between 2000 and 2005, Chinese companies went from accounting for zero percent to 35 percent of billings at J. Walter Thompson in China.

Perhaps no brand typifies Chinese brands' ability to win on their own turf better than Lenovo (formerly Legend), a Chinese PC manufacturer. Lenovo was started in 1984 and initially struggled to keep pace with foreign brands. As recently as 1997 it was losing money and market share to brands like IBM, HP, and Compaq. But within two years it had turned its financial fortunes around with the help of low prices, government contracts, and a vast distribution network, growing more than 100 percent between 1998 and 1999 and grabbing 15 percent market share, about twice that of its closest rival.[87] It protected and grew its market leadership in China, which enabled it to purchase IBM's PC division in 2005. In early 2006, it began selling low-priced PCs bearing the Lenovo name in the United

States. Lenovo's global ambitions illustrate the latest brand trend to emerge in China, that of local brands growing globally. This trend is the topic of the next section.

Locals Going Global

Due to its high-profile acquisition of IBM's PC unit, Lenovo is likely the most well known of the Chinese seeking to build brands abroad. There are many others in China, however, pursuing a similar strategy. Many observers predict that some of these brands will follow in the footsteps of Korea's Samsung, LG, and Hyundai as Asian brands that rose from obscurity to global prominence in a matter of a couple decades. Appliance-maker Haier is a Chinese firm with the potential to do just that. To better compete in overseas markets, Haier increased its R&D spending to 4 percent of revenues. "In the past, we tried to design our products in Qingdao and sell them to the U.S. and Japan," explained CEO Zhang Ruimin. "They didn't meet overseas consumers' needs and didn't sell well."[88] By 2004, Haier had 22 factories overseas and distribution at Wal-Mart, Sears, and Best Buy helped its foreign revenues rise to $1.3 billion, or 13 percent of total revenues. Athletic clothing and equipment maker Li-Ning sought to build its international profile by outfitting many Chinese athletes and the entire Spanish basketball team for the 2004 Athens Olympics, and by acquiring the rights to use NBA players and logos in its marketing.[89] Other Chinese brands to set out into foreign soil include electronics firm TCL, cell phone manufacturer China Kejian, networking equipment maker Huawei, and Tsingtao beer.

These moves abroad are, in part, simply a function of the pressures facing large firms searching for sources of revenue growth beyond an increasingly competitive domestic market. Another cause is official encouragement from the Chinese government, who dictated that between 30 and 50 state firms should be built into "national champions" or "globally competitive" companies by 2010,[90] and therefore exhorted Chinese companies "to set up overseas operations, acquire foreign assets, and transform themselves into multinational corporations."[91] A related reason is the notion of global brand recognition as a source of national pride. One Chinese industrialist had a slogan printed on the wall of one of his factories that captured this source of Chinese companies' global aspirations: "One who earns money in China is a winner; one who earns money overseas is a hero."[92]

Yet the path to global brand leadership was fraught with complications. As of 2006, no Chinese brand could be considered a global brand. In fact, one advertising executive working in China argued that "Chinese companies are light years away" from exporting their brands successfully.[93] Put plainly, Chinese companies were behind the curve when it came to branding compared to global competitors, a fact Haier CEO Zhang readily acknowledged, saying "[Chinese companies] started brand development very late, so we have to catch up in a very short period of time."[94] Companies that did have an international presence, such as Haier and Lenovo, were priced as entry-level bargains, like their Korean predecessors. To "shortcut" their way to brand recognition and respect, some Chinese firms began bidding for foreign brands, as Lenovo did with IBM. Still others, like Haier, invest more heavily in R&D in order to bolster their images with innovation. Despite the difficulties Chinese brands had encountered growing overseas, one consultant remained optimistic about Chinese brands one day taking their place as global brand leaders:

> Market shares will go up and down. Some Chinese companies will lose. It's a learning process. But there is no doubt that world-class Chinese brands will emerge.[95]

Notes

1. For a more detailed discussion of branding in Asia, see Martin Roll, *Asian Brand Strategy: How Asia Builds Strong Brands* (London: Palgrave Macmillan, 2005) and Paul Temporal, *Branding in Asia: The Creation, Development, and Management of Asian Brands for the Global Market* (New York: John Wiley & Sons, 2001).
2. Christine Dugas, "Marketing's New Look," *Business Week,* 26 January 1987, 64–69.
3. Peter Oberlink, "Regional Marketing Starts Taking Hold," *Adweek,* 6 April 1987, 36–37.
4. Thomas Moore, "Different Folks, Different Strokes," *Fortune,* 16 September 1985, 65, 68.
5. Michael J. McCarthy, "In Texas Beer Brawl, Anheuser and Miller Aren't Pulling Punches," *Wall Street Journal,* 5 December 1996, A1, A12.
6. Alix M. Freedman, "National Firms Find That Selling to Local Tastes Is Costly, Complex," *Wall Street Journal,* 9 February 1987, 1.
7. Roberta Bernstein, "Food for Thought," *American Demographics* (May 2000): 39–40.
8. Jennifer L. Aaker, Anne M. Brumbaugh, and Sonya A. Grier, "Nontarget Markets and Viewer Distinctiveness: The Impact of Target Marketing on Advertising Attitudes," *Journal of Consumer*

Psychology 9, no. 3 (2000): 127–140; Sonya A. Grier and Rohit Deshpande, "Social Dimensions of Consumer Distinctiveness: The Influence of Social Status on Group Identity and Advertising Persuasion," *Journal of Marketing Research* 38 (May 2001): 216–224.

9. Michael J. Thomas, Jack R. Bureau, and Narsingh Saxena, "The Relevance of Global Branding," *Journal of Brand Management* 2, no. 5 (1995): 299–307.
10. Shaoming Zou and S. Tamer Cavusgil, "The GMS: A Broad Conceptualization of Global Marketing Strategy and Its Effect on Firm Performance," *Journal of Marketing* 66 (October 2002): 40–56.
11. Vanessa O'Connell, "Exxon 'Centralizes' New Global Campaign," *Wall Street Journal,* 11 July 2001, B6.
12. Dana L. Alden, Jan-Benedict E. M. Steenkamp, and Rajeev Batra, "Brand Positioning Through Advertising in Asia, North America, and Europe: The Role of Global Consumer Culture," *Journal of Marketing* 63 (January 1999): 75–87.
13. Rakeev Batra, Venkatram Ramaswamy, Dana L. Alden, Jan-Benedict E. M. Steenkap, and S. Ramachander, "Effects of Brand Local and Nonlocal Origin on Consumer Attitudes in Developing Countries," *Journal of Consumer Psychology* 9, no. 2 (2000): 83–95; Jan-Benedict E. M. Steenkamp, Rajeev Batra, and Dana L. Alden, "How Perceived Globalness Creates Brand Value," *Journal of International Business Studies* 34 (2003): 53–65.
14. Ian M. Lewis, "Key Issues in Globalizing Brands: Why There Aren't Any Global OTC Medicine Brands," talk presented at the Third Annual Advertising and Promotion Workshop, Advertising Research Foundation, 5–6 February 1991.
15. Corporate Executive Board, "Overcoming Executional Challenges in Global Brand Management," Marketing Leadership Council, Case Book, March 2001.
16. Terry Lefton, "The Global Exchange of Pricelessness," *Brandweek,* November 30, 1998.
17. Ibid.
18. Dawar and Parker, however, show how the use of brand name as an important signal of quality occurs in various countries. See Niraj Dawar and Philip Parker, "Marketing Universals: Consumers' Use of Brand Name, Price, Physical Appearance, and Retailer Reputation as Signals of Quality," *Journal of Marketing* 58 (April 1994): 81–95.
19. Choi Lee and Robert T. Green, "Cross-Cultural Examination of the Fishbein Behavioral Intentions Model," *Journal of International Business Studies* (Second Quarter 1991): 289–305.
20. Dennis Chase, "A Global Comeback," *Advertising Age,* 20 August 1987, 142–214.
21. Theodore Levitt, "The Globalization of Markets," *Harvard Business Review* (May–June 1983): 92–102.
22. Gabriella Stern, "Heinz Aims to Export Taste for Ketchup," *Wall Street Journal,* 20 November 1992, B1.
23. Theresa Howard, "Coca-Cola Hopes Taking New Path Leads to Success," *USA Today,* 6 March 2001, 6B.
24. Robert L. Wehling, "Even at P&G, Only 3 Brands Make Truly Global Grade So Far," *Advertising Age,* 1 January 1998, 8.
25. Shelly Branch, "ACNielsen Gives 43 Brands Global Status," *Wall Street Journal,* 31 October 2001, B8.
26. Frank van den Driest, "Danone: Serving Up Servant Leadership," allaboutbranding.com, March 2006.
27. Michael Porter, *Competitive Advantage* (New York: Free Press, 1985), 4–5.
28. Julia Flynn, "Heineken's Battle to Stay Top Bottle," *Business Week,* 1 August 1994, 60–62.
29. Carla Rapoport, "Nestlé's Brand Building Machine," *Fortune,* 19 September 1994, 147–156.
30. For more information on global marketing strategies, see George S. Yip, *Total Global Strategy* (Englewood Cliffs, NJ: Prentice Hall, 1996).
31. V. T. Bharadwaj, Gautam M. Swaroop, and Ireena Vittal, "Winning the Indian Consumer," *McKinsey Quarterly Special Edition: Fulfilling India's Promise,* 2005.
32. Ginny Parker, "Going Global Can Hit Snags, Vodafone Finds," *Wall Street Journal,* 16 June 2004, B1.
33. "Softbank to Change Vodafone Japan's Name to Softbank Mobile," *TelecomWorldWire,* 18 May 2006.
34. Asihish Banerjee, "Global Campaigns Don't Work; Multinationals Do," *Advertising Age,* 18 April 1994, 23.
35. Jorge A. Monjaras, "Unilever Launches Snuggle in Mexico," *Advertising Age,* 24 February 2003, 20.
36. Patricia Sellers, "Pepsi Opens a Second Front," *Fortune,* 8 August 1994, 70–76.
37. Julie Skur Hill and Joseph M. Winski, "Goodbye Global Ads," *Advertising Age,* 16 November 1987, 22.
38. Vijay Govindarajan and Christopher Trimble, "Serving the Need of the Poor—For Profit," *Across the Board,* December 2001.
39. Rapoport, "Nestlé's Brand Building Machine."
40. Peter Fritsch and Gregory L. White, "Even Rivals Concede GM Has Deftly Steered Road to Success in Brazil," *Wall Street Journal,* 25 February 1999, A1, A8.
41. Mark Maremont, "They're All Screaming for Häagen-Dazs," *Business Week,* 4 October 1991, 121.
42. "Technology's Mr. Predictable," *The Economist,* 24 September 2005.
43. Carol Matlack, "eBay Steams into Europe," *Business Week,* 6 November 2000, 116.
44. William Wells, "Global Advertisers Should Pay Heed to Contextual Variations," *Marketing News,* 13 February 1987, 18.
45. Martin S. Roth, "The Effects of Culture and Socioeconomics on the Performance of Global Brand Image Strategies," *Journal of Marketing Research* 32 (May 1995): 163–175.

46. Joann S. Lublin, "More U.S. Magazines to Travel Abroad," *Wall Street Journal,* 18 January 1990, B1.
47. Miriam Jordan, "In Rural India, Video Vans Sell Toothpaste and Shampoo," *Wall Street Journal,* 10 January 1996, B1, B5.
48. Emily Nelson and Miriam Jordan, "Seeking New Markets for Tampons, P&G Faces Cultural Barrier, "*Wall Street Journal,* 8 December 2000, A1, A8.
49. Patrick Barwise and Thomas Robertson, "Brand Portfolios," *European Management Journal* 10, no. 3 (September 1992): 277–285.
50. Flynn, "Heineken's Battle."
51. David P. Hamilton, "United It Stands. Fuji Xerox Is a Rarity in World Business: A Joint Venture That Works," *Wall Street Journal,* 26 September 1996, R19.
52. Gail DeGeorge, "They Don't Call It Blockbuster for Nothing," *Business Week,* 19 October 1992, 113–114.
53. Stephanie Anderson Forest, "A Pier 1 in Every Port?" *Business Week,* 31 May 1993, 81.
54. Sellers, "Pepsi Opens Second Front."
55. Richard Gibson, "Gerber Missed the Boat in Quest to Go Global, So It Turned to Sandoz," *Wall Street Journal,* 24 May 1994, A1, A4.
56. Lewis, "Key Issues in Globalizing Brands."
57. Edward H. Meyer, "Consumers around the World: Do They Have the Same Wants and Needs?" *Management Review* (January 1985): 26–29.
58. Stephen A. Greyser, "Let's Talk Sense about Global Marketing," speech given to Asian Advertising Congress, Bangkok, July 1986.
59. Rebecca Fanin, "What Agencies Really Think of Global Theory," *Marketing & Media Decisions* (December 1984): 74–82.
60. George Anders, "Ad Agencies and Big Concerns Debate World Brands' Value," *Wall Street Journal,* 14 June 1984, 33.
61. Douglas R. Sease, "Japanese Firms Use U.S. Designers to Tailor Products to Local Tastes," *Wall Street Journal,* 4 March 1986, 1.
62. Maureen Marston, "Transferring Equity across Border," paper presented at the ARF Fourth Annual Advertising and Promotion Workshop, 12–13 February 1992.
63. Joanne Lipman, "Marketers Turn Sour on Global Sales Pitch Harvard Guru Makes," *Wall Street Journal,* 12 May 1988, 1.
64. Michael Flagg, "Coca-Cola Adopts Local-Drinks Strategy in Asia," *Wall Street Journal,* 30 July 2001.
65. Hermann Simon, "Pricing Problems in a Global Setting," *Marketing News,* 9 October 1995, 4.
66. Rahul Jacob, "Asia, Where Big Brands Are Blooming," *Business Week,* 23 August 1993, 55.
67. Hubert Gatignon and Piet Vanden Abeele, "To Standardize or Not to Standardize: Marketing Mix Effectiveness in Europe," MSI Report 95–109 (Cambridge, MA: Marketing Science Institute, 1995).
68. John A. Quelch and Edward J. Hoff, "Customizing Global Marketing," *Harvard Business Review* (May–June 1986): 59–68.
69. Hajo Riesenbeck and Anthony Freeling, "How Global Are Global Brands?" *McKinsey Quarterly* no. 4, 3–18, as referenced in Barwise and Robertson, "Brand Portfolios." See also Dennis M. Sandler and David Shani, "Brand Globally but Advertise Locally? An Empirical Investigation," *Journal of Product & Brand Management* 2, no. 2 (1993): 59–71; Gatignon and Vanden Abeele, "To Standardize or Not to Standardize"; Saeed Samiee and Kendall Roth, "The Influence of Global Marketing Standardization on Performance," *Journal of Marketing* 56 (April 1992): 1–17; and David M. Szymanski, Sundar G. Bharadwaj, and P. Rajan Varadarajan, "Standardization versus Adaptation of International Marketing Strategy: An Empirical Investigation," *Journal of Marketing* 57 (October 1993): 1–17.
70. Ken Wells, "Global Campaigns, After Many Missteps, Finally Pay Dividends," *Wall Street Journal,* 27 August 1992, A1.
71. Sharen Kindel, "A Brush with Success: Colgate Palmolive Company," *Hemisphere,* September 1996, 15.
72. George E. Belch and Michael Belch, *Introduction to Advertising and Promotion Management: An Integrated Marketing Communications Perspective,* 3rd ed. (Chicago, Richard Irwin, 1995).
73. Barwise and Robertson, "Brand Portfolios."
74. Robert Frank, "Potato Chips to Go Global—Or So Pepsi Bets," *Wall Street Journal,* 30 November 1995, B1.
75. Dexter Roberts and Frederik Balfour, "To Get Rich Is Glorious," *BusinessWeek,* 6 February 2006, 46.
76. Clay Chandler, "Little Emperors," *Fortune,* 4 October 2004, 138.
77. Roberts and Balfour, "To Get Rich Is Glorious."
78. Ibid.
79. Leslie Chang, "Cracking China's Market," *Wall Street Journal,* 9 January 2003, B1.
80. Dean Foust, "Taking Off Like 'A Rocket Ship,'" *BusinessWeek,* 3 April 2006, 76.
81. Russell Flannery, "'China Is a Big Prize,'" *Forbes,* 10 May 2004, 163.
82. Leslie Chang, "Cracking China's Market," *Wall Street Journal,* 9 January 2003, B1.
83. Ted C. Fishman, "The Chinese Century," *New York Times,* 4 July 2004, 1.
84. Dexter Roberts, "China's Power Brands," *BusinessWeek,* 8 November 2004, 77.
85. "A Behemoth Kept at Bay," *BusinessWeek,* 3 April 2006, 44.
86. Frederik Balfour, "Ad Agencies Unchained," *BusinessWeek,* 25 April 2005, 50.
87. Dexter Roberts, "How a Legend Lives Up to Its Name," *BusinessWeek,* 15 February 1999.

88. Roberts, "China's Power Brands."
89. Deborah L. Vence, "*Not* Taking Care of Business," *Marketing News,* 15 March 2005, 19.
90. "The Struggle of the Champions," *The Economist,* 8 January 2005, 59.
91. David Barboza, "Name Goods in China but Brand X Elsewhere," *New York Times,* 29 June 2005.
92. David Barboza, "Some Assembly Needed: China as Asia's Factory," *New York Times,* 9 February 2006, C1.
93. Roberts, "China's Power Brands."
94. Gerry Khermouch, "Breaking into the Name Game," *BusinessWeek,* 7 April 2003, 54.
95. Roberts, "China's Power Brands."

15 CLOSING OBSERVATIONS

Preview

This final chapter provides some closing observations concerning strategic brand management. First we'll briefly review the CBBE framework. Next, we highlight managerial guidelines and key themes that emerged in previous chapters and summarize success factors for branding. Following up on some of the discussion from Chapter 1, we then consider some special topics by applying the CBBE framework to addressing specific strategic brand management issues for different types of products. We'll conclude by considering the future of branding. Brand Focus 15.0 presents "The Brand Report Card" to help brand managers understand and rate their brands' performance on key branding dimensions.[1]

Strategic Brand Management Guidelines

Summary of Customer-Based Brand Equity Framework

Strategic brand management uses the design and implementation of marketing programs and activities to build, measure, and manage brand equity. Before we review some guidelines for strategic brand management, let's briefly summarize—one last time!—the customer-based brand equity framework.

The rationale behind the framework is to recognize the importance of the customer in the creation and management of brand equity. As one top marketing executive put it: "Consumers own brands, and your brand is what consumers will permit you to have." Consistent with this view, we defined customer-based brand equity in Chapter 2 as the differential effect that consumers' brand knowledge has on their response to the marketing of that brand. A brand has positive customer-based brand equity if customers react more favorably to a product and the way it is marketed when the brand is identified, than when the brand is attributed to a fictitiously named or unnamed version of the product.

The basic premise of customer-based brand equity is that the power of a brand lies in the minds of consumers, and what they've experienced and learned about the brand over time. More formally, we described brand knowledge in Chapter 3 in terms of an associative network memory model, in which the brand is like a node in memory with a variety of different types of associations linked to it. Brand knowledge has two components: brand awareness and brand image. ***Brand awareness*** is related to the strength of the brand node or trace in memory, as reflected by consumers' ability to recall or recognize the brand under different conditions. Brand awareness has depth and breadth. Its depth describes the likelihood that consumers can recognize or recall the brand. Breadth describes the variety of purchase and consumption situations in which the brand comes to mind. ***Brand image*** is consumer perceptions of and preferences for a brand, measured by the various types of brand associations held in memory. Although brand associations come in many forms, we can usefully distinguish between performance-related and imagery-related attributes and benefits.

Sources of Brand Equity. Customer-based brand equity occurs when the consumer has a high level of awareness and familiarity with the brand and holds some strong, favorable, and unique brand associations in memory. In some cases, brand awareness alone is sufficient to result in more favorable consumer response, for example, in low-involvement decision settings in which consumers lack motivation or ability and are willing to base their choices merely on familiar brands. In other cases, the strength, favorability, and uniqueness of the brand associations play a critical role in determining the differential response making up the brand equity. Conceptually, these three dimensions of brand associations depend on the following factors:

1. *Strength:* The strength of a brand association is a function of both the amount, or quantity, of processing that information initially receives, as well as the nature, or quality, of the processing. The more deeply a person thinks about brand information and relates it to existing brand knowledge, the stronger the resulting brand associations. Two factors strengthening the association to any piece of brand information are the personal relevance of the information and the consistency with which the consumer sees it over time.
2. *Favorability:* Favorable associations for a brand are those that are desirable to customers, successfully delivered by the product, and conveyed by the supporting marketing program. Associations may relate to the product or to other intangible, non-product-related aspects like usage or user imagery. However, consumers will not deem all brand associations important or view them all favorably, nor will they value them equally across different purchase or consumption situations.
3. *Uniqueness:* To create the differential response that leads to customer-based brand equity, marketers need to associate unique, meaningful points of difference to the brand to provide a competitive advantage and a "reason why" consumers should buy it. For other brand associations, however, it may be sufficient to be comparable or roughly equal in favorability to competing associations. These associations function as points of parity in consumers' minds to establish category membership and negate potential points of difference for competitors. In other words, these associations are designed to provide consumers "no reason why not" to choose the brand.

Figure 15-1 summarizes these broad conceptual guidelines for creating desired brand knowledge structures.

Outcomes of Brand Equity. Assuming we can create a positive brand image, with marketing programs that register the brand in memory and link it to strong, favorable, and unique associations, we can realize a number of benefits for the brand, as follows:

- Greater loyalty
- Less vulnerability to competitive marketing actions
- Less vulnerability to marketing crises
- Larger margins

1. **Depth of brand awareness:** Determined by the ease of brand recognition and recall.
2. **Breadth of brand awareness:** Determined by the number of purchase and consumption situations for which the brand comes to mind.
3. **Strong brand associations:** Created by marketing programs that convey relevant information to consumers in a consistent fashion at any one point in time, as well as over time.
4. **Favorable brand associations:** Created when marketing programs effectively deliver product-related and non-product-related benefits that are desired by consumers.
5. **Unique brand associations:** Strong and favorable, create points of difference that distinguish the brand from other brands. Brand associations that are not unique, however, can create valuable points of parity to establish necessary category associations or to neutralize competitive points of difference.

FIGURE 15-1

Determinants of Desired Brand Knowledge Structures

- More inelastic consumer response to price increases
- More elastic consumer response to price decreases
- Greater trade cooperation and support
- Increased marketing communication effectiveness
- Possible licensing opportunities
- Additional brand extension opportunities

Tactical Guidelines

Chapter 1 highlighted the chief ingredients of the CBBE framework in terms of how to build, measure, and manage brand equity. The specific themes and recommendations that we developed in subsequent chapters are as follows.

Building Brand Equity. Tactically, we can build brand equity in three major ways: (1) through the initial choice of the brand elements making up the brand, (2) through marketing activities and the design of the marketing program, and (3) through the leverage of secondary associations that link the brand to other entities like a company, geographic region, other brand, person, or event. Guidelines emerged in Chapters 4 to 7 for each of these approaches, as summarized in Figures 15-2 and 15-3.

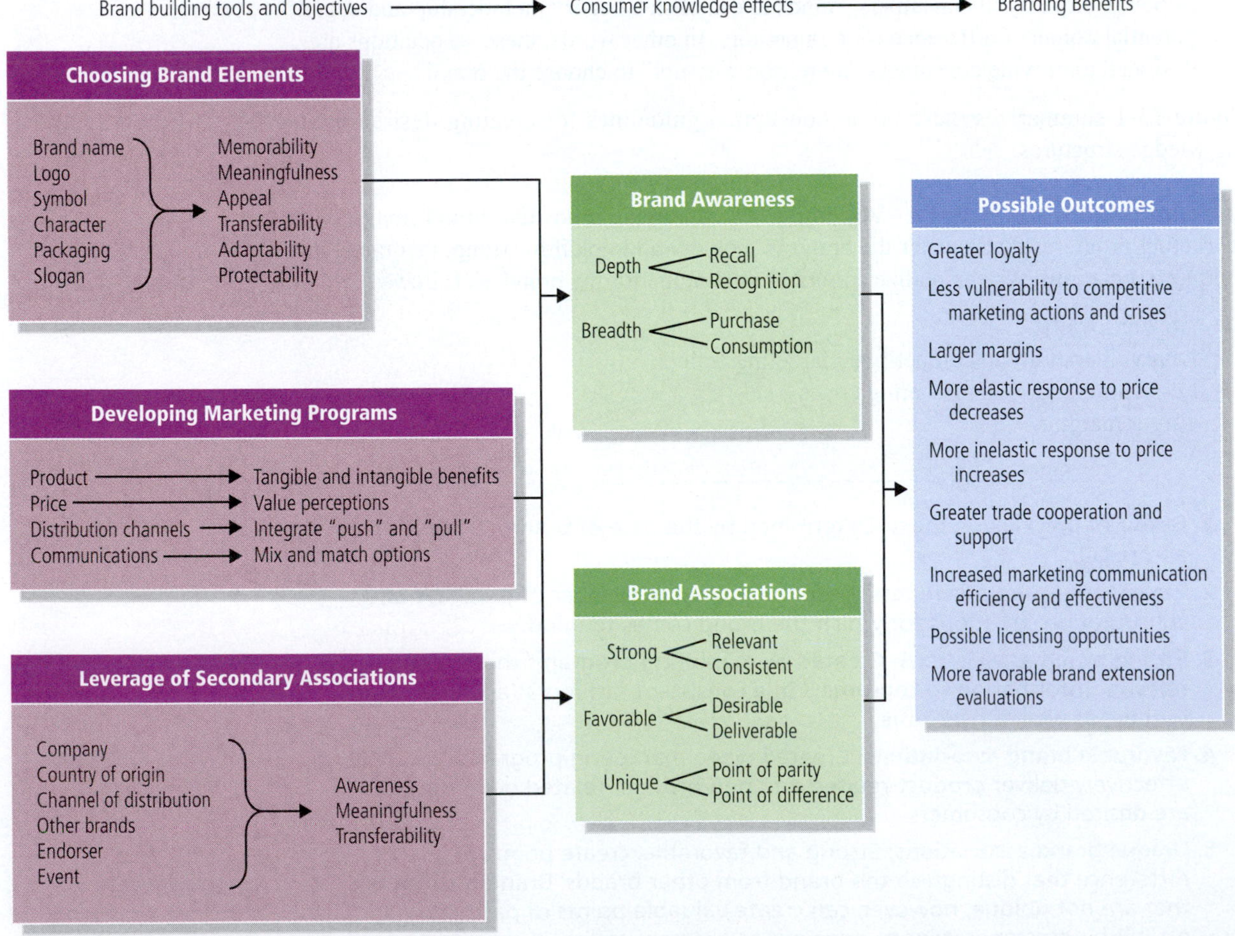

FIGURE 15-2

Building Customer-Based Brand Equity

1. Mix and match brand elements—brand names, logos, symbols, characters, slogans, jingles, and packages—by choosing different brand elements to achieve different objectives and by designing brand elements to be as mutually reinforcing as possible.
2. Ensure a high level of perceived quality and create a rich brand image by linking tangible and intangible product-related and non-product-related associations to the brand.
3. Adopt value-based pricing strategies to set prices and guide discount pricing policies over time that reflect consumers' perceptions of value and willingness to pay a premium.
4. Consider a range of direct and indirect distribution options and blend brand-building push strategies for retailers and other channel members with brand-building pull strategies for consumers.
5. Mix marketing communication options by choosing a broad set of communication options based on their differential ability to affect brand awareness and create, maintain, or strengthen favorable and unique brand associations. Match marketing communication options by ensuring consistency and directly reinforcing some communication options with other communication options.
6. Leverage secondary associations to compensate for otherwise missing dimensions of the marketing program by linking the brand to other entities such as companies, channels of distribution, other brands, characters, spokespeople or other endorsers, or events that reinforce and augment the brand image.

FIGURE 15-3

Guidelines for Building Brand Equity

THEMES. A dominant theme across many of these different ways to build brand equity is the importance of complementarity and consistency. Ensuring ***complementarity*** means choosing different brand elements and supporting marketing activities so that the potential contribution to brand equity of one compensates for the shortcomings of others. For example, some brand elements may primarily enhance awareness through a memorable brand logo, whereas others may facilitate the linkage of brand associations with a meaningful brand name or a clever slogan. Similarly, an ad campaign might create a certain point-of-difference association, whereas a retail promotion creates a vital point-of-parity association. Finally, we can link certain other entities to the brand to leverage secondary associations, provide other sources of brand equity, or further reinforce existing associations.

Thus, it is important to put into place a varied set of brand elements and marketing activities and programs, to create the desired level of awareness and type of image that leads to brand equity. At the same time, a high degree of ***consistency*** across these elements helps to create the highest level of awareness and the strongest and most favorable associations possible. Consistency ensures that diverse brand and marketing mix elements share a common core meaning, perhaps by conveying the same information, such as a benefit association that is reinforced by a highly integrated, well-branded marketing communications program.

Measuring Brand Equity. We can measure brand equity indirectly, by measuring its potential sources, and directly, by measuring its possible outcomes. Measuring sources requires measuring aspects of brand awareness and brand image that can lead to the differential customer response that creates brand equity: breadth and depth of brand awareness; the strength, favorability, and uniqueness of brand associations; the valence

1. Formalize the firm's view of brand equity into a document, the brand equity charter, that provides relevant branding guidelines to marketing managers.
2. Conduct brand inventories to profile how all of the products sold by a company are branded and marketed and conduct brand exploratories to understand what consumers think and feel about a brand as part of periodic brand audits to assess the health of brands, understand their sources of brand equity, and suggest ways to improve and leverage that equity.
3. Conduct consumer tracking studies on a routine basis to provide current information as to how brands are performing with respect to the key sources and outcomes of brand equity as identified by the brand audit.
4. Assemble results of tracking survey and other relevant outcome measures into a brand equity report to be distributed on a regular basis to provide descriptive information as to what is happening with a brand as well as diagnostic information as to why it is happening.
5. Establish a person or department to oversee the implementation of the brand equity charter and brand equity reports to make sure that, as much as possible, product and marketing actions across divisions and geographic boundaries are done in a way that reflects the spirit of the charter and the substance of the report so as to maximize the long-term equity of the brand.

FIGURE 15-4

Guidelines for Measuring Brand Equity

of brand responses; and the nature of brand relationships. Measuring outcomes requires us to estimate the various benefits from creating these sources of brand equity. The brand value chain depicts this relationship more broadly by considering how marketing activity affects these sources of brand equity, and how the resulting outcomes influence the investment community, as well as how various filters or multipliers intervene between the stages.

Marketers need to properly design and implement a ***brand equity measurement system***, a set of research procedures designed to provide timely, accurate, and actionable information for marketers about their brands. Implementing a brand equity measurement system has three steps: (1) conducting brand audits, (2) designing brand tracking studies, and (3) establishing a brand equity management system.

Guidelines in each of these areas are summarized in Figure 15-4.

THEMES. The dominant theme in measuring brand equity is the need to employ a full complement of research techniques and processes that capture as much as possible the richness and complexity of brand equity. We need multiple techniques and measures to tap into all the various sources and outcomes of brand equity, to help interpret brand equity research, and to ensure that we get actionable information at the right time.

Managing Brand Equity. Finally, managing brand equity requires taking a broad, long-term perspective of brands. A broad view of brand equity is critically important, especially when firms are selling multiple products and multiple brands in multiple markets. Here, brand hierarchies must define common and distinct brand elements among various nested products. New product and brand extension strategies also must ensure that we have optimal brand and product portfolios. Finally, we need to manage these brands and products effectively over geographic boundaries and target market segments, by creating brand awareness and a positive brand image in each market in which the brand is sold.

1. Define Brand Hierarchy

A. *Principle of Simplicity:* Employ as few levels as possible.
B. *Principle of Clarity:* Logic and relationship of all brand elements employed must be obvious and transparent.
C. *Principle of Relevance:* Create abstract associations relevant to as many products as possible.
D. *Principle of Differentiation:* Differentiate individual products and brands.
E. *Principle of Growth:* Investments in market penetration or expansion vs. product development should be made according to ROI opportunities.
F. *Principle of Survival:* Brand extensions must achieve brand equity in their categories.
G. *Principle of Synergy:* Brand extensions should enhance the equity of the parent brand.
H. *Principle of Prominence:* Adjust prominence to affect perceptions of product distance.
I. *Principle of Commonality:* Link common products through shared brand elements.

2. Define Brand–Product Matrix

A. *Brand Extensions:* Establish new equity and enhance existing equity.
B. *Brand Portfolio:* Maximize coverage and minimize overlap.

3. Enhance Brand Equity over Time

A. *Brand Reinforcement:* Innovation in product design, manufacturing, and merchandising. Relevance in user and usage imagery.
B. *Brand Revitalization:* "Back to basics" strategy. "Reinvention" strategy.

4. Establish Brand Equity over Market Segments

A. *Identify Differences in Consumer Behavior:* How they purchase and use products. What they know and feel about different brands.
B. *Adjust Branding Program:* Choice of brand elements. Nature of supporting marketing program. Leverage of secondary association.

FIGURE 15-5

Managing Customer-Based Brand Equity

A long-term view of brand equity is necessary because changes in current marketing programs and activities and in the marketing environment can affect consumers' brand knowledge structures, and thus their response to future marketing programs and activities. Managing brands over time requires reinforcing the brand meaning and adjusting the branding program as needed. For brands whose equity has eroded over time, we rely on a number of revitalization strategies.

Figures 15-5 and 15-6 highlight some important guidelines for managing brand equity.

THEMES. The dominant themes in managing brand equity are the importance of maintaining balance in marketing activities and of making moderate levels of change in the marketing program over time. Without some modifications of the marketing program, a brand runs the risk of becoming obsolete or irrelevant to consumers. At the same time, dramatic shifts back and forth in brand strategies can confuse or alienate consumers. Thus, a consistent thread of meaning—which consumers can recognize—should run through the marketing program and reflect the key sources of equity for the brand and its core brand associations.

1. Define the brand hierarchy in terms of the number of levels to use and the relative prominence that brands at different levels will receive when combined to brand any one product.
2. Create global associations relevant to as many brands nested at the level below in the hierarchy as possible but sharply differentiate brands at the same level of the hierarchy.
3. Introduce brand extensions that complement the product mix of the firm, leverage parent brand associations, and enhance parent brand equity.
4. Clearly establish the roles of brands in the brand portfolio, adding, deleting, and modifying brands as necessary.
5. Reinforce brand equity over time through marketing actions that consistently convey the meaning of the brand in terms of what products the brand represents, what benefits it supplies, what needs it satisfies, and why it is superior to competitive brands.
6. Enhance brand equity over time through innovation in product design, manufacturing, and merchandising and continued relevance in user and usage imagery.
7. Identify differences in consumer behavior in different market segments and adjust the branding program accordingly on a cost-benefit basis.

FIGURE 15-6

Guidelines for Managing Brand Equity

What Makes a Strong Brand?

To create a strong brand and maximize brand equity, marketing managers must do the following:

- Understand brand meaning and market appropriate products and services in an appropriate manner.
- Properly position the brand.
- Provide superior delivery of desired benefits.
- Employ a full range of complementary brand elements, supporting marketing activities, and secondary associations.
- Embrace integrated marketing communications and communicate with a consistent voice.
- Measure consumer perceptions of value and develop a pricing strategy accordingly.
- Establish credibility and appropriate brand personality and imagery.
- Maintain innovation and relevance for the brand.
- Strategically design and implement a brand hierarchy and brand portfolio.
- Implement a brand equity management system to ensure that marketing actions properly reflect the brand equity concept.

One of the most skilled brand-builders is Procter & Gamble. Branding Brief 15-1 describes how it has changed its marketing processes and philosophy in recent years to reflect new marketing realities.

On the flip side of the coin, what common branding mistakes prevent firms from creating strong, powerful brands? The "seven deadly sins of brand management" include the following (see Figure 15-7):[2]

1. *Failure to fully understand the meaning of the brand:* Given that consumers "own" brands, it is critical to understand what they think and feel about brands and then plan and implement marketing programs accordingly. Too often, managers convince

1. Failure to fully understand the meaning of the brand
2. Failure to live up to the brand promise
3. Failure to adequately support the brand
4. Failure to be patient with the brand
5. Failure to adequately control the brand
6. Failure to properly balance consistency and change with the brand
7. Failure to understand the complexity of brand equity measurement and management

FIGURE 15-7

Seven Deadly Sins of Brand Management

themselves of the validity of marketing actions—for example, a new brand extension, ad campaign, or price hike—based on a mistaken belief about what consumers know or what marketers would like them to know about the brand. Managers often ignore the full range of associations—both tangible and intangible—that may characterize the brand.

2. *Failure to live up to the brand promise:* A brand should be a promise and a commitment to consumers, but too often that promise is broken. A common mistake is to set brand expectations too high and then fail to live up to them in the marketing program. By overpromising and not delivering, a firm is worse off in many ways than if it had not set expectations at all.
3. *Failure to adequately support the brand:* Creating and maintaining brand knowledge structures requires marketing investments. Too often, managers want to get something for nothing by building brand equity without a willingness to provide proper marketing support or, once brand equity has been built, by expecting the brand to remain strong despite the lack of further investments.
4. *Failure to be patient with the brand:* Brand equity must be carefully and patiently built from the ground up. A firm foundation for brand equity requires that consumers have the proper depth and breadth of awareness and strong, favorable, and unique associations in memory. Too often, managers want to take shortcuts and bypass more basic branding considerations—such as achieving the necessary level of brand awareness—to concentrate on flashier aspects of brand building related to its image.
5. *Failure to adequately control the brand:* All employees of the firm must understand brand equity, and the firm's actions must reflect a broader corporate perspective as well as a more specific product perspective. Too often, firms make decisions haphazardly without a true understanding of the current and desired brand equity and without a recognition of the impact these decisions have on other brands or brand-related activities.
6. *Failure to properly balance consistency and change with the brand:* Managing a brand necessitates striking the difficult, but crucial, balance between maintaining continuity in marketing activities and implementing changes to update the product or image of a brand. Too often, managers are left behind, as a result of not making adjustments in their marketing program to reflect changes in the marketing environment. Or they may make so many changes that the brand becomes a moving target without any meaning to consumers.
7. *Failure to understand the complexity of brand equity measurement and management:* Effective brand management requires discipline, creativity, focus, and the ability to make hundreds of decisions in the best possible manner. Unfortunately, sometimes marketers oversimplify the process and try to equate success in branding with taking one particular action or approach. Brand equity is not optimized as a result.

BRANDING BRIEF 15-1

Reinvigorating Branding at Procter & Gamble

Procter & Gamble has been a leader in marketing for much of its 160-plus years of existence and has been referred to by some as "the single greatest marketing company in the world." P&G, already the world's largest consumer packaged goods company, became even larger with the $57 billion acquisition of Gillette in 2005. After struggling briefly at the turn of the 21st century, under the direction of CEO A. G. Lafley, appointed in 2000, P&G has maintained its leadership in the consumer packaged goods market by following four key strategies.

Renewed Emphasis on R&D

Between 2001 and 2004, P&G updated all its 200 brands, rejuvenating many with the aid of innovations, which enabled the company to increase market share in 70 percent of its businesses. The company leveraged its R&D in launching a number of innovative products in existing categories, including the Swiffer mop, Mr. Clean Magic Eraser, a battery-powered Crest SpinBrush toothbrush, and teeth-whitening Crest Whitestrips. To augment its innovative products, P&G also placed a renewed emphasis on design by appointing its first-ever chief design officer in 2001 and installing a top design officer in each of its global business units. CEO A. G. Lafley emphasized the importance of design in combination with innovation, saying, "When we consciously involved design at the front end—such as with Crest Whitestrips . . . and our whole line of Swiffer quick-clean products—we generated more trial, more repurchase, and more sales."

New Communication Approaches

While P&G increased its ad budget from 8.1 percent of sales in 2001 to 10.7 percent of sales in 2004, it also dramatically shifted 20 percent of this budget away from TV advertising and toward "media-neutral" advertising, which determines media spending without bias toward any particular medium based on precedent. In place of big television buys, P&G has pioneered the use of less obtrusive marketing techniques such as Vocalpoint, a word-of-mouth marketing program that enlists 600,000 mothers, among others, to promote its brands by giving positive testimonials, samples, and coupons to friends and neighbors. Sales in markets where

Special Applications

In Chapter 1 we deliberately defined ***product*** to encompass not only physical goods but also services, retail stores, people, organizations, places, and ideas. While the themes and guidelines for building, measuring, and managing brand equity that we've presented are appropriate for virtually all types of products, here we'll consider in greater detail some specific issues for some less conventional types of products—industrial and business-to-business products, high-technology products, services, retailers, small businesses, and online brands.

Vocalpoint was used during the 2005 Dawn Direct Foam launch were double those in markets that did not use Vocalpoint.

New Research Approaches

P&G conducts approximately 10,000 consumer research projects each year, spending more than $100 million annually. The company significantly changed its research practice after Lafley became CEO, by using qualitative observational research techniques to unlock consumer insights instead of relying heavily on quantitative analysis. Lafley referred to ethnographic research as the "best way to create value," stating, "If you want to understand how a lion hunts, don't go to the zoo. Go to the jungle." In keeping with this view, Lafley required that the top 50 managers at P&G visit with consumers either in their homes or on shopping trips at least once per quarter.

New Branding Philosophy

While it did launch successful new brands such as Swiffer, P&G began pursuing a strategy with less inherent risk: leverage existing assets by investing in well-known "power brands." This strategy arose from the fact that between 1992 and 2002 more than 50 percent of profits and 66 percent of sales growth came from P&G's top 10 global brands. Consequently, P&G focused more on growing core brands from its stable, rather than on adding many new ones. In some cases, as with Mr. Clean, P&G went as far as resurrecting a brand and turning it into a power brand through the launch of a number of innovative new products. As another example, the company took the familiar but faded Old Spice deodorant brand and remade it as a performance brand, building it into the leading deodorant for men in the United States with 20 percent of the market in 2004. P&G often sought to leverage its power brands with vertical extensions into higher-margin categories, as it did with Crest Whitestrips and Mr. Clean AutoDry Car Wash System, which retail for about $25 each.

Sources: A. G. Lafley Interview, "Fast Talk," *Fast Company,* June 2004, 51; Robert Berner, "P&G Has Rivals in a Wringer," *BusinessWeek,* 4 October 2004, 74; Mark Ritson, "P&G's Tactics Point to Marketing's Way Ahead," *Marketing,* 13 April 2005, 19; Bob Garfield, "The Chaos Scenario," *Advertising Age,* 4 April 2005, 1; Nirmalya Kumar, "Kill a Brand, Keep a Customer," *Harvard Business Review,* December 2003, 86.

Industrial and Business-to-Business Products

Industrial goods and business-to-business marketing sometimes call for different branding practices.[3] Here are some basic branding guidelines (see Figure 15-8). Branding Brief 15-2 describes how Siemens has attempted to create a strong corporate industrial brand.

Adopt a corporate or family branding strategy and create a well-defined brand hierarchy. Because companies selling industrial goods often carry a large and complex number of product lines and variations, marketers should devise a logical and well-organized brand hierarchy. Given the breadth and complexity of their product mix, companies selling industrial goods—like GE, Hewlett-Packard, IBM, ABB, BASF, and John Deere—are

1. Adopt a corporate or family branding strategy and create a well-defined brand hierarchy.
2. Link non-product-related imagery associations.
3. Employ a full range of marketing communication options.
4. Leverage equity of other companies that are customers.
5. Segment markets carefully and develop tailored branding and marketing programs.

FIGURE 15-8

Additional Guidelines for Industrial Products

more likely to emphasize corporate or family brands. Thus, a particularly effective branding strategy for industrial goods is to create sub-brands by combining a well-known and respected corporate name with descriptive product modifiers.

Link non-product-related imagery associations. Programs to build brand equity for industrial goods can be different from those for consumer goods because, given the nature of the organizational buying process, product-related associations may play a relatively more important role than non-product-related associations. Industrial brands often emphasize

BRANDING BRIEF 15-2

Business-to-Business Branding at Siemens

Despite the fact that Siemens products have been available in the U.S. market since 1954, research indicated that only 12 percent of U.S. consumers are able to identify the company. Siemens employs over 80,000 U.S. workers, turbines made by its Westinghouse division provide 40 percent of the power in the United States, and more than half of U.S. cars run using Siemens parts. Though it is not a high-visibility corporation, Siemens is a household name in most of the 192 other countries in which it competes.

Siemens began its first corporate advertising campaign in the United States in 1988. But in 2000, CEO Gerhard Schulmeyer expressed disappointment with his company's previous branding efforts in America:

> *We get mad at ourselves. We haven't done the greatest job of branding. No letter could move in this country without our technology, but we never felt a need to tell the people this.*

In 2001, the company set out to raise its image in the eyes of U.S. consumers. This move represented the third step in a plan initiated in 1998 to reinvent Siemens as a high-profile brand, using longtime competitor GE as a model. The company made the United States its primary target for a series of image advertisements that launched in April 2001. Siemens spent $25 million on U.S. media for the campaign, which was part of an estimated $500 million that the company earmarked for U.S. marketing through 2002.

The series began with teaser print ads, which were followed by television spots that used the tagline "Spin the Globe" that emphasized Siemens' global reach in consumer goods. Because they were aiming at increasing sales of its consumer goods, the ads featured Siemens mobile phones. One problem with the company's mobiles, however, was that they were based

functionality and cost/benefit considerations. Nevertheless, even non-performance-related associations can be useful for forming other perceptions of the firm, such as the prestige of a company or the type of other companies that uses the firm's products.

Corporate or family brands must convey credibility and possess favorable global associations. Corporate credibility is often a primary risk reduction heuristic adopted by industrial buyers. For years, one of the key sources of brand equity for IBM was the perception that "you'll never get fired for buying IBM." Once that special cachet faded, the brand found itself in a much more competitive situation. Creating a feeling of security for industrial buyers can thus be an important source of brand equity.

Many industrial firms distinguish themselves on the basis of the customer service they provide, in addition to the quality of their products. For example, Premier Industrial Corporation charges up to 50 percent more than competitors for every one of the 250,000 industrial parts it stocks and distributes, because of its strong commitment to customer service, as exemplified by the following anecdote:

> Early one afternoon in late 1988, Premier Industrial Corp. got a call from the manager of a Caterpillar Inc. tractor plant in Decatur, Illinois. A $10 electrical relay had broken down, idling an entire assembly line. A sales representative for Premier

on European wireless standards different from the dominant standard in the U.S. market, so the company held back from mass marketing them until universal standards developed. Siemens mobile phones never succeeded in competing with top handset companies Nokia, Motorola, Samsung, and Sony Ericsson, however, and were eventually sold to Taiwan's BenQ in 2005.

The company's next big focus in the United States was a program called One Siemens, designed to get the company's units to work together to land big contracts. Bundled contracts that included products and services from a number of Siemens' units were inked to build new hospitals and a sports stadium and totaled $900 million in 2004. Siemens' North America CEO credited the new initiative with generating half that total, which Siemens would not have won otherwise. Still, Siemens' U.S. sales of $16.5 billion in 2004 were only $500 million above its 2000 sales. The company launched a new campaign in 2005 that, while consistent with its One Siemens philosophy, still sought to address the recognition problems that the campaign launched in 2001 was intended to remedy. Keeping the tagline "Spin the Globe," the ads attempted to convey Siemens' breadth by showing all the company's offerings coming together to form structures such as water plants. Echoing the sentiment expressed in 2000 by then-CEO Schulmeyer, Siemens' creative director stated, "Our company is ubiquitous but invisible; we're behind the scenes—that's the dilemma."

Sources: James Cox, "Siemens Cultivates American Accent," *USA Today,* 5 March 2001; Sarah Ellison, "Siemens Woos Youth with New Attitude," *Wall Street Journal,* 15 February 2001; Alfred Kueppers, "Siemens's U.S. Debut Isn't Ideal," *Asian Wall Street Journal,* 19 March 2001, N1; Jack Ewing, "Nokia, Siemens Plan to Join and Conquer," *BusinessWeek,* 19 June 2006; Thomas Clark and Dan Roberts, "Siemens Sets a 30-Month U.S. Strategy," *Financial Times,* 29 July 2004, 25; Diane Anderson, "Siemens Engineers Name Recognition," *Brandweek,* 5 December 2005.

> located a replacement at the company's Los Angeles warehouse and rushed it to a plane headed for St. Louis. By 10:30 that night, a Premier employee had delivered the part, and the line was up and running. "You can't build tractors if you can't move the line," remarked the Caterpillar purchasing analyst. "They really saved us a bundle of money."[4]

As further illustration, creative changes in customer service have similarly built brand equity and allowed Armstrong World Industries to charge higher prices for its floor tiles and Weyerhaeuser's wood-products division to command premiums for its commodity-like two-by-fours. Following IBM's lead, after losing ground in selling its telecommunications hardware, Lucent began to shift into more differentiated value-added services to offer current customers more complete packages and to create new opportunities.[5]

Employ a full range of marketing communication options. Another difference between industrial and consumer products is the way they are sold (see Figure 15-9). Industrial marketing communications tend to convey more detailed product information in a more direct or face-to-face manner. Thus, personal selling plays an important role. At the same time, other communication options can enhance awareness or the formation of brand associations. One effective industrial marketing communication approach is to combine direct hard-sell messages with more indirect image-related messages that convey who and what the company is all about.

Leverage equity of other companies that are customers. Industrial brands can leverage secondary associations differently. For example, communicate credibility by identifying other companies that are customers for the firm's products or services. The challenge in advertising, however, is ensuring that these other companies don't distract from the message about the advertised company and its brands. Even countries can serve in an endorsement strategy. For example, Interlock—a New Zealand brand acquired by ASSA ABLOY that specializes in window hardware—has used the fact that it's the only foreign company in its industry to sell in Japan as an endorsement strategy to sell its products to firms in other countries.

Segment customers carefully and develop tailored branding and marketing programs. Finally, as with any brand, understand how different customer segments view products and brands. For industrial goods, different customer segments such as engineers, accountants, and purchasing managers may exist within as well as across organizations. The associations that serve each as sources of brand equity may differ. It may be particularly important to achieve points of parity with these different

FIGURE 15-9

Alternative Communication Options: Business-to-Business Market

- Media advertising (TV, radio, newspaper, magazines)
- Trade journal advertising
- Directories
- Direct mail
- Brochures and sales literature
- Audiovisual presentation tapes
- Giveaways
- Sponsorship or event marketing
- Exhibitions, trade shows, and conventions
- Publicity or public relations

constituencies, so that key points of difference can come into play. U.K. branding experts de Chernatony and McDonald put it this way:

> In consumer marketing, brands tend to be bought by individuals, while many people are involved in organizational purchasing. The brand marketer is faced with the challenge of not only identifying which managers are involved in the purchasing decision, but also what brand attributes are of particular concern to each of them. The various benefits of the brand, therefore, need to be communicated to all involved, stressing the relevant attributes to particular individuals. For example, the brand's reliable delivery may need to be stressed to the production manager, its low life-cycle costs to the accountant, and so on.[6]

Marketing programs must reflect the role of individuals in the buying center, or the process-initiator, influencer, purchaser, user, and so on. Some individuals within the organization may be more concerned with developing a deep relationship with the company and therefore place greater value on trustworthiness and corporate credibility; others may seek merely to make transactions and therefore place greater value on product performance and expertise.

High-Tech Products

One special category of physical goods, in both consumer and industrial markets, is technologically intensive or "high-tech" products. The main distinguishing feature of high-tech products is that the products themselves change rapidly over time because of innovations and R&D breakthroughs. High-tech products aren't restricted to computer- or microprocessor-related products. Technology has played an important role in the branding and marketing of products as diverse as razor blades for Gillette and athletic shoes for Nike.

The short product life cycles for high-tech products have several significant branding implications (see Figure 15-10 for specific guidelines). Branding Brief 15-3 describes branding developments for Cisco, a successful corporate brand of the past decade.

Establish brand awareness and a rich brand image. Many high-tech companies have learned the hard way the importance of branding their products and not relying on product specifications alone to drive their sales. It's typically not true that "if you build a great product, they will come." You need well-designed and well-funded marketing programs to create brand awareness and a strong brand image. Non-product-related associations concerning brand personality or other imagery may be important, especially in distinguishing near-parity products.

Create corporate credibility associations. One implication of rapid product turnover is the need to create a corporate or family brand with strong credibility associations. Because of the often complex nature of high-tech products and the continual introduction of new products or modifications of existing products, consumer perceptions of the expertise and trustworthiness of the firm are particularly important. In a high-tech setting, trustworthiness also relates

1. Establish brand awareness and a rich brand image.
2. Create corporate credibility associations.
3. Leverage secondary associations of quality.
4. Avoid overbranding products.
5. Selectively introduce new products as new brands and clearly identify the nature of brand extensions.

FIGURE 15-10

Additional Guidelines for High-Tech Products

BRANDING BRIEF 15-3

Sustaining the Cisco Brand

Cisco, the networking equipment manufacturer founded by a group of Stanford computer scientists in 1984, grew to be the market leader in the switchers and routers that directed traffic on the Internet. As a result, the company reaped the rewards of the Internet boom of the late 1990s, growing from $1.3 billion in sales in 1994 to $21.4 billion in 2000. Its stock performed phenomenally, rising 100,000 percent from its 1990 IPO and surpassing Microsoft in market capitalization in 2000. Cisco developed ad campaigns during this period to reinforce its central role on the Internet, including one B-to-B effort which contained a number of facts about the Internet's growth and asked "Are You Ready?" before concluding with the tagline "Empowering the Internet Generation." A Cisco marketing VP at the time stated, "One (goal) is to make the Internet relevant, and the other is to make Cisco synonymous with the Internet."

Being synonymous with the Internet was a boon during the boom times, but a curse when the dot-com bubble burst. Cisco's fortunes faded as companies scaled back their investments in Internet equipment. Revenue growth slowed, leading the company to post a loss in 2001, and its market valuation declined by $430 billion between March 2000 and January 2002. The company faced challenging conditions in which to grow its brand, yet CEO John Chambers remained upbeat, remarking that "Cisco does better during the tough times."

Though the heady days of 70 percent annual growth disappeared, Cisco indeed managed to survive intact, thanks to cost reductions and timely expansions into new networking technologies. It expanded into the increasingly popular voice-over-IP market, earning 40 percent market share by 2003. It also moved into wireless Internet networking markets with the acquisition of Linksys in 2003, which contributed to revenues immediately. To grow in its core networking business, Cisco focused on a major customer issue: security.

to consumers' perceptions of the firm's longevity and staying power. With technology companies, the president or CEO often is a key component of the brand and performs an important brand-building and communication function, in some cases as an advocate of the technology.

Leverage secondary associations of quality. Lacking the ability to judge the quality of high-tech products, consumers may use brand reputation as a means to reduce risk. This means that secondary associations may better communicate product quality. Third-party endorsements from top companies, leading consumer magazines, or industry experts may help to achieve the necessary perceptions of product quality. To garner these endorsements, however, products need to achieve demonstrable differences in product performance, suggesting the importance of innovative product development over time.

Avoid overbranding products. One mistake made by many high-tech firms is to "overbrand" their products by using too many ingredient and endorser brands. For example, in 1995 Silicon Graphics introduced its next-generation 3-D workstation, the Indigo^2 IMPACT, which was divided into performance categories with the following modifiers (in increasing order of performance): "High," "Solid," "Killer," and "Maximum." Given the length of the brand name, customers typically used the most specific modifier in the

As part of a global campaign based on the advantages of a secure network, Cisco sponsored the Euro 2004 soccer championships and ran online and television ads that used the visual metaphor of preventing a goal to reinforce the theme of security. As a result of these measures, Cisco's share of the $92 billion communications equipment market rose from 10 percent in 2001 to to 16 percent in 2004. Sales on the year grew 17 percent to $22 billion and net income rose 24 percent to $5.3 billion.

Cisco developed a new advertising approach in 2005, shifting the focus away from the product itself and instead emphasizing the role of Cisco in everyday life. Print ads for the campaign featured scenes from life and the tagline "Powered by Cisco," for example, an image of a newborn baby with the text "8lbs. 3oz. Powered by Cisco." The ads included a "manifesto" that concluded with a line about the Internet being a "secure, intelligent, ubiquitous network we have all built together. The network powered by Cisco. And shared by everyone."

With Cisco once again reminding consumers of its centrality to the Internet—albeit with a more human tone—and financials again improving in 2005 to $6 billion in profit on sales of $25 billion, the company regained its stride. Emboldened, it embarked on a new goal to broaden its meaning as a provider of voice, video, data and wireless products that connect people via the "Human Network." To make the brand a household name, a $100 million campaign was launched in October 2006 that involved a new logo, TV and print ads, product placement (on "The Office"), Web logs, and chat rooms.

Sources: Diane Anderson, "Cisco Reboots Image with $150M Effort," *Brandweek,* 10 January 2005; Bradley Johnson, "Cisco Ad Budget Soars as It Builds Internet Image," *Advertising Age,* 17 August 1998, 4; Andy Serwer, "There's Something About Cisco," *Fortune,* 15 May 2000, 114; John A. Byrne and Ben Elgin, "Cisco: Behind the Hype," *BusinessWeek,* 21 January 2002, 54; Stephanie N. Mehta, "Cisco Fractures Its Own Fairytale," *Fortune,* 14 May 2001, 104; Peter Burrows, "Cisco's Comeback," *BusinessWeek,* 14 November 2003, 116; Peter Burrows, "Can Cisco Settle for Less Than Sizzling?" *BusinessWeek,* 21 February 2005, 62; Marguerite Reardon, "Cisco Spends Millions on Becoming a Household Name," CNET news.com, October 6, 2006.

product name as a shorthand reference to the computer. For example, customers abbreviated the "Indigo^2 IMPACT Solid" to just "Solid."

When a product is overbranded in this way, brand equity slides down the hierarchy to lower levels at the expense of the family brand or company brand. Though the company made national headlines, the Silicon Graphics master brand was not necessarily as well known as its popular Indigo sub-brands, which became problematic as successors to Indigo were introduced.

Selectively introduce new products as new brands, and clearly identify the nature of brand extensions. Another implication of the abbreviated nature of product life cycles is the importance of optimally designing brand portfolios and brand hierarchies. Several issues are relevant here. First, brand extensions are a common high-tech branding strategy. With new products continually emerging, it would be prohibitively expensive to brand them with new names in each case. Typically, names for new products include modifiers from existing products—for example, alphabetical (Microsoft Windows XP), numerical (Microsoft Xbox 360), time-based (Microsoft Exchange Server 2007), or other schemes—unless they represent dramatic departures or marked product improvements for the brand. Using a new name for a new product is a means to signal to consumers that this particular generation or version of a product is a major departure and significantly different from prior versions.

Thus, family brands are an important means of grouping products. Marketers must clearly distinguish individual items or products within those brand families, however, and define brand migration strategies that reflect product introduction strategies and consumer market trends.

Other brand portfolio issues relate to the importance of retaining some brands. Too often, high-tech firms continually introduce totally new sub-brands, making it difficult for consumers to develop product or brand loyalty to any one brand.

Services

We noted in Chapter 1 that the level of sophistication in service branding has greatly increased in recent years, as suggested by the following guidelines (see Figure 15-11). Branding Brief 15-4 reviews how Singapore Airlines rose above the competition in the last decade.

Maximize service quality by recognizing the myriad ways to affect consumer service perceptions. From a branding perspective, one challenge with services is their intangible nature. A consequence of this intangibility is that consumers may have difficulty forming

BRANDING BRIEF 15-4

Singapore Airlines Soars

Singapore Airlines was founded in 1972 with a severe handicap compared to other airlines: The tiny island nation of Singapore had no domestic air traffic to guarantee travelers. Singapore Airlines therefore targeted the long-haul segment of the market, leveraging Singapore's status as a major business destination to build routes from North America, Europe, and elsewhere in Asia. From the beginning, Singapore Airlines chose to emphasize superior service to differentiate it from other carriers. It introduced the now-famous Singapore Girl, the symbol of warm and hospitable service, to entice travelers in ads billing the airline as "A Great Way to Fly," a tagline it retained for decades. The airline quickly earned an enduring reputation for "pampering" passengers by focusing on the details of in-flight service. It was the first airline to serve hot meals and give passengers free beverages, as well as the first to provide hot towels on takeoff and landing. In 2005, first-class passengers on Singapore flights received Givenchy pajamas and Bulgari "amenity kits."

Singapore Airlines has become one of the world's most admired service brands.

The company's attention to detail was also reflected in its strictly enforced guidelines for what its flight attendants could wear, down to the color of their makeup, which could be one

1. Maximize service quality by recognizing the myriad ways to affect consumer service perceptions.
2. Employ a full range of brand elements to enhance brand recall and signal more tangible aspects of the brand.
3. Create and communicate strong organizational associations.
4. Design corporate communication programs that augment consumers' service encounters and experiences.
5. Establish a brand hierarchy by creating distinct family brands or individual brands as well as meaningful ingredient brands.

FIGURE 15-11

Additional Guidelines for Services

their quality evaluations and may end up basing them on considerations other than their own service experience. Researchers have identified a number of dimensions of service quality:[7]

- *Tangibles:* Physical facilities, equipment, and appearance of personnel
- *Reliability:* Ability to perform the promised service right the first time (standardized facilities and operations)

of only two color combinations. Singapore Airlines even experimented with standardized perfume for its attendants in the late 1990s, creating a scent called Stefan Floridian Waters that all its flight attendants wore. This laser focus on the details ensured that its customers enjoyed a consistent experience every time they encountered the brand.

Singapore Airlines also differentiated by leading the way in technology available on its flights. It was the first airline to offer personal video screens to passengers, and the first to offer video on demand. The age of its fleet, averaging 5.5 years, is much lower than the industry average of 13 years. Other airlines were quick to copy each innovation as Singapore Airlines rolled them out, so the company strove to maintain its pace of innovation in order to stay one step ahead of the competition. For example, the company spent more than $100 million in 2001 to equip the business class section of its planes with full-reclining SpaceBeds that molded to passengers' body countours and that, at 6 feet 6 inches long, were billed as "the biggest beds in business class."

As a result of its dual focus on service and technology, Singapore Airlines has become a success story in the notoriously competitive airline industry, having never had a money-losing year since it started. In 2004, it was the world's most profitable airline, earning $825 million on $7 billion in revenues, and it had a market capitalization second only to Southwest Airlines. Most importantly, Singapore Airlines remains a favorite of consumers, winning more than 500 awards since 2003, such as "World's Best International Airline" from *Travel & Leisure* every year from 2003 to 2006.

Sources: Jonathan Holburt, "Are Brands Becoming the Export 'Ideology' of the 21st Century?" *Advertising Age,* 13 March 2006, 24; Justin Doebele, "The Engineer," *Forbes,* 9 January 2006, 122; Greg Lindsay, "Airworld War," *Advertising Age,* 24 October 2005, 12; Martin Lindstrom, "Follow Your Nose to Marketing Evolution," *Advertising Age,* 23 May 2005, 136.

- *Responsiveness:* Willingness to help customers and provide customer service
- *Competence:* Knowledge and skill of employees
- *Trustworthiness:* Believability and honesty (ability to convey trust and confidence)
- *Empathy:* Caring, individualized attention
- *Courtesy:* Friendliness of customer contact
- *Communication:* Keeping customers informed in language they can understand and listening to what they say

Thus, service quality perceptions depend on a number of specific associations that vary in how directly they relate to the actual service experience. Academic researchers Berry, Parasuraman, and Zeithaml offer 10 recommendations that they maintain are essential for improving service quality across service industries (see Figure 15-12).[8]

1. **Listening:** Understand what customers really want through continuous learning about the expectations and perceptions of customers and noncustomers (e.g., by means of a service quality information system).
2. **Reliability:** Reliability is the single most important dimension of service quality and must be a service priority.
3. **Basic service:** Service companies must deliver the basics and do what they are supposed to do—keep promises, use common sense, listen to customers, keep customers informed, and be determined to deliver value to customers.
4. **Service design:** Develop a holistic view of the service while managing its many details.
5. Recovery: To satisfy customers who encounter a service problem, service companies should encourage customers to complain (and make it easy for them to do so), respond quickly and personally, and develop a problem resolution system.
6. **Surprising customers:** Although reliability is the most important dimension in meeting customers' service expectations, process dimensions (e.g., assurance, responsiveness, and empathy) are most important in exceeding customer expectations, such as by surprising customers with uncommon swiftness, grace, courtesy, competence, commitment, and understanding.
7. **Fair play:** Service companies must make special efforts to be fair and to demonstrate fairness to customers and employees.
8. **Teamwork:** Teamwork is what enables large organizations to deliver service with care and attentiveness by improving employee motivation and capabilities.
9. **Employee research:** Conduct research with employees to reveal why service problems occur and what companies must do to solve problems.
10. **Servant leadership:** Quality service comes from inspired leadership throughout the organization; from excellent service-system design; from the effective use of information and technology; and from a slow-to-change, invisible, all-powerful, internal force called corporate culture.

Source: Leonard L. Berry, A. Parasuraman, and Valarie A. Zeithaml, "Ten Lessons for Improving Service Quality," MSI Report 93–104 (Cambridge, MA: Marketing Science Institute, 1993). Used with permission of Marketing Science Institute.

FIGURE 15-12

Recommendations for Improving Service Quality

Employ a full range of brand elements to enhance brand recall and signal more tangible aspects of the brand. Intangibility also has implications for the choice of brand elements. Because consumers often make service decisions and arrangements away from the actual service location itself (say, at home or at work), brand recall, preferably aided by an easy-to-remember and easy-to-pronounce brand name, becomes critically important. Because a physical product does not exist, packaging in a literal sense is not really relevant, although the physical facilities of the service provider serve as the external "packaging" of a service (primary and secondary signage, environmental design and reception area, apparel, collateral material, and so on).

Other brand elements—logos, symbols, characters, and slogans—must then pick up the slack and complement the brand name to build brand awareness and brand image. These elements often attempt to make the service and some of its key benefits more tangible, concrete, and real—for example, the "friendly skies" of United, the "good hands" of Allstate, and the "bullish" nature of Merrill Lynch. All aspects of the service delivery process can be branded, which is why Allied Moving Lines is concerned about the appearance of its drivers and laborers, why UPS has developed such strong equity with the brown color of its trucks, and why Doubletree hotels offers warm, fresh-baked cookies as a means of symbolizing the company's caring and friendliness.

Create and communicate strong organizational associations. Organizational associations, such as perceptions about the people who make up the organization and who provide the service, are likely to be particularly important brand associations that may directly or indirectly affect evaluations of service quality. Particularly important associations are company credibility and perceived expertise, trustworthiness, and likability. Fidelity's ad campaign in the early 2000s that featured Peter Lynch leveraged its famed analyst's equity in humorous ad executions that created favorable perceptions on all three of these credibility dimensions.

Design communication programs that augment consumers' service encounters and experiences. Service firms must design marketing communication and information programs so that consumers learn more about the brand than the information they glean from their service encounters alone. These programs may include advertising, direct mail, and other communications particularly effective at helping the firm to develop the proper brand personality. The communication programs should be fully integrated and evolve over time. Surprisingly, Citigroup walked away from a strong credibility position for its retail brand when it dropped its "Citi Never Sleeps" ad campaign.

Establish a brand hierarchy by creating distinct family brands or individual brands as well as meaningful ingredient brands. Finally, services also must consider developing a brand hierarchy and brand portfolio that permit positioning and targeting of different market segments. Marketers can brand classes of service vertically on the basis of price and quality. Vertical extensions often require sub-branding strategies in which the corporate name is combined with an individual brand name or modifier. In the hotel and airlines industries, brand lines and portfolios have developed from brand extensions and introductions. For example, United Airlines brands its business class service as Connoisseur Class, its frequent flier program as Mileage Plus, and its short-haul airlines as United Express. As another example, Hilton Hotel has introduced Hilton Garden Inns to target budget-conscious business travelers and compete with the popular Courtyard by Marriott chain.

Retailers

Chapters 5 and 7 reviewed how retailers and other channel intermediaries can affect the brand equity of the products they sell, as well as creating their own brand equity by establishing awareness and associations to their product assortment (breadth and depth), pricing and credit policy, quality of service, and so on. For example, Wal-Mart has made itself perhaps the premier U.S. retail brand by becoming the low-price, high-value provider of a host of everyday consumer products. Consumers may form these associations in many ways, such as on the basis of personal experience, word of mouth, or through advertisements or other indirect means. Following are several guidelines for building brand equity for a retailer that are particularly relevant (see Figure 15-13). Branding Brief 15-5 describes the recent ascension of U.K. retailer Tesco.

Create a brand hierarchy by branding the store as a whole, as well as individual departments, classes of service, or any other noteworthy aspects of the retail service or shopping experience. Establishing a brand hierarchy helps to create synergies in brand development. Retailers also must consider brand portfolio issues and what other retail stores or chains to introduce in order to provide more complete market coverage. For example, Wal-Mart introduced Sam's Club to tap into the growing discount or warehouse retail market.

BRANDING BRIEF 15-5

Branding Success at Tesco

British supermarket Tesco was the second-biggest grocery chain in the United Kingdom in the 1980s, behind the dominant Sainsbury chain. Tesco began upgrading its stores and product selection around 1983, but by 1990 the company had been unable to take market share from Sainsbury. Tesco was still considered a "pile it high and sell it cheap" mass-market retailer and wanted to change this perception. In a brief to its advertising agency in 1989, Tesco expressed a desire "to develop an image campaign which will lift us out of the mold in our particular sector."

Beans.
We sell mung beans, which are good for your blood.
Adzuki beans, which are good for your heart.
Oh, and baked beans...
Which are good for your toast.
TESCO | Every little helps

Tesco received a brand boost by recognizing that "every little helps."

The company's first image campaign, called "Quest for Quality," ran from 1990 to 1992. It starred Dudley Moore as a Tesco employee who looked all over the globe for French free-range chickens and discovered en route other exotic products to add to Tesco shelves. The idea was to surprise consumers with the range of high-quality goods available at Tesco. An instant success, the ad peaked at 89 percent prompted awareness in tracking studies. During the time that the "Quest for Quality" ran, Tesco also invested heavily in improvements for the business by launching 114 initiatives that improved the overall shopping experience, such as baby-changing facilities and a new value product range.

Tesco devised a new campaign featuring 20 commercials, each focusing on a different initiative, that were linked by the tagline "Every Little Helps." These ads conveyed Tesco's new customer-oriented approach of always "doing right by the customer." Prompted awareness of these ads reached 64 percent, and Tesco's revenues and market share rose steadily until Tesco surpassed Sainsbury's as the U.K. market leader in 1995. Company research revealed that 1.3 million new customers started shopping at Tesco between 1990 and 1995.

Another Tesco advertising campaign that helped endear the company to customers was its Computers for Schools cause-related marketing campaign, started in 1992. It quickly became the best-known cause-related campaign in the United Kingdom, with prompted awareness levels near

1. Create a brand hierarchy by branding the store as a whole, as well as individual departments, classes of service, or any other aspects of the retail service or shopping experience.
2. Enhance manufacturers' brand equity by communicating and demonstrating their points of difference and other strong, favorable, and unique brand associations.
3. Establish brand equity at all levels of the brand hierarchy by offering added value in the selection, purchase, or delivery of product offerings.
4. Create multichannel shopping experiences.
5. Avoid overbranding.

FIGURE 15-13

Additional Guidelines for Retailers

50 percent. Customers receive vouchers from Tesco for every £10 spent, which they can donate to the school of their choosing. The chosen school exchanges the vouchers for new computer equipment. Parent-teacher associations and school governors joined together to maximize voucher collection, which further enhanced community involvement in the program. Tesco capitalized on the link between its brand and the Computers for Schools program in 1998, when the company began selling computer hardware. Since the program began, Tesco Computers for Schools has delivered almost $100 million worth of computer equipment to schools in the United Kingdom.

In 1995, the same year it passed Sainsbury's, Tesco introduced its frequent-shopper program, based on the Tesco Clubcard loyalty card. The Clubcard was credited with driving much of Tesco's subsequent success. In addition to driving customer loyalty, the Clubcard enabled Tesco to gather reams of customer data and tailor merchandise assortments and store layouts to specific stores, and customize special offers to specific customers. The Clubcard propelled Tesco's market share rise, which reached 15 percent in 1999. In both 1998 and 1999, other British companies voted Tesco Britain's most admired company. With the help of savvy and sustained marketing efforts, Tesco had transformed itself from an also-ran into a market leader in less than a decade.

In the following years, Tesco continued to apply its winning formula of using customer data to optimize its marketing and dominated the British retail landscape, moving beyond supermarkets to "big-box" retailing of general merchandise. By 2005, it had a 35 percent share of supermarket spending in the United Kingdom, almost twice that of its nearest competitor, and a 14 percent share of total retail sales. The company also used the same strategy to expand overseas. In 2005, Tesco had 648 stores outside the United Kingdom—with plans to enter the U.S. market by 2007—and was the supermarket leader in Poland, Hungary, Thailand, Ireland, and Slovakia. Tesco ranked as Britain's largest company and the sixth-largest retailer in the world in 2006.

Sources: Ashleye Sharpe and Joanna Bamford, "Tesco Stores Ltd.," paper presented at Advertising Effectiveness Awards, 2000; Hamish Pringle and Marjorie Thompson, *Brand Spirit* (New York: John Wiley, 1999); "The Prime Minister Launches the 10th Tesco Computers for Schools Scheme," *M2 Presswire*, 26 January 2001; Elizabeth Rigby, "Prosperous Tesco Takes Retailing to a New Level," *Financial Times*, 21 September 2005, 23; Richard Fletcher, "Leahy Shrugs Off Talk of a 'Brain Drain,'" *Sunday Times* (London), 29 January 2006, 7.

Similarly, individual departments can take on unique sets of associations that appeal to a particular target market. For example, Nordstrom has a number of clothing departments, each designed with distinct images and positions, such as t.b.d. for the latest women's trends, Brass Plum for teen girls, Encore for plus-size women, and Individualist for fashionable women's professional attire. The retailer may brand these departments or even use them as "ingredient brands," designed and supported by a national manufacturer (like Polo shops in major department stores, which sell only that Ralph Lauren brand).

Enhance manufacturer's brand equity. As a second guideline, retailers should exploit as much as possible the brand equity of the manufacturer brands they sell, by communicating and demonstrating their points of difference and other strong, favorable, and unique brand associations. Manufacturers often employ push strategies that encourage retailers to better support their brands. By cooperating with and perhaps even enhancing these programs, retailers should be able to sell products at higher prices and margins, generating greater profits as a result. Consider the marketing push provided by DuPont to help out merchants in the very fragmented retail carpet market.

DuPont Stainmaster Carpet

When DuPont launched Stainmaster carpet, it provided intensive retail support. Dealers received a 12-page catalog describing what DuPont had to offer in merchandising DuPont Stainmaster carpet, as well as cards, brochures, cleaning instructions, and DuPont's *Complete Book of Carpeting.* Store and product identification for dealers included hanging mobiles with Stainmaster logos, large canvas banners to hang outside showrooms, in-store wall and window posters, carpet-identification medallions, sales tags, and photo boards depicting the Stainmaster TV commercials. A key feature was a demonstration unit that allowed customers to dip a

DuPont Stainmaster carpet has benefited from much in-store marketing and merchandising activity.

toothbrush-like swizzle stick, which had one treated and one untreated group of tufts, into various stains and go through the simple stain-removal process to see for themselves how Stainmaster worked. Promotional activities encouraged dealers to hold special events or sales to promote Stainmaster; one chain ran a "Pet Parade" in Los Angeles that featured hundreds of animals—from cats to monkeys—strutting along a length of red carpet made with Stainmaster.

Establish brand equity at all levels of the brand hierarchy by offering added value in the selection, purchase, or delivery of product offerings. Retailers must create their own strong, favorable, and unique associations that go beyond the products they sell. Sharper Image has created a niche as a seller of creative, upscale products and gadgets. Victoria's Secret has gained notoriety as a provider of stylish, feminine clothing. Costco and Price Club created strong discount associations.

To communicate these broader associations, image campaigns often focus on the advantages to consumers of shopping at and buying from the stores in general, rather than on promotions for specific sale items. For example, Radio Shack now advertises that it is the "consumer-friendly" provider of electronic parts, accessories, and specialty equipment through a campaign with the slogan "You've Got Questions. We've Got Answers."

Land Rover Centres

A former president of Land Rover North America once said, car buying is "literally the most horrible retail experience any customer can imagine—why not make it easy and why not make it fun?" Land Rover Centres feature upscale safari-garbed salespeople who are trained to avoid high-pressure sales tactics. The Centres have a premium specialty store look modeled after either a hunting lodge or a ski villa. In addition to showcasing vehicles, they display Land Rover Gear such as a branded line of shirts, gloves, sweatshirts, and coats. Some Centres show videotapes of Land Rovers in the wilds of Africa or have an adjacent short off-road rock course with Hill climbs and descents designed to showcase vehicle capability.[9] In 2006, Land Rover had 96 such centres, representing 60 percent of Land Rover retailers.

Create multichannel shopping experiences. Increasingly, retailers are selling their wares in a variety of channels, such as physical stores, catalogs, and online Web sites. Office Depot recognized the importance of supplementing its 800-plus stores back in 1997 with a strong online and catalog presence. By offering service and convenience—and by not cutting its prices—Office Depot has been able to maintain its market leadership. Regardless of the channel, consumers must have rewarding shopping experiences in searching, choosing,

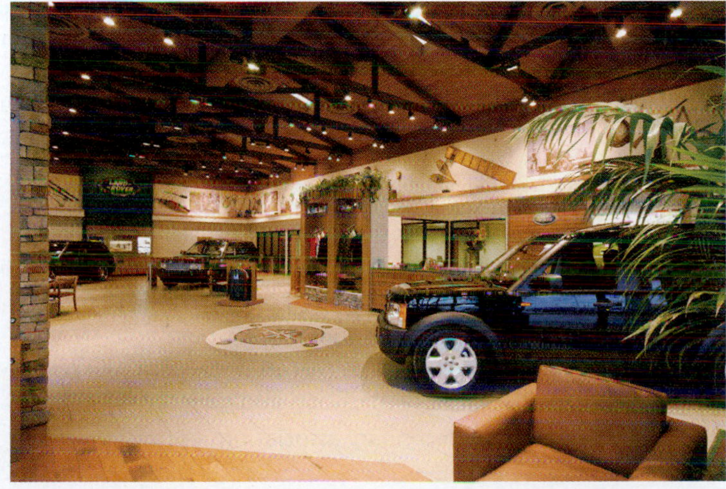

Land Rover Centres create a unique retail experience.

paying for, and receiving products. In some case, these experiences may turn out to be valuable points of difference, or at least necessary points of parity, with respect to competitors.

Avoid overbranding. Finally, if a retailer is selling its own private labels, it is important not to employ too many brands. Retailers are particularly susceptible to "bottom-up branding," in which each department creates its own set of brands. For example, Nordstrom found itself having to support scores of different brands across its different departments, sometimes with little connection among them. Recall from Chapter 5 that one advantage of store brands, however, is that they often represent associations that transfer across categories. The more an abstract association like value or fashionability is desirable and deliverable across categories, the more likely that the marketer can gain efficiencies by concentrating on a few major brands.

Small Businesses

Building brands for a small business is a challenge because of their limited resources and budgets. Unlike major brands that often have more resources at their disposal, small businesses usually do not have the luxury to make mistakes and must design and implement marketing programs much more carefully. Nevertheless, numerous success stories exist of entrepreneurs who have built their brands up essentially from scratch to become powerhouse brands. In 1998, J. Darius Bickoff launched the "vitaminwater" brand as a vitamin-enhanced and flavored alternative to plain bottled water. By 2005 vitaminwater was generating $350 million in annual sales and even had an endorsement deal with rapper 50 Cent for its Formula 50 flavor.[10]

In general, because there are usually limited resources behind the brand, both focus and consistency in marketing programs are critically important. To compensate for fewer funds, creativity is also paramount—finding new ways to market new ideas about products to consumers. The Science of Branding 15-1 contains some provocative notions about how small brands can compete with big ones. Figure 15-14 displays some specific branding guidelines for small businesses, discussed next, and Branding Brief 15-6 describes how Green Mountain Coffee built a strong brand.

Emphasize building one or two strong brands. Given fewer resources, strategically it may be necessary to emphasize building one or two strong brands. A corporate branding strategy can be an efficient means to build brand equity, although the focus may just be on a major family brand. For example, Intuit concentrated its marketing efforts on building the Quicken brand name of software.

Focus the marketing program on one or two key associations. Small businesses often must rely on only one or two key associations as points of difference. They must consistently reinforce these associations across the marketing program and over time. The College Kit, in Hanover, New Hampshire, had a mission to "deliver products, services and marketing messages into the hands and minds of college consumers through creative,

FIGURE 15-14

Additional Guidelines for Small Business

1. Emphasize building one or two strong brands.
2. Focus the marketing program on one or two key associations.
3. Employ a well-integrated set of brand elements that enhances both brand awareness and brand image.
4. Design creative brand-building push campaigns and consumer-involving pull campaigns that capture attention and generate demand.
5. Leverage as many secondary associations as possible.

THE SCIENCE OF BRANDING 15-1

How Smaller Can Be Better

Adam Morgan, in a fascinating book, *Eating the Big Fish: How Challenger Brands Can Compete Against Brand Leaders,* offers eight suggestions for how small brands can better compete:

1. *Break with your immediate past:* Don't be afraid to ask "dumb" questions to challenge convention and view your brand differently.
2. *Build a "lighthouse identity":* Establish values and communicate who and why you are (e.g., Apple).
3. *Assume thought leadership of the category:* Break convention in terms of representation (what you say about yourself), where you say it (medium), and experience (what you do beyond talk).
4. *Create symbols of reevaluation:* A rocket uses half of its fuel in the first mile to break loose from the gravitational pull—you may need to polarize people.
5. *Sacrifice:* Focus your target, message, reach and frequency, distribution, and line extensions and recognize that less can be more.
6. *Overcommit:* Although you may do fewer things, do "big" things when you do them.
7. *Use publicity and advertising to enter popular culture:* Unconventional communications can get people talking.
8. *Be idea centered, not consumer centered:* Sustain challenger momentum by not losing sight of what the brand is about and can be and redefine marketing support and the center of the company to reflect this vision.

Source: Adam Morgan, *Eating the Big Fish: How Challenger Brands Can Compete Against Brand Leaders* (New York: John Wiley & Sons, 1999). Reprinted with permission of John Wiley & Sons, Inc.

connected, sometimes outrageous, and always entertaining programs." Thus, its key associations were "creative," "well-targeted," and "marketing programs for college students."

Employ a well-integrated set of brand elements. Tactically, it is important for small businesses to maximize the contribution of each of the three main ways to build brand equity. First, a distinctive, well-integrated set of brand elements will enhance both brand awareness and brand image, as suggested by the following example.

RUMBA

Seattle's Wall Data made connectivity software between desktop and host computers (various mainframes) that allowed users to avoid rebooting or reconfiguring. In the mid-1990s, Wall Data cleverly branded its family of software products "Rumba" and combined that name with a symbol of a man and woman dancing cheek-to-cheek. It used the slogan "Get Connected" in advertising, promotional materials, and packaging. To further build awareness and image, the company even hosted rumba dance lessons at trade shows. The success of the Rumba product line permitted the later introduction of other sets of software products branded with dance themes, such as "Salsa."

BRANDING BRIEF 15-6

Vermont's Green Mountain Coffee is a compelling demonstration of how a small business can grow to be a big brand.

Green Mountain Coffee Roasters

Bob Stiller founded Green Mountain Coffee Roasters in 1981 when he opened a small café in Waitsfield, Vermont. According to the company, it was not long before tourists who stopped in the café asked whether they could receive Green Mountain Coffee at home, via mail. The company answered this demand by launching its mail-order business. Green Mountain sought out local customers by opening other retail locations in Vermont and Maine. In the company's early years, it used no advertising, instead engaging in extensive sampling.

Stiller took the company public in 1993 and used the proceeds to expand the mail-order operation and open additional retail stores. Green Mountain also invested in technological improvements for its roasting and packaging system, spending $500,000 on a system that removes oxygen from packages of coffee and improves shelf life.

Green Mountain closed its 12 retail locations in 1998 in order to focus on wholesale business. The company's wholesale customers include restaurants, convenience stores, office coffee distributors, and airlines. For at-home customers, Green Mountain retained its mail-order catalog and its Coffee Club home-delivery subscription

Brand elements ideally should be memorable and meaningful, with as much creative potential as possible. Innovative packaging can be a substitute for ad campaigns by capturing attention at the point of purchase. For example, Smartfood popcorn introduced its first product without any advertising, by means of a unique package that served as a strong visual symbol on the shelf and an extensive sampling program that encouraged trial. Proper names or family names, which often characterize small businesses, may provide some distinctiveness but suffer in terms of pronounceability, meaningfulness, memorability, and other branding considerations. If these deficiencies are too great, other brand elements should be explored.

Design creative brand-building push campaigns and consumer-involving pull campaigns that capture attention and generate demand. Small businesses must design creative push and pull programs that capture the attention of consumers and other channel members alike. Clearly, this is a sizable challenge on a limited budget. Unfortunately, without a strong pull campaign creating product interest, retailers may not feel enough motivation to stock and support the brand. Conversely, without a strong push campaign that convinces retailers of the merits of the product, the brand may fail to achieve adequate support or even be stocked at all. Thus, creative and cost-effective push and pull marketing programs must increase the visibility of the brand and get both consumers and retailers talking about it.

Because small businesses often must rely on word of mouth to create strong, favorable, and unique brand associations, public relations and low-cost promotions and sponsorship can be inexpensive means to enhance brand awareness and brand image. For example, Noah Alper, co-founder of Noah's Bagels, reached out to the Jewish community and transplanted New Yorkers in Northern California through well-publicized events and appearances that

service, and in 1998 it began selling coffee and other specialty products online at www.greenmountaincoffee.com. In addition to 60 varieties of Green Mountain Coffee, customers can order from a diverse assortment of products, including coffee grinders, mugs, chocolates, and gift baskets.

Green Mountain, which gives 5 percent of its pretax profits to "socially responsible" causes, grew rapidly as its wholesale business brought it in contact with an ever-widening customer base. Between 1995 and 2000, sales increased at an average rate of 24 percent annually. In 2001, the company sold the equivalent of 10 million cups of coffee every day and maintained relationships with more than 7,000 wholesale customers. That same year, *Forbes* named Stiller as its first-ever "Entrepreneur of the Year." As U.S. consumer demand for organic products continued to grow, so too did Green Mountain's financials. From 2001 to 2005, the company averaged 14 percent revenue growth, with 2005 revenues topping $160 million. That year, Green Mountain forged a deal to supply Newman's Own for its organic coffee brand, which was sold in 650 McDonald's locations in the Northeast. This move pushed Green Mountain stock over $40 per share.

Sources: www.greenmountaincoffee.com; "Green Mountain Coffee Roasters: Towards a New Business Model," Center for Business as an Agent of World Benefit at Case Western Reserve University, 2004; Luisa Kroll, "Entrepreneur of the Year: Java Man," *Forbes,* 29 October 2001, 142; "Green Mountain Coffee, Inc. Founder, President and CEO Named Forbes First 'Entrepreneur of the Year,'" *Business Wire,* 16 October 2001.

promoted the "authentic" nature of the bagel chain. Marketers of the PowerBar, a nutrient-rich, low-fat "energy bar," used selective sponsorship of top marathon runners, cyclists, and tennis players and events like the Boston Marathon to raise awareness and improve image. Selective distribution that targets opinion leaders can also be a cost-effective means to implement a push strategy. For example, brands such as Perrier bottled water and Paul Mitchell and Nexus shampoo were initially introduced to a carefully selected set of outlets before broadening distribution.

Leverage as many secondary associations as possible. Finally, another way for small businesses to build brand equity is to leverage as many secondary associations as possible. Secondary associations are often a cost-effective, shortcut means to build brand equity. Consider any entity with potentially relevant associations, especially those that help to signal quality or credibility. Along those lines, to make the company appear "bigger" than it really is, a well-designed Web site can be invaluable.

Online

Creating a brand online brings a special set of challenges. Many of the guidelines for business-to-business, high-tech, retailing, and small businesses may apply, depending on the nature of the online business. At the same time, a number of other guidelines are worth reinforcing (as summarized in Figure 15-15). Branding Brief 15-7 outlines how MySpace built one of the strongest online brands.

Don't forget the brand-building basics. Remember brand-building basics such as establishing points of parity (convenience, price, and variety) and points of difference (cus-

1. Don't forget the brand-building basics.
2. Create strong brand identity.
3. Generate strong consumer pull.
4. Selectively choose brand partnerships.
5. Maximize relationship marketing.

FIGURE 15-15

Additional Guidelines for Online Brands

tomer service, credibility, and personality). As we noted in earlier chapters, one mistake of many failed dot-com brands was being impatient to build their brands and failing to build from the bottom up.

In research undertaken to understand online service quality, defined as the extent to which a Web site facilitates efficient and effective shopping, purchasing, and delivery, one study

BRANDING BRIEF 15-7

Making Connections at MySpace

In just 2 years, MySpace grew from a relative latecomer to the social-networking Web site world to the dominant player in the category. Friendster, the Web site that formally launched the online social networking era in August 2002, beat MySpace to the Net by 11 months, a near-eternity in Internet time. The idea behind social networking Web sites is deceptively simple: Provide a way for Web surfers to publish profiles of themselves through which to connect with old or current friends and make new ones. Whereas Friendster was unable to sustain its initial momentum, attracting fewer than a million visitors in October 2005, MySpace had more than 20 million visitors that same month.

MySpace has become an overnite sensation on the Web.

Following on the heels of Friendster, MySpace management was able to learn from the first mover's mistakes. Friendster's registered user base quickly grew to 20 million, but the company was unable to keep pace with this growth and the site was beset by technical problems. It also lacked features, not offering users the opportunity to load songs to stream on their profiles, start blogs, post on message boards, or upload more than a handful of pictures. MySpace invested heavily in technology to keep pace with its torrid growth as well as

identified 11 dimensions of perceived e-service quality: access, ease of navigation, efficiency, flexibility, reliability, personalization, security/privacy, responsiveness, assurance/trust, site aesthetics, and price knowledge.[11] Land's End became a top-selling company online by treating its Internet operations as a digital translation of its successful catalog, ensuring that merchandise was presented properly and that excellent customer service prevailed.

Create strong brand identity. Given that consumers aren't physically confronted by brands as they are in a store, brand awareness and recall are critical. Toward that goal, choosing the right URL is an important priority. Because the Internet revolution led to an explosion of .com name registrations, choosing the best new URL is difficult. Keep the basic brand element criteria in mind, with perhaps greater emphasis on brand recall as an objective (1-800-FLOWERS took its brand directly to the Web). A simple but evocative name can be useful, like BabyCenter.com, an information and commerce Web site providing content on pregnancy and babies, an interactive community for parents and parents-to-be, and a store featuring thousands of baby products and supplies.

enabling users to add almost an unlimited amount of content to their pages, in particular streaming audio. This feature allowed professional and aspiring bands to build profiles and share their music with the vast audience of MySpace users. Before long, many bands began debuting their albums on the site, and MySpace started its own record label, appropriately named MySpace Records, in 2005. MySpace also made more of an effort to tie the site into its users' real-life social lives, sponsoring concerts and other events in a number of cities.

MySpace makes its money by selling ad space on its Web site, once again a lucrative business on the Internet. In October 2005, MySpace accounted for 10 percent of all ads viewed online. To avoid annoying its user base, it does not allow invasive pop-up ads or spyware, instead selling banner ads or on-site promotions and allowing products and television shows to create their own MySpace accounts. This latter feature is another difference between MySpace and Friendster. Friendster initially deleted accounts not linked to a real person, barring profiles for pets and products. On MySpace, any profile that wasn't offensive was welcome, and product profiles became marketing tools. For example, Disney created a Pirates of the Caribbean sequel profile to promote the movie that attracted 70,000 "friends" on MySpace. Other major advertisers with profiles include Victoria's Secret, Aquafina, Chili's Bar and Grill, and Jose Cuervo. MySpace makes upwards of $50,000 per month from these major brand profiles.

In July 2005, MySpace's new media business model was validated when an old media giant, News Corporation, purchased MySpace's parent company Intermix Media for $580 million. MySpace's growth continued to accelerate; it signed up new members at a rate of 2 million per week in June 2006, pushing total registered users over 72 million. It garnered more monthly page views than any other Web site except Yahoo!, putting it in league with the Internet elite. MySpace's next step was to expand into 11 countries, mostly in Europe, with a longer-term goal of entering India and China.

Sources: Jessi Hempel, "The MySpace Generation," *BusinessWeek,* 12 December 2005, 86; Allison Fass, "Piggyback," *Forbes,* 19 June 2006; Shawn Gold interview, *Advertising Age,* 5 June 2006, S-4; Tom Braithwaite and Andrew Edgecliffe-Johnson, "MySpace Pushes for International Expansion," *Financial Times,* 20 June 2006, 28.

Generate strong consumer pull. An important lesson for online brands was the need to create demand off-line, to drive consumers online. One way to do this is to use a wide variety of sampling and other trial devices. For example, AOL conducted massive sampling and free giveaways of its CD-ROMs that eventually led to increased consumer adoptions. More broadly, online brands must introduce the best possible integrated marketing communication program, consisting of combinations of public relations; television, radio, and print advertising; sponsorship; and so on.

Selectively choose brand partnerships. Online brands can benefit from establishing a number of brand partners with which they can link. Such linkages can drive traffic, signal credibility, and help to enhance image. Partnerships must be entered selectively, however, to satisfy brand-building and profit criteria. For example, even when CDNOW had its own Cosmic Credit affiliate program that targeted low-volume, nonprofessional sites of music fans, it also initiated a number of higher-profile strategic partnerships by forming alliances with powerful online brands such as AOL and Excite before eventually having their operations run by Amazon.[12]

Maximize relationship marketing. Finally, some of the potential advantages of online brands are customization and interactivity. It is especially important, then, to engage in one-to-one, participatory, experiential, and other forms of relationship marketing. Creating a strong online brand community between the consumer and the brand, as well as with other consumers, can help to achieve brand resonance. For example, one marketing executive at Yahoo! characterized its strategy by saying, "We've really focused our marketing efforts on attracting new users and providing an experience online that makes them stay."[13] Yahoo! attempts to make the Internet experience as fun and entertaining as possible but also practical, useful, and convenient in its range of applications. Online brokerage Ameritrade provides detailed, timely, customized financial information to its clients. Online brands can offer much potentially relevant customer information; for example, Amazon provides professional and customer reviews; purchase circles and overall sales rankings; text samples; and personalized recommendations.

Future Brand Priorities

Our journey to better understand strategic brand management is about over, but it's worth considering a few final questions. How will branding change in the coming years? What are the biggest branding challenges? What will make a successful "twenty-first-century brand?"

The general importance of branding seems unlikely to change for one critical reason: It's highly likely that consumers will continue to value the functions brands provide. In a more and more complex world, well-managed brands can simplify, communicate, reassure, and provide important meaning to consumers. Using the principles reflected in the brand report card and avoiding the seven deadly sins of brand management reviewed earlier should help in the pursuit of brand management. This final section highlights several important considerations in building, measuring, and managing brand equity in the future and concludes by suggesting a broad theme for strategic brand management.

Building Brand Equity

Brand Elements. In a cluttered, competitive marketplace, the brand elements that make up the brand will have to do more and more of the selling job. In a time-compressed marketing world, the fact that a brand name can be noticed and its meaning registered or activated in memory within just a few seconds is a tremendous asset. Creating a powerful brand with inherent marketing value to build awareness and image, as well as serve as a strong foundation to link associations, can provide a firm with a strong competitive advantage.

Although general branding principles should apply in designing a twenty-first-century brand, what may change are some of the means of creating strong brands. For example, brand elements will increasingly use verbal and visual elements that creatively and dramatically help to build brand equity. Meaningful brands with creative potential will benefit from appealing to all the senses. Brands have long used auditory branding devices, for example, the three-note Nabisco jingle, the percolating Maxwell House jingle, and the NBC jingle. Movie studios have always been able to take advantage of their cinematic exposure to use sight, sound, and motion to present their brands (Universal's spinning globe, Paramount's mountain peak, and MGM's roaring lion). With increased technical abilities and improved special effects, marketers will now be able to create brand elements that come to life and capture consumer attention, an important quality given the need to communicate and sell via brands in current markets. Thus, multidimensional forms will play a more important role in audio and video presentations of the brand. A twenty-first-century brand will take advantage of different media to customize the brand presentation, so that each brand element more effectively contributes to brand equity and brand elements more effectively reinforce each other.

Marketing Programs. Strong brands in the twenty-first century also will rise above others by better understanding the needs, wants, and desires of consumers and creating marketing programs that fulfill and even surpass consumer expectations. Successful brands will have a rich but internally cohesive brand image whose associations consumers highly value. Marketing programs will seamlessly reinforce these associations through product, pricing, distribution, and communication strategies that creatively remind consumers of what the brand has to offer. With these marketing programs, consumers will have a clear picture of what the brand represents and why it is special. Consumers will then view the brand as a "trusted friend" and value its dependability and superiority. Marketers will engage in dialogue with consumers, listening to their product joys and frustrations and establishing a rapport and relationship that will transcend mere commercial exchanges. They will develop a deep understanding of what makes their brand successful, retaining enduring core elements while modifying peripheral elements that fail to add value or unnecessarily absorb costs.

Finally, smart marketers in the twenty-first century will create strong brand associations to all possible marketing effects, choosing not just which brand elements will represent the brand but also how to use them in the marketing program.

Measuring Brand Equity

Marketers of successful twenty-first-century brands will create formalized measurement approaches and processes that ensure they continually monitor their sources of brand equity and those of competitors. They'll develop a greater understanding of how different marketing actions affect their sources and outcomes of brand equity and go beyond piecemeal research projects (like periodic advertising campaign evaluations) to devise new and original ways to obtain accurate, comprehensive, and up-to-date information about the status of their brands. By maintaining close contact with the brand, managers will be better able to understand just what makes their brand tick. With greater accountability in marketing activities and programs, managers will better use their brand investments, putting money behind the right brands at the right time and in the right ways.

Managing Brand Equity

It will be essential in building strong twenty-first-century brands to align internal and external brand management. ***Internal brand management*** ensures that employees and marketing partners appreciate and understand basic branding notions and how they can affect the equity of brands. Brand management is not just a separate function within the organization but the responsibility and obligation of all. Firms must put the right structures, processes, incentives, and resources into place, for example, through brand equity charters, reports, and oversight.

Internal brand management is especially critical for a corporate brand, in which every employee directly or indirectly represents the brand and can therefore affect brand equity.[14] It helps to ensure proper external brand management. ***External brand management*** requires understanding the needs, wants, and desires of consumers and creating brand marketing programs that fulfill and even surpass consumer expectations.

Companies must also align bottom-up and top-down marketing management. ***Bottom-up brand management*** requires that marketing managers maximize brand equity for individual products in particular markets, with relatively little regard for other brands and products the firm sells, or for other markets it sells to. Although such close, detailed brand supervision can be advantageous, creating brand equity for every different possible product and market in this way can be an expensive and difficult process and, most important, ignores the possibility of obtaining synergies.

Top-down brand management, on the other hand, captures the big picture and recognizes possible synergies across products and markets to brand products accordingly. This approach would seek common products and markets that could share marketing programs and activities for brands and only develop separate brands and marketing programs as dictated by the consumer or competitive environment.

Unfortunately, if left unmanaged, firms tend to follow the bottom-up approach, marketing many brands inconsistently and incompatibly. Managing brands in a top-down fashion requires centralized and coordinated marketing guidance and actions from high-level marketing supervisors. Firms must pay particular attention to how to best develop and leverage the corporate brand.

Successful brands will effectively blend top-down and bottom-up, and internal and external, brand management activities. Marketers of successful twenty-first-century brands will continually evolve and adapt every aspect of their marketing programs to enhance brand equity. These marketers will develop a deep understanding of what makes their brand successful, retaining enduring core elements while modifying peripheral elements that fail to add value or unnecessarily absorb costs. Marketers of successful twenty-first-century brands also will appreciate how their brands fit in with respect to other brands sold by the firm. They will capitalize on and judiciously exploit the potential of their brand in product development and brand extensions, while at the same time recognizing its limits and boundaries.

Achieving Marketing Balance

These potential brand management tradeoffs suggest a broader issue and challenge with marketing and brand management. The most fundamental challenge of marketing and brand management is reconciling the many potential tradeoffs in marketing decisions.[15] Figure 15-16 lists a number of the different possible tradeoffs or conflicts that can occur in making strategic, tactical, financial, or organizational decisions for a brand. Clearly, tradeoffs are pervasive and marketers must make choices in the context of constrained—and often fairly limited—resources. To illustrate, recall from Chapter 3 the many negatively

Strategic
Retaining customers vs. acquiring customers
Brand expansion vs. brand fortification
Product performance vs. brand image
Points of parity vs. points of difference

Tactical
Push vs. pull
Continuity vs. change
Classic vs. contemporary image
Independent vs. universal image

Financial
Short-run vs. long-run objectives
Sales-generating vs. brand-building activities
Accountable or measurable tactics vs. nonmeasurable tactics
Quality maximization vs. cost minimization

Organizational
Global vs. local
Top down vs. bottom up
Customization vs. standardization
Internal vs. external

FIGURE 15-16

Some Brand Marketing Tradeoffs

correlated attributes and benefits that exist in the minds of consumers, and the challenge these relationships presented for positioning.

One response to these tradeoffs is to adopt an extreme solution and maximize one of the two dimensions in the tradeoff. Many management gurus advocate positions that, in effect, lead to such a singular focus. Such approaches, however, obviously leave the brand vulnerable to the negative consequences of ignoring the other dimension. The reality is that for marketing success, we must typically address both dimensions and achieve a more balanced marketing solution. Marketing balance occurs when marketers attempt to address all possible tradeoffs as much as possible in organizing, planning, and implementing their marketing programs.

There are three means or levels of achieving marketing balance, in increasing order of potential effectiveness:

1. *Alternate:* Identify and recognize the various tradeoffs, but attempt to emphasize one dimension at a time and try to alternate whichever dimension receives emphasis over time, so that neither dimension is ignored. Although it is potentially effective, this approach can produce a pendulum effect. Marketers may overreact to a perceived imbalance in emphasis and overcorrect as a result.
2. *Divide:* Split the difference and do a little of both to cover all the bases. Again, although potentially effective, this approach may suffer if insufficient or inadequate resources are put against the two objectives and the marketing effort does not achieve critical mass. Doing a little of this and a little of that may not yield sufficient impact.
3. *Finesse:* Reconcile the decision tradeoffs, finesse the difference, and achieve synergy between the two dimensions.

Hitting the marketing sweet spot thus may require some well-thought-out moderation and balance throughout the marketing organization and its activities. For example, marketing balance can come from strategically creative advertising that entertains and sells products, like the California Milk Processor Board's "Got Milk?" campaign. It can include equity-building promotions, such as Procter & Gamble's promotion for Ivory soap that reinforced a key attribute of "floating" and a key benefit of "purity" while also moving product. It can introduce robust brand positions such as Apple's "The Power to Be Your Best," which reconciled the seemingly negatively correlated benefits of "easy to use" and "powerful" in the minds of consumers.

THE SCIENCE OF BRANDING 15-2

David Aaker's Brand Equity Model

One of branding's academic pioneers is Berkeley's David Aaker. Aaker defines brand equity as a set of five categories of brand assets and liabilities linked to a brand, its name, and symbol that add to or subtract from the value provided by a product or service to a firm or to that firm's customers, or both. These categories of brand assets are (1) brand loyalty, (2) brand awareness, (3) perceived quality, (4) brand associations, and (5) other proprietary assets (e.g., patents, trademarks, and channel relationships). These assets provide various benefits and value, as shown in Figure 15-17.

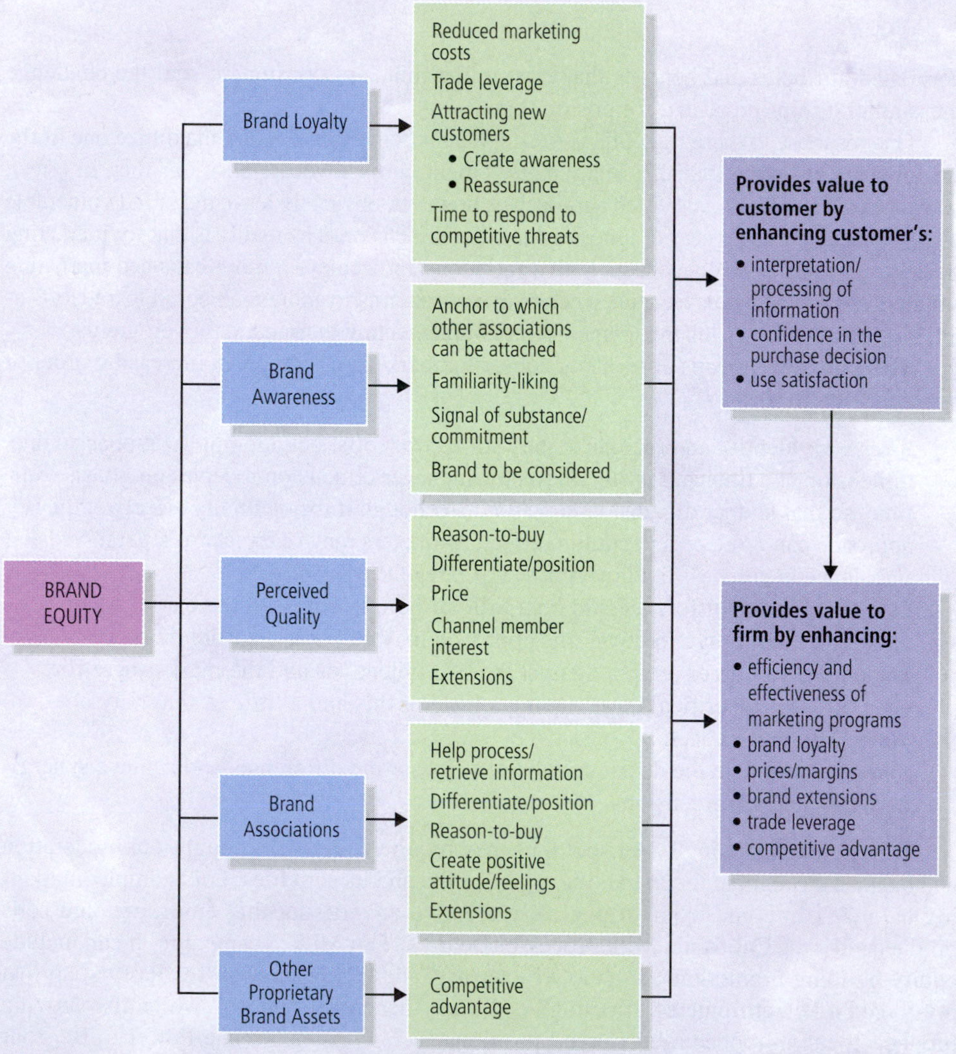

FIGURE 15-17

Aaker's Brand Equity Framework

Aaker describes a number of issues in building, measuring, and managing brand equity. A summary of guidelines emerging from his framework can be found in Figure 15-18. According

1. **Brand identity.** Have an identity for each brand. Consider the perspective of the brand-as-person, brand-as-organization, and brand-as-symbol, as well as the brand-as-product. Identify the core identity. Modify the identity as needed for different market segments and products. Remember that an image is how you are perceived, and an identity is how you aspire to be perceived.
2. **Value proposition.** Know the value proposition for each brand that has a driver role. Consider emotional and symbolic benefits as well as functional benefits. Know how endorser brands will provide credibility. Understand the customer/brand relationship.
3. **Brand position.** For each brand, have a brand position that will provide clear guidance to those implementing a communication program. Recall that a position is the part of the identity that is actively communicated.
4. **Execution.** Execute the communication program so that it not only is on target with the identity and position but achieves brilliance and durability. Generate alternatives and consider options beyond media advertising.
5. **Consistency over time.** Have as a goal a consistent identity, position, and execution over time. Maintain symbols, imagery, and metaphors that work. Understand and resist organizational biases toward changing the identity, position, and execution.
6. **Brand system.** Make sure the brands in the portfolio are consistent and synergistic. Know their roles. Have or develop silver bullets to help support brand identities and positions. Exploit branded features and services. Use sub-brands to clarify and modify. Know the strategic brands.
7. **Brand leverage.** Extend brands and develop co-branding programs only if the brand identity will be both used and reinforced. Identify range brands and, for each, develop an identity and specify how that identity will be different in disparate product contexts. If a brand is moved up or down, take care to manage the integrity of the resulting brand identity.
8. **Tracking brand equity.** Track brand equity over time, including brand awareness, perceived quality, brand loyalty, and especially brand associations. Have specific communication objectives. Especially note areas where the brand identity and positioning and communication objectives are not reflected in the perceptions of the brand.
9. **Brand responsibility.** Have someone in charge of the brand who will create the identity and positions and coordinate the execution over organizational units, media, and markets. Beware when a brand is being used in a business where it is not the cornerstone.
10. **Invest in brands.** Continue investing in brands even when the financial goals are not being met.

FIGURE 15-18

Aaker's Ten Guidelines for Building Strong Brands

(Continued)

to Aaker, a particularly important concept for building brand equity is brand identity. Aaker defines ***brand identity*** as

> a unique set of brand associations that the brand strategist aspires to create or maintain. These associations represent what the brand stands for and imply a promise to customers from the organization members. Brand identity should help establish a relationship between the brand and the customer by generating a value proposition involving functional, emotional, or self-expressive benefits.

Brand identity consists of twelve dimensions organized around four perspectives—the brand-as-product (product scope, product attributes, quality/value, uses, users, country of origin), brand-as-organization (organizational attributes, local versus global), brand-as-person (brand personality, brand–customer relationships), and brand-as-symbol (visual imagery/metaphors and brand heritage).

Brand identity structure includes a core and extended identity. The core identity—the central, timeless essence of the brand—is most likely to remain constant as the brand travels to new markets and products. The extended identity includes brand identity elements, organized into cohesive and meaningful groups.

A particularly important concept for managing brand equity according to Aaker is brand systems. Aaker emphasizes that a key to managing brands in an environment of complexity is to consider them not just as individual performers but as members of a system of brands that must work together to support one another. He notes that the goals of the system are qualitatively different from the goals of individual brand identities and include exploiting commonalities to generate synergy, reducing brand identity damage, achieving clarity of product offerings, facilitating change and adaptation, and allocating resources. Aaker also notes that many brands within a system fall into a natural hierarchy and may play different roles in the system—for example, endorsers, drivers, strategic brands, silver bullets, branded benefits, and sub-brand roles.

Source: David A. Aaker, *Building Strong Brands* (New York: Free Press, 1995). Adapted with the permission of The Free Press, A Division of Simon & Schuster Adult Publishing Group.

Marketing balance can actually be more difficult to achieve than more extreme solutions—it requires greater discipline, care, and thought. To use a golf analogy, the golfer with the smoothest swing is often the one who hits the ball farther and straighter. Marketing balance may not be as "exciting" as more radical solutions, but it can turn out to be much more productive. Marketing balance is all about making marketing work harder, be more versatile, and achieve more objectives. To realize marketing balance, we must create multiple meanings, multiple responses, and multiple effects with marketing activities.

Marketing balance does not imply that marketers should not take chances, should not do different things, or should not do things differently. It *does* imply an acceptance of the fact that marketing is multifaceted and has multiple objectives, markets, and activities. It also recognizes the importance of avoiding oversimplification: Marketers must do many things and do them right. Fundamentally, to achieve marketing balance, marketers must understand and address marketing tradeoffs.

THE SCIENCE OF BRANDING 15-3

Scott Bedbury's Eight Branding Principles

Scott Bedbury, one of the key brand architects behind both the Starbucks and Nike brands in the 1990s, offers his brand philosophy in his book *A New Brand World.* A strong proponent of a consumer-centric approach to branding, Bedbury outlines the following eight branding principles for brand leadership in the twenty-first century.

1. Relying on brand awareness has become marketing's fool's gold.
2. You have to know it before you grow it.
3. Remember the "spandex rule" of branding: Just because you can, doesn't mean you should.
4. Transcend a product-only relationship with consumers.
5. Everything matters.
6. All brands need good parents.
7. Big doesn't have to be bad.
8. Relevance, simplicity, and humanity—rather than technology—will distinguish brands in the future.

Source: Scott Bedbury with Stephen Fenichell, *A New Brand World: Eight Principles for Achieving Brand Leadership in the 21st Century* (New York: Viking Press, 2002). Used with permission of Scott Bedbury.

Review

The challenges and complexities of the modern marketplace make efficient and effective marketing an imperative. The concept of brand equity has been put forth as a means to focus marketing efforts. The businesses that win in the twenty-first century will be those that have marketers who successfully build, measure, and manage brand equity. This final chapter reviewed some of the important guidelines put forth in this text to help in that endeavor.

Effective brand management requires consistent actions and applications of these guidelines across all aspects of the marketing program. Nevertheless, to some extent, rules are made to be broken, and these guidelines should be viewed only as a point of departure in the difficult process of creating a world-class brand. Each branding situation and application is unique and requires careful scrutiny and analysis as how best to apply, or perhaps in some cases ignore, these various recommendations and guidelines. Smart marketers will capitalize on every tool at their disposal—and devise ones that are not—in their relentless pursuit of achieving brand preeminence. To provide further stimulation, The Science of Branding 15-2 and 15-3 summarize some ideas from leading brand strategists David Aaker and Scott Bedbury.

Discussion Questions

1. What do you think makes a strong brand? Can you add any criteria to the list provided?
2. What about deadly sins of brand management? Do you see anything missing from the list of seven in Figure 15-7?

3. Pick one of the special applications of branding and choose a representative brand within that category. How well do the five guidelines for that category apply? Can you think of others not listed?
4. What do you see as the future of branding? How will the roles of brands change? What different strategies might emerge as to how to build, measure, and manage brand equity in the coming years? What do you see as the biggest challenges?
5. Review the different tradeoffs identified as part of achieving marketing balance. Can you identify any other tradeoffs not listed? For each tradeoff, can you identify a company that has excelled in achieving balance on that tradeoff?

BRAND FOCUS 15.0

The Brand Report Card

Rate your brand on a scale of 1 to 10 (1 = extremely poor; 10 = extremely good) for each of the following characteristics.[16] Create a similar report card for your major competitors. Compare and contrast the results with all the relevant participants in the management of your brand. Doing so should help you identify areas that need improvement, recognize areas in which you excel, and learn more about how your particular brand is configured. Be brutally honest in answering the questions—approach them as an outsider and from a consumer perspective.

Score

1.____ Managers understand what the brand means to consumers.
- Have you created detailed, research-driven mental maps of your target customers?
- Have you attempted to define a brand mantra?
- Have you outlined customer-driven boundaries for brand extensions and guidelines for marketing programs?

2.____ The brand is properly positioned.
- Have you established necessary and competitive points of parity?
- Have you established desirable and deliverable points of difference?

3.____ Customers receive superior delivery of the benefits they value most.
- Have you attempted to uncover unmet consumer needs and wants?
- Do you relentlessly focus on maximizing your customers' product and service experiences?

4.____ The brand takes advantage of the full repertoire of branding and marketing activities available to build brand equity.
- Have you strategically chosen and designed your brand name, logo, symbol, slogan packaging, signage, and so forth to build brand awareness and image?
- Have you implemented integrated push and pull strategies that target intermediaries and end customers, respectively?

5.____ Marketing and communications efforts are seamlessly integrated (or as close to it as humanly possible). The brand communicates with one voice.
- Have you considered all the alternative ways to create brand awareness and link brand associations?
- Have you ensured that common meaning is contained throughout your marketing communication program?
- Have you capitalized on the unique capabilities of each communication option?
- Have you been careful to preserve important brand values in your communications over time?

6.____ The brand's pricing strategy is based on consumer perceptions of value.
- Have you estimated the added value perceived by customers?
- Have you optimized price, cost, and quality to meet or exceed consumer expectations?

7.____ The brand uses appropriate imagery to support its personality.
- Have you established credibility by ensuring that the brand and the people behind it are seen as expert, trustworthy, and likable?
- Have you established appropriate user and usage imagery?
- Have you crafted the right brand personality?

8.____ The brand is innovative and relevant.
- Have you invested in product improvements that provide improved benefits and better solutions for your customers?
- Have you stayed up-to-date and in touch with your customers?

9.____ For a multiproduct, multibrand company, the brand hierarchy and brand portfolio are strategically sound.
- For the brand hierarchy, are associations at the highest levels relevant to as many products as possible at the next lower levels and are brands well differentiated at any one level?
- For the brand portfolio, do the brands maximize market coverage while minimizing their overlap at the same time?

10.____ The company has in place a system to monitor brand equity and performance.
- Have you created a brand charter that defines the meaning and equity of the brand and how it should be treated?
- Do you conduct periodic brand audits to assess the health of your brands and to set strategic direction?
- Do you conduct routine tracking studies to evaluate current marketing performance?
- Do you regularly distribute brand equity reports that summarize all brand-relevant research and information to assist marketing decision making?
- Have you assigned people within the organization the responsibility of monitoring and preserving brand equity?

Notes

1. For an application in a franchise setting, see Leyland Pitt, Julie Napoli, and Rian Van Der Merwe, "Managing the Franchised Brand: The Franchisee's Perspective," *Journal of Brand Management* 10 (August 2003): 411–420.
2. Based on Kevin Lane Keller, "The Brand Report Card," *Harvard Business Review* (January/February 2000): 147–157.
3. Kevin Lane Keller and Frederick E. Webster, Jr., "A Roadmap for Branding in Industrial Markets," *Journal of Brand Management* 11 (May 2004): 388–402.
4. Stephen Philips and Amy Dunkin, "King Customer," *Business Week,* 12 March 1990, 88–94.
5. Daniel Lyons, "You Want Fries With That?" *Forbes,* 24 May 2004, 56–57.
6. Leslie de Chernatony and Malcom H. B. McDonald, *Creating Powerful Brands* (Oxford: Butterworth-Heinemann, 1992).
7. A. Parasuraman, Valarie A. Zeithaml, and Leonard L. Berry, "A Conceptual Model of Service Quality and Its Implications for Future Research," *Journal of Marketing* (Fall 1985): 41–50.
8. Leonard L. Berry, A. Parasuraman, and Valarie A. Zeithaml, "Ten Lessons for Improving Service Quality," MSI Report 93–104 (Cambridge, MA: Marketing Science Institute, 1993).
9. Keith Naughton, "The Ralph Lauren of Car Dealers," *Business Week,* 20 November 1995, 151.
10. "Simply Groundbreaking," *Advertising Age,* 5 June 2006, 5.
11. Valarie A. Zeithaml, Parsu Parasuraman, and Arvind Malhotra, "Understanding e-Service Quality," presentation made at MSI Board of Trustees Meeting, "Marketing Knowledge in the Age of e-Commerce," November 2000. See also Parasuraman, Zeithaml, and Berry, "Conceptual Model of Service Quality," as well as William Boulding, Ajay Kalra, and Richard Staelin, "A Dynamic Process Model of Service Quality: From Expectations to Behavioral Intentions," *Journal of Marketing Research* (February 1993): 7–27 for an important extension.
12. Donna L. Hoffman and Thomas P. Novak, "How to Acquire Customers on the Web," *Harvard Business Review* (May–June 2000): 179–188.
13. Debra Thompson, "Branding Hasn't Changed Much," *Marketing Computers,* April 2000.
14. Mary Jo Hatch and Majken Scultz, "Are the Corporate Stars Aligned for Your Corporate Brand?" *Harvard Business Review* (February 2001): 129–134.
15. Kevin Lane Keller and Frederick E. Webster, Jr. "Marketing Balance: Finessing Marketing Trade-Offs," working paper, Tuck School of Business, Dartmouth College, 2002.
16. Based on Kevin Lane Keller, "The Brand Report Card," *Harvard Business Review* (January/February 2000): 147–157.

EPILOGUE

When asked how he beat Jimmy Conners in the 1980 Master's tournament after losing to him in their previous 16 matches, Vitas Gerulaitis quipped:

"Nobody . . . but *nobody* . . . beats Vitas Gerulaitis 17 times in a row."

I guess you have to draw the line somewhere.

May all your brands be winners.

CREDITS

Chapter 1

6, Getty Images/Time Life Pictures; 12 (top), PhotoEdit, Inc.; 12 (bottom), Eaton Corporation; 18, Courtesy of Southwest Airlines; 20, AP Wide World Photos; 21, Yvonne Hemsey/Getty Images, Inc.; 24, Jamie McDonald/Getty Images, Inc.; 25, Picture Desk, Inc./Kobal Collection; 26, Used with permission of R&R Partners; 37, © LeFrank David/CORBIS KIPA, All Rights Reserved.

Chapter 2

62, Used with permission of Tropicana Products, Inc.; 64, PhotoEdit, Inc.; 70, Getty Images, Inc.; 73, Landov LLC; 80, © Jones Soda Company. All Rights Reserved. Used with permission.

Chapter 3

104, © Layne Kennedy/CORBIS, All Rights Reserved; 106, AP Wide World Photos; 108, Used with permission of Subaru of America, Inc. All rights reserved; 109, Courtesy Nivea; 117, Justin Sullivan/Getty Images, Inc.; 124, Photolibrary.Com; 126, SuperStock, Inc.; 133, Used with permission of Rolex; 144, Used with permission of Pepsico.

Chapter 4

148, © Parrot Pascal/CORBIS, All Rights Reserved; 155, Landov LLC; 158, Green Giant® is a registered trademark of General Mills and is used with permission; 160–161, Used with permission of Geico; 164, Generals Mills/AP Wide World; 167, Christopher Harting/© 2007 Hot & Flashy is a Trademark of Blue Q, Massachusetts; 168, © Copyright 2003 Benetton Group S.p.A. Photo: James Mollison; 171, Used with permission of JetBlue, © 2007, JetBlue Airways; 174, General Mills for Business Wire/Getty Images, Inc.

Chapter 5

186, AP Wide World Photos; 188, Matthew Stockman/Getty Images, Inc.; 192, Adrian Dennis/Agence France Presse/Getty Images; 213, PhotoEdit, Inc.; 220, AP Wide Word Photos; 224, Used with permission of Heinz.

Chapter 6

232, Used with permission of Mazda; 240, Used with permission of Ford Motor Company; 244, © David Turnley/CORBIS All Rights Reserved; 245, © James Leynse/ CORBIS All Rights Reserved; 254, Picture Desk, Inc./Kobal Collection; 260, Getty Images, Inc.; 263, Landov LLC.

Chapter 7

286, Used with permission of New Zealand Trade and Enterprise; 296, Courtesy of Daimler Chrysler Corporation; 297, General Mills/Getty Images, Inc.; 299, Paula Bronstein/Getty Images, Inc.; 302, © James Leynse/ CORBIS All Rights Reserved; 305, AP Wide World Photos.

Chapter 8

320, Stephen Chemin/Getty Images, Inc.; 334, Corbis Royalty Free; 336, Pillsbury® is a registered trademark of General Mills and is used with permission; 337 (left, right), America's Milk Processors; 341, Used with permission of IBM; 344, Reproduced with permission of The Procter & Gamble Company; 346, Copyright 2008 General Motors Corp. Used with permission of GM Media Archives.

Chapter 9

366, Joie de Vivre Hospitality; 373, Courtesy of Burton Snowboards.

Chapter 10

422, Howard Deshong/StockFood/Getty Images, Inc.

Chapter 11

436, Pearson Education/PH College; 438, PhotoEdit, Inc.; 440, AP Wide World Photos; 442, AP Wide World Photos; 456, Used with permission of 3M Corporation; 458, General Motors Corp. Used with permission, GM Media Archives; 459, Samantha Sin/Agence France Presse/Getty Images, Inc.; 460, Photo courtesy Clif Bar & Co.; 462, Courtesy L.L. Bean, Inc.; 470, Landov LLC.

Chapter 12

492, Bernard Annebicque/Corbis Sygma; 494, AP Wide World Photos; 496, © NBC. Photographer: Paul Drinkwater. Courtesy NBC/Photofest; 500, Getty Images, Inc.–Photodisc; 502 (top), Used with permission of Procter & Gamble; 502 (bottom), Pierre Tostee ASP/Getty Images, Inc.; 508, Corbis/Reuters America LLC; 510, Landov LLC; 514, Courtesy of Michelin North America, Inc.; 516, AP Wide World Photos; 534, Landov LLC.

Chapter 13

554, AP Wide World Photos; 556, Landov LLC; 560, Tim Ridley © Dorling Kindersley, Courtesy of Burberry's of London; 562, Used with permission of Harley-Davidson Motor Co.; 564, Used with permission of Pepsico; 571, Tim Bieber/Getty Images, Inc.; 572, AP Wide World Photos; 575, Mario Tama/Getty Images, Inc.; 576, Volkswagen of American, Inc.

Chapter 14

603 (top), AP Wide World Photos; 603 (bottom), Landov LLC; 620, Landov LLC.

Chapter 15

652, AP Wide World Photos; 656, Courtesy of Tesco Stores Limited; 658, Used with permission of INVISTA; 659, Glen Davis; 662, Courtesy of Green Mountain Coffee Roasters; 664, Landov LLC.

INDEX

A

B

C

D

E

F

I

J

K

L

M

N

O

P

Q

T

U

V